Welfare Benefits and Tax Credits Handbook

10th edition

Child Poverty Action Group

CPAG promotes action for the prevention and relief of poverty among children and families with children. To achieve this, CPAG aims to raise awareness of the causes, extent, nature and impact of poverty, and strategies for its eradication and prevention; bring about positive policy changes for families with children in poverty; and enable those eligible for income maintenance to have access to their full entitlement. If you are not already supporting us, please consider making a donation, or ask for details of our membership schemes, training courses and publications.

Published by Child Poverty Action Group
94 White Lion Street, London N1 9PF
020 7837 7979

Child Poverty Action Group is a charity registered in England and Wales (registration number 294841) and in Scotland (registration number SC039339). Company limited by guarantee registered in England (registration number 1993854).

A CIP record for this book is available from the British Library

ISBN: 978 1 906076 12 2

Design by Devious Designs
Typeset by David Lewis XML Associates Limited
Printed in the UK by CPI William Clowes Beccles NR34 7TL
Cover photo by Ray Roberts/Photofusion

The authors

Consultant editor: Simon Osborne

Pamela Fitzpatrick is a welfare rights worker at CPAG.

Carolyn George is a freelance trainer and writer on welfare rights.

Rachel Hadwen is a freelance trainer and consultant in welfare rights and related areas. She previously worked for Citizens Advice as a social security specialist.

Daphne Hall is a part-time welfare rights adviser at Bristol City Council and a freelance trainer and writer on welfare rights.

David Malcolm is Head of Social Policy the National Union of Students.

Susan Mitchell is a freelance writer on welfare rights.

Paul Moorhouse has been a welfare rights adviser since 1994. He is currently a freelance trainer and writer.

Simon Osborne is a welfare rights worker at CPAG, based at CPAG in Scotland.

Judith Paterson is CPAG in Scotland's Welfare Rights Co-ordinator.

Peter Turville is a welfare rights worker at Oxfordshire Welfare Rights.

Paula Twigg is Manager of CPAG's Citizens' Rights Office.

Barbara Williamson is a freelance writer on welfare rights.

Mark Willis is a welfare rights worker at CPAG in Scotland.

Stewart Wright is Deputy District Chair of the Social Security and Child Support Appeals Tribunal. From 1999 to 2007 he was Legal Officer at CPAG.

Acknowledgements

The authors would like to thank Miranda Bayliss, Sarah Clarke, Edward Graham, Barbara Gray, Arnie James, Beth Lakhani and Celia Minoughan for their invaluable comments.

We would also like to acknowledge the efforts of the many authors of previous editions of the *National Welfare Benefits Handbook*, the *Rights Guide to Non-Means-Tested Benefits* and the *Jobseeker's Allowance Handbook*, on which this book is based.

Thanks are due to Alison Key and Nikki Johnston for editing and managing the production of the book so efficiently, and to Paula McDiarmid and Pascale Vassie for proofreading the text. Particular thanks are due to Katherine Dawson for producing the index.

We would also like to thank, once again, staff at the Department for Work and Pensions, Child Support Agency, the Revenue, Department for Education and Skills, and the Tax Credit Office for their help and co-operation. In particular, we are grateful to Maria Kolpa of Jobcentre Plus and everyone in the DWP's Housing Benefit Strategy Division LHA Implementation Team.

We would also like to say thank you to the staff at KonnectSoft, David Lewis XML Associates and Clowes for keeping up with our schedules.

The law covered in this book was correct on 1 March 2008 and includes Regulations laid up to this date.

Foreword

The year 2008 marks the sixtieth anniversary of the passing of the National Assistance Act. This should be a year for anti-poverty activists to celebrate, and for all of us who work in it – and rely on it – to praise our welfare state. Many of us know our own families were lifted out of poverty thanks to the post-war reforms that brought about a system of security and social protection that previously families lacked. Those reforms: family allowances to help parents meet the costs of raising children; financial protection when jobs were lost through unemployment, family breakdown, illness or bereavement; the promise of a secure retirement; free healthcare; and access to free full-time education, have transformed our prospects compared with those of our parents and grandparents. They have ensured that many of us escape the poverty, and the fear of poverty, experienced by earlier generations.

But we also know that too many of our children still continue to grow up in poverty. Yet far from seeking to celebrate the modern welfare state, or to extend its mission to end child poverty for ever, its achievements and the principles on which it is founded face a 'drip, drip' diet of criticism, carping and threat. Politicians vie to talk toughest. The right to financial support for one's family is subject to an ever more onerous set of conditions. Fraud and scrounging are exaggerated, while error and complexity increase, leaving families without access to the benefits to which they are entitled. And then, we are surprised when Britain finds itself at the bottom of the Unicef child wellbeing league.

Welfare rights advisers, whose professionalism, dedication and expertise are vital in maximising family incomes to help bring about an end to poverty, are in the frontline of trying to reverse this trend. In providing you with our specialist handbooks, training and online resources, we aim to equip you to do that job more effectively as you advise families on their rights.

But more than that. In this sixtieth anniversary year, as ministers unveil yet more welfare reforms with more demands and coercion, and as we see increasing attempts to divide the 'deserving' from the 'undeserving' poor, we hope to enlist your support as campaigners and advocates for a truly modern welfare state. We ask you to mark the passage of the 1948 Act by working with Child Poverty Action Group to demand a reform programme for the twenty-first century that guarantees a fairer future for every child, and ends child poverty for good.

Kate Green

Child Poverty Action Group Chief Executive

Contents

How to use this *Handbook*

This *Handbook* covers the rules for all welfare benefits and tax credits.

The basic structure of the benefit and tax credit systems is summarised in Chapter 1. This chapter explains the differences between the various types of benefits and tax credits, and includes a quick guide to the benefits and tax credits you can claim depending on your circumstances.

This *Handbook* also aims to give practical help in the areas where disputes are likely to arise between claimants and local authorities, the Department for Work and Pensions (DWP), the Revenue or other government departments. If you are challenging a decision related to your claim it is helpful to refer to the relevant law and official guidance, and references are given in the notes at the end of each chapter.

In this *Handbook* the chapters are organised into seven parts. Part 1 outlines the benefit and tax credit systems. Parts 2–5 are about benefits and Part 6 is about tax credits. Part 7 outlines the immigration and residence rules that apply to both benefits and tax credits. Broadly, all the information about individual benefits, in alphabetical order, is in Part 2, and all the benefit rules that apply to particular groups, or are common to all of the benefits, are in Parts 3–5. Part 6 describes the two different tax credits as well as the rules common to both.

The notes are at the end of each chapter and are numbered in the order they appear in the text. The notes are in abbreviated form, in order to save space, and the relevant abbreviations are listed in Appendix 11.

For example, 'Reg 52(2) JSA Regs' is regulation 52(2) of the Jobseeker's Allowance Regulations 1996. The references are usually to Acts or Regulations, but sometimes they are to caselaw (social security commissioners' or court decisions) and guidance issued by the DWP. Appendix 2 and Appendix 3 suggest where to look for copies of the law and caselaw.

In the text, abbreviations are also used for most of the benefits in order to save space. There is a list of abbreviations used in the text pn pxi. However, an abbreviated term is always given in full the first time it is used in a chapter or section.

The index contains entries in bold type, directing you to the general information on the subject or where the subject is covered more fully. Sub-entries under the bold headings are listed alphabetically and direct you to specific aspects of the subject.

The cross references in the text refer you to other information about the relevant topic.

The main subjects in each chapter are summarised in the contents pages at the front of this book. The main subject headings and page numbers are repeated at the beginning of each chapter.

Contents of this Handbook

Part 1 contains just one chapter introducing the main structure of the benefit and tax credit systems.

Part 2 covers the rules for all the non-means-tested and means-tested benefits.

Part 3 describes the special rules that apply to certain groups of claimants.

Part 4 gives the general rules that apply to all, or most of, the benefits.

Part 5 describes the administration of benefits and how to challenge decisions made about benefits or complain if you have been treated unfairly.

Part 6 covers the rules for tax credits, describes how they are administered and explains how to challenge tax credit decisions.

Part 7 covers the immigration and residence rules that apply to benefits and tax credits.

The benefit and tax credit rates listed in the following sections and throughout this *Handbook* are those applying from April 2008.

Abbreviations

AA	attendance allowance
BL	budgeting loan
CA	carer's allowance
CAB	Citizens Advice Bureau
CCG	community care grant
CL	crisis loan
CSA	Child Support Agency
CRU	Compensation Recovery Unit
CTB	council tax benefit
CTC	child tax credit
DLA care	disability living allowance care component
DLA mobility	disability living allowance mobility component
DWP	Department for Work and Pensions
EC	European Community
ECtHR	European Court of Human Rights
ECJ	European Court of Justice
EEA	European Economic Area
EO	employment officer
ESA	employment and support allowance
EU	European Union
EWC	expected week of childbirth
GP	general practitioner
HB	housing benefit
IB	incapacity benefit
ICA	invalid care allowance
IIDB	industrial injuries disablement benefit
IRS	Independent Review Service
IS	income support
JSA	jobseeker's allowance
MA	maternity allowance
MP	Member of Parliament
MS	Medical Service
NI	national insurance
NICO	National Insurance Contributions Office
PAYE	Pay As You Earn
PC	pension credit
REA	reduced earnings allowance
SAAS	Student Awards Agency for Scotland
SAP	statutory adoption pay
SDA	severe disablement allowance
SF	social fund
SFI	social fund inspector
SFO	social fund officer
SLC	Student Loan Company
SMP	statutory maternity pay
SPP	statutory paternity pay
SSP	statutory sick pay
TCO	Tax Credit Office
TS	Tribunals Service
WTC	working tax credit

Means-tested benefit rates

Income support/income-based jobseeker's allowance

Personal allowances		£pw
Single	Under 25	47.95
	25 or over	60.50
Lone parent	Under 18	47.95
	18 or over	60.50
Couple	Both under 18	47.95
	Both under 18, certain cases	72.35
	One under 18, one 18-24	47.95
	One under 18, one 25 or over	60.50
	One under 18, certain cases	94.95
	Both 18 or over	94.95

Premiums		
Carer		27.75
Disability	Single	25.85
	Couple	36.85
Enhanced disability	Single	12.60
	Couple	18.15
Severe disability	One qualifies	50.35
	Two qualify	100.70
Pensioner	Single (jobseeker's allowance only)	63.55
	Couple	94.40

Children (Pre-6 April 2004 claims with no child tax credit)

Child under 20 personal allowance	52.59
Family premium	16.75
Disabled child premium	48.72
Enhanced disability premium (child)	19.60

Capital limits	Lower	Upper
Standard	6,000	16,000
Care homes	10,000	16,000

Tariff income £1 per £250 between lower and upper limit

Pension credit

Guarantee credit

Standard minimum guarantee	Single	124.05
	Couple	189.35

		£pw
Severe disability addition	One qualifies	50.35
	Two qualify	100.70
Carer addition		27.75
Savings credit		
Threshold	Single	91.20
	Couple	145.80
Maximum	Single	19.71
	Couple	26.13
Capital limits		
Standard		6,000
Care homes		10,000
No upper limit		
Deemed income £1 per £500 above disregard		

Housing benefit and council tax benefit

Personal allowances

Single	Under 25	47.95
	25 or over	60.50
Lone parent	Under 18	47.95
	18 or over	60.50
Couple	Both under 18	72.35
	One or both 18 or over	94.95
Children	Under 20	52.59
Pensioner 60 or over	Single under 65	124.05
	Single 65 or over	143.80
	Couple both under 65	189.35
	Couple one or both 65 or over	215.50
Premiums		
Carer		27.75
Disability	Single	25.85
	Couple	36.85
Disabled child		48.72
Enhanced disability	Single	12.60
	Couple	18.15
	Child	19.60
Severe disability	One qualifies	50.35
	Two qualify	100.70
Family	Ordinary rate	16.75
	Some lone parents	22.20
	Baby addition	10.50

Capital limits		£pw Lower	Upper
Standard		6,000	16,000
Care home (housing benefit only)		10,000	16,000

Tariff income £1 per £250 between lower and upper limit
£1 per £500 for those aged 60 or over
No upper limit or tariff income for those on PC guarantee credit

Note: changes to housing benefit and council tax benefit personal allowances and premiums are expected from October 2008 for people claiming the new employment and support allowance (see CPAG's *Welfare Rights Bulletin* for details).

Social fund payments		
Maternity grant		500.00
Cold weather payment		8.50
Winter fuel payment	60–79	200.00
	80 or over	300.00
	Care home (60–79)	100.00
	Care home (80 or over)	150.00

Non-means-tested benefit rates

	Claimant £pw	Adult dependant £pw
Attendance allowance		
Higher rate	67.00	
Lower rate	44.85	
Bereavement benefits		
Bereavement payment (lump sum)	2,000	
Bereavement allowance/widow's pension (55 or over)	90.70	
Bereavement allowance/widow's pension (45–54)	27.21–84.35	
Widowed parent's allowance/widowed mother's allowance	90.70	
Carer's allowance	50.55	30.20
Child benefit		
Only/eldest child	18.80	
Other child(ren)	12.55	
Child dependant (some existing claimants only)		
Only/eldest child	8.75	
Other child(ren)	11.35	
Disability living allowance		
Care component		
Highest rate	67.00	
Middle rate	44.85	
Lowest rate	17.75	
Mobility component		
Higher rate	46.75	
Lower rate	17.75	
Guardian's allowance	13.45	

	Claimant £pw	Adult dependant £pw
Short-term incapacity benefit		
Lower rate	63.75	39.40
Higher rate	75.40	39.40
Lower rate (over pension age)	81.10	48.65
Higher rate (over pension age)	84.50	48.65
Long-term incapacity benefit	84.50	50.55
Age addition (under 35)	17.75	
Age addition (35–44)	8.90	
Industrial disablement benefit		
Under 18	20%: £16.77 to 100%: £83.85	
18 or over	20%: £27.36 to 100%: £136.80	
Contribution-based jobseeker's allowance		
Under 25	47.95	
25 or over	60.50	
Maternity allowance		
Standard rate	117.18	39.40
Retirement pension		
Category A	90.70	54.35
Category B (widow(er)/surviving civil partner)	90.70	
Category B (spouse/civil partner)	54.35	
Category D	54.35	
Severe disablement allowance	51.05	30.40
Age addition (under 40)	17.75	
Age addition (40–49)	11.40	
Age addition (50–59)	5.70	
Statutory maternity, paternity and adoption pay		
Standard rate	117.18	
Statutory sick pay	75.40	
National insurance contributions		
Lower earnings limit	90.00	
Primary threshold	105.00	
Employee's class 1 rate	11% of £105.01 to £770 1% above £770	
Class 2 rate	2.30	

Tax credit rates

		£ per day	£ per year
Child tax credit			
Family element	Basic	1.50	545
	Baby element	1.50	545
Child element		5.72	2,085
Disability element		6.96	2,540
Severe disability element		2.80	1,020
Working tax credit			
Basic element		4.94	1,800
Couple element		4.85	1,770
Lone parent element		4.85	1,770
30-hour element		2.02	735
Disability element		6.59	2,405
Severe disability element		2.80	1,020
50-plus element	Working 16–29 hours	3.39	1,235
	Working 30 hours or more	5.05	1,840
Childcare element	80% eligible childcare costs to a weekly maximum of:		
	One child	weekly maximum £175	
	Two or more children	weekly maximum £300	
Thresholds			
First income threshold	Working tax credit only or with child tax credit		£6,420
	Child tax credit only		£15,575
First taper			39%
Second income threshold			min. £50,000
Second taper			6.67%
Income disregard			£25,000

Part 1

Introduction

Chapter 1
Introduction

This chapter covers:

1. The benefit and tax credit system

The government department responsible for the overall administration and policy work for most social security benefits, other than housing benefit (HB) and council tax benefit (CTB), is the **Department for Work and Pensions (DWP)**. Tax credits, child benefit and guardian's allowance are dealt with by **Her Majesty's Revenue and Customs** (referred to in this *Handbook* as 'the Revenue'). HB and CTB are administered by **local authorities**.

An executive agency of the DWP, called **Jobcentre Plus**, administers most benefit claims for people under state retirement age (referred to by the DWP as people of 'working age'). The **Pension Service** deals with retirement pension and pension credit, and the **Disability and Carers Service** deals with disability benefits and carer's allowance. **Note:** these two agencies were due to be merged on 1 April 2008 to create a new DWP agency, the **Pension, Disability and Carers Service**, but it is expected that, for the time being, all contact with claimants will continue to be made by the Pension Service and the Disability and Carers Service and their contact details will remain the same.

Another executive agency of the DWP is the **Child Support Agency** (CSA), which administers the child support system. The Government is introducing extensive reforms to child support and will replace the CSA with a new body, the **Child Maintenance and Enforcement Commission** during 2008. An executive agency of the Ministry of Justice, the **Tribunals Service**, is responsible for administering benefit and tax credit appeals.

The main types of benefit and tax credit

Some benefits are paid only if you have limited income and capital. These benefits are known as **means-tested benefits** because there is an investigation into your means before you can be paid them. You do not have to satisfy any national insurance (NI) contribution conditions (see Chapter 31). See pxii for a list of means-tested benefits.

Child tax credit (CTC) and **working tax credit** are also means tested (see Chapters 48 and 49).

Some other benefits (known as 'passported' benefits) are payable if you qualify for particular means-tested benefits or tax credits (see p5). Some benefits are 'discretionary' even if you satisfy a means test.

Non-means-tested benefits do not involve a detailed investigation of your means. You qualify if you satisfy certain basic conditions such as being available for work, disabled or bereaved. It may still be relevant to ask whether you have any earnings or an occupational pension because many of the benefits are designed to compensate for your loss of earnings, but normally your income or capital does not affect your entitlement. You have to satisfy the NI contribution conditions for some non-means-tested benefits (see Chapter 31). See pxv for a list of non-means-tested benefits.

Jobseeker's allowance (JSA) and employment and support allowance (ESA) (a new benefit expected to be introduced in October 2008) are benefits that are both means tested and non-means tested. *Income-based* JSA is means tested and *contribution-based* JSA is non-means tested (see Chapter 15). A third type of JSA, *joint-claim* JSA, is a kind of income-based JSA, but has some special rules about claiming for certain couples.

Similarly, *income-related* ESA is means tested and *contributory* ESA is non-means tested (see Chapter 7). A third type of ESA, ESA in *youth* is similar to contributory ESA, but has neither NI contribution conditions nor a means test.

If you qualify for the non-means-tested element of either JSA or ESA you may also qualify for the means-tested elements if:

- you qualify for any of the premiums that can be added to your basic personal allowance (see p771); *or*
- you need help with your mortgage interest or other types of housing costs (see Chapter 34).

This *Handbook* also covers the rules for **statutory sick pay, statutory maternity pay, statutory paternity pay** and **statutory adoption pay,** which are paid without any means test by your employer, rather than by the DWP.

You may be entitled to a combination of non-means-tested and means-tested benefits. For example, you might receive retirement pension topped up by pension credit. In addition, you might also qualify for help with your rent (HB) and your council tax (CTB).

Passported benefits

Some benefits and tax credits act as a 'passport' to other benefits. These are:

Passported benefit	*Passports*
Free school meals	Income support Income-based jobseeker's allowance Some recipients of child tax credit Guarantee credit of pension credit (England and Wales only)
Health benefits	Income support Income-based jobseeker's allowance Some recipients of child tax credit Some recipients of working tax credit Guarantee credit of pension credit
Sure Start maternity grant	Income support Income-based jobseeker's allowance Pension credit (either or both credits) Some recipients of child tax credit (see p513) Some recipients of working tax credit (see p513)
Social fund funeral expenses payment	Income support Income-based jobseeker's allowance Pension credit (either or both credits) Some recipients of child tax credit (see p515) Some recipients of working tax credit (see p515) Housing benefit Council tax benefit
Social fund cold weather payment, community care grant and budgeting loan	Income support Income-based jobseeker's allowance Pension credit (either or both credits)

It is understood that income-related employment and support allowance will be a passport in the same way as income support (except for free school meals, where the passport will be CTC). See www.cpag.org.uk/esa or CPAG's *Welfare Rights Bulletin* for updates.

2. Which benefits and tax credits should you claim

You may be able to claim a combination of non-means-tested benefits, means-tested benefits and tax credits. You should check to see:

- if you are entitled to any 'earnings replacement' benefits; *then*

- if you can get any benefits because of your circumstances – eg, because you are disabled or are looking after children; *and finally*
- whether you qualify for any means-tested benefits or tax credits to top up your benefit and other income.

Qualifying for some of the non-means-tested benefits means you qualify for some of the means-tested benefits at a higher rate. It is worth getting help to ensure you are claiming all the benefits to which you are entitled. See Appendix 2 for information about where you can go for advice and assistance. See below for ideas of benefits you might claim in certain circumstances.

Remember:

- when you claim, ask for your claim to be backdated if relevant (see p964);
- if getting one of the non-means-tested benefits you are claiming qualifies you for another benefit, claim the other benefit at the same time (see p968).

The following table is an overview of the possible benefits and tax credits to which you may be entitled depending on your circumstances. You may find that more than one of the circumstances applies to you – eg, you may have a child, a disability, a mortgage and work part time. Refer to each separate circumstance that applies.

Summaries of the rules for each benefit/tax credit are provided in the text following this table. Refer to the relevant chapters for full details.

Whatever category you are in, you might get the following benefits/tax credits if you do not have enough money to live on. These can be paid on their own, or in addition to other benefits:

- income support (IS) or income-based jobseeker's allowance (JSA), if not in full-time paid work;
- working tax credit (WTC), if in full-time paid work;
- pension credit (PC), if in or out of full-time paid work.

Your circumstance	*Benefits/tax credits to which you may be entitled*
Bereaved	Bereavement payment
	Widowed parent's allowance
	Bereavement allowance
	Funeral expenses payment
Carer	Carer's allowance
Responsible for a child	Child tax credit
	Child benefit
	Guardian's allowance
	Statutory maternity pay
	Statutory paternity pay
	Statutory adoption pay

	Maternity allowance
	Health benefits
	Cold weather payment
Disabled	Disability living allowance
	Attendance allowance
	Industrial injuries benefits
	Cold weather payment
Incapable of work	Incapacity benefit
	Non-contributory incapacity benefit
	Statutory sick pay
	Severe disablement allowance
	Cold weather payment
	Employment and support allowance
Have a mortgage	Income support
	Income-based jobseeker's allowance
	Pension credit
	Council tax benefit
Not enough money to meet certain needs	Community care grant
	Budgeting loan
	Crisis loan
Pensioner	State retirement pension
	Pension credit
	Winter fuel payment
	Cold weather payment
Pregnant	Statutory maternity pay
	Maternity allowance
	Sure Start maternity grant
	Health benefits
Tenant	Housing benefit
	Council tax benefit
Unemployed and seeking work	Contribution-based jobseeker's allowance
	Income-based jobseeker's allowance

Attendance allowance

- Attendance allowance (AA) is not means tested and is for those aged 65 or over when they claim who need help with personal care (see Chapter 6).
- If you receive this benefit you may also be entitled to disability-related premiums if you claim housing benefit (HB) and/or council tax benefit (CT or your partner claims IS, income-based JSA, income-related employmen support allowance (ESA) (expected from October 2008), or an ad amount if you claim PC (see Chapter 33).

- If you get AA at any rate, your carer may qualify for carer's allowance (CA) (but your carer should check whether this will affect any IS/income-based JSA/ income-related ESA/HB/CTB or PC you may be getting – see below).

Bereavement allowance

- Bereavement allowance is paid for up to 52 weeks for people who were 45 or over but under pension age when their spouse or civil partner died.
- You cannot get bereavement allowance and widowed parent's allowance at the same time (see Chapter 2).

Bereavement payment

- Bereavement payment is a one-off lump-sum payment for people who were under pension age when their spouse or civil partner died or whose late spouse or civil partner was not entitled to state retirement pension (see Chapter 2).

Budgeting loan

- You may get an interest-free loan to help you with particular expenses. You have to be in receipt of a qualifying benefit when you claim and throughout the previous 26 weeks (see Chapter 21).

Carer's allowance

- CA is paid if you are providing 35 hours or more care per week for a person who is entitled to disability living allowance (DLA) care component at the middle or highest rate, or AA (see Chapter 3).
- If you get CA you qualify for a carer's premium if you claim IS, income-based JSA, income-related ESA (expected from October 2008), HB and/or CTB, or a carer's additional amount if you claim PC, but the CA counts as income for these benefits. However, before you claim CA check whether this will affect the person for whom you are caring – if s/he gets a benefit that includes a severe disability premium or additional amount, this could be stopped if you claim CA (see Chapter 33).

Child benefit

- Child benefit is not means tested and is paid regardless of whether or not you are working (see Chapter 4).

Child tax credit

- Child tax credit (CTC) is paid whether you are in or out of work. The amount you may get depends on a means test (see Chapter 48).

Christmas bonus

- You qualify for a Christmas bonus of £10 if you receive any of the following qualifying benefits for at least part of the 'relevant week' (even if the benefit is paid later):
  - AA;
  - DLA;
  - CA;
  - disablement benefit (only if it includes unemployability supplement or constant attendance allowance);
  - long-term incapacity benefit (IB);
  - severe disablement allowance;
  - retirement pension;
  - PC;
  - widowed mother's allowance, widowed parent's allowance or widow's pension;
  - industrial death benefit for widows or widowers;
  - mobility supplement;
  - war disablement pension (only if you are at least 65 before the end of the relevant week);
  - war widow's or surviving civil partner's pension;
  - ESA, which includes either the support or the work-related activity component (when the ESA take effect – see Chapter 7).
- The 'relevant week' is usually the week beginning with the first Monday in December.
- You may also claim an extra bonus for your partner (a further £10) if s/he has not received a bonus in her/his own right, and:
  - you are both at least pension age (60 for women and 65 for men) and you are entitled, or may be treated as entitled, to an increase of one of the qualifying benefits in respect of her/him; *or*
  - you are both at least 60 and the only qualifying benefit you get is PC.
- The bonus is not taxable and has no effect on other benefits or tax credits.
- It is paid automatically. However, you should contact the DWP if you have not obtained your bonus within a year. Otherwise, your right is lost.

Cold weather payment

- Social fund cold weather payments are paid automatically if you are getting IS or income-based JSA that includes a qualifying premium or you have a child under five, or you are getting PC (see Chapter 22).

Community care grant

- You may get a grant specifically to help you live independently in the community. You have to be in receipt of a qualifying benefit when you claim (see Chapter 21).

Contribution-based jobseeker's allowance

- Contribution-based JSA is paid for 26 weeks if you satisfy the national insurance (NI) contribution conditions. It is not means tested but earnings can affect the amount of benefit you receive (see Chapter 15).
- You must show that you are available for and actively seeking work and you must have a current jobseeker's agreement with Jobcentre Plus.

Council tax benefit

- If you are liable for council tax and are on a low income you may get CTB. It is paid whether you are in or out of work (see Chapter 5).
- If you are the only person liable for council tax on your home and you have an adult on a low income living with you, you might be able to get 'second adult rebate' instead of CTB, no matter how much income or capital you have. It is paid whether you are in or out of work (see Chapter 5).

Crisis loan

- A crisis loan may be payable if you have had an emergency or disaster and you do not have enough money to meet immediate short-term needs. You do not have to be in receipt of a benefit to get this loan but have to be likely to be able to repay it (see Chapter 21).

Disability living allowance

- DLA is not means tested and is paid where you need help with your mobility and/or your personal care. You must be under 65 when you first claim (see Chapter 6).
- If you receive this benefit you may also be entitled to disability-related premiums if you claim IS, income-based JSA, HB and/or CTB, income-related ESA (expected from October 2008), or an additional amount if you claim PC (see Chapter 33).
- If you get DLA care component at the middle or highest rate your carer may qualify for CA (but your carer should check whether this will affect any IS/income-based JSA/income-related ESA/HB/CTB or PC you are getting – see p8).

Employment and support allowance

- ESA is a new benefit for people who have 'limited capability for work' because of ill health or a disability. At the time this *Handbook* was written, ESA was expected to be introduced in October 2008. ESA will replace incapacity benefit (IB) and IS on the basis of incapacity for work for new claimants.
- Contributory ESA is paid if you satisfy the NI contribution conditions, but you do not have to pass a means test.
- Income-related ESA is paid if you pass the means test, but you do not have to satisfy NI contribution conditions.

- ESA in youth is neither contributory nor means-tested but you must be aged under 20 (or in some circumstances aged under 25) when the period of limited capability for work began.
- It is possible to receive contributory ESA (or ESA in youth) topped up with income-related ESA (see Chapter 7).

Funeral expenses payment

- To get help with the cost of a funeral through the social fund you have to receive a qualifying benefit (see Chapter 22).

Guardian's allowance

- Guardian's allowance is paid to you if you are looking after a child who is effectively an orphan (see Chapter 8).

Health benefits

- Health benefits include free prescriptions, dental treatment, and help under the Healthy Start scheme. If you get a qualifying benefit you have a 'passported' entitlement to health benefits. Alternatively, you may qualify on low-income grounds (see Chapter 9).

Housing benefit

- If you have rent to pay and are on a low income you may get HB. It is paid whether you are in or out of work (see Chapter 10).

Incapacity benefit

- You have to satisfy the NI contribution conditions to be paid IB unless you became incapable of work in youth (see Chapter 12).
- ESA (expected to be introduced in October 2008) will replace new claims for IB.

Income-based jobseeker's allowance

- Income-based JSA is means tested and non-contributory. It is paid for as long as you satisfy the conditions of entitlement. It can be paid in addition to contribution-based JSA if you have any additional needs – eg, a disability or eligible housing costs (see Chapter 15).
- You must show that you are available for and actively seeking work and you must have a current jobseeker's agreement with Jobcentre Plus. If you work less than 16 hours a week you may be required to take up a full-time job (see Chapter 15).
- Some mortgage payments can be met by this benefit and if you are eligible you may have to serve a waiting period before you get this assistance (see Chapter 34).

Income support

- To qualify you have to fit into one of the categories of eligible claimants (eg, lone parents or disabled people) (see Chapter 13).
- IS can be paid in addition to other benefits to top up your income to a certain level.
- Some mortgage payments can be met by this benefit and if you are eligible you may have to serve a waiting period before you get this assistance (see Chapter 34).

Industrial injuries benefits

- Industrial injuries benefits are paid if you are disabled as a result of being injured or contracting a disease at work (see Chapter 14).
- If you receive this benefit you may also be entitled to disability-related premiums if you claim IS, income-based JSA, HB and/or CTB (see Chapter 33).

Maternity allowance

- If you are pregnant or have recently had a baby and you are not entitled to statutory maternity pay (SMP) you may be eligible for maternity allowance (MA) – eg, if you are self-employed (see Chapter 17).

Non-contributory incapacity benefit

- If you do not qualify for IB on the basis of your NI contribution record, you may qualify if you became incapacitated in youth (see Chapter 12).
- ESA in youth (expected to be introduced in October 2008) will replace new claims for non-contributory IB.

Pension credit

- The guarantee credit of PC is paid to both men and women aged 60 or over and acts to top up a low income; it is means tested. The savings credit of PC is paid to men and women aged 65 or over (or whose partner is 65 or over) and acts as a reward for making provisions for retirement, such as savings, above the basic state pension (see Chapter 18).
- Some mortgage payments can be met by this benefit (see Chapter 34).

Severe disablement allowance

- Severe disablement allowance (SDA) was abolished for new claimants on 6 April 2001 but some claimants with entitlement before that date remain eligible to receive it (see Chapter 20).

State retirement pension

- State retirement pension is paid to women from the age of 60 and to men from the age of 65. It is based on the amount of your NI contributions (or your partner's in the case of a Category B pension) (see Chapter 19).

Statutory adoption pay

- Statutory adoption pay is paid if you are, or have been, an employee who satisfies the continuous employment and earnings conditions. It is paid for up to 39 weeks when a child is placed, or is expected to be placed, with you for adoption (see Chapter 23).

Statutory maternity pay

- SMP is paid if you are an employee who satisfies the continuous employment and earnings conditions. It is paid for up to 39 weeks (see Chapter 23).
- If you are not entitled to SMP you may be eligible for MA – eg, if you are self-employed (see Chapter 23).

Statutory paternity pay

- Statutory paternity pay is paid if you are, or have been, an employee who satisfies the continuous employment and earnings conditions. It is paid for two weeks if your partner has just given birth or you have adopted a child (see Chapter 23).

Statutory sick pay

- Statutory sick pay (SSP) is paid to employees for the first 28 weeks of incapacity (see Chapter 24).

Sure Start maternity grant

- To get a Sure Start maternity grant you have to receive a qualifying benefit (see Chapter 22).

Widowed parent's allowance

- Widowed parent's allowance is for widows, widowers and surviving civil partners with children, and for widows or surviving civil partners who are pregnant.
- You cannot get both widowed parent's allowance and bereavement allowance at the same time (see Chapter 2).

Winter fuel payment

- Social fund winter fuel payments are for people aged 60 or over, regardless of their means (see Chapter 22).

Working tax credit

- Working tax credit (WTC) is paid if you work 16 hours or more a week (or in some cases 30 hours or more a week) and have a low income (see Chapter 49).

3. Financial help when starting work

If you or your partner start working full time (16 hours or more a week) or increase your earnings, and as a result stop claiming certain benefits, you might be entitled to some financial support to help your transition into work after a period of time on benefit. You may be entitled to one or more of the following, depending on your circumstances:

- **child maintenance bonus**, but these are gradually being phased out (see p757);
- **mortgage interest run-on** (see p823);
- **extended payments of housing benefit and council tax benefit** (see p222 and p97);
- **job grant** of £100 if you are single or a member of a couple without children or £250 if you are a lone parent or a member of a couple with children. You qualify if you start work of at least 16 hours a week (or your partner starts work of at least 24 hours a week) after you have received, continuously for the previous 26 weeks, income support (IS), jobseeker's allowance (JSA), incapacity benefit (IB), or severe disablement allowance. Some other payments may also count. You must expect the work to last five weeks or more;
- a payment from the **Adviser Discretion Fund** of up to £100 (or more if the cost of need is higher), at the discretion of your personal adviser at the Jobcentre Plus office, to help overcome barriers to work – eg, initial travel and childcare costs or work clothes. You must be on a New Deal scheme or receiving JSA, IS, IB, carer's allowance, SDA, pension credit or bereavement allowance for 26 weeks or more;
- **return-to-work credit** of £40 a week for the first year for people moving from IB into full-time work and earning less than £15,000 a year;
- **in-work credit** of £40 a week for the first year in a new job for lone parents (£60 for lone parents and couples in London) who have received IS or JSA for 12 months or more. You cannot receive both an in-work credit and a return-to-work credit.

The New Deal schemes also provide help with other costs such as childcare and training. For further details of the various financial incentives to move into full-time work see Inclusion's *Welfare to Work Handbook* or contact your local Jobcentre Plus office.

4. Other financial help

This *Handbook* is mainly concerned with information about social security benefits and tax credits. However, there is other financial help to which you may be entitled, especially if you are on a low income, have children, have an illness, disability or other special needs, or are an older person.

More detail on such help can be found in CPAG's *Paying for Care Handbook* and in the *Disability Rights Handbook*, published by Disability Alliance.

Education benefits

Free school meals

Children are entitled to free school meals if their families receive:

- income support (see Chapter 13) or income-based jobseeker's allowance (see Chapter 15);
- child tax credit (CTC) (but not working tax credit) and whose annual taxable income is £15,575 or less;
- guarantee credit of pension credit (PC) (England and Wales only). PC claimants in Scotland may qualify if they receive CTC, as above.

Also entitled are:

- 16–18-year-olds receiving the above benefits or tax credit in their own right;
- asylum seekers in receipt of support provided under Part VI of the Immigration and Asylum Act 1999.

Education maintenance allowance

Education maintenance allowances are means-tested payments for young people aged 16,17 or 18 who stay on in further education. The payments are made direct to the young person and are conditional upon regular course attendance. They are payable for two to three years. The young person may receive a weekly allowance of either £10, £20 or £30 depending on the household income. S/he may also receive bonuses if s/he remains on her/his course and does well against learning objectives set out in her/his education maintenance allowance contract. A further bonus may be payable if s/he returns to study for a second year.

Education maintenance allowances do not count as income for any benefits or tax credits the parent may be getting, so the young person can get an allowance and the parent's child benefit and CTC are unaffected. The education maintenance allowance is also not affected by any income the young person has from part-time work.

For further details, see www.direct.gov.uk, www.emascotland.com or www.wales.gov.uk.

Clothing grants

Local authorities can give grants for school uniforms and other school clothes. Each authority determines its own eligibility rules. Some school governing bodies or parents' associations also provide help with school clothing.

School transport

Local authorities must provide free transport to school for pupils under 16 where it is considered necessary to enable that pupil to get to the 'nearest suitable school'.

Other support for students

To find out what help is available to finance your studies, contact your local authority or college. Also see CPAG's *Student Support and Benefits Handbook for England and Wales* and *Benefits for Students in Scotland Handbook*.

Housing grants

Local authority grants

Your local authority may be able to provide you with a grant to help with the cost of improving your home. The main types of grant available are:

- renovation grants;
- disabled facilities grants;
- home repair assistance.

For more details, see CPAG's *Paying for Care Handbook*.

Home energy efficiency scheme

This scheme provides grants for insulating and draught-proofing your home.

For more details, see CPAG's *Paying for Care Handbook*, or contact the Energy Action Grants Agency, Archbold Terrace, Jesmond, Newcastle upon Tyne NE2 1DB (freephone 0800 072 0150) or at www.eagagroup.com.

Help from social services

Local authority social services departments have statutory duties to provide a range of practical and financial help to families, children, young people, older people, people with disabilities and asylum seekers.

If you are an asylum seeker, see Chapter 58.

For more details, see CPAG's *Paying for Care Handbook*.

Special funds for sick or disabled people

A variety of help is available for people with an illness or disability to assist with things like paying for care services in their own home, equipment, holidays, furniture and transport needs, and for people with haemophilia or HIV contracted via haemophilia treatment.

For more information, see CPAG's *Paying for Care Handbook* and the *Disability Rights Handbook*, published by Disability Alliance.

Charities

There are many charities that provide various types of help to people in need. Your local authority social services department or local advice centre may know of appropriate charities that could assist you, or you can consult publications, such as the *A Guide to Grants for Individuals in Need* and the *Charities Digest*, in your local library.

Part 2

Benefits

Chapter 2

Bereavement benefits

This chapter contains the rules about bereavement benefits. It covers:

If your spouse or civil partner has died, you may qualify for bereavement benefits. The three main benefits, collectively known as bereavement benefits, are:

- **bereavement payment** – a lump-sum payment of £2,000;
- **widowed parent's allowance** – a weekly benefit paid to widows or surviving civil partners who are pregnant or have children and to widowers who have children; *and*
- **bereavement allowance** – a weekly benefit paid for up to 52 weeks to widows, widowers or surviving civil partners who are at least 45 years of age when their spouse or civil partner dies.

You can only qualify for bereavement benefits if your late spouse or civil partner either satisfied the national insurance contribution conditions or died as the result of an industrial accident or disease. Your entitlement to bereavement benefits is not affected by any work that you do, nor by any income or savings that you have.

To qualify for bereavement benefits you must be a widow, widower or surviving civil partner (see p26). If you do not know whether your spouse or civil partner is dead, see p30.

Bereavement benefits replaced the old system of widows' benefits, which were only payable to women. If you are a woman whose husband died before 9 April 2001 you may still qualify for widows' benefits (see p31).

There are some groups of claimants to whom special rules apply (see p31).

1. Bereavement payment

A bereavement payment is a one-off, lump-sum payment which you can be paid in addition to widowed parent's allowance or bereavement allowance.

Who can claim a bereavement payment

You qualify for a bereavement payment if:[1]

- you are either:
  - a widow or widower and your spouse died on or after 9 April 2001 (see p26 for the meaning of widow and widower); *or*
  - from 5 December 2005, a surviving civil partner (see p26); *and*
- your late spouse or civil partner either:
  - satisfied the national insurance (NI) contribution conditions (see p737); *or*
  - died as the result of an industrial injury or disease (see p30); *and either*
- you were under pension age when your spouse or civil partner died (ie, under 60 for women, 65 for men); *or*
- if you were over pension age (ie, 60 or over for a woman, 65 or over for a man), your spouse or civil partner was not entitled to a Category A retirement pension when s/he died*; and*
- you claim within 12 months of your spouse's or civil partner's death (however, from 24 September 2007, if you are over pension age you are not required to make a claim to qualify – see below), but see p37 if you were not aware that your spouse or civil partner had died, and p21 if you and your spouse or civil partner were not in Great Britain (GB) when s/he died.

From 24 September 2007, if you are over pension age you do not need to make a claim in order to qualify for a bereavement payment.[2] However, the DWP states that this rule is currently more generous than intended and an amendment to the regulations is planned (probably in October 2008 – see CPAG's *Welfare Rights Bulletin* for updates). This would ensure that you can only qualify for a bereavement payment without making a claim if you were over pension age when your spouse or civil partner died and if both you and your late spouse or civil partner were receiving retirement pensions when s/he died. If you are in this situation, it is intended that you will be able to establish your entitlement to a bereavement payment even if it is more than 12 months since your spouse or civil partner died. But, until such an amendment comes into force, it is arguable that if you are over pension age (even if you were not when your spouse or civil partner died) there is no time limit for claiming a bereavement payment and you may qualify even if it is more than 12 months since your spouse or civil partner died.

Disqualification

Your entitlement to a bereavement payment is not affected if you marry or enter into a civil partnership after the death of your late spouse or civil partner. However, a bereavement payment will not be paid to you if, at the time of your spouse's or civil partner's death, you were cohabiting (see p30).[3]

If your spouse or civil partner was not in GB at the time s/he died you cannot qualify for a bereavement payment unless:[4]

- you were in GB on the date of your spouse's or civil partner's death; *or*
- you returned to GB within four weeks of her/his death. In this circumstance, if you are required to make a claim for a bereavement payment in order to qualify (see above) and you did not claim it within 12 months of your spouse's or civil partner's death, but you claimed within 12 months of your return to GB, it may be possible to argue that you can still qualify for a bereavement payment; *or*
- your spouse's or civil partner's NI contribution record is sufficient for you to satisfy the contribution conditions for widowed parent's allowance and bereavement allowance (see p738).

The rules about your age

There is no lower age limit for entitlement to a bereavement payment. Anyone who is legally old enough to marry or form a civil partnership may qualify.

For the upper age limit for qualifying for a bereavement payment, see p20.

Claiming for others

A bereavement payment is a lump-sum payment and there are no additions made to it for any of your dependants.

The amount of bereavement payment

A bereavement payment is a lump sum of £2,000.[5]

See p33 for details of how to claim a bereavement payment.

2. Widowed parent's allowance

Widowed parent's allowance is a weekly benefit. You cannot receive widowed parent's allowance and bereavement allowance at the same time, but you may become entitled to bereavement allowance after your entitlement to widowed parent's allowance ends (see p24).

In addition to your widowed parent's allowance you may also qualify for a bereavement payment (see p20).

Who can claim widowed parent's allowance

You qualify for widowed parent's allowance if:[6]

- you are either:
  - a widow or widower (see p26) whose spouse died on or after 9 April 2001; *or*
  - from 5 December 2005, a surviving civil partner (see p26); *or*
  - a widower whose wife died before 9 April 2001 (if you are a widow whose husband died before this date see p31); *and*
- you are under pension age (ie, under 60 for women, 65 for men); *and*
- your late spouse or civil partner either:
  - satisfied the national insurance (NI) contribution conditions (see p738); *or*
  - died as the result of an industrial injury or disease (see p30); *and*
- you are either:
  - entitled to child benefit (or treated as entitled to child benefit if the child has been absent from Great Britain[7]) for at least one eligible child (see p22); *or*
  - a widow and you are pregnant by your late husband; *or*
  - a widow or a surviving civil partner and you were residing with your late husband or civil partner immediately before her/his death and you are pregnant as a result of artificial insemination by a donor or in vitro fertilisation which was carried out before her/his death.

A 'child'

The term 'child' in this chapter means both a 'child' and a 'qualifying young person'. For who counts as a 'child' or 'qualifying young person', see p57. The definitions for the purpose of widowed parent's allowance are the same as the definitions for child benefit purposes.

Eligible children

A child only counts as an eligible child if *either*:[8]

- s/he is your and your late spouse's (or late civil partner's) son or daughter; *or*
- you were residing with your late spouse or civil partner immediately before s/he died and you were entitled, or treated as entitled, to child benefit for the child at that time; *or*
- immediately before s/he died, your late spouse or civil partner was entitled, or treated as entitled, to child benefit for the child;

and either:

- the child is living with you (see p63); *or*
- you are contributing to the cost of supporting her/him. The payments you make must be at least equal to the amount of any child benefit payable for that child (see p68) plus £13.45.

The latter condition (ie, that you satisfy one of the last two bullet points) is to be revoked but, at the time of writing, it was not known when this change will be introduced. In effect, however, this revocation will only reduce the amount of the contribution that you are required to pay to qualify for widowed parent's allowance if your child is not living with you. This is because, in order to qualify for widowed parent's allowance, you will still normally need to be entitled (or treated as entitled) to child benefit for an eligible child and to qualify for child benefit the child must either be living with you or you must be contributing to the cost of supporting her/him (see p63).[9] See CPAG's *Welfare Rights Bulletin* for updates.

You or your late spouse or civil partner can be treated as entitled to child benefit for a child if you would have been entitled to it had you claimed it, and had the child not been abroad.[10]

If you and your spouse or civil partner were living apart at the time of her/his death, you can still be considered to have been residing with her/him if your separation was only intended to be temporary.[11] See p693 for the meaning of 'residing with'.

There are special rules which may allow your late spouse or civil partner to be treated as entitled to child benefit if, prior to your marriage or civil partnership, you were previously widowed or your civil partner had died. If you might need to rely on this rule, seek advice.[12]

Disqualification and suspension

Entitlement to widowed parent's allowance ends if you marry or enter into a civil partnership, and you are not able to re-qualify for it even if you subsequently get divorced or if your civil partnership is dissolved. It is suspended during any period in which you are cohabiting (see p30) but is reinstated if you stop cohabiting.[13]

The rules about your age

There is no lower age limit for widowed parent's allowance. Anyone who is legally old enough to have married or formed a civil partnership may qualify. Widowed parent's allowance cannot be paid once you reach pension age (ie, 60 for women, 65 for men) but you may then qualify for a Category A or B retirement pension (see p465).

Claiming for others

Increases for your dependent children, which were abolished on 6 April 2003, could be claimed if you were entitled to basic widowed parent's allowance (and not just the additional earnings-related payment of widowed parent's allowance). You were only entitled to an increase for a child if s/he was an eligible child (see p22) and you were entitled to child benefit for her/him, (or, in some circumstances, you could be treated as entitled to child benefit while getting a family benefit from another country).[14] See p692 for the circumstances when, even if you are entitled to child benefit for a child, you are treated as if you are not.

If you were entitled to an increase for a dependent child on 5 April 2003 you may be able to continue to receive it after that date (see p691).

You cannot claim an increase in widowed parent's allowance for an adult dependant. (See pp26 and 30 for the effect of marriage, entering into a civil partnership and co-habitation on your entitlement to bereavement benefits.)

The amount of widowed parent's allowance

Widowed parent's allowance is made up of:

- a basic widowed parent's allowance (which may be paid at a reduced rate if your late spouse's or civil partner's NI record was incomplete – see below);
- an additional earnings-related payment based on your late spouse's or civil partner's earnings under the additional state pension scheme, if her/his NI contribution record qualifies you for this (see p476). You may be entitled to this even if her/his contribution record is not sufficient for you to qualify for basic widowed parent's allowance.[15]

	£pw
Basic widowed parent's allowance (full rate)	90.70
Increase for child dependant (but see p23):	
– eldest eligible child (for whom child benefit is paid)	8.75
– other eligible children (each)	11.35

If you are entitled to widowed parent's allowance you will also be entitled to a Christmas bonus (see p9).

See p33 for details of how to claim widowed parent's allowance.

Reduction in the basic widowed parent's allowance

You may receive a reduced rate of the basic widowed parent's allowance if your spouse's or civil partner's contribution record was incomplete (see p739).[16] If so, you may be able to increase your entitlement by paying Class 3 contributions on your spouse's or civil partner's behalf (which you may do even though s/he has died – see p725 for further details and p727 for the time limits for making such payments). Write to the Contributor Caseworker at the National Insurance Contributions Office in Newcastle (see Appendix 1), quoting your own NI number as well as your late spouse's or civil partner's, and ask whether you could benefit from this rule.

3. **Bereavement allowance**

Bereavement allowance is a weekly benefit paid for up to 52 weeks. You cannot receive both widowed parent's allowance and bereavement allowance at the same time, but you may qualify for bereavement allowance when your entitlement to widowed parent's allowance stops.

In addition to qualifying for bereavement allowance, you may also be entitled to a bereavement payment (see p20).

Who can claim bereavement allowance

You qualify for bereavement allowance if:[17]

- you are either:
  - a widow or widower and your spouse died on or after 9 April 2001 (see p26 for the meaning of widow and widower); *or*
  - from 5 December 2005, a surviving civil partner (see p26); *and*
- you were at least 45 years old when your spouse or civil partner died (see below); *and*
- you are under pension age (ie, under 60 for women, 65 for men); *and*
- not more than 52 weeks have passed since your spouse or civil partner died; *and*
- your late spouse or civil partner either:
  - satisfied the national insurance (NI) contribution conditions (see p738); *or*
  - died as the result of an industrial injury or disease (see p30).

Disqualification and suspension

Bereavement allowance ceases if you marry or form a civil partnership and you cannot re-qualify for it even if you subsequently get divorced or your civil partnership is dissolved. It is suspended while you are cohabiting but will be reinstated if you stop cohabiting (see p30).[18]

The rules about your age

You must be 45 or over at the time your spouse or civil partner died to qualify for bereavement allowance.

You cannot receive bereavement allowance if you are over pension age (ie, 60 or over for women or 65 or over for men). However, you may qualify for retirement pension based on your own or your late spouse's or civil partner's NI contributions (see Chapter 19).

Claiming for others

You cannot get an increase in your bereavement allowance for your dependants.

The amount of bereavement allowance

The full rate of bereavement allowance is £90.70 a week.[19]

Your bereavement allowance may be reduced, by the amounts below if:

- your late spouse's or civil partner's NI contribution record was incomplete; *or*
- you were under 55 when s/he died.

Your late spouse's or civil partner's contribution record

If your late spouse's or civil partner's NI contribution record was not complete, the amount of basic bereavement allowance you receive is reduced proportionately (see p739). Just as for widowed parent's allowance, you may be able to increase your entitlement by paying Class 3 contributions on your spouse's or civil partner's behalf (see p24).

Your age

Your bereavement allowance is reduced if you were under 55 when your spouse or civil partner died.[20] For each year, or part of a year, by which you were under 55 your bereavement allowance is reduced by 7 per cent. This percentage reduction remains the same for as long as you receive bereavement allowance.

The full rate of bereavement allowance is £90.70. So, if your spouse or civil partner had a complete NI contribution record the amount you would receive is as follows.

Age when spouse or civil partner died	*Rate of bereavement allowance (£pw)*
54	84.35
53	78.00
52	71.65
51	65.30
50	58.96
49	52.61
48	46.26
47	39.91
46	33.56
45	27.21

4. **Definition of terms**

Who counts as a widow, widower or surviving civil partner

In order to qualify for bereavement benefits you must be a widow, widower or surviving civil partner. If you have been bereaved more than once, your entitlement to bereavement benefits depends on the contribution record of your most recent spouse or civil partner.

If, following the death of your spouse or civil partner you marry or enter into a civil partnership, you are no longer a widow, widower or a surviving civil partner and lose all entitlement to widowed parent's allowance and bereavement allowance based on your previous spouse's or civil partner's contribution record.[21]

If you are cohabiting, see p30.

Widows and widowers

You are a widow or widower if you were married to your spouse at the date of her/his death and the marriage was considered valid under UK law. See p29 for details about invalid marriages.

In Scotland (but not the rest of Great Britain (GB)) you can also be a widow or widower if you were married 'by cohabitation with habit and repute' even if you did not go through a formal wedding ceremony. However, this only applies if your cohabitation with habit and repute began before 4 May 2006.[22] If so, to establish the existence of a marriage by cohabitation with habit and repute your relationship must have been more than simply living together, as there must have been something about it which meant that it could be inferred that you and your partner consented to marriage and nothing existed which would have prevented a valid marriage taking place (eg, either party already being married to someone else).[23] In addition, your relationship must have been such that other people generally believed that you were married.[24] If your cohabitation with habit and repute began on or after 4 May 2006 you will not be treated as married and therefore, will not count as a widow or widower if your partner dies (unless, in certain circumstances, you contracted a marriage abroad which you have since realised was invalid. If so, seek advice).

There is no equivalent to the Scottish marriage by cohabitation with habit and repute in the rest of GB. In one case, however, the Court of Appeal decided that a woman who was not actually married to her partner could be presumed to be validly married following a Sikh ceremony of marriage (held in England) and a long period of cohabitation. Although the temple in which the couple held their marriage ceremony was not registered for marriages, she believed herself to be married. The Court decided that she still counted as the man's widow.[25]

Surviving civil partners

You are a surviving civil partner if at the time of your partner's death you were civil partners and the civil partnership was valid under UK law. Civil partnerships were introduced in the UK from 5 December 2005. See p29 for details about invalid civil partnerships.

To count as civil partners you must have been registered as such in the UK or, in certain circumstances, have registered a legal relationship abroad (ie, under the law of another country). If your civil partnership was registered abroad, at a place such as a British consulate or as a result of a connection to the armed forces, you may also count as civil partners. If your partnership was registered abroad and you are uncertain about your rights, seek advice (see Appendix 2).[26]

Separation, divorce and dissolution

If you were divorced when your ex-spouse died, you are not a widow or widower. But in England and Wales, a divorce becomes effective only when the decree absolute is pronounced. So, if you were in the process of obtaining a divorce, you are still entitled to bereavement benefits if your spouse died before the decree was made absolute. In Scotland you are divorced when a decree of divorce is issued.

If you were living apart from your spouse when s/he died but without being divorced from her/him you are a widow or widower. This applies even if you were judicially separated as long as you were not actually divorced.

If your civil partnership had been dissolved when your civil partner died you will not be considered to be a surviving civil partner. A civil partnership is dissolved in England and Wales when a final dissolution order is issued or, in Scotland, when a decree of dissolution is granted. If you were separated from your civil partner when s/he died, but your civil partnership had not been dissolved you will still count as a surviving civil partner.

Your entitlement to bereavement benefits will be affected if the DWP disputes the validity of an earlier divorce or dissolution of a civil partnership. In this circumstance, seek advice.

Polygamous marriages

If your marriage was polygamous, you are not normally entitled to bereavement benefit following the death of your spouse. This is because, as a general rule, the law in England, Wales and Scotland does not treat a man and a woman as legally married unless their marriage is a monogamous one.[27]

A marriage is only considered polygamous if the law of the country where the marriage takes place permits either party to have another wife or husband.[28] Usually it is the husband who is allowed to have more than one wife but the rules apply in the same way if it is the wife who is permitted two or more husbands.[29] However, a polygamous marriage can give rise to an entitlement to bereavement benefits:

- if it is only potentially polygamous (ie, if neither the husband nor the wife has ever had more than one spouse); *or*
- when it is formerly polygamous (ie, if the husband or wife have had other spouses in the past but all such spouses have now died or been divorced),

but not on any day when it is actually polygamous (ie, the husband has more than one wife or the wife more than one husband).

This means that you are treated as a widow or widower if, on the day s/he died, neither you nor your spouse had any other husband or wife.

If you are refused bereavement benefits because your marriage was or is polygamous, you should take advice. The law on polygamous marriages is complex and it is possible that even if you think your marriage is polygamous, the law will not agree with you.

This depends on whether you were your spouse's first wife or husband and on where you and your spouse were 'domiciled' at the time of your marriage and any subsequent marriage. 'Domicile' is a difficult legal concept but, in very general terms, it means the country in which you have chosen to make your permanent home.[30] Domicile is not the same as 'presence' (see p1357), 'residence' (see p1357), 'ordinary residence' (see p1357) or nationality.

In particular, no one who is domiciled in England and Wales is allowed to contract a polygamous marriage anywhere in the world even if the local law allows it.[31]

Decision makers refer any questions about whether a marriage is to be treated as monogamous or polygamous to a special section of the DWP.

If the DWP considers that you were polygamously married because it disputes the validity of an earlier divorce, seek advice.

Example

At the time of their wedding, Shaznaz and her husband were domiciled in Pakistan and were married under Islamic law. After the wedding they came to live in England and made their permanent home here and had no intention of returning to live in Pakistan at any time. Later her husband returned temporarily to Pakistan and married a second wife. As her husband was domiciled in England rather than Pakistan at the time of the second marriage, English law does not recognise the second marriage and, therefore, regards Shaznaz as her late husband's only wife. Provided she meets the other conditions of entitlement, she is entitled to bereavement benefits.[32] If her husband had re-acquired domicile in Pakistan at the time of his second marriage, and his second wife was still alive, both marriages would be polygamous, and neither wife could claim bereavement benefits.[33]

A tribunal of commissioners has decided that it is not unlawful to deny bereavement benefits to widows of marriages that were actually polygamous at the time of the spouse's death.[34]

Void and voidable marriages and civil partnerships

Sometimes the law treats a marriage or civil partnership as invalid even though you have been through a marriage or registration ceremony.

A **void** marriage or civil partnership (eg, one where at least one of the partners was not eligible to marry or form a civil partnership) is invalid and from a legal point of view is treated as if it never existed (although for most practical purposes, it is necessary to confirm the position by getting a court order).[35]

A **voidable** marriage or civil partnership (eg, in England and Wales, a marriage that has not been consummated is voidable) can be annulled, and in England and Wales is treated as having been valid until a decree absolute of annulment is pronounced.[36]

As with polygamous marriages (see p28), questions about the validity of marriages or civil partnerships can be deceptively difficult. The DWP has a special unit that decides questions in this area. If it claims that your marriage or civil partnership was invalid, you should seek advice (see Appendix 2).

Proving that your spouse or civil partner is dead

It is up to you to prove to the DWP decision maker that your spouse or civil partner is dead and that you were married or were civil partners when s/he died.

Normally this is not a problem. When you register the death you get an extra death certificate for social security purposes, called a Certificate of Registration of Death. If you complete the form on the back and forward it to the DWP, you are sent the claim form for bereavement benefits. See p33 for further information about claiming bereavement benefits.

If your spouse's or civil partner's whereabouts are unknown

It may be difficult to establish your entitlement to bereavement benefits if your spouse or civil partner is missing and you think that s/he has died. In these circumstances, you can request that a decision maker at the DWP determines that your spouse or civil partner has died or can be presumed to have died.[37] If you are in this situation, seek advice.

See p37 for details of backdating bereavement benefits if you were unaware of your spouse's or civil partner's death.

Cohabitation

A bereavement payment will not be paid to you if you are cohabiting at the time of your spouse's or civil partner's death. In this chapter 'cohabiting' means:

- living with someone of the opposite sex as husband and wife; *or*
- living with someone of the same sex as if you are civil partners.

Your widowed parent's allowance or bereavement allowance is suspended if you are cohabiting, but becomes payable again if the cohabitation ends.[38]

Deciding whether or not you are cohabiting may not be straightforward. For information about whether you count as cohabiting, see p704.

If the DWP decides that you are cohabiting and you do not agree, you can challenge its decision (see Chapters 41 and 42).

Industrial accident or disease

The meaning of 'industrial accident or disease' is discussed on p314. To qualify for bereavement benefits the industrial accident or disease must have been a cause of death, but it need not have been a direct cause or the only cause.[39]

5. **Special benefit rules**

There are some groups of claimants to whom special rules apply. These are covered below and in Chapters 26 and 58. Special rules apply to:

- widows whose husbands died before 9 April 2001 (see below);
- widowers whose wives died before 9 April 2001 (see p32);
- people who have obtained a gender recognition certificate (see p32);
- people who are abroad (see p1349);
- people who are in prison or detention (see p625).

Widows whose husbands died before 9 April 2001

If your husband died before 9 April 2001 you are not entitled to bereavement benefits but instead may claim widows' benefits. Widows' benefits consist of widow's payment, widowed mother's allowance and widow's pension.

For an explanation of the main qualifying conditions for widows' benefits see the 2nd edition of this *Handbook* and see the table at the beginning of this edition for the current rates of widows' benefits.

You could only qualify for a **widow's payment** if you made a claim within three months of your husband's death (or within a longer period if you were not aware that he had died – see p128 of CPAG's *Welfare Benefits Handbook* 2000/01).

If you satisfy the qualifying conditions for **widowed mother's allowance**, you can continue to receive this for as long as you have an eligible child, as there is no upper age limit. Just as for widowed parent's allowance, a 'child' is someone who counts as a child or qualifying young person for child benefit purposes and it is the child benefit rules that are in force at the time for which payment is made or sought that are relevant. So, for example, changes to the child benefit rules from 10 April 2006, which allow child benefit to be paid for a qualifying young person until the age of 20, will apply to widowed mother's allowance from that date.

If your entitlement to widowed mother's allowance ends, or if you are not entitled to widowed mother's allowance, you may qualify for a **widow's pension**. This can be paid until you reach 65, if you satisfy the qualifying conditions.

If you were entitled to widows' benefits and invalidity benefit prior to 12 April 1995, you may benefit from transitional rules – see p132 of CPAG's *Welfare Benefits Handbook* 2000/01 for details.

Widows' benefits and retirement pension

If your husband died before 9 April 2001 and you are 60 or over you may be entitled to both retirement pension and either widow's pension or widowed mother's allowance. Because of the overlapping benefit rules you cannot receive both benefits in full at the same time but see p132 of CPAG's *Welfare Benefits Handbook* 2000/01 if you are in this position.

You may qualify for retirement pension on the basis of being a widow (see Chapter 19). Once you qualify for retirement pension, unlike widow's pension and widowed mother's allowance, your entitlement to it does not end if you marry or form a civil partnership. So it may be financially beneficial to delay marriage or the formation of a civil partnership until after pension age (see p466).

Widowers whose wives died before 9 April 2001

If you are a man and your wife died before 9 April 2001 you may be in a less favourable position than a woman whose husband died before 9 April 2001. This is because a woman whose husband died before 9 April 2001 may qualify for widows' benefits but you cannot. Although you can claim widowed parent's allowance this can only be paid until you reach 65. In contrast, a woman in the same position could claim widowed mother's allowance, which is payable after pension age if the other qualifying conditions are met.

The fact that there were no widowers' benefits equivalent to the widows' benefits available to women has been challenged on the basis that it breached the non-discrimination principle contained in the European Convention on Human Rights (ECHR).[40] For a discussion of the decisions in these cases and their consequences see CPAG's *Welfare Rights Bulletin* 198.

If you are a man and you are over pension age you may qualify for a Category B retirement pension based on your late wife's NI contribution record (see p466) or if you are incapable of work you may qualify for incapacity benefit under the special rules for widowers (see p277).

People who have obtained a gender recognition certificate

If you have been living in the opposite gender or have changed gender and you have obtained a full gender recognition certificate, your entitlement to bereavement and widows' benefits may be affected. (An interim gender recognition certificate does not affect your benefit entitlement.) The following is a summary of some of the rules. If you are likely to be affected by them, seek advice.[41]

- You must dissolve or annul any existing marriage or civil partnership in order to obtain a full gender recognition certificate. Once you have done so, you will not be entitled to bereavement benefits on the basis of your ex-spouse's or former civil partner's contribution record if s/he subsequently dies.
- If you were still married or in a civil partnership at the time of your spouse's or civil partner's death, you may qualify for bereavement benefits even if, after the death, you obtain a full gender recognition certificate. However, on the issue of a full certificate any entitlement to:
  - widow's pension will end;
  - widowed mother's allowance will end but you will instead qualify for widowed parent's allowance.

- Your pension age will change to 60 if you have been recognised as a woman, or 65 if you have been recognised as a man.[42]

6. Claims and backdating

To be entitled to bereavement benefits you must usually make a claim (but see below for an exception).[43] The rules on claiming are outlined below. For more details on claims, see Chapter 38. It may be possible to claim in advance (see p35) or to get your claim backdated (see p36). If you wish, you may amend or withdraw your claim before it is assessed by writing to the DWP.

Making a claim

From 24 September 2007, if you are over pension age (ie, 60 or over if you are a woman, 65 or over, if you are a man) you do not need to make a claim in order to qualify for a bereavement payment. (**Note:** this may help you to qualify for a bereavement payment if it is more than 12 months since your spouse or civil partner died – see p20). However, as detailed on p20, the DWP states that this rule is currently more generous than intended and an amendment is planned.

In the interim, if you were over pension age when your spouse or civil partner died and you were both receiving retirement pension when s/he died, you do not need to complete a claim form for a bereavement payment although it is advisable to ensure the DWP is aware of the death. The DWP prefers that you do this by telephoning the Pension Service (see Appendix 1). If you are over pension age, but either you were under pension age when your spouse or civil partner died, or you and your spouse or civil partner were not both receiving retirement pension when s/he died, then although it is not currently a condition of entitlement to a bereavement payment that you make a claim, the DWP will ask you to complete a claim form (Form BB1) and send it to the DWP office that covers your local area (see below) in order for your entitlement to be considered.

If you want to claim widowed parent's allowance or bereavement allowance, or you are under pension age and want to claim a bereavement payment, your claim *must* be in writing and must usually be made on the correct application form (a BB1 form). This form serves as a claim for a bereavement payment, widowed parent's allowance and bereavement allowance and can be obtained by telephoning Jobcentre Plus (tel: 0800 055 6688 or 0800 012 1888 for Welsh speakers; textphone 0800 023 4888) or can be downloaded from the Jobcentre Plus website (www.jobcentreplus.gov.uk).

In certain circumstances, the decision maker may accept a written application which is not on the correct form (see p959).[44] Your completed claim should be sent to the DWP office which covers your local area (usually this will be a regional benefit delivery centre). If an envelope with the relevant address is not included with the form, you can obtain the address from your local Jobcentre Plus or DWP office, or by telephoning Jobcentre Plus (see above). If you are 60 or over you may also be able to make your claim by taking or sending it to a designated local authority or English county council office or other 'alternative office' (see p958 for details). It is advisable to keep a copy of your claim form in case queries arise.

For more details about making a claim, see p955.

Information to support your claim

When you claim bereavement benefits, you must satisfy what is known as the 'national insurance (NI) number requirement' (unless you are not required to make a claim because you are over pension age and are just entitled to a bereavement payment – see above). In most cases this means you must provide your NI number.[45] See p962 for further details.

You can also be asked to supply 'certificates, documents, information and evidence' considered relevant to your claim, such as your spouse's or civil partner's death certificate or the Certificate of Registration of Death (see p30 if you do not have proof of whether your spouse or civil partner has died), and your marriage or civil partnership certificate, if you have one.[46] A commissioner's decision has given guidance on assessing evidence from countries where reliable documentary proof of life events such as marriage may not be available.[47] It is best to send evidence or documents relating to your claim to the office handling the claim. If you are 60 or over, a designated local authority or English county council office or other 'alternative office' may also be able to accept evidence and documents from you in connection with your claim (see p958).

The DWP may not need to verify evidence used by the local authority in connection with your housing or council tax benefit claim (see p961).

If you are asked to provide evidence or documents which you do not have, ask what other evidence would be acceptable. Ask the DWP to explain what is required and why, and complain if you feel any requests for information are unreasonable.

See p961 for further of evidence which may be required to support your claim.

Who should claim

You must normally claim bereavement benefits yourself. However, bereavement benefits can be claimed by another adult on your behalf if you are not able to act for yourself. This person is known as your 'appointee' (see p955 for details).

The date of your claim

From 24 September 2007, if you are over pension age, you do not need to make a claim in order to qualify for a bereavement payment (but see p20). However, to qualify for widowed parent's allowance, bereavement allowance, and, if you are under pension age, for a bereavement payment you must make a claim. The date of your claim is important as it determines the date from which you will be paid widowed parent's allowance or bereavement allowance (see p38) and, if you are under pension age, whether you will qualify for a bereavement payment. The date of your claim is normally the date it is received at a DWP or Jobcentre Plus office or, if you are 60 or over and submit your claim to a designated local authority, English county council or other 'alternative office' (see p958), the date it is received by that office.[48] A claim can be counted as having been received even on a day when the office is closed if that is the day it would have normally been delivered.[49]

If the claim you submit is incomplete or not on the correct form you may be asked to provide further information or to complete the correct form. As long as this additional information or form is received by the DWP within a month of it being sent back to you (or longer if the decision maker thinks that the delay is reasonable), your claim can be treated as made on the date that the initial claim was received.[50]

In some circumstances you can claim before you qualify for bereavement benefits (see below) or the date of your claim can be backdated (see p36).

See p37 if you claim late because you did not know that your spouse or civil partner had died.

If you claim the wrong benefit

The decision maker may treat a claim for retirement pension as a claim for bereavement benefits.[51] This may help you qualify for a bereavement payment although, from 24 September 2007, if you are pension age or over, you may qualify for a bereavement payment even if you have not made a claim (see p20). A claim for retirement pension may also allow you to get your widowed parent's allowance or bereavement allowance backdated for more than the normal three months (see p36). If your retirement pension claim is accepted as a claim for widowed parent's allowance or bereavement allowance, your claim can be backdated for up to three months from the date of your retirement pension claim if you satisfy the qualifying conditions over that period.

See p963 for details of interchanging claims in this way.

Claiming in advance

You can claim bereavement benefits up to three months before you expect to qualify. In most circumstances you will not know of your need to claim benefit in advance, but this may be relevant if, for example, you know that you will no longer be cohabiting.[52]

How your claim is dealt with

In certain circumstances your entitlement to a bereavement payment will be dealt with by the Pension Service (see p33). Otherwise, your claim is dealt with by the DWP office that covers your local area (usually this will be a regional benefit delivery centre), although that office may refer certain questions on your claim to other offices. Queries about your claim should be made to the office covering your area.

You may be able to claim an interim payment while waiting for a decision on your claim (see p986) or to claim means-tested benefits or tax credits if your income is low (see p39). You may also be able to apply for a crisis loan if you need money to tide you over (see Chapter 21).

See p970 for more information on the processing of claims.

Backdating your claim

A claim for a **bereavement payment** must usually be made within 12 months of your spouse's or civil partner's death, unless:

- your spouse died before 1 April 2003 when it had to be made within three months of her/his death (but see p21 if you and your spouse or civil partner were not in GB when s/he died); *or*
- you were not aware that your spouse or civil partner had died (see p37); *or*
- from 24 September 2007, you are pension age or over (ie, at least 60 for a woman, 65 for a man), when it is not necessary for you to make a claim to qualify (see p20 for details, including details of a possible amendment to this rule).

There is no time limit for claiming **widowed parent's allowance** or **bereavement allowance** and payment of these benefits can be backdated for up to three months before the date that you make your claim, if you satisfy the qualifying conditions over that period. You do not need to show reasons why your claim was late (see p964). So, as long as you claim widowed parent's allowance or bereavement allowance within three months of your spouse's or civil partner's death you will not lose any money. If you were not aware of your spouse's or civil partner's death you may be able to get your claim backdated further (see p37). However, it is important to remember that bereavement allowance is only payable for the 52-week period running from the date your spouse or civil partner died.

If you might have qualified for benefit earlier but did not claim because you were given the wrong information or were misled by the DWP you could ask for an *ex gratia* payment (see p1186) or complain to the Independent Case Examiner or Ombudsman via your MP (see pp1181 and 1184).

See p35 if you claimed retirement pension instead of bereavement benefits.

See p965 for more details about backdating claims.

If you were unaware of your spouse's or civil partner's death

If you were not aware that your spouse or civil partner had died then, in the following circumstances, the time limit for claiming a bereavement payment and the normal three-month time limit on backdating of widowed parent's allowance and bereavement allowance can be extended.

If you claim within 12 months of your spouse's or civil partner's death

From 11 April 2005 (or for civil partners, from 5 December 2005), if:[53]

- the death of your spouse or civil partner has been difficult to establish but s/he has been found to have died or is presumed by the DWP to have died (whether or not her/his body has been found or identified); *and*
- you claim bereavement benefit within 12 months of your spouse's or civil partner's death or presumed death,

your claim can be backdated to the date s/he died or is presumed to have died, as long as you meet the other conditions of entitlement over that period.

If it is more than 12 months since your spouse or civil partner died

The time limit for claiming may be extended further if it is more than 12 months since your spouse or civil partner died or since the date that s/he is presumed to have died and *either:*

- your spouse's or civil partner's body has not been found or identified (or if it has you were not aware of this when you asked the decision maker at the DWP to decide whether s/he had died); *and*
- the decision maker has decided that your spouse or civil partner has died or that it can be presumed s/he is dead; *and*
- you claim bereavement benefits within 12 months of the decision maker's decision;

or

- your spouse's or civil partner's body has been found or identified and you learn of this within 12 months of the discovery or identification; *and*
- you claim bereavement benefits within 12 months of finding out about her/his death.

Bereavement benefits can be backdated to the date that the decision maker has determined was the date of your spouse's or civil partner's death in the former situation. In the latter circumstances, bereavement benefits can only be backdated for a maximum of two years. This is because you must claim within 12 months of finding out about your spouse's or civil partner's death and, in turn, you must have learnt about your spouse's or civil partner's death within 12 months of her/his body being identified.[54]

7. Getting paid

A **bereavement payment** is a lump-sum one-off payment.

Widowed parent's allowance and **bereavement allowance** are weekly benefits and so cannot be paid for periods of less than a week. Payment of widowed parent's allowance or bereavement allowance is normally made by direct credit transfer into your bank (or similar account).[55] If you are unable to open or manage an account payment can be made by cheque (see p978).

Payments are normally made either four-weekly in arrears or weekly in advance on a Tuesday, although the DWP may choose another day as your normal payday.[56] If you qualify for widowed parent's allowance or bereavement allowance, payments will normally run from the first payday after the date of your claim (see p34), unless the date of your claim is on your payday, when they will run from that day.[57]

If the amount of benefit to which you are entitled is less than £5 a week a decision maker at the DWP can decide how often you are paid, although you must be paid at least once a year.[58]

Payment of bereavement benefits may be made to someone else on your behalf if you are unable to act for yourself (called your 'appointee' – see p955).

If your entitlement to widowed parent's allowance or bereavement allowance ends, payment of benefit will continue up to, but not including, the following payday (ie, the following Tuesday unless the DWP has chosen another day as your normal payday). However, if your entitlement ends on a payday your benefit will be paid up to, but not including, that day.

If your benefit is not paid into your account or your benefit cheque is lost or stolen, see p983. If payment of your widowed parent's allowance or bereavement allowance is suspended, see p984.

You may not be paid widowed parent's allowance or bereavement allowance if you have been sanctioned for benefit offences (see p1047).

Delays and complaints

If payments of your bereavement benefits are delayed, you might be able to get an interim payment. See p986 for further details.

If you experience delays, or wish to complain about how your claim has been dealt with, see Chapter 46. You might be able to claim compensation (see p1186).

Change of circumstances

You must report any change in your circumstances which the DWP has informed you that you must tell it about (but it is important to remember that the DWP might not inform you of all the changes you need to tell it about). It is your duty also to report changes which you might reasonably be expected to know might affect your entitlement to, the amount of, or the payment of your benefit.[59] You should report such changes promptly either by writing to or telephoning the office handling your claim (unless the DWP has decided that you can tell it about the change another way). In some cases, the decision maker might say you must report changes in writing. In practice, it is *always* advisable to report the change in writing or to confirm a telephone conversation in writing and keep a copy of your letter in case of a dispute in the future. If you do not promptly report any such change, any resulting overpayment may be recoverable from you (see Chapter 39). If you are considered deliberately to have acted falsely or dishonestly, you may also be guilty of an offence (see Chapter 40).

Widowed parent's allowance and bereavement allowance are normally awarded for an indefinite period, unless your circumstances are likely to change shortly after the award.[60] For payment of benefit to be stopped or adjusted, the decision on your entitlement must first be revised or superseded (see Chapter 41). If, following a change in your circumstances, the decision on your claim is superseded and your entitlement to benefit is affected, the date from which the new decision takes effect depends on whether or not it is advantageous to you and whether you reported the change in time (see p1080 for further details).

Overpayments and fraud

If you are overpaid bereavement benefits, you might have to repay them. The rules on overpayments are covered in Chapter 39.

If you have been accused of fraud, see Chapter 40.

8. Challenging bereavement benefit decisions

You can apply for a revision or supersession of a bereavement benefit decision, or appeal against it (see Chapters 41 and 42).

Certain decisions are not open to appeal, although you can request that such decisions be revised or superseded (see p1097).[61]

9. Tax, tax credits and other benefits

The lump-sum bereavement payment is not taxable. Widowed parent's allowance and bereavement allowance are taxable apart from any increase to widowed parent's allowance for children.[62]

Tax credits

If your income is low and you work for sufficient hours each week (see Chapter 50) you may qualify for working tax credit (WTC – see Chapter 49) as well as bereavement benefits. If you have at least one dependent child you may also qualify for child tax credit (CTC – see Chapter 48). Bereavement payment is ignored when calculating your entitlement to WTC and CTC. Widowed parent's allowance counts as pension income for WTC and CTC (and it may be possible to ignore some of your pension income – see p1263 for details). Bereavement allowance counts in full as benefit income (see p1258). If you are at least 50 and are entitled to WTC, receipt of widowed parent's allowance or bereavement allowance may help you to qualify for a 50-plus element within your WTC (see p1239).[63]

Means-tested benefits

If you have a low income, in addition to bereavement benefits, you may be entitled to means-tested benefits. A bereavement payment is counted as capital for the purposes of all means-tested benefits. Widowed parent's allowance and bereavement allowance (less any tax payable on them) are counted as income. However, £10 of your weekly widowed parent's allowance is ignored when calculating your entitlement to income-based jobseeker's allowance[64] (JSA – see Chapter 15), income support[65] (IS – see Chapter 13) and pension credit (PC – see Chapter 18).[66]

£15 of your weekly widowed parent's allowance or widowed mother's allowance (see p31) is ignored when calculating your entitlement to housing benefit[67] (HB – see Chapter 10) and council tax benefit[68] (CTB – see Chapter 5). However, if you are getting both widowed parent's allowance and only the savings credit of PC, the income used to calculate your HB and CTB is that used by the DWP to calculate your entitlement to PC (which includes only a £10 disregard from your widowed parent's allowance).

Bereavement allowance is counted in full as income when calculating your entitlement to income-based JSA, IS, HB, CTB and PC.

If your partner was entitled to HB when s/he died and you claim HB within a month of her/his death, your HB claim can be treated as made on the date your partner died (see p204). The same rule applies for CTB. In some circumstances you can get your HB or CTB claim backdated further (see pp207 and 92).

Non-means-tested benefits

Your entitlement to non-means-tested benefits is not affected by your entitlement to a bereavement payment.

Widowed parent's allowance and bereavement allowance are affected by the overlapping benefit rules and so you may not qualify for these benefits if another earnings replacement benefit is being paid to you (see p981).

If you are still receiving an increase in your widowed parent's allowance for a child or young person (see p23), the amount of that increase is adjusted if you receive child benefit for her/him paid at the rate for the eldest eligible child (see p23).

You cannot receive both guardian's allowance for a child or young person and an increase in your widowed parent's allowance for the same child or young person.[69]

Once you reach pension age you may qualify for a Category A or B retirement pension on the basis of your late spouse's or civil partner's national insurance (NI) contribution record (see p465).

When your bereavement benefit stops you may qualify for NI credits for incapacity benefit and JSA (see p731 for details).[70]

Passports and other sources of help

If you are on a low income, you might be entitled to certain health service benefits (see Chapter 9), free school meals for your children (see p15) or for other sources of help (see p14). You may also qualify for a social fund payment (see Chapters 21 and 22), and in particular to a grant for funeral expenses from the social fund (see p515).

For advice about preparing funerals and registering deaths, obtain DWP leaflet D49, *What to Do After a Death in England and Wales* or *What to Do After a Death in Scotland,* published by the Scottish Executive Justice Department.

Notes

1. **Bereavement payment**
   1 ss36 and 60(2) and (3) SSCBA 1992; regs 3(da) and 19(3A) SS(C&P) Regs
   2 Reg 3(da) SS(C&P) Regs
   3 s36(2) SSCBA 1992
   4 Reg 4(2B) SSB(PA) Regs
   5 Sch 4 Part II SSCBA 1992

2. **Widowed parent's allowance**
   6 ss39A and 60(2) and (3) SSCBA 1992
   7 Reg 16ZA SS(WB&RP) Regs
   8 ss39A(3), 77(5) and 122(5) SSCBA 1992
   9 s39A(3) SSCBA 1992, as it is to be amended by s51 WRA 2007
   10 Reg 16ZA SS(WB&RP) Regs
   11 Reg 2(4) SSB(PRT) Regs
   12 Reg 16ZA(2) SS(WB&RP) Regs
   13 s39A(4) and (5)(b) SSCBA 1992
   14 ss80(5) and 81 SSCBA 1992; Art 3 TCA(No.3)O; reg 4A(4) SSB(Dep) Regs
   15 Reg 6(2) SS(WB&RP) Regs
   16 Reg 6 SS(WB&RP) Regs

3. **Bereavement allowance**
   17 ss39B and 60(2) and (3) SSCBA 1992
   18 s39B(4) and (5) SSCBA 1992
   19 ss39C and 44 SSCBA 1992
   20 s39C(5) SSCBA 1992

4. **Definition of terms**
   21 ss39A(4) and 39B(4) SSCBA 1992
   22 R(G) 5/83; s3 Family Law (Scotland) Act 2006; Family Law (Scotland) Act 2006 (Commencement, Transitional Provisions and Savings) Order 2006 No.212
   23 R(G) 1/71
   24 CSG/7/1995; CSG/681/2003
   25 *CAO v Bath, The Times*, 28 October 1999 (CA), reported as R(G) 1/00; but see also R(G)2/70
   26 s1 CPA 2004
   27 *Hyde v Hyde* [1866]; reg 2 SSFA(PM) Regs
   28 Reg 1(2) SSFA(PM) Regs

29 Reg 1(4) SSFA(PM) Regs; s6 IA 1978
30 R(S) 2/92
31 s11(3) MCA 1973
32 R(G) 1/95
33 R(G) 1/93
34 R(P) 2/06
35 R(G) 2/63
36 R(G) 1/73
37 paras 10469-94 DMG
38 ss39A(5) and 39B(5) SSCBA 1992
39 CI/142/1949; R(I) 14/51

5. **Special benefit rules**

40 *Willis v United Kingdom*, No.36042/97, unreported, 11 June 2002 (ECtHR); *Runkee and White v United Kingdom*, Nos. 42949/98 and 53134/99, unreported 10 May 2007, (ECtHR)
41 ss4 and 5 and Sch 5 paras 3-5 GRA 2004
42 But see also *Richards v Secretary of State for Work and Pensions* C-423/04, unreported, 27 April 2006 (ECJ); R(P) 1/07; *Grant v United Kingdom*, No.32570/03, unreported, 23 May 2006 (ECtHR); CP/3485/2003

6. **Claims and backdating**

43 s1 SSAA 1992
44 Reg 4(1) SS(C&P) Regs
45 s1(1A) and (1B) SSAA 1992
46 Reg 7(1) SS(C&P) Regs
47 CP/4062/2004
48 Reg 6(1) SS(C&P) Regs
49 R(SB) 8/89
50 Regs 4(7) and 6(1) SS(C&P) Regs
51 Reg 9(1) and Sch 1 Part I SS(C&P) Regs
52 Reg 13 SS(C&P) Regs
53 Reg 19(3B) SS(C&P) Regs
54 CG/7235/1995

7. **Getting paid**

55 Reg 21 SS(C&P) Regs
56 Reg 22(1) and (3) and Sch 6 para 6 SS(C&P) Regs
57 Reg 16(1) SS(C&P) Regs
58 Reg 22(2) SS(C&P) Regs
59 Reg 32(1)-(1C) SS(C&P) Regs
60 Reg 17 SS(C&P) Regs

8. **Challenging bereavement benefit decisions**

61 s12(1) and Sch 2 SSA 1998; regs 3(8) and 6(2)(d) SS&CS(DA) Regs

9. **Tax, tax credits and other benefits**

62 ss577-79, 661 and 676 IT(EP)A 2003
63 Reg 18(9) WTC(EMR) Regs
64 Reg 103 and Sch 7 para 17(e) JSA Regs
65 Reg 40 and Sch 9 para 16(h) IS Regs
66 Sch IV para 7 SPC Regs
67 Reg 40 and Sch 5 para 16 HB Regs; reg 29 and Sch 5 paras 7 and 8 HB(SPC) Regs
68 Reg 30 and Sch 4 para 17 CTB Regs; reg 19 and Sch 3 paras 7 and 8 CTB(SPC) Regs
69 Reg 7(4) SS(OB) Regs
70 Reg 8C SS(Cr) Regs

Chapter 3

Carer's allowance

This chapter covers:

Carer's allowance (CA) is paid to people who care for someone who is severely disabled. You do not have to have paid national insurance contributions to qualify for CA. Although your entitlement depends on the level of any earnings that you have, it is not affected by the level of your savings. Before 1 April 2003 CA was called invalid care allowance.[1]

1. Who can claim carer's allowance

You qualify for carer's allowance (CA) if:[2]

- you satisfy the residence conditions (see p1358);
- you are not a 'person subject to immigration control' (see p1334);[3]
- you are caring for a person receiving either the highest or middle rate of disability living allowance (DLA) care component (see p107), attendance allowance (AA) (see p117) or constant attendance allowance in respect of industrial or war disablement (see p326). You do not have to be the person's relative, nor do you have to live with her/him;
- the care you give is regular and substantial (see p44);
- you are not gainfully employed or in full-time education (see pp45 and 45);
- you are aged 16 or over.

There are some groups of claimants to whom special rules apply (see p46).

Note:[4]

- Only one person can qualify for CA for caring for the same disabled person. If you cannot agree on who this should be, the DWP decides.
- If you care for two or more disabled people you can still only qualify for one award of CA.

Regularly and substantially caring

To qualify for CA you must be engaged in caring for a disabled person 'regularly and substantially'. You satisfy this requirement during any week in which you are (or are likely to be) engaged and regularly engaged in caring for her/him for 35 hours or more.[5] For CA, a week runs from Sunday to Saturday.[6] Caring might include supervision as well as assistance. If some of the time is spent preparing for the disabled person to come to stay with you, or clearing up after her/his visit, this can also count towards the 35 hours.[7]

Note:

- You cannot average the hours in one week with those in another – eg, if you care 35 hours or more in some weeks and less than 35 in others.[8] The rules require that you care for at least 35 hours in the week in question.
- If you are caring for two or more disabled people, you can only qualify for CA if you are caring for at least one of them for 35 hours or more a week.[9] You cannot add together the hours you are caring for all of them to make up the 35.

Breaks from caring

Once you have been caring for a disabled person for a while, temporary breaks in your care do not lead to the loss of your benefit. If you have been providing care for at least 35 hours a week in 22 of the last 26 weeks (or for at least 14 of the last 26 weeks, and the reason you did not provide care for 22 weeks was that either you or the disabled person were in hospital or in a similar institution), you can still get CA. Weeks before you claimed CA can be counted. Effectively, you can have four weeks' break from caring in any period of six months, or 12 weeks' break if one of you was in hospital or in a similar institution for at least eight weeks.[10] See p612 for the meaning of 'similar institution'.

CA stops if the DLA, AA or constant attendance allowance of the person for whom you are caring stops because s/he is in hospital or certain other special sorts of accommodation (see Chapter 26).[11]

If the person receiving care dies

If the person you care for dies, you continue to be entitled to CA for a further eight weeks, even though you are no longer providing care, as long as you satisfy the other qualifying conditions. The eight-week period runs from the Sunday following the death unless the death occurred on a Sunday, when it runs from that day.[12]

Gainfully employed

You cannot qualify for CA if you are 'gainfully employed'. You count as gainfully employed if your earnings in the previous week (from employment and/or self-employment) were more than £95. For the way earnings are calculated, see p832.[13] Your earnings are ignored if you are working during a period when you are not actually caring for the disabled person – eg, because s/he is in hospital or you are on your four weeks' break from caring (see p44).[14]

Full-time education

If you are in 'full-time education' you cannot get CA. The rules on what counts as full-time education for CA are different from those for other benefits (see p590).[15]

2. The rules about your age

You can claim carer's allowance (CA) if you are aged 16 or over.[16] There is no upper age limit.

Note: if you qualify for retirement pension as well as CA you are not paid both benefits in full because of the overlapping benefit rules (see p981).

Age rules before 1994 and 2002

Before 28 October 2002: To qualify for invalid care allowance (ICA) (now called CA) after your 65th birthday you had to have been entitled to it before you were 65. If you were, after you reached 65 some of the qualifying conditions were relaxed and you could continue to get ICA even if you no longer cared for the disabled person or you started gainful employment (see above). If you were aged 65 or over and entitled to ICA (or you would have been entitled but for the overlapping benefit rules – see p981) immediately before 28 October 2002, you can continue to receive CA on this basis.[17]

Before 28 October 1994: There were different upper age limits for claiming ICA for men and women (60 for women, 65 for men). This discrimination was found to be unlawful and the upper age limit was changed to 65 for both men and women from 28 October 1994 (until 28 October 2002). Women who were 65 before 28 October 1994 and who would have qualified for ICA but for the discriminatory age rules may still be able to claim now, whether or not they claimed before, even if they no longer care for a disabled person or are gainfully employed.[18] If you are in this situation, seek advice.

3. Claiming for others

If you are the person providing care you can claim the basic rate of carer's allowance (CA) for yourself. If s/he resides with you, you can also claim an increase for your spouse or civil partner, or for someone who cares for a child or young person for whom you get child benefit (see Chapter 29). If you have been entitled to an increase in your CA for your partner for at least six months and you are both 18 or over but under 60, the benefit rules state that your partner may be required to take part in a work-focused interview and your benefit can be reduced if s/he fails to do so without good cause (see p972). However the DWP states that, in practice, it does not require partners to attend such interviews in connection with CA claims.

You may choose not to claim increases to which you may be entitled if, for example, this would take you over the income limit for income support or income-based jobseeker's allowance (but see p52).

Increases for dependent children

Increases for your dependent children, whichcould be claimed with CA, were abolished on 6 April 2003. However, if you were entitled to an increase in your CA for a dependent child on 5 April 2003 you may be able to continue to receive it after that date (see p691).

4. The amount of benefit

The amount of carer's allowance (CA) you get depends on whether you are claiming for any dependants (see p45).[19]

	£pw
Claimant	50.55
Adult dependant	30.20
Child dependant (first child)	8.75
Child dependant (each subsequent child)	11.35

While receiving CA, you are credited with Class 1 national insurance contributions (see p729).

5. Special benefit rules

Special rules may apply to you if:

- you have come from or are going abroad (see Chapter 58);
- you, or the person you are caring for, are in hospital (see p614);
- the person you are caring for goes into a care home or other special accommodation (see p621);
- you, or the person you are caring for, is a prisoner (see p625).

6. Claims and backdating

The rules about claiming and backdating are in Chapter 38. This section tells you about the specific rules that apply to carer's allowance (CA). If you are claiming a means-tested benefit see p52 before you decide whether to also claim CA, as the effect of CA on your other benefits (and possibly those of the person for whom you care) means it is not always advisable for you to claim it.

If the person for whom you are caring has recently been awarded the highest or middle rate care component of disability living allowance (DLA), attendance allowance (AA) or constant attendance allowance and you choose to claim CA, you should claim within three months of the decision to award this benefit to her/him, or you may lose benefit (see p50).

Making a claim

A claim for CA must be made in writing and must be on Form DS700 (unless you get retirement pension, in which case you can use a shorter form – Form DS700(SP). You must complete the form and provide any information or evidence required (see p48). In certain circumstances, the DWP may accept a written application not on the approved form (see p959).

CA forms can be obtained from your local Jobcentre Plus or other DWP office or can be printed from www.direct.gov.uk/carers. You can also ring either the Carer's Allowance Unit on 01253 856123 (textphone 01772 899489), your local DWP telephone contact centre (see p956) or the Benefit Enquiry Line on 0800 882200 (textphone 0800 243355) to obtain a claim form.

You should send your completed claim form to the Carer's Allowance Unit, Palatine House, Lancaster Road, Preston PR1 1HB. You may also be able to make your claim by taking or sending it to an 'alternative office' – see p958 for details.

Alternatively, you can claim CA by completing an online application form and submitting it to the DWP over the internet as long as the DWP accepts this form of communication from you (see below).

Whichever procedure you follow, it is advisable to keep a copy of your claim form in case queries arise.

See p955 for the detailed rules on making a claim.

Using the internet

As well as sending claims and information by post, in certain circumstances you may use the internet to:[20]

- make a claim for CA;
- make a claim for an increase in your CA for an adult dependant;
- notify the DWP of a change in your circumstances.

You can do this by logging on to www.direct.gov.uk/carers, looking up CA, following the links for the CA e-service and completing the claim form or relevant change of circumstances form online. After submitting the relevant form you are given a transaction number. You should keep a record of this in case problems arise, as it can be used to trace your claim or notification. Although in many circumstances the decision maker has the power not to accept the above information or a claim from you when it is sent online, as long as you submit the information or claim through the website (rather than by email), using the forms on the site when appropriate, and follow the procedure given on the website for submitting the information or claim, this would be unusual.

Note: at the time of publication it was not possible to send any documents or papers to support your claim over the internet. You have to forward these separately to the DWP by post.

Information to support your claim

When you claim CA, you must satisfy the 'national insurance (NI) number requirement'. In most cases this means you must provide your NI number, as well as that of any adult dependant for whom you are claiming (see p962). You may also be asked to provide proof of your idenity (see p962).

You can also be asked to supply 'certificates, documents, information and evidence' considered relevant to your claim.[21] You must provide the information or evidence wihin one month. A decision maker can allow you longer than this if s/he thinks it is reasonable. The one-month time limit runs from the date of the request, *not* the date you made your claim for CA.

It is best to send evidence or documents relating to your claim to the Carer's Allowance Unit. However, evidence and documents can also be taken or sent to your local DWP or Jobcentre Plus office, or to an 'alternative office' (see p958).

The CA claim forms (including the internet form) contain a declaration to be completed by the person you care for, or the person acting for her/him. This asks for confirmation that you provide 35 hours' care a week and explains that her/his benefit may be affected if your claim is successful. Her/his benefit is only affected if s/he receives a severe disability premium in her/his income support (IS), income-based jobseeker's allowance (JSA), housing benefit or council tax benefit, or an additional amount for severe disability in her/his pension credit (PC) – see p784. Even if this declaration is not completed, the DWP should still make a decision on your claim, although failure to return it is likely to lead to a delay in the decision and, if it raises questions about the level of care you provide, may result in a refusal of your claim.

Who should claim

You must normally claim CA on your own behalf. However, CA can be claimed by another adult on your behalf if you are unable to act for yourself. This person is called your 'appointee' (see p955 for further details).

Before deciding whether to claim, you should be aware of how CA affects your entitlement to means-tested benefits and that of the person for whom you care (see p52).

The date of your claim

The date of your claim is important as it determines the date from which you are awarded CA. In some cases you can claim in advance (see below) and sometimes your claim can be backdated (see p50). If you want this to be done you should make this clear when you claim or the DWP might not consider it.

Your **'date of claim'** is usually the date on which your completed claim form is received at the DWP or a designated 'alternative office' (see p958).[22]

However, if you make a claim for CA in writing, but not on the approved form (see p47), or if the claim form you submit is incomplete, you may be asked to provide further information or to complete the approved form properly. As long as this additional information or form is returned within a month of it being sent back to you (or longer if the decision maker thinks it is reasonable – see p959), the decision maker must treat your claim as made on the date that your initial written claim or form was received.[23] If you submit your claim online via the government website (see p47), your date of claim is usually the date it is received, although a decision maker has the discretion to treat it as having been received on an earlier or later date than this.[24]

If you claim the wrong benefit

If you claim IS when you should have claimed CA , either in addition to or instead of IS, a decision maker can treat your IS claim as a claim for CA (see p963).[25] This rule may enable you to get round the strict time limits on backdating (see p50). Decision makers are not obliged to treat an IS claim as a claim for CA, and there is no right of appeal against a decision not to do so. The only legal challenge is by judicial review.[26]

Claiming in advance

You can claim CA up to three months before you qualify. This gives the DWP time to ensure you receive benefit as soon as you are entitled.[27] The decision maker can award benefit from a future date if s/he believes that you will satisfy all the CA qualifying conditions on that date. You may want to consider claiming in advance – eg, if you are currently earning more than £95 a week but you plan to stop work or reduce your hours.

How your claim is dealt with

A decision on your claim is made by a decision maker at the Carer's Allowance Unit. The DWP aims to deal with new claims for CA within three weeks.

Backdating your claim

It is very important to claim in time. A claim for CA can usually only be backdated for a maximum of three months.[28] You must satisfy the qualifying conditions over that period. You do not have to show any reasons why your claim was late. The general rules on backdating are covered on p964.

Your claim can be backdated for more than three months if:[29]

- you claim CA within three months of a decision to award a 'qualifying benefit' to the person for whom you care (including a decision made by an appeal tribunal, commissioner or court). Your CA is backdated to the date from which the qualifying benefit is payable. This does not apply if the decision awarding the qualifying benefit was made following a renewal claim where a fixed period award has ended or is due to end. In this case, the normal backdating rule applies and your CA can be backdated for up to three months. **Note:** if the person for whom you care has made a renewal claim for a qualifying benefit, you may need to make a claim for CA within 10 days to protect your position, in case the award of the qualifying benefit expires before a decision is made on the renewal claim. Your initial CA claim will be refused, but if you claim again within three months of the qualifying benefit being awarded, your CA is backdated to the date of your original claim;[30]
- your CA stopped because the 'qualifying benefit' of the person for whom you care was reduced or stopped (including where a fixed term award for the qualifying benefit came to an end) or where payment of the qualifying benefit stopped because the person for whom you care goes into hospital, or is being provided with accommodation in a care home or other special accommodation (see p618). If you make a further claim within three months of the decision to reinstate the qualifying benefit, or of payment starting again, your CA is backdated to the date that your earlier claim ended or the date from which the qualifying benefit was re-awarded or became payable again, whichever is later.

A **'qualifying benefit'** is either the middle/highest rate DLA care component, AA or constant attendance allowance.

If you might have qualified for benefit earlier but did not claim because you were given the wrong information by the DWP or because you were misled by it, you could ask for an *ex gratia* payment (see p1186) or complain to the Ombudsman via your MP (see p1184).

7. Getting paid

Payment of carer's allowance (CA) is normally made by direct credit transfer into your bank (or similar) account.[31] If you are unable to open or manage an account, payment can be made by cheque (see p978). If you are unable to act for yourself, CA can be paid to someone else on your behalf, called your appointee (see p955).

CA is paid either weekly in advance or at four-weekly intervals.[32] You are normally paid on Mondays. However, if the person for whom you are caring receives constant attendance allowance with her/his industrial injuries disablement benefit or war pension, you are paid on Wednesdays.[33] If you are entitled to CA, payments normally run from the first payday (ie, Monday or Wednesday) after the date of your claim, unless the date of your claim is on your payday, when they run from that day.

Note:

- CA awards can be made for a fixed period or indefinitely;[34]
- deductions can be made from your CA to repay certain loans (see p992);
- you might not be paid CA if you have been sanctioned for benefit offences (see p1047).

If your cheque is lost or stolen or you have forgotten your PIN, see p983. If payment of your CA is suspended, see p984.

Delays and complaints

If payment of your CA is delayed, you might be able to get an interim payment. See p986 for further details.

If you experience delays, see p1186. If you wish to complain about how your claim has been dealt with, see p1181. You might be able to claim compensation (see p1186).

Change of circumstances

The DWP should inform you of the main kinds of changes in your circumstances that you need to report, but might not actually list them all. In any case, it is your duty to report any change in your circumstances which might affect your right to CA, or the amount or payment of your benefit. You should do this promptly in writing or by telephone to the Carer's Allowance Unit (although in individual cases notification might be accepted in a form other than in writing or by telephone). In some cases, however, the decision maker might say you must report changes in writing. You can also send notification of your change of circumstances via the Government's website (see p47), as long as the DWP accepts this form of communication from you.[35]

Although you may be able to report changes of circumstances by telephone or some other means, it is always advisable to write, or to confirm a telephone conversation in writing, so that there is a clear record of the information you have given, and to keep a copy of the letter you send in case problems arise.

If you do not report any such change promptly, any resulting overpayment may be recoverable from you (see Chapter 39). If you are considered deliberately to have acted falsely or dishonestly, you may also be guilty of an offence (see Chapter 40).

When there has been a relevant change of circumstances, a decision maker looks at your claim again and makes a new decision, called a supersession (see p1074).

If the decision on your claim is superseded and your entitlement to benefit is affected, the date from which the new decision takes effect depends on whether or not it is advantageous to you and whether you reported the change in time (see p1080 for further details).

Overpayments and fraud

If you are overpaid CA, you might have to repay it. See Chapter 39.

If you have been accused of fraud, see Chapter 40.

8. Challenging a carer's allowance decision

You can apply for a revision or supersession of a carer's allowance (CA) decision, or appeal against it (see Chapters 41 and 42). You may not be paid CA if you have been sanctioned for benefit offences (see p997).

9. Tax, tax credits and other benefits

Carer's allowance (CA) is taxable except for any increases for children.[36]

Tax credits

If your income is low you may qualify for child tax credit (CTC) (if you have at least one dependent child – see Chapter 48) and working tax credit (WTC) (if you or your partner, if you have one, are in qualifying remunerative work – see Chapters 49 and 50). Remember, however, that you cannot get CA if you are in gainful employment (see p45). CA is counted in full as income for both these tax credits. If you are receiving CA and you are 50 or over, this may help you qualify for the 50-plus element of WTC.

Means-tested benefits

You may qualify for income support (IS) or pension credit (PC) in addition to your CA. If you receive CA, you come within one of the groups of people who can claim IS (see p292).[37] Even if you are not receiving CA, you may still come within one of the groups (see p294).[38]

If you and your partner are claiming income-based jobseeker's allowance (JSA) and you are a member of a 'joint-claim couple' (see p381) you are not required to be available for work, to actively seek work or to enter into a jobseeker's agreement if you are a carer who is entitled to claim IS (see p295). However, in these circumstances you should consider claiming IS or PC instead of income-based JSA.

If your income is low you may also qualify for housing benefit (HB) and council tax benefit (CTB).

Before you claim CA, you should consider how your claim might affect your entitlement (and that of the person you care for) to means-tested benefits. In particular, you should be aware of the following points.

- If you receive CA (or are entitled but do not receive it because of the overlapping benefit rules – see p981) you get a carer's premium included in your IS, income-based JSA, HB or CTB (carer's additional amount with PC) – see p789.[39] However, CA counts in full as income (less any tax payable on it) when calculating your entitlement.[40] This means that if you are getting IS, income-based JSA or PC, claiming CA normally reduces your entitlement to those benefits and only increases your overall income by the amount of the carer's premium/additional amount.
- CA counts as qualifying income for the savings credit of PC. So claiming CA may also affect your entitlement to the savings credit. How your entitlement is affected depends on the amount of other qualifying income you have.
- If you work, the situation may be slightly different. This is because if you get CA, and so receive a carer's premium/additional amount, £20 of your earnings can be disregarded (rather than the standard £5 or £10 – see Chapter 36) when working out your entitlement. See pp855 and 887 for details of an additional earnings disregard for HB and CTB. (**Note:** the rule for calculating your earnings for entitlement to CA is different.)
- Claiming CA may mean that your income is too high for you to qualify for means-tested benefits, even if the carer's premium/additional amount is awarded. In this situation, losing entitlement to IS, income-based JSA or the guarantee credit of PC can mean your entitlement to HB and CTB is reduced and you no longer qualify for benefits like free school meals for your children and social fund payments. You need to calculate whether the increase in your weekly income compensates you for the loss of these benefits. If in doubt, seek advice.
- If the person you care for gets one of the means-tested benefits and the middle or highest rate care component of disability living allowance or attendance allowance, s/he may receive a severe disability premium/additional amount in her/his IS, income-based JSA, PC, HB or CTB (see p784). If you are entitled to and receive CA, s/he loses entitlement to that premium/additional amount. You therefore need to discuss whether or not a claim for CA is a good idea. It is

important to bear in mind that the severe disability premium/additional amount is worth more than the carer's premium.

- For IS, income-based JSA and, if you are under 60, HB and CTB, if you choose not to claim CA, the DWP may treat you as if you receive it and reduce your benefit accordingly. This is because you can be treated as if you receive income that you deliberately fail to apply for (see p873). For this 'notional income' rule to apply, however, there has to be no doubt that you would qualify for CA and this may be difficult for the DWP to establish, particularly if, for example, you have not claimed or been awarded CA already. If you are affected by this rule, seek advice.
- For means-tested benefits, you can also be treated as if you receive income which you deliberately deprive yourself of in order to qualify for, or increase your entitlement to, benefit (see pp873 and 894). For this rule to apply the deprivation must be to gain benefit for yourself or your family. So if the person you care for is not a member of your family, you should not be treated as having deprived yourself of income if you stop claiming CA solely so that s/he can qualify for a severe disability premium.[41] However, in this situation, if you are claiming IS, income-based JSA or (if you are under 60) HB or CTB, the DWP may still consider whether you have failed to apply for income that would be available to you.

Non-means-tested benefits

CA is subject to the overlapping benefit rules, which means that you may not be paid CA in full if another earnings-replacement benefit is paid to you (see p981).

For each week you receive CA you can receive a national insurance (NI) credit (but your contribution record may be protected anyway through home responsibilities protection – see p733). You may also be able to build up your entitlement to additional state pension if you are entitled to CA or to home responsibilities protection as a carer (see p733).

Even if you are receiving another earnings-replacement benefit it may still be worth claiming CA if this would help you qualify for a carer's premium in your means-tested benefit (see p52) or for credited NI contributions.

Passports and other sources of help

If you get CA (or would get it but for the overlapping benefit rules), you are entitled to a Christmas bonus (see p9).

If you are on a low income, you might be entitled to certain health service benefits such as free prescriptions (see Chapter 9). You may also qualify for a social fund payment (see Chapters 21 and 22) and for free school meals for any children that you have (see p15).

Notes

1 Art 2 RR(CA)O

1. **Who can claim carer's allowance**
2 s70 SSCBA 1992; regs 3 and 9(1) SS(ICA) Regs
3 s115 IAA 1999
4 s70(7) SSCBA 1992
5 Reg 4(1) SS(ICA) Regs
6 s122 SSCBA 1992
7 CG/6/1990
8 R(G) 3/91
9 Reg 4(1A) SS(ICA) Regs
10 Reg 4(2) SS(ICA) Regs
11 *Secretary of State for Work and Pensions v Pridding* [2002] EWCA Civ 306, *The Times*, 3 April 2002
12 s70(1A) SSCBA 1992
13 Reg 8(1) SS(ICA) Regs
14 Reg 8(2) SS(ICA) Regs
15 Reg 5 SS(ICA) Regs

2. **The rules about your age**
16 s70(3) SSCBA 1992
17 Art 4 RR(CA)O
18 Reg 10A SS(ICA) Regs; *Secretary of State v Thomas* [1993] QB 747; R(G) 2/94; CG/5425/95; para 60063 DMG

4. **The amount of benefit**
19 Sch 4 SSCBA 1992

6. **Claims and backdating**
20 Regs 4ZC and 32ZA and Sch 9ZC SS(C&P) Regs
21 Reg 7(1) SS(C&P) Regs
22 Reg 6(1)(a) and (1ZA) SS(C&P) Regs
23 Reg 6(1)(b) SS(C&P) Regs
24 Reg 4ZC and Sch 9ZC para 4(1) and (2) SS(C&P) Regs
25 Reg 9(1) and Sch 1 SS(C&P) Regs
26 R(A) 3/81
27 Reg 13 SS(C&P) Regs
28 Reg 19 SS(C&P) Regs
29 Reg 6(16)-(22), (33) and (34) SS(C&P) Regs
30 Reg 6(16)-(18) SS(C&P) Regs

7. **Getting paid**
31 Reg 21 SS(C&P) Regs
32 Reg 22(1) SS(C&P) Regs
33 Reg 22(3) and Sch 6 SS(C&P) Regs
34 Reg 17 SS(C&P) Regs
35 Regs 32 and 32ZA SS(C&P) Regs

9. **Tax, tax credits and other benefits**
36 ss660, 661 and 676 IT(EP)A 2003
37 Reg 4ZA and Sch 1B para 4(b) IS Regs
38 Reg 4ZA and Sch 1B para 4(a) IS Regs; R(IS) 8/02
39 **IS** Sch 2 para 14ZA IS Regs
JSA Sch 1 para 17 JSA Regs
HB Sch 3 para 17 HB Regs; Sch 3 para 9 HB(SPC) Regs
CTB Sch 1 para 17 CTB Regs; Sch 1 para 9 CTB(SPC) Regs
40 **IS** Reg 40 IS Regs
JSA Reg 103 JSA Regs
HB Reg 40 HB Regs; reg 29 HB(SPC) Regs
CTB Reg 30 CTB Regs; reg 19 CTB(SPC) Regs
41 para 28611 DMG

4

Chapter 4

Child benefit

This chapter contains the rules about child benefit. It covers:

Child benefit is a benefit paid to people who are responsible for a child or qualifying young person (also referred to as a child in this chapter). If you qualify for it, child benefit is paid for each child for whom you are responsible, with a higher amount paid for your eldest eligible child. You do not have to be a parent of a child to qualify for child benefit for her/him and the child does not necessarily have to live with you. It is not necessary to have paid national insurance contributions to qualify for child benefit and your entitlement to child benefit is not affected by any income or savings that you have.

The Revenue is responsible for the administration and payment of child benefit.

1. Who can claim child benefit

You qualify for child benefit for a child if:[1]

- s/he counts as a 'child' or 'qualifying young person' (see p57). **Note:** in the rest of this chapter the term 'child' is used for both child and qualifying young person; *and*
- you are responsible for the child because *either*:
  - the child lives with you (see p63); *or*
  - you contribute to the cost of supporting the child (see p64) at a rate of at least the amount of child benefit for that child; *and*
- you have priority over other potential claimants (see p65); *and*

- you and the child satisfy the presence and residence conditions (including for you, if you claim child benefit on or after 1 May 2004, the 'right to reside' test – see pp1359 and 1361); *and*
- you are not a 'person subject to immigration control', although there are exceptions to this (see p1334).

See p67 for details of when child benefit will not be paid.

There are some groups of claimants and children to whom special rules apply (see p69). If your child has died, see p75.

Who counts as a 'child'

Anyone aged under 16 counts as a **'child'** for child benefit purposes, whether they go to school or not. As long as you meet the other qualifying conditions, child benefit can be paid for them.[2] Child benefit can then continue be paid for a child after s/he reaches 16 for as long as s/he counts as a 'qualifying young person'.

Who counts as a 'qualifying young person'

A **'qualifying young person'** is someone who:[3]

- is aged 16 and has left relevant education (see p59) or training. In this circumstance s/he can count as a qualifying young person up to and including the 31 August after her/his 16th birthday; *or*
- is aged 16 or 17 and:
  - has left education or training; *and*
  - is registered for work, education or training; *and*
  - is not in remunerative work; *and*
  - is within her/his extension period (see p59); *or*
- is aged 16 or over and under 20 (but see below if s/he is a 19-year-old) and either:
  - is on a course of full-time non-advanced education (see p60); *or*
  - is on approved training (see p61); *and*
  - began, or was enrolled or accepted on that course of full-time non-advanced education or approved training before reaching 19 (see p62 for details of interruptions in education or training that can be ignored); *or*
- is aged 16 or over and under 20 (but see below if s/he is a 19-year-old) and has either:
  - finished a course of full-time non-advanced education (see p60), and is enrolled or accepted on another such course; *or*
  - finished a course of full-time non-advanced education or approved training (see p61), and is enrolled or accepted on a course of approved training;

  this does not apply if the course is provided as a result of her/his employment; *or*

- is aged 16 or over and under 20 (but see below if s/he is a 19-year-old) and has left relevant education (see p59) or approved training and has not passed the end of the week which includes her/his 'terminal date' (also referred to in this chapter as the 'terminal date rule' – see p62).

If your child counts as a qualifying young person on more than one of the above grounds, s/he will be considered to be a qualifying young person until the last date that applies.[4]

If you stop being entitled to child benefit for your child because s/he no longer counts as a qualifying young person, but s/he later satisfies one of the above conditions again and so counts as a qualifying young person once more, child benefit can again become payable for her/him if you make a new claim (but see p62 if there is just an interruption in your child being able to fulfil the above conditions).

In the rest of this chapter we use the term 'child' to mean both young people aged under 16 and qualifying young people aged 16 or over.

19-year-olds

If your child is 19 you are only entitled to child benefit for her/him if s/he counts as a qualifying young person. A 19-year-old counts as a qualifying young person if:[5]

- s/he is on a course of full-time non-advanced education or approved training (see pp60 and 61) which is not provided because of her/his job and s/he either:
  - started the course before becoming 19; *or*
  - started the course while 19 but s/he was enrolled or accepted on it before reaching 19 (if s/he was not, see below).

  In this situation, as long as you meet the other qualifying conditions, you will normally continue to be entitled to child benefit for her/him until the end of the week which includes the first terminal date falling after the end of the course or training (unless s/he is 20 before that date – see p62);
- s/he has either finished one course of full-time non-advanced education and is enrolled or accepted on another, or has finished one course of full-time non-advanced education or approved training and is enrolled or accepted on a course of approved training. It is not necessary for your child to have been enrolled or accepted on the course before becoming 19, but the courses must not be provided because of her/his employment.

If a young person who is continuing in education or training, starts a new course of full-time non-advanced education or approved training *after* reaching 19, and was not enrolled or accepted on that course before becoming 19, the Revenue's intention is that s/he will still count as a qualifying young person while on the new course as long as there have been no gaps between her/his old and new courses of education or training, or as long as the only gaps are normal academic holidays or interruptions which can be ignored (see p62). However, if there has been a longer break between the old and new course, the Revenue states that s/he will not count as a qualifying young person on the grounds of being in full-time non-advanced education or approved training while on the new course.

However, in this situation even if the Revenue does not accept that your child counts as a qualifying young person while on the new course, s/he can count as a qualifying young person from the date s/he is enrolled or accepted on the course until the date the new course starts. Also, as long as s/he is under 20, it may be possible to argue that s/he should count as a qualifying young person for a period after s/he leaves such a course under the 'terminal date rule' (see p62).[6]

If you satisfy the other qualifying conditions, but are refused child benefit for your 19-year-old in these circumstances, seek advice.

Relevant education

Relevant education is defined as education which is full time and non-advanced. For the meaning of non-advanced education see p61. For the purpose of deciding if your child is in relevant education, the Revenue considers that the definition of 'full time' given on p60 applies, but this is not actually stated in the legislation. It may, therefore, be possible to argue, for example, that unsupervised as well as supervised study should be counted when assessing if such a course is full time.

The extension period

If a child is 16 or 17 and has left education or training, s/he continues to count as a qualifying young person, and so child benefit can continue to be paid for her/him, during an **'extension period'** if:[7]

- s/he is registered as available for work, education or training with the Careers Service, Connexions Service, Ministry of Defence or with a similar body in Northern Ireland or, in some circumstances, in another European Economic Area state; *and*
- s/he is not in remunerative work (ie, s/he is not working for 24 hours a week or more for payment, or in expectation of payment); *and*
- s/he is not in education or training; *and*
- you were entitled to child benefit for her/him immediately before the extension period started; *and*
- you apply in writing within three months of the date your child's education or training finished.

In this context, 'education' and 'training' are not defined and so may mean any kind of education or training.

The extension period starts from the Monday after your child's course of education or training ends and lasts for 20 weeks from that date. If your child reaches 18 during the extension period, unless s/he counts as a qualifying young person on another ground (see p57), your child benefit for her/him will end from the first child benefit payday on or after s/he reaches 18.[8]

If there is an interruption in your child's ability to satisfy the above conditions, see p62.

See p67 for circumstances when child benefit will not be paid.

Full-time non-advanced education

If your child is 16 or over but under 20 s/he can count as a qualifying young person if s/he is attending a full-time course of non-advanced education, or if s/he is enrolled or accepted on such a course. For either of these circumstances to apply:[9]

- the course must not be provided as a result of your child's employment or because of an office s/he holds (but see below); *and*
- the course must either be provided:
  - at a school or college; *or*
  - elsewhere (such as at home) but only if a decision maker approves the education and s/he was being educated in this way before reaching 16.

In addition, for your child to count as a qualifying young person on the ground that s/he is attending a full-time non-advanced course, s/he must normally have either started, or been enrolled or accepted on it before s/he reached 19 (but see p58).

If your child finishes a course of full-time non-advanced education before s/he is 20, s/he will continue to count as a qualifying young person, and so you can still qualify for child benefit for her/him, until the end of the week which includes the first terminal date after her/his course ends (or until s/he is 20 if this is earlier – see p62).

You may also still qualify for child benefit for her/him if she counts as a qualifying young person on another ground (see p57).[10]

Note: your child cannot count as a qualifying young person on the ground of being in full-time non-advanced education if s/he is on a course of education provided as a result of her/his job. However, as long as s/he is under 20, it may be arguable that s/he *can* count as a qualifying young person for a period after s/he leaves such a course under the 'terminal date rule', as the rules regarding terminal dates do not exclude education that is provided under an employment contract (see p62, but see p68 if your child is working).

See p62 if your child's education is interrupted.

Full-time education

For the purpose of defining full-time non-advanced education, a course of education counts as full time if it is for an average of more than 12 hours a week during term time, including tuition, supervised study, exams and practical work, but excluding meal breaks and unsupervised study.[11]

'Supervised' study requires the close proximity of a teacher or tutor to enforce discipline, and provide encouragement and help.[12]

Non-advanced education

The main examples of advanced and non-advanced courses are set out below.[13] There may be others.

Non-advanced courses	*Advanced courses*
GCSEs	a university degree
AS and A levels	NVQ level 4
NVQ level 3 and below	Higher National Diploma (HND)
SVQ level 3 and below	Diploma of Higher Education
National Diploma or Ordinary National Diploma (OND)	a teaching qualification
Scottish National Qualifications (higher or advanced higher level)	Scottish Qualifications Authority Higher National Diploma or Higher National Certificate
National Certificate of Edexcel	SVQ level 4 and above
BTEC Nationals	BTEC Higher Nationals

Approved training

If your child is aged 16 or over but under 20, s/he can count as a qualifying young person if:[14]

- s/he is on a course of approved training, which s/he either started or was enrolled or accepted on before s/he reached 19 (but see p58); *or*
- s/he was on a course of full-time non-advanced education or approved training and is now enrolled or accepted on a course of approved training.

For either of these circumstances to apply the training must not be provided under a contract of employment (but see p62).

Approved training is any of the following training courses:[15]

- in England, Entry to Employment or Programme-Led Apprenticeships;
- in Scotland, Get Ready for Work, Skillseekers or Modern Apprenticeships;
- in Wales, Skillbuild, Skillbuild+ or Foundation Modern Apprenticeships.

See p62 if your child's training is interrupted.

If your child leaves approved training before reaching 20, s/he can continue to be considered a qualifying young person, and so you can still qualify for child benefit for her/him, until the end of the week which includes the first 'terminal date' after s/he leaves (or until s/he reaches 20 if that is earlier). You may also still qualify for child benefit for her/him if she counts as a qualifying young person on another ground (see p57).[16]

Note: although your child will not count as a qualifying young person on the ground of being on approved training if the training is provided under her/his employment contract, s/he may count as a qualifying young person for a period after such training ends under the 'terminal date rule', as long as s/he is under 20. This is because the rules regarding terminal dates do not exclude training provided under an employment contract (see p62, but see below if your child is working).

The 'terminal date rule'

If your child leaves relevant education or approved training before reaching 20, s/he continues to count as a qualifying young person until either:[17]

- the first Sunday on or after her/his 'terminal date' (see below); *or*
- if s/he reaches 20 on or before that date, the Sunday on or after her/his 20th birthday (unless her/his 20th birthday is on a Monday when s/he will count as a qualifying young person until the Sunday before her/his birthday).

This means that unless s/he continues to count as a qualifying young person on another ground, the general rule is that you will stop receiving child benefit for her/him on that date.

Your child's '**terminal date**' is the first of the following dates that falls after the date her/his relevant education or approved training finished:

- the last day in February; *or*
- 31 May; *or*
- 31 August; *or*
- 30 November.

A child who will return to sit an external examination in connection with her/his course of relevant education is treated as still being in such education until the date of the last exam.[18]

A child who has taken the Higher or Advanced Higher Certificate in Scotland can be treated as being in relevant education until the date that a comparable course in England or Wales would end, if this is later.[19] This is because exams are often taken earlier in Scotland than in England and Wales.

Interruptions

If there is a break in your child being able to satisfy the conditions for being a qualifying young person (see p57), the interruption can be ignored:[20]

- for up to six months (whether or not the interruption began before or after the child was 16) if it is found to be 'reasonable' in the circumstances; *or*
- indefinitely if it is caused by your child having a physical or mental illness or disability and the length of the absence is found to be reasonable given the circumstances.

In practical terms, this means your child can still be considered to be a qualifying young person during the interruption.

The Revenue states that this rule is only supposed to apply when there is an interruption in your child's ability to attend a course of education or training (eg, because of ill-health).

However, it is arguable that this rule can also apply to 16/17-year-olds during the extension period. So, if there is an interruption in your child's ability to meet any of the conditions for entitlement during the extension period (which are explained on p59), and that interruption is reasonable, it may be possible to argue that your child benefit for her/him should continue.

However, an interruption cannot be ignored if, immediately after the interruption, your child starts, or is likely to start:[21]

- a training course which is not 'approved training'; *or*
- a course of advanced education; *or*
- education connected to her/his employment.

Responsible for a child

You are only entitled to child benefit for a child if you are responsible for her/him. You count as responsible for a child in any week in which:[22]

- you have the child living with you (see below); *or*
- you contribute to the cost of providing for the child (see p64).

A child 'living with' you

To be living with you, the child 'must live in the same house or other residence as [you] and also be carrying on there with [you] a settled course of daily living'.[23] This does not mean the same as 'residing together' or 'presence under the same roof'.[24] A child may be 'living with' you even while away. There are special rules if your child is looked after by a local authority (see p69).

Absence from home

If the child is absent from home, s/he is still treated as living with you as long as s/he has not been away for more than 56 days in the last 16 weeks.[25] In calculating whether a child has been absent from home for 56 days, certain days of absence are ignored. These are days when the child is away only to:[26]

- receive education or training (the Revenue states that this rule applies only if the child is away receiving full-time non-advanced education or approved training, but this is not explicitly stated in the regulations); *or*
- stay in certain forms of residential accommodation, if this is necessary because of a disability the child has or because her/his health would be 'significantly impaired or further impaired' if s/he were not staying in the accommodation (but see p64); *or*
- receive inpatient treatment in a hospital or similar institution (but see p64).

In the latter two situations a maximum of 12 consecutive weeks' absence can be ignored, unless you are regularly incurring expenditure in respect of the child, when the period of absence can be ignored indefinitely.[27] (As long as you are making visits, or giving the child pocket money, this condition is likely to be satisfied.) Two or more periods in hospital or residential accommodation separated by 28 days or less are treated as one when calculating the 12-week period.

If the child's absence is not solely for one of the three reasons listed on p63 her/his days of absence cannot be ignored and s/he will no longer be considered to be living with you if s/he has been away for more than 56 days in the last 16 weeks.

However, even if a child is not living with you, you may still qualify for child benefit for her/him if you are contributing to the child's maintenance.

See p1360 if your child is abroad.

Example

Amy's son was in hospital for 18 weeks and while he was there she regularly took him food, drinks and comics. On being discharged, he went to stay with his grandmother for a month to convalesce before returning home. Amy is entitled to child benefit for her son while he was away. Although he was in hospital for over 12 weeks, she regularly incurred expenditure for him and so she is treated as if he was still living with her for the time he was an inpatient. Amy's son also counts as still living with her for the period he was staying with his grandmother as he was not considered to be absent from home for more than 56 days in the previous 16 weeks. The period he was in hospital is ignored when calculating the 56-day period.

Contributing to the cost of supporting a child

If a child is not living with you, you can still qualify for child benefit if you contribute to the cost of supporting her/him. To satisfy this condition you must contribute at least the amount of child benefit payable for the child (see p68).[28]

Contributions must be regular, although the odd hiccup may be ignored.[29] Payments in kind rather than cash may be accepted.[30] If you reside with your spouse or civil partner, any contribution made by one of you may be treated as a contribution by the other.[31] Similarly, if you and another person (or persons) each contribute less than the amount of child benefit payable for the child, but your total contributions are at least equal to the amount of child benefit payable, one of you is treated as contributing the whole sum. If you do not agree on which one of you it is to be, the Revenue decides.[32] If you qualify for child benefit on this basis, once benefit has been awarded, you alone must actually contribute at least the amount of child benefit paid for the child in order to continue to be entitled.

See p693 for the way the amount of contribution is calculated in difficult cases.

Priority between claimants

Potentially, it is possible for more than one person to be entitled to child benefit for the same child – eg, when a child is living with one parent and maintained by the other. However, only one person can be awarded child benefit for a particular child. There is an order of priority which governs who receives child benefit when two or more people would otherwise be entitled.[33]

No one is entitled to child benefit without making a claim and the priority rules do not apply unless at least two people have claimed child benefit for the same child and both of them would qualify for it.[34]

Then, claimants take priority in the following order:[35]

- a person with whom the child lives;
- a wife, where a husband and wife are residing together (see p67);
- a parent (including a step-parent and adoptive parent, but in this context, the rules do not allow the civil partner of the child's parent to count as a step-parent);[36]
- the mother (including a stepmother) where the parents are unmarried and are residing together (see p67). In this context, the rules do not allow the civil partner of the child's mother to count as a stepmother;
- in any other case, a person agreed by those entitled;
- if there is no agreement, a person selected by a decision maker at the Revenue (in which case there is no appeal against the decision[37] – but see p1097).

Even if the new claim takes priority over an existing claim, child benefit continues to be paid on the existing claim for the three weeks following the week in which the new claim is made, unless the existing claimant withdraws her/his claim prior to this.[38] In addition, even if your claim has priority you normally cannot receive child benefit for a period during which it has already been paid to someone else for the same child – see p74 for details.

If you have claimed child benefit but you want someone who has equal or lower priority to you to receive child benefit instead of you, you should write to or telephone the Child Benefit Office (see Appendix 1).[39]

It may be important to concede priority if you spend periods abroad, as entitlement to child benefit normally stops if you have been abroad for more than eight weeks (or 12 weeks in some circumstances, see p1359).

Separation and the priority rules

Problems can arise when there are competing child benefit claims for a child from a mother and father who have just separated. If the mother was receiving child benefit before the separation and the child continues to live with her, she continues to be entitled to child benefit. If the mother was receiving child benefit before the separation and the child goes to live with the father, as long as he has made a valid claim for child benefit his claim should have priority if:[40]

- the father and mother are no longer considered to be residing together. If their separation is permanent this should normally be from the date that they separate (see p67); *or*
- the mother either withdraws her child benefit claim or elects that he receive it instead; *or*
- the child is no longer treated as living with her/his mother (normally after the child has been away from her for 56 days, see p63).

However, in this situation, even if the father's claim has priority, the mother will continue to be entitled to child benefit instead of him for the three weeks following the week in which the father makes his claim, unless she either withdraws her claim before this, or she stops qualifying for child benefit for another reason. Also, the father cannot normally receive child benefit for a period during which it has already been paid to the mother (but see p74 for exceptions to this rule).

Shared care

When the care of a child is shared between two parents who are both entitled to child benefit but cannot agree on who should receive it, the Revenue must exercise its discretion to decide to whom it is reasonable to pay the benefit. This will usually involve considering which parent has the greater responsibility of care. In reaching its decision, the Revenue might consider issues such as the number of hours each parent has responsibility for the child each week, the terms of any court orders, where the child's possessions are kept, at which address the child is registered with schools and doctors, the contributions each parent makes towards the cost of bringing up the child (although this may not be conclusive if the resources of one parent are greater than the other), and the impact that the decision might have on each parent. These are just examples of what might be considered, as each case will depend on its circumstances.

In reaching its decision, the Revenue is also entitled to take into account the existence of other children of the relationship for whom child benefit is paid. For example, the High Court held that where two parents had nearly equal responsibility for the care of their two children, it was not unreasonable for the decision maker to decide that each parent should receive child benefit in respect of one child.[41]

In looking at the division of care between parents, the Revenue should take a refined approach. In a case in which a father was the main carer of two children in term time, but the father and mother each had the children for half the school holidays, the Court held that in such situations it may be necessary for the decision maker to consider paying each of the parents child benefit for one child during the school holidays to produce an equitable result.[42]

'Residing together'

It may be important to know whether a couple who are responsible for a child are 'residing together' (or 'residing with' each other)[43] because:

- if a married couple are residing together, the wife's claim has priority over the husband's;
- if an unmarried couple are residing together, the mother's claim has priority;
- you may not be entitled to child benefit for a child who is married or in a civil partnership if s/he is residing with her spouse or civil partner (see below).

The rules on whether a couple are residing together are not the same for child benefit as for other benefits.

If you are married, in a civil partnership or are a parent of a child, even if you are apart, you and your spouse or civil partner, or you and the other parent of your child, are still treated as residing together if:[44]

- the absence from each other is not likely to be permanent; *or*
- the reason for the absence is only because one or both of you has a mental health problem and is receiving care or treatment as an inpatient in a hospital or a similar institution, whether this is likely to be temporary or permanent.

Even if you have not lived together, you can be treated as residing together if your absence from each other is not likely to be permanent.[45]

It is possible to be absent from one another while you are living under the same roof if you are maintaining separate households.[46]

When child benefit is not paid

You are not entitled to child benefit for a child if:[47]

- s/he is married or in a civil partnership, unless the child is not residing with her/his spouse or civil partner, or her/his spouse or civil partner is in relevant education or approved training. But the child's spouse or civil partner can never be the claimant even in these circumstances; *or*
- s/he is cohabiting (see p68), unless her/his partner is in relevant education or approved training (but in this circumstance her/his partner can never be the claimant); *or*
- s/he receives, in her/his own right:
  - incapacity benefit (if this is paid on the basis of her/his incapacity for work in youth);
  - income support (see Chapter 13);
  - income-based jobseeker's allowance (see Chapter 15);
  - working tax credit (see Chapter 49) or child tax credit (see Chapter 48); *or*
- s/he has spent more than eight consecutive weeks either:
  - in prison or other custody; *or*
  - being looked after by the local authority (but see p69).

A child will be considered to be **cohabiting** if s/he and someone of the opposite sex live together as if they were husband and wife, or if s/he and someone of the same sex live together as if they were civil partners.

16–19-year-olds who work

If your child is under 16, your entitlement to child benefit for her/him is unaffected by any work that s/he does.

If your child is 16 or over but under 20, and s/he only counts as a qualifying young person under the 'terminal date' rule (see p62) or because s/he is within an extension period (see p59), you cannot receive child benefit for her/him if s/he works for 24 hours a week or more if the work is done for payment or in expectation of payment.[48]

However, if your child is a qualifying young person on any of the other grounds listed on p57 – eg, because s/he is on a course of full-time non-advanced education or enrolled or accepted on such a course, any work s/he does should not affect your entitlement to child benefit.

2. The rules about your age

There is no upper or lower age limit for entitlement to child benefit.

3. Claiming for others

Child benefit can be claimed for each child for whom you are responsible. No increase in child benefit is paid for any other dependants that you have.

4. The amount of benefit

Child benefit is payable at the following weekly rates.[49]

	£pw
Eldest eligible child:	18.80
Other children (each)	12.55

The general rule is that a higher rate of child benefit is normally paid for the eldest (or only) child in a family.[50]

If you live with your partner and each of you has children from a previous relationship for whom you receive separate child benefit, you will not both receive the higher rate of child benefit. Instead, the higher rate is paid to the person who has the eldest child. (In this context, partner means spouse, civil partner or someone with whom you are living as if you were husband and wife or civil partners.)

Entitlement to child benefit does not qualify you for national insurance credits. However, if you qualify for child benefit you (or, in some circumstances, someone you reside with and with whom you share the responsibility for the child) may be able to qualify for home responsibilities protection (see p733) and may be able to build up entitlement to additional state pension (see p476).[51]

5. **Special benefit rules**

There are some groups of claimants to whom special rules apply. These are covered below and in Chapters 26 and 58. Special rules apply to:

- children being looked after by a local authority, or who are in prison or detention (see below);
- children who go or come from abroad (see pp1349 and 1359);
- people subject to immigration control (see p1333);
- people in prison (see p626).

Prison, detention or looked after by the local authority

If a child is away from home and, for at least one day a week in the last eight consecutive weeks, is either:[52]

- being looked after by a local authority and is provided with accommodation under the Children Act 1989 or the Children (Scotland) Act 1995 and at least part of the cost of either the accommodation or the child's maintenance is being paid out of local authority or public funds (but see p70); *or*
- subject to a supervision requirement and living in residential accommodation under s44 Social Work (Scotland) Act 1968 (**Note:** although the child benefit rules refer to s44, it has been repealed and a supervision requirement is now made under the Children (Scotland) Act 1995); *or*
- in prison or another form of detention such as a detention centre or young offenders' institution,

child benefit is not usually payable for her/him after the eight-week period.

However, there are some exceptions to this rule.

We refer to children in the situations above as being 'looked after by the local authority', 'subject to a supervision requirement' and 'in prision' respectively.

Exceptions

- You are not excluded from entitlement to child benefit for a child on the grounds that s/he is being looked after by the local authority if the child is placed in residential accommodation by the local authority solely because of a disability which s/he has, or on the grounds that her/his health would be significantly impaired or further impaired were s/he not in the accommodation.[53] In these circumstances, however, see p63.

- As child benefit only stops after the child has been looked after by the local authority, subject to a supervision requirement or in prison for at least one day a week in the last eight consecutive weeks, if the child ceases to be in one of these situations for at least a week (ie, from Monday to Sunday), the eight-week period should start again if s/he is subsequently looked after by the local authority, subject to a supervision requirement or placed in prison once more.
- You continue to get child benefit after the first eight weeks as long as the child 'ordinarily' lives with you throughout at least one whole day each week (which, in practice means at least two nights – see below) even if s/he is not actually at home in that particular week.[54]
- After the first eight weeks' absence, even if the child continues to be looked after by the local authority, subject to a supervision requirement or in prison and does not 'ordinarily' live with you for at least one day a week, you still qualify for child benefit when the child comes to stay with you if s/he comes to stay for a week or more.[55]
- If the child is detained in a hospital or a similar institution because of mental health problems the general rule is that you continue to be entitled to child benefit for her/him unless s/he was taken there from prison or another place of detention and is still within the term of her/his sentence.[56]
- If the child has been detained in custody but at the conclusion of criminal proceedings is not sentenced to a term of imprisonment or detention, or detention and training, you are entitled to child benefit for her/him for the period of her/his earlier detention.[57]

A **'week'** means seven days beginning with a Monday.[58] A **'day'** means from midnight to midnight.[59] Because the child must live with you 'throughout' the day,[60] this means that, in practice, s/he has to stay with you for two nights to be regarded as living with you for one day.

Fostering and adoption

- *You* cannot qualify for child benefit for a child if, for any day in a week, the local authority has arranged for the child to be placed with you under placement, looking after or fostering arrangements and the local authority is paying you an allowance towards the cost of the child's accommodation or maintenance under s23 Children Act 1989 or s26 Children (Scotland) Act 1995.[61]
- *No one* can qualify for child benefit for a child if s/he has been placed for adoption in the house of her/his prospective adopters if they are receiving

payments from the local authority for the child's accommodation or maintenance under the above provisions.[62]

If these circumstances do not apply – eg, if the local authority is not making payments under the provisions mentioned, the normal rules on entitlement to child benefit apply, including the rules on children who are being looked after by the local authority described on p69 (and the exceptions to these rules described on p69).

Your entitlement to child benefit is not affected if you are looking after a child under private fostering arrangements.

6. Claims and backdating

To be entitled to child benefit you must make a claim for it.[63] The rules for claiming are explained in brief below. The more detailed rules are explained in Chapter 38. It may be possible to claim child benefit in advance (see p73) or to get your claim backdated (see p73).

Making a claim

A claim for child benefit must be made in writing on the correct form – Form CH2, which can be obtained from the Child Benefit Office (see Appendix 1) or from the Revenue website (see Appendix 1). Your local Revenue enquiry centre or Jobcentre Plus office may also hold stocks of the form. Alternatively, there is an interactive, computer-based version of Form CH2 available on the Revenue's website (follow the 'do it online' link). This form must be completed on screen, printed off, signed and sent by post. A decision maker at the Revenue has the discretion to accept a written claim which is not on the correct form if it is sufficient in the circumstances (see p959).[64]

Your child benefit claim should be sent to the Child Benefit Office (see Appendix 1). Claims can also be taken or sent to a Revenue enquiry centre or a Jobcentre Plus office. Keep a copy of your claim in case queries arise. You may amend or withdraw your claim before it is assessed by writing to the Child Benefit Office.

For more details about making a claim see p955.

Information to support your claim

When you claim child benefit you must satisfy the 'national insurance (NI) number requirement' (see p962). This means that, in most cases, you must provide your NI number when making a claim for child benefit. You can also be asked to supply 'certificates, documents, information and evidence' considered relevant to your claim.[65]

The Revenue will usually need to see an original copy of your child's birth or adoption certificate, which you can either send to the Child Benefit Office or take to your local Revenue enquiry centre or Jobcentre Plus office.[66]

If you are asked to provide evidence or documents which you do not have, ask what other evidence would be acceptable. Ask the Revenue to explain what is required and why, and complain if you feel any requests for information are unreasonable.

Who should claim

You must normally make a claim for child benefit yourself. However, child benefit can be claimed by another adult on your behalf if you are unable to act for yourself. This person is known as your 'appointee' (see p955).

If someone else makes a claim for child benefit for the same child on her/his own behalf you are only entitled to child benefit for that child if you have priority over the other claimant. See p65 for details of priority between claimants.

The date of your claim

The date of your claim is important as it determines the date from which you will be paid child benefit (see p74). The date of your claim is normally the date it is received at either the Child Benefit Office, a Revenue enquiry centre, a Jobcentre Plus office or at the Revenue's office at Comben House, Merseyside.[67]

If the claim you submit is incomplete or not on the correct form, you may be asked to provide further information or to complete the correct form. As long as this additional information or form is submitted within a month of it being sent back to you (or longer if the decision maker thinks the delay is reasonable), your claim is treated as made on the date that the initial claim was received at one of the above offices.[68]

In some circumstances you can claim before you qualify for child benefit (see p73), or the date of your claim can be backdated (see p73).

If you claim the wrong benefit

The decision maker has the discretion to treat a claim for guardian's allowance (see Chapter 8) as a claim for child benefit for the same child.[69] If, before 7 April 2003, you claimed maternity allowance (as long as this was claimed after your baby was born) or an increase in incapacity benefit (IB), widowed mother's allowance, widowed parent's allowance, retirement pension, severe disablement allowance (SDA), or carer's allowance (CA) for a child dependant, the decision maker may also treat this as a claim for child benefit for the same child. Although increases in non-means-tested benefits for children were abolished from 6 April 2003, some people will continue to receive them (see p691).

If your claim for one of the above benefits is accepted as a claim for child benefit, your claim can be backdated for up to three months before the date you claimed that benefit, if you satisfy the qualifying conditions for child benefit over that period. This may allow you to get your claim for child benefit backdated for more than the usual three months. However, see p74 if someone else has been getting child benefit for the child.

See p963 for further details of interchanging claims in this way.

Claiming in advance

You cannot claim child benefit before a child is born because you will not know the precise date of birth. In other situations you can claim up to three months before you expect to be entitled – eg, when a child is returning from care.[70]

How your claim is dealt with

Your claim is dealt with by the Child Benefit Office and queries about your claim should be made to that office.

You may be able to claim an interim payment while waiting for a decision on your claim (see p986) or claim means-tested benefits or tax credits if your income is low (see p76).

See p970 for more information about the processing of claims.

Backdating your claim

You should make a claim for child benefit within three months of becoming entitled to it. If you claim late, you can only receive up to three months' arrears of benefit (although there are special rules if you were getting child benefit and move between Great Britain and Northern Ireland or if you have been recognised as a refugee – see p1348).[71] You do not have to show any reason why your claim was late. However, if someone else who is also entitled to child benefit for the same child has already been receiving it, you are not entitled to arrears. Instead, if your claim takes priority (see p65), you will be paid child benefit from the fourth week after the week in which you claim, unless the other person withdraws her/his claim prior to this (but see p74 if someone else has already been paid child benefit for the same child).[72]

If you might have qualified for child benefit earlier but did not claim because you were given the wrong information or misled by the DWP or the Revenue, you could ask for an *ex gratia* payment (see p1186) or complain to the Independent Case Examiner or to the Ombudsman via your MP (see pp1183 and 1184).

See p72 for details of when a claim for another benefit can be treated as a claim for child benefit.

See p965 for more details about the backdating of claims.

7. Getting paid

Child benefit is a weekly benefit, which means that it cannot be paid for periods of less than a week. If you qualify for child benefit, your benefit is paid from the Monday after the date of your claim (see p72).[73] However, if the date of your claim is a Monday it is arguable that payment should actually begin from that day. As your date of claim can be backdated for up to three months, if you claim within three months of your child's birth and you satisfy the qualifying conditions, child benefit will normally be paid from the Monday after your child was born.[74]

If you are making a claim for child benefit and someone else who is also entitled to child benefit for the same child is already receiving it, you will only receive child benefit if your claim has priority over that of the existing claimant's (see p65). In these circumstances, your benefit normally starts from the beginning of the fourth week after the week in which you claim, unless the existing claimant withdraws her/his claim prior to this. However, even if your claim has priority you cannot receive child benefit for a period for which it has already been paid to someone else for the same child, unless:[75]

- the Revenue (or where the decision has been made following an appeal, the appeal tribunal, or social security commissioner) has decided that the child benefit paid is recoverable because of the person's failure to disclose or her/his misrepresentation of any material fact (see p1009) and no appeal against that decision has been made within the time limit; *or*
- even though the Revenue has decided that the benefit was not recoverable or had not made a decision on its recoverablity, the money has been repaid.

Child benefit is normally paid by direct credit transfer into your bank account (or similar account). If you are unable to open or manage an account, payment can be made by cheque(see p979).[76]

Although the decision maker has discretion to choose any day of the week as your normal payday, child benefit is generally paid every four weeks on a Monday (unless the decision maker has arranged for you to be paid on a Tuesday) for three weeks in arrears and one week in advance.[77] In some circumstances, weekly payments of child benefit can be made including if:[78]

- you are a lone parent; *or*
- you or your spouse/civil partner or partner (the person with whom you are living as husband and wife/civil partners) are entitled to income-based jobseeker's allowance or income support (see Chapters 15 and 13); *or*
- the decision maker is satisfied that four-weekly payment 'is causing hardship'.

Payment can also be made to someone else on your behalf, called your 'appointee' (see p955), if you are unable to act for yourself.

If your entitlement to child benefit ends, payment of benefit normally continues up to, but not including, the following Monday. However, if your entitlement ends on a Monday your benefit will normally be paid up to, but not including, that day. If your benefit is not paid into your account or a benefit cheque is lost or stolen, see p983. If payment of your child benefit is suspended, see p984.

Delays and complaints

If payment of your child benefit is delayed, you might be able to get an interim payment. See p986 for further details.

If you experience delays, or wish to complain about how your claim has been dealt with, see Chapter 46. You might be able to claim compensation (see p1186).

Change of circumstances

You must report any change in your circumstances that the Revenue has informed you that you must tell it about (although the Revenue might not inform you of all the changes you need to tell it about). Also, it is also your duty to report any change which you might reasonably be expected to know might affect your right to, the payment of, or the amount of your benefit.[79] You should report such changes promptly. If you do not, any resulting overpayment may be recoverable from you (see Chapter 39). If you are considered deliberately to have acted falsely or dishonestly, you may also be guilty of an offence (see Chapter 40). You should write to the Child Benefit Office to report a change in your circumstances. However, if you have reported a change verbally to a Revenue enquiry centre or Jobcentre Plus office, in some circumstances this may be sufficient. If you report a change verbally it is advisable to make a note of the time and date of your conversation, the name of the person you informed and confirm your conversation in writing to the Child Benefit Office, keeping a copy of your letter in case problems arise.

You can also use the forms available on the Revenue's website (see Appendix 1) to report a change of circumstances.

Child benefit is normally awarded for an indefinite period (unless your circumstances are likely to change shortly after the award).[80] In order for payment of child benefit to be stopped or adjusted, the decision on your entitlement must first be revised or superseded (see Chapter 41).[81] If, following a change in your circumstances, the decision on your claim is superseded and your entitlement to benefit is affected, the date from which the new decision takes effect depends on whether or not it is advantageous to you and whether you reported the change in time (see p1080 for further details).

If your child dies

If your child dies and you were entitled to child benefit for her/him in the week in which s/he died (or you would have been had s/he not died in the same week that s/he was born), child benefit will continue to be paid for a period of eight weeks, or until the Monday after s/he would have been 20, if this falls within the eight-week period. If it was your partner who was getting child benefit for the child and s/he also dies, you will be entitled to child benefit for the eight-week period. This only applies if you were living with your partner at the time s/he died. In this context, partner means your spouse, civil partner or someone with whom you were living as husband and wife or as civil partners.[82]

Overpayments and fraud

If you are overpaid child benefit, you might have to repay it. The rules on overpayments are covered in Chapter 39.

If you have been accused of fraud, see Chapter 40.

8. Challenging a child benefit decision

You can apply for a revision or supersession of a child benefit decision, or appeal against it (see Chapters 41 and 42). Certain decisions, such as who should receive child benefit when two people whose claims have equal priority cannot agree (see p65), cannot be appealed. However, you may ask for such decisions to be revised or superseded (see p1097).[83]

9. Tax, tax credits and other benefits

Child benefit is not taxable.[84]

Tax credits

If your income is low you may qualify for working tax credit (if you or your partner, if you have one, are in full-time paid work – see p1222) and child tax credit (CTC – see Chapter 48). Child benefit is ignored when calculating your entitlement to tax credits.[85]

Means-tested benefits

If you have a low income you may be entitled to means-tested benefits which can be paid in addition to child benefit.

Income support and income-based jobseeker's allowance

From 6 April 2004, if you have been awarded CTC or if you make a new claim for income support (IS) or income-based jobseeker's allowance (JSA), any child benefit you receive is ignored when calculating your entitlement to IS and income-based JSA.[86]

If you have been getting IS or income-based JSA since before 6 April 2004 with an amount for a child included in your claim and have not yet been awarded CTC, your child benefit is taken into account in full as income when calculating your entitlement to IS or income-based JSA. However, if you get child benefit for a child under one year old and still get IS or income-based JSA for the child rather than CTC, £10.50 of your child benefit is ignored when calculating your entitlement to IS or income-based JSA (even if you have more than one child).[87]

Pension credit

Child benefit is ignored when calculating entitlement to pension credit (PC).[88]

Housing benefit and council tax benefit

Child benefit is ignored when calculating your entitlement to housing benefit (HB – see Chapter 10) and council tax benefit (CTB – see Chapter 5) if:

- you are getting IS, income-based JSA or the guarantee credit of PC (as in this situation you will be passported on to the maximum rate of HB and CTB – see p190); *or*
- you are getting the savings credit of PC; *or*
- you or your partner are aged 60 or over.

Child benefit is taken into acccount in full as income for HB and CTB if you and your partner are aged under 60 and you are not getting IS or income-based JSA.[89]

Non-means-tested benefits

If you are entitled to another non-means-tested benefit, you may be receiving an increase in that benefit for a child. These increases for children were abolished on 6 April 2003, but some people continue to be entitled to them (see p691). However, the increase is reduced if you also receive child benefit for that child paid at the rate for the eldest eligible child (ie, £18.80) – see p983.

Your entitlement to any other non-means-tested benefit is not affected by your entitlement to child benefit.

Passports and other sources of help

If you are on a low income, you might be entitled to certain health service benefits, such as free prescriptions (see Chapter 9). You may also qualify for a social fund payment (see Chapters 21 and 22) and for free school meals for your child(ren)(see p15).

Young people between the ages of 16 and 19 who are in non-advanced education may qualify for an educational maintenance allowance or other financial help with their studies (see p15).

In 2005 the Government introduced a child trust fund scheme.[90] Details of the scheme are published on the Revenue's website.

Notes

1. **Who can claim child benefit**
 1 ss141, 142, 143, 144, and 146 SSCBA 1992; s115 IAA 1999; reg 23 CB Regs
 2 s142(1) SSCBA 1992
 3 s142(2) SSCBA 1992; regs 2-7 CB Regs
 4 Reg 2(2) CB Regs
 5 Reg 3(2) and (4) CB Regs
 6 This is because in the rules on terminal dates there is no requirement that a course of education or training must be started before a person is 19.
 7 Reg 5 CB Regs
 8 Reg 14 CB&GA(Admin) Regs; reg 5(3) CB Regs
 9 Reg 3(2)(a) and (3) CB Regs
 10 Regs 2(2), 3, 4, 5, 6 and 7 CB Regs
 11 Reg 1(3) CB Regs
 12 R(F) 1/93, but see also *Flemming v Secretary of State for Work and Pensions* [2002] EWCA Civ 641, reported as R(G) 2/02
 13 Reg 1(3) CB Regs
 14 Reg 3(2)(c), (d) and (4) CB Regs
 15 Reg 1(3) CB Regs
 16 Regs 2(2) and 7 CB Regs
 17 Reg 7(2) CB Regs
 18 Reg 7(2)2.1 CB Regs
 19 Reg 7(2)1.3 CB Regs
 20 Reg 6(2) and (3) CB Regs
 21 Reg 6(4) CB Regs
 22 s143 SSCBA 1992
 23 R(F) 2/81
 24 R(F) 2/79
 25 s143(2) SSCBA 1992
 26 s143(3) SSCBA 1992; reg 9 CB Regs
 27 s143(3)(b) and (c) and (4) SSCBA 1992; reg 10 CB Regs
 28 s143(1)(b) SSCBA 1992
 29 R(U) 14/62
 30 R(U) 3/66
 31 Reg 11(4) CB Regs
 32 Reg 11 CB Regs
 33 s144(3) and Sch 10 SSCBA 1992
 34 s13(1) SSAA 1992
 35 Sch 10 SSCBA 1992
 36 s147(3) SSCBA 1992
 37 Sch 2 para 4 SSA 1998
 38 Sch 10 para 1 SSCBA 1992
 39 Regs 14and 15 CB Regs
 40 CF/1771/2003
 41 *R (on the application of Ford) v Board of Inland Revenue* [2005] EWHC Admin 1109, 19 May 2005; see also *R (Chester) v Secretary of State for Social Security* [2001] EWHC Admin 1119, 7 December 2001, unreported
 42 *R (Chester) v Secretary of State for Social Security* [2001] EWHC Admin 1119, 7 December 2001, unreported
 43 *Grove v Insurance Officer*, reported as an appendix to R(F) 4/85
 44 s147(4) SSCBA 1992; reg 34 CB Regs
 45 R(F) 4/85
 46 R(F) 3/81
 47 Sch 9 paras 1 and 3 SSCBA 1992; regs 8, 12,13 and 16 CB Regs
 48 Regs 1(3), 5(2)(c) and 7(3) CB Regs

4. **The amount of benefit**
 49 Reg 2(1) CB(R) Regs
 50 Reg 2(1) and (2) CB(R) Regs
 51 s44A SSCBA 1992

5. **Special benefit rules**
 52 s147(2) and Sch 9 para 1 SSCBA 1992; regs 16-19 CB Regs
 53 Regs 9 and 18(b) CB Regs
 54 Reg 16(1)(b)(iv) CB Regs
 55 Reg 16(1)(b)(i)-(iii) CB Regs
 56 Reg 17(2)-(5) CB Regs
 57 Regs 1(3) and 17(1) CB Regs
 58 s147(1) SSCBA 1992
 59 R(F) 3/85
 60 Reg 16(2) CB Regs
 61 Reg 16(3) CB Regs
 62 Reg 16(4) and (5) CB Regs

6. **Claims and backdating**
 63 s13 SSAA 1992
 64 Reg 5 CB&GA(Admin) Regs
 65 Reg 7 CB&GA(Admin) Regs
 66 Regs 3(2) and 5(5) CB&GA(AA) Regs
 67 Reg 5(3) CB&GA(Admin) Regs
 68 Reg 10 CB&GA(Admin) Regs
 69 Reg 11 CB&GA(Admin) Regs
 70 Reg 12 CB&GA(Admin) Regs
 71 Reg 6 CB&GA(Admin) Regs
 72 Sch 10 para 1 SSCBA 1992

7. **Getting paid**
73 Reg 13 CB&GA(Admin) Regs
74 s147 SSCBA 1992
75 Sch 10, para 1 SSCBA 1992; s13(2) SSAA 1992; reg 38 CB Regs
76 Regs 16 and 17 CB&GA(Admin) Regs
77 Reg 18(2) CB&GA(Admin) Regs
78 Regs 18(3), 19 and 20(1) and (2) CB&GA(Admin) Regs
79 Reg 23 CB&GA(Admin) Regs
80 Reg 15 CB&GA(Admin) Regs
81 Reg 15 CB&GA(Admin) Regs
82 s145A SSCBA 1992; reg 20 CB Regs

8. **Challenging a child benefit decision**
83 s12(1) and Sch 2 SSA 1998; regs 9 and 13(2) CB&GA(DA) Regs

9. **Tax, tax credits and other benefits**
84 s677 IT(EP)A 2003
85 Reg 7 TC(DCI) Regs
86 Sch 9 para 5B IS Regs; Sch 7 para 6B JSA Regs
87 Reg 40 IS Regs; reg 103 JSA Regs; regs 1, 7 and 8 SS(WTCCTC)(CA) Regs
88 Regs 9 and 15(1)(j) SPC Regs
89 **HB** Reg 40 HB Regs; regs 27 and 29 HB(SPC) Regs
CTB Reg 30 CTB Regs; regs 17 and 19 CTB(SPC) Regs
90 Child Trust Funds Act 2004; Child Trust Funds Regulations 2004 No.1450

5

Chapter 5

Council tax benefit

This chapter covers:

Council tax benefit (CTB) is paid to people with a low income who pay council tax. It is paid whether or not the claimant is available for or in full-time paid work and may be paid in addition to other benefits and tax credits. CTB is paid by local authorities, although it is a national scheme and the rules are mainly determined by DWP regulations.

There are two types of CTB:

- **main CTB**, based on your council tax liability and your (and any partner's and dependants') assumed needs and resources; *and*
- alternative maximum CTB, known as **second adult rebate**, not based on your needs or resources but on the circumstances of certain other adults ('second adults') living with you.

If you are eligible for both types of CTB, you are paid whichever is the higher.

You might be able to claim discretionary housing payments to top up your CTB. See p222 for further information.

If you stop getting income support, income-based jobseeker's allowance, incapacity benefit or severe disablement allowance because you start work or increase your hours or earnings, you may be entitled to extended payments of CTB. See p94 for further information.

You do not have to have paid national insurance contributions to qualify for CTB.

The rules for CTB are often the same as for housing benefit (HB). In this chapter, where the rules are the same or similar, reference is made to the chapter on HB. Footnotes in that chapter contain references to both the HB and CTB legislation where applicable.

If you are 60 or over

The CTB rules for people who are 60 or over who are not (and whose partners are not) getting IS or income-based JSA are different (and more generous) than those for other claimants.

If you turn 60, you should check to see if you qualify for CTB even if you did not do so before that age. The different rules for income, capital and applicable amounts are covered in other chapters, but a summary of the income and capital rules is given on p178.

1. Who can claim council tax benefit

Main council tax benefit

You qualify for main council tax benefit (CTB) if:[1]

- you are liable for council tax in respect of the home where you are 'resident' (see p83); *and*
- your income is low enough (see Chapter 36); *and*
- unless you or your partner are getting the guarantee credit of pension credit (PC), your savings and other capital are worth £16,000 or less (see Chapter 37). There is no capital limit if you or your partner are getting the guarantee credit of PC;[2] *and*
- you are not a full-time student (although there are certain limited exceptions – see p587). This rule does not apply if you are 60 or over and neither you nor your partner are getting income support (IS) or income-based jobseeker's allowance (JSA);[3] *and*
- you satisfy the the 'right to reside test' (see p1361) and the 'habitual residence test' (see p1367); *and*
- you are not a 'person subject to immigration control' (see p1334). There are exceptions to this rule.

There are some groups of claimants to whom special rules apply (see p91).

Second adult rebate

Second adult rebate is designed to help you if you have certain other residents (referred to as second adults) in your home who do not share liability for council tax with you and who do not pay rent to you.

You qualify for a second adult rebate if:[4]

- you are liable for council tax in respect of the home where you are 'resident' (see p83); *and*

- you are the only person liable for the council tax on the home (with certain exceptions – see p83); *and*
- no one living in your home pays you rent (with certain expections – see p83); *and*
- you have one or more 'second adults' (see below) living with you who are on a low income; *and*
- you satisfy the 'right to reside test' (see p1361) and the 'habitual residence test' (see p1367); *and*
- you are not a 'person subject to immigration control' (see p1334). There are exceptions to this rule.

Note: second adult rebate is based on the circumstances of the 'second adult(s)' living with you. The whole of *your* income and capital is ignored when you claim second adult rebate. So you can get it even if *you* have a high income and/or capital worth more than £16,000.[5] However, at the time this *Handbook* was written, there *was* a capital limit for people aged 60 or over not getting IS, income-based JSA or the guarantee credit of PC. The rules are to be amended to correct this. See CPAG's *Welfare Rights Bulletin* for updates.

For second adult rebate it does not matter if you are a student.

Second adult rebate is an alternative type of CTB that can be paid instead of, but not as well as, main CTB. Whenever you claim CTB the local authority must assess you for both types and award whichever is the greater.[6]

Who counts as a second adult

You must have at least one 'second adult' residing with you to qualify for second adult rebate. In practice, residents classified as second adults are mainly the same people as those treated as non-dependants for main CTB purposes (see p86). However, someone residing with you does *not* count as a second adult if:[7]

- s/he is aged under 18;[8] *or*
- s/he has what is known as a 'status discount' (and is ignored for council tax purposes) – eg, full-time students and people who are severely mentally impaired;[9] *or*
- s/he is your partner with whom you are jointly liable for council tax;[10] *or*
- s/he is jointly liable to pay the council tax with you – eg, s/he is a joint owner or tenant. Although you cannot get second adult rebate for her/him, s/he may be able to claim CTB for her/his own share of the bill).[11]

No one who resides with you counts as a second adult (and you therefore cannot get second adult rebate) if:

- you are a member of a couple or polygamous marriage, unless both you and your partner (or in the case of a polygamous marriage, at least two of the members) have status discounts;[12] *or*

- you are living with one or more other people, all of whom are jointly liable for council tax with you (eg, as joint owners or tenants) and at least two of those who are jointly liable do *not* have status discounts.[13]

Residents liable to pay rent

You cannot qualify for second adult rebate if a second adult who resides with you is liable to pay you rent for occupying your home. Any people paying you rent who do not count as second adults are ignored for these purposes.[14] Some local authorities consider you not entitled to second adult rebate if *any* resident is liable to pay you rent. You should argue that if a person paying you rent does not come within the description of second adult, s/he does not prevent you receiving second adult rebate.

Liability to pay council tax

See CPAG's *Council Tax Handbook* for the rules about council tax. If you are jointly liable to pay council tax this may affect the amount of main CTB or second adult rebate you receive (see pp86 and 91).

Where you are resident

For CTB purposes, you are a resident in the home where you have your 'sole or main residence'.[15] This is the same criterion as for liability for council tax, so any decision on your sole or main residence should be the same for CTB purposes.[16] Your main residence is the property that a reasonable onlooker with knowledge of the facts would regard as your home.[17] **Note:** you cannot qualify for CTB if you are a prisoner on temporary release.[18]

Temporary absence from home

A property can count as your sole or main residence even if you spend substantial periods of time away from it, if you consider it to be the main place where you live.[19] However, if you are absent from home for more than a set temporary period, you cannot qualify for CTB.[20]

The rules about temporary absence from your home are broadly the same as those for housing benefit (HB) (see pp185 and 187).

Council tax benefit for more than one home

Unlike for HB, there are no rules on when you can and cannot get CTB for more than one home. However, if you occupy more than one property as a home (eg, because you have a large family) and you are liable for council tax on both, you can argue that you are a resident in, and qualify for CTB for, both properties.[21] However, if you choose to split your time between two homes (eg, your normal home and a holiday home), you can only get CTB for the property that is your sole or main residence.

2. The rules about your age

You must be aged 18 or over to qualify for council tax benefit (CTB). If you are under 18 you cannot be liable for council tax, so you do not need to claim CTB.

If you are 60 or over and neither you nor your partner are getting income support or income-based jobseeker's allowance, more generous rules apply.

3. Claiming for others

You claim council tax benefit for your family (see Chapter 30).

4. The amount of benefit

Calculating main council tax benefit

The amount of main council tax benefit (CTB) you get depends on:

- your 'applicable amount' (see Chapter 33). This is made up of personal allowances and premiums for any special needs;
- your 'maximum CTB' (see p85); *and*
- how much income and capital you have (see Chapters 36 and 37).

If you do not qualify for CTB currently, you may qualify when:

- the benefit rates go up every April; *or*
- you or your partner turn:
  - 60. Your applicable amount is then higher. If neither you nor your partner are on income support (IS) or income-based jobseeker's allowance (JSA), the income and capital rules are also more generous; *or*
  - 65. Your personal allowance is increased by the equivalent of the amount of the maximum savings credit of pension credit (PC), whether or not you receive this, if neither you nor your partner are on IS or income-based JSA.

In addition, if your income is too high for you to qualify for CTB currently, you might qualify once you or a member of your family becomes entitled to another benefit (a 'qualifying benefit'). See p92 for further information.

If you need extra financial assistance to meet your council tax, you might be entitled to discretionary housing payments (see p222).

Remember that if you:

- stop getting IS, income-based JSA, incapacity benefit or severe disablement allowance because of starting work or increasing your hours or your earnings, you may be entitled to extended payments of CTB (see p94);

- stop getting IS or income-based JSA because you are moving onto PC, you may be able to continue to receive CTB at the same rate for four weeks. The rules are the same as for housing benefit (HB)(see p211);
- have been incapable of work but move into work or training, you might count as a 'welfare to work beneficiary' (see p666). This means you retain entitlement to the disability or higher pensioner premium (see pp779 and 783) if you become incapable of work again within 104 weeks.

If you are on income support, income-based jobseeker's allowance or the guarantee credit of pension credit

Being on IS, income-based JSA or the guarantee credit of PC is an automatic passport to maximum CTB (once you have made a claim). You do not need to work out applicable amounts, income or capital. CTB = maximum CTB. **Note:** the new income-related employment and support allowance (see Chapter 7) will also be an automatic passport to maximum CTB.

For these purposes, you are treated as on income-based JSA:[22]

- when you satisfy the conditions of entitlement but are not being paid it because of a sanction (see Chapter 16);
- on your waiting days (see p366); *and*
- when it is not paid because of the 'loss of benefit' rules (see p1047).

If you are not on income support, income-based jobseeker's allowance or the guarantee credit of pension credit

- **Step one:** check that your capital is not too high (see Chapter 37).
- **Step two:** work out your maximum CTB (see below).
- **Step three:** work out your applicable amount (see Chapter 33).
- **Step four:** work out your income (see Chapter 36 but also p592 if you are a student and p881 if you are getting the savings credit of PC).
- **Step five:** calculate CTB:
  - If your income is **less than or equal to** your applicable amount, CTB = 'maximum CTB'.
  - If your income is **more than** your applicable amount, work out the difference. CTB = 'maximum CTB' minus 20 per cent of the difference between your income and your applicable amount.

Maximum council tax benefit

Maximum CTB is your net weekly liability for council tax after deducting:[23]

- any disability reduction, discount or transitional reduction;
- any non-dependant deductions (see p88).

Net weekly liability for council tax

Net weekly liability is assessed by dividing your annual council tax liability by the number of days in the financial year (365 or 366) and then multiplying this by seven.[24]

Example

Cara's net council tax liability is £810

Divide this by 365 = £2.219178

Multiply this by 7. Cara's net weekly liability = £15.534246

DWP guidance recommends that the figures should not be rounded until the final annual amount of CTB is worked out, and that calculations should usually be done to six decimal places.[25] When notifying you of your CTB a rounded figure can be specified.[26]

Joint liability

If you are a member of a couple and are jointly liable for council tax, one of you must claim CTB for both of you.[27] If you are also jointly liable with one or more other residents, you can claim on a two-person share of the bill. See p702 for who counts as a couple.

If you are (or count as) a single person and are jointly liable for council tax, the local authority calculates your maximum CTB by dividing the total net liability for council tax by the number of liable people. Any liable person who is a student not entitled to CTB is ignored.[28]

Example

Ravi, Maxine and Bill share a flat. They are jointly liable for a net annual council tax bill of £600. £600 divided by 3 = £200. They can each make a separate claim for CTB on £200 liability. Ravi and Maxine become a couple. Either of them can make a claim for CTB on £400 liability (a two-person share), with Bill making a separate claim on £200 liability (a one-person share).

Bill becomes a full-time student and is therefore excluded from entitlement to CTB. Ravi and Maxine can now claim CTB on the full £600 liability.

Under the council tax rules, a person who is jointly and severally liable for council tax can be held responsible for the full amount of council tax due on the property while receiving CTB only on her/his share. Note, however, that students who share with non-students are not jointly and severally liable for council tax with the non-students.[29]

Deductions for non-dependants

If other people normally live with you in your home who are not part of your family for benefit purposes (see p700) and are not liable for council tax ('**non-dependants**'), a set deduction is usually made from your CTB.[30] This is because it is assumed the non-dependant makes a contribution towards your outgoings, whether or not s/he does so. Examples of non-dependants are adult sons or daughters, or elderly relatives who share your home.

The rules for whether a person is a non-dependant are the same as for HB (see p196). However, the categories of people who are not non-dependants are slightly different.

People who are not non-dependants

The following people do *not* count as non-dependants, and no non-dependant deduction is made for them, even if they normally live with you:[31]

- a member of your family for benefit purposes (see p700);
- if you are in a polygamous marriage, a partner of yours and any child or qualifying young person in your household for whom you or a partner is responsible (see p710);
- a child or qualifying young person living with you who is not a member of your household (see p712);
- someone who is employed by a charitable or voluntary organisation as a resident carer for you or your partner and who you pay for the service. This can also apply if a public body pays on your behalf;
- someone who is jointly liable to pay council tax in respect of your home;
- someone who is liable to pay rent on a commercial basis (see p182) to you or your partner. However, although no non-dependant deduction can be made for her/him, the rent s/he pays can count as your income (see pp865 and 890).

If the person comes within the last two categories above, s/he can still be treated as your non-dependant if:[32]

- you or your partner are her/his landlord, s/he resides with you and s/he is:
  - a close relative of yours or your partner; *or*
  - the agreement to pay rent or council tax is not a commercial one. The meaning of these terms is the same as for HB (see p182); *or*
- you or your partner are her/his landlord and the agreement to pay rent or council tax has been created to take advantage of the CTB scheme. This does not apply if s/he had a legitimate liability to pay you or your partner within the eight weeks prior to entering into the agreement.
  For the meaning of 'taking advantage', see p184. **Note:** just because someone is taking advantage of the HB scheme does not mean that s/he is taking advantage of the CTB scheme. The local authority should consider the two schemes separately; *or*
- s/he is jointly liable with you for council tax on the home and within the last eight weeks was a non-dependant of one or more residents there, who were liable for the tax. This does not apply if you can persuade the local authority that the liability to pay council tax was not made to take advantage of the CTB scheme.

When no non-dependant deduction is made

The rules on when no non-dependant deduction is made are the same as for HB (see p198) except that:[33]

- all non-dependants on IS or income-based JSA are ignored and not just those under 25; *and*
- no deduction is made for the following people with what are known as status discounts:
  - people 18 or over for whom child benefit is payable and recent school and college-leavers under 20;
  - student nurses, foreign language assistants, apprentices and foreign spouses or dependants of students;
  - people who are 'severely mentally impaired'(see below);
  - people in detention;
  - certain carers; *and*
  - members of visiting armed forces, members of international headquarters and defence organisations and their dependants;
- no non-dependant deduction is ever made for a full-time student – even if s/he works during the summer vacation.

A person counts as **'severely mentally impaired'** if a doctor has certified that s/he has a severe impairment of intelligence and social functioning which appears to be permanent.[34] S/he must also be entitled to a qualifying benefit.[35] See CPAG's *Council Tax Handbook* for further information.

The amount of deductions

If you have a non-dependant living with you who is 18 or over and for whom a deduction must be made, a fixed amount is deducted from your CTB, whatever s/he pays you. Unless your non-dependant is in full-time paid work, a £2.30 deduction is made each week. If your non-dependant is in full-time paid work, the amount of the deduction depends on her/his gross weekly income as follows.[36]

Circumstances of the non-dependant	*Deduction*
18 or over and in full-time paid work with a weekly gross income of:	
– £369 or more	£6.95
– £296–£368.99	£5.80
– £172–£295.99	£4.60
– Under £172	£2.30
Others aged 18 or over (for whom a deduction is made)	£2.30

The rules on full-time paid work are covered in Chapter 27.

Remember:

- a non-dependant who is not in (or treated as in) full-time paid work does not attract the higher levels of deduction even if her/his income is £172 or more;
- if someone is on IS or income-based JSA (see p85) for more than three days in a benefit week, s/he does not count as in full-time paid work in that week. This means no deduction is made.[37]

As with HB, your CTB can be assessed using the income and capital of a non-dependant, instead of your own, if you are trying to take advantage of the CTB scheme (see p200).

Only one deduction is made for a non-dependant couple (or members of a polygamous marriage). The deduction made is the highest that would have been made if they were treated as individuals and based on their joint income, even if only one of them is in full-time paid work.[38]

If you share liability for the council tax with others, the amount of the non-dependant deduction is divided equally between you, even if the others are not claiming CTB.[39] However, if the local authority thinks that the non-dependant deduction only belongs to one of you, the whole deduction is made from that person's CTB. If you are a member of couple and share liability with someone, your CTB is reduced by two-thirds of the non-dependant deduction.

Discretionary housing payments

If you need extra financial assistance to meet your housing costs (including your council tax), you might be able to claim discretionary housing payments to top up your CTB. See p222 for further information.

Extra benefit for war pensioners

The local authority has the power to pay extra CTB to people getting certain war pensions. See p200 for further information.

Calculating second adult rebate

The amount of second adult rebate you get is a percentage of your council tax liability (see below), based on the gross income of the second adult. The percentages are:[40]

Income of second adult(s)	*Second adult rebate*
Second adult (or all second adults) on IS/income-based JSA/PC	25%
Second adult(s) total gross weekly income:	
– Under £169	15%
– £169–£219.99	7.5%
– £220 or more	Nil

Student dwellings Occupiers are either students excluded from entitlement to main CTB or on IS/income-based JSA/PC. At least one must be a student and at least one on IS/income-based JSA/PC.	100%

For the 100 per cent rebate, someone counts as a student excluded from entitlement to main CTB if s/he would be excluded if s/he were under age 60.[41]

Unless you qualify for a 100 per cent rebate, the maximum second adult rebate you can get is always 25 per cent of your council tax liability, even where you would have received a 50 per cent discount, or would have been exempt altogether were it not for the presence of two or more second adults in your home.

Council tax liability used for a second adult rebate

Second adult rebate is based on your gross council tax liability, after any reductions for disability and, in the case of 100 per cent rebate, any discounts, have been applied.[42] **Note:** this is not the same figure as used for main CTB. However, the procedure for converting annual to weekly amounts is the same (see p85). Where you have received a discount it must be added back on to the net amount of council tax payable to arrive at the figure used in the second adult rebate calculation. This is only done for the purposes of the CTB calculation – you still receive your discount in practice.

Assessment of second adult income

To obtain a second adult rebate, you must give the local authority details of the gross income of any second adults living with you. Where there is more than one second adult, their combined gross income is used.[43]

Gross income includes the second adult's:

- earnings;
- non-earned income, including social security benefits;
- actual income from capital (as opposed to, for example, 'tariff income'). The capital itself is ignored.

Gross income does *not* include:[44]

- any income of a second adult on IS, income-based JSA or PC;
- any attendance allowance or disability living allowance;
- certain payments from the MacFarlane Trusts, the Eileen Trust, the Skipton Fund, the London Bombings Relief Charitable Fund, the Fund and the Independent Living Funds;
- the income of any person with a status discount (see p82), except where that person has a partner who is not ignored for discount purposes (in which case

the gross income of both partners, less disregarded income, is taken into account).

A basic problem with second adult rebate is that it involves looking at the income of someone who may not always wish to give you that information. If you have difficulty establishing the income of your second adult(s) you may find that the local authority automatically assumes the highest income and that you are not entitled to CTB. If you cannot persuade your second adult(s) to give details of her/his income to you, they may be prepared to tell the local authority directly. Failing this, you could try finding out the going rate for the type of work they do, or social security benefits they receive, and ask the local authority to make a reasonable estimate based on that. The local authority should not assume the worst. It should assess what the likely level of your second adult's income is on the evidence available.[45]

Second adult rebates and jointly liable claimants

In contrast to main CTB, where there is more than one resident liable for the council tax in your dwelling, any second adult rebate is always calculated on the (pre-discounted) liability for your dwelling as a whole. Unless you are jointly liable with your partner, every jointly liable person must make her/his own separate claim in order to get a share of the second adult rebate. Any second adult rebate is then split equally between all the jointly liable residents.[46] However, if you are jointly liable with your partner, one of you claims on behalf of both and receives the entire second adult rebate (or if you are sharing with other liable residents, a couple's share).[47]

Discretionary housing payments

You cannot claim discretionary housing payments to top up your second adult rebate unless you would have been entitled to CTB if you had not received a second adult rebate. See p222 for further information.

5. Special benefit rules

There are some groups of claimants to whom special rules apply. These are covered in Chapters 25, 26 and 58. Special rules apply to:

- people subject to immigration control (see p1334);
- students (see p587);
- people in care homes and other special accommodation (see p621);
- prisoners (see p624).

6. Claims and backdating

The rules for claiming council tax benefit (CTB) are the same as for housing benefit (HB). See p200 for full details, substituting CTB where it says HB. The different rules for CTB are covered below. Remember that:

- you can claim CTB even if you have already paid your council tax bill in advance;
- if you are in arrears with your council tax bill, this does not affect your right to claim CTB. You may even be able to get your claim backdated (see below and p206);
- if you want to claim discretionary housing payments, you must claim separately. See p223 for further information.

Claiming in advance

The rules about advance claims for CTB are generally the same as for HB (see p205). You can also claim CTB up to eight weeks before you become liable for council tax and you are treated as having claimed on the day your liability begins.[48]

Council tax benefit after an award of a 'qualifying benefit'

You might not be entitled to CTB currently, but would be once you or a member of your family become entitled to another 'qualifying benefit' – eg, disability living allowance or carer's allowance. Alternatively, you might be entitled to a higher rate of benefit once the qualifying benefit is awarded. If you are already entitled to CTB when the qualifying benefit is awarded, see pp1070 and 1077. If you only qualify for CTB when the qualifying benefit is awarded, see p205.

Backdating your claim

The rules about late claims and backdated CTB are the same as for HB (see p206). In addition, if you did not claim CTB because your name was not put on the council tax bill, you should argue that you have good cause for a late claim because you did not realise you were liable for council tax as the local authority had failed (via the council tax bill) to inform you of this.

There is a special rule if your local authority has not set its council tax rate by the beginning of the financial year.[49] As long as you claim within one month of the council tax being set or imposed, your claim is backdated to 1 April, or the date you first became entitled to CTB, if that is later.

Notice of the decision

You receive separate decision notices for HB and CTB. However, the information which must be included is the same (see p208) except that those items specifically relating to rent are excluded in a CTB decision notice and, instead, it must show your weekly council tax liability rounded to the nearest penny.[50] Among other things, it should also include:

- if you have been assessed for, and are entitled to, both main CTB and second adult rebate, the amount of benefit entitlement in each case and the fact that you can only be paid the higher amount;[51]
- if you have been assessed for a second adult rebate, the gross income of any second adult(s) used to determine the rate of CTB, including where any second adult is on income support, income-based jobseeker's allowance or pension credit.[52]

7. Getting paid

There is no minimum entitlement to council tax benefit (CTB). This means that you are paid CTB however low your entitlement is.

Your **entitlement to CTB starts:**[53]

- if you became liable for council tax in the first of the weeks for which you are claiming, from the Monday of that week; *or*
- in all other cases, from the Monday following your date of claim (or following the date from which you are claiming if your claim is backdated).

The rules for when your **entitlement to CTB ends** are the same as for housing benefit (HB) (see p209). **Note:** you must let the local authority know about certain changes in your circumstances and the local authority can review your claim regularly.

Payment of CTB is normally made by reducing your annual council tax bill. Your weekly benefit is converted to a daily figure by dividing by seven and then multiplying the answer by the number of days between your first day of entitlement and the following 31 March.

If you are jointly liable for council tax with one or more other residents, apart from your partner, remember that any CTB they receive is also credited to the same bill as your own. You need to take this into account when agreeing with them how any remaining balance of council tax liability should be shared between you.

Where your CTB cannot be used to reduce your bill (eg, you have already paid it in full), payment can be made direct to you.[54] Usually you must ask for the money. If you do not, your CTB is likely to be credited against your next year's bill.[55] However, if you are no longer liable for council tax in an authority's area, it must send you any outstanding CTB within 14 days if possible.[56] Payment is normally made to you or to your appointee, if you have one (see p214).[57]

Continuing payments

There are two situations when your CTB can continue to be paid even though your entitlement may otherwise have changed. If you stop claiming:

- income support (IS) or income-based jobseeker's allowance (JSA) because you are moving onto pension credit (PC) you may be able to continue to receive CTB at the same rate for four weeks. The rules are the same as for HB (see p211);
- IS, income-based JSA, incapacity benefit (IB) or severe disablement allowance (SDA) because of starting work or increasing your hours or your earnings, you may be entitled to extended payments of CTB (see below).

Extended payments on starting work

If you are on IS, income-based JSA, IB or SDA and your entitlement ends because you start work, or increase your hours or pay, you may be entitled to continue to receive the same amount of CTB as you did before your entitlement ended. This is paid for up to four weeks. If you pay rent, you may also be entitled to extended payments of HB. For information about extended payments, see p211. The rules are the same as for HB.

Note: your entitlement to CTB also ends in the circumstances described above and you must make a new claim – ie, to continue to get CTB after the extended payments end (see p209). If you do not notify within a four-week time limit, or make a new claim, you could be overpaid CTB and you may have to repay it. See pp1021 and 1033 for further information. The Government says, however, that the rules are to be amended in October 2008. Your entitlement to CTB will no longer end and you will not have to make a fresh claim. Instead, this will be dealt with as a normal change of circumstances. See CPAG's *Welfare Rights Bulletin* for updates.

Amount of extended payments

The weekly amount of your extended payment of CTB is the amount of CTB you got in the last week before your entitlement to IS, income-based JSA, IB or SDA ceased.[58] The rules on how long the payment lasts are the same as for extended payments of HB (see p212). However, you *are* paid extended payments of CTB during rent-free periods. If you move, you get the maximum CTB (see p85) applicable to your new address minus any non-dependant deductions (see p86) that applied at your old address.[59] However, if you are getting extended payments because you stopped getting IB or SDA, you are paid the amount of weekly CTB payable in your last week of entitlement if this is lower.[60]

If you were being paid discretionary housing payments (see p222), ask for these to continue for the extended payment period.

If you claim CTB on the basis of your income from work and your new entitlement is higher than your extended payment, you can be paid up to the level of your new entitlement.

Suspending benefit

Local authorities have powers to suspend and terminate benefit (see p984).

Delays and complaints

The rules are the same as for HB (see p216).

Payments on death

If a claimant dies, any outstanding CTB can be paid to her/his personal representative or, if there is none, to the next of kin aged 16 or over.[61] A written application for this must be sent to the local authority within 12 months of the death.

Change of circumstances

It is your duty to report any changes in circumstances which might affect your right to, or the amount of, your CTB or payment of your benefit.[62] You should do this promptly in writing to the office handling your claim (although in individual cases notification may be accepted in a form other than in writing). If your local authority allows you to claim CTB by telephone, you can also report a change of circumstances by telephone (unless it says you must report it in writing). Note that if your local authority authorises it, you can report changes electronically (eg, by email).[63] However, it is always best to report a change in writing and to keep a copy in case of a dispute in the future.

If you do not report a change promptly in writing, any resulting overpayment may be recoverable from you (see Chapter 39). If you are considered deliberately to have acted falsely or dishonestly, you may also be guilty of an offence (see Chapter 40).

The rules are the same as for HB (see p217) except that:

- you do not need to notify any changes in rent for council tax purposes, nor do you have to tell the local authority the amount of council tax you pay;[64]
- if you are getting second adult rebate, you must give written notice of any changes in the number of adults living in your home and any changes to their gross income.[65]

There are additional changes you have to report if you are getting PC. The rules are the same as for HB (see p218).

When changes in circumstances take effect

The rules about when changes in circumstance take effect are generally the same as those for HB (see p219), but there are some differences. As with HB, normally, a change affects your CTB from the Monday after it occurs.[66] However, the following changes affect your benefit from the date they occur:[67]

- a change in the amount of your council tax;
- changes to the CTB regulations;
- the fact that you have become part of a couple;
- the death of, or separation from, your partner.

If two or more changes occur in the same week and each takes effect from a different date under the above rules, they are all taken into account from the date of the first change.[68]

Overpayments and fraud

If you are overpaid CTB, you might have to repay it. The rules on overpayments are covered in Chapter 39.

If you have been accused of fraud, see Chapter 40. You might get a reduced amount of CTB if you have been sanctioned for benefit offences (see p1049).

8. Challenging a council tax benefit decision

You can apply for a revision or supersession of a council tax benefit decision or appeal against it (see Chapters 41 and 42).

9. Tax, tax credits and other benefits

Council tax benefit (CTB) is not taxable.

Tax credits

If you are in work you may be able to claim working tax credit (WTC). Whether or not you are in work, you may be able to claim child tax credit (CTC). WTC counts as income when working out your CTB. So does CTC, unless you are 60 or over and neither you nor your partner are getting income support (IS) or income-based jobseeker's allowance (JSA).

Means-tested benefits

If you pay rent, you may be able to claim housing benefit (HB) as well as CTB. If you are on a low income, you may be able to claim other means-tested benefits to top this up. Entitlement to IS, income-based JSA or the guarantee credit of pension credit acts as an automatic passport to maximum CTB (see p85). **Note:** income-related employment and support allowance (see Chapter 7) will also be an automatic passport to maximum CTB.

Non-means-tested benefits

The non-means-tested benefits in this *Handbook* (other than attendance allowance (AA), disability living allowance (DLA), guardian's allowance and, if you are 60 or over and neither you nor your partner are getting IS or income-based JSA, child benefit) are taken into account as income when working out the amount of CTB you get. However, it can still be worth claiming these benefits. If you, your partner or your child(ren) qualify for certain non-means-tested benefits (including AA, DLA and child benefit) you also qualify for certain premiums (see p775) and potentially a higher rate of CTB. If you think you might qualify you should seek advice to see if you would be better off.

You may only qualify for CTB once you or a member of your family are awarded another benefit, known as a 'qualifying benefit'. You may be entitled to a higher rate of CTB once the qualifying benefit is awarded. See p92 for information.

Passports and other sources of help

If you are on a low income, you might qualify for certain health benefits, such as free prescriptions (see Chapter 9). You may also qualify for other sources of help (see p14), or a funeral expenses payment, maternity grant or another payment from the social fund (see Chapters 21 and 22).

Financial help on starting work

If you stop getting IS, income-based JSA, incapacity benefit or severe disablement allowance because you start work or your hours or earnings in your existing job increase, you may be entitled to extended payments of HB or CTB. This means you can usually continue to get the same amount of benefit for four weeks (see p94). You may also be able to get a child maintenance bonus (see p757), mortgage interest run-on (if you have a home loan – see p823) and a job grant (see p14). See p14 for information about other financial help you might get.

Notes

1. **Who can claim council tax benefit**
1 s131(1)(a) and (3)-(5) SSCBA 1992
2 Reg 16 CTB(SPC) Regs
3 Reg 45 CTB Regs
4 s131(1)(b), (3) and (6) SSCBA 1992
5 Sch 5 para 46(1) CTB Regs; reg 16 CTB(SPC) Regs
6 s131(9) SSCBA 1992; CH/48/2006
7 s131(7) SSCBA 1992
8 s6(5) LGFA 1992
9 Sch 1 LGFA 1992
10 Reg 63(a) CTB Regs; reg 47(a) CTB(SPC) Regs
11 Reg 63(c) CTB Regs; reg 47(c) CTB(SPC) Regs
12 Reg 63(b) CTB Regs; reg 47(b) CTB(SPC) Regs
13 Reg 63(d) CTB Regs; reg 47(d) CTB(SPC) Regs
14 s131(6)(a) and (7) SSCBA 1992
15 s131(11) SSCBA 1992; s6(5) LGFA 1992; reg 2(1) CTB Regs; reg 2(1) CTB(SPC) Regs
16 R(H) 3/08
17 *Williams v Horsham District Council* [2004] unreported, EWCA Civ 39, 21 January 2004
18 Reg 8(5) and (6)(c) CTB Regs; reg 8(5) and (6)(c) CTB(SPC) Regs
19 *Ward v Kingston upon Hull MBC* [1993] RA 71 (QBD)
20 s131(3)(b) SSCBA 1992; reg 8 CTB Regs; reg 8 CTB(SPC) Regs
21 R(H) 3/08

4. **The amount of benefit**
22 Reg 2(4) CTB Regs; reg 2(4) CTB(SPC) Regs
23 Reg 57(1) and (2) CTB Regs; reg 40(1) and (2) CTB(SPC) Regs
24 Reg 57(1) CTB Regs; reg 40(1) CTB(SPC) Regs
25 Annex B A5 GM
26 Sch 8 paras 9-10 CTB Regs; Sch 7 paras 9-10 CTB(SPC) Regs
27 Reg 57(4) CTB Regs; reg 40(4) CTB(SPC) Regs
28 Reg 57(3) CTB Regs; reg 40(3) CTB(SPC) Regs
29 **EW** ss6(4) and 9(2) LGFA 1992
S ss75 and 77 LGFA 1992
Both Sch 1 para 4(2) LGFA 1992
Note that the definition of student is different from that for CTB.
30 Regs 3 and 57(1) CTB Regs; regs 3 and 40(1) CTB(SPC) Regs
31 Reg 3(2) CTB Regs; reg 3(2) CTB(SPC) Regs
32 Reg 3(3) CTB Regs; reg 3(3) CTB(SPC) Regs
33 Reg 58(6)-(8) CTB Regs; reg 42(6)-(8) CTB(SPC) Regs
34 Sch 1(2) LGFA 1992
35 Reg 3 CT(DD)O
36 Reg 58(1),(2) and (9) CTB Regs; reg 42(1),(2) and (9) CTB(SPC) Regs
37 Reg 6(6) CTB Regs; reg 6(6) CTB(SPC) Regs
38 Reg 58(3) and (4) CTB Regs; reg 42(3) and (4) CTB(SPC) Regs
39 Reg 58(5) CTB Regs; reg 42(5) CTB(SPC) Regs
40 Reg 62 and Sch 2 para 1 CTB Regs; reg 46 and Sch 6 para 1 CTB(SPC) Regs
41 Sch 2 para 1(1)(b) CTB Regs; Sch 6 para 1(1)(b) CTB(SPC) Regs
42 Reg 62 and Sch 2 para 1(2) CTB Regs; reg 46 and Sch 6 para 1(2) CTB(SPC) Regs
43 Reg 62 and Sch 2 para 1 Table CTB Regs; reg 46 and Sch 6 para 1 Table CTB(SPC) Regs
44 Reg 62and Sch 2 paras 1 (Table) 2 and 3 CTB Regs; reg 46 and Sch 6 paras 1 (Table) 2 and 3 CTB(SPC) Regs
45 CH/48/2006
46 Reg 62(2)CTB Regs; reg 46(2) CTB(SPC) Regs
47 Reg 62(3) CTB Regs; reg 46(3) CTB(SPC) Regs

6. **Claims and backdating**
48 Reg 69(10) CTB Regs; reg 53(10) CTB(SPC) Regs
49 Reg 69(11) CTB Regs; reg 53(11) CTB(SPC) Regs
50 Sch 8 paras 9(a) and 10(a) CTB Regs; Sch 7 paras 9(1)(a) and 10(a) CTB(SPC) Regs

51 Sch 8 paras 12(b), 14(b) and 15 CTB Regs; Sch 7 paras 12(b), 14(b) and 15 CTB(SPC) Regs
52 Sch 8 para 13(c) and (e) CTB Regs; Sch 7 para 13(c) and (e) CTB(SPC) Regs

7. **Getting paid**

53 Reg 64 CTB Regs; reg 48 CTB(SPC) Regs
54 Reg 77(1)(b) and (3) CTB Regs; reg 62(1)(b) and (3) CTB(SPC) Regs
55 Reg 77(3)(a)(ii) CTB Regs; reg 62(3)(a)(ii) CTB(SPC) Regs
56 Reg 77(3)(b) CTB Regs; reg 62(3)(b) CTB(SPC) Regs
57 Reg 78 CTB Regs; reg 63 CTB(SPC) Regs
58 Schs 6 para 3 and 7 para 2 CTB Regs; Sch 5 para 2 CTB(SPC) Regs
59 Schs 6 paras 4 and 5 and 7 paras 3-5 CTB Regs; Sch 5 paras 3-5 CTB(SPC) Regs
60 Sch 7 para 4(b) CTB Regs; Sch 5 para 4(b) CTB(SPC) Regs
61 Reg 80 CTB Regs; reg 65 CTB(SPC) Regs
62 Reg 74(1) CTB Regs; reg 59(1) CTB(SPC) Regs; reg 4 SS(NCC) Regs
63 Reg 74A and Sch 9 CTB Regs; reg 59A and Sch 8 CTB(SPC) Regs
64 Reg 74(3) CTB Regs; reg 59(3) CTB(SPC) Regs
65 Reg 74(5) CTB Regs; reg 59(5) CTB(SPC) Regs
66 Reg 67(1) CTB Regs; reg 50(1) CTB(SPC) Regs
67 Reg 67(2)-(6) CTB Regs; reg 50(2)-(6) CTB(SPC) Regs
68 Reg 67(7) CTB Regs; reg 50(7) CTB(SPC) Regs

Chapter 6

Disability living allowance and attendance allowance

This chapter covers:

Disability living allowance (DLA) is a benefit for those who are under 65 when they claim. It has both mobility and care components. Although there are separate components, DLA is a single benefit for which you only have to make one claim. Each component can be paid at different rates. Attendance allowance (AA) is a benefit for those who are aged 65 or over when they claim.

You do not have to have paid national insurance contributions to qualify for DLA or AA.

There are some groups of claimants to whom special rules apply (see p120).

1. Disability living allowance mobility component

Disability living allowance mobility component (DLA mobility) is for people who have difficulties with walking. There are two rates: higher rate and lower rate.

Who can claim

You qualify for DLA mobility if:[1]

- you satisfy the residence conditions (see p1358);
- you are not a 'person subject to immigration control', although there are exceptions to this rule (see p1334);
- you satisfy the age rules (see p117) – ie:
  - for the *higher rate* of DLA mobility you must be aged three or over, but under 65;
  - for the *lower rate* of DLA mobility you must be aged five or over, but under 65;
- you are not in hospital (although sometimes DLA mobility is paid in hospital) (see p613);
- you are likely to be able, from time to time, to benefit from enhanced facilities for locomotion (see below);
- you satisfy the **'disability'** conditions – ie:
  - for the *higher rate* of DLA mobility:
    - you have a disability from a physical cause that means you are unable, or virtually unable, to walk (see p102); *or*
    - you are both deaf and blind (see p104); *or*
    - you were born without feet, are a double amputee or otherwise without both legs (see p104); *or*
    - you are 'severely mentally impaired', and have severe behavioural problems, and qualify for the highest rate of DLA care component (DLA care) (see p104);
  - for the *lower rate* of DLA mobility you must show that, although you are able to walk you are so severely disabled, physically or mentally, that, ignoring any ability to use familiar routes, you are unable to take advantage of your walking abilities outdoors without guidance or supervision from another person most of the time (see p105).[2] There is also an extra test if you are claiming on behalf of a child under 16 (see p118);
  - for *both rates* you must satisfy one of the disability conditions throughout the three months before the start of your award and be likely to satisfy it for the next six months (unless you are terminally ill – see p107). But see p123 if a previous award had ended and you are reclaiming.

To 'benefit from enhanced facilities for locomotion'

To qualify for either rate of DLA mobility you must be able to 'benefit from enhanced facilities for locomotion'. This means you must be able to take advantage of outdoor journeys. It is not essential that you are interested in or enjoy going out, provided it would be beneficial for you to do so.[3] For example, you can get DLA mobility even if you have to be carried out to a car for a ride.

Disability conditions for higher rate mobility component

'Unable or virtually unable to walk'

You are eligible for higher mobility if 'your physical condition as a whole is such that, without having regard to circumstances peculiar to [you] as to the place of residence or as to the place of, or nature of, employment:

- you are unable to walk; *or*
- your ability to walk out of doors is so limited, as regards:
  - the distance over which; *and/or*
  - the speed at which; *and/or*
  - the length of time for which; *and/or*
  - the manner in which you can make progress on foot without severe discomfort,

  that you are virtually unable to walk; *or*
- the exertion required to walk would constitute a danger to your life or would be likely to lead to a serious deterioration in your health'.[4]

Your personal circumstances should not be taken into account. It is not, for instance, relevant if you live a long way from your nearest bus stop,[5] or if you are no longer able to use public transport.

Physical disability

To qualify for higher mobility your inability, or virtual inability, to walk must have a physical cause.[6] There may be a physical cause, such as pain or dizziness, even if there is no medically diagnosed reason for this. It does not matter if the original cause was mental so long as there is a current physical cause. For example, someone who has severe depression and whose muscles have atrophied, so that s/he is now virtually unable to walk could qualify. Where there is a combination of physical and mental factors, the physical contribution must be more than minimal. If you have myalgic encephalomyelitis (ME) or chronic fatigue syndrome, this should be accepted as having a physical origin unless there is evidence that your mobility restrictions have a purely psychological cause.[7] Inability to make progress on foot because of behavioural problems can qualify if you can show that the cause is physical – eg, Downs Syndrome or autism, both of which are accepted as disorders of development of the brain.[8]

Unable to walk

You are unable to walk if you cannot move your body along by alternate, weightbearing steps of the feet.[9]

Prostheses, aids and medication

Your ability to walk is considered after taking into account any prosthesis or artificial aid you habitually wear or use, or that would be suitable for you.[10] You may not qualify if you are able to walk with a stick or crutches. However, someone with one leg and no artificial limb suitable for her/him to use is regarded as 'unable to walk', even if s/he can get around on crutches.[11] If you have no feet you qualify automatically (see p104).[12]

Your walking is assessed taking account of any medication you normally and reasonably use (eg, it may not be practical to carry a bulky nebuliser).[13] But you should not be expected to undergo surgery, and if you do not take the prescribed medicines or treatment your walking should be assessed as you are now, not how you might be if you accepted the treatment.[14]

Outdoors

The test is whether you can walk outdoors, not indoors. If you have problems with your balance on uneven pavements and roads, or you have a lung or other condition which is made worse by wind or rain, these are relevant factors.[15]

Distance

The law does not require a specific distance to be used when determining your inability to walk. In practice, you may well be refused benefit if you state that you can walk more than 50 metres. However, your walking speed, the time it takes you to cover the distance and your manner of walking are also relevant and you should give details about these on the form.[16]

Without severe discomfort

Any walking you can achieve only with severe discomfort should be ignored when considering whether you are virtually unable to walk.[17] If, when you walk, you feel severe discomfort – eg, pain or breathlessness brought on by walking[18] – you should make this clear. You may be able to walk a distance without severe discomfort, followed by a further distance which does cause you severe discomfort, and then have to stop altogether. In this case it would be incorrect to decide that discomfort became severe only when it was so great as to prevent you walking.[19] The correct test is 'how far the person can walk before severe discomfort is occasioned by going any further'. But further walking (ie, without severe discomfort) after a brief rest stop could be taken into account.[20] If you are already in severe discomfort before you start to walk, even if the pain gets no worse, you should count as virtually unable to walk so long as your disability affects the physical act of walking. For example, someone with an injured foot qualified in this way.[21] You do not, however, count as virtually unable to walk if something unconnected with walking causes the discomfort. For example, someone whose skin blistered in sunlight was held not to be virtually unable to walk even though he was in severe discomfort outdoors.[22]

The exertion required to walk

You can qualify for higher mobility if walking is dangerous to your health. The 'exertion required to walk' must lead to a danger to life or a serious deterioration in health. However, a person with ME, who needed a few days' rest after walking, did not satisfy the test. You need to show that you would never recover, or recovery would take a significant period of time (eg,12 months) or would require some form of medical intervention.[23]

Blind and deaf

You are treated as being unable to walk if:

- the degree of disablement resulting from your loss of vision is 100 per cent; *and*
- the degree of disablement resulting from your loss of hearing is 80 per cent on a scale where 100 per cent represents absolute deafness;[24] *and*
- the combined effects of the blindness and deafness mean that you are unable to walk to any intended or required destination while out of doors, without the help of another person.[25]

The Regulations do not specify how to assess the degree of disablement, but caselaw suggests that the industrial injury provisions should be used.[26] These state that 100 per cent disablement through 'loss of vision' means 'loss of sight to such an extent as to render the claimant unable to perform any work for which eyesight is essential'.[27] This is the same definition as that used when someone is registered as blind.

If your level of hearing loss, averaged between both ears at 1, 2 and 3 kHz is at least 87decibels, you will satisfy the 80 per cent disablement test.[28] You may be required to undertake a hearing test. The assessment of your hearing ability takes into account any hearing aid you use or could reasonably be expected to use.[29]

People without feet

If you do not have legs or feet (missing from the ankle or above) you are automatically treated as being unable to walk.[30] This is so even if you can walk with prostheses.

Severe mental impairment and behavioural problems

There is another route to *higher rate* DLA mobility for those with severe behavioural difficulties.

You qualify if:

- you are **'severely mentally impaired'** – ie, you have arrested or incomplete development of the brain, which results in severe impairment of intelligence and social functioning; *and*
- you display severe behavioural problems – ie:
  - you exhibit extreme disruptive behaviour; *and*
  - you regularly require someone else to intervene and physically restrain you in order to prevent you causing injury to yourself or others or damage to property; *and*

- you are so unpredictable that another person has to be present and watching over you whenever you are awake; *and*
- you qualify for the highest rate of DLA care.[31]

If you do not meet all of the above elements of the severe mental impairment test – eg, you may not be sufficiently unsettled at night to get the highest rate DLA care, there is nothing to stop you trying to qualify for higher mobility on the basis that you are virtually unable to walk (see p102). You could argue that your disability prevents you from walking effectively, causing so many refusals to walk that you can be said to be virtually unable to walk.[32]

Arrested or incomplete development

You can only be regarded as having 'arrested or incomplete development of the brain' if this is something that occured before the brain reached its final development. Medical opinion suggests this is at or before the age of 30. Someone with Alzheimer's disease, a degenerative condition which occurs after the brain has fully developed, would not qualify under this route.[33] In the case of an illness such as schizophrenia you may qualify via the 'severe mental impairment' route, but the age at which your illness began is significant and you also need to have a severe impairment of intelligence *and* of social functioning.[34]

Severe impairment of intelligence

If your IQ is 55 or less it is generally accepted as a 'severe impairment of intelligence'. However, some people may have a higher IQ but be unable to apply it practically.[35] Your 'degree of judgement in relation to everyday living' should also be taken into account.[36] For example, an autistic child with no awareness of danger may have severely impaired intelligence even if her/his IQ is over 55.[37]

Physical restraint

Physical restraint may involve as little as a hand on the arm. You do not need to show that any force is used.[38] If the presence of those who watch over you is enough to prevent you from being disruptive altogether or a specially adapted environment allows you to be safely left alone, you may not pass the test.[39]

Disability condition for lower rate mobility component

You qualify for *lower rate* DLA mobility if you are 'so severely disabled physically or mentally' that you cannot walk outdoors 'without guidance or supervision from another person most of the time'.[40]

Any walking that you can accomplish on familiar routes is ignored for the purposes of this test – but inability to walk, whether on familiar or unfamiliar routes, should be considered.[41] If you experience pain or discomfort as a result of walking, but you do not satisfy the 'virtually unable to walk' test for *higher rate* DLA mobility (see p102), you do not necessarily qualify for *lower rate* DLA mobility. Qualification for lower rate DLA mobility is based on an assessment of your need for supervision or guidance rather than your physical ability to walk.[42]

'Guidance' and 'supervision' clearly overlap and some forms of assistance could be treated as either guidance or supervision (see below).

Fear and anxiety

You can qualify for the lower rate on the basis of mental as well as physical disablement. If you have an anxiety disorder and you are mentally disabled to the extent that you need the help of an escort to overcome your fear of going outside, you may satisfy the 'guidance or supervision' requirement.[43] If no amount of reassurance can persuade you to go outside, you would not qualify.[44] However, if you can just manage a walk into your garden this may be enough to qualify.[45]

Any fear or anxiety that stops you going out on your own must arise from a mental disability in order to count. Fear and anxiety arising from a physical disability, such as an ordinary rational fear of having to cope with incontinence while alone, is not sufficient, although you may still have a physical need for supervision.[46] If your physical disability causes you such fear or anxiety that you can be said to be mentally disabled and therefore need a companion outside, you may qualify.

Guidance

'Guidance' can take a number of different forms. It can mean physically leading or directing you, giving oral suggestion or persuasion, helping you avoid obstacles or places which upset you, or leading or persuading you when you become disorientated or have a panic attack.

If you are visually impaired and use a guide dog or a long cane you may still need guidance to follow directions, avoid obstacles or help you cross roads. A profoundly deaf person, whose primary method of communication is sign language, may require guidance in unfamiliar places if s/he is unable to ask for or follow directions.[47] Even though the deaf person's companion may only intervene occasionally, s/he will still be guiding or supervising 'most of the time' because otherwise the deaf person would not know when to change direction. However, deaf people may not qualify if they are 'capable of studying maps, reading street signs or communicating with passers by.[48]

Supervision

'Supervision' can also take different forms. It can be precautionary–accompanying and watching over you, in order to monitor your physical, mental or emotional state in case you need more positive action to encourage you to continue walking. It can also be monitoring the route ahead for obstacles, dangers, places or situations which might upset you. Supervision can take more active forms, such as encouraging, persuading or cajoling you, talking to you to take your mind off your fears,[49] or distracting you from possibly alarming situations through conversation.[50]

Unlike the 'continual supervision' condition for DLA care, supervision need not be required to prevent 'substantial danger'.[51] If you qualify for DLA care because you require continual supervision you may also qualify for lower rate DLA mobility.[52] However, you will not be automatically passported onto lower rate mobility. Your eligibility must be assessed on the mobility criteria alone.[53]

The supervision does not need to actually improve your walking ability, but should enable you to 'take advantage of the faculty of walking'. If you need to have someone with you because, for example, you are at risk of fits or seizures or a severe asthma attack,[54] even though you have no difficulty getting about, you can qualify for lower rate mobility.[55]

Terminal illness

Terminal illness is defined in the same way for the mobility component as for DLA care (see p121). However, if you are terminally ill you will not automatically qualify for DLA mobility. The only special treatment given is that, where a claim is made specifically on the basis that you are terminally ill, you do not have to satisfy the three-month backward qualifying condition.[56] The forward qualifying condition is modified to last for the period you are expected to live, rather than the usual six months.

2. Disability living allowance care component

Disability living allowance care component (DLA care) is for people with attention or supervision needs.

Who can claim

You qualify for DLA care if:[57]

- you satisfy the residence conditions (see p1358);
- you are not a 'person subject to immigration control', although there are some exceptions (see p1334);
- you are under the age of 65 when you first claim (see p117);
- you are not in hospital (see p611) or certain types of accommodation (see p617);
- you satisfy the '**disability**' conditions, for either:
  - the lowest rate of the care component (see 108); *or*
  - the middle rate of the care component (see 108); *or*
  - the highest rate of the care component (see p108); *or*
  - you are terminally ill (see p121);
- you have satisfied the disability condition throughout the three months immediately before your award begins (see p123 if you are re-claiming

within two years) and you are likely to continue to satisfy the disability conditions for the next six months *or* you are terminally ill.

Children under 16 also have to satisfy an extra disability test (see p118).

Disability conditions for lowest rate care component

You qualify for the lowest rate of DLA care if:[58]

- you are 16 or over and you are so severely disabled physically or mentally that you cannot prepare a cooked main meal for yourself if you have the ingredients (the 'cooking test' – see p109); *or*
- you are so severely disabled physically or mentally that you require (see p111), in connection with your bodily functions, attention from another person for a significant portion of the day, whether during a single period or a number of periods (see pp112 and 114).

Disability conditions for middle rate care component

To qualify for the middle rate of DLA care you must show that you are so severely disabled physically or mentally that you require (see p111):[59]

- frequent attention from another person throughout the day in connection with your bodily functions (see p112); *or*
- continual supervision throughout the day in order to avoid substantial danger to yourself or others (see p115); *or*
- prolonged or repeated attention at night (see p115) in connection with your bodily functions (see p112); *or*
- another person to be awake at night for a prolonged period or at frequent intervals to watch over you (see p116) in order to avoid substantial danger to yourself or others.

This means you must have either daytime or night-time attention or supervision needs.

Disability conditions for highest rate care component

To qualify for the highest rate of DLA care you must be so severely disabled physically or mentally that:

- you require frequent attention throughout the day in connection with your bodily functions, *or* continual supervision throughout the day to avoid substantial danger to yourself or others; *and*
- you require prolonged or repeated attention at night in connection with your bodily functions, *or* in order to avoid substantial danger to yourself or others you require another person to be awake at night for a prolonged period or at frequent intervals to watch over you;[60] *or*
- you are terminally ill (see p121).[61]

This means you must have both daytime and night-time requirements, *or* you must be terminally ill.

'So severely disabled physically or mentally'

To qualify, you must be 'so severely disabled physically or mentally' that you need attention or supervision. There is no requirement that you must have a specific medical condition – ie, one which has been named by a doctor. What is important is that you have a disability (ie, have some functional incapacity or impairment) as a result of which you have care needs.[62] However, medical evidence might still be important in deciding whether you have a disability and what your care needs are.[63]

Problems sometimes arise where, for example, a child has behavioural problems that have not been attributed to a disability. A tribunal of commisioners has ruled that what is key is whether you have the physical or mental power to control the behaviour.[64] Issues have also arisen regarding children with enuresis. One commissioner has held that immaturity (ie, unexceptional developmental delay) is not a disability,[65] but it is arguable that this no longer stands in light of this tribunal of commissioners' decision.

There is no extra test of severity; your disability is regarded as severe if you satisfy one of the disability tests.[66]

Care needs resulting from any medical condition caused or made worse by alcohol should be taken into account, whether or not you can control your drinking. The transitory effects of intoxication, such as incontinence or vomiting, can also be considered for the care component (and lower rate, but not higher rate, mobility component) if the consumption of alcohol is because of a medical condition that means you cannot realistically stop drinking.[67]

The cooking test

You qualify for the lowest rate DLA care if you can show that you are so severely disabled, physically or mentally, that you cannot prepare a cooked main meal for yourself if you have the ingredients. This test does not apply to children under the age of 16.[68] The meal in question is a labour-intensive main meal for one person, freshly cooked on a traditional cooker (but note that the mere fact that you use a microwave would not be proof that you cannot prepare a cooked main meal).[69] It is a hypothetical test about what you can reasonably do – it does not matter what you actually do or do not do.[70]

It is not enough to argue that you simply do not know how to cook. The test assumes that those who do not know how are at least willing to learn.[71]

The test is a broad view of your ability – it does not necessarily matter if there are some days when your ability is more or less than it is the rest of the time.[72]

You need to show that your disability makes you unable to perform the tasks that are needed to cook such a main meal. You need to explain about your ability to plan a meal and to prepare and cook it – eg, to:

- peel and chop vegetables;
- use taps;
- use cooking utensils;
- use a cooker;
- lift hot or heavy pans;
- drain vegetables;
- tell if food is cooked properly.

In order to cook a main meal you need to be able to manage both physical tasks (eg, lifting, carrying, bending, and using kitchen equipment) and mental tasks such as concentrating and planning.

- If you have a visual impairment you should qualify if you are unable to read labels or cooking instructions, check whether vegetables have been adequately prepared and washed or see whether food is properly cooked.
- If you have a mental condition and so lack the motivation or concentration to cook, you should satisfy the test.[73]
- You may qualify if you can perform some of the individual cooking tasks (eg, chopping meat or vegetables) but overall you do not have the stamina to prepare an entire meal. For example, if you have chronic back pain and cannot stand for long periods, it may not be reasonable to expect you to prepare a meal and wait for it to cook while sitting down.[74]
- You may qualify if breathing difficulties in a hot, steamy kitchen or nausea stop you cooking.[75]

Kitchen aids and adaptations

There is some confusion about whether the availability of cooking aids and adaptations is a relevant consideration for the cooking test. Since this is simply a hypothetical test of what you can or cannot reasonably do, you could argue that it is not appropriate, or reasonable, to consider whether your kitchen is, or could be, specially adapted.[76] It would certainly be incorrect to expect you to use a microwave to heat up convenience food.[77] However, cooking aids and adaptations may be taken into account if it is 'reasonable' to do so – eg, if you could readily obtain them.[78] If it is suggested you use a slotted spoon instead of draining vegetables from the pan, explain any difficulties you might still have lifting pans of water on and off the cooker. In another case it was ruled that although a perching stool may be useful to relieve fatigue or discomfort, you still need to be sufficiently agile and mobile to cook a meal.[79]

Reasonableness

Only those who could 'reasonably' be expected to prepare a cooked main meal should be regarded as being able to do so. What is reasonable depends on the circumstances of your case. For example, if you have blackouts or seizures it may be dangerous for you to cook. In one case, a person with haemophilia was judged to be at some risk and to experience some anxiety when cooking, but not to the extent that it was unreasonable for him to prepare a cooked main meal.[80]

Attention and supervision

'Requires'

In order to satisfy the attention or supervision conditions (see p107) you have to show that you 'require' this assistance from another person. This means that the assistance must be 'reasonably required' rather than 'medically required'.[81] For example, if you are incontinent and need help changing your bedding, that help should count as 'reasonably required' even if not actually required to help protect your skin.

The correct test is 'whether the attention is reasonably required to enable the severely disabled person as far as reasonably possible to live a normal life'.[82] Having a social life, taking part in recreation and cultural activities are part of normal life, and it is reasonable to want to do them.[83] It is, therefore, reasonable for a blind person to have someone read newspapers, describe television pictures, or guide her/him during social outings. Similarly, it is reasonable for a person with learning disabilities to have assistance in order to travel to, or take part in, social and recreational pursuits. What is reasonable in each case depends on the age and interests of the disabled person.[84]

Reasonably requires supervision

The requirement for supervision need only be reasonable. You are not expected to avoid doing everything that carries a risk of harm in order to avoid the need for supervision. You can avoid most risks by staying in a chair all day but that may be totally unreasonable.[85] It is not reasonable to expect you to avoid all situations in which you might fall.[86]

In considering your need for continual supervision (see p115), the fact that such supervision is actually provided should be regarded as strong evidence that it is required. As one chief commissioner said: 'Mothers would be unlikely to exhaust themselves by providing it unnecessarily for years.'[87]

If such supervision is not provided, because you live alone, then you may be told that your choice is 'a strong indication that ... [continual] ... supervision is not required'.[88] But this always depends on the facts of your particular case. You may reasonably require supervision even if you do not receive it. You should be very clear about the difficulties you have when your needs are not met, and about what help you think you need.[89]

Refusing medical treatment

Refusing medical treatment may affect the assessment. If you would be able to cope with less help were you to accept treatment you have been offered by your doctor, the help you need may not be regarded as reasonably required. You should argue that it is reasonable for you not to take the treatment – eg, because of the side effects. Refusing invasive surgery should be accepted. It should also be accepted as reasonable if your psychiatric condition causes you to refuse treatment.[90]

Attention

The attention you require must be in connection with **'bodily functions'**. These have been defined as the normal action of any organ of the body, or a number of organs acting together.[91] Thus, movement of the limbs is a bodily function that is used in walking. Eating is made up of the bodily functions of the jaw, mouth, stomach and alimentary tract. But the activity must be a normal action or purpose of that organ or set of organs so shopping or cleaning do not qualify because they are 'not functions of organs of the body, but merely things which a body can do if the relevant bodily functions... are working normally.'[92]

The attention is in connection with the bodily function if it is a substitute method of providing what the bodily function would provide if it were not totally or partially impaired.[93] For example, guiding a blind person so that s/he is able to walk outside should be treated as attention with the bodily function of 'seeing', rather than of 'walking'. A guide assists with 'seeing' by acting 'as the eyes' of a blind person.

'Attention' is 'a service of a close and intimate nature ... involving personal contact carried out in the presence of the disabled person'. The attention must need to be given in the physical presence of the disabled person.[94] It must also be in connection with the bodily function. So helping someone to drink counts; carrying the drinks to where they are sitting does not.[95] Although attention must usually involve personal contact, it need not take the form of *physical* contact. Contact established by the spoken word may count if, for example, you are blind.[96] Thus, reading, describing or giving verbal instructions can be attention. Similarly, if you would neglect yourself unless cajoled or stimulated to do routine tasks you may require attention in the form of active stimulation.[97] Spoken reassurance counts as long as the carer is required to be physically in the same place as the disabled person. Reassurance provided over the telephone and other types of support not required to be given in the physical presence of the disabled person cannot qualify as attention,[98] although they may indicate a need for attention where help cannot be provided otherwise.[99]

Attention or supervision?

'Attention' involves a service of an 'active nature'[100] whereas **'supervision'** is passive and 'may be precautionary or anticipatory, yet never result in intervention'.[101] However, where supervision does lead to intervention, this constitutes attention, so you should not regard the two categories as completely separate. For example, if you need to be supervised because you are likely to fall and injure yourself, you receive attention every time your carer gives you a steadying hand or warns you of an obstacle you are about to trip over.[102] If that attention is frequent you qualify for middle rate DLA care, even if the supervision is not 'continual' throughout the day. Sometimes an act can be both supervision and attention. It is, therefore, important to emphasise the full extent of your needs without trying to fit them neatly into either 'attention' or 'supervision' categories at the expense of leaving things out.

Communication

A tribunal of commissioners has ruled that communication is made up of a 'bundle' of bodily functions. This can include functions of the brain such as language processing, or the senses such as hearing. But you need to identify what bodily function is impaired and what attention is needed from another person in connection with that bodily function.[103] If you are profoundly deaf you may need an interpreter because you cannot hear spoken language,[104] or extra effort may be required to initiate a two-way conversation.[105]

Help to explain written information to a deaf person with poor literacy skills[106] or to someone with a learning disability may also qualify.[107]

Domestic duties

Attention must normally be carried out in the presence of the disabled person.[108] A period of attention can also include incidental activities which could take place outside the presence of the claimant. For example, if a carer strips a soiled bed at night, the additional tasks of wringing out the sheets, putting sheets to soak or hanging them up to dry could count as attention if done on the spot, as would cleaning a soiled carpet or furniture after an episode of incontinence.[109] Taking the washing away or doing the cleaning at a different time would not qualify as attention.

Other domestic tasks can usually be performed by a carer outside your presence and, therefore, do not normally count as attention. But it is different if you do your own domestic tasks with the help of a carer. If you are blind and someone helps you to cook for yourself by reading cooking instructions to you, this is assistance with the bodily function of 'seeing' and can count as attention.[110] Similarly, if you have a learning disability and go shopping, you may need help to communicate your requirements. There are, however, conflicting commissioners' decisions on whether assistance of this kind, which enables someone to perform her/his own domestic tasks, is attention that is reasonably required.[111] You should argue if a disabled person, given help, is able to shop or cook for her/himself, that this is part of what constitutes a 'normal life' (see definition of 'requires' on p111).[112]

Childcare

The assistance given to disabled parents to enable them to look after their children can also count as attention.[113] It will help if you can identify the bodily function in connection with which the parent needs attention. For example, lifting or holding babies so that their mother can feed them is a sufficiently intimate service.[114] Similarly, assisting a disabled mother to take part in outdoor activities with her children can allow her to lead a normal social life.[115] When assessing the *parent's* care needs a distinction must be made between help provided to the parent, which counts as attention, and that given directly to the child, which does not count.[116]

Special diets

Attention only counts if it needs to be given in the physical presence of the disabled person, so it will often be difficult to include help with food preparation. Arguably though, this type of help may, nonetheless, count as attention if it forms part of a broader sequence of care tasks. For example, the various parts of the process of regulating the blood sugar levels of a diabetic child, some of which require personal contact and some of which do not, should nonetheless *all* be treated as attention because they are integral elements of an overall regime.[117]

Night and day

An adult who needs help going to the toilet at 3am, a time when most people are asleep, clearly needs that help at night. Problems can sometimes arise when children or adults need supervision or attention in the late evening or early morning.

'**Night**' has been defined as 'that period of inactivity, or that principal period of inactivity, through which each household goes in the dark hours' beginning when 'the household, as it were, closes down for the night'.[118] The pattern of activities of the particular household needs to be taken into account. If a carer stays up into the small hours to help you but would otherwise go to bed earlier, that should count as night care.[119] Similarly if a carer gets up early in the morning to help you but would otherwise get up later with the rest of the household, that should count as night care.[120] If you live alone and go to bed unusually late or get up unusually early, your 'night' may be assumed to begin at a more average time of 11pm or to end at 7am.[121]

The definition of 'night' for a child is the same as for an adult, so that attention given to a child in the evening before the adults have gone to bed counts only towards satisfaction of the day condition.[122]

'Attention... for a significant portion of the day'

If you can show that you need attention for a 'significant portion of the day' you qualify for lowest rate DLA care.[123] A significant portion of the day can be either during a single period or a number of periods.

You may qualify for lowest rate DLA care if you only need help for *part* of the day, rather than *throughout* the day (see p115) – eg, you need help with activities connected with getting up, such as dressing and washing, at the beginning of the day and with activities connected with going to bed, such as undressing and washing, at the end of the day, but are otherwise able to care for yourself without help. Help at night does not count for the lower rate.[124]

The term **'a significant portion of the day'** is often taken to mean an hour or thereabouts.[125] But if your carer spends less time than that in total but has to give help for a brief period on a number of small occasions then that might qualify.[126] Or if your carer does not have much time available or the help s/he gives is in spells of particularly concentrated activity, less than an hour's help may be enough. Factors like the amount, importance or effect of the attention could count towards its significance.[127]

Frequent attention throughout the day

To satisfy the day attention condition you need to show that attention is required **frequently throughout the day.**[128] A frequent need might include help with toileting (whether that be to reach the toilet, use a commode, or deal with zips and buttons), or help to walk within your own home. These are both examples of activities which most people would reasonably engage in with some frequency during the course of a normal day. Most people who satisfy the 'frequency' condition do so by virtue of a range of different types of care needs which, when added together, occur frequently and throughout the day. For this test, it is the pattern of the needs across the day which is crucial. If you only need help at the beginning and end of the day you are unlikely to satisfy the test. The help you need must be both **'frequent'**, meaning 'several times – not once or twice'[129] and required 'at intervals spread over the day'.[130] However, even if the spread is uneven and there are lengthy periods when you do not need help, this should not necessarily disqualify you.[131]

Prolonged or repeated attention at night

The help that needs to be given in the night has to be either prolonged or repeated.[132] The DWP regards 20 minutes of attention as **'prolonged'**.[133] **'Repeated'** simply means twice or more.[134]

Because sleeping is a 'bodily function', soothing a child back to sleep counts as giving attention in connection with a bodily function.[135]

Continual supervision

You satisfy the **daytime supervision** condition if you require another person to provide 'continual supervision' throughout the day to prevent the risk of substantial danger, either to yourself or to others.[136] This supervision test consists of four parts.[137]

- **There must be a substantial danger to yourself or someone else as a result of your medical condition.** What constitutes a 'substantial danger' must be decided on the facts of each case. For example, if an elderly person falls, this is more likely to constitute a 'substantial danger' than if a younger person falls but only sustains minor bruises. What causes the fall may also be relevant. A person who loses consciousness would not be able to do anything to save her/himself.

- **The substantial danger must be one against which it is reasonable to guard.** This involves weighing the remoteness of the risk and the seriousness of the consequences should it arise. While the risk of a house catching fire may be remote, the consequences of leaving a disabled person who is unable to move alone in a house which did catch fire would be catastrophic. Similarly, the consequences of allowing a child to run out onto the road could be dire even though such an incident may be isolated.[138] Thus, it can be argued that you reasonably require continual supervision.[139] In assessing the likelihood of danger, the decision maker must look not only at what has happened in the past but at what may happen in the future.[140]
- **There must be a need for the supervision.** What should count as supervision is the level of supervision you 'reasonably require' (see p111). Although you may not receive much supervision (perhaps because you live alone), you may still qualify if you can show you ought to be receiving it. If you have mental health problems you may need supervision to help prevent you harming yourself. It is wrong to assume, without fully investigating your case, that if you really were at risk of harming yourself you would be a hospital inpatient.[141] Further, if you are at risk of committing suicide, it would also be wrong to suggest that no amount of supervision would prevent a determined suicide attempt and supervision is, therefore, not required. The correct approach is to decide whether supervision would result in 'a real reduction in the risk of harm to the claimant'.[142]
- **The supervision must be continual.** This is something less than 'continuous', but supervision which is required only occasionally or spasmodically is insufficient. The 'characteristic nature of supervision is overseeing or watching over considered with reference to its frequency or regularity of occurrence'.[143] Supervision can be precautionary and anticipatory. It does not necessarily involve direct intervention.

  If you are liable to epileptic fits without warning you may need continual supervision, although attention for the period between the fits is not required.[144] Even if you have warning of the fits so that you can prevent yourself from falling, you may require continual supervision if you suffer from prolonged periods of confusion afterwards.[145] If you are a parent with a young child you may need supervision so that there is someone to look after your child when you have a fit.

Watching over

You satisfy the night-time supervision condition if you need someone to be awake to watch over you at night to prevent the risk of substantial danger to yourself or others.[146] The person watching over you has to be awake for a 'prolonged period' or 'at frequent intervals'. DWP guidance suggests a 'prolonged period' may mean 20 minutes or more[147] and the term 'at frequent intervals' means more than twice.

3. Attendance allowance

Attendance allowance (AA) is a benefit for people aged 65 and over with attention or supervision needs. There is a higher rate and a lower rate, the rules of which are similar to those for the highest and middle rates of the disability living allowance care component (DLA care) respectively (see p108). Unlike DLA, AA does not have a mobility component.

Who can claim

You qualify for AA if:[148]

- you satisfy the residence conditions (see p1358);
- you are not a 'person subject to immigration control', although there are exceptions to this (see p1334);
- you are 65 or over when you first claim (see below);
- you are not in hospital (see p611) or in certain types of accommodation (see p617);
- you satisfy the '**disability**' conditions – ie:
  - you meet one or more of the day or night conditions (see p108); *and*
  - you meet the condition(s) throughout a period of six months, ending within at least two years of the date on which your award begins (see p124 if you are re-claiming within two years); *or*
  - you are terminally ill (see p121).

The disability conditions

The disability conditions for AA are the same as those for the middle or highest rates of DLA care. There is no equivalent in AA of the lowest rate of DLA care. You get lower rate AA if you satisfy the disability conditions for middle rate DLA care (see p108). You get higher rate AA if you satisfy the disability conditions for highest rate DLA care (see p108).

4. The rules about your age

Disability living allowance mobility component (DLA mobility) has lower and upper age limits, as described below. DLA care component (DLA care) has an upper age limit of 65.

Children aged under 16 must satisfy an additional test for DLA care and the lower rate of DLA mobility. They cannot claim the lower rate of DLA care by the 'cooking test' route.

You cannot claim attendance allowance (AA) if you are under 65.

Age limits for children

Children can get the higher rate of DLA mobility from the age of three onwards and the lower rate of DLA mobility from the age of five.[149] The three months before the child reaches the age at which s/he can get DLA mobility can form the qualifying period (see p107), enabling payment to be made from her/his birthday.

There is no lower age limit for DLA care. However, as with other claimants, a baby has to meet the qualifying conditions for three months before the allowance becomes payable, unless s/he is terminally ill.

Children under the age of 16 cannot qualify for the lowest rate of DLA care via the cooking test (see p109). A child can only qualify for lowest rate of DLA care if s/he requires attention for a 'significant portion of the day' (see p114).

There is also an additional test for children for the lower rate of DLA mobility and for DLA care.

The additional test for children

For the lower rate of DLA mobility, in addition to the usual guidance or supervision condition (see p106), you must also show that *either*:

- the child requires substantially more guidance or supervision (see p106) than children of her/his age in normal physical and mental health would; *or*
- children of the same age in normal physical and mental health would not require such guidance or supervision.[150]

This extra test does not apply to the higher rate of DLA mobility.

For DLA care, you must show that *either*:

- the child has attention or supervision requirements 'substantially in excess of the normal requirements' of a child of the same age; *or*
- the child has substantial attention or supervision requirements which younger children in normal physical and mental health may also have, but which children of the same age and in normal physical and mental health would not have.[151]

The extra test does not apply if you are claiming DLA care for a child who is terminally ill.[152]

As all young children require assistance throughout the day, it can be difficult to explain how you are providing attention or supervision which is 'substantially in excess' of what is normally required (see p127 for tips on filling out the children's claim form). It may be either because of the extra time you devote to these tasks, or 'by virtue of the quality or degree of attention or supervision which is required'.[153] For example, non-disabled children may need their food cut up, whereas disabled children may also need their food spooned into their mouths, or they may require you to be in the same room at all times, whereas you could supervise a non-disabled child from a different room.

For the lower rate DLA mobility test, able-bodied children may only require adults to accompany them, children with, for example, visual impairments or learning disabilities may need adults physically to hold or guide them, or to watch over them much more attentively (see p127 for tips on answering the mobility questions on the children's claim form). Similarly, a young deaf child may need someone to stay within touching distance or maintain eye contact, whereas a hearing child would not.[154]

The comparison should be with an 'average child' – ie, a child of average intelligence whose behaviour is neither particularly good nor bad.[155]

Aged over 65

You can claim AA if you are aged 65 or over. If you are approaching your 65th birthday, it is usually better to claim DLA since DLA has a mobility component and an additional lowest rate care component.

Normally, the upper age limit for claiming either rate of DLA mobility is 65. You must make your claim and be sufficiently disabled to qualify before the date of your 65th birthday, but you need not have completed the three-month qualifying period by then.[156]

Although you must be under 65 to qualify, once DLA mobility is awarded it can be paid beyond the age of 65. However, if your condition worsens or improves after you reach the age of 65, you cannot qualify for either rate of DLA mobility or the lower rate of DLA care for the first time.[157] You can renew a DLA mobility award or the lowest rate of DLA care award that expires after age 65, but you must reclaim within a year of the previous award ending.[158]

You can also be awarded either rate of DLA mobility or the lowest rate of DLA care after reaching the age of 65 if you have an existing award of another component of DLA and ask for a revision or supersession of that award after you are 65. You must show that you have satisfied the disability conditions for the new component since you were 64 or earlier. The qualifying period is three months for DLA mobility or six months for DLA care, unless you had already completed a three-month qualifying period by the time you turned 65.[159]

If your condition worsens, you can move up to the middle or highest rate of DLA care. You have to show that you have met the qualifying conditions for the middle or highest rate for six months before it can be awarded, not three months. This is because the rules about qualifying periods for those in receipt of DLA care over the age of 65 are the same as for AA.[160] If it has been over a year since your previous award ended, you must claim AA instead of DLA care.

5. The amount of benefit[161]

Disability living allowance mobility component (DLA mobility) is paid at two weekly rates:

- the *lower rate* of DLA mobility is £17.75;
- the *higher rate* of DLA mobility is £46.75.

DLA care component (DLA care) is paid at three weekly rates:
- the *lowest rate* of DLA care is £17.75;
- the *middle rate* of DLA care is £44.85;
- the *highest rate* of DLA care is £67.00.

Attendance allowance (AA) is paid at two weekly rates:
- the *lower rate* of AA is £44.85;
- the *higher rate* of AA is £67.00.

In addition, you are entitled to a Christmas bonus (see p9). You are not credited with national insurance contributions by virtue of receiving DLA or AA.

6. Special benefit rules

There are some groups of claimants to whom special rules apply. These are covered on p120 and in Chapters 26 and 58. Special rules apply to:
- people on renal dialysis (see below);
- people who are terminally ill (see p121);
- people subject to immigration control (see Chapter 58);
- people who have gone abroad (see Chapter 57);
- people in care homes (see p618);
- people in hospital (see p611);
- people in hospices (see p611);
- people in prison (see p625).

People on renal dialysis

Special rules may apply if you are undergoing renal dialysis on a kidney machine[162] that entitles you to the middle rate of disability living allowance care component (DLA care) or the lower rate of attendance allowance (AA).

To qualify, you need to have treatment regularly for two or more sessions a week. You also need to show that either you require, or the dialysis is of a type which requires, the attendance or supervision of another person.

These rules also apply if you dialyse in hospital as an outpatient and have no help from any member of the staff. Others who dialyse in hospital do not qualify by this special route but you can count these spells of hospital dialysis towards the qualifying periods. This helps those who alternate between dialysis in hospital and at home to get AA or DLA care more quickly for the times they dialyse at home. Even if you do not qualify under this route you may qualify for DLA care (see p107) or AA (see p117) under the ordinary conditions.

People who are terminally ill

You are regarded as **'terminally ill'** if you have a progressive disease and can reasonably be expected to die within six months as a result of that disease.[163] This does not mean that it must be more likely than not that you will die within this period. It simply means that death within six months would not be unexpected.

A terminally ill claimant is automatically treated as satisfying the conditions for the highest rate of DLA care and there is no requirement to satisfy the three-month qualifying period.[164] Similarly, the higher rate of AA is paid straight away without you having to serve the six-month qualifying period.[165] If you are terminally ill, you do not automatically get DLA mobility component (DLA mobility). You must satisfy the usual disability conditions for DLA mobility but you do not need to serve the usual three-month qualifying period.[166]

The DWP aims to deal with these claims within eight working days. They are referred to as 'claims under the special rules'.

The special rules apply only if your claim is made on that basis, or if an application for revision or supersession on an existing claim is made on that basis.[167]

Someone else is allowed to make a claim, or apply for a revision or supersession, on behalf of a terminally ill person without her/his knowledge or authority.[168]

The DWP can supersede your award if your condition or prognosis improves so that you are no longer regarded as 'terminally ill'.

Since September 2006, special rules awards have been made for a fixed period of three years. If there is already a mobility award in place, the length of the special rules award may be adjusted to finish at the same time as the mobility award. Since October 2007, existing special rules awards in place for more than three years have been subject to a 'review exercise'. If you are under the age of 65 your award will be reviewed. If you are aged 65–84 your award may be reviewed as part of a sample exercise. If you are over 85, you are exempt from this.

7. Claims and backdating

The success of a disability living allowance (DLA) or attendance allowance (AA) claim can often depend on how well you have completed the claim form.

A claim for AA or DLA should be made on the relevant DWP claim form – Form AA1 or DLA1. You can obtain the claim pack by contacting your local disability benefits centre, or by ringing the DWP freephone Benefit Enquiry Line for people with disabilities on 0800 882 200 (textphone 0800 243 355). Alternatively, you can request a claim form by sending in the tear-off coupon from leaflet DS702 for AA, or DS704 for DLA. You will then be sent a claim form by post (it may be wise to keep a record of the date you asked for it). The claim form is date-stamped and you have six weeks from the date of your request to return it.[169]

Claim packs are also available from Citizens Advice Bureaux, other advice agencies and on the DWP website (see Appendix 1). These packs are not date-stamped so you must send in the completed form as soon as possible to secure your date of claim. This is the date on which your form is received by the DWP (see p123). Keep a copy of your claim in case queries arise. The law allows you to return your claim form to any DWP office or 'alternative' office (see p958) but, in practice, you should send the completed claim pack to the disability benefits centre covering your area. You can also download or complete a form online on the DWP website (see p123 for date of claim).

Claims under the special rules for terminally ill people are made in a different way (see below).

In certain circumstances the Secretary of State may accept a written application which is not on the correct form (see p959).[170]

Information to support your claim

When you claim DLA or AA, you must satisfy the national insurance (NI) number requirement. In most cases this means you must provide your NI number. These requirements do not apply if you are claiming DLA on behalf of a child under 16.[171] See p962 for further details.

Who should claim

A claim for DLA or AA is normally made by the disabled person her/himself. A claim for a child under 16 or a person unable to manage her/his own affairs is made by the disabled person's appointee (see pp131 and 955).

Claiming for terminally ill people

If a claim is being made on the basis that a person is terminally ill (see p121), it may be made without that person's knowledge or authority. This applies equally to claims for AA, DLA care component (DLA care) or DLA mobility component (DLA mobility) (although in this latter case, as explained on p107, terminal illness only exempts the claimant from the rules about qualifying periods).[172]

These claims are known as 'claims under the special rules'. People claiming under these rules need to provide Form DS1500, completed by their GP or consultant, detailing their medical condition. They do not need to fill in the parts of the claim form relating to their need for personal care. If they wish to claim DLA mobility, they do need to answer the relevant questions.

It is possible for someone acting on behalf of a terminally ill person to request a revision or supersession of an unfavourable decision, and even to appeal to a tribunal, without that person's knowledge or permission.[173]

When the decision maker receives the DS1500 s/he makes an assessment on whether the person meets the special rules. If s/he decides s/he does not, the person can claim in the normal way or appeal the decision.

The date of your claim

The date of your claim is the date your request for a claim pack is received by the DWP, providing you return the properly completed form within six weeks of the date of your request.[174] If the DWP has issued a form without date-stamping it, write and explain when and where it was issued and ask for the claim to be treated as made on that date.[175] There is also discretion to extend the six-week deadline, so if you return the form late explain why.

If you are using a claim form issued by an advice agency or downloaded from the internet, your date of claim is the date your completed form is received by the DWP. If you submit a claim online it is treated as made on the date it is accepted by the system.[176]

If you claim the wrong benefit

A claim for DLA can be treated as a claim for AA and vice versa (see p963).[177] A claim for an increase of industrial injuries disablement benefit where constant attendance is needed can be treated as a claim for DLA or AA and vice versa (see p963).[178]

Claiming in advance

A claim for DLA or AA can be made before you have satisfied the three-month qualifying period for DLA[179] (see pp100 and 107) or the six-month qualifying period for AA[180] (see p117). As long as you claim no more than three months before you would qualify for DLA or six months before you would qualify for AA, and you satisfy the other qualifying conditions, you can be awarded DLA or AA in advance of your date of entitlement.

Renewal claims

DLA and AA can be awarded for fixed periods (see p130). Renewal claims are usually invited up to six months before your old award expires. It is important that you send back your completed renewal claim form before your old award expires as no backdating is possible.

Decision makers normally treat your renewal claim as a new claim beginning on the day after your old award runs out.[181] However, they may use the information you give in the renewal claim to revise or supersede your existing award, in which case your entitlement may be changed earlier.[182] If you think you have a strong case for an increased award, you should return your renewal form early and ask for a revision or supersession. If this is not the case, it is advisable to return the form nearer the date your current award runs out.

Reclaiming under age 65

If your award has ended and you reclaim within two years – eg, because your condition has deteriorated, you do not have to serve the standard three-month qualifying period again, provided you meet all the other qualifying conditions for the rate you previously received.[183] This is because the qualifying period is taken to be the last three months of your previous award.[184] If you reclaim a different rate, you do have to serve the standard qualifying period.

Reclaiming over age 65

If your DLA award ended after you reached 65 and you reclaim the same rate within one year, you can be paid without having to serve the standard qualifying period again. The qualifying period is three months for DLA mobility or six months for DLA care, unless you already completed a three-month qualifying period by the time you turned 65.[185] To reclaim another rate (see p119), you do have to serve the qualifying period again. If it has been over a year since your previous award ended, you must claim AA instead of DLA care, and you will not be able to reclaim DLA mobility.[186]

If your AA award has ended, you can reclaim the same rate within two years without having to serve the standard six-month qualifying period again.[187]

Completing the claim form

Make sure you get the correct form. There are two DLA claim packs – one for those under the age of 16 (DLA1 Child) and one for those aged 16 and over (DLA1) – and one AA claim pack (AA1). See p124 for tips on filling in your claim form.

If you find it difficult to complete the form, the DWP can help you complete it by telephone, or in some circumstances can send a visiting officer to do so. Most advice agencies can also help you.

Attendance allowance claims

The AA claim form is short and has just one page for day needs and one for night needs. Try and include all the information that is relevant and use extra pages if necessary. Sometimes the decision maker will phone you to ask for further information. If you do not want to be phoned, write this clearly on the form.

Disability living allowance claims

The DLA claim form is long and has several pages on different aspects of care and mobility. Fill in all the pages that are relevant. If the same difficulties apply on more than one page repeat the information or refer back to where you put it earlier in the form. There is space to include details of people who know about your difficulties. This could include carers and support workers as well as medical professionals.

The claim pack for adults

The DLA form asks you questions about your mobility problems, your supervision and attention needs, and your ability to cook a main meal. Do not worry if a lot of the questions do not apply to you. You can, for example, qualify for the lowest rate of DLA care because of the problems you have cooking a main meal (see p109), which only takes up one page of the claim pack.

You should give as much detail as you can. Do not feel bound by the size of the boxes. If you need extra space to explain your situation in full, use a separate piece of paper.

There is a statement to be completed by someone who knows you. If your doctor fills this in s/he should not charge you. If you do not have anyone who can complete it, leave it blank.

Unmet care needs

It can be difficult if you do not receive any help from another person to describe your attention or supervision needs. Many disabled people struggle to perform daily tasks on their own. If you do not have a carer you should still describe your problems. You should ask yourself whether certain activities cause you pain, or make you dizzy, tired or breathless. If you take a long time to perform particular tasks you should explain this. You should also say if you are not able to perform a particular activity adequately – eg, if you cannot bend down you may not be able to reach your feet when washing.

Aids and adaptations

If a decision maker thinks that you can use a particular aid or adaptation s/he may decide you do not need attention or supervision. For example, if you have a commode the decision maker may conclude you do not need someone to help you get to the toilet at night. You should, therefore, try to explain how useful any equipment actually is and whether you still need help from another person in spite of the equipment. If, for instance, you have had a bath rail fitted, but find it very difficult to climb in or out of a bath, you should explain this.

Frequency, variability and duration

You are asked throughout the form to estimate how long you need help for, how many times a day, and how many days a week.

- The questions about 'how long' you need help for are important if you need attention for a 'significant portion of the day' (see p114) or you need 'prolonged' attention at night (see p115).
- The questions about 'how many times a day' you need help are important if you need 'frequent attention throughout the day' (see p115) or 'watching over' at frequent intervals during the night (see p116).
- The questions about 'how many days a week' you need help are designed to assess your overall needs, particularly if you have a variable or fluctuating condition. If your condition does not vary but you only receive help on certain days you should still say that you need help seven days a week. It is the help you need, not the help you actually get, that counts. If you need attention or supervision or have difficulties walking most days of the week, your needs are

taken into account. However, if you only have problems a few days a week, you will not necessarily be refused DLA.[188] In this case, explain fully the help you need on your 'bad' days but include the help you need on your 'good' days as well so that you are giving an overall picture.

It can sometimes be helpful to keep a diary of your needs over a period of a week or more and send this in.

Walking outdoors

The section on 'walking outdoors' is for the higher rate of DLA mobility. If walking causes you 'severe discomfort' you may be regarded as being virtually unable to walk (see p102).

- You are asked to say how far you can walk before you feel discomfort and how long on average it takes you to walk this distance. If you are not sure how to answer this you should get someone to walk outdoors with you to measure the distance you can walk without severe discomfort and the time it takes you to walk this far. It may help to give an example of the distance – eg, 'I can walk past five houses – about 40 metres'. Bear in mind that if you can walk a further distance without severe discomfort after a brief rest it is the total distance that counts.
- You should explain what sort of discomfort you experience, such as pain or breathlessness.
- You should also describe your manner of walking. For example, you may have problems with balance, or you may walk with a limp, drag your feet, or shuffle.
- If you need to stop to rest you should try to explain how far you can walk before you need to stop, and for how long you need to rest.

Guidance or supervision

If you are able to walk but need guidance or supervision outdoors, at least in unfamiliar places, you may qualify for the lower rate of DLA mobility (see p105). The section on 'having someone with you when you are outdoors' relates directly to this qualifying condition. Explain clearly what your companion does or might need to do to help you – eg, whether s/he physically leads you, gives directions or helps you avoid obstacles, or whether s/he monitors your condition or the route ahead, or encourages or calms you. Say why you need your companion to do these things. If you need supervision because you are at risk of danger, the questions on 'falls or stumbles', 'someone keeping an eye on you', and 'dizzy spells, fits, seizures or something like this', which relate primarily to the 'continual supervision' test for the care component (see p115), may also help you qualify for the lower rate of the mobility component.

Mental disabilities

There is a section on 'the way you feel about your mental health'. This relates to both supervision and attention needs. There is also a section on 'communicating with other people', where you should mention problems casued by anxiety, intrusive thoughts or anger, as well as questions throughout the claim pack that ask if someone has to 'tell you or encourage you' to perform a particular activity. These questions are also designed for people with mental disabilities who may need reminding or persuading to attend to their bodily functions. The section on 'the help you need when you go out during the day or in the evening' may also be appropriate for people with mental disabilities who need assistance to undertake social, leisure and recreational activities.

Sensory impairments

The section on 'communicating with other people' applies to deaf claimants who may need an interpreter or other help with communicating or reading, or blind people who need to have newspapers or correspondence read to them (see p111). Blind people who need someone to tell them if they have stains on their clothes or if their hands are clean should explain these problems in the 'dressing' and 'washing' sections. It is especially important that people with sensory impairments complete the section on 'the help you need when you go out during the day or in the evening' to explain the help needed to undertake social and recreational activities . If you are working and need extra help at work, include this.

The claim pack for children

The claim pack for children is substantially different from the adult form. However, some issues, such as how to answer the questions on frequency, variability and duration of needs, are similar to those faced by people filling in the adult pack (see p124). You should, therefore, read the section on the adult claim pack, as well as this section, if you are completing a child's pack. You should consider the following issues, which are specific to claiming for children.

When the child is in bed at night

Only the needs your child has after the rest of the household has gone to bed count as night-time needs (see p114).

Mobility

The form reminds you that children can only qualify for DLA mobility from the age of three, but points out that problems with getting around may indicate care or supervision needs. It can be difficult to explain how a disabled child requires 'substantially more' guidance or supervision (see p118) outdoors in order to qualify for the lower rate of DLA mobility (see p105). This is because most young children do not go out, at least in unfamiliar places, on their own. A child with a sensory impairment or learning disability may require much more direct or close supervision than a non-disabled child.[189] Whereas a non-disabled child may be allowed to walk in the presence of an adult, a disabled child may require an adult physically to hold or guide her/him. Also, a 'familiar route' to a non-disabled child may be a hazardous obstacle course to a child whose sight is impaired.

Extra attention or supervision

When explaining about your child's 'extra' requirements you should bear in mind that they must be 'substantially in excess' of that required by a non-disabled child (see p118).[190]

For example, you may let a non-disabled child play outdoors in the street and instruct her/him not to cross roads. You may be able to supervise the child indirectly without having to watch her/him all the time. However, you may have to supervise directly a child with sensory impairments or behavioural problems, or confine her/him indoors. Or perhaps a child with attention deficit disorder would need to be accompanied to school or to local shops, whereas a non-disabled child would be allowed to go on her/his own.[191]

About the child's development

The questions on development are extremely important to show that disabled children need extra care or supervision.

Disabled children may need extra help in order to develop daily living skills, language and social skills. For example, babies with sensory impairments may require more physical stimulation to aid parental bonding and develop communication skills. Children learn spontaneously through play, but a disabled child may need help to use toys, or may need to be coaxed to explore her/his environment. Children with learning or sensory disabilities require extra help to develop daily living or language skills. They may also develop these skills later than non-disabled children.

If you have no experience of bringing up children you may not know exactly when a child should be crawling, walking, speaking and feeding her/himself. If you are not sure, you should ask your health visitor or paediatrician. For example, most children pick up and eat food by 8 to 12 months. Therefore, if you are still feeding a child after 12 months you are providing attention that a non-disabled child of the same age would not need.

Decision makers tend to take a mechanical view of child development and assume that children adapt to particular disabilities by set ages. This leads to fixed-period awards that expire when a child reaches a certain age. However, it is wrong to assume that all disabled children respond to the problems they face in the same way. In one case a child with photosensitive epilepsy was known to watch television even though he was not supposed to. It could not be said that he was 'old enough to know better', as there was evidence that he persisted in doing things that were known to be bad for him.[192]

School-age children

Disabled children, particularly those with sensory impairments or learning disabilities, usually require extra help with their school work. Extra help in the classroom or with homework can count towards a child's attention needs, provided you can show it is in connection with a bodily function (see p112).[193] A commissioner has suggested that straightforward teaching would probably not be suffiently intimate to qualify.[194] A statement of special educational needs may provide useful supporting evidence of the extra help needed with her/his studies.

Communicating

Pre-lingual deaf children, whose first language is British Sign Language, may need help to understand or communicate in written or spoken English. Blind children will not only need help to understand written information, but may also need help to learn Braille. Children with behavioural problems may need help to express themselves or understand other people.

How your claim is dealt with

Claims are initially dealt with at regional disability benefits centres. A decision maker can award DLA or AA on the basis of your claim form alone but may choose to contact someone you have named on the form for more information. It is a good idea to include details of all the medical professionals and other people who know and understand your needs so that the decision maker knows who to contact. If s/he cannot get enough information s/he may also arrange for you to be given a medical examination by a doctor acting on behalf of the DWP. The doctor will sometimes visit you at home.

If you refuse to attend a medical examination 'without good cause', the decision maker has to decide your claim against you.[195]

The decision maker may telephone you to ask for further information. If you do not want to be telephoned, write this clearly on the claim form.

The DWP aims to deal with new claims for DLA within 39 working days and new claims for AA within 22 working days. Claims made under the 'special rules' for terminal illness (see p121) should be decided within eight working days.

Backdating your claim

It is very important to claim in time. A claim for DLA or AA cannot be backdated.[196]

If you might have qualified for benefit earlier but did not claim because you were given the wrong information or misled by the DWP you could ask for an *ex gratia* payment (see p1186) or complain to the Ombudsman via your MP (see p1184).

8. Getting paid

Payment of disability living allowance (DLA) or attendance allowance (AA) is normally made by credit transfer ('direct payment') into a bank (or similar) account. You still have the option of opening an account that allows you to collect your benefit at a post office (see p978).[197] If you are unable to open or manage an account, it may be possible to be paid by cheque. For more information about these payment methods, see p978.

AA and DLA are normally paid every four weeks.[198] In practice, they are normally paid in arrears. AA can be paid weekly in advance. If you are claiming DLA under the special rules for terminal illness, it can be paid weekly.

If you leave hospital or a care home and expect to return within 28 days, DLA and AA can be paid at a daily rate for days at home (see Chapter 26).[199]

DLA and AA are normally paid on Wednesdays, but the Secretary of State can vary the payday.[200]

If you are claiming other DWP benefits, DLA or AA may be paid in a single payment with them instead.

The higher rate of DLA mobility component (DLA mobility) can be paid directly to Motability if you are purchasing a car through the scheme (see p134).

Payment can also be made to someone else on your behalf, called your 'appointee' (see p955), if you are unable to act for yourself. Direct deductions cannot be made from DLA or AA to repay debts (see Chapter 38). If payment of your DLA or AA is suspended, see p984.

Length of awards

Awards of DLA or AA can be made for either fixed or indefinite periods.[201] The length of an award depends on how long a decision maker estimates your current needs may last. If you have an indefinite award (previously called a life award), you will not have to make a renewal claim at any stage, but it is always open to the DWP to reduce or stop your award if it has grounds to revise or supersede it.[202]

In practice, awards are usually made for at least six months because of the DLA requirement that you should satisfy the disability conditions for the next six months. However, there is no legal minimum length for an award.[203] If you think benefit should be awarded for longer, perhaps because your condition is such that your care or mobility needs will not decrease, or because you need a longer award of DLA mobility to take advantage of the Motability scheme (see p134), you should consider asking for a revision (see p1065). You should, however, bear in mind that, if you challenge the length of your award, the rate of your award may also be reconsidered. If your award is for a limited period you will be invited to make a renewal claim six months before the award runs out (see p123). Special rules awards are made for three years (see p121).

Although DLA has two components there can only be a single DLA award, consisting of one or both components. You can have an indefinite award of one component combined with a limited period award of the other. However, you cannot be awarded both components for two different fixed periods – both award periods must be aligned to end on the same day.[204]

Payment to children

DLA for a child under the age of 16 is usually paid to an adult with whom the child is living, whom the Secretary of State appoints to act on her/his behalf (often called an 'appointee'). This is normally the child's mother or father.[205] Children cannot make valid claims on their own behalf.[206]

The allowance can continue to be paid to the appointee in some circumstances when the child and appointee are not living together, including during a temporary separation of up to 12 weeks, or when the child is absent at a boarding school or in hospital (although other rules may mean that payment stops – see p611). DLA ceases to be paid to the appointee immediately when the child is being looked after by a local authority or any similar arrangement, unless the arrangement is not intended to last for more than 12 weeks.[207]

Delays and complaints

If payment of your DLA or AA is delayed, you might be able to get an interim payment. See p986 for further details.

If you experience delays or wish to complain about how your claim has been dealt with, see Chapter 46. You might be able to claim compensation (see p1186).

Change of circumstances

It is your duty to report any change in your circumstances that might affect your right to, the amount of, or payment of your benefit.[208] You should do this promptly by writing to or telephoning the Disability and Contact Processing Unit (although in individual cases notification might be accepted in a form other than in writing or by telephone). In some cases, however, the decision maker might say you must report changes in writing. In any case, you might want to report the change in writing and keep a copy in case of a dispute in the future. If you do not promptly report any such change, any resulting overpayment may be recoverable from you (see Chapter 39). If you are considered deliberately to have acted falsely or dishonestly, you may also be guilty of an offence (see Chapter 40).

If your condition deteriorates so that you become eligible for a higher rate or another component, benefit can be backdated to the first pay day after the end of the three-month (for DLA) or six-month (for AA) qualifying period, as long as you tell the DWP no later than a month after completing the qualifying period. If payment of (but not entitlement to) DLA or AA has stopped – eg, while you are in hospital or a care home – you should still notify the DWP so that the correct rate is paid when payment resumes. If you do not report a change of circumstances within the month, benefit can still be backdated if you do so within 13 months and there were 'special circumstances' that meant it was not practical to report the change earlier.[209]

If your condition improves so that you should drop down a rate, lose a component or lose benefit altogether, the new decision normally takes effect

....

from the date you tell the DWP of the improvement, or from the date of the decision if the DWP changed it without you asking. It would only take effect from an earlier date (and cause an overpayment) if you should have realised earlier that the change should have been reported. The DWP recognises that it is difficult for claimants to realise when a gradual improvement begins to affect benefit entitlement.[210]

Overpayments and fraud

If you have been overpaid DLA or AA, you might have to repay it. The rules on overpayments are covered in Chapter 39.

If you have been accused of fraud, see Chapter 40.

Right payment programme

Since May 2007 the DWP has been checking existing DLA awards as part of a 'right payment programme'. AA recipients are not currently having their awards checked.

The programme applies to people on all rates of DLA, including those originally awarded DLA 'for life' or indefinitely. You are exempt if your award has been looked at in the last 12 months, if you have been awarded benefit under the 'special rules' (see p121) or if no DLA is being paid – eg, because you are in hospital (see Chapter 26).

The DWP contacts you by sending a postal questionnaire (DLA300). You have a duty to supply any information requested that may affect benefit entitlement.[211] If you do not respond , the DWP may notify you that your benefit may be suspended if you do not reply within a further month.[212] This one-month limit can be extended if necessary to arrange for someone to help you complete the questionnaire.[213] If, after your benefit has been suspended for a month, you still have not complied, your award can be terminated.[214]

As part of the initial investigation into an existing award the DWP can require you to have a medical examination.[215] If you fail, without good cause, to have a medical examination on two consecutive occasions, your benefit can be suspended.[216] If, after your benefit has been suspended for one month, you still have not had a medical examination, your benefit can be terminated.[217]

9. Challenging a decision

If you disagree with a disability living allowance or attendance allowance decision you can challenge it by a revision (see p1065), supersession (see p1074), or appeal (see p1094).

10. Tax, tax credits and other benefits

Tax

Attendance allowance (AA) and disability living allowance (DLA) are not taxable.[218]

Tax credits

DLA and AA are ignored as income when calculating child tax credit (CTC) and working tax credit (WTC). An award of AA or DLA at any rate counts as a qualifying benefit for the disability element of WTC, which you may get if you are working. A disability element is included in CTC for each child who gets DLA (any rate). If s/he gets the highest rate of the DLA care component (DLA care), you may get a severe disability element in CTC. If you or your partner get the highest rate of DLA care or the higher rate of AA, a severe disability element is included in WTC. See Chapter 51 for more information.

Means-tested benefits

Neither AA nor any rate of DLA is taken into account as income when calculating income support (IS), income-based jobseeker's allowance (JSA), housing benefit (HB), council tax benefit (CTB) or the guarantee credit or savings credit of pension credit (PC). DLA and AA are paid on top of these benefits.

If you or your partner are entitled to AA or DLA, your IS, income-based JSA, HB and CTB include the disability premium, or higher pensioner premium if either of you are aged over 60 (see p775). If you or your partner are entitled to the highest rate DLA care and aged under 60, you also get an enhanced disability premium (see p781). A severe disability premium is included in IS, income-based JSA, HB or CTB, or an addition for severe disability is included in the guarantee credit of PC if you receive AA or the highest or middle rate of the DLA care component and meet the other conditions for that premium. For further information, see p784.

If your child is entitled to DLA, HB/CTB includes a disabled child premium. If s/he gets the highest rate of DLA care, HB/CTB includes an enhanced disability premium. These premiums are also included in IS and income-based JSA if you do not yet get CTC.

If you or your partner are entitled to AA or DLA care, non-dependant deductions (see p815) are not made from any housing costs you claim (ie, HB, CTB and mortgage interest payments included in IS, income-based JSA and the guarantee credit of PC).

Non-means-tested benefits

DLA and AA may be paid in addition to any other non-means-tested benefits described in this *Handbook* except that:

- AA and DLA care overlap with constant attendance allowance under the industrial injuries scheme (see p326) or war pensions scheme;[219] *and*
- DLA mobility component (DLA mobility) overlaps with the war pensioners' mobility supplement payable under the war pensions scheme.[220]

If you are receiving highest or middle rate of DLA care or AA and someone regularly looks after you, that person may be entitled to carer's allowance (see Chapter 3).

If you get the highest rate of DLA care you are automatically treated as being incapable of work under the personal capability assessment (see p668), and the long-term rate of incapacity benefit is payable after 28 weeks instead of 52 weeks.

Passports and other sources of help

If you are on a low income, you might be entitled to certain health service benefits such as free prescriptions (see Chapter 9). You may also qualify for other sources of help (see p14) or a social fund payment (see Chapters 21 and 22) or free school meals (see p15).

If you get the higher rate DLA mobility, you or your carer can be exempt from paying vehicle excise duty (road tax) on a car used solely by you or for your purposes. Contact the Disability Contact and Processing Unit (see Appendix 1) for an application form.

If you get the higher rate DLA mobility you should qualify for the Blue Badge scheme of parking concessions, which operates throughout Great Britain and in the European Economic Area (with certain local variations). You should contact your local authority for further information.

If any member of your household receives AA or DLA at any rate you can get a grant from the Warm Front scheme (Warm Deal in Scotland; Warm Homes in Northern Ireland) (formerly the Home Energy Efficiency Scheme) for home insulation and other heating improvements (see p16). To obtain further information, contact freephone (for textphone users add 18001 as a prefix):

- England: 0800 316 6011;
- Scotland: 0800 316 1653;
- Wales: 0800 316 2815;
- Northern Ireland: 0800 181 667.

If you are aged over 16 and under 66 and you are getting the highest rate DLA care you may be eligible for money from the Independent Living Funds to finance care provision (see p16).

Motability

Motability is a charity that runs a scheme to help you lease or buy a car if you receive the higher rate DLA mobility for a period of 12 months or more (see p100).

DLA mobility is paid direct to Motability.[221] You may also have to make a down payment. If you drive more than 12,000 miles a year you may have to make further annual payments. For further information, write to Motability, Goodman House, Station Approach, Harlow, Essex CM20 2ET, telephone 0845 456 4566 or visit www.motability.co.uk. Motability produces leaflets on its schemes for car leasing and hire purchase of new cars, used cars and electric wheelchairs.

Notes

1. Disability living allowance mobility component

1 s73 SSCBA 1992
2 s73(1)(d) SSCBA 1992
3 CM/5/1986
4 Reg 12(1)(a) SS(DLA) Regs
5 R(M) 3/78
6 Reg 12(1)(a) SS(DLA) Regs; R(M) 2/78; R(DLA) 4/06
7 CDLA/2822/1999; CDLA/4329/1999
8 R(M) 3/86; CSDLA/202/2007
9 R(M) 2/89; CDLA/97/2001
10 Reg 12(4) SS(DLA) Regs
11 R(M) 2/89
12 Reg 12(1)(b) SS(DLA) Regs
13 CDLA/3188/2002
14 R(M) 1/95; CSDLA/171/1998
15 CM/208/1989; CSDLA/0044/2002
16 CDLA/1389/1997
17 R(M) 1/81
18 R(M) 1/83
19 CM/627/1993
20 CDLA/608/1994; R(DLA) 4/03
21 R(DLA) 4/04
22 *Hewitt and Diment v CAO* 29 June 1998 (CA), reported as R(DLA) 6/99
23 R(M) 1/98; CDLA/3941/2005 interpreted 'exertion' to mean the activity of walking 'however slight the exertion'.
24 Reg 12(2) SS(DLA) Regs
25 Reg 12(3) SS(DLA) Regs
26 R(DLA) 3/95
27 Sch 2 SS(GB) Regs
28 Reg 34 (2) and Sch 3 Part II SS(IIPD) Regs
29 Reg 12(2) SS(DLA) Regs
30 Reg 12(1)(b) SS(DLA) Regs
31 s73(3) SSCBA 1992; reg 12(5) and (6) SS(DLA) Regs
32 R(M) 3/86; CSDLA/202/2007
33 R(DLA) 2/96
34 R(DLA) 3/98
35 *M (a child) v CAO* 29 October 1999 (CA), reported as R(DLA) 1/00
36 CDLA/95/1995
37 CDLA/3215/2001
38 CDLA/2054/1998
39 R(DLA) 7/02; R(DLA) 9/02; CDLA/3244/2001
40 s73(1)(d) SSCBA 1992
41 R(DLA) 6/03
42 CDLA/42/1994
43 CDLA/42/1994; R(DLA) 3/04
44 There are conflicting decisions on whether a person who needs guidance or supervision, but cannot take advantage of the faculty of walking, can qualify. See CDLA/2364/1995 and CDLA/42/1994.
45 CDLA/2142/2005
46 Reg 12(7) and (8) SS(DLA) Regs; R(DLA) 3/04; CDLA/2409/2003; R(DLA) 6/05
47 R(DLA) 4/01
48 R(DLA) 4/01
49 R(DLA) 3/04
50 CDLA/42/1994
51 CDLA/42/1994
52 CDLA/52/1994; CDLA/3360/1995; CSDLA/591/1997; CDLA/2643/1998
53 R(DLA) 4/01
54 R(DLA) 6/05
55 R(DLA) 4/01
56 s73(12) SSCBA 1992

2. **Disability living allowance care component**

57 s72 SSCBA 1992
58 s72(1)(a) SSCBA 1992
59 s72(1)(b) and (c) SSCBA 1992
60 s72(4)(a) SSCBA 1992
61 s72(5) SSCBA 1992
62 R(DLA) 3/06 tribunal of commissioners
63 CDLA/4475/04
64 R(DLA) 3/06 tribunal of commissioners
65 R(DLA) 1/05
66 R(DLA) 10/02 approved by R(DLA) 3/06 tribunal of commissioners
67 R(DLA) 6/06 tribunal of commissioners
68 s72(1a)(a) SSCBA 1992
69 CDLA/1215/05; CDLA/2367/2004
70 R(DLA) 7/03
71 *R v Secretary of State for Social Security ex parte Armstrong* [1996] (CA)
72 *Moyna v Secretary of State for Work and Pensions* [2003] (HL), reported as R(DLA) 7/03
73 CSDLA/80/1996
74 CDLA/7374/1995; R(DLA) 8/02
75 CDLA/20/1994; CDLA/4214/2002; CSDLA/859/2003 held that the effect of being nauseous does not affect the capacity to carry out the tasks in cooking following R(DLA) 7/03, which the commissioner argued meant the test of reasonableness no longer applies to the cooking test. However, CDLA/1256/2007 held that it does, citing CDLA/1271/04 in support.
76 R(DLA) 2/95, which nonetheless allows for the use of 'certain devices to assist' which may form part of 'normal reasonable facilities' for cooking. However, CDLA/1212/2005 held, following R(DLA) 7/03 (cooking test is a notional test and a thought experiment), that it is not relevant to the tests whether a claimant does or does not have a microwave oven or other standard equipment.
77 CDLA/20/1994; R(DLA) 2/95 insists on a traditional cooker, but note CDLA/770/2000, which allows fresh food to be prepared in a microwave. See also CDLA/3778/2002.
78 CDLA/17329/1996 and CDLA/770/2000, both of which would appear to give more weight to the use of special cooking aids than R(DLA) 2/95; see CPAG's *Welfare Rights Bulletin* 163
79 CDLA/1714/2005
80 R(DLA) 1/97
81 R(A) 3/86 and *Mallinson v Secretary of State for Social Security* 21 April 1994 (HL), reported as R(A) 3/94
82 *Secretary of State for Social Security v Fairey* (aka *Halliday*) 21 May 1997 (HL), reported as R(A) 2/98
83 *Secretary of State for Social Security v Fairey* (aka *Halliday*) 21 May 1997 (HL), reported as R(A) 2/98
84 *Secretary of State for Social Security v Fairey* (aka *Halliday*) 21 May 1997 (HL), reported as R(A) 2/98
85 R(A) 3/89
86 R(A) 5/90
87 R(A) 1/73
88 CDLA/899/1994
89 See for example, R(A) 3/86 and *R v Secretary of State for Social Services ex parte Connolly* [1986] 1 WLR 421 (CA)
90 R(DLA) 10/02
91 *R v National Insurance Commissioner ex parte Secretary of State for Social Services* [1981] 1 WLR 1017 (CA), also reported as R(A) 2/80
92 R(DLA) 1/07 tribunal of commissioners
93 *Mallinson v Secretary of State for Social Security* 21 April 1994 (HL), reported as R(A) 3/94
94 *R v National Insurance Commissioner ex parte Secretary of State for Social Services* [1981] 1 WLR 1017 (CA), also reported as R(A) 2/80; reg 10C SS (DLA) Regs
95 R(A) 1/06
96 *Mallinson v Secretary of State for Social Security* 21 April 1994 (HL), reported as R(A) 3/94
97 CA/177/1988; CDLA/14696/1996; R(DLA) 1/07 tribunal of commissioners
98 Reg 10C SS(DLA) Regs; reg 8BA SS(AA) Regs
99 CDLA/4333/2004
100 R(A) 3/74
101 R(A) 2/75
102 CA/86/1987
103 R(DLA) 1/07 tribunal of commissioners
104 *R v Social Security Commissioner ex parte Butler* February 1984, unreported and *Secretary of State for Social Security v Fairey* (aka *Halliday*) 21 May 1997 (HL), reported as R(A) 2/98
105 R(DLA) 1/02, R(DLA) 2/02 and R(DLA) 3/02 review the issue in the light of *Fairey* 15 June 1995 (CA)
106 R(DLA) 2/02
107 CDLA/3607/2001

108 *R v National Insurance Commissioner ex parte Secretary of State for Social Services* [1981] 1 WLR 1017 (CA), also reported as R(A) 2/80
109 *Cockburn v CAO and Another* 21 May 1997 (HL), reported as R(A) 2/98; *Ramsden v Secretary of State for Work and Pensions* 31 January 2003 (CA), reported as R(DLA) 2/03
110 CDLA/267/1994
111 CDLA/267/1994, CDLA/11652/1995, CDLA/3711/1995, CDLA/12381/1996, CDLA/16996/1996,CDLA/16129/1996 and CDLA/4352/1999 are useful, but conflict with CSDLA/281/1996 and CSDLA/314/1997. See CPAG's *Welfare Rights Bulletin* 145 for an analysis of this issue.
112 *Secretary of State for Social Security v Fairey* (aka *Halliday*) 21 May 1997 (HL), reported as R(A) 2/98
113 CDLA/16129/1996, CDLA/16996/1996 and CDLA/4352/1999 are helpful, but conflict with CSDLA/314/1997
114 CDLA/4352/1999 and CDLA/5216/1998, the latter being more restrictive.
115 CDLA/4352/1999
116 CDLA/5216/1998
117 R(DLA) 1/98
118 *R v National Insurance Commissioner ex parte Secretary of State for Social Services* [1974] 1 WLR 1290 (DC), also reported as R(A) 4/74
119 CDLA/2852/2002
120 CDLA/997/2003
121 R(A) 1/04
122 R(A) 1/78
123 s72(1)(a)(i) SSCBA 1992
124 R(DLA) 8/02
125 CDLA/58/1993
126 CSDLA/29/1994
127 *Ramsden v Secretary of State for Work and Pensions* 31 January 2003 (CA), reported as R(DLA) 2/03
128 s72(1)(b) SSCBA 1992
129 *R v National Insurance Commissioner ex parte Secretary of State for Social Services* [1981] 1 WLR 1017 (CA), also reported as R(A) 2/80. However, in R(DLA) 5/05, following R(DLA) 7/03, a commissioner took the view that this refers to the minimum meaning of the words and not necessarily to how they should always be applied in the context of the qualifying conditions for DLA. He preferred the phrase 'frequent ... throughout' the day to be looked at as a whole and given its ordinary, everyday meaning, taking account of all relevant factors.
130 CA/281/1989
131 CA/140/1985
132 s72(1)(c)(i) SSCBA 1992
133 R(DLA) 5/05
134 *R v National Insurance Commissioner ex parte Secretary of State for Social Services* [1981] 1 WLR 1017 (CA), also reported as R(A) 2/80. However, in R(DLA) 5/05, following R(DLA) 7/03, a commissioner took the view that this refers to the minimum meaning of the words and not necessarily to how they should always be applied in the context of the qualifying conditions for DLA. He preferred the word 'prolonged' to be looked at as a whole and given its ordinary, everyday meaning, taking account of all relevant factors.
135 R(A) 3/78
136 ss64(2)(b) and 72(1)(b)(ii) SSCBA 1992
137 R(A) 1/83
138 CA/15/1979, approved in R(A) 1/83
139 R(A) 2/89
140 CA/33/1984
141 R(A) 2/75
142 *Moran v Secretary of State for Social Services, The Times,* 14 March 1987 (CA), reported as R(A) 1/88
143 R(A) 5/81
144 R(A) 2/91
145 R(A) 3/92
146 s72(1)(c)(ii) SSCBA 1992
147 para 61165 DMG

3. **Attendance allowance**
148 ss64, 65 and 66 SSCBA 1992; reg 3 SS(AA) Regs

4. **The rules about your age**
149 s73(1A) SSCBA 1992
150 s73(4A) SSCBA 1992
151 s72(1A)(b) SSCBA 1992
152 R(DLA) 1/99
153 CA/92/1992; CSDLA/76/1998; CDLA/4806/2002; CSDLA/91/2003; CDLA/4100/2004. See CPAG's *Welfare Rights Bulletin* 147 for an analysis of the extra test for children.
154 CDLA/2268/1999
155 CA/92/1992
156 s75(1) SSCBA 1992; reg 3 SS(DLA) Regs
157 Sch 1 paras 2-7 SS(DLA) Regs
158 Sch 1 para 1 SS(DLA) Regs; see also CSDLA/388/2000

159 Sch 1 para 3 SS(DLA) Regs
160 Sch 1 para 3(2)(b) SS(DLA) Regs

5. **The amount of benefit**
161 Sch 4 SSCBA 1992; reg 4 SS(DLA) Regs

6. **Special benefit rules**
162 Reg 5 SS(AA) Regs; reg 7 SS(DLA) Regs
163 s66(1) and (2) SSCBA 1992
164 s72(5) SSCBA 1992
165 s66(1) SSCBA 1992
166 s73(12) SSCBA 1992
167 Regs 3(9)(b) and 6(6)(c) SS&CS(D&A) Regs
168 ss66(2)(b) and 76(3) SSCBA 1992

7. **Claims and backdating**
169 Reg 6(8), (8A) and (9) SS(C&P) Regs
170 Reg 4(1) SS(C&P) Regs
171 Reg 1A SS(DLA) Regs
172 ss66(2)(b) and 76(3) SSCBA 1992; s1(3) SSAA 1992
173 s66(2)(b) SSCBA 1992
174 Reg 6(8), (8A) and (9) SS(C&P) Regs
175 Reg 6(8a) SS(C&P) Regs
176 Sch 9ZC para 4(3) SS(C&P) Regs
177 Reg 9(1) and Sch 1 SS(C&P) Regs
178 Reg 9(1) and Sch 1 SS(C&P) Regs
179 Reg 13A(1) SS(C&P) Regs
180 s65(6) SSCBA 1992
181 Reg 13C SS(C&P) Regs
182 CDLA/14895/1996
183 Regs 6 and 11 SS(DLA) Regs
184 Regs 6 and 11 SS(DLA) Regs
185 Reg 6(3) and (4) SS(DLA) Regs
186 Regs 6 and 11 and Sch 1 paras 3 and 5 SS(DLA) Regs
187 Reg 3 SS(AA) Regs
188 R(A) 2/74; see also *Moyna v Secretary of State for Work and Pensions* 31 July 2003 (HL), reported as R(DLA) 7/03
189 CDLA/2268/1999
190 CA/92/1992; CSDLA/91/2003
191 CDLA/4806/2002
192 CDLA/339/1994
193 *Secretary of State for Work and Pensions v Hughes (a minor)*, reported as R(DLA) 1/04
194 CDLA/1983/06
195 s19(3) SSA 1998
196 ss65(4) and 76(1) SSCBA 1992

8. **Getting paid**
197 Reg 21 SS(C&P) Regs
198 Reg 22 SS(C&P) Regs
199 Reg 25 SS(C&P) Regs
200 Reg 22(3) and Sch 6 SS(C&P) Regs
201 ss65(1)(a) and 71(3) SSCBA 1992
202 s67(1) WRPA 1999
203 R(DLA) 11/02
204 s71(3) SSCBA 1992
205 Reg 43 SS(C&P) Regs
206 CDLA/1326/1995
207 Reg 43 SS(C&P) Regs
208 Reg 32(1A) and (1B) SS(C&P) Regs
209 Reg 7(9) SS&CS(DA) Regs
210 Reg 7(2)(c) SS&CS(DA) Regs
211 Reg 32(1) SS(C&P) Regs
212 Reg 17 SS&CS(DA) Regs
213 Reg 17(4)(a)(ii) SS&CS(DA) Regs
214 Reg 18 SS&CS(DA) Regs
215 Reg 19(1) SS&CS(DA) Regs
216 Reg 19(2) SS&CS(DA) Regs
217 Reg 19(3) and (4) SS&CS(DA) Regs

10. **Tax, tax credits and other benefits**
218 s677 IT(EP)A 2003
219 Sch 1 para 5 SS(OB) Regs
220 Reg 42(1)(b)(ii) SS(C&P) Regs
221 Regs 44, 45 and 46 SS(C&P) Regs

Chapter 7

Employment and support allowance

This chapter covers:

Employment and support allowance (ESA) is a new benefit that, at the time this *Handbook* was written, was due to be introduced in October 2008. It is a benefit for people who have 'limited capability for work' (ie, it is unreasonable to require them to work) because of illness or disability, and who are not entitled to statutory sick pay.

ESA will replace incapacity benefit (IB) and income support (IS) on the basis of incapacity for work for new claimants. People already claiming IB or IS (or severe disablement allowance) for incapacity for work when ESA is introduced are expected to continue to receive these benefits (in particular during 2008/09), although the Government plans eventually to transfer all claimants to ESA.

There are two types of ESA. **Contributory ESA** is paid if you satisfy the national insurance (NI) conditions. There is no means test.

Some young people may be able to get contributory ESA without satisfying the NI conditions, although there are specific rules on age and full-time education. This is referred to in this chapter as ESA in youth.

Income-related ESA is paid if you pass the means test. You do not have to satisfy the NI conditions. It is possible to receive contributory ESA (including ESA in youth) topped up with income-related ESA.

Note: at the time this *Handbook* was written, the rules had not been finalised. This chapter, therefore, provides an outline of the main rules that had been made and of those that were expected to be made. For more information and updates, see www.cpag.org.uk/esa or CPAG's *Welfare Rights Bulletin*.

1. Who can claim employment and support allowance

You qualify for employment and support allowance (ESA) if:[1]

- you have 'limited capability for work' (see p147); *and*
- you are aged 16 or over but under pension age (60 for women, 65 for men); *and*
- you are in Great Britain (see p146 if you go abroad); *and*
- you are not entitled in your own right to income support (IS) or jobseeker's allowance (JSA), including if you are part of a couple entitled to joint-claim JSA; *and*
- you are not entitled to statutory sick pay; *and*
- you satisfy the extra rules for contributory ESA (see p141, and for ESA in youth see p141) or income-related ESA (see p141).

You are not usually entitled to ESA for the first three days of your claim (see below). You cannot get ESA and certain other benefits at the same time (see p151).

Most claimants of ESA (except those in the 'support group' – see p145) are required to take part in work-focused interviews, including work-focused health-related assessments (see p973).

There are some groups of claimants to whom special benefit rules will apply (see p146).

Period of limited capability for work and waiting days

You are not entitled to ESA for three 'waiting days' at the beginning of your 'period of limited capability for work'.[2] The rules on this period had not been finalised at the time this *Handbook* was written, but exceptions may be made in specified cases – eg, if you were previously entitled to another benefit such as JSA. Also, separate periods may be 'linked' to form one period if they are separated by less than a set number of days.

Disqualification from benefit

The rules on when you can be disqualified from ESA had not been finalised at the time this *Handbook* was written.[3] They are, however, expected to say that you can be disqualified from receiving ESA for up to six weeks if:

- you have 'limited capability for work' because of your own misconduct; *or*
- you continue to have 'limited capability for work' because you have failed without 'good cause' to follow medical advice; *or*
- you fail without 'good cause' to follow any 'prescribed rules of behaviour'.

Extra rules for contributory employment and support allowance

To get contributory ESA, in addition to satisfying the basic rules of entitlement (see p140), you must either satisfy the national insurance contribution conditions (see p735) or the rules for ESA in youth (see below).[4]

Employment and support allowance in youth

You can get ESA in youth if, in addition to satisfying the basic rules of entitlement (see p140):[5]

- you were aged under 20 (or in some circumstances aged under 25) when the 'period of limited capability for work' that applies to your claim for ESA began; *and*
- you are not receiving 'full-time education'; *and*
- you have had 'limited capability for work' for a consecutive period of at least 196 days (these may fall before your 16th birthday); *and*
- you satisfy rules on residence and/or presence in Great Britain.

At the time this *Handbook* was written, these rules, including on 'full-time education' and residence and presence, had not been finalised. The residence and presence rules are expected to be similar to those that apply to incapacity benefit (IB) for incapacity in youth (see p1358). The rules on when you can get ESA in youth are expected to be similar to those that apply for IB for incapacity in youth (see p266). It is also expected that the rules will say that, in some circumstances, once you have qualified under these rules, you can re-qualify for ESA in youth even though you are now aged over 20 (or 25). Again, they are expected to be similar to the IB for incapacity in youth rules. See www.cpag.org.uk/esa or CPAG's *Welfare Rights Bulletin* for updates.

Extra rules for income-related employment and support allowance

In addition to satisfying the basic rules of entitlement (see p140), you can get income-related ESA if:[6]

- your income is less than your applicable amount (see Chapter 33); *and*
- your capital is not over the limit (this is expected to be £16,000 – ie, the same as for IS); *and*
- you are not entitled to pension credit (PC); *and*
- your partner is not entitled to income-related ESA, income-based JSA, IS or PC in her/his own right; *and*
- neither you nor your partner if you are in a couple (see p702) are engaged in 'remunerative work'; *and*
- you are not receiving 'education'; *and*
- you are not a 'person subject to immigration control' (see p1334).[7]

It is also expected that you will need to satisfy the right to reside and habitual residence tests in the same way as for IS (see Chapter 59). The rules on income and capital are also expected to be similar to those that apply to IS (see Chapters 36 and 37). The definition of 'remunerative work' and the circumstances in which you are regarded as receiving 'education' have yet to be decided, although it is expected that exceptions will be made – eg, for some students with disabilities. See www.cpag.org.uk/esa or CPAG's *Welfare Rights Bulletin* for updates.

2. The rules about your age

In order to satisfy the basic rules for employment and support allowance (ESA) you must be aged at least 16 but under pension age. Pension age is 60 for women and 65 for men.

For ESA in youth, you must have been aged under 20 (or in some circumstances under 25) when your 'period of limited capability for work' began (see p140).

3. Claiming for others

Contributory employment and support allowance (ESA) does not include extra amounts for your partner or children.[8]

Income-related ESA does include an amount for your partner – the applicable amount that forms part of the calculation of your benefit includes a personal allowance for a couple (see p702 for when you count as a couple). It does not include amounts for children.[9]

If you get an amount for your spouse or partner in your income-related ESA, s/he may have to take part in work-focused interviews (ie, as well as you). However, at the time this *Handbook* was written, the rules providing for this had not been made. See www.cpag.org.uk/esa or CPAG's *Welfare Rights Bulletin* for updates.

4. The amount of benefit

You are paid a limited amount of employment and support allowance (ESA) during an initial 'assessment phase' (in most cases this is expected to last 13 weeks) and are paid more thereafter.

There are no age-related additions or additions for dependants.

ESA continues for as long as you remain entitled and are below pension age. The exact amount of ESA you are paid depends on:

- whether you are claiming contributory ESA or income-related ESA;
- whether you are in the assessment phase;

- which of the two possible additional components you get after the assessment phase. These are the 'support component' (see p145) and the 'work-related activity component' (see p145).

ESA is worked out as follows.

- In the the assessment phase, for **contributory ESA** you get a basic allowance (see below), for **income-related ESA**, what you get depends on your applicable amount and income (see p144).
- After the assessment phase is over, you get an additional component added. In income-related ESA, it is added to your applicable amount and, as in the assessment phase, your income is subtracted from your applicable amount.
- If ESA is topped up by income-related ESA, the total amount of ESA payable is the amount of entitlement to income-related ESA.

In certain circumstances your ESA may be reduced. For contributory ESA, this is expected to be if you receive certain pension payments and if you are a local councillor and your net councillor's allowances exceed a set limit. These rules, however, had not been confirmed at the time this *Handbook* was written.

For either type of ESA, your benefit may also be reduced if the work-related activity component (see p145) applies to you and you do not comply with the requirement to attend work-focused interviews and associated activity (see p145).

Contributory employment and support allowance[10]

The first weeks of your entitlement (in most cases this is expected to be the first 13 weeks) are known as the '**assessment phase**'. This is the period during which the DWP gathers further information relevant to your claim (including assessing whether you have 'limited capability for work'). During this period, you are entitled only to a set rate of benefit, called the '**basic allowance**'. This is expected to be set at the level of contribution-based jobseeker's allowance to which someone of your age would be entitled – ie, £47.95 if you are under 25, £60.50 if aged 25 or over.

After the assessment phase, your basic allowance is paid at the level of contribution-based JSA payable to someone aged 25 or over (no matter what your age) – ie, £60.50.

In addition to the basic allowance, you are paid one of two possible additional components: the 'support component' or the 'work-related activity component' (see p145). If the DWP is still assessing you after the time for the usual assessment phase has ended, you continue to receive the basic allowance, but when you are eventually awarded the additional component, it is backdated to the point at which the assessment phase normally ends.

It is expected that, in certain circumstances, eg if you were previously entitled to ESA and are claiming again, the assessment phase will not apply and you will be able to receive your full entitlement to ESA straight away. Otherwise, the assessment phase applies, including when you are transferring to ESA from statutory sick pay.

Contributory ESA can be topped up with income-related ESA.

Your benefit may be reduced if you receive certain kinds of pension payments (eg, personal or occupational pension is taken into account). At the time this *Handbook* was written, however, these rules had not been finalised, but it is expected that they will be the same as those for incapacity benefit (see p276).[11] See www.cpag.org.uk/esa or CPAG's *Welfare Rights Bulletin* for updates.

Income-related employment and support allowance[12]

As with contributory ESA, in most cases there is an initial '**assessment phase**' (see p143), but instead of a basic allowance during this period, your ESA tops up your income. The amount you get depends on your needs (your 'applicable amount') and how much income you have. At the time this *Handbook* was written, however, these rules had not been finalised.

Your applicable amount consists of:

- a personal allowance (see p771); *and*
- premiums (see p775). **Note:** it is expected that only the enhanced disability, severe disability, carer's and pensioner premiums will apply; *and*
- housing costs, mainly for mortgage interest payments, although some other costs can be included (the rules are expected to be similar to those that apply for income support (see Chapter 34).

The rules on how your income and entitlement to income-related ESA are calculated are expected to be similar to those that apply for IS (see p299 and Chapter 36). Basically, your income is subtracted from your applicable amount and any remaining sum is your entitlement to income-related ESA. If you would not be entitled to ESA until either of the two additional components described below are added, you may be given an 'advance award' under which you will be paid from the point that the additional component is awarded.[13]

After the assessment phase, as with contributory ESA, one of the two additional components (support component or work-related activity component) is added to your personal allowance, premiums and housing costs to give a new applicable amount, from which your income is subtracted. Again, the calculation is expected to work in much the same way as for IS.

Income-related ESA can top up contributory ESA. This can happen if the amount of entitlement to income-related ESA is greater than the amount of entitlement to contributory ESA. If this is the case, your ESA will consist of both contributory ESA and (the remainder) of income-related ESA.[14]

Support component[15]

The support component is one of the additional components that can be included as part of your entitlement to ESA.

At the time this *Handbook* was written, the amount of this component was not known, but it is expected to be paid at a higher level than the work-related activity component.

You are entitled to the support component if:

- the assessment phase has ended; *and*
- you are assessed as having 'limited capability for work-related activity'.

It is not known if further conditions will have to be satisfied.

If you are assessed as having 'limited capability for work-related activity', you are regarded as being in the '**support group**' for ESA. As well as being entitled to the support component, you do not have to take part in work-focused interviews or associated activity as a condition of getting benefit. The intention is that where paper evidence (eg, medical evidence from your doctor) already shows that you should be in the support group, that decision will be made without you having to attend a medical examination.[16]

The rules on when you are regarded as having 'limited capability for work-related activity' have not yet been finalised. See www.cpag.org.uk/esa or CPAG's *Welfare Rights Bulletin* for updates. In order to qualify, however, your mental or physical condition must be such that one or more statements (or 'descriptors') describing a severe limitation in certain activities (eg, walking, continence, maintaining personal hygiene, learning and communication) could be applied to you. You may be required to complete a questionnaire and/or attend a medical examination. It is expected that in certain circumstances you will automatically qualify. These are likely to include if:

- you have a terminal illness (ie, your death can reasonably be expected within six months);
- you are receiving treatment by way of intravenous, intraperitoneal or intrathecal chemotherapy;
- due to specific disease or disablement there would be a substantial risk to the mental or physical health of any person, were you found not to have limited capability for work;
- you are pregnant and there would be a serious risk of damage to your health or your baby's health if you do not refrain from work-related activity.

Work-related activity component[17]

A work-related activity component can be included as part of your entitlement to ESA.

At the time this *Handbook* was written, the amount of this component was not known.

You are entitled to the work-related activity component if:

- the assessment phase has ended; *and*
- you are not assessed as having 'limited capability for work-related activity' (ie, you are not entitled to the support component – see p145); *and*
- you comply with the requirement to attend work-focused interviews and associated activity under the Pathways to Work scheme (see p973). If you do not, you may have the component reduced by 50 per cent and eventually removed completely.

5. Special benefit rules

In addition to the main rules described on pp140 and 141, there are some groups of claimants to whom special benefit rules are expected to apply. At the time this *Handbook* was written, however, most of these rules had not been made. See www.cpag.org.uk/esa or CPAG's *Welfare Right Bulletin* for updates.

Special rules are expected to apply to:

- people in prison or detention;[18]
- people going abroad.[19] The rules for contributory employment and support allowance (ESA) are expected to be similar to those for incapacity benefit (see p1350) and the rules for income-related ESA are expected to be similar to those for income support (see p1350). (**Note:** rules regarding people coming from abroad are part of the main rules described on pp140–142.)

6. Claims and backdating

It is expected that the rules on claiming employment and support allowance (ESA) will be broadly similar to the main rules for incapacity benefit (IB) and income support (IS) for incapacity for work (see Chapter 38). This means, in most cases, you will be expected to start your claim by making a telephone call to a Jobcentre Plus contact centre (although paper claim forms should also be available if it is not suitable for you to use the telephone). In most cases (unless you are recognised as exempt straight away) you will be required to attend a medical examination to assess whether you have 'limited capability for work' and 'limited capability for work-related activity'. Also, you will usually be required to attend compulsory work-focused interviews under the Pathways to Work scheme. The date for the first of these interviews will usually be eight weeks after you claim.

It is expected that the rules on the date of your claim will be similar to those for IB (see p281) and IS (see p304). However, it is understood that rules will be introduced to allow both contributory and income-related ESA to be backdated automatically for three months (as with IB – see p282), although at the time of writing this had not been confirmed.

The DWP has the power to make rules (not made at the time this *Handbook* was written) to say that if you make a new claim for IB, IS for incapacity for work or severe disablement allowance on or after the day ESA is introduced, this can be treated as a claim for ESA.[20]

7. Getting paid

At the time this *Handbook* was written, the relevant rules on getting paid had not been made. It is expected though that, in general, the main rules about payment of benefit, including your duty to report changes in circumstances, will apply (see p970). It is not yet known how the rules on overlapping benefits (see p981) will apply.

8. Limited capability for work

One of the basic rules of entitlement to employment and support allowance (ESA) is that you must be assessed as having 'limited capability for work'. This means that because of your mental or physical condition it is unreasonable to require you to work.

Note: the test of 'limited capability for work' is due to apply only to claimants of ESA. Existing claimants of incapacity benefit (IB) and income support will still be subject to the test of 'incapacity for work' (see Chapter 28) for the time being. It is understood that existing claimants aged under 25 will be subject to the test of 'limited capability for work' from 2009 and all other existing claimants from 2010.

Work you may do while claiming

Rules are expected to say that, in general, you cannot 'work' and be entitled to ESA at the same time.[21] These rules had not been made at the time this *Handbook* was written. However, they are expected to be very similar to the rules that apply to working and being 'incapable of work' for IB purposes. In particular, it is understood that you can undertake 'permitted work' (see p663) and that the same earnings limits will apply to such work for both types of ESA as they do for IB (although this had not been confirmed at the time of writing).[22]

The test of limited capability for work

The test of 'limited capability for work' is expected to be known as the **'work capability assessment'**.

The details of the test were not finalised at the time this *Handbook* was written.[23] See www.cpag.org.uk/esa or CPAG's *Welfare Rights Bulletin* for updates.

Overall, the test is an assessment of:

- 'whether a person's capability for work is limited by his physical or mental condition; *and, if so*
- whether the limitation is such that it is not reasonable to require him to work'.[24]

The work capability assessment rules are expected to specify that that meant, 'an assessment of the extent to which a person who has some specific disease or bodily or mental disablement', is capable of performing specified activities.

There will be two main ways of satisfying the assessment:

- scoring sufficient points in the assessment (see p981);
- scoring insufficient points because an 'exceptional circumstance' applies to you (see p150).

Apart from these, you may also be *treated* as having limited capability for work (see p149).

The work capability assessment procedure

This is expected to be similar to the procedure used for assessing incapacity for work under the personal capability assessment (see p674). In particular, it is expected that information will be sought from your doctor and, unless you are to be treated as having limited capability for work (see below), you will be sent a questionnaire (an ESA 50) to complete. In most cases, you will then be required to attend a medical examination with a doctor (or other approved healthcare professional) from the DWP Medical Service. As in the personal capability assessment, you may fail the work capability assessment if you do not return the questionnaire and attend the medical. The rules on this are expected to be very similar to those that apply to the personal capability assessment (see pp674 and 678).

Unlike in the personal capability assessment, the doctor (or other approved healthcare professional) will also carry out two other tests:[25]

- an assessment of whether you have 'limited capability for work-related activity' – ie, whether you should be in the support group (see p145); *and*
- a 'work-focused health-related assessment' – ie, to compile medical information on your employability.

Although not actually about your limited capability for work, the rules are expected to say that you must take part in these tests. If you do not, and you are not considered to have good cause for not taking part, you may be found not to be in the support group (regarding the test of 'limited capability for work-related activity') or subject to a reduction in your benefit (regarding the 'work-focused health-related assessment')(see p977).

Treated as having limited capability for work[26]

Rules were not finalised at the time this *Handbook* was written, but they are likely to say that you are treated as having limited capability for work if:

- you have applied for ESA but the work capability assessment has not yet been carried out, as long as you provide medical certificates. However, if you have failed the assessment in the last six months, this will only apply to you if you have a new condition, your condition has significantly worsened or, having been treated as failing the assessment because you did not provide information, you have now provided it; *or*
- a specific circumstance applies to you. These are expected to include if:
  - you are terminally ill;
  - you are receiving intravenous, intraperitoneal or intrathecal chemotherapy;
  - you have a specific disease or bodily or mental disability and because of this there would be a severe risk to the health of any person if you are not found to have limited capability for work;
  - you have been given official notice to refrain from work because you are a carrier of, or have been in contact with, an infectious disease;
  - you are pregnant and there is a serious risk to your health or your baby's health if you do not refrain from work;
  - you are pregnant or have recently given birth, you would not be entitled to either maternity allowance (MA) or statutory maternity pay, you have a medical certificate giving the expected or actual date of birth, and you are within the period beginning with the first day of the sixth week before the expected week of childbirth (or the actual day of childbirth if earlier) and ending on the 14th day after you have the baby;
  - you are an inpatient in hospital;
  - you are receiving certain regular treatment (haemodialysis for chronic renal failure, plasmapherisis or radiotherapy, or total parenteral nutrition for gross impairment of enteric function);
  - you are in the MA period;[27]
  - you are in the support group for ESA (see p145). (Although not mentioned in the draft rules, it is understood that the DWP plans to add this provision.)

Scoring points[28]

The assessment is carried out without referring to any job and does not take into account your education or training, or any language or literacy problems. It is a test of your ability to perform certain activities. There are two lists of activities: one physical, one mental. Under each activity, there is a further list of statements, called 'descriptors', which describe different levels of difficulty in carrying out the activity. Attached to each descriptor is a points score. You are awarded the highest scoring descriptor in each activity that applies to you, taking into account your ability when wearing or using any aid, appliance or prosthesis you normally use.

The details of the activities and descriptors were not finalised at the time this *Handbook* was written.

To satisfy the test by scoring points, you must score a total of 15 points or more. The points can be scored in one or more activities, and scores from the physical and mental activities can be combined. For example, you can score nine points in the physical test and six points in the mental test, which combined give 15 and so satisfy the test.

Good days and bad days, pain and tiredness

It is not clear how such matters are to be treated for ESA. Arguably, however, many of the considerations that apply to the personal capability assessment (see p672) should also apply to the work capability assessment for ESA.

Exceptional circumstances[29]

If you do not otherwise satisfy the work capability assessment, it is expected that you will be treated as doing so if you have a severe uncontrolled or uncontrollable life-threatening disease, and there is medical evidence to show this. There must be reasonable cause for the disease not to be controllable by a recognised therapeutic procedure.

9. Challenging an employment and support allowance decision

The rules on challenging employment and support allowance (ESA) decisions had not been finalised at the time this *Handbook* was written. See www.cpag.org.uk/esa or CPAG's *Welfare Rights Bulletin* for updates.

It is expected that, in general, you will be able to challenge a decision by applying for a revision or supersession (see Chapter 41), or by making an appeal (see Chapter 42). For example, you should have the right of appeal against decisions on such matters as whether you satisfy the conditions for ESA, whether you are entitled to the support component or the work-related activity component, and whether you have 'limited capability for work'. The Government has said that there will be a right of appeal against any decision that attracts a 'financial sanction' and against all decisions that have a 'financial impact', such as whether or not you are placed in the support group.[30]

At time of writing it was unclear whether, if you are found not to have limited capability for work and appeal against that decision, you would be able to get income-related ESA at a reduced rate pending the decision on your appeal.

10. **Tax, tax credits and other benefits**

Tax

Contributory employment and support allowance (ESA) and ESA in youth are taxable; income-related ESA is not.[31]

Tax credits

If you have at least one dependent child you may qualify for child tax credit (see Chapter 48). If you are getting contributory ESA and your partner works, you may as a couple be entitled to working tax credit (see Chapter 49). At the time this Handbook was written it was expected that ESA would count as a 'qualifying benefit' for the disability element of working tax credit in the same way that incapacity benefit does. It was also expected that income-related ESA will be added to the list of benefits that act as a passport to the maximum rate of tax credits – see www.cpag.org.uk/esa or CPAG's *Wefare Rights Bulletin* for updates.

Means-tested benefits

The rules on who can get ESA (see p140) mean you can only get ESA and some means-tested benefits together. Remember that contributory ESA can be topped up by income-related ESA.

You cannot yourself claim ESA and **income support** (IS) at the same time. If you partner gets IS in her/his own right, you cannot get income-related ESA. If it would be possible for you to claim either ESA or IS – eg, if you are ill, disabled, a lone parent or a carer, you will need to decide which benefit to claim. You may wish to seek advice about this, as your choice will affect things like how much benefit you get at different times, and the sort of work-focused interviews you are required to attend.

You cannot yourself claim ESA and **jobseeker's allowance** (JSA), including as part of a joint-claim couple, at the same time. If your *partner* is entitled in her/his own right to income-based JSA and it is not joint-claim JSA (eg, because you have a dependent child), you can get contributory ESA at the same time.

You cannot claim income-related ESA if your partner gets **pension credit**.

You can get ESA and **housing benefit/council tax benefit** at the same time.

Non-means-tested benefits

At the time this *Handbook* was written, it was not known how the rules on overlapping benefits (see p981) would apply to ESA.

You will not be entitled to ESA if you are entitled to **statutory sick pay**.[32] Rules may say that you can still get contributory ESA if you get **statutory maternity pay (SMP)** or **statutory adoption pay (SAP)**, if the amount is less than the ESA, in which case your ESA is reduced by the amount of the SMP or SAP you get. These rules, however, had not been made at the time this *Handbook* was written.

You cannot yourself claim ESA and **JSA** at the same time. If you partner is entitled to contribution-based JSA, you can claim ESA, although it is expected that it would be taken into account when assessing your income for ESA.

Notes

1. **Who can claim employment and support allowance**
   1 ss1 and 20(1) WRA 2007
   2 Sch 2 paras 2-4 WRA 2007; Explanatory Notes to WRA 2007, para 301
   3 s18 WRA 2007
   4 Sch 1 paras 1-4 WRA 2007
   5 Sch 1 para 4 WRA 2007; Explanatory Notes to WRA, para 294
   6 Sch 1 para 6 WRA 2007
   7 Sch 3 para 19 WRA 2007

3. **Claiming for others**
   8 s2 WRA 2007
   9 s4 WRA 2007; Explanatory Notes to WRA, para 56

4. **The amount of benefit**
   10 s2 WRA 2007; Explanatory Notes to WRA, paras 52-53
   11 s3 WRA 2007; Explanatory Notes to WRA, para 54
   12 s4 WRA 2007; Explanatory Notes to WRA, paras 55-58
   13 s5 WRA 2007
   14 s6 WRA 2007
   15 ss2(2) and 4(4) WRA 2007; ESA(LCWRA)
   16 House of Commons *Hansard*, Welfare Reform Bill Standing Committee, 19 October 2006, col124
   17 ss2(3) and 4(5) WRA 2007

5. **Special benefit rules**
   18 ss4(3) and 18(4)(b) WRA 2007
   19 Sch 2 paras 5, 6 and 8 WRA 2007

6. **Claims and backdating**
   20 Sch 4 para 3 WRA 2007

8. **Limited capability for work**
   21 Sch 2 para 10 WRA 2007
   22 Email from DWP to Gary Vaux at Hertfordshire County Council, 19 December 2007; email from Gary Vaux to DWP, 17 January 2008
   23 ESA(LCWR) Regs
   24 s8(1) WRA 2007
   25 ss9 and 11 WRA 2007
   26 Regs 4, 9 and 10 and 13 ESA(LCWR) Regs
   27 Email from DWP to CPAG, 15 January 2008
   28 Reg 3 ESA(LCWR) Regs
   29 Reg 12 ESA(LCWR) Regs

9. **Challenging an employment and support allowance decision**
   30 House of Commons *Hansard*, Welfare Reform Bill Standing Committee, 19 October 2006, col137

10. **Tax, tax credits and other benefits**
   31 ss658(4), 661(1) and 677 IT(EP)A 2003
   32 s20 WRA 2007

Chapter 8

Guardian's allowance

This chapter covers:

You may be entitled to guardian's allowance if you look after a child or qualifying young person who is effectively an orphan. To qualify for guardian's allowance it is not necessary for you to be a child's legal guardian or for both of the child's parents to have died. You may qualify if one parent has died and the other is in prison or her/his whereabouts are unknown. You do not need to have paid national insurance contributions to qualify for guardian's allowance. Your entitlement is not affected by whether or not you work, or by any savings or income you have. The Revenue is responsible for the administration and payment of guardian's allowance.

Child benefit, disability living allowance and child tax credit are also available for children (see Chapters 4, 6 and 48).

1. Who can claim guardian's allowance

You qualify for a guardian's allowance if:[1]

- you are entitled, or treated as entitled, to child benefit for a 'child' or a 'qualifying young person' (see p154). In this chapter the term 'child' is used to refer to both a child and a qualifying young person; *and*
- the child is an 'eligible child' (see p155); *and either*
  - the child is living with you (see p63). A child who is absent from home may still be treated as living with you in the circumstances described on p63; *or*

  - you or, if you are residing with your spouse or civil partner, you and/or your spouse or civil partner make contributions to the cost of providing for the child at the rate of at least £13.45 a week in addition to any payment you are making to qualify you for child benefit for the child (see below and p64); *and*
- the residence conditions are satisfied (see p1360).

Even if you are not making contributions to the cost of providing for the child, you can be treated as if you are if you give a written undertaking to make the contributions once benefit is paid to you. Any decision to pay you guardian's allowance on this basis may be revised if you do not actually make contributions once benefit is paid to you.[2]

If a child for whom you get guardian's allowance dies, see p160.

There are some groups of claimants to whom special rules apply (see p157).

Treated as entitled to child benefit

In order to qualify for guardian's allowance you must either be entitled, or treated as entitled, to child benefit for the child (see Chapter 4). If you are not actually entitled to child benefit for the child, you are treated as being entitled to it:[3]

- if you are residing with your spouse and s/he is entitled to child benefit for the child (this rule does not apply to civil partners). However, if a husband and wife reside together and both would be entitled to guardian's allowance for the same child, benefit is awarded to the wife rather than the husband; *or*
- for a week in which you are living in Great Britain and would have been entitled to child benefit for the child had you (or your spouse or civil partner, if you reside with her/him) not been getting a family benefit from another country; *or*
- for a week in which you (or your spouse or civil partner, if you reside with her/him) would have been entitled to child benefit had the child been born at the end of the week before her/his actual birth; *or*
- for the week before the first week that guardian's allowance is paid to you, if you would have been entitled to guardian's allowance for that week had child benefit been paid.

As both child benefit and guardian's allowance are normally paid from the Monday after you become entitled, the latter two provisions ensure that you do not have to wait a further week to qualify for guardian's allowance.

A 'child' or 'qualifying young person'

The rules on who counts as a 'child' or a 'qualifying young person' for the purposes of guardian's allowance are the same as those for child benefit – see p57 for details. In this chapter the term 'child' is used to refer to both children and qualifying young people.

'Eligible' children

A child is an **'eligible child'** if:[4]

- both the child's parents have died (see below if the child is adopted or has a step-parent); *or*
- one of the child's parents has died and at the time of the death you did not know the whereabouts of the other parent and all your reasonable efforts to trace her/him have been unsuccessful (see below); *or*
- one of the child's parents is dead and the other is sentenced to a term of imprisonment, or is detained in hospital by a court order (but see p156).

Parents, adoptive parents and step-parents

The general rule is that a parent of a child may not claim guardian's allowance for that child.[5]

If a child is adopted, her/his adoptive parents count as parents.[6] Guardian's allowance may be payable if both adoptive parents have died, or if one has died and the other is in prison or her/his whereabouts are unknown. If a child has been adopted by only one person, a claim can be made for guardian's allowance if that person dies.

If a child has been adopted, her/his biological parents are not precluded from entitlement and, in the above circumstances, may claim guardian's allowance.[7]

However, adoptive parents may continue to receive guardian's allowance if they were entitled to it immediately before the adoption.[8]

If, when a child was born, her/his parents were unmarried, guardian's allowance is payable after the death of the mother, provided that paternity has not been clearly established.[9] Guardian's allowance is also payable if a child's biological or adoptive parents were divorced (or their civil partnership had been dissolved), one parent has died and, at the time of her/his death, the other parent did not have custody of the child (and s/he did not hold a residence order in respect of the child) and was not maintaining the child (and was not liable for maintenance for the child under a court order or under a child support maintenance assessment or calculation). However, you cannot qualify for guardian's allowance if you are the surviving parent of the child.[10]

A step-parent does not count as a parent for guardian's allowance and so may be entitled to guardian's allowance for a stepchild.

Missing parents

If one of the child's parents is dead you may qualify for guardian's allowance if, at the date of the death, you did not know the whereabouts of the other parent and since then you have failed to discover her/his whereabouts despite making reasonable efforts to do so.[11] Reasonable efforts include asking known relatives and friends and checking old addresses. However, this may not apply if you can show that there is a danger that you or the child might experience harm or undue distress if you try to trace the missing parent.[12]

If contact has been made with a surviving parent since the death of the other parent (but prior to the decision on the claim), guardian's allowance cannot be paid, as the whereabouts of the surviving parent have been known.[13] This applies even if the contact was only fleeting, such as at the funeral. In this situation you cannot qualify for guardian's allowance even if the surviving parent subsequently disappears.

If such contact has not been made, the position is less clear. If you are able to communicate with the surviving parent in some way, this is likely to be sufficient to show that the whereabouts of that parent are known.[14] 'Whereabouts' are not the same as an address, so merely showing that you do not know where the surviving parent actually lives may not be sufficient if you know the locality in which s/he is based. However, the locality must be sufficiently defined – if all that is known is that the surviving parent is in a large urban area, you could argue that her/his whereabouts are unknown.

Prison sentences

If one of the child's parents is dead and the other is in prison, you are only entitled to guardian's allowance if the surviving parent:[15]

- is serving a sentence of imprisonment or detention and has at least two years of that sentence remaining from the date of the death; *or*
- is detained in hospital by order of a court under particular legislation.

A sentence of imprisonment or detention includes detention in a young offenders' institution and detention and training orders, but does not include any period of imprisonment for contempt of court. There are detailed rules for calculating whether the length of a sentence amounts to two years, so if you are affected by these rules seek advice.

2. **The rules about your age**

There is no upper or lower age limit for entitlement to guardian's allowance.

3. **Claiming for others**

Guardian's allowance is payable for each eligible child. No additional guardian's allowance is paid for any other dependants you have.

4. **The amount of benefit**

Guardian's allowance of £13.45 a week is payable for each eligible child.[16]

Entitlement to guardian's allowance does not qualify you for national insurance (NI) credits. However, if you also receive child benefit you (or, in some circumstances someone you reside with whom you share responsibility for a child) may be able to qualify for home responsibilities protection (see p733).

5. Special benefit rules

There are some groups of claimants to whom special rules apply. These are covered in Chapters 26 and 58. Special rules apply to:

- people going abroad (see p1349);
- people coming from abroad (see p1360);
- eligible children who are in legal custody (see p626);
- eligible children whose parents were born outside the UK (see p1360).

6. Claims and backdating

In order to be entitled to guardian's allowance you must make a claim for it.[17] The rules for claiming are described briefly below and explained in more detail in Chapter 38. You may claim guardian's allowance before you become entitled to it, or your claim can be backdated (see p159).

Making a claim

Claims for guardian's allowance should be made in writing on Form BG1, which can be obtained from the Guardian's Allowance Unit (telephone: 0845 302 1464; textphone: 0845 302 1474), or the Revenue's website (see Appendix 1). Some local Revenue enquiry centres or Jobcentre Plus offices may also stock the form. The Revenue decision maker has the discretion to accept a written claim which is not on the correct form if it is sufficient in the circumstances (see p959).[18] You can submit your claim to the Guardian's Allowance Unit, Child Benefit Office (Washington), PO Box 1, Newcastle upon Tyne NE88 1AA, or to a Revenue enquiry office or a Jobcentre Plus office.

Keep a copy of your claim in case queries arise.

You may amend or withdraw your claim before it is assessed by writing to the Guardian's Allowance Unit. See p955 for more details about making a claim.

Information to support your claim

When you claim guardian's allowance you must satisfy what is known as the 'national insurance (NI) number requirement' (see p962). This means that, in most cases, you must provide your NI number when making a claim. You can also be asked to supply 'certificates, documents, information and evidence' considered relevant to your claim.[19] For example, you may be asked to supply the birth certificate(s) of the child(ren) for whom you are claiming.

If you are asked to provide evidence or documents which you do not have, ask what other evidence would be acceptable. Ask the Revenue to explain what is required and why, and complain if you believe any requests for information are unreasonable.

Who should claim

You must normally claim guardian's allowance yourself. However, if you are unable to manage your own affairs, another person can claim guardian's allowance for you by becoming your 'appointee' (see p955).

If you are a married woman and you live with your husband it is you, rather than your husband, who will be entitled to guardian's allowance.

The date of your claim

The date of your claim is important as it determines the date from which you will be paid guardian's allowance (see p159). The date of your claim is normally the date it is received at either the Child Benefit Office, the Revenue's office at Comben House, Merseyside, a Revenue enquiry centre or a Jobcentre Plus office.[20]

If you submit a written claim which is incomplete or not on the correct form you may be asked to provide further information or to complete the correct form. As long as this additional information or form is submitted within a month of it being sent back to you (or longer, if the decision maker thinks that the delay is reasonable), your claim is treated as having been made on the date the initial claim was received at one of the above offices.[21]

In some circumstances, you can claim before you qualify for guardian's allowance or the date of your claim can be backdated (see p159).

If you claim the wrong benefit

The decision maker can treat a claim for child benefit for a child as a claim for guardian's allowance for the same child.[22] This may allow you to get your claim for guardian's allowance backdated for more than the normal three months. If your child benefit claim is accepted as a claim for guardian's allowance, your claim can be backdated for up to three months from the date you claimed child benefit, if you satisfy the qualifying conditions over that period.

See p963 for details of interchanging claims in this way.

Claiming in advance

You can claim guardian's allowance up to three months before you expect to qualify for it – eg, if you know you will be taking responsibility for a child.[23] It is helpful to claim in advance if you can, as the Revenue can then gather the information it needs and decide your claim in good time.

How your claim is dealt with

Your claim is dealt with by the Guardian's Allowance Unit of the Child Benefit Office and queries about your claim should be made to that office.

You may be able to claim an interim payment while waiting for a decision on your claim (see p986) or to claim means-tested benefits and tax credits if your income is low (see p161). See p970 for more information about the processing of claims.

Backdating claims

Your claim for guardian's allowance can be backdated for up to three months from the date that you make your claim if you satisfy the qualifying conditions over that period.[24] You do not have to show any reasons why your claim was late. The rules on backdating are covered on p965. (There are special rules if you were getting guardian's allowance and move between Great Britain and Northern Ireland or if you have been recognised as a refugee.[25])

If you might have qualified for benefit for an even earlier period but did not claim because you were given the wrong information or were misled by the Revenue or the DWP you could ask for an *ex gratia* payment (see p1186) or complain to the Ombudsman via your MP (see p1184).

If you claimed child benefit instead of guardian's allowance, see p158.

7. Getting paid

Guardian's allowance is a weekly benefit and so cannot be paid for a period of less than a week. Payment of guardian's allowance is normally made by direct credit transfer into your bank account or similar account. If you are unable to open or manage an account, payment can be made by cheque (see p979). If you also receive child benefit, guardian's allowance is paid at the same time and in the same way as your child benefit (see p74).[26]

Payment of guardian's allowance starts from the first Monday after the date of your claim (see p158), unless your date of claim is a Monday, when it starts on that day.[27] For details of when your date of claim can be backdated, see above.

If your entitlement to guardian's allowance ends, payment will continue up to, but not including, the following payday (which will normally be either Monday or Tuesday) unless your entitlement ends on a payday, when your benefit will be paid up to, but not including, that day.[28] If your benefit is not paid into your account or your benefit cheque is lost or stolen, see p983. If payment of your guardian's allowance is suspended, see p984.

Delays and complaints

If payment of your guardian's allowance is delayed, you might be able to get an interim payment. See p986 for further details. If you experience delays, or wish to complain about how your claim has been dealt with, see Chapter 46. You might be able to claim compensation (see p1186).

Change of circumstances

You must report any change in your circumstances that the Revenue has informed you that you must tell it about (although the Revenue might not inform you of all the changes you need to tell it about). Also, it is your duty to report any change in your circumstances that you might reasonably be expected to know might affect your right to, the amount of, or the payment of your benefit.[29] You should report such changes promptly. If you do not, any resulting overpayment may be recoverable from you (see Chapter 39). If you are considered deliberately to have acted falsely or dishonestly, you may also be guilty of an offence (see Chapter 40). You should write to the Guardian's Allowance Unit to report a change in your circumstances. However, if you have reported a change verbally or have reported a change to a Revenue enquiry centre or Jobcentre Plus office, in some circumstances this may be sufficient.[30]

If you report a change verbally, it is advisable to note the time and date of your conversation, the name of the person you informed, and confirm your conversation in writing to the Guardian's Allowance Unit, keeping a copy of your letter in case problems arise. The rules about when your benefit will be adjusted following a change in your circumstances are the same as those for child benefit (see p75).

If a child dies

If a child for whom you are receiving child benefit dies, you can qualify for guardian's allowance for the eight-week period that child benefit remains in payment for that child (see p75), as long as you meet the normal qualifying conditions for guardian's allowance over that time (other than the condition that the child either must be living with you, or you must be contributing to her/his maintenance).[31]

Overpayments and fraud

If you are overpaid guardian's allowance, you might have to repay it. The rules on overpayments are covered in Chapter 39.

If you have been accused of fraud, see Chapter 40.

8. Challenging a guardian's allowance decision

You can apply for a revision or supersession of a guardian's allowance decision, or appeal against it – see Chapters 41 and 42.

9. Tax, tax credits and other benefits

Guardian's allowance is not taxable.[32]

Means-tested benefits and tax credits

If you have a low income you may be entitled to means-tested benefits, which can be paid in addition to guardian's allowance. Guardian's allowance is ignored when calculating your entitlement to income-based jobseeker's allowance[33] (see Chapter 15), income support[34] (see Chapter 13), pension credit[35] (see Chapter 18), housing benefit[36] (see Chapter 10), council tax benefit[37] (see Chapter 5), working tax credit (see Chapter 49) and child tax credit[38] (see Chapter 48).

Non-means-tested benefits

Although increases in non-means-tested benefits for children were abolished on 6 April 2003, some people continue to be entitled to them (see p691). You cannot get an increase in a non-means-tested benefit for a child for whom you get guardian's allowance because of the overlapping benefit rules (see p983).[39] Otherwise, guardian's allowance can be paid in addition to any other non-means-tested benefit.

Passports and other sources of help

If you are looking after a child but you are not the child's parent and you do not qualify for guardian's allowance, you could consider approaching the local authority social services department for a fostering allowance.

If you are on a low income, you may be entitled to certain health service benefits (see Chapter 9). You may also qualify for a social fund payment (see Chapters 21 and 22), free school meals for your children (see p15) or for other sources of help (see p14).

Notes

1. **Who can claim guardian's allowance**
   1 ss77 and 122(5) SSCBA 1992
   2 Reg 5 SSB(Dep) Regs
   3 ss77(9) and 122(4) SSCBA 1992; reg 4A SSB(Dep) Regs
   4 s77(2) SSCBA 1992; reg 7 GA(Gen) Regs
   5 s77(10) SSCBA 1992
   6 Reg 4 GA(Gen) Regs
   7 s77(10) SSCBA 1992; R(G) 4/83 (appendix)
   8 s77(10) and (11) SSCBA 1992
   9 Reg 5 GA(Gen) Regs
   10 s77(10) SSCBA 1992; reg 6 GA(Gen) Regs
   11 s77(2)(b) SSCBA 1992
   12 Child Benefit Technical Manual 12090
   13 CG/60/1992; R(G) 2/83; CSG/8/1992
   14 CG/60/1992; CF/2735/2003
   15 Reg 7 GA(Gen) Regs

4. **The amount of benefit**
   16 Sch 4 Part III SSCBA 1992

6. **Claims and backdating**
   17 s1 SSAA 1992
   18 Reg 5 CB&GA(Admin) Regs
   19 Reg 7 CB&GA(Admin) Regs
   20 Reg 5(3) CB&GA(Admin) Regs
   21 Reg 10 CB&GA(Admin) Regs
   22 Reg 11 CB&GA(Admin) Regs
   23 Reg 12 CB&GA(Admin) Regs
   24 Reg 6(1) CB&GA(Admin) Regs
   25 Reg 6(2) CB&GA(Admin) Regs

7. **Getting paid**
   26 Regs 16(2),17(5) and 18(4) CB&GA(Admin) Regs
   27 Reg 13 CB&GA(Admin) Regs
   28 Reg 14 CB&GA(Admin) Regs
   29 Reg 23 CB&GA(Admin) Regs
   30 Reg 23(4) and (5) CB&GA(Admin) Regs
   31 s145A(4) SSCBA 1992

9. **Tax, tax credits and other benefits**
   32 s677 IT(EP)A 2003
   33 Sch 7 para 6A JSA Regs
   34 Sch 9 para 5A IS Regs
   35 Reg 15(1)(g) SPC Regs
   36 Sch 5 para 50 HB Regs; regs 27 and 29 HB(SPC) Regs
   37 Sch 4 para 51 CTB Regs; regs 17 and 19 CTB(SPC) Regs
   38 Reg 7 TC(DCI) Regs
   39 Reg 7(4) SS(OB) Regs

Chapter 9

Health benefits

This chapter covers:

1. Charges and exemptions

Although the NHS generally provides free health care, there are fixed charges for some items and services such as prescriptions, dental treatment, sight tests, glasses, wigs and fabric supports.

You are exempt from these charges, however, if:[1]

- you, or a member of your family (see p700), are receiving income support (IS), income-based jobseeker's allowance (JSA) or the guarantee credit of pension credit (PC);
- you or your partner are receiving:
  - child tax credit (CTC – see Chapter 48); *or*
  - CTC and working tax credit (WTC – see Chapter 49); *or*
  - WTC including a disability or severe disability element (see p1237); *and*

  your gross annual income, as calculated by the Revenue for tax credit purposes at the time of your tax credit award, does not exceed £15,050. Members of your family for tax credit purposes (see p1196) are also exempt from charges if you satisfy these conditions;
- you are a permanent resident in a care home and your place is being partly or wholly funded by a local authority (see p618). If your place is *not* being funded by a local authority, you may qualify for help with health charges under the low income scheme (see p171) or on other grounds;

- you are a hospital inpatient, in which case all medication and NHS treatment is provided free of charge (including glasses and contact lenses if prescribed through the Hospital Eye Service). If you are an outpatient, medication taken and treatment given while you are in the hospital is also provided without charge (but you may be charged for dentures and bridges);
- you are an asylum seeker, or a dependant of an asylum seeker, who is receiving asylum support (see p1345);
- you are a war disablement pensioner and need the relevant item or service because of your war disability;
- you are aged 16 or 17 and are being financially maintained by a local authority in England or Wales after being looked after by a local authority (see p610);
- you are receiving support from a local authority in Scotland under s29(1) Children (Scotland) Act 1995, after leaving care;
- you are in prison or a young offenders' institution.

You may also be exempt from some charges because of your age or health condition.

If you are not exempt on any of the above grounds, you may be entitled to full or partial remission of charges on the grounds of low income (see p171).

2. **Prescriptions**

Free prescriptions

Prescriptions are free in Wales. Otherwise you qualify for free prescriptions if:[2]

- you are in one of the exempt groups listed above; *or*
- your income is low enough (see p174); *or*
- you are aged 60 or over; *or*
- you are aged under 16, or under 19 and are in full-time education; *or*
- you are pregnant, or have given birth in the last 12 months; *or*
- your prescription was issued to you while you were in prison; *or*
- you have:
  - a continuing physical disability which prevents you leaving your home except with the help of another person;
  - epilepsy requiring continuous anti-convulsive therapy;
  - a permanent fistula, including a caecostomy, ileostomy, laryngostomy or colostomy, needing continuous surgical dressing or an appliance;
  - diabetes mellitus (except where treatment is by diet alone);
  - diabetes insipidus and other forms of hypopituitarism;
  - myxoedema;
  - hypoparathyroidism;

- forms of hypoadrenalism (including Addison's disease), for which specific substitution therapy is essential; *or*
- myasthenia gravis.

Reduced-cost prescriptions

You cannot get reduced-cost prescriptions under the low income scheme.

If you are not exempt from charges, and you need more than three prescription items in three months (four months in Scotland) or 14 items (10 items in Scotland) in a year, you can save money by buying a pre-payment certificate.

You apply for a certificate on Form FP95 in England or EC95 in Scotland, which you can get from chemists, some doctors' surgeries and relevant health bodies. In England, you can also apply using a credit or debit card on 0845 850 0030 or via the Prescription Pricing Division website at www.ppa.nhs.uk. You can also pay in monthly instalments by direct debit. A refund can be claimed in certain circumstances if you buy a pre-payment certificate and then qualify for free prescriptions.

3. Dental treatment and dentures

Free treatment

NHS check-ups are free in Scotland. Otherwise, you qualify for free NHS dental treatment (including check-ups) and appliances (including dentures) if, when your treatment is arranged or charges are made:[3]

- you are in one of the exempt groups listed on p163; *or*
- your income is low enough (see p172); *or*
- you are under 18, or under 19 and in full-time education; *or*
- for examinations only in Wales, you are under 25 or are 60 or over; *or*
- you are pregnant or have given birth within the last 12 months; *or*
- you are a patient of the Community Dental Service (this service is available for people who have difficulty getting treatment because of a disability or for other reasons – contact your health authority for details) or an NHS Hospital Dental Service. Note, however, that there may be a charge for dentures and bridges.

Reduced-cost treatment

If you do not qualify for free treatment, you may qualify for reduced-cost treatment and appliances on the ground of low income. See p171 for details.

4. **Sight tests and glasses**

Free sight tests

NHS sight tests are free in Scotland. Otherwise, you qualify for a free NHS sight test if:[4]

- you are in one of the exempt groups listed on p163; *or*
- your income is low enough (see p174); *or*
- you are aged 60 or over; *or*
- you are under 16, or under 19 and in full-time education; *or*
- you are registered blind or partially sighted; *or*
- you have been prescribed complex or powerful lenses (ie, one lens which has a power in any one meridian of at least plus or minus ten dioptres, or which is a prism-controlled bifocal lens); *or*
- you have been diagnosed as having diabetes or glaucoma or are at risk of getting glaucoma; *or*
- you are aged 40 or over and are the parent, brother, sister or child of someone with glaucoma; *or*
- you are a patient of the Hospital Eye Service.

Reduced-cost sight tests

If you do not qualify for a free sight test, you may be entitled to a reduced-cost sight test on low income grounds.[5] See p171 for details. There is no set charge for a sight test, so it is worth shopping around if you are not entitled to a free test.

Vouchers for glasses and contact lenses

If you are given a prescription for glasses following an eye test, you are entitled to a voucher that you can use to buy (or repair) glasses or contact lenses if:[6]

- you are in one of the exempt groups listed on p163; *or*
- your income is low enough (see p174); *or*
- you are under 16, or under 19 and in full-time education; *or*
- you are a Hospital Eye Service patient needing frequent changes of glasses or contact lenses; *or*
- you have been prescribed complex or powerful lenses (see above).

You are entitled to a voucher if:[7]

- you require glasses or contact lenses for the first time; *or*
- your new prescription differs from your old one; *or*
- your old glasses have worn out through fair wear and tear; *or*
- you are under 16; *or*
- because of illness (or disability in Scotland) you have lost or damaged your glasses or contact lenses and the cost of repair or replacement is not covered by insurance or warranty; *and*

- you, or a member of your family, are exempt from charges because you are receiving income support (IS), income-based jobseeker's allowance (JSA), the guarantee credit of pension credit (PC) or tax credits (see p163); *or*
- your income is low enough (see p174); *or*
- you have been prescribed complex lenses (see p166).

Vouchers are issued by opticians or a hospital (if it has prescribed you with complex lenses or you need to change your lenses frequently). Each voucher has a coded value depending on the type of lenses (or repair) you need.[8] You can redeem the voucher at any supplier when you buy glasses (or have them repaired) or contact lenses. Vouchers are, however, only valid for six months[9] and they may not cover the full cost of the glasses or lenses you choose to buy. Prices vary and you may need to shop around if you do not want to pay the extra cost.

Reduced-value vouchers

You may be entitled to a reduced-value voucher on the grounds of low income. See p171 for details.

5. Fares to hospital

Full help

You qualify for full help with your fares to attend a hospital or any other establishment for NHS treatment or services if:[10]

- you are in one of the exempt groups listed on p163; *or*
- your income is low enough (see p174); *or*
- you are a patient at a genito-urinary medicine clinic more than 15 miles from your home (more than five miles if you need to attend on a weekly basis); *or*
- you live in the Isles of Scilly or the Scottish Islands or Highlands and have to travel more than a specified distance for hospital treatment.

The law allows help with the cost of travelling by the cheapest means of transport available and, where necessary, the cost of overnight accommodation. This usually means standard-class public transport. If you have to go by car or taxi, you should be paid your mileage allowance, road and toll charges or taxi fares. The travel expenses of an escort can also be met if you need to be accompanied for a medical reason. Special rules (including maximum costs) apply if you live in the Isles of Scilly or the Scottish Islands or Highlands.[11]

You should claim at the hospital (ask for the office which deals with claims). You may be able to request payment in advance of travelling, where this is necessary or, alternatively, you could apply for a social fund crisis loan from the DWP (see p503).

If you are travelling abroad to receive NHS treatment, you are entitled to payment for the cost of travel to and from the airport, ferry port or international train station if you are in one of the above groups. You are also entitled to payment or repayment of onward travelling expenses to the treatment centre, whether or not you fall within one of the above groups. The amount and mode of transport and payment is determined by the health authority or board prior to travel.

If you are receiving IS, income-based JSA or PC and are visiting a close relative or partner, you may be eligible for a social fund community care grant to help with your fares (see p493).

Partial help

You may qualify for partial help with your hospital fares on the grounds of low income. See p171 for details.

6. Healthy Start food and vitamins

If you qualify for Healthy Start food and vitamins, you get free vitamins as well as fixed-value vouchers that can be used to buy specified types of food.

Healthy Start food

You qualify for Healthy Start food vouchers if you are:[12]

- **pregnant** and have been for more than 10 weeks, and you are:
  - 18 or over and are entitled to (or a member of the family (see p700) of someone who is entitled to) income support (IS), income-based jobseeker's allowance (JSA) or child tax credit (CTC), provided in the latter case that gross income for CTC purposes does not exceed £15,575 and there is no entitlement to working tax credit (WTC); *or*
  - under 18, whether or not you qualify for any benefits or tax credits (but not if you are excluded from these because you are a 'person subject to immigration control' – see p1334); *or*
- **a mother** who has 'parental responsibility' for a child and:
  - you are 18 or over and either your child is under one or it is less than a year since her/his expected date of birth. This means you can continue to qualify for vouchers for a period after your child is one – ie, if s/he was born prematurely. You must be entitled to (or a member of the family (see p700) of someone who is entitled to) IS, income-based JSA or CTC, provided in the latter case that gross income for CTC purposes does not exceed £15,575 and there is no entitlement to WTC; *or*
  - it is less than four months since your baby's expected date of birth and you have not yet notified Healthy Start that s/he was born. Once you notify the

birth you may then qualify under the rule above. You must have been getting IS, income-based JSA or CTC (provided in the latter case that gross income for CTC purposes did not exceed £15,575 and there was no entitlement to WTC) before your baby was born.

'Parental responsibility' means parental responsibility as defined in s3(1) Children Act 1989 (in England or Wales) or s1(1) Children (Scotland) Act 1995 (in Scotland).[13]

If you qualify for vouchers for more than one child under this rule (eg, you have twins), you get a voucher for each. If you do not have parental responsibility but would otherwise qualify for vouchers, your child qualifies instead of you;

- **a child under four** who is a member of the family of someone who is entitled to IS, income-based JSA or CTC provided, in the latter case, that the person's gross income at the time of the CTC award does not exceed £15,575 for CTC purposes and s/he is not entitled to WTC.

Note: for these purposes, you are treated as not entitled to WTC during the four-week WTC run-on (see p1229).

In practice this means that each week you get one voucher for each of your children aged between one and four, two vouchers for each of your children under one (or within one year of their expected date of birth), plus one voucher if you are pregnant. Each voucher is worth £3.[14]

Example

Vera is 17 weeks pregnant. She has three children, twin girls aged two and a boy aged seven. She is getting IS. She qualifies for a voucher because she is more than 10 weeks pregnant. Her twins each qualify for a voucher as they are under four. Her son does not qualify for a voucher. Vera gets three vouchers each week totaling £9. When the baby is born, Vera will still be entitled to a voucher because she will be a mother of a child under one. The baby will also be entitled to a voucher. She will then get four vouchers each week totaling £12.

Vouchers can be exchanged for Healthy Start food at registered food outlets. If there is no registered food outlet within a reasonable distance of your home, you are paid an amount equal to the value of the vouchers to which you are entitled.[15]

'Healthy Start food' means liquid cow's milk and cow's milk-based infant formula, fresh fruit and vegetables including loose, pre-packed, whole, sliced, chopped or mixed fruit or vegetables (but not fruit or vegetables to which salt, sugar, herbs or other flavouring has been added).[16]

Note: if you are an asylum seeker receiving asylum support (see p1345), you receive extra money to help you buy healthy food if you are pregnant or have a child under three.

Claims

You must make an initial claim for Healthy Start food vouchers in writing and must provide specified information and evidence.[17] You should complete the form in the Healthy Start leaflet (HS01), available from maternity clinics and some doctors' surgeries or from 0845 6076823. Information about Healthy Start and a claim form are also available at www.healthystart.nhs.uk. The form must be countersigned by a health professional (eg, a midwife or health visitor) who certifies when your baby is due (if you are pregnant) and that you have been given appropriate advice about healthy eating and breastfeeding. If you are under 16, your claim must also be signed by your parent or carer.

If you are getting Healthy Start food vouchers while you are pregnant and then inform Healthy Start of your baby's birth by telephone while s/he is under four months old, you can get extra vouchers for her/him from her/his date of birth.[18] You need to make a claim for CTC for her/him (or add her/him to your existing claim), to ensure that you continue to get the vouchers.

You receive your vouchers by post every four weeks. If you do not get vouchers to which you think you are entitled, or have any other problems with these, you should contact the Healthy Start helpline on 0845 6076823.

Healthy Start vitamins

If you qualify for Healthy Start food vouchers (see p168), you also qualify for Healthy Start vitamins.[19] Mothers and pregnant women are entitled to 56 vitamin tablets and children under four to 10 millilitres of vitamin drops every eight weeks. Your Primary Care Trust, health board or health trust (eg, your NHS maternity or child health clinic or health centre) is responsible for giving you your free vitamins. Ask your local health professional what the local arrangements are.

You do not have to make a separate claim for Healthy Start vitamins. However, you must show evidence to the vitamin supplier that you are entitled (ie, the letter to which your most recent Healthy Start vouchers were attached) and, if requested, proof of your child's age.[20]

Free milk for children in daycare

Children under five are entitled to 189–200 millilitres of free milk on each day they are looked after for two hours or more:[21]

- by a registered childminder or daycare provider; *or*
- in a school, playcentre or workplace nursery which is exempt from registration; *or*
- in local authority daycare.

Children under one are allowed fresh or dried milk.

Note: this is provided by the welfare food scheme *not* by Healthy Start.

7. The low income scheme

You (and members of your family) may be entitled to full or partial remission of NHS charges on the grounds of low income if you are not exempt on other grounds. The low income scheme is administered by the NHS Business Services Authority (see Appendix 1).

To qualify for help under the scheme, you must have capital of less than £16,000 (£17,250 in Wales), or £21,500 (£22,000 in Wales) if you live permanently in a care home (see p910).[22] Your capital is calculated as for other means-tested benefits (see Chapter 36). Tariff income from capital is calculated as for IS, unless you are a permanent resident in a care home (see p172).

To determine whether you qualify for help under the low income scheme, your 'requirements' (see p172) are compared with your 'income' (see below). If your income does not exceed your requirements by more than 50 per cent of the current cost of a prescription (at the time of writing this was £3.55), you are exempt from charges.[23] If your income exceeds your requirements by more than this amount, you are entitled to partial remission of charges as follows.[24]

- Dental charges and charges for wigs and fabric supports which are higher than three times the amount by which your income exceeds your requirements (your 'excess income') are remitted.
- The cost of a sight test is reduced to the amount of your excess income, if lower, plus the amount by which the cost exceeds the NHS sight test fee.
- The value of a voucher for glasses or lenses is reduced by twice your excess income.
- The amount you can claim for hospital fares is reduced by the amount of your excess income.

You cannot get partial help with the cost of prescriptions under the low income scheme (but see p165 for pre-payment certificates).

Calculating your requirements

Your 'requirements' are similar to the income support (IS) 'applicable amount' (see Chapter 33). The most significant elements and differences are set out below. **Note:** there are no exclusions or reductions for people who are subject to immigration control or not habitually resident in the UK, or for students, people engaged in a trade dispute or people without accommodation.

Your **'requirements'** are made up of the following elements.[25]

- **Personal allowance(s):**

Single person aged under 25	£47.95
Single person aged 25–59 and lone parent aged under 60	£60.50
Single person and lone parent, aged 60 or over	£124.05

Couples, both partners aged under 60	£94.95
Couples, one or both partners aged 60 or over	£189.35

- **Premiums:** the disability, enhanced disability, severe disability, bereavement and carer's premiums are added to your requirements if you would qualify for them under IS rules (see p775). A disability premium can be included if you or your partner have been incapable of work for 28 weeks rather than 52 weeks.
- **Amounts for children:** your requirements do not include any amounts for children.
- **Weekly council tax *less* any council tax benefit** (see Chapter 5).
- **Weekly rent *less* any housing benefit** (HB) (see Chapter 10) and any non-dependant deductions applicable under the rules on IS housing costs (see p815). Deductions for fuel and ineligible service charges are made in accordance with HB rules.
- **Weekly mortgage interest and capital payments on loans** secured on a home, or to buy a home, or to adapt a home for the special needs of a disabled person, **and payments on an endowment policy** relating to the purchase of a home. Deductions are made for non-dependants.
- **If you live permanently in a care home** (see Chapter 26), your 'requirements' are your weekly accommodation charge, including meals and services, and a personal expenses allowance. Remember that if your place is being funded by a local authority (fully or in part), you are exempt from charges (see p163).

Calculating your income

Your income is calculated as for IS (see p844), with the following modifications.[26]

- Your income is normally taken into account in the week in which it is paid. If you are affected by a trade dispute, your normal earnings are taken into account.
- You are entitled to an earnings disregard of £20 if you would qualfy for a disability premium (see p779), or you or your partner are aged 60 or over.
- Regular liable relative payments count as weekly income. Irregular payments are averaged over the 13 weeks prior to your claim. Lump-sum payments are treated as capital.
- Student loans and grants are divided by 52, unless you are in your final year or are doing a one-year course, in which case the loan is divided by the number of weeks you are studying. The £10 disregard from student loans only applies if you are eligible for a premium (see p779), you receive an allowance because of deafness, or you are not a student but your partner is. In addition, in England and Wales, sums in excess of a specified amount of a maintenance grant (and if you are a Scottish student studying in England, any 'additional loan'), and any loan paid under Reg 10 Education (Student Loans) (Scotland) Regulations

2000, are disregarded. Also, in England and Scotland, where a voluntary payment is taken into account up to £20 of it is disregarded.

- Insurance policy payments for housing costs not met by IS count as income, but payments for unsecured loans for repairs and improvements (including premiums) are ignored.
- The capital limit for tariff income is £13,000 (£17,250 in Wales) if you are permanently in residential or nursing care. Remember that if your place is being funded by a local authority (fully or in part), you are exempt from charges (see p163).
- The savings credit of pension credit is ignored as income.

8. Claims and refunds

Claiming full help with health costs

- If you are exempt from charges on the grounds of your **age**, **receipt of a qualifying benefit** or because you are a **full-time student under 19**, you should complete the back of the prescription form, or complete the appropriate form at your dentist, optician or hospital.
- If you are exempt because you receive **tax credits** (see p163), you should be sent an exemption certificate (normally valid for up to 15 months) automatically. This could be up to six weeks after you are awarded tax credits. If you have not yet been sent your exemption certificate, you can sign the prescription form, or other appropriate form to say you do not have to pay and use your tax credits award letter as proof of this.
- If you are exempt from charges because you are **pregnant** or have **given birth** in the last 12 months, you should obtain an exemption certificate by completing a form, which you can get from your doctor, midwife or health visitor.
- If you are entitled to free prescriptions because you have a **prescribed condition**, you should apply for an exemption certificate on Form FP92A (EC92A in Scotland), which you can get from your doctor, hospital or pharmacist.
- If you are exempt from charges because you are an **asylum seeker** and you are not receiving asylum support, you should apply to the NHS Business Services Authority (see Appendix 1) for an HC2 exemption certificate by completing an HC1 application form, which you can get from a Jobcentre Plus office or NHS hospital. If you are receiving asylum support, see p174.
- If you are exempt because you live in a **care home** or you are **16 or 17 and were formerly looked after by a local authority** you need an HC2 certificate, but you can apply for one on a special short form HC1(SC).

- If you are exempt because you are a **war disablement pensioner**, you should contact the Veterans Agency Treatment Group (Norcross, Blackpool FY5 3WP).

Claiming under the low income scheme

To apply for remission of charges on the grounds of low income, you must complete Form HC1, obtainable from Jobcentre Plus offices or NHS hospitals. You can also request a form online at www.ppa.nhs.uk. Send the completed form to the NHS Business Services Authority (see Appendix 1).

If your income is low enough to qualify for free services you are sent an HC2 certificate. If you qualify for partial remission of charges, you are sent an HC3 certificate. Another person can apply on your behalf if you are unable to act. Certificates are normally valid for 12 months. However, they are valid for:[27]

- five years, if you are a single person aged 65 or over or one of a couple where one partner is aged 60 or over and the other is aged 65 or over, and you do not receive earnings, or payments from an occupational pension, a personal pension, or an annuity, and you do not have a dependent child or young person as part of your household; *or*
- six months from the date of claim, if you are an asylum seeker receiving asylum support, in which case a certificate is issued by the Border and Immigration Agency. If you have queries, telephone 0845 602 1739.

If you are a full-time student, your certificate normally lasts until the end of your course or the start of the next academic year.

You should make a repeat claim on Form HC1 shortly before the expiry date. If you have a five-year certificate, you must notify the issuing authority of any changes in your circumstances. In other cases, changes of circumstances (eg, starting work) do not affect the validity of a certificate but, if the change could result in increased help, you can re-apply for a fresh assessment before the certificate expires.

Proof of entitlement

You are normally asked for proof that you are entitled to full or partial help with charges, although you should not be denied an item or service if you are unable to provide the required evidence. If you have an HC2 or HC3 certificate you should show this to the dentist, optician, hospital or pharmacist (you may also have to enter details on the appropriate form). In other cases, you may need to show evidence of your date of birth, student status, FP92 exemption certificate or tax credit exemption certificate.

If you receive help to which you were not entitled, you can be issued with a penalty notice requiring you to pay the charge you should have paid plus a penalty of five times that charge (up to a maximum of £100), unless you can show that you did not act 'wrongfully' or with 'any lack of care'. The penalty can be increased by up to £50 if you do not pay it within 28 days, and court proceedings can be taken to recover the debt. Anyone wrongly claiming help with charges on your behalf can themselves be liable to pay a penalty charge. You can also be prosecuted if you wrongly obtain help on the basis of a false statement or representation.[28]

Delays and problems

For general queries, telephone 0845 850 1166. You can ask for a formal review of the decision on your claim by writing to the Review Section, NHS Business Services Authority, PO Box 993, Newcastle Upon Tyne NE99 2TZ. You can also request a review online at www.ppa.nhs.uk.

If there are delays in obtaining a certificate, you can complain to the customer services manager. If necessary, you could pay for the treatment or items you need then try and obtain a refund (see below).

Refunds

If you pay for an item or service which you could have got free, or at reduced cost, you can apply for a refund. You should do this within three months of paying the charge, although the time limit can in some cases be extended if you can show good cause for applying late (eg, you were ill).[29] **Note:** in Scotland, if you got a prepayment certificate before 1 April 2008 (when prescription charges went down) and it is valid for at least a month after that date, you can apply for a partial refund.

You should apply for a refund of a prescription charge on Form FP57 (EC57 in Scotland), which you must obtain when you pay as one cannot be supplied later. For other items and services, you should apply for a refund on Form HC5. You can get the forms by telephoning 0845 850 1166, or from a Jobcentre Plus office or NHS hospital. You must submit a receipt or other documents to show that you have paid the charge. If you need an HC2 or HC3 certificate and have not applied for one, you should also send a Form HC1 with your application for a refund.

9. Healthcare equipment

Healthcare equipment, such as special footwear, leg appliances, wigs, surgical supports, wheelchairs, commodes, incontinence pads, hearing aids and low vision aids can be provided by health authorities, hospitals and GPs, either free of charge or on prescription (see p164). Equipment for daily living can also be provided by social services departments, but may be subject to a reasonable charge.

Notes

1. Charges and exemptions

1 Regs 3-5 NHS(TERC) Regs; regs 3 and 4 NHS(TERC)(S) Regs; regs 3-5 NHS(TERC)(W) Regs

2. Prescriptions

2 NHS(FP&CDA)(W) Regs; Regs 4-6 NHS(TERC) Regs; regs 3 and 4 NHS(TERC)(S) Regs; reg 7 NHS(CDA) Regs; reg 7 NHS(CDA)(S) Regs

3. Dental treatment and dentures

3 Regs 3-5 NHS(TERC) Regs; regs 3 and 4 NHS(TERC)(S) Regs; regs 3-5 NHS(TERC)(W) Regs; Sch 2 NHS(DC) Regs; Sch 2 NHS(DC)(S) Regs; reg 3 and Sch 5 NHS(DC)(W) Regs; Schs 12 and 12ZA NHSA 1977

4. Sight tests and glasses

4 Reg 13 NHS(GOS) Regs; reg 3 NHS(OCP) Regs
5 Reg 3 NHS(OCP) Regs
6 Regs 8 and 15 NHS(OCP) Regs; regs 8 and 15 NHS(OCP)(S) Regs
7 Regs 9 and 15 NHS(OCP) Regs; regs 9 and 15 and NHS(OCP)(S) Regs
8 Schs 1-3 NHS(OCP) Regs; Schs 1-3 NHS(OCP)(S) Regs
9 Reg 12(1) NHS(OCP) Regs; reg 12(1) NHS(OCP)(S) Regs

5. Fares to hospital

10 Regs 3, 5 and 6 NHS(TERC) Regs; regs 3-5 NHS(TERC)(S) Regs; regs 3, 5 and 6 NHS(TERC)(W) Regs
11 Reg 5B NHS(TERC) Regs; reg 7 NHS(TERC)(S) Regs

6. Healthy Start food and vitamins

12 Reg 3 HSS&WF(A) Regs
13 Reg 2(1) HSS&WF(A) Regs
14 Regs 2(1), 8 and 9 HSS&WF(A) Regs
15 Reg 5(2) HSS&WF(A) Regs
16 Regs 2(1) and 5(1) and Sch 3 HSS&WF(A) Regs; HSS(DHSF)(W) Regs
17 Reg 4 and Sch 2 HSS&WF(A) Regs
18 Reg 4(2) HSS&WF(A) Regs
19 Reg 3 HSS&WF(A) Regs
20 Reg 8A HSS&WF(A) Regs
21 Reg 18 WF Regs

7. The low income scheme

22 Sch 1 Table A NHS(TERC) Regs; Sch 1 Table A NHS(TERC)(S) Regs; Sch 1 Table A NHS(TERC)(W) Regs
23 Reg 5(2)(e) NHS(TERC) Regs; reg 4(2)(c) NHS(TERC)(S) Regs; reg 5(2)(e) NHS(TERC)(W) Regs
24 Reg 6 NHS(TERC) Regs; reg 5 NHS(TERC)(S) Regs; reg 6 NHS(TERC)(W) Regs; regs 1, 3, 7, 14 and 19 NHS(OCP) Regs; regs 1, 14 and 19 NHS(OCP)(S) Regs
25 Reg 17 and Sch 1 Part II NHS(TERC) Regs; reg 8 and Sch 1 Part II NHS(TERC)(S) Regs; reg 16 and Sch 1 Table B NHS(TERC)(W) Regs
26 Reg 16 and Sch 1 Part I NHS(TERC) Regs; reg 8 and Sch 1 Part 1 NHS(TERC)(S) Regs; reg 15 and Sch 1 Table A NHS(TERC)(W) Regs

8. Claims and refunds

27 Reg 8 NHS(TERC) Regs; reg 10 NHS(TERC)(S) Regs; reg 8 NHS(TERC)(W) Regs
28 ss122A, 122B and 122C NHSA 1977; ss99ZA and 99ZB NHS(S)A 1978
29 Reg 11 (NHS)(TERC) Regs; reg 11 NHS(TERC)(S) Regs; reg 10 NHS(TERC)(W) Regs; reg 10 (NHS)(CDA) Regs; regs 10 and 11 (NHS)(CDA)(S) Regs; regs 6 and 20 NHS(OCP) Regs; reg 20 NHS(OCP)(S) Regs

Chapter 10

Housing benefit and discretionary housing payments

This chapter covers:

Housing benefit (HB) is paid to people with a low income who pay rent. It is paid whether or not you are available for or in full-time paid work, and may be paid in addition to other benefits or tax credits. HB is paid by local authorities, although it is a national scheme and the rules are mainly determined by DWP regulations.

You do not have to have paid national insurance contributions to qualify for HB.

You might be able to claim discretionary housing payments to top up your HB. See p222 for further information.

If you stop getting income support, income-based jobseeker's allowance, incapacity benefit or severe disablement allowance because you start work or increase your hours or earnings, you may be entitled toextended payments of HB. See p211 for further information.

1. Who can claim housing benefit

You qualify for housing benefit (HB) if:[1]

- your income is low enough (see Chapter 36);
- unless you or your partner are getting the guarantee credit of pension credit (PC), your savings and other capital are worth £16,000 or less (see Chapter 37). There is no capital limit if you or your partner are getting the guarantee credit of PC;[2]
- the payments you make can be met by HB (see p179);
- you or your partner count as liable to pay rent (see p180);
- the payments you make are for the home in which you normally live (see p184), or you are only temporarily absent from it;
- you satisfy the 'right to reside test' (see p1361) and the 'habitual residence test' (see p1367); *and*
- you are not a 'person subject to immigration control' (see p1334). There are exceptions to this rule.

There are some groups of claimants to whom special rules apply (see p200).

If you are 60 or over

The HB rules for people who are 60 or over who are not (and whose partners are not) getting income support (IS) or income-based jobseeker's allowance (JSA) are different (and more generous) than those for other HB claimants, so you should check to see if you qualify for HB when you or your partner turn 60, even if you did not do so before that age. The different rules for income, capital and applicable amounts are covered in Chapters 36, 37 and 33, but a summary of the income and capital rules is given below.

Income and capital

If you are **on the guarantee credit of PC**, for HB purposes all of your income and capital is ignored.[3] This means there is no capital limit if you get the guarantee credit of PC and you automatically qualify for maximum HB.

If you are **on the savings credit of PC but not the guarantee credit**:[4]

- the local authority uses the assessment of income and capital that the DWP used for working out your PC entitlement (the 'assessed income figure') as the basis for working out your income and capital for HB. The local authority may modify this figure to take certain income into account – eg, the amount of savings credit you receive is taken into account as income for HB;
- if your capital rises above £16,000 while you are on HB and there is an assessed income period in force (see p458), the local authority then calculates your capital according to the HB rules for those who are 60 or over and not on IS or

income-based JSA. If the calculation confirms you have capital over £16,000, you are no longer entitled to HB.

You cannot appeal against the local authority's use of the 'assessed income figure'.[5] If you disagree with the DWP assessment of your income and capital, you need to lodge your appeal with the DWP, not the local authority. However, if the local authority modifies your 'assessed income figure', you do have a right of appeal against the modification. You may, therefore, need to appeal against both decisions in some circumstances. If you lodge an appeal with the local authority and the situation is ambiguous, the local authority should advise you to also lodge an appeal with the DWP.[6]

If you are **not on either the guarantee credit or the savings credit of PC**, the local authority works out your capital and income using the HB rules for those who are 60 or over and not on IS or income-based JSA.

Payments that can be met by housing benefit

HB can meet rent that you pay to your landlord. It can also meet other types of payment, such as payments as a licensee, and payments for bed and breakfast and hostel accommodation. In this *Handbook*, we refer to any payments you make as 'rent'. Some types of payment cannot be met by HB (see p180).

HB can meet:[7]

- rent paid in respect of a tenancy. This can include rent or ground rent payable in respect of a lease of 21 years or less.[8] If your lease is for longer than 21 years, the rent or ground rent might be met by IS, income-based JSA or PC – see p807;
- payments in respect of a licence or other permission to occupy premises;
- 'mesne profits' (in Scotland, 'violent profits'), including payments made if you remain in occupation when a tenancy has been ended;
- other payments for the use and occupation of premises (including boat licence and mooring permit fees if you live in a houseboat[9]);
- payments for eligible service charges (see p194);
- rent, including mooring charges, for a houseboat;
- site rent for a caravan or mobile home (but not a tent, although that might be met through IS, income-based JSA or PC – see p807);
- rent paid on a garage or land (unless used for business purposes). Either you must be making a reasonable effort to end your liability for it, or you must have been unable to rent your home without it;[10]
- contributions made by a resident of a charity's almshouse;
- payments made under a rental purchase agreement under which the purchase price is paid in more than one instalment and you do not finally own your home until all, or an agreed part of, the purchase price has been paid;
- in Scotland, payments in respect of croft land.

The payment must be in return for your occupation of the home. This usually means that the payments must be made to the person who has the right to let you occupy it, or someone acting on her/his behalf. Payments to someone else might qualify for HB; this depends on, for example, whether you have a valid tenancy agreement with that person.[11]

Payments that cannot be met by housing benefit

HB cannot meet payments:[12]

- by an owner or under a long tenancy – ie, you own your accommodation or have a lease of more than 21 years – unless you have a shared ownership tenancy (ie, buying part of your house or flat and renting the rest), in which case you can get HB on the part you rent. You are treated as the owner of the property if you have the right to sell it, even though you may not be able to do so without the consent of other joint owners;[13]
- you make for a dwelling owned (or part-owned) by your partner;
- by a Crown tenant. Some landlords of Crown tenants have rent rebate schemes that are similar to HB;[14]
- under a co-ownership scheme under which you receive a payment related to the value of the accommodation when you leave;
- under a hire purchase (eg, for the purchase of a mobile home), credit sale or a conditional sale agreement except to the extent that it is in respect of land.

In all of the above cases (other than the second) the payments might be met by IS, income-based JSA or PC instead. In the second case, the payments you make to your partner cannot be met by IS, income-based JSA or PC, but certain loans and other housing costs you (or your partner) have might be met by those benefits. See Chapter 34 for further information.

In addition, HB cannot meet payments if you are getting IS or income-based JSA for these.[15] If you are now getting your housing costs met through IS or income-based JSA but were previously getting HB for the same accommodation, your HB continues for your first four weeks on IS or income-based JSA, but this is deducted from your IS or income-based JSA.[16] Remember that if you buy a home and immediately before that you were renting accommodation and getting HB, you might not get your full housing costs met (see p805).

Note: if you live in a care home, you usually cannot get HB for the rent you pay to the home (see p624).

Liability to pay rent

You count as liable to pay rent if:[17]

- you or your partner are liable; *or*
- you are treated as liable. You are treated as liable if:

- you have to pay rent in order to remain living in your home because the liable person is not doing so, and:[18]
  - your former partner is liable to make the payments. It does not matter whether or not the landlord is prepared to transfer the tenancy to you or wants to evict you. If you are a local authority tenant and the local authority refuses to accept your HB claim, point out that the eligibility rules for HB and for transferring local authority tenancies are quite separate; *or*
  - you are not the former partner of the liable person and it is reasonable to treat you as liable. If the local authority refuses to exercise this discretion in your favour, request a revision or appeal (see Chapters 41 and 42); *or*
- your landlord allows you a rent-free period as compensation for undertaking repairs or redecoration which s/he would otherwise have had to carry out. You must have actually carried out the work. This only applies for a maximum of eight benefit weeks in respect of any one rent-free period. If you expect the work to last longer, you should arrange with your landlord to schedule the work in periods of eight weeks or less, separated by at least one complete benefit week where you resume paying rent; *or*
- you are the partner of a full-time student who is treated as not liable to pay rent (see p182). This means that you can qualify for HB even if your partner cannot do so.

Even if you fall into one of these categories, you can still be treated as not being liable to pay rent and so not entitled to HB in certain circumstances (see p182).

If you pay your rent in advance, you are still treated as liable to pay it, even where you paid it before claiming HB.[19]

What 'liable' means

For you to be 'liable' to pay rent, your agreement must be legally enforceable.[20] It is not enough if you only have a moral obligation, such as a promise to pay something whenever you can afford to do so. You can count as liable to pay rent even if someone else has been paying it on your behalf, or where your landlord has failed to provide notice of an address for the purposes of s48 Landlord and Tenant Act 1987 so rent is treated as not being due.[21] You can be liable to pay rent by yourself or you can be jointly liable to do so (see p182).

If you have a **written agreement** with your landlord, the local authority uses this to decide if you are liable to pay rent and whether the liability is a genuine part of the agreement between you. Even if the local authority accepts this, it might still treat you as not liable to pay rent (see p182).[22]

Your agreement can be enforceable even if it is **not in writing**. If you have made a firm promise to pay money to your landlord in return for your occupation of the property, that should be treated as sufficient to allow you to claim HB. If the local authority refuses to accept that you have a legal liability unless you produce a written agreement, a rent book or some other evidence in writing of the agreement, argue that this is wrong and seek a revision or appeal (see Chapters 41 and 42).[23]

16/17-year-olds

People under 18 can be liable to pay rent and, therefore, entitled to HB. This applies where there is an intention to create legal relations, regardless of the precise wording of the agreement.

If you are aged under 16, an adult or social services department is generally responsible for the rent. However, HB departments should not make decisions on HB entitlement based on what services they think the social services department ought to provide.

Joint liability

If you are a member of a couple (see p702) and are jointly liable for the rent, only one of you can claim HB (see p204).[24]

The way a group of single people living together and paying rent to their landlord is treated depends on how many of you are liable under the agreement. If all, or some of you, have joint liability for the rent, you can each make a separate claim and be paid HB on your share (unless the local authority thinks the joint tenancy has been created to take advantage of the HB scheme – see p184).

People treated as not liable to pay rent

Even if you or your partner are actually liable to pay rent, or you are treated as liable, you cannot qualify for HB if you are treated as though you are not liable to do so. You are treated as not liable to pay rent if you:

- are a full-time **student** and you do not come into one of the categories of those who can get HB (see p588).[25] This does not apply if you are 60 or over and neither you nor your partner are getting IS or income-based JSA;
- do **not satisfy the habitual residence test** (see p1367).[26]

In addition, you are treated as not liable to pay rent if:[27]

- you are a member of, and are fully maintained by, a **religious order**;
- you are living in a **care home** or an **independent hospital** (but see p624);[28]
- you **pay rent to someone you live with and that person is a close relative** (see below) of yours or your partner.[29] You are regarded as living with your landlord if you share some accommodation with her/him, other than a bathroom, toilet or a hall or passageway.[30] It does not matter if you use the accommodation at different times or if you pay to use it;[31]
- your **agreement to pay rent is not on a commercial basis.**[32] In deciding whether or not your agreement is commercial, the local authority must look at the whole agreement, taking into account all the circumstances. It must consider, among other things:[33]

  - whether your agreement includes terms which are not legally enforceable. DWP guidance suggests that this might arise, for example, where a tenant does household chores. But if you do chores in exchange for a lower rent, it could be considered commercial;
  - your agreement to pay rent. The rent need not necessarily be a market rent. Your agreement can count as commercial even if your landlord is not collecting the full contractual rent from you – eg, where it is not being met by HB because of the rent restriction rules (see Chapter 11);
  - your relationship to your landlord. Just because you are a relative of, or have a close friendship with, her/him, or s/he provides you with care and support, does not mean that your agreement is non-commercial;
- you are **renting from**:
  - your ex-partner and the home is your former joint home; *or*
  - your partner's ex-partner and the home is your partner's former joint home with her/his ex-partner;
- you or your partner are **responsible for a child of your landlord**.[34] Being responsible for a child means more than caring for her/him. It only applies in situations where the child is included in your HB claim (see p709).[35]
- you, your partner, your ex-partner, your partner's ex-partner or a close relative of yours or your partner who lives with you is either:
  - a **director or employee of a company which is your landlord**; *or*
  - a **trustee or beneficiary of a trust which is your landlord.**

  However, you should be treated as liable if you can show the arrangement was not intended to take advantage of the HB scheme (see p184);
- you are renting accommodation from a trustee of a trust, of which your child or your partner's child is a **beneficiary**;
- you were **previously the non-dependant** (see p196) of someone who lived, and continues to live, in the accommodation. This should not apply to you if you can show that the agreement was not created to take advantage of the HB scheme (see p184);[36]
- you or your current partner **previously owned (or had a long tenancy** in – ie, a lease of more than 21 years) **the accommodation** and less than five years have passed since you last owned it (or the tenancy ceased).[37]

  This rule does not apply if you can show that you could not have continued to remain in the accommodation without giving up ownership (or the tenancy). Whether you were legally or practically compelled to give up ownership or the tenancy is relevant, but your motivation for doing so is not;[38]
- you or your partner are employed by your landlord and are **occupying your accommodation as a condition of employment**. This should not apply if you continue to live in the accommodation after ceasing employment;
- where none of the above apply, but the local authority considers that your **liability to pay rent has been created to take advantage of the HB scheme**.

'Close relative'

A 'close relative' is a parent, parent-in-law (including a civil partner's parent), son, son-in-law (including a son's civil partner), daughter, daughter-in-law (including a daughter's civil partner), brother, sister, step-parent (including a parent's civil partner), stepson (including a civil partner's son), stepdaughter (including a civil partner's daughter), or the partners of any of these.[39] It also includes half-brothers and sisters.[40] Relations with in-laws or step-relatives are severed by divorce (or dissolution of a civil partnership) but arguably not by death – eg, a step-child is still a step-child after the death of her/his mother.[41]

Agreements taking advantage of the housing benefit scheme

In order for your agreement to count as 'taking advantage of the housing benefit scheme', it must be shown that it amounts to an abuse of the scheme or to taking improper advantage of it, and that the main reason for you entering the agreement was to obtain HB.[42] All the circumstances should be taken into account in deciding if this is the case, including what your landlord has to say.[43] An agreement can count as taking advantage of the HB scheme even if it was created from the best of motives.[44]

Your agreement does not take advantage of the HB scheme just because your landlord is your parent[45] or because you hope to be able to claim HB to help you with your rent – ie, if your main purpose is to get accommodation for yourself, not to obtain HB.[46] In particular, you should not be seen as taking advantage of the HB scheme just because you seek to find out the eligible rent (see p192) from the rent officer before moving in.

Tenants of a landlord who deliberately charges high rents to try and get them paid by HB may fall foul of this provision, even if they had no such intention themselves. However, the fact that a landlord sets a high rent does not in itself mean that the liability takes advantage of the HB scheme.[47] If your landlord is going to evict you if you cannot get HB, this suggests that the agreement does not take advantage of the HB scheme.[48]

If the local authority refuses you HB on the basis that you are taking advantage of the HB scheme, you can request a revision or appeal (see Chapters 41 and 42).

Occupying accommodation as your home

HB is paid for the home in which you normally live.[49] You cannot usually be paid for any other home. There are special rules if you:

- have just moved into your home (see p185);
- are temporarily away from home (see p185);
- are liable to pay rent on more than one home (see p187);
- are in certain other situations (see p188).

If you have to live in an approved bail or probation hostel or are a prisoner on temporary release, you are not treated as occupying the accommodation you are staying in as your home.[50] This means that you cannot qualify for HB towards any rent you pay there.

Moving home

If you have **just moved into your home** but were liable to pay rent before moving in, you can get HB on your new home for a period of up to four weeks before you moved in.[51] Before moving, you must either have claimed HB or have notified the local authority of the move to the new home. If you have given up your previous home and have no other home, you can argue that the date you move in is the date you move your furniture and belongings in.[52] You qualify if your delay in moving was reasonable, *and*:

- you were waiting for a social fund payment for a need connected with the move – eg, removal expenses or to help you set up home. This only applies if:
  - you have a child of five or under living with you; *or*
  - you are 60 or over and neither you nor your partner are getting IS or income-based JSA; *or*
  - you are under 60 (or you or your partner are getting IS or income-based JSA) and you qualify for one of the pensioner premiums or a disability, severe disability or disabled child premium (see pp778–784); *or*
- you were waiting for adaptations to be finished to meet needs you or a member of your family for benefit purposes have because of a disability. The adaptations must involve a change to the fabric or structure of the dwelling, not just decorating or furnishing (eg, carpeting) it;[53] *or*
- you became liable to make payments on your new home while you were a hospital patient or in 'residential accommodation' (see p187).

Your HB is not actually paid until you move in. If an earlier claim for HB you made before you moved in was turned down, you must claim again within four weeks of moving to qualify.

In addition, if you are **not liable to pay rent in your new accommodation** (this includes, for example, prison), you can get HB for up to four weeks for your former home if you:[54]

- were liable for rent on it immediately before moving into your new accommodation and continue to be liable; *and*
- could not reasonably have avoided liability for rent on your former home.

If you are obliged to pay rent for your old home as well as your new accommodation, you can only get HB for one of these unless you are covered by the rules described on p187.[55]

Temporary absence from home

If you are temporarily away from your normal home, have not rented it and intend to return, your HB can continue to be paid for a period. You can argue that you count as temporarily absent from home even if you have not yet stayed there – eg, you move your furniture and belongings in, but then have to go into hospital.[56]

You can get HB for **13 weeks** for your normal home while you are away, whatever the reason. You must be unlikely to be away for longer than this.[57]

You can get HB for **52 weeks** for your normal home if you are unlikely to be away for longer than this (or in exceptional circumstances, unlikely to be away for substantially longer than this) and:[58]

- you are a remand prisoner held in custody pending trial or sentence. You are treated as still in custody if you are a prisoner on temporary release. Once you are sentenced, you no longer qualify for HB under this rule, but might instead qualify under the 13-week rule. However, the 13 weeks run from the date you were first in prison. So any time you spend in prison awaiting trial or sentence counts towards the 13 weeks;[59]
- you are required to live in an approved bail hostel or an address away from your normal home as a condition of bail;
- you are resident in a hospital or similar institution as a patient;
- you, your partner or a dependent child are undergoing medical treatment or medically-approved convalescence in the UK or abroad, other than in 'residential accommodation' (see p187);
- you are providing, or receiving, 'medically approved' care (ie, certified by a medical practitioner) in the UK or abroad. If you are receiving the care, you cannot be in 'residential accommodation' (see p187);
- you are caring for a child whose parent or guardian is away from home receiving medically approved care or medical treatment;
- you are undertaking a training course in the UK or abroad which is provided by, or on behalf of, or approved by a government department, the Secretary of State, Scottish Enterprise or Highlands and Islands Enterprise;
- you are a student. For HB, but not CTB, you must not fall into the first category under 'Other situations' on p188 nor be entitled to HB on two homes (see p187);
- you are in 'residential accommodation' (see p187) for short-term respite care. However, if you are in the home for a trial period to see if you wish to move there permanently, you can only get HB for up to 13 weeks.[60] On the date you enter the accommodation, you must intend to return home if it is not suitable.[61] If the home does not suit your needs, you can have further trial periods in other homes so long as you are not away from home for more than 52 weeks;
- you are away from home through fear of violence. You need not have experienced actual violence, but you must be in fear of violence in your home or from a former family member. The former category includes violence by neighbours and racial attacks on your home. See p187 if you need to claim for two homes and p188 if you do not intend to return to your former home.

Unless you are in residential accommodation for a trial period (see p186), your intention to return and whether or not you are unlikely to be away for longer than 13/52 weeks should be considered, initially based on the circumstances on the date you leave your home.[62] If at any time after that date you no longer intend to return or it becomes likely that you will be away from home for more than the 13/52 weeks, your entitlement can be reconsidered.[63]

The 13 and 52 weeks both run from the date you leave home. If, for example, you have been away from home for 10 weeks and then have grounds to continue to get HB for 52 weeks, you only get HB for the balance: 42 weeks. However, a new period of absence starts if you return home for even a short stay. A stay of at least 24 hours may be enough.[64] This does not apply, however, if you are a prisoner on temporary release .[65]

'Residential accommodation'

For these purposes, 'residential accommodation' means a care home, an independent hospital or an Abbeyfield Home.[66] It includes establishments managed or provided by bodies incorporated by Royal Charter or constituted by an Act of Parliament, other than by local social services.

Housing benefit for more than one home

You can usually only get HB for one home. However, if you have to pay rent for two homes, you can get HB for both:

- for up to **four weeks** if:[67]
  - you have moved into a new home and you could not reasonably avoid having to pay rent on your old home.[68] The local authority must consider the reasons why you had to move quickly. For example, if you were forced to move quickly to take advantage of better accommodation you may not have been able to avoid leaving without giving notice; *or*
  - you qualify for HB on a new home because a move was delayed while you were adapting your new home for the disability needs of a member of your family (see p185). You can get HB on both homes for the four weeks prior to the date you move. The adaptations must involve a change to the fabric or structure of the dwelling, not just decorating or furnishing (eg, carpeting) it;[69]
- for up to **52 weeks**, if you have left your home because of a fear of violence (see p186 for what counts as violence). You must intend to return to your former home, and it must be reasonable for you to receive HB for both homes;[70]
- **indefinitely**, if:[71]
  - you are a member of a couple and you or your partner are a student who is not excluded from HB (see p588) or a trainee on a government course, and it is necessary for you to live apart, and it is reasonable for you to receive HB for both homes;

- your family is large and the local authority has housed you in more than one home.

Other situations

If you have left your home because of a **fear of violence** (see p186 for what counts as violence) and cannot be paid HB for two homes (see p187) or while temporarily absent from home (see p186) – eg, you do not intend to return to your former home – you can get HB for four weeks for your former home.[72] This only applies if your liability to pay rent was unavoidable (eg, you should have given your landlord notice, but had to leave in a hurry because of the violence).

If you have **two homes**, and you are only liable to pay for one of them, you are treated as occupying the home for which you pay and therefore get HB for that home, even when you are not there. This applies if:

- you are a single claimant (including a lone parent), and you are either a student eligible for HB (see p588) or on a training course (see p186), and you live in one home during periods of study or training and another home at other times (eg for vacations);[73] *or*
- you had to move into temporary accommodation because essential repairs are being carried out on your main home.[74] 'Essential repairs' means basic works rather than luxuries, but they need not be crucial to make the house habitable.[75]

Note: you cannot get HB under this rule if you pay rent for both homes, or if you pay rent for one and a mortgage on the other.

2. The rules about your age

There are no lower or upper age limits for claiming housing benefit (HB). However, if you are:

- under 16, there may be a question about whether you have a legally enforceable liability for rent (see p182);
- 16 or 17 and have been looked after by a local authority, you cannot usually claim HB. Instead, your local authority should support and accommodate you. See p609 for further information;
- 60 or over and neither you nor your partner are getting income support or income-based jobseeker's allowance, more generous rules apply.

If you are a single claimant under 25 and are living in private rented accommodation, the amount of your rent that can be met by HB might be restricted to the 'single room rent' or the local housing allowance for one-bedroom shared accommodation (see Chapter 11).

3. **Claiming for others**

You claim housing benefit for your family (see Chapter 30).

4. **The amount of benefit**

The amount of housing benefit (HB) you get depends on:

- your 'applicable amount' (see Chapter 33). This is made up of personal allowances and premiums for any special needs;
- your 'maximum HB' (see below); *and*
- how much income and capital you have (see Chapters 36 and 37).

Maximum HB

Your **'maximum HB'** is your 'eligible rent' (see p192), calculated on a weekly basis, minus any deductions made for your non-dependants (see p196).[76] The amount depends on whether your 'eligible rent' is restricted under any of the rent restriction schemes (see Chapter 11).

Example

Mr and Mrs Feinstein and their adult son live together in a flat rented from the local council. Mr Feinstein is the sole tenant. The rent is £75 a week. This does not include any service charges. Their son earns £120 a week gross.

Eligible rent is £75 (the contractual rent)	£75.00
Minus non-dependant deduction (see p196)	£17.00
Maximum housing benefit	**£58.00**

If you do not qualify for HB currently, you may qualify when:

- the benefit rates go up every April; *or*
- you or your partner turn:
  - 60. Your applicable amount is then higher. If neither you nor your partner are on income support (IS) or income-based jobseeker's allowance (JSA), the income and capital rules are also more generous; *or*
  - 65. Your personal allowance is increased by the equivalent of the amount of the maximum savings credit of pension credit (PC), whether or not you receive this, if neither you nor your partner are on IS or income-based JSA.

In addition, if your income is too high for you to qualify for HB currently, you might qualify once you, or a member of your family, become entitled to another benefit (a 'qualifying benefit'). See p205 for further information.

If you need extra financial assistance to meet your housing costs, you might be entitled to discretionary housing payments (see p222).

Remember that if you:

- stop getting IS, income-based JSA, incapacity benefit or severe disablement allowance because of starting work or increasing your hours or your earnings, you may be entitled to extended payments of HB (see p211);
- stop getting IS or income-based JSA because you are moving onto PC, you may be able to continue to receive HB at the same rate for four weeks (see p211);
- have been incapable of work but move into work or training, you might count as a 'welfare to work' beneficiary (see p666). This means you retain entitlement to the disability or higher pensioner premium (see pp779 and 783) if you become incapable of work again within 104 weeks.

You might get a reduced amount of HB if:

- your HB is restricted under the 'loss of benefit for benefit offences' rules (see p1047); *or*
- you live in a pilot area and have been evicted for anti-social behaviour (see p220).

If you are on income support, income-based jobseeker's allowance or the guarantee credit of pension credit

Being on IS, income-based JSA or the guarantee credit of PC is an automatic passport to maximum HB (once you have made a claim for HB). You therefore do not need to work out your applicable amount, income or capital.[77] In these circumstances HB = 'maximum HB' (see p189). **Note:** income-related employment and support allowance (see Chapter 7) will also be a passport to maximum HB.

For these purposes, you are treated as on income-based JSA:[78]

- when you satisfy the conditions of entitlement but are not being paid it because of a sanction (see Chapter 16);
- on your waiting days (see p366); *and*
- when it is not paid because of the 'loss of benefit' rules (see p1047).

Example

Glen and his partner Craig are joint housing association tenants. Glen's aunt, aged 50, lives with them. They pay rent of £100 a week. They receive income-based JSA while they are looking for work. Glen's aunt receives IS. Glen claims HB.

Eligible rent is £100 a week.

Glen's aunt counts as a non-dependant and the appropriate deduction for her is £7.40 a week (see p196).

Therefore, Glen's maximum HB is £92.60 week (£100.00 – £7.40).

Because they receive income-based JSA, Glen's HB is £92.60 week.

If you are not on income support, income-based jobseeker's allowance or the guarantee credit of pension credit

- **Step one:** check that your capital is not too high (see Chapter 37).
- **Step two:** work out your 'maximum HB' (see p189).
- **Step three:** work out your applicable amount (see Chapter 33).
- **Step four:** work out your income (see Chapter 36, but also p589 if you are a student and p881 if you are getting the savings credit of PC).
- **Step five:** calculate HB:
  - If your **income is less than or equal to your applicable amount**, HB = 'maximum HB'.
  - If your **income is greater than your applicable amount**, work out the difference. HB = 'maximum HB' minus 65 per cent of the difference between your income and your applicable amount.

Examples

Mr Jopling is aged 45. He is unemployed. Mrs Jopling is aged 46. She works 21 hours a week. She is paid £165 a week after deductions of tax and national insurance contributions. The couple are joint private tenants who pay £120 rent a week. Mrs Jopling claims HB. Her eligible rent is £108 a week because rent restriction rules have been applied.

Mr and Mrs Jopling have no non-dependants. Therefore, her maximum HB is £108 a week.

Mrs Jopling's applicable amount is £94.95 (the standard rate for a couple).

Her income to be taken into account is £155 a week (because £10 of her earnings are disregarded – see p855).

The difference between her income and her applicable amount is therefore £60.05 a week.

65% x £60.05 = £39.03 a week.

Mrs Jopling's HB is therefore £108 – £39.03 = £68.97 a week.

Mr Haralambous is 67 years old. He receives the savings credit of PC, totalling £17.33 a week. His weekly income from his private and state pensions is £130 – this is too high to qualify for the guarantee credit of PC. His total weekly income is therefore £147.33 (£130 + £17.33). He is a sole tenant of his council flat and has no non-dependants. His rent of £100 a week includes his heating and hot water. His eligible rent is £82.75 a week because £15.45 and £1.80 are deducted from his contractual rent for heating and hot water. This is also his maximum HB because he does not have any non-dependants.

His applicable amount is £143.80 (adult personal allowance for a single person aged 65 or over).

The difference between his income and his applicable amount is £3.53.

65% x £3.53 = £2.29 a week.

Mr Haralambous's HB is therefore £82.75 – £2.29 = £80.46 a week.

Eligible rent

Your 'eligible rent' is the amount of your rent used for the purpose of calculating your HB. It can be different than the actual amount of rent you pay. Unless any of the rent restriction rules apply to you, your eligible rent is your contractual rent, minus any ineligible charges (see p193).[79] If any of the rent restriction rules apply to you, your eligible rent is usually your 'maximum rent' as determined under those rules (ie, your contractual rent, minus any amount above the level to which your rent is restricted. See Chapter 11 for details of all the rent restriction schemes and how your 'maximum rent' (and, therefore, your eligible rent) is worked out. **Note:** the rent restriction rules do *not* apply if you are a tenant of the local authority who pays your HB.

The local authority has general powers to decrease your eligible rent to an amount it considers appropriate (see p234).

Remember the following.

- If you are in shared accommodation, your eligible rent might be apportioned between you and the people with whom you share (see below).
- If the rent you pay covers both residential and other accommodation (eg, for business use), your HB only covers the rent you pay for the residential accommodation.[80]

If you live in shared accommodation

Unless the 'local housing allowance' rules apply to you (see p235), if you share accommodation with others who are not members of your family for HB purposes and are jointly liable for the rent with them, the local authority apportions the eligible rent between you. It considers:[81]

- the number of jointly liable people in the property (including any students who are treated as not liable to pay rent);[82] *and*
- the proportion of the rent actually paid by each liable person; *and*
- any other relevant circumstances, such as:
  - the number of rooms occupied by each jointly liable person;
  - whether any formal or informal agreement exists between you regarding the use and occupation of the home; *and*
  - if one of the jointly liable people has left the accommodation, the demands being made by the landlord on those who remain, or the possibility of finding other accommodation.

In some circumstances, it could be appropriate to apportion the whole of the rent to you even if you are jointly liable.[83]

Where the rent includes any ineligible service charges, these are apportioned between you on the same basis as the rent. If only one of you is liable for the rent that person is treated as the tenant and the other(s) might count as a non-dependant(s) (see p196).

Example

Sarah and Maude are friends who rent a housing association flat. They are joint tenants and pay rent of £100 a week. Sarah claims HB. The eligible rent is apportioned between them and Sarah's HB is based on £50 (£100 divided by 2).

Note: if the 'local housing allowance' rules apply to you, the eligible rent is not apportioned if you share accommodation with others who are not members of your family. However, the local authority *does* apportion your 'cap rent' (see p238).[84]

Ineligible charges

Unless the 'local reference rent' or 'local housing allowance' rules apply to you, the local authority deducts ineligible charges when it works out your eligible rent. However, ineligible charges are excluded when the rent officer makes determinations (for the 'local reference rent' rules) and sets the 'local housing allowances'.

Ineligible charges include:

- water charges:[85]
- most fuel charges (see below); *and*
- some service charges (see p195), including charges for meals (see p195).

Remember that in addition, you cannot get HB for:

- payments for any part of your accommodation that is used exclusively for business purposes;[86]
- rent supplements charged to clear your rent arrears.[87]

Fuel charges

Fuel charges are ineligible unless they are for communal areas (see p194).[88] If your fuel charge is:

- specified on your rent book or is **readily identifiable** from your agreement with your landlord the full amount of the charge is ineligible.[89] If your fuel charge is specified but it is considered to be unrealistically low in relation to the fuel provided, the charge is treated as unspecified and a flat-rate amount is ineligible instead (see p194). This is also the case if your total fuel charge is specified but contains an unknown amount for communal areas. If you are a council tenant, the regulations assume your fuel charges are always specified or readily identifiable, since the local authority is also your landlord.[90]
- **not readily identifiable**, a flat-rate amount is ineligible. The flat-rate fuel amounts are:[91]

Where you and your family occupy more than one room:	
For heating (other than hot water)	£15.45
For hot water	£1.80
For lighting	£1.25
For cooking	£1.80
Where you and your family occupy one room only:	
For heating alone, or heating combined with either hot water or lighting or both	£9.25
For cooking	£1.80

These amounts are added together where fuel is supplied for more than one purpose. If you are a joint tenant, all the amounts are apportioned according to your share of the rent (see p192).

If flat-rate fuel amounts have been used in calculating your HB, the local authority must notify you about this and explain that if you can produce evidence from which the actual or approximate amount of your fuel charge can be estimated, the flat-rate amounts may be varied accordingly.[92]

The DWP says that the amounts for one room should apply where you occupy one room only, including cases where the room or other communal areas are shared (such as a kitchen or communal lounge).[93] You should also argue that they apply where you are forced to live in one room because the other room(s) in your accommodation are, in practice, unfit to live in – eg, because of severe mould or dampness.

Fuel for communal areas

If you pay a service charge for the use of fuel in communal areas, and that charge is separately identified from any other charge for fuel used within your accommodation, it may be included as part of your eligible rent.[94] Communal areas include access areas like halls and passageways, but not rooms in common use except those in sheltered accommodation – eg, a shared TV lounge or dining room.[95] If you pay a charge for the provision of a heating system (eg, regular boiler maintenance) this is also eligible where the amount is separately identified from any other fuel charge you pay.[96]

Service charges

Many service charges are covered by HB, but only if payment is a condition of occupying the accommodation rather than an optional extra.[97] Eligible and ineligible service charges are listed on p195. If the local authority regards any of the eligible charges as excessive it estimates a reasonable amount given the cost of comparable services.[98] If you are in supported accommodation, see p196.

Eligible services

The following services are eligible for HB:

- services for the provision of adequate accommodation including general management costs, gardens, children's play areas, lifts, entry phones, communal telephone costs, portering and rubbish removal.[99] TV and radio relay charges are covered, including free-to-view UK channels;[100]
- laundry facilities (eg, a laundry room in an apartment block), but not charges for the provision of personal laundry;[101]
- furniture and household equipment, but not if there is an agreement that the furniture will eventually become yours;[102]
- cleaning of rooms and windows in communal areas and the outside of windows where neither you nor any member of your household is able to clean them yourself, unless payment for these is made by your local authority or the National Assembly for Wales.[103]

Ineligible services

The following services are not eligible for HB:[104]

- food, including prepared meals (see below);
- sports facilities;
- TV rental, licence and subscription fees (but see above);
- transport;
- personal laundry service;
- provision of an emergency alarm system;
- medical expenses;
- nursing and personal care;
- counselling and other support services;
- any other charge not connected with providing adequate accommodation and not specifically included in the list of eligible charges above.

The amount of the charge specified in your rent agreement is not eligible for HB, though local authorities can substitute their own estimate where they consider the amount to be unreasonably low.[105]

Where the amount is not specified in your rent agreement, the local authority estimates how much is fairly attributable to the service, given the cost of comparable services.[106]

Charges for meals

Where your housing costs include an amount for meals, set amounts are ineligible regardless of the actual cost.[107] These are:

Where at least three meals a day are provided:

For the claimant and each additional member of the family aged 16 or over	£21.60
For each additional member of the family aged under 16	£10.90

Where breakfast only is provided:

For the claimant and each additional member of the family, regardless of age	£2.65
In all other cases (part-board):	
For the claimant and each additional member of the family aged 16 or over	£14.35
For each additional member of the family aged under 16	£7.20

For these purposes, a person is treated as having reached the age of 16 on the first Monday in September following her/his 16th birthday.

The standard amounts are ineligible for everyone who has meals paid for by you – including meals for someone who is not part of your family, such as a non-dependant.[108]

Service charges in supported accommodation

If you live in supported accommodation, HB can help with your rent. However, HB is not available for the support services provided with your accommodation. Instead, the local authority's Supporting People team funds your landlord (eg, a registered social landlord or voluntary organisation) to provide these.

In some cases, the local authority can charge you for the support services you get. Your local authority uses its means test to determine how much you have to pay. See CPAG's *Paying for Care Handbook* for further information.

Calculating a weekly amount of housing benefit

HB is always paid for a specific benefit week – a period of seven consecutive days beginning with a Monday and ending on a Sunday.[109] If you pay rent at different intervals (eg, monthly or daily) the amount has to be converted to a weekly figure before HB can be calculated.[110]

Rent-free periods

If you have a regular rent-free period (eg, you pay rent on a 48-week rent year) you get no HB during your rent-free period. Your applicable amount, weekly income, non-dependant deductions, the set deductions for meals and fuel charges and the minimum amount payable (but not your eligible rent) are adjusted.[111]

Note: this does not apply if your landlord has temporarily waived the rent in return for you doing repairs (see p181).

Deductions for non-dependants

If other people normally live with you in your home who are not part of your family for benefit purposes (see p700) (called **'non-dependants'**), a set deduction is usually made from your HB.[112] This is because it is assumed the non-dependant makes a contribution towards your outgoings, whether or not s/he does so. Examples of non-dependants are adult sons or daughters, or elderly relatives who share your home. A person does *not* normally live with you if s/he has not been there long enough to regard your home as her/his normal home.[113]

A person can only be treated as **living with you** if s/he shares some accommodation with you.[114] A person who is separately liable to pay rent to your landlord does not count as living with you, nor does a person who only shares a bathroom, lavatory, or a communal area such as a hall, passageway or a room in common use in sheltered accommodation. However, if any other areas of the house are shared, such as the kitchen, the other person is treated as living with you. This is the case even if you only use it at different times and you maintain different households (see p703 for the meaning of 'household').[115]

A number of factors should be taken into account to decide whether a person is **normally living with you**, including:[116]

- the relationship between you;
- how much time s/he spends at your address;
- where s/he has her/his post sent;
- where s/he keeps most of her/his clothes and personal belongings;
- whether her/his stay or absence from your address is temporary or permanent;
- whether s/he has another place that could be regarded as home or whether s/he just travels around.

People who are not non-dependants

The following people do not count as non-dependants, and no non-dependant deduction is made for them, even if they normally live with you:[117]

- a member of your family for benefit purposes (see p700);
- a child or qualifying young person living with you who is not a member of your household (see p712);
- someone who is employed by a charitable or voluntary organisation as a resident carer for you or your partner and who you pay for the service. This can also apply if a public body pays on your behalf;
- any person, or a member of their household, to whom you or your partner are liable to pay rent on a commercial basis;
- someone who jointly occupies your home and is either a co-owner or jointly liable with you or your partner to make payments in respect of occupying it. You do not jointly occupy the home with someone unless you made a joint agreement with your landlord to occupy the home. The fact that you live in the same home does not make you joint occupiers;[118]
- someone who is liable to pay rent on a commercial basis to you or your partner. However, although no non-dependant deduction can be made for her/him, the rent s/he pays can count as your income (see pp865 and 890).

If the person comes within the last three categories above, s/he *does* count as a non-dependant if s/he is treated as not liable for rent under the rules explained on p182 (unless s/he is a student or has failed the 'habitual residence test' or is a 'person subject to immigration control').[119]

When no non-dependant deduction is made

Even if you have a non-dependant living with you, no non-dependant deduction is made for her/him if either you or your partner:[120]

- are registered blind or have regained your eyesight within the last 28 weeks; *or*
- receive attendance allowance (AA) (or equivalent benefits paid because of injury at work or a war injury) or the care component of disability living allowance (DLA).

No deduction is made in respect of any non-dependant who is:[121]

- staying with you but whose normal home is elsewhere;
- receiving a training allowance in connection with a youth training scheme under specific provisions;[122]
- a full-time student during her/his period of study. Unless you or your partner are 65 or over and neither of you are on IS or income-based JSA, this only applies during the summer vacation if the student is not in full-time work;
- in hospital for more than 52 weeks. Separate stays in hospital which are not more than 28 days apart are added together when calculating the 52 weeks;
- in prison;
- under 18 years old;[123]
- under 25 and on IS/income-based JSA. S/he can be treated as on income-based JSA for these purposes (see p190);[124]
- on PC.[125]

The amount of deductions

If you have a non-dependant living with you who is 18 or over, and for whom a deduction must be made, a fixed amount is deducted from your HB, whatever s/he pays you. Unless your non-dependant is in full-time paid work, a £7.40 deduction is made each week. If your non-dependant is in full-time paid work, the amount of the deduction depends on her/his gross weekly income as follows:[126]

Circumstances of the non-dependant	*Deduction*
Aged 18 or over and in full-time paid work with a weekly gross income of:	
– £369 or more	£47.75
– £296–£368.99	£43.50
– £223–£295.99	£38.20
– £172–£222.99	£23.35
– £116–£171.99	£17.00
All others (for whom a deduction is made)	£ 7.40

The rules on full-time paid work are covered in Chapter 27. Remember the following.

- A non-dependant who is not in (or is treated as not in) full-time paid work does not attract the higher levels of deduction even if her/his weekly gross income is £116 or more.
- If someone is on IS or income-based JSA (see p190) for more than three days in a benefit week, s/he does not count as being in full-time paid work in that week.[127] This means the lower deduction (£7.40) is made (or no deduction is made, if s/he is under 25).

Gross income includes wages before tax and national insurance are deducted, plus any other income the non-dependant has (apart from AA, constant attendance allowance, DLA and payments from any of the Macfarlane Trusts, the Eileen Trust, the Skipton Fund and the London Bombings Relief Charitable Fund, the Fund and the Independent Living Funds[128]).

You should try to provide information to show which deduction applies. If you cannot, ask the local authority to consider the circumstances – eg, if your non-dependant is doing a job which is normally very low paid. The local authority should not assume that your non-dependant is earning the highest amount, but should assess what the likely level of her/his earnings are on the evidence available.[129]

A deduction is made from your eligible rent for every non-dependant living in your household except in the case of a non-dependant couple (see below).

If you are 65 or over

If you or your partner are 65 or over and a non-dependant moves in with you, and so a deduction should be made, or there has been a change of circumstances in respect of a non-dependant, the effect of this can be delayed for 26 weeks (see p220).

Non-dependant couples

Only one deduction is made for a couple (see p702) (or the members of a polygamous marriage) who are non-dependants. The deduction made is the highest that would have been made if they were treated as individuals.[130] For the purpose of deciding which income band applies (see p198), their joint income counts, even if only one of them is in full-time work.[131]

Non-dependants of joint occupiers

If you share a non-dependant with any other joint occupiers, the deduction is divided between you, taking into account the proportion of housing costs paid by each. No apportionment is made between the members of a couple (or polygamous marriage).[132] If the person is a non-dependant of only one of you, the full deduction is made from only that person's benefit.

Income and capital of a non-dependant is greater than yours

Normally, the income and capital of any non-dependant is only relevant in deciding which non-dependant deduction applies. However, your HB entitlement is assessed on the basis of your non-dependant's income and capital rather than your own if:[133]

- you are not on IS/income-based JSA; *and*
- the income and capital of your non-dependant are both greater than yours; *and*
- the local authority is satisfied you have made an arrangement with your non-dependant to take advantage of the HB scheme (see p184).

Any income and capital normally treated as belonging to you is completely ignored, but the rest of the calculation proceeds as normal.

Discretionary housing payments

If you need extra financial assistance to meet your housing costs (including your council tax) you might be able to claim discretionary housing payments to top up your HB. See p222 for further information.

Extra benefit for war pensioners

The local authority has the power to pay extra HB to people getting certain war pensions, by disregarding some or all of the pension as income, rather than just disregarding £10.[134] If the authority uses this power it must apply the income disregard to all people in receipt of these pensions. See pp861 and 889 for further information.

5. Special benefit rules

There are some groups of claimants to whom special rules apply. These are covered in Chapters 25, 26 and 58. Special rules apply to:

- students (see p587);
- people subject to immigration control (see p1334);
- prisoners (see p627);
- people in care homes and other special accommodation (see p621).

6. Claims and backdating

You should claim housing benefit (HB) as soon as you think you might be entitled or you may lose benefit. The rules about backdating are explained on p206. If you are claiming because your entitlement ended when you or your partner started work (or increased your hours or your pay) and stopped getting income support (IS), income-based jobseeker's allowance (JSA), incapacity benefit (IB) or severe disablement allowance, see pp209 and 213.

If you want to claim discretionary housing payments, you must claim separately. See p223 for further information.

Making a claim

Unless you are allowed to claim by telephone (see p202) or are claiming pension credit (PC) by telephone, all claims for HB must be made in writing on a properly completed claim form.[135] You must provide any information and evidence required on the form. You can claim in some other written form (eg, by letter) so long as the written information and evidence you provide is sufficient. Claim forms are available from your local authority.[136] If your local authority has authorised it (by a Chief Executive's Direction), you can also claim by electronic communication – eg, online or by email.[137]

In addition, if you are claiming:

- IS or income-based JSA, there is an HB and council tax benefit (CTB) claim form in the IS/JSA claim pack. This is also available from the DWP website (see Appendix 1). If you are claiming IS or income-based JSA via a contact centre, your HB and CTB claims are usually completed at the same time;
- PC by telephone, the DWP completes a claim form for you and you are given a copy to check and sign.[138] If you request a PC claim form, a claim form for HB and CTB is included. In both cases, you may be asked to provide further information – eg, if you have children or are working or have non-dependants living with you.

The local authority may ask you to complete its own form. You should do this as soon as possible. It should not ask you to complete its own form if you claim HB when you claim PC – see above.

Send your claim as soon as you can so you do not lose benefit. Keep a copy in case queries arise. Remember that the local authority might ask you for other information and evidence (see p203).

You may amend or withdraw your claim in writing at any time before a decision has been made on it. Unless you can claim HB (or are claiming PC) by telephone, amendments must be made in writing and are treated as though they were part of your original claim.[139] If you can claim HB (or are claiming PC) by telephone, you can also amend your claim by telephone. A notice to withdraw your claim takes effect from the day it is received.[140]

If you are claiming HB or CTB within 12 weeks of a previous entitlement ending, you may be able to make a 'rapid re-claim' (see p202).

Telephone claims

You can claim HB by telephone if your local authority has published a number for this purpose.[141] The local authority may then provide a written statement of your circumstances. For your claim to be valid, you have to approve this statement. Note that even if you cannot claim by telephone, if you telephone to ask to be sent a claim form and you return it within one month, your claim is backdated to the date of your phone call (see p204).

Note: the local authority may ask you for other information and evidence (see p203).

Making sure your claim is valid

Your claim is 'defective' if you:[142]

- do not complete your claim form properly or you claim by letter and do not provide sufficient information and evidence;
- are allowed to, and claim by, telephone and do not provide all the information required by the local authority during the telephone call;
- are claiming PC by telephone and do not provide all the information required by the DWP during the telephone call.

It is very important that you provide any information or evidence required. Until you do, you may not count as having made a valid claim.

If you have:[143]

- not completed the claim form properly, the local authority can return it to you to do so;[144] *or*
- claimed by letter, the local authority can send you a claim form to complete properly;[145] *or*
- claimed HB (or are claiming PC) by telephone, the local authority must give you an opportunity to provide the information required.

If you return the form properly completed or provide the information or evidence within one month, your claim is treated as though it was received on the date of your original claim.[146] The local authority can allow you longer than one month if it thinks this reasonable.

Note: if your claim is not accepted as valid, you should be given a decision saying so. You can appeal against the decision.

Rapid re-claim

You may be able to complete a shortened HB and CTB claim form – known as 'rapid re-claim' – if you are claiming within 12 weeks of a previous entitlement to HB or CTB ending.[147] This only applies if:

- you are also re-claiming IS, JSA or IB; *and*
- you are entitled to IS, income-based JSA or IB; *and*

- your circumstances have not changed since the last time you were claiming HB or CTB.

You are given the shortened form by the Jobcentre Plus office with the claim form for IS, JSA or IB. You must send your HB and CTB claim to the local authority, *not* to the DWP. If you fill in the form properly, the local authority should be able to make a decision on your HB or CTB claim without asking you for further information. However, if you do not do so, or any of your details have changed since the last time you claimed HB or CTB, the local authority may send you a full HB or CTB form to complete or ask you for further information.

Where to make your claim

If you claim **in writing**, you must usually send or give your HB claim to the local authority's designated office for the receipt of HB and CTB claims.[148] The address is usually on the claim form or a notice accompanying it. You can also send or give your claim to:[149]

- if you or your partner are claiming IS, IB, PC or JSA, either your DWP office *or* to the local authority's designated office for HB/CTB claims. If you send your HB/CTB claim to the DWP, unless your HB/CTB claim is on the same form as your IS, IB or JSA claim, the DWP must forward it to the local authority within two working days of the date your HB/CTB claim was received or as soon as practicable after that.[150]
  It may be wise to send your HB/CTB form directly to the local authority. If you do this, the local authority verifies your entitlement to IS, IB or income-based JSA before assessing your HB. This may speed up your HB/CTB claim; *or*
- if you are at least the qualifying age for PC (60), any authorised office.

You can also send or give your claim to a county council office if your local authority has arranged for claims to be received there.[151]

If your local authority has authorised it (by a Chief Executive's Direction) and you are claiming **online or by email**, check the correct address for this with your local authority.[152]

Keep a copy of your claim form wherever possible. Ask for confirmation that you have delivered it to the relevant office.

If you are allowed to claim **by telephone** (see p202), you must make your claim to the telephone number published for this purpose.[153]

Information to support your claim

Where possible, your claim for HB should be accompanied by all the information and evidence needed to assess it,[154] but you should not delay your claim just because you do not have all the evidence ready to send. Even if you provide all the information required with your claim, the local authority might ask you for further evidence or information. You must then supply this within one month – or longer if the local authority thinks this is reasonable.[155]

Unless you are living in a hostel, you and your partner must satisfy the national insurance (NI) number requirement (see p962). If you have claimed HB in association with a claim for PC, IS or income-based JSA and the DWP has accepted that you satisfy the NI number requirement, the local authority can accept that it is also satisfied for HB purposes.[156] If your claim is for contribution-based JSA or IB, the local authority may still need to verify your partner's NI number and identity.

The local authority may ask you to provide information after you are awarded HB. If you fail to do so, your HB could be suspended or even terminated.

Who should claim

If you are a single person or a lone parent, you make a claim for HB on your own behalf. If you are one of a couple you can decide between you who should claim. See p702 for who counts as a couple. The choice of claimant may affect the level of HB you receive – eg, if one of you is a full-time student and not entitled to HB (see p588). If you are considering changing the claim into your partner's name, you should check whether this could result in you becoming subject to harsher rent restriction rules (see Chapter 11). It is only if you cannot agree who should be the claimant that the local authority can decide for you.[157]

If a person is either temporarily or permanently unable to manage her/his own affairs, the local authority must accept a claim made by someone formally appointed to act legally on her/his behalf – eg, someone appointed with power of attorney, a deputy appointed by the Court of Protection or, in Scotland, a judicial factor or any guardian appointed under the Adults with Incapacity (Scotland) Act 2000 administering the person's estate.[158]

If no one has been formally appointed to look after a claimant's affairs, the local authority can decide to make someone aged over 18 an appointee who can act on her/his behalf.[159] For the purpose of the claim, an appointee has the responsibility of exercising all rights and duties as though s/he were the claimant.[160]

You can write to ask to be an appointee, and can resign after giving four weeks' notice. The local authority may terminate any appointment at any time.[161] If someone is given a formal legal appointment, that person automatically takes over from the person appointed by the local authority.[162]

The date of your claim

Your date of claim is important because it affects the date from which your HB starts (see p209). However, in some cases, you can claim in advance (see p205) and in some cases your claim can be backdated (see p205).

Your **'date of claim'** is usually the earliest of:[163]

- the date you first notify a designated office, DWP office or authorised office (see p203) (or county council office, if the local authority has arranged for claims there) that you want to claim HB (eg, by telephone or in person or where someone does this on your behalf), if a properly completed claim form is received in one of those offices within one month of it being sent or given to you. The one-month period can be extended if the local authority thinks it is reasonable; *or*
- the date your valid claim is received by the designated office, DWP office or authorised office (see p203) (or county council office, if the local authority has arranged for claims there).

There are exceptions to the rule. If:[164]

- you or your partner have successfully claimed IS, income-based JSA or the guarantee credit of PC and your HB claim is made within one month of your IS, income-based JSA or PC claim being received by the DWP, your HB claim is treated as having been made on the first day of entitlement to IS, income-based JSA or PC (including the three waiting days for JSA);
- you or your partner are on IS, income-based JSA or the guarantee credit of PC and have just become liable to pay rent and your HB claim reaches the local authority's designated office or DWP office within one month of you becoming liable, it is treated as being made on the date that you first became liable;
- you have separated from your partner or s/he has died and s/he was claiming HB for you on the date this happened and you claim within one month of this, your claim is treated as having been made on the date you separated or your partner died.

Claiming in advance

You can claim HB in advance if:

- you become liable for rent for the first time but cannot move into your accommodation until after your liability begins. You must claim HB as soon as you are liable. Then, once you have moved in, you may be able to receive HB for up to four weeks prior to moving in. See p185 for further information;
- you are not entitled to HB now, but will become entitled within 13 weeks of claiming (17 weeks, if you or your partner will be 60 or over within 17 weeks), unless the reason you do not qualify straight away is because you fail the 'habitual residence test' (see p1367). The local authority can treat your claim as having been made in the benefit week immediately before you are first entitled.[165] If this happens, you do not need to make a further claim later.

Housing benefit after an award of a 'qualifying benefit'

You might not be entitled to HB currently, but would be once you or a member of your family become entitled to another 'qualifying benefit' – eg, disability living allowance or carer's allowance. Alternatively, you might be entitled to a higher rate of benefit once the 'qualifying benefit' is awarded. If you are already entitled to HB when the qualifying benefit is awarded, see pp1070, 1077 and 1085.

If you only qualify for HB (or CTB) when the qualifying benefit is awarded, the rules operate in an unfair way. You should, therefore, claim HB (or CTB) while waiting to hear about the claim for a qualifying benefit. Then:

- ask the local authority to check whether you are entitled to HB (or CTB) on the basis of your circumstances, regardless of whether you are entitled to a qualifying benefit. If you are, it should award HB (or CTB). If you later get a qualifying benefit your award should be revised or superseded (see pp1070 and 1077);
- if you do not qualify for HB (or CTB) until awarded a qualifying benefit, ask the local authority to wait to make a decision on your claim until the award of qualifying benefit is made. This is what is known as 'stockpiling' your claim.

If the local authority refuses to stockpile your claim, you can try to argue that its failure to delay making a decision on your claim was an 'error of law' and, therefore, that there are grounds for an 'any time' revision (see p1068).[166] If you are refused HB (or CTB) but have since been awarded a qualifying benefit, claim again and ask for your claim to be backdated. You should argue that you have good cause for your late claim (see p207). If you lose benefit because of the way the rules operate, ask your local authority for an *ex gratia* payment to cover the period before your fresh HB (or CTB) claim.

Backdating your claim

It is very important to claim in time. A claim for HB can be backdated:

- if you are 60 or over and neither you nor your partner are on IS or income-based JSA, for up to 12 months. You only need to show that you qualified for HB during that period;[167] *or*
- in all other cases, for up to 52 weeks. However, you must show that you qualified for HB during that period and prove you have continuous 'good cause' for your failure to claim throughout the whole time for which you want to claim.[168]

Note: the Government says it intends to reduce the maximum amount of time a claim can be backdated to three months. See CPAG's *Welfare Rights Bulletin* for updates.

Any backdated HB is calculated based on your circumstances and the HB rules as they were over the backdating period.

You must claim for a past period for backdated HB to be considered. You should do this as soon as possible. HB can only be backdated from the date of your request, not from the date of your original claim for HB, if earlier.

If you would have been entitled to HB for an earlier period, you could:

- ask for an 'any time' revision if there are grounds (see p1068);
- ask for an *ex gratia* payment from the local authority if you were given wrong information or misled by it (see p1186);
- complain to the Ombudsman (see p1185).

If you only qualify for HB when a 'qualifying benefit' is awarded, see p206.

Good cause for claiming late

You count as having 'good cause' for your late claim if you can show there is something that would probably have caused a reasonable person of your age and experience to act (or fail to act) as you did, having regard to all the circumstances (including your state of health and the information which you received and which you might have obtained).[169] It is your mental age, not your chronological age that is relevant.[170] If you have a mental health problem that makes you act unreasonably, then that must be borne in mind.[171]

The following are examples of situations where you might have good cause for making a late claim.

- You sought advice about your rights but were misled by someone on whom you were entitled to rely. You are entitled to rely on officers from the local authority or the DWP, or independent advisers such as solicitors, Citizens Advice Bureaux, trade union officials or accountants.[172] Relying on the advice of work colleagues, friends, or even a doctor, is not enough.[173] The inquiries that you made need not have been specific, provided the situation is such that you ought to have been told about your possible entitlement.
- You did not seek advice about your rights because you misunderstood them (eg, you reasonably believed you did not need to make a claim), or you mistakenly thought that you understood them, or you mistakenly thought that you had no entitlement and there was nothing for you to enquire about.[174] Generally, you are expected to find out about your rights but if it was reasonable for you to form one of these views, you can still have good cause.
- The delay was due to some factor beyond your control, such as the failure of the post, or the failure of someone you asked to help with your claim, provided you have checked whether the claim has arrived in good time.[175]
- You are unable to claim because of physical or mental ill health.[176] However, you might reasonably be expected to seek the assistance of friends or relatives if available.
- You have difficulty communicating in English, or understanding documents, or have little knowledge of the benefits system. These matters should be taken into account but are not usually good cause in themselves.[177]
- You only qualify for HB or CTB when a 'qualifying benefit' is awarded (see p205).

Notice of the decision

If you are a person affected by an HB decision you must be notified of it by the local authority within 14 days or as soon as 'reasonably practicable'.[178] You can request reasons for a decision. Your request must be in writing and it must be signed by you.[179]

You are a person affected by a decision if you are:[180]

- a claimant;
- someone acting for a claimant who is unable to act for her/himself – eg, an appointee;
- someone from whom the local authority decides to recover an overpayment (including a landlord); *or*
- a landlord or agent, where the decision concerns whether or not to make a direct payment of HB to you.[181]

Information a decision notice should contain

The local authority must include a minimum amount of information in its decision notice, and may also include other relevant information.[182] If the decision is one against which you have a right of appeal (see p1095) you must be informed of:[183]

- your right to appeal against the decision; *and*
- your right to a written statement of reasons for the decision (if this is not already included – see p1061).

Other information that must be provided varies with the particular circumstances of your case. In any local authority decision, you should be informed of (where relevant):[184]

- the normal weekly amount of HB to which you are entitled, including the amount and category of any non-dependant deductions and of any notional fuel deductions. You must be told why fuel deductions have been made, and that they can be varied if you provide evidence of the actual amount involved;
- your weekly eligible rent (see p192);
- if you are a private tenant, the day your HB will be paid and whether payment will be made weekly or monthly;
- the date on which your entitlement starts;
- if you are not receiving IS or income-based JSA or you are on PC but are only entitled to the savings credit, how your applicable amount is calculated;
- if you are not receiving IS or income-based JSA, how your income has been assessed;
- if you are on PC but are only entitled to the savings credit:
  - the amount of the savings credit taken into account;
  - the amount of income and capital notified to the local authority by the DWP which has been taken into account. The local authority must also tell you about any modifications it makes to your income or capital;

  - the amount of capital the local authority has taken into account, if the DWP notified the local authority that your capital was less than £16,000 but it has increased to more than that figure while an assessed income period was in force (see p458);
- if your level of HB is less than the minimum amount payable, that this is the reason why you have no entitlement;
- if your claim was successful, your duty to notify the local authority of any change in circumstances which might affect your entitlement and what kinds of changes should be reported;
- if your claim was unsuccessful, a statement explaining exactly why you are not entitled;
- if it has been decided to pay your HB direct to your landlord, information saying how much is to be paid to your landlord and when payments will start, and also that where recovery of an overpayment is made from a landlord (see p1029) and recovery is made from a tenant other than the one who was overpaid, that tenant is treated as if the full payment of HB had been made;[185]
- if the income and capital of a non-dependant has been used instead of yours to calculate your HB (see p200), additional information saying that this has happened and why.

7. Getting paid

No housing benefit (HB) is payable if the amount would be less than 50 pence a week.[186]

When your entitlement starts

Your entitlement to HB starts:[187]

- if you became liable for rent in the first of the weeks for which you are claiming, from the Monday of that week. This includes where you become liable for daily payments in a hostel, accommodation provided by the local authority because you are homeless or on a short-term lease; *or*
- in all other cases, from the Monday following your date of claim (or following the date from which you are claiming if your claim is backdated).

A benefit week is a period of seven days running from Monday to Sunday.[188] This means that if you claim HB in the same week in which your liability for rent begins or you became liable for rent in the first of the weeks in respect of which you are claiming, your HB starts on the same day your liability actually begins.[189]

When your entitlement ends

Your entitlement to HB ends if your circumstances change in a way that means you no longer satisfy the rules described in this chapter. In addition, your entitlement to HB ends, even if you would otherwise continue to qualify, if you or your partner started work (including self-employment) or increased your earnings from or hours of work and:[190]

- had been continuously entitled to and in receipt of income support (IS) or income-based jobseeker's allowance (JSA) (including joint-claim JSA) or a combination of these for at least 26 weeks and entitlement ended because of the earnings or work. The 26 weeks includes periods of less than five weeks when you counted as in full-time paid work because you were on an employment zone programme; *or*
- had been continuously entitled to and in receipt of either incapacity benefit (IB) or severe disablement allowance (SDA) or a combination of these for 26 weeks and entitlement ended because of the earnings or work. This only applies if neither you nor your partner:
  – are getting pension credit (PC); *and*
  – were entitled to or in receipt of IS.

In both cases, the work (or increase in hours or pay) must be expected to last for five weeks or more.

Entitlement ends even if you would be entitled to HB on the basis of your income from work. Your entitlement ends at the end of the benefit week in which entitlement to IS, income-based JSA, IB or SDA ceases. You *must* make a fresh claim for HB to continue to qualify. In order to ensure your claim is continuous, you must claim within a strict time limit (see p213).

In all of these situations, you might qualify for extended payments of HB and council tax benefit (CTB) – see p211.

If you stop claiming IS or income-based JSA, for any other reason, this in itself does *not* end your entitlement to HB.[191] However, your new circumstances could affect the amount of, or your entitlement to, HB. You do not have to make a fresh claim for HB in this situation, but you do have to report the change in your circumstances to the local authority. It can do a revision or supersession (see Chapter 41).

Note: the Government says that the rules are to be amended in October 2008. You or your partner starting work, or increasing your earnings from or hours of work, in the circumstances described above will no longer end your entitlement to HB and you will no longer have to make a fresh claim. Instead, this will be dealt with as a normal change of circumstances. See CPAG's *Welfare Rights Bulletin* for updates.

Continuing payments

There are two situations when your HB can continue to be paid at the same rate, even though your entitlement might otherwise have changed. If you stop claiming:

- IS or income-based JSA because you are moving onto PC, you may be able to continue to receive HB at the same rate for four weeks (see below);
- IS, income-based JSA, IB or SDA because of starting work or increasing your hours or your earnings, you may be entitled to extended payments of HB (see p211).

Continuing payments on claiming pension credit

To avoid problems caused by delays in reassessing your HB when you move from IS or income-based JSA onto PC, so long as you otherwise continue to qualify for HB, you continue to receive it at the same rate as before this happened (but see below) for:[192]

- a period of four weeks from the day after your IS or income-based JSA ceases; *or*
- if the four-week period ends before the last day of a benefit week, until the end of the benefit week in which the end of the four-week period falls.

You qualify for continuing payments if:[193]

- your partner has claimed PC and the DWP has certified this; *or*
- your IS ceased because you turned 60 or, if you were getting income-based JSA beyond that age, this ceased because you turned 65. The DWP must certify this and that you are required to claim or have claimed PC (or are treated as having done so).

Your maximum HB (see p189) is recalculated if your rent increases or there is a change in the non-dependant deductions (see p196) that should be made.[194]

Extended payments on starting work

If you are on IS, income-based JSA, IB or SDA and your entitlement ends because you start work or increase your hours or pay, you may be entitled to continue to receive the same amount of HB as you did before your entitlement ended. These extended payments of HB are paid for up to four weeks. You may also be entitled to extended payments of CTB.

Note: the Government says that the rules are to be amended in October 2008.

Who can claim extended payments

You qualify for extended payments of HB if:

- the DWP has certified that you or your partner:[195]
  - were entitled to and in receipt of IS or income-based JSA and your entitlement ended because you or your partner started work (including self-employed work) or increased your earnings from, or hours of, work. Mortgage interest run-on ceasing (see p823) does not count for these purposes; *and*
  - had been continuously entitled to, and in receipt of, either IS or JSA or a combination of these for 26 weeks. This includes periods of less than five weeks when you counted as in full-time paid work (see p648) because you were on an employment zone programme; *or*

- unless you are getting PC, you or your partner:[196]
  - were *not* entitled to or in receipt of IS; *and*
  - were entitled to and in receipt of IB or SDA and your entitlement ended because you or your partner started work (including self-employment) or increased your earnings from, or hours of, work; *and*
  - had been continuously entitled to, and in receipt of, either SDA or IB or a combination of these for 26 weeks.

You only qualify for extended payments of HB if, in addition, you (or your partner) notify the local authority or a DWP office for claims for IS, income-based JSA or PC that:[197]

- you (or your partner) have started, or are about to start, full-time paid work (see p648) or increase your hours or earnings; *and*
- you expect the work (or increase in hours or pay) to last for five weeks or more.

You must notify the local authority or DWP within four weeks of starting work or of the increase in your hours or pay. The time limit is very strict. If you miss it, try to claim HB on the basis of your income and ask for your claim to be backdated (see p206).

If you move home, you can still qualify for extended payments of HB, so long as the day you moved was in the same week, or the week before, you or your partner started work or increased your earnings from or hours of work.[198]

Your entitlement to HB also ends in the circumstances described above and you must make a new claim – ie, to continue to get HB after the extended payments end (see p209). If you do not notify within the four-week time limit, or make a new claim, you could be overpaid HB and you might have to repay it.

Amount of the extended payments

The weekly amount of your extended payments is the amount of HB payable in your last week of your IS, income-based JSA, IB or SDA claim (ignoring rent-free weeks).[199] This amount is paid for four weeks unless:[200]

- any of the weeks count as rent-free periods (see p196); *or*
- you move to local authority accommodation (but see p213); *or*
- your liability to pay rent ceases altogether within the four weeks.

If you were being paid discretionary housing payments (see p222), ask for these to continue for the extended payment period.

If you move house (unless you move into local authority accommodation), you continue to get the weekly amount of HB payable on your old home.[201] No account is taken of changes in circumstances over the extended payment period – eg, non-dependants (see p196), rent increases, increases in income, rent-free weeks.

If you move into local authority accommodation, the amount of the extended payments is the eligible rent (see p192) at your new address minus any non-dependant deductions (see p196) which applied at the old address.[202] However, if you are getting extended payments because you stopped getting IB or SDA, you are paid the amount of weekly HB payable in your last week of entitlement if this is lower.[203]

Even if you get extended payments, you may still qualify for HB on two homes (see p187).[204]

If you claim HB on the basis of your income from work, and your new entitlement is higher than your extended payment, you can be paid up to the level of your new entitlement (see below).

Claims

You do not have to make a claim for extended payments of HB.[205] Provided you let your local authority and DWP office know you are starting work, or increasing your hours or earnings within the time limit (see p212), extended payments of HB and CTB should be made automatically.

Challenging a decision

You can apply for a revision or supersession of an extended payments decision or appeal against it (see Chapters 41 and 42). However, if you disagree with what the DWP has certified (eg, whether or not you were entitled to and in receipt of IS or income-based JSA continuously), you need to take this up with the DWP.[206]

In-work claims for housing benefit

You are treated as entitled to and getting HB:[207]

- during the four weeks for which you are paid extended payments; *or*
- until your liability to pay rent ends, if this is sooner.

If you claim HB again within the period above that applies to you, or within the four weeks after, your HB entitlement will be continuous. This means if you have a form of transitional protection that requires continuous entitlement, your transitional protection continues.

If your new entitlement to HB on the basis of your income from work is more than the amount of your extended payments (eg, where your rent increases or a non-dependant with a high income moves out), HB can be paid up to the level of your new HB entitlement.[208]

Your new HB claim is dealt with as a priority if you claim within 14 days of the day after the day your IS or income-based JSA ceased.[209] You only get priority if you notified the local authority or DWP (see p212) within 14 days of this happening.

How your benefit is paid

If your landlord is the housing authority responsible for the payment of HB, you receive HB in the form of a reduction in your rent. This is called a rent rebate.[210]

If you are a private tenant (or a housing association tenant), you receive HB in the form of a rent allowance which is usually paid to you although, in some cases, it may be paid direct to your landlord or to someone acting on your behalf (see below).[211]

Although rent allowances are normally paid in the form of a cheque, the local authority has the discretion to pay you by whatever method it chooses but, in doing so, it must have regard to your 'reasonable needs and convenience'.[212] It should not insist on payment into a bank account if you do not have one, nor make you collect it if it is difficult to reach the office by public transport.[213] If it does, you can complain to your local councillor. If that has no effect, ask your MP to take the matter up with the local authority (see p1183), and also complain to the Ombudsman (see p1185).

If the local authority refuses to replace a payment which has never arrived, you could threaten to sue in the county court. If payment of your HB is suspended, see p984.

Payment to someone acting on your behalf

Where an appointee or some other person legally empowered to act for a claimant has claimed HB on her/his behalf, that person can also receive the payments.[214]

If you are able to claim HB for yourself, you can still nominate an agent to receive or collect it for you. To do this you must make a written request to the local authority. Anyone you nominate must be aged 18 or over.[215]

If a claimant dies, any unpaid HB may be paid to her/his personal representative or, where there is none, to her/his next of kin aged 16 or over.[216] For payment to be made, a written application must be received by the local authority within 12 months of the claimant's death. The time limit can be extended at the local authority's discretion. Where HB was being paid to the landlord prior to the claimant's death, the local authority can pay any outstanding HB to clear remaining rent due.

Payment direct to a landlord

Your HB can be paid directly to your landlord (or the person to whom you pay rent) in specific circumstances. Your landlord could contact the local authority about this.[217] The local authority can suspend payment of your HB while it makes enquires as to who should be paid your HB.[218] If the local authority is suspicious of your landlord, see p216.

If you have just claimed HB or the local authority has done a supersession of your award, and the local authority thinks you have not already paid your rent and that it would be in the interests of the 'efficient administration' of HB, it can make the first cheque payable to your landlord (although it is sent to you).[219]

Both you and your landlord should be notified if HB is to be paid to your landlord. If it is *not* in your interests to have HB paid directly to your landlord it is worth trying to persuade the local authority to withhold it rather than paying it to your landlord. *Always* consider seeking advice before you do so.

When payment must be made to your landlord

The local authority *must* pay your HB, including payments on account (see p217),[220] directly to your landlord (or the person to whom you pay rent) if:

- you or your partner are on IS, JSA or PC and the DWP has decided to pay part of your benefit to your landlord for arrears (see p991);[221] *or*
- you have rent arrears equivalent to eight weeks' rent or more, unless the local authority considers it to be in your overriding interest not to make direct payments.[222] Once your arrears have been reduced to less than eight weeks' rent, compulsory direct payments stop. The local authority may then choose to continue direct payments on a discretionary basis (see below).

Note: if the local housing allowance rules apply to you (see p235), the maximum the local authority can pay to your landlord is the amount of rent and arrears of rent you are liable to pay even if the amount of HB to which you are entitled is higher than your rent liability.[223]

Payment to your landlord on a discretionary basis

Unless the local housing allowance rules apply to you (see p235), the local authority may pay your HB directly to your landlord (or the person to whom you pay rent):[224]

- if you have requested or agreed to direct payments; *or*
- without your agreement, if it decides that direct payments are in the best interests of yourself and your family.

If the local housing allowance rules apply to you (see p235), the local authority may pay your HB directly to your landlord if it:[225]

- thinks you are likely to have difficulty managing your own financial affairs or that it is improbable that you will pay your rent. The local authority can pay your rent direct to your landlord (for a maximum of eight weeks) while it considers the situation; *or*
- has already made direct payments during your current award of HB in any of the situations when payments must be made (see above).

If the local housing allowance rules apply to you (see p235), the maximum the local authority can pay to your landlord is the amount of rent and arrears of rent you are liable to pay.[226] This applies even if the amount of HB to which you are entitled is higher than your rent liability.

Whether or not the local housing allowance rules apply to you, the local authority may also pay your HB directly to your landlord (or the person to whom you pay rent) without your agreement if you have left the address for which you were getting HB and there are rent arrears. In this case, direct payments of any unpaid HB due in respect of that accommodation can be made, up to the total of the outstanding arrears.[227]

When the local authority is suspicious about a landlord

If HB is being paid to a landlord, or a request is made for payment to a landlord, and the local authority suspects impropriety on the part of the landlord, it may require a landlord (or her/his agent) to provide information.[228] This must be supplied in typewritten or printed form (or in handwritten or electronic form if the local authority agrees) within four weeks. A further four weeks can be allowed if a written request for an extension of time is made within four weeks of the request for information.[229] The local authority may also refuse to make direct payments where it 'is not satisfied that the landlord is a fit and proper person'.[230]

However, direct payments may be made if:[231]

- the requirements for discretionary direct payments are met; *and*
- the local authority is satisfied that it is in the best interests of you and your family.

If the local authority decides not to make payments to your landlord, it can make payments to you (including sending you a cheque payable to the landlord) or to a trusted third party, such as a social worker or solicitor.[232]

Time of payment

HB is normally paid to you in arrears at intervals of a week, two weeks, four weeks or a month, depending on when your rent is normally due. It can also be paid at longer intervals if you agree.[233] Different rules apply if HB is paid direct to your landlord.[234]

If your rent allowance is less than £1 a week, the local authority can choose to pay your benefit up to six months in arrears.[235]

You can insist on two-weekly payments if your rent allowance is more than £2 a week unless HB is paid direct to your landlord.[236] The local authority can pay your rent allowance weekly either to avoid an overpayment or where you are liable to pay rent weekly and it is in your interests for HB to be paid weekly.[237]

Suspending benefit

Local authorities have powers to suspend and terminate benefit. See p984 for details.

Delays and complaints

The local authority must make a decision on your claim, tell you in writing what the decision is, and pay you any HB to which you are entitled within 14 days, or, if that is not reasonably practicable, as soon as possible after that.[238] If you consider a delay is unreasonable, write to the HB manager and threaten to complain to the Ombudsman (see p1185). In serious cases you may want to seek advice on whether you have grounds for judicial review (see p1129).

Interim payments

If you are a private (or housing association) tenant and the local authority has not been able to assess your HB within the required period, you should receive a payment on account (known as an interim payment) while your claim is being sorted out.[239] The local authority should automatically do this. You do not have to request an interim payment.[240]

Some local authorities treat interim payments as though they are discretionary. However, the local authority *must* pay you an amount which it considers reasonable, given what it knows about your circumstances.[241]

Interim payments can only be refused if it is clear that you will not be entitled to HB or the reason for the delay is that you have been asked for information or evidence in support of your claim and you have failed, without good cause, to provide it (see p203).[242] If the delay has been caused by a third party (eg, the rent officer, your bank or employer) this does not affect your right to an interim payment. If your local authority has not made a payment on account, you should complain. You could also complain to the Ombudsman (see p1185).

If the local authority makes a payment on account, it should notify you of the amount and that it can recover any overpayment which occurs if your actual HB entitlement is different from the interim amount.[243]

If your interim payment is less than your true entitlement, your future HB can be adjusted to take account of the underpayment.[244]

Change of circumstances

It is your duty to report any change in your circumstances which might affect your right to, the amount of, or payment of, your HB.[245] You should do this promptly in writing to the office handling your claim (although in individual cases notification might be accepted in a form other than in writing). If your local authority allows you to claim HB by telephone (see p202), you can also report a change of circumstances by telephone (unless it says you must report it in writing). It is always best to report a change in writing and keep a copy in case of a dispute in the future. **Note:** if your local authority authorises it, you can report changes electronically (eg, by email).[246]

If you do not report any such change promptly in writing, any resulting overpayment may be recoverable from you (see Chapter 39). If you are considered deliberately to have acted falsely or dishonestly, you may also be guilty of an offence (see Chapter 40). Remember:

- the local authority must tell you in writing about the changes you have to report;[247]

- it is important to report changes to the right department. Your duty to notify changes is to the HB department, not to the local authority as a whole;[248]
- if your benefit is paid to someone else on your behalf, the duty to report any relevant changes extends to her/him as well.[249]

If in doubt, always report changes in circumstances. If you think that the local authority might not have taken a change into account, you should check with it.

If you do not get pension credit

If you do not get PC, you must always report:[250]

- any change to your rent, unless you are a local authority tenant;
- entitlement to IS or income-based JSA ending. You should not assume that the DWP does this on your behalf. Make sure that you make a fresh claim for HB if you are still on a low income after coming off IS, income-based JSA, IB or SDA because of increased hours of work or earnings. You should check to see if you qualify for extended payments of HB and CTB (see p211). Note that you do not need to make a fresh claim if your entitlement to IS or income-based JSA ends for another reason;
- a member of your family is no longer a child for benefit purposes (see p709).

Examples of other changes you must also report are:

- if you do not get IS or income-based JSA, your family income or capital;
- the number of boarders or sub-tenants you have or in the payments made by them;
- the number of, or circumstances of, any non-dependants that may affect the level of deductions made to your benefit (see p196);
- your status (eg, marriage, civil partnership, cohabitation, separation or divorce).

If you get pension credit

If you get PC you must report:[251]

- any change to your tenancy, apart from changes in your rent if you are a local authority tenant;
- any changes affecting a non-dependant normally living with you or with whom you normally live;
- any absence from your home which is, or is likely to be, for more than 13 weeks.

If you are only getting the savings credit of PC, you must also report:[252]

- changes affecting a child who lives with you which could affect how much HB you get. You need not report changes in the child's age;
- any changes to your capital which do or could take it above £16,000;

- any change in the income or capital of a non-dependant of yours, if your HB has been assessed on the basis of this instead of your own (see p200), and whether s/he has stopped or resumed living with you;
- any change in the income or capital of your partner that has not been taken into account since the determination of your PC award, and whether your partner has stopped or resumed living with you.

If you are on PC, these are the only changes you have to report to the local authority.[253] Other relevant changes in your circumstances should be passed on to the local authority by the DWP.

Other changes

There may be other changes which the local authority requires you to report, depending on the particular circumstances of your case. The need to report these additional changes must be drawn to your attention at the time you claim and also if you are asked for further information.[254] This is important because you only have a duty to report changes which you 'might reasonably be expected to know' could affect your HB.[255]

You do not have to report:[256]

- any changes in your rent if you are a local authority tenant;
- changes in the ages of members of your family, or of non-dependants, unless the change results in a young person ceasing to count as a member of your family for benefit purposes.[257]

When changes in circumstances take effect

If you claim HB and then report a change in circumstances before the local authority has assessed your claim, your application is assessed on the basis of the revised information you have provided.

If a change of circumstance takes place once benefit has been awarded, the local authority must establish the date on which that change actually occurred.[258] Where you have ceased to be entitled to another social security benefit, the date the change occurred must always be taken as the day after your last day of entitlement to that benefit.[259]

In most cases, a change takes effect from the start of the benefit week after the one in which the change actually occurred.[260] This applies whether or not a decision is advantageous to you. This means that, on whatever day of the week the change actually occurs, the change is implemented as from the following Monday. However, if you are liable to pay rent on a daily basis – eg, in a hostel, and the change means you are no longer entitled to HB, it takes effect on the day it actually occurs.[261]

Exceptions to the rule

There are a number of exceptions to the general rule described above. These include where:

- the change is one you are required to notify to the local authority (other than one relating to you having to take part in a work-focused interview – see p971 – or if you are on PC, one of the exceptions to the rules described below) and it is advantageous to you, you must notify the change within one month of it taking place.[262] The one-month period can be extended in certain circumstances (see p1082). If you notify the change outside the one-month period (or any longer period allowed by the local authority) the date of notification is treated as if that is the date the change occurred;
- a payment of income (or arrears of income) for a past period, other than benefit or arrears of benefit, is taken into account from the date it would have been taken into account had it been paid to you on time.[263] Note that arrears of some benefits, working tax credit, child tax credit and discretionary housing payments count as capital and can be disregarded for a period after they are paid (see pp921 and 940);
- you or your partner are at least 65 and either a non-dependant comes to live with you, or there is a change in respect of a non-dependant, so that a higher non-dependant deduction should be made.[264] The effect of this can be delayed for 26 weeks. This does not apply if you or your partner are getting IS or income-based JSA.

Note: there are also exceptions if there is a change in your rent,[265] and where the change is that you move to a new home or become (or cease to be) entitled to HB for more than one home.[266]

There are additional exceptions to the rules described above if you are on PC and the amount of this changes because of a change in your circumstances or the correction of an official error (see p1068), and this means there is a change in the amount of HB you can be paid. This includes where you are only getting the savings credit of PC and the change is as a result of a change in the DWP assessment of your income or savings.[267]

Special rules apply if two or more changes occurring in the same benefit week would normally take effect in different benefit weeks.[268]

Overpayments and fraud

If you are overpaid HB, you might have to repay it. The rules on overpayments are covered in Chapter 39.

If you have been accused of fraud, see Chapter 40. You might get a reduced amount of HB if you have been sanctioned for benefit offences.

Eviction for anti-social behaviour

If you live in a pilot scheme area, your HB may be paid at a reduced rate (or not at all) during a 'restriction period' if you have been evicted for anti-social behaviour and certain other conditions apply, including that you have failed without good cause to comply with a warning notice to take specified action.[269] The restriction period can last for up to five years. The pilot scheme areas are Blackburn, Blackpool, Dover, Manchester, New Forest, Newham, South Gloucestershire and Wirral.

8. Challenging a housing benefit decision

You can apply for a revision or a supersession of a housing benefit decision, or appeal against it (see Chapters 41 and 42).

9. Tax, tax credits and other benefits

Housing benefit (HB) is not taxable.

Tax credits

If you are in work you might be able to claim working tax credit (WTC). Whether or not you are in work, you might be able to claim child tax credit (CTC). WTC counts as income in working out your HB. So does CTC, unless you are 60 or over and neither you nor your partner are getting income support (IS) or income-based jobseeker's allowance (JSA).

Means-tested benefits

If you pay council tax, you may be able to claim council tax benefit (CTB) as well as HB. If you are on a low income, you may be able to claim other means-tested benefits to top this up. Entitlement to IS, income-based JSA or the guarantee credit of pension credit acts as an automatic passport to maximum HB (see p190).

Non-means-tested benefits

The non-means-tested benefits in this *Handbook* (other than attendance allowance (AA), disability living allowance (DLA), guardian's allowance and, if you are 60 or over and neither you nor your partner are getting IS or income-based JSA, child benefit) are taken into account as income when working out the amount of HB you get. However, it can still be worth claiming these benefits. If you, your partner or your child(ren) qualify for certain non-means-tested benefits (including AA, DLA and child benefit) you also qualify for certain premiums (see p775) and potentially a higher rate of HB. If you think you might qualify you should seek advice to see if you would be better off.

You may only qualify for HB once you or a member of your family are awarded another benefit, known as a 'qualifying benefit'. You may be entitled to a higher rate of HB once the qualifying benefit is awarded. See p205 for information.

Passports and other sources of help

If you are on a low income, you might qualify for certain health benefits such as free prescriptions (see Chapter 9). You may also qualify for other sources of help (see p14) or a social fund payment, maternity grant or funeral expenses payment (see Chapters 21 and 22).

Financial help on starting work

If you stop getting IS, income-based JSA, incapacity benefit or severe disablement allowance because you start work or your hours or earnings in your exisiting job increase, you may be entitled to extended payments of HB or CTB. This means you can usually continue to get the same amount of benefit for four weeks (see p211). You might also be able to get child maintenance bonus (see p757), mortgage interest run-on (if you have a home loan – see p823) and a job grant (see p14). See p14 for information about other financial help you might get.

10. **Discretionary housing payments**

Discretionary housing payments are extra payments that can be made by your local authority to help meet your rent or council tax liability. They do not count as housing benefit (HB) or council tax benefit (CTB).

You do not have a 'right' to discretionary housing payments. They are paid from a cash-limited budget allocated to your local authority by the Government.

Who can claim discretionary housing payments

A local authority can pay you discretionary housing payments if:[270]
- you are entitled to HB or CTB; *and*
- you appear to require some financial assistance in addition to your HB or CTB to meet your housing costs (including council tax).

Local authorities have discretion on whether to pay you, what amount to pay you (with certain limits) and over what period to pay you.[271]

Payments not met by discretionary housing payments

Discretionary housing payments cannot be made to you if your need for financial assistance arises as a consequence of:[272]
- ineligible service charges under the HB scheme (see p195);
- water and sewerage charges;
- council tax liability if you are entitled to HB but not CTB;
- liabilities that can be met by HB if you are entitled to CTB but not HB;
- council tax liability if you are only entitled to the second adult rebate and are not or would not have been entitled to CTB if you had not received the rebate;

- your rent payments being increased to cover arrears of rent, service charges or other unpaid charge;
- a reduced benefit decision because you refused to co-operate in pursuing maintenance for your child(ren) (see p748);
- your benefit being reduced because you refused to attend a work-focused interview (see p971);
- your jobseeker's allowance (JSA) being stopped or reduced because you left your work voluntarily (see p402) or you lost your job because of misconduct (see Chapter 16);
- your benefit being suspended (see p984);
- a reduction in the amount of your HB or CTB because an overpayment is being recovered;
- your benefit being restricted:
  - because a court has decided that you failed to comply with a community order without a reasonable excuse (see p997); *or*
  - under the 'loss of benefit for benefit offences' rules (see p1047); *or*
  - because you live in a pilot area and have been evicted for anti-social behaviour (see p220).

The amount of discretionary housing payments

Discretionary housing payments are normally paid in weekly amounts. It is up to the local authority to decide for how long you can be paid and how far your payments can be backdated.[273] You cannot be paid more than:[274]

- in the case of an amount to assist you to meet your council tax liabilities, your weekly council tax liability;
- in the case of an amount to meet payments in respect of your home, other than council tax, an amount to meet your rent and other amounts listed on p179 (payments which can be met by HB) less any amounts paid for ineligible service charges and rent-free periods.

Claims

A claim for discretionary housing payments is separate from your claim for HB or CTB. You claim from your local authority and you should ask it how to make a claim. The local authority may accept a claim from you, or from someone acting on your behalf, as long as you are entitled to HB or CTB.[275] Your local authority does not have to insist your claim is made in writing but it decides what 'form or manner' your claim should take.[276]

You must provide grounds for your claim and provide any other information that the local authority specifies.[277] If you want your claim to be backdated, tell the local authority.

Getting paid

You must be given written notice of the local authority's decision on your claim and the reasons for its decision as soon as is 'reasonably practical'.[278] It can pay you or, if reasonable, someone else where appropriate.[279]

Change of circumstances

As with HB, it is your duty to report any change in your circumstances that might affect your right to, the amount of, or payment of your benefit (see p217).

Challenging a discretionary housing payment decision

You do not have a right of appeal to an independent appeal tribunal against a discretionary housing payment decision. However, you do have the right to ask the local authority for a review of its decision.[280] You are entitled to written notice and reasons for the review decision as soon as is 'reasonably practicable'.[281] You might be able to challenge a review decision by judicial review (see p1129).

Tax, tax credits and other benefits

Discretionary housing payments are not taxable.

Discretionary hardship payments are disregarded as income and capital for income support, JSA, HB and CTB, working tax credit and child tax credit purposes.[282]

Notes

Between 7 April 2008 and 6 April 2009 there are two versions of the HB regulations. The footnotes contain references to both. If you were getting HB immediately before 1 April 2007 (unless the Pathfinder local housing allowance rules applied), the old versions continue to apply to you until 6 April 2009, or until the first of the following occurs. The local authority:

- has to apply to the rent officer for determinations;
- would have had to apply to the rent officer for determinations but for the fact that there are existing determinations it can use;
- works out a new 'eligible rent' where no rent restriction rules apply;
- works out a new 'eligible rent' under the pre-January 1996 rules.

In addition, the new versions apply if you claim HB or move home on or after 7 April 2008.

1. **Who can claim housing benefit**

1 s130 SSCBA 1992; s115 IAA 1999; reg 10 HB Regs; reg 10 HB(SPC) Regs
2 Reg 26 HB(SPC) Regs
3 **HB** Reg 26 HB(SPC) Regs
CTB Reg 16 CTB(SPC) Regs
4 **HB** Reg 27 HB(SPC) Regs
CTB Reg 17 CTB(SPC) Regs
5 Sch para 6 HB&CTB(DA) Regs
6 para 1103 *Housing Benefit and Council Tax Benefit Pension Credit Handbook*
7 Regs 11(1) and 12(1) HB Regs; regs 11(1) and 12(1) HB(SPC) Regs
8 CH/3110/2003; R(H) 3/07
9 CH/844/2002
10 Reg 2(4)(a) HB Regs; reg 2(4)(a) HB(SPC) Regs
11 *R v Cambridge CC ex parte Thomas,* 10 February 1995 (QBD); CH/2959/2006
12 Reg 12(2) HB Regs; reg 12(2) HB(SPC) Regs
13 Reg 2(1), definition of 'long tenancy' and 'owner' HB Regs; reg 2(1), definition of 'long tenancy' and 'owner' HB(SPC) Regs; CH 2258/2004; *Burton v New Forest District Council* [2004] EWCA Civ 1510, reported as R(H) 7/05; R(H) 3/07; CH/3586/2005; R(H) 8/07
14 Para A4/4.200-4.201 GM
15 Reg 11(2) HB Regs
16 Reg 11(4) HB Regs
17 Reg 8(1) HB Regs; reg 8(1) HB(SPC) Regs
18 CSHB/606/2005
19 Reg 8(2) HB Regs; reg 8(2) HB(SPC) Regs
20 *R v Rugby BC HBRB ex parte Harrison* [1994] 28 HLR 36 (QBD)
21 CH/3579/2003; CH 257/2005
22 R(H) 3/03
23 *R v Poole BC ex parte Ross* [1995] 28 HLR 351 (QBD); *R v Warrington BC ex parte Williams* [1997] 29 HLR 872 (QBD)
24 s134(2) SSCBA 1992; reg 82(1) HB Regs; reg 63(1) HB(SPC) Regs
25 Reg 56 HB Regs
26 Reg 10 HB Regs; reg 10 HB(SPC) Regs
27 Reg 9(1) HB Regs; reg 9(1) HB(SPC) Regs
28 Reg 9(4) HB Regs; reg 9(4) HB(SPC) Regs; CH/1326/2004; CH/1328/2004
29 CH/542/2006; R(H) 5/06 decided that the rule did not conflict with the Human Rights Act.
30 Reg 3(4) HB Regs; reg 3(4) HB(SPC) Regs
31 *Thamesdown BC v Goonery* [1995] 1 CLY 2600 (CA)
32 R(H) 1/03; CH/1171/2002; CH/2899/2005
33 Reg 9(2) HB Regs; reg 9(2) HB(SPC) Regs; *R v Poole BC ex parte Ross* [1995] 28 HLR 351 (QBD); CH/1076/2002; CH/296/2004; CH/1097/2004; para A3/3.258-65 GM
34 *R (Tucker) v Secretary of State* [2001] EWCA Div 1646, unreported (EWCA). The Court decided that the rule did not conflict with the Human Rights Act.
35 para A3/3.269 GM
36 Reg 9(3) HB Regs; reg 9(3) HB(SPC) Regs
37 Reg 2(1) HB Regs and reg 2(1) HB(SPC) Regs. Both, definition of 'owner' and 'long tenancy'. CH/1278/2002; CH/0296/2003
38 CH/3853/2001; CH/396/2002; R(H) 6/07
39 **HB** Reg 2(1) HB Regs; reg 2(1) HB(SPC) Regs
CTB Reg 2(1) CTB Regs; reg 2(1) CTB(SPC) Regs
40 R(SB) 27/87; paras A3/3.240-41 GM
41 paras A3/3.243-45 GM
42 *R v Solihull MBC ex parte Simpson* [1995] 1 FLR 140 (CA); CH/39/2007
43 *R (Mackay) v Barking and Dagenham HBRB* [2001] EWHC Admin 234 (HC)
44 CH/2258/2004
45 *R (Mackay) v Barking and Dagenham HBRB* [2001] EWHC Admin 234 (HC)
46 *R v Sutton LBC HBRB ex parte Keegan* [1992] 27 HLR 92 (QBD)
47 *R v Manchester CC ex parte Baragrove Properties Ltd* [1991] 23 HLR 337 (QBD); *R v Gloucestershire CC ex parte Dadds* [1997] 29 HLR 700 (QBD); CH/39/2007
48 *R v Poole BC ex parte Ross* [1995] 28 HLR 351 (QBD)
49 s130(1) SSCBA 1992; reg 7(1) and (2) HB Regs; reg 7(1) and (2) HB(SPC) Regs
50 Reg 7(5), (14) and (15)(c) HB Regs; reg 7(5), (14) and (15)(c) HB(SPC) Regs
51 Reg 7(8) HB Regs; reg 7(8) HB(SPC) Regs
52 R(H) 9/05
53 CH/1363/2006; R(H) 4/07
54 Reg 7(7) HB Regs; reg 7(7) HB(SPC) Regs; para A3/3.430 GM
55 CH/2201/2002
56 R(H) 9/05

57 **HB** Reg 7(13) HB Regs; reg 7(13) HB(SPC) Regs
CTB Reg 8(2) and (3)(b) CTB Regs; reg 8(2) and (3)(b) CTB(SPC) Regs
58 **HB** Reg 7(16) HB Regs; reg 7(16) HB(SPC) Regs
CTB Reg 8(2), (3)(c) and (4) CTB Regs; reg 8(2), (3)(c) and (4) CTB(SPC) Regs
59 **HB** Reg 7(14) and (15)(b) HB Regs; reg 7(14) and (15)(b) HB(SPC) Regs
CTB Reg 8(5) and (6)(b) CTB Regs; reg 8(5) and (6)(b) CTB(SPC) Regs
Both CSH/499/2006
60 **HB** Reg 7(11) HB Regs; reg 7(11) HB(SPC) Regs
CTB Reg 8(3)(a) CTB Regs; reg 8(3)(a) CTB(SPC) Regs
61 *Secretary of State for Work and Pensions v Selby District Council and Bowman* [2006] EWCA Civ 271, 13 February 2006, reported as R(H) 4/06
62 CH/1237/2004
63 CH/3893/2004
64 *R v Penwith DC ex parte Burt* [1988] 22 HLR 292 (QBD); para A3/3.460 GM
65 **HB** Reg 7(14) and (15)(a) HB Regs; reg 7(14) and (15)(a) HB(SPC) Regs
CTB Reg 8(5) and (6)(a) CTB Regs; reg 8(5) and (6)(a) CTB(SPC) Regs
66 Reg 7(18) HB Regs; reg 7(18) HB(SPC) Regs
67 Reg 7(6)(d) and (e) HB Regs; reg 7(6)(d) and (e) HB(SPC) Regs
68 CH/1911/2006
69 R(H) 4/07
70 Reg 7(6)(a) HB Regs; reg 7(6)(a) HB(SPC) Regs
71 Reg 7(6)(b) and (c) HB Regs; reg 7(6)(b) and (c) HB(SPC) Regs
72 Reg 7(10) HB Regs; reg 7(10) HB(SPC) Regs
73 Reg 7(3) HB Regs; reg 7(3) HB(SPC) Regs
74 Reg 7(4) HB Regs; reg 7(4) HB(SPC) Regs
75 R(SB) 10/81

4. **The amount of benefit**

76 Reg 70 HB Regs, and reg 70 HB Regs as substituted by reg 12 HB(LHA&IS)A Regs; reg 50 HB(SPC) Regs, and reg 50 HB(SPC) Regs as substituted by reg 12 HB(SPC)(LHA&IS)A Regs
77 **HB** s130(3) SSCBA 1992; Schs 5 para 4 and 6 para 5 HB Regs; reg 26 HB(SPC) Regs
CTB Schs 4 para 4 and 5 para 5 CTB Regs; reg 16 CTB(SPC) Regs
Both *R v Penwith DC ex parte Menear* [1991] 24 HLR 120 (QBD); *R v South Ribble DC HBRB ex parte Hamilton* [2000] 33 HLR 104 (CA)
78 **HB** Reg 2(3) HB Regs; reg 2(3) HB(SPC) Regs
CTB Reg 2(4) CTB Regs; reg 2(4) CTB(SPC) Regs
79 Regs 12(3)(b) and 12B(2) HB Regs; regs 12(3)(b) and 12B(2) HB(SPC) Regs
80 Regs 12(4), 12B(3) and 12C(2) HB Regs; regs 12(4), 12B(3) and 12C(2) HB(SPC) Regs; reg 12(4) HB Regs and reg 12(4) HB(SPC) Regs as set out in Sch 3 para 5 HB&CTB(CP) Regs and as set out in Sch 3 para 5 HB&CTB(CP) Regs as substituted by reg 6 HB(LHA,M&C)A Regs
81 Regs 12(5), 12B(4) and 12C(2) HB Regs; regs 12(5), 12B(4) and 12C(2) HB(SPC) Regs; reg 12(5) HB Regs and reg 12(5) HB(SPC) Regs as inserted by Sch 3 para 5 HB&CTB(CP) Regs; CH/3376/2002
82 *R (Naghshbandi) v Camden LBC* [2002] EWCA Civ 1038, *The Times,* 5 August, unreported (CA)
83 CH/3376/2002
84 Reg 13D(12) HB Regs; reg 13D(12) HB(SPC) Regs
85 Regs 12(3)(b) and 12B(2) HB Regs; regs 12(3)(b) and 12B(2) HB(SPC) Regs; regs 12(3)(b) and 12B(2) HB Regs and regs 12(3)(b) and 12B(2) HB(SPC) Regs as set out in Sch 3 para 5 HB&CTB(CP) Regs and as set out in Sch 3 para 5 HB&CTB(CP) Regs as substituted by reg 6 HB(LHA,M&C)A Regs; *R v Bristol City Council ex parte Jacobs* [1999] 32 HLR 82 (QBD)
86 Regs 12(4), 12B(3) and 12C(2) HB Regs; regs 12(4), 12B(3) and 12C(2) HB(SPC) Regs; reg 12(4) HB Regs and reg 12(4) HB(SPC) Regs as set out in Sch 3 para 5 HB&CTB(CP) Regs and as set out in Sch 3 para 5 HB&CTB(CP) Regs as substituted by reg 6 HB(LHA,M&C)A Regs
87 Reg 11(3) HB Regs and reg 11(3) HB Regs as amended by reg 4 HB(LHA&IS)A Regs; reg 11(2) HB(SPC) Regs
88 Sch 1 para 5 HB Regs; Sch 1 para 5 HB(SPC) Regs

89 Sch 1 para 6(1)HB Regs; Sch 1 para 6(1) HB(SPC) Regs
90 Sch 1 para 6(1)(a)HB Regs; Sch 1 para 6(1)(a) HB(SPC) Regs
91 Sch 1 para 6(2) and (3) HB Regs; Sch 1 para 6(2) and (3) HB(SPC) Regs
92 Schs 1 para 6(4) and 9 para 9(b) HB Regs; Schs 1 para 6(4) and 8 para 9(1)(b) HB(SPC) Regs
93 para A4/4.233 GM
94 Sch 1 paras 5 and 6(1)(b) HB Regs; Sch 1 paras 5 and 6(1)(b) HB(SPC) Regs
95 Sch 1 para 8 HB Regs; Sch 1 para 8 HB(SPC) Regs
96 Sch 1 para 8 HB Regs; Sch 1 para 8 HB(SPC) Regs
97 Reg 12(1)(e) HB Regs; reg 12(1)(e) HB(SPC) Regs
98 Sch 1 para 4 HB Regs; Sch 1 para 4 HB(SPC) Regs
99 para A4/4.730 GM
100 Sch 1 para 1(a)(iii)HB Regs; Sch 1 para 1(a)(iii) HB(SPC) Regs
101 Sch 1 para 1(a)(ii)HB Regs; Sch 1 para 1(a)(ii) HB(SPC) Regs
102 Sch 1 para 1(b)HB Regs; Sch 1 para 1(b) HB(SPC) Regs
103 Sch 1 para 1(a)(iv)HB Regs; Sch 1 para 1(a)(iv) HB(SPC) Regs
104 Regs 12(3)(b)(ii) and 12B(2)(b) and Sch 1 para 1 HB Regs; regs 12(3)(b)(ii) and 12B(2)(b)and Sch 1 para 1 HB(SPC) Regs; reg 12(3)(b) HB Regs and reg 12(3)(b) HB(SPC) Regs as substituted by Sch 3 para 5 HB&CTB(CP) Regs
105 Regs 12(3)(b)(iii) and 12B(2)(c) and Sch 1 para 3(2) HB Regs; regs 12(3)(b)(iii) and 12B(2)(c) and Sch 1 para 3(2) HB(SPC) Regs; reg 12(3)(c) HB Regs and reg 12(3)(c) HB(SPC) Regs as substituted by Sch 3 para 5 HB&CTB(CP) Regs
106 Sch 1 para 3 HB Regs; Sch 1 para 3 HB(SPC) Regs
107 Sch 1 paras 1(a)(i) and 2(1) HB Regs; Sch 1 paras 1(a)(i) and 2(1) HB(SPC) Regs
108 Sch 1 para 2(6) and (7) HB Regs; Sch 1 para 2(6) and (7) HB(SPC) Regs
109 Reg 2(1) HB Regs; reg 2(1) HB(SPC) Regs
110 Reg 80 HB Regs, and reg 80 HB Regs as substituted by reg 16 HB(LHA&IS)A Regs; reg 61 HB(SPC) Regs, and reg 61 HB(SPC) Regs as substituted by reg 16 HB(SPC)(LHA&IS)A Regs
111 Reg 81(3) and Sch 1 para 7(2) HB Regs, and reg 81(3) HB Regs as substituted by reg 16 HB(LHA&IS)A Regs; reg 62(3) and Sch 1 para 7(2) HB(SPC) Regs, and reg 62(3) HB(SPC) Regs as substituted by reg 16 HB(SPC)(LHA&IS)A Regs
112 **HB** Regs 3(1) and 70 HB Regs, and reg 70 HB Regs as substituted by reg 12 HB(LHA&IS)A Regs; regs 3(1) and 50 HB(SPC) Regs, and reg 50 HB(SPC) Regs as substituted by reg 12 HB(SPC)(LHA&IS)A Regs
CTB Regs 3(1) and 57(1) CTB Regs; regs 3(1) and 40(1) CTB(SPC) Regs
113 CIS/14850/1996
114 Reg 3(4) and Sch 1 para 8 HB Regs and reg 3(4) HB Regs as amended by reg 4 HB(LHA&IS)A Regs; reg 3(4) and Sch 1 para 8 HB(SPC) Regs and reg 3(4) HB(SPC) Regs as amended by reg 4 HB(SPC)(LHA&IS)A Regs
115 *Thamesdown BC v Goonery* [1995] ICLY 2600 (CA)
116 Para A5/5.521 GM
117 **HB** Reg 3(2) HB Regs; reg 3(2) HB(SPC) Regs
CTB Reg 3(2) CTB Regs; reg 3(2) CTB(SPC) Regs
118 *R v Chesterfield BC ex parte Fullwood* [1993] 26 HLR 126 (CA)
119 Reg 3(3) HB Regs; reg 3(3) HB(SPC) Regs
120 **HB** Regs 2(1), definition of 'attendance allowance' and 74(6) HB Regs, and reg 74(6) HB Regs as substituted by reg 14 HB(LHA&IS)A Regs; regs 2(1), definition of 'attendance allowance' and 55(6) HB(SPC) Regs, and reg 55(6) HB(SPC) Regs as substituted by reg 14 HB(SPC)(LHA&IS)A Regs
CTB Regs 2(1), definition of 'attendance allowance' and 58(6) CTB Regs; regs 2(1), definition of 'attendance allowance' and 42(6) CTB(SPC) Regs
121 **HB** Reg 74(7) HB Regs, and reg 74(7) HB Regs as substituted by reg 14 HB(LHA&IS)A Regs; reg 55(7) HB(SPC) Regs and reg 74(7) HB(SPC) Regs as substituted by reg 14 HB(SPC)(LHA&IS)A Regs
CTB Reg 58(7) CTB Regs; reg 42(7) CTB(SPC) Regs
122 s2 ETA 1973 and s2 Enterprise and New Towns (Scotland) Act 1990

123 **HB** Reg 74(1) HB Regs, and reg 74(1) HB Regs as substituted by reg 14 HB(LHA&IS)A Regs; reg 55(1) HB(SPC) Regs, and reg 74(1) HB(SPC) Regs as substituted by reg 14 HB(SPC)(LHA&IS)A Regs
CTB Reg 58(1) CTB Regs; reg 42(1) CTB(SPC) Regs

124 Regs 2(3) and 74(8) HB Regs, and reg 74(8) HB Regs as substituted by reg 14 HB(LHA&IS)A Regs; regs 2(3) and 55(8) HB(SPC) Regs, and reg 55(8) as substituted by reg 14 HB(SPC)(LHA&IS)A Regs

125 **HB** Reg 74(10) HB Regs, and reg 74(10) HB Regs as substituted by reg 14 HB(LHA&IS)A Regs; reg 55(9) HB(SPC) Regs and reg 55(9) HB(SPC) Regs as substituted by reg 14 HB(SPC)(LHA&IS)A Regs
CTB Reg 58(8) CTB Regs; reg 42(8) CTB(SPC) Regs

126 Reg 74(1) and (2) HB Regs, and reg 74(1) and (2) HB Regs as substituted by reg 14 HB(LHA&IS)A Regs; reg 55(1) and (2) HB(SPC) Regs, and reg 55(1) and (2) HB(SPC) Regs as substituted by reg 14 HB(SPC)(LHA&IS)A Regs

127 **HB** Reg 6(6) HB Regs; reg 6(6) HB(SPC) Regs
CTB Reg 6(6) CTB Regs; reg 6(6) CTB(SPC) Regs

128 **HB** Reg 74(9) HB Regs, and reg 74(9) HB Regs as substituted by reg 14 HB(LHA&IS)A Regs; reg 55(10) HB(SPC) Regs, and reg 55(10) HB(SPC Regs as substituted by reg 14 HB(SPC)(LHA&IS)A Regs
CTB Reg 58(9) CTB Regs; reg 42(9) CTB(SPC) Regs

129 CH/48/2006

130 **HB** Reg 74(3) HB Regs, and reg 74(3) HB Regs as substituted by reg 14 HB(LHA&IS)A Regs; reg 55(3) HB(SPC) Regs and reg 55(3) HB(SPC) Regs as substituted by reg 14 HB(SPC)(LHA&IS)A Regs
CTB Reg 58(3) CTB Regs; reg 42(3) CTB(SPC) Regs

131 **HB** Reg 74(4) HB Regs, and reg 74(4) HB Regs as substituted by reg 14 HB(LHA&IS)A Regs; reg 55(4) HB(SPC) Regs, and reg 55(4) HB(SPC Regs as substituted by reg 14 HB(SPC)(LHA&IS)A Regs
CTB Reg 58(4) CTB Regs; reg 42(4) CTB(SPC) Regs

132 Reg 74(5) HB Regs, and reg 74(5) HB Regs as substituted by reg 14 HB(LHA&IS)A Regs; reg 55(5) HB(SPC) Regs, and reg 55(5) HB(SPC) Regs as substituted by reg 14 HB(SPC)(LHA&IS)A Regs

133 **HB** Reg 26 HB Regs; reg 24 HB(SPC) Regs
CTB Reg 16 CTB Regs; reg 14 CTB(SPC) Regs

134 **HB** s134(8) and (14) SSAA 1992
CTB s139(6) and (11) SSAA 1992
Both Sch Housing Benefit and Council Tax Benefit (War Pension Disregards) Regulations 2007 No.1619

6. **Claims and backdating**

135 **HB** Reg 83(1) and (9) HB Regs; reg 64(2) and (10) HB(SPC) Regs
CTB Reg 69(1) and (9) CTB Regs; reg 53(1) and (9) CTB(SPC) Regs

136 **HB** Reg 83(2) HB Regs; reg 64(3) HB(SPC) Regs
CTB Reg 69(2) CTB Regs; reg 53(2) CTB(SPC) Regs

137 **HB** Reg 83A and Sch 11 HB Regs; reg 64A and Sch 10 HB(SPC) Regs
CTB Reg 69A and Sch 9 CTB Regs; reg 53A and Sch 8 CTB(SPC) Regs

138 **HB** Reg 64(5B) HB(SPC) Regs
CTB Reg 53(4B) CTB(SPC) Regs

139 **HB** Reg 87(1) HB Regs; reg 68(1) HB(SPC) Regs
CTB Reg 73(1) CTB Regs; reg 58(1) CTB(SPC) Regs

140 **HB** Reg 87(2) HB Regs; reg 68(2) HB(SPC) Regs
CTB Reg 73(2) CTB Regs; reg 58(2) CTB(SPC) Regs

141 **HB** Reg 83(4A) and (4B) HB Regs; reg 64(5A) and (5C) HB(SPC) Regs
CTB Reg 69(4A) and (4B) CTB Regs; reg 53(4A) and (4C) CTB(SPC) Regs

142 **HB** Reg 83(4C) and (6) HB Regs; reg 64(5D) and (7) HB(SPC) Regs
CTB Reg 69(4D) and (6) CTB Regs; reg 53(4D) and (6) CTB(SPC) Regs

143 **HB** Reg 83(4D) and (7) HB Regs; reg 64(5E) and (8) HB(SPC) Regs
CTB Reg 69(4D) and (7) CTB Regs; reg 53(4E) and (7) CTB(SPC) Regs

144 **HB** Reg 83(7) HB Regs; reg 64(8) HB(SPC) Regs
CTB Reg 69(7) CTB Regs; reg 53(7) CTB(SPC) Regs

145 **HB** Reg 83(7)(b) HB Regs; reg 64(8)(b) HB(SPC) Regs
CTB Reg 69(7)(b) CTB Regs; reg 53(7)(b) CTB(SPC) Regs
146 **HB** Reg 83(4E) and (8) HB Regs; reg 64(5F) and (9) HB(SPC) Regs
CTB Reg 69(4E) and (8) CTB Regs; reg 53(4F) and (8) CTB(SPC) Regs
147 paras A2/2.560-65 GM
148 **HB** Reg 83(4)(b) HB Regs; reg 64(5)(b) HB(SPC) Regs
CTB Reg 69(4)(b) CTB Regs; reg 53(4)(b) CTB(SPC) Regs
149 **HB** Regs 2, definition of 'appropriate DWP office', and 83(4)(a) and (d)-(f) and (13) HB Regs; regs 2, definition of 'appropriate DWP office', and 64(5)(a) and (d)-(f) and (14) HB(SPC) Regs
CTB Regs 2, definition of 'appropriate DWP office', and 69(4)(a) and (d)-(f) and (15) CTB Regs; regs 2, definition of 'appropriate DWP office', and 53(4)(a) and (d)-(f) and (15) CTB(SPC) Regs
150 **HB** Reg 83(4)(c) HB Regs; reg 64(5)(c) HB(SPC) Regs
CTB Reg 69(4)(c) CTB Regs; reg 53(4)(c) CTB(SPC) Regs
151 **HB** Reg 83(4)(g) HB Regs; reg 64(5)(g) HB(SPC) Regs
CTB Reg 69(4)(g) CTB Regs; reg 53(4)(g) CTB(SPC) Regs
152 **HB** Reg 83A and Sch 11 HB Regs; reg 64A and Sch 10 HB(SPC) Regs
CTB Reg 69A and Sch 9 CTB Regs; reg 53A and Sch 8 CTB(SPC) Regs
153 **HB** Reg 83(4A) HB Regs; reg 64(5A) HB(SPC) Regs
CTB Reg 69(4A) CTB Regs; reg 53(4A) CTB(SPC) Regs
154 **HB** Reg 83(1), (4C) and (9) HB Regs; reg 64(2), (5D) and (10) HB(SPC) Regs
CTB Reg 69(1), (4C) and (9) CTB Regs; reg 53(1), (4D) and (9) CTB(SPC) Regs
155 **HB** Reg 86(1) HB Regs; reg 67(1) HB(SPC) Regs
CTB Reg 72(1) CTB Regs (this erroneously states four weeks, but it is to be amended); reg 57(1) CTB(SPC) Regs
156 para A1/1.300 GM
157 **HB** Reg 82(1) HB Regs; reg 63(1) HB(SPC) Regs
CTB Reg 68(1) CTB Regs; reg 52(1) CTB(SPC) Regs
Both CH/2995/2006
158 **HB** Reg 82(2) HB Regs; reg 63(2) HB(SPC) Regs
CTB Reg 68(2) CTB Regs; reg 52(2) CTB(SPC) Regs
159 **HB** Reg 82(3) and (5) HB Regs; reg 63(3) and (5) HB(SPC) Regs
CTB Reg 68(3) and (5) CTB Regs; reg 52(3) and (5) CTB(SPC) Regs
160 **HB** Reg 82(6) HB Regs; reg 63(6) HB(SPC) Regs
CTB Reg 68(6) CTB Regs; reg 52(6) CTB(SPC) Regs
161 **HB** Reg 82(4) HB Regs; reg 63(4) HB(SPC) Regs
CTB Reg 68(4) CTB Regs; reg 52(4) CTB(SPC) Regs
162 **HB** Reg 82(4)(c) HB Regs; reg 63(4)(c) HB(SPC) Regs
CTB Reg 68(4)(c) CTB Regs; reg 52(4)(c) CTB(SPC) Regs
163 **HB** Regs 83(5)(d) and (e) and 85(1) HB Regs; regs 64(6)(d) and (e) and 66(1) HB(SPC) Regs
CTB Regs 69(5)(d) and (e) and 71(1) CTB Regs (this erroneously states four weeks, but it is to be amended); regs 53(5)(d) and (e) and 55(1) CTB(SPC) Regs
164 **HB** Reg 83(5)(a)-(c) HB Regs; reg 64(6)(a)-(c) HB(SPC) Regs
CTB Reg 69(5)(a)-(c) CTB Regs; reg 53(5)(a)-(c) CTB(SPC) Regs
165 **HB** Reg 83(10) and (11) HB Regs; reg 64(11) and (12) HB(SPC) Regs
CTB Reg 69(12) and (13) CTB Regs; reg 53(12) CTB(SPC) Regs
166 CG/1479/1999; CIS/217/1999
167 **HB** Reg 64(1) HB(SPC) Regs
CTB Regs 53(1ZA) and 56 CTB(SPC) Regs
168 **HB** Reg 83(12) HB Regs
CTB Reg 69(14) CTB Regs
169 R(S) 2/63 (T); CH/2659/2002; CH/474/2002; CH/393/2003; A2/Annex A GM
170 CH/393/2003
171 CH/474/2002
172 R(SB) 6/83; CS/50/1950; R(U) 9/74; CI/146/1991; CI/142/1993; *R v Canterbury CC ex parte Goodman*, 11 July 1995, unreported (QBD); CFC/39/1993
173 R(U) 5/56; R(S) 5/56
174 CI/37/1995
175 R(P) 2/85
176 R(S) 10/59; R(SB) 17/83
177 R(G) 1/75
178 Reg 90 HB Regs; reg 71 HB(SPC) Regs; reg 10 HB&CTB(DA) Regs

179 Reg 90(2) HB Regs; reg 71(2) HB(SPC) Regs; reg 10 HB&CTB(DA) Regs
180 Reg 3 HB&CTB(DA)Regs
181 CH/180/2006
182 **HB** Reg 90 and Sch 9 HB Regs; reg 71 and Sch 8 HB(SPC) Regs
CTB Reg 76 and Sch 8 CTB Regs; reg 61 and Sch 7 CTB(SPC) Regs
183 Reg 10(1) HB&CTB(DA) Regs
184 **HB** Sch 9 paras 9-15 HB Regs; Sch 8 paras 9-15 HB(SPC) Regs
CTB Sch 8 paras 9-16 CTB Regs; Sch 7 paras 9-16 CTB(SPC) Regs
185 Sch 9 paras 11 and 12HB Regs; Sch 8 paras 11 and 12 HB(SPC) Regs

7. **Getting paid**
186 Reg 75 HB Regs; reg 56 HB(SPC) Regs
187 Reg 76 HB Regs; Reg 57 HB(SPC) Regs; R(H) 7/07
188 **HB** Reg 2(1) HB Regs; reg 2(1) HB(SPC) Regs
CTB Reg 2(1) CTB Regs; reg 2(1) CTB(SPC) Regs
189 Reg 80(2), (4)(a), (5) and (9) HB Regs, and reg 80(2), (3)(a), (4) and (8) HB Regs as substituted by reg 16 HB(LHA)A Regs; reg 61(2), (4)(a), (5) and (9) HB(SPC) Regs, and reg 61(2), (3)(a), (4) and (8) HB(SPC) Regs as substituted by reg 16 HB(SPC)(LHA)A Regs
190 **HB** Regs 77 and 78 HB Regs; reg 58 HB(SPC) Regs
CTB Regs 65 and 66 CTB Regs; reg 49 CTB(SPC) Regs
191 CH/3736/2006
192 **HB** Reg 54(3)-(5) HB(SPC) Regs
CTB reg 45(3)-(5) CTB(SPC) Regs
193 **HB** Reg 54(1) and (2) HB(SPC) Regs
CTB Reg 45(1) and (2) CTB(SPC) Regs
194 **HB** Reg 54(6) HB(SPC) Regs
CTB Reg 45(6) CTB(SPC) Regs
195 **HB** Regs 5 and 72 and Sch 7 para 1 HB Regs
CTB Regs 5 and 60 and Sch 6 para 1 CTB Regs
196 **HB** Reg 73 HB Regs; reg 53 HB(SPC) Regs
CTB Reg 61 CTB Regs; reg 44 CTB(SPC) Regs
197 **HB** Reg 2(1), definition of 'appropriate DWP office', and Schs 7 para 2 and 8 para 1 HB Regs; reg 2(1), definition of 'appropriate DWP office', and Sch 7 para 1 HB(SPC) Regs
CTB Reg 2(1), definition of 'appropriate DWP office', and Schs 6 para 2 and 7 para 1 CTB Regs; reg 2(1), definition of 'appropriate DWP office', and Sch 5 para 1 CTB(SPC) Regs
198 **HB** Regs 72(1)(b) and 73(1)(b) HB Regs; reg 53(1)(b) HB(SPC) Regs
CTB Regs 60(1)(b) and 61(1)(b) CTB Regs; reg 44(1)(b) CTB(SPC) Regs
Both CH/1762/2004
199 Schs 7 para 3 and 8 para 2 HB Regs and Schs 7 para 3 and 8 para 2 HB Regs as amended by reg 19 HB(LHA&IS)A Regs; Sch 7 para 2 HB(SPC) Regs and Sch 7 para 2 HB(SPC) Regs as amended by reg 19 HB(SPC)(LHA&IS)A Regs
200 Regs 72(6)and (8) and 73(6) and (7) and Schs 7 para 3(5) and 8 para 2(5) HB Regs; reg 53(6) and (7) and Sch 7 para 2(5) HB(SPC) Regs
201 Schs 7 paras 5-8 and 8 paras 4-6 HB Regs; Sch 7 paras 4-6 HB(SPC) Regs
202 Schs 7 para 7(b) and 8 para 6(b) HB Regs; Sch 7 para 6(b) HB(SPC) Regs
203 Sch 8 para 6(b)(ii) HB Regs; Sch 7 para 6(b)(ii) HB(SPC) Regs
204 Schs 7 para 9 and 8 para 8 HB Regs; Sch 7 para 8 HB(SPC) Regs
205 **HB** Regs 72(2) and 73(2) HB Regs; reg 53(2) HB(SPC) Regs
CTB Regs 60(2) and 61(2) CTB Regs; reg 44(2) CTB(SPC) Regs
206 CH/5553/2002
207 **HB** Regs 72(6) and (8) and 73(6) and (7) HB Regs; reg 53(6) and (7) HB(SPC) Regs
CTB Regs 60(6) and 61(6) CTB Regs; reg 44(6) CTB(SPC) Regs
208 **HB** Schs 7 para 10 and 8 para 9 HB Regs; Sch 7 para 9 HB(SPC) Regs
CTB Schs 6 para 6 and 7 para 6 CTB Regs; Sch 5 para 6 CTB(SPC) Regs
209 **HB** Reg 89(3) HB Regs; reg 70(3) HB(SPC) Regs
CTB Reg 75(3) CTB Regs; reg 60(3) CTB(SPC) Regs
210 s134(1A) SSAA 1992
211 s134(1B) SSAA 1992; regs 91A and 94(1) HB Regs; regs 72A and 75(1) HB(SPC) Regs
212 Reg 91(1)(b) HB Regs; reg 72(1)(b) HB(SPC) Regs
213 para A6/6.120 GM

214 **HB** Reg 94(2) HB Regs; reg 75(2) HB(SPC) Regs
CTB Reg 78(2) CTB Regs; reg 63(2) CTB(SPC) Regs
215 Reg 94(3) HB Regs; reg 75(3) HB(SPC) Regs
216 **HB** Reg 97 HB Regs; reg 78 HB(SPC) Regs
CTB Reg 80 CTB Regs; reg 65 CTB(SPC) Regs
217 *R v Haringey LBC ex parte Azad Ayub* [1992] 25 HLR 566 (QBD)
218 R(H) 1/08
219 Reg 96(2) HB Regs; reg 77(2) HB(SPC) Regs
220 *R v Haringey LBC ex parte Azad Ayub* [1992] 25 HLR 566 (QBD)
221 Reg 95(1)(a) HB Regs; reg 76(1)(a) HB(SPC) Regs; Sch 9 SS(C&P) Regs
222 Reg 95(1)(b) HB Regs; reg 76(1)(b) HB(SPC) Regs
223 Reg 95(2A) HB Regs; reg 76(2A) HB(SPC) Regs
224 Reg 96(1)(a) and (b) and (3A)(a) HB Regs; reg 77(1)(a) and (b) and (3A)(a) HB(SPC) Regs
225 Reg 96(3A)(b) HB Regs; reg 77(3A)(b) HB(SPC) Regs
226 Reg 95(2A) HB Regs; reg 76(2A) HB(SPC) Regs
227 Regs 95(2A) and 96(1)(c) HB Regs; regs 76(2A) and 77(1)(c) HB(SPC) Regs
228 s126A SSAA 1992; regs 118 and 119 HB Regs; regs 99 and 100 HB(SPC) Regs
229 Reg 120 HB Regs; reg 101 HB(SPC) Regs
230 Regs 95(3)and 96(3) HB Regs; regs 76(3) and 77(3) HB(SPC) Regs
231 Reg 96(3) HB Regs and reg 96(3) HB Regs as amended by reg 17 HB(LHA&IS)A Regs; reg 77(3) HB(SPC) Regs and reg 77(3) HB(SPC) Regs as amended by reg 17 HB(SPC)(LHA&IS)A Regs
232 para A6/6.211 GM
233 Reg 92(1) and (6) HB Regs; reg 73(1) and (6) HB(SPC) Regs
234 Reg 92(3) and (4) HB Regs; reg 73(3) and (4) HB(SPC) Regs
235 Reg 91(2) HB Regs; reg 72(2) HB(SPC) Regs
236 Reg 92(5) HB Regs; reg 73(5) HB(SPC) Regs
237 Reg 92(6) HB Regs; reg 73(6) HB(SPC) Regs
238 **HB** Regs 89(2), 90(1) and 91(3) HB Regs; regs 70(2), 71(1) and 72(3) HB(SPC) Regs
CTB Regs 75(2), 76(1)(a) and 77(3)(b) and (c) CTB Regs; regs 60(2), 61(2)(a) and 62(3)(b) and (c) CTB(SPC) Regs
239 Reg 93(1) HB Regs; reg 74(1) HB(SPC) Regs
240 *R v Haringey LBC ex parte Azad Ayub* [1992] 25 HLR 566 (QBD)
241 paras A6/6.158 GM
242 Reg 93(1) HB Regs; reg 74(1) HB(SPC) Regs; *R v Haringey LBC ex parte Azad Ayub* [1992] 25 HLR 566 (QBD)
243 Reg 93(2) HB Regs; reg 74(2) HB(SPC) Regs
244 Reg 93(3) HB Regs; reg 74(3) HB(SPC) Regs
245 Reg 88(1) HB Regs; reg 69(1) HB(SPC) Regs; reg 4 SS(NCC) Regs
246 Reg 88A and Sch 11 HB Regs; reg 69A and Sch 10 HB(SPC) Regs
247 **HB** Sch 9 paras 9(1)(g) and 10(a) HB Regs; Sch 8 paras 9(1)(g) and 10(a) HB(SPC) Regs
CTB Sch 8 paras 9(1)(e), 10(a), 13 (f) and 15 CTB Regs; Sch 7 paras 9(1)(e), 10(a), 13(f) and 15 CTB(SPC) Regs
248 **HB** Regs 2(1), 86(3) and 88(1) HB Regs; regs 2(1), 67(3) and 69(1) HB(SPC) Regs
CTB Regs 2(1), 72(3) and 74(1) CTB Regs; regs 2(1), 57(3) and 59(1) CTB(SPC) Regs
249 **HB** Reg 88(1) HB Regs; reg 69(1) HB(SPC) Regs
CTB Reg 74(1) CTB Regs; reg 59(1) CTB(SPC) Regs
250 **HB** Reg 88(1), (3)(a) and (d) and (4) HB Regs; reg 69(1) and (4)(a) HB(SPC) Regs
CTB Reg 74(1), (3)(d), (4) and (5) CTB Regs; reg 59(1), (4) and (5) CTB(SPC) Regs
251 **HB** Reg 69(6) HB(SPC) Regs
CTB Reg 59(7) CTB(SPC) Regs
252 **HB** Reg 69(7) HB(SPC) Regs
CTB Reg 59(8) CTB(SPC) Regs
253 **HB** Reg 69(8) HB(SPC) Regs
CTB Reg 59(9) CTB(SPC) Regs
254 **HB** Regs 86(3) and 90 and Sch 9 HB Regs; regs 67(3) and 71 and Sch 8 HB(SPC) Regs
CTB Regs 72(3) and 76 and Sch 8 CTB Regs; regs 57(3) and 61 and Sch 7 CTB(SPC) Regs
255 **HB** Reg 88(1) HB Regs; reg 69(1) HB(SPC) Regs
CTB Reg 74(1) CTB Regs; reg 59(1) CTB(SPC) Regs

256 **HB** Reg 88(3) HB Regs; reg 69(3) HB(SPC) Regs
CTB Reg 74(3) CTB Regs; reg 59(3) CTB(SPC) Regs
257 **HB** Reg 88(4) HB Regs; reg 69(4) HB(SPC) Regs
CTB Reg 74(4) CTB Regs; reg 59(4) CTB(SPC) Regs
258 **HB** Reg 79 HB Regs; reg 59 HB(SPC) Regs
CTB Reg 67 CTB Regs; reg 50 CTB(SPC) Regs
Both Reg 8 HB&CTB(DA) Regs
259 **HB** Reg 79(1) HB Regs and reg 79(1) HB Regs, as amended by reg 15 HB(LHA&IS)A Regs; reg 59(1) HB(SPC) Regs and reg 59(1) HB(SPC) Regs, as amended by reg 15 HB(SPC)(LHA&IS)A Regs
CTB Reg 67(1) CTB Regs; reg 50(1) CTB(SPC) Regs
260 **HB** Reg 79(1) HB Regs and reg 79(1) HB Regs, as amended by reg 15 HB(LHA&IS)A Regs; reg 59(1) HB(SPC) Regs and reg 59(1) HB(SPC) Regs, as amended by reg 15 HB(SPC)(LHA&IS)A Regs
CTB Reg 67(1) CTB Regs; reg 50(1) CTB(SPC) Regs
Both Reg 8(2) HB&CTB(DA) Regs
261 Reg 79(8) HB Regs; reg 59(8) HB(SPC) Regs
262 Reg 8(3) HB&CTB(DA) Regs
263 **HB** Reg 79(6) and (7) HB Regs; reg 59 (6) and (7) HB(SPC) Regs
CTB Reg 67(8) and (9) CTB Regs; reg 50(8) and (9) CTB(SPC) Regs
264 **HB** Reg 59(10)-(13) HB(SPC) Regs
CTB Reg 50(10)-(13) CTB(SPC) Regs
265 Reg 79(2) and (8) HB Regs; reg 59(2) and (8) HB(SPC) Regs
266 Reg 79(2A), (2B), (8) and (9) HB Regs; reg 59(2A), (2B), (8) and (9) HB(SPC) Regs
267 **HB** Reg 60 HB(SPC) Regs
CTB Reg 51 CTB(SPC) Regs
268 Reg 79(4) and (8) HB Regs; reg 59(4) and (8) HB(SPC) Regs
269 s130B SSCBA 1992; The Housing Benefit (Loss of Benefit) (Pilot Scheme) Regulations 2007 No.2202; The Housing Benefit (Loss of Benefit) (Pilot Scheme) (Supplementary) Regulations 2007 No.2474

10. **Discretionary housing payments**
270 s69 CSPSSA 2000; reg 2(1) DFA Regs
271 Reg 2(2) DFA Regs
272 Reg 3 DFA Regs
273 Reg 5 DFA Regs
274 Reg 4 DFA Regs
275 Reg 6 DFA Regs
276 Reg 6(1)(a) DFA Regs
277 Reg 7 DFA Regs
278 Reg 6(3) DFA Regs
279 Reg 6(2) DFA Regs
280 Reg 8 DFA Regs
281 Reg 6(3) DFA Regs
282 **IS** Schs 9 para 71 and 10 para 7(1)(d) IS Regs
JSA Schs 7 para 71 and 8 para 12(1)(d) JSA Regs
HB Schs 5 para 62 and 6 para 9(1)(d) HB Regs
CTB Schs 4 para 62 and 5 para 9(1)(d) CTB Regs
TCReg 7 Table 3 para 9 TC(DCI) Regs

Chapter 11

Housing benefit rent restrictions

This chapter covers:

The rent used to calculate your housing benefit (HB) may be restricted if you are a private tenant or the tenant of a registered social landlord (a housing association). The rules described in this chapter do not apply if you are the tenant of the local authority who pays you HB.

There are three sets of rent restriction rules:

- the local housing allowance rules;
- the local reference rent rules; *and*
- the pre-January 1996 rules.

If rent restriction rules apply to you, the local authority uses these to work out the amount of rent to use to calculate your HB. Your HB is calculated using this figure, *not* the rent that you are supposed to pay, and there could be a shortfall. You might be able to get discretionary housing payments to help with this (see p222).

The amount of HB that is payable (whether rent restriction rules apply or not) depends on your applicable amount, income and capital, and on your 'maximum HB'. Your maximum HB is your weekly 'eligible rent' minus deductions for any non-dependants. If rent restriction rules apply, your eligible rent is usually your maximum rent (see pp238, 247 and 253). For full details of the calculation, see Chapter 10.

1. Which rent restriction rules apply

The local housing allowance rules, piloted in 18 Pathfinder areas from 2003, are being introduced nationwide from 7 April 2008. The Government's intention is that if your housing benefit (HB) was being restricted under any of the rules that applied before 7 April 2008, it will continue to be restricted under those rules until there is a break in your claim or you move to a new home (see pp241, 242 and 249). If rent restriction rules still apply to you, your HB will be restricted under the rules that are then applicable. If you are considering a move, or there will be a break in your HB claim, you should check whether the rules that will apply to you are more or less favourable than before. In some cases, you can apply to the local authority to find out the rent figure that will be used to calculate your HB (see p254).

If you make a **new claim for HB on or after 7 April 2008** (or you have a current claim and **move on or after 7 April 2008**) and you are not a tenant of the local authority who pays you HB (eg, you are a private or housing association tenant), the following applies.

- The rent restriction rules do *not* apply if you have an 'excluded tenancy' (see p235).
- The pre-January 1996 rules apply if you live in 'exempt accommodation' (see p249) or you are an 'exempt claimant' (see p249).
- The local reference rent rules apply (see p242) if you live in a hostel, houseboat, mobile home or caravan or your rent includes board and attendance. They *may* apply if your landlord is a registered social landlord (a housing association) or your tenancy is a former local authority or new town letting which has been transferred to a new owner.
- In all other cases, the local housing allowance rules apply (see p235).

Discretion to decrease eligible rent

Whether or not any of the rent restriction rules apply to you, the local authority has discretion to decrease your eligible rent to an amount it considers 'appropriate'.[1] It should have evidence which justifies it doing so and must exercise its discretion properly. All the circumstances should be taken into account, including your health and financial circumstances,[2] the special housing-related needs of anyone occupying your home and whether alternative accommodation is available to HB claimants.[3] Local authorities should rarely use their powers to decrease your HB in this way. If your HB is reduced under this rule you should ask for a revision or appeal (see Chapters 41 and 42).

2. Excluded tenancies

If you have an excluded tenancy, the rent restriction rules do not apply to you. The following are 'excluded tenancies':[4]

- a regulated or protected tenancy (ie, a tenancy entered into before 15 January 1989 or, in Scotland, 2 January 1989);
- a tenancy in an approved bail hostel or probation hostel. In any case, if you are required to live in such a hostel, you cannot claim HB towards the rent you pay to the hostel (see p184);
- a housing action trust tenancy;
- a former local authority or new town letting which has been transferred to a new owner, unless there has been a rent increase since the transfer; *and*
  - the local authority considers your rent to be unreasonably high; *or*
  - if the transfer took place before 7 October 2002 only, the local authority considers your accommodation to be unreasonably large.

  If this is the case, the local reference rent rules apply (see p242);
- a registered housing association letting, unless the local authority considers your accommodation to be unreasonably large or your rent unreasonably high. If it does, the local reference rent rules apply (see p242);
- a shared ownership tenancy, unless this is with a private landlord, in which case the local housing allowance rules may apply.

3. The local housing allowance rules

The local housing allowance rules apply to most private tenants. They apply (unless you have an 'excluded tenancy' or the local reference rent or the pre-January 1996 rules apply) if, on or after 7 April 2008, you:[5]

- claim housing benefit (HB); *or*
- move to a new home while you are entitled to HB; *or*
- live in a former Pathfinder area and the pilot local housing allowance rules applied to you before that date. However, you may have transitional protection (see p241).

Note: if you were claiming HB before 7 April 2008 and your rent was restricted under any of the rules that then applied, these can continue to apply instead of the local housing allowance rules until you move to a new home, or there is a break in your HB claim (see pp242, 249 and p241).

The local housing allowance rules can apply if you have a shared ownership tenancy and this is with a private landlord.

Which local housing allowance is appropriate?

The local housing allowance that is appropriate for you depends on the area where you live and the category of dwelling that applies to you. Local housing allowances for each category of dwelling are set by the rent officer and are based on the median of local market rents for assured tenancies in a 'broad rental market area'.[6] Local housing allowances are set by the rent officer monthly and are made public.[7]

'Broad rental market area'[8]

A 'broad rental market area' is two or more distinct areas of residential accommodation. Each must adjoin at least one of the others. In addition, it must be an area where you could reasonably be expected to live where there are a variety of kinds of residential accommodation and types of tenancy, and taking into account the facilities and services for health, education, recreation, banking and shopping, and the travel distance by public and private transport.

Categories of dwelling

The category of dwelling that applies to you depends on how many bedrooms you are allowed under the size criteria, and whether you are in shared accommodation.

Under the **size criteria**, you are allowed one bedroom for each of the following occupiers (each coming only into the first category for which s/he is eligible):[9]

- a couple (see p702);
- a person who is not a child (ie, someone aged 16 or over);
- two children of the same sex;
- two children under 10;
- a child.

'Occupiers' means you and anyone else living in the dwelling (other than a joint tenant who is not a member of your household).[10] This can include people who are not part of your family for benefit purposes (eg, your non-dependants). However, if you share the care of a child, the child is considered to be occupying the home of the parent with whom s/he normally lives.[11]

The rent officer sets a local housing allowance for one-bedroom shared accommodation, one-bedroom self-contained accommodation and for dwellings where the tenant has the use of only two, three, four and five bedrooms.[12] The local authority must ask the rent officer to set a local housing allowance for larger dwellings if this is needed.[13]

Example

Bill and Sarah have two sons and one daughter, all under age 10. Sarah's nephew, aged 20, lives with them. They are allowed four bedrooms: one for Bill and Sarah, one for their sons, one for their daughter and one for Sarah's nephew. The appropriate local housing allowance is that for a dwellling with four bedrooms.

One-bedroom shared accommodation

The local housing allowance for one-bedroom shared accommodation (the local authority may call this 'Category A') is appropriate if:[14]

- you are a single claimant under 25 (a 'young individual') and you do not have a non-dependant living with you (see p196). This applies even if you do not live in shared accommodation. See below for exceptions; *or*
- you (and your partner) are only allowed one bedroom under the size criteria (ie, you are a single claimant or a member of a couple without children, and you do not have a non-dependant living with you). This only applies if you live in shared accommodation – ie, you do not have the exclusive use of at least two rooms, or the exclusive use of at least one room, a bathroom and a toilet and a kitchen or facilities for cooking. See below for exceptions.

However, the local housing allowance for one-bedroom self-contained accommodation (see below) is instead appropriate (even if you live in shared accommodation) if you (or your partner):

- qualify for a severe disability premium as part of your applicable amount (see p784); *or*
- are under the age of 22 and were in the care of, or under the supervision of, a local authority under specific legal provisions after you turned 16 or were provided with accommodation by the local authority under s20 Children Act 1989.[15]

One-bedroom self-contained accommodation

The local housing allowance for one-bedroom self-contained accommodation (the local authority may call this 'Category B') is appropriate if you are allowed one bedroom under the size criteria (ie, you are a single claimant or are a member of a couple without children and you do not have a non-dependant living with you). You must be renting accommodation where you have:[16]

- the exclusive use of at least two rooms; *or*
- the exclusive use of one room as well as the exclusive use of a bathroom and a toilet, a kitchen or facilities for cooking.

'Room' means a bedroom or a 'room suitable for living in' (other than one you share with someone who is not a member of your household, a non-dependant or someone who pays rent to you or your partner).

Note: if you are a single claimant under 25 who does not qualify for a severe disability premium and is not under 22 and formerly in care (see above), the local housing allowance for one-bedroom shared accommodation is instead appropriate, even if you do not live in shared accommodation.

Dwellings with two or more bedrooms

Unless the local housing allowance for one-bedroom shared or one-bedroom self-contained accommodation is appropriate, the appropriate local housing allowance is the one for the category of dwelling with the number of bedrooms you are allowed under the size criteria (see p236).[17] So this category applies – eg, if you are a lone parent or a member of a couple with children, or if you have a non-dependant living with you.

Maximum rent

Your 'maximum rent' for HB purposes is the appropriate local housing allowance for you, or if lower, your 'cap rent' plus £15.[18] The local authority might call this your 'maximum rent (LHA)'. The 'eligible rent' used to calculate your HB (see p192) is your 'maximum rent'.[19]

Your **'cap rent'** is the rent you are liable, or treated as liable, to pay for your home.[20] If you share accommodation with others who are not members of your family for HB purposes and you are jointly liable for the rent with them, the local authority apportions the 'cap rent' between you.

Example

Phil, aged 28, shares a private-rented house with four friends. Phil claims HB. The rent is £300 a week. His 'cap rent' is £60 (£300 divided by 5).

The local authority has general powers to decrease your 'cap rent' to an amount it considers appropriate (see p234 – the rules are the same as for 'eligible rent').

Example

Hannah, aged 28, is a joint tenant of a private flat with three friends. The rent for the flat is is £200 a week. Hannah works part time and earns £100 a week after deductions of tax and national insurance contributions. Hannah claims HB.

The local housing allowance appropriate for Hannah is that for one-bedroom shared accommodation (£75). Hannah's 'cap rent' is £50 (£200 divided by 4). Her 'maximum rent' (and her 'eligible rent') is, therefore, £65 (£50 + £5) because this is lower than the local housing allowance.

Hannah has no non-dependants. Therefore, her 'maximum HB' (see p189) is £65.

Her applicable amount is £60.50 (the standard amount for a single person 25 or over).

Her income to be taken into account is £95 a week (£5 of her earnings are disregarded – see p854).

The difference between her income and her applicable amount is, therefore, £34.50 a week.

65% x £34.50 = £22.42 a week.

Hannah's HB is therefore £65 – £22.42 = £42.58 a week.

Your 'maximum rent' is based on the local housing allowance that is appropriate when your claim is assessed. Your HB is paid on this basis until the next time the local authority assesses your claim (usually annually), even if the allowance or your rent changes.[21] When the local authority reassesses your claim it uses the local housing allowance that is then appropriate. Some changes of circumstance can lead to an earlier re-assessment – eg, if:[22]

- there is a change in the category of dwelling that applies to you (see p236) – ie, you are allowed more or fewer bedrooms; *or*
- a member of your family (or a relative of you or your partner who lives in the same accommodation as you without a separate right to do so) dies; *or*
- you move to a new home.

Your 'maximum rent' is then based on the local housing allowance that is appropriate for you on the date of the change.[23] However, if a member of your family (or a relative) has died, any *decrease* can be delayed for a period (see p240).

Example

Cleo rents a three-bedroom house from a private landlord. She pays £170 a week rent. She lives there with her son, aged 18, who is doing his A levels. The appropriate local housing allowance is that for two-bedroom accommodation. When she claims income support (IS) and HB on 12 April 2008 the local housing allowance for two-bedroom accommodation is £105 and for three-bedroom accommodation is £155. Cleo's maximum rent (and eligible rent) is the local housing allowance for two-bedroom accommodation. Cleo has no non-dependants, so her maximum HB, and therefore her HB, is £105 a week.

Cleo's Aunt Sue comes to live with her on 20 July 2008. As there has been a change in the category of dwelling that applies to Cleo (this is now for three-bedroom accommodation), the local authority reassesses her claim. The local housing allowance for three-bedroom accommodation has increased to £158. Cleo's maximum rent (and eligible rent) is £158. Aunt Sue in on incapacity benefit so a non-dependant deduction of £7.40 must be made. Cleo's maximum HB and, therefore, her HB is £150.60 a week (£158 – £7.40).

Notes:

- If the rent you pay is lower than your maximum rent (and, therefore, your HB is higher than your rent) you can keep the difference. The extra HB does not affect your other benefits.
- If you live in a former Pathfinder area you may have transitional protection (see p241).

- If you are considering renting accommodation to which the local housing allowance rules apply and and no local housing allowance has been set for the size of property you need, you can ask the local authority to apply for one (see p254).

Delay before a rent restriction is applied

A rent restriction can be delayed if:

- a member of your family (or a relative of you or your partner who lived in the same accommodation as you without a separate right to do so) dies and you still live there (temporary absences of up to 13 weeks are allowed). In this case, unless your eligible rent for HB purposes under the normal local housing allowance rule is the same or higher:[24]
  - no restriction is made for 12 months from the date of death if no eligible rent applied at the time of death (ie, you were not yet claiming HB). Your eligible rent is your contractual rent, minus any ineligible charges (see p193). If you are in shared accommodation, this can be apportioned between you and the people with whom you share. It only covers the rent you pay for residential accommodation; *or*
  - any eligible rent which applied on the day before the death continues to apply for 12 months from the date of death.
- you, or a member of your family (or a relative of you or your partner who lives in the same dwelling as you without a separate right to do so) could meet the costs of the dwelling when you took them on (this could include other bills as well as the rent). No restriction is made for 13 weeks provided neither you nor your partner received HB in the 52 weeks before your current award of HB.[25] Your eligible rent is your contractual rent, minus ineligible charges (see p193). If you are in shared accommodation, this can be apportioned between you and the people with whom you share. It only covers the rent you pay for residential accommodation.

Note: your eligible rent can change before the end of the 12-month/13-week period if your eligible rent as calculated under the normal local housing allowance rules is now the same or higher, or you move to a new home or another member of your family (or relative) dies.[26]

Relative

For these purposes, 'relative' means a close relative (see p182) or a grandparent, grandchild, uncle, aunt, nephew or niece.[27]

Example

Mr and Mrs Connor and their four-year-old son live in a three-bedroom flat. They pay rent of £170 a week. Until her recent death, Mr Connor's mother lived with them. Mr Connor's maximum rent (and hence his eligible rent) was being restricted to the local housing allowance for a three-bedroom property (£150).

When he notifies the local authority of the death of his mother, his new maximum rent (and eligible rent) is the local housing allowance for a two-bedroom property (£105). However, the decrease is delayed for 12 months.

Mr Connor is getting income support. Before his mother's death his HB was £142.60 a week (£150 minus a non-dependant deduction of £7.40).

For 12 months from his mother's date of death, his HB is £150 a week.

Note: if you live in a former Pathfinder area, different rules apply where a member of your family or a relative has died and where you or a member of the family/ relative could meet the costs of the dwelling when you took them on (see below).[28]

Challenging a rent restriction

You cannot appeal against the amount of the local housing allowance. However, you can appeal against local authority decisions made in connection with the local housing allowance – eg, whether you are a 'young individual' or whether someone occupies accommodation with you.

Transitional rules

The local housing allowance rules were piloted in 18 Pathfinder areas from late 2003 until 7 April 2008. The pilot rules were more generous than the current rules. If you live in a former Pathfinder area you may have transitional protection if, before 7 April 2008:[29]

- your HB was calculated on the basis of the local housing allowance; *or*
- a rent restriction was delayed because of the death of a member of your family (or a relative); *or*
- a rent restriction was delayed for 13 weeks because you or a member of your family (or a relative) could meet the costs of your dwelling when you took them on.

If you have transitional protection and a member of your family (or a relative of yours or your partner's who lives in the same accommodation as you without a separate right to do so) dies before 7 April 2009, a consequent rent restriction can also be delayed.[30] Transitional protection can continue after 7 April 2009.[31]

Former Pathfinder areas[32]

Argyll and Bute; Blackpool; Brighton and Hove; Conwy; Coventry; East Riding of Yorkshire; Edinburgh; Guildford; Leeds; London Borough of Lewisham; Northeast Lincolnshire; Norwich; Pembrokeshore; Salford; South Norfolk; St Helens; Teignbridge; Wandsworth

4. The local reference rent rules

Unless you have an 'excluded tenancy' (see p235) or the pre-January 1996 rules apply (see p249), the local reference rent rules apply to you if, on or after 7 April 2008, you claim housing benefit (HB) or move to a new home while you are entitled to HB and:[33]

- your landlord is a registered social landlord (ie, a registered housing association). However,this only applies if the local authority considers your accommodation to be unreasonably large or your rent unreasonably high. Otherwise, you have an 'excluded tenancy' (see p235); *or*
- your tenancy was a local authority or new town letting, but it has been transferred to a new owner. However, this only applies if there has been a rent increase since the transfer; *and*
  - the local authority considers your rent to be unreasonably high; *or*
  - if the transfer took place before 7 October 2002, the local authority considers your accommodation to be unreasonably large.

  Otherwise, you have an 'excluded tenancy (see p235); *or*
- you live in a hostel, a houseboat, a mobile home or a caravan; *or*
- your rent includes board and attendance.

These rules can also apply to other private tenants, but only if you were entitled to HB immediately before 7 April 2008 under the local reference rent rules that then applied. See below for further information.

If you were getting housing benefit before 7 April 2008

Even if you are not someone to whom the current local reference rent rules apply (eg, you rent a private house or flat), if you were entitled to HB immediately before 7 April 2008 and the local reference rent rules applied to you, they continue to do so until you make a new claim for HB (ie, after a break in your claim) or you move to a new home.[34] If rent restriction rules still apply to you, your HB will be restricted under the rules that are then applicable. See CPAG's *Welfare Benefits and Tax Credits Handbook* 2007/08 for details of the old rules.

The local reference rent rules continue to apply to you, even following any of the changes of circumstance listed on p243, and then when the local authority has to apply to the rent officer for determinations every 52 weeks thereafter.[35]

However, if none of these changes have occurred (and you have not made a new claim for HB or moved) and the only reason the local authority has to apply to the rent officer for determinations is because it is more than 52 weeks since it last did so, you can argue that the rent restriction rules no longer apply to you and your eligible rent must be worked out under the normal rules (see p192).[36] **Note:** this is not the Government's intention and the local authority is likely to say that the local reference rent rules continue to apply to you in this situation.

Rent officer determinations

If the local reference rent rules apply, your 'maximum rent' (see p247) is based on rent officer determinations. The rent officer makes determinations about the rent for your home, comparing it with the rent for other private sector tenancies in the area. The determinations are significantly high rent, size-related rent and exceptionally high rent. The lowest of these is what is known as the 'claim-related rent' (see p245). The rent officer also makes determinations that indicate the average rents for specific types of accommodation in the locality: the local reference rent (see p245) and a single room rent (see p246).

Localities and neighbourhoods

A '**locality**' is two or more neighbourhoods, including the one where your home is. Each must adjoin at least one of the others. In addition, it must be an area where you could reasonably be expected to live (and where there are a variety of kinds of residential accommodation and types of tenancy) taking into account the facilities and services for health, education, recreation, banking and shopping in (or accessible to) the neighbourhood where your home is, and the travel distance by public and private transport.[37]

A '**neighbourhood**' is:[38]

- if you live in a town or city, the part of the town or city where your home is located which is a distinct area of residential accommodation; *or*
- if you do not live in a town or city, the area surrounding your home which is a distinct area of residential accommodation which includes homes of the same size as yours (or of a size you are allowed under the size criteria – see p244).

When the local authority must apply for determinations

The local authority must apply to the rent officer and ask her/him to make determinations if:[39]

- you make a new claim for HB or move to a new home while you are entitled to HB, but only if the local reference rent rules apply (see p242);
- a previous reference to the rent officer was made in respect of your claim more than 52 weeks ago (but see p242); *or*
- there has been one of the following changes of circumstances since a rent officer determination:[40]
  - the number of occupiers has changed (except in a hostel);
  - there has been a substantial change in the condition of the dwelling or the terms of the tenancy (other than a rent increase);
  - there has been an increase in the rent under a term of the tenancy, unless the previous determination was a significantly high, size-related or exceptionally high rent determination (see p244);[41]

 - a size-related rent determination (see p244) was made and there has since been a change in the composition of the household, or a child living with you has reached the age of 10 or 16; *or*
- your HB was being restricted under the local housing allowance rules, but these no longer apply – eg, if the home you rent was sold to a housing association and the local reference rent rules apply instead.

The local authority *cannot* apply to the rent officer for determinations if:

- a rent officer determination has been made for the same tenancy (or a tenancy in the same dwelling) on substantially the same terms within the last 52 weeks.[42] This means that a determination made for a previous tenant may be valid for your HB claim. A new referral *is* needed if you are a young individual and no single room rent determination has yet been made (see p246);
- you live in a hostel and a rent officer determination has been made for similar accommodation in the hostel, sleeping the same number of people as yours, within the last 12 months and there has been no change of circumstances in respect of that accommodation.[43]

Significantly high and exceptionally high rent determinations

If your rent is significantly higher than that paid for similar tenancies and dwellings in the vicinity, the rent officer determines an amount your landlord might reasonably be paid for your tenancy (a '**significantly high rent determination**').[44] For these purposes, a '**vicinity**' is the immediate area around your home.

If the rent officer considers the 'rent payable' for your home to be exceptionally high, s/he determines the highest amount your landlord might reasonably be paid for an assured tenancy in the neighbourhood (see p243) which is the same size as your home (or the size you are allowed under the size criteria) – an '**exceptionally high rent determination**'.[45]

'Rent payable' means:

- the size-related rent determination; *or*
- if there is no such determination, the significantly high rent determination; *or*
- in any other case, the rent you are supposed to pay.

Size-related rent determination

If your accommodation is larger than you are allowed under the 'size criteria', the rent officer determines an amount your landlord might reasonably be paid for a similar tenancy in the vicinity of an appropriate size for you.[46] For these purposes, '**vicinity**' means the immediate area around your home, or where there is no dwelling in that area of a size you are allowed under the size criteria, the nearest area where there is one.[47]

Under the '**size criteria**', the rent officer (ignoring, for example, your kitchen, bathroom and toilet) allows you one bedroom, or room 'suitable for living in', for each of the following occupiers (each coming only into the first category for which s/he is eligible):[48]

- a couple (see p702);
- a person who is not a child (ie, someone aged 16 or over);
- two children of the same sex;
- two children under 10;
- a child.

In addition, you are allowed the following number of rooms 'suitable for living in':

Number of occupiers	*Number of rooms*
Less than 4	1
4 to 6	2
7 or more	3

A person counts as an 'occupier' if the local authority includes her/him on the form used to refer your tenancy to the rent officer.[49] This can include people who are not part of your family for benefit purposes (eg, your non-dependants). However, if you share the care of a child, the child is considered to be occupying the home of only one parent – the parent with whom the child normally lives.[50]

If any of the rooms in your home are not suitable for living in (eg, because of their size or lack of ventilation), you should argue that they should be ignored.

Example

Alice and Len have three children: two sons, 12 and 14, and a daughter, 17. They are allowed one room for themselves, one for their sons and one for their daughter – three bedrooms (or rooms 'suitable for living in') as well as two other rooms 'suitable for living in'. They are therefore allowed five rooms, as well as a kitchen, bathroom and toilet.

Note: if you are a single person under 25, the rent officer must also identify a single room rent. See p246 for further information.

Claim-related rent

The rent officer also identifies what is known as the claim-related rent. This is the lowest of the above determinations or, if no such determination was made, the rent you are supposed to pay.[51]

Local reference rent

The local reference rent is the midpoint of 'reasonable market rents' for assured tenancies in the locality (see p243) appropriate to the size of property that you are living in (or the size you are allowed under the size criteria – see p244).[52] It is only provided if your rent, or the lowest of the rent officer determinations (excluding the single room rent), exceeds it.

Single room rent

If you are a single claimant under the age of 25 (a 'young individual') in most cases, the rent officer identifies a single room rent.[53] Your 'maximum rent' (see p247) is based on this figure unless you have a non-dependant living with you (see p196), or you:[54]

- qualify for a severe disability premium as part of your applicable amount (see p784); *or*
- are a housing association tenant; *or*
- are under the age of 22 and:
  - were in the care of or under the supervision of a local authority under specific legal provisions after you turned 16; *or*
  - were provided with accommodation by the local authority under s20 Children Act 1989.

Even if your 'maximum rent' is not based on the single room rent, the other local reference rent rules described in this chapter can still apply.

The **single room rent** is the midpoint of 'reasonable market rents' for accommodation in the locality (see p243), in which the tenant has exclusive use of one bedroom only and other than that only shares a living room, kitchen, a toilet and bathroom and makes no payment for board and attendance.[55]

Service charges in rent officer determinations

The local authority notifies the rent officer of the amount of rent you are supposed to pay, whether this includes service charges and the amount of the charges that can and cannot be met by HB (see p193).[56] The claim-related rent (see p245) does not include ineligible charges unless you live in one-room accommodation and the landlord provides substantial board and attendance. In this case the claim-related rent and local reference rent (though not the single room rent) include charges for meals.[57]

Notification to the local authority

The rent officer notifies the local authority of the claim-related rent and, if lower, the local reference rent or single room rent.[58] This must be done within five working days of the local authority's request for determinations (25 days if the rent officer intends to visit the property) or as soon as is practicable after that.[59] If the rent officer needs further information, the five (or 25) days run from the date this is received.

Maximum rent

If the 'local reference rent' rules apply, your 'maximum rent' for HB purposes, and therefore your 'eligible rent' (see p192), is usually the lowest of these determinations, even if the rent you pay is higher.[60]

Your 'maximum rent' is:[61]

- the lowest of the claim-related rent, the local reference rent or, if you are a single person under 25 and it is relevant, the single room rent (see p246); *or*
- if you have been continuously entitled to, and in receipt of, HB for the same property since 5 October 1997 and you are 25 or over, the local reference rent (plus half the difference between the local reference rent and the claim-related rent).[62] If you or your partner are a 'welfare to work' beneficiary (see p666) breaks in your claim of up to 52 weeks are ignored.

Example

Jo and Louis are a couple who rent a three-bedroom mobile home with a living room and separate dining room. They pay rent of £120 a week. The rent officer decides that the accommodation is too big and that the rent is too high so makes significantly high and size-related rent determinations. He notifies the local authority of a claim-related rent of £90 and a local reference rent of £80. Jo and Louis's 'maximum rent' is £80 a week.

Once your 'maximum rent' is set, your HB is paid on the basis of this until the next time the local authority makes a reference to the rent officer about your claim (usually annually). However, if you negotiate with your landlord and s/he agrees a new rent which is lower than the maximum rent, your HB is re-calculated using your new rent.[63]

Note:

- If you are in shared accommodation, your 'maximum rent' can be apportioned between you and the people with whom you share. It only covers the rent you pay for residential accommodation.[64]
- A rent restriction can be delayed in some circumstances (see below).
- If you are considering renting accommodation to which the local reference rent rules apply and you are likely to claim HB, you can apply to the local authority for a pre-tenancy determination (see p254).

Delay before a rent restriction is applied

A rent restriction can be delayed in some circumstances.

- If a member of your family (or a relative of yours or your partner who lives in the same accommodation as you without a separate right to do so) dies and you still live there (temporary absences of up to 13 weeks are allowed). In this case:[65]

  - no restriction applies for 12 months from the date of death if no 'maximum rent' applied at the time of the death; *or*
  - any 'maximum rent' which applied at the time of death continues to do so for the 12 months from the date of death.
- If you, or a member of your family (or a relative of yours or your partner who lives in the same dwelling as you without a separate right to do so) could meet the costs of the dwelling when you took them on (this could include other bills as well as the rent), no restriction can be made for 13 weeks provided neither you nor your partner received HB in the 52 weeks before your current award of HB.[66]

For these purposes, **'relative'** means a close relative (see p182) or a grandparent, grandchild, uncle, aunt, nephew or niece.[67]

Challenging a rent restriction

You cannot appeal against the rent officer's determinations. However, the local authority *can* ask for them to be redetermined on your behalf.[68] You must apply to the local authority in writing no later than one month after the date you are notified of its decision on your HB claim. The local authority must then apply to the rent officer for a redetermination and pass any representations you make or evidence you supply to her/him within seven days. In practice, if you seek a revision or appeal against an HB decision and this relates in whole or in part to the rent officer's determinations, the local authority should apply for a redetermination.[69]

It is not easy to challenge rent officers, but it may be possible in some circumstances. If, for example, the rent officer has said your rent is significantly high, you may be able to get her/him to reconsider by providing evidence of similar tenancies where tenants who are not on HB are paying the same rent as you. The rent officer must get the advice of one or two other rent officers and notify the local authority of her/his decision within 20 working days.[70]

The rent officer's redetermination might reduce your maximum rent so you need to consider your position carefully before requesting a redetermination (or asking for a revision or an appeal). You could end up with less HB as a result. However, if the redetermination:[71]

- reduces your maximum rent (see p247), it only applies from the Monday after the date of redetermination, so you have not been overpaid;
- increases your maximum rent, it applies from the date of the original decision and you should be paid any HB arrears.

The local authority has the power to ask for a rent officer redetermination, even if you have not done so.[72] In this case, you can ask for a further redetermination. Otherwise, you are limited to one request for a rent officer determination.[73]

If the local authority discovers an error in the referral to the rent officer (eg, if it made a mistake about the number of occupiers) or if the rent officer discovers an error (other than in the application of professional judgement), the local authority must apply for a substitute determination.[74] If there has been a property-related error (eg, about the number of rooms or the provision of services or furniture) the rent officer can send a substitute determination automatically.[75]

You can seek a redetermination in either of these situations.

Note: you *can* appeal against local authority decisions made in connection with rent officer decisions – eg, whether you are a 'young individual'. If you are in doubt, you may want to appeal *and* ask for a redetermination.

5. The pre-January 1996 rules

Prior to January 1996 the the rent restriction rules were less harsh than the rules that replaced them. These pre-January 1996 rules apply if you live in 'exempt accommodation') or you are an 'exempt claimant'.

Exempt accommodation

The 'pre-January 1996' rules apply to you if you live in 'exempt accommodation'.[76] You live in 'exempt accommodation' if it is:[77]

- temporary accommodationfor people without a settled way of life, funded by the Resettlement Agency; *or*
- accommodation provided by a housing association, non-metropolitan county council, registered charity or voluntary organisation where that body, or a person acting on its behalf, also provides you with care, support or supervision.[78] The care and support must be more than a token or minimal amount.[79] **Note:** if the person (or body) providing the care, support or supervision has a contract with the local authority Supporting People team to provide these, but is not providing the accommodation, the decision maker is likely to say it is not exempt accommodation.[80]

Exempt claimants

The pre-January 1996 rules apply to you if you are an 'exempt claimant' – ie:[81]

- you have been continuously entitled to and in receipt of housing benefit (HB) since 1 January 1996; *and*
- you continue to occupy the same property as your home (except if you are forced to move because fire, flood or natural catastrophe makes it uninhabitable).

The rules suggest that breaks in your claim of up to four weeks are ignored (52 weeks if you or your partner are a 'welfare to work' beneficiary (see p666).

However, the DWP says it did not intend there to be a linking rule, and that a break in your claim of a week or more should mean that you are no longer an 'exempt claimant'.[82]

If you are thinking of making *any* changes to your claim, you should check whether this would mean you are no longer an 'exempt claimant' and therefore the local reference rent or the local housing allowance rules apply. You are definitely no longer an 'exempt claimant', for example, if you make a new claim for HB separated by more than four weeks (or 52 weeks) from a previous claim (but see above) or you move (including moving rooms within the same house).[83]

The rules suggest that an exemption can be transferred to you if you claim HB because:[84]

- an exempt claimant dies and you are a member of her/his family, or any relative (see p248) occupying the same accommodation without a separate right to do so. You must continue to occupy the same property and claim within four weeks of the death;
- your partner (who was exempt) has been detained in custody and is not entitled to HB under the temporary absence rules (see p185). You must continue to occupy the same property and claim within four weeks of the imprisonment;
- your former partner (who was exempt) has left the dwelling and you are no longer living together as husband and wife. This should also apply if you are no longer living together as civil partners. You must continue to occupy the same property and claim within four weeks of the date s/he left.

The exemption can only be transferred if either the exempt claimant was in receipt of HB at the time s/he died (or left the dwelling), or had become a 'welfare to work' beneficiary (see p666) within the previous 52 weeks.[85]

Note: the DWP says it did not intend to allow an exemption to be transferred.[86]

When your rent can be restricted

The local authority must restrict your 'eligible rent' if it decides your accommodation is unreasonably large or your rent is unreasonably high (see below).[87] If you are in a 'protected group' (see p252), this only applies if:[88]

- cheaper suitable alternative accommodation is available to you; *and*
- it is reasonable to expect you to move.

Note: a rent restriction can be delayed in some circumstances (see p253).

Is your accommodation unreasonably large?

Your accommodation can count as unreasonably large if it is larger than is reasonably needed for you and anyone who also occupies the accommodation (including non-dependants and sub-tenants), taking account of suitable alternative accommodation occupied by other households of the same size.[89] The important question is the size of home that you need, rather than the size of home that you want.[90]

The needs of everyone living in your accommodation, whether or not they are part of your family, must be considered. For example, you might need additional space because someone has a disability, or lives elsewhere but regularly comes to visit you.

Is your rent unreasonably high?

Your rent can count as too high if it is unreasonably high compared with that for suitable alternative accommodation elsewhere.[91] 'Rent' includes, among other things, any service charges or licence fees you have to pay.[92]

When deciding whether your rent is unreasonably high, the local authority may ask a rent officer to assess a reasonable rent for your property, but the figures are not binding. *It* (not the rent officer) must decide whether your rent is unreasonably high, using different criteria from that used by the rent officer.[93]

It is not enough for the local authority to argue that your rent is merely higher than that for suitable alternative accommodation; it must be unreasonably higher.[94] In making this comparison, the local authority must consider the full range of rents that could be paid for such accommodation and not just the cheapest.[95] If your rent is within the range[96] or just above it,[97] the local authority may find it difficult to justify finding your rent to be unreasonably high.

What is suitable alternative accommodation?

It is not sufficient for the local authority to show that cheaper or smaller alternative accommodation exists; it must also be **'suitable'** for the age and health of all the people that the local authority must take into account, having regard to the nature of the accommodation and the facilities available.[98] The local authority must consider these factors, even if you do not raise your housing needs yourself.[99]

The people that the local authority must consider are:[100]

- you;
- members of your family for HB purposes; *and*
- any relative (see p247) of you or your partner who lives in the same dwelling as you without a separate right to do so.

The local authority must compare your home with **'alternative accommodation'**.

- It cannot just compare homes with the same number of bedrooms; some effort must be made to establish what other facilities are available.[101]
- It must compare your home with other properties offering the same security of tenure. For example, if you have an assured tenancy, the local authority may not rely on comparisons with accommodation that is let on assured shorthold tenancies, or with council or housing association properties.[102]

- It does not have to exclude properties which you cannot take because the landlord wants a deposit that you cannot afford.[103] However, if you are in a 'protected group', you might be able to argue that the accommodation is not available to you (see below).
- It should not make comparisons with other parts of the country where accommodation costs differ widely from local ones, but it may compare your property with one in a less expensive area within a city.[104]

Are you in a protected group?

If the local authority decides that your rent, or the size of your accommodation, is unreasonable, it must consider whether you are in a 'protected group'.[105] If you are, it cannot restrict your rent unless cheaper suitable alternative accommodation is available and it is reasonable to expect you to move.

You are in a protected group if any of the people the local authority must consider:

- are aged 60 or over; *or*
- satisfy any of the tests of being incapable of work for social security purposes (see p661);[106] *or*
- have a child (this includes a qualifying young person) living with them for whom they are responsible (see p710).

Is cheaper suitable alternative accommodation available?

The local authority must prove that suitable alternative accommodation (see p251) exists and is actually available to you. It does not need to refer to specific properties, but must have sufficient evidence to demonstrate the existence of an active housing market comprising accommodation of a suitable type, rent and location for you.[107]

In considering whether accommodation is **'available'**, the local authority must have regard to personal factors, such as whether you can afford to pay a deposit.[108] If the local authority produces a list of properties which are available to you, try to show that they are not available due to your personal circumstances.[109]

Is it reasonable to expect you to move?

The local authority must show that it is reasonable to expect you to move. It must take into account the adverse effects of a move on:[110]

- your ability to retain your job; *and*
- the education of any child or young person living with you. In considering this, the local authority must justify any decision that it is reasonable to make the child travel to or move school.[111]

The local authority may say that it does not need to consider any other factors, such as your health.[112] You can argue that this is wrong, since the Regulations only say that the local authority *must* take into account the two factors above. For example, if you are elderly and have lived in a house for a long time, you should argue that it is unreasonable to expect you to move because you are used to living there and are settled.

Maximum rent

Your 'maximum rent' for HB purposes (and your 'eligible rent' – see p192) is normally your contractual rent minus ineligible services. If you are in shared accommodation, this can be apportioned between you and the people with whom you share. It only covers the rent you pay for residential accommodation.[113]

However, if the local authority decides your 'eligible rent' should be restricted, It reduces it to the amount it considers appropriate.[114] It must take into account the cost of suitable alternative accommodation and other circumstances that are reasonably relevant to the decision (eg, pregnancy, the difficulty of finding other suitable accommodation and whether the local authority would have to rehouse you if you had to move).[115]

The local authority should not be unduly influenced by the amount of subsidy it is paid by the government, but it can take this into account when deciding on a reasonable level of rent. It cannot be reduced below that payable for suitable alternative accommodation.[116]

Delay before a rent restriction is applied

No restriction can be made for 12 months from the date of the death of a member of your family (or a relative (see p248) who lives in the same dwelling as you without a separate right to do so).[117] If you or a member of your family for HB purposes (or a relative of you or your partner who lives in the same dwelling as you without a separate right to do so) could meet the costs of the dwelling when you took them on (this could include other bills as well as the rent), no restriction can be made for 13 weeks provided you did not receive HB in the 52 weeks before your current award of HB.[118]

Rent increases

If your landlord increases your rent, the local authority cannot increase your 'eligible rent' by the full amount if it decides that:[119]

- the increase is unreasonably high compared with increases in suitable alternative accommodation. It must consider the amount of the increase as well as, for example, the quality of the accommodation, your age and state of health, whether you would have to move if the increase is not met and how a move would affect you;[120] *or*
- the increase is unreasonable because a previous increase has occurred within the preceding 12 months.

If the local authority considers a rent increase to have been unreasonable, it may either refuse to meet all of that increase or only so much of it as it considers appropriate. If your rent has been increased for the second time in under 12 months but it is still below the market level for suitable alternative accommodation, or the increase reflects improvements made to your accommodation, press for the full amount to be allowed.

Challenging a rent restriction

If you disagree with the local authority's decision to apply a rent restriction, or with the amount of the restriction, you can ask for a revision or appeal (see Chapters 41 and 42).

6. If you are considering renting accommodation

If you are considering renting accommodation privately, and are likely to claim housing benefit (HB), you might want to find out the rent figure that will be used to calculate it.

If the local housing allowance rules apply to you and an appropriate **local housing allowance** (see p236) has not yet been set, you can ask the local authority to apply to the rent officer for one.[121] The rent officer must then set one as soon as reasonably practicable.[122] You must apply in writing on the form approved by your local authority. Both you and your prospective landlord must sign it.[123]

If the local reference rent rules apply to you, you can apply to the local authority for a **pre-tenancy determination**.[124] You can also apply if you are already receiving HB and your tenancy is due for renewal. Your current tenancy agreement must have started at least 11 months before your request.[125] The procedure is as follows.

- You must apply in writing on the form approved by your local authority. Both you and your prospective landlord must sign it.[126] The local authority must forward your request to the rent officer within two days of receipt.[127]
- The rent officer must send you, the prospective landlord and the local authority her/his determinations within five working days (unless s/he needs more information from the local authority) or as soon as is practicable after that.[128] If the rent officer needs further information, the five days runs from the date this is received.

A pre-tenancy determination is usually valid for a year.[129] So if someone else applied for a pre-tenancy determination for your accommodation in the previous 12 months, it also applies to you.

You cannot appeal against a pre-tenancy determination. However, if you accept the tenancy and claim HB, you can ask for it to be redetermined. If you subsequently negotiate a lower rent with your landlord, which is lower than your 'maximum rent', your HB is re-calculated using your new rent.[130]

Notes

Between 7 April 2008 and 6 April 2009 there are two versions of the HB regulations. The footnotes contain references to both. If you were getting HB immediately before 1 April 2007 (unless the Pathfinder local housing allowance rules applied), the old versions continue to apply to you until 6 April 2009, or until the first of the following occurs. The local authority:
- has to apply to the rent officer for determinations;
- would have had to apply to the rent officer for determinations but for the fact that there are existing determinations it can use;
- works out a new 'eligible rent' where no rent restriction rules apply;
- works out a new 'eligible rent' under the pre-January 1996 rules.

In addition, the new versions apply if you claim HB or move home on or after 7 April 2008.

1. Which rent restriction rules apply

1 Regs 12(7), 12B(6), 12C(2) and (3) and 13D(12) HB Regs; regs 12(7), 12B(6), 12C(2) and 13D(12) HB(SPC) Regs
2 *R on the application ofLaali v Westminster* CC [2002] HLR 179 (HC)
3 *R v Macclesfield BC HBRB ex parte Temsemani* [1999] unreported (QBD); A4 Annex B GM

2. Excluded tenancies

4 Regs 13C(5)(c) and 14(4)(b) and Sch 2 paras 3-12 HB Regs and reg 14(2)(b) and Sch 2 paras 3-13 HB Regs as substituted by regs 8 and 18 HB(LHA&IS)A Regs; regs 13C(5)(c) and 14(4)(b) and Sch 2 paras 3-12 HB(SPC) Regs and reg 14(2)(b) and Sch 2 paras 3-13 HB Regs as substituted by regs 8 and 18 HB(SPC)(LHA&IS)A Regs

3. The local housing allowance rules

5 Reg 13C(1), (2)(a)-(c), (4A)(a) and (5) HB Regs; reg 13C(1), (2)(a)-(c), (4A)(a) and (5) HB(SPC) Regs
6 Reg 13D(1) HB Regs; reg 13D(1) HB(SPC) Regs; Art 4B(2A) and (4) and Sch 3B RO(HBF)O; Art 4B(2A) and (4) and Sch 3B RO(HBF)(S)O
7 Reg 13E HB Regs; reg 13E HB(SPC) Regs; Art 4B(2A) RO(HBF)O; Art 4B(2A) RO(HBF)(S)O
8 Sch 3B para 4 RO(HBF)O; Sch 3B para 4 RO(HBF)(S)O
9 Reg 13D(3) HB Regs; reg 13D(3) HB(SPC) Regs
10 Reg 13D(12) HB Regs; reg 13D(12) HB(SPC) Regs. Both, definition of 'occupiers'.
11 *R v Swale Borough Council HBRB ex parte Marchant* [1999] 1 FLR 1087 (QBD), [2000] 1 FLR 246 (CA)
12 Sch 3B para 1 RO(HBF)O; Sch 3B para 1 RO(HBF)(S)O
13 Reg 13D(7) HB Regs; reg 13D(7) HB(SPC) Regs
14 Reg 13D(2)(a) HB Regs; reg 13D(2)(a) HB(SPC) Regs
15 Reg 2(1)HB Regs, definition of 'young individual'; reg 13D(12) HB(SPC) Regs, definition of 'care leaver'

16 Reg 13D(2)(b) HB Regs; reg 13D(2)(b) HB(SPC) Regs
17 Reg 13D(2)(c) HB Regs; reg 13D(2)(c) HB(SPC) Regs
18 Reg 13D(5) and (6) HB Regs; reg 13D(5) and (6) HB(SPC) Regs
19 Reg 12D(2)(a) HB Regs; reg 12D(2)(a) HB(SPC) Regs
20 Reg 13D(4) and (12) HB Regs; reg 13D(4)and (12) HB(SPC) Regs
21 Regs 12D(2) and 13C(3), (4) and (6) HB Regs; regs 12D(2) and 13C(3), (4) and (6) HB(SPC) Regs
22 Regs 2, definition of 'linked person', 12D(2)(b) and 13C(2)(d) HB Regs; regs 2, definition of 'linked person', 12D(2)(b) and 13C(2)(d) HB(SPC) Regs
23 Reg 13D(1) and (12) HB Regs; reg 13D(1) and (12) HB(SPC) Regs. Both, definition of 'relevant date'.
24 Regs 2(1), definition of 'reckonable rent' and 12D(3), (4) and (8) HB Regs; regs 2(1), definition of 'reckonable rent' and 12D(3), (4) and (8) HB(SPC) Regs
25 Reg 12D(5), (6) and (8) HB Regs; reg 12D(5), (6) and (8) HB(SPC) Regs
26 Reg 12D(7) HB Regs; reg 12D(7) HB(SPC) Regs
27 Reg 2(1) HB Regs; reg 2(1) HB(SPC) Regs
28 Reg 12D as modified and regs 12E-12K as inserted by Sch 10 para 6 HB Regs; reg 12D as modified and regs 12E-12K as inserted by Sch 9 para 6 HB(SPC) Regs
29 Regs 12E-12G as inserted by Sch 10 para 6 HB Regs; regs 12E-12G as inserted by Sch 9 para 6 HB(SPC) Regs
30 Reg 12H as inserted by Sch 10 para 6 HB Regs; reg 12H as inserted by Sch 9 para 6 HB(SPC) Regs
31 Regs 12I-12K as inserted by Sch 10 para 6 HB Regs; regs 12I-12K as inserted by Sch 9 para 6 HB(SPC) Regs
32 Sch 10 Part 1 HB Regs; Sch 9 Part 1 HB(SPC) Regs

4. **The local reference rent rules**

33 Regs 13(1), 13C(5)(a)-(e) and (6) and 14(1) HB Regs as substituted by regs 6-8 HB(LHA&IS)A Regs; regs 13(1), 13C(5)(a)-(e) and (6) and 14(1) HB(SPC) Regs as substituted by regs 6-8 HB(SPC)(LHA&IS)A Regs
34 Reg 13C(2)(a)-(c) HB Regs; reg 13C(2)(a)-(c) HB(SPC) Regs
35 Regs 13(1) and 14(1)(c), (f) and (g) and (8) HB Regs as substituted by regs 6 and 8 HB(LHA&IS)A Regs; regs 13(1) and 14(1)(c), (f) and (g) and (8) HB(SPC) Regs as substituted by regs 6 and 8 HB(SPC)(LHA&IS)A Regs
36 Reg 1(5), (6)(a) and (b) and (7) HB(LHA&IS)A Regs; reg 1(5), (6)(a) and (b) and (7) HB(SPC)(LHA&IS)A Regs bring the new versions of the regulations into effect. The new local reference rent rules then only apply where a local authority is required to apply to the rent officer for determinations. It must do so under reg 14(1)(f) and (g) HB Regs as substituted by reg 8 HB(LHA&IS)A Regs only if 52 weeks have passed since the local authority made an application under the substituted reg 14 HB Regs, not if the last application was made under the former version. The same would apply under the HB(SPC) Regs.
37 Sch 1 para 4(6) RO(HBF)O;Sch 1 para 4(6) RO(HBF)(S)O; *R (Heffernan) v The Rent Service* [2006] EWHC 2478 Admin, 10 October 2006, unreported
38 Sch 1 para 3(5) RO(HBF)O;Sch 1 para 3(5) RO(HBF)(S)O
39 Reg 14(1) HB Regs and reg 14(1) HB Regs as substituted by reg 8 HB(LHS&IS)A Regs; reg 14(1) HB(SPC) Regs and reg 14(1) HB(SPC) Regs as substituted by reg 8 HB(SPC)(LHS&IS)A Regs
40 Sch 2 para 2(3)(a)-(d) HB Regs and Sch 2 para 2(3)(a)-(d) HB Regs as substituted by reg 18 HB(LHA&IS)A Regs; Sch 2 para 2(3)(a)-(d) HB(SPC) Regs and Sch 2 para 2(3)(a)-(d) HB(SPC) Regs as substituted by reg 18 HB(SPC)(LHA&IS)A Regs
41 CH/1556/2006
42 Sch 2 para 2(1) and (2) HB Regs and Sch 2 para 2(1) and (2) HB Regs as substituted by reg 18 HB(LHA&IS)A Regs; Sch 2 para 2(1) and (2) HB(SPC) Regs and Sch 2 para 2(1) and (2) HB(SPC) Regs as substituted by reg 18 HB(SPC)(LHA&IS)A Regs
43 Reg 14(4)(a)and (8) HB Regs and reg 14(2)(a) and (7) HB Regs as substituted by reg 8 HB(LHA&IS)A Regs; reg 14(4)(a) and (8) HB(SPC) Regs and reg 14(2)(a) and (7) HB(SPC) Regs as substituted by reg 8 HB(SPC)(LHA&IS)A Regs
44 Sch 1 para 1 RO(HBF)O; Sch 1 para 1 RO(HBF)(S)O

45 Sch 1 para 3 RO(HBF)O; Sch 1 para 3 RO(HBF)(S)O
46 Sch 1 para 2 RO(HBF)O; Sch 1 para 2 RO(HBF)(S)O 1997
47 Sch 1 para 1(4) RO(HBF)O; Sch 1 para 1(4) RO(HBF)(S)O
48 Sch 2 RO(HBF)O; Sch 2 RO(HBF)(S)O
49 Art 2(1) RO(HBF)O; Art 2(1) RO(HBF)(S)O
Both definition of 'occupier'
50 *R v Swale Borough Council HBRB ex parte Marchant* [1999] 1 FLR 1087 (QBD), [2000] 1 FLR 246 (CA)
51 Sch 1 para 6 RO(HBF)O and Sch 1 para 6 RO(HBF)O as amended by Art 9 RO(HBF)AO; Sch 1 para 6 RO(HBF)(S)O and Sch 1 para 6 RO(HBF)(S)O as amended by Art 18 RO(HBF)AO
52 Sch 1 para 4 RO(HBF)O; Sch 1 para 4 RO(HBF)(S)O
53 Reg 13(4) HB Regs and reg 13(5) HB Regs as substituted by reg 6 HB(LHA&IS)A Regs
54 Regs 2(1), definition of 'young individual' and 13(5) HB Regs and regs 2(1), definition of 'young individual' and 13(6) HB Regs as substituted by reg 6 HB(LHA&IS)A Regs
55 Sch 1 para 5 RO(HBF)O; Sch 1 para 5 RO(HBF)(S)O
56 Reg 114A(6) and (8)(a) HB Regs; reg 114A(6) and (8)(a) HB(SPC) Regs
57 Sch 1 paras 5(2)(c) and 7(1)(a)(ii)RO(HBF)O and Sch 1 para 7(1) RO(HBF)O as substituted by Art 8 RO(HBF)AO; Sch 1 paras 5(2)(c) and 7(1)(a)(ii) RO(HBF)(S)O and Sch 1 para 7(1) RO(HBF)O as substituted by Art 17 RO(HBF)AO
58 Sch 1 para 9 RO(HBF)O and Sch 1 para 9 RO(HBF)O as amended by Art 9 RO(HBF)AO; Sch 1 para 9 RO(HBF)(S)O and Sch 1 para 9 RO(HBF)(S)O as amended by Art 18 RO(HBF)AO
59 Art 2(1) RO(HBF)O; Art 2(1) RO(HBF)(S)O
Both definition of 'relevant period'
60 Regs 12(3)(a) and 12C HB Regs; regs 12(3)(a) and 12C HB(SPC) Regs
61 Reg 13(2), (4) and (6) HB Regs and reg 13(2), (3) and (5) HB Regs as substituted by reg 6 HB(LHA&IS)A Regs; reg 13(2), (4) and (6) HB(SPC) Regs and reg 13(2) and (3) HB(SPC) Regs as substituted by reg 6 HB(SPC)(LHA&IS)A Regs
62 Reg 13(4) HB Regs as substituted by reg 6 HB(LHA&IS)A Regs; reg 13(4) HB(SPC) Regs as substituted by reg 6 HB(SPC)(LHA&IS)A Regs; Sch 3 para 8 HB&CTB(CP) Regs and Sch 3 para 8 HB&CTB(CP) Regs as substituted by reg 6(3) HB(LHA,M&C)A Regs
63 Regs 13(8) and 13ZB(1) HB Regs; reg 13(6) and 13ZB(1) HB(SPC) Regs
64 Regs 12(4) and(5) and 12C(2) and (3) HB Regs; regs 12(4) and (5) and 12C(2) HB(SPC) Regs
65 Regs 2, definition of 'linked person', 13(11), (12), (16) and (17) and 13ZA(1) and (2) HB Regs; regs 2, definition of 'linked person', 13(11), (12), (16) and (17) and 13ZA(1) and (2) HB(SPC) Regs
66 Regs 13(14)-(17) and 13ZA(3) and (4) HB Regs; regs 13(14)-(17) and 13ZA(3) and (4) HB(SPC) Regs
67 Reg 2(1) HB Regs; reg 2(1) HB(SPC) Regs
68 Reg 16 HB Regs and reg 16 HB Regs as substituted by reg 9 HB(LHA&IS)A Regs; reg 16 HB(SPC) Regs and reg 16 HB(SPC) Regs as substituted by reg 9 HB(SPC)(LHA&IS)A Regs
69 Reg 16(1)(b) HB Regs and reg 16(1)(b) HB Regs as substituted by reg 9 HB(LHA&IS)A Regs; reg 16(1)(b) HB(SPC) Regs and reg 16(1)(b) HB(SPC) Regs as substituted by reg 9 HB(SPC)(LHA&IS)A Regs
70 Arts 2(1), definition of 'relevant period' and 4 and Sch 3 RO(HBF)O; Arts 2(1), definition of 'relevant period' and 4 and Sch 3 RO(HBF)(S)O
71 Regs 16(5) and 79(1) HB Regs and reg 16(5) HB Regs as substituted by reg 9 HB(LHA&IS)A Regs; regs 16(5) and 59(1) HB(SPC) Regs and reg 16(5) HB(SPC) Regs as substituted by reg 9 HB(SPC)(LHA&IS)A Regs; reg 8(2) and (6) HB&CTB(DA) Regs
72 Reg 15 HB Regs and reg 15 HB Regs as substituted by reg 9 HB(LHA&IS)A Regs; reg 15 HB(SPC) Regs and reg 15 HB(SPC) Regs as substituted by reg 9 HB(SPC)(LHA&IS)A Regs
73 Reg 16(3) and (4) HB Regs and reg 16(3) and (4) HB Regs as substituted by reg 9 HB(LHA&IS)A Regs; reg 16(3) and (4) HB(SPC) Regs and reg 16(3) and (4) HB(SPC) Regs as substituted by reg 9 HB(SPC)(LHA&IS)A Regs

74 Reg 17 HB Regs and reg 17 HB Regs as substituted by reg 9 HB(LHA&IS)A Regs; reg 17 HB(SPC) Regs and reg 17 HB(SPC) Regs as substituted by reg 9 HB(SPC)(LHA&IS)A Regs
75 HB/CTB Circular G5/2005

5. **The pre-January 1996 rules**

76 Regs 13C(5)(b) HB Regs; reg 13C(5)(b) HB(SPC) Regs; Sch 3 para 4(1)(b) HB&CTB(CP) Regs and Sch 3 para 4(1)(b) HB&CTB(CP) Regs as substituted by reg 6 HB(LHA,M&C)A Regs
77 Sch 3 para 4(10) HB&CTB(CP) Regs and Sch 3 para 4(10) HB&CTB(CP) Regs as substituted by reg 6 HB(LHA,M&C)A Regs; CH/1289/2007
78 R(H) 7/07; CH/779/2007; CH/1246/2007
79 R(H) 8/07; CH/1289/2007
80 R(H) 2/07
81 Reg 13C(2)(a)-(c) HB Regs; reg 13C(2)(a)-(c) HB(SPC) Regs; Sch 3 para 4(1)(a), (2), (3) and (4) HB&CTB(CP) Regs and Sch 3 para 4(1)(a), (2), (3) and (4) HB&CTB(CP) Regs as substituted by reg 6 HB(LHA,M&C)A Regs
82 Reg 13C HB Regs; reg 13C HB(SPC) Regs
83 Reg 13C(2)(a)-(c) HB Regs; reg 13C(2)(a)-(c) HB(SPC) Regs
84 Sch 3 para 4(5), (6), (9) and (10) HB&CTB(CP) Regs and Sch 3 para 4(5), (6), (9) and (10) HB&CTB(CP) Regs as substituted by reg 6 HB(LHA,M&C)A Regs
All Definitions of 'relevant date' and 'previous beneficiary'
85 Sch 3 para 4(10) HB&CTB(CP) Regs and Sch 3 para 4(10) HB&CTB(CP) Regs as substituted by reg 6 HB(LHA,M&C)A Regs
All Definition of 'previous beneficiary'
86 Reg 13C HB Regs; reg 13C HB(SPC) Regs
87 Reg 13(3) HB Regs and reg 13(3) HB(SPC) Regs as set out in Sch 3 para 5(2) HB&CTB(CP) Regs and reg 13(3) HB Regs and reg 13(3) HB(SPC) Regs as set out in Sch 3 para 5(2) HB&CTB(CP) Regs as substituted by reg 6 HB(LHA,M&C)A Regs
88 Reg 13(4) HB Regs and reg 13(4) HB(SPC) Regs as set out in Sch 3 para 5(2) HB&CTB(CP) Regs and reg 13(4) HB Regs and reg 13(4) HB(SPC) Regs as set out in Sch 3 para 5(2) HB&CTB(CP) Regs as substituted by reg 6 HB(LHA,M&C)A Regs
89 Reg 13(3)(a) HB Regs and reg 13(3)(a) HB(SPC) Regs as set out in Sch 3 para 5(2) HB&CTB(CP) Regs and reg 13(3)(a) HB Regs and reg 13(3)(a) HB(SPC) Regs as set out in Sch 3 para 5(2) HB&CTB(CP) Regs as substituted by reg 6 HB(LHA,M&C)A Regs
90 *R v Kensington and Chelsea RBC HBRB ex parte Pirie* [1997] 26 March, unreported (QBD)
91 Reg 13(3)(b) HB Regs and reg 13(3)(b) HB(SPC) Regs as set out in Sch 3 para 5(2) HB&CTB(CP) Regs and reg 13(3)(b) HB Regs and reg 13(3)(b) HB(SPC) Regs as set out in Sch 3 para 5(2) HB&CTB(CP) Regs as substituted by reg 6 HB(LHA,M&C)A Regs
92 *R v Beverley District Council HBRB ex parte Hare* [1995] 27 HLR 637 (QBD)
93 *R v Kensington and Chelsea RBC HBRB ex parte Sheikh*, 14 January 1997, unreported (QBD)
94 *R v Kensington and Chelsea RBC ex parte Abou-Jaoude*, 10 May 1996, unreported (QBD)
95 *Macleod v Banff and Buchan District HBRB* [1988] SLT 753 (CS); *Malcolm v Tweedale District HBRB* [1994] SLT 1212 (CS); CH/4970/2002
96 *R v Kensington and Chelsea RBC ex parte Abou-Jaoude*, 10 May 1996, ureported (QBD)
97 *R v Coventry CC ex parte Waite*, 7 July 1995, unreported (QBD)
98 Reg 13(9) HB Regs and reg 13(9) HB(SPC) Regs as set out in Sch 3 para 5(2) HB&CTB(CP) Regs and reg 13(9) HB Regs and reg 13(9) HB(SPC) Regs as set out in Sch 3 para 5(2) HB&CTB(CP) Regs as substituted by reg 6 HB(LHA,M&C)A Regs
99 R(H) 2/05
100 Reg 13(10) and (11) HB Regs and reg 13(10) and (11) HB(SPC) Regs as set out in Sch 3 para 5(2) HB&CTB(CP) Regs and reg 13(10) and (11) HB Regs and reg 13(10) and (11) HB(SPC) Regs as set out in Sch 3 para 5(2) HB&CTB(CP) Regs as substituted by reg 6 HB(LHA,M&C)A Regs

101 *R v Lambeth LBC HBRB ex parte Harrington*, 22 November 1996, unreported (QBD)
102 Reg 13(9)(a) HB Regs and reg 13(9)(a) HB(SPC) Regs as set out in Sch 3 para 5(2) HB&CTB(CP) Regs and reg 13(9)(a) HB Regs and reg 13(9)(a) HB(SPC) Regs as set out in Sch 3 para 5(2) HB&CTB(CP) Regs as substituted by reg 6 HB(LHA,M&C)A Regs; *R v Kensington and Chelsea RBC ex parte Pirie,* 26 March 1997, unreported (QBD)*; R v Coventry CC ex parte Waite*, 7 July 1995, unreported (QBD)
103 *R v Waltham Forest LBC ex parte Holder* [1996] 29 HLR 71 (QBD); *R v Slough BC ex parte Green*, 15 November 1996, unreported (QBD)
104 *R v Waltham Forest LBC ex parte Holder* [1996] 29 HLR 71 (QBD)*; R v Kensington and Chelsea RBC HBRB ex parte Sheikh*, 14 January 1997, unreported (QBD)
105 Reg 13(4) HB Regs and reg 13(4) HB(SPC) Regs as set out in Sch 3 para 5(2) HB&CTB(CP) Regs and reg 13(4) HB Regs and reg 13(4) HB(SPC) Regs as set out in Sch 3 para 5(2) HB&CTB(CP) Regs as substituted by reg 6 HB(LHA,M&C)A Regs
106 R(H) 3/06
107 *R v East Devon DC HBRB ex parte Gibson* [1993] 25 HLR 487 (QBD); CH/4306/2003
108 *R v Waltham Forest LBC ex parte Holder* [1996] 29 HLR 71 (QBD)
109 *R v Oadby and Wigston DC ex parte Dickman* [1995] 28 HLR 806 (QBD)
110 Reg 13(9)(b) HB Regs and reg 13(9)(b) HB(SPC) Regs as set out in Sch 3 para 5(2) HB&CTB(CP) Regs and reg 13(9)(b) HB Regs and reg 13(9)(b) HB(SPC) Regs as set out in Sch 3 para 5(2) HB&CTB(CP) Regs as substituted by reg 6 HB(LHA,M&C)A Regs
111 *R v Kensington and Chelsea RBC HBRB ex parte Sheikh*, 14 January 1997, unreported (QBD)
112 *R v Kensington and Chelsea RBC HBRB ex parte Carney* [1997] Crown Office Digest 124 (QBD)
113 Reg 12(3)-(5) HB Regs and reg 12(3)-(5) HB(SPC) Regs as set out in Sch 3 para 5(1) HB&CTB(CP) Regs and reg 12(3)-(5) HB Regs and reg 12(3)-(5) HB(SPC) Regs as set out in Sch 3 para 5(1) HB&CTB(CP) Regs as substituted by reg 6 HB(LHA,M&C)A Regs
114 Reg 13(3) HB Regs and reg 13(3) HB(SPC) Regs as set out in Sch 3 para 5(1) HB&CTB(CP) Regs and reg 13(3) HB Regs and reg 13(3) HB(SPC) Regs as set out in Sch 3 para 5(1) HB&CTB(CP) Regs as substituted by reg 6 HB(LHA,M&C)A Regs
115 *R v City of Westminster HBRB ex parte Mehanne* [1992] 2 All ER 317 (CA)
116 *R v Brent LBC HBRB ex parte Connery* [1989] 22 HLR 40 (QBD)
117 Reg 13(5) HB Regs and reg 13(5) HB(SPC) Regs as set out in Sch 3 para 5(2) HB&CTB(CP) Regs and reg 13(5) HB Regs and reg 13(5) HB(SPC) Regs as set out in Sch 3 para 5(2) HB&CTB(CP) Regs as substituted by reg 6 HB(LHA,M&C)A Regs
118 Reg 13(7) and (8) HB Regs and reg 13(7) and (8) HB(SPC) Regs as set out in Sch 3 para 5(2) HB&CTB(CP) Regs and reg 13(7) and (8) HB Regs and reg 13(7) and (8) HB(SPC) Regs as set out in Sch 3 para 5(2) HB&CTB(CP) Regs as substituted by reg 6 HB(LHA,M&C)A Regs
119 Reg 13ZA HB Regs and reg 13ZA HB(SPC) Regs as set out in Sch 3 para 5(3) HB&CTB(CP) Regs and reg 13ZA HB Regs and reg 13ZA HB(SPC) Regs as set out in Sch 3 para 5(3) HB&CTB(CP) Regs as substituted by reg 6 HB(LHA,M&C)A Regs
120 CH/2214/2003

6. **If you are considering renting accommodation**

121 Reg 13D(8) HB Regs; reg 13D(8) HB(SPC) Regs
122 Art 4B(4A) RO(HBF)O; Art 4B(4A) RO(HBF)(S)O
123 Reg 13D(9) HB Regs; reg 13D(9) HB(SPC) Regs
124 Reg 14(1)(e), and (4) HB Regs and reg 14(1)(e) and (2) HB Regs as substituted by reg 8 HB(LHA&IS)A Regs; reg 14(1)(e) and (4) HB(SPC) Regs and reg 14(1)(e) and (2) HB(SPC) Regs as substituted by reg 8 HB(SPC)(LHA&IS)A Regs
125 Reg 14(10) HB Regs and reg 14(8) HB Regs as substituted by reg 8 HB(LHA&IS)A Regs; reg 14(10) HB(SPC) Regs and reg 14(8) HB(SPC) Regs as substituted by reg 8 HB(SPC)(LHA&IS)A Regs
All definition of 'prospective occupier'

126 Reg 14(1)(e) HB Regs and reg 14(1)(e) and (8), definition of 'specified matters' HB Regs as substituted by reg 8 HB(LHA&IS)A Regs; reg 14(1)(e) HB(SPC) Regs and reg 14 (1)(e) and (8), definition of 'specified matters' HB(SPC) Regs as substituted by reg 8 HB(SPC)(LHA&IS)A Regs
127 Reg 14(6) HB Regs and reg 14(5) HB Regs as substituted by reg 8 HB(LHA&IS)A Regs; reg 14(6) HB(SPC) Regs and reg 14(5) HB(SPC) Regs as substituted by reg 8 HB(SPC)(LHA&IS)A Regs
128 Art 2(1) RO(HBF)O; Art 2(1) RO(HBF)(S)O
Both definition of 'relevant period'
129 Reg 14(5)(b) and Sch 2 para 2(2)(b) HB Regs and reg 14(4)(b) and Sch 2 para 2(2)(b) HB Regs as substituted by reg 8 HB(LHA&IS)A Regs; reg 14(5)(b) and Sch 2 para 2(2)(b) HB(SPC) Regs and reg 14(4)(b) and Sch 2 para 2(2)(b) HB(SPC) Regs as substituted by reg 8 HB(SPC)(LHA&IS)A Regs
130 Regs 13(9) and (10) and 13ZB(2)-(4) HB Regs; regs 13(9) and (10) and 13ZB(2)-(4) HB(SPC) Regs

Chapter 12

Incapacity benefit

This chapter covers:

Incapacity benefit (IB) is paid to people who are incapable of work and who either:

- have paid or been credited with sufficient national insurance (NI) contributions; *or*
- became incapable of work in youth.

There are special rules which also allow some widows and widowers to qualify for IB.

Your entitlement to IB does not depend on whether or not you are employed (although you must be incapable of work) and is not affected by any savings you have. However, your entitlement can be affected by some types of income you receive, such as certain pension payments (see p276).

If you are employed but are off work sick you normally receive statutory sick pay (SSP) from your employer for the first 28 weeks of your incapacity for work (see Chapter 24). After that, if you satisfy the qualifying conditions, you can claim IB from the DWP. If you are not entitled to SSP you may qualify for IB from the start of your incapacity for work.

IB is payable at three rates: a lower short-term rate, a higher short-term rate and a long-term rate. The rate paid depends on how long you have been incapable of work (see p273 for details).

See Chapter 28 for details of how your incapacity for work is assessed.

Employment and support allowance

It is expected that in October 2008 the Government will introduce a new benefit, employment and support allowance (ESA). At the time this *Handbook* was written full details were not available but, in general, from the date ESA is introduced you will not be able to make a new claim for IB. Instead, people too ill to work will need to claim ESA (they can still claim SSP first). ESA will be paid on the basis of 'limited capability for work'. It will have a contributory element with age rules and NI conditions similar to those for IB. See Chapter 7 for more details.

It is expected that people already on IB at the point of change will continue to receive it until the Government decides to transfer existing claims to ESA. It is not yet known when this will be, but it is not expected to happen during 2008/09. For updates on ESA, see www.cpag.org.uk/esa or CPAG's *Welfare Rights Bulletin*.

1. Who can claim incapacity benefit

You qualify for incapacity benefit (IB) if:[1]

- you are assessed as, or treated as, incapable of work (see below and 661); *and*
- you are within a 'period of incapacity for work' (see p264); *and*
- for short-term IB you are not more than five years above pension age and for long-term IB you are not over pension age (see p271). For the meaning of short-term IB and long-term IB see p273; *and*
- you are not entitled to statutory sick pay (SSP – see Chapter 24); *and either*
- you have paid (or been credited with) sufficient national insurance (NI) contributions (see p735); *or*
- you qualify as someone who became incapable of work in youth (see p266); *or*
- you are no more than five years over pension age (60 for a woman, 65 for a man), your period of incapacity for work began before you reached pension age, and you would qualify for a Category B retirement pension as a widow, widower or surviving civil partner, or a Category A retirement pension had you not deferred claiming it or 'de-retired' (see Chapter 19). (**Note:** this provision only allows you to qualify for short-term IB); *or*
- your spouse died before 9 April 2001 and you qualify as a widow or widower (see p277).

There are some groups of claimants to whom special rules apply (see p277).

Incapable of work

In order to qualify for IB you must be incapable of work or treated as incapable of work. Whether you are incapable of work is determined by the **own occupation test** or the **personal capability assessment** described in Chapter 28. See p263 for the details of when you can be treated as incapable of work. In some circumstances even if you are incapable of work you are treated as if you are not and so will not qualify for IB (see below).

Treated as incapable of work

You are treated as incapable of work on days on which:

- you are deemed to be incapable of work without having to satisfy the own occupation test or the personal capability assessment (see p665); *or*
- you are exempt from the personal capability assessment (see p669); *or*
- having failed the personal capability assessment, you are in 'exceptional circumstances' (see p673); *or*
- you are entitled to maternity allowance (MA) and have not been disqualified from receiving it (see p437).[2] (**Note:** you cannot be paid both MA and IB in full because of the overlapping benefit rules – see p981 – but days on MA count towards the periods required to qualify for the higher short-term rate and long-term rate of IB – see p273); *or*
- you are making a new claim which is linked (see p264) to a previous award of IB, and in that previous award you were incorrectly awarded NI credits (ie, through official error) regarding the second contribution condition;[3] *or*
- you work at night in the circumstances described below.

See p266 if you were getting SSP and you are claiming IB on the basis that you became incapable of work in youth.

If you work at night

If you work night shifts you may end one shift and start another on the same day (a day runs from midnight to midnight). If you are incapable of working on only one of those shifts it would normally be difficult to show that the day is a day of incapacity for work. This is because you are normally treated as capable of work on a day on which you do some work. For this reason, there are special rules to help people who work a shift that spans midnight.[4]

- If you worked a different number of hours before and after midnight, you are treated as incapable of work on the day that you work the least hours if you are incapable of work for the rest of that day.
- If you worked the same number of hours before and after midnight, you are treated as incapable of work on the first day of that shift if the shift falls at the end of a period of incapacity for work (see p264), or on the second day of that shift if the shift falls at the beginning of a period of incapacity for work.

Treated as not incapable of work

Even if it has been decided that you are incapable of work, you will be treated as capable of work (and so will not be entitled to IB) in any weeks in which you actually do work, unless that work can be ignored. See p662 for details.

Also, even if you are incapable of work you are treated as capable of work on certain other days including those on which:[5]

- you have not made a claim for IB (or if you have made a late claim, days for which IB was disallowed because your claim was late); *or*
- you have been disqualified from receiving IB during a period of absence from Great Britain (GB) or a period when you are imprisoned or detained in legal custody, if that disqualification is for more than six weeks; *or*
- you are on a training course for which you get a training allowance unless *either*
  - you finished (or stopped attending) the course before your claim for IB, *or*
  - the allowance you receive is only to cover your meal or travel expenses; *or*
  - you are on the Adult Learning Option scheme and the allowance you receive is not intended to cover your basic living expenses (ie, food, ordinary clothing or footwear, household fuel, rent covered by housing benefit, council tax, water charges, or any housing costs covered by income support or jobseeker's allowance);

  However, days when you are on a training course count as days of incapacity for work for the purpose of qualifying for IB while temporarily absent from GB; *or*
- you are receiving statutory maternity pay (SMP) or statutory adoption pay (SAP – see Chapter 23) (but days on SMP or SAP sometimes count towards the periods required to qualify for the higher rate of short-term IB, or long-term IB – see pp273 and 288);[6]
- you do not satisfy the 'NI number requirement' when making your claim (see p962).[7]

Period of incapacity for work

You are only entitled to IB for any day on which you are incapable of work which forms part of a 'period of incapacity for work'.

A **'period of incapacity for work'** is either:

- a period of four or more consecutive days when you are incapable of work;[8] *or*
- if you are having plasmapheresis, chemotherapy or radiotherapy, or regular weekly kidney dialysis or total parenteral nutrition, a period of two days when you are incapable of work. These days do not have to be consecutive as long as they are within a period of seven consecutive days.[9] In these circumstances, you are treated as incapable of work on the days that you have this treatment.[10]

Two or more periods of incapacity for work can sometimes be linked together to form a single period – see below.

The linking rules

Two or more periods of incapacity for work separated by eight weeks or less are linked together to form a single period.[11] If you are a 'welfare to work' beneficiary (see p666), two periods of incapacity for work can be linked in this way if they are separated by 104 weeks or less.

You are not entitled to IB for the periods between the linked periods of incapacity for work,[12] but if periods are linked in this way it means that:

- the question of whether or not you satisfy the contribution conditions is decided at the beginning of the first period of incapacity for work;
- you do not have to serve a further three waiting days before being entitled to payment of IB (see p270);
- for the purpose of calculating the date from which you become entitled to the higher rate of short-term or long-term IB, previous periods when you were entitled to IB in a linked period of incapacity for work can be counted;
- you can continue to qualify for IB on the grounds that you were incapable of work in youth, if this is the basis on which you qualified before, and if you still have not paid or been credited with sufficient NI contributions to qualify otherwise.

Tax credits and the linking rules

If you claim IB after stopping full-time paid work (defined on p1222), any day during the two-year period ending with the day after you finished work is treated as a day of incapacity for work if:[13]

- you were incapable of work on the day after you stopped work; *and*
- you were previously entitled to the higher rate of short-term IB or long-term IB at some time in the two-year period ending with the day after you finish work; *and*
- you were entitled to the disability element of working tax credit (WTC – see p1237) on the day before you stopped work, or you would have been had your (and your partner's, if you have one) income not been too high; *and*
- you were paid WTC or the child, disabled child or severely disabled child element of child tax credit (CTC) for the day before you stopped work; *and*
- it is one for which you were both entitled to the disability element of WTC (or you would have been had your income not been too high); *and*
- it is one for which you were paid WTC, or the child, disabled child or severely disabled child element of CTC.

This rule does not enable you to qualify for IB for the period you were working, but is intended to help you to return to the rate of IB you were receiving before you started work.

For IB linking rules for periods when you were entitled to disabled person's tax credit (now abolished), see p266 of CPAG's *Welfare Benefits and Tax Credits Handbook* 2005/06.

Training for work and the linking rules

If you have been on a training for work course (see below) and:[14]

- you were entitled to the higher rate of short-term or long-term IB at some time in the eight weeks before you started your training; *and*
- your training has stopped and on the day after it stopped you were incapable of work; *and*
- this day falls within two years of the last day on which you were entitled to IB,

any day on which you were doing such training counts as a day of incapacity for work if you subsequently claim IB again. Although this rule will not help you to qualify for IB while you are on the course, it can help you to return to the rate of IB you were receiving before the training started.

'Training for work' means training provided under the Employment and Training Act 1973 or, in Scotland, the Enterprise and New Towns (Scotland) Act 1990, or one which you attend for 16 hours or more a week if the primary purpose of the training is teaching occupational or vocational skills.[15]

Incapable of work in youth

If you do not qualify for IB on the basis of your NI contribution record you may still qualify if you became incapable of work in youth.

You will qualify for IB on the basis of incapacity in youth if:[16]

- you are aged 16 or over; *and*
- you have been incapable of work for at least 196 consecutive days (see below); *and*
- you were under 20 (or, in some circumstances, under 25 – see p267) when your period of incapacity for work started and you claim in time (see p267); *and*
- you satisfy the residence and presence conditions (see p1358); *and*
- you are not a 'person subject to immigration control', although there are exceptions to this rule (see p1333); *and*
- if you are under 19, you are not in full-time education (see p269).

If you previously qualified for IB on the basis of your incapacity for work in youth but your entitlement ended, you may be able to requalify for IB on the same basis if you become incapable of work again even if you are over 20 (or 25) (see p269).

If you were under 20 on 6 April 2001 and were getting severe disablement allowance (SDA), your SDA would have stopped on 5 April 2002. You would then have automatically qualified for long-term IB on the basis of your incapacity for work in youth.

The 196-day qualifying period

In order to qualify for IB as someone who became incapable of work in youth, you must have been incapable of work, or treated as incapable of work, for at least the 196 days immediately before the first day on which your entitlement can begin.

See Chapter 28 for details of when you are considered incapable of work and p263 for details of when you can be treated as incapable of work. Days on which you were entitled to SSP can also count towards the 196-day qualifying period.[17]

The 196 days must be consecutive and for this purpose Sundays count, so that 196 days is 28 weeks. The linking rules described on p264 do not apply and any break in your incapacity for work within the qualifying period means that the 196 days must begin again. Entitlement to the lower rate of short-term IB only begins once you have served the 196-day qualifying period.

Although you must be at least 16 to qualify for IB on the basis of your incapacity for work in youth, days when you are incapable of work that fall before your 16th birthday can still be counted when calculating the 196-day period.

You should include a backdated medical certificate covering the period of your incapacity for work when you make your claim.

If you have a break in your claim, you do not have to serve the 196-day qualifying period again before being paid IB on a new claim if your new period of incapacity for work is linked to your earlier period of incapacity for work (see p264).[18]

Age

You must have been under 20 when your period of incapacity for work started (or under 25 in the circumstances given below). It is not necessary for you to be under 20 (or 25) on the date of your claim for IB. The DWP usually says that if you are over 20 (or 25) and you fail to claim within three months of the end of your 196-day qualifying period (which must begin before your 20th (or 25th) birthday), you will not be able to qualify for IB on the basis of incapacity in youth. However, it is arguable that the rules themselves do not clearly say this.

Once you qualify for IB on the grounds of your incapacity for work in youth you can continue to receive it even after you reach 20 (or 25) as long as your period of incapacity for work continues. If there is a break in your period of incapacity for work, as long as the linking rules described on p264 allow your present period of incapacity for work to be linked to one in which you qualified for IB on the grounds of your incapacity for work in youth, you can requalify for IB on this basis.

You can also requalify for IB after your 20th (or 25th) birthday in the circumstances detailed on p269.

Under-25-year-olds

The age condition is relaxed to include some people over the age of 20 who have been studying or training and who have not paid or been credited with sufficient NI contributions to qualify for IB otherwise.

If you are under 25 when your period of incapacity for work starts, you can still qualify for IB on the basis of your incapacity for work in youth if, in addition to the main conditions described on p266:[19]

- you registered on a course of full-time advanced or secondary education, or on a course of vocational or work-based training (see below), at least three months before you became 20; *and*
- not more than an academic term passed between the date you registered on that course and attended it; *and*
- you started the course at least three months before you reached 20; *and*
- you finished the course some time after the start of the last two complete tax years which fall before the benefit year in which you claim IB (see p736).

You are still treated as attending a course of education or training if your attendance is interrupted because of illness or a domestic emergency.[20]

Education and training

For the meaning of **'advanced education'**, see p579.

'Secondary education' is a course of education below advanced level which you attend at a recognised educational establishment, such as a school or college, or which you attend elsewhere if the Secretary of State is satisfied that the education you receive is equivalent to that given at a recognised educational establishment.[21]

'Full-time' education is not defined and so it can be argued that it should be given its ordinary and natural meaning, and could include periods of unsupervised as well as supervised study.

However, if you are on a part-time course because you have a disability which means that you cannot attend full time, then you are treated as if you are attending a full-time course.[22]

'Vocational training' includes training described as 'training for work' on p266, and also includes any training which is provided by someone recognised by the Secretary of State and which is for people with a mental or physical disability, if the main purpose of the training is to teach occupational or vocational skills.

'Work-based training' is vocational training which you do on an employer's premises.

Attending more than one course

The rules on course attendance are not entirely clear if you have attended more than one course, each with different finishing dates. If you satisfy the above conditions for under-25-year-olds for more than one course, it is the end date of the last of those that is relevant. However, if you started one course at least three months before you reached 20 and started another course less than three months before your 20th birthday, and so you meet the above conditions in relation to the first but not the second course, the position is less clear. If there is a gap between the two courses (other than just a normal end-of-term holiday) it is the date on which the first course ends which governs your entitlement.

If there is no gap between the courses (other than an end-of-term holiday) the DWP states that the intention is that the above time limits apply to the end of the second course. The Regulations may not achieve this, however, and arguably the time limits for claiming relate to the end of the course which you started at least three months before you reached 20, rather than to the end of any subsequent course. In these circumstances, you may be entitled to IB once your first course of education or training ends, even if you are still attending a subsequent course, as long as you meet the other qualifying conditions. If you are refused IB in these circumstances, seek advice. **Note:** you may not qualify for IB if you are on a training course for which you get a training allowance (see p263).

Under 19 and in full-time education

If you are under 19 and on a full-time course of education you cannot qualify for IB on the basis of being incapable of work in youth (but see below if the course you attend is designed for people with disabilities). For this purpose you are considered to be in full-time education if you attend a course for 21 hours or more a week.[23] Temporary interruptions in your education are disregarded. If you are under 19 and studying for less than 21 hours a week (or 19 or over and studying either full or part time), you can qualify for IB as long as you meet the other conditions of entitlement.

Courses for people with disabilities

When calculating whether you are studying for 21 hours a week or more, only the instruction or tuition you receive which would be suitable for someone of the same age or sex as you who did not have a physical or mental disability is counted.[24] Both the course content and the method of teaching must be considered when deciding whether the education is suitable for someone without a disability.[25] If part of your course is suitable for people without disabilities but part is not (eg, because some of it makes use of information in Braille), only the part of the course that is suitable for students who do not have a disability is counted.

Requalifying on the basis of your incapacity for work in youth

If you previously qualified for IB on the basis of your incapacity for work in youth, there are rules that allow you to requalify for IB on this basis even if you are over 20 (or 25).

If your present period of incapacity for work is linked to an earlier period when you received IB on the grounds of your incapacity for work in youth, you can requalify on this basis (see p264 for when periods can be linked). If your periods of incapacity for work are linked in this way your previous period on IB is counted when assessing whether you qualify for the higher rate of short-term IB or long-term IB.

If your present period of incapacity for work cannot be linked with an earlier one, you can still qualify for IB on the basis of your incapacity for work in youth in the circumstances detailed below. In these circumstances you will return to the lower rate of short-term IB even if you were previously receiving the higher rate of short-term IB or long-term IB. You can qualify for IB in this way if:[26]

- you were previously entitled to IB on the basis of your incapacity for work in youth; *and*
- your last claim for IB did not end because you were either found to be capable of work or because it was decided that you could be treated as capable of work (see p263); *and*
- you are 20 or over (or 25 or over, if you would otherwise qualify under the rules for people between 20 and 25 – see p267); *and either*
- your last claim for IB ended only because you were planning to take up employment or training in the circumstances detailed below (whether or not you actually did so); *or*
- your last claim for IB ended only because you were absent from GB in the circumstances detailed below.

Taking up employment or training

If your last claim for IB only ended because you planned to take up employment or training, you can requalify if you meet the above conditions and:

- any earnings that you received over the period from when your last IB claim ended until your current period of incapacity for work began were so low that you do not meet the first NI contribution condition for IB (see p735); *and*
- you re-claim IB not more than 56 days after the day you stopped work.

In certain circumstances, receipt of disabled person's tax credit (which was abolished from April 2003) allowed you to requalify for IB in youth on this ground even if you had not reclaimed IB within 56 days of stopping work. See p271 of CPAG's *Welfare Benefits and Tax Credits Handbook* 2005/06 for details.

Absence from Great Britain

If your last claim for IB only ended because you went abroad, you can requalify if you meet the above conditions and:

- you have been incapable of work for at least 196 consecutive days since you returned to GB; *and*
- you reclaim IB within three months of the end of that 196-day period.

Waiting days

You are not normally entitled to IB for the first three days in your period of incapacity for work. These are called 'waiting days'.[27]

However, you do not have to serve these three waiting days, and so can qualify for IB from the first day of your period of incapacity for work, if:[28]

- your period of incapacity for work can be linked to a previous one (see p264); *or*

- you were previously receiving SSP and your period of incapacity for work falls within the 57 days after your entitlement to SSP ended; *or*
- you get IB on the grounds of your incapacity for work in youth (see p266); *or*
- you were discharged from the armed forces and particular circumstances apply.

Disqualification from benefit

You can be disqualified from receiving IB for up to six weeks if:[29]

- you are incapable of work because of your own misconduct. This means conduct which is blameworthy or wrong, and does not include playing dangerous sports or having an accident. Involuntary alcoholism is not 'misconduct', but drunkenness is;[30]
- you refuse suitable treatment without good cause (see below). You are not required to subject yourself to 'invasive' treatment – eg, surgery (unless it is very minor), inoculation or vaccination;
- you fail to refrain from behaviour calculated to slow down your recovery without good cause;
- you are away from home without leaving details of where you can be found without good cause. This is because you may need to attend a medical examination or be seen by a visiting officer from the DWP. If you are going away (eg, to stay at a friend's or relative's house) write to the DWP giving details of the period you will be away, and where you are going (but see p1350 if you are going abroad).

'**Good cause**' in this context is not defined by the legislation. The decision maker should consider all the circumstances when deciding whether you have good cause. You may have good cause, for example, for refusing medical treatment on religious grounds.

If you disagree with the disqualification, or with the period of it, you can appeal.

2. The rules about your age

Lower age limit

In order to qualify for incapacity benefit (IB) on the grounds of being incapable of work in youth (see p266) you must be 16 or over.

If you qualify for IB on the basis of your national insurance (NI) contribution record there is no lower age limit, but you must have paid or been credited with NI contributions over a period of at least two years (see p737). You do not have to start paying NI contributions on earnings until you are 16 years of age.

Upper age limit

You are not entitled to long-term IB after you reach pension age.[31] Pension age is 60 for a woman and 65 for a man.

If you are not more than five years over pension age you are entitled to short-term IB if:

- you would have been entitled to a Category A or, on the basis of your late spouse's or late civil partner's NI contributions, a Category B retirement pension had you not deferred claiming it or 'de-retired' (see p468); *and*
- your period of incapacity for work began before you reached pension age; *and*
- the period of 364 days during which IB is paid at the short-term rate has not yet run out.[32]

See p274 for details of the amount of IB paid after you reach pension age and p288 for details of whether you may be better off claiming your retirement pension or remaining on IB after reaching pension age.

3. Claiming for others

If you are getting incapacity benefit (IB) (either the short-term or long-term rates) you may be entitled to an increase for your adult dependant – ie, your spouse, civil partner or someone who looks after your child (see p686).[33] Your entitlement to an increase may be affected by certain income your adult dependant receives (see p690). This earnings rule is more generous for long-term IB than for short-term IB. This means that if your adult dependant has too much income to entitle you to an increase when you are receiving short-term IB, you may become entitled once you begin to be paid at the long-term rate. If so, you must make a separate claim for this increase within three months of becoming entitled to the long-term rate. If you do not, only three months' arrears are paid.[34]

For details of whether your partner may be required to take part in a work-focused interview, see p972. Your benefit may be reduced if s/he fails to do so without good cause.[35]

Increases for your dependent children that could be claimed with the higher rate of short-term IB or long-term IB (or, if you were over pension age, with the lower rate of short-term IB) were abolished on 6 April 2003. However, if you were entitled to an increase for a dependent child on 5 April 2003 you may be able to continue to receive it after that date (see p691). If your partner has certain kinds of income your entitlement to an increase for a child may be affected (see p691).

4. The amount of benefit

Rates of incapacity benefit

Incapacity benefit (IB) is paid at three rates. The rate you receive depends on the length of time you have either been entitled to IB, or treated as entitled to IB (see below). Days on which you are disqualified from receiving IB (see p271) are not counted.[36] You receive:

- the lower rate of short-term IB for the first 28 weeks of entitlement;
- the higher rate of short-term IB after 28 weeks of entitlement (ie, from the 197th day of entitlement);
- long-term IB after 52 weeks of entitlement (ie, from the 365th day of entitlement);
- an amount equivalent to the long-term rate after 28 weeks of entitlement, if you are terminally ill or receiving the highest rate of disability living allowance (DLA) care component (see Chapter 7). The definition of 'terminally ill' is the same as for DLA (see p121).[37]

Treated as entitled to incapacity benefit

For the purpose of determining the rate of benefit you receive, you are treated as entitled to IB on:[38]

- the first three days of your 'period of incapacity for work' (you cannot always receive IB for these days, which are called 'waiting days' – see p270);
- days on which you are entitled to maternity allowance (see Chapter 17);
- days on which you are entitled to statutory maternity pay (SMP) or statutory adoption pay (SAP) but only if:
  - you are incapable of work, and on the day before your SMP or SAP started you were within a period of incapacity for work (see p264) or were receiving statutory sick pay (SSP); *and*
  - the days are not days on which you are treated as capable of work for IB purposes (see p263); *and*
  - you satisfy the contribution conditions for IB on the first day in your period of incapacity for work or on a day on which you were receiving SSP;
- days on which you satisfied the contribution conditions for IB and were entitled to SSP, as long as your period of entitlement to SSP ended not more than 57 days before your current period of incapacity for work began (see p287);
- certain days of sickness absence from duty if you were a member of the armed forces.

Amount paid

The full weekly rates of IB are as follows, but in certain circumstances your IB may be reduced (see below).

	Under pension age £pw	*Pension age or over £pw*
Long-term IB		
Claimant	84.50	n/a
Adult dependant	50.55	n/a
Child dependant:		
– eldest eligible child	8.75	n/a
– each other child	11.35	n/a
Short-term IB (higher rate)		
Claimant	75.40	84.50
Adult dependant	39.40	48.65
Child dependant:		
– eldest eligible child	8.75	8.75
– each other child	11.35	11.35
Short-term IB (lower rate)		
Claimant	63.75	81.10
Adult dependant	39.40	48.65
Child dependant:		
– eldest eligible child	n/a	8.75
– each other child	n/a	11.35

If you are terminally ill or you are getting the highest rate of the DLA care component, your IB can be paid at a rate which is equivalent to the long-term rate of IB after you have been entitled to short-term IB for 196 days.[39]

See p272 and Chapter 29 for details of the qualifying conditions for payment of an increase in your IB for dependants.

If IB is payable for a period of less than a week it is paid at a daily rate of one-seventh of the weekly amount.

If you are entitled to long-term IB, you may also be entitled to:

- an age-related addition (see p275); *and*
- a Christmas bonus (see p9).

Your IB will be reduced if:

- you receive certain pension payments or certain payments from the Pension Protection Fund (see p276 for details and for details of exceptions);
- you are a local councillor and your net councillor's allowances exceed £88.50 a week (see p829);[40]

- you are over pension age (60 for women, 65 for men) and are entitled to short-term IB (you cannot qualify for long-term IB if you are over pension age) and your retirement pension, had you claimed it, would have been reduced because your national insurance (NI) contribution record is incomplete. In this situation your short-term IB will be reduced by the same proportion (see p739). However, as for people under pension age, if you are terminally ill or you are getting the highest rate of the DLA care component you can receive the equivalent of the long-term rate of IB after the first 196 days of entitlement to short-term IB, if this would be more favourable to you than receiving the higher rate of short-term IB.[41]

The amount of your benefit may also be reduced if you or, in some cases your partner, are required to take part in a work-focused interview and fail to do so (see p975) or if your partner is required to take part because you get an increase in your IB for her/him (see p972).

In some circumstances deductions from your benefit may be made to repay certain loans (see p992) and, if you get income support (IS) or pension credit (PC) with your IB, deductions may be made from your IB and paid directly to other third parties. This may happen if your IS or PC alone is insufficient to meet those payments (see p988).

For each week you receive IB you are entitled to NI contribution credits (see p728).

Certain people who are entitled to long-term IB throughout a tax year may also build up entitlement to additional state pension (see p476 for details).[42]

Age-related additions

Once you are entitled to long-term IB you are paid an age-related addition to your benefit if you were under 45 *either*:[43]

- on the first day of your period of incapacity for work (see p264); *or*
- on the first day of any previous periods of incapacity for work linked to your current one (see p264); *or*
- on the first day of your period of entitlement to SSP (see p557), if you were previously on SSP and your current period of incapacity for work started not more than 57 days after your SSP stopped.

Special rules apply to certain widows or if you are a serving member of the armed forces.[44]

This age-related addition is paid at two rates depending on your age on the relevant day.

Age	*£pw*
Under 35	17.75
Under 45	8.90

If you receive a guaranteed minimum pension from a contracted-out occupational pension scheme (which may be from your late spouse's or late civil partner's pension scheme) the amount of your age addition will be reduced by the amount of your guaranteed minimum pension.[45]

Reduction in incapacity benefit for pension payments

If your entitlement to IB started on or after 6 April 2001 your benefit may be reduced if you receive certain kinds of pension payments (but see p277 if you receive the highest rate of DLA care component).

If the total amount of the gross pension payments you receive amounts to more than £85 a week, your IB is reduced by half the amount of pension payments paid above £85 a week.[46]

Example

Ebadur is entitled to IB from 30 April 2005. He is receiving two pensions, a personal pension of £52 a week gross and a public service pension of £43 a week gross. The pensions total £95 a week. As these amount to £10 more than £85, his IB is reduced by £5 a week (50 per cent of £10).

Your benefit is reduced proportionately if you get IB for a period of less than a week. If the total gross pension payments you receive amount to £85 or less each week then your IB is unaffected.

Pensions that are taken into account

Pension payments that are taken into account are periodic payments made under:[47]

- any personal, occupational, or public service pension scheme; *and*
- any permanant health insurance policy arranged by your employer that provides payments in connection with ill health or disability after your employment ends. However, if you contributed more than 50 per cent of the pension premiums the amount you receive from this kind of pension will be ignored; *and*
- the Pension Protection Fund.

Other types of pension payments (including one-off lump-sum payments) are ignored for the purpose of calculating your entitlement to IB. The following types of payment are also ignored and so will not affect your IB:

- any part of your pension paid direct to an ex-spouse or ex-civil partner by the pension scheme trustees under a court order;[48]
- any payments you receive as a result of the death of the pension holder[49] (but see p276 if you get an age addition with your IB and a guaranteed minimum pension from your late spouse's or civil partner's contracted-out occupational pension scheme).

If you are entitled to the highest rate of DLA care component (see Chapter 6) all pension payments you receive are ignored and so do not affect your entitlement to IB.[50]

If you were entitled to incapacity benefit before 6 April 2001

If you were entitled to IB before 6 April 2001 and you have continued to be entitled to IB since that time, any pension payments you receive will not affect your IB.[51] However, see p276 if you get an age addition with your IB and a guaranteed minimum pension from a contracted-out occupational pension scheme.

If you break your claim for IB but later requalify, pension payments you receive can still be ignored if your period(s) of incapacity for work can be linked (see p264).

5. Special benefit rules

There are some groups of claimants to whom special rules apply. These are covered below and in Chapters 25, 26 and 58. Special rules apply to:

- widows and widowers (see below);
- people who have been incapable of work since 12 April 1995 (see p278);
- people going abroad (see p1350);
- people in prison or detention (see p625).

Widows and widowers

If you are a widow or widower and your spouse died before 9 April 2001, you may qualify for incapacity benefit (IB) even if you do not satisfy the national insurance (NI) contribution conditions. If so, you can be paid long-term IB even if you have not received short-term IB first.

If you are a widow you are entitled under these rules if:[52]

- your husband died before 9 April 2001; *and*
- you were not entitled to widowed mother's allowance after your husband died or you are no longer entitled to widowed mother's allowance; *and*

- the date when your husband died or your widowed mother's allowance stopped was after 5 April 1979; *and*
- you are incapable of work and your current period of incapacity for work (see p264) began either before your husband died or before your widowed mother's allowance stopped, and has lasted for at least 364 days (or 196 days if you are terminally ill, see p121); *and*
- you would have been entitled to widow's pension if you had been over 45 when your husband died or when your widowed mother's allowance stopped, or you receive a reduced widow's pension because of your age at the relevant time (see p31); *and*
- you would not otherwise be entitled to any rate of IB – eg, because you have not paid or been credited with sufficient contributions.

In these circumstances, you receive the long-term rate of IB or, if you are receiving a reduced rate of widow's pension, you receive that and the difference between the rate of widow's pension you receive and the long-term rate of IB.[53]

If you are a widower you are entitled if:[54]

- your wife died after 5 April 1979 but before 9 April 2001; *and*
- you were incapable of work when she died or you became incapable of work within 13 weeks of the day after her death; *and*
- your period of incapacity for work has lasted for at least 364 days (or 196 days if you are terminally ill – see p121); *and*
- you would not otherwise be entitled to any rate of IB – eg, because you have not paid or been credited with sufficient contributions.

In these circumstances you receive the long-term rate of IB. If you are a widower who has a qualifying child you may also qualify for widowed parent's allowance (see p21). However, the overlapping benefit rules mean that you cannot receive both widowed parent's allowance and IB in full (see p981).

Days in receipt of statutory sick pay (see Chapter 24) count towards the 364-day (or 196-day) period of incapacity for work for both widows and widowers.

You cannot qualify for long-term IB under these provisions if you are over pension age, but you may qualify for a Category A pension under these rules instead.[55]

Your entitlement to long-term IB on the basis of being a widow or widower ends following the issue of a full gender recognition certificate.[56]

People incapable of work since 12 April 1995

IB was introduced on 13 April 1995 and replaced sickness benefit and invalidity benefit. Some people who were getting invalidity benefit immediately before IB was introduced, including some who qualified on the basis of an industrial injury, are still protected by transitional rules and receive 'transitional long-term IB' (see the 8th edition of CPAG's *Welfare Benefits and Tax Credits Handbook* for further details).[57]

6. **Claims and backdating**

To be entitled to incapacity benefit (IB) you must make a claim for it.[58] The main rules for claiming are described in Chapter 38. The following section explains the specific rules for IB.

If you are claiming IB you may be required to attend work-focused interviews and, if you fail to take part in such an interview, your benefit may be reduced (see p971). If you are making a new claim (and in some areas even if you have already made your claim) you may be required to take part in a more intensive work-focused interview procedure under the Pathways to Work scheme (see p973).[59]

It may be possible to claim in advance (see p282) or to get your claim backdated (see p282).

If you wish, you may amend or withdraw your claim in writing before it is assessed.

Making a claim

A claim for IB must be made in writing on the appropriate form. The decision maker at the DWP may accept a written application that is not on the correct form if this is sufficient in the circumstances (see p959).[60] You must also make a written claim for an increase for a dependant (see Chapter 29).

It is always advisable to keep a copy of your claim form in case queries arise.

You will usually be expected to start your claim (particularly if you are under 60) either by:

- telephoning a DWP contact centre – the DWP will complete a claim form with you and send it for you to sign (see p956); *or*
- submitting a short electronic form at www.dwp.gov.uk/eservice. You give basic details on this form and give a convenient time for someone from the DWP to telephone you in order to complete a full claim form. Submitting the electronic form indicates that you want to start claiming IB and is not the same as actually making a claim, so if you do not get a quick reply, seek advice.

If you are 60 or over, the DWP may send you a claim form to complete (Form SC1) rather than completing a claim form with you over the telephone.

Although it is best to use the telephone or internet to start your claim if you can (particularly if you are under 60), if you cannot or do not want to do so, the DWP should still be able to deal with your claim in other ways. For example, the DWP should accept a paper claim form, either on Form SC1 or, if you are claiming on the grounds of being incapable of work in youth, Form IB(Y)1 (although an SC1 claim form can be treated as a claim for IB on the basis of incapacity in youth).[61] You may be able obtain these claim forms from your local DWP or Jobcentre Plus office. They are also available on the Jobcentre Plus website.

If you complete either Form SC1 or IB(Y)1, you should send it to the DWP office covering your local area (usually, this will be a regional benefit delivery centre). The address should be in the telephone directory or you may be able to obtain it from your local Jobcentre Plus office. You may instead send or take your claim form to a designated local authority office or other 'alternative office', or if you live in England a designated office of a county council (see p958).

If you intend to make your claim by completing an SC1 or IB(Y)1 form, in some cases it may be worth telephoning your local DWP or Jobcentre Plus office (or your designated local authority or county council office or other 'alternative office') to tell them you intend to claim IB. As long as your form is received within a month of your telephone call, the date of your IB claim will be the date of your call (see p281). However, in practice this will normally only be necessary if your claim form is likely to be received more than three months after the date from which you want to claim IB, as a claim for IB can be backdated for up to three months anyway if you satisfy the qualifying conditions over that period (see p282).

If you are employed

If you are employed you should normally be paid statutory sick pay (SSP – see Chapter 24) for the first 28 weeks of your incapacity for work. If your employer thinks that you are not entitled to SSP or if your entitlement to SSP has run out, your employer should complete and give you an SSP1 form and you should claim IB from your local DWP or Jobcentre Plus office as described above. You will normally be expected to include the SSP1 form and a medical certificate with your claim. If you disagree with your employer's decision to refuse to pay you SSP or to stop paying you SSP, you can refer the matter to the Revenue (see p1151), but do not delay claiming IB while you do so. If you have asked the Revenue to decide whether you should qualify for SSP, explain this to the DWP when you make your IB claim. See p282 if you are claiming IB after your employer has refused your claim for SSP.

Information to support your claim

When you claim IB, you and any adult dependant for whom you are claiming must satisfy the national insurance number requirement (see p962).

You can also be asked to supply 'certificates, documents, information and evidence' considered relevant to your claim.[62] For example, you will normally be expected to provide medical evidence of your incapacity for work (see p281). Evidence or documents relating to your claim may be taken or sent to your local DWP or Jobcentre Plus office. Designated local authority or county council offices, or certain other 'alternative offices' may also be able to accept evidence and documents from you in connection with your claim (see p958).

If you are asked to provide evidence or documents that you do not have, ask what other evidence would be acceptable. Always ask the DWP to explain what is required and why, and complain if you think any requests for information are unreasonable.

Medical evidence

For the first seven days of your incapacity for work the DWP should accept a self-certificate. After seven days you need to provide proof of your incapacity for work in the form of a medical certificate from your doctor. If it is unreasonable to expect you to provide a medical certificate (MED 3) from a doctor, the DWP should accept other evidence if this is sufficient to show that you should not work because of some specific disease or bodily or mental disablement.[63] If you have been (or are likely to be) unfit for work for more than seven days you should send the medical certificate with the claim form.

When making a decision on your claim, the decision maker may refer your case to a medical practitioner (normally a Medical Service doctor or other approved healthcare professional – see p661) for a report and a medical examination. If you fail to attend a medical examination without good cause your claim can be refused.[64]

Who should claim

You must normally claim IB on your own behalf. However, IB can be claimed by another adult on your behalf if you are not able to act for yourself. This person is your 'appointee' (see p955 for further details).

The date of your claim

The date of your claim is important as it determines the date from which you will be paid IB (see p284). The date of your claim is normally the earlier of:

- the date you first notified a DWP or Jobcentre Plus office (if you prefer, you can also notify a designated local authority or English county council office or other 'alternative office' (see p958) of your intention to make a claim, and submit the claim to that office) of your intention to make a claim (eg, by telephoning the contact centre or submitting an electronic form), as long as your properly completed claim form (see p279) is received by one of those offices within a month of that date (see below if you are aged 60 over); *or*
- the date your properly completed claim form or signed statement is received at a DWP or Jobcentre Plus office (or other certain other office).[65]

If you submit a claim form which is not properly completed or you make a written claim but it is not on the correct form, you may be asked to provide further information or complete the correct form. As long as the DWP or Jobcentre Plus office receives this additional information or form within a month of it being sent back to you (or longer if the decision maker thinks that the delay is reasonable), your claim is treated as properly made on the date the initial claim was received (see p959).[66]

A claim can be counted as having been received at the office even on a day when the office is closed if that is the day it would have normally been delivered.[67]

In some circumstances you can claim before you qualify for IB or the date of your claim can be backdated (see below).

If you claim the wrong benefit

If you are employed and have claimed SSP but your employer decides that you are not entitled to SSP, and you claim IB within three months of being notified of your employer's decision in writing, your claim for IB is treated as having been made on the date of your claim for SSP.[68]

A claim for maternity allowance (MA) may be treated as a claim for IB.[69] If your MA claim is accepted as a claim for IB, your IB can be backdated for up to three months before the date you claimed MA if you satisfy the qualifying conditions over that period. See p963 for details of interchanging claims in this way.

Claiming in advance

You can claim IB up to three months before you expect to qualify for it.[70] It is helpful to claim in advance if you can, as it can allow the DWP time to gather the information it may need to decide your claim.

How your claim is dealt with

Your claim is dealt with by the DWP office that covers your local area and queries about your claim should be made to that office.

You may be able to claim an interim payment while waiting for a decision on your claim (see p986), or to claim means-tested benefits if your income is low (see p286), or apply for a crisis loan to tide you over until benefit is paid (see p503).

See p970 for more information about the processing of claims.

Backdating your claim

A claim for IB can be backdated for up to three months as long as you satisfy the qualifying conditions over that period. You do not have to show reasons why your claim was late.[71]

If you were previously entitled to IB but your benefit was stopped because you were not thought to be incapable of work and:

- when your IB stopped you had made a claim for disability living allowance (DLA), or constant attendance allowance and the claim had not been decided; *and*
- your claim for that benefit was successful and you were awarded the highest rate of the DLA care component, or constant attendance allowance paid at a rate that is higher than the 'lower weekly rate' (which means that you are exempt from the personal capability assessment); *and*
- you make a further claim for IB within three months of the decision to award you the other benefit,

your later claim for IB can be backdated either to the date that your previous claim for IB stopped, or to the date from which you were awarded the other benefit, whichever is later.[72]

If you might have qualified for benefit earlier but did not claim because you were given the wrong information or were misled by the DWP you could ask for an *ex gratia* payment (see p1186) or complain to the Ombudsman via your MP (see p1184).

If you have claimed SSP or MA instead of IB, see p282.

See p965 for more details about the backdating of claims.

Starting work when your claim ends

When your IB ends you are given a form by the DWP. If you are starting work or returning to your job you should give this form to your employer.

If you start work within a month of your entitlement to IB stopping, you may be able to benefit from the rules for 'welfare to work' beneficiaries (see p666). If you are a 'welfare to work' beneficiary and you become incapable of work again within your 104-week linking period, you can return to the same level of IB that you were previously receiving (see p666).

Even if you do not qualify as a 'welfare to work' beneficiary, if you return to work but fall sick again within eight weeks of the end of your previous period of incapacity for work (see p264), you can then claim IB and not SSP.

Linking periods of incapacity for work in this way may be beneficial because IB paid at the higher short-term rate or the long-term rate is more than SSP, and can include additions for dependants. If you do go off work again within your linked period your employer should give you Form SSP1, which you should submit with your claim for IB.

Certain people may qualify for a return-to-work credit or in-work credit when they start work. Ask at your local Jobcentre Plus office about these schemes.

You may be able to claim an extended payment of housing benefit and council tax benefit if your entitlement to IB stops because you either start work, your hours of work increase or your earnings go up (see p211). Certain IB claimants may also qualify for a job grant on starting work (see p14).

When you return to work you may also be entitled to tax credits or means-tested benefits if your income is low (see Chapter 1).

7. Getting paid

Incapacity benefit (IB) is a daily benefit, which means that it can be paid for periods of less than a week. The daily rate is one-seventh of the weekly amount.

IB is normally paid by direct credit transfer into your bank (or similar) account. If you are unable to open or manage an account, payment can be made by cheque (see p978).[73]

If you satisfy the qualifying conditions, you are paid IB from the date of your claim, although you normally receive payment of IB fortnightly in arrears unless:

- immediately before you claimed IB you were claiming income support (IS – see Chapter 13) because you were too ill or disabled to work and IS was being paid to you weekly, in which case IB is paid weekly in arrears;[74] *or*
- you have been continuously entitled to IB since 13 April 1995 and were entitled to sickness benefit or invalidity benefit (which were replaced by IB) on 12 April 1995, in which case IB is paid weekly in arrears;[75] *or*
- the amount you are due is less than £1 a week, in which case it may be paid four-weekly in arrears, but see below if your IB is reduced because of pension payments you receive;[76] *or*
- your IB is reduced to less than £5 a week because of pension payments that you receive (see p276), in which case the DWP decision maker can decide how often you are paid, although you must be paid at least once a year.[77]

Payment may be made to someone else on your behalf if you are unable to act for yourself (called your 'appointee' – see p955).

If your IB has been reduced because you (or your partner) failed to take part in a work-focused interview, see p976.

See p274 for other reasons why your IB may be reduced.

Your IB may be suspended and eventually stopped if you are asked by the DWP to provide a medical certificate and you do not do so.[78]

If payment of your IB is suspended, see p984.

If your benefit cheque is missing, see p983.

Delays and complaints

If payment of your IB is delayed, you might be able to get an interim payment. See p986 for further details.

If you experience delays (see p1186), or wish to complain about how your claim has been dealt with, see p1181. You might be able to claim compensation (see p1186).

Change of circumstances

You must report any change in your circumstances that the DWP has informed you that you should tell it about (but it is important to remember that the DWP might not inform you of all the changes you need to tell it about). It is also your duty to report changes which you might reasonably be expected to know might affect your entitlement to, the amount of, or the payment of, your benefit.[79] You should report such changes promptly, either by writing to, or telephoning, the office handling your claim, unless the DWP has decided that you can tell it about the change in another way. In some cases, the decision maker might say you *must* report changes in writing. In practice, it is *always* advisable to report the change in writing, or to confirm a telephone conversation in writing and keep a copy of your letter, in case of a dispute in the future. If you do not promptly report any such change, any resulting overpayment may be recoverable from you (see Chapter 39). If you are considered deliberately to have acted falsely or dishonestly, you may also be guilty of an offence (see Chapter 40).

IB is normally awarded for an indefinite period, unless your circumstances are likely to change shortly after the award.[80] In order for payment of IB to be stopped or adjusted, the decision on your entitlement must first be revised or superseded. The rules about when a decision on your IB claim can be revised or superseded, and about the date from which a new decision takes effect, are described in Chapter 41. For example, if the Medical Service has provided a new medical report to the DWP see p1077, or if a decision on your entitlement to IB has been superseded because it has been decided you can be treated as incapable of work because you are exempt from the personal capability assessment,[81] see p1084.

Overpayments and fraud

If you are overpaid IB, you might have to repay it. The rules on overpayments are covered in Chapter 39.

If you have been accused of fraud, see Chapter 40. You may not be paid IB if you have been sanctioned for benefit offences (see p1047).

8. Challenging an incapacity benefit decision

You can apply for a revision or supersession of an incapacity benefit (IB) decision, or appeal against it (see Chapters 41 and 42).

If you are appealing a question that relates to whether you are incapable of work under the personal capability assessment, your appeal will be heard by an appeal tribunal. This must include at least one medically qualified and one legally qualified person.[82] The chair of the tribunal may refer you for a medical examination if this is necessary to help the tribunal decide whether you are incapable of work.[83] See p681 for advice on appeals relating to your incapacity for work. If you make a fresh claim for IB while waiting for your appeal to be decided, the decision on that claim can be revised on the basis of the appeal tribunal's eventual decision.[84]

Certain decisions cannot be appealed, although you can request that they be revised or superseded (see p1097).

9. Tax, tax credits and other benefits

The general rule is that incapacity benefit (IB) is taxable apart from the following, which are tax free:[85]

- the lower rate of short-term IB;
- transitional long-term IB (see p278) paid because you were receiving invalidity benefit on 12 April 1995; *and*
- any increase in your IB paid for one or more child dependants.

Tax credits

In addition to IB you may qualify for child tax credit (CTC – see Chapter 48) if you have at least one dependent child. If your partner works, or if you are receiving the lower rate of short-term IB and were in full-time paid work (see Chapter 50) immediately (or, arguably, during the four-week 'run-on period') before your IB began, you may qualify for working tax credit (WTC – see Chapter 49). However, the higher rate of short-term IB and long-term IB count in full as income for CTC and WTC. The lower rate of short-term IB (and transitional long-term IB – see p279) are ignored when calculating your entitlement to CTC and WTC.[86]

If your partner works and you pay for childcare, your entitlement to the higher rate of short-term or long-term IB can help you qualify for a childcare element with WTC (see p1240).

Your past entitlement to IB may help you qualify for WTC if you now work for at least 16 hours a week. It may also qualify you for the disability element and, if you or your partner are at least 50, the 50-plus element of WTC (see pp1237 and 1239 for details).[87]

As you normally cannot qualify for CTC for a young person who is receiving IB in her/his own right (see p1200), an overpayment of CTC may arise if a backdated payment of IB is made to a young person.

Means-tested benefits

If you have a low income, in addition to IB you may be entitled to income support (IS) if you are under 60 (see Chapter 13), or pension credit (PC) if you are 60 or over (see Chapter 18). You may also be entitled to housing benefit (HB – see Chapter 10) and council tax benefit (CTB – see Chapter 5). If you live with a partner s/he may be entitled to income-based jobseeker's allowance (JSA – see Chapter 15). If you are a member of a 'joint-claim couple' for JSA (see p381) you will not be required to be available for work, to actively seek work or to enter into a jobseeker's agreement if you are incapable of work, or treated as incapable of work. IB counts in full as income for all these benefits (less any tax payable on it) although it is not treated as qualifying income for the savings credit of PC.

If you are receiving IB at the long-term rate (or if your IB is paid at a rate equivalent to the long-term rate because you are terminally ill) and you are under 60, you qualify for a disability premium for IS, income-based JSA, HB and CTB (see p779). Your entitlement to long-term IB (or to IB paid at a rate equivalent to the long-term rate because you are terminally ill) can also qualify your partner for a higher pensioner premium within her/his income-based JSA (if either of you is 60 or over) or IS (if you are 60 or over but s/he is not). In some circumstances, if you are entitled to IB, certain childcare costs may be deducted from your partner's earnings and/or from your own earnings, if you have any, when calculating your entitlement to HB and CTB (see p856). In some cases, your earnings and any WTC and CTC you or your partner receive can be added together before applying this deduction.

You may be able to claim an extended payment of HB and CTB if your entitlement to IB stops because you either start work, your hours of work increase or your earnings go up (see p211).

Non-means-tested benefits

IB is affected by the overlapping benefit rules, which means that you may not qualify for IB in full if another earnings-replacement benefit is paid to you (see p981).

Statutory sick pay

You cannot receive IB if you are receiving statutory sick pay (SSP).[88] However, provided:

- your period of entitlement to SSP ended not more than 57 days before your current period of incapacity for work; *and*
- you would have satisfied the contribution conditions for IB (see p735),

any week during which you received a whole week's SSP counts as seven days of short-term IB for the purpose of satisfying the qualifying periods for long-term, and the higher rate of short-term, IB if you claim IB after your SSP ends.[89]

Odd days of entitlement to SSP are also taken into account.[90]

Days on which you receive SSP can also count towards the 196 days for which you must be incapable of work in order to qualify for IB on the grounds of your incapacity for work in youth (see p266).

Statutory adoption pay and statutory maternity pay

Days within the maternity pay period (see p536) and the adoption pay period can count towards the qualifying period for long-term, or the higher rate of short-term, IB (see p273).

If you are entitled to statutory maternity pay (SMP) or statutory adoption pay (SAP) and either the higher short-term rate of IB or long-term IB, your IB will be reduced by the gross amount of SMP or SAP to which you are entitled. If you are only entitled to the lower short-term rate of IB you will not qualify for IB while you are entitled to SMP or SAP.[91]

Jobseeker's allowance

You cannot normally qualify for JSA and IB at the same time. This is because you must be capable of work to qualify for JSA (although short periods of sickness can be ignored – see p345) and incapable of work to qualify for IB.[92]

A period of incapacity for work can sometimes link two or more 'jobseeking periods' – ie, periods during which you are entitled to JSA (see p340).

If a decision maker decides you are no longer entitled to IB, perhaps because s/he considers you are capable of work, you will often not receive notification of this until after the date your entitlement ends. If you subsequently claim JSA you may be able to get the JSA claim backdated for up to a month, so that you do not lose out in these circumstances (see p966).

Retirement pension

You cannot receive IB if you are receiving Category A retirement pension or Category B retirement pension as a widow or widower.

If you received the age-related addition to long-term IB at any point during the eight weeks (104 weeks if you are a 'welfare to work' beneficiary – see p666) before you reach pension age, an equivalent amount is added to your retirement pension.[93]

Short-term IB is paid at a higher rate after you reach pension age (but see p275 if, had you claimed it, your retirement pension would have been reduced because your national insurance contribution record was incomplete).

The circumstances in which it may be advisable to remain on short-term IB rather than claim your retirement pension include:

- if you have sufficient income from other sources to pay income tax during the first six months of your entitlement to short-term IB when, unlike retirement pensions, IB is not taxable; *or*
- if you are not entitled to a full-rate retirement pension and you are terminally ill or getting the highest rate of disability living allowance care component, if the amount of IB paid after 196 days would be higher than the rate of retirement pension to which you are entitled.

Passports and other sources of help

If you are on a low income, you might be entitled to certain health service benefits, such as free prescriptions (see Chapter 9). You may also qualify for a social fund payment (see Chapters 21 and 22) and free school meals for any children you have (see p15) or for other sources of help (see p14).

Certain IB claimants in pilot areas may be entitled to return-to work credit or in-work credit when they start work, or to a job preparation premium. Certain IB claimants may also qualify for a job grant on starting work (see p14). Ask about these schemes at your local Jobcentre Plus office.

Notes

1. **Who can claim incapacity benefit**
   1 s30A and Sch 12 para 1 SSCBA 1992
   2 s30C(2) SSCBA 1992
   3 Reg 4A(2) SS(IB) Regs
   4 Reg 5 SS(IB) Regs
   5 Reg 4 SS(IB) Regs
   6 s171ZP(1) and Sch 13 para 1 SSCBA 1992; regs 7A and 7B SS(IB) Regs
   7 Reg 4(1)(a)(iv) SS(IB) Regs
   8 s30C(1)(b) SSCBA 1992
   9 Reg 6 SS(IB) Regs
   10 Reg 13 SS(IFW) Regs
   11 s30C(1)(c) SSCBA 1992
   12 *CAO v Astle* [1999] *Journal of Social Security Law*, Vol 6, Issue 4
   13 s30C(5), (5A) and (5B) SSCBA 1992
   14 s30C(6) SSCBA 1992
   15 s30C(6) SSCBA 1992; reg 3 SS(IB) Regs
   16 s30A(1)(b)and (2A) SSCBA 1992
   17 Reg 4A SS(IB) Regs
   18 s30A(2A)(c) SSCBA 1992
   19 Reg 15 SS(IB) Regs
   20 Reg 15(4) SS(IB) Regs
   21 Reg 15(5) SS(IB) Regs
   22 Reg 15(5) SS(IB) Regs
   23 Reg 17(2) SS(IB) Regs
   24 Reg 17(3) SS(IB) Regs
   25 R(S) 2/87
   26 Reg 18 SS(IB) Regs
   27 s30A(3) SSCBA 1992
   28 s30A(3) and Sch 12 para 4 SSCBA 1992; reg 2 SSCBA (MHMFIB) Regs; reg 7C SS(IB) Regs
   29 s171E SSCBA 1992; reg 18 SS(IFW) Regs
   30 R(S) 2/53

2. **The rules about your age**
   31 s30A(5) SSCBA 1992
   32 s30A(2)(b) SSCBA 1992

3. **Claiming for others**
   33 s86A SSCBA 1992; reg 9 SS(IB-ID) Regs
   34 Reg 19(2) and (3) SS(C&P) Regs
   35 Regs 2 and 3 SS(JPIP) Regs

4. **The amount of benefit**
   36 s30D(4) SSCBA 1992
   37 s30B(4) SSCBA 1992
   38 s30D SSCBA 1992; reg 3 SSCBA (MHMFIB) Regs; regs 7, 7A, 7B and 7C SS(IB) Regs
   39 s30B(4) SSCBA 1992
   40 s30E SSCBA 1992; regs 8 and 9 SS(IB) Regs
   41 s30B(3) and (4) SSCBA 1992
   42 s44A SSCBA 1992
   43 s30B(7) SSCBA 1992; regs 10 and 11 SS(IB) Regs
   44 Regs 12 and 13 SS(IB) Regs
   45 s46(3) Pension Schemes Act 1993
   46 s30DD SSCBA 1992; R(IB)3/05
   47 s30DD(5) SSCBA 1992; regs 20 and 21 SS(IB) Regs
   48 R(IB) 1/04; paras 56144-46 DMG
   49 Reg 21 SS(IB) Regs
   50 Reg 26 SS(IB) Regs
   51 Reg 6 SS(IB)MA Regs

5. **Special benefit rules**
52 s40 SSCBA 1992
53 s40(5) SSCBA 1992
54 s41 SSCBA 1992
55 ss40(6) and 41(5) SSCBA 1992
56 Sch 5 para 6 GRA 2004
57 SS(IB)(T) Regs

6. **Claims and backdating**
58 s1 SSAA 1992
59 SS(IBWFI) Regs. See CPAG's *Welfare Rights Bulletin* 177 p7 and 180 p5 for details
60 Reg 4(1) SS(C&P) Regs
61 CIB/1410/2005
62 Reg 7(1) SS(C&P) Regs
63 Regs 2 and 5 SS(ME) Regs
64 s19 SSA 1998
65 Reg 6(1), (1D) and (1E) SS(C&P) Regs
66 Regs 4(7) and 6(1) SS(C&P) Regs
67 R(SB) 8/89; CIB/2805/2003
68 Reg 10(1) and (2) SS(C&P) Regs
69 Reg 9 and Sch 1 Part I SS(C&P) Regs
70 Reg 13 SS(C&P) Regs
71 Reg 19(1)and Sch 4 SS(C&P) Regs; CIB/2805/2003
72 Reg 6(23) and (24) SS(C&P) Regs

7. **Getting paid**
73 Reg 21 SS(C&P) Regs
74 Reg 24(2)(b) SS(C&P) Regs
75 Reg 24(2)(a) SS(C&P) Regs
76 Reg 24(3) SS(C&P) Regs
77 Reg 24(3A) SS(C&P) Regs
78 Reg 17 SS&CS(DA) Regs
79 Reg 32 SS(C&P) Regs
80 Reg 17 SS(C&P) Regs
81 Reg 7(11) SS&CS(DA) Regs

8. **Challenging an incapacity benefit decision**
82 Reg 36 SS&CS(DA) Regs
83 s20 SSA 1998; reg 41 SS&CS(DA) Regs
84 Reg 3(5A) SS&CS(DA) Regs

9. **Tax, tax credits and other benefits**
85 ss660-64 and 676 IT(EP)A 2003
86 Reg 7 TC(DCI) Regs
87 Regs 9 and 18 WTC(EMR) Regs
88 Sch 12 para 1 SSCBA 1992
89 s30D(3) SSCBA 1992; reg 7 SS(IB) Regs
90 Reg 7(2)(b) SS(IB) Regs
91 s171ZP(1) and Sch 13 para 1 SSCBA 1992; regs 7A and 7B SS(IB) Regs
92 Reg 55 JSA Regs
93 s47(1) SSCBA 1992; reg 3A SS(WB&RP) Regs

Chapter 13

Income support

This chapter covers:

Income support (IS) is a benefit for people with a low income. It is not paid to unemployed people who have to be available for and actively seeking work. They may be able to claim jobseeker's allowance instead. IS is not paid to people in full-time paid work (see Chapter 27), who may be able to claim working tax credit.

You do not have to have paid national insurance (NI) contributions to qualify for IS.

In some situations, while you are on IS you are credited with Class 1 NI contributions (see p727 for further details), or you may qualify for 'home responsibilities protection' (see p733).

Employment and support allowance

IS paid on the grounds of incacapity for work and incapacity benefit (IB) are to be replaced with employment and support allowance (ESA). This is expected to be in October 2008. ESA will be an integrated contributory and means-tested benefit (see Chapter 7 for further information). It will be paid to new claimants only; existing IS and IB claimants will remain on those benefits. However, the current IS rules may be subject to change. See www.cpag.org.uk/esa or CPAG's *Welfare Rights Bulletin* for updates.

1. Who can claim income support

You qualify for income support (IS) if:[1]

- you fit into one of the groups of people who can claim IS (see below);
- neither you nor your partner count as in full-time paid work (see p296 and Chapter 27). You can claim if you are temporarily away from full-time work – eg, you are sick or on unpaid parental or paternity leave (see p294) or if you have recently returned to work after a trade dispute (see p654). If you have just taken up full-time paid work you may be able to claim IS for the first four weeks – known as 'mortgage interest run-on' (see p823);
- you are not studying full time. There are exceptions to this rule (see p582). See p577 if you are at school or college. See p584 if you are studying part time;
- you are not entitled to contribution-based jobseeker's allowance (JSA) and neither you nor your partner are entitled to income-based JSA (either individually or as a 'joint-claim couple'). **Note:** when the rules on the new employment and support allowance (ESA) take effect (see Chapter 7), in order to qualify for IS you must not be entitled to ESA and your partner must not be entitled to income-related ESA;
- your partner is not entitled to pension credit (PC);
- you are at least 16 and are under 60. If you are 60 or over, you may be able to claim PC;
- your income is less than your applicable amount (see p299);
- your savings and other capital are worth £16,000 or less. Some capital (in particular, your home) is ignored (see Chapter 37); *and*
- you satisfy the 'habitual residence test' and the 'right to reside test', and are present in Great Britain. To find out if you are exempt from the tests, see Chapter 59. To see if you can claim IS during a temporary absence abroad, see p1350; *and*
- you are not a 'person subject to immigration control' (see p1334).[2] There are exceptions to this rule, but for some of these, you are only entitled to an urgent cases payment (see p297).

There are some groups of claimants to whom special rules apply (see p300). In addition, if you do not satisfy the normal rules for IS, you may be able to get an urgent cases payment of IS (see p297).

In some cases, you (or your partner if you have one) may be required to attend a work-focused interview. See p297 for further information.

Groups of people who can claim income support

You can claim IS if you satisfy the other rules for getting IS described above and fit into one of the groups described below.[3] If you fit into one of the groups on any day in a benefit week, you count as doing so for the whole week.

Sick and disabled people[4]

Employment and support allowance

IS paid on the grounds of incacapity for work and incapacity benefit (IB) are to be replaced with employment and support allowance (ESA). This is expected to be in October 2008. ESA will be an integrated contributory and means-tested benefit (see Chapter 7 for further information). It will be paid to new claimants only; existing IS and IB claimants will remain on those benefits. However, the current IS rules may be subject to change. See www.cpag.org.uk/esa or CPAG's *Welfare Rights Bulletin* for updates.

- You are incapable of work because of illness or disability and you:
  - are entitled to statutory sick pay (see Chapter 24); *or*
  - satisfy the 'own occupation test' (see p667) or the 'personal capability assessment' for IB (see p668); *or*
  - are treated as incapable of work by a decision maker – eg, because you have a severe condition or an infectious disease, or are blind (see p662); *or*
  - are treated as capable of work because you are disqualified from receiving IB because of misconduct or failure to accept treatment (see p271).
- You are appealing a decision that you are not entitled to a benefit (eg, IS or IB) because you are not treated as incapable of work under:
  - the own occupation test – see p667 (if you continue to send in medical certificates during the period of your appeal); *or*
  - the personal capability assessment – see p668 (but you might be paid at a reduced rate – see p294).

  You *must appeal* to fit into this group of people who can get IS. You must appeal against the decision refusing you benefit or national insurance credits, not the determination that says you are fit for work. You can get IS from the date you are treated as capable of work until your appeal has been finally determined.[5]

  You do *not* come within this group of people who can claim IS if:
  - you simply ask for a revision (see p1065); *or*
  - you are appealing any other type of decision about your incapacity for work – eg, if you are treated as capable of work because you failed to attend a medical without good cause (see p678).

  If you are in these situations, you cannot get IS unless you come within any of the other groups of people who can claim described in this chapter.
- You are mentally or physically disabled and because of this your earnings or the number of hours you work are reduced to 75 per cent or less of that for a person without your disability in the same or a comparable job.
- You are registered blind (certified blind in Scotland). If you regain your sight you continue to be treated as blind for 28 weeks after you have been taken off the register.
- You are someone who counts as not in full-time work while living in a care home, an Abbeyfield home or an independent hospital (see p655).

If you are appealing about the personal capability assessment

If you are claiming IS while appealing about the personal capability assessment and you do not come within any of the other groups of people who can claim IS described in this chapter, you are given a 'benefit penalty'.[6] Your IS is reduced by 20 per cent of the personal allowance for a single claimant of your age (see p773).

If you are given a benefit penalty, you may be better off claiming JSA (see p683 for more information about claiming JSA in this situation). Your claim for JSA should not influence the decision on your appeal about your incapacity for work.

If your appeal is successful, any reduction in the amount of your benefit, for example because you lost the disability premium (see p779), must be repaid to you.

People with childcare responsibilities and carers[7]

- You are a lone parent who is responsible for a child under 16 who lives in your household (see pp710 and 712).[8] Once your only or youngest child turns 16, you cannot claim IS unless you fit into one of the other groups of people who can claim. **Note:** the Government may lower this age to 12 in 2008 and to seven by 2010. See CPAG's *Welfare Rights Bulletin* for updates.
- You are entitled to and on 'parental leave' from work under the rules in the Maternity and Parental Leave etc. Regulations 1999; *and*
  - during the period for which you are claiming IS, you are not entitled to a payment of any kind from your employer; *and*
  - you and your child(ren) live in the same household (see p 712); *and*
  - you were entitled to working tax credit (WTC), child tax credit (CTC) payable at a higher rate than the family element, housing benefit (HB) or council tax benefit (CTB) on the day before your parental leave began.
- You are entitled to and on paternity leave;[9] *and*
  - not entitled to statutory paternity pay (see p528) or to a payment of any kind from your employer during the period for which you are claiming IS; *or*
  - you were entitled to WTC, CTC payable at a higher rate than the family element, HB or CTB on the day before your paternity leave began.
- You are fostering a child under 16 through a local authority or voluntary organisation and are not a member of a couple (see p702).
- You are looking after a child under 16 because her/his parent or the person who usually looks after her/him is temporarily away or ill.[10]
- You are responsible for a child under 16 who lives in your household (see pp710 and 712) and your partner is temporarily out of the UK.
- You are pregnant; *and*
  - incapable of work because of your pregnancy. You only have to show that you are incapable of work, not that there is a serious risk to your health or that of your baby;[11] *or*
  - there are 11 weeks or less before the week your baby is due.
- You had a baby not more than 15 weeks ago.

- You are looking after your partner, or a child (this includes a 'qualifying young person') for whom you are responsible and who lives in your household (see pp710 and 712), who is temporarily ill.
- You are a carer, and either:
  - you receive carer's allowance (CA), or would receive it had it not been restricted under the 'loss of benefit for benefit offences' rules (see p1047); *or*
  - the person for whom you care:
    - has claimed attendance allowance (AA) or disability living allowance (DLA). You are entitled to IS for up to 26 weeks from the date of the claim for AA/DLA or until the claim is decided, whichever comes first; *or*
    - receives AA or the highest or middle rate care component of DLA; *or*
    - has been awarded AA or the highest or middle rate care component of DLA on an advance claim but it has not yet gone into payment.

  You must be 'regularly and substantially engaged' in providing care. For CA, this means for at least 35 hours a week. However, to qualify for IS if you do not receive CA, the decision maker must look at the quality and quantity of care you provide. This could be less than 35 hours a week.[12]

  If you cease meeting these conditions or stop being a carer, you can continue to claim IS for a further eight weeks. After that, you cannot get IS unless you fit into one of the other groups of people who can claim described in this chapter.

Pupils, students and people on training courses[13]

- You are a person in 'relevant education' who can qualify for IS (see p576).
- You are a student who can claim IS (see p582).
- You are aged 16 to 24 and on a training course being provided by the Learning and Skills Council for England, the National Assembly for Wales, or in Scotland, by a local enterprise company. This does not apply if you are a child for child benefit purposes (see p57).

  Some participants on training schemes have the legal status of employees (and are normally given contracts of employment). If you are an employee, you do not qualify for IS if you are in full-time paid work (see p648). You might qualify for WTC instead (see Chapter 49).

  If you receive a training allowance while on a course, your income may be too high for you to qualify for IS. However, you are likely to qualify if, for example, you are on a lower rate of training allowance, qualify for a disability premium (see p779).

Others[14]

- You have to go to court or tribunal as a JP, juror, witness or party to the proceedings.
- You have beenremanded in custody, or committed in custody but only until your trial or until you have been sentenced (see p627). You can only get IS for

your housing costs (see Chapter 34). If you pay rent, you may qualify for HB (see p186) and if you pay council tax, you may qualify for CTB (see p83).

- You have been accepted by the Home Office as a refugee and you were officially notified of this on or before 14 June 2007 (but only from the date of your claim for asylum to the date the decision was made). This enables you to claim backdated IS (see p1347).
- You are a refugee who is learning English in order to obtain employment. You must be on a course for more than 15 hours a week and, at the time the course started, you must have been in Britain for a year or less. You can get IS for up to nine months.
- You are a 'person subject to immigration control', but you are entitled to the urgent cases rate of IS (see p1344).
- You are not treated as in full-time work because you qualify for 'mortgage interest run-on' (see pp823 and 655).
- You are involved in a trade dispute or have been back to work for 15 days or less following a trade dispute (see p634).

Full-time paid work

You cannot usually get IS if you or your partner are in full-time paid work. If you are the IS claimant, this means 16 hours or more each week. For your partner, this means 24 hours or more each week. If you both work less than this, you can get IS. In some situations you are treated as *not* in full-time work even if you work more than 16/24 hours (see p654). In others, you are treated as in full-time work when you are not (see p653). See p650 for details of how your hours are calculated and p649 for what counts as paid work.

If you or your partner normally work 16/24 hours or more but are off sick or on maternity, paternity or adoption leave you do not count as in full-time paid work.[15] You may, therefore, be able to claim IS if you fit into one of the groups of people who can claim. You might also qualify for WTC. **Note:** when the ESA rules take effect, you may have to claim ESA if you are away from work because you are sick (see Chapter 7).

If you or your partner have just taken up full-time paid work, you may be able to claim IS for help with your housing costs for the first four weeks. This is known as 'mortgage interest run-on' (see p823).

If you work less than 16 hours and your partner works at least 16 hours but less than 24 hours each week, you and your partner might be able to claim WTC. In some cases, you might be able to claim both WTC and IS. See p657 for further information. You should seek advice to see how you would be better off financially.

If your partner is 60 or over and either of you is working 16/24 hours or more each week, your partner might be able to claim PC or WTC (or both if your income is low enough). There is no full-time paid work rule for PC but earnings are taken into account when working out how much PC you can get.

Note: if you are claiming IS because you are incapable of work (see p293), you should consult the DWP *before* you do any work, even if this is for less than 16/24 hours or the work is unpaid. If you work, you might be treated as capable of work. If this happens, you cannot claim IS unless you fit into one of the other groups of people who can claim described in this chapter. See p662 for further information about work you may do while you are incapable of work.

Work-focused interviews

In many situations when you claim IS, you must attend a work-focused interview. This is so even if you are a lone parent. If you fail to do so without good cause:

- when you first claim IS, you might not count as making a valid claim;
- when you are already getting IS, you might be paid IS at a reduced rate.

If you have a partner, s/he can be required to attend a work-focused interview if you and s/he are both 18 or over but under 60. If your partner fails to attend an interview without good cause, your IS might be paid at a reduced rate.

See pp971–978 for further information about work-focused interviews.

Urgent cases payments

Urgent cases payments are payments of IS at a reduced rate (see p1344). You may be able to get these if you are:[16]

- a 'person subject to immigration control' (see p1334) and meet certain conditions; *or*
- treated as having income which was due to be paid to you but which has not been paid (see p874). The income you are treated as possessing must not be readily available to you and the decision maker must be satisfied that if you do not get an urgent cases payment, you, your partner or any child(ren) for whom you are responsible and who live in your household (see pp710 and 712) will experience hardship.[17] If you were due to receive a *benefit* but it has not been paid you are *not* treated as possessing it.

Urgent cases payments are calculated in a special way (see p1344). An urgent cases payment is a payment of IS, so you are automatically eligible for some other benefits (see p309). Even if your partner is entitled to ordinary IS you can claim urgent cases payments instead if the amount you receive would be higher. You do not have to make a separate claim for urgent cases payments.[18]

2. The rules about your age

You must be at least 16 to qualify for income support (IS). If you are 16 or 17, there are some issues to bear in mind (see p300). If you do not qualify for IS, check if you qualify for jobseeker's allowance (JSA) instead (see p371). Even if you cannot get IS or JSA you may qualify for housing benefit and council tax benefit.

You cannot claim IS if you are 60 or over. Instead, you can claim pension credit.

3. Claiming for others

You claim income support (IS) for yourself and your partner, if you have one. See p702 for who counts as a couple. If you do not fit into one of the groups of people who can claim IS (see p292) but your partner does, s/he could be the claimant. Whichever one of you claims IS, the other should seek advice about how to protect her/his national insurance record. See Chapter 31 for more details about national insurance credits.

In some cases, you need to know who counts as a member of your 'family' for IS purposes. Member of the **'family'** means your partner and any child who is a member of your household and for whom you count as 'responsible' (see below).[19]

Children

There are some situations when you must show that you are 'responsible' for a child who is living in your household – eg, you may need to show that you are a lone parent in order to fit into one of the groups of people who can claim IS. For information about when you count as responsible for a child and when s/he counts as living in your household, see p709.

You should remember the following.

- You can count as responsible for any child under 16, and for any qualifying young person – referred to as 'children' in this *Handbook* (see p710). You do not have to be the child's parent.[20]
- You can continue to count as responsible for children who have left school or training until the 'terminal date' (see p62) and during what is known as the 'extension period' (see p59).
- A young person claiming IS or jobseeker's allowance in her/his own right does not count as your child for IS purposes, nor do certain 16/17-year-olds who are no longer being looked after by a local authority (see p610).
- In some situations, a child does not count as a member of your household even if s/he normally does, or continues to count as a member of your household while s/he is temporarily away from home (see p712).

4. The amount of benefit

Income support (IS) tops up your income to a level that is set by the Government and which changes every April. The amount you get depends on your needs (your 'applicable amount') and on how much income and capital you have.[21] For the rules on income see Chapter 36, and on capital, Chapter 37. There are three steps involved in working out your IS (see below).

You may get a reduced amount of IS if:

- you refuse to co-operate with pursuing maintenance for your children (see p747); *or*
- you are claiming IS while appealing a decision of the DWP which says that you are capable of work under the personal capability assessment (see p294). This does not apply if you fit into one of the other groups of people who can claim IS (see p292); *or*
- you are getting an urgent cases payment of IS (see p297); *or*
- you (or in some cases your partner) were required to attend a work-focused interview and failed to do so without good cause (see pp971and 972); *or*
- a court has decided that you failed to comply with a community order without a reasonable excuse (see p997), or your IS has been restricted under the 'loss of benefit for benefit offences' rules (see p1047).

Step one: calculate your applicable amount

Your applicable amount consists of:

- **a personal allowance** (see p771); *plus*
- **premiums** (see p775) for any special needs; *plus*
- **housing costs**, principally for mortgage interest payments (see Chapter 34).

Personal allowances and premiums are increased every April. If you do not qualify for IS currently, you might qualify when the rates go up.

If you have children

If you claim IS and are getting child tax credit (CTC), IS does not include allowances and premiums for your children. CTC does not count as income for IS, nor does child benefit. If you were getting IS on 5 April 2004 and this included allowances and premiums for your children but you were not yet entitled to CTC, you will be transferred onto CTC sometime in the future. Until then, you will continue to get allowances and premiums for your children. See p709 for further information.

Step two: calculate your income

This is the amount you have coming in each week from, for instance, other benefits, part-time earnings, working tax credit and maintenance (see Chapter

36). If you have capital over £6,000 (£10,000 if you live in a care home) it also includes your tariff income (see p866).

Step three: deduct income from applicable amount

Example

Mr and Mrs Hughes, aged 27 and 29, have a daughter aged eight. Mr Hughes has been incapable of work for two years. He gets long-term rate incapacity benefit (IB) of £99.15. Mrs Hughes gets child benefit and CTC. The couple have no housing costs to be covered by IS. Their applicable amount is:

Personal allowance	£94.95
Disability premium	£36.85
Total	£131.80

Their income to be taken into account is £99.15 (IB). Child benefit and CTC are ignored. Their IS is £131.80 (applicable amount) *minus* £99.15 (income) = £32.65.

If your income is too high for you to qualify for IS currently, you might qualify once you or a member of your family become entitled to another benefit (a 'qualifying benefit'). You should make your claim for IS at the same time as your claim for the qualifying benefit (see p968).

Different rules for calculating your benefit can apply if you are in one of the groups to whom special rules apply (see below).

5. **Special benefit rules**

There are some groups of claimants to whom special rules apply. Special rules apply to:

- 16/17-year-olds (see below);
- people from abroad (see Chapter 58);
- students (see Chapter 25)
- people without accommodation, involved in a trade dispute, in hospital or who are prisoners (see Chapter 26).

Your income support (IS) may be affected if you (or your partner or child(ren) live in a care home (see p617).

16/17-year-olds

If you are 16 or 17 you are entitled to IS in your own right if you satisfy the normal rules of entitlement described in this chapter.[22] You must fit within one of the groups of people who can claim IS listed on pp292–296.[23] You should not have your claim refused or be turned away by the DWP simply because of your age.

However, you should remember the following.

- If you have been looked after by a local authority in England or Wales on or after 1 October 2001, you usually cannot claim IS. Instead, your local authority should support and accommodate you. Similar rules apply in Scotland. See p611 for exceptions to the rules.
- If you count as in 'relevant education', you are only entitled to IS in specified circumstances (see p577).[24] If you are a 'qualifying young person' for child benefit purposes and are living with someone who counts as responsible for you, s/he might be able to claim child benefit and child tax credit (CTC) for you. If you count as someone's child for IS or income-based jobseeker's allowance (JSA) purposes and s/he is claiming, you cannot claim IS yourself.[25]
- Your IS personal allowance depends on your (and your partner's) age and circumstances (see p773).
- In certain circumstances, you may satisfy the rules for both IS and income-based JSA, but you cannot claim both.[26] It is usually better to claim IS to avoid the requirement to be available for and actively seeking work and training and the attendant risk of benefit sanctions (see Chapter 16). You can still look for work if you want to. If you claim IS rather than JSA, however, you might not receive national insurance credits (see Chapter 31).
- You should check to see if you are entitled to any of the other benefits or tax credits in this *Handbook*. See p5 for some ideas about what you might be able to claim.

If you are not entitled to IS, you may be entitled to income-based JSA if you satisfy the special rules which apply to 16/17-year-olds (see p371).

6. Claims and backdating

You must usually claim on the first day you want your benefit to start. See p304 for more information about your date of claim. The rules about claiming and backdating are in Chapter 38. This section tells you about the specific rules that apply to income support (IS).

If you do not live with your child(ren)'s other parent, you might be required to provide information to the Child Support Agency that is needed to make a maintenance calculation or assessment (see p746).

Future changes

The Government plans to introduce a 'skills screen' when people claim IS to identify any basic literacy, numeracy or language needs they have. Claimants will also be signposted to the Adult Advancement and Careers Service, which will advise them about entitlement to training. See CPAG's *Welfare Rights Bulletin* for updates.

Making a claim

To be entitled to IS, you must normally make a claim.[27] A claim for IS must be in writing and on the form approved by the DWP, which is free of charge.[28] You must complete the form in accordance with the instructions on it and provide any information or evidence required (see p303). Bear the following in mind.

- You can make initial contact by telephone or letter. You may also be able to start a claim online at www.dwp.gov.uk/eservice. The date of your initial contact is important because it usually determines the date on which your claim is treated as made. See p304 for further information about your date of claim.
- If you want to withdraw or amend your claim, notify the DWP before it makes its decision (see p959).[29]

In practice you are usually required to start your claim by telephoning a 'contact centre'. Your local Jobcentre Plus office has this number, and it may also be displayed in local advice centres and libraries. The centre takes basic details, then calls you back to go through the details of your claim. Also, the date of an initial work-focused interview (see p971) is set, unless it is agreed that you do not need to attend one. You are then sent a statement recording these details, which you are asked to sign, and details of the evidence and information you should bring with you to the interview (or forward to the DWP). The signed statement of details forms your official claim, instead of an old-style claim form.

It is best for you to start your claim in this way if you can. However, if you cannot or do not want to use the telephone to start your claim, the Jobcentre Plus office can still deal with your claim in other ways. You might, for example, be invited for a face-to-face interview to gather the relevant details, or in some cases an old-style claim form might be accepted. You may also be able to claim at an alternative office (see p958). Seek advice if you are unable to use a telephone and the Jobcentre Plus office will not let you start your claim in any other way.

Old-style claim forms are available from Jobcentre Plus offices and online on the Jobcentre Plus website (see Appendix 1). They might be available at your local Citizens Advice Bureau, welfare rights service or advice centre. If you obtain a claim form, it is still important to telephone your local DWP or Jobcentre Plus office to let them know you want to claim IS to ensure your date of claim is the earliest possible date (see p304). If you do not, you might lose benefit. Be ready to give your national insurance number. You should complete the form and return it to the relevant office within one month of your initial contact.

If you are claiming IS within 12 weeks of a previous claim, you might be given a shortened claim form. This is known as 'rapid re-claim'.

Note: keep a copy of your completed claim forms and the evidence and information you provide in case queries arise.

Housing benefit and council tax benefit

You have to make a separate claim to your local authority for housing benefit (HB) and for council tax benefit (CTB). When you claim IS via a contact centre, your HB and CTB claims are usually completed at the same time or you may be given a claim form with your IS claim form (or it is available on the Jobcentre Plus website – see Appendix 1). If you are making a 'rapid re-claim' for IS, you may also be able to make a rapid re-claim for HB and CTB. See pp200 and 92 for further information about claiming HB and CTB.

Information to support your claim

When you claim IS, you must satisfy the national insurance (NI) number requirement. In most cases this means you must provide your NI number as well as that of your partner (see p962). You may also be asked to provide proof of your identity (see p962) and information to support your claim (see below).

Providing information with your claim

It is important that you provide any information or evidence required – known as the 'evidence requirement'. Until you do, you may not count as having made a valid claim and you could lose benefit.[30] See p960 for further information about the evidence requirement and to see if you are exempt.

Note that if:

- you are claiming IS because you are incapable of work and do not have an employer or are not already getting incapacity benefit (IB) or severe disablement allowance, you are usually also asked to claim IB;
- you have a mortgage, you are given an additional form to give to your lender. It provides details about your mortgage and returns the form to the DWP;
- it is not possible to assess your housing costs (see Chapter 34) accurately or your entitlement to the severe disability premium (see p784) the decision maker can exclude these from your IS until they can be calculated.[31]

Information and evidence you must supply after you claim

Even if you have provided all that is required, a decision maker might need additional evidence or information to enable her/him to make a decision about your claim. You can be asked to supply any certificates, documents, information or evidence considered relevant to your claim or to an issue arising from your claim.[32]

You must provide the information or evidence within one month of the request. A decision maker can allow you longer than this if s/he thinks it is reasonable. The one-month time limit runs from the date of the decision maker's request for the additional information, *not* the date you made your IS claim.

Who should claim

If you are a single person or a lone parent you claim on your own behalf. If you are one of a couple, you must choose which one of you claims for you both. See p702 for who counts as a couple. Where you have a choice about who can claim and you cannot agree, a decision maker decides.[33] If you are a member of a couple claiming backdated IS after one of you is awarded refugee status (see p1347), the claim must be made by the refugee.[34] **Note:** you can only claim backdated IS under this rule if you were accepted by the Home Office as a refugee and were officially notified of this on or before 14 June 2007.

You can change which partner claims, provided the partner previously claiming agrees.[35] It can be worth swapping who claims, for example, if:

- it would entitle you to a disability premium (see p779);
- one of you:
  - is about to go abroad or otherwise lose entitlement – eg, become a student;
  - fits into one of the groups of people who can claim IS but the other does not (see p292). You should both seek advice about how to protect your NI record;
  - is working less than 16 hours a week and the other is working between 16 and 24 hours a week (see p648 for what counts as full-time paid work). In this case, you and your partner might also be able to claim working tax credit (WTC – see p657). You should seek advice to see how you would be better off financially.

If you cannot make your claim yourself (eg, you are mentally ill or have dementia), an 'appointee' (see p955) can claim on your behalf.

The date of your claim

You are usually not entitled to IS for any day before your 'date of claim'.[36] However, in some cases you can claim in advance (see p305) and sometimes your date of claim can be backdated (see p305). If you want this to be done you should make this clear when you claim or the DWP might not consider it.

Your **'date of claim'** is usually the earliest of:[37]

- the date you first contact a benefit office (eg, you ask to claim IS in person, by telephone or letter or you submit a defective claim) or someone does this on your behalf so long as a properly completed claim and all the information and evidence required (see p303) are provided within one month; *or*
- the date your properly completed claim and all the information and evidence required are received in the benefit office (or if you may claim at an alternative office (see p958), that office).

If you claim the wrong benefit

If you claim WTC and you are refused because neither you nor your partner are in full-time paid work for WTC purposes (see Chapter 50), your claim for IS can be backdated to the date you claimed WTC.[38] However, you must claim IS within 14 days of the decision refusing your WTC claim. You can ask for your IS claim to start on a later date instead – eg, where your income is too high currently but is due to decrease.

If you claim IS and you should have claimed carer's allowance (CA) instead of or in addition to IS, a decision maker can treat your IS claim as a claim for CA.[39] This could help you qualify for backdated carer's premium (see p789).

Claiming in advance

If you do not qualify for IS from the date of your claim (unless this is because you fail the habitual residence test – see p1367), but will do so within the next three months, you can be awarded IS from the first date on which you qualify.[40] This gives the DWP time to ensure you receive benefit as soon as you are entitled. You should let the DWP know you want to claim in advance when you claim. You might have to persuade the DWP that it can accept a claim in advance.

You might not be entitled to IS currently, but would be once you or a member of your family become entitled to another 'qualifying benefit' – eg, disability living allowance or CA. You should make your claim for IS at the same time as the claim for the qualifying benefit. If you are:

- refused IS, claim again when you get a decision about the qualifying benefit and ask for your IS to be backdated to the date of your first IS claim or to the date from which the qualifying benefit is paid, if that is later. See p968 for further information;
- awarded IS, you might be entitled to a higher rate once the outcome of the claim for the qualifying benefit is known. Seek a revision or a supersession if you think this applies to you. See p1085 for further information.

How your claim is dealt with

It is very unlikely that you will get an immediate decision on your claim because the facts need to be checked and your benefit calculated. If you think it is taking too long to deal with your claim, see p307.

Backdating your claim

It is very important to claim in time. A claim for IS can be backdated for a maximum of three months but only in exceptional circumstances. See p964 for the general rules on backdating. There are exceptions to the rule. Your claim can be backdated for more than three months if:

- you are claiming backdated IS after being awarded a qualifying benefit and an earlier IS claim had been refused because you did not at that time get a qualifying benefit (see p968);[41]
- you claimed WTC when you should have claimed IS (see p304).

If you might have qualified for benefit earlier but did not claim because you were given the wrong information by the DWP or because you were misled by it you could ask for an *ex gratia* payment (see p1186) or complain to the Ombudsman via your MP (see p1184).

7. **Getting paid**

Income support (IS) is usually paid by direct payment into your bank (or similar) account (see p978).[42] In some cases, you may instead be paid by cheque. You can indicate which method of payment you prefer when you claim IS, although a decision maker decides how IS is paid and you cannot appeal against this decision. Payment can be made to someone else on your behalf, called your 'appointee' (see p955). In some circumstances part of your IS can be deducted and paid to other people and organisations on your behalf (see p987).

IS is a weekly benefit. However, if you are only entitled to IS for part of a week, you are only paid for the part-week.[43]

If you are entitled to less than 10 pence a week you are not paid IS at all, unless you are receiving another social security benefit which can be paid with IS.[44] If you are entitled to less than £1 a week a decision maker can decide to pay you quarterly in arrears.[45]

You are paid in advance if you are:[46]

- receiving widows' or bereavement benefits (but only if you are not providing or required to provide medical evidence of incapacity for work); *or*
- returning to work after a trade dispute .

If you are paid in advance, your entitlement to IS usually begins on the first payday of any widows' or bereavement benefit to which you are entitled (or would be entitled if you had sufficient national insurance contributions) following the date of your claim for IS. For example, widowed parent's allowance is paid on a Tuesday. If you claim IS on a Wednesday you are entitled to IS in advance from the following Tuesday. But if you claim on a Tuesday, you get it from that day.

You are paid in arrears if you are not in one of the above groups, although your entitlement to IS usually starts from the date of your claim (see p304).[47] You might be able to get a crisis loan to tide you over while you are waiting to be paid your IS (see p503).

Once your entitlement has been worked out, a decision maker decides how often and on what day you are paid unless you are entitled to incapacity benefit (IB), severe disablement allowance, or widows' or bereavement benefits.[48] If you are entitled to one of these (or would be if you satisfied the contribution conditions), you are paid IS on the same day of the week as that other benefit and at the same intervals.[49] If you are incapable of work and not getting IB you are paid fortnightly in arrears.[50]

If your cheque is lost or stolen or you have forgotten your PIN, see p983. If payment of your IS is suspended, see p984.

Note: the Government says it intends to amend the rules and pay all claimants their IS at least fortnightly in arrears. The day you are paid will depend on your national insurance number. See CPAG's *Welfare Rights Bulletin* for updates.

Delays and complaints

If payment of your IS is delayed, you might be able to get an interim payment (see p986). You may also be eligible for a crisis loan (see p503).

If you experience delays, or wish to complain about how your claim has been dealt with, see p1181. You might be able to claim compensation (see p1186).

Change of circumstances

The DWP should inform you of the main kinds of changes in your circumstances that you need to report, but might not actually list them all. In any case, it is your duty to report any change in your circumstances which might affect your right to or the amount of your IS, or payment of your benefit. You should do this promptly in writing or by telephone (although in some cases notification might be accepted in a form other than in writing or by telephone). In some cases, however, the decision maker might say you must report changes in writing. In any case, it is always best to report the change in writing and keep a copy in case of a dispute in the future.

You should report changes to the benefit office handling your claim. This could be your Jobcentre Plus office or a benefit delivery centre or regional processing centre. Check with the Jobcentre Plus office if you are in any doubt.

If you do not report any such change promptly, any resulting overpayment may be recoverable from you (see Chapter 39). If you are considered deliberately to have acted falsely or dishonestly, you may also be guilty of an offence (see Chapter 40). A change of circumstances could mean that you qualify for more or less IS, or even that you are no longer entitled.

If you have a mortgage, the DWP can ask your lender about any changes in the amount you owe. If you have this information (eg, from an annual statement you receive from your lender) you must also advise the DWP just in case your lender fails to do so. Make sure the DWP takes this information into account so you are not overpaid IS.

When there has been a relevant change of circumstances, a decision maker looks at your claim again and makes a new decision, called a 'supersession' (see p1074). Your IS is then adjusted from the date this new decision takes effect (see p308). When this is depends on whether the new decision is to your advantage, and whether you reported the change in time. See p1080 for information about when a supersession takes effect.

When your income support is adjusted

As a general rule, your IS is adjusted as follows.[51]

- If you are paid IS in arrears, your IS is adjusted from the beginning of the week in which the change of circumstances takes effect (see p1080).
- If you are paid IS in advance, your IS is adjusted from the date the change of circumstances takes effect if this is the day you are paid benefit. If it is not, your IS is adjusted from the next week.

There are exceptions to the rules above.

- If a decision is to your advantage, but you failed to notify the DWP of a change within the time limit (see p1080), your IS is adjusted:[52]
  - if you are paid in arrears, from the beginning of the week in which you notified the change; *or*
  - if you are paid in advance, from the day on which you notified the change, if this is the day you are paid benefit. If it is not, your IS is adjusted from the next week.
- Your IS is adjusted from the date of the change of circumstances (or the day on which this is expected to take place) if:[53]
  - you are paid IS in arrears and the change of circumstances means you no longer qualify for IS. However, the ordinary rule (see p307) applies if the reason you no longer qualify is that your income is too high;
  - a child (see p298) only stays with you for part of the week and the rest of the week is in care or custody;
  - you are going into or coming out of prison (see p624);
  - you, or your partner or child for whom you are responsible (see p298) comes home from hospital for a stay of less than a week;
  - you or your partner are no longer treated as being involved in a trade dispute because you are incapable of work or in your maternity period (see p634);
  - you claim IB or bereavement benefits and, as a result, the day of the week you are paid benefit changes (see p306);
  - you only live in a care home for part of the week and are entitled to disability living allowance when you are staying elsewhere. This means that you can be paid, for example, the severe disability and enhanced disability premiums when you are staying away from the care home.
- If you have income that is counted as paid on a particular day (see p879) and this changes (or such a change is expected), your IS is adjusted from the day the income counts as being paid.[54]
- If a decision has been made that you failed to take part in a work-focused interview without 'good cause' (see p976), your IS is adjusted from the week after that decision.[55]

If a change of circumstances means the amount of your IS should go down but the decision maker certifies that it is not practical to adjust your IS on the days outlined above, your IS is adjusted from the beginning of the week following the week in which the new decision is made (or in which the change is expected to occur if this has not yet happened).[56] This does not apply if the change is that you have claimed IB or bereavement benefits, or if there is a change in income that counts as paid on a particular day. **Note:** this rule may change when the employment and support allowance rules take effect (see Chapter 7).

Overpayments and fraud

If you are overpaid IS, you may have to repay it. See Chapter 39.

If you have been accused of fraud, see Chapter 40. You might get a reduced amount of IS if you have been sanctioned for benefit offences (see p1047).

8. Challenging an income support decision

You can apply for a revision or supersession of an income support decision, or appeal against it (see Chapters 41 and 42).

9. Tax, tax credits and other benefits

Income support (IS) is not taxable except if you are involved in a trade dispute and you are claiming it in respect of your partner.

Tax credits

If you work less than 16 hours a week and your partner works at least 16 hours but less than 24 hours a week, you and your partner may be able to claim working tax credit. However, before deciding whether to claim you should seek advice to see how you would be better off financially. See p657 for further information.

Whether or not you are in work, you might be able to claim child tax credit (CTC). CTC is not taken into account as income in working out your IS.

Means-tested benefits

If you pay rent or council tax you may be entitled to housing benefit (HB) and council tax benefit (CTB), as well as IS.

You might be able to choose whether to claim IS or income-based jobseeker's allowance. If you have a partner and s/he is 60 or over, s/he may be able to claim pension credit for you instead of you claiming IS. See p395 for further information.

Non-means-tested benefits

The non-means-tested benefits in this *Handbook* (other than attendance allowance (AA), disability living allowance (DLA), guardian's allowance and, if you are getting CTC, child benefit) are taken into account as income when working out the amount of IS you get. However, it can still be worth claiming these benefits. If you or your partner qualify for certain non-means-tested benefits (including AA and DLA) you also qualify for certain premiums (see p775) and, therefore, a higher rate of IS.

You might only qualify for IS once you or a member of your family are awarded another benefit, known as a 'qualifying benefit'. To make sure you do not lose out while awaiting the outcome of a claim for a qualifying benefit, claim IS at the same time. If your IS claim is refused, once the qualifying benefit is awarded claim IS again and ask for it to be backdated to the date of your first claim. See p968 for details.

Passports and other sources of help

If you are entitled to IS you also qualify for health benefits such as free prescriptions (see Chapter 9) and education benefits such as free school meals (see p15). You may also qualify for social fund payments (see Chapters 21 and 22).

Financial help on starting work

If you stop getting IS because you or your partner start work, or your earnings or hours in your existing job increase, you may be able to get a child maintenance bonus (see p757), mortgage interest run-on (if you have a home loan – see p823), extended payments of HB or CTB (if you pay rent or council tax – see pp211 and 94) and a job grant (see p14). See p14 for information about other financial help you might get.

Notes

1. **Who can claim income support**
  1 s124 SSCBA 1992
  2 s115 IAA 1999
  3 Reg 4ZA and Sch 1B IS Regs
  4 Sch 1B paras 7-9, 13 and 24-27 IS Regs
  5 CIS/2654/1999
  6 Reg 22A IS Regs
  7 Sch 1B paras 1-6, 14, 14A, 14B and 23 IS Regs
  8 CIS/2260/2002
  9 The rules on paternity leave are in Part 2 Paternity and Adoption Regulations 2002 No.2788
  10 CIS/866/2004
  11 CIS/0542/2001
  12 R(IS) 8/02
  13 Sch 1B paras 10-12, 15 and 28 IS Regs
  14 Sch 1B paras 9A and 18-22 IS Regs
  15 Reg 5(3A) IS Regs
  16 Reg 70(2) IS Regs
  17 Reg 70(4) IS Regs
  18 para 31350 DMG

3. **Claiming for others**
  19 s137(1) SSCBA 1992
  20 s137(1) SSCBA 1992; reg 14 IS Regs

4. **The amount of benefit**
  21 s124(4) SSCBA 1992

5. **Special benefit rules**
  22 s124(1)(a) SSCBA 1992
  23 s124(1)(e) SSCBA 1992; Sch 1B IS Regs
  24 s124(1)(d) SSCBA 1992; reg 13 IS Regs
  25 s134(2) SSCBA 1992
  26 s124(1)(f) SSCBA 1992; s3(1)(b) JSA 1995; reg 61(1)(c) JSA Regs

6. **Claims and backdating**
  27 s1 SSAA 1992
  28 Reg 4(1A) and (5) SS(C&P) Regs
  29 Reg 5(2) SS(C&P) Regs
  30 Regs 4(1A) and (9) and 6(1A) SS(C&P) Regs
  31 Reg 13 SS&CS(DA) Regs
  32 Reg 7 SS(C&P) Regs
  33 Reg 4(3) SS(C&P) Regs
  34 Reg 4(3C) SS(C&P) Regs
  35 Reg 4(4) SS(C&P) Regs
  36 Reg 19(1) and Sch 4 para 6 SS(C&P) Regs
  37 Reg 6(1ZA) and (1A) SS(C&P) Regs; R(IS) 10/06
  38 Reg 6(28) SS(C&P) Regs
  39 Reg 9(1) and Sch 1 SS(C&P) Regs
  40 Reg 13(1) and (9) SS(C&P) Regs
  41 Reg 6(16)-(18) SS(C&P) Regs

7. **Getting paid**
  42 Reg 21 SS(C&P) Regs
  43 s124(5) and (6) SSCBA 1992; reg 73 IS Regs
  44 Reg 26(4) SS(C&P) Regs
  45 Sch 7 para 5 SS(C&P) Regs
  46 Reg 26(1) and Sch 7 paras 2, 3 and 6(2) SS(C&P) Regs
  47 Sch 7 paras 1, 3 and 6(1) SS(C&P) Regs
  48 Sch 7 para 3(2) SS(C&P) Regs
  49 Sch 7 para 3(1) SS(C&P) Regs
  50 Sch 7 para 3(1A) SS(C&P) Regs
  51 Reg 7and Sch 3A para 1 SS&CS(DA) Regs
  52 Reg 7(2)(b) SS&CS(DA) Regs
  53 Sch 3A paras 2 and 3 SS&CS(DA) Regs
  54 Sch 3A para 4 SS&CS(DA) Regs
  55 Reg 7(25) SS&CS(DA) Regs
  56 Sch 3A para 5 SS&CS(DA) Regs

Chapter 14

Industrial injuries benefits

This chapter covers:

Industrial injuries benefits are paid if you are disabled as a result of an accident at work or a disease caused by your job. The main benefit is **disablement benefit** (see p324). You may also qualify for **reduced earnings allowance** (see p326) or **retirement allowance** (see p330).

You do not have to have paid national insurance contributions to get industrial injuries benefits.

1. Who can get industrial injuries benefits

For all industrial injuries benefits (except industrial death benefit) you must satisfy the **'industrial injury condition'** – ie:[1]

- you have had a 'personal injury' in an 'industrial accident' (see p314) or you have a 'prescribed industrial disease' (see p318); *and*
- at the time of the injury you were an employed earner (see p313); *and*
- as a result of that accident or disease you have had a 'loss of faculty' (see p320); *and*
- as a result of that 'loss of faculty' you are 'disabled'.

You are not covered by the scheme if your disability was caused by an industrial accident which happened before, or by a disease the onset of which was before 5 July 1948. However, you may still be able to claim allowances under either the

Workman's Compensation (Supplementation) Scheme 1982 or the Pneumoconiosis, Byssinosis and Miscellaneous Diseases Scheme 1983.

You can only qualify for reduced earnings allowance (REA – see p326) and retirement allowance (see p330) if your accident or disease occurred before October 1990.

For information about industrial death benefit if your spouse died before April 1988, see the 17th edition of CPAG's *Rights Guide to Non-Means-Tested Benefits*.

If you have been injured by your work, you may also have the right to sue your employer. Legal help may be available and you may be able to get a free consultation with a solicitor. Your right to compensation from your employer is separate from your rights to benefit under the industrial injuries scheme (although your compensation may be reduced if you have received benefits from the DWP – see p997).

Employed earners

You can claim industrial injuries benefits only if you were an 'employed earner' whose accident or disease was caused by your employed earner's employment.[2] You are an employed earner if you are gainfully employed under a contract of service. This means that there is some obligation by an employer to pay you remuneration as an employee for tasks that you are bound to perform for the employer under the contract of employment.[3] Therefore, if you are self-employed you are excluded from the scheme, as are most trainees on government training schemes.

Entitlement to industrial injuries benefits is not dependent on you having paid national insurance contributions. However, payment of contributions is a way of deciding whether or not you are an employed earner.

If you pay, or ought to pay, Class 1 contributions (see p722) as an employed earner you can qualify for industrial injuries benefits. This includes those paying Class 1 (and, in the case of volunteer development workers, Class 2 – see p724) contributions while abroad.[4] You can qualify if your earnings are too low to pay contributions; mostly this is because of part-time work but can also apply to those who are too young to pay contributions. Finally, you are also treated as being an employed earner if you are an apprentice, mine inspector or rescue worker, special constable, taxi driver, office cleaner, agency worker, minister of religion, lecturer, member of an aircrew, mariner, or in some situations an offshore oil or gas worker.[5]

You are treated as *not* being an employed earner if:[6]

- you are employed by your spouse or civil partner and either your employment is not for the purpose of her/his employment or your earnings are normally below the lower earnings limit (see p722). So a man employed by his wife to help run her shop, and earning less than £90 a week (the current lower earnings limit), is not an employed earner; *or*

- you are employed by a close relative (parent, step-parent, grandparent, son, daughter, stepchild, grandchild, brother, sister, half-brother or half-sister) in a private house where you both live, and your employment is not for your relative's trade or business carried out there; *or*
- you are a member of visiting armed forces, or a civilian employed by them, unless you are normally resident in the UK.

Personal injury

Personal injury includes the obvious, such as broken legs or arms,[7] but also covers the less obvious, such as strains and psychological injury.[8] So an assault at work causing slight physical injury might cause a far greater injury to the mind by resulting in agoraphobia or a breakdown. In difficult cases, the question is whether or not you have suffered a physiological or psychological change for the worse. It is not enough just to be in pain if the pain is merely a symptom of an existing condition and does not make that condition substantially worse.[9] The damage must be to you or part of you. Dislocation of an artificial hip joint counts as a personal injury,[10] but damage to a pair of spectacles[11] or an artificial leg[12] does not.

Accident

The term '**accident**' has been defined as an unlooked-for occurrence or mishap.[13] However, an accident need only be unexpected from the worker's point of view. It does not matter that it could have been anticipated by an expert.[14] If you do a heavy or dangerous job where accidents are common, a resulting injury is just as much an accident as if your job is sedentary and comparatively safe. If your heavy lifting or work-related stress causes a heart attack, it is the heart attack which is the accident, not the heavy lifting or stress.[15] Deliberate acts by third parties can be accidents – eg, assaults on security workers or on staff in shops and hospitals.[16] However, if you start a fight at work and injure your hand punching somebody, that is not an industrial accident.

An accident will be 'industrial' if you can show a connection with your work. For accidents this connection is established if the accident arose 'out of and in the course of your employment'.[17] It is important to realise that despite the name, it is not only industrial workers who can have 'industrial accidents'; all employees can. For example, if you are an office worker and a badly loaded filing cabinet tilts and falls on you, this would count as an 'industrial accident'. The term 'industrial accident' conjures up images of a very dramatic event, but any accident sustained while you are doing your job can qualify – eg, spilling a hot drink and scalding yourself can be an industrial accident. An illness brought on by conversation could count as being caused by an industrial accident.[18]

Accident or process?

One of the most difficult problems is to distinguish between an 'accident', for which benefit is payable, and a 'process', for which it is not (unless it causes a 'prescribed disease' – see p318). Clearly, to fall from a ladder and break your leg is an 'accident'. Equally clearly, to work for many years as a heavy manual worker and have a sore back is a cumulative 'process' as would be the breathing in of dust over many years.[19] However, sometimes a series of events, over a period of time, can be viewed as an 'accident' for the purposes of the benefit.[20] The cumulative effect of a series of incidents can also result in an accident.[21] Furthermore, you should not be excluded from entitlement to benefit simply because you cannot identify which of the incidents caused the injury.[22]

Example

Cyril's job is trimming excess rubber from hot water bottles with a pair of scissors. A particularly hard batch of rubber comes through and each cut requires greater strength. Over two or three days he suffers a strain injury in his hand. The series of cuts constitutes a series of 'accidents' that meets the definition.

It is easier to establish the series of events as an accident if the period of time is fairly short,[23] or is noticed at an identifiable moment.[24] An accident is proved if you can establish that an identifiable occurrence must have happened, even if it is impossible to prove when.[25]

In the course of employment

The accident (see p314) must arise 'in the course of employment'. It has been said that:

> an accident befalls a person in the course of his or her employment if it occurs while he or she is doing what a person so employed may reasonably do within a time during which he is employed, and at a place where he may reasonably be during that time to do that thing.[26]

Difficulties arise when work rules are broken, or when you do something not directly connected with work.

Generally speaking, when you arrive at your employer's factory or shop, and are on her/his private property, you are 'in the course of your employment'. You do not have to have clocked in or have reported to your actual workplace. If you arrive early to get ready for work or to have a meal in the canteen[27] you are covered, although if you arrive early to fit in a game of pool you are not.[28] You are probably covered during breaks from working if you remain on the employer's property,[29] but probably not if you go elsewhere. So if, during a tea break, you go to a local shop to buy a snack, you are outside the course of your employment.[30] If you are allowed to have a snack either at home or at work while still on duty (as may happen with a police officer) you are covered.[31]

While at work most activities are considered to be 'in the course of employment'.[32] Smoking,[33] chatting[34] or passing sweets[35] are all 'reasonably incidental' to the employment, provided they are not done in breach of instructions.[36] Even if you were doing something in breach of instructions you are still covered if what you were doing was done for the purposes of, or in connection with, your employment.[37]

Examples

Clara works as a labourer in a paper factory where there is an absolute ban on riding on the load of a forklift truck. She is seen riding on the load, falls off and is injured. Usually she would not be covered, but she saw the load was slipping and rode on the truck in order to hold it on. This was done for the purposes of her employment and so, this time, she is covered.

Maureen is a supervisor in an office where central heating has been removed, but not replaced or the holes patched. It is cold and her staff are threatening not to work in the draught. The employer does not respond to her pleas for help. She goes onto the roof to patch the holes with papers and falls through one of them. She is 'in the course of employment' even though the employer would have disapproved of her activities.

Even if you are at home you may, depending on the requirements of your contract, be covered. This may even include a person on sick leave.[38]

In putting forward your claim (see p331) or arguing your case at an appeal (see Chapter 42), you should consider all aspects of your employment, including the wording of your contract and the degree of flexibility in the arrangements between you and your employer.[39]

Accidents while travelling

As more people are injured on journeys to and from work than are injured at work itself, accidents while travelling have been a source of much dispute. You are not in the course of your employment (see p315) during ordinary journeys to and from work, unless you are travelling on transport operated by or on behalf of your employer, or arranged by your employer, and not in the ordinary course of public transport service.[40]

Many employees have no set place of work – eg, lorry drivers, local authority home helps, gas and electricity company employees. Obviously a lorry driver is at work when driving her/his lorry, but gas company workers travelling directly from home to their first job of the day are not always in the course of employment (see p315), even if driving a company van. It depends on the circumstances, including the rules for the use of the van.[41] A home help has been found to be in the course of her employment travelling between jobs, but not going to the first job or from the last. This is because she became engaged in her employment once she started at the first job and remained engaged until the end of the day.[42]

Some employees with no fixed hours of work may be regarded as covered from the moment of leaving home.[43] Recent cases have eased the rules on travelling – eg, to conferences or meetings. You must look at all the factors in a common sense way when deciding whether or not you were in the course of your employment. So a police officer who had to travel about 40 miles from home to a training course was in the course of his employment while travelling.[44] Provided you go reasonably directly, with no marked deviation from a proper route, and do not embark on activities unrelated to the journey, you may be covered.

One important factor in deciding whether you are in the course of your employment is whether you receive wages for travelling.[45] However, if you receive a flat-rate travelling allowance as compensation for having to work at a workplace other than your normal base, this may not be enough to make your journey to your alternative workplace part of your work.[46]

Out of employment

As well as arising in the course of your employment (see p315), the accident (see p314) must arise 'out of' your employment, so that it can be said that in some way the employment contributed to it. The fact that you suffered a displaced retina at work is not sufficient to show it arose 'out of' the employment, but medical evidence which shows that it was caused by sudden head movements while inspecting a production line enables you to establish that an industrial accident (see p314) took place. An unexplained fracture while walking at work is not an industrial accident,[47] but it is if you slip and the fracture occurs while you are falling onto the ground. You are covered even if you are more susceptible to injury because, for example, your bones are brittle[48] or your eyes are weak.

Example

Joe, a farm worker, suffers sudden pain in the groin while doing his normal job of digging. It is found that a previous hernia, which had been surgically repaired, has given way again. The decision maker says that this could have happened at any time and so did not arise 'out of' the employment. Joe's doctor says it could have happened at any time but probably did so at that time because of the heavy digging. A tribunal awards him benefit.

An accident also arises out of your employment if it arises in the course of employment (see p315) *and* it is caused by:[49]

- another's misconduct, skylarking or negligence; *or*
- the behaviour or presence of an animal (including a bird, fish or insect); *or*
- your being struck by any object or by lightning; *and*

- you did not directly or indirectly induce or contribute to the accident happening by your conduct outside the employment or by any act not incidental to the employment.

An accident is deemed to arise out of and in the course of your employment if you are helping people in an emergency, or trying to save property at or near where you are employed.[50] A milkman was covered when he was helping to put out a fire at a customer's home.[51]

Prescribed industrial disease

It is necessary for the disease to be a **'prescribed industrial disease'**. This means it is on a list[52] set out in regulations of diseases which are known to have a link to a particular occupation, called a 'prescribed occupation' (see below).[53] Each prescribed disease has a statutory definition and you must fit within that definition. It is not sufficient simply to have a medical diagnosis that you suffer from a particular condition.[54] From time to time new diseases are added to the list. However, you cannot claim for a disease for any period prior to it being added to the list.[55] Each prescribed industrial disease has a letter and number to identify it – eg, prescribed disease A12 is carpal tunnel syndrome and prescribed disease D1 is pneumoconiosis. The complete list is in Appendix 8. Whether or not you have a prescribed industrial disease is known as the 'diagnosis question'.[56]

If the DWP accepts that you have a prescribed industrial disease, other diseases which result from it (eg, amnesia resulting from methyl bromide poisoning, prescribed disease C12) are included when assessing your 'loss of faculty' and disablement.[57] See p320 for further information on how your disablement is assessed.

Prescribed occupations

Different diseases are 'prescribed' for different types of jobs because different jobs have different health risks. To qualify for benefit on grounds of a prescribed industrial disease it is not enough to have a disease which happens to be on the list. You must also prove:

- that you have worked in one or more of the jobs for which that disease is prescribed ('prescribed occupations'); *and*
- that your job caused the disease.

If the DWP refuses to accept that you have worked in a prescribed occupation you should take advice, preferably from your trade union if you have one, or from an advice agency. An expert's report may help to prove your case.

Time limits

For most prescribed diseases you do not have to have worked in a prescribed occupation for any minimum length of time. You can also claim at any time, even if it is many years since you worked in that occupation. However, there are exceptions to these general rules. If you have occupational deafness (prescribed disease A10) you must have worked in a prescribed occupation for 10 years and claim within five years of having done so.[58] If you have occupational asthma (prescribed disease D7) you must claim within 10 years of working in a prescribed occupation.[59] If you have coal miners' chronic bronchitis or emphysema (prescribed disease D12) you must have been working in a prescribed occupation for 20 years.[60] If you have cataract (prescribed disease A2) you must have worked in a prescribed occupation for five years or more in aggregate.[61] Commissioners have ruled in two cases that, in calculating periods of exposure, account may be made of self-employment.[62] However, from 10 July 2000, regulations specify that only periods of employment rather than self-employment can be used to calculate the relevant periods. These regulations do not apply to claims made prior to 10 October 2000.[63]

Cause

You must prove that the prescribed disease is because of your occupation. For some diseases it is assumed that if you have the disease within one month of last working in the prescribed occupation (see p318), the occupation caused the disease.[64] The decision maker can get evidence to rebut this, but it has to be very clear and establish that, on the balance of probabilities, there was a non-industrial cause. If there is doubt it should go in the claimant's favour.[65] With carpal tunnel syndrome (prescribed disease A12), and dermatitis (prescribed disease D5) there is no such presumption.

The presumption operates with slightly different time conditions for occupational deafness (prescribed disease A10), tuberculosis (prescribed disease B5), pneumoconiosis (prescribed disease D1), byssinosis (prescribed disease D2), and chronic bronchitis and emphysema (prescribed disease D12). The connection for carpal tunnel syndrome and dermatitis, therefore, has to be proved. The DWP investigates the connection issue, and you may need to ask your GP or consultant for a report linking the disease to your occupation. However, it is not necessary to prove the link beyond any reasonable doubt and to rule out all other possibilities. It is necessary only to establish the link 'on a balance of probabilities'; in other words, it is more likely than not that there is a connection.

Example

Connie, a hospital cleaner, uses a new cleaning material. A rash develops on her hands and she has to give up her job. The medical evidence shows that the cleaning material could have caused the problem but so could several things with which Connie had been in contact outside work. There is a strong argument that the cleaning material caused the rash because the rash developed so soon after using it.

Onset and recrudescence

The **'onset'** (date of starting) of a prescribed disease is taken as the date of the first day you had a relevant 'loss of faculty' (see below). In deafness cases it is the later of either the date you first experienced the loss of faculty or the date you successfully claimed benefit.[66]

In diseases other than deafness, asthma and respiratory conditions, you can improve and then worsen again. It is important to know whether it is a **'recrudescence'** (fresh outbreak of the existing disease) or a completely new attack. The first enables an immediate supersession;[67] with the second, you have to wait for 15 weeks before disablement benefit can be claimed. If a further attack commences during a current period of assessment, it is assumed to be a recrudescence unless the contrary is proved.

Loss of faculty and disablement

In addition to showing the link between your injury or disease and your occupation, you also need to establish that you have had a 'loss of faculty' and are 'disabled'.

'Loss of faculty' is the damage or impairment of part of the body or mind caused by the industrial accident or disease. **'Disability'** is the inability to do something that is caused by that damage or impairment. **'Disablement'** is the total of all of your disabilities which, taken together, amount to a disablement. This disablement is expressed as a percentage.

In assessing your disablement, there are three disablement questions.[68]

- Has the relevant industrial accident (see p314) or prescribed disease (see p318) resulted in a loss of faculty (see below)?
- What is the extent of disablement resulting from a loss of faculty (this is expressed as a percentage – see p321)?
- What period is to be taken into account by the assessment (see p324)?

These questions are decided by decision makers.

Has the relevant accident or disease resulted in a loss of faculty?

A **'loss of faculty'** is an 'impairment of the proper functioning of part of the body or mind'[69] caused by an accident or disease. A 'loss of faculty' is not the same as disablement. It includes disfigurement even if the disfigurement is not accompanied by a loss of physical faculty.[70] A decision that there has been a personal injury resulting from an industrial accident (see p314) does not itself prevent a decision maker or tribunal from finding that there is no loss of faculty but this is rare.[71]

What is the extent of disablement?

In order to qualify for disablement benefit (see p324), generally you must reach a threshold of at least 14 per cent disablement. However, a finding of at least 1 per cent may permit a claim for REA (see p326).

The extent of your disablement is assessed on a percentage basis. Any assessment between 14 and 19 per cent is treated as being 20 per cent (except for those entitled to disablement gratuities).[72] If the total disablement from all industrial accidents and diseases is more than 20 per cent, it is rounded to the nearest multiple of 10 per cent with multiples of 5 per cent being rounded upwards.[73]

Some assessments of disablement are set out in regulations.[74] These are known as 'prescribed degrees of disablement' and include various amputations (eg, loss of a hand or a leg) and degrees of hearing loss (see Appendix 7). However, even in these cases the decision makers must take into account the real disablement resulting from an injury, and increase or decrease the figure to arrive at a reasonable assessment[75] – eg, the loss of a right hand is more disabling for a right-handed person than for a left-handed person. Impaired function of the pleura, pericardium or peritoneum caused by diffuse mesothelioma automatically has an assessment of 100 per cent disablement.[76]

Apart from age, sex and physical and mental condition, the personal circumstances of a claimant must be ignored, so that particular problems you may have, like the location of your office, or the distance to the nearest bus stop, are not taken into account.

Your disablement should be assessed by comparing you with a person of the same age and sex whose physical and mental condition is normal.[77]

When there is no prescribed degree of disablement (see above), and these form the vast majority of cases, the authorities assess you on the basis of their experience but may refer to the prescribed percentages to help them decide.[78] Although you may suggest that your assessment should be a particular percentage, by analogy with the percentage figures in the regulations, those assessing your claim come to their own medical judgement.[79] One point in favour of claimants is that 100 per cent is given to people who are far from totally disabled (eg, those with no disabilities other than total deafness) and presumably other assessments should reflect this. Commissioners have held that a percentage disablement awarded by a tribunal will only be wrong if it is wildly wrong or the tribunal has reached an impossible conclusion on the evidence.[80]

It is important that you are very straightforward with the examining doctor. The authorities have checks to establish that your symptoms are consistent with the injury, and that your movements are consistent with the disablement you claim you have. Therefore, how you walk into the room and how you undress are looked at as carefully as how you respond to the examination. Do make sure, though, that those who are examining you are aware of all the things that you now cannot do as a result of your injury or disease.

Offsets if your disability has more than one cause

If a disability has more than one cause, the rules for assessment are complex. If a disability is congenital or arose before an industrial one, it is deducted from the total disability.[81] The reduction is often called the '**offset**'. The procedure on offsets is complex and frequently leads to disputes. Mistakes are sometimes made because the decision maker incorrectly offsets for medical conditions which were not causing any disability.

Examples

Sam loses a hand, which would normally be 60 per cent, but he had previously lost the index finger. So 14 per cent is deducted, leaving 46 per cent (rounded up to 50 per cent).

Sian has a back injury as a result of an industrial accident. A decision maker has reduced her assessment by 5 per cent on the grounds of a pre-existing disability of which she knew nothing. Many people have spines that are slightly curved due to lifting things. The decision maker may have looked at an X-ray, correctly considered that her curved spine was not due to the relevant accident and then incorrectly reduced her assessment.

In the second example, the decision maker should have considered whether the pre-existing loss of faculty (see p320), the curved spine, really had (or would have) led to disablement which would have occurred even if the industrial accident (see p314) had not happened. S/he should have considered, among other things, whether the loss of faculty led to disablement before the industrial accident occurred. There is no physical disablement if you do not have any pain or restriction of movement and it is, therefore, wrong to reduce your assessment unless there is a good reason for deciding that disablement would have arisen during the period of assessment even if the industrial accident had not occurred.

In the second example, depending on the medical opinion:

- there might be no offset (see above); *or*
- it might be proper to make a life award (see p324) with some uniform offset over the whole period in respect of the future back problems Sian would have been likely to have; *or*
- it might be proper to make a stepped assessment, making no offset initially but bringing one in at some future date, or applying different levels of offset for different parts of the period covered by the award.[82]

No reduction is made if 100 per cent is a reasonable assessment for the industrial accident.[83]

The decision maker should also bear in mind that even if you did have a pre-existing problem which caused a disability, the accident may worsen the effects of it, as well as cause a new problem. In such a case, the assessment should reflect the increase in the original problem as well as the new disability.[84]

If another disability arose after an industrial accident, the decision maker first has to assess the disablement arising from the purely industrial injury. If it is less than 11 per cent any disability from the other cause is ignored; if it is more than 11 per cent any extra disablement caused by the effect of the industrial injury on the other disability is added.[85]

Examples

Ali loses a little finger in an industrial accident and is assessed as 7 per cent disabled as a result. He then loses the other fingers of that hand in a non-industrial accident. He continues to be assessed as 7 per cent disabled because of the industrial accident.

Paul loses the middle, ring and little fingers of one hand in an industrial accident and is assessed as 30 per cent disabled as a result. He then loses the index finger of that hand in a non-industrial accident. His total disablement is now 50 per cent. But loss of the index finger only would have been 14 per cent. The disablement resulting from his industrial accident may, therefore, be reassessed at 36 per cent (50 per cent *minus* 14 per cent) which is rounded up to 40 per cent.

Two or more industrial accidents or diseases

If you have more than one industrial accident, the percentages of disablement (see p320 and Appendix 7) can be added together and may entitle you to benefit, even if neither accident would do so on its own. If you have two or more industrial accidents you may end up in a situation where the second or later accident is made worse by the interaction with the effect of the previous accident(s). The assessment process can allow for this.[86] Your most recent assessment should include an increase for any such interaction.[87] The same would apply where an industrial disease (see p318) interacts with the effects of an industrial accident.

Example

Steve has a fall at work and seriously injures his left leg. He receives a life assessment of 10 per cent. Years later, he has a further fall and seriously injures the other leg. He is assessed as 10 per cent disabled for that accident, with a further 5 per cent for the extra disability he has as a result of the interaction between the two injuries. The total of 25 per cent is rounded up, resulting in payment of a 30 per cent pension.

There are special rules if you have pneumoconiosis. The rules allow for certain conditions to be taken into account in order to increase the assessment even though these conditions did not arise from the pneumoconiosis. Any effect of tuberculosis is assessed with the effects of the pneumoconiosis.[88] If your disability is assessed at 50 per cent because of the pneumoconiosis, any additional disability because of chronic bronchitis or emphysema is added.[89] If you have made such a claim for pneumoconiosis you cannot then make an separate claim for chronic bronchitis or emphysema.[90]

The period taken into account by the assessment

The decision maker or appeal tribunal makes an assessment (see p321) for a period 'during which the claimant has suffered and may be expected to continue to suffer from the relevant loss of faculty'. Percentage assessments are usually made for six months, or for one or two years, or are given for life,[91] but definite dates must be given.

An assessment is either final or provisional.[92] You get a provisional assessment when there is doubt about what will happen in the future, and you are automatically called for another assessment at the end of the period.[93] Life assessments are final.

If you are given a final assessment for a fixed period this means that the authorities believe you will no longer be affected by your accident or disease by the end of that period. If you think that the effects of the accident or disease will last for longer, you should consider an appeal against that assessment (see p1098).

If your condition deteriorates during a period of assessment, or if you still have a disability at the end of a period for which you have been given a final assessment, you should apply for a supersession (see p1074).

An assessment of disablement for occupational deafness is for life.[94]

2. **Industrial injuries disablement benefit**

The main industrial injuries benefit is industrial injuries disablement benefit (IIDB). There are also a number of benefits which are paid as increases to IIDB. The most important are:

- constant attendance allowance (see p326); *and*
- exceptionally severe disablement allowance (see p326).

Who can claim industrial injuries disablement benefit

You qualify for IIDB if:[95]

- you satisfy the industrial injury condition (see p312) as a result of one or more industrial accidents (see p314) or prescribed diseases (see p318);
- your resulting disablement is assessed as being at least 14 per cent (1 per cent in the case of pneumoconiosis, byssinosis and diffuse mesothelioma) (see p321 and Appendix 7);
- 90 days (excluding Sundays) have elapsed since the date of the accident or of the onset of the prescribed disease or injury (those who have the prescribed disease of mesothelioma can be paid without serving this waiting period).

There are some groups of claimants for whom special rules apply (see p331).

Disqualification

You may be disqualified for misconduct on similar grounds as for incapacity benefit (see p271).[96]

The rules about your age

You must be old enough to be an employed earner. If you are aged under 18 you receive a lower rate of benefit.

Claiming for others

There are no increases for dependants unless you are getting unemployability supplement (a benefit that was abolished for new claims after 5 April 1987).

The amount of benefit

The amount of benefit you get depends on the extent of your disablement (see p321 for how this is assessed).[97]

Extent of disablement	*Benefit per week Claimant aged under 18 without dependants*	*Benefit per week Any other claimant*
	£	£
100%	83.85	136.80
90%	75.47	123.12
80%	67.08	109.44
70%	58.70	95.76
60%	50.31	82.08
50%	41.93	68.40
40%	35.54	54.72
30%	25.16	41.04
11%–20%	16.77	27.36

Since 1 October 1986, IIDB has been paid only if the assessment of your disablement is at least 14 per cent,[98] except in the cases of pneumoconiosis, byssinosis and diffuse mesothelioma, when benefit is paid if the assessment is at least 1 per cent.[99]

Until 1 October 1986, IIDB was paid in respect of any assessment of disablement of at least 1 per cent. The old rules are still in force for assessments following claims made before that date.[100] If you are getting a payment as a result of such a small percentage assessment, see p176 of the 17th edition of CPAG's *Rights Guide to Non-Means-Tested Benefits*.

You might be able to get an increase of benefit (see p326). In addition, if you are getting unemployability supplement (a benefit that was abolished for new claims after 5 April 1987) or constant attendance allowance (see below) you are entitled to a Christmas bonus (see p9).

Increases of industrial injuries disablement benefit

You get increased IIDB if you qualify for constant attendance allowance or exceptionally severe disablement allowance.

Constant attendance allowance

You qualify for constant attendance allowance if:[101]

- you are entitled to a basic industrial injuries disablement pension based on a degree of disablement assessed at 100 per cent; *and*
- you require constant attendance as a result of the relevant loss of faculty (see p320).

Disablement as a result of pre-1948 industrial accidents and diseases, war injuries and injuries incurred while on police or fire duty, may be taken into account in considering the degree of your disablement.[102]

There are two rates:

- The **higher weekly rate** of £109.60 is paid if you are 'so exceptionally severely disabled as to be entirely, or almost entirely, dependent on (constant) attendance for the necessities of life, and [are] likely to remain so dependent for a prolonged period and the attendance so required is whole-time'.[103]
- The **lower weekly rate** of £54.80 is paid if you are 'to a substantial extent dependent on (constant) attendance for the necessities of life and [are] likely to remain so dependent for a prolonged period'. This may be increased up to £82.20 a week if 'the extent of such attendance is greater by reason of the beneficiary's exceptionally severe disablement'. If attendance is part time only, the amount payable is 'such sum as may be reasonable in the circumstances' (usually £27.40 a week).[104] Some claimants may be better off claiming the care component of disability living allowance (see p107) or the ordinary attendance allowance instead (see p117).

Exceptionally severe disablement allowance

This is paid at the weekly rate of £54.80 if:

- you are entitled to constant attendance allowance (or would be if you were not in hospital) at a rate in excess of £54.80 a week; *and*
- you are likely to remain so permanently.[105]

3. Reduced earnings allowance

Reduced earnings allowance (REA) is available only if you had an accident or started to have a disease before 1 October 1990. A successful first claim can still be made now if you had such an accident or disease before that date.

The amount of REA you get depends on whether your current earnings, or earnings in a job which it is considered you could do, are less than the current earnings in your previous 'regular occupation' (see p329).

Who can get reduced earnings allowance

You qualify for REA if:[106]

- you satisfy the industrial injury condition (see p312) because of an industrial accident (see p314) before 1 October 1990 or an industrial disease (see p318), the onset of which was before that date (see p320); *and*
- your resulting disablement is assessed as being at least 1 per cent (see p320 and Appendix 7); *and*
- as a result of a relevant loss of faculty *either*:
  - you are incapable and likely to remain permanently incapable of following your regular occupation (see p328) and are incapable of following employment of an equivalent standard (see p329) which is suitable in your case (the 'permanent condition' – see p328); *or*
  - you are, and have been at all times since the end of the 90-day qualifying period for disablement benefit, incapable of following your regular occupation or employment of an equivalent standard (see p329) which is suitable in your case ('the continuing condition' – see p328); *and either*
- you are under pension age (but see below); *or*
- you have not given up regular employment (see p329); *and*
- you have not been in receipt of REA since 1 October 1990 and subsequently ceased to be entitled to it for at least one day (see p329).

Some claimants have been successful in claiming REA after pension age and retaining REA rather than moving onto the lower rate of retirement allowance (see p330). This is on the basis that the law allows a person who is over pension age and claiming REA for the first time to be paid REA rather than retirement allowance.[107]

In addition to those rules of entitlement, if you were entitled to REA on either 10 April 1988 or 9 April 1989 and on that date you were over pension age and were retired, or were treated as retired, you remain entitled to the allowance for life. For the meaning of 'retired or treated as retired' in this context, see p69 of the 12th edition of CPAG's *Rights Guide to Non-Means-Tested Benefits*.

There are some groups of claimants for whom special rules apply (see p331).

Reduced earnings

Although REA compensates for loss of earnings, the fact that you are losing money as a result of an industrial accident or disease is not, in itself, enough. You must meet either the permanent or continuing conditions outlined on p328.

The permanent condition

Only incapacity at the time of your claim and in the future are relevant. The phrase 'likely to remain permanently incapable' relates only to your 'regular occupation' (see below) and not to 'employment of an equivalent standard' (see p329). So you do not need to prove at a tribunal that you are likely to remain incapable of employment of an equivalent standard; just that you are not likely to be able to perform your normal job.

If you have pneumoconiosis, and you are advised not to work by a decision maker, you are deemed not to be able to work unless the decision maker proves otherwise.[108]

If your condition could be improved by an operation, and you refuse to have it, the decision maker may disqualify you, but only if the operation is a very minor one.[109] You have the right to refuse a more serious operation.

The continuing condition

Only incapacity at the time of your claim and in the past are relevant, so there is less scope for argument than when assessing the future. However, if you returned to work but were 'sheltered' by your workmates, you can still argue that you were 'incapable' of following your regular occupation (see below). Specific provision is made so that, if you have worked since the end of the 90-day period, but this work was approved by the Secretary of State or done on the advice of a doctor for rehabilitation, testing or training, it can be disregarded. So, also, is employment before obtaining surgical treatment, and six months of employment thereafter.[110] If you have given up work because of your pneumoconiosis on the advice of a decision maker you are deemed to have been continuously incapable of following that regular occupation.[111]

Regular occupation

Deciding what your 'regular occupation' is involves looking at your work history (part time[112] as well as full time) and the content of the job, as opposed to its title. For example, a docker still employed to work as a docker but unable to earn as much because he is unable to do the full range of his duties was found incapable of his regular occupation.[113]

If an accident happens when you have just started a new job, that job may well be treated as your regular occupation. Your intentions and prospects need to be considered.[114] But a stop-gap occupation, taken on during poor health, would not be treated as your regular occupation.[115] If you are a full-time student, any part-time work counts as your regular occupation.[116] If your earnings are derived from several jobs you may face problems. Any employment which is subsidiary to your usual or main job does not count. If you would have been fairly sure to have been promoted by the time of your claim, but for the accident, then the promoted position may count as the regular occupation. It is possible to make a number of separate claims for REA. If you had a number of industrial accidents and had to downgrade your employment each time, you can be compensated for each accident. The crucial point is whether each accident has led to a change in your regular occupation.[117]

If you have a prescribed disease (see p318) and, because of this, gave up a job before you applied for benefit, it may count as your regular occupation.[118]

Suitable employment of an equivalent standard

Suitability is judged by looking at your education, experience, training, work history and general health.[119] Only employed earner's employment can be treated as suitable, so self-employed work is not considered.[120] The question then is whether the employment is of an equivalent standard. The test is objective; the normal earnings of people employed in what is considered suitable employment are compared with with the normal earnings of those employed in the regular occupation.[121] The earnings in both occupations have to be assessed taking into account bonuses, overtime if normally paid[122] and benefits in kind.

If your regular occupation (see p328) was part time, full-time work is not of an equivalent standard even if you are medically fit to do it. Like must be compared with like. However, if there are no jobs of the same number of hours, different work for a similar number of hours may be regarded as equivalent.[123]

Regular employment

If you are over pension age, you are only entitled to REA if you are in 'regular employment'. During any period when you are not entitled to REA because you have given up 'regular employment', you receive retirement allowance instead (see p330). This is paid to you at a much lower rate. If you have obtained a full gender recognition certificate then the person's gender becomes the acquired gender.[124] Therefore, a man who is issued with a gender recognition certificate as a woman will convert to REA at 60. A woman who is issued with a gender recognition certificate as a man will convert to REA at 65.

The definition of 'regular employment' was changed from 24 March 1996. **'Regular employment'** since then means working for an average of 10 hours or more a week within a period of five or more weeks of such employment.[125]

The rules about your age

You need to be old enough to be an employed earner. REA is paid until you reach pension age and it is then replaced with retirement allowance (see p330). If you are now over pension age but have never claimed REA even though you meet the conditions for entitlement, you do not appear to be excluded under the regulations from claiming REA. The DWP is currently making awards of REA on such claims. If you are considering making a claim for REA and you are about to reach pension age you should seek advice before delaying a claim for REA.

Claiming for others

There are no increases for dependants.

The amount of benefit

The amount of REA you get is the amount by which your current earnings, or earnings in a job which it is considered you could do, are less than the current earnings in your previous regular occupation (see p328).[126] Earnings include overtime.

For most claimants this is a fairly routine calculation. However, if you are unemployed:

- the DWP's doctors are asked for your limitations;
- the DWP disability employment advisers are asked to say what job they think you could do; *and*
- the Jobcentre Plus is asked to quote a wage which such a job would command in your area.

You should look carefully at all the elements of the calculation and assess whether the jobs quoted are realistic for you to do, whether the wages seem correct and if a proper allowance has been given for you as an individual.

Once the first assessment has been made, the amount is usually increased in line with earnings in that industry or workplace, unless that regular occupation (see p328) has ceased to exist.[127] In that case, it is calculated as rising in line with the nearest 'occupational group' as defined by the DWP. You can ask for a fresh assessment to take into account your normal prospects of advancement, though here you have to show that promotion would have happened, say at the end of a period of employment or training, not just that it may have happened if you had been particularly diligent.[128]

The maximum amount of reduced earnings allowance

The maximum amount you may receive for any one award is £54.72 a week.[129] The total you can received from industrial injuries disablement benefit (IIDB) and REA (whether for one or more awards) is 140 per cent of the standard rate of IIDB.[130]

If you were over pension age and retired before 6 April 1987 your allowance will be reduced if it would otherwise mean you would be receiving more than 100 per cent disablement benefit.[131]

4. Retirement allowance

Retirement allowance is a reduced rate of reduced earnings allowance (REA – see p326) for people over pension age, paid for life.

You qualify for retirement allowance if:[132]

- you are over pension age (60 for women and 65 for men);
- you have given up regular employment (see p329);
- you were entitled to REA at a rate of at least £2 a week (in total, if you had more than one award) immediately before you gave up regular employment (see p329);
- you are not entitled to REA.

There are some groups of claimants to whom special rules apply (see below). You must be over pension age to qualify and there are no increases for dependants.

The amount of retirement allowance you get is £13.68 a week or 25 per cent of the amount of REA you were receiving, whichever is the lower.

5. Special benefit rules

Special rules apply to prisoners (see Chapter 26). Industrial injuries disablement benefit is paid for up to one year of any sentence in addition to any period on remand.[133] There are also special rules for some people going abroad (see Chapter 58).

6. Claims and backdating

Making a claim

A claim for benefit should usually be made on the appropriate form available from your local DWP office or the DWP website. There are a number of different claim forms depending on the benefit claimed and on the type of accident or disease. In certain circumstances, the Secretary of State may accept a written application which is not on the correct form (see p959).[134]

You can apply for a declaration that you have had an industrial accident, even if you do not wish to claim any benefit. You do this by contacting your local DWP office. This may be wise if you have had an accident but are not sure whether you wish to proceed with a claim for benefit.[135]

Keep a copy of your claim in case queries arise.

Information to support your claim

When you claim industrial injuries benefits, you must satisfy the national insurance (NI) number requirement. In most cases this means you must provide your NI number as well as your partner's. See p962 for further details.

Who should claim

You claim for yourself unless you are unable to act on your own. In such cases it may be appropriate for an 'appointee' to make the claim (see p955).

The date of your claim

The date of your claim is the date it is received at the appropriate DWP office.

If you claim the wrong benefit

In some circumstances, it is possible for a claim for one benefit to be treated as a claim for a different benefit (see p963). However, for industrial injuries benefits it is only possible to 'interchange' constant attendance allowance with disability living allowance and attendance allowance. There is no right of appeal against a refusal.

Claiming in advance

An advance claim can be made for IIDB if you have had an accident or have a prescribed disease and you are within the 90-day waiting period, otherwise it is not possible to claim industrial injuries benefits in advance.

Renewal claims

Assessments can be provisional or final, and for a limited period or for life. A provisional assessment means that the decision maker considers your medical condition has not yet settled down, and might get worse or better. At the end of a provisional assessment you will be invited to be re-examined. A final assessment means that the medical authorities consider your condition has settled down and your case is dealt with once and for all. At the end of a period of award you therefore need to apply for a renewal of benefit.

If you are awarded disablement benefit for a particular disease, you may recover at some point but subsequently have a further attack. If there is a continuation or recrudescence of the old disease you do not have to wait 15 weeks before gaining entitlement to disablement benefit.

Backdating claims

It is very important to claim in time. Your claim can be backdated for up to three months if you satisfy the qualifying conditions over that period. You do not have to show any reasons why your claim was late. The rules on backdating are covered on p964.

If you might have qualified for benefit earlier but did not claim because you were given the wrong information or were misled by the DWP you could ask for an *ex gratia* payment (see p1186) or complain to the Ombudsman via your MP (see p1184).

7. Getting paid

Industrial injuries benefits are weekly benefits paid in advance by credit transfer into a bank or similar account.

Payment can also be made to someone else on your behalf – called your 'appointee' (see p955).

If your order book is lost or stolen, see p983. If payment of your industrial injuries benefit is suspended, see p984.

Delays and complaints

If payment of your industrial injuries benefit is delayed, you might be able to get an interim payment. See p986 for further details.

If you experience delays or wish to complain about how your claim has been dealt with, see p1180. You might be able to claim compensation (see p1186).

Change of circumstances

The DWP should inform you of the main kinds of changes in your circumstances that you need to report to it, but might not actually list them all. In any case, it is your duty to report *any* change in your circumstances which you might reasonably be expected to know could affect your right to, the amount of, or the payment of your benefit.[136] You should notify changes to the office handling your claim in writing or by telephone (although in individual cases notification might be accepted in a different form). In some cases, however, the decision maker may say you must report changes in writing. In any case, you may want to report the change in writing and keep a copy in case of a dispute in the future. If you do not promptly report any such change in writing, any resulting overpayment may be recoverable from you (see Chapter 39). If you are considered deliberately to have acted falsely or dishonestly, you may also be guilty of an offence (see Chapter 40).

Overpayments and fraud

If you are overpaid industrial injuries benefits, you might have to repay them. The rules on overpayments are covered in Chapter 39.

If you have been accused of fraud, see Chapter 40.

8. Challenging an industrial injuries benefit decision

You can apply for a revision or a supersession of an industrial injuries benefit decision, or appeal against it (see Chapters 41 and 42).

9. Tax, tax credits and other benefits

Industrial injuries benefits are not taxable.[137]

Tax credits

Industrial injuries benefits are ignored as income for tax credits.

Means-tested benefits

Industrial injuries disablement benefit, reduced earnings allowance and retirement allowance are taken into account in full for income support (IS), income-based jobseeker's allowance (JSA), housing benefit, council tax benefit and pension credit (PC).

Non-means-tested benefits

In general, the overlapping benefits rule does not apply to industrial injuries benefits and it is possible for them to overlap – eg, to receive full disablement benefit as well as full incapacity benefit (IB).

Carer's allowance (see Chapter 3) may be paid to someone who is 'regularly and substantially caring' for you while you are receiving constant attendance allowance (see p326).

If you were receiving sickness benefit or IB because of an industrial accident or disease on 12 April 1995 you can continue to qualify for IB, even though you do not satisfy the contribution conditions, provided that you remain incapable of work because of the accident or disease.[138]

Passports and other sources of help

If you have (or are a dependant of someone who has died and who had) pneumoconiosis (including asbestosis, silicosis and kaolinosis), byssinosis, diffuse mesothelioma, diffuse pleural thickening, or primary carcinoma of the lung if accompanied by asbestosis or diffuse pleural thickening, and you cannot get compensation from your employer (eg, because s/he has ceased trading), or you do not have a realistic chance of obtaining damages from that employer, you may be able to get a one-off lump-sum payment in addition to any industrial injuries benefit.

If you are on a low income, you might be entitled to certain health benefits, such as free prescriptions (see Chapter 9). You may also qualify for a social fund payment (see Chapters 21 and 22). If you are getting IS, the guarantee credit of PC or income-based JSA, your child(ren) qualify for free school meals (see p15). You may also be entitled to health benefits and free school meals if you are getting tax credits.

If your spouse or civil partner died as a result of an industrial accident or disease you may qualify for a bereavement benefit even though the national insurance contribution conditions are not satisfied (see p25).[139]

Notes

1. **Who can get industrial injuries benefits**

1 s94(1) SSCBA 1992
2 ss94(1) and 108(1) SSCBA 1992
3 s2(1) SSCBA 1992; *Vandyk v Minister of Pensions and National Insurance* [1955] QB 29
4 Reg 10C(6) SSB(PA) Regs
5 Regs 2, 4 and 6 SS(EEEIIP) Regs
6 Reg 3 SS(EEEIIP) Regs
7 CI/257/1949; CI/159/1950
8 R(I) 22/59
9 R(I) 1/76
10 R(I) 8/81
11 R(I) 1/82
12 R(I) 7/56
13 *Fenton v Thorley* [1903] AC 443 (HL)
14 CI/123/1949
15 *Jones v Secretary of State for Social Services* [1972] AC 944 (HL), also reported as an appendix to R(I) 3/69, and CI/2842/2006
16 *Trim Joint District School Board of Management v Kelly* [1914] AC 667 (HL)
17 s94(1) SSCBA 1992
18 CI/105/1998; CI/142/2006
19 *Roberts v Dorothea Slate Quarries Co. Ltd* [1948] 2 All ER 201 (HL)
20 R(I) 24/54; R(I) 43/55
21 CI/3370/1999
22 *Mullen v Secretary of State for Work and Pensions* [2002] SC 251; SLT 149; SCLR 475; GWD 3-121, IH (2 Div)
23 R(I) 43/61; R(I) 4/62
24 R(I) 18/54
25 CI/159/1950
26 *Moore v Manchester Liners Ltd* [1910] AC 498 at p500 (HL)
27 *R v National Insurance Commissioner ex parte East* [1976] ICR 206 (DC), also reported as an appendix to R(I) 16/75
28 R(I) 1/59
29 *R v Industrial Injuries Commissioner ex parte AEU* [1966] 2 QB 31 (CA), also reported as an appendix to R(I) 4/66
30 R(I) 10/81
31 *R v National Insurance Commissioner ex parte Reed* (DC), reported as an appendix to R(I) 7/80
32 s94(3) SSCBA 1992
33 *R v Industrial Injuries Commissioner ex parte AEU* [1966] 2 QB 31 (CA), also reported as an appendix to R(I) 4/66
34 R(I) 46/53
35 R(I) 17/63
36 *R v Industrial Injuries Commissioner ex parte AEU* [1966] 2 QB 31 (CA), also reported as an appendix to R(I) 4/66
37 s98 SSCBA 1992
38 In R(I)1/99 a Benefits Agency officer, assaulted by a claimant while at home on sick leave, was found to have been injured 'in the course of her employment'. Although this case was subsequently overturned by the Court of Appeal, the Court ruled that a person might be in the course of his employment if at the relevant time he was carrying out some duty he was contracted to do; *CAO v Rhodes*, [1999] ICR 178
39 *Nancollas v Insurance Officer* [1985] 1 All ER 833 (CA), also reported as an appendix to R(I) 7/85
40 s99 SSCBA 1992
41 R(I) 1/88
42 R(I) 12/75
43 R(I) 4/70
44 *Nancollas v Insurance Officer* [1985] 1 All ER 833 (CA), also reported as an appendix to R(I) 7/85
45 *Smith v Stages* [1989] 2 WLR 529 (HL)
46 R(I) 1/91
47 R(I) 6/82

48 R(I) 12/52
49 s101 SSCBA 1992
50 s100 SSCBA 1992
51 R(I) 6/63
52 Sch 2 SS(IIPD) Regs
53 ss108(1) and 109(1) SSCBA 1992; reg 2 SS(IIPD) Regs
54 R(I) 3/03
55 R(I)2/03 and R(I)4/96
56 Reg 12 SS&CS(DA) Regs
57 Reg 3 SS(IIPD) Regs
58 Regs 2(c) and 25 SS(IIPD) Regs. Although at one time it was held that the time limit in respect of occupational deafness had been imposed unlawfully, it was made valid retrospectively by Sch 6 para 4(3) SSA 1990.
59 Reg 36 SS(IIPD) Regs
60 Sch 1 SS(IIPD) Regs
61 Reg 2(e) SS(IIPD) Regs
62 CI/286/1995; CSI/89/1996
63 Reg 25(2)(a) SS(IIPD) Regs
64 There is no such presumption for any disease falling under the C category of disease. Reg 4(1) SS(IIPD) Regs
65 Reg 4 SS(IIPD) Regs; R(I) 38/52
66 Reg 6(2)(c) SS(IIPD) Regs
67 Reg 7 SS(IIPD) Regs
68 s45(1)(a) and (b) SSAA 1992
69 *Jones v Secretary of State for Social Services* [1972] AC 944 (HL), also reported as an appendix to R(I) 3/69
70 CI/499/2000; s122(1) SSCBA 1992
71 s30 SSA 1998
72 s103(3) SSCBA 1992
73 s103(2) and (3) SSCBA 1992; regs 15A and 15B SS(IIPD) Regs, as amended
74 Sch 2 SS(GB) Regs; Sch 3 SS(IIPD) Regs
75 Reg 11(6) SS(GB) Regs
76 Reg 20A SS(IIPD) Regs
77 Sch 6 para 1 SSCBA 1992
78 Reg 11(8) SS(GB) Regs; R(I) 5/95; R(I) 1/04
79 CI/636/1993, although the commissioner said that where there are specific submissions backed with expert medical evidence on the percentage assessment, it would be an error of law to arrive at a different figure without giving reasons for this.
80 R(I) 2/06
81 Reg 11(3) SS(GB) Regs
82 CI/34/1993
83 Reg 11(7) SS(GB) Regs
84 R(I) 3/91, which contains a definitive survey of the situations where reg 11 SS(GB) Regs comes into play.
85 Reg 11(4) SS(GB) Regs
86 Reg 11(5) SS(GB) Regs
87 R(I) 3/91
88 Reg 21 SS(IIPD) Regs
89 Reg 22 SS(IIPD) Regs
90 Reg 2(d) SS(IIPD) Regs
91 Sch 6 para 6 SSCBA 1992
92 Sch 6 para 7 SSCBA 1992
93 Sch 6 para 6(2)(b) SSCBA 1992
94 Reg 29 SS(IIPD) Regs

2. **Industrial injuries disablement benefit**

95 ss103 and 108 SSCBA 1992
96 Reg 40 SS(GB) Regs
97 Sch 4 SSCBA 1992
98 s103(1) and Sch 7 para 9(1) SSCBA 1992
99 Reg 20(1) SS(IIPD) Regs
100 Sch 7 para 9(1)(a) SSCBA 1992; reg 14 SS(II&D)MP Regs
101 s104 SSCBA 1992
102 Reg 20 SS(GB) Regs
103 Sch 4 SSCBA 1992; reg 19(b) SS(GB) Regs
104 Sch 4 SSCBA 1992; reg 19(a) SS(GB) Regs
105 s105 SSCBA 1992

3. **Reduced earnings allowance**

106 Sch 7 paras 11 and 12(1), (2) and (7) SSCBA 1992
107 Sch 7 paras 11 and 13(1) SSCBA 1992
108 Reg 23(a) SS(IIPD) Regs
109 Reg 40 SS(GB) Regs; R(I) 2/86
110 Reg 17 SS(GB) Regs
111 Reg 23(b) SS(IIPD) Regs
112 *R v National Insurance Commissioner ex parte Mellors* [1971] 2 QB 401 (CA), also reported as an appendix to R(I) 7/69
113 R(I) 28/51
114 R(I) 65/54
115 CI/80/1949
116 Reg 2 SS(II&D)MP Regs
117 *Hagan v Secretary of State for Social Security* [2001] EWCA Civ 1452, reported in R(I) 2/02
118 Reg 17 SS(IIPD) Regs
119 R(I) 22/61
120 Sch 7 para 11(5)(b) SSCBA 1992
121 *R v National Insurance Commissioner ex parte Mellors* [1971] 2 QB 401, [1971] 1 All ER 740
122 R(I) 7/51; R(I) 1/72
123 R(I) 3/83
124 s9 GRA 2004
125 Reg 2 SS(IIRE) Regs; R(I) 3/93
126 Sch 7 para 11(10) SSCBA 1992
127 Sch 7 para 11(14) SSCBA 1992
128 R(I) 8/67

129 Sch 7 para 11(10) SSCBA 1992
130 Sch 7 para 11(10) SSCBA 1992
131 Sch 7 para 11(11) SSCBA 1992

4. **Retirement allowance**
132 Sch 7 para 13 SSCBA 1992

5. **Special benefit rules**
133 Reg 2(6) and (7) SS(GB) Regs

6. **Claims and backdating**
134 Reg 4(1) SS(C&P) Regs
135 s29 SSA 1998

7. **Getting paid**
136 Reg 32(1A) and (1B) SS(C&P) Regs

9. **Tax, tax credits and other benefits**
137 s617 ICTA 1988
138 Regs 14, 17 and 21 SS(IB)(T) Regs
139 s60(2) and (3) SSCBA 1992

15

Chapter 15

Jobseeker's allowance: main rules

This chapter covers:

Jobseeker's allowance (JSA) is for people who are unemployed (or who work but do not count as in full-time paid work) and who are looking for full-time work. You must normally satisfy what are known as the 'labour market conditions' (see p339). JSA is not paid to people in full-time paid work (see Chapter 27) who may be able to claim working tax credit instead.

There are two main types of JSA. **Contribution-based JSA** is paid if you satisfy the national insurance (NI) contributions conditions. **Income-based JSA** is paid if you pass the means test.

A third type of JSA, **joint-claim JSA**, is very similar to income-based JSA. It is paid if you are a member of a 'joint-claim couple'. Both of you must usually satisfy all the conditions for getting JSA (see p342 for who is exempt). Most of the rules are the same as for income-based JSA, although there are important differences for claims. See p381 for further details. Unless otherwise stated, references in this *Handbook* to income-based JSA are also references to joint-claim JSA. We only refer to joint-claim JSA where the rules are significantly different.

You do not have to have paid NI contributions to qualify for income-based JSA. While you are on JSA you are entitled to NI contribution credits (see p727).

It is possible to receive contribution-based JSA with an income-based JSA top-up. There are some situations where you might want to claim income support or pension credit instead (see p395).

Even if you are entitled to JSA, you may find you are not paid if you are 'sanctioned' – eg, if you lose your job through misconduct or fail to take up a job or training scheme opportunity. If this happens, you might qualify for hardship payments. You might also qualify for hardship payments if there is doubt whether you satisfy the labour market conditions. See Chapter 16 for further information.

1. Who can claim jobseeker's allowance

You qualify for jobseeker's allowance (JSA) if you:[1]

- do not count as being in full-time paid work (see p344 and Chapter 27), and if you are claiming income-based JSA, nor does your partner. If you have just taken up full-time paid work you may be able to claim income support (IS) for the first four weeks – known as 'mortgage interest run-on' (see p823); *and*
- are capable of work. However, in certain circumstances, people who are sick or who have gone abroad for NHS hospital treatment can get JSA (see p344). (**Note:** when the employment and support allowance (ESA) rules take effect, to qualify for JSA you must not have 'limited capability for work'. See Chapter 7 and www.cpag.org.uk/esa or CPAG's *Welfare Rights Bulletin* for updates); *and*
- are not in 'relevant education' (see p576). In addition, if you are a full-time student you usually cannot get JSA. See p345 for further information; *and*
- satisfy what are known as the 'labour market conditions' – ie, you must:
  - be 'available for work' (see p347); *and*
  - be 'actively seeking work' (see p357); *and*
  - have a current 'jobseeker's agreement' with the DWP (see p361); *and*
- are below pensionable age (60 for women and 65 for men); *and*
- are not getting income support (IS); *and*
- are in Great Britain (GB). JSA can continue to be paid in limited circumstances while you are temporarily away (see p1352) and contribution-based JSA can be 'exported' if you are unemployed and looking for work in a European Economic Area country (see p1391).

In addition, you must satisfy extra rules. For contribution-based JSA see p341. For income-based JSA (or joint-claim JSA) see p341.

You are usually not entitled to JSA for the first three days of your 'jobseeking period' (see below). These are known as 'waiting days' (see p366).

There are some groups of claimants to whom special rules apply (see p369). In addition, if you do not satisfy the normal rules for getting JSA, you may be able to get an urgent cases payment of JSA (see p364).

Jobseeking periods

A **'jobseeking period'** is the period during which you either meet the basic conditions of entitlement for JSA (see above), or do not satisfy the labour market conditions but receive hardship payments (see p422).[2] **Note:** if you are a man aged 60–65, special rules apply under which, in some circumstances, your jobseeking period continues even though you do not satisfy the labour market conditions.[3]

It is not necessary to satisfy the extra rules for contribution-based or income-based JSA for a jobseeking period to exist.

Linked jobseeking periods

In some cases, a jobseeking period may be linked with an earlier one. Also, certain periods in which you satisfy other conditions ('linked periods' – see below) can be linked to a jobseeking period. This means that:[4]

- the question of whether you satisfy the national insurance (NI) contribution conditions for contribution-based JSA (see p735) is decided by looking at your situation at the beginning of the first jobseeking period (or a period linked to a jobseeking period if earlier) and not at the beginning of your current claim;[5]
- you do not have to serve another three waiting days (see p366) to get JSA;
- if the jobseeking periods together are longer than 182 days, you cannot get any more contribution-based JSA (see p367);
- if the jobseeking periods together are at least two years, you might be able to get JSA while attending a qualifying course (see p346).

Two jobseeking periods are treated as linked if they are separated by one or any combination of the following:[6]

- any period of no more than 12 weeks; *or*
- a period during which you are doing jury service; *or*
- a 'linked period' (see below); *or*
- any period of no more than 12 weeks which comes between two 'linked periods' or between a jobseeking period and a 'linked period'.

Linked periods

A 'linked period' is any period during which you are:[7]

– entitled to carer's allowance (CA) but only if this allows you to get contribution-based JSA when you would not otherwise satisfy the contribution conditions; *or*

– incapable of work or treated as incapable of work (see p661); *or*

– getting maternity allowance; *or*

– undergoing training, including on the New Deal, and receiving a training allowance; *or*

– on the self-employed employment option of the New Deal; *or*

– not entitled to JSA because you count as being in full-time paid work (see p344) or your earnings or income are too high as a result of you being on the environment task force or voluntary sector option of the New Deal for young people, or the 'intensive activity period' of the New Deal for people aged 25 to 60 or an employment zone programme (see p412).

What is not counted as part of a jobseeking period

The following do not count as part of a jobseeking period:[8]

- days for which you do not claim (or are not treated as claiming) JSA;
- days for which you lost your entitlement to JSA because you failed, without good cause, to attend the Jobcentre Plus office when required or to sign on (see p389);
- a period for which you claimed backdated benefit, but which has been refused (see p385);
- any week (Sunday to Saturday) for which you are not entitled to JSA because you were involved in a trade dispute for all or part of that week (see p634);
- days on which you are not entitled to JSA because you have not provided your or your partner's NI number (see p380).

Extra rules for contribution-based jobseeker's allowance

To get contribution-based JSA, in addition to satisfying the basic rules of entitlement (see p339), you must:[9]

- satisfy the contribution conditions (see p735). This depends on your record of NI contributions and credits in the two tax years immediately before the benefit year in which your jobseeking period begins (or in which a period linked to a jobseeking period begins if earlier); *and*
- not have earnings above a specified amount – known as the 'prescribed amount' (see p839). **Note:** if you have earnings below this amount, your JSA is reduced to take account of them.

Extra rules for income-based jobseeker's allowance

If you do not qualify for contribution-based JSA, or if you do but need additional benefit (for your partner or housing costs), you can qualify for income-based JSA if:[10]

- your income is less than your applicable amount (see p368); *and*
- your savings and other capital are worth £16,000 or less. Some capital (in particular your home) is ignored (see Chapter 37); *and*
- you are not claiming and entitled to pension credit (PC), nor is your partner if you have one; *and*
  - if you are *not* a 'joint-claim couple', your partner is not claiming and entitled to either IS or income-based JSA; *or*
  - if you *are* a 'joint-claim couple' (see p381), neither you nor your partner are claiming and entitled to IS.

If you or your partner can qualify for IS or PC check if this would make you better off than if you were to claim income-based JSA.

Note: when the ESA rules take effect you cannot qualify for income-based JSA if you or your partner are claiming and entitled to income-related ESA, or

if you are a 'joint-claim couple', either of you are claiming and entitled to that benefit (see Chapter 7); *and*
- no one else is claiming IS or income-based JSA for you as part of their family (see p366); *and*
- you (or if you are a 'joint-claim couple', at least one of you) are aged 18 or over but if you are a 16/17-year-old you might get income-based JSA if you satisfy special rules (see p371); *and*
- you satisfy the 'habitual residence test' and the 'right to reside test'. To find out if you are exempt from the tests, see Chapter 59; *and*
- you are not a person subject to immigration control (see p1334). There are exceptions to this rule, but for some of these, you are only entitled to an urgent cases payment (see p1334).

Exemptions for 'joint-claim couples'

If you are a member of a 'joint-claim couple' (see p381) and one of you satisfies all the rules for claiming JSA, the two of you can still qualify for joint-claim JSA even if the other does not satisfy the labour market conditions or is not in GB. The one who does not satisfy the rules must be below pensionable age, not count as being in full-time paid work (see p344) and fit into one of the exempt groups below.[11] You must still make a joint claim for JSA. Even if you are in an exempt group, you can be required to attend a work-focused interview.[12]

Exempt groups

You fit into an exempt group if, for at least one day in a benefit week, you are:[13]
- studying full time. You count as studying full time for these purposes if you are:
  - a 'qualifying young person' for child benefit purposes (see p57) or are a full-time student (see p579); *and*
    - you were when you and your partner claimed JSA; *or*
    - when you and your partner claimed JSA you had been allocated a place on a full-time course of study from the next academic year or term or had applied for such a place and had not yet received a decision; *or*
    - you applied to commence a full-time course of study within one month of the last day of a previous course or within one month of the day you received examination results from one. This does not apply to applications for courses of study beyond the level of a first degree course; *or*
  - someone who can claim IS while in 'relevant education', other than a refugee learning English (see p577).

  You can only fit into this exempt group for one joint claim, unless another one is made because the first ceased when one of you started full-time paid work or was summoned to do jury service or was within any of the linked periods on p340;[14] *or*

- a carer who can claim IS (see p294). If you cease meeting this condition or stop being a carer, you continue to fit into an exempt group for a further eight weeks; *or*
- incapable of work because of illness or disability – ie, you:
  - are entitled to statutory sick pay (SSP); *or*
  - satisfy the own occupation test or the personal capability assessment for incapacity benefit (IB – see pp667 and 668); *or*
  - are treated as incapable of work by a decision maker – eg, you have a severe condition or have an infectious disease or are blind (see p662); *or*
  - are incapable of work but are treated as capable of work – eg, because you are disqualified from receiving IB due to misconduct or failure to accept treatment (see p271); *or*
- treated as not being in full-time paid work while living in a care home, an Abbeyfield home or an independent hospital (see p655); *or*
- mentally or physically disabled and because of this, your earnings or the number of hours you work are reduced to 75 per cent or less of that for a person without your disability in the same or a comparable job; *or*
- a disabled student (see p582); *or*
- registered blind (certified blind in Scotland). If you regain your sight, you continue to be exempt for 28 weeks after being taken off the register; *or*
- incapable of work because of your pregnancy. You only have to show that you are incapable of work, not that there is a serious risk to your health or that of your baby;[15] *or*
- aged 60 or over. In practice, this only applies if you are a man aged 60 or over but under 65. In this situation you might be better off if you claim PC rather than JSA; *or*
- a refugee learning English in order to obtain employment. You must be on a course for more than 15 hours a week and, at the time the course started, you must have been in GB for a year or less. You can only be exempt for nine months on this ground; *or*
- required to go to court or tribunal as a justice of the peace (JP), juror, witness or party to the proceedings; *or*
- not a 'qualifying young person' for child benefit purposes (see p57) and are aged 16–24 years and on a training course provided by the Learning and Skills Council for England, the National Assembly for Wales or in Scotland by a local enterprise company; *or*
- involved in a trade dispute (see p634).

If you fit into one of the exempt groups above (other than the first one, studying full time), you should also qualify for IS; in this case you can choose whether to claim IS or JSA. If you are 60 or over, you might be able to claim PC. See p395 for further information before deciding what to do.

Full-time paid work

You cannot usually get JSA if you are in full-time paid work. You cannot get income-based JSA if either you or your partner are in full-time paid work. If you are the JSA claimant, this means 16 hours or more each week.[16] For your partner, this means 24 hours or more each week.

If you are a member of a 'joint-claim couple', you cannot get joint-claim JSA if either of you is in full-time paid work. If one of you is working fewer than 16 hours a week, the other can then work up to 24 hours a week. The person working 16 to 24 hours does not have to claim joint-claim JSA.

In some situations you are treated as *not* in full-time work even if you work more than 16/24 hours (see p654). In others, you are treated as in full-time work when you are not (see p653). See p650 for details of how your hours are calculated and p649 for what counts as paid work.

If your partner normally works 16/24 hours or more but is off sick or on maternity, paternity or adoption leave s/he does not count as in full-time paid work.[17] You may, therefore, be able to claim JSA. You might also qualify for working tax credit (WTC).

If you work less than 16 hours and your partner works at least 16 hours but less than 24 hours each week, you and your partner might be able to claim WTC. In some cases, you might be able to claim both WTC and JSA. See p657 for further information. You should seek advice to see how you would be better off financially.

If you or your partner are 60 or over and either of you is working 16/24 hours or more each week, you might be able to claim PC or WTC (or both if your income is low enough). There is no full-time paid work rule for PC, but earnings are taken into account in working out how much you can get.

Note: if you or your partner have just taken up full-time paid work, you may be able to claim IS for help with your housing costs for the first four weeks. This is known as 'mortgage interest run-on' (see p823).

Capable of work

To qualify for JSA, you must be capable of work.[18] There are two tests for deciding whether you are capable or incapable of work – the 'own occupation test' and the 'personal capability assessment'. See Chapter 28 for further details. If a decision maker has decided for the purpose of some other benefit that you are capable (or incapable) under the tests, you are automatically treated as being capable (or incapable) of work for JSA.[19] You still have to show that you are available for work if you are ill or have a disability, but there are some special rules to help you do this (see p353). Note that even if you have been found incapable of work under the personal capability assessment, you can claim JSA and be treated as capable of work in some circumstances.[20]

Note: when the ESA rules take effect, to qualify for JSA you must not have 'limited capability for work' (see Chapter 7).

Periods of sickness when you can claim jobseeker's allowance

Even if you are incapable of work, you do not have to stop claiming JSA in some situations. You are treated as being capable of work and as available for and actively seeking work (see pp347 and 357) if the only reason why you would not otherwise qualify for JSA is that:

- you are unable to work because you are sick (for up to two weeks – see below). This does not apply if you have stated in writing that you are going to claim or have claimed IB, severe disablement allowance (SDA) or IS;[21] *or*
- you are incapable of work and temporarily absent from GB for the purpose of getting NHS hospital treatment under certain provisions. This does not apply if you have stated in writing before the period of temporary absence abroad begins that you have claimed IB, SDA or IS immediately before the beginning of the period.[22] You can be paid JSA indefinitely under this rule.

You have to make a written declaration that you will be incapable of work from a specific date or for a specific period, on a special form available at the Jobcentre Plus office.[23]

Note: the provisions under which arrangements for undergoing NHS hospital treatment abroad are made currently only apply in England and Wales, not in Scotland.

Two-week periods of sickness

You are allowed up to two two-week periods of sickness in a 'jobseeking period' (see p340) or if your jobseeking period has lasted more than 12 months, in any successive 12-month periods.[24] If you are sick more often than this, or for a longer period, you must claim IB and/or IS (PC if you are 60 or over) instead of JSA for the time you are unable to work.

The rules on two-week periods of sickness do not apply to you if you were getting IB, SDA, SSP or IS (if paid because you were sick and including a disability premium) in the eight weeks before you were sick.[25] Instead, you can claim benefit as being incapable of work without having to serve any 'waiting days' (see pp270 and 561).

Note: the Government intends to introduce rules that will mean that you must continue to claim JSA for the two-week periods you are allowed before you can claim IB.

Getting a training allowance

Provided you are not a child or qualifying young person for child benefit purposes (see p57), if you are receiving training and getting a training allowance you can get income-based JSA without having to satisfy the labour market conditions.[26]

This also applies if you would have been getting a training allowance if a court had not decided that you failed to comply with a community order without a reasonable excuse (see p997). For these purposes, 'training' does not include training for people aged 16–24 provided by the Learning and Skills Council for England, the National Assembly for Wales or by Scottish Enterprise or Highlands and Islands Enterprise. However, if this is the type of training you are receiving, you might qualify for IS (see p295).

Training allowance

'**Training allowance**' means an allowance payable to you for your maintenance or in respect of a member of your family (see p366) out of public funds by a government department or by, or on behalf of, the Secretary of State, Scottish Enterprise, Scottish Highlands and Islands Enterprise, the Learning and Skills Council for England or the National Assembly for Wales.[27] It must be payable for the period or part of a period of a course of training or instruction provided by or under arrangements made with that department, or approved by it.

Full-time training and study

You cannot usually get JSA if you are studying full time because you are treated as unavailable for work (see p352). To find out if you can claim JSA while studying full time, see p583. You might be able to get JSA while studying part time (see p584).

In some situations, you *can* take a full-time '**qualifying course**'and continue to get JSA. While you are on the course, you are treated as available for and actively seeking work. You can get JSA while attending a 'qualifying course' if:[28]

- you are aged 25 or over; *and*
- you had been 'receiving benefit' (see below) during a jobseeking period (see p339) for at least two years at the time the course starts. In working out whether you have been 'receiving benefit' for two years, the rules for linking jobseeking periods apply (see p340); *and*
- an employment officer (EO) approves your attendance; *and*
- you satisfy the conditions for being treated as available for and actively seeking work (see pp350 and 360).

Once you have started the course, the course becomes compulsory. This means that if you abandon it without 'good cause' or are dismissed because of misconduct, you could be sanctioned (see p412).

Qualifying courses and receiving benefit[29]

A '**qualifying course**' is a course of further or higher education which is employment-related and lasts no more than 12 consecutive months. A course of a higher standard thatn this can also be a qualifying course if your EO agrees.

'Receiving benefit' means getting JSA or IS as an unemployed person or NI credits for unemployment or because you are 60 or over. It also means getting IS as an asylum seeker, but only if you have been accepted as having refugee status or have been granted exceptional leave to remain in the UK, and you were getting IS as an asylum seeker, or were subsequently paid backdated IS, at some time in the 12 weeks before the start of the 'jobseeking period' (see p339), which includes the date that your course starts. Note that this can only apply if were accepted by the Home Office as a refugee and officially notified of this on or before 14 June 2007.

Available for work

To qualify for JSA you must be available for work. To be available for work you must be 'willing and able' to take up work 'immediately'.[30]

In some circumstances you can be treated as being available for work even if you are not actually available (see p349). Special rules allow you to count as available for work for the first 13 weeks of a period when you are laid off or on short-time working (see p370). If you are not available or treated as available for work, you cannot get JSA, but you may be able to get hardship payments (see p422). Check to see if you qualify for any of the other benefits in this *Handbook*.

The DWP can decide that you are not available for work without having to show that you have turned down a job.[31] However, the fact that you turn down a job does not necessarily mean that you are not available.

In some situations you can restrict your availability (see p354). However, you must have a 'reasonable prospect' of getting work unless the restrictions are reasonable in view of your physical or mental condition (see p353).

Willing and able to take up work immediately

Being **willing** to work is essentially a test of your attitude – your desire and willingness to work. What you do in practice to display this willingness is usually dealt with under the rules for actively seeking work (see p357).

You must be prepared to take up work as an employed person – being only available for self-employment is not sufficient.[32] However, this means that you do not count as being unavailable for work if you refuse to work as a self-employed person.

In order to be **able** to work it must be lawful for you to work in GB.[33] Your immigration status may affect this – eg, if a condition of your entry is that you do not work. In addition there must be nothing to prevent you from receiving job offers (eg, because you are away from home for more than a short time) and nothing to prevent you acting on them straight away (eg, because you are involved in other commitments you cannot abandon easily).

Being able to take up work **immediately** means that you must usually be able to start work without any delay, with little more than the time needed to get washed and dressed and have breakfast.[34] You can be allowed more time than this in the following situations. You only need to be available for work:

- on **one week's notice** if you are doing voluntary work or have caring responsibilities.[35] You must be willing and able to attend an interview in connection with opportunities for work on 48 hours' notice.
  '**Voluntary work**' is work which is done for a charity or other not-for-profit organisation or for anyone other than a member of your family (see p366) for which you receive no payment other than for your reasonable expenses.
  '**Caring responsibilities**' means responsibility for looking after a child under 16, someone over pension age or someone who needs care because of her/his mental or physical condition who is a member of your household (see p703 on the meaning of household) or a close relative (see below);
- on **24 hours' notice** if you are providing a service, whether paid or not, but do not qualify as a carer or a volunteer.[36] This includes services you provide for family or friends on an entirely non-commercial basis, such as giving someone a regular lift to work in your car.[37] It could also include activities that are of service to the community in general – eg, people doing community orders (see below), tribunal members (eg, appeal and employment tribunals) and people who are working.[38]
- **after your notice period** has passed if you are working part time. This applies if you have a duty to give your employer notice that you are leaving work under employment law.[39] If you must give longer notice than this under the terms of your contract of employment, argue that a longer notice period should apply.

Note: if you have said that you are only available to work at certain times you are *not* required to be able to take up employment at times that you are not available.[40] However, you must be willing and able to take up the offer as soon as you reach the next period in your pattern of availability (see p356).

'Close relative' means partner, parent, step-parent, parent-in-law, parent of a civil partner, grandparent, son, step-son, son-in-law, son of a civil partner, daughter, step-daughter, daughter-in-law, daughter of a civil partner, brother, sister, grandchild or the partner of any of these.[41]

If you are an **offender** you may be required, as part of your punishment, to do unpaid work in the community. You count as being available for work if arrangements are made so that you can be notified of a vacancy or interview and you can leave the unpaid work in order to take up a job within 24 hours.[42] If you are required to attend a course you have to be available for work immediately because this is unlikely to count as providing a service. To be considered available for work you should make sure that you can be contacted at short notice and are allowed to leave the course to attend an interview if required to do so. An offender who is released early from prison under the Home Detention Curfew Scheme can be available for work during daytime hours.

Treated as being available for work

Even if you are not actually available for work, you can be treated as if you are for short periods during your claim. When you can be treated as being available for work and the length of the period depends on the circumstances.[43] You must still satisfy the other conditions of entitlement to JSA. Remember that special rules allow you to count as available for work for up to 13 weeks of being laid off or on short-time working (see p370).

General rules

You are treated as available for work:[44]

- at the **beginning of your claim**, from your date of claim until the day of the week on which your signing day falls if, in respect of all the days concerned, you are available in line with any agreed restrictions on your availability (see p352) and:[45]
  - you have an agreed 'pattern of availability' (ie, the particular days and hours you are available for work) or are allowed to restrict your availability because of a physical or mental condition, caring responsibilities or because you are on short-time working;[46] *or*
  - you do not have an agreed 'pattern of availability' and are available for work for eight hours each day;
- during the **last week of your claim**, until the day your entitlement to JSA ends (except where your claim ends on the day of the week you would sign on if it were a signing-on week);
- if you are **sick** for a two-week period or are temporarily absent from GB for the purpose of getting NHS hospital treatment (see p345);
- if you were **recently found capable of work**, but only if your time limit for claiming JSA is extended because you were not told your entitlement to IS or IB had ended so could not claim JSA in time.

Studying and training

In some cases, you can study or take part in training courses while on JSA so long as you satisfy the rules of entitlement. See p576 for further information about studying and claiming JSA. Some people getting training allowances do not have to satisfy the labour market conditions (see p345).

In some situations, you would not normally count as being available for work while studying. However, you do:[47]

- for one period of up to two weeks in any 12 months, when you are:

- a full-time student (see p579) **on an employment-related course** which has been approved in advance by your EO. See below for more generous rules if you are on a 'qualifying course'; *or*
- **attending a residential work camp** in GB, organised by a charity, local authority or voluntary organisation for the benefit of the community or the environment;[48]

- if you are attending a compulsory residential course as part of an **Open University course** (for up to one week for each course);
- if you are attending a residential training programme run by **the Venture Trust** (for one programme only for a maximum of four weeks in any 12-month period).

Special rules apply if you are attending a **'qualifying course'** with the approval of an EO (see p346). You are treated as being available for work in any week:[49]

- which falls entirely or partly in term time, so long as you provide written evidence, within five days of it being requested, confirming that you are attending and making satisfactory progress on the course. This must be signed by you and by the college or educational establishment;
- in which you are taking exams relating to the course; *or*
- which falls entirely in a vacation, if you are willing and able to take up any 'casual employment' immediately. **'Casual employment'** means employment that you can leave without giving notice or if you must give notice, that you can leave before the end of the vacation.

Temporary absence from Great Britain

You are treated as available for work when you are temporarily absent from GB and:[50]

- you are taking a child who is a member of your household (see p712) and for whom you are responsible (see p710) abroad temporarily for medical treatment (for a maximum of eight weeks). The treatment must be under the supervision of a person qualified in medical, physiotherapeutic or similar practices;[51] *or*
- you are attending a job interview, provided you have told your EO in advance and confirmed it in writing if required to do so (for a maximum of seven days); *or*
- you are a member of a couple and the pensioner, enhanced pensioner, higher pensioner, disability or severe disability premium is being paid for your partner (see Chapter 33) and you are both away from GB (for a maximum of four weeks); *or*
- you are abroad for the purpose of getting NHS hospital treatment (see p345); *or*
- on the date of the JSA claim, you are a member of a 'joint-claim couple' (see p381) and on the day the other member of the couple makes the claim for JSA, you are:

– in Northern Ireland (for a maximum of four weeks) but only if you are unlikely to be away for more than 52 weeks; *or*
– attending a job interview (for a maximum of seven days).

If you are looking after a child because your partner is temporarily absent from the UK, see below.

Other

You are treated as available for work:[52]

- if you are **looking after a child under 16**. This only applies (for a maximum of eight weeks) if you are:
  – a member of a couple and looking after a child under 16 who is a member of your household and for whom you are responsible (see p710) while your partner is temporarily absent from the UK; *or*
  – looking after a child under 16 on a full-time basis because the person who normally looks after the child is ill or temporarily away from home or looking after a member of the family who is ill;
- if you have been **discharged from detention** in prison, a remand centre or a youth custody institution (for one week from the date of discharge);[53]
- during **temporary police detention** (legal custody in Scotland) of up to 96 hours, but not if you come within the definition of 'prisoner' (see p627);
- if you are required to **attend a court or tribunal** as a justice of the peace, juror, witness or party to any proceedings (but not if you come within the definition of 'prisoner' – see p627) (for a maximum of eight weeks). You must have notified your EO beforehand;[54]
- if you are engaged in crewing or launching a lifeboat, are carrying out duties as a part-time firefighter or are engaged during an emergency as a member of an organised group which is helping to save lives, prevent injury or a serious threat to the health of others, or protect property;[55]
- if you are dealing with circumstances arising from:
  – a domestic emergency affecting you or a close friend or close relative (see p348); *or*
  – the death, serious illness or funeral of a close friend or close relative (see p348); *or*
  – the death of someone for whom you were caring.

  You can only be treated as being available in these circumstances for up to a week at a time and for no more than four occasions in any 12-month period. You are only treated as available during the time it takes to deal with the matter.

If you are selected as a **juror** you must attend court when asked to do so. You should not presume that if you lose JSA this will be made up by the court. Before you go on jury service, the court sends you a certificate of loss of earnings. You should show it to the DWP and it will tell you how being on jury service affects your claim. You might instead be able to claim IS.

Treated as being unavailable for work

Even if you are (or can be treated as) available for employment, you are nevertheless treated as unavailable for work if:[56]

- you are a full-time student, *unless* you are:
  - on a 'qualifying course' (see p350); *or*
  - a member of a couple who are both students, it is the summer vacation, one of you is responsible for a child (see p710) and you satisfy all the normal rules on being available for work. If you are a lone parent, you can argue this rule also applies to you;[57] *or*
  - treated as being available for work because you are on an employment-related course or on a residential training programme run by the Venture Trust (see p349);
- you are on temporary release from prison;
- you are receiving maternity allowance or statutory maternity pay;
- you are on paternity leave, or ordinary or additional adoption leave;
- it is the beginning of your claim, from the date of claim until the day of the week on which your signing day falls, unless you come under the rule for being treated as being available for that period (see p349).

Unavailable for part of a week

A situation may arise which makes you unavailable for work for a short period during a benefit week – eg, because you were away from home. If this happens to you and you have put restrictions on the times that you are available (see p356):[58]

- your JSA is not affected, if the period you are not available comes entirely outside your 'pattern of availability' (ie, the particular days and hours that you are available for work); *or*
- you lose JSA for the whole of that benefit week if all or part of the period you are not available comes within your 'pattern of availability'.

If this happens to you and you have *not* put any restrictions on the hours that you are available, you may find that you lose benefit for that week because you are not available to take up work immediately.[59] For this reason it is best to avoid signing a jobseeker's agreement with totally unrestricted hours.

Note: if you were arrested and held by the police for a short time but then released, you can be treated as available for work for up to 96 hours while you were detained (see p351).

Restrictions on availability for work

If you have a physical or mental condition, you can restrict your availability in any way if the restrictions are reasonable (see p353). Otherwise, if you can prove that you still have a reasonable prospect of securing employment (see below), you can make some restrictions on the work you are available to do. These are:[60]

- the **type of work** you are prepared to do (see p354);
- the **hours** you are prepared to work (see p355);
- the **times** you are prepared to work (see p356);
- the **terms and conditions** of employment you are prepared to accept, including the rate of pay (see p356);
- the **location** of the job.

Note: if you and the DWP have not agreed in advance that there are certain types of work which you cannot, or are unwilling, to do, it may prove difficult to justify turning down such a job if it is offered to you later.

A 'reasonable prospect' of securing employment

You must show that you have a reasonable prospect of securing employment despite any restrictions you are allowed to place on your availability.[61] If you impose more than one type of restriction, it is the cumulative effect on your job prospects that is considered. The DWP must consider all the evidence and in particular:[62]

- your skills, qualifications and experience; *and*
- the type and number of job vacancies within daily travelling distance of your home; *and*
- the length of time you have been unemployed; *and*
- the job applications which you have made and their outcome; *and*
- whether you are willing to move home to take up a job, but only where you are placing restrictions on the type of job you are prepared to do.

Your job prospects may be poor. However, if you do not put any restrictions on the work you will take, you are accepted as being available no matter how poor your prospects of finding work may be. You should therefore think carefully if it is sensible to apply restrictions if this applies to you.

Physical or mental condition

You can restrict your availability for work in any way if the restrictions are reasonable in view of your physical or mental condition.[63] If the restrictions you impose are reasonable ones for you, you do not have to show that you have reasonable prospects of securing employment (see above).

You are normally expected to provide medical evidence, but if you have no prospects of work at all, you should consider whether you really are capable of work. If not, it may be in your interest to claim IB, IS or PC instead of JSA. If you have been found fit for work following a personal capability assessment and are appealing against the decision, see p683 for information about claiming JSA during this period.

If you also place restrictions on your availability for work that are *not* connected with your physical or mental condition, you must show that you have a reasonable prospect of securing employment with all your restrictions. You should, therefore, think carefully before placing additional restrictions on your availability.

The type of work you are prepared to do

The general rule is that you have to be available for any type of employment, but you are allowed to place restrictions on the sort of job you are prepared to do so long as you have a reasonable prospect of securing employment (see p353).[64] In addition, special rules allow you to make restrictions:

- during your 'permitted period' if you have one (see below);
- if you have been laid off or are working part time (see p369);
- because of your physical or mental condition (see p353);
- because of a sincerely held religious belief or conscientious objection (see p354).

Permitted periods

A **'permitted period'** is a period of between one and 13 weeks from the date you claim JSA during which you are allowed to be available only for vacancies in your normal line of work (your 'usual occupation') and which pay at least what you would normally receive.[65] Any other restrictions you place on your availability must be consistent with the conditions of work that are normal in your usual occupation.

The term 'usual occupation' is not defined in the rules. If you have followed an occupation for a long time, this can count as your usual occupation.[66] If you had only recently started a new occupation before claiming JSA, it may still count as your usual occupation if you intend to follow that type of employment in future.[67]

Not everyone is allowed a permitted period. Whether or not you are allowed one and, if so, how long it lasts, are matters that you and the EO need to discuss when arriving at your jobseeker's agreement (see p361).[68]

The DWP must consider the following factors:[69]

- your 'usual occupation' and any relevant skills or qualifications you may have; *and*
- the length of time you have spent training for or have worked in the occupation or since you have worked in the occupation; *and*
- the availability and location of jobs in that area of work.

A permitted period can be, and often is, less than 13 weeks.

Religious or conscientious objection

You do not have to be available for work that offends a sincerely held religious belief or a sincere conscientious objection – eg, a job in a company associated with live animal exports if you have a conscientious objection to these.[70] You must still have reasonable prospects of securing employment despite those restrictions (see p353).[71]

The hours you are prepared to work

The general rule is that in order to qualify as being available for work:[72]

- you must be prepared to take a job which would involve working for *at least* 40 hours a week; *and*
- you must also be prepared to work for less than 40 hours a week if required to do so. In practice, this means that you must be prepared to work part time.

You are allowed to restrict the number of hours you are prepared to work if:

- this is reasonable in view of your physical or mental condition (see p353); *or*
- you are a short-time worker (see p369); *or*
- you have caring responsibilities (see below).

You must be prepared to work for the maximum number of hours for which you are available or for a lower number.

You are allowed to refuse a job formally notified to you which would be for less than 24 hours a week (16 hours a week, if it is agreed you need only be available for less than 24 hours a week – eg, because you have responsibilities as a carer – see below).[73] This is because you can show 'good cause' for refusing to apply and cannot be sanctioned (see p410).

Caring responsibilities

You may restrict the total hours for which you are available to less than 40 hours a week if:[74]

- you are caring for a child under 16, a person over pension age or someone who needs care because of a physical or mental condition. S/he must either be in the same household as you, or a close relative (see p348). 'Household' is not defined, but see p703; *and*
- you are available for employment for as many hours as your caring responsibilities permit and for at least 16 hours a week; *and*
- you have a reasonable chance of securing employment (see p353) despite the restricted hours you are prepared to work.

When deciding whether you qualify under this rule, the DWP must consider relevant factors. These include the particular hours and days you spend caring, whether your caring responsibilities are shared with someone else and the age and physical and mental condition of the person being cared for.[75]

If you are a carer and you cannot make yourself available for work at least 16 hours a week, consider claiming IS or, if you are 60 or over, PC rather than JSA.

The times you are prepared to work

The general rule is that in order to qualify as being available for work, you must be prepared to work at any time of the day or on any day of the week. However, you are allowed to put restrictions on the times you are prepared to work if:[76]

- the total hours during which you are prepared to work are at least 40 a week (unless you are someone who is allowed to restrict your hours);
- you have agreed with the DWP a 'pattern of availability' (ie, the particular days and hours that you are available for work) and this has been recorded in your jobseeker's agreement (see p361);[77] *and*
- you still have reasonable prospects of securing employment despite the restrictions (see p353) and they do not *considerably* reduce your prospects of securing employment.

If you are doing voluntary work and you have placed restrictions on the total number of hours you are available to work, any voluntary work (see p348) you do within your 'pattern of availability' must be ignored for the purpose of deciding if you are available, so long as you are willing and able to rearrange the voluntary work within:[78]

- one week's notice, in order to take up any job whose hours fall within your pattern of availability;
- 48 hours' notice, to attend an interview in connection with an opportunity for work at a time that falls within your pattern of availability.

There is a similar rule if you are a part-time student (see p586).

The terms and conditions of employment you will accept

You can make restrictions on the terms and conditions of employment you are prepared to accept (including the rate of pay – but see below) so long as you can show you still have reasonable prospects of securing employment despite those restrictions (see p353).[79]

The rate of pay you are prepared to accept

You can only restrict the rate of pay you are willing to accept in three situations. You can restrict it:

- if you have a 'permitted period' (see p354), to the rate you are accustomed to receive in your usual occupation during your permitted period;[80]
- for six months from the date you claimed JSA, so long as you still have reasonable prospects of securing employment (see p353);[81]
- indefinitely, if this is reasonable in view of your physical or mental condition (see p353).[82]

It is *vital* that the wage or salary you say you are willing to accept should not be higher than the going rate for the jobs you have said you are looking for.

Remember that you should not be expected to work for a rate of pay below the national minimum wage (see p430).

The location of the job

You can make restrictions on the localities within which you are available for work so long as you can show you still have reasonable prospects of securing employment in the selected areas (see p353).[83]

Actively seeking work

In order to qualify for JSA you must be actively seeking work. In some cases you can be treated as if you are (see p359).[84] Special rules apply if you have been allowed a 'permitted period' (see p354).

To be actively seeking work:

- you must take, in each benefit week, such 'steps' as you can reasonably be expected to have to take in order to have the best prospects of securing employment;[85]
- you are expected to take more than two steps during a week unless taking one or two steps is all that it is reasonable for you to do.[86] Note that it is possible that in some weeks there may be no steps at all that you can reasonably be expected to take.[87]

The normal actively seeking work rule is adapted to cover any part-week at the beginning of your claim. You satisfy the test so long as you take such steps as are reasonable in the part-week to ensure you have the best chance of getting a job.[88]

Your jobseeker's agreement (see p361) says what steps you have agreed to take to find work, but you do not necessarily have to take all the steps each week to prove you are actively seeking work.[89] The test for whether you have been actively seeking work is what you *did*, not what you did not do.

In order to check that you are actively seeking work, the DWP asks you to give details of the steps you have taken when you sign on (see p386). It is, therefore, extremely important that you keep records of your attempts to get a job.

You might not count as actively seeking work if it is considered that you should be taking more steps or ones that give you a better chance of finding work. You may be asked at an interview to change the steps you must take. In this case, the EO may propose a change in your jobseeker's agreement (see p363).

What counts as a 'step'

Anything you do that might lead to your being offered employment should count as a step. Steps include:[90]

- applying for jobs in writing, personally or by phone;
- seeking information from advertisements, advertisers, agencies or employers;
- registering with an agency or appointing someone else to help you find work – eg, an agent if you are looking for work in the entertainment field;

- preparing a CV;
- asking a previous employer for a reference;
- preparing a list of or looking for information about employers who may be able to offer you a job;
- looking for information about an occupation with a view to finding a job in that occupation;
- getting specialist advice on how to improve your chances of finding a job – eg, from a disability employment adviser.

There are many other things that could count as steps – eg, looking for suitable job vacancies at the Jobcentre Plus office, searching for jobs on the Jobcentre Plus website and making enquiries about jobs by internet or email. If you are using the internet or email, remember to keep a record as proof.

When the DWP decides whether you have been actively seeking work in a week, it must disregard a step if (unless there are reasons beyond your control) you:[91]

- act in a violent or abusive manner; *or*
- spoil an application if the step is completing a job application; *or*
- undermine your prospects of getting a job by your behaviour or appearance.

In these circumstances, the DWP might issue a jobseeker's direction (see p406) and sanction you if you fail to comply with it.

Deciding what steps are reasonable

When the DWP decides what steps are reasonable, all the circumstances in your individual case must be considered, including:[92]

- your skills, qualifications and abilities;
- any physical or mental limitations you may have;
- how long you have been unemployed, and your work experience;
- the steps you have taken in previous weeks and how those steps have improved your chances of finding a job;
- the availability and location of job vacancies;
- any time you have spent:
  - launching or crewing a lifeboat or acting as a part-time firefighter, undertaking duties as a member of the Territorial Army or reserve force, attending an outward bound course or taking part in an organised group helping in an emergency;
  - undertaking voluntary work and the extent to which it may have improved your chances of finding a paid job;
  - improving your chances of finding a job by training to use aids to overcome any physical or mental disabilities you may have or, if you are blind, training to use a guide dog;

  - as a part-time student on an employment-related course or time you have spent on an employment or training programme for which no training allowance is paid, if this is for less than three days a week;
- any circumstances which have resulted in you being treated as being available for work (see p349);
- whether you have applied for, taken part in or accepted a place on a course funded by the Government or European Community, which is designed to help you select, train for, obtain or retain employment or self-employment;
- if you are homeless, the fact that you have no accommodation and the steps which you need to take and did take to find a home. It should be accepted that being homeless may limit the steps you can take to look for work and that you need time to look for somewhere to live.

If your chances of getting work are poor, there may only be a limited number of steps you can take each week but it may be reasonable for the DWP to expect you to pursue all of them every week. If your chances of getting work are good, there may be many steps you could take each week but it would not be reasonable for the DWP to expect you to take all of them.[93]

Actively seeking work during your 'permitted period'

If you have been allowed a 'permitted period' (see p354) you count as actively seeking work during that period even if you are only looking for jobs in your normal line of work or at your normal level of pay, or both.[94] If you have been self-employed in your usual occupation at any time within the 12 months before you claim JSA you count as actively seeking work if you are seeking self-employment in that occupation.

Treated as actively seeking work

Even if you are not actively seeking work you can be treated as if you are in some circumstances.

- You can count as actively seeking work while you are laid off or working short time (see p369).[95]
- You are allowed two weeks (longer in some circumstances) during which you are seen as actively seeking work while away from home (see p360).
- Other situations where you can be treated as actively seeking work generally mirror those where you are treated as 'available for work' and have the same maximum lengths (see p349).[96] However, in most cases you are only considered to be actively seeking work if the situation affects you for at least three days in the benefit week. There are differences.
  - You are treated as actively seeking work in any week which is part of a period in which you are taking active steps to become self-employed under a scheme to assist people to do so.[97] This only applies during a single period lasting no more than eight weeks in any period of entitlement to JSA, starting

with the week in which you are accepted on a place under the scheme. The scheme must be provided or funded by a specified government agency.
- You are treated as actively seeking work for any week in which you spend at least three days on a government sponsored employment or training course or programme for which you are not paid a training allowance.[98]

If you are attending a **'qualifying course'**with the approval of an EO (see p345) and are treated as being available for work (see p350), you are also treated as actively seeking work.[99] If this is in any week which falls entirely in a vacation, you must take such steps as can reasonably be expected in order to have the best prospects of securing 'casual employment' (see p350).

Absence from home

While you are on JSA, you can be treated as actively seeking work while away from home – eg, on holiday.[100] You still have to be available for work, so you are expected to give an assurance that you are willing and able to cut your absence short if notified of a job. In any 12-month period, you can be away from home for up to:[101]

- three weeks, if during each week you spend at least three days on an outward bound course; *or*
- if you are blind, two weeks, plus up to four other weeks spent attending training in the use of guide dogs for at least three days a week; *or*
- two weeks, in any other case.

If you are away for longer than this and so cannot be treated as actively seeking work, you must show that you are looking for work while you are away.

If you are considering going away from home, remember the following.

- You must inform the DWP before you go away; your EO can require you to give notice in writing.
- You must be available for work (see p347) and able to receive information about job offers. You must, therefore, provide details of how you can be contacted or how you plan to contact the DWP while you are away.[102]
- You must usually be in GB to qualify for JSA. To see if you can get JSA while temporarily away see p1352, and p350 to see if you can be treated as available for work. If you are unemployed and want to look for work in a European Economic Area country, see p1391 to see if you can export your contribution-based JSA. See p345 if you are going to be temporarily absent from GB for the purpose of getting NHS hospital treatment. Even if you cannot get JSA while you are away, you might be able to get national insurance credits (see p728).
- When you return home you must sign on (see p386) the very next day your Jobcentre Plus office is open even if that is not your usual signing on day. If you do not, you may lose benefit for the whole of the period you were away unless you can show that you had 'good cause' for failing to sign on (see p389).

The jobseeker's agreement

To qualify for JSA you must agree and sign a 'jobseeker's agreement'. It enables the DWP to monitor and direct your search for a job and gives you a chance to put any restrictions on your availability for work that are agreed on record. It is discussed with you during your interview (see p380).

Until you have agreed the contents of the jobseeker's agreement with your EO, your claim for JSA is not passed to a decision maker to decide whether you are entitled to JSA. However, see below for situations when you can be treated as having signed an agreement.

The agreement is not valid until it has been signed by you and the EO.[103] You must be given a copy.[104] To find out when your agreement can be backdated, see p363. For what happens if you cannot agree, see p362.

If a decision on your claim is delayed or JSA is refused because you have not entered into a jobseeker's agreement you may be able to get hardship payments (see p422).

What is in the jobseeker's agreement

A jobseeker's agreement must contain specific information such as your name, the date of the agreement and the type of job you are looking for. It must also include:[105]

- unless you say that you are prepared to work at any time, the total number of hours that you are available for work each week, with a breakdown of what hours you are available on each day. This is what is known as your 'pattern of availability'. For information on restricting the number of hours and the times for which you are available, see pp355 and 356;
- other restrictions you are placing on the work you are prepared to do – eg, the level of pay or the distance you are prepared to travel (see p352);
- the steps you are to take to seek work (see p357) or action you will take to improve your chances of work (eg, attendance on relevant courses);
- if you have been allowed a 'permitted period' (see p354), the dates on which it starts and ends;
- a statement of your rights if you and the EO cannot agree on what should be in the agreement.

The agreement also advises you to keep a record of what you do to find work and that if you do not do enough, your JSA might be affected.

Your jobseeker's agreement is not binding on you or the DWP; there is no penalty if you fail to keep it.[106] However, whether or not you keep to your jobseeker's agreement, the DWP might still decide that you are not available for or actively seeking work. If you have done everything in your jobseeker's agreement, argue that you should not be accused of not actively seeking work.[107]

Treated as signing a jobseeker's agreement

You can be treated as signing a jobseeker's agreement:[108]

- for the period from your date of claim until the date of your interview with a visiting EO, where you are allowed to make a claim for JSA by post (see p380);
- if you stop claiming JSA before your interview;
- for as long as you are treated as being available for work because of circumstances which arose between the date of your claim and your interview;
- if there are circumstances affecting the normal procedures for claiming, awarding or paying JSA (eg, a computer failure at the DWP, a strike by staff or severe weather) which make it impracticable or difficult for you to comply with them;[109]
- where you sign on after a period of claiming JSA while getting a training allowance (and so not having to be available for work), from the date your training course ends until your interview;
- for the period of your temporary absence from GB if you are a member of a 'joint-claim couple' (see p381) and on the date that the other member of the couple makes a claim for JSA you are:
  - in Northern Ireland (for a maximum of four weeks) but only if you are unlikely to be away for more than 52 weeks; *or*
  - attending a job interview (for a maximum of seven days).

Disputes about a jobseeker's agreement

Your EO is not allowed to sign your jobseeker's agreement unless s/he is satisfied that you would qualify as being available for and actively seeking work if you complied with its terms.[110] If s/he thinks you are placing unreasonable restrictions on your availability for work or that the steps you are proposing to take to actively to seek work are not sufficient, s/he will not sign the agreement.

If this situation arises the EO may refer a proposed jobseeker's agreement to a decision maker. If you ask your EO to do so, s/he must refer the proposed agreement to a decision maker immediately.[111]

The decision maker decides:[112]

- whether it is reasonable to expect you to have to comply with it; *and*
- whether you would qualify as being available for and actively seeking work if you were to comply with it.

The decision maker may also direct the EO to enter into a jobseeker's agreement on whatever terms s/he considers appropriate and may also order that if the agreement is entered into, it should be backdated.[113]

The decision maker must make a decision within 14 days of the agreement being referred, unless to do so would be impracticable, and must notify you of the decision.[114] If you are happy with the decision, you have to see your EO and sign the agreement. If you are unhappy with it, you can ask for the decision to be revised or superseded, or appeal to an appeal tribunal (see pp1065, 1074 and Chapter 42).

If your proposed jobseeker's agreement is referred to a decision maker, you should immediately apply for hardship payments (see p422). See Chapter 46 for information about dealing with delays and making complaints.

If the decision maker decides in your favour, your jobseeker's agreement is normally backdated and you are paid arrears of JSA from the date of your claim. However, if the decision maker decides against you, you are unlikely to get any backdating. You therefore risk losing benefit if you refuse to sign the jobseeker's agreement and insist on its referral to a decision maker.

Rather than refuse to sign the jobseeker's agreement, you might do better to sign it and then write to the DWP saying that you would like to change it (see below). You should not lose JSA so long as you comply with the original jobseeker's agreement while the variation is being considered. It is important you make it clear that you intend to do so. If there is a doubt whether you are available for or actively seeking work, your JSA could be suspended (see p984).

Backdating the jobseeker's agreement

A jobseeker's agreement is automatically backdated to the first day from which you claimed JSA so long as you and your EO can agree about what it should contain and it is not referred to a decision maker.[115] This includes any date to which your claim has been backdated (see p966).

If the agreement is referred to a decision maker it is only backdated if s/he makes a direction ordering this.[116] When deciding whether to make a direction, s/he must consider all the relevant circumstances including the following factors:[117]

- whether it was reasonable for you to refuse to accept the agreement proposed by the EO; *and*
- whether the terms of any alternative agreement which you may have proposed are reasonable; *and*
- whether you have subsequently said that you would be prepared to accept the agreement proposed by the EO; *and*
- the date on which you were first prepared to enter into an agreement which the decision maker considers to be reasonable; *and*
- the fact that the first opportunity you had to sign a jobseeker's agreement was later than the date of your claim for JSA.

Changing your jobseeker's agreement

The terms of your jobseeker's agreement can be changed by agreement between you and your EO. Any change must be in writing and signed by you and the EO.[118]

Both you and the EO can propose changes at any time. You should put your proposals in writing, giving full details of the changes you want to make and your reasons. An EO cannot agree to a change unless s/he considers that the terms mean that you satisfy the labour market conditions.[119] If you and the EO:

- agree the proposed changes, you must be given a copy of the new jobseeker's agreement;[120]
- do not agree the proposed changes, these can be referred to a decision maker.[121] They *must* be referred to a decision maker if you request this. If the decision maker believes that both your and the EO's proposals are reasonable and you would qualify as being available for and actively seeking work, the DWP says s/he should change the agreement along the lines proposed by you.[122]

When a referral to a decision maker is made

When a proposed change to a jobseeker's agreement is referred to a decision maker, your existing agreement remains in force until a decision is made. Your JSA might be suspended if you do not stick to the terms of the agreement, if this causes a doubt about whether you are available for or actively seeking work.

The decision maker can direct a change of the jobseeker's agreement and the terms on which you and the EO must agree to change it. S/he can also say when the new agreement takes effect.[123] If a change you proposed is accepted and it makes the terms of the agreement less restrictive, you can argue that the new agreement should take effect from the date on which you proposed the change.[124]

If you fail to sign the new agreement within 21 days, the decision maker can bring your jobseeker's agreement to an end.[125] If this happens, you no longer get JSA, including during any revision or appeal period, unless you qualify for hardship payments (see p422).

If you are unhappy with the decision maker's decision you can request a revision or appeal to an appeal tribunal (see p1065 and Chapter 42). If your appeal is eventually allowed, the original jobseeker's agreement revives and you are owed arrears even if the tribunal or commissioner directs another change in the agreement.[126]

Urgent cases payments

Urgent cases payments are payments of JSA at a reduced rate (see p1344). You may be able to get these if you are:[127]

- a 'person subject to immigration control' (see p1334) and meet certain conditions; *or*
- treated as having income which was due to be paid to you but which has not been paid (see p874). The income you are treated as having must not be readily available to you and the decision maker must be satisfied that if you do not get an urgent cases payment, you, your partner or any children for whom you are responsible and who live in your household (see p366) will experience hardship.[128] If you were due to receive a *benefit* but it has not been paid you are *not* treated as having it.

Urgent cases payments are calculated in a special way (see p1344). An urgent cases payment is a payment of income-based JSA so you are automatically eligible for some other benefits (see p396). Even if you or your partner are entitled to ordinary income-based JSA you can claim urgent cases payments instead if the amount you receive would be higher. You do not have to make a separate claim for urgent cases payments.[129]

There may be situations when you come under the rules for an urgent cases payment and hardship payments (see p422) for the same period. If so, your JSA is assessed at a particularly low rate.

2. The rules about your age

There is no minimum age for entitlement to **contribution-based jobseeker's allowance (JSA)** but in practice, because you can only qualify if you have paid or been credited with sufficient national insurance (NI) contributions in the two tax years before the benefit year in which you claim, you are unlikely to qualify before the age of 18.

You cannot usually qualify for **income-based JSA** until you are 18. There are special rules that can help you qualify if you are 16 or 17 (see p371). If you do not qualify, see if you might qualify for income support (IS) instead. Even if you cannot get JSA or IS you may qualify for housing benefit.

You cannot usually qualify for **joint-claim JSA** unless you and your partner are both 18. If only one of you is 18 or over, the other must qualify for income-based JSA in her/his own right as a 16/17-year-old (see p371).[130]

You cannot claim JSA if you are pension age or over (currently 60 for a woman and 65 for a man). In practice there is usually no point in remaining on income-based JSA if you are a man aged 60 or over, as from that time you qualify for pension credit (PC) on the grounds of age without having to sign on as unemployed. You also receive automatic NI credits (see p731). You (and your partner) should be no worse off on PC than on income-based JSA. See p395 for further information.

3. Claiming for others

If you claim **contribution-based jobseeker's allowance** (JSA) you can only claim for yourself. You cannot claim any additions for your partner or your children.

You and your partner must usually both claim **joint-claim JSA** if you are what is known as a 'joint-claim couple' (see p381).

You claim **income-based JSA** (but not joint-claim JSA) for yourself and your partner, if you have one. If you are a member of a couple who does not have to claim joint-claim JSA, you or your partner may claim income-based JSA for you both. See p702 for who counts as a couple. Whichever one of you claims, the other can make a claim for credits in order to protect her/his national insurance record (see p728).

In some cases, you need to know who counts as a member of your 'family' for JSA purposes. Member of the 'family' means your partner and any child who is a member of your household and for whom you count as 'responsible' (see below).[131]

Children

There are some situations in which you must show that you are 'responsible' (see p710) for a child who is living in your household. You should remember the following.

- You can count as responsible for any child under 16, and for any qualifying young person – referred to as 'children' in this *Handbook* (see p710). You do not have to be the child's parent.[132]
- You can continue to count as responsible for children who have left school or training until the 'terminal date' (see p62) and during what is known as the 'extension period' (see p59).
- A young person claiming income support or JSA in her/his own right does not count as your child for JSA purposes, nor do certain 16/17-year-olds who are no longer being looked after by a local authority (see p610).
- In some situations, a child does not count as a member of your household even if s/he normally does, or continues to count as a member of your household while s/he is temporarily away from home (see p712).[133]

Note: there are different rules about children for the purpose of deciding whether you must claim joint-claim JSA. See p381 for further information.

4. The amount of benefit

The amount of jobseeker's allowance (JSA) you get depends on whether you are claiming contribution-based JSA or income-based JSA.

Waiting days

You are not entitled to either income-based or contribution-based JSA for the first three days ('waiting days') of any jobseeking period (see p339) unless:[134]

- your claim is linked to a previous claim for JSA (see p340). For 'joint-claim couples' this includes a previous claim made by either of you separately; *or*
- you (or for 'joint-claim couples' only, either of you) have been entitled to income support (IS), incapacity benefit or carer's allowance within the 12 weeks before you become entitled to JSA.

- you are the member of a 'joint-claim couple' nominated to be paid JSA and are in receipt of a training allowance; *or*
- you are 16 or 17 and getting JSA under the severe hardship rules (see p373).

In addition, you do not have to serve any waiting days if you swap from claiming IS to claiming JSA, or you and your partner swap which of you claims IS or JSA for both of you, and the new claim is for JSA.[135]

If you receive income-based JSA you are entitled to maximum housing benefit and/or council tax benefit during any waiting days (see pp84 and 190).

Amount of contribution-based jobseeker's allowance

Contribution-based JSA is paid at the following weekly rates.[136]

Age of claimant	*£pw*
Under 18	47.95
18–24	47.95
25 and over	60.50

You are not paid an allowance for your partner or children.

These amounts are reduced penny for penny if you receive certain pension payments of more than £50 in any week.[137] Contribution-based JSA may also be reduced penny for penny by any part-time earnings. For more on how earnings and pension payments affect contribution-based JSA, see p840. Other types of income and any capital including any earnings and capital of your partner do not affect your contribution-based JSA.[138]

Contribution-based JSA is only paid for a limited period. You can claim income-based JSA (including joint-claim JSA) to top up your contribution-based JSA if you satisfy the means test.

Duration of contribution-based jobseeker's allowance

You cannot receive more than 182 days of contribution-based JSA in any jobseeking period (see p339) or in two or more jobseeking periods where entitlement is based on national insurance contributions in the same two contribution years.[139] However, you can have another 182 days of contribution-based JSA for a later claim if:[140]

- you satisfy the contribution conditions; *and*
- at least one of the two contribution years used to decide whether you satisfy the contribution conditions is later than the second contribution year used to decide your previous entitlement.

Each day for which you are entitled to contribution-based JSA, even if you are not paid, counts towards the 182-day total. Because JSA is a weekly benefit, you are entitled on Saturdays and Sundays.

Days when you are entitled to contribution-based JSA but are not paid include days you:

- satisfy the contribution conditions for contribution-based JSA but:[141]
  - you have been sanctioned (see Chapter 16); *or*
  - your JSA is not payable because a court has decided that you failed to comply with a community order without a reasonable excuse (see p997) or because of the 'loss of benefit for benefit offences' rules (see p1047); *or*
- meet conditions of entitlement but a pension, or a combination of a pension and earnings, means that the amount paid is reduced to nil (see p839); *or*
- are refused contribution-based JSA because you do not meet the labour market conditions *and* you are receiving a hardship payment (see p424).[142]

Days when you are not entitled to JSA, and which do *not* count towards the 182-day total include:

- waiting days (see p366);
- days in any benefit week where you are not entitled to JSA because you earn more than the prescribed amount (see p839);
- days when you are refused contribution-based JSA because you do not meet the labour market conditions and you are *not* getting a hardship payment.

Amount of income-based jobseeker's allowance

Income-based JSA tops up your income to a level set by the Government that changes every April. The amount you get depends on your needs (your 'applicable amount') and on how much income and capital you have.[143] For the rules on income see Chapter 36 and on capital, Chapter 37.

Your applicable amount consists of:

- a **personal allowance** (see p771); *and*
- **premiums** (see p775) for any special needs; *and*
- **housing costs,** principally for mortgage interest payments (see Chapter 34).

The way income-based JSA is calculated is the same as for IS (see pp299–300).

If you have children

If you claim income-based JSA and are getting child tax credit (CTC), income-based JSA does not include allowances and premiums for your children. CTC does not count as income for income-based JSA, nor does child benefit.

If you were getting income-based JSA on 5 April 2004 and this included allowances and premiums for your children, but you were not yet entitled to CTC, you will be transferred onto CTC sometime in the future. Until then, you will continue to get allowances and premiums for your children. See p709 for further information.

You might get a reduced amount of JSA if:

- you refuse to co-operate in pursuing mainatenace for your child(ren)(see p748); *or*
- you are getting an urgent cases payment of JSA (see p364); *or*
- you are required to make a joint claim for JSA but your partner has not fulfilled all the eligibility conditions (see p382) or has been sanctioned (see Chapter 16); *or*
- you have a partner, you are both 18 or over but under 60 and your partner has failed to attend a work-focused interview without good cause (see p972); *or*
- you are receiving a hardship payment of income-based JSA (see Chapter 16); *or*
- a court has decided that you failed to comply with a community order without a reasonable excuse (see p997) or your JSA has been restricted under the 'loss of benefit for benefit offences' rules (see p1047).

Different rules for calculating your JSA can sometimes apply if you are in one of the groups to whom special rules apply.

5. Special benefit rules

There are some groups of claimants to whom special rules apply. These are:

- workers who are laid off or working short time (see below);
- 16/17-year-olds (see p371);
- people from abroad (see Chapter 58);
- people who are studying (see Chapter 25);
- people without accommodation, involved in a trade dispute or in hospital (see Chapter 26).

Your jobseeker's allowance (JSA) might be affected if you (or your partner or child(ren) live in a care home (see p617).

Laid-off and short-time workers

If, because of 'temporary adverse industrial conditions' you have a job but:[144]

- your work and wages have been suspended, you count as being **laid off** (eg, you are a farm worker whose work is suspended because of a scare about food safety);
- your hours of work have been reduced, you count as being on **short-time working** (eg, you are a secretary in a solicitor's office whose hours are reduced because the property market is flat and there is no conveyancing to be done).

Special rules allow you to be seen as being available for and actively seeking work (see pp347 and 357) for up to 13 weeks if you have been laid off or put on short-time working even though you are still subject to your normal employment contract and so have a duty to return to work or to working full time as soon as your employer calls on you to do so.

The days you claim JSA count towards your 182 days of contribution-based JSA entitlement. So, if you think that you are likely to become fully unemployed in the foreseeable future, and you are not claiming income-based JSA, you might gain more JSA overall by not claiming it until you become fully unemployed. However, if your earnings drop below the lower earnings limit (see p722) you cease to be treated as paying national insurance (NI) contributions. You may then wish to sign on for JSA which entitles you to NI credits (see p728).

Availability for work

You count as being available for work for the first 13 weeks of a period of being laid off or of short-time working so long as:[145]

- you are willing and able to:
  - return immediately to the job from which you were laid off or to full-time working in the job in which you are being kept on short time; *and*
  - take up immediately (subject to the rules on p347) any 'casual employment' which is within daily travelling distance of your home. If you are a short-time worker, this only has to be during the hours when you are not working in your normal job; *and*
- in the case of short-time working only, the weekly total of the number of hours during which you are working and the number of hours during which you are available for 'casual employment' is at least 40 hours (unless you are restricting your hours of availability to less than 40 because of a physical or mental condition or because of caring responsibilities – see pp353 and 355).

A **'week'** for this purpose means any period of seven consecutive days.[146] **'Casual employment'** is work which the employer is prepared for you to leave without giving any notice.[147]

You are not entitled to a 'permitted period' (see p354) unless you lose your job completely during the first 13 weeks of your JSA claim.[148] In this case, you are allowed a permitted period but it must end by a date no more than 13 weeks after the start of your JSA claim.

Actively seeking work

You are treated as actively seeking work during any benefit week in which you are subject to the special rules on availability described above, for at least three days. You must take all the steps which you can reasonably be expected to take which give you the best prospects of finding 'casual employment'.[149]

16/17-year-olds

You can qualify for JSA if you are aged 16 or 17 in some circumstances. You can qualify for:

- **contribution-based** JSA (see p341) if you satisfy the contribution conditions;
- **income-based** JSA if you satisfy the basic rules of entitlement and you are entitled under the rules described below. This includes severe hardship payments (see p373);
- **joint-claim** JSA, if you satisfy the basic rules of entitlement, only one of you is 18 or over and the other would be entitled to income-based JSA under the rules described below. This includes severe hardship payments (see p373).

If you are claiming any type of JSA, you can apply for ordinary hardship payments if you are sanctioned or there is a doubt about you meeting the labour market conditions (see p422).

When you cannot qualify for income-based jobseeker's allowance

You cannot qualify for JSA if you:

- are a member of the family (see p366) of someone who is claiming income support (IS) or income-based JSA;[150] *or*
- were formerly looked after by a local authority, having been in care after your 14th birthday for at least 13 weeks. See p609 for further information and exceptions to the rules.

In addition, remember that in most cases, you cannot claim JSA if you are in 'relevant education' (see p576).

Entitlement to income-based jobseeker's allowance

You can qualify for income-based JSA while you are 16 or 17 if you are a person who can claim:

- at any time before age 18 (see below); *or*
- during the child benefit extension period (see below); *or*
- during other limited periods (see p373); *or*
- on a discretionary basis. This applies if you do not qualify for income-based JSA under the rules listed above but would otherwise experience severe hardship (see p373). In this case you are paid severe hardship payments.

You must satisfy all the other rules of entitlement to income-based JSA (see pp339 and 341). You must register for work and training and must usually show that you are actively seeking both of these. There are special rules for calculating your JSA applicable amount if you are a member of a couple (see p773).

Qualifying at any time before age 18

You can qualify for income-based JSA at any time before you are 18 if you satisfy the normal conditions of entitlement and:[151]

- you come within one of the groups of people who can claim IS (see p292). In this case, you may be able to choose whether to claim JSA or IS; *or*
- you are one of a couple and you are responsible for a child under 16 who is a member of your household (see p366).

Qualifying during the child benefit 'extension period'

You qualify for income-based JSA during the child benefit 'extension period' – a period of 20 weeks after leaving school or college (see p59) if:[152]

- you are married or in a civil partnership and your partner is:
  - 18 or over; *or*
  - under 18, does not qualify for contribution-based JSA, was not formerly looked after by a local authority, having been in care after her/his 14th birthday for at least 13 weeks (see p609) and:
    - is registered for work and training; *or*
    - is treated as being responsible for a child under 16 who is a member of her/his household (see p366); *or*
    - is laid off or on short-time working and is available for work under the special rules described on p369; *or*
    - is temporarily absent from Great Britain and is taking a child for whom you are responsible and who is a member of your household (see p366) abroad for treatment (for the first eight weeks of the absence); *or*
    - is incapable of work and training because of a physical or mental condition and a doctor confirms s/he is likely to remain incapable for a period of at least 12 months; *or*
    - fits into certain of the groups of people who can claim IS, that is, people with childcare responsibilities and carers (other than those on parental or paternity leave), including those who can claim while pregnant (see p294), pupils, students and people on training courses (see p295), people who are blind, or who are refugees learning English, or who are subject to immigration control but entitled to the urgent cases rate of IS (see p295).

  Satisfying these rules helps you to qualify for the highest rate of personal allowance for a couple. In many of these cases your partner can claim either JSA or IS, but this allows you to be the claimant instead; *or*
- you are an orphan with no one acting as your parent (including foster parents, a local authority or a voluntary organisation if you are being looked after by them, or any other person with parental responsibility for you); *or*
- you are living away from your parents and any person acting as your parent and:
  - immediately before you were 16 you were in custody, or being looked after by a local authority who placed you with someone other than a close relative (see p788); *or*
  - instead you are living elsewhere:

  - as part of a programme of resettlement or rehabilitation under the supervision of the probation service or a local authority; *or*
  - to avoid physical or sexual abuse; *or*
  - because you need special accommodation because of mental or physical illness or disability; *or*
- your parents are unable to support you financially and they are in custody or unable to enter Great Britain (eg, because of the immigration rules) or 'chronically sick or mentally or physically disabled'; *or*
- this is because you are estranged from them (see p578) or you are in physical or moral danger or there is a serious risk to your physical or mental health.

Qualifying during other limited periods

Even if you are not someone who qualifies for income-based JSA at any time before you are 18 (see p371), you may be able to claim it for a limited period.

- You can qualify after the end of the child benefit 'extension period' (see p59) if:[153]
  - you are in one of the groups of people who can claim income-based JSA during that period (see p372) and you are discharged from custody or detention after it ends. You can get income-based JSA for up to eight weeks from the day after you were discharged;
  - you have to live away from your parents and anyone acting as your parent following a stay in accommodation provided by a local authority. You can claim income-based JSA for up to eight weeks from the date of leaving the accommodation, whether before or after the end of the child benefit 'extension period'. If you leave the accommodation less than eight weeks before the end of the 'extension period', you are first entitled to income-based JSA under the rules on p372, and then your benefit can continue under this rule until the end of the eight-week period. Remember that some people cannot claim JSA when they leave local authority care (see p610).
- You can claim during any period that you are laid off or are on short-time working and are available for work under the special rules described on p369.[154]
- If you have never been sanctioned (unless this was for failing to carry out a jobseeker's direction) and have accepted an offer to enlist in the armed forces within eight weeks of the offer being made and were not in employment or training when it was made, you can qualify for income-based JSA until you are due to enlist (or you turn 18 if this is sooner). See Chapter 16 for further information about sanctions.[155]

Qualifying for severe hardship payments

If you do not qualify for income-based JSA under any of the rules for 16/17-year-olds above or for IS, you can still be paid income-based JSA on a discretionary basis if you would otherwise experience severe hardship (see p374).[156] These are referred to as 'severe hardship payments' in this *Handbook*.

If it is decided that you are in severe hardship or will experience severe hardship, a 'severe hardship direction' is issued. You must have one to get severe hardship payments. If you are one of a couple and you are only getting income-based JSA at one of the lower rates (see p773), you may be eligible for a couple rate if a 'severe hardship direction' is made in respect of your partner.

Remember that:

- severe hardship payments are payments of JSA so you are automatically eligible for other benefits (see p396);
- there are special rules about sanctions that only apply to severe hardship payments (see p421).

All your circumstances should be considered when deciding whether you are experiencing or likely to experience severe hardship. The factors that should be taken into account include:[157]

- your financial circumstances, including your income, capital and outgoings;
- whether the person you live with is on a means-tested benefit;
- whether you are homeless or at risk of homelessness if severe hardship payments are not paid, whether you have any health problems, are pregnant or are vulnerable and at risk for any reason and whether you have access to food and accommodation.

A severe hardship direction normally lasts for eight weeks but it can be longer or shorter than this.[158] For example, a short-term direction should be made if you are starting work or training soon or evidence to support your application is not easily available.[159]

When your severe hardship direction ends, you can apply for it to be renewed. If it is, you can continue to get severe hardship payments. However, if your severe hardship direction is revoked, you can no longer get these payments. A direction can (but does not have to) be revoked if:[160]

- your circumstances have changed and you would no longer experience severe hardship if you did not receive severe hardship payments; *or*
- the direction was given in ignorance of, or because of a mistake about, a material fact and but for this, it would not have been given. This could give rise to a recoverable overpayment (see Chapter 39);[161] *or*
- you failed to follow up an opportunity of a place on a training scheme or rejected an offer of a place and cannot show good cause for having done so. 'Good cause' is not defined in the rules. If your severe hardship direction is revoked on this ground, you can apply for another one straight away but if one is made, your severe hardship payments are reduced for a two-week period. See p419 for further information about severe hardship payment sanctions.

Labour market conditions

If you are 16 or 17, in general you are subject to the same labour market conditions as people aged 18 or over.[162] However, there are some important differences.

Availability for work

Usually you can restrict your availability to jobs where the employer provides 'suitable training' (but see below for exceptions).[163] You do not have to show that you have a reasonable prospect of securing employment (see p353) despite this restriction.

You *cannot* restrict your availability to jobs offering suitable training if:

- you have been sanctioned either under the normal rules or under the special rules for severe hardship payments (see Chapter 16), unless the sanction was for failing to carry out a jobseeker's direction;
- you are claiming JSA under the special rules for people laid off or on short-time working (see p369);
- you are claiming under the special rules for people waiting to enlist in the armed forces (see p373).

Deciding whether training is **'suitable training'**[164] involves considering factors such as your personal abilities and skills, your preference and the preference of your training provider, the level of qualification you are aiming for, the length of the training, how easily you can travel to the training and how soon the training will begin.

If you have only worked for a short time but you received training for that type of work or obtained relevant qualifications, you could argue that you have a usual occupation and so should be given a 'permitted period' (see p354).

Actively seeking work

If you are 16 or 17:[165]

- you are required to actively seek both work *and* training;
- you are expected to take more than one step during a week (usually at least one to find work and one to find training) unless taking one step is all that it is reasonable for you to do;
- in addition to the normal list of activities that count as a step (see p357), the activities of seeking training and seeking full-time education also count.

For this purpose training means 'suitable training' (see above).

These exceptions do not apply if you are claiming under the special rules for people laid off or on short-time working or for people waiting to enlist in the armed forces (see pp369 and 373). The first two exceptions do not apply if you have been sanctioned either under the normal JSA rules or under the additional rules for severe hardship payments (see Chapter 16), unless the sanction was for failing to carry out a jobseeker's direction.

Jobseeker's agreement

If you are 16 or 17, in general, your jobseeker's agreement is the same as those for people aged 18 or over, although it places emphasis on training. However, it must explain the rules about sanctions for claimants under 18 (see p419), unless you are claiming JSA because you are laid off or on short-time working (see p369) or you have accepted an offer to enlist in the armed forces.[166] It should also include details of what you agreed with the Careers Service or the Connexions Service about your training or employment options.

Claiming jobseeker's allowance if you are 16 or 17

To claim JSA, including severe hardship payments, you must first register for both work and training with the Careers Service or the Connexions Service.[167] They will give you a referral form to take to the Jobcentre Plus office where you are interviewed.

You do not have to register with the Careers Service or Connexions Service if:

- you are claiming under the special rules for people laid off or on short-time working (see p369) or if you have accepted an offer to enlist in the armed forces (see p373);[168] *or*
- there is an emergency at the Careers Services or Connexions Service or you would experience hardship because of the extra time it would take to register there.[169] If this applies, you must register with the Jobcentre Plus office on a temporary basis.

If you are claiming severe hardship payments, remember to state this when you claim JSA. Always insist on your right to make a claim under the severe hardship rules and refuse to be turned away. Try to take as much evidence as you can to your interview to show that you would experience severe hardship without payments. Be ready to explain fully why your parents are not supporting you or why they should not be expected to continue to do so and, if relevant, why it could be damaging if they were to be contacted.

If you are claiming JSA (other than severe hardship payments) the normal rules about claims and payments apply (see p378).

How your claim for severe hardship payments is dealt with

You must have a 'severe hardship direction' to qualify for severe hardship payments. Authorised staff in the Jobcentre Plus office can consider whether to issue one but must refer your case to the Under-Eighteens Support Team (UEST – see Appendix 1) for a decision if their decision is likely to be negative.[170] It should make a decision within 24 hours.

If you say your parents cannot or will not support you, the DWP should accept this. You should not be refused a severe hardship direction just because you are living at home. The DWP may say that it wants to contact a responsible third party, such as a relative, social worker, youth worker or recognised voluntary worker, to corroborate what you have said.[171] It should only do this if what you have said is self-contradictory or inherently improbable. It must always ask your permission before it does so. However, if you refuse this without good reason, your case is referred directly to the UEST. If you have written evidence from, or are accompanied by, a responsible third party, further enquiries of, or contact with, your parents may not be necessary.

If there is difficulty in obtaining evidence from your parents or a third party, the interviewing officer should consider a short-term direction. You can then receive severe hardship payments while further enquiries are made.

Once a severe hardship direction is issued, the normal rules and procedures for claiming income-based JSA apply. Severe hardship payments are paid in arrears, but if payment is due immediately, a 'counter payment' can be made. If you need money urgently you could apply for a social fund crisis loan (see Chapter 21).

Challenging a jobseeker's allowance decision

You can challenge a decision about whether you satisfy the rules for entitlement to JSA in the usual way. See p394 and Chapters 41 and 42 for further information.

For severe hardship payments only, you *cannot* appeal against the decision whether:[172]

- you would experience severe hardship;
- to issue or revoke a severe hardship direction or how long it should last.

However, you have a right to ask for a revision or seek a supersession of a decision against which you do not have a right of appeal (see pp1065 and 1074). You do not have to show specific grounds in this situation. Any reasons you give for disagreeing with the decision should be considered. You can also ask for a 'review' of a decision not to issue a severe hardship direction.[173]

You can also complain to your MP. You might be able to apply for a judicial review (see p1129). If, for example, you obtain more evidence of your hardship, you could also make a new claim.

Sanctions

The normal rules on sanctions apply if you are claiming contribution-based JSA. If you are aged 16 or 17 and receiving income-based JSA (including severe hardship payments – see p373), you can be sanctioned in the same way as other claimants if you have:

- left a job voluntarily without just cause (see p402); *or*
- lost a job because of misconduct (see p401).

See Chapter 16 for further information about the normal rules on sanctions. Where the sanctions are for other reasons, special rules apply if you are 16 or 17 years old or are getting severe hardship payments (see p420).

6. Claims and backdating

You must usually claim on the first day you want your benefit to start. See p383 for more information about your date of claim. The rules about claims and backdating are in Chapter 38. This section tells you about the specific rules that apply to jobseeker's allowance (JSA).

While you are getting JSA, you must show that you are available for and actively seeking work. For this reason, as well as completing claim forms, you are expected to attend:

- an interview when you claim (see p380); *and*
- an interview when you sign on fortnightly (see p386); *and*
- further interviews as required (see p388).

If you fail to sign on or attend an interview, your entitlement to JSA could end (see p389).

If you are claiming income-based JSA and do not live with your child(ren)'s other parent, you might be required to provide information to the Child Support Agency, needed to make a maintenance calculation or assessment (see p746).

JSA is administered by the DWP. Two types of officer deal with JSA claims – decision makers and employment officers (EOs) (see p1057).

Future changes

The Government plans to introduce a 'skills screen' when people start a claim for JSA to identify any basic literacy, numeracy or language needs they have. Where there are skills gaps, claimants will be encouraged to attend a full 'skills health check' which may result in a referral for training. 'Skills health checks' will be compulsory for those who have been claiming JSA for six months. See CPAG's *Welfare Rights Bulletin* for updates.

Making a claim

To be entitled to JSA, you must normally make a claim.[174] A claim for JSA must be in writing and on the form approved by the DWP.[175] You must complete the form in accordance with the instructions on it and provide any information or evidence required (see p380). Bear the following in mind.

- You can make initial contact by telephone or letter. You may also be able to start a claim online at www.dwp.gov.uk/eservice. The date of your initial contact is important because it usually determines the date on which your claim is treated as being made. See p383 for further information about your date of claim.
- If you are 16 or 17 years old, you normally have to register for work and training at the Careers Service or Connexions Service (see p376).

- If you want to withdraw or amend your claim, notify the Jobcentre Plus office before it makes its decision.[176]

In practice, you are usually required to start your claim by telephoning a 'contact centre'. Your local Jobcentre Plus office has this number, and it may also be displayed in local advice centres and libraries. The centre takes basic details, then calls you back to go through the details of your claim. Also, the date of an interview (see p380) is set. You are then sent a statement recording those details, which you are asked to sign, and details of the evidence and information you should bring with you to the interview. The signed statement of details forms your official claim, instead of the old-style claim form. You may also be given a form to complete about the work for which you are available and how you are actively seeking work. The information you give forms the basis of your jobseeker's agreement.

It is best for you to start your claim in this way if you can. However, if you cannot or do not want to use the telephone to start your claim, the DWP says that the Jobcentre Plus office can still deal with your claim in other ways. You might, for example, be invited for a face-to-face interview to gather the relevant details, or in some cases an old-style claim form may be accepted. JSA claim forms are only available from Jobcentre Plus offices. Seek advice if you are unable to use a telephone and the Jobcentre Plus office will not let you start your claim in any other way.

If you are claiming JSA within 12 weeks of a previous claim, you might be given a shortened claim form. This is known as 'rapid re-claim'.

Remember to keep a copy of your completed claim forms and the evidence and information you provide in case queries arise.

Housing benefit and council tax benefit

You have to make a separate claim to your local authority for housing benefit (HB) and council tax benefit (CTB). When you claim JSA via a contact centre, your HB and CTB claims are usually completed at the same time. If you claim JSA on an old style-claim form, you may given HB and CTB claim forms (or these are available on the Jobcentre Plus website). If you are making a 'rapid re-claim' for JSA, you may also be able to make a 'rapid reclaim' for HB and CTB. See pp200 and 92 for further information about claiming HB and CTB.

Claiming national insurance credits

If you are claiming national insurance (NI) credits but not JSA (see p728), the normal claim procedures for getting JSA apply to you. You must make your application in writing and arrange an appointment for an interview (see p380).

The interview

You (or if you are claiming joint-claim JSA, both of you) must usually attend an interview to discuss what work you are looking for and what you intend to do to find it. If attending the Jobcentre Plus office would mean that you would have to be away from home for too long, you might be allowed to send in your forms by post and your jobseeker's agreement is treated as existing until your interview is carried out by a 'visiting employment officer'. This is known as a **'postal claim'**.

If you have been sent a claim form to complete, you should do this before your interview. If you do not provide all the evidence and information required, your interview might not go ahead unless you are exempt from the evidence requirement (p960).

You are interviewed by an EO. The aims of the interview are:

- to help you back into work as quickly as possible;
- to make sure that you are eligible to claim JSA;
- to draw up a jobseeker's agreement (see p361).

The interview forms the basis of the jobseeker's agreement which both you and the EO must sign. The EO may refer you to a job vacancy immediately but a jobseeker's agreement should still be completed to establish entitlement in case you do not get a job.

The interview also covers what you were doing before you became unemployed and, in particular, why you left your previous job. If the EO thinks that you may have left voluntarily or been dismissed for misconduct (and therefore might be liable to be sanctioned – see Chapter 16) you are asked to complete a form explaining your side of the story.

Information to support your claim

When you claim JSA you must satisfy the NI number requirement. In most cases this means that you must provide your NI number as well as your partner's (see p962). You may also be asked to provide proof of your identity (see p962) and information to support your claim (see below).

Providing information with your claim

It is very important that you provide any information or evidence required – known as the 'evidence requirement'. Until you do, you may not count as having made a valid claim and you could lose benefit. See p960 for further information about the evidence requirement and to see if you are exempt.

If you have a mortgage you are given an additional form to give to your lender. It provides details about your mortgage and returns it to the DWP.

Information and evidence you must supply after you claim

Even if you have provided all that is required, a decision maker might need additional evidence or information to enable her/him to make a decision about your claim. You can be asked to supply any certificates, documents, information or evidence considered relevant to your claim or to an issue arising from your claim.[177] You must do this within seven days of the request. A decision maker can allow you longer than this if s/he thinks it is reasonable. The seven-day time limit runs from the date of the decision maker's request for the additional information, *not* the date you made your JSA claim. If you do not provide the information, the decision maker is likely to decide your claim in the way most adverse to you.

Who should claim

For **contribution-based JSA**, you claim on your own behalf.

For **income-based JSA**, if you are a single person or a lone parent you claim on your own behalf. Unless you must make a joint claim for JSA (see below), if you are a member of a couple you must choose which one of you claims for you both. See p702 for who counts as a couple. If you cannot agree who should claim, a decision maker decides.[178] If you are not the person claiming JSA, you may wish to claim NI credits to protect your NI record (see p728) or to gain help from back-to-work schemes.

Joint claims for jobseeker's allowance

You must make a joint claim for JSA if you are a member of a couple (see p702) and:[179]

- at least one of you is 18 or over and was born after 28 October 1947; *and*
- neither of you is responsible for children in the circumstances listed below.

You are known as a **'joint-claim couple'**. If you are a joint-claim couple both of you must usually:

- claim JSA; *and*
- satisfy all the rules for getting income-based JSA (see pp339 and 341).

For exceptions to these rules, see pp342 and 382. Remember that you cannot count as a joint-claim couple, even if you complete your JSA claim form as if you were, unless you come under the rules described above.[180]

Responsible for children

You do not have to claim joint-claim JSA if you or your partner count as being responsible for a child (this includes a 'qualifying young person'). For these purposes, you count as being responsible for a child if:[181]

- you are entitled to child benefit for her/him; *or*
- no one is receiving child benefit for her/him but:
  - you count as responsible because s/he usually lives with you; *or*
  - you are the only person who has claimed child benefit for her/him but your claim has not yet been decided; *or*

- someone else is responsible for her/him but s/he is staying with you so that s/he can attend school; *or*
- you are looking after her/him for the local authority or a voluntary organisation (or in Scotland only, s/he has been boarded out with you) under specific provisions; *or*
- you are looking after her/him with a view to adoption.

Even if you do not get child benefit for your child and none of the other rules above apply, if you share actual responsibility for the child (eg, with your ex-partner) and are a 'substantial minority carer' (ie, you have the child with you for at least 104 nights a year), following a court decision it may be arguable that you should still be regarded as responsible for the child.[182] Seek advice and see CPAG's *Welfare Rights Bulletins* 185 pp9–11 and 194 pp5–6.

If you and your partner **become responsible** for a child while you are claiming joint-claim JSA you must provide the DWP with evidence of this if required.[183] You and your partner must notify the DWP which of you is to continue claiming income-based JSA for you both. Your claim for JSA then continues without interruption.

If you and your partner **stop being responsible** for any children while you are claiming income-based JSA, or they have all died or have reached the age of 16 and are not qualifying young people for child benefit purposes (see p57), you and your partner must then claim joint-claim JSA.[184] Your claim for JSA can continue without interruption if the DWP has sufficient information to award you joint-claim JSA and you or your partner have told the DWP which of you has been nominated to receive payment for you both.

If your partner does not claim jobseeker's allowance

If you are a member of a joint-claim couple and you satisfy all the rules for getting income-based JSA (see pp339 and 341), in certain circumstances you can qualify for JSA even if your partner has not made a joint claim with you. This is the case if your partner:[185]

- failed to attend the interview (see p380); *or*
- failed to meet the labour market conditions; *or*
- is subject to immigration control (see p1334); *or*
- is temporarily absent from Great Britain; *or*
- has failed to satisfy the 'habitual residence test' or the 'right to reside test' (see Chapter 59); *or*
- is over pension age (60 for women and 65 for men). In this situation, you both might be better off if your partner were to claim pension credit for you rather than JSA; *or*
- works 16 or more but under 24 hours a week; *or*
- has claimed maternity allowance or statutory maternity pay; *or*
- is pregnant and there are 11 weeks or less before the week the baby is due; *or*

- was pregnant and her pregnancy ended not more than 15 weeks ago (ie, when her baby was born, or she had a miscarriage); *or*
- is receiving an unemployment benefit from another country under a reciprocal agreement (see p1354); *or*
- is receiving statutory sick pay and was working 16 hours or more a week immediately before s/he became incapable of work.

In the first three cases your JSA entitlement is calculated as if you were a single claimant.[186] In the fourth case your JSA entitlement is calculated for both of you in the normal manner for the first four weeks (seven days if the absence is to attend an interview for employment); after that it is calculated as if you were a single claimant.[187] In the remaining cases, JSA entitlement is calculated for both of you in the normal manner. In all other respects you are treated as a couple and, therefore, any income or capital of your partner is taken into account.

The date of your claim

You are usually not entitled to JSA for any day before your date of claim.[188] However, in some cases you can claim in advance (see p384) and sometimes your claim can be backdated (see p385). If you want this to be done, you should make this clear when you claim or the DWP might not consider it.

Your **'date of claim'** is usually:

- if you (and your partner if you are a 'joint-claim couple') attend your interview (see p380) at the time specified by the DWP and provide a properly completed claim form with all the information and evidence required (see p380), the date you first contact the Jobcentre Plus office – eg, by telephone;[189] *or*
- if you are allowed a postal claim (see p380), the earliest of:[190]
  - the date you first contact the Jobcentre Plus office, so long as a properly completed claim form with all the information and evidence required (see p380) is provided within one month of your first contact; *or*
  - the date on which a properly completed claim form with all the information and evidence required (see p380) is received at the Jobcentre Plus office;
- if you are a 'joint-claim couple' and only one of you is required to attend an interview, the earliest of:[191]
  - the date on which a properly completed claim form with all the information and evidence required (see p380) is received at the Jobcentre Plus office, so long as the person who is required to attend an interview does so; *or*
  - the date you or your partner first contact the Jobcentre Plus office, so long as a properly completed claim form with all the information and evidence required (see p380) is provided within one month of your first contact.

If you (or you or your partner if you are a 'joint-claim couple') **fail to attend an interview** at the time specified by the DWP and cannot show good cause for this, the rules above do not apply. If, without good cause, you fail to attend an interview or attend at the wrong time, so long as a properly completed claim form with all the information and evidence required is provided (see p380), your date of claim is, unless you are a 'joint-claim couple', the date you eventually go to the Jobcentre Plus office.[192] If you are a 'joint-claim couple', your date of claim is:[193]

- if you are both required to attend an interview, the date one of you eventually goes to the Jobcentre Plus office. However, in this situation, you can only get the single person's rate of JSA (see p382); *or*
- if only one of you is required to attend an interview, the date the person who is required to attend eventually goes to the Jobcentre Plus office.

'Good cause' is not defined. All relevant circumstances must be considered. These may relate to your abilities or to external factors. The general test is whether there is some factor that would probably cause a reasonable person of your age and experience to act, or fail to act, as you did.[194]

The DWP can extend the time you have to provide a properly completed claim form by up to one month from the date you first contacted the Jobcentre Plus office to claim JSA.[195] This is discretionary, so you should provide your claim form as required (see above) wherever possible.

If you are a member of a couple and one of you claims contribution-based JSA but is not entitled to it and a subsequent income-based JSA claim is made by your partner (or you and your partner if you are a joint-claim couple), the date of claim for income-based JSA is the date of the earlier claim for contribution-based JSA.[196] If your partner has been claiming contribution-based JSA, this expires and you claim income-based JSA, the date of claim for your income-based JSA is the day after your partner's entitlement expires.[197]

If you claim the wrong benefit

If you claim working tax credit (WTC) and you are refused because neither you nor your partner are in full-time paid work for WTC purposes (see Chapter 50), your claim for JSA can be backdated to the date you claimed WTC.[198] However, you must claim JSA within 14 days of the decision refusing your WTC claim. You can ask for your JSA claim to start on a later date instead – eg, where your income is too high currently, but is due to decrease.

Claiming in advance

If you do not qualify for JSA from the date of your claim (unless this is because you fail the habitual residence test – see p1367), but will do so within the next three months, you can be awarded JSA from the first date on which you will qualify.[199] This gives the DWP time to ensure you receive benefit as soon as you are entitled. You should let the DWP know you want to claim in advance when you claim and at your interview. You might have to persuade the DWP that it can accept a claim in advance.

You might not be entitled to JSA currently, but would be once you or a member of your family (see p366) become entitled to another 'qualifying benefit' – eg, disability living allowance or carer's allowance. You should make your claim for JSA at the same time as the claim for the qualifying benefit. If you are:

- refused JSA, claim again when you get a decision about the qualifying benefit and ask for your JSA to be backdated to the date of your first JSA claim or to the date from which the qualifying benefit is paid, if that is later. See p968 for further information;
- awarded JSA, you might be entitled to a higher rate once the outcome of the claim for the qualifying benefit is known. Seek a revision or a supersession if you think this applies to you. See p1085 for further information.

How your claim is dealt with

It is very unlikely that you will get an immediate decision on your claim. For contribution-based JSA your NI contribution record needs to be checked. For income-based JSA your benefit needs to be calculated. If the delay is caused by doubt as to whether you meet the labour market conditions you may be able to receive hardship payments (see p422). If you think it is taking too long to deal with your claim, see p392.

Backdating your claim

It is very important to claim in time. A claim for JSA can be backdated for a maximum of three months, but only in exceptional circumstances. The general rules on backdating are covered on p964. There are special backdating rules if you are making a new claim for JSA after you failed to sign on or attend an interview (see p391).

There are exceptions to the rule. Your claim can be backdated more than three months if:

- you are claiming JSA after being awarded a qualifying benefit and an earlier JSA claim had been refused because you did not at that time get a qualifying benefit (see p968); *or*
- you claimed WTC when you should have claimed JSA (see p384).

If you might have qualified for benefit earlier but did not claim because you were given the wrong information or misled by the DWP you could ask for an extra statutory payment (see p1186) or complain to the Ombudsman (see p1184).

If you want to get your jobseeker's agreement backdated, see p363.

After your claim has been accepted

Once your claim for JSA has been accepted, in order to continue to receive JSA you have to:

- sign on regularly at the Jobcentre Plus office and attend regular interviews; *and*
- attend further interviews as required (see p388).

Note:

- If you have a partner, and you are both under 60, your partner might be required to attend a work-focused interview (see p972). If s/he fails to do so without good cause, your income-based JSA might be paid at a reduced rate.
- In some cases, if you fail to provide information when required to do so, your JSA could be suspended or even terminated (see p985).
- If you live in a pilot scheme area, you may have to attend a 'rights and responsibilities' seminar if you have not found work after eight weeks on JSA.

Signing on and regular interviews

Unless you are allowed to sign on by post (see p387), while you are getting JSA you (and if you are a joint-claim couple, both of you) must normally attend the Jobcentre Plus office in order to sign a declaration that:[200]

- you have been available for and actively seeking work or could be treated as if you were (see pp347 and 357); *and*
- there has been no change in your circumstances which might affect the amount of or your right to JSA (other than those you may have already notified to the DWP).

Generally, you must sign on every fortnight. This is the case even if you are paid weekly. You can be notified of the time and place you should attend by phone, post or electronic means.[201] To find out if you must sign on more frequently, see p386. If you are told you are not entitled to JSA, you can argue that you no longer have to sign on – eg, while you are appealing against the decision.[202] However, if your appeal is successful, in order to be paid arrears you need to show that you have satisfied the labour market conditions since the last time that you signed on, which can often be difficult. So it is always best to continue to sign on to protect your position.

Each time you sign on, you are interviewed. The aims of the interview are to:

- keep a regular check on what you are doing to find work and make sure that your jobseeker's agreement remains up-to-date and relevant. You should take your records of your attempts to find work with you;
- discuss any difficulties you are experiencing and identify any help and support which the DWP can give you;
- check whether there have been any relevant changes in your circumstances;
- refer you to job, training or employment scheme vacancies (see p387).

You may be referred to an EO for a more in-depth interview if what you say raises a doubt as to whether you remain entitled to JSA.

More frequent signing on

You may be required to sign on weekly for six weeks after your first 'restart interview' (see p388). You may be required to sign on and attend interviews more frequently than once every two weeks if you are suspected of fraud or you are of no fixed abode.

Because decisions about how often you have to sign on and attend interviews are made by EOs, you do not have a right of appeal. However, you can ask for the frequency to be altered – eg, if your circumstances change or the cost of travel causes hardship. If you are told that you are suspected of fraud, see Chapter 40.

Signing on by post

The DWP might allow you to sign on by post – eg, if you live a long way from the Jobcentre Plus office, or you have a mental or physical disability which restricts your mobility. Even so:

- you must attend for your interview (see p380) and further interviews as required (see p388). You could try to get an interview arranged with a visiting EO nearer your home if attending at the Jobcentre Plus office would result in your being away from home for a long time;
- you must send a signed declaration and show that you are available for and actively seeking work (see pp347 and 357). If this is not received within five working days of your postal signing date, your entitlement to JSA ends unless you can show 'good cause' for the delay (see p389). If you cannot show this, you must make a fresh claim for JSA and attend a new interview (see p380).

Proving you are actively seeking work

It is very important to keep careful records of the steps you take to get a job.

- Make a note every time you do anything which might count as a 'step' towards actively seeking work (see p357). Include the dates and times, who you spoke to and what was said.
- Keep copies of any letters or emails you send and of any advertisements to which you reply.
- Tell the EO if you have difficulty reading or writing, or with the English language. You can get a friend or relative to help you compile your record (and to help you look for jobs). The DWP may be prepared to accept an oral report. You could keep a written record in your first language and take an interpreter or ask for an interpreter to be provided if you cannot take anyone with you.

Referral to job, training or employment programme vacancies

While you are claiming JSA, the DWP may refer you to a job vacancy. You should always be offered the vacancies with the highest rates of pay before those paying lower rates. Bear in mind that the law now gives some workers minimum rights regarding rate of pay, hours, rest breaks and holidays (see p429) and you should not be expected to accept jobs that do not meet those standards.

If you are not considered ready for a job you are likely to be referred to a place on a training scheme or employment or New Deal programme. Some of these are compulsory. If you are on a compulsory programme you can be sanctioned for failing to attend, or for leaving early (see p412). A scheme or programme that is not compulsory may become so if you are issued with a jobseeker's direction (see p406).

You risk being sanctioned if, without good cause, you refuse to apply for a notified job vacancy (see p406). Alternatively, you could be issued with a jobseeker's direction and risk being sanctioned if you refuse or fail to carry it out (see p406). A refusal to apply for a job or vacancy on a scheme or programme may also raise doubts about whether you are available for work (see p347).

Referral to a disability employment adviser

If you have a disability which impedes your search for work you may be eligible for specialist help from the DWP, including referral to a disability employment adviser. Every Jobcentre Plus office has a disability adviser who is responsible for good practice relating to disabled people.

You may want to ask to be referred to an adviser if, for example:

- you feel that the normal service from the Jobcentre Plus office is not meeting your needs; *or*
- your health problem or disability has worsened significantly, or you have a new disability or health problem and need specialist help; *or*
- you need new skills in order to do a job; *or*
- you need practical help with looking for a job (eg, help in getting interviews or identifying specialist equipment); *or*
- you are not clear about the effect your disability has on the job options that are open to you.

Further interviews

If you remain unemployed for a period of time you must attend a number of other interviews.

- You are normally asked to attend an interview **after you have been claiming JSA for 13 weeks** (or at the end of your permitted period – see p354), and at regular intervals thereafter, linked to the length of time you have to be unemployed to qualify for various schemes to help you get back into work. You might be required to sign on weekly for six weeks after your first interview.

  At the interview, an EO reviews your situation, the type of work you are looking for and the steps you are taking to find it. You may be asked to agree to a change of your jobseeker's agreement (see p363) to record any change in the type of work for which you are looking or steps you will take to find it.
- You can be called for an interview **at any time** – eg, if the DWP thinks that you need more help with your search for work or there is a question about whether you fulfil the labour market conditions.

Travel expenses

Your travel expenses to and from the Jobcentre Plus office to **sign on** are *not* reimbursed. If this causes you hardship, you should ask if you can sign on by post.

You *can* have your travel costs reimbursed if you are given an appointment for an **interview** on a day other than the day you normally attend to sign on, or if you have to attend a different office on your normal signing on day and you incur additional costs.[203] If you are signing on by post but are required to visit the Jobcentre Plus office for an interview you are also entitled to a refund of travel costs.

Failure to sign on or attend an interview

Your entitlement to JSA can end if you fail to sign on, whether by going to the Jobcentre Plus office or by post, or you fail to attend an interview when required to do so. Your benefit can be suspended while a decision maker is considering the matter (see p984).

Unless you can show 'good cause' for your failure within five working days (see below) your entitlement to JSA ends if you fail to:[204]

- attend at a place specified by an EO in a notification:
  - at the right time, but you do attend sometime on the right day and it is not the first time that you have been late. The DWP must have sent you a written notice warning you that your JSA could cease if you fail to attend your next appointment; *or*
  - on the right day. The rules do not make any explicit provision for you to be given a warning in the way that they do for the situation where you attend late but on the right day.

  Notification can be in writing, by telephone or email. If you can show you did not receive the notification, this means that you have not failed to attend and your entitlement to JSA should, therefore, not end. The law normally assumes that when a letter has been sent correctly addressed and with the full postage paid, it will be received. So if notification was sent to you, you need to put forward a good case to show why this assumption should not be made – eg, you have always responded properly to other notifications when these were received from the Jobcentre Plus office or there are problems with your postal address.[205]

  If the requirement to attend is for a training scheme or employment programme, your entitlement does not end. However, you can be sanctioned instead (see p412); *or*
- sign a declaration, whether this is at the Jobcentre Plus office or by post.[206]

'Good cause'

You may be able to avoid your entitlement to JSA ending if, within five working days of your failure to attend or sign on, you provide an explanation which shows that you had 'good cause' for the failure.[207] The decision maker decides whether you have good cause and you have the right to appeal against her/his decision. You have **automatic good cause** for a failure to attend if:[208]

- you have caring responsibilities or are engaged in voluntary work and you were given less than 48 hours' notice or you are providing a service and you were given less than 24 hours' notice (see p347); *or*
- on the day you failed to attend you were someone who was treated as being available for employment in the circumstances listed on pp349–352, although there are limited exceptions to this rule;[209] *or*
- the day you failed to attend was in a week during which you were treated as actively seeking work because of an absence from home (see p360).

If you do not have automatic good cause, you may still have **good cause for other reasons**. When deciding good cause, the decision maker must take into account *all* the circumstances of your case, including whether you misunderstood what you had to do because of language, learning or literacy difficulties or because you were misled by an EO. In addition, the decision maker must take into account:

- if you failed to attend:[210]
  - whether you (or someone for whom you are caring) were attending a medical or dental appointment which it would have been unreasonable to expect you to rearrange;
  - any transport difficulties;
  - any religious reasons why you could not attend;
  - whether you were attending a job interview;
- if you failed to sign on, adverse postal conditions (for postal claimants only).[211]

When your entitlement to jobseeker's allowance ends

If you fail to attend an interview or to sign on, you lose JSA for the period between the date on which your entitlement ends and the date on which you are treated as having claimed again.

The date on which your entitlement to JSA ends is the *earliest* of the following days:[212]

- the day after the last day for which you have provided information which shows you continue to be entitled to JSA (eg, at your regular fortnightly interview). In many cases this means the day after the last day on which you signed on;
- if you failed to attend or attend at the wrong time, the day on which you should have attended;
- if you failed to sign on, the day on which you should have done so.

The date on which you are treated as having claimed JSA again is normally the first day on which you contact the Jobcentre Plus office again. But if this was the same day as the failure to attend (ie, you came on the right day but were late for the appointment) you are treated as having made your fresh claim on the *following* day.[213] See below to see if your new claim can be backdated.

The effect of this is that, if you fail to sign on, you may lose JSA for the full two weeks for which you would have been paid if you had signed on at the right time. In addition, you lose JSA for the days between the day you missed signing on and the day you next contact the Jobcentre Plus office. If you have missed signing, it is possible to provide the necessary information at a later date.[214] So as soon as you contact the Jobcentre Plus office again, ask it to accept the information you would have provided on the signing day. If this is accepted, the decision maker should revise the decision that stopped your benefit so that you are paid up to the date you failed to sign on.

Backdating your new claim

Where your entitlement to JSA has ceased because you failed to attend an interview or to sign on and you have to make a new claim, it may be possible to get your new claim backdated and so avoid some, or all, of the loss of JSA. Your claim can be backdated:

- under any of the normal rules (see p964); *or*
- under the special rules described below.

Your claim can be backdated to the day after your entitlement to JSA ended if:[215]

- you failed to attend because of one of the circumstances listed on pp349–352 which allow you to be treated as being available for employment and you make a new claim for JSA no later than the day after those circumstances cease to apply. There are limited exceptions to this rule;[216] *or*
- you failed to attend because you were away from home while eligible to be treated as actively seeking work because of an absence from home (see p360), and you make a new claim for JSA no later than the day after you returned home; *or*
- you are normally allowed to sign on by post, you did not receive the instruction to attend the Jobcentre Plus office and you made a new claim for JSA immediately you were informed that you had failed to attend the appointment.

7. Getting paid

Jobseeker's allowance (JSA) is usually paid by direct payment into your bank (or similar) account (see p978). In some cases, you may instead be paid by cheque. You can indicate which method of payment you prefer when you claim JSA, although a decision maker decides how JSA is paid. You cannot appeal against this decision.

If you and your partner are a 'joint-claim couple' you must nominate which one of you receives payment for you both. Where you cannot agree, a decision maker decides.[217] Even if you are not the person nominated to receive the JSA, if you separate from your partner and s/he cannot be traced, you can be paid any arrears of JSA that are due.[218]

In some circumstances, part of your JSA can be deducted and paid to other people and organisations on your behalf (see p987).

JSA is a weekly benefit.[219] Most questions about entitlement are decided in relation to a particular **'benefit week'** – ie, the period of seven days ending on the day of the week on which you sign on.[220]

JSA is normally paid fortnightly in arrears, although the DWP can decide to make other arrangements in particular cases.[221] You are usually paid for the last two benefit weeks up to and including the day you (and your partner if you are a 'joint-claim couple') sign on. If you do not sign on, you are not paid (and see p389).

If you are entitled to less than 10p a week you are not paid JSA at all,[222] but you are still eligible for national insurance (NI) credits (see p728). If you are entitled to less than £1 a week, a decision maker can decide to pay you quarterly in arrears.[223]

If your cheque is lost or stolen or you have forgotten your PIN, see p983. If payment of your JSA is suspended, see p984.

Delays and complaints

If payment of your JSA is delayed, you might be able to get an interim payment (see p986). You may also be eligible for a crisis loan (see p503).

If you experience delays, or wish to complain about how your claim has been dealt with, see Chapter 46. You might be able to claim compensation (see p1186).

Change of circumstances

The DWP should inform you of the main kinds of changes in your circumstances that you need to report, but might not actually list them all. In any case, it is your duty to report any change in your circumstances which might affect the amount of, your right to, or payment of, JSA as well as any such change that is likely to occur.[224] You should do this promptly in writing or by telephone (although in individual cases notification might be accepted in a form other than in writing or by telephone). In some cases, however, the decision maker might say that you must report changes in writing. In any case, it is always best to report the change in writing and keep a copy in case of a dispute in the future.

If you do not notify any such change promptly, any resulting overpayment may be recoverable from you (see Chapter 39). If you are considered deliberately to have acted falsely or dishonestly, you may also be guilty of an offence (see Chapter 40).

If you have a mortgage, the DWP can ask your lender about any changes in the amount you owe during your JSA claim. If you have this information – eg, from an annual statement you receive from your lender, you must also advise the DWP in case your lender fails to do so. Make sure the DWP takes this information into account so you are not overpaid JSA.

When there has been a relevant change of circumstances, a decision maker looks at your claim again and makes a new decision, called a 'supersession' (see p1074). Your JSA is then adjusted from the date this new decision takes effect (see below). When this is depends on whether the new decision is to your advantage, and whether you reported the change in time. See p1080 for information about when a supersession takes effect. A change of circumstances could mean that you qualify for more or less JSA, or even that you are no longer entitled.

When your jobseeker's allowance is adjusted

As a general rule, your JSA is adjusted from the first day of the benefit week in which the change occurs or is expected to do so.[225] See p1080 for further information about the general rule.

There are exceptions to the rule.

- If a decision is to your advantage, but you failed to notify the DWP of a change within the time limit (see p1080), your JSA is adjusted:[226]
  - if you are paid in arrears, from the first day of the benefit week in which you notified the change; *or*
  - if you are paid in advance, from the day on which you notified the change, if this is the day you are paid benefit. If it is not, your JSA is adjusted from the next week.
- Your JSA is adjusted from the date of the change of circumstances (or the day on which this is expected to take place) if:[227]
  - the change of circumstances means you no longer qualify for JSA. However, the ordinary rule applies if the reason that you no longer qualify is that your income is too high;
  - a child (see p366) only stays with you for part of the week and for the rest of the week is in care or in custody;
  - if you are a 'joint-claim couple', you cease to be a couple;
  - your partner or child for whom you are responsible (see p366) comes home from hospital for a stay of less than a week.

  This also applies if your circumstances change back again.
- If you have income that is counted as being paid on a particular day (see p879) and this changes (or such a change is expected), your JSA is adjusted from the day the income counts as being paid.[228] But this does not apply to an adjustment to your contribution-based JSA due to a change in your occupational pension.

If a change of circumstances means the amount of your JSA should go down (or is expected to go down) but a decision maker accepts it would not be practicable to adjust your JSA on the days outlined above, your JSA is adjusted from the first day of the benefit week following the one in which the change occurred.[229]

Overpayments and fraud

If you are overpaid JSA, you might have to repay it. The rules on overpayments are covered in Chapter 39.

If you have been accused of fraud, see Chapter 40. You might get a reduced amount of JSA if you have been sanctioned for benefit offences (see p1047).

8. Challenging a jobseeker's allowance decision

You can apply for a revision or a supersession of a jobseeker's allowance (JSA) decision, or appeal against it (see Chapters 41 and 42). Remember that if you are told you are not entitled to JSA, you can argue that you no longer have to sign on – eg, while you are appealing against the decision.[230] However, it is always best to continue to sign on to protect your position.

You cannot seek a revision or a supersession of an employment officer's (EO's) decision or appeal against it. If you disagree with an EO's decision, see p1063.

9. Tax, tax credits and other benefits

Jobseeker's allowance (JSA) is taxable.[231] The maximum amount of JSA that is taxable is:

- if you are claiming for yourself, an amount equal to the appropriate personal allowance for a person of your age (see p771); *or*
- if you are a member of a couple, an amount equal to the income-based JSA personal allowance for an adult couple (half this amount if your partner is unable to claim JSA because s/he is involved in a trade dispute).

The tax is not deducted while JSA is being paid but reduces the refund you would otherwise receive through Pay As You Earn (PAYE) when you return to work. Any tax refunds of PAYE payments are paid to you at the end of the tax year to which they relate. Any other tax refund is paid only when you stop getting JSA.

Tax credits

If you work less than 16 hours each week and your partner works at least 16 hours but less than 24 hours each week, you and your partner might be able to claim working tax credit. However, before deciding whether to claim you should seek advice to see how you would be better off financially. See p657 for further information.

Whether or not you are in work, you might be able to claim child tax credit (CTC). CTC does not count as income for income-based JSA purposes.

Means-tested benefits

If you pay rent or council tax you may be entitled to housing benefit (HB) and council tax benefit (CTB) as well as JSA. If you are getting contribution-based JSA, you may also be entitled to income-based JSA to top this up. Your contribution-based JSA counts as income for the purposes of those benefits.

If you are a man aged 60–64, you might be able to claim pension credit (PC) instead of income-based JSA. You may be better off doing so if you have savings or other capital (see below).

Claiming income support or pension credit

You cannot claim both JSA and income support (IS) at the same time, nor income-based JSA and PC at the same time. If you have a partner, s/he can claim IS or PC and you can claim contribution-based JSA (but not income-based JSA).

You therefore need to choose whether to claim income-based JSA or IS (or PC) in some situations. You should consider the following when deciding.

- The rates of IS, the guarantee credit of PC and income-based JSA are usually the same but you do not have to sign on, or look for work or risk being sanctioned if you are claiming IS or PC (nor does your partner).
- You may want to claim JSA instead of IS in order to receive national insurance (NI) contribution credits (see p728). You might not be entitled to NI credits if you claim IS.
- If you are sanctioned, you or your partner should claim IS or PC if eligible. You cannot get hardship payments (see p422) if you or your partner come within one of the groups of people who can claim IS, even if you do not claim it.
- If you claim PC:
  - there is no capital limit and the tariff income rules are more generous;
  - you can qualify for the savings credit of PC if you or your partner are 65 or over;
  - there is no rule that prevents you or your partner doing full-time paid work (known as 'remunerative work'), although any earnings from work are taken into account in working out how much PC you can get;
  - the HB and CTB rules are more generous.

Non-means-tested benefits

The non-means-tested benefits in this *Handbook* (other than attendance allowance (AA), disability living allowance (DLA), guardian's allowance and if you are getting CTC, child benefit) are taken into account when working out the amount of income-based JSA you can get. However, it can be worth claiming these benefits. If you or your partner qualify for certain non-means-tested benefits (including AA and DLA) you also qualify for certain premiums (see p775) and, therefore, a higher rate of income-based JSA.

You might only qualify for income-based JSA once you or a member of your family are awarded another benefit known as a 'qualifying benefit'. To make sure you do not lose out while awaiting the outcome of a claim for a qualifying benefit, claim JSA at the same time. If your claim for income-based JSA is refused, once the qualifying benefit is awarded claim JSA again and ask for it to be backdated to the date of your first claim. See p968 for further details.

Contribution-based JSA is affected by the overlapping benefit rules (see p981).

Passports and other sources of help

If you are entitled to income-based JSA you also qualify for health benefits such as free prescriptions (see Chapter 9) and education benefits such as free school meals (see p15). You may also qualify for social fund payments (see Chapters 21 and 22).

Financial help on starting work

If you stop getting JSA because you or your partner start work, or your earnings or your hours in your existing job increase, you might be able to get child maintenance bonus (see p757), mortgage interest run-on (if you have a home loan – see p823), extended payments of HB or CTB (if you pay rent or council tax – see pp211 and 94) and a job grant (see p14). See p14 for information about other financial help you might get.

Notes

1. **Who can claim jobseeker's allowance**

1 ss1-3 and 3A JSA 1995
2 Reg 47(1) and (2) JSA Regs
3 Reg 49 JSA Regs
4 Sch 1 para 3 JSA 1995
5 s2(1) and (4) JSA 1995
6 Reg 48 JSA Regs
7 Reg 48(2) and (3) JSA Regs
8 Reg 47(3) JSA Regs
9 s2 JSA 1995
10 ss3, 3A and 13 JSA 1995
11 Reg 3D JSA Regs; Sch 1 para 8A JSA 1995
12 Reg 8 SS(JPI) Regs
13 Sch A1 JSA Regs
14 Reg 3D(3) and (4) JSA Regs
15 CIS/0542/2001
16 Reg 51 JSA Regs
17 Reg 52(1) JSA Regs
18 s1(2)(f) JSA 1995
19 Sch 1 para 2 JSA 1995; reg 10 SS&CS(DA) Regs; reg 6(3) SS(IFW) Regs
20 Reg 17A SS(IFW) Regs
21 Reg 55(1) JSA Regs
22 Reg 55A(1) JSA Regs
23 Regs 55(2) and 55A(2) JSA Regs
24 Reg 55(3) JSA Regs
25 Reg 55(4) JSA Regs
26 Reg 170 JSA Regs
27 Reg 1(3) JSA Regs. Note that the definition was not amended when the Department for Education and Skills was renamed the Department for Children, Schools and Families.
28 Reg 17A(2), (3) and (5) JSA Regs

29 Reg 17A(7)-(8) JSA Regs
30 s6(1) JSA 1995; regs 6 and 10 JSA Regs
31 R(U) 44/53
32 s6(1) JSA 1995
33 *Shaukat Ali v CAO,* appendix to R(U) 1/85
34 *Secretary of State for Social Security v David,* 15 December 2000 (CA), reported as R(JSA) 3/01
35 Regs 4 and 5(1)(b) and (6) JSA Regs
36 Reg 5(2) JSA Regs
37 C(U) 96/1994
38 para 21277 DMG
39 Reg 5(3) JSA Regs; para 21299 DMG
40 Reg 5(4) JSA Regs
41 Reg 4 JSA Regs
42 paras 21287-93 DMG
43 Reg 14(2)-(3) JSA Regs
44 Reg 14(1)(i), (j), (l), (ll) and (o) JSA Regs
45 Reg 14(2A) JSA Regs
46 R(JSA) 2/07
47 Reg 14(1)(a), (b), (f) and (k) JSA Regs
48 Reg 4 JSA Regs
49 Reg 17A(3) and (7) JSA Regs
50 Reg 14(1)(c), (ll), (m), (n), (nn), (p) and (q) JSA Regs
51 Reg 14(4) JSA Regs
52 Reg 14(1)(d), (e), (g), (h), (r) and (s) and (2) JSA Regs
53 CJSA/5944/1999
54 Reg 14(2B) JSA Regs
55 Reg 14(5) JSA Regs
56 Reg 15 JSA Regs
57 CJSA/2663/2006. If you are a male lone parent, it may be more difficult for you to benefit from this decision.
58 Reg 7(3) JSA Regs
59 *Secretary of State for Social Security v David,* 15 December 2000 (CA), reported as R(JSA) 3/01
60 s6(3) JSA 1995; regs 6, 7 and 8 JSA Regs
61 Reg 10 JSA Regs
62 Reg 10(1) JSA Regs
63 Reg 13(3) JSA Regs
64 Reg 8 JSA Regs
65 s6(5)(7) and (8) JSA 1995; reg 16 JSA Regs
66 para 21399 DMG
67 paras 21403-04 DMG
68 Reg 31(f) JSA Regs
69 Reg 16(2) JSA Regs
70 para 21451 DMG
71 Reg 13(2) JSA Regs
72 Reg 6 JSA Regs
73 Reg 72(5A)(b) JSA Regs
74 Regs 4 and 13(4) JSA Regs
75 Reg 13(5) JSA Regs
76 Reg 7(1) and (2) JSA Regs
77 R(JSA) 2/07
78 Reg 12 JSA Regs
79 Reg 8 JSA Regs
80 Reg 16(1) JSA Regs
81 Regs 8 and 9 JSA Regs
82 Reg 13(3) JSA Regs
83 Reg 8 JSA Regs
84 ss1(2)(c) and 7 JSA 1995
85 s7(1) JSA 1995
86 Reg 18(1) JSA Regs
87 CJSA/2162/2001
88 Reg 18A JSA Regs
89 CJSA/1814/2007
90 Reg 18(2) JSA Regs
91 Reg 18(4) JSA Regs
92 Reg 18(3) JSA Regs
93 paras 21616-20 DMG
94 Reg 20 JSA Regs
95 Reg 21 JSA Regs
96 Reg 19 JSA Regs
97 Reg 19(1)(r) and (3) JSA Regs
98 Reg 19(1)(q) JSA Regs
99 Reg 21A JSA Regs
100 Reg 19(1)(p) JSA Regs
101 Reg 19(2) JSA Regs
102 R(U) 4/66
103 s9(3) JSA 1995
104 s9(4) JSA 1995
105 s9(1) JSA 1995; reg 31 JSA Regs
106 CJSA/1814/2007
107 CJSA/2162/2001
108 Reg 34 JSA Regs
109 CJSA/935/1999
110 s9(5) JSA 1995
111 s9(6) JSA 1995
112 s9(6)(a) and (b) JSA 1995
113 s9(7)(b) and (c) JSA 1995
114 s9(7)(a) and (8)(b) JSA 1995; reg 33 JSA Regs
115 Reg 35 JSA Regs
116 s9(7)(c) JSA 1995
117 s9(8)(a) JSA 1995; reg 32 JSA Regs
118 s10(1) and (2) JSA 1995
119 s10(4) JSA 1995
120 s10(3) JSA 1995
121 s10(5) JSA 1995
122 s10(7)(a) JSA 1995; reg 39 JSA Regs; para 21951 DMG
123 s10(6)(b) and (d) JSA 1995
124 R(JSA) 2/07
125 s10(6)(c) JSA 1995; reg 38 JSA Regs
126 CJSA/4435/1998
127 Reg 147 JSA Regs
128 Reg 147(6) JSA Regs
129 para 31350 DMG

2. **The rules about your age**
130 s3A(1)(e)(ii) JSA 1995; reg 58 JSA Regs

3. **Claiming for others**
131 s35(1) JSA 1995
132 s35 JSA 1995; reg 77 JSA Regs
133 Reg 78 JSA Regs

4. **The amount of benefit**
134 Sch 1 para 4 JSA 1995; reg 46 JSA Regs
135 Reg 14A SS&CS(DA) Regs
136 s4(1) and (2) JSA 1995; reg 79 JSA Regs
137 ss4(1)and 35(1) JSA 1995; reg 81(1) JSA Regs
138 Reg 80(2) JSA Regs
139 s5(1) JSA 1995
140 s5(2) JSA 1995
141 Reg 47(4)(b)(ii) JSA Regs
142 Reg 47(2) and (4)(c) JSA Regs
143 ss4(3) and (3A) and 13 JSA 1995

5. **Special benefit rules**
144 Reg 4 JSA Regs
145 Reg 17(1)-(3) JSA Regs
146 Reg 17(5) JSA Regs
147 Reg 4 JSA Regs
148 Reg 17(4) JSA Regs
149 Reg 21 JSA Regs
150 ss3(1)(c) and (d) and 3A(1)(b) and (c) JSA 1995
151 ss3(1)(f)(iii) and 3A(1)(e)(ii) JSA 1995; reg 61(1)(b) and (c) and (2)(b) JSA Regs
152 ss3(1)(f)(iii) and 3A(1)(e)(ii) JSA 1995; regs 57 and 59 JSA Regs
153 ss3(1)(f)(iii) and 3A(1)(e)(ii) JSA 1995; reg 60 JSA Regs
154 Reg 61(1)(a) and (2)(a) JSA Regs
155 Reg 61(1)(f) and (2)(e) JSA Regs
156 ss3(1)(f)(ii), 3A(1)(e)(i) and 16 JSA 1995
157 paras 39-63, 96-116 and 209-10 'Making a Severe Hardship Decision' (internal DWP guidance available at www.dwp.gov.uk/advisers/jsa_for_16-17year_olds.pdf)
158 s16(2) and (4) JSA 1995
159 paras 133-4 'Making a Severe Hardship Decision' (internal DWP guidance available at www.dwp.gov.uk/advisers/jsa_for_16-17year_olds.pdf)
160 s16(3) JSA 1995
161 s71A SSAA 1992
162 Regs 64-66 JSA Regs
163 Reg 64(2) and (3) JSA Regs
164 Reg 57(1) JSA Regs
165 Regs 65 and 65A JSA Regs
166 Reg 66 JSA Regs
167 Reg 62 JSA Regs
168 Reg62(1) JSA Regs
169 Reg 62(2) and (3) JSA Regs
170 para 117 'Making a Severe Hardship Decision' (internal DWP guidance available at www.dwp.gov.uk/advisers/jsa_for_16-17year_olds.pdf)
171 paras 5-37 'Making a Severe Hardship Decision' (internal DWP guidance available at www.dwp.gov.uk/advisers/jsa_for_16-17year_olds.pdf)
172 Sch 2 para 1(a) SSA 1998
173 paras 120-1 'Making a Severe Hardship Decision' (internal DWP guidance available at www.dwp.gov.uk/advisers/jsa_for_16-17year_olds.pdf)

6. **Claims and backdating**
174 s1 SSAA 1992; reg 3(g) SS(C&P) Regs
175 Regs 4(1A) and (6) SS(C&P) Regs
176 Reg 5 SS(C&P) Regs
177 Reg 24 JSA Regs
178 Reg 4(3B)(a) SS(C&P) Regs
179 s1(2B) and (4) JSA 1995; reg 3A(1) JSA Regs
180 CJSA/2633/2004
181 s1(4) JSA 1995; reg 3A(1) JSA Regs
182 *Hockenjos v Secretary of State for Social Security* [2004] EWCA Civ 1749, 21 December 2004, reported as R(JSA) 1/05 and R(JSA) 2/05
183 Sch 1 para 9A JSA 1995; reg 3B JSA Regs
184 Sch 1 paras 9B and 9C JSA 1995; reg 3C JSA Regs
185 s1(2C) JSA 1995; reg 3E JSA Regs
186 Sch 5 paras 10(2)(b), 13A and 17A JSA Regs
187 Sch 5A para 7 JSA Regs
188 Reg 19(1) and Sch 4 para 1 SS(C&P) Regs
189 Reg 6(4ZB)(a) and (4A)(a)(i) SS(C&P) Regs
190 Reg 6(4A)(b) SS(C&P) Regs
191 Reg 6(4ZC)(a) and (b) SS(C&P) Regs
192 Reg 6(4A)(a)(ii) SS(C&P) Regs
193 Reg 6(4ZB)(b) and (4ZC)(c) SS(C&P) Regs
194 CS/371/1949
195 Reg 6(4AB) SS(C&P) Regs
196 Reg 4(3B)(b) SS(C&P) Regs
197 Reg 4(3B)(c) SS(C&P) Regs
198 Reg 6(28) SS(C&P) Regs
199 Reg 13(1) and (9) SS(C&P) Regs
200 s8 JSA 1995; reg 24(6) JSA Regs
201 Regs 23 and 23A JSA Regs
202 CJSA/1080/2002
203 paras 30-35 Ch 13 ESG I vol
204 s8(2) JSA 1995; regs 25 and 27 JSA Regs
205 Regs 23 and 23A JSA Regs; s7 IA 1978; R(JSA) 1/04

206 *Secretary of State for Work and Pensions v Michael Ferguson* [2003] EWCA Civ 536, reported as R(JSA) 6/03
207 Reg 27 JSA Regs
208 Reg 30 JSA Regs
209 The exceptions are those treated as available under reg 14(1)(h)-(j) and (nn)-(q) JSA Regs
210 Reg 28 JSA Regs
211 Reg 29 JSA Regs
212 Reg 26 JSA Regs; *Secretary of State for Work and Pensions v Michael Ferguson* [2003] EWCA Civ 536, reported as R(JSA) 6/03; R(JSA) 2/04
213 Reg 6(4C) SS(C&P) Regs
214 R(JSA) 2/04
215 Reg 6(4B) SS(C&P) Regs
216 The exceptions are those treated as available under reg 14(1)(h)-(j) and (nn)-(q) JSA Regs

7. **Getting paid**
217 s3B JSA 1995
218 Reg 30A SS(C&P) Regs
219 s1(3) JSA 1995
220 Reg 1(3) JSA Regs
221 Reg 26A SS(C&P) Regs
222 Reg 87A JSA Regs
223 Reg 26A(3) SS(C&P) Regs
224 Reg 24(7) JSA Regs; reg 3 SS(NCC) Regs
225 Reg 7 and Sch 3A para 7 SS&CS(DA) Regs
226 Reg 7(2)(b) SS&CS(DA) Regs
227 Sch 3A paras 8 and 9 SS&CS(DA) Regs
228 Sch 3A para 10 SS&CS(DA) Regs
229 Sch 3A para 11 SS&CS(DA) Regs

8. **Challenging a jobseeker's allowance decision**
230 CJSA/1080/2002

9. **Tax, tax credits and other benefits**
231 ss671-75 IT(EP)A 2003

Chapter 16

Jobseeker's allowance: sanctions and hardship payments

This chapter covers:

Even if you are entitled to jobseeker's allowance (JSA) you may find that you are not paid for a period if a decision maker decides you should be sanctioned. If you are sanctioned:

- the length of time for which you are sanctioned (the 'sanction period') can be fixed or variable (see p415). During the sanction period, JSA is usually not paid or is paid at a reduced rate;
- special rules apply if you are 16 or 17 (see p419);
- if you disagree that you should be sanctioned, or with the sanction period, you can challenge the decision (see p421);
- you may be able to get hardship payments (see p422).

The days in your sanction period count towards your 182 days of entitlement to contribution-based JSA (see p367) even though you are not actually paid any benefit. You are treated as on income-based JSA if you are not being paid it because of a sanction, so you remain entitled to maximum housing benefit and council tax benefit.[1]

If you are sanctioned, check whether you (or if you are a member of a 'joint-claim couple', your partner) can claim income support (IS) or pension credit (PC) instead. If you are not a member of a joint-claim couple and you have a partner s/he may qualify for JSA, IS or PC instead of you.

Note: additional rules apply if a court has decided you failed to comply with a community order without reasonable excuse (see p997) or you have been sanctioned because of benefit offences (see p1047).

1. Employment-related sanctions

You can be sanctioned if you:[2]

- lose a job because of 'misconduct' (see below); *or*
- leave a job voluntarily (see p402); *or*
- refuse or fail to carry out a jobseeker's direction (see p406); *or*
- fail to apply for or accept a job (see p406); *or*
- 'neglect to avail' yourself of a job (see p407).

Employment for these purposes does not include self-employment, or self-employment on an employment programme or the 'intensive activity period' (instead the rules for training sanctions apply – see p412).[3] However, employment on the employed option of the New Deal for Young People *is* included. When considering whether you should be sanctioned, the decision maker should only look at your last employment preceding your claim and your subsequent actions.[4]

For information about challenging a sanction decision, see p421.

Losing a job because of misconduct

You can be sanctioned if you lose your job through misconduct.[5] This includes where you are suspended from work for misconduct[6] or if you resigned rather than be dismissed.[7] You cannot be sanctioned for misconduct in self-employment.

The sanction period is variable (see p417).

What is misconduct?

'Misconduct' is not defined in the rules. However, bear the following in mind.

- You are guilty of misconduct only if your actions or omissions are 'blameworthy'. This does not mean that it has to be established that you did anything dishonest or that you deliberately did something wrong; serious carelessness or negligence may be enough.[8]
- Everyone makes mistakes or is inefficient from time to time. So, for example, if you are a naturally slow worker who, despite making every effort, cannot produce the output required by your employer, you are not guilty of misconduct even if the poor performance may justify your dismissal.[9]
- The misconduct has to have some connection with your employment. It does not have to take place during working hours to count as misconduct.

However, a sanction cannot be imposed if the actions or omissions took place before your employment began – eg, you said or failed to say something when applying for the job.[10]
- Some behaviour is clearly misconduct – eg, dishonesty (whether or not connected with your work) if it causes your employer to dismiss you because s/he no longer trusts you.[11]
- Some behaviour is not necessarily misconduct.
  - Bad time-keeping and failing to report in time that you are sick might amount to misconduct – eg, if you were persistently late or failed to report that you were sick on a number of occasions.
  - A refusal to carry out a reasonable instruction by an employer is not misconduct if you had a good reason for refusing or your refusal was due to a genuine misunderstanding.[12]
  - Breaking rules covering personal conduct might be misconduct, depending on the seriousness of the breach. A breach of a trivial rule might not be misconduct.[13]
  - A refusal to work overtime is misconduct if you were under a duty to work overtime when required and the request to do it was reasonable.

Although evidence from your employer is taken into account, the fact that s/he did not describe your actions as 'misconduct' does not guarantee that you can escape a sanction. However, this should go heavily in your favour.

Whether misconduct caused the loss of employment

Your misconduct need not be the only cause of the loss of your employment, but it must be an immediate and substantial reason for you losing your job.[14] If your misconduct was not the real reason for your dismissal (eg, your employer used this as an excuse to dismiss you but really only wanted to reduce numbers of staff) you should not be sanctioned.

It is not relevant that your dismissal was unreasonable or an over-reaction on your employer's part. However, you should seek advice to see whether you might have a case for unfair dismissal at an employment tribunal.

If there was misconduct, the exact way in which you lost your employment is not important. You may be summarily dismissed, be dismissed with notice or resign as an alternative to possible dismissal.[15]

Leaving your job voluntarily

You can be sanctioned if you leave your job 'voluntarily' without 'just cause' (see p404).[16] A sanction can only be imposed if:
- you were in employment (not self-employment); *and*
- you were not in a 'trial period' (see p408).

The decision maker has to show that you left your employment voluntarily but, once this is shown, you must then show that you had 'just cause' for leaving if you want to avoid a sanction.

The sanction period is variable (see p417).

Whether you left voluntarily

'Voluntarily' is not defined in the rules, but the DWP says it means that you have brought your employment to an end by your own acts and of your own free will.[17] You have not left your employment voluntarily if you had no choice in the matter or there is convincing evidence (eg, medical evidence from your GP) that you were not responsible for your actions.

If you resign because you genuinely believe that your employer is about to end your employment or because you were given the 'choice' of resignation or dismissal, you have not left your job voluntarily. However, the DWP may then consider whether you lost your job through misconduct (see p401).

You are likely to be treated as leaving your job voluntarily if you resign giving notice. However, when deciding the length of the sanction period, the decision maker should take into account whether you:[18]

- were willing to work your notice (but your employer would not let you) and might have had a better chance of finding other work while you were still in the job;
- tried to withdraw your notice, even if this was not accepted.

Your employer may have given you notice to end your employment but then cancelled or suspended it, allowing you to continue in the same employment. If you decide not to continue in the employment and it is clear that you have a genuine choice to remain, you are likely to be treated as leaving voluntarily.[19] However, the circumstances may be such as to amount to 'just cause' (see p404) or to justify a reduction in the sanction period (see p417).

Volunteering for redundancy

You do not count as leaving your job voluntarily if you volunteer or accept your employer's proposal for redundancy.[20] This only applies where there is a redundancy situation at your workplace – eg, where a whole factory or department is closing down or where there is a cut in the number of people needed to carry out certain tasks.[21]

You have not left employment voluntarily if your job was abolished, even if you were offered or you could have applied for alternative jobs with the same employer. However, if you refuse other work, you might be sanctioned for another reason – eg, refusing employment or 'neglecting to avail' yourself of an opportunity of employment (see pp406 and 407).

There is no special rule to help you if you take early retirement (see p405).

Change in terms and conditions of employment

If your employer ends your contract of employment, you have *not* left a job voluntarily.[22] A change in your terms or conditions by your employer can mean that s/he has ended your existing contract of employment – eg, if a change is imposed without your agreement and the new terms are a lot less favourable than before. If you leave your employment as a result, you can try to argue that you have not left your job voluntarily but have been dismissed, or that you had 'just cause' for leaving.

'Just cause' for leaving your job

If the decision maker says that you left your job voluntarily, it is up to you to show that you had 'just cause' for doing so. 'Just cause' is not defined in the rules. It is not the same as 'good cause', which applies to other sanctions.

To have 'just cause' for leaving your job you must show that you acted reasonably in leaving and also that the circumstances of your case make it proper that public funds should support you.[23] You cannot argue you had 'just cause' simply because the conditions of your employment were poor, but see p429 if there was a breach in the law on minimum working conditions. You are expected if at all possible to take steps through the proper channels to sort out any problems – eg, by raising them with your employer or using the grievance procedure, rather than leaving immediately[24] and to look for another job seriously before giving one up.

Your chances of getting other employment, including self-employment, should be taken into account. If these were good and this is combined with strong reasons for leaving your job, you *may* have acted reasonably in leaving your job and have 'just cause'.[25]

Even if it is decided that you do not have 'just cause' for leaving your job, these factors may work in your favour in reducing the sanction period.

You may have 'just cause' for leaving a job in the following situations.

- You genuinely did not know or were mistaken about the **conditions of the job** (eg, it was beyond your physical or mental capacity, or was harmful to your health), you gave it a fair trial before leaving and it was reasonable for you to have left when you did.[26]
- You leave your job for **personal or domestic reasons** – eg, you give up work to look after a sick relative.[27] If you leave your job to move with your partner who has taken a job elsewhere, you can try to argue that you have 'just cause' or that the length of the sanction period should be limited.[28] Relevant factors may include how important it was to your partner's career to make the move and how good your chances are of finding work in the new area.

  The circumstances must usually have become very pressing or urgent to justify leaving your job before looking for alternative employment. It could be helpful to show that you tried to negotiate an arrangement with your employer to resolve the problem – eg, a reduction in your hours or time off work.

- Your employer makes a **change in the terms and conditions of your employment** which does not amount to an ending of your contract of employment. You are expected to use any grievance procedure first.
  Decision makers are not allowed to take 'any matter relating to the level of remuneration' into account when deciding whether or not you have 'just cause' for leaving your job (but see p430 if your employer is paying below the national minimum wage).[29] This appears to mean that if you leave your job because your employer cuts your wages unilaterally you are not able to show 'just cause'. However, a cut in pay can mean your existing contract of employment has ended and, therefore, you have been dismissed rather than having left your job.
- You left your job because of a **firm offer of alternative employment**, but claimed jobseeker's allowance (JSA) because the offer fell through. You should be treated as having 'just cause' for leaving unless the offer was cancelled before you left your previous employment or you changed your mind and did not take the new job and you could have stayed in the existing employment, or did not ask your employer if you could stay.[30]

Taking retirement

Some employers lay down a general retirement age but allow you to apply for permission to leave before that age (known as 'early retirement'). Under employment rules, you have a right to ask to work beyond that age. If the age that your employer has set is below 65, you may be able to challenge this under the age discrimination laws.

If you do take early retirement or do not take advantage of an opportunity to continue working after retirement age, you might be regarded as having left your job voluntarily.[31] However, you might be able to show 'just cause' if, for example, you can show that the work was getting too much for you because of your age or you would have been employed on worse terms and conditions than before.

Employers sometimes institute special early retirement schemes which run for a limited period, often in order to deal with a redundancy situation. In that case, you come under the special rules about redundancy (see p403). Employers often try to avoid using the word redundancy and you may have to prove to the decision maker that a redundancy situation existed.

If you take early retirement under some other special scheme, you cannot show 'just cause' merely because your action was in your employer's interest.[32] However, this might be an argument for reducing the length of the sanction period, particularly if you worked in the public sector and could say that your action was in the public interest.[33]

Refusing or failing to carry out a jobseeker's direction

You can be sanctioned if you refuse or fail to carry out a reasonable jobseeker's direction (see below), without 'good cause' (see p409).[34]

The sanction period is fixed at two or four weeks (see p416).

A jobseeker's direction

A **'jobseeker's direction'** is a written notice from your employment officer (EO) telling you to take specific action to find a job or increase your chances of being employed.[35] For example, you might be directed to apply for a specific job vacancy, to attend a training course, or to improve your appearance or behaviour so as to present yourself better to potential employers. You are normally given an opportunity to take the action voluntarily before any direction is given. It must be clear that you are being given a jobseeker's direction.

A jobseeker's direction can be given at any time and more than once. It states the time within which you are expected to comply with it and checks are made to ensure that you have done so. Each refusal to carry out a direction could result in you being sanctioned.

Is a jobseeker's direction 'reasonable'?

A jobseeker's direction must be reasonable. It would not be reasonable, for example, if it would not help you find a job or increase your chances of being employed, was at odds with your sincere conscientious or religious beliefs or might unlawfully discriminate on grounds such as gender, religion or nationality.

Any jobseeker's direction must be relevant to *your* needs and to the circumstances of the local labour market. If the EO accepts that a jobseeker's direction was unreasonable, or could not be carried out in the time required, s/he cancels the direction.

A jobseeker's direction might require you to apply for a job that is for less than 24 hours a week if it improves your prospects of finding further work.[36] However, you can argue that you have good cause for refusing or failing to carry it out, or that the direction is unreasonable, as you should not be sanctioned for refusing to apply for, or accept, a notified job vacancy for less than 24 hours a week (16 hours a week in some circumstances) — see p410.

Failing to apply for or to accept a job

You can be sanctioned if you are notified by the DWP of a job vacancy and you do not apply for it or refuse to accept it when offered to you.[37] This does not apply if you can show 'good cause' (see p409).

If you repeatedly fail to take jobs that are offered to you, a decision maker may also decide you are not available for or actively seeking work (see pp347 and 357) and refuse you JSA altogether.

The sanction period is variable (see p417).

Notification of a job vacancy

To be sanctioned, you must have been notified of a job vacancy by the DWP, orally, in writing or by other means. You should argue that no sanction should be imposed if you did not receive the notification. A job advert that is simply displayed in a Jobcentre Plus office or on the Jobcentre Plus website does not by itself amount to a notification by the DWP. However, if you identify a vacancy yourself and then discuss it with a DWP adviser, the DWP may say you have been 'notified'.[38]

You must be given sufficient information to enable you to pursue the vacancy or to make an informed decision on whether to pursue it.[39] You risk being sanctioned if you do not apply for the job, do not attend for interview or refuse the job if it is offered to you.

If you are notified of a vacancy and are unsure about what your financial situation would be, check the amount of benefits and tax credits for which you would qualify if you took the job – eg, working tax credit, council tax benefit and housing benefit. If you need help with the calculations, seek advice from one of the agencies listed in Appendix 2. Remember that you may not be able to show 'good cause' for refusing a job because of your income or the rate of pay (see p411).

Treated as refusing to apply for or to accept a job

The DWP might treat you as having refused to apply for or accept a job if:[40]

- you fail to complete the job application form properly or give inappropriate answers to questions on the form. However, if you submit your application to the DWP and it does not pass this on to a potential employer, you can argue that you did not fail to apply for the job; *or*
- you fail to attend or are late for a job interview, or you go to the wrong place through your own negligence; *or*
- you behave in such a way that you lose the chance of getting the job. This should only apply to things you actually said or did (or refused to do) and not just because a prospective employer disliked your appearance or manner; *or*
- you accept a job but fail to start it or impose unreasonable conditions so that the offer is withdrawn.

You can be expected to apply for and accept temporary work. You cannot escape a sanction on the grounds that a job is temporary, but the decision maker should take the date the job would have ended into account when deciding the period of any sanction (see p417).

'Neglecting to avail' yourself of a job

You can be sanctioned if you fail to take up ('neglect to avail' yourself of) a reasonable opportunity of employment without 'good cause' (see p409).[41] You do not have to be notified of a vacancy by the DWP for this sanction to apply.

You count as 'neglecting to avail' yourself of an opportunity if you have the chance to return to a job with a former employer but you fail to take it up. However, this rule does not apply if the 'opportunity' is for further work with an employer you have been working for during a 'trial period' (see below).

The sanction period is variable (see p417).

When this sanction applies

In practice, this sanction usually applies in situations where you were not in a trial period (see below) and you do not return to work with your former employer after what was originally intended to be a temporary break – eg, if you decide not to resume work after maternity leave or you refuse an offer of alternative employment in a redundancy situation. A sanction should only be imposed if the job vacancy was in a 'qualifying former employment' (see below). This is because you automatically have good cause for 'neglecting to avail' yourself of the job if it is *not* a qualifying former employment (see p410).[42]

The DWP is likely to apply a sanction if, for example, you knew you had a reasonable chance of getting the job and did not take the necessary steps to get it.[43] It cannot apply the sanction if the job was vacant because of a stoppage of work caused by a trade dispute.[44]

Qualifying former employment

A job counts as a 'qualifying former employment' if:[45]

- it is with an employer you previously worked for or an employer who took over the business from your former employer; *and*
- it is not more than a year between the date you last worked for the employer and the date the question of a sanction arises; *and*
- the terms and conditions are not less favourable than those of the job you had when you last worked for the employer.

The date on which you last worked for the employer is the date you last attended work, not the last date for which you were paid.

Trial periods

In certain circumstances you may take a job for a 'trial period' and leave it without the risk of being sanctioned for leaving voluntarily or for 'neglecting to avail' yourself of a reasonable opportunity of employment (see pp402 and 407).[46] You *must* leave the employment within the trial period to avoid being sanctioned. You do not have to have agreed with the DWP that you were taking up the employment on a trial basis. **Note:** if you leave shortly after the trial period and are sanctioned, you can argue for a shorter sanction period.[47]

If you are dismissed or you leave the job as an alternative to being dismissed, you might still be sanctioned if this was because of misconduct (see p401).

The trial period rule applies if, for at least 13 weeks before the day you begin employment, you have not:[48]

- worked (including as a self-employed person); *or*
- been a full-time student (see p579) or in 'relevant education' (see p576). You do not count as a full-time student if you were in receipt of a training allowance.[49]

A **'trial period'** is the period of eight weeks starting with the beginning of your fifth week and ending at the end of your 12th week in the job. However, for this purpose, weeks in which you work for fewer than 16 hours are ignored.[50] The DWP includes periods when you are not actually working but you are required by contract to be in a certain place in order to carry out a job.[51] Periods when you are off work sick or on holiday, even if you are paid, do not count when calculating the number of hours.

To be sure you are covered by this rule, you must work at least some of the fifth week and leave before you have worked all of the 12th. In calculating the fifth and the 12th weeks, the 'week' starts on the day you begin work and ends at midnight seven days later.[52]

If you do not claim JSA for more than 12 consecutive weeks (ie, until after the trial period), a new 'jobseeking period' (see p339) begins when you next claim. This means:

- you have to serve a further three waiting days (see p366) before getting JSA; *and*
- you may not qualify for contribution-based JSA if you no longer satisfy the contribution conditions (see p735).

Employment-related sanctions and 'good cause'

A sanction cannot be imposed if you have 'good cause' for:

- refusing or failing to carry out a reasonable 'jobseeker's direction' (see p406);
- failing to apply for, or refusing to accept, a job (see p406);
- 'neglecting to avail' yourself of a job opportunity (see p407).

The factors which may mean you have 'good cause' depend on the sanction. The decision maker must take all the circumstances into account. Some circumstances:

- count as 'good cause' (see p410);
- must be taken into account when deciding whether you have 'good cause' (see p410);
- do not count as 'good cause' (see p411).

A different 'good cause' rule applies when a sanction is connected with a training scheme or employment programme. There are some special rules for 16/17-year olds (see p419). Remember that you can be sanctioned for leaving a job voluntarily without 'just cause' rather than 'good cause'.

Circumstances that count as good cause

You have 'good cause' if:

- you refuse to apply for or accept a job involving fewer than 24 hours work a week (16 hours if you have been allowed to restrict your availability for work to less than 24 hours a week – see p355).[53] This ground does not apply if you refuse or fail to carry out a jobseeker's direction. However, you may be able to challenge the direction as unreasonable (see p406);
- you do not accept a job that is vacant because of a trade dispute – ie, you are not required to be a strike-breaker;[54]
- you are within your 'permitted period' (see p354) and have restricted the type of work for which you are available to your usual occupation or to at least your usual rate of pay, and you refuse a job that does not meet these conditions;[55]
- you have trained for a particular type of work for at least two calendar months. You do not have to accept work in any other kind of employment for four weeks after your training ends. A 'week' for these purposes means any period of seven consecutive days.[56] 'Training' for these purposes is not defined and should be given its ordinary everyday meaning;
- you have 'neglected to avail' yourself of an opportunity of employment, unless it is a 'qualifying former employment' (see p408);[57]
- you have been laid off or are on short-time working and have been accepted as available only for casual employment (see p370), and you refuse to take some other type of work;[58]
- you come under the rules that exempt you from having to be able to start work immediately (see p347), or you have said that you are only available to work at certain times and you are not required to take up employment at times when you are not available (see p348), and you refuse to take a job where you would have to do so;[59]
- you fail or refuse to apply for, or accept, a notified job vacancy, or 'neglect to avail' yourself of an opportunity of employment with a qualifying former employer (see p407) while on a 'qualifying course' as a full-time student (see p346) and:[60]
  - this happens in the four weeks before the end of the course or your examinations; *or*
  - it is other than casual employment during your vacation, unless it is permanent full-time paid work (16 hours or more a week).

Circumstances that must be taken into account

If you do not have automatic good cause, the decision maker must take certain circumstances into account when deciding whether you have 'good cause'.[61] These include:

- any discrepancy between the restrictions you have been allowed to place on your availability for work and the requirements of the job, although minor differences might not count;

- any of your conditions or personal circumstances that suggest that a particular job or carrying out a jobseeker's direction would be likely to cause you excessive physical or mental stress or significant harm to your health;
- any sincerely held religious or conscientious objection;
- any caring responsibilities (see p355) that make it unreasonable for you to do the job or carry out a jobseeker's direction;
- the travelling time involved between your home and the place of work (or a place mentioned in a jobseeker's direction), but see below;
- certain expenses that would be unavoidably incurred, if they would amount to an unreasonably high proportion of the income you would receive.[62]

These are not the only circumstances that can be taken into account. Account should also be taken of any other factor that appears relevant. See, in particular, p429 for when the terms of a job on offer break the laws on minimum working conditions.

Circumstances that do not count as good cause

You cannot refuse to apply for a job simply because of the rate of pay offered.[63] However, see p430 if the rate of pay is below the minimum wage.

In addition, you cannot show good cause if you refuse or fail to apply for a job or to carry out a jobseeker's direction because of:[64]

- your income or outgoings or those of any member of your household (see p703), either as they are now or as they would be if you took the job or carried out the direction. For these purposes, 'outgoings' do not include any expenses taken into account that would be an unreasonably high proportion of your income (see above).
  You cannot, for example, argue that you need a high wage because you have a large mortgage or an expensive lifestyle. You might be able to show good cause if:[65]
  - you have been allowed to place restrictions on the rate of pay you would accept because of your physical or mental condition (see p353), or under the rules about a 'permitted period' (see p354); *or*
  - the job you have refused to accept would have been paid on a commission-only basis; *or*
- unless it is unreasonable because of your health or caring responsibilities (see p355),the travelling time between your home and the place of work (or a place mentioned in a jobseeker's direction) if this is less than:[66]
  - one hour either way, during the first 13 weeks you are entitled to JSA; *or*
  - one and a half hours either way, in all other cases.

2. New Deal, training scheme and employment programme-related sanctions

If attendance on a training scheme or employment programme is compulsory, you can be sanctioned if you:[67]

- lose your place because of '**misconduct**' (see p401). References to an employer should be read as references to your scheme or programme provider; *or*
- **give up or fail to attend without 'good cause'** (see p414). You are treated as failing to attend if you have been absent without authorisation, even if the absence is only for one day.[68] You might be treated as failing to attend if you arrive late and are not allowed to attend;[69] *or*
- are **notified of a place and fail to apply for or accept it** when offered to you without 'good cause' (see p414). See the information in the section about failing to apply for or accept a job on p406. References to an employer should be read as references to your scheme or programme provider; *or*
- **'neglect to avail'** yourself of a reasonable opportunity of a place without 'good cause' (see p414). You do not have to be notified by the DWP for this sanction to apply.

The sanction period is fixed (one, two or four weeks, or 26 weeks for some New Deal sanctions). See p416 for further information.

For information about scheme and programme-related sanctions and good cause see p414, and on challenging a sanction decision, see p421.

Compulsory training schemes and employment programmes

Compulsory training schemes and employment programmes include many of the New Deal options. At the time this *Handbook* was written, the following training schemes and employment programmes were compulsory for the purposes of the rules about sanctions.[70]

Training schemes

Work-Based Learning for Young People (Skillseekers in Scotland)

New Deal schemes

The full-time education and training option of the New Deal for Young People
The self-employed employment option of the New Deal for Young People
The voluntary sector option of the New Deal for Young People
The environment task force option of the New Deal for Young People
The intensive activity period of the New Deal for people aged 25 or over but less than 60

Other employment programmes

Gateway to Work
Employment zone programmes (some of these are in pilot areas only)
Jobseeker Mandatory Activity Pilot (in pilot areas only)

In addition, if you are on a 'qualifying course' and are, therefore, treated as available for work (see p350), your course counts as compulsory and you can be sanctioned if you give up your place or fail to attend the course without good cause, or you lose your place through misconduct.[71]

Schemes can be added to or removed from the list of compulsory training schemes and employment programmes. You should seek advice if you are in any doubt about whether a scheme or programme is compulsory.

Although other training schemes and initiatives to help you find work are not compulsory, your employment officer (EO) can compel you to attend one by issuing a jobseeker's direction (see p406).

Note: the Government plans to introduce a 'skills screen' when people start a claim for jobseeker's allowance (JSA) to identify any basic literacy, numeracy or language needs they have. Where there are skills gaps, claimants will be encouraged to attend a full 'skills health check', which may result in a referral for training. Skills health checks will be compulsory for those who have been claiming JSA for six months. See CPAG's *Welfare Rights Bulletin* for updates.

New Deal schemes

Whether and when you can be required to attend any particular New Deal scheme depends on your age and the length of time you have been unemployed.[72] In certain situations it is possible to join a New Deal scheme earlier than the compulsory date, but if you subsequently agree to embark on any options they become compulsory and you could be sanctioned for leaving them. During the 'gateway' period when you first enter the New Deal, if you fail without good cause to attend set interviews, your JSA claim is terminated under the rules about failing to attend interviews (see p389). If you claim again, you go back on to the 'gateway' where you left off.

If you refuse to start an option on a compulsory New Deal programme once you have received your official referral letter, or if you leave an option without good cause or are dismissed for misconduct, you can be sanctioned.

Remember the following.

- If you are self-employed while on a New Deal option or the intensive activity period any sanction related to this self-employment is a New Deal sanction.[73]
- If you are on the employed option of the New Deal, employment-related sanctions apply, not New Deal sanctions.

Scheme and programme-related sanctions and 'good cause'

A training scheme or employment programme sanction cannot be imposed if you have 'good cause' for:

- giving up or failing to attend; *or*
- failing to apply for or accept a place; *or*
- 'neglecting to avail' yourself of a place.

There are some special rules for 16/17-year olds (see p419).

When deciding whether you have 'good cause', the decision maker must consider all the circumstances of your case, but certain circumstances always count as good cause.[74] You may also have good cause in other situations. The decision maker should consider all the reasons you put forward. The rules do not specify any particular factors to be taken into account.

Circumstances that count as good cause

You have 'good cause' if:[75]

- you had a disease or physical/mental disability that meant you were unable to attend, or your health (or that of others) would have been at risk if you had done so;
- you gave up a place and your continued participation would have put your health and safety at risk;
- your failure to participate in the scheme or programme resulted from a sincerely held religious or conscientious objection;[76]
- your travelling time to and from the scheme or programme would have exceeded one hour in each direction. If there are no appropriate schemes within an hour's travelling distance, you may be expected to travel for over one hour. You may have good cause if travel is difficult – eg, because of a disability or poor health, or if the distance involved is very long;
- you are on a 'qualifying' full-time educational course (see p346) and you:[77]
  - fail to attend or abandon the course because it was unsuitable for you or you lacked the ability to do it, or it is less than four weeks since you started it; *or*
  - fail to apply for or attend an employment programme if this was at a time that would have prevented you from attending the qualifying course;
- you had caring responsibilities (see p355) and no close relative (see p348) of the person cared for or member of that person's household was available to provide the care, and it was not practical to make other arrangements;
- you were arranging or attending the funeral of a close relative or a close friend;
- you had to deal with a domestic emergency;
- you were crewing or launching a lifeboat, working as a part-time firefighter or doing work as part of an organised group for the benefit of others in an emergency.

For **New Deal scheme sanctions** only, if you fail to start or leave any of the options early you have good cause if you were not given a written notification by the DWP about the scheme in question that warned you about when you could be sanctioned and that payment of your JSA could cease or be reduced.[78]

3. Deciding if you should be sanctioned

If there is a possibility that you will be sanctioned, make sure you give full details of your side of the story when you claim jobseeker's allowance (JSA). If you:

- **left or were dismissed** from a job and it appears there may have been misconduct or you may have left your job voluntarily without just cause, your former employer is asked for a statement. You should be given an adequate chance to comment on what s/he says.[79] Your remarks may be passed to her/him for further comments. Make sure you explain why you disagree with the allegation of misconduct or why you had 'just cause' (see p404) for leaving your job. If you are going to an employment tribunal (eg, to claim unfair dismissal), you should say so. Discuss your reply with whoever is advising you on this, as you may be asked questions at the employment tribunal hearing by your former employer about what you have said;
- **refused to apply for or accept a job**, what the potential employer says might be taken into account. Make sure you explain what enquiries you made about the nature of the job, and your reasons for not applying for or accepting it;
- **refuse or fail to carry out a jobseeker's direction**, you are asked for your reasons. If the direction is not cancelled, your case is referred to a decision maker to decide whether you should be sanctioned.

For **training scheme and employment programme-related sanctions**, your scheme or programme provider is asked for a statement. Before a sanction is imposed, you should be given an adequate chance to comment on any statements made against you.[80]

4. Sanction periods and amount payable

If it is decided that a sanction should be applied, a decision maker must decide the length of the sanction period. A sanction period may be for a fixed or variable period.

For information about the amount of jobseeker's allowance (JSA) payable if you are sanctioned, see p418. If your JSA is not paid or is paid at a reduced rate, you might be able to get hardship payments (see p422).

If you disagree that you should be sanctioned or with the length of the sanction period, you can challenge the decision (see p421).

Note: there are some special rules for 16/17-year olds (see p419).

Sanction	*Period*
Losing a job because of misconduct (see p401)	Variable: 1–26 weeks
Leaving a job voluntarily (see p402)	Variable: 1–26 weeks
Failing to apply for or accept a job (see p406)	Variable: 1–26 weeks
'Neglecting to avail' yourself of a job opportunity (see p407)	Variable: 1–26 weeks
Failing to carry out a jobseeker's direction (see p406)	Fixed: 2 or 4 weeks
New Deal sanctions (see p412)	Fixed: 2, 4 or 26 weeks
Gateway to Work sanctions (see p412)	Fixed: 2 weeks
Jobseeker Mandatory Activity Pilot (in pilot areas)	Fixed: 1 week
Other training scheme/employment programme-related sanctions (see p412)	Fixed: 2 or 4 weeks

Once a sanction period has begun, it continues unbroken until the sanction period comes to an end.[81] This means that if you take a job or training for a short period but then claim again during the period of the sanction, you are still caught by the sanction.

Fixed sanction periods

A fixed-period sanction is either:[82]

- two weeks; *or*
- four weeks if you have already had a fixed-period sanction within the past 12 months; *or*
- 26 weeks for some New Deal sanctions (see p417).

Note: in pilot areas only, if you fail to take part in the Jobseeker Mandatory Activity Pilot the fixed period sanction is one week.

Sanctions other than for New Deal schemes

Unless it is a New Deal sanction (see p417) or a Jobseeker Mandatory Activity Pilot sanction, a sanction is imposed for two weeks (or four weeks if it is not a Gateway to Work sanction and you are sanctioned within 12 months of a previous fixed-period sanction).[83] The 12 months run from the first day of the previous sanction to the date of the decision imposing the current sanction.

If you are given a four-week sanction but later the first (two-week) sanction is removed (eg, by a tribunal), ask a decision maker to reduce the four-week sanction period to two weeks.[84] If s/he fails to do so, appeal. If you have already appealed against the second sanction, the tribunal should take the removal of the first sanction into account.[85]

New Deal scheme sanctions

A fixed-period New Deal scheme sanction is imposed for two weeks.[86] However, other than for sanctions relating to a Gateway to Work programme, the period is:

- four weeks if you have already had a sanction imposed within the last 12 months and both sanctions relate to the intensive activity period of the New Deal or both sanctions relate to other New Deal schemes;[87] *or*
- 26 weeks if you are given a sanction on three or more occasions, each sanction has been within 12 months of the previous one and all of the sanctions relate to the intensive activity period of the New Deal or all of the sanctions relate to other New Deal schemes.[88]

  If this is the first time a 26-week sanction period is applied to you, and the DWP notifies you that you no longer have to participate in the scheme, you can get income-based JSA again even if your 26-week sanction period has not ended.[89] Your income-based JSA starts on the later of:
  - the date from which you no longer have to participate in the New Deal scheme; *or*
  - the date four weeks after your JSA ceased.

Any other sanctions given in the previous 12 months do not affect the period of a New Deal scheme sanction.

Variable sanction period

A variable sanction can be any length from one week to 26 weeks.[90] Sanction periods are usually complete weeks, but there is nothing in the rules to prevent them including part weeks. However, a sanction of at least one week must be imposed, even if the decision maker thinks that the appropriate sanction period is less than one week.

Deciding for how long you should be sanctioned

In deciding the length of the sanction period, the decision maker can take into account anything that provides some reason for your conduct. You should be given a chance to provide information and evidence.[91] The rationale behind sanctions is that your conduct should not result in unnecessary expenditure of public funds. However, bear the following in mind.

- A 26-week sanction period is not the starting point; it is the maximum. A one-week sanction is the starting point, which can then be adjusted by referring to any aggravating or mitigating factors.[92]
- A 26-week sanction period should only be imposed in the most serious cases. A lot of caselaw on variable sanction periods was decided when the minimum period of a sanction was one day and the maximum six weeks, and when payment of benefit was reduced rather than stopped altogether. Although the principles still apply, they should be applied less harshly.

- There should be a difference in the sanction imposed where you have simply failed to apply for a job vacancy, as opposed to refusing to accept an offer of employment or losing your job through misconduct, particularly if you were unlikely to get the job.[93]

Decision makers must consider:[94]
- how long the employment you left or failed to take up was likely to have lasted, if this was less than 26 weeks. The decision maker should not impose a sanction for a period longer than the job would have lasted;
- if you left a job:
  - because of misconduct but your employer is prepared to take you back, the date you are to resume work. The decision maker should end the sanction period on that date;
  - voluntarily and the job was for 16 hours or less a week, the rate of pay and hours of work in that job. If the job did not provide an adequate income, this is a mitigating factor;
  - voluntarily or 'neglected to avail' yourself of a reasonable opportunity of employment, any physical or mental stress connected with the job.

The decision maker should also take account of any time during which you were not receiving JSA since the date you, for example, stopped work. The DWP says that having calculated the length of the sanction period that is appropriate in your case, the decision maker subtracts days you were not receiving JSA.[95] The result of this deduction may be that the sanction period is reduced to nothing, so you are not sanctioned if more than 26 weeks have passed between you leaving your last job and claiming JSA.

Amount of jobseeker's allowance payable

JSA is **not paid** during the sanction period if you are sanctioned and you are a single person or a member of a couple (other than a joint-claim couple), or if you are a member of a joint-claim couple and both of you are sanctioned.[96]

JSA is **paid at a reduced rate** during the sanction period if you are a member of a 'joint-claim couple' and only one of you is sanctioned.[97] In this situation, the JSA is paid to the person who has not been sanctioned. The person who has not been sanctioned is paid at the rate of:[98]
- contribution-based JSA, if s/he satisfies the rules for claiming it; *or*
- hardship payments, if you and your partner qualify (see p427); *or*
- in any other case, income-based JSA calculated as if s/he is a single person (see p368). However, any income or capital either of you have is taken into account in the calculation.

Unless you are on Work-Based Learning for Young People (Skillseekers in Scotland), JSA is **paid at the full rate** that applies to you if you (or if you are a member of a joint-claim couple, one of you) are getting a training allowance.[99]

If your JSA is not paid or is paid at a reduced rate, you might be able to get hardship payments (see p422). You should also check to see if you (or your partner) qualify for income support or pension credit instead of JSA. If you are a member of a couple (other than a joint-claim couple) your partner might be able to claim JSA instead of you.

5. **Special rules for 16/17-year-olds**

If you are aged 16 or 17, you can be sanctioned in the same way as claimants aged 18 and over if you are receiving:

- contribution-based jobseeker's allowance (JSA);[100] *or*
- income-based JSA, including under the severe hardship rules (see p373); *and*
  - have left a job voluntarily without 'just cause' (see p402); *or*
  - have lost a job because of misconduct (see p401).

If the sanctions are for other reasons, including where they are training related, special rules apply to 16/17-year-olds for good cause (see below) and for sanction periods (see p420). If you are 16 or 17, you may apply for hardship payments (see p422) in the same way as people aged 18 and over.

Good cause

Certain sanctions do not apply if you can show 'good cause' for acting or failing to act as you did. When deciding whether you have good cause, the decision maker should consider the factors that apply to sanctions for people aged 18 and over (see pp409 and 414). You might also have good cause under additional rules applying to training-related sanctions and to employment-related sanctions for 16/17-year-olds.

Training-related sanctions

If you give up or fail to attend a compulsory training scheme or employment programme (see p412) or fail to accept or 'neglect to avail' yourself of a place on one, you cannot be sanctioned if you can show 'good cause'. In addition to any other ground on which you can argue 'good cause' (see p414), you have this automatically if:[101]

- it is the first time that you have acted or failed to act in a way that could lead to a training-related sanction (under the normal or severe hardship payment rules); *and*
- you were a 'new jobseeker' (see p420):

- when you first started the scheme or programme, if a sanction is being considered because you gave up a place; *or*
- at the time of the act or omission, if the sanction is for another reason.

You are a '**new jobseeker**' for these purposes if, since you left full-time education, you have *never*:[102]

- worked for 16 hours or more a week or done a complete training course; *or*
- lost a place on a training scheme or employment programme because of misconduct, or failed to complete a training course or given up a place on a scheme or programme unless you had good cause.

If you are getting **severe hardship payments** (see p373), different rules for training-related sanctions apply.[103] You are only sanctioned if it is the second time you have done something connected with a training scheme that deserves a sanction.

Employment-related sanctions

If you have neglected to avail yourself of a reasonable opportunity of a job (see p407), or refused or failed to apply for a notified job vacancy (see p406), in addition to any other ground on which you can argue good cause (see p409) you have automatic good cause if your employer did not offer you suitable training (see p375).[104] This rule does not apply if:

- your JSA (including under the severe hardship rules) has been reduced in the past for the same reasons or because of a training-related sanction; *or*
- your JSA has been stopped in the past because you lost a job because of misconduct or left a job voluntarily without 'just cause' (see pp401 and 402); *or*
- you are claiming under the special rules for 16/17-year-olds who are on short-time working, have been laid off or who have accepted a firm offer to join the armed forces (see p373).

Sanction periods and amount of jobseeker's allowance payable

A fixed sanction period of two weeks applies where:[105]

- a fixed-period sanction (of whatever length) would be applied to you if you were 18 or over (see p416); *or*
- you fail to apply for, or to accept, a job (see p406) or 'neglect to avail' yourself of a job opportunity (see p407).

During the sanction period you continue to be paid benefit, but at a reduced rate. If you stop claiming JSA before the two weeks is over and then claim again, you are paid JSA at the reduced rate for the remainder of the two-week period. If you reach the age of 18 before the end of your two-week sanction, the sanction ends and you are paid the full rate of JSA for an 18-year-old.

If you are getting **severe hardship payments** (see p373), and you get a training-related sanction, your JSA is paid at a reduced rate for two weeks.[106] If your severe hardship direction is revoked (see p374) you can apply for severe hardship payments again immediately but they are paid at a reduced rate for two weeks.

Note: if you are being sanctioned for any other reason, the ordinary sanction periods apply (see p415). You might qualify for hardship payments (see p422).

Reduced rates of jobseeker's allowance

Your JSA is reduced by 40 per cent of the single person's (or lone parent's) personal allowance, even if you are a member of a couple, or by 20 per cent if you or any member of your family (see p366) are pregnant or seriously ill.[107] 'Seriously ill' is not defined.

6. Challenging a sanction decision

If you disagree with a sanction decision, you can challenge it.[108] You can challenge:

- the decision to give you a sanction; *and*
- the length of the sanction period.

You can apply for a revision or supersession of a sanction decision, or appeal against it in the usual way. See Chapters 41 and 42 for further information.

If you are sanctioned for failing to comply with a jobseeker's direction (see p406) you can challenge this on the basis that the direction that led to the sanction was not reasonable or that you have 'good cause' for not complying with it (see p409).

Appeals

It is often worth appealing to a tribunal. Even if the tribunal agrees that a sanction should be applied, it can reduce the length of a variable sanction period. However, an appeal tribunal could decide to extend your sanction period or that the circumstances justify a different sanction. You should seek advice if you are worried this might happen in your case.

An appeal gives you a chance to challenge your former employer's version of events. Note that employers can be invited to attend appeal hearings, but rarely do so. See p1133 for further information about the evidence tribunals can consider.

If you do not attend a hearing and fresh allegations are made against you, the tribunal should consider an adjournment to allow you to attend or to answer the allegations in writing. If a presenting officer is at the hearing, s/he should normally request one.[109] However, there is no guarantee this will happen so you should attend if you can.

Relationship with unfair dismissal and other proceedings

Sometimes the same facts have to be considered by other bodies – eg, employment tribunals and the criminal courts. The questions and legal tests that other bodies use may not be the same as those which apply to jobseeker's allowance (JSA).

The benefit decision-making authorities and employment tribunals are entirely independent of each other – decisions by one are not binding on the other. This means, for example, that a finding by an employment tribunal that a dismissal was fair does not prevent a decision maker or an appeal tribunal from concluding that you did not lose your job through misconduct.[110]

Similarly, although appeal tribunals normally accept a criminal conviction as proof that you have done what is alleged, it must still go on to consider whether this was connected with your employment, whether it amounts to misconduct and whether the misconduct was the reason you lost your employment.

A decision maker or appeal tribunal does not have to wait for the outcome of other proceedings before making a decision.[111] They are more likely to do so if there is a conflict of evidence.

7. Hardship payments

Hardship payments are reduced-rate payments of income-based jobseeker's allowance (JSA) that are made in limited circumstances. You can get hardship payments if you have been sanctioned, and also in other situations. In addition:

- you must be in a 'vulnerable group' (see p425); *or*
- if you are not in a vulnerable group, a decision maker must be satisfied that you or your partner would experience hardship if you are not paid (see p426).

For information about the amount of hardship payments, see p427.

When you can get hardship payments

You can qualify for hardship payments:

- at the beginning of a claim if you are waiting for a decision about whether you satisfy the labour market conditions (see p423);
- if you do not qualify for JSA because you do not satisfy the labour market conditions (see p424);
- if your benefit is suspended because of a doubt about whether you continue to satisfy the labour market conditions (see p424);
- if you have been sanctioned (see p424).

You cannot qualify for hardship payments if you or your partner are entitled to income support (IS) or come within one of the groups of people who can claim IS.[112] In this case, you or your partner can claim IS instead of hardship payments.

If you or your partner are 60 or over, you (or your partner) might be able to claim pension credit (PC) instead of hardship payments.

Whether or not you qualify for hardship payments, you may be able to claim an interim payment of JSA (see p986).

If, after receiving hardship payments, you are awarded full income-based JSA, IS or PC for the same period, the income-based JSA, IS or PC is reduced by the amount of hardship payments you were paid.[113]

At the beginning of a claim

You qualify for hardship payments at the beginning of a claim for JSA if you are waiting for a decision about whether you (or if you are a member of a joint-claim couple, you or your partner) are available for work or actively seeking work, or about your jobseeker's agreement.[114] If there is any other reason for the delay in deciding your claim you are not eligible.

You get hardship payments until the decision maker makes a decision on your claim, so long as you continue to satisfy the other conditions for getting income-based JSA (see p341).

If you cannot qualify for hardship payments, you might be able to get a crisis loan. See p503 for further information.

If you are in a vulnerable group

If you are in a vulnerable group (see p425) you get hardship payments from the later of:

- the fourth day of your jobseeking period (ie, after the three waiting days) or the date of your claim if the waiting days rule does not apply (see p366); *or*
- the date from which a decision maker decides that you count as in a vulnerable group.

Normally you can only get hardship payments from the day that you make a 'hardship statement', but a payment can be made for a period before the date of the statement if the decision maker is satisfied that you have experienced hardship because of a lack of resources during that period.[115] You cannot, however, get hardship payments for any period before your claim for JSA is made, unless it is a period for which a backdated claim is accepted.

If you are not in a vulnerable group

If you are not in a vulnerable group (see p425) you get hardship payments from the later of:[116]

- the 18th day after your claim for JSA or the 15th day after your claim if the waiting days rule does not apply (see p366); *or*
- the date you submitted your hardship statement (see p428).

The labour market conditions are not satisfied

If a decision maker decides that you (or if you are a member of a joint-claim couple, you or your partner) are not available for work, not actively seeking work or that you do not have a valid jobseeker's agreement (known as the 'labour market conditions'), you can qualify for hardship payments, but only if you are **in a vulnerable group** (see p425).[117] This does not apply if you (or if you are a joint-claim couple, either of you) are treated as unavailable for work for one of the reasons listed on p352.

You get hardship payments indefinitely from the day the decision maker decides that you do not satisfy the labour market conditions. You must continue to satisfy the other conditions for getting JSA (see p339).

Jobseeker's allowance is suspended

You can qualify for hardship payments if your JSA is suspended because there is doubt about whether you (or if you are a member of a joint-claim couple, you or your partner) are meeting the labour market conditions.[118]

You get hardship payments until the decision maker makes a decision, so long as you satisfy the other conditions for getting income-based JSA (see p341). If you are a member of a joint-claim couple, both of you must satisfy these conditions (or one of you if the other is in an exempt group – see p342). If the decision maker eventually decides that you do not satisfy the labour market conditions, you can only continue to get hardship payments if you are in a vulnerable group (see above).

If you are **in a vulnerable group** (see p425), you get hardship payments from the date that the suspension begins.

If you are **not in a vulnerable group**, you cannot get hardship payments until the 15th day of the suspension.[119] If you are subject to successive 14-day suspensions (eg, at each signing day the employment officer doubts that you took sufficient steps to find work) and so never reach the 15th day of any suspension period and receive payment, seek advice as this may be unlawful.

Jobseeker's allowance is not paid because you have been sanctioned

If you are sanctioned, you can qualify for hardship payments during the sanction period.[120]

If you are **in a vulnerable group** (see p425) you get hardship payments from the first day of the sanction period. If you are **not in a vulnerable group** you cannot get hardship payments until the 15th day of the sanction. This means that if the sanction period is for two weeks or less you do not get benefit for the sanction period at all unless you are in a vulnerable group. If during a sanction period another sanction is imposed for a different reason, you cannot get hardship payments for the first 14 days of the period of the new sanction.[121]

Hardship payments continue until the end of the sanction period so long as:

- if you are a single person or a member of a couple (but not a joint-claim couple), you satisfy the other conditions for getting income-based JSA; *or*
- if you are a member of a joint-claim couple, you both satisfy the other conditions for getting income-based JSA, or one of you does and the other is someone who does not have to. See p342 for further information about exemptions for joint-claim couples.

New Deal sanctions

If you (or if you are a joint-claim couple, you or your partner) are sanctioned for failing to take up or attend or for leaving a compulsory New Deal scheme, without good cause, you cannot receive hardship payments unless you are in a vulnerable group, no matter how long the sanction period lasts.[122] If you cease to be required to participate in an option, you may qualify for hardship payments if the sanction has already lasted 14 days. If a 26-week sanction period has been set but you subsequently complete an option without being sanctioned again, see p417.

Hardship and vulnerable groups

Even if you come within one of the situations when hardship payments can be made, you cannot get them unless the decision maker is satisfied that you are in a vulnerable group or that you or your partner would experience hardship if payments were not made.[123] Hardship payments can be made sooner if you are in a vulnerable group. In some situations, you can only get hardship payments if you are in a vulnerable group.

Vulnerable groups

You are in a vulnerable group if:[124]

- you or your partner are **pregnant** and would experience hardship if no payment were made;
- you are a member of a couple and one of you is **responsible for a child under 16 or a qualifying young person** who would experience hardship if no payment were made. See p710 for when you count as responsible for a child or young person;
- you are not a member of a couple and are **responsible for a qualifying young person** who would experience hardship if no payment were made. See p710 for when you count as responsible for a young person. If you are responsible for a child under 16 you can claim IS and cannot claim hardship payments;
- your income-based JSA includes a **disability premium** (see p779) or would include one if your claim were to succeed and the person for whom the premium is paid would experience hardship if no payment were made;
- you or your partner have a **chronic medical condition** and as a result your (or your partner's) functional capacity is 'limited or restricted by physical impairment', and the decision maker is satisfied that:
  - it has lasted or is likely to last for at least 26 weeks; *and*

- the health of the person with the condition will decline further than that of a 'normal healthy adult' within the next two weeks and that person would experience hardship if no payment were made.

The decision maker first considers whether the medical condition makes you or your partner incapable of work (see p661) and therefore entitled to IS.[125] In this case, you cannot claim hardship payments and should claim IS instead;

- you and/or your partner:
  - are **caring for someone** who:
    - is getting attendance allowance (AA) or the highest or middle rate of the care component of disability living allowance (DLA) or has claimed one of these benefits, but only for up to 26 weeks from the date of the claim or until the claim is decided, whichever is first; *or*
    - has been awarded AA or the highest or middle rate of DLA care component but it has not yet been paid; *and*
  - would not be able to continue caring if no hardship payment were made. You do not have to show that the person you are caring for would experience hardship.

  The care must be provided for a considerable portion of each week. This rule does not apply if the person who is being cared for is in a care home, an Abbeyfield Home or an independent hospital;[126]
- you or your partner are a **16/17-year-old** who can claim income-based JSA (see p371) and would experience hardship if no payment were made (or if you are a joint-claim couple, the couple will experience hardship);
- you or your partner are claiming JSA on the basis of a **severe hardship direction** (see p373). You do not have to show that you would experience hardship. However, you do not count as in a vulnerable group if the person subject to the direction does not satisfy the labour market conditions (see p374); *or*
- you (or if you are a joint-claim couple, at least one of you) are under 21 at the date of your hardship statement and within the last three years were **being looked after by the local authority**, were someone the local authority had a duty to keep in touch with under the Children Act 1989, or you qualified for advice and assistance. Remember that if you are 16 or 17 and were being looked after by a local authority when you reached 16, you usually cannot claim income-based JSA. Instead, your local authority should support and accommodate you. See p609 for further information and exceptions to the rule.

Deciding hardship

'Hardship' is not defined in the rules. The DWP says that it means 'severe suffering or privation' (meaning 'a lack of the necessities of life').[127] When deciding whether or not someone would experience hardship, the decision maker must consider:[128]

- whether you, or a member of your family (see p366) qualify for a disability premium (see p779) or the disability element or severe disability element of child tax credit (CTC) (see p1234);
- the resources likely to be available to you or a member of your family (see p366) if no hardship payments are made, how far these fall short of the amount of hardship payments to which you would be entitled (see p427) and the length of time this is likely to be the case;
- whether there is a 'substantial risk' that you or a member of your family (see p366) would be without essential items (eg, food, clothes, heating and accommodation) or whether they would be available at considerably reduced levels and, if so, for how long.

If your claim is refused, you should always consider applying for a revision or appealing (see Chapters 41 and 42).

Available resources

When deciding whether you have resources available to you, the decision maker normally takes into account income and capital that is disregarded when calculating income-based JSA – eg, DLA or savings below £6,000 (see p910). Also included are any resources that may be available from someone in your household who is not a member of your family.

You should only be treated as having resources that are likely to be actually available to you. For example, you may have savings in a bank account but they are subject to a notice period for withdrawal and so you may face hardship until you get access to your capital.

The rules about your age

You cannot usually qualify for hardship payments until you are 18. However, if you are aged 16 or 17, you can claim if you come into any of the categories of 16/17-year-olds who qualify for income-based JSA (see p371). If you are 16 or 17, and have been sanctioned, in many situations you do not need to claim hardship payments because you continue to get income-based JSA but at a reduced rate (see p420).

The amount of hardship payments

The weekly amount of hardship payments you get depends on your needs. Your personal allowance, premiums and housing costs are calculated as for income-based JSA (see p368). The normal disregards for capital and income are applied when calculating your hardship payments. However, your applicable amount is normally reduced by 40 per cent of:[129]

- if you are not a member of a couple, the appropriate personal allowance for a single person of your age;

- if you are a member of a couple (other than a joint-claim couple), the appropriate personal allowance for a single person:
  - aged 16–24, if both of you are aged 16 or 17, or if one of you is between 18 and 24 years old and the other is a 16/17-year-old who does not qualify for income-based JSA;
  - aged 25 or over, in all other cases, so long as one of you is 18 or over;
- if you are a joint-claim couple, the appropriate personal allowance for a single person:
  - aged 18–24, if one of you is between 18 and 24 years old and the other is a 16/17-year-old who can claim income-based JSA (other than severe hardship payments);
  - aged 25 or over, in all other cases, so long as one of you is 18 or over.

The reduction is only 20 per cent if you or a member of your family (see p366) are pregnant or seriously ill. 'Seriously ill' is not defined in the rules, but the DWP says it means an important, significant or severe illness (it does not have to be long term or permanent).[130]

Claiming hardship payments

Because hardship payments are not a separate benefit, you do not have to make a claim for them. But in order to be satisfied that you are in hardship, the decision maker needs to know a great deal more about your circumstances than you are likely to have stated when you claimed income-based JSA. You cannot get hardship payments until you (or if you are a joint-claim couple, either of you) have made and signed a **'hardship statement'**.[131]

Your hardship statement is normally recorded at an interview. You are asked about your personal circumstances and medical conditions, what savings you have, what other benefits you are getting, what other money you have coming in and how much you owe. You are asked to give permission for the DWP to contact your GP if further medical evidence is required.

Although you cannot receive hardship payments until you have made your hardship statement, there is no general rule to prevent you from receiving these for a period before the date on which you made the statement. A special rule applies where you qualify for hardship payments because you are waiting for a decision at the beginning of your JSA claim (see p423).

The likelihood of being able to convince the decision maker that you are experiencing hardship increases over time. You should make a fresh hardship claim at any time you are without the normal payment of JSA.

Getting paid

While you are receiving hardship payments, you normally have to make a 'hardship declaration' at the Jobcentre Plus office each time you sign on, to confirm that you are still in hardship.[132] If it seems that you are no longer in hardship, the decision maker can revise or supersede the decision to award you hardship payments.

Challenging a hardship payment decision

If you are refused hardship payments you have a right of appeal to an appeal tribunal (see Chapter 42) but this takes time and you may be able to get matters resolved more quickly if you ask first for the decision to be revised (see p1065). To help you do this, you can ask for a written statement of reasons for the decision if this has not already been provided (see p1061).

Remember to tell the DWP if your circumstances worsen while you are seeking a revision or appealing. Ask the DWP to consider whether hardship payments can now be paid based on your new circumstances. If you have a partner, check to see if s/he can claim IS, PC or JSA instead of you.

Tax, tax credits and other benefits

Hardship payments are taxable in the same way as any other type of JSA (see p394).

Claiming other benefits or tax credits

As hardship payments are paid at a reduced rate, if you have a partner, you should consider whether s/he could claim JSA (or IS or PC) instead of you. If so, you should continue to claim hardship payments until her/his claim has been decided (to cover the period while the claim is being processed). However, you should let the DWP know that this is what you are doing so that there is no overpayment. If your partner's claim for benefit is accepted, your entitlement to hardship payments ends. You may wish to continue to sign on to protect your national insurance record (see p728).

If you have children, check to see if you qualify for child tax credit. If your partner counts as in full-time paid work for working tax credit (WTC) purposes (see Chapter 50), check to see if you might be better off claiming WTC.

Passported benefits

Hardship payments are a type of income-based JSA and you are still entitled to full housing benefit and council tax benefit, payments from the social fund[133] and other passported benefits in the usual way (see p396).

8. Laws about minimum working conditions

Employers are required to provide certain minimum working conditions. These rules are relevant to the jobseeker's allowance (JSA) rules about sanctions and being available for work. A brief summary of the rules follows.

The Working Time Regulations

These regulations are designed to protect the health and safety of workers. The main rules are:

- a limit on the hours in the average working week;
- minimum annual holiday entitlement;
- entitlement to breaks from work (both daily breaks and a longer break once a week) and to rest periods while at work;
- special protection for night workers.

This *Handbook* cannot cover the detailed rules nor the complicated system of exceptions to them. You should seek specialist advice if you think your employer is breaking these rules.

The National Minimum Wage Act

This Act provides that the minimum hourly rate of pay in any job should be:

- if you are aged 22 or over, £5.52 (£5.73 from October 2008);
- if you are aged 18–21, £4.60 (£4.77 from October 2008);
- if you are under age 18 and not of compulsory school age, £3.40 (£3.53 from October 2008).

The effect on jobseeker's allowance

The rules about minimum working conditions can affect your claim for JSA if you leave a job and also if you are looking for work.

Leaving a job voluntarily

If you give up a job because you believe that your employer is not complying with the legal requirements described above, you cannot necessarily argue 'just cause' (see p404). This is because of the principle that leaving a job must always be seen as the last resort and you should first do everything else possible to resolve problems before giving up your job.

If all else fails or if you feel that the hours you are being expected to work or the amount of pay you are receiving is intolerable, you might decide to give up work. In that case the laws about minimum working conditions could help you to show 'just cause'. You should point out that the intention of the Working Time Regulations is to protect the health and safety of workers, so conditions that do not comply with them should be regarded as unacceptable.

In considering 'just cause', no account should be taken of the 'level of remuneration' of the job in question (see p405). However, the DWP says this does not apply if you left your job because you tried to get your employer to pay the national minimum wage and your employer is not doing so.[134]

Placing restrictions on your availability

It should be possible for you to place a restriction on your availability for work – ie, that you will not accept a job, the terms of which do not comply with the legal requirements (eg, where an employer is offering a job at less than the minimum wage). You can try to argue that the rule that says you must still have reasonable prospects of finding work despite the restriction (see p353) should not apply as the DWP ought to assume that all employers will obey the law.

Refusing to apply for a job

You should try to argue that you have 'good cause' (see p409) for not applying for any job where the terms do not comply with the legal requirements. You need to be careful to make sure that this is so, particularly where the Working Time Regulations are concerned, in view of the many exceptions and opt-outs that might apply. If the terms offered break the rules about the hour limit on the average working week, it is possible that the DWP might suggest that you should agree to an 'individual opt-out'. You should argue that this would be unreasonable, as the working time rules are intended to protect the health and safety of workers. The DWP says you *do* have good cause for refusing a job if you do so because it does not pay at least the national minimum wage that applies to you.[135]

Notes

1 Reg 2(3)(a) HB Regs; reg 2(3)(a) HB(SPC) Regs

1. **Employment-related sanctions**

2 ss19(5)(a), (6) and 20A(2)(a) and (d)-(g) JSA 1995
3 Reg 75(4) JSA Regs
4 CJSA/3304/1999
5 ss19(6)(a) and 20A(2)(d) JSA 1995
6 R(U) 10/71
7 R(U) 2/76
8 R(U) 8/57, para 6
9 para 34106 DMG
10 R(U) 26/56; R(U) 1/58; para 34194 DMG
11 R(U) 10/53
12 R(U) 14/56
13 R(U) 24/56
14 R(U) 1/57; R(U) 14/57; CU/34/1992
15 R(U) 2/76
16 ss19(6)(b) and 20A(2)(e) JSA 1995
17 para 34241 DMG
18 R(U) 1/96; R(U) 27/59
19 para 34256 DMG
20 ss19(7) and 20A(9) JSA 1995; reg 71 JSA Regs; R(U) 3/91
21 Reg 71(2) JSA Regs
22 R(U) 25/52
23 *Crewe v Social Security Commissioner* [1982] 1 WLR 1209 (CA), also reported as R(U) 3/81; R(U) 20/64(T); R(U) 4/87
24 R(U) 20/64(T)
25 paras 34379-83 DMG; R(U) 4/73
26 para 34290 DMG; R(U) 3/73
27 R(U) 14/52
28 R(U) 19/52; R(U) 4/87; CJSA/2507/2005
29 ss19(9) and 20A(9) JSA 1995
30 paras 34384-86 DMG
31 R(U) 26/51; R(U) 20/64; R(U) 4/70; R(U) 1/81
32 R(U) 3/81

33 R(U) 4/87
34 ss19(5)(a) and 20A(2)(a) JSA 1995
35 ss19(10)(b) and 20A(9) JSA 1995
36 para 34651 DMG
37 ss19(6)(c) and 20A(2)(f) JSA 1995
38 para 34399 DMG
39 R(U) 32/52
40 para 34400 DMG; CJSA/2082/2002; CJSA/2692/1999
41 ss19(6)(d) and 20A(2)(g) JSA 1995
42 Reg 72(8) JSA Regs
43 paras 34591-92 DMG
44 s20(1) JSA 1995
45 Reg 72(9) JSA Regs
46 ss20(3)and 20B(3) JSA 1995
47 CJSA/1703/2006
48 Reg 74 JSA Regs
49 Reg 1(3) JSA Regs, definition of 'full-time student'
50 Reg 74(4) JSA Regs
51 para 34237 DMG
52 Reg 75(2) JSA Regs
53 Reg 72(5A) JSA Regs
54 ss20(1) and 20B(1) JSA 1995
55 Reg 72(5)(a) JSA Regs
56 Reg 72(4) JSA Regs
57 ss19(6)(d) and 20A(2)(g) JSA 1995; reg 72(8) and (9) JSA Regs
58 Reg 72(5)(a) JSA Regs
59 Reg 72(5)(b) JSA Regs
60 Reg 72(3A) and (3B) JSA Regs
61 Reg 72(2) JSA Regs
62 paras 34504-12 and 34684-88 DMG
63 ss19(9) and 20A(9) JSA 1995
64 Reg 72(6) JSA Regs
65 Reg 72(7) JSA Regs
66 Reg 72(6)(b) JSA Regs

2. **New Deal, training scheme and employment programme-related sanctions**

67 ss19(5) and 20A(2)(b) and (c) JSA 1995
68 para 34743 DMG
69 R(JSA) 2/06
70 Regs 1(3), definition of 'the New Deal options' and 75(1) JSA Regs
71 Reg 75(1)(b)(iii) JSA Regs
72 paras 14100-380 DMG
73 Reg 75(4) JSA Regs
74 The list in reg 73(2) JSA Regs is without prejudice to any other circumstances in which someone might be regarded as having good cause. R(JSA) 2/06 suggests otherwise, but it is submitted that in this respect the decision is wrong.
75 Reg 73(2) JSA Regs
76 R(JSA) 7/03 discusses the meaning of 'conscientious objection' in this context.
77 Reg 73(2B) and (4) JSA Regs
78 Reg 73(2A) JSA Regs

3. **Deciding if you should be sanctioned**

79 paras 34077-82 and 34228-31 DMG
80 para 34738 DMG

4. **Sanction periods and amount payable**

81 R(U) 24/56
82 ss19(2) and 20A(3) JSA 1995; reg 69(1) JSA Regs
83 Reg 69(1)(a) and (b) JSA Regs
84 Reg 3(6) SS&CS(DA) Regs
85 CJSA/2375/2000
86 Reg 69(1)(a) JSA Regs
87 Reg 69(1)(b) JSA Regs
88 Reg 69(1)(c) and (d) JSA Regs
89 Reg 69(3) and (4) JSA Regs
90 ss19(3) and 20A(4) JSA 1995
91 R(U) 8/74(T)
92 CJSA/1703/2006
93 CJSA/3875/2002
94 Reg 70 JSA Regs
95 paras 34045-46 DMG
96 ss19(1) and 20A(5)(a) JSA 1995
97 s20A(5)(b) and (7) JSA 1995
98 s20A(6) JSA 1995; reg 74BJSA Regs
99 Reg 74A JSA Regs

5. **Special rules for 16/17-year-olds**

100 Reg 57 JSA Regs, definition of 'young person'
101 Reg 67(1) JSA Regs
102 Reg 67(3) JSA Regs
103 ss16(3)(b), 17(3) and 20(2)(b) JSA 1995; reg 63 JSA Regs
104 Reg 67(2) JSA Regs
105 Reg 68 JSA Regs
106 ss16(3)(b), 17(3) and 20(2)(b) JSA 1995; reg 63 JSA Regs
107 Regs 63(1) and (3) and 68(1) and (2) JSA Regs

6. **Challenging a sanction decision**

108 Sch 3 para 3(d) SSA 1998
109 paras 34082, 34231 and 34739 DMG
110 R(U) 2/74
111 R(U) 10/54

7. **Hardship payments**

112 Regs 140(3) and 146A(3) JSA Regs
113 Regs 146 and 146H JSA Regs; reg 5 SS(PAOR) Regs
114 Regs 141(2), 142(2), 146C(2) and 146D(2) JSA Regs
115 Regs 141(3) and 146C(3) JSA Regs
116 Regs 142(2) and 146D(2) JSA Regs
117 Regs 141(4) and 146C(4) JSA Regs

118 Regs 141(5), 142(3), 146C(5) and 146D(3) JSA Regs
119 Regs 142(4) and 146D(4) JSA Regs
120 Regs 141(6), 142(5), 146C(6) and 146D(5) JSA Regs
121 para 35304 DMG
122 Regs 140(4A), 140A, 146A(5) and 146B JSA Regs
123 Regs 140(1) and (2) and 146A(1) and (2) JSA Regs
124 Regs 140(1) and 146A(1) JSA Regs
125 para 35073 DMG
126 Regs 140(4) and 146A(4) JSA Regs
127 para 35155 DMG
128 Regs 140(5) and 146A(6) JSA Regs
129 Regs 145 and 146G JSA Regs
130 R(SB) 19/82; para 35315 DMG
131 Regs 143 and 146E JSA Regs
132 Regs 144 and 146F JSA Regs
133 SF Dirs 8 and 25

8. **Laws about minimum working conditions**

134 para 34284 DMG
135 para 34437 DMG

Chapter 17

Maternity allowance

This chapter covers:

If you are pregnant or have recently given birth, and you are not entitled to statutory maternity pay (SMP – see Chapter 23), you may qualify for maternity allowance (MA). MA is paid by the DWP for a maximum of 39 weeks.

You do not have to have paid national insurance contributions to qualify for MA. Although you must satisfy an employment and an earnings condition, your entitlement to MA is not affected by any other income or savings you may have.

You cannot receive MA for any week in which you are entitled to SMP. So, for example, you may get MA rather than SMP if you are self-employed, or if you do not satisfy the earnings condition or continuous employment rule for SMP.

If you do not qualify for MA (or SMP), you may be entitled to statutory sick pay (unless you are within the periods mentioned on p563), or incapacity benefit (see Chapter 12) or, from when it is introduced, employment and support allowance (see Chapter 7).

Definitions of some of the terms used in this chapter are given on p442.

Note: the Government plans to increase the maximum period of payment of MA to 52 weeks. The date for this change has not yet been decided, but it is unlikely it will affect people whose baby is due before April 2010.[1] See CPAG's *Welfare Rights Bulletin* for updates.

1. Who can claim maternity allowance

You qualify for maternity allowance (MA) if:[2]

- you are pregnant or have recently given birth, and you are within your 'maternity allowance period' (see below);
- you satisfy the employment condition (see below);
- you satisfy the earnings condition (see below);
- you are not entitled to statutory maternity pay (SMP).

In certain circumstances you may be disqualified from receiving MA – eg, you may be disqualified if you work during your MA period. See p437 for details.

Maternity allowance period

MA is payable for a period of up to 39 consecutive weeks - known as the **'maternity allowance period'**.[3] The earliest date on which your MA period can start is from the beginning of the 11th week before the expected week of childbirth (EWC – see p442), unless your baby is born before this, and the latest is the day after your baby is born. Within these limits, the rules for when your MA period starts are the same as those for SMP (see p536) except that:[4]

- if you are not working at the beginning of the 11th week before your EWC, your MA period will start from the beginning of that week; *and*
- if you are not entitled to MA during the 11th week before your EWC, but you become entitled to it before your baby is born (perhaps because you then meet the earnings or employment condition), as long as you have stopped work, the earliest day on which your MA period can start is the day you become entitled to MA and the latest is the day after the birth.

Employment condition

In order to qualify for MA you must have worked as an employee and/or been self-employed for at least 26 weeks in the 66 weeks immediately before your EWC (see p442). This 66-week period is known as the **'test period'**.[5] If you work for just part of a week, the whole of that week counts towards the 26-week requirement. The 26 weeks do not need to be consecutive and you do not need to have worked for the same employer for the whole period. You need only show that you have been employed and/or self-employed for any part of each of the 26 weeks.

Some women can take periods of employment in other European Economic Area countries (including A8 and A2 states – see p1383) into account when calculating the number of weeks in which they have been employed (see p1389).

Earnings condition

To qualify for MA your average weekly earnings (or, if you are self-employed, the average weekly earnings you are treated as having) must be at least equal to the

MA threshold of £30 a week (see below for how your average earnings are calculated).[6]

Earnings from employment

If you are employed, your gross earnings are used to calculate your average weekly earnings. What counts as earnings for MA purposes is the same as for SMP (see p532).[7] Any backdated pay rises which are paid for the period over which your earnings are averaged (see below) are included, as are any payments which the Revenue has retrospectively treated as earnings for that period under backdated tax legislation.[8]

Earnings from self-employment

If you are self-employed you are treated as earning the following amount each week and this figure is used to calculate your average weekly earnings, irrespective of the amount you actually earn:[9]

- for each week that you hold a national insurance (NI) small earnings exception certificate (see p724), you are treated as having weekly earnings equal to the MA threshold of £30 a week; *and*
- for each week for which you have paid a Class 2 NI contribution, you are treated as having weekly earnings of an amount 90 per cent of which is equal to the maximum amount of MA that can be paid for that week. From 7 April 2008, as the maximum amount of MA that can be paid is £117.18, you are treated as having earnings of £130.20 a week. (For weeks between 9 April 2007 and 6 April 2008 you would have been treated as having weekly earnings of £125.28.) If you have paid a Class 2 contribution for at least 13 weeks in your 66-week test period you will qualify for MA of £117.18 a week.[10]

Calculating average earnings

Your average weekly earnings are calculated as follows.

- If you have paid Class 2 contributions as a self-employed person for at least 13 of the weeks in your 66-week test period, add together your earnings in the first 13 weeks in your test period and divide the total by 13. In this situation you will qualify for MA of £117.18 a week.
- If you have not paid Class 2 contributions in at least 13 weeks in your 66-week test period – eg, because you were not self-employed or your earnings from self-employment were not high enough, add together your earnings in the 13 weeks in your 66-week test period (see p442) when your earnings are highest and divide the total by 13.[11]

In both cases, the 13 weeks do not need to be consecutive and if you have more than one job, the earnings from all your jobs, including earnings you are treated as having from self-employment, are counted.[12] If you are not paid weekly, work out your weekly earnings by dividing the payments you receive by the nearest number of weeks in the period for which they are paid.[13]

More than one job

If you are receiving SMP from one job, you cannot receive MA for the same week on the basis of another job you have or from self-employment.

Disqualification from benefit

You will be disqualified from receiving MA for a period if:[14]

- you work for more than 10 days during your MA period. When calculating whether you have worked for more than 10 days, both employed and self-employed work counts and the 10 days do not need to be consecutive. If you work for part of a day it counts as a full day. (Any payment your receive for the 10 days' work does not affect your MA);
- without good cause, you fail to take 'due care of your health' or to answer 'reasonable enquiries' from the DWP about whether you are doing so. The enquiries should not relate to any medical examination, treatment or advice you have or have not been given;
- prior to the birth of your baby you fail to attend a medical examination without good cause. You must have been given written notice of the examination at least three days beforehand by the DWP or someone acting on its behalf.

The question of whether or not you have good cause for your behaviour depends on your circumstances.

The DWP can disqualify you for as long as is reasonable given the circumstances. However, if you are disqualified because:

- you have worked for more than 10 days in your MA period, the disqualification must be for at least the number of days that you worked in excess of those 10 days;
- you have not attended a medical examination, the disqualification cannot continue once you have given birth.

If you disagree with the DWP, you can challenge its decision on whether you have good cause or on the length of the disqualification period (see p442).

Note: if you are employed and on maternity leave, working for more than 10 days may affect your continued entitlement to leave (and so affect your entitlement to MA). If you do not want to bring your period of maternity leave to an end, seek employment advice before agreeing to such work.

2. The rules about your age

There are no upper or lower age limits for receiving maternity allowance.

3. Claiming for others

You may be entitled to an increase in your maternity allowance for an adult dependant (see Chapter 29).

4. The amount of benefit[15]

	£ per week
Claimant	the lesser of 117.18 or 90% of earnings
Adult dependant	39.40
Maternity allowance threshold	30.00

You will only qualify for maternity allowance (MA) if your average weekly earnings are at least equal to the MA threshold (see p443).[16] See p436 for how your average earnings are calculated. The amount of MA you receive is either 90 per cent of your average weekly earnings or £117.18 a week, whichever is less. MA is only payable during your 'maternity allowance period' (see p435).

If you satisfy the contribution conditions for incapacity benefit (IB) and your MA is less than the amount of IB you would qualify for, see p444 (but note the information given on the introduction of employment and support allowance).

5. Special benefit rules

There are some groups of claimants to whom special rules apply. These are covered below and in Chapters 26 and 58. Special rules apply to you if:

- you are in prison or legal custody (see p625);
- you go abroad (see p1352).

There are also special rules if you have returned from abroad where you worked in the 12 months immediately before the end of the 15th week before your expected week of childbirth and you are ordinarily resident in Great Britain.[17]

6. Claims and backdating

To be entitled to maternity allowance (MA) you must make a claim for it.[18] The rules on claiming are described below and in Chapter 38. It may be possible to claim in advance (see p440) or to get your claim backdated (see p441).

If you are (or have recently been) employed, you may be entitled to statutory maternity pay (SMP – see Chapter 23) from your employer (or ex-employer). You cannot qualify for MA if you are entitled to SMP. If your employer (or ex-employer) has decided you are not entitled to SMP, claim MA. If you disagree with the decision, ask the Revenue to make a decision on your entitlement (see Chapter 43). The employer should give you Form SMP1 which you should send to the DWP to support your claim for MA. If you are challenging the SMP decision, make a copy of the SMP1 for the Revenue. The DWP will normally ask the Revenue to decide your entitlement to SMP before it makes a decision on your MA claim.

Making a claim

A claim for MA must be made in writing on the appropriate application form (MA1). Your local antenatal clinic or any Jobcentre Plus office may have the form, or you can get one from www.jobcentreplus.gov.uk or by telephoning Jobcentre Plus (see p956). The decision maker at the DWP may accept a written application that is not on the correct form if this is sufficient in the circumstances (see p959).[19] Your claim will not be accepted unless it is received after the 15th week before your expected week of childbirth (EWC).[20]

If you want an increase for an adult dependant (see Chapter 29), you must make a claim for this by filling in the relevant section of the MA1 form.

You should send your claim, together with an SMP1 form from your employer (if applicable – see above), to the DWP office which covers your local area (usually this will be a regional benefit delivery centre). If an envelope with the relevant address is not included with the form, you can get the address by telephoning Jobcentre Plus, or from your local Jobcentre Plus or DWP office.

It is advisable to keep a copy of your claim in case queries arise.

Information to support your claim

When you claim MA, you and any adult dependant for whom you are claiming must satisfy the national insurance number requirement (see p962). You must also provide medical evidence, normally a certificate from your doctor or a registered midwife, giving the expected date of birth of your child and, if you are claiming MA after your baby is born, giving the date of the baby's birth (Form MAT B1).[21] This certificate will not be accepted as evidence of your EWC if it is issued before the 20th week before your EWC. If you cannot obtain a MAT B1, the DWP can accept other medical evidence of the expected date of birth or actual date of birth, if this is sufficient – eg, a birth certificate.

If you have been employed the DWP will expect you to provide pay slips or some other written proof of your earnings and an SMP1 form from any employer for whom you worked during the 15th week before your EWC (see p439).

Do not delay sending in your claim for MA because you are waiting for your MAT B1, SMP1, or evidence of your earnings. You can send these in later, when you get them.

Who should claim

If you are unable to manage your own affairs, another person can claim MA for you as your 'appointee' (see p955).

The date of your claim

The date of your claim is normally the date it is received at a DWP office.[22]

If the claim you submit is incomplete or not on the correct form you may be asked to provide further information or to complete the correct form. As long as the DWP receives this additional information from you within a month of it being sent back to you (or longer if the decision maker thinks that the delay is reasonable), your claim is treated as made on the date the initial claim was received at the DWP office (see p959).[23] In some circumstances you can claim before you qualify for MA, or the date of your claim can be backdated (see p441).

If you claim the wrong benefit

A claim for incapacity benefit (IB – see Chapter 12) may be treated as a claim for MA and vice versa (see p964).[24] This may allow you to get your claim for MA backdated for more than the normal three months. If your employer (or former employer) has decided that you are not entitled to SMP and you claim MA within three months of being notified of your employer's decision in writing, your claim for MA is treated as having been made either on the date on which you gave the employer notice of when you wanted the maternity pay period to start or at the beginning of the 14th week before your EWC, whichever is later.[25]

Claiming in advance

You cannot make a claim for MA until after the 15th week before your EWC (ie, until week 26 of pregnancy) but you should claim as soon as possible after that.[26] However, it may be worth waiting a few weeks before claiming if this means you will have higher average earnings and this would increase the amount of your MA. If you plan to stop work after the 11th week before the EWC and you claim while you are still working, the DWP will send you Form BM25A, notifying you of your entitlement and asking to be informed of the actual date you stop work.

How your claim is dealt with

Your claim is dealt with by the DWP office that covers your local area, and queries about your claim should be made to that office.

You may be able to claim an interim payment if you are waiting for a decision on your claim (see p986) or a crisis loan to tide you over until benefit is paid (see p503). You could also claim means-tested benefits if your income is low (see p443).

See p970 for more information about the processing of claims.

Backdating your claim

A claim for MA can be backdated for up to three months if you satisfy the normal MA qualifying conditions. You do not have to show any reasons why your claim was late.[27]

If you might have qualified for benefit earlier but did not claim because you were given the wrong information or misled by the DWP you could ask for an *ex gratia* payment (see p1186) or complain to the Independent Case Examiner or to the Ombudsman via your MP (see pp1181 and 1184).

If you have claimed IB instead of MA or if you have been refused SMP, see p440.

7. Getting paid

Maternity allowance (MA) can be paid from the start of the MA period (see p435) for up to 39 weeks. It is a daily benefit, which means that it can be paid for periods of less than a week. The daily rate is one-seventh of the weekly amount.[28]

MA is normally paid by direct credit transfer into your bank (or similar) account. If you are unable to open or manage an account, payment can be made by cheque (see p979 for details).[29]

Payments are normally made each Friday for payment from the previous Sunday.[30] You are entitled to national insurance contribution credits for each week you receive MA (because you will normally be treated as incapable of work in those weeks – see p728).

If your benefit is not paid into your account or your benefit cheque is lost or stolen, see p983. If payment of your MA is suspended, see p984.

Delays and complaints

If payment of your MA is delayed, you might be able to get an interim payment (see p986).

If you experience delays, or wish to complain about how your claim has been dealt with, see Chapter 46. You might be able to claim compensation (see p1186).

Change of circumstances

You must report any change in your circumstances which the DWP has informed you that you must tell it about (but it is important to remember that the DWP might not inform you of all the changes you need to tell it about). It is your duty to also report *any* change which you might reasonably be expected to know might affect your entitlement to, the amount of, or the payment of, your benefit. You should report such changes promptly either by writing to, or by telephoning, the office handling your claim, unless the DWP has decided you can tell it about the change another way. In some cases, the decision maker might say you must report changes in writing.[31] In practice, it is *always* advisable to report the change in writing or to confirm a telephone conversation in writing and keep a copy of your letter in case of a future dispute. If you do not promptly report any such change, any resulting overpayment may be recoverable from you (see Chapter 39). If you are considered deliberately to have acted falsely or dishonestly, you may also be guilty of an offence (see Chapter 40).

If the change affects your entitlement to MA, a decision maker will look at your claim again and make a new decision (see p1074). The date from which the new decision takes effect depends on whether or not it is advantageous to you and whether you reported the change in time (see p1080 for further details).

Overpayments and fraud

If you are overpaid MA, you might have to repay it. The rules on overpayments are covered in Chapter 39.

If you have been accused of fraud, see Chapter 40.

8. Challenging a maternity allowance decision

You can apply for a revision or supersession of a maternity allowance decision, or appeal against it (see Chapters 41 and 42). Certain decisions cannot be appealed, although you can request that they be revised or superseded (see p1097).

9. Definitions of terms

- The '**expected week of childbirth**'(sometimes called the '**expected week of confinement**') is the week, starting on a Sunday, in which your baby is due to be born.
- The '**maternity allowance period**' is the period of up to 39 weeks during which maternity allowance (MA) is paid. See p435 for when it can start.
- The '**test period**' is the period of 66 weeks immediately before the week in which your baby is due, which is used to calculate entitlement to MA.

- The **'maternity allowance threshold'** is the minimum level of average earnings you need to qualify for MA.

Example

Rita's baby is due on Saturday 19 July 2008. The following dates apply.

- The 'expected week of childbirth' begins on the Sunday before – ie, Sunday 13 July 2008.
- The first week before the 'expected week of childbirth' begins on Sunday 6 July 2008, the second on Sunday 29 June 2008 and so on.
- The 11th week before the 'expected week of childbirth' begins on Sunday 27 April 2008. This is important because it is normally the earliest date from which Rita can be paid MA (or statutory maternity pay).
- The 66-week 'test period' runs from Sunday 8 April 2007 to Saturday 12 July 2008.

Appendix 5 contains a table of relevant dates for all the weeks in 2008/09.

10. Tax, tax credits and other benefits

Maternity allowance (MA) is not taxable.[32]

Tax credits

If you have a partner who is in full-time paid work you may qualify for working tax credit (WTC – see Chapter 49) in addition to your MA. In some circumstances, you may also qualify for WTC if you are receiving MA or you are either on ordinary maternity leave or within the first 13 weeks of your additional maternity leave (see p1229 for details).

If you are entitled to WTC, you may be able to get help with the cost of childcare for your new baby even before you return to work (see p1240).

If you have a dependent child you may also qualify for child tax credit (CTC – see Chapter 48).

MA is ignored when calculating your entitlement to tax credits.

Means-tested benefits

If you have a low income you may be able to get income support (IS – see Chapter 13) while you are on maternity leave (see p294). If your partner is 60 or over s/he may instead qualify for pension credit for you (PC – see Chapter 18).

If you have a low income you may also be entitled to housing benefit (HB – see Chapter 10) and council tax benefit (CTB – see Chapter 5). If you are getting MA you may be able to get an allowance for childcare costs deducted from your earnings when calculating your entitlement to HB and CTB – see p856.

You cannot claim jobseeker's allowance (JSA) if you are getting MA because you are treated as unavailable for work, but your partner may qualify.[33] If you and your partner would normally have to make a joint claim for JSA (see p381) then:

- if you are incapable of work because of your pregnancy, you do not need to meet the labour market conditions – only your partner must; *or*
- your partner can receive JSA for you both without you needing to make a joint claim if you are getting MA (or statutory maternity pay), or from the 11th week before your expected week of childbirth until 15 weeks after the baby is born.

The MA you get is taken into account in full when calculating your entitlement to IS, income-based JSA, HB and CTB.

For PC, any MA you receive counts as benefit income but is ignored when calculating your qualifying income for the savings credit of PC (see Chapter 18).[34]

Non-means-tested benefits

MA is affected by the overlapping benefit rules (see p981).

You cannot get contribution-based JSA (see Chapter 15) or statutory sick pay (SSP) if you are receiving MA. See p563 for how your SSP entitlement is affected if you are pregnant.

Incapacity benefit

If you are pregnant you can be treated as incapable of work for incapacity benefit (IB) purposes (and so you may qualify for IB) while you are entitled to MA (see p263) or in the circumstances explained on p665.[35] If you are entitled to both MA and IB and the amount of IB you are entitled to is more than your MA, you receive the higher amount of benefit. You cannot receive both benefits in full because of the overlapping benefit rules. Decision makers are advised that you do not need to submit a separate claim for IB in this situation (see p964).[36]

Days on which you were entitled to MA count when calculating whether you are entitled to the higher rate of short-term IB or long-term IB.

Note: the introduction of employment and support allowance (see Chapter 7), planned for October 2008, will affect these rules. See CPAG's *Welfare Rights Bulletin* for updates.

Passports and other sources of help

If you have been awarded IS, income-based JSA, PC, the disability or severe disability element of WTC, or CTC paid at a higher rate than the family element, you may be entitled to a Sure Start maternity grant of £500 per child from the social fund (see p513). You might be able to get other help from the discretionary social fund (see Chapter 21).

For the qualifying conditions for free school meals for children, see p15.

For information on your possible entitlement to certain health service benefits and Healthy Start welfare food vouchers, see Chapter 9.

Note: the Government plans to introduce a 'health in pregnancy grant' of £190 in April 2009. This will be payable to all pregnant women after the 24th week of pregnancy as long they have had specific health advice from a health care professional.

Notes

1 ss35(2) and 165 SSCBA 1992

1. **Who can claim maternity allowance**
2 s35 SSCBA 1992
3 s35(2) and 165 SSCBA 1992; reg 2(2) SMP Regs
4 s35(2) and 165 SSCBA 1992; reg 2 SMP Regs; reg 3 SS(MatA) Regs
5 s35(1)(b) SSCBA 1992
6 ss35(1)(c) and (6A) and 35A(4) SSCBA 1992
7 s35A(4)(a) SSCBA 1992; reg 2 SS(MatA)(E) Regs
8 Regs 2(1)(za) and 6(2) SS(MatA)(E) Regs
9 Reg 3 SS(MatA)(E) Regs
10 s35A(5)(c), (5A) and (5B) SSCBA 1992; reg 5 SS(MatA)(E) Regs
11 Reg 6(1) SS(MatA)(E) Regs
12 Reg 4(1) SS(MatA)(E) Regs
13 Reg 6(3) SS(MatA)(E) Regs
14 Reg 2 SS(MatA) Regs

4. **The amount of benefit**
15 ss35(1) and 35A SSCBA 1992
16 s35(1)(c) SSCBA 1992

5. **Special benefit rules**
17 SS(MatA)(WA) Regs

6. **Claims and backdating**
18 s1 SSAA 1992
19 Reg 4(1) SS(C&P) Regs
20 Reg 14(1) SS(C&P) Regs
21 Reg 2(3) SS(ME) Regs
22 Reg 6(1) SS(C&P) Regs
23 Regs 4(7) and 6(1) SS(C&P) Regs
24 Reg 9 and Sch 1 Part I SS(C&P) Regs
25 Reg 10(3) and (4) SS(C&P) Regs
26 Reg 14 SS(C&P) Regs
27 Reg 19(2) SS(C&P) Regs

7. **Getting paid**
28 s35(5) SSCBA 1992
29 Reg 21 SS(C&P) Regs
30 Reg 24(4) SS(C&P) Regs
31 Reg 32(1)-(1B) SS(C&P) Regs

10. **Tax, tax credits and other benefits**
32 s677 IT(EP)A 2003
33 Reg 15(c) JSA Regs
34 Regs 9 and 15(1) SPC Regs
35 s30C(2) SSCBA 1992; reg 14 SS(IFW) Regs
36 para 56115 DMG

Chapter 18

Pension credit

This chapter covers:

Pension credit (PC) is a benefit for people aged 60 or over. The purpose of PC is to ensure that pensioners have a guaranteed level of income and are rewarded for having made provisions for retirement, such as savings, above the basic state pension.

PC consists of two elements:

- guarantee credit;
- savings credit.

You may be entitled to either or both of these elements.

PC is administered by the Pension Service, an executive agency of the DWP.

1. Who can claim pension credit

Guarantee credit

You are entitled to a guarantee credit if:[1]

- you are 60 or over (see p447);[2]
- you are in Great Britain (GB) (with exceptions for periods of temporary absence) and satisfy the 'habitual residence' test and the 'right to reside' test (see Chapter 59);[3]
- you have no income or your income is below the appropriate minimum guarantee (see p448);[4]

- you are not a 'person subject to immigration control', although there are exceptions to this rule (see p1334).[5]

Savings credit

You are entitled to a savings credit if:[6]

- you or your partner are 65 or over (see below);[7]
- you are in GB (with exceptions for periods of temporary absence) and satisfy the 'habitual residence' test and the 'right to reside' test (see Chapter 59);[8]
- you are not a 'person subject to immigration control', although there are exceptions to this rule (see p1334);[9]
- you have 'qualifying income' that exceeds the 'savings credit threshold' but is not too high to produce a nil award (see p450).[10]

2. The rules about your age

Entitlement to pension credit is linked to the minimum qualifying age at which a woman can receive state pension, which is currently 60.[11] However, this age will rise steadily to 65 between 2010 and 2020. Once it is equalised, the age for both men and women will rise to 68 between 2024 and 2046.

Additionally, you or your partner must be 65 or over in order to qualify for the savings credit element.[12]

3. Claiming for others

You claim for yourself and your partner (if you have one) and for each additional spouse in a polygamous marriage. If you have a child for whom you are responsible, you should claim child tax credit (see Chapter 48) as there are no child amounts payable with pension credit. See Chapter 30 for who counts as your family.

4. The amount of credit

How much pension credit (PC) you receive depends on whether you are single or a member of a couple, or have any disabilities, any caring responsibilities or any eligible housing costs. The maximum amount of guarantee credit you could receive is reduced by your income (subject to any applicable disregards). For savings credit the rules are slightly more complicated (see p450). For information on income and capital, see Chapters 36 and 37. However, for the details on qualifying income for savings credit, see p450.

Guarantee credit

Your maximum guarantee credit is known as the 'appropriate minimum guarantee'[13] and is made up of:

- standard minimum guarantee; *and*
- where applicable, additional amounts.

Standard minimum guarantee

If you do not have any additional needs you will receive an award of PC, which will ensure that your weekly income is brought up to one of the following standard minimum guarantee levels.

Single person[14]	£124.05
Couple[15]	£189.35
Each additional spouse in a polygamous marriage[16]	£65.30

Additional amounts

If you have additional needs, such as a disability, caring responsibilities or housing costs, your award will bring your income to the level of the standard minimum guarantee plus additional amounts. These broadly correspond to the premiums and housing costs payable with IS, with an additional transitional amount to ensure that those in receipt of IS or income-based jobseeker's allowance (JSA) at the time they first become entitled to PC are not worse off as a result of the change.

The additional amounts are:

Severe disability[17] The qualifying rules for this amount are broadly the same as for the IS severe disability premium (see p784).	£50.35	£100.70 (if both partners qualify)
Carer[18] The rules are the same as those for the IS carer's premium (see p789).	£27.75	£27.75 (for each partner who qualifies)
Housing costs[19] These provisions are covered in Chapter 34 and broadly mirror those for IS, but with some exceptions.	See Chapter 34	
Transitional[20]	See below	

Transitional amount[21]

If you are in receipt of IS or income-based JSA when you first become entitled to PC, in order to ensure that you are not worse off by moving onto PC, you appropriate minimum guarantee may include a 'transitional amount'. You will be eligible for this extra amount if, on the day you first become entitled to PC, your IS or income-based JSA applicable amount (less any amounts for dependent children or any residential allowance) exceeds your appropriate minimum guarantee.

The transitional amount will reduce over time by any increase in your appropriate minimum guarantee and will cease when you or your partner stop being entitled to PC (disregarding any break in entitlement of less than eight weeks).[22]

The guarantee credit calculation

Step one: calculate your appropriate minimum guarantee

This consists of:

- standard minimum guarantee for you and your partner, if you have one; *plus*
- additional amounts for any special needs and/or housing costs.

Step two: calculate your income[23]

This is the amount you have coming in each week from, for example, some state benefits, private pensions and earnings. Not all income counts (eg, disability living allowance (DLA), attendance allowance (AA), child tax credit and child benefit) and some income is subject to disregards (see Chapter 36, but also see p458 for assessed income periods). If you have capital over £6,000 (£10,000 if you live in a care home) you will be treated as having £1 for every £500 (or part of £500) capital that exceeds £6,000 (£10,000 if you live in a care home).[24]

Step three: deduct income from appropriate minimum guarantee

The amount of your guarantee credit is your appropriate minimum guarantee less any relevant income you have.[25] If your income is above the appropriate minimum guarantee you will not qualify for any guarantee credit, but you might qualify for some savings credit. Additionally, you may qualify for guarantee credit if you or your partner become entitled to a qualifying benefit, like AA, which would increase the amount of your appropriate minimum guarantee.

Examples

Barbara is single and aged 68. She is in receipt of AA. She lives alone and no one gets carer's allowance for looking after her. She lives in rented accommodation.

Her appropriate minimum guarantee is:

Standard minimum guarantee (single person rate)	£124.05
Severe disability additional amount	£50.35
Total	£174.40

Her weekly income is her basic state pension of £62. AA is ignored as income.

She is therefore entitled to £112.40 guarantee credit to bring her total income up to £174.40.

She is not entitled to any savings credit as she does not have any qualifying income above the savings credit threshold (see p450).

She will also be entitled to maximum housing benefit (HB) and council tax benefit (CTB) and any other passports that may apply.

Maria and Geoff are a couple. Maria is 62 and Geoff is 67. Their 24-year-old daughter lives with them and she is in receipt of income-based JSA. They have eligible weekly housing costs of £40. Maria receives the middle rate care component of DLA and Geoff gets AA.

Their appropriate minimum guarantee is:

Standard minimum guarantee (couple rate)	£189.35
Eligible housing costs	£40.00
Total	£229.35

Their joint weekly income for calculating PC is £238.05, made up of basic state pension of £145.05 (Maria £54.35, Geoff £90.70), occupational pension of £90 and £3 deemed income from £7,500 savings. DLA and AA are ignored as income.

They are not entitled to any guarantee credit because their income exceeds their appropriate minimum guarantee of £229.35. Their appropriate minimum guarantee does not include a severe disability addition because their 24-year-old daughter lives with them. However, they are entitled to some savings credit as they have qualifying income above the savings credit threshold (see below).

Savings credit

In order to qualify for this element of PC you must have qualifying income above the **'savings credit threshold'** of:[26]

Single person	£91.20
Couple	£145.80

'Qualifying income' for the purposes of entitlement to savings credit is all income that counts for guarantee credit (see Chapters 36 and 37) except:[27]

- working tax credit;
- incapacity benefit (IB);
- contribution-based JSA;
- severe disablement allowance;
- maternity allowance;
- maintenance payments for you, or your partner, from a spouse or former spouse.

The amount of savings credit to which you are entitled is subject to a maximum figure known as the '**maximum savings credit**'[28] and these are different for a single claimant and a couple.

Single person	£19.71
Couple	£26.13

The savings credit calculation[29]

If you have already calculated whether you are entitled to the guarantee credit you will already have worked out the amounts in Steps one and two. If you are entitled to the guarantee credit, you only need to follow Steps one to four below.

Step one: calculate your total income figure
This is any income that counts for PC purposes and includes qualifying income.

Step two: calculate your appropriate minimum guarantee
This is the standard minimum guarantee plus any additional amounts.

Step three: calculate 60 per cent of any qualifying income you have which is above the savings credit threshold that applies to you (subject to the maximum savings credit payable)
This is 60 per cent of all your income that counts for the guarantee credit, other than non-qualifying income listed on p450, above the savings credit threshold of £91.20 (if you are single) or £145.80 (if you are a couple). The figure you calculate is the maximum savings credit you can receive, but it is subject to a cap: you cannot get more than £19.71 if you are single, or £26.13 if you are a couple.

Step four: compare total income with appropriate minimum guarantee
If your total income (Step one) is less than your appropriate minimum guarantee (Step two) **the amount at Step three will be your savings credit**. If your total income is more than your appropriate minimum guarantee, go to Step five.

Step five: calculate 40 per cent of total income that exceeds your appropriate minimum guarantee
This is 40 per cent of your total income, not just qualifying income, above your appropriate minimum guarantee.

Step six: deduct amount at Step five from amount at Step three
This is your savings credit.

If you cannot deduct it because it is more than the amount at Step three, you will not get any savings credit.

Examples

Terry and Julie are a couple over 65. They have a total weekly income of £175.05 made up of £145.05 basic state pension and £30 personal pension – all of this is qualifying income.

Step one: their total income is £175.05.

Step two: their appropriate minimum guarantee is £189.35 (standard minimum guarantee with no additional amounts).

Step three: their total qualifying income of £175.05 exceeds the savings credit threshold of £145.80 by £29.25.

£29.25 x 60% = £17.55.

Step four: their total income (Step one) is less than their appropriate minimum guarantee (Step two) so the amount in Step three (£17.55) is their savings credit.

They would also qualify for a guarantee credit of £14.30 to bring their income to the standard minimum guarantee (£189.35) for a couple. Their total income would then be £206.90 (£175.05 + £14.30 guarantee credit + £17.55 savings credit).

They may also be entitled to maximum HB and CTB and other passports (see p461).

Angelina and Michael are a couple. Michael is 67 and Angelina is 58. They have a total weekly income of £239.20 made up of £90.70 state pension, £60 private pension, £84.50 IB for Angelina, and £4 deemed income from £8,000 savings. They have eligible housing costs of £15 a week.

Step one: their total income is £239.20.

Step two: their appropriate minimum guarantee is £204.35 (£189.35 standard minimum guarantee + housing costs of £15).

Step three: their total qualifying income of £154.70 (state pension, private pension, and deemed income from savings) exceeds the savings credit threshold of £145.80 by £8.90. 60 per cent of £8.90 is £5.34. The £84.50 IB is not qualifying income.

Step four: their total income (Step one) is more than their appropriate minimum guarantee (Step two) so proceed to Step five.

Step five: their total income of £239.20 exceeds their appropriate minimum guarantee of £204.35 by £34.85.

£34.85 x 40% = £13.94.

Step six: the amount at Step five (£13.94) cannot be deducted from the amount of Step three (£5.34) so they are not entitled to savings credit.

They are also not entitled to a guarantee credit as their income is greater than their appropriate minimum guarantee.

5. Special benefit rules

There are some groups of claimants to whom special rules apply which can affect the calculation of, and entitlement to, pension credit (PC). These are covered in Chapters 26 and 58. Special rules apply to:

- 'people subject to immigration control' (see p1333);
- people in hospital (see p611);
- people in care homes (see p617);
- prisoners (see p624).

You are not entitled to any PC if you are a member of, and are fully maintained by, a religious order.[30]

6. Claims and backdating

The rules about claiming and backdating are covered in Chapter 38. This section explains specific rules that apply to pension credit (PC) – it tells you how you (or your partner) can make a claim for PC, the details you need to provide, when to claim and the date your claim will start from.

Making a claim

A claim can be made by telephone, in writing on an approved form (or other manner accepted as sufficient by the Secretery of State) or in person.[31]

The claim must be made to a DWP office, a local authority housing benefit (HB) or council tax benefit (CTB) office or, in England, a county council or 'alternative office' (see p958). Claims made to a local authority or alternative office must be in writing.

A **telephone claim** must be made to the Pension Service on 0800 99 1234 (textphone 0800 169 0133) from 8am to 8pm, Monday to Friday and 9am to 1pm on Saturday. If English is not your first language, someone can telephone on your behalf and say you want to apply using another language and a member of staff and an interpreter will call you back at an agreed time to help you apply. You will be asked about your circumstances, including information about any income or savings and any housing costs you or your partner may have. Claims can be made entirely by telephone, without the need for a claim form to be signed. Where further information or verification is needed, a letter is sent for you to complete, sign and return with any requested verification. Once the claim has been decided (whether entirely by telephone or after obtaining further information), you will be sent a statement of details, setting out the information upon which the award is based. You will be asked to check this and report any omissions or changes. An award notice will also be sent to you setting out how your award of PC is made up. If you choose not to apply by telephone, a claim form will be sent to you to complete.

A written claim can be requested on the tear-off slip at the back of leaflet PC1L (available at www.pensions.gov.uk), or in writing, stating that you want to apply for PC. The tear-off slip or letter should be sent to: Freepost RRKJ-AEXK-JRLB The

Pension Service, PO Box 16, Gateshead, NE92 1BA. As long as you send your properly completed form back within one month, your date of claim will be the date your letter or tear-off slip arrived at the Gateshead address.

At the time of writing, it is not possible to make an online application via www.pensions.gov.uk/pensioncredit. However, you can complete the form online, print it out, sign it and send by post. You can also print it out and complete it by hand.

If you are under 65 and have been awarded the guarantee credit, when you turn 65 you will be contacted to assess whether you are entitled to any savings credit and whether you should be given an assessed income period. The Pension Service will either telephone you and complete the form over the telephone or send you the form to complete. You must provide the information requested as part of this review within one month of being asked to do so.[32]

If you claim PC by telephone you can usually also claim HB and/or CTB at the same time. In this case, a three-page HB/CTB form can be completed over the phone and is sent to you to check and sign. In some cases, you may be sent a supplementary form(s) that you must also complete and sign – this might happen if you have a non-dependant living with you and/or you pay rent to a private landlord or housing association. You should send the HB/CTB form(s) to your local authority.

From October 2008, however, the Pension Service intends to send the relevant information automatically to the local authority. If you request a PC claim form, a 26-page HB/CTB form is included in the PC claim pack. You should complete the HB/CTB form and send it to your local authority. For details of the date from which your HB and/or CTB starts, see p204.

Information and evidence to support your claim

When you claim you must satisfy the national insurance number requirement in order to be entitled to PC.[33] In most cases, you and your partner must satisfy this condition (see p962 for further details). You may also be required to provide any additional information and evidence relevant to your claim – eg, specific details of any personal pension scheme to which you belong.[34] Additionally, you may be required to provide, within one month of being notified of the requirement, information and evidence of any likely future changes in circumstances that are needed to enable the decision maker to decide whether to apply an assessed income period and, if so, the length of that period.[35] If the claim was made in writing to the local authority or in England, to the county council, the local authority or county council can accept and obtain information and evidence, and give advice about the PC claim.

For claims made in the advance period (the four months before you reach the qualifying age) the one-month time limit starts from the day after the advance period ends.[36]

Who should claim

If you are a single person, you must claim on your own behalf. If you are one of a couple, you must choose which one of you claims for you both (see p702). If you have a choice about who can claim but you cannot agree, a decision maker decides.[37]

You can swap who claims as long as the partner previously claiming agrees. It may be worthwhile doing so, for example, if one of you is about to go abroad.

An 'appointee' can claim on your behalf if you cannot claim for yourself – eg, if you have a mental health condition (see p955).

The date of your claim

You are normally not entitled to PC on any day before your 'date of claim'. However, you can claim PC in advance before you qualify (see below) and your date of claim can be backdated (see p456).

Your **'date of your claim'** (unless the backdating rules apply) is:[38]

- the date your written or telephone claim, properly completed with all the required information and evidence, is received at the appropriate office (the DWP, local authority HB/CTB office or county council); *or*
- the date your 'defective claim' (ie, not properly completed with all the required information and evidence) is received at the appropriate office and you correct the defect within one month (or a longer period that the DWP considers reasonable) of being notified of the defect; *or*
- the date you contact the appropriate office of your intention to claim, and you submit a properly completed claim with all the required information and evidence within one month of this date.

If you are making an advance claim for PC before you have reached the qualifying age and your claim is defective, you may correct it at any time before the end of the advance period.[39]

Claiming in advance

You can make an advance claim for PC to give the DWP time to ensure you receive your benefit as soon as you become entitled. However, you cannot make an advance claim if the reason you do not qualify straight away is because you fail the habitual residence test (see p1368). PC can be claimed up to four months before you qualify, whether this is before you reach the qualifying age[40] and know you will be entitled when you reach that age, *or* after you reach the qualifying age when you know you will have a future entitlement – eg, because of a drop in income. The date of claim is the date you qualify.[41]

How your claim is dealt with

Your claim is dealt with by the Pension Service. It may request further information in connection with your claim and aims to do this by telephone or post. In some cases, it may arrange a date for an interview or a home visit.

Backdating your claim

It is important that you claim in time because PC can only be backdated for up to a limited period – currently 12 months (but the Government intends to reduce the backdating period to three months from October 2008). Your claim can be backdated if you satisfy the qualifying conditions over the period for which you require backdating – you do not have to show why your claim was late.[42] If you want your claim to be backdated it is important that you request this as claims are not automatically backdated. You can do so on Part 10 of the application form. If you make a telephone claim, you should be asked about the date from which you want your claim to start.

If you claim backdated PC after being awarded a qualifying benefit and an earlier PC claim was refused because you did not at that time get a qualifying benefit, your PC can be backdated to the date of your earlier PC claim or the date when the qualifying benefit was first payable, whichever is later (see p968 for more information on qualifying benefits).[43]

For general rules on backdating, see Chapter 38.

7. Getting paid

You can be paid pension credit (PC) by direct credit transfer into a bank, building society or post office card account or by cheque.

PC is a weekly benefit. You can be paid for a part-week if you:

- were entitled to income support (IS) or income-based jobseeker's allowance (JSA) immediately before your first day of PC entitlement; *and*
- your PC entitlement is likely to continue throughout the first full benefit week that follows the part-week.

Although the rules allow for payments via direct credit transfer to be made within seven days of 'each successive period of entitlement',[44] in practice PC is paid weekly in advance on Mondays or on the same day as any retirement pension is paid.[45] If you were entitled to IS immediately before 6 October 2003 and your IS was paid in arrears then your PC will also be paid in arrears.[46]

If you are entitled to less than 10 pence a week you are not paid PC, unless you are receiving another social security benefit that can be paid with PC,[47] although you will still have an underlying entitlement. If your entitlement is less than £1 a week a decision maker can decide to pay you quarterly in arrears.

Unless you fit into the exceptions below or your PC award falls on the first day in your benefit week, your PC is payable in the benefit week following your claim.[48] The **'benefit week'** runs for seven days starting from Monday or the day of the week any state retirement pension is paid.[49] Therefore, if the first day of your benefit week is a Monday and you claim PC on a Tuesday, it will be paid the following Monday.

Exceptions:[50]

- If you were entitled to IS or income-based JSA immediately before reaching the qualifying age (see p447) and have been awarded PC from that date, your entitlement to guarantee credit will begin from the first day of the PC award.
- If you were entitled to income-based JSA after reaching the qualifying age and have been awarded PC from the day after your income-based JSA ended, your guarantee credit will begin from the first day of the PC award (this will only apply to men because of the different qualifying ages for PC and JSA).

Delays and complaints

If you are dissatisfied with the way your claim has been handled, you may wish to complain (see Chapter 46). You may be able to claim compensation (see p1186).

If payment of your PC is delayed, you may be able to get an interim payment (see p986) or a social fund crisis loan (see p503) to help you until your benefit is paid.

Change of circumstances

The DWP should inform you of the main kinds of changes in your circumstances that you need to report, but might not actually list them all. In any case, it is your duty to report *any* change in your circumstances which you might reasonably be expected to know could affect your right to, the amount of, or the payment of your benefit. You should notify changes promptly to the office handling your claim.[51]

See p458 for circumstances that do not need to be reported during the assessed income period. You report a change promptly in writing or by telephone to the office handling your claim. In some cases, however, the decision maker may say you must report changes in writing. In any case, you may want to report the change in writing and keep a copy in case of a dispute in the future. If you fail to report any changes promptly an overpayment may result which may be recoverable from you (see Chapter 39). If you are considered deliberately to have acted falsely or dishonestly, you may also be guilty of an offence (see Chapter 40). If your circumstances change you may be entitled to more or less PC or even none at all.

If there are any changes to the amount of housing costs you owe or the interest payable, your lender is required to report these to the DWP. If you have this information you must also inform the DWP just in case your lender fails to do so.

To avoid an overpayment, make sure that the DWP takes this information into account.

Where there has been a relevant change of circumstances, your claim is looked at again by a decision maker and a new decision is made – this is called a 'supersession' (see p1074). Your PC is then adjusted from the date the new decision takes effect. When this is depends on whether the new decision is advantageous to you and whether you reported the change in time. See p1079 for more details on when a supersession takes effect.

When your pension credit is adjusted

Generally, your PC is adjusted from the day the change occurs or is expected to occur, if this is the day you are paid benefit. If it is not, your PC is adjusted from the start of the next benefit week.[52]

However, there are a few exceptions to this general rule.[53]

Assessed income period[54]

An assessed income period is a set period during which you are not required to report any changes in certain types of your income, known as 'retirement provision'.

'Retirement provision' means income from:[55]

- retirement pension (other than one payable under the Social Security Contributions and Benefits Act 1992);
- an annuity (other than retirement pension income);
- capital.

The effect of this is that if you have an increase in, or subsequently start to receive, your 'retirement provision' during your assessed income period you do not have to report this to the DWP. All other income changes that affect your PC entitlement must be reported to the DWP as soon as they occur.

An assessed income period will only be set if you or your partner are 65 or over. An assessed income period will not be made if:

- you are a member of a couple and one of you is under 60; *or*
- you have been awarded PC or your PC has been increased because an element of your 'retirement provision' that is due to be paid has temporarily stopped; *or*
- you have failed to provide sufficient information, as requested by the DWP at the end of the assessed income period, to enable the DWP to determine whether your 'retirement provision' will vary throughout the 12 months that follow the day the previous assessed income period ends.[56]

An assessed income period can be set for five years[57] (or seven years[58] if you or your partner were awarded PC from 6 October 2003 and were 65 on or before that date – this is to avoid a build-up of reassessments in 2008). If the amount assessed as your 'retirement provision' seems unlikely to represent your typical 'retirement provision' throughout the following 12 months an assessed income period may be made for less than five years or not at all. [59] If you have asked for your claim to be backdated (see p456), in reaching a decision on whether your retirement provision is likely to be typical throughout the 12 months, the decision maker will look at the 12 months starting with the date from when your claim is backdated, as opposed to the date you make your claim.[60]

Deemed increases in retirement provision

If the terms of your retirement provision provide for periodic increases and the date and amount of such increases, and the DWP is informed of these, the increase will be in line with these terms.[61] Otherwise, the increase will be in line with the social security uprating for additional pensions.[62] There will be no deemed increase if your retirement provision arrangements do not provide for periodic increases in the amount payable.[63] If your retirement provision includes income from capital it will be deemed not to change unless it is capital that counts as having a tariff income.[64] In that case, it may be deemed to increase or decrease in line with any changes made to the tariff income rules – presently £1 for every £500 (or part of £500) over £6,000 (£10,000 if you live in a care home).

If the adjustment to your retirement provision results in a change in the amount of PC to which you are entitled, the DWP amends your PC payment automatically[65] to take effect from the start of the benefit week where the increase or uprating date also falls on that day. In all other cases, it takes effect from the start of the next benefit week.[66] However, if the period for which the first increase in retirement provision is paid is not the same length as the period of the last regular payment, the adjustment takes effect from the date of the second payment of the increased amount if that falls on the same day as the start of the benefit week; otherwise, from the start of the next benefit week. For example, your occupational pension is paid at the end of each month. Your last payment was made on 31 March 2008. An annual increase of 1.8 per cent takes effect on 16 April 2008 and is first included in the payment on 30 April 2008. The period from 16 April to 30 April (15 days) is not the same length as the last regular payment (one month) so any resulting adjustment to the PC is not applied until the start of the benefit week following the second payment of the increased amount.

Decreases in retirement provision

If your retirement provision decreases during an assessed income period you can report this and your PC will be adjusted. This will not end the period, rather your PC award is adjusted via a supersession.[67] It is in your interests to report decreases in order to gain from any increased PC during a current assessed income period, otherwise you will have to wait until the reassessment at the end of the period where any PC adjustment would only apply from the start of your next assessed income period.

When an assessed income period ends

Certain circumstances will bring your assessed income period to an end. These are where:

- you become a member of a couple;[68]
- you cease to be a member of a couple;[69]
- you reach (or, if you are a couple, the other member of the couple reaches) the age of 65;[70]
- you are no longer entitled to PC;[71]
- you are single and enter a care home on a permanent basis;[72]
- payments of retirement pension due to you stop temporarily or are less than the amount due and your PC award is superseded as a result.[73]

Overpayments and fraud

If you are overpaid PC, you might have to repay some or all of it. The rules on recovery are the same as those for IS and these are covered in Chapter 39. If you have been accused of fraud, see Chapter 40. Your PC might be reduced if you have been sanctioned for benefit offences (see p1047).

8. Challenging a pension credit decision

The same rules on revisions, supersessions and appeals apply to pension credit as for other benefits (see Chapters 41 and 42).

9. Tax, tax credits and other benefits

Pension credit (PC) is not taxable.

Tax credits

PC acts as a passport to tax credits, although you need to make a separate claim for tax credits. If you have responsibility for a child you may be entitled to child tax credit (CTC). CTC does not count as income when calculating PC.[74]

If you are working 16 hours or more a week you might also be entitled to working tax credit (WTC – see Chapter 49). Because PC has no 16-hour work rule, it may be possible to get WTC and PC if your income is low enough, but any WTC you receive will count as income when calculating your PC entitlement.[75]

Means-tested benefits

If you pay rent and/or council tax you may qualify for housing benefit (HB – see p177) and/or council tax benefit (CTB – see p80).

If you receive the guarantee credit you automatically qualify for maximum HB and/or CTB but you still have to make a separate claim. If you are only entitled to the savings credit element your HB/CTB claim is subject to a standard calculation. The Pension Service provides the local authority with the assessed income figure (this is the figure the DWP used for working out your PC entitlement). The local authority modifies this figure to take certain income into account – eg, savings credit.[76] Although savings credit counts as income for HB and CTB, the HB/CTB applicable amount for people 65 or over is increased by an amount equal to the maximum savings credit (see p450) to minimise any loss in HB/CTB as a result of having more qualifying income (see Chapter 33).

The £16,000 capital limit does not apply if you receive the guarantee credit (with or without the savings credit). In all other cases it continues to apply, including if you receive just the savings credit.

If you are a man aged between 60 and 65 you can choose between claiming income-based jobseeker's allowance (JSA) or PC. This is because income-based JSA is paid to those who are below pensionable age and this is 65 for a man and 60 for a woman, whereas the qualifying age for PC is linked to the pensionable age for a woman. When deciding which benefit to claim you will need to be aware of the different rules governing these two benefits to ensure that you will be better off. For example, there is no capital limit or 16-hour work rule for PC but there is for income-based JSA. Furthermore, to benefit from the HB/CTB rules that came into effect on 6 October 2003 neither you nor your partner must be in receipt of IS or income-based JSA. You should, therefore, seek advice from your local advice centre. See Chapters 36 and 37 for more details of the treatment of income and capital.

Non-means-tested benefits

The non-means-tested benefits in this *Handbook* (other than attendance allowance, disability living allowance, bereavement payment, guardian's allowance, constant attendance allowance, exceptionally severe disablement allowance, statutory sick pay, statutory maternity pay, statutory paternity pay, statutory adoption pay and child benefit) are taken into account as income when calculating any entitlement to PC (see Chapter 36).

However, qualifying for certain non-means-tested benefits can help you qualify for more PC. For example, if you get carer's allowance you may be entitled to a carer's additional amount within your appropriate minimum guarantee.

Passports and other sources of help

If you are entitled to PC you may also be eligible for the following (but some are only accessible if you are getting the guarantee credit of PC):

- health benefits if you are getting the guarantee credit of PC (see Chapter 9);

- free school meals if you are getting the guarantee credit of PC (this only applies in England and Wales – claimants in Scotland can qualify via CTC if they are getting CTC (but not WTC) and have an annual taxable income of £15,575 or less);
- social fund payments (both discretionary and regulated) if you receive either or both elements of PC (see Chapters 21 and 22);
- home insulation grants and discretionary grants from the local authority towards the cost of home improvements (see p16).

Notes

1. **Who can claim pension credit**
1 s2 SPCA 2002
2 s1(6) SPCA 2002
3 s1(2)(a) SPCA 2002; regs 2-4 SPC Regs
4 s2(2) SPCA 2002; reg 6 SPC Regs
5 s4(2) SPCA 2002
6 s3 SPCA 2002
7 s3(1) SPCA 2002
8 s1(2)(a) SPCA 2002; regs 2-4 SPC Regs
9 s4(2) SPCA 2002
10 s3(2) SPCA 2002

2. **The rules about your age**
11 s1(6) SPCA 2002
12 s3(1) SPCA 2002

4. **The amount of credit**
13 s2(3) SPCA 2002
14 Reg 6(1)(b) SPC Regs
15 Reg 6(1)(a) SPC Regs
16 Reg 6 and Sch 3 para 1(5) SPC Regs
17 Reg 6(4) and (5) SPC Regs
18 Reg 6(6)(a) SPC Regs
19 Reg 6(6)(c) SPC Regs
20 Reg 6(6)(b) SPC Regs
21 Reg 6(6)(b) and Sch 1 para 6 SPC Regs
22 Sch 1 para 6(8)-(9) SPC Regs
23 s15 SPCA 2002; regs 14-24 SPC Regs
24 Reg 15(6) SPC Regs
25 s2(2) SPCA 2002
26 Reg 7(2) SPC Regs
27 Reg 9 SPC Regs
28 s3(7) SPCA 2002; reg 7(1)(a) SPC Regs
29 s3(3) SPCA 2002; reg 7(1)(b)-(c) SPC Regs

5. **Special benefit rules**
30 ss2(9) and 3(8) SPCA 2002; regs 6(2)(b) and 7(3)(b) SPC Regs

6. **Claims and backdating**
31 Reg 4D SS(C&P) Regs
32 Reg 7(1B) SS(C&P) Regs
33 s1(1A) and (1B) SSAA 1992
34 Reg 7(4) SS(C&P) Regs
35 Reg 7(1A) and (1B) SS(C&P) Regs
36 Reg 7(1C) SS(C&P) Regs
37 Reg 4D(7) SS(C&P) Regs
38 Reg 4F SS(C&P) Regs
39 Regs 4D(12) and 4E(3) SS(C&P) Regs
40 Regs 4E and 13D(4) SS(C&P) Regs
41 Reg 13D SS(C&P) Regs
42 Reg 19(1) and Sch 4 para 12 SS(C&P) Regs
43 Reg 6(16) SS(C&P) Regs

7. **Getting paid**
44 Regs 21(3) and 26B(4) SS(C&P) Regs
45 Reg 26B SS(C&P) Regs
46 Reg 36(6) SPC(CTMP) Regs
47 Reg 13 SPC Regs
48 Reg 16A(1) SS(C&P) Regs
49 Reg 16A(4) SS(C&P) Regs
50 Reg 16A(2) SS(C&P) Regs
51 Reg 32(1A) and (1B) SS(C&P) Regs
52 Reg 7 and Sch 3B para 1(b) SS&CS(DA) Regs
53 Reg 7and Sch 3B SS&CS(DA) Regs
54 ss6-10 SPCA 2002; regs 10-12 SPC Regs
55 s7(6) SPCA 2002
56 Reg 10(1) SPC Regs
57 s9 SPCA 2002

58 Reg 37 SPC(CTMP) Regs
59 s9(2) SPCA 2002
60 Memo DMG SPC 29
61 Reg 10(4) SPC Regs
62 Reg 10(6) SPC Regs
63 Reg 10(2)(a) SPC Regs
64 Reg 10(2)(b) and (7) SPC Regs
65 s10 SPCA 2002
66 Reg 10(5)-(7) SPC Regs
67 s8 SPCA 2002
68 s9(4)(a) SPCA 2002
69 s9(4)(b) SPCA 2002
70 s9(4)(c) and (d) SPCA 2002
71 Reg 12(a) SPC Regs
72 Reg 12(c) SPC Regs
73 Reg 12(b) SPC Regs

9. **Tax, tax credits and other benefits**
74 s7(2) TCA 2002; reg 4(d) TC(ITDR) Regs
75 s15(1)(b) SPCA 2002
76 **HB** Reg 27 HB(SPC) Regs
CTB Reg 17 CTB(SPC) Regs

Chapter 19

Retirement pensions

This chapter covers:

There are three main categories of retirement pension:

- Category A retirement pension, based on your own national insurance (NI) contribution record;
- Category B retirement pension, based on your spouse's or civil partner's (or late spouse or civil partner's) NI record;
- Category D retirement pension, a non-contributory pension payable to those over 80.

Note: the Pensions Act 2007 will introduce major changes to the amount of pension paid, the age at which a person will become entitled to a pension and the amount of contributions required to be paid in order to qualify for a pension. See Chapter 31 for further details and CPAG's *Welfare Rights Bulletin* for updates.

1. Who can claim retirement pensions

You can get a retirement pension when you reach 'pensionable age'. **'Pensionable age'** is currently 65 for a man and 60 for a woman.[1] This rule discriminates on grounds of sex but is not contrary to European Community (EC) law (see p1166). However, pensionable age for women will be increased from 60 to 65 between 2010 and 2020 (see p469). You do not automatically become entitled to your retirement pension just by reaching pensionable age. You must claim. If you do not claim you are treated as having deferred your retirement (see p467). If you are claiming a dependant's increase in your pension (see p686) you will need to claim separately on the appropriate form.[2]

You do not have to retire and you can choose whether or not to give up work. If you decide to carry on working, your earnings do not reduce the pension you receive (although if your spouse or civil partner is still working you may not get an increase in your pension for her/him – see p687).

If you are getting transitional long-term incapacity benefit (see p278) you should take advice before claiming (see p479). Do not wait for more than three months after reaching pensionable age before making a decision or you may lose out (see p964).

There are some groups of claimants to whom special rules apply (see p472).

Following the introduction of the Gender Recognition Act in April 2005, if you have applied to the Gender Recognition Panel and you are granted a full gender recognition certificate your entitlement to retirement pensions can change. When you get your certificate, benefit will be paid on the basis of your acquired gender. Therefore, if your acquired gender is female you will qualify for a pension at 60 and if your acquired gender is male you will qualify for a pension at 65.

Category A retirement pension

You qualify for a Category A pension if:[3]

- you satisfy the contribution conditions (see p738) on the basis of your own contribution record. If you do not satisfy the contribution conditions, you may qualify based on the contributions of your late or former spouse or civil partner; *and*
- you are over pensionable age.

Category B retirement pension for a spouse or civil partner

You qualify for a Category B pension if:[4]

- you were married or had a civil partner when you reached pensionable age (or married or formed a civil partnership after that age);
- you and your spouse or civil partner are over pensionable age;
- your spouse or civil partner satisfies the contribution conditions (see p738); *and*
- your spouse or civil partner is entitled to a Category A retirement pension.

If your spouse or civil partner was receiving an increase of Category A retirement pension for you before you receive this pension, that increase is replaced by this pension, which is normally paid at the same rate.[5]

Note: if you are a man, or a woman with a civil partner, you cannot get a Category B retirement pension under this rule if your wife or civil partner was born before 6 April 1950.[6]

Category B retirement pension for widows, widowers or surviving civil partners

You qualify for a Category B pension if:[7]

- you are a widow, widower or surviving civil partner; *and*
- your late spouse or civil partner:
  - satisfied the contribution conditions (see p738); *or*
  - died as a result of an industrial injury or disease (see p19).

In addition you must satisfy one of the following conditions.

- When your spouse or civil partner died you had reached pensionable age.[8] If you are a widower or a surviving civil partner, you cannot qualify under this rule if you reach pensionable age before 6 April 2010.
- For widowers and surviving civil partners only, when your wife or civil partner died, both of you had reached pensionable age.[9] You can only qualify under this rule if you reach pensionable age before 6 April 2010. In the case of widowers only, your wife must have died on or after 6 April 1979.
- Before you reached pensionable age, you were entitled, or treated as entitled, to widow's pension (or if you are a man, you would have been entitled to widow's pension had you been a woman) because of your late spouse's death.[10] You cannot qualify under this rule if your spouse died on or after 9 April 2001. If you are a widower, you cannot qualify under this rule of you reach pensionable age before 6 April 2010.
- Since your late spouse or civil partner died you have not remarried or formed a civil partnership, and because of her/his death, you were entitled to (or treated as entitled to):[11]
  - widowed parent's allowance, immediately before you reached pensionable age or at any time when over the age of 45; *or*
  - bereavement allowance at any time before you reached pensionable age.

Although payment of bereavement benefits is suspended when you are cohabiting (see p30), you can still qualify for Category B retirement pension from pensionable age. However, you must claim the pension. If you do not, the DWP continues to treat you as entitled to bereavement benefits (and therefore continues to suspend payment during cohabitation) until your 65th birthday (see p474).[12]

When Category B retirement pension can be paid

Once you qualify for a Category B retirement pension, it is paid for life. It does not cease if you live with a new partner, re-marry or form a civil partnership.[13] If you are approaching pensionable age and considering re-marriage you should assess your position and, if necessary, take advice. There may be financial benefits in postponing any wedding so that you are still a widow, widower or surviving civil partner immediately before attaining pensionable age. You should seek financial advice before deciding what to do.

Category D retirement pension

You qualify for a Category D pension if:[14]

- you are aged 80 or over;
- you were ordinarily resident in Great Britain (GB – see p1357) on the day you reached the age of 80;
- you have been resident in GB for a period of at least 10 years in any continuous period of 20 years immediately before you attained the age of 80; *and*
- you are entitled either to no other retirement pension or to an amount of retirement pension less than the current rate of a Category D retirement pension.

Graduated retirement benefit

'Graduated retirement benefit' is an increase in the weekly rate of retirement pension. However, although described as an increase in pension rate, graduated retirement benefit can be paid to a person over pension age who is not entitled to a retirement pension because s/he does not satisfy the national insurance (NI) contribution conditions. Between 1961 and 6 April 1975, those paying flat-rate Class 1 contributions also paid graduated contributions and they receive a small annual increase in respect of these payments.[15]

You are also entitled to an age addition of 25p a week if you are over 80 and receiving graduated retirement benefit but not (for some reason) receiving any other retirement pension.[16]

If you are a widow, you may add half of your husband's entitlement to your own. Similarly, a widower entitled to a Category B retirement pension (or who would be if he did not have a Category A retirement pension) may also add half his wife's entitlement to his own.[17] From 5 December 2005 this rule has also applied to surviving civil partners.

Graduated retirement benefit may be paid even if you are not entitled to any retirement pension. If you are entitled to only a very small amount, however, you receive a lump-sum payment instead of weekly payments. It is increased if you defer entitlement to a retirement pension (see below).[18]

The contribution conditions for graduated retirement benefit discriminate against women on the grounds of their sex, but are probably not contrary to EC law (see p1166).

Deferring your retirement pension

After you reach pensionable age, you are allowed to defer entitlement to a Category A or Category B retirement pension. In return for doing so, you later become entitled to a higher rate of pension.

Your pension is increased for each week you defer entitlement. The same applies to graduated retirement benefit (see p467).[19] The rules were changed in April 2005[20] to encourage more people to defer their pensions. Prior to this date you could only defer your pension for a maximum period of five years. By doing so your pension would be increased by one-seventh of 1 per cent.[21] Therefore, if you deferred entitlement for the whole five-year period, you received slightly over 37 per cent extra retirement pension each week. For periods you defer your pension after April 2005 your pension will be increased by one-fifth of 1 per cent for each week of deferment. There is no longer a five-year limit for deferral. If you defer your pension for at least 12 months you can receive a one-off lump sum based on the amount of pension that you would have received plus interest.[22] The Pension Service publishes a leaflet, *Your Guide to State Pension Deferral: putting off your state pension to get extra state pension or a lump-sum payment later* (SPD1), available from www.thepensionservice.gov.uk.

The benefits that are increased in this way include any additional pension under the additional state pension scheme (see p477), an incapacity increase and any increase resulting from your late spouse or civil partner's deferment, but not increases for dependants or age additions.[23]

If you are a widow and your husband had deferred his entitlement to a pension, you become entitled to the increase he would have gained through his deferment provided you do not re-marry before you reach the age of 60. If you are a widower, you become entitled to an increase from your wife's deferment if you were over pensionable age when she died.[24]

You do not receive an increase in pension for any period that you receive any other contributory benefit, severe disablement allowance, carer's allowance or maternity allowance,[25] nor for any day when you would have been disqualified from receiving a Category A or B retirement pension because you were in prison.[26]

In particular, this rule applies to graduated retirement benefit (see p467).[27] As payments of graduated retirement benefit are usually very small, this can mean that an increment to a Category A or B retirement pension worth many pounds can be lost because of payments of graduated retirement benefit of as little as a few pence a week. This is a problem that particularly affects married women, but everyone should think carefully and, if necessary, take advice before claiming graduated retirement benefit unless they are claiming their retirement pension at the same time (particularly since the graduated retirement benefit is itself increased if you defer claiming it).

If you are receiving a means-tested benefit, deferring your retirement pension may also lead to a problem under the notional income rules. These sometimes entitle the DWP to treat you as if you were claiming your pension, even though you are not, when your entitlement to benefit is calculated. For further details of the notional income rules, see p873.

De-retirement

You can defer your retirement pension (see p467) simply by not claiming it but, once you have become entitled, you may only defer by notifying the DWP of your intention by telephoning or writing to the Pension Service.[28] This is what is known as **'de-retiring'**. You may de-retire in this way at any time during the first five years after you reach pensionable age.[29] You can also cancel your deferment at any time, but you cannot then de-retire a second time.[30]

If you are married and entitled to a Category A retirement pension and you have a spouse who is entitled to a Category B pension by virtue of your contributions, you cannot de-retire without the consent of your spouse unless that consent is unreasonably withheld.[31]

2. **The rules about your age**

Category A or B pension can be claimed when you reach pensionable age (65 for men, 60 for women). Category D pension can be claimed if you are over 80.

Pensionable age for women will be increased from 60 to 65 between 2010 and 2020.[32] These changes will affect women who were born after 5 April 1950. Women born after 5 April 1955 will reach pensionable age at 65 and those born between 6 April 1950 and 5 April 1955 will reach it at an age between 60 and 65. If you are in the latter category, the precise date on which you will reach pensionable age depends on your date of birth. Appendix 6 contains a table with further details.

If you are a married man who was born after 5 April 1945 or a widower whose late wife was born after 5 April 1950, the rules for Category B retirement pension will be the same as those which currently apply to women.[33] The discriminatory rules about increases to a Category A retirement pension for a dependent adult are also to be abolished from 6 April 2010.[34]

Note: the Pensions Act 2007 will make significant changes to the rules on the age when you become entitled to a pension. The Act allows for state pension age to increase by one year per decade between 2020 and 2050.

3. **Claiming for others**

You may qualify for an increase in your retirement pension if you have any dependants (see Chapter 29).

4. **The amount of benefit**

Category A retirement pension[35]

	£pw
Claimant	90.70
Adult dependant	54.35

In addition, you may receive:
- an age addition of 25p a week if you are over 80;
- graduated retirement benefit based on earnings between 1961 and 1975 (see p467);
- an additional state pension if you reached pensionable age after 5 April 1979 (see p477);
- a higher pension if you deferred entitlement to pension (see p467);
- an amount equal to the age-related addition to long-term incapacity benefit if you were receiving this within eight weeks (104 weeks if you are a welfare-to-work beneficiary – see p666) of reaching pensionable age (see p464).[36] If you have an additional state pension, this amount is set off against it;[37]
- a Christmas bonus (see p9).

You may receive less than the standard amount of pension if you only partially satisfy the contribution conditions (see p738). If so, it may be possible to improve your contribution record by paying Class 3 contributions (see p725). These can be paid even after you reach pensionable age but you should do so as soon as possible or you may lose the opportunity (see p726).

In addition, if you are married or a civil partner and you are entitled to both a Category A pension at a reduced rate on the basis of your own contributions and a Category B pension on your spouse or civil partner's contributions (see below), there are special rules which allow your pension to be increased to the maximum of £54.35.[38]

Category B retirement pension for a spouse or civil partner[39]

	£pw
Claimant	54.35

In addition, you may receive:
- an age addition of 25p a week if you are over 80;
- a higher pension from deferring entitlement to pension (see p467);
- a Christmas bonus (see p9).

You may receive less than the standard rate because your spouse or civil partner only partially satisfies the contribution conditions (see p738, but see also p726). If so, it may be possible for her/him to improve her/his contribution record (or for you to improve your own and become entitled to a Category A retirement pension in your own right) by paying Class 3 contributions (see p725). These can be paid even after you reach pensionable age, but you should do so as soon as possible or you may lose the opportunity (see p726).

Category B retirement pension for widows, widowers or civil partners[40]

	£pw
Claimant	90.70

In addition, you may receive:
- an age addition of 25p a week if you are over 80;
- graduated retirement benefit based on your late spouse's/civil partner's graduated contributions between 1961 and 1975 (see below);
- a higher pension if your late spouse/civil partner deferred entitlement to pension (see p467);
- an additional state pension based on earnings after 5 April 1979 (see p476);
- a Christmas bonus (see p9).

You may receive less than the standard amount of pension because your spouse or civil partner only partially satisfied the contribution conditions (see p739). If so, it may be possible to improve her/his contribution record by paying Class 3 contributions (see p725). These can be paid even after your spouse or civil partner's death but you should do so as soon as possible or you may lose the opportunity (see p727).

Category D retirement pension[41]

	£pw
Claimant	54.35

In addition, you receive:
- an age addition of 25p a week because you are over 80;
- a Christmas bonus (see p9).

Graduated retirement benefit

The amount of graduated retirement benefit you can receive depends upon the amount of special graduated contributions paid on earnings between 1961 and 1975 (see p467).

5. Special benefit rules

Divorced people and former civil partners

There are special rules that may help you qualify for a Category A retirement pension if you are divorced or have ended a civil partnership and you cannot qualify on the basis of your own contributions.[42] In practice, these rules mean that if your former spouse or civil partner had a full contribution record, you can use it to replace your own, *either*:

- for all the years in your working life up to and including the one in which you were divorced; *or*
- for all the years during which you were married; *or*
- for all the years during which you were a civil partner up to and including the year in which your civil partnership was dissolved.

If your former spouse or civil partner's contribution record was incomplete, you are not necessarily treated as satisfying the second contribution condition for all of those years. But this may still be more than you would qualify for on the basis of your own contributions. These rules apply if:[43]

- you have been divorced or your civil partnership ended; *or*
- your marriage was not void (see p29) and has been annulled by a court; *and either*
- your decree absolute of divorce or nullity is dated after you reach pensionable age; *or*
- your decree absolute of divorce or nullity is dated before you reach pensionable age and you do not remarry before you reach that age; *or*
- your civil partnership is dissolved before you reach pensionable age.

If you are in one of these categories, you are treated as satisfying the first contribution condition (see p738) for a Category A retirement pension if your former spouse or civil partner did so in any year of her/his working life (see p739) up to and including the year in which your marriage or civil partnership ended.[44]

In addition, you can use your former spouse's or civil partner's contribution record instead of your own in order to increase the number of years in which you satisfy the second contribution condition (see p738).[45]

People coming from or going abroad

If you have lived elsewhere than the UK during your working life, your pension may be affected. For example, it may be paid at a reduced rate. However, there are reciprocal arrangements with many countries which may assist you. Equally, if you have worked in another European Economic Area state you may benefit from European Community law (see p1382).

6. Claims and backdating

Making a claim

Normally the DWP sends you a claim form (BR1) about four months before you reach pensionable age. If you wish to claim an increase in your pension for a dependant you must complete the appropriate form. The DWP has a tele-claim service for pensions, available for people who are within four months of pension age to claim their retirement pension over the telephone. The service is available from 8am to 8pm Monday to Friday on 0845 300 1084. You can also request a forecast of the amount of pension that you will receive, by phoning 0845 300 0168. However, until autumn 2008 the pension forecast service is limited to people who will reach pension age before 6 April 2010.

It is possible to make and amend a claim for retirement pension or graduated retirement pension by telephone.[46]

If you have not received a form three months before you want to receive the pension, ask for one from your local DWP office. Claim forms should be returned to your local DWP office.

You can defer claiming your Category A or Category B retirement pension during the first five years after you reach pensionable age. In return for doing so, you later become entitled to a higher rate of pension. See p467 for further details. You can also de-retire after claiming (see p468).

Keep a copy of your claim in case queries arise.

Information to support your claim

When you claim retirement pension, you must satisfy the national insurance (NI) number requirement. In most cases this means you must provide your NI number (as well as your partner's, if you are claiming a dependant's addition). See p962 for further details.

Proving your age

It is up to you to prove that you have reached pensionable age. For most claimants it is sufficient to produce your birth certificate, but problems can occur if you were born in a country which did not have a formal system of registering births. Other evidence which can prove your birth date includes:

- passport or identity card;
- school or health records;
- army records;
- statements from people who know you.

The date of your claim

The date of your claim is the date it is received by the appropriate DWP office.

If you claim the wrong benefit

In certain circumstances if you have claimed the wrong benefit, it is possible for your claim to be interchanged with another benefit.[47] For retirement pensions this interchange is only possible with widows' benefits or bereavement benefits.

Claiming in advance

Claims for retirement pensions may be made up to, but no more than, four months in advance.[48] You should take advantage of this, as it can take a long time to sort out your contribution record.

Exceptions to the rule on claiming[49]

Provided you meet the other conditions of entitlement, you need not claim Category D retirement pension if you were 'ordinarily resident' in Great Britain (see p1357) on your 80th birthday and you are already receiving another retirement pension.

If you are a widow, you need not claim your Category A or B retirement pension if *either*:

- you are over 65 when you stop getting widowed mother's allowance; *or*
- you are getting a widow's pension immediately before your 65th birthday.[50]

In either of these situations, your retirement pension should be paid to you automatically as soon as you stop getting widowed mother's allowance or reach 65. However, it may be advantageous to you to claim your retirement pension – eg, because you are cohabiting.

You need not claim your Category A retirement pension if you are entitled to another retirement pension and you get divorced or your civil partnership is dissolved.[51] You need not claim your Category B retirement pension if you are entitled to either or both a Category A retirement pension or graduated retirement benefit and you marry or enter into a civil partnership.[52]

How your claim is dealt with

The DWP aims to process 95 per cent of claims within 60 days and more complex cases within 85 days.[53]

Backdating your claim

The maximum period for backdating is 12 months. However, you cannot backdate your claim for any period before the date you would have first become entitled to your pension.[54] It is very important to claim in time. You do not have to show any reasons why your claim was late. The rules on backdating are covered on p964. In some limited circumstances where you were not notified that your contribution record was insufficient for the years 1996 to 2002, it is possible for the claim to be backdated beyond the 12-month period to 1 October 1998.[55]

If you might have qualified for benefit earlier but did not claim because you were given the wrong information by the DWP or because you were misled by it, you could ask for an *ex gratia* payment (see p1186) or complain to the Ombudsman via your MP (see p1183).

7. Getting paid

Pensions are usually paid by credit transfer into a bank or similar account. You can choose to be paid by direct credit transfer either four-weekly or quarterly in arrears (see p978 for details).

Payment can also be made to someone else on your behalf, called your appointee (see p955).

If payment of your retirement pension is suspended, see p984.

Delays and complaints

If payment of your retirement pension is delayed, you might be able to get an interim payment (see p986).

If you experience delays, or wish to complain about how your claim has been dealt with, see p1186. You might be able to claim compensation (see p1186).

Change of circumstances

The DWP should inform you of the main kinds of changes in your circumstances you need to report, but might not actually list them all. In any case, it is your duty to report *any* change in your circumstances which you might reasonably be expected to know could affect your right to, the amount of, or the payment of your benefit.[56] You should notify changes promptly in writing or by telephone to the office handling your claim (although in individual cases notification might be accepted in another form). In some cases, however, the decision maker might say you must report changes in writing. In any case, you might want to report the change in writing and keep a copy in case of a dispute in the future. If you do not promptly report any such change in writing, any resulting overpayment may be recoverable from you (see Chapter 39). If you are considered deliberately to have acted falsely or dishonestly, you may also be guilty of an offence (see Chapter 40).

Overpayments and fraud

If you are overpaid retirement pension, you might have to repay it. The rules on overpayments are covered in Chapter 39.

If you have been accused of fraud, see Chapter 40.

8. Challenging a retirement pension decision

You can apply for a revision or supersession of a retirement pension decision, or appeal against it (see Chapters 41 and 42).

9. The additional state pension scheme

Introduction

Most employees pay national insurance (NI) contributions that give entitlement to the basic state retirement pension. Those employees, but not the self-employed, can also earn additional pension. The additional state pension provides for earnings-related pensions to be paid to people who have paid (or whose late spouses/civil partners have paid) Class 1 contributions in excess of the minimum required for entitlement to those benefits.

The rules for the additional state pension were subject to major changes from April 2002. Prior to this, the additional state pension was calculated under the state earnings-related pension scheme (SERPS). The rules since April 2002 are based on the state second pension – a simplified and more generous version of SERPS. In particular, under the new scheme certain low-paid employees are deemed to have a minimum level of earnings.

You are not in the additional state pension scheme if you are either contracted out by your employer (see below) or a member of an appropriate personal pension scheme (see p477).

If you were receiving invalidity benefit immediately before it was abolished in April 1995 and were receiving an earnings-related addition to your basic invalidity pension (for which you would have had to have paid Class 1 contributions at some point between April 1978 and April 1991), you will continue to receive the same amount as an addition to your incapacity benefit (IB). However, unlike the rest of your IB, this earnings-related component is not uprated for inflation each year and its real value will therefore diminish over time.

If a couple divorces it is possible to apply to the court for a share of any additional pension.[57]

Contracting out of the additional state pension scheme

You may be contracted out of the additional state pension scheme by your employer if your employment counts for the purpose of either a salary-related occupational pension (where the pension you eventually get is linked to your final salary) or if your employer makes certain minimum payments to a contracted-out money purchase scheme (where the pension you eventually get depends on what your pension fund can afford to buy in the open market when you come to retire). To enable you to be contracted out, either sort of scheme must be covered by a certificate from the Revenue.[58]

The effect of being contracted out is that you and your employer pay NI contributions at a lower rate than other employees and their employers (see p722).[59] This means that you do not build up any entitlement to pensions under the additional state pension scheme (although, until April 1991, you did as an addition to invalidity pension).[60] However, you will have to contribute to your employer's scheme and will receive a benefit from that.

An employer cannot compel you to be a member of any particular scheme, so you can opt out and join an appropriate pension scheme of your choice (see p477).[61]

Appropriate personal and stakeholder pension schemes

If a personal pension scheme satisfies certain conditions, the trustees or managers of the scheme may obtain an appropriate scheme certificate from the Revenue.[62]

If you choose to become a member of an appropriate personal pension scheme, the Secretary of State pays to the scheme the difference between your contracted-in NI contributions and those you would have paid had you been contracted out.[63] The main difference is that it is your decision to join the scheme and not your employer's.

Since 6 April 2001 it has been possible to use a stakeholder pension scheme to contract out of the additional state pension scheme. The advantage of doing this is that strict rules about charges and penalties apply to stakeholder pensions.

If you are employed and earn above the lower earnings limit, your employer must offer you access to a stakeholder pension scheme even if it does not offer an occupational pension scheme. You will then be able to make contributions by deductions from your pay. There are exceptions for employers who have fewer than five employees, who offer an occupational pension scheme to all employees within a year of their joining or who contribute at least 3 per cent of salary to certain types of approved personal pensions.

If you contract out of the additional state pension scheme by either method, you are then treated as not contributing to the additional state pension and must build up your personal pension or stakeholder pension instead.

Calculating the additional state pension

The additional pension is calculated by adding together:

- the amount of additional pension accrued under the rules up to 6 April 2002 (under the previous scheme of SERPS); *and*
- the amount of additional pension accrued under the additional state pension (the state second pension).

For Category A retirement pension, the additional pension depends on your earnings factor (see p735) in each relevant year in which you have paid contributions. For bereavement benefit or Category B retirement pensions, the additional pension depends on your spouse's (or civil partner's) earnings factor in each relevant year for which s/he has paid contributions.[64] In certain circumstances, a widow or widower may be entitled to an additional pension based both on her/his own contributions and those of her/his spouse.

You can write to the Revenue Contributions Office asking for a pensions forecast. You should receive a reply stating how much additional pension it thinks you are entitled to at current values and an estimate of the additional pension which you will receive if you continue working. For further details on calculating the additional state pension, see *A Guide to State Pensions* (NP46), available from the Pension Service.

Claimants who reached pensionable age before 6 April 1999

If you reached pensionable age before 6 April 1999 (ie, if you are a man who was born before 6 April 1934 or a woman who was born before 6 April 1939) the rules were generally more favourable. For an example of how this worked in practice, see the 21st edition of CPAG's *Rights Guide to Non-Means-Tested Benefits*, p244.

Payment to widows, widowers and surviving civil partners

At present, a widow, widower or surviving civil partner who is eligible for a basic state retirement pension based on her/his spouse/civil partner's contributions can, in certain circumstances, also receive any additional state pension based on her/his spouse/civil partner's contributions.

Under plans introduced in 1986 by the previous government, it was originally intended that people whose spouses/civil partners died after 5 April 2000 would only inherit a maximum of 50 per cent of that spouse's additional state pension entitlement. However, because of a major failure by the (then) DSS to advise people about the change, the present government decided not to implement the change to inherited additional state pensions from SERPS until 6 October 2002 and to phase the reduction over a period of 10 years rather than introduce an immediate 50 per cent cut. This phased reduction only applies to the additional pension inherited under the SERPS scheme. Any additional pension derived from the state second pension scheme will only be inheritable at 50 per cent. The percentage of the deceased person's additional state pension entitlement from SERPS which can be inherited by her/his surviving spouse will be reduced if the deceased person reached pensionable age from 5 October 2002 as follows:[65]

Date when deceased person reached pensionable age	*Maximum % of additional pension passing to surviving spouse or civil partner*
6.10.02 to 5.10.04	90
6.10.04 to 5.10.06	80
6.10.06 to 5.10.08	70
6.10.08 to 5.10.10	60
6.10.10 onwards	50

Note: it is the date on which the deceased person reached pensionable age which is important for this purpose, not the date on which s/he died.

People who are able to prove that they were given incorrect or incomplete information about the reduction in inherited SERPS additional pension and who have experienced financial loss as a result may also be able to claim compensation for maladministration (see p1186).

The maximum amount of inherited additional pension from state second pension is 50 per cent.

10. **Tax, tax credits and other benefits**

Retirement pensions are taxable.[66]

Tax credits

Retirement pensions are partially taken into account for tax credits (see Chapter 51).

Means-tested benefits

It is possible to get a retirement pension and also pension credit (PC – see Chapter 18) and other means-tested benefits such as housing benefit and/or council tax benefit.

Retirement pensions are taken fully into account for the purposes of means-tested benefits, but pensioners receive a higher rate of some means-tested benefits.

Non-means-tested benefits

If you were entitled to invalidity benefit on 12 April 1995 you can continue to receive transitional long-term incapacity benefit (IB) if you were over pension age on that date. There may be advantages in doing this as IB is not taxable and award of this benefit can lead to payment of some other means-tested benefits at a higher rate.

Retirement pensions are affected by the overlapping benefit rules (see p981).

Retirement benefit overlaps with jobseeker's allowance, IB, severe disablement allowance, carer's allowance, widowed parent's allowance and bereavement allowance.

There are special rules if you are entitled to both a Category A and Category B retirement pension (see p470).

Passports and other sources of help

People over 60 get free prescriptions and eye tests regardless of income. If you are on a low income, you may also qualify for other sources of help (see Chapter 1) or a social fund payment (see Chapters 21 and 22). If you are getting PC you may qualify for free dental treatment and school meals (see p15).

Notes

1. **Who can claim retirement pensions**
   1 s122(1) SSCBA 1992; Sch 4 PA 1995
   2 Reg 2(3) SS(C&P) Regs
   3 ss44(1) and 48 SSCBA 1992
   4 s48A and Sch 3 Part I para 5 SSCBA 1992
   5 Reg 10 SS(OB) Regs
   6 Sch 4 para 3(2) PA 1995; Sch 24 para 25(6) CPA 2004
   7 ss48B, 48BB, 48C and 60(2) and (3) and Sch 3 Part I para 5 SSCBA 1992
   8 s48B(1) and (1A) SSCBA 1992; Sch 4 para 3(3) PA 1995
   9 s51SSCBA 1992; Sch 4 para 3(3) PA 1995; Sch 24 para 28(b) CPA 2004
   10 s48B(4)-(8)SSCBA 1992; Sch 4 para 3(3) PA 1995; reg 7 SS(WB&RP) Regs
   11 s48BBSSCBA 1992; reg 7A SS(WB&RP) Regs
   12 ss38(3), 39A(5) and 39B(5) SSCBA 1992; reg 3 SS(C&P) Regs
   13 ss48C(1)and 51(4) SSCBA 1992
   14 s78(3) SSCBA 1992; reg 10 SS(WB&RP) Regs
   15 s36 NIA 1965, as kept in force by Sch 1 SS(GRB) No.2 Regs; Art 7(1) SSBU(No.2)O 1991
   16 Reg 17(1)(h) and (3) SS(WB&RP) Regs
   17 s37 NIA 1965, as kept in force by Sch 1 SS(GRB) No.2 Regs
   18 s36(4) NIA 1965, as kept in force by Sch 1 SS(GRB) No.2 Regs
   19 Sch 2 SS(GRB) No.2 Regs
   20 s55 and Sch 5 SSCBA 5 1992
   21 Sch 5 paras 1 and 2 SSCBA 1992
   22 Sch 5 para A1 SSCBA 1992; SS(DRPSAPGRB)(MP)Regs
   23 Sch 5 para 2(5) SSCBA 1992
   24 Sch 5 para 4 SSCBA 1992
   25 Reg 4(1)(b)(i) SS(WB&RP) Regs
   26 Reg 4(1)(a) SS(WB&RP) Regs
   27 Reg 4(1)(b)(ii) SS(WB&RP) Regs
   28 s54 SSCBA 1992; reg 2(3) SS(WB&RP) Regs
   29 s54(1) SSCBA
   30 Reg 2(2)(a) SS(WB&RP) Regs
   31 s54(3) SSCBA; reg 2(2)(b) SS(WB&RP) Regs

2. **The rules about your age**
   32 s126 and Sch 4 PA 1995
   33 ss48A-48C SSCBA 1992, as inserted by Sch 4 para 3 PA 1995
   34 s83A SSCBA 1992, as inserted by Sch 4 para 2 PA 1995

4. **The amount of benefit**
   35 ss44(4) and 45 SSCBA 1992
   36 ss34(3) and 47(1) SSCBA 1992; reg 3A SS(WB&RP) Regs

37 s47(2) SSCBA 1992
38 s51A SSCBA 1992
39 s48A and Sch 4 SSCBA 1992
40 s48B SSCBA 1992
41 s78(6) and Sch 4 para 7 SSCBA 1992

5. **Special benefit rules**
42 s48 SSCBA
43 Reg 1(3) SS(WB&RP) Regs
44 Reg 8(2) and (3) SS(WB&RP) Regs
45 Reg 8(2) and (4) SS(WB&RP) Regs

6. **Claims and backdating**
46 Social Security (Claims and Payments and Payments on Account, Overpayments and Recovery) Amendment Regulations 2005 No.34
47 Reg 9(1) and Sch 1 SS(C&P) Regs
48 Reg 15 SS(C&P) Regs
49 Reg 3 SS(C&P) Regs
50 However, it may be worth claiming your Category A retirement pension as soon as you reach 60 if your contribution record, or the combined record of you and your late husband, is better than your late husband's record taken on its own.
51 Reg 3(ca) SS(C&P) Regs
52 Reg 3(cb) SS(C&P) Regs
53 Pension Service Annual Report (2006/07)
54 Reg 19 and Sch 4 para 13 SS(C&P) Regs
55 Reg 6(31) and (32) SS(C&P) Regs

7. **Getting paid**
56 Reg 32(1B) SS(C&P) Regs

9. **The additional state pension scheme**
57 s47 WRPA 1999
58 s7(3) and (4) PSA 1993
59 s41 PSA 1993
60 s46 PSA 1993
61 ss160 and 161 PSA 1993
62 s7 PSA 1993
63 ss43(1)and 45(1) PSA 1993
64 ss48A-48C SSCBA 1992
65 Social Security (Inherited SERPS) Regulations 2001 No.1085

10. **Tax, tax credits and other benefits**
66 s617 ICTA 1988

Chapter 20

Severe disablement allowance

This chapter covers the transitional rules on severe disablement allowance (SDA). It contains:

SDA was abolished on 6 April 2001, but certain people entitled before that date can continue to receive it.

Note: the introduction of employment and support allowance (see Chapter 7) planned for October 2008 may affect SDA, although details were not available at the time of publication. See www.cpag.org.uk/esa or CPAG's *Welfare Rights Bulletin* for updates.

1. Who is still entitled

You can only be entitled to severe disablement allowance (SDA) now if:[1]

- you were aged 20 or over on 6 April 2001; *and*
- your current period of incapacity for work started before 6 April 2001 (see p483); *and*
- you have been entitled to SDA on any day of incapacity for work in your current period of incapacity for work and you continue to meet the qualifying conditions for SDA (see p483).

See p483 for when two or more periods of incapacity for work can be linked.

To qualify for SDA now, you need to have been entitled to it for at least one day before 6 April 2001 in your current period of incapacity for work. A claim for SDA could be backdated for up to three months. However, as a claim for incapacity benefit (IB) or maternity allowance (MA) can be treated as a claim for SDA (see p963), you may be able to qualify for SDA now if you claimed IB or MA no more than three months after 5 April 2001.

Age on 6 April 2001

You are only entitled to SDA now if you were aged 20 or over on 6 April 2001. If you were under 20 on 6 April 2001 and you qualified for SDA, you were only entitled to receive it for one year after that date. On 6 April 2002 you would have been transferred on to long-term IB on the basis of your incapacity in youth (see p266).

Period of incapacity for work

For details of how incapacity for work is assessed for the purpose of SDA, see Chapter 28. See p264 for the meaning of 'period of incapacity for work'.

Linking rules

If you can link a past period of incapacity for work in which you were entitled to SDA to your present period of incapacity for work, you may still be entitled to receive SDA now, even if you were not actually receiving SDA immediately before 6 April 2001, or if your entitlement ceases for a time after that date. The rules on when two or more periods can be linked are largely the same as for IB (see p264).[2]

Qualifying conditions

To be entitled to SDA now you must continue to satisfy the usual qualifying conditions for it. See Chapter 4 of the 2000/01 edition of the *Welfare Benefits Handbook* for these.

You and, in some circumstances, your partner may be required to attend work-focused interviews (see pp971 and 972).

2. The amount of benefit

For the current rate of severe disablement allowance (SDA) see pxvi.

You may be entitled to an increase in your SDA for an adult dependant or for a dependent child or young person (see Chapter 29). Increases for dependent children and young people have been abolished from 6 April 2003, but some people can continue to qualify for them after that date (see p691).

Notes

1. **Who is still entitled**
   1 Art 4 WRPA(No.9)O
   2 s68(10) and (10A) SSCBA 1992; Art4 WRPA(No.9)O

Chapter 21

Social fund: discretionary payments

This chapter covers:

The social fund (SF) makes two types of payments to people in need.

- Sure Start maternity grants, funeral expenses, cold weather payments and winter fuel payments are available from the **regulated social fund**. You are legally entitled to a payment if you satisfy the conditions of entitlement laid down in regulations. See Chapter 22.
- Community care grants, budgeting loans and crisis loans are available from the **discretionary social fund** to meet a variety of other needs. You are eligible for a payment if you satisfy the qualifying rules, but payments are discretionary and budget-limited. The discretionary SF is covered in this chapter. SF reviews are covered in Chapter 44.

1. General matters

The discretionary social fund (SF) is different from most other social security provision because:

- it is strictly budget-limited and there is no legal entitlement to a payment;
- most payments are in the form of loans, recoverable by deductions from weekly benefit; *and*
- there is no right of appeal to an independent tribunal, although there is an internal review system and the right to request a further review by a quasi-independent social fund inspector (see p1160).

The discretionary nature and restricted scope of this part of the SF scheme has been heavily criticised. It nevertheless remains an important source of help for many people.

Legal framework

Payments can be made from the discretionary SF in the form of:

- community care grants (CCGs) to meet needs relating to community care;
- budgeting loans (BLs) to meet intermittent expenses;
- crisis loans (CLs) to meet immediate, short-term needs.[1]

Decisions are made on behalf of the Secretary of State by 'appropriate officers', more commonly referred to as decision makers, based in local DWP offices.[2] The social fund service is in the process of being centralised. The aim is to have just 20 offices by April 2008.

Legally binding 'directions' set out the eligibility conditions for each type of payment, the procedure for reviews, and the criteria for managing district budgets.[3]

The rules on the procedural aspects of applying for a grant, loan or review and the acceptance and recovery of loans are set out in regulations.[4]

Court decisions create binding caselaw, although they are sometimes only relevant to the particular case in question. Social fund inspector (SFI) decisions do not create binding caselaw but can be useful guidance (see p1162).

Legislation on the SF, together with commentary, can be found in *Social Security Legislation, Volume II* (see Appendix 3). The SF Directions can be found in the *Social Fund Guide* (see p486).

Budgetary control

The Government sets the total budget for the discretionary SF each year (which runs from April). Each DWP district is then allocated a fixed sum for grants and another for loans.[5] However, the Government intends to change this to a single national loans budget.

An area decision maker is responsible for planning and monitoring expenditure on a monthly basis and issuing guidance to decision makers on what needs the budget can afford to meet (see p486).[6] There is, however, no monthly limit on expenditure. The directions only prohibit expenditure in excess of the annual district budget.[7] It is possible for the Secretary of State to allocate additional funds to a district in the course of a year – eg, where there has been severe flooding.[8]

Decision makers must have regard to the budget when deciding whether to make a payment and how much to award.[9] The budget is only one factor they must take into account, however, and refusing an application solely on budgetary grounds, without considering the urgency and priority of the application, would be unlawful, unless the district budget is exhausted. The High Court has ruled that when an application for a CCG is considered, need and priority should be assessed before budgetary considerations are taken into account and this is now reflected in official guidance.[10]

The SF directions require the district budget to be managed so that as far as possible, high-priority applications for CCGs and CLs can be met and the maximum amounts payable for BL applications can be maintained throughout the year.[11] The aim is to achieve consistent decision making.

Guidance

In addition to the legal framework there are several forms of guidance available. These are not legally binding, but decision makers must take them into account.

The *Social Fund Guide* (see Appendix 3), in addition to the legally binding directions, contains guidance by the Secretary of State on how to interpret the law and directions and on administering the Social Fund.[12]

Local guidance specifies what level of priority the budget can afford to meet in respect of CCGs and CLs and identifies the maximum BL payable for an application of the lowest weighting (see p501).[13] The local guidance is reviewed and can be revised monthly. Copies of the guidance should be available from your DWP office.

Decisions of the SFIs (see p1160) are a useful guide to interpretation and decision making. The SF Independent Review Service (IRS – see Appendix 1) publishes a *Journal* three times a year which includes a digest of decisions (also available on the IRS website).

Advice by the SF Commissioner, who is responsible for the IRS, contains guidance to SFIs on specific areas of the law, which they are expected to follow. The guidance is published on the IRS website and in the *Journal*.

Applications

Where and how to apply

An application for a payment from the discretionary SF should normally be made to your local Jobcentre Plus office. If you are moving out of care and claiming a CCG, you should apply to the office which covers the area to which you are moving, unless you are only claiming removal expenses and/or fares. If you are applying for a CL, you can apply to the office nearest to where your need arises.

Applications for CCGs and BLs must be made in writing, either on an approved form (SF300 for CCGs and SF500 for BLs), or in some other written form which is accepted as sufficient by the Secretary of State.[14] An application for a CL is encouraged to be made by telephone but can be made in writing on Form SF401.[15] If a CL is awarded following a verbal application, you must provide satisfactory evidence of your identity and confirm the details of your application in writing before you are paid. If a CL is refused following a verbal application, you should still receive a written decision together with notification of your right to request a review. If you have difficulty making yourself understood on the telephone, you should be offered an immediate office interview instead.[16]

You can get the application forms from your local DWP office, or download them from the DWP website (see Appendix 1).

You are expected to apply for the grant or loan that is most appropriate to your circumstances. You should always apply for a CCG rather than a loan if you may be eligible. However, the decision maker has discretion to decide that an application for a CL should be treated as an application for a CCG and vice versa, if information in the application warrants it.[17] Information in a BL application may also be treated as an application for a CCG or CL.[18]

An application can be made on your behalf by another person, so long as you give your written consent (this is not necessary, however, if an appointee is acting for you).[19]

Your application is treated as made on the day it is received by the DWP.[20] If your application was incomplete and you comply with a request for additional information, your application is treated as made on the day it was originally received.[21] You are not normally required to produce corroborating evidence and should not be asked for evidence for which you have to pay.[22] It is sometimes helpful, however, to submit supporting evidence which confirms the existence and urgency of your need.

Repeat applications

If you have been awarded or refused a CCG or CL for an item or service, you cannot get a CCG or CL for the same item or service if you re-apply for it within 26 weeks of a previous application, unless there has been a relevant change of circumstances.[23] This rule does not apply to BLs. A relevant change in circumstances could be a change in your personal circumstances, or, for example, an increase in the amount available from the district budget.[24]

You should also note the following points.

- Applications by different partners are not covered by the above rule. The second application must be made by the same person who made the first application for the rule to apply.[25]
- The rule should not apply if your first application was incomplete, or you withdrew it before a decision was made, or you declined or did not respond to an offer.[26]
- Only payments for the 'same item or service' are excluded. An application for the same or a similar or related item should not be excluded if it is for a different need (eg, an application for a bed for one child is different to an application for a bed for another child, while an application for bedding may be different to an application for sheets, pillow cases and eiderdown). Applications for different items of clothing or for travel expenses for different periods should not be caught by the rule.[27]

Decisions

Although awards are discretionary, decision makers must act in accordance with the SF directions and take account of the national and local guidance (see p486).[28] They are also told to 'take particular care that their decisions are not in any way affected by bias or prejudice on such grounds as colour, ethnic or national origin, sexual orientation, sex or religion'.[29]

The consistency and standard of decision making have been heavily criticised. In part, this is a reflection of the contradictory nature of the SF's aim to meet need within a strictly limited budget.

You should receive a written decision on your application, with an explanation for a refusal or part refusal, together with a notification of your right to request a review (see p1156).

There are no legal time limits within which the DWP must make decisions, but the *Social Fund Guide* instructs decision makers to decide applications 'without delay' once they have all the necessary information and never to delay a decision until the need has passed.[30]Applications for a CL should, where possible, be dealt with on the day the need arises.[31] If there are unreasonable delays, you should complain to the district manager and, if necessary, consider asking your MP to take up your case with the manager or the Ombudsman (see p1183).

Payments and overpayments

Payment should normally be made to you, but the DWP can decide to pay a supplier directly[32] and, where appropriate, pay you in the form of food vouchers, travel warrants, cash or instalments. You can request a review of a decision to pay a supplier directly.

If you misrepresent or fail to disclose any material fact, any payment you receive in consequence is recoverable from you.[33] For more details about overpayments and recovery, see Chapter 39. You must be notified in writing of any overpayment decision and you have the right to request a review (see Chapter 44).[34]

Tax

Social fund loans and grants are not taxable.

Other benefits and tax credits

Payments from the discretionary SF are disregarded as income and capital for the purposes of means-tested benefits and tax credits, and do not affect entitlement to any non-means-tested benefits.

2. Community care grants

Community care grants (CCGs) are non-repayable grants to help people live independently in the community. There is no legal entitlement to a CCG, but you do have the right to request a review if you are not satisfied with a decision (see Chapter 44).

Eligibility

To be eligible for a CCG, you must satisfy all of the following conditions, which are laid down in legally binding directions.

- **You must be in receipt of income support (IS), income-based jobseeker's allowance (JSA) (including payments on account and hardship payments) or pension credit (PC) (guarantee or savings credit) when your application for a CCG is treated as made** (see p487).[35] The only exception to this rule is if you are due to leave institutional or residential care (see p490) within six weeks of the date your application for a CCG is made and you are likely to get IS, income-based JSA or PC when you leave. If you receive a backdated award of IS, income-based JSA or PC which covers the date you applied for CCG, you are eligible for a CCG. You are not eligible, however, if you apply for a CCG on one of the three 'waiting days' for JSA (see p366) unless you are moving out of institutional or residential care (see p490). You are treated as being 'in receipt of' IS, income-based JSA or PC if it is being paid to you, or to an appointee on your behalf.[36] The High Court has held that you are not 'in receipt of IS/income-based JSA' if your partner or another member of your family is the claimant.[37] If you are a member of a 'joint-claim couple' (see p381), you are only eligible for a CCG if you are the partner being paid JSA.[38]
- **You must not have too much capital.**[39] Any CCG awarded is reduced by the amount of capital you have in excess of £500 (£1,000 if you or your partner are 60 or over). Capital is calculated as for IS, income-based JSA or PC, depending on which benefit you are receiving (see Chapter 37). Payments made from the Family Fund to you, your partner or child, and refugee integration loans are ignored. Capital held by your children should be disregarded. Capital below the above limits should not be taken into account as a resource from which a need could be met (see p496).
- **You or your partner must not be involved in a trade dispute,**[40] unless your claim is for travel expenses to visit a sick person. See p493 for details.
- **You mustnot be a 'person subject to immigration control'** (there are exceptions to this rule) – see p1334.
- **The CCG must not be for an excluded item**[41] (see p495).
- **You must be awarded a CCG of at least £30,**[42] unless your award is for daily living expenses or travel expenses.
- **You must need a CCG for one or more of the following purposes:**[43]
  - to help you, or a member of your family, or other person for whom you or a member of your family will be providing care, to establish yourself (or her/himself) in the community following a stay in institutional or residential accommodation in which you (or s/he) received care (see p490);
  - to help you, or a member of your family, or other person for whom you or a member of your family will be providing care, to remain in the community

rather than enter institutional or residential accommodation in which you (or s/he) will receive care (see below);
- to help you to set up home in the community as part of a planned resettlement programme following a period during which you have been without a settled way of life (see p491);
- to ease exceptional pressures on you and your family (see p492);
- to allow you, or your partner, to care for a prisoner or young offender on temporary release (see p493);
- to help you, or one or more members of your family, with travel expenses within the UK in certain circumstances (see p493).

None of the above terms are defined in the *Social Fund Guide* and so are open to interpretation.

Qualifying conditions

As well as meeting the eligibility conditions, you must also show that you meet the following qualifying conditions.

Moving out of institutional or residential accommodation

A CCG can be paid to help you, or a member of your family, or other person for whom you or a member of your family will be providing care, to establish yourself (or her/himself) in the community, following a stay in institutional or residential accommodation in which you (or s/he) received care.[44]

Interpretation

- See p493 for the meaning of 'family'.
- 'Institutional or residential accommodation' means accommodation where residents receive a significant and substantial amount of care, supervision or protection because they are unable to live independently in the community or might be a danger to others in the community.[45] Examples of accommodation given are hospitals, care homes, foster care, hostels, prisons and youth centres.[46] Decision makers are told to treat applications from discharged prisoners with particular urgency and sensitivity, bearing in mind the pressures they face and the risk of re-offending.[47] If you cannot establish that you lived in institutional or residential accommodation, you may still be eligible for a CCG to help you remain in the community, or for planned resettlement (see p491).
- You should be eligible if you are establishing yourself in the community for the first time because, for example, you have always lived in care, or you have recently arrived in the UK and have been in a refugee camp overseas or a refugee hostel in the UK (the High Court has ruled that 'the community' is restricted to the UK).[48] The High Court has said that you must be actually or imminently in the community to qualify.[49]

- A 'stay in' institutional or residential accommodation normally means at least three months, or a pattern of frequent or regular admission.[50] The High Court has ruled, however, that undue importance should not be attached to the reference to three months[51] and the SF Commissioner advises that a stay of less than three months can satisfy the direction.[52]

Staying out of institutional or residential accommodation

A CCG can be paid to help you, or a member of your family, or other person for whom you or a member of your family will be providing care, to remain in the community, rather than enter institutional or residential accommodation in which you (or s/he) will receive care.[53]

Interpretation

- See p490 for guidance on the meaning of 'institutional or residential accommodation'.
- See p493 for the meaning of 'family'.
- There is no requirement that a CCG must be able to 'prevent' you going into institutional or residential accommodation. The legal test is whether a CCG will 'help' you remain in the community. Decision makers should consider whether a CCG would improve your independent life in the community and, therefore, reduce the risk of or delay your admission into care.[54] Going into hospital, even for a short admission, should count as entering care in this context.[55] The risk of care does not have to be immediate, but should be more than a remote possibility (if it is immediate, the application should be given higher priority).[56] If your condition makes you liable to repeated stays in care, you could still get a CCG if it could reduce the frequency or length of such stays.
- Actual or potential risk to physical or mental health because of a lack of items such as basic furniture, cooking facilities, clothes, bedding and heaters can be used to argue that a CCG for such items will lessen the risk of entry into hospital or other types of institutional or residential accommodation.

Planned resettlement

A CCG can be paid to help you set up home in the community as part of a planned resettlement programme.[57]

Interpretation

- A programme of resettlement involves help to set up home and help with matters such as budgeting skills, literacy skills, careers guidance and benefits advice. 'Setting up home' involves more than just moving into a new property and may still be in process (or even begin) some time after a move has occurred.[58]

- People without a settled way of life might have been in a night shelter, hostel, emergency shelter, temporary supported lodging scheme, or temporary accommodation provided for asylum seekers, or sleeping rough, but this is not an exhaustive list.[59] It could also, for example, cover people moving between the houses of friends or relatives.[60]
- Planned resettlement programmes may be run by local authorities, voluntary organisations, housing associations and registered charities.[61] Again, this is not an exhaustive list and you can argue you are part of a programme planned by any other organisation or person (including yourself), even if they are unconnected to your accommodation.[62] Decision makers are told they may need to check that a resettlement programme exists at the accommodation you are moving from and that you are on such a programme.[63]
- If you cannot qualify for a CCG under this section, you may still be eligible for a CCG to help you move out of, or stay out of, institutional or residential accommodation (see pp490 and 491).

Easing exceptional pressures on families

A CCG can be paid to ease exceptional pressures on you and your family.[64] The scope for applications on this basis is very wide.

When making your application, always fully explain all the pressures your family is experiencing and how a CCG will ease those pressures and help you to continue living independently in the community.

Exceptional pressures

The following points may be relevant.[65]

- 'Exceptional' means something greater than the normal range of pressures experienced by most families.
- The overall effect of the different pressures on a family should be assessed, including their cumulative impact. You should always, therefore, list all the pressures affecting your family and explain their overall effect.
- Whether the pressures were foreseeable or are common is irrelevant, although higher priority should be given to a new, unforeseeable need.
- The breakdown of a relationship, particularly involving domestic violence, is a common source of exceptional stress, as is disability.
- Low income, lone parenthood and poor or overcrowded living conditions can be the source of exceptional pressures.
- Pressures that arise from a sudden event (eg, a disaster or fire) can be exceptional and traumatic. Pressures which have existed for a long time do not necessarily become easier to handle.
- There does not have to be any risk of a person going into care for exceptional pressures to exist.

- Mental stress, anxiety, depression, disability and illness are all sources and symptoms of exceptional pressures. The fact that an applicant does not appear stressed at an interview does not mean that exceptional pressures do not exist.
- Exceptional pressures experienced by children are valid – eg, health risk or discomfort arising from lack of clothes or facilities in the home.
- Refugees moving into the community from temporary accommodation provided by the Border and Immigration Agency may face exceptional family pressures.
- Letters of support from professionals can help your case.

Family

The law refers to 'easing exceptional pressures on a person and his family'. This implies that people not living in a family are excluded. This interpretation was endorsed in a High Court case.[66]

The SF Commissioner advises that a family could include:

- couples (with or without children, married or unmarried and with same- or different-sex partners);
- 'nuclear' and extended families;
- relationships of long-term interdependence, even where there are no blood or marriage ties;
- a woman who has been pregnant for 24 weeks or more.[67]

Prisoners on temporary release

A CCG can be paid to allow you or your partner to care for a prisoner or young offender on temporary release.[68]

Amount

You will normally be awarded one-seventh of your IS, income-based JSA or PC personal allowance for each day you are caring for a prisoner or young offender. If the prisoner is your partner, the suggested amount is one-seventh of the difference between your personal allowance and the couple rate.[69] The £30 minimum rule (see p489) does not apply.[70]

Travel expenses

A CCG can be paid to assist you and/or a member of your family with travel expenses in the UK (including overnight accommodation charges) to:[71]

- visit someone who is ill (in hospital or elsewhere); *or*
- attend a relative's funeral; *or*
- ease a domestic crisis (not defined); *or*
- visit a child who is with the other parent pending a court decision; *or*
- move to suitable accommodation.

Amount

A CCG for travel expenses should be calculated as follows:[72]

- the cost of standard rate public transport (excluding air fares); *or*
- the cost of petrol, either up to the cost of public transport if available or in full if public transport is not available or you are unable to use it; *or*
- taxi fares, if public transport is unavailable or you or your partner cannot use public transport and have no access to private transport; *plus*
- the cost of an escort's fare if you cannot travel alone; *plus*
- the reasonable cost of necessary overnight accommodation.

The £30 minimum rule (see p489) does not apply to a CCG for travel expenses.[73]

Excluded items

The social fund (SF) Directions exclude payment for the items listed below.[74]

Items excluded from community care grants and crisis loans

- A need which occurs outside the UK. This rule may constitute unlawful discrimination in the case of European Economic Area nationals (see p1382).
- An educational or training need, including clothing and tools.
- 'Distinctive' school uniform, or any equipment or sports clothes for school use. You may, however, be eligible for a budgeting loan (BL) (see p498). You may also be eligible for a grant for school uniform from your local authority.
- Travel expenses to and from school. You may, however, be eligible for a BL (see p498). You may also be eligible for help from your local authority.
- School meals taken during school holidays by children who are entitled to free school meals.
- Expenses in connection with court proceedings (including a community service order) – eg, legal fees, court fees, fines, costs, damages and travel expenses. You can, however, get a crisis loan (CL) for emergency travel expenses (see p508).
- Removal charges where you are permanently re-housed following a compulsory purchase order, a redevelopment or closing order, or where there is a compulsory exchange of tenancies or you are permanently re-housed as homeless under the Housing Acts. In all these circumstances, your local authority may help you. Alternatively you may be eligible for a BL (see p498).
- The cost of domestic assistance or respite care. This would include the cost of home care or short breaks in residential care.
- Repairs to property owned by public sector housing bodies including local authorities, most housing associations, housing co-operatives and housing trusts.
- Medical, surgical, optical, aural or dental items or services. A medical item does not include an everyday item needed because of a medical condition – eg, cotton sheets and non-allergic bedding (when a person is allergic to synthetic),

built-up shoes, special beds, incontinence pads. If an item is not in ordinary, everyday use, it should only be treated as a medical item if its sole purpose is to cure, alleviate, treat, diagnose or prevent a medical condition. Wheelchairs (or parts for them) and stairlifts should not be excluded under this test, but you can be refused a payment if help is available from the NHS, social services or elsewhere.[75]

- Work-related expenses. This includes fares when seeking work and the cost of work clothes.[76] You may be able to get help with fares to interviews from Jobcentre Plus. Alternatively you may be eligible for a BL (see p498).
- Debts to government departments. These could include national insurance arrears, income tax liabilities and customs charges.
- Investments.
- Council tax, and council water charges.
- Housing costs (other than those listed below), including:
  - repairs and improvements to your home, including garage, garden and outbuildings (but see below for minor repairs and improvements);
  - deposits to secure accommodation;
  - mortgage payments, rent, service charges, water and sewerage charges and any other accommodation charges.

  Note: repairs and improvements are only excluded if they relate to the structure or permanent fixtures of your home (eg, windows) as opposed to movable items (eg, stairlifts).[77]

Housing costs that are not excluded[78]

You can be awarded:

- a CCG or CL for minor repairs and improvements ('minor' is not defined but relevant factors include the nature and extent of the work, the time needed to complete it and the cost of materials and labour[79]);
- a CCG for overnight accommodation as part of a travel expenses payment (see p493);
- a CL for rent in advance for fresh accommodation where the landlord is not a local authority;
- a CL for housing costs not met by housing benefit, IS or income-based JSA or not eligible for direct deductions from IS, income-based JSA, or PC (see p988) – eg, emptying cesspits or septic tanks;
- a CL for board and lodging or hostel charges.

A BL is also payable for rent in advance, removal expenses, and the improvement, maintenance and security of the home (see p498).

Additional items excluded from community care grants[80]

- The cost of purchasing, renting or installing a telephone and of any call charges. You may, however, be eligible for help from your local authority social services department if you are chronically sick or disabled.

- Any expenses which the local authority has a statutory duty to meet (discretionary powers do not trigger the exclusion, nor should statutory duties not undertaken by the local authority).
- The cost of any fuel and standing charges.
- Any daily living expenses, such as food and groceries, except where incurred in caring for a prisoner on temporary release or where the maximum amount for a CL has already been awarded (see p508).
- Any item worth less than £30, or several items which together are worth less than £30 (unless the award is for daily living expenses or travel expenses).[81]

Maternity and funeral expenses

The discretionary SF cannot meet maternity and funeral expenses as these are provided for by the regulated SF (see Chapter 22).[82] Although maternity and funeral expenses are not defined, they do not include items such as clothing for a pregnant woman or a growing (as opposed to newborn) baby, funeral clothing and headstones.[83] The SF Commissioner's Advice states that only maternity expenses to meet the immediate needs of a recently born baby (and not the mother) are excluded from the discretionary SF.[84] A CCG could, therefore, be paid for items such as highchairs, stair gates, prams and even a cot or carrycot if the baby used something else to sleep in immediately after birth.

What to claim for

You can claim for help with any expenses which are not excluded (see p494). Examples include:

- furniture, cookers, beds, bedding and household equipment, floor covering, curtains, heaters;
- moving expenses, including removal costs, fares and storage charges;
- connection charges when setting up or moving home;
- items which will improve your living conditions, such as minor repairs, redecoration and refurbishment, installation of a pre-payment meter, washing machine;
- clothing and footwear;
- maternity and funeral expenses that are arguably not covered by the regulated SF (see above);
- items needed because of disability (including wheelchairs, stair lifts, special clothing, an orthopaedic mattress, or an upright armchair).

Decision making and priorities

When deciding an application for a CCG, the law requires decision makers to have regard to all the circumstances of each case and, in particular:[85]

- the nature, extent and urgency of the need;
- the existence of resources which could meet the need;
- whether any other person or body could wholly or partly meet the need;

- the district budget (see p485);
- the SF directions (see p485);
- national and local guidance (see p486).

The High Court has ruled that need and the priority of an application (see below) should be assessed before budgetary considerations are taken into account.[86] Decision makers must have regard to the district grants budget, however, when they decide whether to award a CCG and how much to pay.

Decision makers should exercise their discretion sensitively and with imagination and avoid a rigid interpretation of the guidance.[87]

The *Social Fund Guide* suggests that applications for CCGs are prioritised as follows.[88]

- High priority should normally be given if a CCG will have a substantial effect in the immediately foreseeable future in resolving or improving the circumstances of the applicant and meeting one of the purposes for which a CCG can be awarded (see p489).
- Medium priority should normally be given if a CCG will have a noticeable (but not substantial or immediate) effect in achieving the above aims.
- Low priority should normally be given if a CCG will only have a minor effect in meeting the above aims.

Circumstances which may affect priority include:[89]

- mental or physical disability and illness and general frailty;
- physical or social abuse or neglect;
- a long period of sleeping rough;
- unstable family circumstances;
- behavioural problems – eg, because of drug or alcohol misuse.

Higher priority should be given where an award of an item would significantly reduce the risk of you going into care, or would immediately alleviate exceptional pressure on your family in a substantial and noticeable way, or where the lack of an item would seriously undermine you becoming established in the community.[90]

Local guidance (see p486) specifies which level of priority can be met by the budget but invariably this tends to be high priority only.

When deciding whether there are other resources which could meet your need, decision makers should not take into account any capital you have below £500 (£1,000 if you or your partner are 60 or over), or your IS, income-based JSA or PC. Any other income you have should only be taken into account if it is available to meet your needs and is not required to meet other expenses. Attendance allowance and the care component of disability living allowance (DLA) should be treated as required to meet disability-related expenses, unless there is evidence to the contrary (the mobility component of DLA must always be disregarded).[91]

Amount and payment

The amount you request should normally be allowed if it is within the broad range of prices for an item of serviceable quality, taking into account prices charged in national catalogue outlets and high street chain retailers.[92] It is not normally necessary to submit written estimates from a supplier, although you may be asked for one if you are asking for removal expenses.[93] You may be offered less than the appropriate amount if the budget is under exceptional pressure but the amount must still be sufficient to cover the cost of the item or service needed.[94] There is no legal maximum award but the minimum in most cases is £30 (see p489). If you are dissatisfied with the amount you have been awarded, you should consider requesting a review (see p1156).

An award should normally be paid to you but can also be paid directly to a supplier on your behalf. This should only happen in exceptional circumstances – eg, where there is firm evidence that the grant will not be used for its intended purpose.[95]

Tactics

- Always apply for a CCG if you are eligible, rather than a loan. Despite the restrictive nature of the SF, the eligibility conditions for a CCG are wide. You can apply for help with anything other than an excluded item (see p494), and the purposes for which a CCG can be awarded (see p489) can cover a wide range of circumstances. Bear in mind the rules about repeat applications (see p487).
- When completing the application form (SF300), you should give specific details of each of the items you need and its cost (or an estimate of the cost).
- Your application must establish that you need a CCG for one of the purposes set out on p489. Explain how the payment you are requesting will help the relevant person to become established or remain in the community, or will help ease exceptional pressures on you and your family.
- Explain how your application fits in with the guidance on high priorities (see p497). You can obtain a copy of the local guidance from your local DWP office (see p486) and refer to it if appropriate. You could also submit supporting evidence – eg, from a doctor or social worker.
- If you are dissatisfied with a decision, you should consider asking for a review (see p1156).

3. Budgeting loans

Budgeting loans (BLs) are interest-free loans intended to help people with intermittent expenses which are difficult to budget for after a period on income support (IS), income-based jobseeker's allowance (JSA) or pension credit (PC). There is no legal entitlement to a BL, but unlike community care grants (CCGs) and crisis loans (CLs) (see pp488 and 503), decision making is based on legally binding rules about who is in your household, rather than discretion.

Although you have the right to request a review (see p487), if you are refused a BL or are given less than you asked for, a decision is only likely to be changed if it was based on incorrect information about your circumstances, or if the amount you are allowed to borrow has increased (see p1159).

Eligibility

To be eligible for a BL, you must satisfy all of the following conditions, which are laid down in legally binding Directions.

- **You must be in receipt of IS, income-based JSA(including payments on account and hardship payments) or PC (guarantee or savings credit** – see Chapter 18) **when your BL application is determined.**[96] You are treated as being in receipt of IS, income-based JSA or PC if it is being paid to you, or to an appointee on your behalf.[97] You are eligible if you receive a backdated award of IS or income-based JSA covering the date your application is determined.[98] The High Court has held that you are not 'in receipt of' IS or income-based JSA if your partner or another member of your family is the claimant.[99] If you are a member of a 'joint-claim couple' (see p381), you are only eligible for a BL if you are the partner being paid JSA.[100]
- **You and/or your partner, between you, must have been receiving IS, income-based JSA (including payments on account and hardship payments) or PC throughout the 26 weeks before the date on which your application is determined, disregarding any number of breaks of 28 days or less.**[101] A period covered by a payment of arrears should count, as should any benefit received while in Northern Ireland.[102] The three waiting days at the start of a jobseeking period (see p366) do not count.[103] More than one partner could help you satisfy the qualifying period.
- **You must not have too much capital.**[104] Any BL award is reduced by the amount of capital you have in excess of £1,000 (£2,000 if you or your partner are 60 or over). Capital is calculated as for IS, income-based JSA or PC, depending on which benefit you are receiving (see Chapter 37). Payments made from the Family Fund to you, your partner or child, and refugee integration loans are ignored.[105] Capital held by your child(ren) should be disregarded.
- **You, or your partner, must not be involved in a trade dispute** (see p633).[106]
- **You must not be a 'person subject to immigration control'** (there are exceptions to this rule) – see p1334.
- **The loan must be for one or more of the following categories of allowable expenses:**[107]

- furniture and household equipment;
- clothing and footwear;
- rent in advance and/or removal expenses to secure fresh accommodation;
- improvement, maintenance and security of the home;
- travelling expenses;
- expenses associated with seeking or re-entering work;
- hire purchase (HP) and other debts for any of the above items.

You are required to tick the category of expense for which you need the loan on the application form. You are not required to specify the particular items you need (eg, bed, winter coat). The exclusions which apply to CCGs and CLs (see p494) do not apply to BLs.

- **The loan must be a minimum of £100 and a maximum of £1,500 (less any outstanding social fund (SF) loans you and your partner have).**[108] You must state how much you are asking for on your application.
- **You must be likely to be able to repay the loan** (see p501).[109]

Decision making and priorities

When deciding a BL application, the law requires decision makers to consider:[110]

- the prescribed factual criteria relating to the applicant's personal circumstances (see p598);
- the existence of resources which could meet the need;
- the district budget (see p484);
- the SF directions;
- national and local guidance (see p486);
- the likelihood of repayment and the time it would take.

In practice, decisions are determined by two factors.

- **The 'weighting' of your application.** This is dependent on who is in your household. See p501 for more details.
- **The baseline figure.** This is the amount determined by the Secretary of State that a single person should receive. The maximum payable for applications with a higher weighting is calculated by multiplying this baseline figure by the weighting of the application. If, for example, the baseline figure is £300, the maximum payable for an application with a weighting of one and one-third will be £400. The baseline figure may vary over the course of the year.

The actual amount you can borrow also depends on the amount you can repay within 104 weeks and whether you already have any outstanding BLs (see p502 for details).

Although decisions are legally made by decision makers, decision making is largely an automated process, with weightings and awards automatically calculated by computer.

The weighting of applications

The weighting of your application is as follows:[111]

- single people have a weighting of one;
- couples without children have a weighting of one and one-third;
- families (including lone parents) with children have a weighting of two and one-third.

The baseline figure is set by the Secretary of State and included in local guidance.[112]

Amount

The actual amount of BL you will be offered depends on the following factors.[113]

- **The amount you request.** You will not be offered more than you ask for, but you may be offered less because of the factors below.
- **The legal minimum and maximum amounts and the capital rules.** You cannot be offered a loan of less than £100 or more than £1,500 (less any outstanding SF loans). The amount of your award will also be reduced if you have too much capital (see p489).
- **The weighting of your application** (see above) and the maximum amount payable by the district budget for an application of that weighting.
- **The amount of any outstanding BL debt you or your partner have.**
  - If you have no outstanding BLs, you will be offered the maximum amount appropriate to the weighting of your application, or the amount you have requested, if this is lower.
  - If you do have an outstanding BL debt, the maximum amount you can borrow is reduced by the amount of your outstanding BL debt.
- **The amount you are likely to be able to repay.** Generally this is the amount you can repay within 104 weeks (see below for details).[114]

Repayments

All loans must be repaid to the DWP.[115]

The decision maker will give you up to three different options for repaying a loan, depending on whether you have any other SF loans outstanding and your other financial commitments. S/he may offer an option of a higher loan with an increased repayment rate, but you cannot be asked to repay at a rate higher than 20 per cent of your IS/income-based JSA applicable amount or PC appropriate minimum guarantee plus any child tax credt or child benefit you receive. The loan must be repaid within 104 weeks.[116]

You will receive a written decision on your application for a BL with details of any loan offers and repayment terms. You have 14 days from the date the decision was sent to return the declaration agreeing to one of the offers made to you (the time limit can be extended for 'special reasons').[117]

Methods of repayment

Both BLs and CLs are nearly always recovered by direct deductions from benefit, although you can make a payment at any time to pay off, partially or wholly, the debt. Deductions can only be made from the following benefits:[118]

- IS;
- PC;
- JSA (contributory or income-based);
- incapacity benefit;
- severe disablement allowance;
- carer's allowance;
- disablement benefit, reduced earnings allowance and industrial death benefit;
- bereavement benefits (excluding the lump-sum bereavement payment) and widows' benefits;
- retirement pensions;
- maternity allowance.

Increases of benefit for age and dependants, and additional benefit under the additional state pension scheme, are also subject to deduction.

Deductions from benefit can be made even where an order for bankruptcy or sequestration has been made.[119]

A loan can be legally recovered from:

- you (the applicant) or the person who the loan was for;[120]
- your partner, if you are living together as a couple as defined for IS purposes (see p702);[121]
- a 'liable relative' (see p753) or a person who has given a sponsorship undertaking (see p1341).[122]

Challenging repayment terms

You cannot request a review of a decision relating to repayment terms or recovery.[123] If you have accepted a loan, however, and the repayment terms are causing hardship (eg, because your financial situation has deteriorated), you can ask the DWP to reschedule the loan by lowering the weekly repayment rate.

Tactics

- Always apply for a CCG, if you are eligible (see p489), rather than a BL. Note that your application for a BL will *not* normally be considered for a CCG (see p486).
- When completing the BL application form (SF500), give details requested about your debts and commitments, as these will affect the standard repayment rate of any loan offer (see p501).
- State how much you are applying for. Bear in mind the minimum and maximum amounts (see p500) and the capital rules (see p489). The local guidance, obtainable from your local DWP office (see p486), should indicate

the maximum BL applicable to your situation (see p500). You can use this figure to work out roughly how much you are likely to be offered, depending on your circumstances (see p501).

- If you are dissatisfied with a BL decision, you can request a review (see p1156). You should note, however, that a decision is only likely to be revised if it was based on an error about your circumstances or if there has been an increase in the maximum loan available (see p500).
- You can reapply for a BL at any time. There is no rule preventing repeat applications for the same or different items of expenditure. You may become eligible if your household circumstances change (see p501) or there is an increase in the maximum loan available.
- Consider the repayment terms carefully before accepting a BL. Deductions of significant amounts from your weekly benefit may leave you seriously short of money. However, BLs are at least interest-free. If you accept a BL but later find that the repayment terms are causing you hardship, ask for the loan to be re-scheduled (ie, for repayments to be reduced).

4. **Crisis loans**

Crisis loans (CLs) are interest-free loans which are intended to help people with their immediate short-term needs in a crisis. Unlike budgeting loans (BLs), you do not have to be in receipt of benefit to qualify. There is no legal entitlement to a CL, but you do have the right to request a review if you are refused a payment or given less than you asked for (see p1156).

Eligibility

To be eligible for a CL, you must satisfy all of the following conditions, which are laid down in legally binding directions.

- **You must be aged 16 or over.**[124]
- **You must be without sufficient resources to meet the immediate short-term needs of yourself and/or your family** (see p504 for details).[125]
- **You must not be an excluded person** (see p505).[126]
- **You must not be a 'person subject to immigration control'** (there are exceptions to this rule) – see p1334.
- **The CL must not be for an excluded item** (see p506).[127]
- **The CL must be to help you meet:**[128]
  - expenses in an emergency, or as a consequence of a disaster, where a CL is the only means by which serious damage or serious risk to the health and safety of yourself or a member of your family may be prevented (see p506); *or*

  - rent in advance payable to a landlord who is not a local authority and where a community care grant (CCG) is being awarded following a stay in institutional or residential accommodation (see p508).
- **The loan cannot exceed £1,500** (less any outstanding social fund (SF) loans you and your partner have).[129] There are also more specific maximum amounts relating to items, services and living expenses (see p508 for details). There is no legal minimum amount of CL.
- **You must be likely to be able to repay the loan** (see p509).[130]

Resources

You must be without sufficient resources to meet the immediate short-term needs of yourself and/or your family. All resources which are actually available to you, or could be obtained in time to meet the need, should be taken into account.[131] Resources available on credit should only be taken into account if you are not on income support (IS), income-based jobseeker's allowance (JSA) or pension credit (PC) and can afford the required repayments.[132]

The following resources should be disregarded:[133]

- other SF payments, housing benefit (HB) and the mobility component of disability living allowance;
- any run-on payments of HB, council tax benefit or mortgage interest;
- refugee integration loans;
- the value of your home, premises acquired for occupation within the next six months, and premises occupied by a relative or your ex-partner;
- the value of any reversionary interest – ie, an interest in property or capital which you will only be able to enjoy in the future when a specified event occurs;
- your business assets;
- any sum paid to you because of damage to, or loss of, your home or personal possessions and intended for their repair or replacement;
- any sum acquired on the express condition that it is used for essential repairs or improvements to your home;
- any compensation award set aside for the replacement of lost livelihood;
- personal possessions, except those acquired for the purpose of qualifying for a CL;
- any payments from the Independent Living Funds, the Macfarlane Trust, the Variant Creutzfeldt Jakob Disease Trusts and the Skipton Fund;
- payments made under s17 Children Act (s22 Children (Scotland) Act), unless they are for the same need as the CL.

Decision makers are also advised to disregard other resources if it is reasonable to do so.[134] You could argue that money set aside to meet forthcoming bills (eg, council tax, fuel bills) is not available and should be disregarded. The SF Commissioner advises social fund inspectors (SFIs) to start from the premise that

IS premiums, other benefits and capital are not available to meet the need, unless there is clear evidence to the contrary.[135]

Decision makers are told not to refer routinely applicants to employers, relatives or close friends unless there is reason to believe their help will be forthcoming.[136] They are also reminded that social services do not normally meet financial needs.[137] The possibility of getting a BL should not be used as a reason for refusing a CL.[138]

Excluded people

People excluded in all circumstances

The following people are excluded by the SF directions from getting a CL in all circumstances:[139]

- people in hospital and care homes (independent or local authority), *unless* their discharge is planned to take place within the next two weeks. (**Note:** people in care homes in Scotland are only excluded if they are receiving nursing or personal care);
- prisoners and people lawfully detained, including those released on temporary licence (but not those released on parole or on bail pending a court hearing);[140]
- members of religious orders who are fully maintained by the order;
- people in 'relevant education' (see p576) who are not entitled to IS or income-based JSA.

People excluded in some circumstances

The following people are excluded by the directions from getting a CL except in very limited circumstances:[141]

- full-time students not on IS, income-based JSA or PC (including payments on account) can only get a CL for expenses arising out of a disaster;
- someone who is a 'person subject to immigration control'(see p1333) can only get a CL for expenses arising out of a disaster (**Note:** if you are an overstayer, subject to a deportation order, or an illegal entrant, you should not apply for a CL before getting advice about regularising your status);
- people involved in a trade dispute (see p633);
- people subject to certain JSA disallowances or sanctions (see below).

People subject to jobseeker's allowance disallowances or sanctions[142]

If you have been refused JSA because you do not satisfy the labour market conditions or you have been sanctioned (see p401), you only have restricted access to a CL. Restricted access means you can only get a CL for expenses arising from a disaster, or for items needed for cooking or space heating (including fireguards).

The restriction usually lasts for two weeks (four weeks if you have a four-week New Deal sanction) and for the same weeks that your JSA is not payable. If you have failed to take part in a work-focused interview where this is required, your access to a CL is restricted until you comply. However, the restriction does not apply to some lone parents (see p975), or if you are receiving a JSA hardship payment (though in the latter case, the amount payable for living expenses is restricted – see p508). Your partner can apply for a CL if you are subject to a disallowance or sanction, but the amount payable for living expenses is restricted (see p508).

Excluded items

You cannot get a CL for any of the items listed on p494.

In addition, you cannot get a CL for the following:[143]

- telephone purchase, installation, call and rental charges;
- mobility needs (this does not include travel expenses);
- holidays;
- television or radio, TV licence, aerial, TV rental;
- garaging, parking, purchase and running costs of any motor vehicle except where payment is being considered for emergency travel expenses.

See p496 if you need help with maternity or funeral expenses.

Emergencies and disasters

Most CLs can only be awarded in an emergency or following a disaster. The SF Commissioner's Advice defines an emergency as 'an unforeseen circumstance or pressing need, either of which requires immediate remedy or action' and a disaster as 'an event that causes great distress or destruction'.[144] Both the risk of an emergency, as well as an emergency or disaster that has already occurred could trigger a payment. You should always explain why a particular situation constitutes an emergency or disaster for you or your family. The consequences, rather than the causes, of the crisis should be the key issue.[145] Self-inflicted crises are not excluded and decision makers should not deny you a CL based on their judgements about your behaviour. Loss of money in the past should not prejudice the payment of a CL needed because of a further loss.

A CL has to be the only means of preventing serious damage or serious risk to health or safety. If a decision maker suggests there are 'other means', which you believe are impractical or unavailable, ask for a review. The burden of proof is on the decision maker (or SFI) to show that there are other means which are actually available to you.[146] 'Health' and 'safety' are not defined, but health includes both physical and mental health, while safety relates to actual or potential danger.[147] Lack of adequate cooking, heating or sleeping facilities could seriously undermine your health, particularly if you already have health problems.[148]

Any supporting evidence from a doctor or social worker will help your case.

Survival for a period without money or a CL does not mean that a CL is not the only means of preventing serious damage or risk to your health or safety.

If you have been refused a BL, decision makers must consider whether the refusal has contributed to the emergency or disaster.[149]

Decision making and priorities

When deciding an application for a CL, the law requires decision makers to have regard to all the circumstances of each case and, in particular:[150]

- the nature, extent and urgency of the need;
- the existence of resources which could meet the need;
- whether any other person or body could wholly or partly meet the need;
- the district budget (see p485);
- the SF directions (see p485);
- national and local guidance (see p486);
- the likelihood of repayment and the time it would take.

The High Court has ruled that need and the priority of an application should be assessed before budgetary considerations are taken into account.[151] The *Social Fund Guide* states that an application for a CL to prevent serious damage or risk to health or safety will by its nature be high priority.[152]

Unlike BL decision making, decision makers must exercise individual discretion when deciding an application for a CL. Decision makers should take account of all the circumstances of each individual case and exercise their discretion flexibly. They should avoid a rigid interpretation of the guidance.

The *Social Fund Guide* gives examples of situations where a CL may be appropriate (see below). They are not exhaustive, however, and you can apply for a loan in any situation so long as you satisfy the eligibility conditions (see p503).

Living expenses for a short period

A CL could be awarded to meet day-to-day living expenses if:

- you are waiting for your first benefit payment or wages;[153]
- you are facing hardship because your employer has imposed a compulsory unpaid holiday;[154]
- you have lost money or you have lost a cheque and replacement is delayed or not made (see p983 on lost payments);[155]
- you cannot get IS or income-based JSA because your capital is over the prescribed limit (see p910) but you cannot realise your assets immediately;[156]
- you are homeless and need living expenses (the *Social Fund Guide* stresses the risk to physical and mental health brought about by sleeping rough and prolonged homelessness);
- you have been discharged from prison and have insufficient money to meet your needs until your first payment of benefit (this can apply even if you have been paid a discharge grant).[157]

A CL should only cover living expenses for more than 14 days in exceptional circumstances – eg, a continuing crisis, loss of money which would normally cover you until your next income is due, or no money because of misfortune or mismanagement.[158]

Other needs

A CL could also be awarded to meet the following needs:

- emergency travel expenses if you are stranded away from home, or emergency fares to hospital;[159]
- fuel reconnection charges[160] (if you need a CL to pay for a powercard or token, an amount to meet fuel arrears should be awarded separately from amounts for current consumption);[161]
- up to four weeks' rent (up to the level of your likely HB) payable in advance to a landlord other than a local authority, where a CCG is also awarded to help you return to the community;[162]
- disasters – eg, fire or flood (see p506);[163]
- other urgent needs for which you cannot get a BL because you have not been receiving IS, income-based JSA or PC for 26 weeks.[164]

Amount

There is no legal minimum. There is a general legal maximum of £1,500 less any outstanding SF loan(s) you have. You also cannot be awarded more than you can afford to repay,[165] usually calculated by multiplying your weekly repayment rate by 104 (see p509). If you already have one or more loans you may find you are offered less than you asked for.

There are also more specific legal maximums for items, services and living expenses.

Items and services:[166] The maximum you can get is the reasonable cost of purchase (including delivery and installation) or the cost of repair, if cheaper. You should not normally be required to provide estimates and decision makers are not expected to check the amount requested against a price list.[167]

Living expenses:[168]

- The normal maximum you can get is 75 per cent of the appropriate IS or income-based JSA personal allowance for you *and* any partner (see pp702 and 773) plus £52.59 for each child.
- If you have been disallowed JSA because you have been sanctioned (see Chapter 16), or have failed to satisfy the labour market conditions, the maximum CL payable to your partner for living expenses is restricted to 75 per cent of her/his JSA personal allowance (see p773) plus £52.59 for each child.
- If you are getting a hardship payment of JSA (see p422), the maximum CL you can get for living expenses is the lesser of:

- 75 per cent of the normal income-based JSA personal allowance for you and any partner (see pp702 and 773) plus £52.59 for each child;
- the hardship rate of income-based JSA payable for you and any family.

Repayments

All CLs must be repaid to the DWP. The rate of repayment, the repayment period and the method of recovery are not subject to review.[169] You can, however, request a change in your repayment terms (see below).

The rate and period of repayment

The guidance says that the loan must be repaid within 104 weeks and the total debt to the SF must not exceed £1,500. When considering your ability to repay, the decision maker will also take into account any existing debts you have.

Methods of repayment

Crisis loans can be recovered by weekly deductions from most benefits. The rules are the same as for BLs (see p501).

Challenging repayment terms

You cannot request a review of a decision relating to the rate of repayment or the recovery of loans. You can request a change in your repayment terms, however, by writing to the DWP, either before accepting a loan, or at any time after accepting a loan (rescheduling), explaining why the repayment terms are unacceptable (eg, because they will cause you more hardship). You should give details of your financial commitments and any relevant changes in your financial circumstances.

Tactics

- Always apply for a CCG (see p488) if you are eligible, rather than a CL. Your application for a CL should be considered for a CCG if it contains information to indicate that a grant may be appropriate (see p488). You could also consider applying for a BL if you are eligible (see p498).
- You are encouraged to apply for a CL on the telephone but can insist on a written application – see p486. Always insist that your application is formally determined by an SF decision maker and that you are given a written decision. It is common for DWP counter staff to 'advise' potential applicants that they will not be given a loan.
- Ensure that full details of your needs and circumstances are included in a written application and are explained to any interviewing officer. You should explain how you satisfy the eligibility rules (see p503), including the condition that a CL is the only way you can avoid a serious risk to your health (see p508). Bear in mind the rules on repeat applications on p487.

- If you claim on the telephone you will normally receive a decision at the same time. If not, you should insist on, and normally receive, a decision on the day your need arises. If there are unreasonable delays, you should complain to the district manager and, if necessary, ask your MP or an advice agency to intervene. Decisions should be based on your circumstances when you apply and a decision should never be delayed on the basis that the need will pass.
- If you are dissatisfied with the decision, consider requesting a review (see p1156). Insist on the review being carried out speedily. You can challenge the repayment terms of a loan if they are causing you hardship (see p509).
- If you are refused a CL on the grounds that another section should pay an interim payment, ask the member of staff to check that the payment is being made. If it is not, ask for a review.

Notes

1. **General matters**

1 s138 SSCBA 1992
2 s139(1) SSCBA 1992;
3 ss138 and 140 SSCBA 1992; s66 SSAA 1992; SF Dirs
4 SF(App) Regs; SF(AR) Regs; SF(RDB) Regs; SF(Misc) Regs
5 s168 SSAA 1992
6 SF Dir 41; part 5 paras 37-48 SFG
7 SF Dir42
8 s168(3)(c) and (d) SSAA 1992; part 5 paras 6 and 7 SFG
9 s140(1)(e) SSCBA 1992
10 *R v SFI ex parte Taylor* [1998] COD 152 (HC); SF Commissioner's Advice on 'Approach to Budgets' 28 October 2003
11 SF Dirs 40 and 41
12 s140(2) SSCBA 1992; s66(7) and (7A) SSAA 1992
13 SF Dir 41
14 Reg 2(1) SF(App) Regs
15 Reg 2A SF(App) Regs
16 part 3 para 24 SFG
17 s140(4)(aa) SSCBA 1992; SF Dir 49; part 3 para 20 SFG
18 part 1 para 18 SFG
19 Reg 2(4) SF(App) Regs
20 Reg 3(a) SF(App) Regs
21 Reg 3(b) SF(App) Regs
22 part 2 paras 31-32 and part 3 paras 33-34 SFG
23 s140(4)(a) SSCBA 1992; SF Dir 7
24 part 2 para 58 and part 3 para 127 SFG
25 s140(4)(a) SSCBA 1992; SF Commissioner's Advice on 'Direction 7 (Repeat Applications)' 1 December 2001
26 part 2 para 56 and part 3 para 125 SFG
27 SF Commissioner's Advice on 'Direction 7 (Same Item or Service)' 1 December 2001
28 s140 SSCBA 1992
29 part 1 para 13 SFG
30 part 2 para 18 and part 3 para 14 SFG
31 part 3 para 18 SFG
32 s138(3) SSCBA 1992
33 s71ZA SSAA 1992; SF Dir 43
34 SF Dir 44

2. **Community care grants**

35 SF Dir 25
36 SF Dir (General)
37 *R v SFI ex parte Davey* 19 October 1998, unreported (HC)
38 SF Dir (General); part 2 para 45 SFG
39 SF Dir 27
40 SF Dir 26
41 SF Dir 29
42 SF Dir 28

43 SF Dir 4
44 SF Dir 4(a)(i)
45 part 2 para 100 SFG
46 part 2 para 107 SFG
47 part 2 para 141 SFG
48 *R v SFI ex parte Mohammed* [1993] COD 263 (HC)
49 *R v Secretary of State for Social Security ex parte Healey* [1991] COD 68 (HC)
50 part 2 para 102 SFG
51 *R v SFI ex parte Sherwin* [1991] COD 68 (HC)
52 SF Commissioner's Advice on 'Direction 4(a)(i)' 1 May 2001
53 SF Dir 4(a)(ii)
54 part 2 para 171 SFG; SF Commissioner's Advice on 'Direction 4(a)(ii)' 1 October 2003
55 SF Commissioner's Advice on 'Direction 4(a)(ii)' 1 October 2003
56 part 2 para 168 SFG
57 SF Dir 4(a)(v)
58 SF Commissioner's Advice on 'Direction 4(a)(v)' 1 May 2003
59 part 2 para 308 SFG
60 SF Commissioner's Advice to SFIs, *IRS Journal*, Winter 2001/02
61 part 2 para 311 SFG
62 SF Commissioner's Advice on 'Direction 4(a)(v)' 1 May 2003
63 part 2 para 313 SFG
64 SF Dir 4(a)(iii)
65 part 2 paras 227-230 SFG
66 *R v Secretary of State for Social Security ex parte Healey* [1991] COD 68 (HC)
67 SF Commissioner's Advice on 'Direction 4(a)(iii)' 4 February 2002
68 SF Dir 4(a)(iv)
69 part 2 para 303 SFG
70 SF Dir 28(b)
71 SF Dir 4(b)
72 part 2 paras 338-41 SFG
73 SF Dir 28(b)
74 SF Dirs 23 and 29
75 CSB/1482/1985; *R v SFI ex parte Connick* 8 June 1993, unreported (HC); part 3 paras 148-153 SFG; SF Commissioner's Advice on 'Excluded Items' 18 June 2001
76 part 3 para 154 SFG
77 SF Commissioner's Advice on 'Housing Costs (General)' 1 March 2003
78 SF Dir 29(d) and Dir 23(2f)
79 part 2 para 84 and part 3 para 144 SFG
80 SF Dir 29
81 SF Dir 28
82 s138(1)(b) SSCBA 1992; *R v SFI ex parte Harper* [1998] COD 221 (HC)
83 part 2 paras 68-76 and part 3 paras 165-173 SFG
84 SF Commissioner's Advice on 'Maternity Expenses' 2 January 2002
85 s140 SSCBA 1992
86 *R v SFI ex parte Taylor* [1998] COD 152 (HC)
87 part 2 para 13 SFG
88 part 2 paras 348-50 SFG
89 part 2 para 352 SFG
90 part 2 para 353 SFG
91 SF Commissioner's Advice on 'Capital Resources' 18 June 2003 and 'Income Resources' 14 October 2003
92 part 2 paras 369 SFG
93 part 2 para 125 SFG
94 part 2 paras 374-75 SFG
95 part 2 paras 318-19 and part 3 paras 221-22 SFG

3. **Budgeting loans**

96 SF Dir 8(1)(a)
97 SF Dir (General)
98 part 4 para 29 SFG
99 *R v SFI ex parte Davey* 19 October 1998, unreported (HC)
100 part 4 para 33 SFG
101 SF Dir 8(1)(c)and 8(2)
102 part 4 paras 29-30 SFG
103 SF Dir 8(3)
104 SF Dir 9
105 SF Dir 9(3)
106 SF Dir 8(1)(b)
107 SF Dir 2
108 SF Dir 10
109 SF Dir 11
110 s140(1A) SSCBA 1992
111 SF Dir 52
112 SF Dir 41(d)
113 SF Dir 53
114 part 4 para 74 SFG
115 s78(1) SSAA 1992
116 part 4 paras 74-82 SFG
117 Reg 2 SF(Misc) Regs
118 Reg 3 SF(RDB) Regs
119 *Mulvey v Secretary of State for Social Security* [1997] SC 105 (HL); *R v Secretary of State for Social Security ex parte Taylor and Chapman*, *The Times*, 5 February 1996 (HC); s78(3A) and (3B) SSAA 1992
120 s78(3)(a) SSAA 1992
121 s78(3)(b) SSAA 1992
122 s78(3)(c) SSAA 1992
123 s38(13) SSA 1998

4. **Crisis loans**
124 SF Dir 14(a)
125 SF Dir 14(b)
126 SF Dirs 15-17
127 SF Dir 23
128 SF Dir 3
129 SF Dir 21
130 SF Dir 22
131 part 3 para 45 SFG
132 part 3 para 46 SFG
133 part 3 paras 47-57 SFG
134 part 3 paras 47 and 58 SFG
135 SF Commissioner's Advice on 'Crisis Loans and Resources' 18 June 2001
136 part 3 para 61 SFG
137 part 3 para 62 SFG
138 SF Commissioner's Advice on 'Direction 3 – Only Means' 29 April 2001
139 SF Dir 15
140 part 3 paras 64-68 SFG
141 SF Dirs 16 and 17
142 SF Dir 17
143 SF Dir 23(2)
144 SF Commissioner's Advice on 'Direction 3 – Emergency/Disaster' 11 August 2003
145 SF Commissioner's Advice on 'Direction 3 – Emergency/Disaster' 11 August 2003
146 SF Commissioner's Advice on 'Direction 3 – Only Means' 29 April 2002
147 SF Commissioner's Advice on 'Direction 3 – Serious Risk' 11 August 2003
148 SF Commissioner's Advice on 'Direction 3 – Serious Risk' 11 August 2003
149 SF Dir 3(2)
150 s140 SSCBA 1992
151 *R v SFI ex parte Taylor* [1998] COD 152 (HC)
152 part 3 para 225 SFG
153 part 3 para 190 SFG
154 part 3 para 191 SFG
155 part 3 paras 183-84 SFG
156 part 3 paras 192-93 SFG
157 part 3 paras 205-07 SFG
158 part 3 paras 185-87 SFG
159 part 3 paras 181-82 and 194-95 SFG
160 part 3 para 196 SFG
161 part 3 paras 240-42 SFG
162 part 3 para 202 SFG
163 part 3 para 177 SFG
164 part 3 para 209 SFG
165 SF Dir 22
166 SF Dir 21
167 part 3 para 252 SFG
168 SF Dirs 18 and 20
169 s78(1) and (2) SSAA 1992

Chapter 22

Social fund: regulated payments

This chapter covers:

Unlike the discretionary social fund (see Chapter 21), the regulated social fund makes payments to people who satisfy conditions of entitlement which are laid down in regulations. As with most other benefits, decisions can be challenged by appealing to a tribunal (see Chapter 42).

1. Sure Start maternity grants

You are entitled to a Sure Start maternity grant if you satisfy all of the following rules.

- You or your partner have been awarded one of the following qualifying benefits in respect of the day you claim a maternity grant:
  - income support (IS);
  - income-based jobseeker's allowance (including hardship payments);
  - child tax credit paid at a rate exceeding the family element (see p1235);
  - working tax credit including the disability or severe disability element (see p1237);
  - pension credit (guarantee or savings credit – see Chapter 18).[1]

  You are eligible if you receive a backdated award of a qualifying benefit covering the date you claim a maternity grant. If you are waiting for a decision on a claim for a qualifying benefit, the DWP may defer making a decision on your maternity grant claim until the qualifying benefit claim has been decided. If your claim for a maternity grant is refused while you are waiting for a decision on a claim for a qualifying benefit, you should reclaim a maternity grant within three months of being awarded the qualifying benefit (see p968). **Note:** if you do not claim a maternity grant within the time limits (see p515), a backdated award of a qualifying benefit will not qualify you for a grant. If you are not entitled to a qualifying benefit in your own right because you are under 16 (or under 19 and in 'relevant education' – see p576), a member of your family can claim a maternity grant for you if s/he is getting a qualifying benefit in respect of you.

- One of the following applies:[2]
  - you or a member of your family are pregnant or have given birth in the last three months (including stillbirth after 24 weeks of pregnancy[3]);
  - you or your partner have adopted a child who is less than 12 months old when you claim a maternity expenses payment. Following a Court of Appeal decision, if you or your partner have a residence order for a child you should be treated in the same way as you would if you had adopted that child;[4]
  - you and your spouse have been granted a parental order allowing you to have a child by a surrogate mother.

  In the last two cases, you are entitled to a payment even if one has already been made to the birth mother or a member of her family.[5]
- You or your partner are not involved in a trade dispute (see p633), unless specified circumstances apply (see p633).[6]
- You claim within the time limits (see p515).
- You have received health and welfare advice from a health professional (see below).
- You are not a 'person subject to immigration control' (there are exceptions to this rule) – see p1334.

The terms 'partner' and 'family' in the above rules have almost the same meanings as they do for IS purposes (see p700).[7]

The rules about your age

There are no special rules on age.

Amount[8]

You are entitled to a grant of £500 for each child or expected child. The payment is not affected by any capital you have.

Claiming and getting paid

You should claim on Form SF100, which you can get from your local Jobcentre Plus office or from the DWP's website (see Appendix 1). There are strict time limits for claiming (see p515). The back of your claim form must be signed by a health professional (ie, midwife, health visitor or doctor) to confirm that you have received health and welfare advice on your baby or your maternal health.

Your date of claim is normally the date your form is received by the DWP.[9] If you make a written claim in some other way, you should be sent the appropriate form to complete. If you return it within one month, or such longer period as the Secretary of State considers reasonable, your date of claim is the date the DWP received your initial application.[10] See p513 for when your claim can be backdated if you are subsequently awarded a qualifying benefit.

If you claim before the birth, you need to submit a maternity certificate (MATB1), a note from your doctor or midwife or an ante-natal clinic appointment card showing your expected date of childbirth. If you claim after your child is born, you are usually asked for a maternity, birth or adoption certificate.

The rules on getting paid and the recovery of overpayments are as for most other benefits (see pp978 and 1019).

Time limits[11]

You can claim a maternity grant at any time from 11 weeks before the first day of your expected week of childbirth until three months after the actual date of the birth. If you adopt a child, have a residence order for a child, or have a child by a surrogate mother, you can claim up to three months following the date of the adoption, residence order or parental order. There is no provision for claiming outside the time limits.

Challenging a decision

Decisions can be challenged by revision, supersession or appeal. The rules are the same as for most other benefits (see Chapters 41 and 42).

---

2. Funeral expenses payments

You qualify for a funeral expenses payment if you satisfy all of the following rules.

- You or your partner (see p518) have been awarded one of the following qualifying benefits in respect of the day you claim a funeral payment:[12]
  - income support (IS);
  - income-based jobseeker's allowance (including hardship payments);
  - housing benefit (HB);
  - council tax benefit (including second adult rebate where you are the 'second adult' – see p81);
  - child tax credit paid at a rate which exceeds the family element (see p1234);
  - working tax credit which includes the disability or severe disability element (see p1236);
  - pension credit (guarantee or savings credit – see Chapter 18).

  You are eligible if you receive a backdated award of a qualifying benefit which covers the date you claim a funeral payment. If you are waiting for a decision on a claim for a qualifying benefit, the DWP may defer making a decision on a claim for a funeral payment until the qualifying benefit claim has been decided.[13] If your claim for a funeral payment is refused while you are waiting for a decision on a claim for a qualifying benefit, you should reclaim within three months of being awarded the qualifying benefit (see p968). **Note:** if you do not claim a funeral payment within the time limit (see p521), a backdated award of a qualifying benefit will not qualify you for a grant.

- You or your partner are in one of the categories of eligible people, listed below, who can be treated as responsible for the funeral expenses.
- You or your partner accept responsibility for funeral expenses (see p518).[14] If you are claiming as a close relative or close friend (see p518), it must also be reasonable for you to accept responsibility (see p518).
- The funeral (ie, burial or cremation)[15] takes place in the UK, unless you or your partner are covered by specified European Community (EC) legislation, in which case the funeral can take place in any European Economic Area (EEA) state or Switzerland (see p519).[16]
- A social fund funeral payment has not already been made in respect of the deceased (but the amount of a previous award can be revised up to the maximum allowed under the rules).[17]
- The deceased was 'ordinarily resident' in the UK when s/he died.[18] See p1357 for the meaning of 'ordinarily resident'.
- You are not a 'person subject to immigration control' (there are exceptions to this rule) – see p1334.
- You claim within the time limits (see p521).

Eligible people

You are only eligible for a funeral payment if you or your partner fall into one of the following categories of people who can be treated as responsible for the funeral costs.[19] See p518 for definitions of the terms used.

- You were the 'partner' of the deceased when s/he died.
- The deceased was a 'child' for whom you were responsible when s/he died and there is no 'absent parent', or there is an absent parent but s/he (or her/his partner) was getting a qualifying benefit (see p515) when the child died. If there is an absent parent who was not getting a qualifying benefit when the child died, you may qualify for a payment as a close relative of the deceased under the rules below. If the deceased was a stillborn child, you are eligible for a funeral payment if you were the parent or the parent's partner, and it does not matter whether there is an absent parent.
- You were a parent, son or daughter of the deceased and it is reasonable for you to accept responsibility for the funeral expenses (see p518).
- You were another 'close relative' or a 'close friend' of the deceased and it is reasonable for you to accept responsibility for the funeral expenses (see p518).

You cannot get a payment, however, if there is a parent, son or daughter of the deceased who could accept responsibility for the funeral expenses and it is reasonable for her/him to do so.[20]

Exclusion of certain close relatives and friends

If you claim as a 'close relative' or 'close friend' of the deceased (see p518), you cannot get a payment if:

- the deceased had a partner (unless that partner died before the funeral without making a claim for a funeral payment);[21]
- the deceased was a child or stillborn child and a responsible person or parent is able to claim a funeral payment under the rules set out on p516;[22]
- there is a parent, son or daughter of the deceased, apart from:[23]
  - anyone under the age of 18;
  - anyone aged 18 or 19 who counts as a qualifying young person for child benefit purposes (see p56);
  - anyone who (or whose partner) has been awarded a qualifying benefit (see p515);
  - anyone estranged from the deceased when s/he died (estranged is not defined but has connotations of emotional disharmony);[24]
  - students aged 18 doing a full-time course of advanced education (see p579), or aged 19 to pension age doing any full-time course (see Chapter 25);
  - members of a religious order which fully maintains them;
  - prisoners (including those in youth custody or a remand centre) who (or whose partners) were getting a qualifying benefit immediately before being detained;
  - inpatients receiving free treatment in a hospital or similar institution, who (or whose partners) were getting a qualifying benefit immediately before becoming a patient;
  - asylum seekers receiving asylum support from the Border and Immigration Agency or a local authority (see p1345);
  - anyone who is ordinarily resident (see p1357) outside the UK;
- there is a close relative of the deceased who was in *closer contact* with the deceased than you were, taking into account the nature and extent of such contact;[25]
- there is a close relative of the deceased who was in *equally close contact* with the deceased as you were and who (or whose partner) is not getting a qualifying benefit (see p515).[26]

Note: the last two bullet points do not apply if the close relative was under the age of 18 when the deceased died, or was a student, member of a religious order, prisoner, inpatient or asylum seeker as set out above, or was ordinarily resident outside the UK.[27]

The DWP (not you) must establish there is another close relative who is not getting a qualifying benefit, if you are refused a payment on this ground.[28]

Examples

Jane is not entitled to a funeral payment because, although she looked after her brother for many years before he died, he had a son who is not getting a qualifying benefit (see p515). Although the son rarely saw his father, they were not estranged.

Yuri is entitled to a funeral payment when his close friend Robert dies because although Robert had two surviving close relatives, a son and a sister-in-law, the son is getting HB and Yuri was in closer contact with Robert than either of them were.

Definitions[29]

Child is defined as for IS purposes (see p709). You are 'responsible' for a child if you get, or could get, child benefit for her/him (see p710).

Stillborn child means a child born dead after 24 weeks of pregnancy.

Absent parent means a parent of a deceased child, where the child:
– was not living in that parent's household at the date of death; *and*
– was living with another person who was responsible for her/him.

Close relative means parent, parent-in-law, son, son-in-law, daughter, daughter-in-law, step-parent, stepson, stepson-in-law, stepdaughter, stepdaughter-in-law, brother, brother-in-law, sister, sister-in-law.

Close friend is not defined in the law. It can include a relative who is not a close relative (eg, a grandparent or grandchild).[30]

Partner has the same meaning as for IS (see p702). You also count as a partner, however, if you were living in a care home (see p617) when the deceased died, *and*:
– you and your spouse or civil partner were living in the same home; *or*
– you were a member of a couple before one or both of you moved into such a home.[31]

This rule is designed to enable a surviving partner to claim a funeral payment where one or both partners were in a home at the date of death.

Accepting responsibility for funeral costs

To qualify for a funeral payment, you or your partner must 'accept responsibility' for funeral expenses.[32] The key factor is whether you are liable to pay the costs of a funeral, rather than whether you have made the arrangements.[33] If the funeral director's account or contract is in your name, you should normally be treated as having accepted responsibility. If the account or contract is in someone else's name (or another person has paid the bill), you can still be 'responsible' if:

- s/he is acting as your agent – eg, because you are too distressed to act on your own behalf;[34] *or*

- s/he transfers liability to you, prior to full payment, with the consent of the funeral director.[35]

If you are a close relative (see p518) or close friend of the deceased, it must also be 'reasonable' for you to accept responsibility for the funeral expenses, in the light of the nature and extent of your contact with the deceased.[36] In one case, it was held reasonable for a person to have accepted responsibility for his father's funeral even though he had not seen him for 24 years. This did not erase the contact they had had in the previous 30 years.[37]

European Economic Area nationals

You can get a funeral payment for a funeral that takes place in any member state of the EEA or Switzerland (see p1383) if:[38]

- you are a 'worker'; *or*
- you are a member of the family of a 'worker' – ie:
  - the worker's spouse or civil partner;
  - the worker's, spouse's or civil partner's children, grandchildren and other descendants who are either under 21 or dependent;
  - dependent relatives of the worker, spouse or civil partner in the ascending line (eg, parents, grandparents); *or*
- you have the right to reside in the UK .

For more details on the benefit rights of EEA nationals, see p1382.

If you have ever been refused a payment for a funeral that took place in an EEA state and you satisfied the above rules, you should ask for a revision (see p1068).

The rules about your age

There are no special rules on age.

Amount of the payment

You are entitled to a payment that is sufficient to cover:[39]

- the necessary costs of purchasing a new burial plot with the exclusive right of burial in it and necessary burial fees. The burial of ashes following cremation is not, however, covered;[40]
- the necessary cremation fees, including medical references and certificates and the fee for removing a pacemaker (restricted to £20 if not carried out by a doctor);[41]
- the costs of documentation necessary for the release of the deceased's assets;[42]
- the reasonable cost of transport for the portion of journeys in excess of 80 kilometres (50 miles), undertaken to:
  - transport the body within the UK to a funeral director's premises or to a place of rest;[43]

  - transport the coffin and bearers in a hearse and the mourners in another vehicle from the funeral director's premises or place of rest to the funeral.[44] The cost of this plus burial in an existing plot cannot exceed the cost of such transport plus the purchase and burial costs of a new plot.[45]
- the necessary expenses of one return journey for the responsible person to arrange or attend the funeral. The maximum allowed is the cost of a return journey from home to the place where the burial or cremation costs are incurred;[46]
- up to £700 for any other funeral expenses (eg, funeral director's fees, religious costs, flowers, other transport costs).[47]

Note:
- The cost of any items or services provided under a pre-paid funeral plan or equivalent arrangement cannot be met. Expenses not covered by the plan can be met if they fall into the above categories, but the maximum allowed under the last category is restricted to £120.[48]
- Costs relating to religious requirements cannot be included in the amount allowed for burial and transport.[49]
- If the amount awarded does not cover your funeral expenses, you could try making an application for a community care grant (eg, for the cost of a headstone), but see p496.

Deductions from awards

The following are deducted from an award of a funeral payment:
- the deceased's assets available to you or a member of your family (defined as for IS purposes – see p909) without probate or letters of administration.[50] Assets at the date of death count, even if you have spent or distributed them prior to your claim for a funeral payment.[51] Arrears of the deceased's attendance allowance (and probably other benefits) paid to you as next-of-kin also count;[52]
- a lump sum legally due to you or a member of your family from an insurance policy, occupational pension scheme, burial club or equivalent source on the death of the deceased;[53]
- any contribution towards funeral expenses made to you or a member of your family by a charity, or a relative of yours or of the deceased;[54]
- a funeral grant paid by the Government for a war disablement pensioner;[55]
- an amount paid or payable under a pre-paid funeral plan or equivalent arrangement (whether or not the plan was fully paid).[56]

Any capital you have apart from the above has no effect on the amount of the funeral payment. Any payments from the Macfarlane Trust, the Macfarlane (Special Payments) Trusts, the Fund, the Eileen Trust, the CJD Trusts, the Skipton Fund or the London Bombings Relief Charitable Fund (see p16) are not deducted from an award of a funeral payment.[57]

Claiming and getting paid

You should claim on Form SF200, which you can get from your local Jobcentre Plus office or from the DWP's website (see Appendix 1). There are strict time limits for claiming (see below). When completing the form, bear in mind the rules about accepting responsibility for the funeral expenses and your contact with the deceased.

Your date of claim is normally the date the form is received by the DWP.[58] If you do not complete the SF200 properly or apply in writing but not on the form, you should be sent the form to complete or correct. If you submit it within one month, or such longer period as the Secretary of State considers reasonable, your claim is treated as made on the date you originally applied.[59] See p515 for when your claim can be backdated if you are subsequently awarded a qualifying benefit.

Payment is normally made directly to the funeral director, unless you have already paid the bill.[60]

The rules relating to the recovery of overpayments are as for other benefits (see p1006) but see below for recovery from the deceased's estate.

Time limits

You can claim at any time from the date of death up to three months after the date of the funeral.[61] There is no provision for late claims. See above for details of the date your claim is treated as made.

Recovery from the deceased's estate

The Secretary of State is entitled to recover funeral expenses payments from the deceased's estate and normally seeks to do so.[62] Funeral expenses are a first charge on the estate and have priority over anything else (although there may be insufficient assets for full repayment).[63]

Challenging a decision

Decisions can be challenged by revision, supersession or appeal. The rules are the same as for most other benefits (see Chapters 41 and 42 for details).

3. Cold weather payments

You qualify for a cold weather payment if:

- a period of cold weather has been forecast or recorded for the area in which your normal home is situated (see p522);[64] *and*
- you have been awarded pension credit (guarantee or savings credit) for at least one day during the period of cold weather, *or* you have been awarded income

support (IS) or income-based jobseeker's allowance (JSA) for at least one day during the period of cold weather and:
  - your IS or income-based JSA includes a disability, severe disability, enhanced disability, disabled child, pensioner, or higher pensioner premium (see p775); *or*
  - you are responsible for a child under five; *or*
  - you are getting child tax credit which includes a disability or severe disability element (see p1234);[65] *and*
- you are not living in a care home (see Chapter 26);[66] *and*
- you are not a 'person subject to immigration control' (there are exceptions to this rule) – see p1334.

A period of cold weather

This is a period of seven consecutive days during which the average of the mean daily temperature, as forecast or recorded for that period at your designated local weather station, is equal to or below 0 degrees celsius.[67]

The rules about your age

There are no special rules about your age.

Amount of the payment

The sum of £8.50 is paid for each week of cold weather.[68]

Claiming and getting paid

You do not need to make a claim for a cold weather payment. The DWP should automatically pay you if you qualify. Your district DWP should publicise when there are periods of cold weather in your area. If you do not receive payment and you think you are entitled, contact your local Jobcentre Plus office. The rules relating to the recovery of overpayments are as for other benefits (see p1006).

Time limits

There are no time limits for claiming a cold weather payment, as there is no requirement to submit a claim.

Challenging a decision

If you do not receive a payment to which you think you are entitled, you should submit a written claim and ask for a written decision. If you are refused, you can request a revision or appeal (see Chapters 41 and 42).

4. **Winter fuel payments**

You qualify for a winter fuel payment if:[69]

- you are aged 60 or over in the week beginning on the third Monday in September (the '**qualifying week**'); *and*
- you are ordinarily resident in Great Britain (see p1357);
  Note: you may be entitled to a payment if you are currently residing in another European Economic Area country or in Switzerland (see Chapter 61); *and*
- if a claim is required, you claim in time (see p524); *and*
- you are not excluded from a payment under the rules below.

Exclusions

You are excluded from entitlement to a payment if, during the qualifying week (see above):[70]

- you are serving a custodial sentence;
- you have been receiving free inpatient treatment for more than 52 weeks in a hospital or similar institution (see p611);
- you are receiving pension credit (PC) or income-based jobseeker's allowance (JSA) and you are living in residential care. You count as '**living in residential care**' if you are living in a care home (ie, an independent home which is registered or exempt from registration, or a local authority home which provides board) throughout the qualifying week and the 12 preceding weeks, disregarding temporary absences;[71]
- you are a 'person subject to immigration control', although there are exceptions to this rule (see p1334).

The rules about your age

You must be aged 60 or over in the qualifying week (see above).

Amount

Subject to the rules below, you are entitled to a winter fuel payment of:

- £200 if you are aged 60–79 (inclusive) in the qualifying week (see above); *or*
- £300 if you are aged 80 or over in the qualifying week.[72]

If you do not get PC or income-based JSA and you share your accommodation with another qualifying person (whether as a partner or a friend) you will get £100 if you are both aged 60–79 or £150 if you are both aged 80 or over. If only one of you is aged 80 or over that person will get £200 and the other person £100. If you do get PC or income-based JSA you (and your partner if you have one) will get £200 if one or both of you is aged 60–79, or £300 if one or both of you is aged 80 or over regardless of whether there is anyone else in your household who qualifies.[73]

If you are living in residential care (see p523) in the qualifying week and are not getting PC or income-based JSA, you are entitled to a payment of £100 if you are aged 60–79, or £150 if you are aged 80 or over.[74]

Additional amount for 2008/09

The Government has announced an additional one-off payment in 2008/09 of £100 for over-80s households and £50 for over-60s households.

Claiming and getting paid

You should automatically receive a payment without having to make a claim if you received a payment the previous year, or you are getting a state retirement pension or any other social security benefit (apart from child benefit, housing benefit or council tax benefit) in the qualifying week.[75]

Otherwise, you must claim a winter fuel payment before 31 March following the qualifying week.[76] To ensure you receive your payment before Christmas, you should submit your claim before the qualifying week. A claim can be accepted in any written format but it is best to use the designated form, which you can get by ringing the winter fuel payment helpline on 08459 151515 (local rate) (textphone: 08456 015613), or from the DWP's website (see Appendix 1).

If you are a member of a couple and your partner is receiving IS, the payment can be made to either of you (even if your partner is under 60).[77]

The Government aims to make payments between mid-November and Christmas.

Claiming for previous winters

During the first three years of the scheme, men aged 60 to 64 in the qualifying week were only eligible for payments if they were in receipt of IS or income-based JSA. In 1999 this was held to be unlawful discrimination.[78] If you missed out on payments because of this discriminatory rule, you can obtain a special form from the helpline see above) to claim backdated payments for 1997/98, 1998/99, and 1999/2000. For details see Chapter 22 of the 2006/07 edition of this *Handbook*.

Challenging a decision

Decisions can be challenged by revision, supersession or appeal in the same way as other benefits (see Chapters 41 and 42). To get a decision, you may have to submit a written claim and request a written decision. Backdated payments for previous winters are not covered by the regulations and it is unclear whether there is a right of appeal against refusal of a payment for previous years. If you think you have been wrongly refused a backdated payment, you should request a written explanation and seek advice if you are unhappy with the response.

Notes

1. **Sure Start maternity grants**
   1 Reg 5(1)(a) SFM&FE Regs
   2 Reg 5(1)(b) SFM&FE Regs
   3 Reg 3(1) SFM&FE Regs
   4 *Francis v Secretary of State for Work and Pensions* [2005] EWCA Civ 1303, 10 November 2005
   5 Reg 4(2) SFM&FE Regs
   6 Reg 6 SFM&FE Regs
   7 Reg 3(1) and (2) SFM&FE Regs
   8 Reg 5(2) SFM&FE Regs
   9 Reg 6(1)(a) SS(C&P) Regs
   10 Regs 4(7) and 6(1)(b) SS(C&P) Regs
   11 Reg 19 and Sch 4 para 8 SS(C&P) Regs

2. **Funeral expenses payments**
   12 Reg 7(3) and (4) SFM&FE Regs
   13 DMG Memo Vol JSA/IS 22
   14 Reg 7(7) SFM&FE Regs
   15 Reg 7(9)(b) SFM&FE Regs
   16 Reg 7(9)(a) SFM&FE Regs
   17 Reg 4(3) and (4) SFM&FE Regs
   18 Reg 7(5) SFM&FE Regs
   19 Reg 7(8)(a)-(e) SFM&FE Regs
   20 Reg 7(8)(e) SFM&FE Regs; R(IS) 7/04
   21 Regs 7(8)(e) and 8(4) SFM&FE Regs
   22 Reg 7(8)(e) SFM&FE Regs; R(IS) 7/04
   23 Reg 8(1) and (2) SFM&FE Regs
   24 R(SB) 2/87
   25 Reg 8(7)(a) SFM&FE Regs
   26 Reg 8(7)(b) SFM&FE Regs
   27 Reg 8(8) SFM&FE Regs
   28 *Kerr v Department for Social Development (NI)* 6 May 2004 (HL)
   29 Reg 3(1) SFM&FE Regs
   30 CIS/788/2003
   31 Reg 3(2) SFM&FE Regs
   32 Reg 7(7) SFM&FE Regs
   33 CSB/488/1982
   34 CIS/12344/1996; R(IS)6/98
   35 CIS/85/1991
   36 Reg 7(8)(e) SFM&FE Regs
   37 CIS/12783/1996
   38 Reg 7(10) SFM&FE Regs
   39 Reg 9(1) and (2) SFM&FE Regs
   40 Reg 9(3)(a) SFM&FE Regs; CIS/16192/1996
   41 Reg 9(3)(b) SFM&FE Regs
   42 Reg 9(3)(c) SFM&FE Regs
   43 Reg 9(3)(d) SFM&FE Regs
   44 Reg 9(3)(e) SFM&FE Regs
   45 Reg 9(8) SFM&FE Regs
   46 Reg 9(3)(f) SFM&FE Regs
   47 Reg 9(3)(g) SFM&FE Regs
   48 Reg 9(10) SFM&FE Regs
   49 Reg 9(7) SFM&FE Regs
   50 Reg 10(1)(a) SFM&FE Regs
   51 R(IS) 14/91
   52 R(IS) 12/93
   53 Reg 10(1)(b) SFM&FE Regs
   54 Reg 10(1)(c) SFM&FE Regs
   55 Reg 10(1)(d) SFM&FE Regs
   56 Reg 10(1)(e) SFM&FE Regs
   57 Reg 10(2) SFM&FE Regs
   58 Reg 6(1)(a) SS(C&P) Regs
   59 Regs 4(7) and 6(1)(b) SS(C&P) Regs
   60 Reg 35(2) SS(C&P) Regs
   61 Sch 4 para 9 SS(C&P) Regs
   62 s78(4) SSAA 1992; CIS/616/1990
   63 R(SB) 18/84

3. **Cold weather payments**
   64 Reg 2(1) and (2) SFCWP Regs
   65 Reg 1A(1) SFCWP Regs
   66 Reg 1A(2) SFCWP Regs
   67 Reg 1(2) and Schs 1 and 2 SFCWP Regs
   68 Reg 3 SFCWP Regs

4. **Winter fuel payments**
   69 Reg 2 SFWFP Regs
   70 Reg 3 SFWFP Regs
   71 Reg 1(2) and (3) SFWFP Regs
   72 Reg 2 SFWFP Regs
   73 Reg 2(1)(ii)(aa), (2) and (3) SFWFP Regs
   74 Reg 2(2)(b) SFWFP Regs
   75 Reg 4 SFWFP Regs
   76 Reg 3(1)(b) and (2) SFWFP Regs
   77 Reg 36(2) SS(C&P) Regs
   78 *Taylor* C-382/98, 16 December 1999 (ECJ)

23

Chapter 23

Statutory maternity, paternity and adoption pay

This chapter covers:

Statutory maternity pay (SMP), statutory paternity pay (SPP) and statutory adoption pay (SAP) are payments made to employees by their employers.

You may be entitled to:

- **SMP** if you are pregnant or have recently given birth. If you do not qualify for SMP you may qualify for maternity allowance (MA) instead (see Chapter 17);
- **SPP** if you are the father of a baby, if your partner has recently given birth or if s/he is adopting a child, or if you are jointly adopting a child with her/him (see p529 for the meaning of 'partner'); *or*
- **SAP** if you are adopting or jointly adopting a child.

The table on p528 details which benefit you may qualify for, given your circumstances.

SMP and SAP are paid for a maximum of 39 weeks. SPP is paid for one or two weeks. You do not have to have paid national insurance contributions to qualify for SMP, SPP or SAP, although there is an employment and an earnings condition for each. Your entitlement to SMP, SPP and SAP is not affected by any other income or savings that you may have.

If you qualify for SMP, SPP or SAP, each is the minimum amount of pay that the law requires employers to pay you during maternity, adoption or paternity leave. However, many employees are entitled to higher amounts of pay under their contracts.

To qualify for SMP, SPP or SAP, you do not need to intend to return to work after your maternity, paternity or adoption leave. If you qualified for it, you do not have to repay SMP, SPP or SAP, even if you do not return to work.

Definitions of some of the terms used in this chapter are on p548.

If you are adopting a child from abroad, see p539.

Future changes

The Government plans to increase the payment period for SMP and SAP to 52 weeks and to introduce 'additional SPP', which will be payable for a period of up to six months in the year after the birth or adoption. Entitlement to additional SPP will depend on your partner returning to work before using up all her/his SMP, MA or SAP.[1] The date for these changes has not yet been decided, but it is unlikely they will affect people whose baby is due before April 2010 or who expect a child to be placed with them before that date – see CPAG's *Welfare Rights Bulletin* for updates.

1. Who is entitled

The table on p528 details which statutory payment you may qualify for, given your circumstances.

If you are jointly adopting a child with your partner (see p529 for the meaning of partner), you can choose whether to request statutory paternity pay (SPP) or statutory adoption pay (SAP) from your employer. Although the amount of SPP and SAP is the same, SAP is payable for up to 39 weeks while SPP is only paid for up to two. In this situation, your partner may be able to qualify for SPP while you get SAP or vice versa. However, you both cannot qualify for SAP for the same adoption and you cannot receive SPP for any week you are entitled to SAP.[2] While only women can qualify for statutory maternity pay (SMP), men or women can qualify for SAP or SPP. The qualifying conditions for SMP, SPP and SAP are described below.

If you are pregnant or have recently given birth and do not qualify for SMP or maternity allowance (MA) you may be entitled to statutory sick pay (SSP) (unless you are within the periods mentioned on p563) or to incapacity benefit (IB – see Chapter 12). But see p262 for future changes affecting IB.

There are some groups of people to whom special rules apply (see p538).

Event	*Circumstances*	*Benefit you may qualify for*
Adoption	You are the sole adopter	SAP
	You and your partner are jointly adopting a child	SAP or SPP (adoption)
	Your partner is the adopter	SPP (adoption)
Birth	You are the mother of the baby	SMP or MA
	You are the father of the baby or the partner of the mother	SPP (birth)

Statutory maternity pay

You qualify for SMP if:[3]

- you are pregnant and within the 11 weeks before your 'expected week of childbirth' (EWC – see p548), or you have recently given birth; *and*
- you satisfy the continuous employment rule (see p530); *and*
- you satisfy the earnings condition (see p532); *and*
- you have given your employer the appropriate notice and information (see p542); *and*
- you are not working for the employer paying you SMP (but see p534); *and*
- you do not work for other employers after the birth (but see p534 for an exception).

Statutory paternity pay

SPP can be paid in respect of an adoption (referred to in this chapter as SPP (adoption)) and in respect of a birth (referred to as SPP (birth)). If a reference in the chapter is to SPP, the rules described relate to both SPP (adoption) and SPP (birth).

See p527 for details of the relationship between SPP and SAP. See p550 if you are entitled to SSP.

You qualify for SPP if:[4]

- you satisfy the continuous employment rule (see p530); *and*
- you satisfy the earnings condition (see p532); *and*
- you have given your employer the required notice and information (see p544); *and*
- you are not working for the employer paying you SPP (but see p534); *and*
- you do not do any work for other employers (but see p534 for an exception).

In addition, the following must apply.

For SPP (adoption):

- your partner is adopting a child, or you and your partner are jointly adopting a child (see p529 for the meaning of partner); *and*

- the person adopting the child (the adopter) is doing so under UK law (but see p539 if the child is adopted from abroad); *and*
- you have, or you expect to have (along with the adopter or the other adopter) the main responsibility for the upbringing of the child; *and*
- while receiving SPP you intend to care for the child or to support the person adopting the child; *and*
- you have not elected to receive SAP.

For SPP (birth):

- while receiving SPP you intend to care for the child or to support the child's mother; *and either*
- you are the child's father and you will have responsibility for her/his upbringing; *or*
- the child's mother is your partner and you will have (apart from the mother's responsibility), the main responsibility for the child's upbringing (see below for the meaning of partner).

Who counts as a partner

For the purpose of SPP you count as the partner of the adopter or of the child's mother if *either*:[5]

- you are her/his spouse or civil partner; *or*
- you live with her/him and the child in an 'enduring family relationship', but in this situation, a parent, grandparent, sister, brother, aunt, uncle, half-sister or half-brother cannot count as your partner, and if you are adopted neither can your adoptive parents, nor vice versa.

Note: the rules on who can jointly adopt a child are different from the rules on who counts as a partner for SPP.

Statutory adoption pay

See p527 for details of the relationship between SPP and SAP. See p550 if you are entitled to statutory sick pay.

You qualify for SAP if:[6]

- a child has been, or is expected to be, placed with you for adoption under UK law (but see p539 if the child is adopted from abroad); *and*
- you satisfy the continuous employment rule (see p530); *and*
- you satisfy the earnings condition (see p532); *and*
- you have given your employer the required notice and information (see p545); *and*
- you have not elected to receive SPP; *and*
- your co-adopter is not claiming SAP, if the child has been placed with both you and your co-adopter for adoption; *and*

- you are not working for the employer paying you SAP (but see p534); *and*
- you do not do any work for other employers (but see p534 for an exception).

Continuous employment rule

To satisfy the continuous employment rule:[7]

- you must have been employed by your employer (see below) for a continuous period of at least 26 weeks ending with:
  - for **SMP** and **SPP** (birth), the 15th week before the EWC (see p548); *or*
  - for **SPP** (adoption) and **SAP**, the week in which you are notified that you have (or, for SPP, you or the adopter has) been matched with a child for adoption (see p548); *and*
- for **SPP** you must also have been continuously employed by that same employer:
  - from the end of the 15th week before the EWC to the day that the child is born, for SPP (birth); *or*
  - from the end of the week in which you were notified of being matched with a child until the day the child is placed with you for adoption, for SPP (adoption).

See p531 if there have been breaks in your employment.

For both **SMP** and **SPP** (birth), if the baby is born in or before the 15th week before the EWC, you satisfy the continuous employment rule if you would have done so had the baby been born on the expected date.[8]

For **SMP**, if you are employed for only part of the 15th week before your EWC, the whole week still counts towards your period of continuous employment. Similarly, for **SAP**, if you are employed for only part of the week in which you receive the notification of a match, the whole week still counts.[9]

In respect of adoptions, the date you are notified of a match is the date you receive the adoption agency's notification rather than the date it is sent.[10]

See p538 if your employer has dismissed you 'solely or mainly' to avoid paying you SMP, SPP or SAP.

Employed by an employer

To satisfy the continuous employment rule, you must have been continuously employed by an employer who was liable to pay secondary Class 1 national insurance (NI) contributions for you, or who would have been liable to pay them had your earnings been high enough (see p722).[11] If you are under 16, you count as employed if your employer would have been liable to pay secondary Class 1 NI contributions on your earnings had you been older.

The question of whether you are an employee is similar to the question of whether you are an 'employed earner' for NI purposes (see p718).

You do not need to have a written contract of employment to count as an employee. Your employer cannot restrict your right to SMP, SPP or SAP by its own rules or contract with you and cannot require you to contribute towards the cost of SMP, SPP or SAP.[12] Periods of employment for the same employer in another European Economic Area state may count towards your period of continuous employment.[13] However, even if you are an employee you may not be entitled to SMP, SPP or SAP if your employer is based outside Great Britain (see p538).[14]

Breaks in employment

For **SMP**, **SPP** and **SAP**, if you return to work for the same employer following a break in your contract of employment, certain weeks when you were not employed can still count towards your 26 weeks of continuous employment. These include weeks in which, for all or part of the week, you were:[15]

- incapable of work because of sickness or injury, unless your incapacity lasted for more than 26 consecutive weeks;
- absent because your employer temporarily had no work to offer you (eg, you are an agency worker and the agency is unable to find you work in any particular week);
- absent from work in circumstances such that, by arrangement or custom, you are regarded as continuing in employment (eg, public holidays, annual shutdown, or certain teachers employed on term-by-term contracts);
- for SMP only, absent from work wholly or partly because of pregnancy or childbirth if there was not more than 26 weeks between your contracts with your employer, and you were employed by your employer both before and after you had your baby but not during the period of your absence;
- for SMP only, absent from work while on paternity, adoption or parental leave.

If it is your employer's practice to offer work for separate periods of six months or less, at least twice a year, to people who have worked for them before (eg, if you are a supply teacher or agency worker), then in some circumstances you do not have to have returned to work in order to benefit from the above rules.[16]

The Revenue may say that even if you are still employed by your employer during periods when you are off work, you will only be considered to be in continuous employment for the period of your absence in the circumstances given above. This would mean, for example, that if you are off work sick but remain employed while you are absent, only a period of up to 26 weeks' absence would count towards your continuous employment. However, it is arguable that periods when you are off work, because of sickness or maternity leave, for example, can still count towards your continuous employment irrespective of the length of your absence as long as you continued to be employed by your employer over these periods.

If your employment is legally transferred from one employer to another your employment is unbroken.[17]

See p638 if your continuity of employment is affected by a strike and p538 if you have been dismissed by your employer.

Reinstatement and re-engagement

If you have been reinstated or re-engaged following an unfair dismissal claim or as a result of a statutory dispute resolution procedure any period between your dismissal and reinstatement or re-engagement counts towards your 26 weeks' continuous employment.[18]

The earnings condition

To qualify for SMP, SPP or SAP your average gross weekly earnings during the 'relevant period' (see p533) must be at least equal to the lower earnings limit for NI contributions.[19]

- For **SMP** or **SPP** (birth), unless your baby is born prior to or during the 15th week before the EWC, it is the lower earnings limit in force at the end of the 15th week before the EWC that is used (see p548).[20]
- For **SAP** and **SPP** (adoption), it is the lower earnings limit in force at the end of the week in which you or the adopter are notified by the adoption agency of being matched with the child (see p548).

For the tax year 2008/09 the lower earnings limit is £90 a week (see Appendix 9 for the amounts for other years).

If your average weekly earnings during the relevant period fall below the lower earnings limit (eg, because you are sick and receiving just SSP) you will not qualify for SMP, SPP or SAP.

See p538 if you have been dismissed because of your pregnancy.

What counts as earnings

As well as your gross wages, bonuses and any overtime pay you receive during the relevant period, your earnings include payments such as:[21]

- SSP, SMP, SAP and SPP;
- arrears of pay following reinstatement or re-engagement in your job or a continuation of your contract of employment under the Employment Rights Act 1996;
- money which retrospectively has been treated as earnings as a result of backdated tax legislation.

Certain payments (eg, redundancy payments and return to work credit) are ignored.[22]

Pay rises

For **SMP**, if you are awarded a pay rise which affects your wages for any part of the period which runs from the first day of your relevant period (see p533) until the last day of your statutory maternity leave, your employer should reassess your average earnings over the relevant period to take account of this increase (even if the pay rise did not actually increase your wages for any week in the relevant period). If you would have been awarded a pay rise but for being on maternity leave, then you are still treated as receiving it. For these purposes 'statutory maternity leave' includes both ordinary and additional maternity leave under the Employment Rights Act 1996. Your employer should recalculate your average weekly earnings as if your earnings in each of the weeks of your relevant period included the increase, and pay any arrears of SMP due to you.[23] If you become entitled to SMP as a result of the pay rise, your employer should deduct any payments of MA that you have received for the same period from the SMP you are owed.[24]

Prior to 6 April 2005, the regulations stated that backdated pay rises should be included in the calculation of your average earnings for SMP *only* if they were paid for the relevant period. The rules were changed as a result of a ruling by the European Court of Justice.[25] If, prior to 6 April 2005, a pay rise was not included in the assessment of your average weekly earnings for SMP, but it affected your wages for any part of the period running from the first day of your relevant period until the last day of your statutory maternity leave, you may be entitled to arrears of SMP. The Revenue has issued guidance to employers on this issue which may be helpful to you, but this guidance is an interpretation of the law and not a statement of the legislation itself.[26] If you consider that you may have been underpaid SMP, but you are outside the time limits mentioned in the Revenue's guidance, seek independent advice.

For **SPP** and **SAP**, any part of a backdated pay rise which is paid for the relevant period should be included in the calculation of your average earnings. Your employer should recalculate your average weekly earnings following the rise and pay any arrears of SPP or SAP due to you.[27]

Meaning of the 'relevant period'[28]

For **SMP** and **SPP** (birth) the **'relevant period'** for calculating your average earnings is the period between:

- your last normal payday that falls either:
  - in or before the 15th week before the EWC (see p548); *or*
  - prior to the Sunday immediately before the baby was born (or, if s/he was born on a Sunday, prior to that day),

  whichever is earlier; *and*
- the day after your last normal payday falling at least eight weeks before that.

For **SAP** and **SPP** (adoption), the relevant period is the period between:

- your last normal payday that falls in or before the week in which you or the adopter are notified of being matched with a child for adoption (see p548). For this purpose a week runs from Sunday to Saturday; *and*
- the day after your last normal payday falling at least eight weeks before that.

In practice this normally means an average based on two months' earnings.[29]

Working during your statutory maternity, paternity or adoption pay period

Working for the employer who is paying you

In order to qualify for SMP or SAP you must have ceased working for the employer paying you SMP or SAP. Ceasing work normally just means starting your period of maternity or adoption leave – there is no requirement that you have to give up your job to qualify – and you can still do up to 10 days' work for your employer during your maternity or adoption pay period without your SMP or SAP being affected. These 10 days, called 'keeping in touch days', do not have to be consecutive but if you work for only part of a day it will still count as a full day of work.

If you work for more than 10 days during the maternity or adoption pay period (see p536) for the employer who is paying you SMP or SAP, you lose a week's SMP or SAP for every week in which you do any work in excess of those 10 days. This applies even if you only work for part of the week. If during the paternity pay period you do *any* work for the employer who is paying you SPP, your employer is not liable to pay you SPP for the week in which you work. These rules apply even if you are working for the employer under a different contract than the one you had before your maternity, paternity or adoption pay period began.[30]

Note that if you intend to work for more than 10 days for the employer who is paying you SMP or SAP, this may affect your continued entitlement to statutory maternity or adoption leave (and so may also affect your entitlement to SMP and SAP for the remainder of the maternity or adoption pay period); if you do not want to bring your period of leave to an end, seek employment advice before agreeing to such work.

For SMP, if you return to work for your employer but you are subsequently off work sick during the maternity pay period you will be entitled to SMP rather than SSP for each week in which you are off work for a whole week. If, after your maternity pay period has ended, you are still off work for medical reasons you may qualify for incapacity benefit (IB – see Chapter 12) or possibly SSP (see Chapter 24), but see p262 for future changes affecting IB.

Working for another employer

The general rule is that if you work for another employer (who is not liable to pay you SMP, SPP or SAP) while on maternity, paternity or adoption leave you lose your entitlement to SMP, SPP or SAP for the week in which you work and for the remainder of your maternity, paternity or adoption pay period.[31]

However, this rule is subject to two exceptions.

- For SMP, if the work is done while you are on maternity leave but before your baby is born, your entitlement to SMP is unaffected.[32]
- Your SMP, SPP or SAP is not affected by any work that you do for an employer who is not liable to pay you SMP, SPP or SAP if you were also employed by that employer:

- in the 15th week before the EWC, for SMP and SPP (birth); *or*
- in the week in which you or the adopter were notified that you had been matched with a child for adoption, for SPP (adoption) and SAP.[33]

You should notify the employer paying you SMP, SPP, or SAP of any work that you do for another employer within seven days of the first day in your maternity, paternity or adoption pay period on which you do such work. For SPP and SAP, your employer has the right to request this information in writing.[34]

2. The rules about your age

There are no upper or lower age limits for statutory maternity pay, statutory paternity pay or statutory adoption pay (SAP). However, as you must be at least 21 years old to adopt a child, you can only qualify for SAP if you are at least 21.

3. Claiming for others

You are not entitled to an increase in statutory maternity pay, statutory paternity pay or statutory adoption pay for any dependants that you have.

4. The amount of benefit

	Period of payment	*Amount*
SMP	First six weeks	90% of average weekly earnings
	Remaining 33 weeks (see below)	Lesser of £117.18 or 90% of average weekly earnings
SPP	Two weeks	Lesser of £117.18 or 90% of average weekly earnings
SAP	39 weeks	Lesser of £117.18 or 90% of average weekly earnings

Statutory maternity pay

Statutory maternity pay (SMP) lasts for up to 39 weeks. For the first six weeks it is paid at the 'earnings-related' rate of 90 per cent of your average weekly earnings in the relevant period (see p533), and for the remaining 33 weeks you receive either £117.18 a week or the earnings-related rate, whichever is lower.[35]

If you are on maternity leave, you should claim national insurance (NI) credits for any week in which your maternity pay falls below the lower earnings limit (see p730) by writing to the Contributor Group at the NI Contributions Office (see Appendix 1). It is very important to do this. If you do not, your future entitlement to contributory benefits such as retirement pension may be affected.

Statutory paternity pay and statutory adoption pay

Both statutory paternity pay (SPP) and statutory adoption pay (SAP) are paid at the same rate. The amount you receive is either 90 per cent of your average weekly earnings calculated over the relevant period (see p533) or £117.18 a week, whichever is less.[36]

Period of payment

Statutory maternity pay[37]

SMP is paid for a period of up to 39 weeks – called the '**maternity pay period**'.

The earliest your maternity pay period can begin is at the start of the 11th week before the expected week of childbirth (EWC), unless your baby is born before this and the latest is the day after your baby is born. Within these limits, when your SMP starts is normally up to you. However, if you are off work with a pregnancy-related absence in the period falling on or after the start of the fourth week before your EWC and not later than the day after you have your baby, your SMP will start on the day after the first day of such absence in that period. This does not apply if your absence is not pregnancy-related.

Once your maternity pay period has begun, the actual date of your baby's birth will not affect your SMP. If the birth takes place earlier than expected, it does not entitle you to more than the 39 weeks' maximum period of SMP – the maternity pay period simply starts and ends sooner.

See p538 if you give up or lose your job.

Statutory paternity pay

SPP can be paid for a maximum of two consecutive weeks – called the '**paternity pay period**' – although you can choose to receive it for just one week, if you prefer.[38] The earliest SPP can be paid is from the child's date of birth, for SPP (birth), or the date of the child's placement for adoption, for SPP (adoption), and the latest is eight weeks after those dates. If the child is born before the EWC (see p548), the latest SPP (birth) can be paid is eight weeks after the first day of the EWC.[39]

As long as you request that your SPP be paid within this period and you give your employer sufficient notice of when you want it to be paid (see p544), you can choose to start your SPP either on:[40]

- a particular date; *or*
- the day of the baby's birth, or the day of the child's placement for adoption (without specifying an actual date). If you are at work on that day, your paternity pay period will begin on the next day; *or*

- a day falling a certain number of days after that (without specifying an actual date).

See p534 if you work for the employer paying you SPP or for another employer during your paternity pay period. See p538 if you give up or lose your job.

Statutory adoption pay

The maximum period for which you can be paid SAP is 39 weeks – called the **'adoption pay period'**.[41]

The earliest date on which the adoption pay period can normally begin is 14 days before the day you expect the child to be placed with you and the latest it can normally start is on the date of placement. As long as you request that your SAP starts within these time limits and give your employer the required period of notice (see p545), you can choose whether you want your adoption pay period to begin either:[42]

- on a particular date (but if the child is placed with you before that date, then the adoption pay period will begin on the date of placement); *or*
- on the day of placement (without specifying an actual date). If it turns out that you are working on that day your adoption pay period will begin on the next day.

Your adoption pay period may end early if the child either:[43]

- is returned to the adoption agency after being placed with you; *or*
- dies, if this happens after being placed with you for adoption; *or*
- is not actually placed with you but your adoption pay period has already begun.

In these circumstances, your adoption pay period will end eight weeks after the end of the week the child is returned, or dies, or that you are notified that the placement is not to take place, if this is earlier than it would have otherwise ended. In this situation a week runs from Sunday to Saturday.

See p534 if you work for the employer paying you SAP or for another employer during your adoption pay period. See p538 if you give up or lose your job.

More than one job

If you satisfy the conditions of entitlement to SMP, SPP or SAP with more than one employer (or under two or more contracts with the same employer), you can get benefit from each job (although if your earnings from any of your jobs are aggregated for calculating your liability to pay NI contributions, those jobs are counted as one and the amount of SMP, SPP or SAP your employers have to pay is apportioned between them).[44]

If you are both employed and self-employed and you receive SMP from your employer, you will not be entitled to maternity allowance for the same week for the same pregnancy on the basis of your self-employment.[45]

5. Special benefit rules

There are some groups of people to whom special rules apply. These are covered below and in Chapter 26. Special rules apply to you if:

- you are in prison or detention (see p625);
- you are outside Great Britain (GB – see below);
- you give up your job or have been dismissed (see below);
- you have been involved in a trade dispute (see p638);
- your baby is stillborn, you have had a multiple birth or adopted more than one child (see p539);
- you have adopted a child from abroad (see p539).

People outside Great Britain

Your entitlement to statutory maternity pay (SMP), statutory paternity pay (SPP) or statutory adoption pay (SAP) is not affected by any absence from GB as long as you count as an employee and you meet the other qualifying conditions. If you are employed abroad you can still count as an employee in certain circumstances.[46]

However, you do not count as an employee if your employer is not present or resident in GB, or does not run a business in GB, or is exempt from the social security legislation by international treaty.[47]

If you give up your job or are dismissed

Special rules may apply to you if you give up your job or are dismissed by your employer. Your employer is still liable to pay you SMP, SPP or SAP if:

- after your maternity, paternity or adoption pay period (see p536) has started, you give up your job, are dismissed or your job ends. Your employer will continue to be liable to pay you SMP, SPP or SAP until your maternity, paternity or adoption pay period finishes (but see p547 if your employer is insolvent);[48] *or*
- your employer dismisses you at any time if the dismissal was 'solely or mainly' to avoid paying SMP, SPP or SAP and you had been employed by that employer for at least eight continuous weeks. In these circumstances the amount of SMP, SPP or SAP to which you may be entitled (see p535) is calculated using your average earnings for the eight-week period ending with the last day for which you were paid;[49] *or*
- you satisfy qualifying conditions for SMP, SPP or SAP and your job ends for any reason at any time after:[50]

- the beginning of the 15th week before your expected week of childbirth (EWC), for SMP; *or*
- the day on which the child is born, for SPP (birth); *or*
- the day on which the child is placed for adoption, for SPP (adoption); *or*
- the beginning of the week in which you were notified of being matched with a child for adoption, for SAP.

For SMP, if your job ends at any time after the start of the 15th week before your EWC, or for SAP, if it ends before the adoption pay period is due to start, you are not required to have given your employer notice of your intention to take maternity or adoption leave, although you will still need to give your employer information to support your entitlement as detailed on p542 – eg, evidence of the expected date of birth, for SMP.[51]

If you qualify for SMP but your job ends before your maternity pay period was due to start, your SMP will start at the beginning of the 11th week before your EWC or, if your job ends after this, on the day after you finish work, unless your baby is born before these dates.[52] If you qualify for SAP but your job ends before your adoption pay period was due to start, it will start 14 days before the expected date of placement, or if your job ends after this, on the day after you finish work, unless your child is placed with you before this.[53]

If you are dismissed while pregnant or on maternity, paternity or adoption leave, seek advice about your right to claim unfair dismissal.

If you start work for another employer after giving up your job or being dismissed, see p534.

Stillbirths, multiple births and adoptions

If your baby is stillborn after the end of the 24th week of pregnancy, SMP or SPP (birth) is payable in the same way as for a live birth.[54] If the baby is stillborn earlier, this is treated as a miscarriage and SMP or SPP (birth) is not payable. Statutory sick pay (SSP – see Chapter 24) or incapacity benefit (IB – see Chapter 12) may be paid if you are incapable of work (but see p262 for future changes affecting IB). If the baby is born alive but then dies (even after only a moment), then this is a live birth and you can get SMP or SPP (birth) even if it happens in or before the 24th week of pregnancy.

No additional SMP, SPP or SAP is payable if you or your partner give birth to more than one baby, or have more than one child placed with you for adoption, unless this happens as part of a different adoption arrangement.[55]

If you are adopting a child from abroad

You may qualify for SPP (adoption) or SAP for an overseas adoption. In order to qualify you must satisfy the normal rules of entitlement for SPP (adoption) or SAP described in this chapter with the modifications explained below. As you will not have been matched with a child for adoption by UK authorities under UK law, it is primarily the rules that refer to the date of placement and the date of notification of being matched for adoption (both of which do not apply to overseas adoptions) that are modified. If such a placement is made under UK law the normal rules of entitlement to SPP and SAP apply.

Continuous employment and overseas adoptions

To qualify for SPP (adoption) or SAP for an overseas adoption, you must have been employed by your employer for a continuous period of at least 26 weeks.[56] In addition, for SPP (adoption) you must have been continuously employed by the same employer from the end of a week in which you met the 26-week continuous employment rule, or from the end of the week in which official notification regarding the adoption was sent to you, if that is later, up to the date the child enters GB.

Earnings condition and overseas adoptions

To satisfy the earnings condition (see p532) the relevant period for calculating your average weekly earnings is the period between:

- your last normal payday in or before a week in which you met the 26-week continuous employment rule, or the week in which official notification regarding the adoption was sent to you or the adopter (see p548), if that is later; *and*
- the day after the last normal payday falling at least eight weeks before that.

Your average earnings over this period must have been at least equal to the NI lower earnings limit (see p722). The lower earnings limit that is used is either the one that was in force at the end of the week in which official notification regarding the adoption was sent to you or, if this is later, the one that was in force at the end of the week in which you met the 26-week continuous employment rule.[57]

Working for another employer and overseas adoptions

If, during your paternity or adoption pay period, you work for another employer who is not liable to pay you SPP or SAP, you will lose your entitlement to SPP or SAP for the week in which you work and any subsequent week unless you were working for that employer in the week in which you received official notification regarding the adoption (see p548).[58]

Period of payment for overseas adoptions

The earliest that SPP can be paid is from the date the child enters GB and the latest is eight weeks after that.

As long as payment falls within this period and you have given your employer the correct period of notice (see pp541 and 544) you can either choose a particular date on which you want your SPP to start or you can ask that it starts on the day the child enters GB without giving an actual date.[59]

If you are claiming SAP, as long as you have given your employer the correct period of notice (see below) you can ask your employer to start paying SAP from either:[60]

- a specific date (which is no later than 28 days after the date that the child enters GB); *or*
- the day the child enters GB (without giving an actual date).

If you give up your job or are dismissed

For SAP, if your job ends, for any reason, before your adoption pay period has begun your employer is still liable to pay you SAP for an overseas adoption as long as you satisfy the qualifying conditions. However, if your adoption pay period begins more than six months after your job ends the Revenue should pay your SAP instead, unless you subsequently become entitled to SAP from another employer within the adoption pay period, when that new employer will then take over responsibility for paying your SAP.[61]

Claiming statutory paternity pay for an overseas adoption

In order to qualify for SPP you must give your employer the notice and information described on p544. However, instead of giving your employer notice of the date of placement or expected placement of the child and of the date of notification of being matched with the child for adoption, you must instead give your employer:[62]

- a declaration stating that you have received official notification (see p548) regarding the adoption; *and*
- notice of the date that you expect the child to enter GB or the date s/he did enter GB if s/he has already done so.

You may use Form SC5 to provide the above information to your employer, available from the Revenue's website at www.hmrc.gov.uk.

Claiming statutory adoption pay for an overseas adoption

In order to qualify for SAP you must give your employer the following notice and information at least 28 days before your adoption pay period is due to start or, if that is not practicable, as soon as is reasonably practicable after that date:[63]

- a copy of the official notification regarding the adoption (see p548);
- a declaration that you wish to receive SAP, not SPP;
- the date that you expect the child to enter GB or, if s/he has already arrived, the date s/he entered GB.

Additional information to be provided for an overseas adoption

In addition to the information outlined above, to qualify for SPP and SAP for an overseas adoption you must inform your employer of:[64]

- the date on which you or the adopter received official notification regarding the adoption (see p548). You should notify your employer of this either within 28 days of:
  - receiving the official notification; *or*
  - being employed by your employer for 26 continuous weeks, if that is later; *and*
- the date of the child's arrival in GB, within 28 days of her/his arrival. For SAP, but not for SPP, you must also give evidence of the child's arrival to your employer (eg, airline tickets or the child's passport showing the date of entry).

If, after you have given the above information, your employer decides that you are not entitled to SPP or SAP s/he must provide you with details of the decision and the reasons for it within 28 days of the date you provided the information.[65]

6. Claims and backdating

Making a claim

It is not necessary for you to complete a claim form to qualify for statutory maternity pay (SMP), statutory paternity pay (SPP) or statutory adoption pay (SAP). Instead you must just give your employer certain notice and information. Your employer must then make a decision on your entitlement. The rules are detailed below and on pp544 and 545.

Notification sent to your employer in a properly addressed and pre-paid letter is treated as having been given on the day it is put in the post.[66]

It is important to remember that there are different notice requirements for entitlement to statutory maternity, paternity and adoption leave. In addition, if your employer offers its own maternity, paternity or adoption pay scheme in addition to SMP, SPP or SAP, the notice requirements for this scheme may also be different. Check this with your employer.

If the Revenue requests information from you in connection with your entitlement, see p1151.

Notice and information for statutory maternity pay

In order to qualify for SMP you must give your employer:

- notice (in writing if your employer requests this) of the date from which you expect your employer to pay you SMP. This notice must be given at least 28 days before you expect payment to start or, if that is not practicable, as soon as reasonably practicable after that.[67] See p536 for when it is possible for your SMP to start; *and*
- evidence of the expected date of birth. You must provide this evidence no more than three weeks after the start of your maternity pay period. This time

limit can be extended to the end of the 13th week of the maternity pay period if you have good cause for the delay.[68]

The meanings of 'as soon as reasonably practicable' and 'good cause' are not defined in the regulations – you would have to show that any delay was reasonable given your circumstances.

If you give your employer less notice than this or you do not provide the above evidence within the time limit your employer may not pay you SMP. If you think your employer's decision is wrong you can challenge it (see p547).

The details of the expected date of birth are on Form MAT B1, which is issued by your doctor or a registered midwife. The earliest you can be issued with a MAT B1 form is the start of the 20th week before your expected week of childbirth (EWC). Your employer needs to be given this form. If you do not have a MAT B1 your employer can accept other medical evidence, but it must be substantially like Form MAT B1.[69]

If your employment ends in or after the 15th week before your baby is due see p539.

If your baby is born prematurely

If your baby is born prematurely, before the date you planned to start your maternity pay period, you may not have been able to give your employer any notice, or sufficient notice, of the date you wanted your SMP to start. Even if you did give your employer the correct notice, your maternity pay period will normally begin on the day after you had your baby, rather than the day that you planned.

To qualify for SMP you must inform your employer (in writing if your employer requests this) of the date on which your baby was born if either:

- your baby is born during or before the 15th week before your EWC; *or*
- you had informed your employer of the date from which you wanted your SMP to start, but the baby was born before that date.

You must do this within four weeks of the birth or, if that is not practicable, as soon as reasonably practicable after that.[70]

In addition, if your baby is born before you intended to start your maternity pay period you must give your employer evidence of the week in which you had the baby (eg, a birth certificate, or a MATB1 form, if the child's date of birth is given on this) as well as evidence of what was the expected date of birth, within three weeks of the start of your maternity pay period. This time limit can be extended to the end of the 13th week of the maternity pay period if you have good cause for the delay.[71]

Notice and information for statutory paternity pay

In order to qualify for SPP you must tell your employer in writing:

- when you would like your SPP to start. See p536 for when it is possible for your benefit to start; *and*
- whether you want to get SPP for one week or two.

You must give your employer this information at least 28 days before your paternity pay period is due to start, or if that is not practicable, as soon as is reasonably practicable after that date (see p546).[72]

Within the same time limit you must also give your employer the following information, in writing.

For SPP (birth):

- the EWC (or the date of birth, if the child has already been born); *and*
- a declaration stating that:
  - you will care for the child or support the child's mother while getting SPP; *and either*
  - you are the child's father and will have responsibility for her/his upbringing; *or*
  - you are the spouse, civil partner or partner of the child's mother and, apart from the mother's responsibility, you will have the main responsibility for the upbringing of the child.

For SPP (adoption):

- the date you expect the child to be placed for adoption (or the date s/he was placed, if the placement has already happened); *and*
- the date on which the adopter was notified that the child had been matched with her/him for adoption (see p548); *and*
- a declaration stating that:
  - you and your spouse, civil partner or partner are jointly adopting a child, or your spouse, civil partner or partner is adopting a child; *and*
  - you have, or expect to have, the main responsibility for the upbringing of the child (apart from the responsibility of the adopter or co-adopter); *and*
  - while getting SPP you intend to care for the child or support the child's adopter; *and*
  - you elect to be paid SPP rather than SAP.

You may use Form SC3 for SPP (birth), or Form SC4 for SPP (adoption), to provide the above information to your employer, available on the Revenue's website at www.hmrc.gov.uk.

If you give your employer less notice than this, or you do not provide the above information within the time limit, your SPP can begin later, once the necessary time limit for providing the notice or information has passed, as long as payment would still fall within the eight-week period in which SPP can be paid (see p536).

In addition, if you notified your employer that you want to start your paternity pay period:

- on the day the child is born or is placed with you for adoption, or on a day falling a certain number of days after the birth or placement, you need to tell your employer the date the child was born or the date on which the placement occurred, as soon as is reasonably practicable after that date;[73]
- on a specific date, but the child is not born or placed with you until after that date, you must give your employer notice of the new date on which you want your paternity pay period to start, as soon as is reasonably practicable.[74]

Notice and information for statutory adoption pay

In order to qualify for SAP you must give your employer:[75]

- notice (in writing if your employer requests this) of:
  - when you want your SAP to start (see p537 for when it is possible for your benefit to start);
  - the date on which you expect the child to be placed with you for adoption;
- a written declaration that you want to receive SAP rather than SPP; *and*
- documents from the adoption agency giving:
  - its name and address and your name and address; *and*
  - the date on which the child is expected to be (or was) placed with you; *and*
  - the date on which it informed you that the child would be placed with you for adoption.

  The adoption agency should provide you with a 'matching certificate' which will give this information.

This notice and information must be given at least 28 days before your adoption pay period is due to start or, if that is not practicable, as soon as is reasonably practicable after that date (see p546), otherwise your employer may not pay you SAP. In this situation it may be possible to argue that your SAP should start later, once the necessary time limit for providing the notice or information has passed, as long as payment would still fall within the adoption pay period (see p537). This may mean, however, that you might not be entitled to SAP for a full 39 weeks. If you are in this position, seek advice. If you think your employer's decision is wrong you can challenge it (see p547).

In addition to the above notice, if you choose to start your adoption pay period on the day the child is placed with you then you must give your employer further notice of the date on which the placement occurs, as soon as is reasonably practicable.[76]

If your employment ends before your adoption pay period begins, see p538.

Who should claim

If you are entitled to SMP, SPP or SAP but are not well enough to deal with your own affairs, the Revenue can appoint someone else to act for you.[77] This person is your 'appointee' (see p955). An application for someone to be your appointee can be made to your local Revenue enquiry centre. You can find out the address and telephone number from the Revenue's website (www.hmrc.gov.uk) or from the telephone directory.

If you claim the wrong benefit

If you are sick with a pregnancy-related illness in the four weeks before the week your baby is due, your employer can start your maternity leave (even if it is sooner than you had planned) and pay you SMP rather than SSP. It cannot do this if your illness is *not* pregnancy-related.[78]

See p440 for details of when you can get a claim for maternity allowance backdated if your employer has informed you that you are not entitled to SMP.

Backdating your entitlement

In order to qualify for **SMP**, **SPP** or **SAP** you must normally give your employer at least 28 days' notice of when you want your benefit to start. If you are not able to do so, your notice must be given as soon as is reasonably practicable after that date. If your employer accepts that you gave notice as soon as was practicable, your SMP, SPP or SAP should be paid from the day you have chosen to start your maternity, paternity or adoption pay period (see p536). In order to qualify you will also have to give your employer the information and evidence detailed on pp542–545 within the time limits outlined on those pages.

What amounts to '**as soon as is reasonably practicable**' is not defined in the regulations – you would have to show that your delay was reasonable given your circumstances. If you disagree with your employer's decision you can ask the Revenue to consider your entitlement (see p547).

7. Getting paid

Your employer usually pays statutory maternity pay (SMP), statutory paternity pay (SPP) or statutory adoption pay (SAP) in the same way as your normal wage or salary.[79] If you are also entitled to contractual maternity, paternity or adoption pay from your employer, SMP, SPP or SAP will form part of your payments. If your employer is liable to make payments to you under your contract, any payment of SMP, SPP or SAP you receive for the same period will go towards discharging your employer's contractual liability.[80] Your employer cannot pay you SMP, SPP or SAP by making a payment in kind, or by providing board and lodging, a service or some other facility.[81]

If you become entitled to SMP as a result of a pay rise or because payments you received were retrospectively treated as earnings under backdated tax legislation, your employer should deduct any payments of maternity allowance (MA) that you received for the same period from the SMP you are owed.[82]

See p536 for the period over which you can be paid SMP, SPP or SAP.

If your employer is liable to pay you SMP, SPP or SAP but is insolvent, the Revenue should pay you.[83] The Revenue will also pay you if you are entitled to SAP for a period after you were imprisoned or in detention (see p626), or for a period during which you were in detention if you were subsequently released without charge, found not guilty or given a non-custodial sentence.[84]

Delays and complaints

See Chapter 43 for details of how you can ask the Revenue to make a decision on your entitlement to SMP, SPP or SAP if your employer cannot, or will not, pay you. If the Revenue (or tax commissioners) decides that you are entitled to benefit, your employer may be required to pay you within a certain time (see p1155).

See p1182 if the Revenue is deciding on your entitlement to SMP, SPP or SAP and you wish to complain about its delay in dealing with your application.

Change of circumstances

You have to keep your employer informed of any change of circumstances which may affect your entitlement, such as starting work for someone else during the maternity, paternity or adoption pay period (see p548).[85]

Overpayments

The rules about overpayments and recovery of overpaid benefit explained in Chapter 39 do not apply to SMP, SPP or SAP.

However, if your employer pays you SMP, SPP or SAP and later decides that you were not entitled to it, it may attempt to recover the sum considered overpaid by making a deduction from your wages. If this happens you should seek advice.

See below if you wish to challenge your employer's decision that you are not entitled to SMP, SPP or SAP.

If your employer decides that you have been paid SMP in error, you should consider claiming MA immediately. You may be able to get this backdated (see p440).

8. Challenging your employer's decision

If you disagree with your employer's decision on your entitlement to statutory maternity pay, statutory paternity pay or statutory adoption pay, or if your employer has failed to make a decision, you can ask the Revenue to make a formal decision on your entitlement, and if you are unhappy with it, you can appeal against the Revenue's decision. For details, see Chapter 43.

9. Definitions of terms

- The '**expected week of childbirth**' (**EWC**) (sometimes called the 'expected week of confinement') is the week, starting on a Sunday, in which your baby is due to be born.
- The '**relevant period**' is the period which is used to calculate your average earnings for statutory maternity pay (SMP), statutory paternity pay (SPP) and statutory adoption pay (SAP). See p533 for how the period is worked out.
- '**SPP (birth)**' means SPP which you qualify for on the basis either of your partner giving birth to a child, or you being the father of a child.
- '**SPP (adoption)**' is SPP that you qualify for on the basis that a child has been, or is to be, placed with your partner for adoption, or with you and your partner for joint adoption.
- '**maternity pay period**' is the period of up to 39 weeks during which SMP is payable. See p536for when it can start.
- The '**adoption pay period**' is the period of up to 39 weeks when statutory adoption pay is payable. See p537for when it can start.
- The '**paternity pay period**' is the period of one or two weeks when SPP is payable. See p536 for when it can start.
- You are '**matched for adoption**' when an adoption agency decides that you would be a suitable adoptive parent for a particular child. The adoption agency should be able to provide you with a **matching certificate** to verify that you have been matched with a child for adoption.
- '**Overseas adoption**' is one in which the child enters Great Britain for the purpose of the adoption and the adoption does not involve the placement of the child under UK law.
- '**Official notification**' regarding the adoption is a written notification issued by or on behalf of the Welsh Assembly, Scottish Ministers or the Secretary of State informing you that it has issued, or is going to issue, a certificate to the overseas authority confirming that you are approved for adoption (sometimes called a Certificate of Eligibility and Suitability to Adopt).

Example

Rita's baby is due on Saturday 19 July 2008. The following dates apply.

– The 'expected week of childbirth' begins on the Sunday before – ie, Sunday 13 July 2008.

– The first week before the 'expected week of childbirth' begins on Sunday 6 July 2008, the second on Sunday 29 June 2008 and so on.

- The 11th week before the 'expected week of childbirth' begins on Sunday 27 April 2008. This is important because it is normally the earliest date from which Rita can be paid SMP (or maternity allowance).
- The 15th week before the 'expected week of childbirth' runs from Sunday 30 March to Saturday 5 April 2008.

Appendix 5 contains a table of relevant dates for all the weeks in 2008/09.

10. Tax, tax credits and other benefits

Statutory maternity pay (SMP), statutory paternity pay (SPP) and statutory adoption pay (SAP) are treated as earnings and you pay tax and national insurance (NI) contributions as appropriate.[86]

Tax credits

If you have a partner who is in full-time paid work (see p1222), in addition to your SMP, SPP or SAP, you may qualify for working tax credit (WTC – see Chapter 49). In some circumstances you may also qualify for WTC if you are receiving SMP, SPP or SAP, or you are either on ordinary maternity, paternity or adoption leave or within the first 13 weeks of your additional maternity or adoption leave period (see p1229 for details).

If you are entitled to WTC, you may be able to get help with the cost of childcare for your new baby or the child placed with you for adoption even before you return to work (see p1240).

If you have a dependent child you may also qualify for child tax credit (CTC – see Chapter 48).

The first £100 of your weekly SMP, SPP or SAP is ignored when calculating your entitlement to WTC and CTC, and any SMP, SPP or SAP you receive over £100 is counted as employment income.

Means-tested benefits

If you have a low income and are under 60, you may be able to get income support (IS – see Chapter 13) while you are on maternity, paternity or adoption leave. See p294 for details of whether you may qualify for IS while on leave. If you are 60 or over you may instead qualify for pension credit (PC – see Chapter 18). If you have a low income you may also be entitled to housing benefit (HB – see Chapter 10) and council tax benefit (CTB – see Chapter 5). If you are getting SMP, SPP or SAP you may be able to get an allowance for childcare costs deducted from your earnings when calculating your entitlement to HB and CTB (see p856).

You cannot claim jobseeker's allowance (JSA) if you are getting SMP, or if you are on paternity, or ordinary or additional adoption leave, because you are treated as unavailable for work, but your partner may qualify.[87] If you are a member of a couple who would normally have to make a joint claim for JSA (see p381) then:

- your partner can get JSA for you both without you needing to make a joint claim if you are getting SMP (or maternity allowance), or from the 11th week before your expected week of childbirth until 15 weeks after the baby is born;
- otherwise, if you are incapable of work because of your pregnancy you do not need to meet the labour market conditions – only your partner must.

Your net SMP, SPP or SAP (after deductions for Class 1 NI, tax and half of any occupational or personal pension payments), is taken into account in full for IS and income-based JSA.

SMP, SPP and SAP are treated as earnings for PC, HB and CTB. This means that when calculating your entitlement to PC, HB and CTB, it may be possible to deduct certain work-related expenses from your SMP, SPP or SAP (see pp847 and 882) as well as any tax, NI and half of any occupational or personal pension payments you pay. You may also be entitled to an earnings disregard (see pp854 and 885).

Non-means-tested benefits

You cannot get contribution-based JSA if you are receiving SMP (see Chapter 15), or if you are on paternity, or ordinary or additional adoption leave. You cannot get statutory sick pay (SSP) when you are receiving SMP. See p563 for how your SSP entitlement is affected if you are pregnant. You cannot receive SPP or SAP for any week in which you are entitled to SSP.[88]

Incapacity benefit

While you are pregnant you can be treated as incapable of work for incapacity benefit (IB) purposes (and so you may qualify for IB) in the circumstances explained on p665.[89]

You can qualify for SMP or SAP and for the higher rate of short-term or long-term IB at the same time, but your IB (including any increase for a dependant) will be reduced by the gross amount of SMP or SAP you receive. If you are only entitled to the lower rate of short-term IB you will not qualify for IB while you are entitled to SMP or SAP.[90]

Days on which you were entitled to SMP or SAP in the circumstances described on p273 count when calculating whether you were entitled to the higher rate of short-term IB or long-term IB.

Note: the introduction of employment and support allowance, which is planned for October 2008, will affect these rules (see Chapter 7 and CPAG's *Welfare Rights Bulletin* for updates).

Passports and other sources of help

If you are receiving IS, income-based JSA, PC, the disability or severe disability element of WTC, or CTC paid at a higher rate than the family element you may be entitled to a Sure Start maternity grant of £500 per child from the social fund. You might be able to get other help from the discretionary social fund (see Chapters 21 and 22).

For information on your entitlement to free prescriptions, free NHS dental treatment and Healthy Start food vouchers, see Chapter 9. For information on whether you are entitled to free school meals for your children, see p15.

Note: the Government plans to introduce a 'health in pregnancy grant' of approximately £190 in April 2009. This will be payable to all pregnant women after the 24th week of pregnancy as long they have had specific health advice from a healthcare professional.

Notes

1 ss6-10 Work and Families Act 2006

1. Who is entitled

2 ss171ZB(4) and 171ZL(4) SSCBA 1992
3 ss164 and 165 SSCBA 1992
4 ss171ZA(2) and (3), 171ZB(2) and (3), 171ZC and 171ZE(4)-(7) SSCBA 1992; regs 4 and 11 SPPSAP(G) Regs; reg 4(2)(b) and (c) PAL Regs
5 Regs 4 and 11 SPPSAP(G) Regs; reg 2 PAL Regs
6 s171ZL(2)-(4) SSCBA 1992; reg 3(2) SPPSAP(G) Regs
7 **SMP** s164(2)(a) SSCBA 1992
SPP ss171ZA(2)(b) and (d) and (3) and 171ZB(2)(b) and (d) and (3) SSCBA 1992
SAP s171ZL(2)(b) and (3) SSCBA 1992
8 Reg 4(2)(a) SMP Regs; reg 5 SPPSAP(G) Regs
9 Reg 11(4) SMP Regs; reg 33(4) SPPSAP(G) Regs
10 ss171ZB(2) and (3) and 171ZL(2) and (3) SSCBA 1992; reg 2(2) SPPSAP(G) Regs
11 ss171(1), 171ZJ(1) and (2) and 171ZS(1) and (2) SSCBA 1992; reg 17 SMP Regs; reg 32 SPPSAP(G) Regs; Sch 8 paras 10(4) and 11(4) EE(A) Regs
12 ss164(6) and (7), 171ZF and 171ZO SSCBA 1992
13 Regs 2 and 5 SMP(PAM) Regs; regs 3, 5 and 6 SPPSAP(PAM) Regs; reg 3 SPP(A)&SAP(AO)(PAM) Regs
14 Reg 17(3) SMP Regs; reg 32(3) SPPSAP(G) Regs
15 Reg 11(1) SMP Regs; reg 33 SPPSAP(G) Regs
16 Reg 11(3A) and (4) SMP Regs; reg 33(3) and (4) SPPSAP(G) Regs
17 Reg 14 SMP Regs; reg 36 SPPSAP(G) Regs
18 Reg 12 SMP Regs; reg 34 SPPSAP(G) Regs
19 ss164(2)(b), 171(4),171ZA(2)(c), 171ZB(2)(c), 171ZJ(6)-(8), 171ZL(2)(d) and 171ZS(6)-(8) SSCBA 1992
20 ss164(2)(b) and 171ZA(2)(c) and (3) SSCBA 1992; reg 4(2)(b) SMP Regs; reg 5(b) SPPSAP(G) Regs
21 Reg 20 SMP Regs; reg 39 SPPSAP(G) Regs

22 Reg 20(2)(a) SMP Regs; reg 39(2)(a) SPPSAP(G) Regs
23 Reg 21(7) SMP Regs
24 Reg 21B SMP Regs
25 *Alabaster v Woolwich plc and Secretary of State for Social Security* [2002] EWCA Civ 211; *Alabaster v Woolwich plc and Secretary of State for Social Security* C-147/02 2004 (ECJ); *Alabaster v Barclays Bank PLC and Secretary of State for Social Security* [2005] EWCA Civ 508
26 Revenue *Employer's Bulletin* Issue 21, October 2005 (www.hmrc.gov.uk/employers-bulletin/archive/empbull21.htm#5) and E15 *Employer Helpbook*
27 Reg 40(7) SPPSAP(G) Regs
28 Reg 21 SMP Regs; reg 40 SPPSAP(G) Regs
29 Reg 21(5) and (6) SMP Regs; reg 40(5) and (6) SPPSAP(G) Regs
30 ss165(4) and (5), 171ZE(5) and (6) and 171ZN(3) and (4) SSCBA 1992; reg 10 SMP Regs; reg 27A SPPSAP(G) Regs
31 ss165(6), 171ZE(7) and 171ZN(5) SSCBA 1992; reg 8(2) SMP Regs; regs 17(1) and 26(1) SPPSAP(G) Regs
32 s165(6) SSCBA 1992
33 Reg 8(1) SMP Regs; regs 10, 16 and 25 SPPSAP(G) Regs
34 Reg 24 SMP Regs; regs 17(2) and (3) and 26(2) and (3) SPPSAP(G) Regs

4. **The amount of benefit**

35 s166 SSCBA 1992
36 Regs 2 and 3 SPPSAP(WR) Regs
37 s165 SSCBA 1992; reg 2 SMP Regs; reg 1(2) SMPSS(MA) Regs
38 s171ZE(2) SSCBA 1992; regs 6(3) and 12(3) SPPSAP(G) Regs
39 s171ZE(3) SSCBA 1992; regs 8 and 14 SPPSAP(G) Regs
40 Regs 6 and 12 SPPSAP(G) Regs
41 Reg 21 SPPSAP(G) Regs; reg 2 SPPSAP(G)(A) Regs
42 s171ZN(2) SSCBA 1992; reg 21 SPPSAP(G) Regs
43 Reg 22 SPPSAP(G) Regs
44 ss164(3), 171ZD(1) and 171ZM(1) SSCBA 1992; reg 18 SMP Regs; reg 38 SPPSAP(G) Regs
45 s35(1)(d) SSCBA 1992

5. **Special benefit rules**

46 Regs 2, 2A, 7 and 8 SMP(PAM) Regs; regs 3, 4, 8 and 9 SPPSAP(PAM) Regs
47 Reg 3 SMP(PAM) Regs; reg 17(3) SMP Regs; reg 2 SPPSAP(PAM) Regs; reg 32(3) SPPSAP(G) Regs
48 ss164(2)(a) and (3), 171ZD and 171ZM SSCBA 1992
49 ss164(8), 171ZD(2) and 171ZM(2) SSCBA 1992; reg 3(1) SMP Regs; regs 20 and 30 SPPSAP(G) Regs
50 ss164(2)(a),171ZA(2)(b) and (d), 171ZB(2)(b) and (d) and 171ZL(2)(b) and (3) SSCBA 1992
51 Reg 23(4) and (5) SMP Regs; reg 29 SPPSAP(G) Regs
52 s165(2) SSCBA 1992; reg 2(5) SMP Regs
53 s165(2) SSCBA, 1992; reg 29 SPPSAP(G) Regs
54 ss171(1) and 171ZA(5) SSCBA 1992
55 ss171(1), 171ZA(4), 171ZB(6) 171ZL(5) SSCBA 1992
56 ss171ZB(2) and (3)and 171ZL(2) and (3) SSCBA 1992 as modified by regs 2 and 3 and Schs 1 and 2 SSCBA(AAO) Regs
57 ss171ZB(2) and (3) and 171ZL(2) and (3) SSCBA 1992 as modified by regs 2 and 3 and Schs 1 and 2 SSCBA(AAO) Regs; reg 40 SPPSAP(G) Regs as modified by reg 3 SPP(A)&SAP(AO)(No.2) Regs
58 Regs 10 and 16 SPP(A)&SAP(AO)(No.2) Regs
59 s171ZE(2) and (3) SSCBA 1992 as modified by reg 2 and Sch 1 SSCBA(AAO) Regs; regs 6 and 8 SPP(A)&SAP(AO)(No.2) Regs
60 Reg 12 SPP(A)&SAP(AO)(No.2) Regs
61 Reg 17 SPP(A)&SAP(AO)(No.2) Regs
62 Reg 9 SPP(A)&SAP(AO)(No.2) Regs
63 Reg 15 SPP(A)&SAP(AO)(No.2) Regs
64 Regs 7, 14 and 15(1)(c) SPP(A)&SAP(AO)(No.2) Regs
65 Reg 11 SPPSAP(A) Regs as modified by reg 3(4) and (5) Statutory Paternity Pay (Adoption) and Statutory Adoption Pay (Adoptions from Overseas) (Administration) Regulations 2003 No.1192

6. **Claims and backdating**

66 Regs 22(4) and 23(3) SMP Regs; reg 47 SPPSAP(G) Regs
67 s164(4) and (5) SSCBA 1992
68 Reg 22 SMP Regs
69 Reg 2 SMP(ME) Regs
70 Reg 23 SMP Regs
71 Reg 22(1) and (2) SMP Regs
72 s171ZC(1) and (2) SSCBA 1992; regs 9 and 15 SPPSAP(G) Regs

73 Regs 7(1) and 13(1) SPPSAP(G) Regs
74 Regs 7(2) and 13(2) SPPSAP(G) Regs
75 s171ZL(6) and (7) SSCBA 1992; regs 23 and 24 SPPSAP(G) Regs
76 Reg 23 SPPSAP(G) Regs
77 Reg 31 SMP Regs; reg 46 SPPSAP(G) Regs
78 Sch 11 para 2(h) SSCBA 1992; reg 2(4) SMP Regs

7. **Getting paid**

79 Reg 27 SMP Regs; reg 41 SPPSAP(G) Regs
80 ss171ZG(2)and 171ZP(5) and Sch 13 para 3 SSCBA 1992
81 Reg 27 SMP Regs; reg 41 SPPSAP(G) Regs
82 Reg 21B SMP Regs
83 Reg 7(3) SMP Regs; reg 43(2) SPPSAP(G) Regs
84 Reg 44 SPPSAP(G) Regs
85 Reg 24 SMP Regs; regs 17(2) and 26(2) SPPSAP(G) Regs

10. **Tax, tax credits and other benefits**

86 s4(1)(a)(ii)-(iv) SSCBA 1992
87 Reg 15(bc) and (c) JSA Regs
88 Regs 18(a) and 27(1)(a) SPPSAP(G) Regs
89 Reg 14 SS(IFW) Regs
90 s171ZP and Sch 13 para 1 SSCBA 1992; reg 7A(4) and 7B(4) SS(IB) Regs

Chapter 24

Statutory sick pay

This chapter covers:

Statutory sick pay (SSP) can be paid to certain employees for up to 28 weeks of incapacity for work. If you are not an employee you do not qualify for SSP (but see p555 if you have been dismissed by your employer). If you are unemployed or self-employed you may qualify for incapacity benefit (IB) or income support (IS) instead (but see below for future changes). SSP is administered and paid by your employer. Your contract of employment may mean that your employer must also pay you occupational sick pay. But SSP is a legal minimum and, if you qualify for it, your employer is not allowed to pay you less.

It is not necessary for you to have paid national insurance contributions to qualify for SSP and your entitlement is not affected by any savings that you have.

Employment and support allowance

IS paid on the basis of incapacity for work and IB are to be replaced by employment and support allowance. This change, which is planned for October 2008, initially will affect only new claimants – with existing IS and IB claimants remaining on those benefits for the time being. See Chapter 7 for details and www.cpag.org.uk/esa or CPAG's *Welfare Rights Bulletin* for updates.

1. Who is entitled to statutory sick pay

You qualify for statutory sick pay (SSP) if:[1]

- you are an employee (see below); *and*
- you are incapable of work (see below); *and*
- you are within a period of incapacity for work (see p556); *and*
- you are within your period of entitlement to SSP (see p557); *and*
- the day is a qualifying day (see p560); *and*
- your normal earnings are equal to or more than the lower earnings limit for national insurance (NI) contributions (see p559).

There are some groups of people to whom special rules apply (see p563). Certain people do not qualify for SSP (see p558). See below if your employer has dismissed you solely or mainly to avoid paying SSP.

Employees

To be entitled to SSP you must be an employee. This does not mean that you must have a written contract of employment. It is the fact that you are employed that matters rather than any documents that you have (though documents are useful for evidence in case of a dispute). Your right to SSP cannot be taken away by any document, whether you sign it or not, and if your employer sacks you to avoid paying SSP, it is still liable to pay it after your contract has ended (see below).[2] The question of whether you are an employee for SSP purposes is similar to the question of whether you are an 'employed earner' for NI purposes (see p718).

However, even if you are an employee, your employer does not have to pay you SSP if it is neither resident nor present in Great Britain (GB), or does not have a place of business in GB, or if it is exempt from the social security legislation because of an international treaty.[3]

See p558 for details of employees who are not entitled to SSP.

Dismissal from work

If your employer dismisses you solely or mainly to avoid having to pay you SSP it is still liable to pay you SSP. In these circumstances your employer should continue to pay you SSP until whichever of the following occurs first:[4]

- your period of entitlement to SSP ends; *or*
- until your contract would have ended had you not been dismissed.

Incapable of work

In order to qualify for SSP you must be 'incapable of work'. However, the usual tests of incapacity for work (see Chapter 28) do not apply to SSP.[5]

To be **'incapable of work'** for SSP purposes, you must either be:[6]

- incapable of doing work which you could reasonably be expected to do under the terms of your contract because you have a specific disease (see p667) or bodily or mental disablement; *or*
- treated as incapable of such work (see p556).

The Revenue relies on employers to administer SSP, but it offers advice to employers on issues of incapacity for work. The Revenue suggests that if your employer doubts that you are incapable of work it may seek medical advice from the company's medical officer, your doctor (although this would only be with your permission) or from the Revenue's own Medical Service (MS).

If your employer requests the Revenue's help in deciding whether you are capable of work, the MS will normally contact your doctor and you may be asked to attend a medical examination with the MS. This can only be done with your consent but, since your employer could simply refuse payment, you are unlikely to gain much by not consenting.

Your employer is then given the MS's view on whether you are capable of work, but is not given any medical report or other explanation. It is still for your employer to decide whether to pay SSP.

Treated as incapable of work

Even if you are not actually incapable of work, your employer (or the Revenue – see p568) has the discretion to treat you as incapable of work if:[7]

- you have been officially excluded from work, or prevented from working because either you are a carrier of or you have been in contact with someone who has a specified disease under public health legislation; *or*
- you are under medical care in connection with a specific disease or bodily or mental disablement; *and*
  - a doctor has stated that you should not work as a precautionary measure or in order to convalesce; *and*
  - you do not work for your normal employer.

If you are incapable of work for just part of a day you must be treated as incapable of work for the whole day as long as you do not do any work on that day. If you are a shift worker and you are incapable of work for part of a day but you do some work on that day you should still be treated as incapable of work for the whole day if you only finish a shift that began the day before and you do not do any work on a shift that starts on that day and ends the next.

Period of incapacity for work

For SSP to be paid to you, you must also be within a 'period of incapacity for work'. A **'period of incapacity for work'** is defined as four or more consecutive days of incapacity for work (see p555).[8] This means that you can only qualify for SSP if you are incapable of work (or can be treated as incapable of work) for at least four days in a row. Every day of the week (including Sunday[9]) counts for this purpose even if it is not a day on which you would normally work. If you are incapable of work on a day that falls before or after the period covered by your contract, such days can still be included in your period of incapacity for work (but see p560 if you have not started work yet).[10]

Two periods of incapacity for work can be 'linked' and treated as a single period if they are separated by eight weeks or less.[11]

For incapacity benefit (IB) purposes, a period of incapacity for work can be two or more days in any week if you are receiving certain types of regular treatment such as dialysis (see p264). For SSP, this rule does not apply. If this prevents you getting SSP and you are receiving one of these forms of treatment, you may qualify for IB instead (see Chapter 12). However, see p554 for details of future changes affecting IB.

Period of entitlement to statutory sick pay

You only qualify for SSP if you are within 'a period of entitlement'. In certain circumstances a period of entitlement cannot arise and so you will not qualify for SSP (see p558).

When entitlement to statutory sick pay starts

A period of entitlement to SSP normally starts on the first day of your period of incapacity for work, unless:

- your contract of employment starts either during your period of incapacity for work or between two linked periods of incapacity for work; *or*
- your incapacity for work began before 1 October 2006 and you were either aged 65 or over when it started or you were under 16 on 1 October 2006.[12]

When entitlement to statutory sick pay ends

A period of entitlement to SSP ends (and so your SSP will stop) when *any* of the circumstances detailed below apply to you:[13]

- your incapacity for work ends;
- you reach your maximum 28 weeks' entitlement to SSP from a particular employer (see p562);[14]
- your contract of employment ends (unless it has been brought to an end by your employer solely or mainly to avoid liability to pay SSP – see p555);
- in certain circumstances, when you are pregnant or have just had a baby (see p563);
- you reach the third anniversary of the start of the period of entitlement (see below);
- you are imprisoned or detained in legal custody (see p625).

Periods of entitlement with the same employer and in some circumstances with different employers (see p562), separated by eight weeks or less, are linked and treated as a single period.[15] This is why it is possible not to have exhausted your 28 weeks' entitlement to SSP over a period of three years. (However, the Government is proposing to abolish the rules allowing you to link periods of entitlement with different employers – see p562.)

If your period of entitlement to SSP ends and you are still incapable of work, see p566 for details of other benefits that you might claim.

If your period of entitlement to SSP ends and you are still incapable of work, you are not entitled to SSP from your employer again until your current period of incapacity ends and a new one arises. In practice, this means that more than eight weeks must elapse between the date you recover and the date when you fall ill again (but see p558 if you got IB in the intervening period).

If your employer stops paying you SSP on the grounds that it considers that your period of entitlement has ended you should be provided with a statement (on Form SSP1 or on your employer's own computerised form which should be provided with the SSP1 form) giving you the reasons for this. There are time limits for providing such information.[16]

If you do not agree with your employer's decision to stop your SSP, see p568.

When statutory sick pay will not be paid

In certain circumstances a period of entitlement to SSP cannot arise. As a result, you will not qualify for any SSP during your period of incapacity for work.[17]

A period of entitlement cannot arise if:

- your normal weekly earnings are below the lower earnings limit (see p559); *or*
- at some time during the 57 days before the date on which your period of entitlement would have started you qualified for either:
  - IB, or you would have done had you satisfied the contribution conditions; *or*
  - severe disablement allowance (SDA).

  In order to have qualified for these benefits you would have had to have claimed them. (You will not be disentitled to SSP on the grounds that you previously qualified for IB if you are now not entitled to IB and you are over pension age – ie, at least 60 if you are a woman , or 65 if you are a man); *or*
- you are a 'welfare to work' beneficiary (see p666), who was previously getting IB or SDA and your period of entitlement would have started within your 104-week linking period (see p666). This does not apply if you are over pension age and not entitled to IB, otherwise in these circumstances you should be able to qualify for either IB or SDA again while you are incapable of work (see p264); *or*
- at the time when your period of entitlement would have begun there is a strike at your workplace (but see p638); *or*
- you have not yet started work under your contract of employment (unless you had an earlier contract with the same employer which ended within the last eight weeks); *or*

- at the time when your period of entitlement would have begun you are within a maternity pay period (see p548) or maternity allowance (MA) period (see p435) because you are pregnant or have just given birth (see p563); *or*
- you are not entitled to statutory maternity pay (SMP) or MA and you are within the period immediately before and after you give birth (see p563); *or*
- you are in prison or legal custody (see p625).

You are also not entitled to SSP (because a period of entitlement cannot arise) if you are employed by an agency and you have a fixed-term contract that lasts for three months or less.[18] This does not apply if you actually work for the agency for more than three months, or if your contract can be linked to an earlier one with the same agency and the combined period of the contracts exceeds 13 weeks. Contracts can be linked if the period between one ending and another starting is eight weeks or less. **Note**: the Government is proposing to amend the law so that agency workers on short-term contracts *can* qualify for SSP. At the time of writing, it was not known when this change would be introduced. See CPAG's *Welfare Rights Bulletin* for updates.

If your employer decides not to pay you SSP on any of the above grounds, it should provide you with a statement (on Form SSP1 or on its own computerised form which it should provide with the Form SSP1) giving you the reasons for this. There are time limits for providing this information.[19] If you do not agree with your employer's decision, see p568.

If you are not entitled to SSP, see p566 for details of other benefits to which you might be entitled.

People with low earnings

You cannot get SSP if your 'normal weekly earnings' are less than the lower earnings limit for NI contributions, currently £90 a week (see p722).

Your **'normal weekly earnings'** are calculated by averaging your gross earnings from your employer (ie, before tax and NI contributions are deducted) over the period which runs between:[20]

- your last normal payday before your period of entitlement to SSP began (see below); *and*
- the day after the last normal payday which falls at least eight weeks before this.

Only payments actually made in this period count.[21]

As well as your wages, your gross earnings include certain other payments, such as:[22]

- SSP, SMP, statutory paternity pay and statutory adoption pay;
- maternity pay;
- arrears of pay following reinstatement or re-engagement in your job or a continuation of a contract of employment under the Employment Rights Act 1996;

- money treated retrospectively as earnings by the Revenue as a result of backdated tax legislation;

Certain payments (eg, redundancy payments and return-to-work credit) are ignored.[23]

If, on average, you receive less than £90 a week, you do not qualify for SSP even if, in theory, you should have been paid more.

There are special rules if you have not been employed sufficiently long to have been paid wages over this eight-week period.[24]

Example

Ernesto works part time and is paid £96 a week. He is going on holiday and his employer pays him two weeks' holiday pay in advance, which he receives during week one. He goes on two weeks' annual leave (weeks two and three). He falls ill in week 10. His SSP is based on the average wages received in weeks two to nine, so the total is £576, not £768. This is divided by eight to give £72. As this is below the lower earnings limit, Ernesto gets no SSP.

See p562 if you have more than one job.

People who have not yet started work

If you have agreed to work for an employer but have not started work when you fall ill you are not entitled to SSP from that employer for any day during the same period of incapacity for work, unless:

- you were employed by the same employer previously; *and*
- not more than eight weeks have passed since your last contract ended.[25]

Qualifying days

You can only be entitled to SSP for 'qualifying days'. '**Qualifying days**' are simply days on which you qualify for payment of SSP, although SSP is not paid for the first three qualifying days. These are known as 'waiting days' (see p561).[26]

Qualifying days are usually those days of the week on which you would normally work if you were not sick. However, other days may be selected as qualifying days by agreement between you and your employer if that would provide a better reflection of your contract of employment (eg, if you work a complicated shift pattern).

For this purpose a week begins on Sunday and there must be a minimum of one qualifying day in each week.[27]

If there is no agreement between you and your employer about which days are qualifying days, or if the only agreement is to treat days of incapacity or days that fall in a period of incapacity for work or a period of entitlement as qualifying days, such an agreement is ignored and the qualifying days are presumed to be:

- the days on which it is agreed that you are required to work; *or*

- Wednesday, if it is agreed that you are not required to work on any day in that week – eg, offshore oil-workers, who may work two weeks 'on' and then two weeks 'off'; *or*
- if you cannot agree on which days you are or are not required to work, every day in the week, except days on which you and your employer agree that no employee works (if you can agree at least to that extent).[28]

'Required to work' means required by the terms of your contract of employment.[29] Days when you can choose whether or not to work do not count – eg, voluntary overtime shifts.

Waiting days

SSP is not paid for the first three qualifying days (see p560) in a period of entitlement.[30] These are called **'waiting days'**. As the waiting days must be qualifying days, they will not necessarily be the first three days of your sickness.

If your period of incapacity for work can be linked to an earlier one you do not have to serve the three waiting days again, but become entitled to SSP from the first qualifying day. Two or more periods of incapacity for work are linked and treated as one if they are separated by eight weeks or less.

2. The rules about your age

From 1 October 2006 there have been no lower or upper age limits for entitlement to statutory sick pay (SSP). From that date, as long as you satisfy the qualifying conditions, you can get SSP no matter what your age. For the rules prior to 1 October 2006, see p560 of the 2007/08 edition of CPAG's *Welfare Benefits and Tax Credits Handbook*.

3. Claiming for others

You cannot receive an increase in statutory sick pay for any dependants.

4. The amount of benefit

Statutory sick pay (SSP) is not paid for the first three qualifying days in a period of entitlement (see p561).[31] After that, it is payable at a rate of £75.40 a week.[32]

SSP is a daily benefit so it can be paid for periods of less than a week. The daily rate is calculated by dividing the weekly amount of SSP by the number of qualifying days you have in that week (a week for these purposes runs from

Sunday to Saturday).[33] The weekly rate of SSP is below the lower earnings limit (see p723) so, if you are not receiving any occupational sick pay, you do not have to pay national insurance (NI) contributions.

You are entitled to Class 1 NI credits for each week that you are entitled to SSP (see p728).[34] You claim them by writing to the Contributor Group at the NI Contributions Office in Newcastle (see Appendix 1), or for assistance you can telephone or visit your local Revenue enquiry centre – you can obtain its details from the telephone directory. It is important that you claim credits in order to protect your contribution record for benefits such as incapacity benefit (IB) and retirement pension.

People with more than one job

If you cannot work, you are entitled to SSP from any job for which you fulfil the qualifying conditions. So, you could get payments of SSP for each of two contracts with the same employer (eg, if you are both a daytime teacher and an evening tutor with an education authority), or payments from two separate employers. However, if the earnings from any of your different jobs are added together when calculating your liability to pay Class 1 NI contributions (which usually means you contribute less than if they had been treated separately – see p723) you can only receive a total of £75.40 from those jobs and your employer's liability to pay you SSP is apportioned accordingly.[35]

It is possible for you to be unable to work on one contract and be entitled to SSP, but at the same time be able to work on a different contract – eg, you perform quite different tasks for each.

Maximum entitlement to statutory sick pay

You are entitled to a maximum of 28 weeks' SSP from any one employer in one period of incapacity for work. Twenty-eight weeks' entitlement is equal to 28 times the weekly rate of SSP.[36]

In calculating the 28-week period, previous periods of entitlement to SSP under the same contract with the same employer are linked to your current one if they are separated by eight weeks or less.[37]

At the time of writing, periods of entitlement with different employers can also be linked if they are separated by eight weeks or less as long as you provide your new employer with a leaver's statement from your past employer detailing the period for which SSP was paid (Form SSP1(L)) within the period required by your employer, or within the period of seven days after your first qualifying day (see p560), whichever is later.[38] The time limit for giving your new employer an SSP1(L) can be extended if you can show good cause for the delay in providing the statement and you provide it not later than the 91st day after your first qualifying day. You should request Form SSP1(L) from an employer if you were entitled to SSP in the eight weeks before your job ended.[39] Linking periods of entitlement in this way allows you to transfer to IB (see Chapter 12) earlier, if you satisfy the qualifying conditions for IB (but, see p554 for details of future changes affecting IB).

However, subject to Parliamentary approval, the Government plans to abolish the rule which allows you to link periods of entitlement to SSP with past and new employers. This change, which is planned for October 2008, means that you would start a new 28-week period of entitlement to SSP with each new employer. See CPAG's *Welfare Rights Bulletin* for updates.

If you are still incapable of work after you have received your maximum 28-week entitlement to SSP, see p566 for details of other benefits that you might claim.

5. Special benefit rules

There are some groups of people to whom special rules apply. These are covered below and in Chapters 26 and 58. Special rules apply to:

- people outside Great Britain (GB) (see below);
- women who are pregnant or who have recently given birth (see below);
- people involved in a trade dispute (see p638);
- people in prison or detention (see p625).

People outside Great Britain

Your entitlement to statutory sick pay (SSP) is not affected by any absence from GB as long as you count as an employee and you meet the other conditions of entitlement to SSP. If you are employed abroad you can still count as an employee in certain circumstances.[40]

However, you do not count as an employee if your employer is not present or resident in GB, or does not run a business in GB, or is exempt from the social security legislation by international treaty.[41]

Women who are pregnant or who have recently given birth

If you are entitled to statutory maternity pay (SMP – see p528) or maternity allowance (MA – see p435) you cannot get SSP during the maternity pay period or the MA period.[42] Within the limits set out on pp435 and 536 (and unless your baby is born early) you have a right to choose when your maternity pay or MA period begins. So, for example, your employer cannot insist that you claim SMP or MA at the earliest possible date in order to limit the period for which it has to pay SSP.

Even if you are not entitled to SMP or MA:

- you cannot get SSP (because a period of entitlement cannot arise) if your period of incapacity for work started at some time during the 18 weeks which run from the first of the following dates:
  - the beginning of the week in which you are incapable of work wholly or partly because of your pregnancy, if this falls on or after the beginning of the fourth week before your 'expected week of childbirth' (see p442); *or*
  - the week in which you had your baby (but see below);[43]
- if SSP is already being paid to you (because your period of entitlement started before the above period, or because your incapacity for work was not initially linked to your pregnancy), your SSP will stop from the first of the following dates:[44]
  - the first day falling on or after the beginning of the fourth week before your 'expected week of childbirth' when you are incapable of work wholly or partly because of your pregnancy; *or*
  - the date on which you have your baby.

If your baby is stillborn before 24 weeks of pregnancy, you qualify for SSP if you satisfy the other conditions of entitlement.

6. Claims and backdating

To qualify for statutory sick pay (SSP), you must notify your employer of your incapacity for work, rather than notifying the DWP or the Revenue. The rules are described below. It may be possible to get your entitlement backdated (see p566).

Making a claim

It is not necessary for you to complete a claim form to qualify for SSP. Instead you must just inform your employer that you are sick (see below). Once you have done this your employer must decide whether you are entitled to SSP. Employers are given guidance on the SSP scheme in leaflet E14 *Employer's Help Book: what to do if your employee is sick*, available on the Revenue's website (www.hmrc.gov.uk).

Telling your employer that you are sick

Employers can decide both the time limits for employees to notify them of their sickness absence and the way that employees should tell them. However, your employer cannot insist that you notify it of your sickness:[45]

- earlier than the first qualifying day (which does not necessarily correspond with your first day of sickness – see p560), or by a specific time on the first qualifying day;
- personally;
- by providing medical evidence;

- more than once a week;
- on a printed form or other document it provides.

Your employer must take reasonable steps to inform you of how and when it requires you to notify it of your absence from work.[46]

The following time limits apply for notifying your employer of your absence.[47]

- You must notify your employer of your absence within the time limit set by your employer, if your employer has taken reasonable steps to inform you of this time limit (unless it requires you to give notice earlier than the first qualifying day).
- If your employer has not taken reasonable steps to inform you, or if it has made no arrangements about the notification it requires, you must notify your employer of your incapacity for work in writing on or before the seventh day after your first qualifying day (see p560).
- This seven-day time limit, or your employer's time limit, can be extended by one month if you have good cause for the delay in informing your employer. What amounts to 'good cause' is not defined in the regulations, but you would have to show that your failure to notify your employer was reasonable given the circumstances.
- If it is not practical for you to inform your employer within that time, the time limit can be extended further as long as you have notified it as soon as is reasonably practicable and you have notified it on or before the 91st day after your first qualifying day.

Notice sent in a properly addressed pre-paid letter is treated as having been given on the day the letter was posted. If you do not notify your employer of your absence within the above time limits you can still be entitled to SSP, it is just that your entitlement will start from a later date.

Information to support your claim

Your employer can require you to provide 'such information as may reasonably be required' for the determination of your claim for SSP.[48]

Medical evidence

For the first seven days of your incapacity for work your employer cannot insist that you obtain a medical certificate, as you are only required to provide a self-certificate as evidence of your incapacity for work.[49] After the first seven days an employer would normally expect you to provide medical certificates from a doctor. If you provide a certificate from someone else, such as an osteopath or chiropractor, this can be accepted if your employer considers it sufficient to show that you are incapable of work. Whatever type of medical evidence you provide, it is up to your employer to decide whether to accept it. See p568 if you want to challenge your employer's decision.

Who should claim

As your employer cannot insist that you personally notify it of your incapacity for work, someone else can notify your employer on your behalf.

If you are not well enough to be able to deal with your own affairs, the Revenue can appoint someone else to act for you. This person is your 'appointee' (see p955). An application for someone to act as your appointee should be made to your local Revenue enquiry centre. You can obtain the address from the telephone directory or from the Revenue's website (www.hmrc.gov.uk).

If you claim the wrong benefit

A claim for another benefit cannot be treated as a request for SSP. However, if you have notified your employer of your sickness, but you are not entitled to SSP, you may be able to get a claim for incapacity benefit (IB) backdated (see p282).[50]

Backdating your entitlement

In order to qualify for SSP you must notify your employer of your sickness (see p564). Even if you have not notified your employer of your sickness promptly your entitlement can still be backdated to your first qualifying day (see p560) if you have notified your employer of your incapacity within the time limits explained on p565 (ie, within the time arranged by your employer, or within seven days if no time limit has been arranged or, in the circumstances described, within either one month or 91 days).

If your entitlement is backdated in this way your SSP should be paid from your fourth qualifying day. (It is not paid for the first three qualifying days, called waiting days, unless your period of incapacity for work is linked to an earlier one – see p561.)

If you notify your employer of your sickness late, but your entitlement cannot be backdated, your entitlement is just delayed. You can still qualify for a total of 28 weeks' payment of SSP (see p562) from the date your entitlement begins if you are off work for that long.[51]

If statutory sick pay ends or is refused

If you do not agree with your employer's decision on your entitlement to SSP, see Chapter 43 for details about how to challenge it.

Whether or not you agree with your employer's decision, you should consider claiming other benefits. If you are incapable of work you should consider claiming IB (see Chapter 12) although the DWP will normally ask the Revenue to make a decision on your entitlement to SSP before they make a decision on your claim for IB. Even if you do not qualify for IB, you should normally still send medical certificates to the Jobcentre Plus or DWP office which covers your local area in order to claim national insurance credits (see p728).

See p568 for details of other benefits you may be entitled to, and p554 for details of future changes affecting IB.

7. Getting paid

Statutory sick pay (SSP) is a daily benefit, which means that if you qualify for it, it can be paid for a period of less than a week. See p561 for the way the daily rate is calculated. SSP is usually paid in the same way as your normal wages or salary. If you have some form of contractual sick pay arrangement with your employer, SSP forms part of your weekly pay. Any payment of SSP goes towards discharging your employer's liability to pay you contractual sick pay for the same period.[52]

Your employer cannot pay you SSP by making a payment in kind or by providing board and lodging, a service or some other facilities.[53]

Deductions that can be made from your wages – eg, union subscriptions, can also be made from your SSP.[54]

Delays and complaints

If your entitlement to SSP has been decided by a Revenue officer or by tax commissioners (see p1153) your employer may be required to pay your SSP within a certain time (see p1155).

See p1155 for details of when payment of SSP can be made by the Revenue if your employer cannot or will not pay you SSP.

Change of circumstances

You should notify your employer of any change in your circumstances that might affect your entitlement to SSP.

Overpayments

The rules on overpayments and recovery of overpaid benefit described in Chapter 39 do not apply to SSP. However, if your employer pays you SSP and later decides that you were not entitled to it, it may attempt to recover the sum it considers overpaid by making a deduction from your wages. If this happens, you should seek advice.

See p568 if you wish to challenge your employer's decision that you are not entitled to SSP.

If your employer decides that you have been paid SSP in error, you should consider claiming incapacity benefit (IB). If you qualify for IB and you make your claim within three months of your employer's decision that you were not entitled to SSP, your IB claim may be backdated (see p282, but see p262 for future changes to IB).[55]

8. Challenging a statutory sick pay decision

If you disagree with your employer's decision on your entitlement to statutory sick pay (SSP), or if your employer has failed to make a decision, you can ask the Revenue to make a formal decision on your entitlement, and if you are unhappy with it, you can appeal against the Revenue's decision. For details of how to challenge such decisions, see Chapter 43.

If your employer will not pay you SSP or stops paying you SSP, see below for details of other benefits that you might claim.

9. Tax, tax credits and other benefits

Statutory sick pay (SSP) is treated like any other earnings and you pay tax and, if you also receive earnings and/or occupational sick pay in the same week, national insurance (NI) contributions by Pay As You Earn in the normal way.[56]

Tax credits

If you have at least one dependent child you may qualify for child tax credit (CTC – see Chapter 48). If you have a partner who is in full-time paid work (see p1222), in addition to your SSP you may qualify for working tax credit (WTC – see Chapter 49). In some circumstances you may also qualify for WTC if you are getting SSP, as you may still count as being in full-time paid work while off work sick (see p1229 for details). It is not necessary for you to have claimed WTC before you became ill, so if you are not getting WTC, perhaps because your income was too high before you went on SSP, check whether you can qualify for it now. If you have been entitled to SSP for 140 days and you satisfy the additional conditions detailed on p1237 you may qualify for the disability element within your WTC. If you qualify for a disability element, on your return to work you can count as in full-time paid work for WTC purposes if you work at least 16 hours a week (see p1223).[57]

For WTC and CTC, any SSP that you receive during the course of the tax year is taken into account as employment income (see Chapter 52).

Means-tested benefits

If you have a low income, as well as SSP you may be entitled to means-tested benefits such as income support (IS – see Chapter 13) if you are under 60, or pension credit (PC – see Chapter 18) if you are 60 or over. You may also be entitled to housing benefit (HB – see Chapter 10) and council tax benefit (CTB – see Chapter 5) in addition to your SSP. If your partner is not in full-time paid work s/he may qualify for jobseeker's allowance (JSA – see Chapter 15). If you are a member of a 'joint-claim couple' for JSA (see p381) you will not be required to be available for work, actively to seek work or to enter into a jobseeker's agreement while you receive SSP (see p342). Alternatively, if you are getting SSP and were working for 16 hours a week or more immediately before you became incapable of work, your partner can qualify for JSA without you needing to make a joint claim with her/him (see p382).

Any of these benefits can be paid in addition to your SSP. However, your net SSP payment (ie, your SSP minus any deductions made for tax, Class 1 NI contributions and half of any contribution you make towards a personal or occupational pension scheme) counts in full as your income when calculating your entitlement to IS and income-based JSA.[58]

SSP is treated as earnings for PC, HB and CTB. This means that when calculating your entitlement to PC, HB and CTB, it may be possible to deduct certain work-related expenses from your SSP (see pp847 and 882) as well as any tax, NI and half of any occupational or personal pension payments you pay. You may also be entitled to an earnings disregard (see pp854 and 885).

If you pay for childcare and you were working for at least 16 hours a week immediately before your SSP started, you may also qualify for a deduction from your earnings for certain childcare charges when calculating your entitlement to HB and CTB (see p856). In some circumstances, your earnings and any WTC and CTC you receive can be added together before applying this deduction.

Non-means-tested benefits

You cannot get incapacity benefit (IB) while you are entitled to SSP.[59] However, if your SSP has run out and you qualify for IB you do not need to serve another three waiting days before your IB is paid.[60] If you satisfied the contribution conditions for IB (see p735) while getting SSP, the time you are on SSP counts towards the 196 days you need to qualify for the higher rate of short-term IB and the 364 days you need to qualify for long-term IB (see p273).[61] If you are claiming IB on the grounds of being incapable of work in youth (see p266), days when you are in receipt of SSP can count towards the 196 consecutive days that you must have been incapable of work in order to qualify for IB.[62] See p554 for future changes which will affect IB.

You cannot qualify for contribution-based JSA, maternity allowance (MA), statutory maternity pay (SMP), statutory paternity pay (SPP) or statutory adoption pay (SAP) while you are getting SSP.[63]

SSP counts as earnings for MA, SMP, SPP, SAP, carer's allowance (CA – see Chapter 3), increases in non-means-tested benefits for dependants (see Chapter 29) and reduced earnings allowance (see p326) and so may affect your entitlement to those benefits.

Payment of SSP does not affect your entitlement to other non-means-tested benefits.

Passports and other sources of help

If you are on a low income, you might be entitled to certain health service benefits (see Chapter 9). You may also qualify for a social fund payment (see Chapters 21 and 22), free school meals for any children that you have (see p15) or for other sources of help (see Chapter 1).

Notes

1. **Who is entitled to statutory sick pay**

1 ss151, 152, 153, 154 and 155 and Schs 11 and 12 SSCBA 1992
2 ss151 and 163(1) SSCBA 1992; regs 4 and 16 SSP Regs
3 Reg 16(2) SSP Regs
4 Reg 4 SSP Regs
5 s171G(1)(b) SSCBA 1992
6 s151(4) SSCBA 1992
7 Reg 2 SSP Regs
8 s152(2) SSCBA 1992
9 s152(5) SSCBA 1992
10 s152(6) SSCBA 1992
11 s152(3) SSCBA 1992
12 s153(2), (7) and (8) SSCBA 1992; s163 and Sch 11 para 2(a) SSCBA 1992 prior to amendments contained in Sch 8 paras 9 and 13 EE(A) Regs
13 s153(2) and (12) SSCBA 1992; reg 3(1), (3) and (4) SSP Regs
14 ss153(2)(b) and 155 SSCBA 1992
15 Reg 3A SSP Regs
16 Reg 15(1A), (3) and (4) SSP Regs
17 s153(3) and Sch 11 SSCBA 1992; reg 3 SSP Regs
18 *Commissioners for HMRC v Thorn Baker Ltd* [2007] EWCA Civ 626 (27 June 2007)
19 Reg 15(1), (1A) and (2) SSP Regs
20 s163(2) SSCBA 1992; regs 17 and 19 SSP Regs
21 CSSP/2/1984; CSSP/3/1984
22 Reg 17 SSP Regs
23 Reg 17(2) SSP Regs
24 Reg 19(7) and (8) SSP Regs
25 Sch 11 para 6 SSCBA 1992
26 ss154 and 155(1) SSCBA 1992
27 s154(3) SSCBA 1992
28 Reg 5(2) and (3) SSP Regs
29 R(SSP) 1/85
30 s155(1) SSCBA 1992

4. **The amount of benefit**

31 s155(1) SSCBA 1992
32 s157 SSCBA 1992
33 s157(3) SSCBA 1992
34 Reg 8B(2)(iii) SS(Cr) Regs
35 Regs 20 and 21 SSP Regs
36 s155(2)-(4) SSCBA 1992
37 Reg 3A SSP Regs
38 Reg 3A SSP Regs
39 Reg 15A SSP Regs

5. **Special benefit rules**

40 s151(1) SSCBA 1992; reg 16(1) SSP Regs; regs 5 and 5A SSP(MAPA) Regs
41 Reg 16 SSP Regs
42 s153(2)(d) and (12) SSCBA 1992
43 Reg 3(5) SSP Regs
44 Reg 3(4) SSP Regs

6. **Claims and backdating**

45 Reg 7(1), (4) and (5) SSP Regs
46 Reg 7(1) and (4) SSP Regs
47 Reg 7(1)-(3) SSP Regs
48 s14(1) SSAA 1992
49 Reg 2(2) Statutory Sick Pay (Medical Evidence) Regulations 1985 No.1604
50 Reg 10(1) and (2) SS(C&P) Regs
51 s156(3) SSCBA 1992

7. **Getting paid**

52 Sch 12 para 2 SSCBA 1992
53 Reg 8 SSP Regs
54 s151(3) SSCBA 1992
55 Reg 10(1) and (2) SS(C&P) Regs

9. **Tax, tax credits and other benefits**

56 s4(1) SSCBA 1992
57 Regs 6 and 9 WTC(EMR) Regs
58 Regs 35(2)(b) and 40(4) and Sch 9 paras 1, 4 and 4A IS Regs; regs 98(2)(c) and 103(6) and Sch 7 paras 1, 4 and 5 JSA Regs
59 Sch 12 para 1 SSCBA 1992
60 Sch 12 para 4 SSCBA 1992
61 s30D(3) SSCBA 1992; reg 7 SS(IB) Regs
62 Reg 4A SS(IB) Regs
63 s153(2)(d) SSCBA 1992; s1 JSA 1995; reg 55(4) JSA Regs; regs 18 and 27 SPPSAP(G) Regs

Part 3

Special benefit rules

Chapter 25

Studying and benefits

This chapter describes the benefit rules that apply if you are studying. It covers:

If you are under 60, full-time or part-time study can have a major impact on your entitlement to benefits. More generous rules apply to people who are 60 or over who are (or whose partner is) not in receipt of income support (IS) or income-based jobseeker's allowance (JSA) (see p576). The rules about studying are different for each benefit. This means you may not be entitled to some benefits, but others are not affected by your study. If you are already claiming a benefit your entitlement may be affected if you start studying. If you are not able to claim benefit while studying, someone else may be able to claim for you.

Scotland has a different education system from England and Wales. The same terms are often used within the education systems of all three countries, but they can have different technical meanings – eg, further, higher and advanced education. Within benefit rules, terms are used to define different levels of education (eg, relevant, non-advanced and advanced), which have a technical meaning for benefit purposes. However, these are terms that are not generally used by education institutions.

Note: only the benefits covered in this chapter are potentially affected if you are studying.

Employment and support allowance

Employment and support allowance (ESA) is due to be introduced in October 2008 (see Chapter 7). At the time of writing, information about how study will affect entitlement to ESA was not available. See www.cpag.org.uk/esa or CPAG's *Welfare Rights Bulletin* for further information.

Students, or students with a partner, aged 60 or over

If you are a student aged 60 (or if you are a student aged under 60 but have a partner aged 60 or over), you (or your partner) may be eligible for pension credit (PC – see Chapter 18), IS (see Chapter 13) or JSA (see Chapter 15). Because students are not excluded from PC and any income from student financial support is treated more generously under PC, you should check to see if you would be better off if you (or your partner) were to claim PC rather than IS or JSA. If you, or your partner, receive PC the more generous rules for calculating housing benefit and council tax may also apply (see p589).

Students from overseas

Most overseas students cannot claim benefits because they are subject to immigration control (see p1333). Even if you are entitled, a successful claim for benefit could affect your right to stay in this country and it is best to get immigration advice before making a claim.

Partners of overseas students

If you are not eligible for benefit, but there are no restrictions on your partner, either as a student or as a 'person subject to immigration control', s/he may be able to claim instead (see p702). However, if s/he receives benefit and you are a 'person subject to immigration control' (see p1333), this may affect your right to remain in the UK under the immigration rules.

1. Income support and jobseeker's allowance

If you are treated as being in 'relevant education' (see below) or a 'full-time student' (see p579), you cannot usually qualify for income support (IS) or contribution-based or income-based jobseeker's allowance (JSA). There are some exceptions, however, which are explained in this section. There are different rules if you are studying part time (see p584).

Relevant education

You count as in **'relevant education'** if you are under 19 and attending a full-time non-advanced course, or if you are 19 and your 19th birthday was on or after 10 April 2006 and you began the course you are currently attending before your 19th birthday.

Definitions

'Full time' means that you attend your course for more than 12 hours a week in normal term time. If your course is for 12 hours or less it does not count as relevant education.[1] You count as a part-time student instead. See p584 to see if you can claim IS or JSA.

A **'non-advanced course'** means any course leading to a qualification below the standard of a degree, NVQ level 4, Higher National Diploma, Diploma of Higher Education, a teaching qualification or similar. See p61 for examples of non-advanced courses.
You also count as in relevant eduction for IS or JSA if you are under 19 and undertaking approved, unwaged training that is not subject to a contract of employment, or are aged 19, your 19th birthday was on or after 10 April 2006 and began the training before your 19th birthday.[2]
'Approved training' includes the following programmes: Entry to Employment and Programme-Led Pathways in England; Get Ready for Work, Skillseekers and Modern Apprenticeships in Scotland; and Skillbuild, Skillbuild+ and Foundation Modern Apprenticeships in Wales.

If you are in relevant education you can only claim IS in some circumstances (see below). You cannot claim JSA.[3]

When you reach your 20th birthday you are no longer treated as in relevant education even if you have not completed your course. From your 20th birthday you are treated as a 'full-time student' (see p579) and you can only receive IS if you are in one of the categories of full-time student who can claim (see p582). This may mean you cannot qualify for IS from your 20th birthday even if you qualify up to that date under the rules below.

If you cannot claim IS or JSA, your parents (or person acting in their place) may be able to claim benefits and tax credits for you (see p578). You should note that the term 'relevant education' does not apply for housing benefit (HB) or council tax benefit (CTB) purposes (see p587).

Care leavers in relevant education

If you are a care leaver aged 16 or 17 (see p610), you can only claim IS or JSA while you are in relevant education if:[4]

- you are a lone parent and treated as responsible for a child; *or*
- you are entitled to the disability or severe disability premium.

Qualifying for income support while in relevant education

You can get IS while in relevant education (see p576) if:[5]

- you are the parent of a child for whom you are treated as responsible (see p63); *or*
- you are entitled to the disability premium or the severe disability premium; *or*
- you have been incapable of work for 28 weeks. Note that where two or more periods of incapacity are separated by periods of no more than eight weeks, they are treated as being continuous; *or*
- you are a student from abroad on limited leave to remain in the UK without recourse to public funds, but you are temporarily without funds for a period of six weeks; *or*

- you are an orphan and have no one acting as your parent; *or*
- you have left local authority care and of necessity you have to live away from your parents and any person acting in their place (see below); *or*
- you have to live away from your parents and any person acting in their place (see below) because:
  - you are estranged from them; *or*
  - you are in physical or moral danger; *or*
  - there is a serious risk to your physical or mental health.

  The physical or moral danger does not have to be caused by your parents. Therefore, a young person who is a refugee and cannot rejoin her/his parents can claim IS while at school;[6] *or*
- you live apart from your parents and any person acting in their place, they are unable to support you *and*:
  - they are in prison; *or*
  - they are unable to come to Britain because they do not have leave to enter under UK immigration law;[7] *or*
  - they are chronically sick, or are mentally or physically disabled. This covers people who could get a disability premium or higher pensioner premium, or have an armed forces grant for car costs because of disability, or are substantially and permanently disabled; *or*
- you are a refugee learning English (see p296).

A **'person acting in place of your parents'** includes a local authority or voluntary organisation if you are being cared for by them, or foster parents, but only until you leave care.[8] It does not include a person who is your sponsor under the immigration laws.[9]

'Estrangement' implies emotional disharmony,[10] where you have no desire to have any prolonged contact with your parents or they feel similarly towards you. It is possible to be estranged even though your parents are providing some financial support or you still have some contact with them. If you are being cared for by a local authority, it is also possible to be estranged from the local authority. If you are, then you could qualify for IS if you have to live away from accommodation provided by a local authority.[11]

Qualifying for jobseeker's allowance while in relevant education

You cannot get JSA while in relevant education.[12] You may be able to claim IS instead if you fit into one of the groups who can claim while in relevant education (see p577) or your parents (or a person acting in their place) may be able to claim benefit and tax credits for you (see below).

When someone else can claim benefits for you

If you cannot claim IS or JSA because you are in relevant education someone else may be able to claim child benefit, child tax credit (CTC) and working tax credit (WTC) because they are treated as 'responsible' for you (see pp691 and 1196).

In some circumstances you may count as both a person who can claim IS while in relevant education and as a person for whom someone else can claim child benefit, CTC and WTC. You should seek advice on which option would mean you are better off financially.

Claiming income support or jobseeker's allowance when you leave relevant education

If you leave school before the legal minimum school-leaving date, you are treated as having stayed on until that date.

Once you have left relevant education, you may be able to claim IS or JSA if you satisfy the rules for getting those benefits (see Chapters 13 and 15). However, when you have reached the official leaving date at the end of your course you continue to be treated as in relevant education during the vacation that follows. The day on which you cease to be treated as in relevant education is called the **'terminal date'** (see p62). While you continue to be treated as in relevant education, you are only entitled to IS in the circumstances outlined on p577 or from your 20th birthday, if it falls after your official leaving date but before the appropriate terminal date.[13]

From the Monday following your terminal date, there are three possibilities.

- You may get IS if you fit into one of the groups of people who can claim (see Chapter 13).
- You may get JSA if you satisfy the qualifying conditions (see Chapter 15 – if you are 16 or 17 you have to satisfy special rules – see p371).
- If you do not get IS or JSA in your own right and you are aged under 18, your parents may be able to continue claiming child benefit for you during the 'child benefit extension period' (see p59).

Calculating income and capital if you are in relevant education

The normal rules for assessing your income and capital apply (see Chapters 36 and 37), except there are special rules for assessing the amount of money available from grants, loans and other financial support for people in education (see p592). **Note:** for the purposes of these special rules, you are treated in the same way as a student.

Full-time students

If you are a full-time student, you cannot usually claim IS or JSA for the duration of your course, including vacations. See p582 for exceptions to this rule. See p583 if you give up, change or take time out of your course and p584 if you are studying part time.

You count as a full-time student if:[14]

- you are not a child or qualifying young person for child benefit purposes (see p57); *and*

- you are under 19 and on a full-time course of 'advanced education'. '**Advanced education**' means degree or postgraduate level qualifications, teaching courses, diplomas of higher education, HND or HNC of the Business Technology Education Council or the Scottish Vocational Education Council and all other courses above advanced GNVQ or equivalent, OND, A levels, a Scottish national qualification (higher or advanced level). See below for what counts as a full-time course; *or*
- you are 19 or over (or 20 or over in certain limited circumstances – see below) but under pension age (60 for women, 65 for men) and on a full-time course of study. If your course is full time you are treated as a full-time student regardless of the level of the course, unless you are aged under 20 and can still be treated as in 'relevant education' (see p576). See below for what counts as a full-time course.

You are treated as a student until either the last day of your course or until you abandon or are dismissed from it.[15] The '**last day of the course**' is the date on which the last day of the final academic year is officially scheduled to fall.[16]

For JSA, the period of study includes periods during which you are doing work connected to the course, even if this is after the normal end of your study.[17]

Full-time courses[18]

If your course is funded by the Learning and Skills Council for England or the National Council for Education and Training in Wales ('the Councils') or Scottish Ministers (see below), the definition of 'full time' depends on your personal pattern of attendance on the course. For all other courses, the term 'full time' applies to the course as a whole, not your personal pattern of attendance. However, for such courses the rules contain no definition of when it is classed as a full-time course.

Courses funded by the Councils or Scottish Ministers

In **England and Wales** your course counts as full time and you will be treated as a full-time student if:

- it is totally or partly funded by the Councils and your personal 'learning agreement' involves more than 16 hours of 'guided learning' each week. Courses funded by the Councils include academic or vocational courses leading to a recognised qualification. The Councils also fund basic literacy and numeracy courses, English as a Second Language programmes, Access and similar courses which prepare you to move on to qualification-bearing courses, and courses developing independent living skills for people with learning difficulties. The number of guided learning hours you do each week is set out in your learning agreement. This is signed by you and the college. The DWP uses this agreement to decide whether or not you are on a full-time course;[19]
- it is not funded by the Councils and is a 'full-time course of study'.

In **Scotland** your course counts as full time and you will be treated as a full-time student if:[20]

- it is totally or partly funded by Scottish Ministers at a college of further education, is not higher education *and* your personal learning document states that your course:
  - involves more than 16 hours a week of classroom-based or workshop-based programmed learning under the guidance of a teacher; *or*
  - involves more than 21 hours study a week, 16 hours or less of which involve classroom-based or workshop-based programmed learning and the rest of which involve using structured learning packages with the help of a teacher.

  The number of hours of 'learning' you do each week is set out in your learning document. This is signed by you and the college. The DWP uses this document to decide whether or not you are on a full-time course;
- it is a course of higher education which is funded in whole or in part by Scottish Ministers;
- it is not funded by Scottish Ministers and is a full-time course of study.

Sandwich courses

A sandwich course may be classed as a full-time course. A sandwich course[21] (excluding a course of initial teacher training) is one that consists of alternate periods of study at your education institution and periods of industrial, professional or commercial placement or work experience organised so that, taking the course as a whole, you attend the periods of study at your education institution for an average of at least 18 weeks a year (19 weeks in Scotland). If your periods of full-time study and work experience alternate within any week of your course, the days of full-time study are aggregated with any weeks of full-time study to determine the number of weeks of full-time study in each year.

If your course includes studying one or more modern languages for at least half of the time spent studying and a period of residence in the country whose language is part of your course, any period of residence overseas during which you are employed counts as a period of work experience.

Health-related courses

If you attend a health-related course (including Project 2000 nurses[22]) for which you are entitled to receive an NHS bursary, you are treated as attending a full-time course.

Modular courses

A modular course is one that consists of two or more modules and your college or university requires you to complete successfully a specific number of modules before it considers you to have completed the course.[23] You will be treated as a full-time student if you are currently attending part of a modular course that would be classed as a full-time course.[24] You will be treated as a full-time student for the period beginning on the day your course is defined as a full-time course and ending on the last day on which you are registered with your college or university as attending or undertaking that part of your course. This includes any vacations in that period, or the vacation immediately following that part of your course, unless that vacation follows the last day on which you are required to attend or undertake your course, or on such earlier date that you finally abandon or are dismissed from that part of the course.[25]

If you have failed examinations or failed to complete successfully a module relating to a period when the course was classed as a full-time course, any period in which you attend or undertake the course in order to re-take those examinations or modules is classed as part of the full-time course and you are treated as a full-time student (even if your college or university registers you as a part-time student during your re-sit period).[26]

Because the rules provide no definition of what is a full-time course (unless funded by the Councils or Scottish Ministers – see p580), you may be able to argue that you are not attending a full-time course, even if:[27]

- you are currently attending or undertaking a modular course on a full-time basis;
- you have transferred to part-time attendance because of exam or module failure; *or*
- you are taking time out of the course (see p602).

If you are in one of these situations, you should obtain advice.

Other courses

If your course does not automatically count as full time under the rules above, whether it counts as a 'full-time course of study' depends on the college or university. Definitions are often based on local custom and practice within education institutions, determined by the demands of course validating bodies or by the fact that full-time courses can attract more resources. The college or university's definition is not absolutely final, but if you want to challenge it you will have to produce a good argument showing why it should not be accepted.[28] If your course is only for a few hours each week, you should argue that it is not full time. However, a course could be full time even though you only have to attend a few lectures a week.[29]

Full-time students who can claim income support

Even if you are a full-time student, you can claim IS if you are:[30]

- a lone parent, including a lone foster parent, of a child under 16; *or*
- a student from abroad and entitled to an urgent cases payment because you are temporarily without funds for a period up to six weeks (see p1344); *or*
- a disabled student[31] and:

  - you qualify for the disability premium or severe disability premium (see pp779 and 784); *or*
  - you have been incapable of work (see p262) for 28 weeks. Two or more periods when you are incapable of work are joined to form a single period if they are separated by less than eight weeks; *or*
  - you qualify for a disabled student's allowance because you are deaf; *or*
- one of a couple who are both full-time students and:
  - you fit into one of the groups of people who can claim IS (see Chapter 13); *and*
  - either one or both of you are responsible for a child or young person (see p63); *and*
  - it is the summer vacation.

  Note: there is a different rule for HB and CTB (see p588); *or*
- a refugee learning English (see p296); *or*
- you are on the Adult Learning Option scheme.

If you are a student who cannot claim IS, check to see if you can claim JSA or pension credit (PC) instead. If you have a partner who is not a full-time student, s/he might be able to claim IS, JSA or PC for you.

Full-time students who can claim jobseeker's allowance

Even if you are a full-time student you can claim JSA if you are:

- one of a couple who are both full-time students and either or both of you is responsible for a child (see p63). (A commissioner has recently decided that the requirement to be a member of a couple unlawfully discriminates against female lone parents, who may therefore also qualify.[32] If you are a male lone parent, however, it may be more difficult for you to benefit from this decision.) This exception only applies during the summer vacation and if you are actually available for work;[33] *or*
- on an employment-related course of up to two weeks that has been approved in advance by the DWP,[34] or a Venture Trust training programme of up to four weeks.[35] In either case, only one course is allowed in any 12-month period; *or*
- aged 25 or over and on an approved employment-related course (see p346), including one under the New Deal for up to nine months; *or*
- waiting to go back to your course, having taken approved time out because of an illness or caring responsibility and that has now come to an end.

If you are a student who cannot claim JSA, check to see if you can claim IS or PC instead. If you have a partner who is not a full-time student, s/he might be able to claim PC, IS or JSA for you.

Housing costs – maintaining two homes

In some cases, if you qualify for IS, income-based JSA or HB, you may be entitled to help with the costs of more than one home if you have to live away from your normal home in order to attend a course. For further details, see pp187 and 801.

Calculating income support or income-based jobseeker's allowance

The normal rules for assessing the income and capital of part-time and full-time students apply (see Chapters 36 and 37), except that there are special rules for assessing the amount of money available from grants, loans and other types of financial support for students (see p592). These rules do not apply to PC. For which student grants or loans do not count as income, see p592.

Part-time students

If you are studying but are not in relevant education (see p576) or attending a full-time course (see p580), you are treated as attending a part-time course and classed as a part-time student.

Claiming income support while studying part time

You can get IS while studying part time if you are not on a full-time course and you satisfy the other rules for getting IS (see Chapter 13).

If you are currently studying part time on a course you previously attended full time, or if you are attending a modular or similar course (see p580) on a part-time basis, the DWP may argue that you are attending a full-time course and should, therefore, be treated as a full-time student. It may be possible to challenge this interpretation.[36] You should seek specialist advice if you are in this situation.

Claiming jobseeker's allowance while studying part time

You count as a part-time student if your course is not full time.[37] In effect, your course is part time if:

- you are under 20 and are not treated as in relevant education (see p576) – ie, you spend 12 hours or less a week in non-advanced education;[38] *or*
- you are on a course funded by the Councils or Scottish Ministers (see p580) and have a learning agreement (learning document in Scotland) from your course stating that your course is for 16 guided learning hours or less (note the slight variation in Scotland – see p580); *or*
- it is not a full-time course of study (see p580).

You can qualify for JSA while studying part time if you meet the labour market conditions (ie, you are available for work, actively seeking work and you have a valid jobseeker's agreement – see Chapter 15). If you have agreed restrictions with the DWP on the hours that you are available for work, there are special rules that can help you claim JSA and study part time (see p586).

When you claim JSA, in addition to the JSA claim form and the *Helping you Back to Work* form, you may be asked to fill in a 'student questionnaire'. Your answers are taken into account when deciding whether you are available for and actively seeking work. The DWP needs to be satisfied that you are genuinely available for and actively seeking work while you are studying part time.

Availability for work and part-time study

Your availability for work should not be affected by your part-time course if your hours of study or training are at times outside your agreed pattern of availability (see p356) – ie, they do not clash with the times you are willing and able to work. If the hours of your course *do* clash with the times you say you are available for work (as set out in your jobseeker's agreement – see p361), you will only be accepted as available for work if either:[39]

- you are able to rearrange the hours of the course or study to fit around your job; *or*
- you are willing and able to give up the course should a job become available.

If you are **under 20** and complete or leave a part-time course, you are not treated as leaving relevant education (see p576) and you, therefore, qualify for benefit straight away, as long as you satisfy the normal rules of entitlement (see p339).

If you are attending an employment-related course as part of the New Deal, you can be treated as available for and actively seeking work (see Chapter 15).

Deciding whether you are available for work

The guidance for decision makers states that a number of factors should be considered when deciding whether you are available for work while you are studying part time. If, for example, it appears you are not willing or able to give up your course or that you cannot confine your study to times that would fit in with employment, you are treated as not being available for work. The factors that may be relevant include:[40]

- where you are studying or training and, if it is away from home, whether you can be contacted if a job becomes available;
- the extent of your efforts to find employment;
- how important the successful completion of the course is to your future career, including whether it will enhance your chances of finding employment;
- whether you gave up a job or training to do the course;
- the days and hours you are required to attend the course;
- whether the times of attendance could be altered to fit in with any job you might obtain or whether successful completion of the course is possible if you miss some of the scheduled attendances;
- the duration of the study or training;
- whether a fee was paid and, if so, the amount and whether any of the fee could be refunded or transferred if you abandoned or interrupted your studies. If you

have paid a fee, it may be more difficult (depending on the amount) to convince the DWP that you are prepared to abandon the course;
- whether you received a grant and, if so, the source, the amount and whether you would have to repay any or all of it if you interrupted or abandoned the course.

The guidance for decision makers states that where a number of claimants are following the same course, some may be able to show that they are available, but others may not.[41] The DWP should not operate a blanket policy of treating all students on the same course as not being available (equally, you cannot assume that you will be treated as available if other people on your course are getting JSA). Each claim should be considered individually. The DWP assumes that you may be less willing to leave a course if you are near the end of the course or as the chance of obtaining a qualification approaches.[42]

Restricted availability for work and part-time study

There are special rules that can help you qualify for JSA if you are a part-time student. These say that in certain circumstances the fact that you are on your course will be ignored when deciding whether you are available for work if the hours of your course fall wholly or partly within the times you say you are available for work. However, you still have to be available for and actively seeking work during the rest of the week when you are not on your course.

These rules apply to you if you are a part-time student, and you are willing and able to rearrange the hours of your course to take up a job and the restrictions on your hours of availability have been agreed with the DWP because:[43]

- of your physical or mental condition (see p353); *or*
- of your caring responsibilities (see p355); *or*
- you are working short time (see p369); *or*
- they leave you available for work for at least 40 hours a week (see p355).

You must also satisfy one of two conditions.

- For the three months immediately before the date you started the course you were unemployed and getting JSA, or incapable of work and getting IS or incapacity benefit (IB – see Chapter 12), or you were on a course of 'training'.
- In the six months before you started the course, you were unemployed and getting JSA, or incapable of work and getting IS or IB for a total of three months altogether, or on a course of 'training' for a total of three months *and* sandwiched between these spells, you were working full time or earning too much to qualify for benefit.

The three-month and six-month periods can only begin after you have reached your terminal date and are treated as having ceased to be in relevant education (see p62).

'**Training**' means training for which young people aged under 18 are eligible, or for which a person aged 18–24 may be eligible, provided or arranged by the Learning and Skills Council for England, the National Council for Education and Training in Wales or a local enterprise council in Scotland.[44]

2. **Housing benefit and council tax benefit**

Whether you can claim housing benefit (HB – see Chapter 10) or council tax benefit (CTB – see Chapter 5) depends on whether you are classed as a full-time or a part-time student. Additional rules apply to claiming and calculating HB. These rules are outlined in this section.

If you have reached the qualifying age for pension credit (PC) (60 for both men and women) and neither you nor your partner are in receipt of income support (IS) or income-based jobseeker's allowance (JSA), the student rules for HB and CTB do not apply and there are no restrictions on you studying and claiming HB/CTB.[45]

Full-time students

If you are a full-time student (see p579), you cannot usually qualify for HB or CTB, but there are some exceptions (see p588).

The rules for deciding if you are a full-time student are the same as for IS and JSA (see p579). Unlike IS and JSA, there is no separate rule in HB/CTB if you are in 'relevant education' (see p576). If you are in relevant education you are treated as a full-time student for HB/CTB. This means you may be able to claim HB/CTB while in relevant education even if you cannot claim IS or JSA.

Part-time students

You may be able to claim HB or CTB if you are studying part time. The rules for deciding if you are a part-time student are the same as for IS and JSA (see p584).

Partners of students

If your partner is not a student, s/he can claim HB/CTB if s/he meets the qualifying rules.[46] The claim is assessed in the normal way, except that (for HB) the rules about being away from term-time accommodation (see p588) apply to the partner's claim.[47] Additionally, the special rules for assessing any income you receive from grants, loans and other types of financial support for students will apply (see p592).

Students and second adult rebate

Full-time students are not precluded from getting second adult rebate and should be assessed in the normal way (see p89).

Council tax and council tax benefit

In England and Wales, if you are living in halls of residence predominantly provided to accommodate students, or in a dwelling wholly occupied by students or other 'relevant persons', you are exempt from having to pay council tax. You cannot, therefore, claim CTB because you are not liable to pay. Different rules apply in Scotland. There is no council tax in Northern Ireland. See CPAG's *Council Tax Handbook* for more details.

Full-time students who can claim housing benefit and council tax benefit

You can claim if:[48]

- you are on IS or income-based JSA; *or*
- you are under 19 and not following a course of higher education (higher education includes degree courses, teacher training, HND, HNC and postgraduate courses) or you are a child or a 'qualifying young person' for child benefit purposes (see p57); *or*
- you and your partner are both full-time students and either or both of you are responsible for a child or qualifying young person (see p57). Note that, unlike IS and JSA, this provision applies throughout the year; *or*
- you are a lone parent with a dependent child or qualifying young person aged under 20 (see p57); *or*
- you are a lone foster parent and the child has been formally placed with you by a local authority or voluntary agency; *or*
- you meet the conditions for the disability premium (see p779), or would do if you were not disqualified from incapacity benefit (see p271); *or*
- you have been incapable of work (see p262) for 28 weeks. Two or more periods when you are incapable of work are joined to form a single period if they are separated by less than eight weeks; *or*
- you meet the conditions for the severe disability premium (see p784); *or*
- you qualify for a disabled student's allowance because you are deaf; *or*
- you are waiting to go back to your course, having taken approved time out because of an illness or caring responsibility and this has now come to an end (see p603).

Note: even if you are a full-time student who fits one of the exception categories listed above, you still cannot receive HB if the circumstances under the two headings below apply to you.

Being away from your term-time accommodation

If you are a full-time student who is eligible for HB (see above) and your main reason for occupying your home is to enable you to attend your course, you cannot get HB on that home for any full week when you are absent from it outside your period of study (see p594).[49]

This rule does not apply if:

- you are away from home because you are in hospital;[50]
- the main reason for occupying your home is *not* to enable you to attend your course but for some other purpose – eg, to provide a home for your children or for yourself because you do not have a home elsewhere where you normally live when you are not attending your course. If this applies, any absences outside your period of study are dealt with under the temporary absence rules (see p185).

Accommodation rented from an educational establishment

If you are a full-time student who can claim HB (see p588), you can receive HB even if you rent your accommodation from your educational establishment.[51] If you are a part-time student, this rule applies if you would be able to claim HB if you were treated as a full-time student.

You cannot, however, get HB if you are a:

- full-time student waiting to go back to your course having taken approved time out because of illness or caring responsibilities (see p603) and your illness or caring responsibilities have not yet ended; *or*
- part-time student receiving IS or JSA.

The above two exceptions do not apply if:

- your educational establishment itself rents the accommodation from a third party other than on a long lease or where the third party is an education authority providing the accommodation as part of its functions; *or*
- the accommodation is owned by a separate legal body – eg, a company established under the Business Expansion Scheme to build halls of residence.

You cannot receive HB if the local authority decides that your educational establishment has arranged for your accommodation to be provided by a person or body other than itself in order to take advantage of the HB scheme.

Living in different accommodation during term time

The rules about claiming HB for two homes are explained on p187.

If you are one of a couple and receive HB for two homes, the assessment of HB for each home is based on your joint income and your applicable amount as a couple.

Calculating housing benefit

If you or your partner get IS, income-based JSA, the guarantee credit of PC or a training allowance, you will be entitled to maximum HB or CTB (see Chapter 10).

If you do not get IS, JSA, the guarantee credit of PC or a training allowance but you or your partner are eligible for HB/CTB, your entitlement is calculated in the same way as for other claimants (see p200), apart from the following additional rule.

Your HB entitlement is calculated differently during your period of study (see p594) than outside it – eg, during most of the summer vacation. For example, your grant or loan income may be taken into account for a different period (see p592 for the treatment of grant and loan income). You may find, therefore, that your HB entitlement is higher, or that you are only entitled to HB outside your period of study and that you need to make a new claim or check that your entitlement is reviewed at that time. If you start your course at another time of year – eg, in January, it is not clear how this rule should apply because your longest vacation may be at some time other than the summer.

The normal rules apply for assessing the income and capital of both full-time and part-time students (see Chapters 35, 36 and 37), except that there are special rules assessing the amount of money available from grants, loans and other types of financial support for students (see p592).

Payments

Students are covered by all the normal rules on the administration and payment of HB (see Chapter 10). However, there are two provisions that can apply specifically to students.

The local authority has the discretion to decide how long your benefit period (see p209) should last.

The local authority may decide to pay a rent allowance once each term, although students have the same right as other claimants to insist on fortnightly payments if their entitlement is more than £2 a week (see p216).

3. **Other benefits and tax credits**

Carer's allowance

You cannot claim carer's allowance (CA – see Chapter 3) if you are in full-time education.[52] If you are attending a university, college or school for 21 hours a week or more you will be treated as being in full-time education. In calculating the 21 hours you include only hours spent in 'supervised study'. You ignore any time spent on meal breaks or unsupervised study undertaken on or off the premises of the educational establishment.[53]

The Court of Appeal has decided[54] that 'supervised study' does not depend on whether your supervisor (ie, teacher, tutor, lecturer) is present with you. If your study is directed to your course of education and the curriculum of your course and it is undertaken to meet the reasonable requirements of your course, it will normally count as supervised study. It will count regardless of whether that study is undertaken on or off the premises of the education institution you attend.

'Unsupervised study' means work beyond the reasonable requirements of your course. In assessing your hours of attendance, evidence from your education institution about the amount of time you are expected to study to complete your course is important. However, your hours of attendance should be judged by the facts in your individual case. You may be able to argue that you intend, expect or actually devote less time to your studies than your education institution considers is necessary to meet the reasonable requirements of the course, or that you are exempt from some requirements of the course because of, for example, a prior qualification.[55]

You will be treated as still in full-time education during vacations and any temporary interruption of the course, but not if you have abandoned the course or been dismissed from it.

Child benefit

Child benefit (see Chapter 4) can be claimed for a person who is under 19 (or under 20 in certain circumstances) and in full-time non-advanced education or training, or during the 'child benefit extension period' (see p59).

Incapacity benefit

You cannot claim incapacity benefit (IB – see Chapter 12) if you are under 19 and in full-time education. Full time means attending a course for 21 hours or more a week.[56] In calculating the 21 hours, any special education or tuition designed for those with a physical or mental disability is ignored (see p269). Temporary interruptions of education are disregarded. Periods of private study are also not included in the 21-hour limit. If you cannot claim IB because you are in full-time education, someone else may be able to claim benefits for you if you are in 'relevant education' (see p576).

If you are under 25 there are special rules that may help you get IB without having to satisfy the national insurance contribution conditions if you have completed a course of full-time advanced or secondary education, or vocational or work-based training, which you started at least three months before your 20th birthday (see p267).

Note: you cannot be treated as capable of work (see Chapter 27) simply because you are studying on either a full-time or part-time course. However, if you are on the Adult Learning Option scheme, see p263.

Employment and support allowance

Employment and support allowance (ESA) is due to be introduced in October 2008 (see Chapter 7). ESA will have a contribution-based component and an income-based component. At the time of writing, however, information was not available on how ESA will be affected by studying. See www.cpag.org.uk/esa or CPAG's *Welfare Rights Bulletin* for further information.

Pension credit

There are no restrictions on claiming pension credit (PC – see Chapter 18) if you study either full time or part time. For income support (IS) there are restrictions if you are under pensionable age (60 for women, 65 for men). The less restrictive rules for PC, therefore, benefit men who are studying full time and are aged between 60 and 65. Additionally, the more generous income and capital rules for PC benefit men and women aged 60 or over who are students or whose partners are students (regardless of their partner's age) as student grants and loans are not taken into account as income (see below).[57]

Social fund payments

You are not excluded from access to a social fund payment simply because you are studying (but see p505 for crisis loans). However, to claim a payment from the social fund (except a crisis loan) you must be in receipt of an appropriate 'qualifying benefit' (see Chapters 21 and 22).

Working tax credit and child tax credit

You are not excluded from claiming a tax credit simply because you are a student. However, special rules apply to calculating your income from a grant, loan or other financial support for students (see p1262).

NHS benefits

You are not excluded from claiming NHS benefits (see Chapter 9) while you are studying.

National insurance credits

You may be able to receive Class 1 credits (see Chapter 31) for any week of a full-time course.

4. Calculating income from grants and loans

The rules in this section apply *only* to the calculation of income support (IS), income-based jobseeker's allowance (JSA), housing benefit (HB) and council tax benefit (CTB). They apply if you are a part-time or a full-time student.

Some income from a grant, a loan and certain other forms of financial support for students is taken into account when calculating your benefit entitlement under the special rules set out below.

Grant and loan income does not affect any contribution-based JSA that you are entitled to claim. These rules do not apply to HB/CTB claimants who are (or whose partner is) aged 60 or over because any student income you have from a grant or loan is not taken into account as income.[58]

The DWP has issued guidance to decision makers concerning the treatment of various types of financial support to students. Often that guidance only covers some of the benefits to which this section refers. For example, guidance may have been issued for HB/CTB purposes but no equivalent guidance has been issued for IS/JSA. Additionally, the legislation and guidance may not cover all sources of student support across the UK, particularly as new sources of support are introduced. You should, therefore, check the current position.

Note: the following information applies to support available to new students from the academic year 2007/08. For the treatment of grant and loan income for students who started their course in previous academic years, see the relevant edition of this *Handbook*.

Student support

There are many types of financial support available to students attending a course at school, sixth-form college, further education college, or who are undergraduates (including students undertaking certain courses below degree level) or postgraduates. These are paid in the form of either a grant or a loan. Some types of grant or loan are available to all students who meet the conditions of entitlement; others are available on a discretionary basis. The support available to students varies, depending on whether you live in England, Wales, Scotland or Northern Ireland. For more detailed information, see CPAG's *Student Support and Benefits Handbook: England, Wales and Northern Ireland* and *Benefits for Students in Scotland Handbook*.

Grants

The term **'grant'**[59] includes any kind of educational grant or award, bursary (such as those paid by the NHS for certain health-related courses), scholarship, studentship, exhibition, or supplementary allowance. It does not include payments from access funds (see p600), education maintenance allowances or similar payments (or the equivalent in Scotland, Wales and Northern Ireland).

You are treated as having a parental or partner's contribution to your grant whether or not it has been paid to you. However, if you are (for IS only) a lone parent, a lone foster parent or (for IS and JSA only) a disabled student, only the amount of contribution you actually receive counts.[60]

Your grant income (or that of your partner) is taken into account as income, but is subject to special rules and disregards. How your grant is treated depends on its source, what it is expected to cover and the period for which it is payable.

General rule on calculating grant income

In most cases, your grant income is assessed over a period starting from the 'benefit week' which coincides with (or immediately follows) the first day of your 'period of study' (see below) and ending with the benefit week, the last day of which coincides with (or immediately precedes) the last day of your period of study. In this context, **'benefit week'** means the week for which benefit is paid.[61]

This means your grant income is apportioned over the number of complete benefit weeks in your period of study. Any part-weeks at the beginning or end of that period will be ignored. **Note:** this rule does not apply to an NHS bursary (see p595).

Your grant income is apportioned as follows.[62]

- If it is payable for your period of study, unless you are attending a sandwich course (see below), over the number of benefit weeks in your period of study.
- If it is payable for a period other than your period of study, over the number of benefit weeks in the period for which the grant is payable.

'Period of study' means:[63]

- for a course of one year or less, from the start of the course to the last day of the course;
- for a course of more than one year, in the first and subsequent years (but not the final year):
  - where the grant is payable for a period of 12 months, from the start of your academic year and ending with the day before the start of your next academic year; *or*
  - in any other case, from the start of your academic year to the last day of your academic year and excluding your normal summer vacation;
- in the final year of a course lasting more than one year, from the start of the academic year and ending with the last day of the course.

Specific types of grant income

If you are attending a **sandwich course** (see p581) your grant income is taken into account over a different period. Any periods spent on placement or work experience in your period of study are excluded and your grant is apportioned over the remaining 'benefit weeks' in your period of study.[64] **Note:** this only applies if your grant is payable for your period of study. If your grant is payable for a different period, it is taken into account over the number of benefit weeks in the period for which it is payable, but excluding any periods spent on placement or work experience.

Postgraduate awards made by research councils and the British Academy are apportioned over the number of benefit weeks in the period for which they are payable (usually a calendar year).

NHS bursaries paid to students in England and Wales are paid in monthly instalments. The bursary (including any supplementary allowances for an adult dependant) should be taken into account over 52 or 53 weeks (benefit weeks sometimes run to 53 weeks, including part-weeks).[65]

If you are studying for an undergraduate diploma or degree or postgraduate qualification in **social work**, you may be eligible for a non-means-tested bursary administered by the General Social Care Council in England, the Care Council for Wales or the Scottish Social Care Council, or an 'incentive grant' from the Social Services Inspectorate in Northern Ireland. The bursary or grant counts in full as grant income.

If you receive a **supplementary allowance** for an adult dependant as part of a student loan (or you could have received one had you taken reasonable steps to apply for one), the allowance is apportioned over the same period as a student loan (see p597). Similarly, if you receive an adult dependant's allowance from any other source (but see p596) and you also receive a student loan (or could have received one had you taken reasonable steps to apply for one), the allowance is apportioned over the same period as a student loan (see p597).[66] However, if you receive a supplementary allowance for an adult dependant as part of an NHS bursary, including an allowance because you are an older student, these allowances are apportioned over 52 or 53 weeks (benefit weeks sometimes run to 53 weeks, including part-weeks).[67] This includes the final year of your course[68] – ie, you are treated as having this income for a period after the last day of your course. Arguably, for IS/JSA only, they should still be ignored once you have completed your course (see p601).

Note: students on health-related courses, except nursing and midwifery diploma courses, may be eligible for supplementary allowances for an adult dependant under both an NHS bursary and (reduced rate) student loan. These separate allowances for an adult dependant will be taken into account over different periods.

If you receive a supplementary allowance from any other source, but you do not receive a student loan (or could not have received one even if you had taken reasonable steps to apply for one) it will be apportioned over the same period as 'basic' grant income (see p593).

In Scotland, a **care leavers' grant** of up to £100 a week towards accommodation can be paid during the long vacation if you are a student, were aged 21 or under at the start of your course and had been in the care or custody of a local authority. This payment is taken fully into account as income for each week for which it is paid.

The **Scottish young person's bursary** is treated in the same way as the student loan (see p597).

A Scottish **mature student's bursary** is taken into account as grant income except an amount paid for childcare is ignored (see below).

Grant income that is ignored

These disregards apply only to the grant you receive for your period of study and not to any supplementary allowances for dependants you may be paid during the long vacation.[69]

The following grant income is ignored:[70]

- any allowance for tuition and examination fees;
- disabled students' allowance;
- any allowance to meet the cost of attending a residential course away from your normal student accommodation during term time;
- any allowance for the cost of your normal home (away from college) but, for IS and JSA, only if your rent is not met by HB;
- any amount for a partner or child abroad;
- for IS/JSA only, any amount intended to maintain a dependent child;
- any amount intended for the childcare costs of a dependent child;
- parents' learning allowance;
- higher education grant;[71]
- special support grant;[72]
- if you have been required to make a contribution to your own grant (eg, because you have other income, such as maintenance), an amount equivalent to that contribution is disregarded.[73] In the case of a couple, the amount of any contribution that one member has been assessed to pay to her/his partner who is a student is disregarded from the non-student's income;[74]
- an education maintenance allowance or similar payments, including a Care to Learn payment, an Assembly learning grant or Passport to Study grant.[75]

In addition to the amounts ignored under the rules above, the following fixed sums are ignored.

- A fixed amount of £370 for books and equipment (2007/08 academic year – see below). If your grant includes a specific amount to cover the cost of books and equipment, that amount will be ignored in addition to this fixed amount.
- A fixed amount of £290 for the cost of travel (2007/08 academic year – see below). If your actual travel costs are higher than any sum specified in your grant for travel (which is ignored under the rules above) plus this fixed amount, the additional costs are not ignored and will be taken into account.[76]

Note: if you also receive a student loan, the above two fixed sums are ignored when calculating your loan income (see p598).

Note: for the purpose of these fixed amounts, the 2007/08 academic year began on 1 August 2007 if your period of study (see p594) began on or after 1 August 2007 but before 1 September 2007. If your period of study began on or after 1 September 2007, the fixed sums apply from that date. At the time of writing, the amounts for 2008/09 were not available. See CPAG's *Welfare Rights Bulletin* for updates.

Loans

A loan is treated as income but is subject to special rules and disregards. Note that some supplementary allowances paid under the student loan provisions are paid as non-repayable grants and are treated as grant income (see p593). Loans paid for tuition fees are disregarded.

Calculating income from a student loan

For full-time students, how your, or your partner's, student loan[77] is treated depends on whether your course lasts for one year or less, or for a longer period. The maximum amount of available loan is taken into account even if you do not apply for a loan or for the maximum amount.[78]

A student loan paid to a student on a Postgraduate Certificate of Education course is treated in the same way as student loans and supplementary allowances for undergraduate students.

If you attend a nursing or midwifery diploma course, no loan income should be taken into account as a student loan is not available for these courses. If you are on another health-related course only the lower maximum loan rate should be taken into account.

Your loan (including any additional weeks' allowance) is treated as explained below.

Academic year

The rules give a definition of an 'academic year' for the purposes of calculating student loan income. This definition may be different from the actual academic year of the education institution you attend.

'Academic year' means a period of 12 months beginning on 1 January, 1 April, 1 July or 1 September according to whether your course begins in the winter, the spring, the summer or the autumn respectively. If you are required to begin attending your course during August or September and to continue attending through the autumn, the 'academic year' of your course is treated as beginning in the autumn rather than summer – ie, from 1 September.[79]

Benefit weeks

Loan income will be apportioned over a period of 'benefit weeks'.

The first appropriate benefit week may fall before the start of your actual academic year and the last benefit week may fall either before or after the last day of your academic year (academic years vary between education institutions). This may mean your benefit is recalculated several times depending on when your actual academic year falls in relation to the relevant benefit weeks. You will need to make a new claim or check that your entitlement is revised at these times.

If you are required to start attending your course in August, or your course is for less than one academic year, the period will begin with the benefit week which coincides with, or immediately follows, the first day of the course.[80]

If your 'academic year' starts other than on 1 September, your loan payable for that 'academic year' is apportioned equally between the benefit weeks in the period beginning with the first day of that 'academic year' and ending with the last day of that 'academic year'. Excluded from that are any benefit weeks falling entirely within the quarter during which, in the opinion of the decision maker, your longest vacation falls.[81]

'Quarter' means one of the periods from 1 January to 31 March, 1 April to 30 June, 1 July to 31 August, or 1 September to 31 December.[82]

In the first, or only, year of your course your loan income (calculated under the rules below) is ignored for each benefit week that falls before the start of your 'period of study' (the first day of the first term). This is because you cannot be treated as a student until you actually start your course.[83]

Loan income that is ignored

The following loan income is ignored:[84]

- loans paid for tuition fees (known as a 'fee loan' or a 'fee contribution loan');[85]
- loans paid to some part-time students in higher education. This income is ignored because it is less than the fixed amounts disregarded for travel, books and equipment (see below);[86]
- if you have been required to make a contribution to your own loan (eg, because you have other income, such as maintenance), an amount equivalent to that contribution is disregarded as income.[87] In the case of a couple, the amount of any contribution that one member has been assessed to pay to her/his partner who is a student is disregarded from the non-student's income.[88]

Once any of the above income has been deducted from your loan income, the following fixed sums are also ignored.

- A fixed amount of £370 for the cost of books and equipment (2007/08 academic year – see below).
- A fixed sum of £290 for the cost of travel (2007/08 academic year – see below).

If your actual costs are higher than these amounts, any additional costs cannot be ignored.[89]

Note: if you also receive a grant, the two fixed sums are ignored from your loan income rather than your grant income (see p596).

Note: for the purpose of these fixed amounts, the 2007/08 academic year began on 1 August 2007 if your period of study (see p594) began on or after 1 August 2007 but before 1 September 2007. If your period of study began on or after 1 September 2007, the fixed sums apply from that date. At the time of writing, the amounts for 2008/09 were not available. See CPAG's *Welfare Rights Bulletin* for updates.

Once the above amounts (including the fixed amounts) have been deducted from your loan income, a further £10 a week is ignored for each week in the period over which your loan income is taken into account (see below). This amount may overlap with other disregards applied to certain war pensions (see p860) and charitable or voluntary payments (see p864). A combined maximum sum of £20 a week can be ignored.

The period over which loan income is taken into account[90]

A course lasting for one academic year or less

Your loan is apportioned over the benefit weeks beginning with the benefit week, the first day of which coincides with or follows the first day of the academic year, and ending with the benefit week, the last day of which coincides with or immediately follows the last day of the course.

A course lasting for more than one academic year

Unless it is your final year (see below), your loan will be taken into account from whichever is the earlier of:

- the first benefit week in September; *or*
- the first benefit week, the first day of which coincides with, or immediately follows, the first day of the autumn term,

and ending with the benefit week that coincides with, or immediately precedes, the last day of June.

Final year of a course

Your loan will be taken into account over the period beginning with either:

- if the final academic year starts on 1 September, the benefit week, the first day of which coincides with or immediately follows the earlier of 1 September or the first day of the autumn term; *or*
- the first benefit week, the first day of which coincides with or immediately follows the first day of the academic year,

and ending with the benefit week that coincides with, or immediately precedes, the last day of the course.

Calculating income from other types of loan

Career development loans paid under s2 Employment and Training Act 1973 are treated as income.[91] However, this income is ignored except where it is paid for, and is used to meet, 'daily living expenses' (see p600).[92]

For JSA and IS, any financial support you receive which is paid in the form of a loan (other than a student loan or a career development loan), including a loan received from an overseas source, does not count as a student loan or a grant.[93] It will be taken into account as 'other income' (see p895). The rules do not say how this income should be treated for HB/CTB but, presumably, the same principle applies.

Payments from access funds

Access funds[94] (which include the Learner Support Fund available to some students in further education, the Financial Contingency Fund in Wales, the Access to Learning Fund offered by higher education institutions in England, further education hardship funds and young students' retention fund in Scotland) are administered by colleges and universities. Individual education institutions may call all or part of these funds by other names – ie, access bursary, mature students' bursary and childcare support. Payments from access funds should be distinguished from payments with similar names from other sources – ie, hardship loans.

How a payment from access funds is treated depends on whether it is paid as a single lump-sum payment, in instalments or to bridge the period before you start your course or receive a student loan payment.

A single lump-sum payment[95]

A single lump-sum payment is treated as capital but it will be disregarded for 52 weeks if the payment is made for and used for any items, expenses or charges which you or your partner may incur (other than 'daily living expenses'). However, if the payment is intended for but not used for these items, expenses or charges it is taken into account as capital immediately. A single lump-sum payment made for 'daily living expenses' counts as capital immediately.

'**Daily living expenses**' are:

- food;
- ordinary clothing or footwear (ie, for normal daily use, but not including school uniforms or that used solely for sporting activities);
- household fuel;
- (for JSA/IS only) rent for which HB is payable;
- (for JSA/IS only) housing costs – see Chapter 34;
- (for JSA/IS only) accommodation charges for residential nursing or care – see Chapter 34;
- council tax;
- water charges.

Payments made in instalments[96]

Payments made in instalments are treated as income, but are disregarded in full. However, if the payment is intended and used for 'daily living expenses' (see above), it is taken into account as income for each week it is intended to cover, except for the first £20 a week, which is disregarded. This amount may overlap with other disregards applied to certain war pensions (see p860) and charitable or voluntary payments (see p864). A combined maximum sum of £20 a week can be ignored.

Payments made before the start of a course or before receipt of a student loan[97]

A payment (whether paid as a single payment or in instalments) made on or after whichever is the earlier of:

- 1 September; *or*
- the first day of your course,

which is intended to bridge the period before you receive your student loan, or which is made in anticipation of you becoming a student, is ignored as both income and capital even if it is for 'daily living expenses'.

Other sources of income intended to cover study costs

If you receive a payment from any source, other than a grant or student loan, which is intended to cover items or expenses that would be ignored when calculating grant income, the payment made from that other source for those items or expenses is also ignored. You must show that the payment is necessary for you to be able to attend the course. Any sum paid which is not necessary (or is likely to exceed the sum necessary) for you to attend the course counts as income. For example, if your grant or student loan does not cover all your tuition fees, any money received from another source, such as a parent, intended to make up the difference is ignored as income. However, if the amount you receive is greater than is likely to be necessary to pay the difference, the amount above that sum counts as income.[98]

Student support once you have completed your course

For IS/JSA only, any grant income, student loan, assessed contribution made by a parent or spouse/civil partner as part of the loan or grant, or career development loan that you received no longer counts as income once you have completed the course.[99]

However, as most (but not all) types of student support are not taken into account for a period after your course is due to end, it should also be ignored as income for HB/CTB once you have completed the course.

Presumably, for IS/JSA/HB/CTB any student financial support you have left once you have completed your course will count as capital (see Chapter 37) as there are no provisions to disregard it under the rules about capital.

5. Giving up, changing or taking time out from your course

If you complete one course and start a different course you are not treated as a student in any period between the courses.[100]

If you are in any of the circumstances below you should seek specialist advice.

If you abandon your course or are dismissed from it you can claim income support (IS) or jobseeker's allowance (JSA) from the day after that date so long as you satisfy the other rules for getting these benefits (see Chapters 13 and 15).

If you are on a sandwich course (see p581), or your course includes a compulsory or optional period on placement, you count as a full-time student during the sandwich or placement period even if you have been unable to find a placement or your placement comes to an end prematurely.[101]

If you attend a course at an educational institution that provides training or instruction to enable you to take examinations set and marked by an entirely different and unconnected body (ie, a professional institution) and you abandon or take time out from it because you fail the examinations set by the other body (or you finish the course at the educational institution but fail the exams), you may be able to argue that you are not a student from the date you left the course at your educational institution even if you intend to re-sit the examinations set by the other body at a later date.[102]

If you are taking time out of your course for any other reason (including to study for and re-sit exams – but see above) and for however long a period, you cannot claim IS or JSA during your period of absence,[103] except in the limited circumstances below (but if you are taking time out from a modular or similar course see also p581).

You may retain entitlement to some student support on a statutory or discretionary basis – eg, through student loans or hardship funds. You should seek specialist advice.

Changing from full-time to part-time attendance

If, for personal reasons, you have to change from full-time to part-time attendance on a 'traditional' full-time course, you may be able to argue that you have abandoned your full-time course and are registered on a part-time course and, therefore, that you are not a full-time student.[104]

If, because of exam failure or any other reason, you change to a different course, or your college requires you to change the level of course (eg, from A level to GCSE) and this involves a change from full-time to part-time study, you should argue that you are a part-time student.[105]

However, changing your attendance may affect your entitlement to any student support you may be receiving. You should seek advice on this before acting.

Time out to be a carer

You cannot get IS or JSA while you are caring for someone. However, you can claim JSA, housing benefit (HB) and council tax benefit (CTB), but not IS, when your caring responsibilities have come to an end.[106] **Note:** the rules do not provide a definition of caring responsibilities or when they come to an end. You can then claim for a maximum period of one year until whichever is the earlier of:

- the day you rejoin your course; *or*
- the first day from which your educational institution has agreed you can rejoin your course,

provided you are not eligible for a student grant or loan during this period. This means that you may not qualify for benefit for the whole of the period after your caring responsibilities end until the date you actually rejoin your course.

Time out because of illness

You cannot get IS or JSA while you are ill. However, you might be able to claim IS if you count as a 'disabled student' (see p582) – ie, when you have been ill for 28 weeks and are treated as 'incapable of work'. Once your illness has ended, you can claim JSA, HB and CTB, but not IS. The rules are the same as for when caring responsibilities have ended – see above.

Time out because of pregnancy

If you are not a student who can claim IS/JSA and you have to take time out because you are pregnant, the rules say you cannot claim IS until you have given birth and become responsible for a child (see p63). The Court of Appeal[107] has decided that, for JSA, this provision does not *directly* discriminate against women under European Community (EC) law. If you are refused IS/JSA/HB/CTB in these circumstances, it may be possible to argue that the decision *indirectly* discriminates against women under EC law or that it is incompatible with the Human Rights Act (see p1171 and CPAG's *Welfare Rights Bulletin* 194 p4). You should seek specialist advice.

Calculating income from grants and loans

Grants

For IS and JSA, if you leave or are dismissed from your course before it finishes, any grant you have received is taken into account as if you were still a student until whichever is the earlier:[108]

- you repay the grant; *or*

- the academic term or vacation in which you ceased to be a student ends; *or*
- the end of the period covered by the last instalment of your grant.

For HB/CTB it will be taken into account as if you were still a student.[109] Presumably, as grants are often paid in instalments, this means that grant income is taken into account over the period for which your last grant instalment was intended to cover.

Loans

If you abandon or are dismissed from your course before it finishes, there are special rules on how your student loan is treated.

If you abandon your course before you have received the final instalment of your student loan, it is taken into account using the formula:[110]

$$\frac{A - (B \times C)}{D}$$

A = the maximum amount of student loan available to you (see p597) – including any amount, paid as a grant, intended for the maintenance of your dependants – that you would have received had you remained a student until the last day of the academic term in which you abandoned or were dismissed from your course, less any disregards that apply (see p598). This amount is the 'relevant payment'.

B = the number of benefit weeks immediately following that which includes the first day of your 'academic year' (see p597) to the benefit week immediately before that which includes the day on which you abandoned or were dismissed from your course.

C = the weekly amount of student loan for the 'academic year' which would have been taken into account to calculate your benefit under the normal rules (see p597) but without applying the £10 a week disregard (see p598). This applies regardless of whether you were actually receiving benefit before you abandoned, or were dismissed, from your course.

D = the number of benefit weeks beginning with the benefit week which includes the day on which you abandoned or were dismissed from your course and ending with the benefit week which includes the last day of the last 'quarter' (see p599) for which your 'relevant payment' (see A) would have been payable to you had you remained on your course.

Example

Bhavna abandons her three-year degree course at a university outside London on 1 November 2008 during the first term of her second year. Her assumed maximum loan income would have been taken into account for 42 weeks (first complete benefit week in September to last complete benefit week in June). **Note:** the following figures are from 2007/08.

Step A: calculate the relevant payment

Loan instalment paid for first term	£1,503
less deduction for books and travel	£646
Total taken into account	**£857**

Step B: calculate the benefit weeks prior to leaving the course

1.9.08 to 26.10.08 = **8 weeks**

Step C: calculate maximum loan for the academic year

Maximum loan	£4,510
less deduction for books and travel	£646
Total loan	£3,864

Weekly amount (£3,864 divided by 43 weeks) = **£89.86 per week**

Step D: calculate complete benefit weeks from the benefit week including the date of abandonment to the end of the benefit week including the end of the quarter

27.10.08 to 28.12.08 = **9 weeks**

Calculation

$$\frac{857 - (8 \times 89.86)}{9} = £15.34 \text{ per week}$$

Therefore, £15.34 a week will be taken into account for the period from 27.10.08 to 28.12.08 (9 weeks) and nothing thereafter.

Note: this formula can result in a nil loan income figure depending on the exact date in your term that you abandon, or are dismissed from, your course.

If you voluntarily repay your student loan, for JSA/IS you are treated as still having that loan income[111] calculated under the above rules. However, guidance to decision makers says you should not be treated as having any loan income if the Student Loan Company demands you repay the loan instalment immediately.[112]

Notes

1. **Income support and jobseeker's allowance**
   1 **IS** Reg 12(1) IS Regs
   JSA Reg 54 JSA Regs
   Both Regs 3-7 CB Regs
   2 Reg 12 IS Regs
   3 s124(1)(d) SSCBA 1992; s1(2)(g) JSA 1995
   4 Reg 2(1)(b)(i)&(ii) C(LC)SSB Regs; reg 13(2)(a) and (b) IS Regs; Memo JSA/IS 04 para 14
   5 Regs 4ZA and 13(2)(a)-(e) IS Regs
   6 R(IS) 9/94
   7 R(IS) 9/94
   8 CIS/11766/1996
   9 R(IS) 9/94

10 R(SB) 2/87
11 CIS/11441/1995
12 s1(2)(g) JSA 1995; reg 54 JSA Regs
13 **IS** Reg 12 IS Regs
JSA Reg 54(1) and (2) JSA Regs
Both s142 SSCBA 1992; reg 7 CB Regs
14 **IS** Reg 61(1) IS Regs, definition of 'full-time student'
JSA Reg 1(3) JSA Regs, definition of 'full-time student'
15 **IS** Reg 2(1) IS Regs, definition of 'period of study'
JSA Reg 1(3A) JSA Regs
HB Reg 53(2)(b) HB Regs
CTB Reg 43(2)(b) CTB Regs
16 **IS** Reg 61(1) IS Regs, definition of 'last day of the course'
JSA Regs 1(3A)(a)(i) and 15(a) JSA Regs
HB Reg 53(1) HB Regs, definition of 'last day of the course'
CTB Reg 43(1) CTB Regs, definition of 'last day of the course'
17 Reg 4 JSA Regs, definition of 'period of study'
18 **IS** Reg 61(1) IS Regs, definitions of 'full-time course of advanced education' and 'full-time course of study'
JSA Reg 1(3) JSA Regs, definition of 'full-time student' – the definition of 'full-time course' is found within that definition
HB Reg 53(1) HB Regs, definition of 'full-time course of study'
CTB Reg 43(1) CTB Regs, definition of 'full-time course of study'
19 paras 30110-14 DMG
20 **IS** Reg 61 IS Regs definitions of 'full-time course of advanced education' and 'full-time course of study'; paras 30107-08 DMG
JSA Reg 1(3) JSA Regs, definition of 'full-time student' – the definition of 'full-time course' is found within that definition
HB Reg 53(1) HB Regs, definitions of 'full-time course of study' and 'higher education'
CTB Reg 43(1) CTB Regs, definitions of 'full-time course of study' and 'higher education'
21 **IS** Reg 61(1) IS Regs
JSA Reg 1(3) JSA Regs
HB Reg 53(1) HB Regs
CTB Reg 43(1) CTB Regs
All definition of 'sandwich course'
22 R(IS) 19/98
23 **IS** Reg 61(4) IS Regs
JSA Reg 1(3C) JSA Regs
HB Reg 53(4) HB Regs
CTB Reg 43(4) CTB Regs
24 **IS** Reg 61(2)(a) IS Regs
JSA Reg 1(3A)(a) JSA Regs
HB Reg 53(2)(a) HB Regs
CTB Reg 43(2)(a) CTB Regs
25 **IS** Reg 61(3)(b) IS Regs
JSA Reg 1(3B)(b) JSA Regs
HB Reg 53(3)(b) HB Regs
CTB Reg 43(3)(b) CTB Regs
26 **IS** Reg 61(3)(a) IS Regs
JSA Reg 1(3B)(a) JSA Regs
HB Reg 53(3)(a) HB Regs
CTB Reg 43(3)(a) CTB Regs
27 R(IS) 15/98; R(IS) 7/99; CJSA/836/1998; R(IS) 1/00
28 R(SB) 40/83; R(SB) 41/83
29 **IS** Reg 61 IS Regs, definitions of 'full-time course of advanced education' and 'full-time course of study'
JSA Reg 1(3) JSA Regs, definition of 'full-time student' – the definition of 'full-time course' is found within that definition
30 Reg 4ZA and Sch 1B IS Regs
31 Sch 1B paras 10, 11 and 12 IS Regs
32 CJSA/2663/2006
33 Reg 15(a) JSA Regs
34 Reg 14(1)(a) JSA Regs
35 Reg 14(1)(k) JSA Regs
36 CIS/152/1994; R(IS) 15/98; CJSA/836/1998; R(IS) 1/00
37 Reg 1(3) JSA Regs, definition of 'part-time student'
38 Reg 54(3) JSA Regs
39 paras 21240-41 DMG
40 para 21242 DMG
41 para 21243 DMG
42 para 21244 DMG
43 Reg 11 JSA Regs
44 Reg 11(3) JSA Regs

2. Housing benefit and council tax benefit

45 There are no student rules in the HB(SPC) Regs and the CTB(SPC) Regs.
46 **HB** Reg 8(1)(e) HB Regs
CTB Reg 57(3) and (4) CTB Regs
47 Reg 58 HB Regs
48 **HB** Reg 56(2) HB Regs
CTB Reg 45(3) Regs
49 Reg 55(1) HB Regs
50 Reg 55(2) HB Regs
51 Reg 57 HB Regs

3. **Other benefits and tax credits**
52 Reg 5 SS(ICA) Regs
53 Reg 5(2) SS(ICA) Regs
54 R(G) 2/02
55 CG/3189/2004
56 Reg 17 SS(IB) Regs; CS/20/1986
57 s15 SPCA 2002; reg 15 SPC Regs

4. **Calculating income from grants and loans**
58 **HB** Reg 29 HB(SPC) Regs
CTB Reg 19 CTB(SPC) Regs
59 **IS** Reg 61(1) IS Regs
JSA Reg 130 JSA Regs
HB Reg 53(1) HB Regs
CTB Reg 43(1) CTB Regs
All definition of 'grant'
60 **IS** Reg 61(1) IS Regs
JSA Reg 130 JSA Regs
HB Reg 53(1) HB Regs
CTB Reg 43(1) CTB Regs
All definition of 'grant income'
61 Sch 7 para 4 SS(C&P)Regs
62 **IS** Reg 62(3) IS Regs
JSA Reg 131(4) JSA Regs
HB Reg 59(5) HB Regs
CTB Reg 46(5) CTB Regs
63 **IS** Reg 61(1) IS Regs
JSA Reg 1(3) JSA Regs
HB Reg 53 HB Regs
CTB Reg 43 CTB Regs
All definition of 'period of study'
64 **IS** Reg 62(4) IS Regs
JSA Reg 131(6) JSA Regs
HB Reg 59(8) HB Regs
CTB Reg 46(8) CTB Regs
65 **IS** Reg 62(3A) IS Regs
JSA Reg 131(5) JSA Regs
HB Reg 59(6) HB Regs
CTB Reg 46(6) CTB Regs
66 **IS** Reg 62(3B) IS Regs
JSA Reg 131(5A) JSA Regs
HB Reg 59(7) HB Regs
CTB Reg 46(7) CTB Regs
67 **IS** Reg 62(3A) IS Regs
JSA Reg 131(5) JSA Regs
HB Reg 59(6) HB Regs
CTB Reg 46(6) CTB Regs
68 R(IS) 15/95
69 CIS/91/1994
70 **IS** Reg 62(2) and (2A) IS Regs
JSA Reg 131(2) and (3) JSA Regs
HB Reg 59(2) and (3) HB Regs
CTB Reg 46(2) and (3) CTB Regs
71 **IS/JSA** para 30328 DMG
HB/CTB paras C2.165-66 GM
72 **IS/JSA** paras 30329-30 DMG
HB/CTB paras C2.170-73 GM
73 **IS** Reg 67A IS Regs
JSA Reg 137A JSA Regs
HB Reg 67 HB Regs
CTB Reg 54 CTB Regs
74 **IS** Reg 67 IS Regs
JSA Reg 137 JSA Regs
HB Reg 66 HB Regs
CTB Reg 53 CTB Regs
75 **IS** Sch 10 para 63 IS Regs
JSA Sch 8 para 52 JSA Regs
HB Sch 6 para 51 HB Regs
CTB Sch 5 para 53 CTB Regs
76 R(IS) 7/95
77 **IS** Reg 61(1) IS Regs
JSA Reg 130 JSA Regs
HB Reg 53(1) HB Regs
CTB Reg 43(1) CTB Regs
All definition of 'student loan'
78 **IS** Reg 66A(3) IS Regs
JSA Reg 136(3) JSA Regs
HB Reg 64(3) HB Regs
CTB Reg 51(3) and (4) CTB Regs
79 **IS** Reg 61(1) IS Regs
JSA Reg 130 JSA Regs
HB Reg 53(1) HB Regs
CTB Reg 43(1) CTB Regs
All definition of 'academic year'
80 **IS** Reg 66A(2)(a) IS Regs
JSA Reg 136(2)(a) JSA Regs
HB Reg 64(2)(a) HB Regs
CTB Reg 51(2)(a) CTB Regs
81 **IS** Reg 66A(2)(aa) IS Regs
JSA Reg 136(2)(aa) JSA Regs
HB Reg 64(2)(b) HB Regs
CTB Reg 51(2)(b) CTB Regs
82 Reg 2 Education (Student Support) Regulations 2001
83 CIS/3734/2004
84 **IS** Reg 66A(5) IS Regs
JSA Reg 136(5) JSA Regs
HB Reg 64(5) HB Regs
CTB Reg 51(5) CTB Regs
85 **IS** Reg 66C IS Regs
JSA Reg 136B JSA Regs
HB Reg 64A HB Regs
CTB Reg 51A CTB Regs
86 para 30290 DMG
87 **IS** Reg 67A IS Regs
JSA Reg 137A JSA Regs
HB Reg 67 HB Regs
CTB Reg 54 CTB Regs
88 **IS** Reg 67 IS Regs
JSA Reg 137 JSA Regs
HB Reg 66 HB Regs
CTB Reg 53 CTB Regs
89 R(IS) 7/95

90 **IS** Reg 66A(2) IS Regs
JSA Reg 136(2) JSA Regs
HB Reg 64(2) HB Regs
CTB Reg 51(2) CTB Regs
91 **IS** Reg 41(6) IS Regs
JSA Reg 104(5) JSA Regs
HB Reg 41(4) HB Regs
CTB Reg 31(4) CTB Regs
92 **IS** Sch 9 para 13 IS Regs
JSA Sch 7 para 14 JSA Regs
HB Sch 5 para 13 HB Regs
CTB Sch 4 para 14 CTB Regs
93 R(IS) 16/95
94 **IS** Reg 61(1) IS Regs
JSA Reg 130 JSA Regs
HB Reg 53(1) HB Regs
CTB Reg 43(1) CTB Regs
All definition of 'access funds'
95 **IS** Reg 68(3) IS Regs
JSA Reg 138(3) JSA Regs
HB Reg 68(3) HB Regs
CTB Reg 55(3) CTB Regs
96 **IS** Reg 66B IS Regs
JSA Reg 136A JSA Regs
HB Reg 65 HB Regs
CTB Reg 52 CTB Regs
97 **IS** Reg 66B(4) IS Regs
JSA Reg 136A(4) JSA Regs
HB Reg 65(5) HB Regs
CTB Reg 52(4) CTB Regs
98 **IS** Reg 66(1) IS Regs
JSA Reg 135(1) JSA Regs
HB Reg 63 HB Regs
CTB Reg 50 CTB Regs
99 **IS** Sch 9 para 61 IS Regs
JSA Sch 7 para 59 JSA Regs

5. **Giving up, changing or taking time out from your course**

100 CIS/368/1992; R(IS) 6/97
101 R(JSA) 2/02
102 R(IS) 7/99
103 R(IS) 1/96
104 paras 30230-33 DMG; paras C2.41-42 GM
105 CIS/152/1994; R(IS) 15/98
106 **JSA** Reg 1(3D) and (3E) JSA Regs
HB Reg 56(6) and (7) HB Regs
CTB Reg 46(6) and (7) CTB Regs
107 R(JSA) 3/02
108 **IS** Reg 32(6A) IS Regs
JSA Reg 97(7) JSA Regs
109 para 2.425 GM
110 **IS** Reg 40(3A),(3AA) and (3AB) IS Regs
JSA Reg 103(5), (5ZA) and (5ZB) JSA Regs
HB Reg 40(7)-(9) HB Regs
CTB Reg 30(8)-(10) CTB Regs
111 Reg 6(6)(a) SS&CS(DA) Regs
112 para 30470 DMG; para C2.421 GM

Chapter 26

Benefits in hospital, prison and other special circumstances

This chapter covers the special rules that affect:

People coming from or going abroad are covered in Chapter 58. People who are studying are covered in Chapter 25.

There are some special rules if you are a **foster carer.** See the chapters in this *Handbook* about the benefits you want to claim. To find out whether:

- you can be treated as in full-time work, see pp655 and 1227;
- fostering allowances are taken into account as income, see pp835, 863, 895 and 1268;
- you can claim home responsibilities protection, see p733.

1. 16/17-year-olds formerly looked after by a local authority

Unless you were formerly looked after by a local authority, being 16 or 17 does not in itself prevent you qualifying for any of the benefits for people of working age in this *Handbook*, other than council tax benefit (CTB) and statutory adoption pay.

Special rules may affect your entitlement to income support (IS), income-based jobseeker's allowance (JSA) and housing benefit (HB) if you are aged 16 or 17 and were formerly looked after by a local authority. If these rules apply to you:

- your local authority must assess and meet your needs for maintenance, accommodation and support; *and*
- you cannot be treated as a member of the family of a person claiming IS, income-based JSA, HB or CTB.[1]

Local DWP and social services offices should liaise to ensure any disputes about who is responsible for supporting you are quickly resolved. If you are refused both benefit and social services support, you should seek specialist advice.

England or Wales

In England or Wales, even if you are no longer being looked after by a local authority, you cannot get IS, income-based JSA or HB if you are 16 or 17 and:[2]

- you were looked after by a local authority (eg, subject to a care or supervision order, or provided with accommodation under ss20, 23 or 23A Children Act 1989) for at least 13 weeks. The 13-week period must start after your 14th birthday and end after you turn 16;[3] *or*
- you are not subject to a care order, but you were in hospital, or detained in a remand centre, or a young offenders or similar institution when you became 16 and immediately before you were in hospital or detained you were looked after by a local authority for at least 13 weeks since your 14th birthday.[4]

The 13 weeks do not have to be continuous. Pre-planned short-term placements of four weeks or less, after which you return to the care of your parent, or person acting as your parent, do not count towards the 13 weeks.[5]

There are exceptions to the rules. See p611 for details.

Scotland

In Scotland, even if you are no longer being looked after by a local authority, you cannot get IS, income-based JSA or HB if you are 16 or 17 and:[6]

- you were looked after by a local authority (eg, subject to a care or supervision order) and provided with accommodation for at least 13 weeks after the age of 14, and the local authority is obliged to provide you with after-care services under s29(1) Children (Scotland) Act 1995; *and*
- you are not living with your family or another person who has parental responsibility for you (or you are but you are receiving regular financial assistance from the local authority under s29(1) Children (Scotland) Act 1995.

The 13 weeks are calculated in the same way as they are for England and Wales (see above).[7]

There are exceptions to the rules – see p611 for details.

Exceptions

You *can* get IS or income-based JSA (but not HB) if you are in one of the following groups of people who can claim IS (see p292):[8]

- lone parents;
- lone foster parents;
- people incapable of work or appealing against an incapacity for work decision;
- disabled workers;
- disabled or deaf students;
- blind people;
- young people in 'relevant education' who are lone parents or who qualify for a disability premium or severe disability premium (see pp779 and 784).

In England and Wales, you are not excluded from IS, income-based JSA or HB if you have been in a family placement for at least six months and you have left local authority care (unless the placement has broken down).[9]

2. Hospital patients

Some of your benefits are affected after you, your partner or child have been in hospital as a patient for a period. This might also be the case if an adult dependant, someone you care for or a non-dependant has been in hospital as a patient for a period. Until then, your benefits are paid as normal. See p612 for who counts as a patient. For:

- the benefits that are affected after 28 or 84 days, see p613;
- the benefits that are affected after 52 weeks, see p615;
- social fund payments, see p617.

You should always inform the DWP (and local authority) promptly if your benefits may be affected by the rules described below to avoid being overpaid or underpaid benefit.

If necessary, you can arrange for someone else to collect your benefit while you are in hospital. If you are unable to manage your affairs, another person or a hospital can act as your appointee (see p955).

See Chapter 9 for details of how to get help with the cost of your fares to and from hospital. If you are visiting someone in hospital, you may be able to claim a community care grant to cover the cost of your fares (see p488).

Note:

- If you go abroad temporarily for NHS treatment in a hospital or other institution, see pp1350, 1352 and 1352 to see if you can claim income support (IS), jobseeker's allowance (JSA) or pension credit (PC).

- If you are detained in a hospital as a result of a criminal conviction because of a mental disorder, although you are a patient, you might be treated in the same way as if you were a prisoner (see pp625 and 627).

Who counts as a patient

You count as a '**patient**' for benefit purposes if you are being maintained free of charge while undergoing medical or other treatment as an inpatient in a hospital or 'similar institution' and:[10]

- the treatment is funded by the NHS; *or*
- the hospital (or similar institution) is maintained and administered by the Defence Council.

You should *not* count as a patient if you are getting treatment as a private patient, or if you are meeting the cost of your treatment in a private hospital, or if your placement was arranged by a local authority (even if the NHS is contributing to the cost of your nursing care).[11]

If you are in a care home and your nursing needs are more than merely incidental and ancillary to any other care needs you may have, you should qualify for all your accommodation costs to be provided free of charge by the NHS.[12] The primary care trust should make an assessment to see if you come under this rule. If it decides that you do, you should only be treated as a patient from the day of the decision.[13] If the primary care trust has never considered the matter, the DWP might decide itself that you should be treated as a patient.

Hospitals and similar institutions[14]

'Hospitals' include all NHS hospitals, armed forces hospitals and special hospitals such as Broadmoor and Rampton. Prison hospital wings, however, do not count as hospitals.

A 'similar institution' is not defined in the rules, but could include some care homes, hospices and rehabilitation units that provide medical or nursing care.[15]

When you count as a patient

You count as a patient from the day after the day you enter hospital (or a similar institution). You do not count as a patient:

- for attendance allowance (AA) and disability living allowance (DLA) only, on the day you leave;[16] *or*
- for all other benefits, on the day after the day you leave.[17]

Example

Hilda is claiming DLA and IS. She is taken ill and admitted to hospital on 1 January. After successful treatment, she is discharged on 21 January.

For DLA purposes, she counts as a patient from 2 January up to and including 20 January = 19 days.

For IS purposes, she counts as a patient from 2 January up to and including 21 January = 20 days.

After 28 or 84 days

Payment of AA and DLA can be affected after someone has been a patient for 28 (or 84 days). Entitlement to child benefit can be affected after your child has been a patient for 84 days. For information on how carer's allowance and means-tested benefits might then be affected, see p614.

Attendance allowance and disability living allowance

AA and DLA are paid as normal until you have been a patient for 28 days. You cannot be paid AA (including constant attendance allowance – see p326) or DLA after you have been a patient for 28 days.[18] However, if you are being paid DLA for a child under 16, this continues until s/he has been a patient for 84 days.[19]

Payment of AA or DLA can begin again from the payday following discharge from hospital.[20] If you expect to be readmitted within 28 days, you can be paid at a daily rate from the day of your discharge.[21]

There is a 28-day 'linking rule'. This means that:[22]

- different periods spent as a patient separated by 28 days or less are linked together and treated as one period; *and*
- periods spent as a resident in a care home during which AA and the DLA care component are not payable (see p618) link with periods spent as a patient if they are 28 days or less apart. Payment of AA or the DLA care component could, therefore, be affected if you enter hospital from a care home.

Example

Horace is claiming AA. He goes into hospital for an operation on 16 July and is discharged on 30 July. He counts as a patient from 17 July up to and including 29 July = 13 days. His AA is not affected by his stay in hospital.

Horace has to go back into hospital for further treatment on 10 August. He counts as a patient again, from 11 August. As there are 28 days or less between his discharge and re-admission, the two spells in hospital are linked. When he has been a patient for a further 15 days, he cannot be paid AA.

Note:

- If you are awarded AA or DLA while you are a patient, payment cannot begin until you are discharged.[23]
- You can continue to be paid the mobility component of DLA while you are a patient if:[24]

- you had a Motability agreement (see p134) when you became a patient, but only until the agreement ends (unless you immediately renew an agreement under the Wheelchair Scheme). You are paid the amount payable under the agreement; *or*
- you have been a patient since 31 July 1995 (other than under 'section' under the Mental Health Acts). Your mobility component is paid at the lower rate.

- If you are terminally ill, you can be paid AA or DLA while you are in a hospice which is not an NHS or Defence Council hospital or similar institution, so long as the DWP has been informed that you are terminally ill.[25]

Child benefit

Your entitlement to child benefit might be affected once your child has been in hospital for 84 days. Normally, s/he no longer counts as living with you (and you cannot get child benefit for her/him) if s/he has been absent from home for more than 56 days in the last 16 weeks. However, certain absences from home can be ignored, including periods of up to 84 days when your child is receiving inpatient treatment in a hospital or similar institution. See p63 for further information.

Carer's allowance

To qualify for carer's allowance (CA) the person you care for must be receiving AA or the highest or middle rate of DLA care component (see p43). So your entitlement to CA ends when the person you care for is no longer receiving AA or DLA. If the person you care for is discharged and receives AA or the DLA care component, you can reclaim CA if you again satisfy the rules for entitlement. Your claim can be backdated to the date from which the AA or DLA is payable (see the 'qualifying benefit' rules on p968).

Remember that once you have been caring for a disabled person for a period, you are allowed a temporary break in caring which does not affect your CA (see p44). This includes where you (or the person you care for) are a patient. You can remain entitled to CA for up to 12 weeks in any period of 26 weeks. This can be useful where you (or the person you care for) are in and out of hospital. However, once the person you care for has been a patient for a total of 28 days, s/he can no longer be paid AA and DLA (see p613). Your entitlement to CA then ends, even if you have not yet had a break of 12 weeks.

Means-tested benefits

IS, income-based JSA, PC, housing benefit (HB) and council tax benefit (CTB) can be affected after you (or your child) have been a patient for 28 (or 84) days.

- If you are claiming AA or DLA and payment stops, if you are a single claimant you are no longer entitled to the severe disability premium (severe disability additional amount for PC) (see p784). However, if you are getting the severe disability premium/additional amount and are a member of a couple, you are treated as getting AA or DLA if one or both of you are patients. Other than for

PC, your carer is treated as getting CA if s/he would be entitled to, and receiving it, but for the fact that you have been a patient for longer than 28 days. This means that you can continue to qualify for the premium/additional amount, but it is paid at the single person's rate.[26]

- Entitlement to the disability, enhanced disability and higher pensioner premiums of IS, income-based JSA, HB and CTB are not affected by the payment of AA or DLA stopping.[27] However, these premiums can be affected once you or your partner have been a patient for 52 weeks (see p616). If your child's DLA has stopped, see below.
- If you are claiming CA, the carer's premium (carer's additional amount for PC) can continue to be paid for up to eight weeks after CA stops (see p789). If you lose your CA because *you* are a patient, the person you were caring for may become entitled to the severe disability premium/additional amount (see p784).

Children

If a child getting DLA is included in your claim for IS, income-based JSA, HB or CTB, entitlement to the disabled child and enhanced disability premium is not affected by payment of her/his DLA stopping, so long as s/he continues to count as a member of your family (see p700).[28] However, for IS and income-based JSA, these premiums are affected once your child has been a patient for 52 weeks (see p616).

If your child ceases to be regarded as a member of your family (see p700) or child benefit stops because your child is no longer treated as living with you, this may affect whether you can get personal allowances and premiums/additional amounts for your child. See p710 for further information.

Changes to allowances and premiums for children

If you claim IS or income-based JSA and are getting child tax credit (CTC), IS and income-based JSA do not include allowances and premiums for your children. However, if you were getting IS or income-based JSA on 5 April 2004 and a dependent child was included in your claim, allowances and premiums for your children can continue until you are transferred onto CTC. See p709 for further information.

After 52 weeks

Some benefits are affected after you or your partner or child (or an adult dependant or a non-dependant) have been a patient for 52 weeks. Until then, they are paid as normal.

Means-tested benefits

IS and income-based JSA may be paid at a reduced rate if you (or your partner or child) have been a patient for a continuous period of more than 52 weeks. You are paid the normal rate, less:[29]

- any disability premium, enhanced disability premium and higher pensioner premium included in your applicable amount. This applies if you are a single claimant or a lone parent. If you are a member of a couple, this applies if both you and your partner have been patients, or only one of you has been and s/he is the only one for whom the premium was included;
- any disabled child premium and enhanced disability premium included in your applicable amount for your child, if s/he has been a patient.

HB and CTB may be paid at a reduced rate if you (or if you are a member of a couple, both you and your partner) have been a patient for more than 52 weeks. The enhanced disability premium is not included in your applicable amount.[30] Note that your entitlement to the disabled child and enhanced disability premium is not affected if your child has been a patient for more than 52 weeks, so long as s/he continues to count as a member of your family (see below).[31]

Partners and children

You count as a couple while you and your partner are only temporarily apart. However, for IS, JSA, PC and HB, you no longer count as a couple if you are likely to be separated from your partner for more than 52 weeks, or in exceptional circumstances, such as a stay in hospital, substantially more than 52 weeks.[32]

If you no longer count as a couple, your means-tested benefits are assessed as if you are a single claimant. If your child is a patient, s/he may no longer count as a member of your family once s/he has been away from home for a period. If this happens, you can no longer get allowances and premiums for your child with HB and CTB (and IS or income-based JSA, if still included). See p712 for further information.

Paying for your normal home while you are a patient

If you are getting HB or CTB, or help with your housing costs with your IS, income-based JSA or PC, these might no longer be payable once you have been absent from home for more than 52 weeks (see pp185 and 799). Another person might be able to get these instead, if s/he can be treated as liable (see pp180 and 797).

Note:

- There are no 'linking rules' with these provisions. This means that if you are discharged from hospital and then are re-admitted, a new period as a patient starts and you can again be entitled to IS, income-based JSA, HB or CTB premiums and to help with housing costs (paid with IS, income-based JSA or PC).

- You can be treated as occupying a new dwelling, even if you have not yet stayed there, if you move your furniture and belongings in but cannot move yourself in because you have to go into hospital.[33]
- For HB and CTB only, if you are a member of a couple, a deduction of childcare charges from earnings can be made if one of you is in remunerative work and the other is in hospital (see pp856 and 888).

Non-dependants

If you have a non-dependant living with you, non-dependant deductions made for her/him (from your IS/income-based JSA/PC housing costs, HB or CTB) stop once s/he has been a patient for 52 weeks.[34] Your non-dependant counts as a 'patient' if s/he is getting inpatient treatment in a hospital or similar institution. The treatment does not have to be free or provided by the NHS. Separate periods spent as a patient which are not more than 28 days apart are added together when calculating the 52 weeks. See Chapters 5, 10 and 34 for further information about non-dependant deductions.

Non-means-tested benefits

If you are entitled to an increase in a non-means-tested benefit for an adult or child dependant (see Chapter 29), this is no longer payable once you (or both you and your dependant) have been a patient for 52 weeks or more, unless you apply to the DWP to pay the increase on your behalf to:[35]

- your dependant; *or*
- someone else approved by the DWP. The DWP must be satisfied that the payment will be used for the benefit of:
  - your dependant, if you are a patient; *or*
  - your child, if both you and your dependant are patients.

Social fund payments

Some social fund payments are affected if you are a patient. You cannot get a **crisis loan** if you are in hospital, unless your discharge is planned to take place in the next two weeks (see p505). You cannot get a **winter fuel payment** if you have been a patient for more than 52 weeks.

3. People in care homes and other special accommodation

Most benefits are paid as normal if you live in a care home or certain other types of special accommodation. In addition, if you are a permanent resident in a care home and your place is funded by the local authority, you are entitled to free health benefits, even if you are not getting a qualifying benefit or do not qualify under the low income scheme (see Chapter 9).

However, the following benefits might be affected.

- Attendance allowance (AA) and the care component of disability living allowance (DLA) are affected if you are resident in a care home for a period where the costs of certain services you get are borne out of public or local funds (see p618). This may then affect your means-tested benefits and the benefits of the person looking after you (eg, carer's allowance (CA)).
- Means-tested benefits and some social fund payments (ie, winter fuel payments, cold weather payments and crisis loans) are affected if you live in certain types of care home for a period (see p624).

If you are claiming child benefit, this might be affected if the child for whom this is being paid is being looked after by the local authority (see p69). There are exceptions to this rule (see p69).

You should always inform the DWP (and local authority) promptly if your benefits may be affected by the rules described below, to avoid being overpaid or underpaid benefit.

Note: if your place in a care home is funded by the NHS, you may count as a 'patient'. In this case your benefits are affected under the rules for patients (see p611) instead of those for care homes.

Care homes and other special accommodation

There is not sufficient space in this *Handbook* to cover the different kinds of care homes and other special accommodation, and the funding arrangements for those living in them. Further details can be found in CPAG's *Paying for Care Handbook*. What you have to pay for your place depends on whether it is funded by the NHS or by the local authority.

Attendance allowance and disability living allowance care component

You cannot be paid AA and DLA care component once you have been a resident in a care home for a period of 28 days, where the 'costs of any qualifying services' provided for you are borne out of public or local funds under specific provisions.[36] Until then, AA and DLA care component are paid as normal. You count as in a care home if it is an establishment that provides you with accommodation as well as nursing or personal care.[37] **Note:** DLA *mobility* component is paid as normal however long you are a resident in a care home.

Specified provisions

The specified provisions are:[38]

– Part III of the National Assistance Act 1948, Part IV of the Social Work (Scotland) Act 1968, the Mental Health (Care and Treatment) (Scotland) Act 2003, the Community Care and Health (Scotland) Act 2002 and the Mental Health Act 1983; *or*

– any other Acts relating to people with disabilities, or (in the case of DLA only) young people, or education or training (eg, in some special residential schools).

There is a wide range of accommodation and funding arrangements. Local authorities also have powers to provide accommodation under housing legislation and the Local Government Act 1972, in which case AA and DLA are not affected.[39]

'Qualifying services' means the costs of accommodation, board and personal care. The 'costs of any qualifying services' does *not* include the cost of:[40]

- domiciliary services (including personal care) provided to people in a private dwelling;
- improvements to, or furniture or equipment provided for:
  - a private dwelling because of the needs of a disabled person;
  - a care home, for which a grant or payment was made out of public or local funds, except where the grant or payment is of a regular or repeated nature;
- social and recreational activities outside the care home;
- the purchase or running of motor vehicles used in connection with any qualifying service provided in the care home; *and*
- NHS services.

Bear in mind that:

- if the NHS provides nursing services in a care home and your nursing needs are more than merely incidental and ancillary to other care needs, you are treated as a 'patient' for DLA and AA purposes[41] – see p612;
- there is a 28-day 'linking rule' (see p620);
- there are exceptions to the rules – eg, if you are meeting the whole cost of your accommodation yourself (see below);
- if you think the DWP has refused payment of AA or DLA wrongly, you can seek a revision or appeal against the refusal. Remember that the view of a local authority is not binding on tribunals.[42]

Note that if you are awarded AA or the care component of DLA while you are resident in a care home in the circumstances described above, you cannot be paid for as long as you continue to stay in the accommodation.[43]

Exceptions to the rules

There are exceptions to the rules. You can continue to be paid AA and the care component of DLA, even *after* 28 days, if:

- you are are meeting the whole costs of all the 'qualifying services' from your own resources, or with the help of another person or a charity, known as 'self-funding'.[44] This applies whether you are in an independent or local authority home. You count as self-funding *even if*:
  - you are claiming benefits such as IS, pension credit, AA and DLA;
  - a local authority has arranged and contracted to pay for your placement, so long as you are paying the whole costs of all the 'qualifying services';
  - a local authority is temporarily funding your placement while you sell a property – eg, your former home. You must be liable and able to repay the local authority in full when the property is sold (known as 'retrospectively self-funding').[45] This includes where you have entered into what is known as a 'deferred payment agreement' with the local authority. The DWP can suspend payment of your AA or DLA, then resume payment when you repay the local authority funding. Note that the value of your home is disregarded for the first 12 weeks you are permanently in a care home. You are not liable to repay local authority funding provided, and are not retrospectively self-funding, during this period; *or*
- you are terminally ill and are in a hospice which is not an NHS or Defence Council hospital or similar institution, so long as the DWP has been informed that you are terminally ill;[46] *or*
- for DLA only, you are a student and the cost of your accommodation is wholly or partly met from a student grant or loan, or from a grant made to education institutions (eg, from funding councils) under specific legislation;[47] *or*
- you are under 16 and being looked after by a local authority or under 18 and receiving services because of your disability or health. This only applies if you have been placed by the local authority in a private dwelling with a family, a relative of yours or some other suitable person;[48] *or*
- your accommodation is outside the UK and the costs of any qualifying services are being borne by a local authority under specified legislation (eg, at the Peto Institute in Hungary or the Higashi School).[49]

When you count as being a resident in a care home

The general rule is that you do not count as a resident in a care home on the day you enter or the day you leave.[50]Note that if you are a patient in a hospital or similar institution (see p611) and enter a care home you count as a resident in the care home from the day you enter; if you leave a care home and enter a hospital or similar institution as a patient, you do not count as a resident in the care home on the day you leave.[51]

There is a 28-day 'linking rule'. This means that different periods as a resident in a care home which are separated by 28 days or less link together for the purpose of calculating the 28 days for which you can continue to be paid AA or the care component of DLA. Periods spent as a patient in a hospital or similar institution (see p611) also count towards the 28-day limit on payment if they are separated by 28 days or less from periods when you are resident in a care home in the circumstances described above.[52]

It can be important to plan periods of respite care in the light of the linking rules so that you can continue to be paid AA and the DLA care component for as long as possible. This also enables your carer to keep her/his CA.

Payment of AA or DLA can begin again from the payday after you are no longer resident in a care home.[53] If you expect to return within 28 days, you can be paid at a daily rate from when you leave.[54]

How other benefits are affected

Payment of AA or DLA care component stopping affects CA in the same way as for patients. See p614 for further information. Remember that the carer's premium (carer's additional amount for pension credit (PC)) can continue to be paid for up to eight weeks after CA stops (see p789).

If you are claiming income support (IS), income-based jobseeker's allowance (JSA), PC, housing benefit (HB) or council tax benefit (CTB), once payment of AA or DLA care component stops, you are no longer entitled to the severe disability premium (severe disability additional amount for PC) or the enhanced disability premium. You might no longer be entitled to the disability premium or higher pensioner premium, if the only reason you qualified was because you were receiving AA or DLA care component. See Chapter 33 for further information about premiums (and additional amounts for PC).

Note: if you are still being paid AA or DLA care component – eg, because you have not yet been in a care home for 28 days, you may be entitled to a severe disability premium, even if you were not before – eg, if you are no longer treated as living with a non-dependant or a partner.

If your partner or a dependent child or young person is living in a care home, see p623 for how your IS, income-based JSA, PC, HB and CTB are affected.

Means-tested benefits

When the term 'care home' is used below, it means:[55]

- a care home (a care home service in Scotland) as defined in s3 Care Standards Act 2000 and s2(3) Regulation of Care (Scotland) Act 2001;
- an Abbeyfield Home run by the Abbeyfield Society or affiliates of that Society;
- an independent hospital (an independent healthcare service in Scotland) as defined in s2 Care Standards Act 2000 and s2(5)(a) and (b) Regulation of Care (Scotland) Act 2001.

If you are not sure if you live in a relevant home, seek advice.

How benefit is affected

Whether your means-tested benefits are affected depends on whether you (or your partner or child) are temporarily or permanently living in a care home. If, however, you are in a care home (on either basis), your IS, income-based JSA, PC, HB and CTB personal allowances and premiums (standard minimum guarantee and additional amounts for PC) are generally calculated in the usual way, but if payment of your AA or DLA care component stops, you may no longer be entitled to certain premiums (see p621).

Note that:

- if you have a partner you might no longer count as a couple if you (or your partner) are a resident in a care home. If your child is resident in a care home, s/he may no longer count as a member of your family for benefit purposes. See p623 for further information;
- for IS and JSA, in some cases, you do not count as in full-time paid work if you are in employment while living in a care home (see p655);
- for PC, if you have an 'assessed income period' (see p458), it comes to an end if you do not have a partner and are provided with accommodation in a care home (other than in an Abbeyfield Home) on a permanent basis;[56]
- if you are on a placement under the Adult Placement Scheme (a scheme similar to fostering, but for adults) living with an approved carer, the normal conditions of entitlement to HB apply.[57] You can get HB for the rent you pay.

Permanent residence in a care home

For benefits other than CTB, the **tariff income** rules are more generous (see pp910 and 935). This also applies if you live in Polish resettlement accommodation. Some temporary absences from the home are ignored. The threshold for calculating your tariff income is £10,000. For HB, this is only relevant (and only applies) in the limited situations in which you can get HB while living in a care home (see p624). The higher threshold is not needed for CTB; if you are a permanent resident in a care home, you are not liable for council tax there.[58]

HB and CTB and help with your housing costs (paid with IS, income-based JSA or PC) are no longer payable for your former home, once you are a permanent resident in a care home. Housing costs can be paid to another person if s/he can be treated as liable to pay them (see p798). Another person may be able to claim HB as a liable person (see p180).

For CTB, if you become a permanent resident in a care home and your home in the community is unoccupied you can apply for it to be exempt from council tax. See CPAG's *Council Tax Handbook* for details.

If payment of your **AA or DLA care component** stops because you are in a care home, you are no longer entitled to premiums (additional amounts for PC) that depend on receipt of AA or DLA care component (see p621). However, for IS only, if you only live in a care home part of the week and are entitled to DLA when you are staying elsewhere, you can be paid, for example, the severe disability and enhanced disability premiums when you are staying away from the care home, from the date the change occurs (or is expected to occur).[59]

Temporary residence in a care home

If you are a temporary resident in a care home (eg, for respite care or for a trial period) you can continue to get HB and CTB and help with your housing costs (paid with IS, income-based JSA or PC) for your normal home. If you intend to return home, you can get these for:[60]

- up to 13 weeks, for any reason, if you are unlikely to be away from home for longer than this; *or*
- up to 13 weeks, if you are in care for a trial period. On the date you enter the accommodation, you must intend to return home if the accommodation is not suitable.[61] If the home does not suit your needs you can have further trial periods in other homes so long as you are not away from home for more than 52 weeks; *or*
- up to 52 weeks, if you are unlikely to be away for longer than this (or in exceptional circumstances, substantially longer than this) and you are in a care home for short-term respite care.

For these purposes: for HB and CTB, a care home includes those managed or provided by bodies incorporated by Royal Charter or constituted by an Act of Parliament, other than by local social services. For PC, a care home does *not* include an Abbeyfield Home.

There are no linking rules with these provisions. This means that if you go home a new period of temporary absence can begin when you go back into the care home. See pp185 and 799 for further information about temporary absence from home.

Partners and children

If you or your partner move into a care home:

- permanently (for PC only, other than to an Abbeyfield Home), you no longer count as a couple.[62] This also applies if you or your partner are both in care homes permanently, even if you are in the same home and the same room.[63] If you do not count as a couple, your benefit, and that of your partner, is calculated as if you are a single claimant;
- temporarily, you still count as a couple if you intend to live together again. For IS, JSA, PC and HB only, this only applies if you are unlikely to be apart for more than 52 weeks, or in exceptional circumstances, substantially longer than 52 weeks.[64]

  For PC, HB and CTB, this means that once the person in the care home stops getting AA or DLA care component, no severe disability premium (additional amount) can be included in your applicable amount for either of you.

  For IS and income-based JSA only, your applicable amount is calculated in a special way. You receive the amount for two single claimants if this is higher than the amount you receive as a couple (see p785). This can include the severe disability premium in respect of either or both of you, as if you were single claimants, even if you are not normally entitled to it at home.[65]

If your child lives in a care home, entitlement to a personal allowance and premiums for her/him might be affected if you no longer get child benefit for her/him, or s/he is no longer being paid DLA, or if s/he no longer counts as a member of your family. The latter situation can include where your child is not living with you and is in a care home or is being looked after by a local authority. Remember that in some cases you can receive benefit for her/him on the days when s/he comes home. See p712 for further information.

Housing benefit for your care home

You cannot usually get HB for the rent you pay to your care home.[66] For these purposes, a care home does *not* include an Abbeyfield Home. There are limited exceptions to the rules – ie, where you were entitled to HB for your care home when the rules changed at various times in the past and you have what is known as transitional protection. Broadly speaking, you can get HB for the rent you pay if you were entitled to it for residential accommodation under the HB rules before 30 October 1990 or before 1 April 1993.[67] In some cases, this only applies so long as you do not break your claim and continue to live in the same home, disregarding certain temporary absences.

Social fund payments

Some social fund payments are affected if you are in a care home. You cannot get:

- a crisis loan if you are in a care home unless your discharge is planned to take place in the next two weeks (see p505). In Scotland, you are only excluded if you are getting nursing or personal care;
- a cold weather payment if you reside in a care home (see p621 – the meaning is the same as for means-tested benefits) or Polish resettlement accommodation;[68]
- a winter fuel payment if you are are getting PC or income-based JSA and in a care home (see p621 – the meaning is the same as for means-tested benefits) or Polish resettlement accommodation for a period (see p523).

4. Prisoners

Your benefit is almost always affected if you are a prisoner. There are also issues to consider if you are given an alternative sentence to prison. It is important to inform the relevant benefit authorities as soon as you, or a member of your family, enter or leave prison to avoid any underpayment or overpayment of benefit. If you are being held on remand and are then sentenced, it is important to notify the benefit authorities as soon as this happens. You should *not* presume that the prison will do this for you.

Non-means-tested benefits

Most non-means-tested benefits are not payable while you are a prisoner. In some cases, payment of your benefit is only suspended pending the outcome of your trial or sentence (see p626). For benefits that are payable, see p626.

You count as a 'prisoner':

- for statutory sick pay (SSP), statutory maternity pay (SMP), statutory adoption pay (SAP) or statutory paternity pay (SPP) if you are detained in legal custody or sentenced to a term of imprisonment (except where the sentence is suspended);[69]
- for other non-means-tested benefits (other than contribution-based jobseeker's allowance (JSA)) if you are imprisoned or detained in legal custody (in Great Britain or abroad) in connection with criminal proceedings (ie, not for civil offences).[70]

You therefore do *not* count as a prisoner and benefits are payable, provided you satisfy the normal rules of entitlement, if:

- you are on bail, or living in approved premises (eg, a bail or probation hostel);
- you are released on parole, temporary licence, an 'end of custody licence' or under a home detention curfew (electronic tagging).

Note:

- Non-means-tested benefits (other than SSP, SMP, SAP or SPP) are not affected if you are detained as a result of a criminal conviction in a hospital or similar institution, as a person suffering from a mental disorder, unless this is under ss45A or 47 Mental Health Act 1983, s59A Criminal Procedure (Scotland) Act 1995 or s136 Mental Health (Care and Treatment)(Scotland) Act 2003.[71] However, check whether your benefit is instead affected under the special rules for hospital patients.
- You cannot qualify for contribution-based JSA while you are in prison as you are unable to satisfy the labour market conditions (being available for work, actively seeking work and having a current jobseeker's agreement).

Benefits not payable

If you count as a prisoner you cannot be paid:

- attendance allowance (AA), bereavement benefits, disability living allowance (DLA), carer's allowance (CA), incapacity benefit (IB), maternity allowance (MA), reduced earnings allowance (REA), retirement allowance, retirement pension, or severe disablement allowance (SDA).[72]
  This includes where you are detained as a result of a criminal conviction in a hospital or similar institution, as a person suffering from a mental disorder, under ss45A or 47 Mental Health Act 1983, s59A Criminal Procedure (Scotland) Act 1995 or s136 Mental Health (Care and Treatment)(Scotland) Act 2003, but only for the length of your original sentence.[73]

You cannot get an increase in the above benefits for your spouse or civil partner if s/he is a prisoner.[74] You are cannot get an increase in benefit for an adult caring for a child (see p688) if the adult or child is a prisoner.[75]

If you are on remand awaiting trial or sentence, payment is suspended pending the outcome (see below);

- SSP, SMP, SAP or SPP.[76] You are not entitled to SMP and SPP for the whole of your maternity or paternity pay period (see p548), even if you are released from prison during it. However, you are entitled to SAP for any period during which you are detained in custody if you are subsequently released without charge or after being found not guilty, or you are convicted but do not receive a custodial sentence. Payment of SAP should also resume for any period of entitlement subsequent to your release.

Benefits suspended

If you are a remand prisoner awaiting trial or sentence, payment of IB, SDA, AA, DLA, CA, MA, REA, retirement pension, retirement allowance and bereavement benefits is suspended pending the outcome. If you subsequently receive a sentence of imprisonment or detention (including a suspended sentence), you are not paid the benefits for the whole period you are in prison.[77] An increase of these benefits for your spouse or civil partner is similarly not paid if s/he is sentenced to imprisonment or detention.

If you (or your spouse or civil partner) do not receive a sentence of imprisonment or detention or your conviction is quashed, full arrears of any benefit which have been withheld are payable when you are released.[78]

Note: arrears are only payable if the normal conditions of entitlement for benefit were met while you (or your spouse/civil partner) were a remand prisoner. For the purpose of entitlement to an increase in your benefit for a spouse or civil partner, you should be treated as still 'residing with' her/him while s/he is in prison, unless your marriage/partnership has broken down and your separation is likely to be permanent.[79]

Benefits payable

You are paid **disablement benefit** (but not the increases listed on p326) for periods when you are a prisoner. However, you are not paid until you are released and you can only get a maximum of 12 months' arrears.[80] If you are in prison for more than a year, you should be paid for the 12-month period which gives you the most benefit.[81] In addition, you are entitled to full arrears for any period you were on remand, if you are not subsequently sentenced to imprisonment or detention.[82]

You are entitled to **child benefit**[83] and **guardian's allowance**[84] while you are a prisoner. You must continue to be 'responsible' for the child (see p63). If you are in prison for some time, you may want to arrange for child benefit to be paid to the person looking after your child. If *your child* is a prisoner, entitlement to child benefit usually ends after eight weeks.[85] There are exceptions to the rules. See p69 for further information. However, full arrears are payable at the end of any period of remand if your child is not sentenced to imprisonment or detention. Once entitlement to child benefit ends, entitlement to guardian's allowance in respect of the child also ends. Note that if child benefit stops because your child is a prisoner, this may affect whether you can get an increase for her/him with your non-means-tested benefits and personal allowances and premiums for her/him with your means-tested benefits.

Means-tested benefits

For means-tested benefits, you count as a prisoner if:[86]

- you are detained in custody (eg, in prison or a young offenders' institution) awaiting trial or sentence (on remand) or following a sentence of imprisonment; *or*
- you are on temporary release under specific provisions (this does not include parole licence).

You do not count as a prisoner if you are detained in hospital under specific mental health provisions (but see below if this is as a result of a criminal conviction). Check to see if your benefit is instead affected by the special rules for hospital patients. In addition, you do not count as a prisoner if:

- you are released on licence or parole; *or*
- you are on bail or living in approved premises (eg, a bail or probation hostel); *or*
- you are released under a home detention curfew (electronic tagging).

Income support, jobseeker's allowance and pension credit

If you count as a prisoner:

- you cannot qualify for JSA as you are unable to satisfy the labour market conditions (being available for work, actively seeking work and having a current jobseeker's agreement). If you need help with your housing costs for your home, you must claim income support (IS) or pension credit (PC) for this (see p628);
- you can qualify for IS and PC guarantee credit for up to 52 weeks while you are detained in custody awaiting trial or sentence. However, you only get the amount for help with your housing costs (see p628). Once you have been sentenced, you are no longer entitled to any IS or PC;[87]
- you cannot get any PC savings credit;[88]
- you may be entitled to the PC severe disability additional amount if you do not receive a sentence of imprisonment and you are given arrears of AA or DLA on your release (see p631).[89]

Note that if you are detained as a result of a criminal conviction in a hospital or similar institution, as a person suffering from a mental disorder, under ss45A or

47 Mental Health Act 1983, s59A Criminal Procedure (Scotland) Act 1995 or s136 Mental Health (Care and Treatment) (Scotland) Act 2003, although you are a patient, you are treated in a similar way to prisoners. You are not entitled to any IS or PC, but only for the length of your original sentence.[90] Although there is no specific rule, the same applies for JSA, as you are not able to satisfy the labour market conditions.

If you are a prisoner and have a partner or children, or if your partner (or child) is a prisoner, see p629.

Paying for your normal home while you are a prisoner

While you are detained in custody **awaiting trial or sentence** (see p627), you can continue to get housing benefit (HB) and council tax benefit (CTB), and help with your housing costs (paid with IS or PC) for your normal home. These are paid for up to 52 weeks, so long as you intend to return home and you are unlikely to be away for longer than this (or, in exceptional circumstances, substantially longer than this).[91] If you were getting help with your housing costs with income-based JSA before you went into prison, once you are a prisoner you must claim IS or PC for this.

If you are serving a **custodial sentence**, you may be able to get HB and CTB for up to 13 weeks, so long as you are unlikely to be away from your normal home for longer than this – ie, you are serving a short sentence.[92] The 13 weeks runs from the date you were first in prison.[93] So any time you spend in prison awaiting trial or sentence counts towards the 13 weeks. If you are serving a sentence of more than 13 weeks, you may still be entitled to HB and CTB, as prisoners serving short sentences are often released early under a home detention curfew (electronic tagging). If you are serving a sentence of up to a year it is possible to be released within 13 weeks.

You are treated as a prisoner during periods of **temporary release** under specific provisions. This means that even if you return home, you are still treated as if you are away. You cannot get help with your housing costs with IS, JSA or PC and you cannot get HB or CTB.[94] These periods also count towards the 13/52 weeks for which HB and CTB may be payable.

Note:

- You can continue to get HB for a former home for up to four weeks if you are still liable to pay rent for it, and you could not reasonably have avoided this liability.[95]
- Housing costs (paid with IS, JSA or PC) can be paid to another person if s/he can be treated as liable to pay them (see p797). Another person may be able to claim HB as a liable person (see p180).
- If your home is unoccupied while you are a prisoner, you can apply for it to be exempt from council tax, provided you are not in prison for non-payment of a fine or council tax. See CPAG'S *Council Tax Handbook* for details.

Note: if you have a **non-dependant** who is a prisoner, no non-dependant deduction is made for her/him.[96] See pp196 and 815 for further information about non-dependant deductions.

Partners and children

If you have a **partner**, and one of you is a prisoner:

- you no longer count as a couple for IS, JSA or PC purposes;[97]
- you continue to count as a couple:
  - for HB purposes, so long as you intend to live together again and the prisoner is unlikely to be away for substantially longer than 52 weeks;[98]
  - for CTB purposes so long as you are only temporarily apart.[99] Unlike for HB, this is not defined in the rules.

  The one who is not a prisoner, if working, may be able to have childcare costs deducted from earnings (see pp856 and 888).[100]

Once you no longer count as a couple, the one who is *not* a prisoner can claim benefit as a single person or lone parent as applicable.

If your **child** is a prisoner, entitlement to a personal allowance and premiums for her/him might be affected if you no longer get child benefit for her/him or if s/he no longer counts as a member of your family. The latter situation can include where your child is in custody. See p712 for further information.

Social fund payments

Most prisoners are excluded from getting a crisis loan (see p505). You cannot get a winter fuel payment if you are serving a custodial sentence (see p523). You cannot get other social fund payments if you are not getting a qualifying benefit (see Chapters 21 and 22). If you are released on temporary licence, a person caring for you may be able to claim a community care grant to help with living expenses (see p493).

Benefits and alternatives to prison

There are a number of alternatives to prison. While awaiting trial or sentence, you might be on bail, including on the condition that you live in approved premises (eg, a bail hostel) or elsewhere away from home. See p630 for how this affects your benefits. In pilot areas, you might have been given a custodial sentence called intermittent custody, served both in and out of prison (see p630).

You might be given a **community sentence** that involves punishment or supervision in the community.

Although you do not count as a prisoner, you should bear the following in mind.

- There might be a question whether you satisfy the labour market conditions for JSA. Seek advice if you think you have been wrongly refused JSA.

- If you undertake basic skills education and are treated as a full-time student, this may affect your entitlement to benefits (see Chapter 25).
- The notional income rules for means-tested benefits should not apply where you participate in unpaid work as part of your sentence.

If you are not sure how your benefit is affected, seek advice.

Intermittent custody

A custodial sentence called intermittent custody was available in pilot areas until November 2006. It allowed offenders to serve their sentence intermittently (ie, some days in prison and some days out of prison). This meant that they could work, study or be a carer, and also claim and be paid benefits, during the week when they were not in prison. See pp635-36 of CPAG's *Welfare Benefits and Tax Credits Handbook* 2007/08 edition for information about how benefits were affected.

If you are on bail or living in approved premises

Your non-means tested benefits are paid as normal if you on bail or are living in approved premises (eg, a bail or probation hostel) or other accommodation as a condition of bail. However, special rules can apply for means-tested benefits.

If you have a partner and you are are temporarily separated because one of you is living away from home, you still count as a couple for means-tested benefit purposes if you intend to live together again. For IS, JSA, PC and HB, this only applies if you are unlikely to be apart for more than 52 weeks or, in exceptional circumstances, substantially longer than 52 weeks.[101] For IS and income-based JSA only, your applicable amount is calculated in a special way; it is calculated at either the couple rate or double the single rate, whichever is the greater.[102]

Paying for your normal home

If you are required to live away from home in an approved bail or probation hostel, you cannot get HB for the rent you pay for that accommodation.[103] However, you can continue to get HB and CTB and help with your housing costs (paid with IS, JSA or PC) for your normal home. These are paid for up to 13 weeks (so long as you are unlikely to be away for longer than this). If you are required to live in the approved hostel or an address away from home as a condition of bail, these are paid for up to 52 weeks (so long as you intend to return home and you are unlikely to be away for longer than this or in exceptional circumstances, substantially longer than this).[104]

If you are no longer entitled to help with housing costs (paid with IS, JSA or PC) these can be paid to another person if s/he can be treated as liable to pay them (see p797). Another person may be able to claim HB as a liable person (see p180).

Benefits on release

If you are **temporarily released** (on temporary licence), you no longer count as a prisoner for non-means-tested benefits (see p625). You still count for means-tested benefits (see p627). However, someone caring for you might qualify for a community care grant (CCG) for her/his expenses in looking after you (see p493).

When you are **permanently released** from prison, you should claim any benefits to which you are entitled as soon as possible. The prison gives you a discharge form which can help you prove your identity.

- As IS and income-based JSA are generally paid in arrears, you may need to apply for an interim payment (see p986) or a social fund crisis loan to meet your initial expenses.
- You may qualify for a CCG to help you settle back into the community – eg, for clothes, furniture and household equipment. You can apply up to six weeks before you are released if you are, or expect to be, in receipt of IS, income-based JSA or PC (see p488).
- For JSA, you are treated as satisfying the labour market conditions for the first seven days after your release.[105]
- If you were getting a disability premium before you went into prison on the basis that you had been incapable of work for 364 days (196 days if terminally ill), the premium should be included in your IS, HB and CTB when you are released without you having to serve a further qualifying period.[106] However, you have to show that you continued to be incapable of work while in prison. See p781 if you became incapable of work while in prison.
- You may receive a discharge grant from the Prison Service, which counts as capital for IS/income-based JSA purposes.[107] The rules do not say how it should be treated for HB, CTB or PC.
- If you are released from prison early under an 'end of custody licence', you count as on temporary release (see above). As well as a discharge grant, the Prison Service pays a weekly amount for living expenses. You may also get help with the costs of your accommodation.
- If you are released without being sentenced to imprisonment or detention, you should receive any arrears of your non-means-tested benefits that were suspended (see p626). You should also check that you have been credited with any earnings to which you are entitled. See p727 for information about national insurance (NI) contributions and credits. If you are released following the quashing of a conviction you are entitled to credits for the period you were imprisoned or detained (see p732).

Help with travelling expenses

The Prison Service can:

- help you with travelling expenses when you are temporarily or permanently released from prison;

- help a partner or close relative with the cost of visiting you in prison or a friend with the cost of bringing your children to visit you (including the cost of an overnight stay where necessary) if s/he is receiving IS, income-based JSA, PC or tax credits, or health benefits because s/he has a low income. Application forms are available from the establishment being visited and from the Assisted Prison Visits Unit, PO Box 2152, Birmingham B15 1SD (telephone 0845 300 1423 or textphone 0845 304 0800). They are also available on the Prison Service website at www.hmprisonservice.gov.uk/adviceandsupport.

5. People without accommodation

Your entitlement to means-tested benefits (other than income support (IS) and income-based jobseeker's allowance (JSA)) and all non-means-tested benefits, is unaffected if you do not have accommodation. Remember, however, that if you are getting JSA, you must satisfy the labour market conditions (be available for and actively seeking work and have a current jobseeker's agreement) – see p633.

If you become homeless and have no money, you may initially need a social fund crisis loan (see p503) or an interim payment (see p986). It is possible to get help at any time in an emergency (see p987). If you set up home as part of a resettlement programme after you have been homeless, you may be entitled to a community care grant (see p491).

If you are homeless, the local authority may have a duty to assist you with accommodation and advice. A child or young person may be entitled to help from social services.

Income support and income-based jobseeker's allowance

Your IS and income-based JSA are paid at a reduced rate if you are a person 'without accommodation'. This is the normal rate, but without any premiums.[108] This rule was challenged under the Human Rights Act but the Court decided that the rules did not conflict with the Act.[109]

'**Accommodation**' is not defined in the rules and should be interpreted widely and flexibly. The DWP says that to count as having accommodation, you must have:

> 'an effective shelter from the elements which is capable of being heated; and in which occupants can sit, lie down, cook and eat; and which is reasonably suited for continuous occupation.[110] The site of the accommodation may alter from day to day, but it is still accommodation if the structure is habitable.'

This includes, for example, tents, caravans and other substantial shelters. However, the DWP is likely to say that cardboard boxes, bus shelters, sleeping bags[111] and cars[112] do not qualify as accommodation.

Having no fixed address is *not* the same as having no accommodation. If you have accommodation, but are staying in different places on different nights – eg, with different friends or relatives, your IS or income-based JSA should be paid as normal.[113]

If you are temporarily absent from the accommodation you normally occupy as your home, even if you are living a lifestyle as though you have no accommodation (eg, you are sleeping rough), you should be treated as having accommodation.[114]

Available for and actively seeking work

You must satisfy the labour market conditions (be available for and actively seeking work and have a current jobseeker's agreement) to get JSA (see Chapter 15). Being homeless may, of course, reduce your prospects of finding work but personal circumstances which reduce your chances of being employed should not prevent you getting JSA, unless you are placing unreasonable restrictions on your availability.

You can be available for work if you do not have accommodation but it must be possible for you to be contacted at short notice if you are to satisfy the requirement that you are willing and able to take up any job immediately, or at 24 hours' or one week's notice (see p347). You may satisfy this requirement by daily visits to the Jobcentre Plus office, or a drop-in centre or support group where a message can be left for you.

The fact that you are homeless should be taken into account when deciding whether you are actively seeking work. In deciding what steps it is reasonable for you to take to find work, the DWP must take into account the fact that you have no accommodation and the steps you need to take to find a home.

6. **People involved in a trade dispute**

If you (or your partner) are involved in a trade dispute, the benefits that are affected are:

- jobseeker's allowance (JSA – see p634);
- income support (IS – see p634);
- statutory sick pay (SSP), and statutory maternity, paternity and adoption pay (SMP, SPP and SAP) (see p637);
- increases for dependants paid with non-means-tested benefits (see p638); *and*
- some social fund payments (see p638).

There are also some issues to consider if you are claiming housing benefit or council tax benefit (see p640).

If you need financial help when you return to work after a trade dispute, see p640 to see if you qualify for an IS loan for the first 15 days.

Whether or not you are involved in a trade dispute is a complex area of law. If there is any doubt, you should seek specialist advice from your trade union or an advice or law centre.

Jobseeker's allowance and income support

JSA and IS are both affected if you (or your partner) are involved in a trade dispute.

- You are not entitled to JSA (including hardship payments) for the whole of any week (seven days from Sunday) if you are involved in a trade dispute (see below) for one or more days during that week.[115] You may, however, be entitled to IS (see below) or pension credit (see Chapter 18). Weeks when you are not entitled do not count as part of your 'jobseeking period' (see p339).[116] This means, for instance, that they do not count towards your 26 weeks' entitlement to contribution-based JSA.
- If you have a partner and only one of you is involved in a trade dispute, unless you are a joint-claim couple (see p381), the one who is not involved can claim income-based JSA. If you are a joint-claim couple you can both claim income-based JSA;[117] the one involved in the trade dispute does not have to satisfy the 'labour market conditions' (see p342).
- You fit into one of the groups of people who can claim IS while you are involved in a trade dispute and for the first 15 days after you return to work (see p296).[118] Note that if you are not involved in a trade dispute but your partner is, you can claim IS instead of her/him if you fall into one of the other groups of people who can claim IS. If you are in this situation you should seek advice about whether it is in your interests to swap which one of you claims.

You are treated as being in full-time paid work for the first seven days you are involved in a trade dispute. You (and your partner) cannot qualify for income-based JSA or IS for that period.[119] This does not apply if your partner was already entitled to income-based JSA or IS when you became involved in the dispute. If the dispute causes a series of stoppages, this only applies for seven days from the start of the first stoppage.[120] After the seven-day period, you are not treated as being in full-time paid work, but your partner's income-based JSA (or your or your partner's IS) is paid at a reduced rate (see p636).[121]

Trade disputes

A **'trade dispute'** is any dispute between employers and employees or between employees and employees about terms or conditions of employment, or the employment or non-employment of anyone.[122]

You count as **involved in a trade dispute** if:[123]

- you are not working because of a 'stoppage of work' caused by a trade dispute at your 'place of work' (see below). You are treated as involved in the trade dispute until the stoppage ends, even if you are not a party to the dispute or your contract has been terminated as part of the dispute (but see below);[124] *or*
- you withdraw your labour to further a trade dispute, whether or not there is a stoppage of work at your place of work.

For income-based JSA and IS only, a decision can be made on your claim as if you are involved in a trade dispute, pending a decision on whether you are actually involved.[125] You cannot appeal to a tribunal against this decision.[126] The decision maker should then carry out a revision of the decision once full information and evidence is available.

'Stoppage of work' and 'place of work'

A **'stoppage of work'** could be due to a strike, lock-out or any other stoppage caused by a trade dispute. The stoppage does not have to involve everybody, or stop all work.[127] The DWP says that there is no 'stoppage' if normal work continues through the employment of replacement workers or reorganisation.[128]

'Place of work' means the place or premises where you are employed but it does not include a separate department carrying out a different branch of work, which is commonly undertaken as a separate business elsewhere (eg, a colliery canteen worker laid off during a miners' strike was not 'involved in a trade dispute at her place of work').[129] It can be difficult to establish that separate branches are commonly separate businesses and not part of integrated activities.[130]

You **do *not* count as being involved in a trade dispute**:

- if you can prove you are not directly interested in the dispute[131] – ie, you will not be affected by its outcome. This could apply if your terms and conditions will not be affected by the outcome of the dispute or your employment has permanently ended and you will not gain anything from the dispute;[132] *or*
- if you can prove that during a stoppage of work:[133]
  - you have been made redundant; *or*
  - you have become genuinely employed elsewhere (ie, not just to avoid the trade dispute rules[134]); *or*
- if you genuinely resume employment with your employer and then leave for a reason other than the trade dispute (note that your JSA may be sanctioned if you leave – see p402).

For income-based JSA (if your partner is claiming) and IS, even if you are (or count as) involved in a trade dispute, the special rules for those involved in a trade dispute do not apply during a period:[135]

- when you are incapable of work; *or*
- from the sixth week before the week you are due to have a baby to the end of the seventh week after the week the baby is born; *or*
- from the day you return to work with the same employer, even if the dispute is continuing or you are doing a different job.[136]

The amount of income support or income-based jobseeker's allowance

Special rules reduce the amount of IS or income-based JSA that is payable if you or your partner are involved in a trade dispute. Your applicable amount is calculated in a special way and it is assumed that you have a set level of strike pay. Certain income is taken into account even if it would be disregarded were you (or your partner) not involved in a trade dispute. **Note:** if you are entitled to IS of less than £5 a week, you are only paid if you are receiving another benefit with which IS can be paid.[137]

Applicable amount

Your IS or income-based JSA applicable amount is calculated as follows.

- For IS only, if you are a single claimant, or member of a couple without children, and both involved in a trade dispute, your applicable amount amount is reduced to nil.[138]
- For IS only, if you are a lone parent, or a member of a couple with children, and both involved in a trade dispute, your applicable amount only includes:[139]
  - personal allowances for your children (where still applicable);
  - premiums for your children and the family premium (where still applicable); *and*
  - housing costs.

  You are not entitled to a personal allowance or any premiums payable in respect of yourself (or of either of you if you are a member of a couple).
- For JSA only, if you are a single claimant, a lone parent or a member of a couple both involved in a trade dispute, you are not entitled to any JSA (see p634). Check to see if you can qualify for IS or PC instead.
- If you are a member of a couple and only one of you is involved in a trade dispute, your applicable amount only includes:[140]
  - half the normal personal allowance for a couple;
  - half of any premiums paid at the couple rate;
  - any premiums payable solely in respect of the person not involved in the trade dispute;
  - personal allowances and the family and disabled child premiums for any children (where still applicable); *and*
  - housing costs.

  You are not entitled to any premiums payable solely for the person involved in the trade dispute.

Actual and assumed strike pay

If you are involved in a trade dispute, the IS and income-based JSA rules assume that you are getting strike pay, whether or not you actually receive any payments. If you (or you and your partner) are involved in a trade dispute £32.50 is deducted from your IS or income-based JSA as 'assumed strike pay'.[141]

Any payments you or your partner actually receive from a trade union in excess of £32.50 a week count as income. Payments of up to £32.50 are ignored. If you and your partner are both involved in a trade dispute, only £32.50 in total is ignored.[142]

Example

Cliff is on strike. He and his partner Bernice have no children. Their only income is £35 a week strike pay.

Applicable amount	£47.45 (half normal amount)
less income	£2.50 (strike pay over £32.50)
	= £44.95
less	£32.50 (assumed strike pay)
= IS payable	£12.45

Other income and capital

Other income and capital is treated as normal except that the following payments are taken into account in full as income:

- any repayment of income tax paid or due;[143]
- any payment received or due because the person involved in the trade dispute is not working (eg, a loan or grant from social services);[144]
- if your IS or income-based JSA still includes amounts for your children, payments made under the Children Act 1989 or Children (Scotland) Act 1995 to promote the welfare of children;[145]
- charitable or voluntary payments and certain personal injury payments (whether regular or irregular) – see p864, except any payments from the Macfarlane Trusts, the Eileen Trust, the Fund or the Independent Living Funds;[146]
- payments in kind (except payments from the above trusts or funds) paid to the person involved in the trade dispute or to a third party (unless used for items allowable under the notional income/capital rules – see pp874 and 929);[147]
- holiday pay payable more than four weeks after your employment is terminated or interrupted (subject to any earnings disregard);[148]
- an advance of earnings or a loan from an employer (subject to any earnings disregard).[149]

Benefits paid by your employer

SSP, SMP, SPP and SAP are all affected if you are involved in a trade dispute.

Statutory sick pay

You cannot qualify for SSP if you are not within a 'period of entitlement' (see p557). A period of entitlement cannot arise if on the date it would begin there is a stoppage of work due to a trade dispute at your place of work (ie you became incapable of work during the trade dispute), unless you can prove that you did not have a direct interest in the dispute on or before that date.[150] You can continue to qualify for SSP if you were already entitled to SSP when the trade dispute began.

'Stoppage of work' and 'trade dispute' are not defined in the SSP rules. However, an overtime ban or working to grade does not count as a stoppage of work.[151] For information about what might count as a 'stoppage of work' and 'place of work' see p634.

You are not entitled to SSP throughout your period of sickness, even if the trade dispute ends. You might, however, qualify for incapacity benefit or IS.

Statutory maternity, paternity and adoption pay

To qualify for SMP, SPP or SAP, you must have been employed for a continuous period of 26 weeks (the 'continuous employment rule' – see p530). For the purpose of this rule, any week in which you are not working because of a stoppage of work due to a trade dispute at your place of work does not break your continuity of employment.[152] However, unless, you can prove that you at no time had a direct interest in the trade dispute:

- any such week does *not* count towards the total of 26 weeks' employment you need to qualify for SMP, SPP or SAP; *and*
- if you are dismissed during the stoppage of work your continuity of employment is broken.

This could mean that you cannot qualify for SMP, SPP or SAP.

For information about the meaning of 'trade dispute', 'stoppage of work' and 'place of work', see p634. The rules are the same as for JSA.[153]

Increases for dependants

You are not entitled to an increase of incapacity benefit, severe disablement allowance, carer's allowance, maternity allowance or Category A retirement pension for an adult dependant who is involved in a trade dispute.[154] For information about what counts as being involved in a trade dispute, see p634. The rules are the same as for JSA.

If the adult dependant returns to work, you should reclaim the increase for her/him.

Social fund payments

Involvement in a trade dispute has no effect on entitlement to a funeral expenses, cold weather or winter fuel payment. However, other social fund payments are affected. For information about when you count as involved in a trade dispute, see p634. The rules are the same as for JSA.

Note: you do not count as being involved in a trade dispute during a period when you are incapable of work or from the sixth week before the week you are due to have a baby to the end of the seventh week after the week the baby is born.[155]

Sure Start maternity grant

If you or your partner are involved in a trade dispute, you can only qualify for a Sure Start maternity grant if:[156]

- you or your partner are receiving IS or income-based JSA and the trade dispute has been going on for at least six weeks when you claim a maternity grant; *or*
- you or your partner are receiving child tax credit paid at a rate higher than the family element (see p1234) or working tax credit which includes the disability or severe disability element (see pp1237 and 1239), which you claimed before the trade dispute began.

Social fund discretionary payments

If you or your partner are involved in a trade dispute, you cannot qualify for a **community care grant** (CCG) unless this is for travel expenses to visit somebody who is ill. This only applies in the following situations.[157]

- You are involved in a trade dispute and are visiting:
  - your partner in a hospital or similar institution; *or*
  - a dependant in a hospital or similar institution (but only if you have no partner living with you who could get a CCG under these provisions or if s/he is also in hospital); *or*
  - a close relative (not defined) or a member of your household who is critically ill (whether or not s/he is in a hospital or similar institution).
- You (or a dependant) are not involved in a trade dispute, but your partner is, and you (or your dependant) are visiting:
  - a close relative who is in a hospital or similar institution or who is critically ill; *or*
  - someone else in hospital or similar institution who is critically ill, and who was a member of your household before going into hospital or getting ill.

You cannot qualify for a **budgeting loan** if you or your partner are involved in a trade dispute.[158]

If you or your partner are involved in a trade dispute, you can only qualify for a **crisis loan** for:[159]

- expenses arising from a disaster; *or*
- the cost of items needed for cooking (including cooking utensils) or space heating (including fireguards).

Housing benefit and council tax benefit

Housing benefit (HB) and council tax benefit (CTB) are not affected if you or your partner are involved in a trade dispute. However, bear the following in mind.

- You may become entitled to HB or CTB (or an increased amount of these) if your income drops because of a trade dispute.
- When assessing your earnings, the local authority should take into account any reduction in your income because of a trade dispute and not just consider your pre-strike earnings.[160]
- The local authority can average out your earnings over a different period than normal, if this results in a more accurate estimate of your earnings (see p876).

Income support loans on return to work

If you return to work with the same employer, whether or not the trade dispute has ended, you can qualify for IS for the first 15 days back at work, in the form of a loan.[161] You fit into one of the groups of people who can claim IS and are not treated as being in full-time paid work for this period.[162] If you are a member of a couple you are not entitled to IS if your partner is in full-time paid work.[163] See Chapter 27 for what counts as full-time paid work.

Your income and capital are calculated as if you were still involved in the trade dispute, except that the rules about actual and assumed strike pay do not apply, nor do those on the treatment of repayments of income tax (paid or due) and payments you get because the person involved in the trade dispute was not working.[164]

Repayment of the loan

Any IS paid during your first 15 days back at work can be recovered by deductions from your earnings.[165] If this is not practical (eg, because you are currently unemployed) it can be recovered directly from you.[166] The rules specify the amount of earnings you must be left with after deductions are made to repay your IS loan.[167]

Your employer can begin making deductions from your earnings from the first payday after receiving a deduction notice from the DWP. If one month has passed since getting the notice, s/he *must* start making deductions on the next payday.[168] Your employer cannot make a deduction if you satisfy her/him that you did not receive the IS loan. The deduction notice expires automatically after 26 weeks.

You must tell the DWP within 10 days if you leave a job or start another while part of your IS loan remains unpaid.[169] It is a criminal offence to fail to do so.[170] It is also a criminal offence for your employer to fail to keep records of deductions and supply the DWP with these.[171] If your employer fails to make a deduction (or makes too low a deduction) which should have been made from your pay, the DWP can recover the amount from your employer instead.[172]

Notes

1. 16/17-year-olds formerly looked after by a local authority

1 **IS** Reg 14(2)(c) IS Regs
JSA Reg 76(2)(d) JSA Regs
HB Reg 19(2)(c) HB Regs; reg 19(2)(c) HB(SPC) Regs
CTB Reg 9(2)(c) CTB Regs; reg 9(2)(c) CTB(SPC) Regs
2 **IS** Reg 4ZA(3A) IS Regs
JSA Reg 57 JSA Regs, definition of 'young person'
Both s6(1) C(LC)A 2000
3 s6 C(LC)A 2000; regs 3 and 4 C(LC)(E) Regs and C(LC)(W) Regs
4 Reg 4(1) and (2) C(LC)(E) Regs and C(LC)(W) Regs
5 Regs 3(3) and 4(3) C(LC)(E) Regs; reg 3(2) C(LC)(W) Regs
6 ss6 and 8(6) C(LC)A 2000; C(LC)SSB(S) Regs
7 Reg 2(4)(a) C(LC)SSB(S) Regs
8 Reg 2 C(LC)SSB Regs; reg 2(3) C(LC)SSB(S) Regs
9 Reg 4(5)-(7) C(LC)(E) Regs; reg 4(4)-(6) C(LC)(W) Regs

2. Hospital patients

10 Reg 2(4) SS(HIP) Regs; NHSA 1977; NHS(S)A 1978; NHSCCA 1990
11 para 18059 DMG
12 R(DLA) 2/06
13 para 18067 DMG
14 paras 18028-33 DMG
15 *White v CAO, The Times,* 2 August 1993 (CA); *Botchett v CAO, The Times,* 8 May 1996, 2 CCLR 121 (CA); *R v North and East Devon Health Authority ex parte Coughlan* [1999] 2 CCLR 285 (CA)
16 Reg 6(2A) SS(AA) Regs; regs 8(2A) and 12A(2A) SS(DLA) Regs
17 Reg 2(5) SS(HIP) Regs
18 Regs 6 and 8(1) SS(AA) Regs; regs 8, 10(1), 12A and 12B(1)(a) SS(DLA) Regs
19 Regs 8, 10(2), 12A and 12B(1)(b) SS(DLA) Regs
20 Reg 16(2) SS(C&P) Regs
21 Reg 25 SS(C&P) Regs
22 Reg 8(2) SS(AA) Regs; regs 10(5) and 12B(3) SS(DLA) Regs
23 Reg 8(3) SS(AA) Regs; regs 10(3) and 12B(2) SS(DLA) Regs
24 Regs 12B(3)-(9) and 12C(1) and (2) SS(DLA) Regs
25 Reg 8(4)-(5) SS(AA) Regs; regs 10(6)-(7) and 12B(9A) and (12) SS(DLA) Regs
26 **IS** Sch 2 paras 13(3A) and 15(5)(b)(i) IS Regs
JSA Sch 1 paras 15(5) and 20(6)(b)(i) JSA Regs
PC Reg 6(5) and Sch 1 para 1(2)(b) SPC Regs
HB Sch 3 paras 14(5) and 20(6)(b)(i) HB Regs; Sch 3 paras 6(7) and 12(1)(b)(i) HB(SPC) Regs
CTB Sch 1 paras 14(5) and 20(6)(b)(i) CTB Regs; Sch 1 paras 6(7) and 12(1)(b)(i) CTB(SPC) Regs
27 **IS** Sch 2 paras 12(1)(d) and 13A(1) IS Regs
JSA Sch 1 paras 14(1)(g)(ii) and 15A(1) JSA Regs
HB Sch 3 paras 13(1)(a)(iii) and 15(1) HB Regs; Sch 3 para 7 HB(SPC) Regs
CTB Sch 1 paras 13(1)(a)(iii) and 15(1) CTB Regs; Sch 1 para 7 CTB(SPC) Regs
28 **IS** Sch 2 paras 13A(1) and 14(1)(a) IS Regs
JSA Sch 1 paras 15A(1) and 16(1)(a) JSA Regs
HB Sch 3 paras 15(1) and 16(a) HB Regs; Sch 3 paras 7 and 8(a) HB(SPC) Regs
CTB Sch 1 paras 15(1) and 16(a) CTB Regs; Sch 1 paras 7 and 8(a) CTB(SPC) Regs
29 **IS** Reg 2(1), definition of 'long-term patient' and Sch 2 paras 10(6), 11(2), 13A(2) and 14(2) IS Regs
JSA Reg 1(3), definition of 'long-term patient' and Sch 1 paras 12(5), 13(2), 15A(2), 16(2), 20F(5), 20G(2) and 20IA(2) JSA Regs
30 **HB** Sch 3 para 15(2) HB Regs
CTB Sch 3 para 15(2) CTB Regs

31 **HB** Sch 3 paras 15(1) and 16(a) HB Regs; Sch 3 paras 7 and 8(a) HB(SPC) Regs
CTB Sch 1 paras 15(1) and 16(a) CTB Regs; Sch 1 paras 7 and 8(a) CTB(SPC) Regs
32 **IS** Reg 16(1) and (2) IS Regs
JSA Reg 78(1)-(2) JSA Regs
PC Reg 5(1)(a) SPC Regs
HB Reg 21(1) and (2) HB Regs; reg 21(1) and (2)HB(SPC) Regs
CTB Reg 11(1) CTB Regs; reg 11(1) CTB(SPC) Regs
33 R(H) 9/05
34 **IS** Sch 3 para 18(7)(g) IS Regs
JSA Sch 2 para 17(7)(g) JSA Regs
PC Sch 2 para 14(7)(e) SPC Regs
HB Reg 74(7)(f) HB Regs; reg 55(7)(f) HB(SPC) Regs
CTB Reg 58(7)(d) CTB Regs; reg 42(7)(d) CTB(SPC) Regs
35 Reg 2(2) and (3) SS(HIP) Regs

3. **People in care homes and other special accommodation**

36 ss67(2) and 72(8) SSCBA 1992; Regs 7 and 8(1) SS(AA) Regs; regs 9 and 10(1) SS(DLA) Regs
37 ss67(3) and 72(9) SSCBA 1992
38 Reg 7(2) SS(AA) Regs; reg 9(2) SS(DLA) Regs
39 CDLA/1465/1998; CDLA/2127/2000
40 ss67(4) and 72(10) SSCBA 1992; reg 7(3) SS(AA) Regs; reg 9(6) SS(DLA) Regs
41 R(DLA) 2/06
42 CA/2985/1997
43 Reg 8(3) SS(AA) Regs; reg 10(3) SS(DLA) Regs
44 Reg 8(6) SS(AA) Regs; reg 10(8) SS(DLA) Regs; *Steane v CAO and Secretary of State*, 24 July 1996 (CA), reported as R(A) 3/96
45 R(A) 1/02; CA/3800/2006; *CAO v Creighton and others*, 15 December 1999 (NICA), reported as R I/00 (AA)
46 Reg 8(4) and (5) SS(AA) Regs; reg 10(6) and (7) SS(DLA) Regs
47 Reg 9(3) SS(DLA) Regs
48 Reg 9(4)(a) and (b) and (5) SS(DLA) Regs
49 Reg 9(4)(c) SS(DLA) Regs
50 Reg 7(4) SS(AA) Regs; reg 9(7) SS(DLA) Regs
51 Reg 7(5)and (6) SS(AA) Regs; reg 9(8) and (9) SS(DLA) Regs
52 Reg 8(2) SS(AA) Regs; reg 10(5) SS(DLA) Regs
53 Reg 16(2) SS(C&P) Regs
54 Reg 25 SS(C&P) Regs
55 **IS** Reg 2(1) IS Regs
JSA Reg 1(3) JSA Regs
PC Reg 1(2) SPC Regs
HB Reg 2(1) HB Regs; reg 2(1) HB(SPC) Regs
CTB Reg 2(1) CTB Regs; reg 2(1) CTB(SPC) Regs
56 Reg 12(c) SPC Regs
57 HB/CTB Circular A20/05
58 **IS** Reg 53(1A), (1B) and (1C) IS Regs
JSA Reg 116(1A), (1B) and (1C) JSA Regs
PC Reg 15(6) and (7) SPC Regs
HB Reg 52(3)-(5), (8) and (9) HB Regs; reg 29(2) and (6) HB(SPC) Regs
59 Sch 3A para 3(h) SS&CS(DA) Regs
60 **IS** Sch 3 para 3(8)-(12) IS Regs
JSA Sch 2 para 3(8)-(12) JSA Regs
PC Sch 2 para 4(8)-(12) SPC Regs
HB Reg 7(11)-(13), (16) and (17) HB Regs; reg 7(11)-(13), (16) and (17) HB(SPC) Regs
CTB Reg 8(2)-(4) CTB Regs; reg 8(2)-(4) CTB(SPC) Regs
61 *Secretary of State for Work and Pensions v Selby District Council and Bowman* [2006] EWCA Civ 271, 13 February 2006, reported as R(H) 4/06
62 **IS** Reg 16(3)(e) IS Regs
JSA Reg 78(3)(d) JSA Regs
PC Reg 5(1)(b) SPC Regs
HB Reg 21(2) HB Regs; reg 21(2) HB(SPC) Regs
CTB Reg 11(1) CTB Regs; reg 11(1) CTB(SPC) Regs
63 Appendix to CIS/4934/1997; CIS/4965/1997; CIS/5232/1997; CIS/3767/1997
64 **IS** Reg 16(1) and (2) IS Regs
JSA Reg 78(1)-(2) JSA Regs
PC Reg 5(1)(a) SPC Regs
HB Reg 21(1) and (2) HB Regs; reg 21(1) and (2) HB(SPC) Regs
CTB Reg 11(1) CTB Regs; reg 11(1) CTB(SPC) Regs
65 CIS/1544/2001
66 Reg 9(1)(k) HB Regs; reg 9(1)(k) HB(SPC) Regs
67 Sch 3 para 9 HB&CTB(CP) Regs
68 Reg 1A(2) and (3) SFCWP Regs

4. **Prisoners**

69 Reg 3(1) SSP Regs; reg 9 SMP Regs; regs 18(c) and 27(1)(c) SPP&SAP(G) Regs
70 s113(1)(b) SSCBA 1992; reg 2(9) and (10) SS(GB) Regs; reg 10(2)(d) and Sch 2 para 7(b)(ii) SSB(Dep) Regs; R(S) 8/79
71 Reg 2(3) SS(GB) Regs

72 s113(1)(b) SSCBA 1992; reg 2 SS(GB) Regs
73 Reg 2(3) and (4) SS(GB) Regs; CSS/239/2007
74 s113(1)(b) SSCBA 1992
75 Reg 10(2)(d) and Sch 2 para 7(b)(ii) SSB(Dep) Regs
76 Reg 3(1) SSP Regs; reg 9 SMP Regs; regs 18(c) and 27(1)(c) SPP&SAP(G) Regs
77 Reg 2(2) and (8)(c) SS(GB) Regs; R(S) 1/71
78 Reg 3 SS(GB) Regs
79 CS/541/1950
80 Regs 2(6) and (7) and 3(1) SS(GB) Regs
81 Reg 2(7) SS(GB) Regs; para 12091 DMG
82 Reg 2(2) and (7) SS(GB) Regs
83 s113(1)(b) SSCBA 1992. Child benefit is not in Parts 2-5 of that Act.
84 Reg 2(5) SS(GB) Regs
85 Sch 9 para 1(a) SSCBA 1992; regs 16 and 17 CB Regs
86 **IS** Reg 21(3) IS Regs
JSA Reg 85(4) JSA Regs
PC Reg 1(2) SPC Regs
HB Reg 7(14) HB Regs; reg 7(14) HB(SPC) Regs
CTB Reg 8(5) CTB Regs; reg 8(5) CTB(SPC) Regs
87 **IS** Schs 1B para 22 and 7 para 8 IS Regs
PC Reg 6(2)(a), (3), (6)(c), (7), (9) and (10) SPC Regs
88 Reg 7(3) SPC Regs
89 Reg 6(3)(b) and (4) SPC Regs
90 **IS** Sch 7 para 2A IS Regs
PC Sch 3 para 2 SPC Regs
91 **IS** Sch 3 para 3(11)(c)(i) and (12) IS Regs
PC Sch 2 para 4(11)(c)(i) and (12) SPC Regs
HB Reg 7(16)(c)(i) and (17) HB Regs; reg 7(16)(c)(i) and (17) HB(SPC) Regs
CTB Reg 8(3)(c) and (4)(a) CTB Regs; reg 8(3)(c) and (4)(a) CTB(SPC) Regs
92 **HB** Reg 7(13) HB Regs; reg 7(13) HB(SPC) Regs
CTB Reg 8(3)(b) CTB Regs; reg 8(3)(b) CTB(SPC) regs
93 CSH/499/2006
94 **IS** Reg 21(3) and Sch 7 para 8(a) IS Regs
JSA Reg 85(4) JSA Regs
PC Regs 1(2) and 6 SPC Regs
HB Reg 7(14) and (15) HB Regs; reg 7(14) and (15) HB(SPC) Regs; R(IS) 17/93; HB Circular A22/04
CTB Reg 8(5) and (6) CTB Regs; reg 8(5) and (6) CTB(SPC) Regs
95 Reg 7(7) HB Regs; reg 7(7) HB(SPC) Regs; paras A3/3.430-32 GM
96 **IS** Sch 3 para 18(7)(g) IS Regs
JSA Sch 2 para 17(7)(g) JSA Regs
PC Sch 2 para 14(7)(e) SPC Regs
HB Reg 74(7)(f) HB Regs; reg 55(7)(f) HB(SPC) Regs
CTB Reg 58(8)(b) CTB Regs; reg 42(8)(b) CTB(SPC) Regs
97 **IS** Reg 16(3)(b) IS Regs
JSA Reg 78(3)(b) JSA Regs
PC Reg 5(1)(c)(ii) and (iii) SPC Regs
98 Reg 21(2) HB Regs; reg 21(2) HB(SPC) Regs
99 Reg 11(1) CTB Regs; reg 11(1) CTB(SPC) Regs
100 **HB** Reg 28 HB Regs; reg 31 HB(SPC) Regs
CTB Reg 18 CTB Regs; reg 21 CTB(SPC) Regs
101 **IS** Reg 16(2) IS Regs
JSA Reg 78(2) JSA Regs
PC Reg 5(1)(a) SPC Regs
HB Reg 21(1) and (2) HB Regs; reg 21(1) and (2) HB(SPC) Regs
CTB Reg 11(1) CTB Regs; reg 11(1) CTB(SPC) Regs
102 **IS** Sch 7 para 9(a)(v) IS Regs
JSA Schs 5 para 5(a)(vi) and 5A para 4(a)(vi) JSA Regs
103 Reg 7(5) HB Regs; reg 7(5) HB(SPC) Regs
104 **IS** Sch 3 para 3(11)(c)(i) and (12) IS Regs
JSA Sch 2 para 2(11)(c)(i) and (12) JSA Regs
PC Sch 2 para 4(11)(c)(i) and (12) SPC Regs
HB Reg 7(16)(c)(i) and (17) HB Regs; reg 7(16)(c)(i) and (17) HB(SPC) Regs
CTB Reg 8(3)(c) and (4)(a) CTB Regs; reg 8(3)(c) and (4)(a) CTB(SPC) Regs
105 Regs 14(1)(h) and 19(1)(h) JSA Regs
106 CIS/15611/1996
107 **IS** Reg 48(7) IS Regs
JSA Reg 110(7) JSA Regs

5. **People without accommodation**
108 **IS** Sch 7 para 6 IS Regs
JSA Schs 5 para 3 and 5A para 2 JSA Regs
109 *R(RJM) v Secretary of State for Work and Pensions* [2007] EWCA Civ 614, 28 June 2007, unreported. The claimant is seeking leave to appeal to the House of Lords.
110 para 24158 DMG
111 para 24159 DMG
112 R(IS) 23/98
113 para 24157 DMG
114 para 24162 DMG

6. **People involved in a trade dispute**
115 ss14 and 35(1), definition of 'week' JSA 1995
116 Reg 47(3)(e) JSA Regs
117 ss15 and 15A JSA 1995; reg 3D and Sch A1 para 17 JSA Regs
118 Sch 1B para 20 IS Regs
119 **IS** Reg 5(4) IS Regs; para 32677 DMG
JSA Reg 52(2) and (2A) JSA Regs; para 32676 DMG
120 paras 32678-79 DMG
121 Reg 6(4)(b) IS Regs; reg 53(g) and (gg) JSA Regs
122 s126 SSCBA 1992; ss14 and 35(1), definition of 'trade dispute' JSA 1995
123 s14(1) and (2) JSA 1995
124 R(U) 1/65; paras 32121-25 and 32160-61 DMG
125 Regs 13(2)(a)(i) and 15(a)(i) SS&CS(DA) Regs
126 Sch 2 paras 13 and 19 SS&CS(DA) Regs
127 R(U) 7/58; R(U) 1/87
128 para 32107 DMG
129 s14(4) and (5) JSA 1995; CU/66/1986(T)
130 R(U) 4/62; R(U) 1/70
131 s14(1)(b) JSA 1995
132 *Presho v Insurance Officer* [1984] (HL) (see R(U) 1/84); *Cartlidge v CAO* [1986] 2 All ER 1 (CA); R(U) 1/87
133 s14(3) JSA 1995
134 R(U) 6/74
135 **IS** s126(1) and (2) SSCBA 1992
JSA Reg 171 JSA Regs
136 **IS** s127(a) SSCBA 1992
JSA s15(4) JSA 1995
137 Reg 26(4) SS(C&P) Regs
138 s126(3)(a) and (d)(i) SSCBA 1992
139 s126(3)(b) and (d)(ii) SSCBA 1992
140 **IS** s126(3)(c) SSCBA 1992
JSA ss15(2)(a) and (b) and 15A(4) and (5) JSA 1995
141 **IS** s126(5)(b) and (7) SSCBA 1992
JSA ss15(2)(d) and 15A(5) JSA 1995; reg 172 JSA Regs
142 **IS** Sch 9 para 34 IS Regs
JSA Sch 7 para 36 JSA Regs
143 **IS** s126(5)(a)(ii) SSCBA 1992; reg 48(2) IS Regs
JSA ss15(2)(c)(i) and 15A(5) JSA 1995; reg 110(2) JSA Regs
144 **IS** s126(5)(a)(i) SSCBA 1992
JSA ss15(2)(c)(ii) and 15A(5) JSA 1995
145 **IS** Reg 41(3) and Schs 9 para 28 and 10 para 17 IS Regs
JSA Reg 104(3) and Schs 7 para 29 and 8 para 22 JSA Regs
146 **IS** Reg 48(9), (10)(a) and (c) and Schs 9 paras 15(3)(b) and 39 and 10 para 22 IS Regs
JSA Reg 110(9) and (10)(a) and (c) and Sch 7 paras 15(3)(b) and 41 and 8 para 27 JSA Regs
147 **IS** Reg 42(4) and Sch 9 para 21 IS Regs
JSA Reg 105(10) and Sch 7 para 22 JSA Regs
148 **IS** Reg 35(1)(d) IS Regs
JSA Reg 98(1)(c) JSA Regs
149 **IS** Reg 48(5) and (6) IS Regs
JSA Reg 110(5) and (6) JSA Regs
150 Sch 11 paras 2(g) and 7 SSCBA 1992
151 R(SSP) 1/86
152 **SMP**Reg 13 SMP Regs
SPP/SAP Reg 35 SPP&SAP(G) Regs; s35 JSA 1995
153 Note, however, that reg 13 SMP Regs was not amended when the JSA 1995 came into force.
154 s91 SSCBA 1992; s14 JSA 1995
155 s126(1) and (2) SSCBA 1992
156 Regs 3(1) and 6 SFM&FE Regs; s126 SSCBA 1992; s14 JSA 1995
157 SF Dir 26; s14 JSA 1995
158 SF Dir 8(1)(b); s14 JSA 1995
159 SF Dir 17(a) and (f); s14 JSA 1995
160 *R v HBRB London Borough of Ealing ex parte Saville* [1986] HLR 349
161 s127 SSCBA 1992
162 Reg 6(4)(b) and Sch 1B para 20 IS Regs
163 s127(b) SSCBA 1992
164 s127(a) SSCBA 1992; regs 35(1)(d), 41(3) and (4), 42(4) and 48(6) and (10) and Schs 9 paras 15, 21, 28 and 39 and 10 para 17 IS Regs
165 s127(c) SSCBA 1992; reg 18 SS(PAOR) Regs
166 Reg 26 SS(PAOR) Regs
167 Reg 22(2)-(4) SS(PAOR) Regs
168 Regs 20, 21 and 22(5)-(6) SS(PAOR) Regs
169 Reg 28 SS(PAOR) Regs
170 Reg 29 SS(PAOR) Regs
171 Regs 27 and 29 SS(PAOR) Regs
172 Reg 27(5) SS(PAOR) Regs

Part 4

Common benefit rules

Chapter 27

Work and benefits

This chapter covers:

This chapter covers the rules about full-time paid work for **income support (IS), jobseeker's allowance (JSA), pension credit, housing benefit (HB) and council tax benefit (CTB)**. The DWP calls this 'remunerative work'.

Entitlement to many benefits is affected by issues to do with work and employment. Most of these rules are specific to the benefit and are included in the relevant chapter in this *Handbook* (see below).

Deciding whether you are an employed earner or self-employed also affects both your national insurance contributions (see Chapter 31) and the way your income from earnings is assessed (see Chapters 35 and 36).

Other benefits and tax credits

Carer's allowance: You cannot qualify if you are gainfully employed. You count as gainfully employed if you earn more than a set amount each week (see p45).

Benefits for incapacity for work: You cannot qualify for benefits based on your incapacity for work (eg, incapacity benefit (IB)) in any week you actually do any work unless this is work you may do while claiming (see p662). Note that this also applies if you are getting IS on the basis that you are incapable of work. This rule may change when the employment and support allowance rules take effect (see Chapter 7).

Industrial injuries benefits: You must have been an employed earner when you had an accident or contracted a disease to be entitled (see p313).

Maternity allowance: You must satisfy an employment condition (see p435).

Statutory sick pay, statutory maternity pay, statutory paternity pay and **statutory adoption pay**: These are linked to you being employed (not self-employed) and in some cases you can get them even if your employment ends (see pp555 and 530).

Working tax credit (WTC): Full-time paid work affects WTC. See Chapter 50 for the rules on full-time paid work for WTC purposes.

In addition:

Benefits for children: You do not qualify for child benefit or guardian's allowance, or for an allowance in your HB or CTB (or if you have not yet claimed child tax credit, in your IS or income-based JSA) for a child who is aged 16 or over who does paid work for 24 hours a week or more.

Adult dependants' additions: Adult dependants' additions are affected by the adult dependant's earnings. See p690 for details.

1. The full-time paid work rule

If you work full time and are paid for the work, you count as being in what the DWP calls 'remunerative work'. This is called 'full-time paid work' in this *Handbook*. See p649 for what counts as paid work and p650 for how your hours are calculated. 'Work' includes self-employment and work which is done from home.

In some circumstances you may be treated as not in full-time paid work even if you are (see p654). In others, you may be treated as if you are in full-time paid work when you are not (see p653).

Full-time paid work affects income support (IS), jobseeker's allowance (JSA), housing benefit (HB), council tax benefit (CTB) and pension credit (PC) in different ways.

- You cannot usually qualify for **IS** or **JSA** if you are in full-time paid work.[1] Your partner's working hours do not affect your entitlement to *contribution-based* JSA, but you cannot get IS or *income-based* JSA if your partner is in full-time paid work.
- Work does not affect your eligibility for **HB, CTB** or **PC**. For HB and CTB, however, if you are in full-time paid work, this can affect the way your income is calculated – eg, whether you can get an additional earnings disregard (see pp855 and 887) or a childcare costs disregard (see pp856 and 888).
- If you have a **non-dependant living with you**, the amount of the non-dependant deduction made from your IS, JSA or PC housing costs and from your HB and CTB can be affected if your non-dependant is in full-time paid work (see pp815, 86 and 196).

Note: when the employment and support allowance (ESA) rules take effect (see Chapter 7), you will not be able to claim income-related ESA if you or your partner are in full-time paid work.[2] At the time this *Handbook* was written, full-time paid work for ESA purposes had not yet been defined. See www.cpag.org.uk/esa or CPAG's *Welfare Rights Bulletin* for updates.

Remember that whether or not you are in full-time or part-time paid work, income from work affects your entitlement to means-tested benefits. This means that, for IS and JSA, although your (or your partner's) hours of work are low enough for you to qualify (or for HB, CTB and PC it does not matter how many hours you work), you might not satisfy the means test.

If you or your partner *are* in full-time paid work you might be able to claim working tax credit (WTC). Different rules on what counts as full-time paid work apply for IS/JSA and WTC. So you may be able to choose whether to claim IS/JSA or WTC. You may be able to claim both IS/JSA/PC and WTC. For IS and JSA, this only applies in some situations – eg, if you are a 'term-time only' worker or you are off sick and getting statutory sick pay. See p657 for information about what you should consider.

Note: you cannot qualify for IS based on your incapacity for work in any week in which you do *any* work (even if this is part time) unless this is work you may do while claiming. See p662 for further information.

What counts as full-time work

You (and, for HB and CTB only, your partner) count as in full-time work if you work 16 hours or more a week.[3] For IS and income-based JSA (but not joint-claim JSA), your partner counts as in full-time paid work if s/he works 24 hours or more a week.[4] Your non-dependant counts as in full-time paid work if s/he works 16 hours or more a week.[5] See p650 for how the hours are calculated.

Note:

- For joint-claim JSA, you do not have to make a joint claim with your partner if s/he works 16 or more but less than 24 hours a week (see p382).[6]
- For HB and CTB, you and your partner may have to work more hours to benefit from an additional earnings disregard (see pp855 and 887).

What counts as paid work

Paid work includes work for which you are paid or expect to be paid – ie, you expect to get payment for the work you are doing, now or at some date in the future, even if no payment is finally made.[7] Some of the initial work necessary to set up a business may not count if it is unpaid preparatory work done with the hope for further work that will be paid.[8] The question of whether or not you are paid or working in expectation of payment has to be decided at the time the work is done, not, for example, at the end of the year or accounting period.[9]

You must have a real likelihood of getting payment, not just a hope or desire to make money – eg, a self-employed writer who has never sold a manuscript and has no publication agreement may be working without real expectation of payment and so is not in full-time paid work even if s/he spends a lot of time writing.[10]

If you have a business but it is not yet making money or has ceased to make a profit, you may count as working in expectation of payment if you are making drawings against future profit or if the business is likely to yield profit in the future. Ultimately, it depends on how viable your business is.[11] If there is no realistic possibility of it yielding a profit, the decision maker is likely to want to know why you are working for nothing.[12]

Paid work includes work for which you receive payment in kind (such as free meals or accommodation or free produce for farmworkers).[13] Note that payments in kind are generally not treated as 'earnings' but as other income which may be disregarded (see pp872 and 883).

How your hours are calculated

When calculating your hours, include all the hours you actually work for which you are paid or which you do in expectation of payment. If you do more than one job, add the total hours from each together. If you routinely do paid overtime, include those hours. If you work casually or intermittently – eg, you are a seasonal worker who works in the summer but you are unemployed the rest of the year, you can argue that it is only the hours you do when you are working that are relevant (but see p651 for information about 'term-time only' workers).[14] Bear in mind that:

- if your hours flucuate, the rules specify how your hours are averaged (see below);
- for IS and JSA only, paid lunch hours and breaks count towards the total hours you work;[15]
- for PC, HB and CTB, the rules do not say how to calculate your hours of work unless these fluctuate. However, for PC, the DWP says you should only count the hours for which you are paid or expect to be paid, including overtime, but not including paid breaks (eg, lunch or tea breaks). It says the word of the person who is doing the work should be accepted unless there is reason for doubt;[16]
- for JSA only, the hours that you or your partner spend caring for someone in the circumstances that allow you to claim IS as a carer (see p295) are ignored unless you are employed and are being paid to act as a carer.[17]

If you are unsure if you are in full-time paid work, see p652. You should appeal if you think your average hours have been calculated unfairly and this means you cannot claim the benefit or tax credit you want. You should work out first whether you are better off claiming IS/JSA or WTC (see p657). Likewise, you should appeal if your non-dependant's hours have been calculated unfairly and the DWP or local authority is making a non-dependant deduction that is too high.

If your hours fluctuate

If your hours fluctuate, an average of your weekly hours is calculated as follows.

- If you have a regular pattern of work, the average hours worked throughout each work 'cycle' is used – eg, if you regularly work three weeks on and one week off, your hours are the average over the four-week period.[18] Note that if you work casually or intermittently – eg, you are a seasonal worker who works in the summer but you are unemployed the rest of the year, you can argue that your work 'cycle' is that part of the year in which you are working and that you do not count as in full-time work when you are unemployed.[19]

- If you have a recognisable cycle of work that lasts for a year with periods where you do not work (eg, in an educational establishment) the 'term-time only' worker rule applies. See below for further information.
- If you do not have a recognisable cycle of work, the average over the five weeks immediately before the date of your claim (or for IS and JSA only, of a supersession decision) is used, or over a longer or a shorter period if this would give a more accurate average.[20] The five-week period may not be appropriate if the average is distorted because, for example, you have done a short period of overtime that is not typical or you have been off sick.[21]
- If you have just started work and no pattern of work is yet established or your working arrangements have changed and your previous work cycle no longer applies, the number of hours or average number of hours you are expected to work each week is used.[22] The decision can be revised or superseded if there is sufficient evidence to calculate the average of the actual hours you have been working.

'Term-time only' workers

If you have a recognisable cycle of work that lasts for a year (eg, in a school or an educational establishment where you have periods of school holidays or similar vacations where you do not work), the 'term-time only' worker rule applies. How the rule works depends on whether you are claiming JSA or IS, PC, HB or CTB. Note that this rule can also apply to other seasonal workers. However, if you work casually or intermittently and are unemployed the rest of the year, you can argue that this rule does not apply to you.[23] If your contract comes to an end before a period of absence from work, you should not count as a term-time only worker, unless you are expected to start work again and there is some commitment by you and your employer that this will happen.[24]

Sometimes it might not be clear whether you have a cycle of work that lasts a year – eg, if you have only started your job recently or have a fixed-term contract that finishes at the end of the school term or are employed on a casual or relief basis.[25] It takes time before it can be said that you have a yearly cycle of work.[26] However, if you have an indefinite contract to work in term-time only, the decision maker is likely to say that you have a yearly work cycle from the start.[27]

Income support, pension credit, housing benefit and council tax benefit

If you only work for part of a year, the average number of hours in the periods when you are actually working (eg, during term-time) determines whether you are in full-time paid work throughout the year.[28] People who work in schools, colleges or similar institutions and have long periods in which they do not work are affected by this rule.

In practice, if the average hours of work you do during term-time means you are in full-time paid work during term-time, you also count as being in full-time paid work over the school holidays, even if you do no work and are not paid. This means:

- if you or your partner count as in full-time paid work, you cannot claim IS during the school holidays. However, you might be able to claim JSA (see below). You should be able to claim WTC if you normally work sufficient hours each week (see Chapter 50);[29]
- if your non-dependant counts as in full-time paid work, higher rate non-dependant deductions may apply.

Jobseeker's allowance

If you only work for part of a year, the average hours over the whole cycle, including periods of no work, are used to decide whether you are in full-time work for the whole year.[30] However, you disregard weeks when you are:

- on paid holiday;
- absent from work because you are off sick or on maternity, paternity or adoption leave;
- absent from work without 'good cause' (see p653).

In practice, if the average hours of work you do over the whole cycle means you are not in full-time paid work, you can claim JSA. However, you may only qualify for income-based JSA during periods when your income is sufficiently low (eg, during unpaid summer holidays). Because the 'term-time only' worker rule is different for WTC, you could also claim WTC if you work sufficient hours each week during term time (see Chapter 50).

Example

Sheila is a school dinner worker. She works 20 hours a week, 38 weeks of the year. She gets four weeks' paid holiday, but otherwise is not paid when she is not working at the school. Her average hours are calculated as follows:

20 hours x 38 weeks = 760 hours. 52 weeks – 4 weeks' paid holiday = 48 weeks.

760 hours divided by 48 weeks = 15.84 average hours a week.

Sheila is not in full-time paid work and can claim JSA if her income is low enough. She might also qualify for WTC.

If you are unsure whether you are in full-time paid work

For IS and JSA, if you are unsure whether you are working for 16/24 hours or more **at the date of your claim**, you should make a further claim in a week when you are more certain. A claim for IS or JSA can only be backdated in limited circumstances (see p966). If you wait to make a second claim until your first claim is decided, you could lose out.

Alternatively, if you are refused WTC because you or your partner do not count as in full-time paid work for WTC purposes and within 14 days of that decision you claim IS or JSA, your claim for IS or JSA can be backdated to the date you claimed WTC.[31]

If your **circumstances change** while you are claiming:

- IS or JSA, you may be uncertain about whether you now count as in full-time paid work (eg, your average weekly hours change or you are now getting regular overtime). If it appears that you are now working 16/24 hours or more each week, report this to the DWP to avoid an overpayment of IS or JSA. You should also check to see if you qualify for WTC;
- HB or CTB, report this to the local authority. A change in your hours of work might affect your entitlement to an additional earnings, or a childcare costs disregard.

If your non-dependant's circumstances change while you are claiming HB or CTB (or help with housing costs in IS, JSA or PC), report this to the local authority (or DWP) to enable your non-dependant deduction to be adjusted.

2. People treated as in full-time paid work

You (or your partner) are treated as being in full-time work:

- if you (or your partner) normally work full time, but you are off work because of a recognised, customary or other holiday and there is a common intention that your employment will be resumed once the holiday is over.[32] Whether you count as on holiday depends on your contractual or legal entitlement to holiday. You can argue that you only count as on holiday if you are paid for it.[33] However, for jobseeker's allowance (JSA), even if you do not count as in full-time paid work because you are on unpaid leave, you are likely to have difficulty persuading the DWP that you are available for and actively seeking work (see Chapter 15).
  Remember that for income support (IS), pension credit, housing benefit and council tax benefit, if you are a full-time 'term-time only' worker and your cycle of work lasts a year, you are treated as in full-time work during the school holidays (see p651);
- if you (or your partner) are away from full-time paid work without 'good cause'.[34] What constitutes 'good cause' for these purposes is not defined in the regulations but all of your circumstances should be taken into account. Whether or not your employer has authorised the absence is not conclusive, although if it is authorised it is likely that you have good cause;

- for **IS** and **JSA**, if you (or your partner) stopped full-time paid work, but you are still within the period covered by payment in lieu of earnings or wages, or certain holiday pay (unless they can be disregarded).[35]
  Note that most earnings and payments *are* disregarded if your employment ends before entitlement to IS or JSA starts; you can claim IS or JSA as soon as you finish work and you are *not* treated as in full-time paid work. They are also disregarded if you are not treated as in full-time paid work, but your employment has not ended, so long as you have not been suspended.
  See p849 for details on final payments;
- for up to seven days if:
  - for **income-based JSA** (not including joint-claim JSA), your partner is involved in a trade dispute and s/he is not entitled to JSA in her/his own right because of this, unless you were receiving income-based JSA when s/he became involved.[36] You cannot get JSA at all if you are the person involved in a trade dispute (see p634);
  - for **joint-claim JSA**, you (or your partner) are involved in a trade dispute, unless you were receiving joint-claim JSA when you or your partner became involved;[37]
  - for **IS**, you or your partner are involved in a trade dispute.[38]

  See Chapter 26 for further information about entitlement to, and the amount of, IS or JSA during a trade dispute.

Your non-dependant can also be treated as in full-time paid work under the rules above.

3. People treated as not in full-time paid work

There are situations when you are treated as not in full-time paid work, even if you actually are. For income support (IS) and jobseeker's allowance (JSA), see below. For housing benefit (HB), council tax benefit (CTB) and pension credit (PC), see p656.

Income support and jobseeker's allowance

You (or your partner) are treated as *not* being in full-time paid work if:[39]

- you (or your partner) are on maternity, paternity or adoption leave or are absent from work because you are sick,[40] even if when you are not on leave or off sick you normally work 16/24 hours or more each week. You might also be able to claim working tax credit (WTC);
- you (or your partner) are working on a government training scheme and are being paid a training allowance;

- you (or your partner) are a volunteer or are working for a charity or voluntary organisation and are giving your services free (except for your expenses);
- you (or your partner) are providing care for someone who is staying with you but who is not normally a member of your household and you receive payments from a health authority, local authority or voluntary organisation for caring for them;
- you (or your partner) are disabled and because of this:
  - your earnings are 75 per cent or less than a person without your disability would reasonably expect to earn, working the same hours in that job, or in a comparable one in the area; *or*
  - you work 75 per cent or less hours than those a person without your disability would reasonably be expected to work in that job or in a comparable job in the area;
- you (or your partner) are a **foster carer** receiving a payment for fostering a child from a local authority, voluntary organisation or a care authority (in Scotland). Note that for WTC purposes, if you are working as a foster carer you can count as being in full-time paid work (see p1227). You may wish to consider how you would be better off financially;
- you (or your partner) work as a part-time firefighter, auxiliary coastguard, member of the Territorial Army or reserve forces, or member of a lifeboat crew;
- you (or your partner) are performing duties as a local authority councillor;
- you (or your partner) are in employment while living in a care home, an Abbeyfield home or an independent hospital. This also applies during temporary absences from the accommodation. You must need care because of your old age, disability, terminal illness or past or present mental disorder, alcohol or drug dependency;
- for **IS**, you qualify for mortgage interest run-on (see p823);
- for **JSA**, your partner (you or your partner in the case of joint-claim JSA) has been involved in a trade dispute for more than seven days (see p634);
- for **IS**, you (or your partner) have been involved in a trade dispute for more than seven days (see p634). This also applies for the first 15 days following your return to work after having been involved in a trade dispute. Note that IS paid following your return to work might be paid as a loan (see p640);
- for **IS**, you (or your partner) are caring for someone (see p295). Any hours of work that you do are ignored, not just the hours that you spend caring;
- for **IS**, you (or your partner) are working as a childminder in your home;
- the work you do is studying in connection with your course of education as a student;[41]
- the only payment you receive, or expect to receive, is a sports award from the Sports Council;
- you are receiving assistance in pursuing self-employment while on an employment zone programme or a programme under s2 Employment and Training Act 1973 or s2 Enterprise and New Towns (Scotland) Act 1990.[42]

Your non-dependant can also be treated as not in full-time paid work under the rules above.

Housing benefit, council tax benefit and pension credit

You (or your partner or non-dependant) are treated as *not* being in full-time paid work if:[43]

- you (or your partner or non-dependant) are on maternity, paternity or adoption leave or are absent from work because you are sick, even if when you are not on leave or off sick you normally work 16 hours or more each week. However, for HB and CTB, you and your partner *can* count as in full-time paid work on such leave to enable you to get an earnings disregard for childcare costs (see pp856 and 888);
- the only payment you (or your partner or non-dependant) receive is a sports award from the Sports Council.

In addition, you (or your partner or non-dependant) are treated as *not* being in full-time paid work in a benefit week, if in that week you (or s/he) are on IS or income-based JSA for more than three days.[44]

4. Self-employed people

Some self-employed people may work long hours for little financial reward, sometimes even making a loss. Nevertheless, if you are in full-time work and the work is done in expectation of payment, it counts as full-time paid work. The DWP counts payments from your business to meet living expenses, whether in cash or in kind, as payment for work unless the drawings are from the business capital.[45] If you simply invest in a business and do not help to run it you are not treated as self-employed.[46]

When calculating the number of hours you work each week, the decision maker counts all those necessary to run your business, including time you spend visiting potential customers, advertising or canvassing, bookkeeping and trips to wholesalers and retailers.[47] The hours spent on services for which you are paid count, but also other time which is essential for your business – eg, preparation time or unsuccessfully soliciting new customers.[48] The decision maker should accept your statement about the hours you work unless there is a reason for doubt.[49] The hours your partner spends helping you in your business do not affect your entitlement to *contribution-based* jobseeker's allowance (JSA), but if your partner works 24 hours a week or more you are not entitled to income support or *income-based* JSA.

5. Working tax credit, income support and jobseeker's allowance

Sometimes it is difficult to show that you count (or do not count) as in full-time paid work. This means that you may be refused both working tax credit (WTC) and income support (IS) or jobseeker's allowance (JSA) because of differences in the rules or because decision makers at the DWP and the Revenue interpret the rules differently. If this happens, appeal against both decisions and ask for the appeals to be heard consecutively so a tribunal can decide which benefit or tax credit is appropriate.

You might be able to claim WTC *or* IS/JSA if you have a partner and s/he works 16 hours or more a week. This is because your partner can work up to 24 hours a week if you are getting IS or income-based JSA.[50] There is no limit on the number of hours your partner can work if you are getting contribution-based JSA.

If you are a **childminder** working from home (for IS), or a **foster carer** (for IS and JSA), you are not treated as in full-time work (see p654). You may, therefore, be able to claim either IS/JSA or WTC if you work 16 hours or more a week. There are also generous rules on the calculation of income (see pp854 and 863).

In some situations you might be able to claim *both* IS or income-based JSA and WTC (eg, if you are a 'term-time only' worker or are off sick and getting statutory sick pay). However, whether you can be paid IS or JSA with WTC depends on your income.

Note:

- WTC counts in full as income for IS and income-based JSA.
- Only taxable JSA counts as income for WTC. Otherwise, IS and JSA are disregarded.[51]

Choosing which benefit or tax credit to claim

If you can choose whether to claim IS, JSA or WTC, you should check which passported benefits you lose or gain (see p5). Also remember to consider the following.

- You get free school meals if you claim IS or income-based JSA or are entitled to child tax credit (CTC) based on an annual income of £15,575 or less and are not getting WTC.
- Child maintenance you receive does not affect WTC and CTC, but can affect IS and income-based JSA.
- If you claim IS or income-based JSA, you can get help with your housing costs (see Chapter 34). These are not taken into account in working out your WTC and CTC.
- There is a capital limit for IS and income-based JSA, but not for WTC and CTC. Instead, income from capital (eg, taxable interest) is taken into account and

the first £300 of the total of this plus pension, foreign and notional income is disregarded (see Chapter 52).

- You can get help with your childcare costs if you claim WTC, but not if you claim IS or JSA.
- If your income in this tax year is higher than in the previous tax year, your awards of WTC and CTC are based on your previous year's income unless your current year's income is more than £25,000 more than this (see p1254).
- If you and your partner are responsible for any children and one of you works at least 16 hours a week, your hours are added together to work out if you can get a 30-hour element in your WTC (see p1237).

Notes

1. **The full-time paid work rule**

1 s124(1)(c) SSCBA 1992; s1(2)(e) JSA 1995
2 s1(2) and Sch 1 para 6(e) and (f) WRA 2007
3 **IS** Reg 5 IS Regs
JSA Reg 51 JSA Regs
HB Reg 6(1) HB Regs; reg 6(1) HB(SPC) Regs
CTB Reg 6(1) CTB Regs; reg 6(1) CTB(SPC) Regs
4 **IS** Reg 5(1A) IS Regs
JSA Reg 51(1)(b) JSA Regs
5 **IS** Regs 2(1) and 5 IS Regs
JSA Reg 51(1)(c) JSA Regs
HB Reg 6(1) HB Regs; reg 6(1) HB(SPC) Regs
CTB Reg 6(1) CTB Regs; reg 6(1) CTB(SPC) Regs
PC Sch 2 para 2(1) SPC Regs
6 Reg 3E(2)(g) JSA Regs
7 R(IS) 5/95; *Fiore v CAO*, 20 June 1995
8 *Kevin Smith v CAO*, 11 October 1994 (CA), reported as R(IS) 21/95
9 *CAO v Ellis*, 15 February 1995 (CA), reported as R(IS) 22/95; CTC/626/2001
10 R(IS) 1/93
11 *CAO v Ellis*, 15 February 1995 (CA), reported as R(IS) 22/95; CIS/434/1994
12 *CAO v Ellis*, 15 February 1995 (CA), reported as R(IS) 22/95
13 CFC/33/1993; R(FIS) 1/83
14 R(JSA) 1/07
15 **IS** Reg 5(7) IS Regs
JSA Reg 51(3)(a) JSA Regs
16 Ch78 App5 paras 21, 23, 30 and 47 DMG
17 Reg 51(3)(c) JSA Regs
18 **IS** Reg 5(2)(b)(i) IS Regs
JSA Reg 51(2)(b)(i) JSA Regs
PC Sch 2 para 2(4) SPC Regs
HB Reg 6(2)(a) HB Regs; reg 6(2)(a) HB(SPC) Regs
CTB Reg 6(2)(a) CTB Regs; reg 6(2)(a) CTB(SPC) Regs
19 R(JSA) 1/07
20 para 20322 DMG
IS Reg 5(2)(b)(ii) IS Regs
JSA Reg 51(2)(b)(ii) JSA Regs
PC Sch 2 para 2(2)(b) SPC Regs
HB Reg 6(2)(b) HB Regs; reg 6(2)(b) HB(SPC) Regs
CTB Reg 6(2)(b) CTB Regs; reg 6(2)(b) CTB(SPC) Regs
21 CFC/2963/2001
22 **IS** Reg 5(2)(a) IS Regs
JSA Reg 51(2)(a) JSA Regs
PC Sch 2 para 2(4) SPC Regs
HB Reg 6(4) HB Regs; reg 6(4) HB(SPC) Regs
CTB Reg 6(4) CTB Regs; reg 6(4) CTB(SPC) Regs
All R(IS) 8/95
23 R(JSA) 1/07
24 CJSA/3832/2006
25 R(JSA) 8/03

26 CIS/914/1997; CJSA/2759/1998
27 R(JSA) 5/02
28 **IS** Regs 2(2)(b)(i) and 5(3B) IS Regs
PC Sch 2 para 2(3) SPC Regs
HB Reg 6(3) HB Regs; reg 6(3) HB(SPC) Regs
CTB Reg 6(3) CTB Regs; reg 6(3) CTB(SPC) Regs
All *Stafford and Banks v CAO* [2001] UKHL 33 (HL), reported as R(IS) 15/01
29 Reg 7 WTC(EMR) Regs
30 Reg 51(2)(b)(i) JSA regs; reg 51(2)(c) JSA Regs disapplied in R(JSA) 4/03; R(JSA) 5/03
31 Reg 6(28) SS(C&P) Regs

2. **People treated as in full-time paid work**
32 **IS** Reg 5(3) IS Regs
JSA Reg 52(1) JSA Regs
PC Sch 2 para 2(5) SPC Regs
HB Reg 6(5) HB Regs; reg 6(5) HB(SPC) Regs
CTB Reg 6(5) CTB Regs; reg 6(5) CTB(SPC) Regs
All R(U) 1/62
33 R(JSA) 5/03; paras 20309 and 20410 and Ch78 App 5 paras 73 and 74 DMG
34 **IS** Reg 5(3) IS Regs
JSA Reg 52(1) JSA Regs
PC Sch 2 para 2(5) SPC Regs
HB Reg 6(5) HB Regs; reg 6(5) HB(SPC) Regs
CTB Reg 6(5) CTB Regs; reg 6(5) CTB(SPC) Regs
35 **IS** Reg 5(5) and (5A) IS Regs
JSA Reg 52(3) and (3A) JSA Regs
36 Reg 52(2) JSA Regs
37 Reg 52(2A) JSA Regs
38 Reg 5(4) IS Regs

3. **People treated as not in full-time paid work**
39 **IS** Regs 5(3A) and 6 IS Regs
JSA Regs 52(1) and 53 JSA Regs
40 CIS/621/2004
41 R(FIS) 1/86; CDWA/1/1992
42 **IS** Reg 2(1) IS Regs, definition of 'self-employment route'
JSA Reg 1(3) JSA Regs, definition of 'self-employment route'
43 **PC** Sch 2 para 2(7) and (8) SPC Regs
HB Reg 6(7) and (8) HB Regs; reg 6(7) and (8) HB(SPC) Regs
CTB Reg 6(7) and (8) CTB Regs; reg 6(7) and (8) CTB(SPC) Regs
44 **PC** Sch 2 para 2(6) SPC Regs
HB Reg 6(6) HB Regs; reg 6(6) HB(SPC) Regs
CTB Reg 6(6) CTB Regs; reg 6(6) CTB(SPC) Regs

4. **Self-employed people**
45 para 20237 DMG
46 CIS/649/1992
47 para 20265 DMG
48 R(FIS) 6/85; *Kazantzis v CAO* [1999], reported as R(IS) 13/99
49 para 20267 DMG

5. **Working tax credit, income support and jobseeker's allowance**
50 **IS** Reg 5(1A) IS Regs
JSA Reg 51(1)(b) JSA Regs
51 Reg 7(3) Table 3 paras 13, 16 and 17 TC(DCI) Regs

Chapter 28

Incapacity for work

This chapter covers:

This chapter explains how the DWP assesses whether you are incapable of work for the purposes of qualifying for:[1]

- incapacity benefit (IB);
- severe disablement allowance;
- income support (IS), if you are claiming this on the basis of being incapable of work;
- the disability premium within IS, housing benefit (HB) and council tax benefit (CTB) if your entitlement to the premium depends on you showing that you have been incapable of work;
- national insurance credits for incapacity.

A determination that you are capable or incapable of work for one of the above benefits also applies to claims for all the others[2] and also applies to a claim for jobseeker's allowance (JSA – see Chapter 15).[3]

The way your incapacity for work is assessed for the purpose of statutory sick pay (SSP) is explained in Chapter 24. The rules described in this chapter do not apply to SSP or to the assessment of your incapacity for work for the purpose of industrial injuries benefits (see Chapter 14).

If you are making a claim for a non-means-tested benefit, such as IB, on the basis of your incapacity for work you should also consider applying for IS, HB and CTB. If you qualify for them, these benefits may be paid in addition to your non-means-tested benefit, although any IB you receive will be treated as income when calculating your entitlement to IS, HB, or CTB. As it may take the DWP some time to decide whether you qualify for a non-means-tested benefit, you should also claim IS if you can, in case your application for IB is refused.

If you are claiming IS on the basis of being incapable of work, or a disability premium within your IS, HB, or CTB and you are not receiving SSP, the DWP or local authority expects you to claim IB. You should do this even if you know that you will not qualify for IB.

Employment and support allowance

At the time this *Handbook* was written, it was expected that in October 2008 the Government would introduce a new benefit, employment and support allowance (ESA). Once ESA is introduced, people making a new claim because they are too ill to work will need to claim ESA instead of IB (although they can still claim SSP). Although ESA will be a benefit for people who are too ill to work, it will not be paid on the basis of 'incapacity for work', but on the basis of 'limited capability for work'. See Chapter 7 for more details.

It is expected that people already on benefit (eg, IB or IS) on the basis of incapacity for work as described in this chapter will continue to receive those benefits on that basis until the Government decides to transfer exisiting claims to ESA, or assesses their current benefit on the basis of 'limited capability for work'. It is not known when this will be, but it is not expected to happen during 2008/09. For updates on ESA, see www.cpag.org.uk/esa or CPAG's *Welfare Rights Bulletin.*

1. Incapacity for work

For all benefits, except statutory sick pay (SSP) and industrial injuries benefits, the question of whether you are incapable of work is determined by one of two tests:

- the 'own occupation test', which applies for the first 28 weeks of your claim if you have a regular occupation when you fall ill (see p668); *or*
- the 'personal capability assessment', which applies after 28 weeks, or from the start of your claim if you do not have a regular occupation when you fall ill.

The DWP's Medical Service

The DWP has contracted a private company (referred to in this *Handbook* as the Medical Service (MS)) to provide a medical service for benefit purposes. The MS is able to use not only doctors, but other approved 'heathcare professionals' such as registered nurses, occupational therapists and physiotherapists, to carry out its work. The MS carries out medical examinations of claimants and provides advice on medical questions relating to incapacity and disability benefits. You may be asked whether you agree to details of your medical condition and history being given to the MS. It is not likely to be in your best interest to refuse to give your authorisation for this as decision makers rely heavily on the MS assessment of your condition when determining whether you are incapable of work, and the MS assessment may be incomplete if they have not been able to obtain information about your medical situation.

In addition, if you refuse to attend a medical examination by an MS examiner, a decision maker can treat you as capable of work, unless you have good cause for your refusal (see p678).

The MS and the DWP must ensure that any information they obtain about you remains confidential.

Treated as incapable of work

In certain circumstances you are treated as incapable of work without having to satisfy the own occupation test or the personal capability assessment.

In particular, you may be:

- deemed to be incapable of work (see p665); *or*
- exempt from the personal capability assessment (see p669); *or*
- treated as incapable of work after failing to satisfy the personal capability assessment because of 'exceptional circumstances' (see p673).

Work you may do while claiming

The general rule is that you cannot work and be incapable of work at the same time. With certain exceptions, even if it has been determined that you are incapable of work, you are treated as capable of work for any week (starting on a Sunday) in which you actually *do* work. (**Note:** this also applies if you work while appealing against a decision on your incapacity.) You are treated as capable of work for the whole week even if you do not work for the whole week. This applies whether or not you are paid for the work.[4]

However, you will only be treated as capable of work on the actual days that you work, rather than for the whole week, if you work:

- during the first week of your claim; *or*
- during the last week that you were incapable of work; *or*
- during any week when you are undergoing plasmapheresis, parenteral chemotherapy, or radiotherapy treatment, or regular weekly renal dialysis or total parenteral nutrition treatment.[5]

If the amount of work you do is so minimal that it can be regarded as trivial or negligible, you should not be treated as capable of work.[6] For example, a man who occasionally helped his florist wife to cut or pack a few flowers was not treated as capable of work as the work he did was considered negligible.[7]

In addition, the following kinds of work are allowed:[8]

- 'approved work' (ie, work on a trial basis for which you are not paid) that has been arranged in writing by the DWP and you are getting incapacity benefit (IB), income support (IS), severe disablement allowance (SDA), or any other benefit or increase (including a disability premium) or national insurance (NI) credits, on the basis of incapacity for work;

- the care of a spouse or civil partner, a partner (if you are a member of an unmarried or same-sex couple), a grandparent, grandchild, uncle, aunt, nephew, niece or a 'close relative' (parent, parent-in-law, son, son-in-law, daughter, daughter-in-law, step-parent, stepson, stepdaughter, brother, sister, or the spouse, civil partner or partner of any of the preceding people[9]);
- domestic work (ie, cooking and cleaning) in your own home;
- work which you do only to protect someone or prevent serious damage to property or livestock during an emergency;
- work as a local councillor;
- work (for a maximum of one day a week) as a member of an appeal tribunal, if you have been appointed because of your experience of disability issues (see p1110), or of the Disability Living Allowance Advisory Board;
- voluntary work if the work is not for a 'close relative' (see above) and if the only payment you receive for the work is to cover your reasonable expenses (but note that the mere fact that you do not accept a wage will not necessarily mean that you are a volunteer);[10]
- work done while receiving assistance in pursuing self-employment under s2 Employment and Training Act 1973 or s2 Enterprise and New Towns (Scotland) Act 1990 (test-trading);
- 'permitted' work (see below).

Permitted work[11]

'Permitted work' is work of any kind, which you can do:

- as part of a **treatment programme** under medical supervision while you are in hospital or regularly attending hospital as an outpatient, as long as you do not earn more than £88.50 a week; *or*
- for an unlimited period, as long as you do not earn more than £20 a week. This is called **permitted work lower limit** (in practice, because of the minimum wage the DWP expects you to be working under five hours a week); *or*
- for an unlimited period, as long as you do not earn more than £88.50 a week and you are in 'supported work' (see p664). This is called **supported permitted work**; *or*
- for up to 52 weeks (or indefinitely in certain circumstances – see below), as long as you work on average for less than 16 hours a week and do not earn more than £ 88.50 a week. This is called **permitted work higher limit**.

For the 16-hour rule see p664. For how your earnings are assessed see Chapter 35.

Permitted work higher limit

You can usually do this for up to 52 weeks. However, if you are exempt from the personal capability assessment under transitional rules or because you have a severe condition (see p669) then you can do this work indefinitely. Otherwise, you can do more permitted work higher limit if:

- since the beginning of the last 52-week period of such work, you have ceased to be entitled to IB or SDA, or (on the basis of incapacity for work) IS, housing benefit (HB), council tax benefit (CTB) or NI credits for a continuous period lasting more than eight weeks; *or*
- at least 52 weeks have passed since you last did such work.

Informing the DWP

There are no special rules about informing the DWP about doing permitted work, but you should inform the DWP as soon as possible if you are doing this work. This is because under general benefit rules you are required to report changes in your circumstances that you might reasonably be expected to know could affect your benefit (see p970).

Note: if the particular activities you carry out in your work suggest to the DWP that you might be capable of work, it may re-assess this.

Supported work

This means work which is supervised by someone employed by a public or local authority, or by a voluntary organisation, whose job it is to find work for people with disabilities. This could include work in a sheltered workshop or with help from social services. The DWP says that you do not have to have the person actually working alongside you, although the support should be ongoing and regular.

16-hour rule

Permitted work (see p663) may sometimes only be disregarded if you do such work for less than 16 hours a week.[12]

It is the average number of hours that you work which is important. Even if you work more than 16 hours in a week you are not treated as capable of work in that week if the average number of hours you normally work is less than 16. If you work for 16 hours or more in a week the decision maker should consider your average hours:

- if you have a normal work cycle, over the period of that cycle;
- otherwise, over the week in question and the four weeks before it.[13]

Only the hours you actually work (as opposed to the hours you are contracted to work) and weeks in which you actually do any work (as opposed to weeks of sickness or holiday) should count.[14]

Although you will not be considered to be capable of work simply because you are doing any of the above types of work, if you are claiming IS the type of work that you do and any earnings you receive may still affect your entitlement. If the work is done for payment or in expectation of payment and you work for 16 hours or more a week, you will not qualify for IS (see p649) unless you can be treated as not being in full-time work (see p649). See p846 for details of how earnings may affect your entitlement to IS.

Deemed incapacity

When either the own occupation test or the personal capability assessment applies to you (see pp667 and 668), you are deemed to be incapable of work:[15]

- if you have been given notice in writing, under specific legislation, to refrain from work because you are a carrier of, or have been in contact with, an infectious disease; *or*
- if you are receiving inpatient treatment (including nursing) at a hospital or in a 'similar institution'; *or*
- on days when you are receiving plasmapheresis, parenteral chemotherapy, or radiotherapy treatment or regular weekly renal dialysis or total parenteral nutrition treatment; *or*
- on days when you are pregnant and there would be a serious risk to your health or your baby's health:
  - when the own occupation test applies to you, if you continue to work in your own occupation; *or*
  - when the personal capability assessment applies, if you work in any occupation; *or*
- if you are pregnant or have recently had a baby; *and*
  - you would not be entitled to either maternity allowance or statutory maternity pay were you to make a claim; *and*
  - you are within the period beginning with the first day of the sixth week before the expected week of childbirth (see p442) or beginning with the actual day of childbirth if that is earlier, and ending on the 14th day after the date you had the baby; *and*
  - you have a medical certificate giving your expected date of childbirth or your actual date of childbirth; *or*
- if you are a 'welfare to work' beneficiary (see p666), in which case you can be treated as incapable of work without having to satisfy the own occupation test or personal capability assessment for up to 91 days if:[16]
  - in your last period of incapacity for work (see p264) you were either assessed under the personal capability assessment (or all-work test) and found to be incapable of work, or you were exempt from the personal capability assessment (or all-work test) for one of the reasons described on p669 (but not for the reasons given in the first two bullet points in that section); *and*
  - you submit a medical certificate to the DWP confirming that you are incapable of work; *and*
  - the days fall within your 104-week linking period or within the first 13 weeks after the end of the 104-week linking period.

The 91 days do not need to be consecutive and so can be separated by days when you work or are not incapable of work. If you are incapable of work for more than 91 days within the above period you will have to satisfy the own occupation test or the personal capability assessment from the 92nd day of your incapacity for work (unless you can be treated as incapable of work for another reason).

'Welfare to work' beneficiary

You are a 'welfare to work' beneficiary if:[17]

- you have stopped receiving a benefit (except SSP) to which you were entitled on the basis of being incapable of work (see p665) after being incapable of work for a period of more than 196 days. The 196 days can include days of incapacity for SSP – known as your 'last period of incapacity for work' (you do not have to have been receiving benefit for all of the 196 days). The 196 days do not need to fall consecutively, as two or more periods of incapacity for work can be linked if they are separated by eight weeks or less – the days within each period of incapacity count towards the 196-day total; *and*
- your benefit stopped on or after 5 October 1998; *and*
- you are within the 104-week period which runs from the first day after the end of that period of incapacity for work (called the 104-week linking period); *and*
- within a month of your entitlement to benefit stopping you start a training course for which you receive a training allowance, or you start work and you are paid for that work or you expect to be paid.

Even if you satisfy these conditions you will not be a 'welfare to work' beneficiary if:

- your 'last period of incapacity for work' (see p264) ended because you were found to be capable of work and either you did not appeal against this or you appealed but did not win your appeal; *or*
- the work that you have started within a month of your benefit stopping is work that you can do while still being considered incapable of work (see p663).

You will have been receiving benefit based on your incapacity for work if you were receiving IB, SDA, IS on the basis of your incapacity for work, NI credits for incapacity for work (see p728), or a disability premium within your IS, HB or CTB paid on the grounds that you are incapable of work.[18]

The 104-week linking period

You are only a 'welfare to work' beneficiary for a fixed 104-week period running from the day after the end of your last 'period of incapacity for work' (see p264). This 104-week period is not affected by whether or not you have periods of incapacity for work within it.

If you are a 'welfare to work' beneficiary, as well as being treated as incapable of work for up to 91 days in the circumstances described on p665, you can immediately return to the same benefit and the same level of benefit that you were receiving before you started work or training, as long as you become incapable of work again within your 104-week linking period. Once your 104-week linking period ends you are no longer considered to be a 'welfare to work' beneficiary. In order to qualify again you will need to satisfy all the rules (see p666).

2. The own occupation test

If you cannot be deemed to be incapable of work (see p665), your incapacity for work will be determined by the 'own occupation test' for the first 28 weeks of your incapacity for work if you have a regular occupation when you become ill or disabled (see below). The **'own occupation test'** is a test of:

> whether [you are] incapable by reason of some specific disease or bodily or mental disablement of doing work which [you] could reasonably be expected to do in the course of the occupation in which [you were] engaged.[19]

'Specific disease' means a disease that has been identified by medical science.[20] A disease is a departure from health capable of identification by its signs and symptoms.[21] If you do not have a specific disease, you may still satisfy the own occupation test if your incapacity for work arises from a bodily or mental disablement.

When the own occupation test applies

The own occupation test applies to you if you have a regular occupation when you become incapable of work. You have a regular occupation if, in the 21 weeks immediately before the start of your period of incapacity for work, you did paid work for more than eight weeks in at least one occupation, for at least 16 hours a week.[22] Paid work includes work done in expectation of payment even if no payment is received. If you have more than one occupation which qualifies under the above rules the test applies to the most recent unless they ended in the same week, in which case you must satisfy the test in each of them.[23]

The own occupation test applies for the first 196 days of your period of incapacity for work (see p668). When calculating this 196-day period you only count days:[24]

- when you were incapable of work; *or*
- when you are treated as incapable of work; *or*
- when you were entitled to statutory sick pay (SSP); *or*
- which fall within a maternity allowance period (see p435).

A '**period of incapacity for work**' in this context means four or more consecutive days of incapacity (unless you are undergoing certain forms of treatment such as renal dialysis – see p665 – when the period of incapacity means two or more days of incapacity in any seven consecutive days).

Any two periods of incapacity for work are linked together if they are separated by a period of eight weeks or less. Your days of incapacity in your earlier period of sickness are added to those in your current period of sickness.

After the first 196 days of incapacity for work, the personal capability assessment applies (see below). The Medical Service (MS) may start the process of a personal capability assessment (see below) even while your incapacity still falls to be assessed under the own occupation test. This could be up to 10 weeks before the own occupation test ceases to apply to you. The intention is to ensure that a decision can be made under the personal capability assessment as soon as it applies to you.[25]

Evidence of incapacity for the own occupation test

For the first seven days of your incapacity for work the DWP usually accepts a self-certification of your sickness. After seven days you are required to provide a medical certificate (Med 3 or 5) from your doctor. If it is unreasonable to expect you to provide a medical certificate, the DWP should accept other evidence if this is sufficient to show that you should not work because of some specific disease or bodily or mental disablement.[26] The decision maker (see p1057) also has the right to request additional information relating to your incapacity for work in your own occupation if this is reasonable.[27]

Either the decision maker or the MS doctor (or other approved healthcare professional) can ask you to attend a medical examination. If you fail to attend, without good cause, you can be treated as capable of work. In these circumstances, if no decision has been made on your claim, it will be refused. If you are already receiving benefit on the basis of incapacity for work your entitlement to benefit will be revised or superseded and your benefit will stop (see p678).

3. The personal capability assessment

After 196 days of incapacity for work, or from the start of your claim if the own occupation test does not apply to you, your incapacity for work is determined by the 'personal capability assessment'. The '**personal capability assessment**' is an assessment of:

> the extent to which a person who has some specific disease or bodily or mental disablement is capable of performing prescribed activities, or is incapable of performing them because of that specific disease or bodily or mental disablement.[28]

See p667 for the meaning of 'specific disease'.

Apart from being deemed incapable of work (see p665), there are three main ways of being incapable of work under the personal capability assessment:

- being **exempt** from the assessment;
- satisfying the assessment by **scoring sufficient points**;
- being treated as satisfying the assessment because an **'exceptional circumstance'** applies.

The assessment is carried out by the Medical Service (MS) but the decision on whether you are incapable of work is taken by a decision maker from the DWP. You will normally be required to be examined by an MS doctor who will prepare an incapacity report for the decision maker. The report gives details of your ability to carry out the prescribed activities.

Treated as incapable of work before the assessment

You are treated as incapable of work until the assessment is carried out, as long as you continue to provide medical certificates.[29] However, if in the last six months you have been found to be capable of work under the own occupation test or the personal capability assessment, you are only treated as incapable of work while waiting for your personal capability assessment if:

- you have a specific disease or physical or mental disability which you did not have when it was decided that you were capable of work; *or*
- your condition has significantly worsened since you were found to be capable of work; *or*
- you were treated as capable of work because you failed to return the incapacity for work questionnaire (see p674) and you have since returned it.

If you cannot be treated as incapable of work while waiting for a personal capability assessment to be carried out, you can claim benefit again on the basis of your incapacity for work but the DWP can delay payment until you have been assessed again and found to be incapable of work. The DWP should not say that you cannot claim again, and it must arrange for another assessment.[30] You may be sent another questionnaire to complete and you may be required to attend another medical, unless the decision maker considers that there is already sufficient evidence to show that, on the balance of probabilities, you are still not incapable of work.[31]

Exempt from the personal capability assessment

You are exempt from the personal capability assessment if one of the following applies to you.[32]

You are exempt under **transitional rules** if you were receiving severe disablement allowance (SDA) on 12 April 1995 and your spell of incapacity for work has continued since then and you continue to send medical certificates to the DWP.

You are also exempt if you have a **severe condition** – ie:

- you are assessed as at least 80 per cent disabled for the purposes of SDA (see Chapter 20);
- you receive the highest rate of the care component of disability living allowance (see p108);
- you are terminally ill (see p107);
- you are registered as blind;
- you have tetraplegia, paraplegia (including uncontrollable involuntary movements or ataxia which render you functionally paraplegic), dementia or are in a persistent vegetative state;
- you are getting disablement benefit (see p324) based on an assessment of at least 80 per cent disablement;
- you are getting constant attendance allowance paid at a rate which is higher than the 'lower weekly rate' (see p326);
- there is 'medical evidence' (see below) to show that you have:
  - a severe learning disability involving severe impairment of intelligence and social functioning caused by the arrested or incomplete physical development of the brain or severe brain damage;
  - a severe and progressive neurological or muscle-wasting disease;
  - an active and progressive form of inflammatory polyarthritis;
  - progressive impairment of cardio-respiratory function which severely and persistently limits effort tolerance;
  - dense paralysis of the upper limb, trunk and lower limb on one side of the body;
  - severe irreversible motor sensory and intellectual deficits from the multiple effects of impairment of function of the brain or nervous system;
  - a severe and progressive immune deficiency state characterised by the occurrence of severe constitutional disease, opportunistic infections or tumour formation;
  - a severe mental illness which severely and adversely affects your mood or behaviour and which severely restricts your social functioning or your awareness of your immediate environment.

The '**medical evidence**' could be:

- evidence from an MS doctor (see p661); *or*
- evidence from any other doctor, a hospital or a similar institution; *or*
- parts of such evidence which is most reliable in the circumstances.[33]

See p665 for other circumstances in which you can be treated as incapable of work under the personal capability assessment.

Scoring points

If you are not exempt, and you cannot be deemed to be incapable of work in the circumstances detailed on p665, you have to satisfy the personal capability assessment in order to be considered incapable of work. This usually means scoring sufficient points, although some people who do not can still be treated as incapable of work (see p673).

The assessment is carried out without refering to any job and does not take into account your education and training, or any language or literacy problems.

The assessment of your incapacity for work under the personal capability assessment is a test of your ability to perform certain activities. There are two lists of activities: one physical and the other mental. The test is set out in full in Appendix 4.

Under each activity, there is a further list of what are called 'descriptors'. These are designed to measure the level of difficulty you have performing the activities to which they relate. Each descriptor has a number of points allocated to it.

To satisfy the test, you have to score either:[34]

- 15 points from the physical activities list; *or*
- 10 points from the mental activities list; *or*
- 15 points if you are combining scores from both the mental and physical activities lists (but see p672).

When calculating your score:

- you can only score points in respect of *one* descriptor within each physical activity (the one you score highest on) but you can score points for every mental descriptor you satisfy, regardless of whether they relate to the same activity;[35]
- you cannot score points in respect of both physical activities 1 (walking) and 2 (walking up and down stairs) – only the highest descriptor you score on from either activity counts.[36]

Physical and mental health problems

The physical descriptors can only apply if your difficulty in performing the activities arises from a specific bodily disease or disablement.[37] The mental health descriptors can only apply to you if your difficulty in performing the activities arises from a mental illness or disablement.[38] However, if your incapacity has a mental origin but results in a specific bodily disablement that restricts your physical functions, you may score points for that under the physical descriptors.[39]

Aids and appliances

Your ability to perform any of the activities is assessed as if you were wearing any prosthesis or other aid or appliance that you normally wear or use.[40] So, for example, if you have an artificial leg and have no problem climbing stairs when you are wearing it, you will score 0 for that activity even though without it you may not be able to climb stairs at all.

Combining scores from the physical and mental activities lists

If you score points in both lists, you can combine your points. When you are combining points in this way, the calculation of the points for mental activities is adjusted so that:

- a score of between 6 and 9 points (inclusive) from the mental activities list counts as 9;
- a score of less than 6 from the mental activities list is completely disregarded.

Example

Carolyn has arthritis in her hands and cannot turn a tap or control knobs on a cooker with one hand (Activity 7, Descriptor (f)). For this she scores 6 points.

In addition she has a depressive mental illness which means that she:

– needs encouragement to get up and dress (Activity 16, Descriptor (a) – 2 points);

– does not care about her appearance and living conditions (Activity 16, Descriptor (d) – 1 point);

– avoids carrying out routine activities because she is convinced they will prove too tiring or stressful (Activity 17, Descriptor (c) – 1 point);

– is unable to cope with changes in daily routine (Activity 17, Descriptor (d) – 1 point).

Carolyn's total score for mental activities is 5. Because this is less than 6, and she is combining scores from both the physical and mental activities lists, her score from the mental activities list is ignored for the purposes of the assessment and her total score is the 6 points she scored for her physical disability. Carolyn is not incapable of work according to the assessment.

Suppose, however, that in addition she feels too frightened to go out on her own (Activity 18, Descriptor (f) – 1 point). Her total score for mental activities is now 6 but because it is to be added to her score from the physical activities list it counts as 9. Her total score is therefore 15 (9 for mental activities + 6 for physical activities). She is incapable of work.

Interpretation of the descriptors

None of the words used in the descriptors are defined and so should be given their ordinary, everyday meaning. Some of the descriptors, however, have been the subject of appeals to the social security commissioners (see p1120) and their interpretations are binding on decision makers and tribunals. For the latest caselaw, see CPAG's *Welfare Benefits and Tax Credits Law Online,* Volume 1 of Sweet & Maxwell's *Social Security: legislation* and CPAG's *Welfare Rights Bulletin* (see Appendix 3).

Good and bad days, pain and tiredness

If your condition fluctuates, so that on good days you can perform an activity but on bad days you cannot, the decision maker (or appeal tribunal – see p1111) should adopt a broad and reasonable approach rather than a literal one. S/he should consider your normal capacity to perform an activity with reasonable regularity taking account of the limits imposed by pain and fatigue. So, if you normally cannot walk up and down a flight of 12 stairs when called to do so, this descriptor applies to you even if you could on occasion manage to do so.

Your ability to perform an activity should be considered in the light of your ability over a period of time that gives a true and fair picture of your condition,[41] not just on a day-by-day basis.[42]

A descriptor should apply to you if you cannot perform the activity most of the time. The decision maker should consider the severity of your condition on your good and bad days, the frequency of your good and bad days, and the unpredictability of the bad days. So, if in a normal week you would have three bad days when you would meet a particular descriptor and four good days when you would nearly meet it, that descriptor may apply to you, especially if your condition is very bad on the bad days.[43]

If you have long periods of remission you may be considered capable of work during those periods. Whether this is the correct approach will depend on the severity of your condition and the length of your periods of ill health and your periods of remission.[44] If your periods of remission are short, for example, you could argue that your ability to perform the activities should be considered across a period of time that is representative of your situation as a whole.

In deciding whether you can normally perform an activity, matters such as pain, fatigue and the increasing difficulty you may have performing an activity on a repeated basis compared with someone in good health should be taken into account.[45] 'Pain' might include nausea and dizziness.[46] The decision maker or tribunal should consider whether you could perform the activity without too much discomfort and whether you can repeat the activity within a reasonable time.[47]

Any risk to your health in performing an activity should be considered, particularly if carrying out the activity is against medical advice. If the risk to your health is sufficiently serious you may be considered incapable of the activity.[48]

Exceptional circumstances

Even if your points score is not sufficiently high, you can still be treated as incapable of work in certain '**exceptional circumstances**'. You are treated as incapable of work if:[49]

- you have a severe uncontrolled or uncontrollable life-threatening disease, and you have medical evidence to show this. There must be a reasonable cause for it not to be controlled by a recognised therapeutic procedure; *or*
- you have a previously undiagnosed, potentially life-threatening condition (eg, cancer or ischaemic heart disease) which is discovered for the first time by the MS doctor; *or*

- you have medical evidence stating that you are likely to undergo a major operation or other major therapeutic procedure within three months of the date of the medical examination carried out by an MS doctor for the purpose of the personal capability assessment (see p676); *or*
- from 8 November 2002, there would be a substantial risk to the mental or physical health of any person were you to be found capable of work.[50] The 'substantial risk' may be that which would arise from the sort of work you would be required to be available for were you to be claiming jobseeker's allowance. But the risk can arise from broad factors such as, in mental disablement cases, apprehension caused by the need to look for work.[51]

The personal capability assessment procedure

The questionnaire

Unless you are exempt (see p669) or you are deemed to be incapable of work (see p665), you are sent an incapacity for work questionnaire (an IB50 form) to complete. When the personal capability assessment is first applied to you during your period of incapacity for work you are also asked to get Form Med 4 from your GP, which you should return with the questionnaire. Although it is advisable, returning the Med 4 form is not compulsory. Even if you do not return it, the decision maker can still proceed with the personal capability assessment.[52]

If the information on your original claim form, or your medical certificates, suggests that you have mental health problems, the DWP will write to your own doctor before sending you a questionnaire to assess whether those problems are severe. If they are, you should be exempt from the personal capability assessment. If the decision maker decides that you are exempt, you are not sent a questionnaire. If your mental health problems are thought to be mild or moderate, a questionnaire is issued in the normal way.

Failing to return the questionnaire

You have six weeks from the date the questionnaire is sent to you to return it. If you have not returned it, a reminder must be sent to you at least four weeks after the questionnaire was sent. You must then be given a further two weeks from the date the reminder was sent to return the questionnaire. If you still have not returned the questionnaire in time you are treated as capable of work unless you can show that you had good cause for not returning it.[53]

When deciding whether you have 'good cause' the decision maker must consider all of the circumstances, including:[54]

- whether you were outside Great Britain at the relevant time;
- your state of health;
- the nature of your disability.

If your benefit stops because you are treated as capable of work as a result of your failure to return the questionnaire, but you have a good reason for not having done so, write to the DWP asking it to revise the decision (see p1065). You should send the completed questionnaire and explain why you were unable to send it in time. You should also make a fresh claim for benefit. If the decision maker decides that you did not have good cause you can appeal (see Chapter 42).

If you are exempt (see p669), or you are deemed to be incapable of work (see p665), you are not required to complete a questionnaire. In addition, if the decision maker has sufficient information to determine whether you are incapable of work then a questionnaire is not required.[55]

Completing the questionnaire

- Read the notes on the form before answering the questions. It may be helpful to draft your answers on a separate sheet of paper first.
- If you have difficulty in writing and have asked someone else to fill in your questionnaire, or have only been able to complete it slowly and with pain, you should explain this on the questionnaire.[56]
- Include details of why you cannot perform particular activities to allow the decision maker to understand fully your condition and how it affects you.
- If you have to appeal, the appeal tribunal may be less likely to believe you have symptoms that you did not mention on the questionnaire. It may be worth letting someone who knows you well check your answers.
- If you have 'good' and 'bad' days (see p672), explain this. Answer the question on the basis of what you can do on your bad days and then give a fuller answer in the space provided, explaining about the good days too. If necessary, give a rough estimate of how often you would be able to perform the activity and how often you would not.
- Compare the draft of your answers with the list in Appendix 4 and work out your score. If your score suggests that you fail the assessment, it may be difficult to persuade the DWP or an appeal tribunal that you should pass it. Your answers should not be exaggerated, but you should check that you have not underestimated any of your problems and that you have given all the detail you can in the space provided.
- If you have difficulties with English or with reading or writing it is vital that you get independent help before you submit the form.
- If someone has helped you fill in the form put in their details at the end where it asks if someone has filled in the form for you – this is an indication of the level of help you need.
- Always make a copy of your answers before you return the original questionnaire to the DWP.

On receiving your completed questionnaire the decision maker considers whether your answers or the information on the Med 4 form which your doctor has completed (see p674) indicate you are exempt from the personal capability assessment (see p673). The DWP may request further information from your doctor about this. If you do not appear to be exempt the decision maker provisionally assesses your score on the personal capability assessment from the information you have given. If your score indicates that you are not incapable of work, your case is referred to the MS (see p676) for a medical examination to be arranged. If your score indicates that you are incapable of work, your case is referred to the MS for 'medical scrutiny'. If it appears that any of the mental health descriptors apply to you, you are asked to attend a medical examination.

Medical scrutiny

A doctor (or other approved healthcare professional) from the MS (see p661) considers the answers you have given on your questionnaire and any other medical evidence that is held. If the MS decides that your answers are consistent with the medical evidence and you score sufficient points to be considered incapable of work, it can refer your case back to the decision maker without examining you. If the medical evidence cannot confirm your level of disability, you are asked to attend a medical examination.

Medical examinations

If you have to attend a medical examination, an appointment is made for you to be examined by an MS doctor (or other approved healthcare professional). The booking for the appointment may be made by telephone. Bear in mind the following.

- If you fail to attend an examination without having good cause you are treated as capable of work (see p678).
- If you cannot attend the medical examination, you should immediately contact the MS to explain why and to ask for another appointment.
- If you are too ill to travel, you should ask to be examined at home.
- You can claim your travel expenses for going to the medical examination. If you have to attend by taxi or minicab (eg, because you are too ill to travel in any other way or there is no public transport available) the DWP will not pay your fares unless you get permission before you travel.
- You can take a friend or adviser to the medical examination with you.

In order to complete a report on your incapacity for work, the doctor (or other approved healthcare professional) asks you about your condition and assesses whether, in her/his opinion, you are incapable of work. S/he considers your degree of incapacity in each of the specific areas of activity set out in Appendix 4. S/he is supposed to consider all the information and reach her/his own judgement on the basis of:

- your answers to the questions on the incapacity for work questionnaire (see p674);
- what you tell her/him;
- the results of the examination and any tests s/he may carry out;

- your appearance and behaviour during the assessment. This does not just mean during the examination itself. For example, when the doctor (or other approved healthcare professional) greets you in the waiting area, s/he can assess your ability to walk and to rise from a chair.

The MS examiner asks about your 'typical' day and uses the information you give to assess your ability to perform activities relevant to the personal capability assessment. If you talk about doing your shopping the examiner may form an opinion on your ability to lift and carry, or if you discuss doing the cleaning this will be relevant to the assessment of your ability to bend and reach. For this reason, if it is painful for you to do such tasks, or you have to use special equipment, you should explain this.

The examiner has to complete an incapacity report indicating which descriptors s/he thinks apply to you. The report is then returned to the decision maker dealing with your claim.

MS examiners are told to carry out mental health assessments when:

- you have a mild or moderate mental health problem;
- you are taking medication which impairs your cognitive function;
- you have an alcohol or drug dependency problem which significantly impairs your mental function;
- you have certain physical or sensory disabilities which impair your cognition and/or your mental function – eg, tinnitus;
- you have mild or moderate learning difficulties;
- a previously unidentified mild or moderate mental health problem is discovered during the assessment.

At the medical examination you should bear in mind the following.

- Tell the MS examiner in as much detail as possible exactly what is wrong with you and how it affects you. If you do not do so, something important may be missed and if you have to appeal, the tribunal may be less willing to accept that you have symptoms which you did not mention.
- Be sure to take with you the medicines and other aids you are taking or using. This may lead the examiner to ask questions which s/he would not otherwise have thought of.
- If you suffer from pain and you anticipate that attending the examination will increase that pain, you may be tempted to take additional painkillers. If possible, it is better not to do this as they may mask your true condition and not allow the MS examiner to see what you are like when you are on your normal dosage of medication. If you have to take additional painkillers you should explain this, and explain what you can and cannot do when on your normal dosage.
- The place where you are examined is likely to be a very artificial environment and there is only limited time. This may affect the judgement of your abilities.

For example, you may be able to bend once or twice on request without pain but you know that if you bend for lengthy periods, or repeatedly, you experience intense discomfort. If that is the case, say so.
- Similarly, if you have good and bad days and you are seen on a good day, be sure to explain how you are on a bad day.
- When asked about the activities you perform on a 'typical day' be sure to explain how your condition affects your ability to carry out day-to-day activities, such as going shopping, doing the chores, washing and dressing and watching TV.
- If you are not fluent in English, it is vital that someone with a good knowledge of English goes with you. Alternatively, the MS should be able to provide (and pay for) an interpreter if you request one.[57]

If, after you the examination, you are unhappy with the way it went, write down what the MS examiner said and did, and what you are unhappy about before your memory fades. This may be helpful for your adviser if there has to be an appeal. If you beleive you were treated unfairly or rudely at the examination, you can make a complaint (ask the MS for a copy of its leaflet on this).

The MS examiner will also carry out a capability report to assess your capabilities and limitations over a range of work-related activities. This report is not used in any way to assess your incapacity for work and is not sent to the decision maker. It is only sent to your personal adviser at Jobcentre Plus to consider when looking at your work prospects.

Failing to attend a medical examination

You must be sent notice of the date and time of your medical examination at least seven days beforehand, unless you have agreed to receive less notice than this. If you then fail to attend, you are treated as capable of work unless you can show that you had 'good cause' for not attending.[58]

In deciding whether you have good cause the decision maker must consider all the circumstances including those detailed on p674. Good cause may also include being too ill or distressed to be examined on that day, or wishing to be examined by someone of the same gender and this is not possible. You may also be able to show that you had good cause if your refusal to attend was based on a firm religious conviction.[59]

If you are treated as capable of work because you fail to attend the medical examination without good cause, your benefit is stopped. You should write to the DWP asking it to revise its decision (see p1065) explaining why you were unable to attend the examination. In case the decision maker does not accept that you had good cause you should also submit a fresh claim for benefit. If the decision maker does not accept that you had good cause you should consider appealing (see Chapter 42).

The decision maker's decision

The report prepared by the MS on your incapacity for work is sent to the DWP decision maker. It is the decision maker, and not the person from the MS, who makes the decision on whether you are incapable of work.[60] The decision maker is free to disagree with the person from the MS, although this is rare.

The decision maker considers the information in the incapacity report from the MS, the information you have given on your questionnaire, the information given by your doctor, and any other related evidence. Using this information s/he assesses your score under the personal capability assessment.

The person who examined you includes in her/his report a suggested date when your incapacity for work should be considered again. There are no detailed guidelines about when individuals should be reassessed.

If you fail the personal capability assessment

If you do not score enough points the decision maker considers whether you can be treated as incapable of work (see p673). If not, you are notified that the DWP considers that you are capable of work. The decision on your entitlement to incapacity benefit (IB), SDA or income support (IS) will be revised or superseded and your benefit will stop. However, your IS should not be stopped if you can still qualify for it for a reason other than your incapacity for work (see p292).

If you have previously passed the personal capability assessment and the DWP is now reassessing you, you should remember that IS, SDA and IB are normally awarded for an indefinite period.[61] If the award is indefinite the decision maker can only stop your benefit by carrying out a revision or supersession in the circumstances detailed on pp1066 and 1075.

If you think you are well enough to work

If you think that you are well enough to work but you do not have a job to return to you should either:

- sign on at your nearest Jobcentre Plus office and claim jobseeker's allowance (JSA – see Chapter 15); *or*
- claim IS if you are entitled to it (see Chapter 13). If you do want to claim IS, you may also want to consider if your national insurance (NI) record will continue to be protected (see p727).

Remember the following.

- The rules on linking periods of incapacity for work (see p264) mean that if you try to go back to work but discover that your health does not permit it, you go straight back onto the same rate of IS, SDA or IB as you were previously getting, as long as you give up work within eight weeks and the DWP accepts that you are incapable of work again.
- For IB and SDA, that eight-week period is extended to two years in certain circumstances (see p264).

- You may be able to get your JSA or new IS claim backdated if your claim is delayed because there was a delay in notifying you of the decision to stop your IS or IB (see p966). However, this is not automatic so you should claim as soon as possible.

If you do not think you are well enough to work

If you think that you are not well enough to work, you can challenge the decision maker's decision on your entitlement to benefit on the basis of your incapacity for work, either on revision or on appeal. The time limits for requesting a revision or appealing against a decision are short (see pp1066 and 1061). You may also be able to claim IS or JSA while appealing. There are advantages and disadvantages with each option.

- If you ask the DWP decision maker to revise the decision, you are only likely to get the decision changed if you provide further evidence to support your argument that you are incapable of work, or if there has been an obvious mistake. See p1066 for details of requesting a revision.
- If you ask for a revision of the decision, unless you qualify for IS for a reason other than your incapacity for work, you will not be able to get IS while waiting for a new decision to be made. If you are in any doubt about whether to ask for a revision, or to appeal, you should appeal.
- If you appeal against the decision, you may qualify for IS while waiting for the appeal to be heard (see p294).[62] Claiming IS while appealing means that you are not required to sign on as available for and actively seeking work.
- However, if you would only qualify for IS on the basis of incapacity for work, you are not entitled to IS again until you have actually appealed, and even then it is paid at a reduced rate. Your IS is reduced by 20 per cent of the personal allowance for a single claimant of your age (see p294 for the rule and p771 for the personal allowance). It is worth checking, therefore, to see if you would be entitled to IS on any other ground (see Chapter 13). Your IS is not reduced if this is the first time that your incapacity for work has been tested and on 12 April 1995 you had been off work sick for 28 weeks or were entitled to IB or SDA.[63] You do not have to send in medical certificates while waiting for your appeal to be heard unless it is a decision under the own occupation test.
- Unless you qualify for IS in the week immediately after the week in which you were found capable of work, you will need to make a fresh claim for IS, even if you had previously been getting it on the basis of incapacity for work.[64] As backdating of an IS claim is not automatic (see p966) this could result in a gap in entitlement. For this reason, it is worth considering appealing and claiming IS on that basis straight away.
- Alternatively, you can appeal against the decision on your entitlement to benefit and claim JSA. This does involve you having to be available for and actively seeking work (see Chapter 15). However, JSA is not paid at a reduced rate during the appeal, claiming it will not jeopardise your appeal, and it is one

way of protecting your NI contribution record while you are waiting for your appeal to be heard. See p683 for more detail.

- If you want to claim on the basis of being incapable of work again, special rules apply if you claim again within six months of failing the personal capability assessment (see p669).

4. Appeals

Once a decision maker has determined you are not incapable of work, the decision on your entitlement to benefit will be revised or superseded and your benefit will normally stop. If you consider that you are incapable of work you should seek advice (see Appendix 2) about appealing against the decision on your benefit entitlement to an appeal tribunal. See Chapter 42 for detailed advice about appealing.

The decision on your incapacity for work

A *determination* that you are not incapable of work is not, in itself, a decision that can be appealed.[65] However, determinations on incapacity for work should be incorporated into a decision on benefit or national insurance (NI) credit entitlement, and you can challenge the determination on your capacity for work by appealing against that decision. If you are claiming income support (IS) on the basis of incapacity for work, you will usually be issued two separate decisions once you have been found capable of work. One will state that you are not entitled to NI credits for the relevant period. The other will state that you are not entitled to IS for the same period. It is important to appeal against the first (usually the credits) decision because an incapacity determination for one benefit is binding on other benefits relating to the same period.[66]

Other things to do when you appeal

Consider seeking advice (see Appendix 2). You should immediately request a copy of the medical evidence that the DWP holds on your file, including a copy of the Medical Service (MS) doctor's (or other approved healthcare professional's) incapacity report. Local DWP offices have been advised that they must provide a copy of the MS report as soon as possible after it has been requested. If you appeal, a copy of the MS incapacity report should be included in the appeal papers the DWP sends to you and the Tribunals Service.

Go and see your own doctor to discuss your capacity for work. In practice, it can be very difficult to win an appeal if you cannot get your GP or consultant to support you. If you have to wait for an appointment with your doctor, and the time limit for appeal is approaching, appeal anyway. You can always withdraw your appeal later if you choose to. If your GP and consultant agree with the decision maker, you should seriously consider your position, as your chance of winning the appeal is not good. But remember that, if you are successful, claiming benefit on the basis of incapacity for work is usually more advantageous to you than claiming alternative benefits.

Remember that there are only certain circumstances in which you can work and still be regarded as incapable of work (see p662) and if you work while you are appealing, you may lose entitlement to benefit even if you actually win your appeal.

The appeal tribunal

If one of the issues to be considered by an appeal tribunal is whether or not you are incapable of work under the personal capability assessment, the tribunal must be made up of at least one legally qualified person and one medically qualified person.[67]

The following may be useful tactics.

- It is best to request an oral hearing of your appeal as this will give the tribunal the opportunity of hearing from you first-hand about how your condition affects you.
- Although not formally required, it is often important that you get medical evidence to support your appeal. This could be from your GP or your consultant if you have one, or from both. It is usually more helpful if such evidence comments on the things at issue in your appeal rather than just sets out your diagnosis and treatment. If your doctor has been treating you on a regular basis for many years, s/he should say so, so that there can be no doubt that s/he is fully aware of your medical history.
- If you are getting IS or income-based jobseeker's allowance (JSA), or if your income is very low, and you are being advised by a solicitor, legal advice centre or law centre, it may be possible to get payment for a medical report through the legal help scheme (see Appendix 2).
- If you have not been able to obtain a medical report in any other way, you can ask the chair of the tribunal to obtain one. This is a discretionary decision for the tribunal. You are not charged, but you do not have any control over who does the medical, and the report is the tribunal's rather than yours.[68] The chair cannot obtain a medical report in advance of the hearing, so there will have to be an adjournment if the tribunal agrees. You should not rely on them doing so, and they will not normally do so if your GP and the MS doctor (or other approved healthcare professional) agree on the diagnosis and disagree only on the effect of your condition on your capacity to work.
- When your appeal concerns your incapacity for work the tribunal cannot carry out its own examination of you.[69] However, it may observe your conduct in the tribunal room – eg, how you walk or sit.

- There is no rule that says the decision maker or appeal tribunal has to agree with the MS report if this conflicts with what you, your GP or consultant says. On the contrary, the decision maker or tribunal should make a reasoned decision based on all the evidence – medical and non-medical. If necessary, point out that the tribunal is at liberty to prefer your own or your doctor's evidence to that of the MS examiner.[70]
- MS medical reports are usually in electronic form. These can frequently have inconsistencies or errors in them. If this is the case make sure you point it out. Tribunals must deal with any discrepancies and take these into account when considering the weight to be given to different sources of evidence.[71]
- It is often useful for a person who lives with you or who knows you well to attend the hearing to describe to the tribunal the day-to-day problems you have.
- You should bring a list of any medication you are taking to the tribunal hearing.

For more about tribunal hearings, see Chapter 42.

Protecting your income and national insurance credits

Incapacity benefit (IB) and severe disablement allowance (SDA) are not paid while your appeal is waiting to be heard. If you have appealed you can still qualify for IS but it may be paid at a reduced rate (see p294). You may qualify for either IS or JSA (see Chapters 13 and 15) while waiting for your appeal to be decided and you will need to consider which benefit you would be better off claiming. Remember the following.

- Claiming JSA may be preferable as it is not reduced, and a successful claim for JSA means that you receive Class 1 NI credits (see p727) while your appeal is waiting to be heard, whatever the outcome.
- If you only claim IS you do not have to sign on as available for and actively seeking work. You get NI credits for the period if you eventually win your appeal, but not if you lose (except in the rare case that you qualify for credits on some other basis). IS may be reduced while you are waiting for your appeal to be heard (see p294). A complete NI contribution record may be important to ensure that you get the maximum pension when you retire and to protect your spouse's or civil partner's entitlement to bereavement benefits should you die.

To be eligible for JSA you have to be capable of work (see p344).[72] The decision maker's decision on capacity for work is binding on the Jobcentre Plus office.[73] This also applies if you later win your appeal and are found to be incapable of work. Your claim for JSA should not influence the decision on your appeal about your incapacity for work. However, remember that there are only certain circumstances in which you can actually work and still be regarded as incapable of work (see p662). So, if you work while you are appealing, you may lose entitlement to benefit even if you actually win your appeal.

To get JSA you must convince the decision maker at the Jobcentre Plus office that you are available for and actively seeking work (see pp347 and 357). To qualify for JSA you will need to be prepared to accept any reasonable work within your limitations. You will not qualify if you say that you are really too sick to work but have been told you have to sign on. You can place restrictions on your availability for work if these are reasonable in the light of your physical or mental condition (see p353).

As the decision on your incapacity for work is binding on the Jobcentre Plus office, if you later win your appeal on your incapacity for work it will mean that the decision on your entitlement to JSA should be revised or superseded and you will not qualify for JSA. If the amount of IS, IB or SDA you would have been entitled to would have been more than the JSA you received, you should qualify for arrears amounting to the difference.

The following points are also relevant.

- The contribution conditions for contribution-based JSA are stricter than for IB. You are not necessarily entitled to the former just because you were getting the latter.
- You may not be entitled to IS (or income-based JSA) if you do not pass the means test (eg, if you have savings or other income) or if, for example, you have a partner who works for 24 or more hours a week. If so, you may have no alternative but to claim contribution-based JSA.

If your condition worsens

If your condition has significantly worsened since the decision maker's decision, or you have a specific disease or disability which was not considered by the decision maker, you should make a fresh claim for IS or IB based on your incapacity for work. In such situations you should be assessed under the personal capability assessment again and should be treated as incapable of work until such an assessment is carried out (see p669).

Notes

1 ss171A(1) and 171G(1) SSCBA 1992
2 s17 SSA 1998; reg 10 SS&CS(DA) Regs
3 Sch 1 para 2 JSA 1995

1. **Incapacity for work**
4 s171D SSCBA 1992; reg 16 SS(IFW) Regs
5 Regs 13(2) and 16(3) SS(IFW) Regs
6 CIB/5298/1997
7 CS/5/1954
8 ss171D and 171F SSCBA 1992; regs 10A, 16 and 17 SS(IFW) Regs
9 Reg 2(1) SS(IFW) Regs
10 Reg 2(1) SS(IFW) Regs
11 Reg 17 SS(IFW) Regs
12 Reg 17(4) and (8) SS(IFW) Regs
13 Reg 17(8) SS(IFW) Regs
14 CIB/1723/2000
15 s171D SSCBA 1992; regs 11-14 SS(IFW) Regs
16 Reg 13A(2) and (4) SS(IFW) Regs
17 Reg 13A SS(IFW) Regs
18 Reg 13A(4) SS(IFW) Regs

2. **The own occupation test**
19 s171B(2) SSCBA 1992
20 CS/57/1982
21 CS/221/1949
22 s171B(1) SSCBA 1992; reg 4(1) SS(IFW) Regs
23 Reg 5 SS(IFW) Regs
24 s171B(3) and (4) SSCBA 1992
25 House of Commons *Hansard,* 22 July 2002, col 1566W
26 Regs 2 and 5 SS(ME) Regs
27 Reg 6(1)(c) SS(IFW) Regs

3. **The personal capability assessment**
28 s171C(2)(a) SSCBA 1992; reg 24 SS(IFW) Regs
29 s171C(3) SSCBA 1992; reg 28 SS(IFW) Regs
30 CIB/3106/2003
31 Reg 6 SS(IFW) Regs
32 Reg 31(3), (4) and (5) SS(IB)(T) Regs; reg 10 SS(IFW) Regs
33 Reg 2(1) SS(IFW) Regs
34 Reg 25(1) SS(IFW) Regs
35 Reg 26(4) SS(IFW) Regs
36 Reg 26(2) SS(IFW) Regs; CIB/14516/1996
37 Reg 25(3)(a) SS(IFW) Regs; CIB/1446/1996
38 Reg 25(3)(b) SS(IFW) Regs
39 CIB/5435/2002
40 Reg 25(2) SS(IFW) Regs
41 CIB/15231/1996
42 CIB/14534/1996
43 CIB/14534/1996
44 CIB/2620/2000
45 CIB/14587/1996; CIB/14722/1996; CIB/13161/1996; CIB/13508/1996
46 CIB/14722/1996
47 CIB/14587/1996
48 CSIB/12/1996
49 Reg 27 SS(IFW) Regs
50 *Howker v Secretary of State for Work and Pensions and the Social Security Advisory Committee* 8 November 2002 (CA), reported as R(IB) 3/03
51 CIB/26/2004; CSIB/33/2004; CIB/143/2007
52 CIB/15325/1996
53 Reg 7 SS(IFW) Regs
54 Reg 9 SS(IFW) Regs
55 Reg 6(2) and (3)(b) SS(IFW) Regs
56 CSIB/17/1996
57 www.dwp.gov.uk/medical/ibh/ibh.pdf – para 4.1.2
58 Reg 8 SS(IFW) Regs
59 R(S) 9/51
60 Reg 11 SS&CS(DA) Regs
61 Reg 17 SS(C&P) Regs; R(S) 1/92
62 Reg 4ZA and Sch IB para 24 IS Regs
63 Reg 4ZA IS Regs
64 Reg 22A(3) IS Regs

4. **Appeals**
65 CIB/2338/2000
66 CIB/2338/2000
67 s7 SSA 1998; reg 36(2)(a)(i) SS&CS(DA) Regs
68 s20 SSA 1998; reg 41 SS&CS(DA) Regs; R(S) 3/84
69 s20 SSA 1998; reg 52 SS&CS(DA) Regs
70 CIB/407/1998; CIB/1149/1998; R(M) 1/93; CIB/3074/2003
71 CIB/511/2005
72 s1 JSA 1995
73 Reg 10 SS&CS(DA) Regs; Sch 1 para 2 JSA 1995

Chapter 29

Claiming for others: non-means-tested benefits

This chapter explains who can be included in your non-means-tested benefit claim. It covers:

1. Increases for your adult dependant

If you are receiving a non-means-tested benefit it may be possible to claim an adult dependant increase either for your '**spouse**' or '**civil partner**', or for an **adult who looks after your child**, but not for both. See p687 for what these terms mean.

Increases for adult dependants can be included in the following benefits:

- incapacity benefit (IB) paid at the long-term or short-term rate (see Chapter 12);
- severe disablement allowance (SDA – see Chapter 20);
- carer's allowance (CA – see Chapter 3);
- Category A retirement pension (see Chapter 19);
- maternity allowance (MA – see Chapter 17).

Whether or not you can get an increase for an adult is determined by which of these benefits you are receiving.

Note: if you make a claim for an adult dependant who is your partner (ie, you are a couple) and your benefit would be increased because of that, your partner may be required to attend a work-focused interview as a condition of you getting the full amount of benefit. See p972 for details.

You can choose not to claim an increase in your non-means-tested benefit for a dependant, but if you are entitled to an increase and are also receiving a means-tested benefit, see p698.

Increase for your spouse or civil partner

Your '**spouse**' is your husband or wife. See p26 for details of who can be recognised as married (p28 if your marriage is polygamous). For same-sex relationships, your '**civil partner**' is someone of the same sex as you with whom you are registered as civil partners.[1] You may be entitled to an increase for your spouse or civil partner if her/his earnings are not too high (see p690). An increase *can* be paid even if your spouse or civil partner is not living with you, as long as you are contributing to her/his maintenance.

You *cannot* qualify for an increase in your benefit for your spouse or civil partner if you are receiving an increase for an adult who cares for your child (see p688).

See p691 for the amount of the increase you receive.

Who can claim

You qualify for extra money for your spouse or civil partner if:[2]

- you make a separate claim for the increase (see p695);[3] *and*
- your spouse or civil partner's earnings, or the payments s/he receives from an occupational or personal pension, are not too high (see p690 for details of this earnings rule); *and*
- you are not getting an increase for a dependent adult who is looking after your child (see p688); *and either*
  - you are residing with your spouse or civil partner (see p693); *or*
  - in some cases only, you are 'contributing to the maintenance' of your spouse or civil partner (see p693) at a weekly rate of at least the amount of the increase (see p691).

Additional conditions for specific benefits

You only qualify for an increase for your spouse or civil partner if, in addition to the above conditions, you satisfy the following.

For **IB** or **SDA**[4] *either*:

- your spouse or civil partner is 60 or over; *or*
- your spouse or civil partner is under 60, and you are 'residing with' (and not merely 'contributing to the maintenance' of) her/him and entitled to child benefit. See p693 for the meaning of 'residing with'.

For **CA** you must reside with (see p693) your spouse or civil partner to get the increase. You cannot qualify just by contributing to her/his maintenance.[5]

For **Category A retirement pension**, you cannot get an increase for your civil partner before 6 April 2010.

If you are a woman, you can only get an increase for your husband in your **Category A retirement pension** if:

- immediately before you became entitled to the Category A retirement pension, you were entitled to IB, including an increase for an adult dependant; *and*
- since then, you have not stopped residing with (see p693) your husband or stopped contributing to his maintenance at a rate at least equal to the rate of the increase and your husband's earnings have not been higher than the rate of the increase.[6]

The discrimination against women is not unlawful because it falls within an exception to the Equal Treatment Directive (see Chapter 45).[7]

If your spouse or civil partner receives benefit

You may not be entitled to an an increase for your spouse or civil partner if s/he is claiming an earnings-replacement benefit (see p981) in her/his own right. This is a frequent source of overpayment and it is very important that when you complete the claim form you give full details of any benefits your spouse is receiving.

Increase for someone who looks after a child

If you are not claiming an increase in your benefit for your spouse or civil partner you may get an increase for an adult dependant who is looking after a child for whom you are responsible. 'Child' here includes a 'qualifying young person' (see p57). You may benefit under these rules if, for example, you live with someone to whom you are not married or in a civil partnership, and one of you stays at home to look after the child. Other people may benefit as well – eg, two people with children who live together for mutual support. You may even get an increase for someone you employ to care for your child.

Who can claim

You qualify for extra money for an adult dependant (who is not your spouse or civil partner) if:[8]

- you make a separate claim for the increase (see p695);[9] *and*
- your dependant's earnings, or any payments s/he receives from an occupational or personal pension, are not too high (see p690 for details of this earnings rule); *and*
- your dependant looks after a child;

and either:

- if you are claiming an increase to **CA**, **MA** or Category A **retirement pension** (this increase is not made to Category B pensions), you are entitled to child benefit for that child (see p692). In some circumstances, even if you are receiving child benefit you will be treated as if you are not (see p692); *or*
- if you are claiming **IB** or **SDA** you are entitled to an increase in that benefit for the child (or you are treated as entitled to such an increase) (see p687);

and either:

- you reside with your dependant (see p693); *or*
- you contribute to the maintenance (see p693) of your dependant at a rate equal to at least the rate of the increase; *or*
- you employ your dependant at a cost to you of at least the standard rate of the increase and the employment started before you became unemployed, incapable of work or retired (whichever applies to you) unless the need for you to employ your dependant arose afterwards; *and*
- you do not also get an increase for your spouse or civil partner; *and*
- your dependant is not absent from Great Britain (GB), unless s/he is residing with you outside GB and you still qualify for benefit.

For **CA** you must reside with (see p693) your dependant to get the increase. You cannot qualify just by contributing to her/his maintenance or employing her/him.[10] If your spouse or civil partner is entitled to a **Category B retirement pension** on the basis of your national insurance (NI) contribution record, you are not entitled to an increase in your Category A retirement pension for an adult dependant who is caring for a child.[11]

Additional conditions for specific benefits

For **CA** you must reside with (see p693) your dependant to get the increase. You cannot qualify just by contributing to her/his maintenance or employing her/him.[12] If your spouse or civil partner is entitled to a **Category B retirement pension** on the basis of your NI contribution record, you are not entitled to an increase in your Category A retirement pension for an adult dependant who is caring for a child.[13]

If your dependant receives benefit

You may not be entitled to the increase if your dependant is claiming an earnings-replacement benefit (see p981) in her/his own right. This is a frequent source of overpayment and it is very important that you give full details of any benefits received by your dependant when you complete the claim form.

The earnings rules

You are not entitled to an increase in your benefit for a spouse/civil partner or for a dependent adult who cares for your child if her/his earnings are too high (but see below if you employ your dependant).

Earnings

Earnings include any payments received from an occupational or personal pension scheme or periodic payments from the Pension Protection Fund (see p838).[14] If your dependant's earnings fluctuate, you do not automatically lose your entitlement to the increase every time s/he earns too much in a particular week (although you have no right to be paid the increase during the following week if that happens).[15] This means that you do not have to make a fresh claim every time your dependant's earnings exceed the limit (although you do have to keep the DWP informed of any such changes). For full details of how earnings are calculated, see p832.

When the increase is not paid

If you are residing with (see p693) an adult dependant and are claiming an increase in **long-term IB, SDA** or **Category A retirement pension**, your increase is not paid if, in the previous week, your dependant earned more than £60.50.[16]

If you are claiming an increase in your **IB** for your spouse/civil partner or adult dependant and s/he is treated as incapable of work while doing 'approved work' (see p665), any payment made to her/him for this work will be ignored.[17]

In any other case (ie, if you are not residing with your dependant or if you are claiming an increase in any other non-means-tested benefit), your increase is not paid if your dependant's earnings in the previous week were more than the standard rate of the increase which you have claimed.[18]

Because the earnings rule is more generous for long-term than for short-term IB, you may not be entitled to an increase during the first year of your entitlement to IB but qualify after you transfer to long-term IB. It is then necessary to make a separate claim for the increase.

If you employ your dependant

If you are claiming an increase for an adult dependant who is not your spouse or civil partner but is looking after a child (see p688), your dependant's earnings do not affect your entitlement to an increase if s/he is employed by you but is not residing with you. If s/he is residing with you (see p693) and you are employing her/him to care for a child, the wages you pay to her/him for this work are ignored.[19]

Amount of increase for an adult dependant

Increases for spouses/civil partners and adult dependants who are caring for a child are paid as follows.[20]

	£pw
Short-term IB (claimant not over pension age)	39.40
Short-term IB (claimant over pension age)	48.65
Long-term IB	50.55
SDA	30.40
MA	39.40
CA	30.20
Category A retirement pension	54.35

If you are over pension age, an increase in your retirement pension or short-term IB may be reduced if your contribution record is incomplete (see p739).[21]

2. Increases for child dependants

You cannot make a new claim for an increase for a child dependant. These increases have been replaced by child tax credit. However, you remain entitled to an increase for a child dependant if you were entitled to one on 5 April 2003 (or your entitlement was backdated to include 5 April).

You will lose this transitional protection if:

- your entitlement to an increase for a child dependant ceases; *or*
- your increase stops being paid for 58 days or more. If the benefit with which you are paid the increase is terminated, your increase will also stop. However, you keep your transitional protection as long as the benefit is awarded to you again and you re-claim the increase within three months of the date the benefit is re-awarded on revision, supersession or appeal.[22]

Earnings limit[23]

If you live together with someone as a couple, your partner's earnings affect your entitlement to an increase for a child. You count as a couple if you live with your spouse or civil partner, or with someone as if you were married or were registered as civil partners. You do not get an increase for your first child for any week if, in the previous week, your partner earned £185 or more. After that you lose entitlement for another child for each complete £25 a week your partner earns in addition to £185.

Amount of increase for a child dependant

The basic rate of the increase is £11.35 for each child.[24] However, if you are in receipt of child benefit at the only or eldest child rate for the same child, the £11.35 is reduced to £8.75.[25]

For all other rules on increases for child dependants see pp746–48 of CPAG's *Welfare Benefits Handbook* 2002/03.

3. Definition of terms

The following definitions apply for the purposes of entitlement to increases for adult dependants.

Who counts as a child

The rules are the same as for child benefit, and include someone who is a 'qualifying young person' (see p56).

Treated as entitled to child benefit

In order to qualify for an increase for an *adult* who is not your spouse or civil partner but is caring for a child, you must either be entitled to child benefit or be treated as entitled to child benefit for that child.

If you do not receive child benefit for a child yourself, you are still treated as doing so if:[26]

- you are residing with your spouse or civil partner and s/he is entitled to child benefit for the child;[27] *or*
- you are residing with (see p693) a parent of the child who is receiving child benefit for the child and the child is living with you; *and either*
  - you are also a parent of the child; *or*
  - you are 'wholly or mainly maintaining' the child; *or*
- you, your spouse or civil partner (or for incapacity benefit (IB) and severe disablement allowance (SDA) only, the child's parent), if you are residing with her/him (see p693), would have been entitled to child benefit for that child had s/he been born at the end of the week before the week in which s/he was born;[28] *or*
- you are in Great Britain and would have been entitled to child benefit if you (or your spouse or civil partner or, for IB and SDA only, the child's parent, if you are residing with her/him – see p693) had not been receiving a family benefit from another country.[29]

Treated as not entitled to child benefit

Except for IB and SDA, even if you are getting child benefit for a child, you are treated as if you are not if you are not the child's parent and:[30]

- the child lives with one of her/his parents and is not living with you; *or*
- the child lives with you and one of her/his parents, but you are not 'wholly or mainly maintaining' the child.

In these circumstances you will not qualify for an increase for an adult dependant if you are claiming this on the grounds that s/he is caring for the child.

'Residing with'

The term **'residing with'** should be given its ordinary meaning. You and your spouse, civil partner or other adult dependant will normally be considered to be residing with each other if you share a home. The arrangement has to have some degree of permanence so you should not be considered to be residing with someone who has come to stay with you for a short period of time.

Temporary absences do not stop two people from being treated as residing with each other.[31] For the purpose of qualifying for an increase for an adult dependant, you are treated as residing with your spouse or civil partner when either or both of you are in hospital, even if the stay in hospital is likely to be permanent.[32]

'Residing with' does not mean the same as 'living with' (see p694) and the rules on whether a couple are residing with each other for the purposes of dependency increases are not the same as for child benefit (see p67).

'Contributing to the maintenance'

If you are not residing with an adult dependant you may still qualify for a dependant's increase for her/him if you are contributing to her/his maintenance at a weekly rate of at least the amount of the increase.

You only qualify for an increase for an adult dependant on this basis if:[33]

- when you were employed, or not incapable of work (see p661), or not a pensioner (whichever applies to you) you were making contributions at this rate, unless the adult only became your dependant later. If you are claiming IB and within a month of you becoming entitled to the increase for an adult dependant the rate of that increase changes (because you reach pension age or start to receive long-term IB), you are treated as satisfying this condition if you were contributing at least the level of the initial increase; *and*
- if the increase is payable at a reduced rate (eg, because of insufficient national insurance contributions – see p739), you continue to contribute at least the amount of the increase which is paid.

'Contributing to the maintenance' means that you are making payments to or on behalf of a person. A weekly payment covers you for the week after it is made, and a monthly payment for the following month.[34] Payments may be in kind, so, for example, money spent on clothing or an outing for a child can be counted.[35]

If you make payments for a spouse/civil partner and one or more children, the total payment is allocated between those dependants in the way that is most advantageous to you (even if you pay under a court order that specifies the amounts in respect of each person).[36] However, a contribution for a spouse or civil partner can only be treated as a contribution for a child and vice versa if your spouse or civil partner is entitled to child benefit for that child. If the payment includes an element of arrears the amount for arrears is ignored.[37]

If you have stopped maintaining a person, you cannot later cover yourself by making a payment in arrears.[38] However, a broad view is taken of an interruption in otherwise regular payments.[39] If you are not paying enough, but think you are, a payment of arrears may be taken into account.[40]

You are treated as though you are making the required contributions if you give a written undertaking to make the contributions as soon as the increase is paid. If on receiving the increase you do not make the contributions, the decision to award the increase can be revised.[41]

'Living with'

'Living with' has the same meaning as it does for child benefit claims (see p63).

4. Special benefit rules

There are some groups of claimants to whom special rules apply. These are covered below and in Chapters 25, 26 and 58. Special rules apply to:

- people (or their dependants) who are in hospital (see p611);
- people (or their dependants) who are in prison or detention (see p624);
- adult dependants involved in trade disputes (see p633);
- people whose marriage is polygamous (see below).

Note: your increase may not be affected in the same way as your basic benefit.

Polygamous marriages

You only qualify for an increase in your non-means-tested benefit for your spouse if you are recognised as having a valid marriage under UK law (see p26). You are not normally treated as having a valid marriage unless your marriage is a monogamous one.[42] This means if your marriage is polygamous you will not generally be entitled to an increase in your benefit for your spouse.[43] Seek further advice if necessary.

Even if you do not qualify for an increase in your non-means-tested benefit for your spouse because your marriage is polygamous, you may still qualify for an increase for her/him if s/he is caring for a child (see p688).

5. Claims, backdating and getting paid

You must make a claim for an increase for a dependant.[44] The rules are described in brief below, but see also Chapter 38, which explains the rules in more detail.

Making a claim

A claim for an increase should be made on the appropriate claim form (this might be a written statement sent to you after starting your claim via a telephone call to a contact centre), although the DWP may accept a written application which is not on the appropriate form if it is sufficient in the circumstances (see p959).[45]

Claim forms for the relevant benefits contain claims for increases for dependants.

Information to support your claim

If you are claiming an increase for an adult dependant you will normally be asked to supply her/his national insurance number (see p962).[46]

When you claim an increase for a dependant you may be asked to supply 'certificates, documents, information and evidence' considered relevant to your claim.[47] This may include, for example, information about your adult dependant's earnings.

If you are asked to provide evidence or documents which you do not have, ask what other evidence would be acceptable. Ask the DWP to explain what is required and why, and complain if you feel any requests for information are unreasonable.

See p961 for further details of evidence that may be required to support your claim.

Who should claim

You must normally claim benefit (including increases for dependants) on your own behalf. However, if your benefit is being claimed by another adult on your behalf because you are not able to act for yourself (called your 'appointee'), the increase in that benefit should also be claimed by your appointee (see p955).

The date of your claim

The date of your claim for an increase for a dependant is normally the date it is received at the DWP office.[48]

If the claim you submit is incomplete or not on the correct form you may be asked to provide further information or to complete the correct form. As long as this additional information or form is returned within a month of it being sent back to you (or longer if the decision maker thinks the delay is reasonable), your claim is treated as being made on the date the initial claim was received at the DWP office.[49]

If you reclaim carer's allowance (CA) after a qualifying benefit was awarded to the person you care for in the circumstances described on p50, your claim for an increase in CA can also be treated as having been made on the date you first claimed the increase or the date from which the qualifying benefit was awarded, if that was later.[50]

It may be possible to claim in advance or your date of claim may be backdated (see below).

If you claim the wrong benefit

If someone has claimed benefit for her/himself (other than a claim for child benefit) and is not entitled to it, but you are entitled to an increase in your non-means-tested benefit for that person, her/his claim can be treated as a claim for an increase in your benefit.[51]

When someone else has claimed an increase in a benefit for an adult dependant but is not entitled to it, that claim may be treated as a claim for an increase in your non-means-tested benefit for the same adult.[52]

If a claim for another benefit is treated as a claim for an increase in your benefit for an adult dependant, this may allow you to backdate your claim for the increase for more than the usual three months (see p696). If you satisfy the qualifying conditions for the increase and for the benefit to which the increase applies you can get the increase backdated for up to three months before the date of the claim for the other benefit.

See p963 for more details on interchanging claims in this way.

Claiming in advance

You can claim an increase in your **retirement pension** up to four months before you expect to qualify for it.[53]

You can claim an increase in your **maternity allowance** (MA) for an adult dependant up to 14 weeks before your expected week of childbirth (see p442 for the meaning of this term) but only if you would have qualified for the increase at the time you make the claim, had MA been in payment.[54]

You can claim an increase for a dependant in any **other non-means-tested benefit** up to three months before you expect to qualify for it.[55]

Backdating your claim

Claims for dependants' increases can be backdated for up to three months from the date you make your claim if you satisfy the conditions of entitlement to the benefit and to the dependant's increase over that period.[56] You do not have to show reasons why your claim was late to qualify for backdated benefit.

If you might have qualified for an increase in your benefit for a dependant earlier but did not claim because you were given the wrong information or were misled by the DWP you could ask for an *ex gratia* payment (see p1186) or complain to the Ombudsman via your MP (see p1183).

See p696 for details of whether you can be treated as having claimed an increase in your benefit for a dependant on the basis of your (or someone else's) claim for another benefit.

See p695 if you have previously claimed CA but your earlier claim was refused. See p964 for more details about the backdating of claims.

Getting paid

If you are claiming an increase for your dependants, that increase is included in the payments of the benefit concerned, and is paid in the same way and on the same day as that benefit. See the relevant benefit chapters for details.

Change of circumstances

The DWP should inform you of the main kinds of changes in your circumstances that you need to report, but might not actually list them all. In any case, it is your duty to report *any* change in our circumstances that you might reasonably be expected to know might affect your right to, the amount of or the payment of your benefit.[57] You should, for example, inform the DWP of a change in your adult dependant's earnings.

You should do this promptly in writing or by telephone to the office handling your claim (although in individual cases notification might be accepted in a form other than in writing, or by telephone). In some cases, however, the decision maker might say that you must report changes in writing. In any case, you might want to report the change in writing and keep a copy in case of a dispute in the future. If you do not promptly report any change which you are required to notify, any resulting overpayment may be recoverable from you (see Chapter 39). If you are considered deliberately to have acted falsely or dishonestly, you may also be guilty of an offence (see Chapter 40).

6. Tax, tax credits and other benefits

Increases of retirement pensions, carer's allowance and incapacity benefit (IB), apart from the lower rate of short-term IB and transitional IB (see p278) for adult dependants, are **taxable**.[58] Other increases are not. Increases are generally taken into account, along with the benefit itself, as income for **tax credits** (see p1257). As with means-tested benefits (see below) that may mean that your income becomes too high to qualify, so affecting your entitlement to payments from the social fund, free school meals and health benefits.

Means-tested benefits

Your entitlement to means-tested benefits (which you may get if you have a low income) includes benefit for your partner and (except for pension credit (PC) and depending on which benefit you are claiming) may include any dependent children who are members of your household (see Chapter 30). This is your 'family' for the purpose of means-tested benefits. Any increase in your non-means-tested benefit for a member of your family is treated as income for means-tested benefits (see p858), although some of your widowed parent's allowance can be ignored when calculating your entitlement to income support (IS), income-based jobseeker's allowance (JSA), PC, housing benefit (HB) and council tax benefit (CTB) (see p860).

If you are receiving a means-tested benefit you may not be better off claiming an increase in your non-means-tested benefit for an adult dependant. If the increase is for a member of your family it will affect the amount of means-tested benefit you receive and may mean your income is too high for you to qualify for that means-tested benefit. If you then lose your entitlement to IS, income-based JSA or PC you may also lose your entitlement to free school meals for your children, community care grants or budgeting loans from the social fund, and health benefits like free prescriptions and Healthy Start food vouchers and vitamins. Your entitlement to HB and CTB may also be reduced. In addition, if you no longer qualify for IS, income-based JSA, PC, HB or CTB, you will not qualify for maternity and funeral expenses payments from the social fund.

However, if you fail to claim an increase in your non-means-tested benefit for an adult dependant to which you are entitled, you may still be treated as receiving the increase for the purpose of calculating your entitlement to IS, income-based JSA, HB or CTB. This is because you can be treated as if you are receiving income which you fail to apply for (called 'notional income') if you would be entitled to it without having to satisfy further conditions (see p873). You should only be treated as having notional income if your entitlement to an increase is straightforward. If you would have to satisfy further conditions to qualify for the increase you should not be treated as receiving it. You should not be treated as having notional income if the increase would not be for a member of your 'family' for means-tested benefit purposes.

Non-means-tested benefits

The overlapping benefit rules (see p981) apply to increases in non-means-tested benefits for dependants. These rules mean you may not be entitled to an increase in more than one benefit for the same child or adult and that you may not qualify for an increase if someone else is receiving an increase for your dependants. You also may not be entitled to an increase for an adult dependant if s/he is claiming an earnings replacement benefit in her/his own right.

Notes

1. **Increases for your adult dependant**
   1 s1 CPA 2004
   2 ss82-85, 86A and 90 SSCBA 1992; regs 8 and 12 and Sch 2 SSB(Dep) Regs; regs 9 and 10 SS(IB-ID) Regs
   3 Reg 2(3) SS(C&P) Regs
   4 s86A SSCBA 1992; reg 9(1) SS(IB-ID) Regs
   5 Sch 2 para 7 SSB(Dep) Regs; s90 SSCBA 1992
   6 s84 SSCBA 1992
   7 *Bramhill v CAO,* C-420/92, 7 July 1994 (ECJ) – the discrimination will end in April 2010 as part of the programme to equalise the rules on pension age and retirement pensions; Sch 4 para 2 PA 1995
   8 ss82(4), 85 and 90 SSCBA 1992; regs 10 and 12 and Sch 2 SSB(Dep) Regs; regs 9, 10 and 14 SS(IB-ID) Regs
   9 Reg 2(3) SS(C&P) Regs
   10 Sch 2 para 7 SSB(Dep) Regs
   11 s85(3) SSCBA 1992
   12 Sch 2 para 7 SSB(Dep) Regs
   13 s85(3) SSCBA 1992
   14 s89 SSCBA 1992; Sch 2 SSB(Dep) Regs
   15 Reg 10 and Sch 2 para 7 SSB(Dep) Regs; reg 10 SS(IB-ID) Regs
   16 Regs 8(2) and (3) and 12 SSB(Dep) Regs; reg 10 SS(IB-ID) Regs
   17 Reg 9(2A) SS(IB-ID) Regs
   18 ss82 and 83(2)(b) SSCBA 1992; reg 12 and Sch 2 para 7 SSB(Dep) Regs; reg 10(1) SS(IB-ID) Regs
   19 Reg 10 and Sch 2 para 7 SSB(Dep) Regs; reg 10 SS(IB-ID) Regs
   20 Sch 4 SSCBA 1992
   21 Reg 6(3) SS(WB&RP) Regs; reg 13 SS(IB-ID) Regs

2. **Increases for child dependants**
   22 Art 3 TCA(No.3)O
   23 s80(4) SSCBA 1992; Sch 2 para 2B SSB(Dep) Regs
   24 Sch 4 SSCBA 1992
   25 Reg 8(2) SS(OB) Regs

3. **Definition of terms**
   26 Reg 4A SSB(Dep) Regs; reg 9(2B) SS(IB-ID) Regs
   27 s122(4) SSCBA 1992
   28 Reg 4A(1)(b) SSB(Dep) Regs; reg 9(2B) SS(IB-ID) Regs
   29 Reg 4A(4) SSB(Dep) Regs; reg 9(2C) SS(IB-ID) Regs
   30 Reg 4B SSB(Dep) Regs
   31 Reg 2(4) SSB(PRT) Regs
   32 Reg 2(2) SSB(PRT) Regs
   33 Reg 11 SSB(Dep) Regs; reg 12 SS(IB-ID) Regs
   34 R(S) 3/74
   35 R(U) 3/66
   36 Reg 3 SSB(Dep) Regs; reg 3 SS(IB-ID) Regs
   37 R(U) 25/58
   38 R(S) 3/74
   39 R(U) 14/62
   40 R(S) 1/59
   41 Reg 5 SSB(Dep) Regs; reg 8 SS(IB-ID) Regs

4. **Special benefit rules**
   42 *Hyde v Hyde* [1886]
   43 Reg 2 SSFA(PM) Regs

5. **Claims, backdating and getting paid**
   44 s1 SSAA 1992
   45 Reg 4(1) SS(C&P) Regs
   46 s1(1A) and (1B) SSAA 1992
   47 Reg 7(1) SS(C&P) Regs
   48 Reg 6(1) SS(C&P) Regs
   49 Regs 4(7) and 6(1) SS(C&P) Regs
   50 Reg 6(29) SS(C&P) Regs
   51 Reg 9(4) SS(C&P) Regs
   52 Reg 9(5) SS(C&P) Regs
   53 Reg 15 SS(C&P) Regs
   54 Reg 14 SS(C&P) Regs
   55 Reg 13 SS(C&P) Regs
   56 Reg 19(2) and (3) SS(C&P) Regs
   57 Reg 32(1A) and (IB) SS(C&P) Regs

6. **Tax, tax credits and other benefits**
   58 s617 ICTA 1988

Chapter 30

Claiming for others: means-tested benefits

This chapter explains who can be included in your claim for any of the means-tested benefits. It covers:

The phrase '**means-tested benefits**' refers to:

- income support (see Chapter 13);
- income-based jobseeker's allowance (JSA – see Chapter 15);
- housing benefit (see Chapter 10); *and*
- council tax benefit (see Chapter 5).

Note: pension credit does not include amounts for children.

In this chapter, unless otherwise stated, references to income-based JSA are intended also to refer to joint-claim JSA.

For claiming for others in non-means tested benefits, see Chapter 29. For claiming for others in child tax credit and working tax credit, see Chapters 48 and 49 respectively.

1. Who is included in your claim

A claim for any of the means-tested benefits will include yourself and, if you have one, your family. Your '**family**' means your partner and your dependent children.

Couples

Your 'family' includes your **partner**, if you have one – ie, if you are a couple. A '**couple**' includes a wife, husband or cohabitee of the opposite sex, and civil partners and cohabitees of the same sex (see p702 for full details).

Children

The rules below are about when **dependent children** (including 'qualifying young persons') can count as part of your family and be included in your claim for means-tested benefits. However, even where your child cannot be included in your claim, there are other circumstances in which it may still be important that you are regarded as being responsible for a child living in your household, or having a child as part of your 'family'. This applies particularly to child benefit (see p63), income support (IS – see p298), income-based jobseeker's allowance (JSA – see p365) and, in some cases, housing costs (see p806).

For all benefits, to count as part of your family the child(ren) must be a member of your household but, even then, certain 16/17-year-old local authority care leavers are excluded (see p610).[1]

The basic rule

If you make a new claim for any of the means-tested benefits in this chapter on or after 6 April 2004, or if your current claim was made before 6 April 2004 but you did not have a dependent child included in the claim until or after that date, dependent children can only be included as part of your family in **housing benefit** (HB) and **council tax benefit** (CTB).[2]

If you make a new claim for **income-based JSA or IS**, or did not have a dependent child included in the claim until 6 April 2004 or after, dependent children cannot be included in your claim.[3] (But see the note in CPAG's *Welfare Rights Bulletin* 186 p12 for some possible doubts about this. The DWP attempted to clarify the rules from 8 September 2005).[4]

Dependent children cannot be included in any claim for **pension credit** (PC).

If you cannot have dependent children included in your claim for IS, income-based JSA or PC, you should claim child tax credit (see Chapter 48) for them instead.

If you are already entitled to IS or income-based JSA, *and*:

- your entitlement to either of those benefits began before 6 April 2004; *and*
- you had a dependent child or children included in the claim,

your dependent children may be included in your claims for these benefits, as well as for HB and CTB – but see p709 for details.

When your benefit is worked out, the needs of your partner and any children included are usually added to yours and so are your partner's income and capital. There are special rules for the treatment of the income and capital of included dependent children (see pp844 and 911).

2. **Couples**

You and your partner are considered to be a 'couple' for mean-tested benefit purposes if you are both 16[5] or over and you are:[6]

- married and living in the same household; *or*
- not married but 'living together as husband and wife'; *or*
- of the same sex, registered as civil partners and living in the same household, *or*
- of the same sex, not registered as civil partners but 'living together as if you were civil partners'.

In these circumstances, you must claim as a couple. Your partner's income and capital are counted when assessing your entitlement and you receive the amount of benefit for couples. If one member of your family is claiming a means-tested benefit, no other member can claim the same benefit for the same period.[7] For income support (IS)/income-based jobseeker's allowance (JSA), housing benefit (HB) and council tax benefit (CTB), partners can choose which of them should be the claimant.[8] The same rule applies to pension credit (PC), but the claimant must be aged 60 or over to qualify.[9]

Note: if you are required to be a 'joint-claim couple' for JSA, both you and your partner will need to be available for and actively seeking work.

For details about how to claim, see p301 (IS), p378 (JSA), p453 (PC), p200 (HB) and p92 (CTB).

Special rules apply if either partner is under 18 (see pp609 and 773).

Note: for PC only, if your partner is not habitually resident in the UK (see p1367) or is a 'person subject to immigration control' (see p1333), you are treated as not being members of the same household,[10] and so cannot count as a couple.

Same-sex couples

If you are same-sex (lesbian or gay) partners, for means-tested benefit purposes you may count as a couple (see above). This rule has applied since 5 December 2005.[11] If you are the civil partner of someone you live with, or live with someone 'as if you were civil partners', you should report this promptly to the office administering your benefit claim, as you will count as a couple for benefit purposes. This could alter your entitlement considerably, including reducing or stopping your benefit if you are already getting it. This is because if you count as a couple your partner's circumstances, including her/his income and capital resources, are taken into account.

It is expected that the DWP and (for HB/CTB) your local authority will, in general, not alter your claim until the first time they come to look at it after 5 December 2005. This could be at the point you tell them that you live with someone 'as civil partners'. But in some circumstances, including if they think you could reasonably have been expected to have told them about your partner before the date they actually looked at your claim again, they may decide to alter your claim from an earlier date.[12] This might mean, in some cases, that you are required to repay an overpayment of benefit. Seek advice if necessary. For overpayments and recovery, see Chapter 39.

Spouse or civil partner

Being **married** to someone does not necessarily mean that you cannot be treated as part of a couple with someone else instead.[13]

You count as **'polygamously married'** if you are married to more than one person and your marriages took place in a country that permits polygamy.[14] There are special rules if you are polygamously married (see p28).[15] Essentially, these specify that any income and capital of a polygamous partner will be taken into account, but an increased sum is allowed to take into account their needs.

You count as someone's **civil partner**if you are both of the same sex and have been registered as her/his civil partner.[16]

Living in the same household

The term **'household'** is not defined. Whether two people should be treated as members of the same household is very much a question of fact. A house can contain a number of separate households and if one person has exclusive occupation of separate accommodation from another s/he will not be considered to be living in the same household. Physical presence together is also not in itself conclusive. There must be a 'particular kind of tie' binding two people together in a domestic establishment. This could, in appropriate circumstances, include a household within, for example, a hotel or boarding house.[17] However, it must also involve two or more people living together as a unit and, as such a unit, enjoying a reasonable level of independence and self-sufficiency. It has been held that a married couple sharing a room in a residential home – because they needed someone else to help with organising their personal care and domestic activities – were not self-sufficient and could not be said to live in a domestic establishment, and therefore did not share a household.[18]

You and another person may be regarded as members of the same household when you think you should not be. If this occurs it is important to try to show that, although you both live in the same house, you maintain separate households.

A separate household might exist if there are:

- independent arrangements for the storage and cooking of food;
- independent financial arrangements;
- separate eating arrangements;
- no evidence of family life;

- separate commitments for housing costs, even if the liability is to another person in the same premises.

You cannot be a member of more than one household at the same time.[19] If two people can be shown to be maintaining separate homes, they cannot be said to be sharing the same household.[20] Even if you have the right to occupy only part of a room, you may have your own household.[21]

Living together as husband and wife or civil partners

If you are **'living together as'** husband and wife or civil partners (ie, cohabiting), you must claim means-tested benefits as a couple.

If you are in a same-sex relationship, for benefit purposes you may be regarded as living together as civil partners or 'as if you were civil partners' from 5 December 2005 – see p702 for more on same-sex couples and benefit. For the 'living together' test, you would only count as living together as if you were civil partners if, were you in a relationship with someone of the opposite sex, you would count as living together as husband and wife.[22] This means that the test (described below is the same for same-sex couples as it is for different-sex couples.

The amount of benefit for a couple is usually less than that for two single people, so it is important to dispute a decision that you are cohabiting if you believe you are not. If you are awarded IS/income-based JSA (and, arguably, PC), the local authority should not make a separate decision about whether you are cohabiting when considering your claim for HB and CTB.[23] However, where fraud is concerned, the local authority can find fraudulent a claim for IS/income-based JSA/PC on which your HB/CTB claim is founded and, therefore, find that you are not entitled to HB/CTB.[24] Also, if you have not been awarded IS, income-based JSA or PC, the local authority has a duty to consider whether you are cohabiting and may reach a different conclusion from that of the DWP.

The factors considered below are used as 'signposts' to determine whether or not you are cohabiting.[25] No one factor need in itself be conclusive, as it is your 'general relationship' as a whole which is of paramount importance[26] and, just as relationships between couples may vary considerably, so each case depends on all its own particular facts and circumstances.

There is no rule, for example, that if your partner stays with you for three nights or more a week you are *automatically* to be treated as a couple who are living together.

Cohabitation – signposts

1. Do you live in the same household?
2. Do you have a sexual relationship?
3. What are your financial arrangements?
4. Is your relationship stable?

5. Do you have children?
6. How do you appear in public?

Living in the same household

In all cases you must spend the major part of your time in the same household (see p703). If one of you has a separate address where you usually live, you should not be considered to be cohabiting. You cannot be a member of more than one household at the same time, so if you are a member of one couple, you cannot also be treated as part of another.

Even if you *do* share a 'household', you may not be cohabiting. It is essential to look at *why* two people are in the same household.[27] For example, where a couple were living in the same household for reasons of 'care, companionship and mutual convenience' they were not 'living together as husband and wife'.[28]

A separated couple living under the same roof should not be treated as a couple if they are maintaining separate households.[29] Where a relationship has only recently broken down, continuing financial support and shared responsibilities and liabilities may be particularly inconclusive, especially if there is evidence of active steps being taken to live apart. The way people live and their attitude of mind may be more significant. Any 'mere hope' of a reconciliation is not a 'reasonable expectation' if at least one partner has accepted that the relationship is at an end.[30]

Note: couples who are still married only have to show that they are living in the same 'household' and, in this type of case, a shared attitude of mind that the relationship is at an end may not be enough to show that there is no shared household.[31]

Being in a sexual relationship

In practice, decision makers may not ask you about the existence of a sexual relationship, in which case they will only have the information if you volunteer it. If you do not have a sexual relationship, you should make this known (and perhaps offer to show your separate sleeping arrangements).

Having a sexual relationship is not sufficient by itself to prove you are cohabiting. If you have never had a sexual relationship there is a strong (but not necessarily conclusive) presumption that you are not cohabiting.[32] A couple who abstain from a sexual relationship before marriage on grounds of principle (eg, religious reasons) should not be counted as cohabiting until they are formally married.[33] Even if the initial decision makers do not go into the question of whether or not there is a sexual relationship, a tribunal (see p1109) has a duty to ask such questions in order to determine whether or not you are cohabiting.[34]

Your financial arrangements

If one partner is supported by the other or household expenses are shared, this may be treated as evidence of cohabitation. However, it is important to consider how they are shared. There is a difference between, on the one hand, paying a fixed weekly contribution or rigidly sharing bills 50/50 and, on the other hand, a free common fund attributable to income and expenditure. The former does not imply cohabitation, the latter might.

The financial relationship between lodger and landlady/landlord often comes under scrutiny. Decision makers sometimes claim that the payments are too high or too low and so indicate that the relationship is not purely financial. It is important to explain how the payments came to be as they are. However low or high the charge may appear, it is the reasoning which led to it at the time which is important. There may be many motives for having a lodger apart from purely commercial ones or cohabitation. It may be that the relationship is entered into so that there is another adult in the house – for company or security, perhaps. Friendship between a lodger and landlady/landlord does not mean that they are cohabiting.

A stable relationship

Marriage and civil partnership are expected to be stable and lasting. It follows that an occasional or brief association should not be regarded as cohabiting. However, the fact that a relationship is stable does not make it cohabitation – eg, you can have a stable landlord/lodger relationship but not be cohabiting.

The way you spend your time together, the activities you do together and the things you do for each other are relevant, so questions such as how you spend your holidays and how you organise the shopping, the laundry and cleaning may be important.

Children

If you have had a child together and live in the same household as the other parent, there is a strong (but not conclusive) presumption of cohabitation.

Your appearance in public

Decision makers may check the electoral roll and claims for national insurance benefits to see if you present yourselves as a couple. Many couples retain their separate identity publicly as unmarried people or people not in a civil partnership. They should, however, be aware that they may be regarded as cohabiting.

Challenging a 'living together' decision

Sometimes benefit is stopped or adjusted because someone regularly stays overnight, even though you might have none of the long-term commitments generally associated with marriage or a civil partnership. But couples with no sexual relationship who live together (eg, as landlord/lodger, tenant or housekeeper, or as flat-sharers) also sometimes fall foul of the rule. People who provide mutual support and share household expenses are not necessarily cohabiting.[35] This is also the case, for example, where friends share a home.

If you disagree with a decision that you are cohabiting, you should challenge the decision (see Chapters 41 and 42), and carefully consider what evidence to gather and submit in relation to each of the six questions on p704 and any other matters that you consider relevant. Possibilities include evidence of the other person having another address[36] (eg, a rent book and other household bills), receipts for board and lodging, statements from friends and relatives, or evidence of a formal separation, divorce proceedings or a dissolution application or order.

You do not have to prove that you are not cohabiting when you first apply for benefit,[37] though you are required to provide the decision maker with any information reasonably required to decide your claim.[38] Neither party has the burden of proof in this situation – a decision should simply be made on all the evidence available.[39] By contrast, if your benefit as a single person is stopped because it is alleged that you are cohabiting, the burden of proof is on the decision maker to prove you are.[40]

If your benefit is stopped because you are cohabiting, you should challenge the decision and/or re-apply immediately if your circumstances change. You should also apply immediately for any other benefits for which you might qualify – eg, HB/CTB, where the local authority may reach a different decision to that of the DWP.[41] You should apply for other benefits for which which you previously automatically qualified if you were on IS or JSA – eg, health benefits (see Chapter 9).

If you are still entitled to a means-tested benefit, even though it is decided that you are cohabiting, you should be paid as a couple.

If your IS, income-based JSA or PC stops and your court order for maintenance is collected by the DWP (see p745), contact the magistrates' (or in Scotland, sheriff's) court immediately to get payments sent direct to you. If the Child Support Agency (or its intended replacement, the Child Maintenance and Enforcement Commission) is collecting a child maintenance assessment for you (see p750), ask it to start paying the money to you.

If you have no money at all, you may be able to get a social fund crisis loan (see p503).

Couples living apart

If you separate *permanently* you can claim as a single person immediately. However, you continue to be treated as a couple while you and your partner are *temporarily* apart.[42] Your former household need not have been in this country.[43] The following rules apply in determining whether you still count as a couple.

- For **IS, income-based JSA, PC and HB**, you count as a couple, even if you or your partner are temporarily living away from your family, unless you:[44]
  - have no intention of resuming living together; *or*
  - are likely to be separated for more than 52 weeks. However, you can still be treated as a couple if you are likely to be separated for more than 52 weeks

provided it is not 'substantially' longer and there are exceptional circumstances such as a stay in hospital, or if there is no control over the length of the absence.

- For **IS, income-based JSA and PC**, you no longer count as a couple if:[45]
  - either of you are in custody;
  - either of you are released on temporary licence from prison;
  - either of you are a compulsory patient detained in hospital under the mental health provisions;
  - either of you are staying permanently in a care home, an Abbeyfield Home or an independent hospital;
  - the claimant is abroad (other than to get NHS treatment) and does not qualify for IS, income-based JSA or PC (see Chapter 58). However, if your partner is temporarily abroad (other than to get NHS treatment) you continue to be treated as a couple, but after four weeks (eight if s/he has taken a child abroad for medical treatment) the amount of IS, income-based JSA or PC you receive is that for a single claimant.[46] You can get IS without signing on if you have children under 16.[47] Your partner's income and capital continue to be treated as yours for as long as the absence is held to be temporary.

  If you are no longer treated as a couple for the purposes of calculating your IS or income-based JSA, you may still be liable to maintain your partner (see p744).
- For **IS and income-based JSA only**, you are still treated as a couple if you are temporarily living apart and one of you is at home or in hospital, or in local authority residential accommodation or in a care home, and the other is:[48]
  - resident in a care home, independent hospital or Abbeyfield Home, but not counted as a patient; *or*
  - in a home for the rehabilitation of alcoholics or drug addicts; *or*
  - in Polish resettlement accommodation; *or*
  - on a government training course and has to live away from home; *or*
  - in a probation or bail hostel.

  Although your income and capital are calculated in the normal way for a couple, your applicable amount is calculated as if each of you were single claimants if this comes to more than your usual couple rate. If you have housing costs (see Chapter 34), your applicable amount includes these as well as any costs of the temporary accommodation of the partner away from home. If you are both away from home, the costs of both sets of temporary accommodation and the family home may be met.[49] If both homes are rented, see p187 for when HB can be paid for more than one home at a time. If you own your home and your partner is staying in rented accommodation, you may get your housing costs met by IS or income-based JSA and your partner can claim HB.

- Where questions of 'intention' are involved (eg, in deciding whether you or your partner intend to resume living with your family), the intention must be unqualified – ie, it must not depend on some factor over which you have no control (eg, the right of entry to the UK being granted by the Home Office[50] or the offer of a suitable job[51]). See p799 if your child is in hospital and you have to stay in lodgings to be nearby.
- See p799 if one or both of you are temporarily in local authority residential accommodation.

3. Claiming for children

As you cannot claim joint-claim jobseeker's allowance (JSA) if you have children, the references to income-based JSA below do not include joint-claim JSA.

In order to claim for a 'child' you must be 'responsible' for her/him and s/he must be living in your 'household' (these terms are explained below). You do not have to be a parent.[52]

Note: the law refers to someone aged under 16 as a 'child' and to someone aged 16-20 as a 'qualifying young person'. In this chapter, the term 'child' is used to refer to both.

A child (including a new child) can only be included in your claim in some cases. From 6 April 2004, a child can be included:[53]

- in your claim for **housing benefit** (HB) or **council tax benefit** (CTB); *or*
- in your claim for **income support** (IS) or **income-based jobseeker's allowance** (JSA) if:
  - your current claim for IS or income-based JSA began before 6 April 2004; *and*
  - you had a dependent child(ren) included in that claim before 6 April 2004 but you have not yet been awarded child tax credit (CTC).

Otherwise, a child cannot be included in your claim. Instead, you will need to claim CTC for her/him (see p1196). (But see the note in CPAG's *Welfare Rights Bulletin* 186 p12 for some possible doubts about this. The DWP attempted to clarify the rules from 8 September 2005.[54])

Note: even where your child cannot be included in your claim, there are circumstances in which it may still be important that you are regarded as being responsible for a child living in your household, or having a child as part of your 'family'. This applies particularly to child benefit (see p63), IS (see p298), income-based JSA (see p365) and, in some cases, housing costs (see p806).

Income support and income-based jobseeker's allowance

Any new claim for IS or income-based JSA does not include an amount for a child (see above).

If you were on IS or income-based JSA before 6 April 2004 and your claim included a dependent child before that date, it may continue to include amounts for all of the children in your family, even those that become part of your family after that date. However, your claim will cease to include amounts for children at some point. The key is the date at which you become entitled to CTC.[55]

However, your IS/income-based JSA claim will cease to include amounts for children at the earliest of:

- the point you make a claim for and are awarded CTC; *or*
- the point the claim for your child is automatically transferred to a CTC claim.

The DWP and the Revenue refer to the process of automatic transfer to CTC claims as 'migration'. Exactly when this process will begin is yet to be announced – see CPAG's *Welfare Rights Bulletin* for updates.

If you were awarded CTC before 6 April 2004, your IS/income-based JSA award will have ceased to have included amounts for a child from that date.[56]

Who counts as a child

A person usually counts as a child (but see below) if:[57]

- s/he is aged under 16; *or*
- s/he is aged 16 or over but under 20 and counts as a 'qualifying young person' for child benefit purposes. This includes, for example, most young people who are at school or college full time doing GCSEs or A levels (or equivalent), or who are doing approved training (but see p56 for full details).

Who is not counted as a child

Someone is *not* counted as a child if:

- s/he is entitled to IS or income-based JSA in her/his own right;[58] *or*
- s/he is aged 16 or 17, left local authority care on or after 1 October 2001 and certain other conditions apply (see p610 for the detail).

Responsibility for a child

You claim IS or income-based JSA, HB or CTB for a child (including a qualifying young person) for whom you are 'responsible' (see p711). **Note:** for IS and income-based JSA, children can in any case *only* be included in certain claims made before 6 April 2004 (see p709).

Where the same benefit is involved, a child can only be the responsibility of one person in any week.[59] There is no provision allowing benefit to be split between parents if a child divides her/his time equally between the homes of two parents. Benefit payable to one person for her/his dependant can be paid to someone else instead,[60] but this is an exceptional measure which only applies if the person paid the benefit is not using it for the child or dependant, or is otherwise squandering it.[61] For HB, rent restrictions will apply, limiting the amount of HB you can claim for the size of the accommodation you may need for a child if someone else is considered to be 'responsible' for her/him (see p244).[62]

The rules are different for different benefits. You are treated as 'responsible' for a child if the following applies.

- For **income-based JSA**, either you get child benefit for the child, or if no one gets child benefit for the child, the child is 'usually living' with you or you are the only person who has applied for the child benefit. However, if you share actual responsibility for the child (eg, with your ex-partner), a court decision means that even if you do not get child benefit for the child, you might be regarded as responsible for the child if you are the **'substantial minority carer'** – ie, you have the child with you for at least 104 nights a year.[63] However, this depends on the child benefit rules unlawfully discriminating against you. Arguably, that may be difficult to show in some cases. If, for example, you are a woman who has separated from a male partner, showing discrimination may be difficult because child benefit is usually awarded to the mother when a different sex-couple separate.[64] Seek advice (see Appendix 2) if necessary.
- For **HB** and **CTB**, the child is 'normally living' with you.[65] This means that s/he spends more time with you than with anyone else.[66] For HB and CTB only, if it is unclear whose household the child lives in, or if s/he spends an equal amount of time with two parents in different homes (this may not mean literally three and a half days with each parent[67]), you are treated as having responsibility if:[68]
  - you get child benefit for the child (see Chapter 4);
  - no one gets child benefit, but you have applied for it;
  - no one has applied for child benefit, or both of you have applied, but you appear to have the most responsibility.

  However, if you are a 'substantial minority carer' (see above), you may be able to argue that you should be regarded as responsible for the child even if you do not get child benefit.[69]
- For **IS only**, you get child benefit for the child (see Chapter 4).[70] Where no one gets child benefit you are 'responsible' if you are the only one who has applied for it. In all other cases the person 'responsible' is the person with whom the child *usually lives*.[71] However, if you are a 'substantial minority carer' (see above), you may be able to argue that you should be regarded as responsible for the child even if you do not get child benefit.[72] If a child for whom you are 'responsible' gets child benefit for another child, you are also 'responsible' for that child.[73]

For **HB** and **CTB**, it is important to look at who gets child benefit only where it is unclear in whose household the child *normally* lives. For **IS**, it is essential to look first at who gets child benefit, and only where this is not decisive is it relevant to look at where the child *usually* lives. This difference may mean that in some situations one parent may be able to claim IS for a child while the other parent can claim income-based JSA, HB or CTB for the same child at the same time.

Living in the same household[74]

These rules apply mainly to **HB** and **CTB** claims. For the purpose of deciding when children can be included in your claim, for **IS** and **income-based JSA** they apply only to those claims where it is still possible to have an amount for a child included (see p709).

If you are counted as responsible for a child, that child is usually treated as a member of your household despite any temporary absence. (For a discussion of what 'household' means, see p703.) However, s/he does *not* count as a member of your household if s/he:

- for **IS, income-based JSA, HB** and **CTB**:
  - has no intention of resuming living with you;
  - is likely to be absent for more than 52 weeks, unless there are exceptional circumstances such as being in hospital or otherwise having no control over the length of absence, and the absence is unlikely to be substantially longer than 52 weeks;
  - is being fostered by you following a formal placement with you by social services. However, you can claim benefit for a child you are fostering privately or where social services have made a less formal arrangement for the child to live with you;
  - is living with you prior to adoption, and has been placed with you by social services or an adoption agency;
  - is boarded out or has been placed with someone else prior to adoption;
  - is in the care of, or being looked after by, the local authority and not living with you. You should receive IS or income-based JSA for her/him for the days when s/he comes home – eg, for the weekend or a holiday.[75] Make sure you tell the decision makers in good time. The local authority can also increase your applicable amount to include the child for HB and CTB for all of that week whether the child returns for all or only part of it;[76]
- for **IS and income-based JSA**:
  - has been in hospital or in a local authority home (for non-temporary accommodation) for more than 12 weeks, and you or other members of your household have not been in regular contact with her/him. The 12 weeks run from the date s/he went into the hospital or home, or from the date you claim IS/income-based JSA, if later.[77] However, if you were getting income-based JSA immediately before your claim for IS, or if you were getting IS immediately before your claim for income-based JSA, the 12 weeks run from the date s/he went into the hospital or home;[78]
  - is in custody. You should receive IS or income-based JSA for any periods your child spends at home;[79]

- has been abroad for more than four weeks, or for more than eight weeks if the absence abroad is to get medical treatment for the child.[80] The four- or eight-week periods run from the day s/he went abroad or from the day you claim IS/income-based JSA, if later. However, if you were getting income-based JSA immediately before your claim for IS, or if you were getting IS immediately before your claim for income-based JSA, the four- or eight-week periods are calculated from the day after the child went abroad;[81]
- is living with you and away from her/his parental or usual home in order to attend school. The child is not treated as a member of your family, but remains a member of her/his parent's household.[82]

When to stop claiming for a child

If you still have amounts for a child included in your claim for IS or income-based JSA, this will cease at the point you become entitled to CTC.

Otherwise, you stop claiming for a child when you no longer fulfil the conditions described above – ie:

- you are no longer *responsible* for her/him (see p710); *or*
- s/he is no longer a *member of your household* (see p712); *or*
- s/he no longer *counts as a child* (see p710).

For example:

- for all benefits, you stop claiming as soon as the child starts normally living elsewhere;
- for **IS**, you stop claiming for a child as soon as someone else starts receiving child benefit for her/him;[83]
- for **IS, income-based JSA, HB and CTB**, you stop claiming if the child becomes entitled to IS or income-based JSA in her/his own right;[84]
- for **IS, income-based JSA, HB** and **CTB**, you claim for a child until s/he is 16, or 20 if s/he counts as a 'qualifying young person' – eg, because s/he is in full-time non-advanced education or approved training (see p576). Children count as in full-time non-advanced education until the 'terminal date' (see p62) or until they get a full-time job if that is earlier. 'Full-time' work for dependent children means at least 24 hours a week.[85]

Notes

1. **Who is included in your claim**
   1 s137(1) SSCBA 1992; s35(1) JSA 1995
   IS Reg 14(2)(c) IS Regs
   JSA Reg 76(2)(d) JSA Regs
   HB Reg 19(2)(c) HB Regs; reg 19(2)(c) HB(SPC) Regs
   CTB Reg 9(2)(c) CTB Regs; reg 9(2)(c) CTB(SPC) Regs
   2 Reg 1 SS(WTCCTC)(CA) Regs
   3 Reg 1(4) and (8) SS(WTCCTC)(CA) Regs
   4 SS(TC)A Regs

2. **Couples**
   5 CFC/7/1992
   6 s137(1) SSCBA 1992
   IS Reg 2(1) IS Regs
   JSA s35(1) JSA 1995; reg 1(3) JSA Regs
   PC s17(1) SPCA 2002; reg 1(2) SPC Regs
   HB Reg 2(1) HB Regs; reg 2(1) HB(SPC) Regs
   CTB Reg 2(1) CTB Regs; reg 2(1) CTB(SPC) Regs
   7 s134(2) SSCBA 1992; s3(1)(d) JSA 1995; s4(1) SPCA 2002
   8 **IS** Reg 4(3) SS(C&P) Regs
   JSA Reg 4(3B) SS(C&P) Regs
   HB Reg 82(1) HB Regs; reg 63(1) HB(SPC) Regs
   CTB Reg 68(1) CTB Regs; reg 52(1) CTB(SPC) Regs
   9 s1(2)(b) and (6) SPCA 2002
   10 Reg 5(1)(h) SPC Regs
   11 s137 SSCBA 1992; s35(1) JSA 1995; s17(1) SPCA 2002, as amended by Sch 24 CPA 2004
   12 **IS/JSA/PC** This is what is understood to be the DWP application of the standard rules on overpayments.
   HB/CTB The Civil Partnership (Pensions, Social Security and Child Support) (Consequential, etc. Provisions) Order 2005 No.2877; HB/CTB Circular A16/05
   13 R(SB) 8/85
   14 **IS** Reg 2(1) IS Regs
   JSA Reg 1(3) JSA Regs
   PC s12 SPCA 2002
   HB Reg 2(1) HB Regs; reg 2(1) HB(SPC) Regs
   CTB Reg 2(1) CTB Regs; reg 2(1) CTB(SPC) Regs
   15 **IS** Regs 18 and 23 IS Regs
   JSA Regs 84 and 88(4) and (5) JSA Regs
   PC Reg 8 and Sch 3 SPC Regs
   HB Regs 23 and 25 HB Regs; regs 22 and 23 HB(SPC) Regs
   CTB Regs 13 and 15 CTB Regs; regs 12 and 13 CTB(SPC) Regs
   16 s1 CPA 2004
   17 *Santos v Santos* [1972] 2 All ER 246; CIS/671/1992; CIS/81/1993
   18 CIS/4935/1997
   19 R(SB) 8/85
   20 R(SB) 4/83
   21 CSB/463/1986
   22 **IS** Reg 2(1) IS Regs
   JSA Reg 1(3) JSA Regs
   PC Reg 1(2) SPC Regs
   HB Reg 2(1) HB Regs; reg 2(1) HB(SPC) Regs
   CTB Reg 2(1) CTB Regs; reg 2(1) CTB(SPC) Regs
   All s137(1A) SSCBA 1992
   23 *R v Penwith District Council HBRB ex parte Menear* 24 HLR 120, 11 October 1991
   24 *R v South Ribble Borough Council HBRB ex parte Hamilton*, 24 January 2000 (CA)
   25 *Crake and Butterworth v SBC* [1982] 1 All ER 498
   26 R(SB) 17/81; R(G) 3/71; CIS/87/1993
   27 *Crake and Butterworth v SBC*, quoted in R(SB) 35/85
   28 R(SB) 35/85
   29 para 11046 DMG
   30 CIS/72/1994
   31 CIS/2900/1998
   32 CIS/87/1993
   33 CSB/150/1985
   34 CIS/87/1993; CIS/2559/2002
   35 CSSB/145/1983
   36 R(SB) 13/82
   37 CIS/317/1994

38 **IS** Reg 7(1) SS(C&P) Regs
JSA Reg 24 JSA Regs
HB Reg 86 HB Regs; reg 67 HB(SPC) Regs
CTB Reg 72 CTB Regs; reg 57 CTB(SPC) Regs
39 CIS/317/1994
40 R(I) 1/71
41 R(H) 9/04
42 **IS** Reg 16(1) IS Regs
JSA Reg 78(1) JSA Regs
PC Reg 5(2) SPC Regs
HB Reg 21(1) HB Regs; reg 21(1) HB(SPC) Regs
CTB Reg 11(1) CTB Regs; reg 11(1) CTB(SPC) Regs
43 CIS/508/1992
44 **IS** Reg 16(1) and (2) IS Regs
JSA Reg 78(2) JSA Regs
PC Reg 5(1)(a) SPC Regs
HB Reg 21(1) and 2) HB Regs; reg 21(1) and (2) HB(SPC) Regs
45 **IS** Reg 16(3) IS Regs
JSA Reg 78(3) JSA Regs
PC Reg 5(1)(b)-(d) and (f) SPC Regs
46 **IS** Sch 7 paras 11 and 11A IS Regs
JSA Sch 5 paras 10 and 11 JSA Regs
47 Sch 1B para 23 IS Regs
48 **IS** Sch 7 para 9 IS Regs
JSA Reg 85 and Sch 5 para 5 JSA Regs
49 **IS** Sch 7 para 9 col (2) IS Regs
JSA Reg 85 and Sch 5 para 5 col (2) JSA Regs
50 CIS/508/1992; CIS/13805/1996
51 CIS/484/1993

3. **Claiming for children**

52 s137 SSCBA 1992; s35 JSA 1995; reg 77 JSA Regs
53 Reg 1 SS(WTCCTC)(CA) Regs
54 SS(TC)A Regs
55 Reg 1(3) and (7) SS(WTCCTC)(CA) Regs
56 Reg 1(2) and (6) SS(WTCCTC)(CA) Regs
57 **All benefits** s137 SSCBA 1992
IS Reg 14 IS Regs
JSA s35 JSA 1995; regs 1(3) and 76 JSA Regs
HB Reg 19 HB Regs; reg 19 HB(SPC) Regs
CTB Reg 9 CTB Regs; reg 9 CTB(SPC) Regs
58 **IS** Reg 14(2) IS Regs
JSA Reg 76(2) JSA Regs
HB Reg 19(2) HB Regs; reg 19(2) HB(SPC) Regs
CTB Reg 9(2) CTB Regs; reg 9(2) CTB(SPC) Regs
59 **IS/HB/CTB** s134(2) SSCBA 1992
IS Reg 15(4) IS Regs
JSA s3(1)(d) JSA 1995; reg 77(5) JSA Regs
HB Reg 20(3) HB Regs; reg 20(3) HB(SPC) Regs
CTB Reg 10(3) CTB Regs; reg 10(3) CTB(SPC) Regs
60 Reg 34 SS(C&P) Regs
61 *Barber v Secretary of State for Work and Pensions* [2002] EWHC Admin 1915, 17 July 2002, unreported
62 *R v Swale Borough Council, ex parte Marchant, The Times*, 17 November 1999 (CA)
63 Reg 77 JSA Regs, as applied in *Hockenjos v Secretary of State for Social Security* [2004] EWCA Civ 1749, reported as R(JSA) 1/05
64 CJSA/2507/2002
65 **HB** Reg 20(1) HB Regs; reg 20(1) HB(SPC) Regs
CTB Reg 10(1) CTB Regs; reg 10(1) CTB(SPC) Regs
66 CFC/1537/1995
67 CFC/1537/1995
68 **HB** Reg 20(2) HB Regs; reg 20(2) HB(SPC) Regs
CTB Reg 10(2) CTB Regs; reg 10(2) CTB(SPC) Regs
69 *Hockenjos v Secretary of State for Social Security* [2004] EWCA Civ 1749, reported as R(JSA) 1/05, applies only to JSA. However, it may support arguments concerning HB/CTB based on the Human Rights Act.
70 **IS** Reg 15(1) IS Reg
JSA Reg 77(1) JSA Regs
71 **IS** Reg 15(2) IS Regs
JSA Reg 77(3) JSA Regs
72 *Hockenjos v Secretary of State for Social Security* [2004] EWCA Civ 1749, reported as R(JSA) 1/05, applies only to JSA. However, it may support arguments concerning IS based on the Human Rights Act.
73 **IS** Reg 15(1A) IS Regs
JSA Reg 77(2) JSA Regs
74 **IS** Reg 16 IS Regs
JSA Reg 78 JSA Regs
HB Reg 21 HB Regs; reg 21 HB(SPC) Regs
CTB Reg 11 CTB Regs; reg 11 CTB(SPC) Regs
75 **IS** Regs 15(3) and 16(6) IS Regs
JSA Regs 77(4) and 78(7) JSA Regs

76 **HB** Reg 21(5) HB Regs; reg 21(5) HB(SPC) Regs
CTB Reg 11(4) CTB Regs; reg 11(4) CTB(SPC) Regs
77 **IS** Reg 16(5)(b) IS Regs
JSA Reg 78(5)(c) JSA Regs
78 **IS** Reg 16(5A) IS Regs
JSA Reg 78(6) JSA Regs
79 **IS** Regs 15(3) and 16(6) IS Regs
JSA Regs 77(4) and 78(5)(l) and (7) JSA Regs
80 **IS** Reg 16(5a) and (aa) IS Regs
JSA Reg 78(5)(a) and (b) JSA Regs
81 **IS** Reg 16(5A) IS Regs
JSA Reg 78(6) JSA Regs
82 **IS** Reg 16(7) IS Regs
JSA Reg 78(8) JSA Regs
83 Reg 15 IS Regs
84 **IS** Reg 14(2)(b) IS Regs
JSA Reg 76(2)(b) JSA Regs
HB Reg 19(2) HB Regs; reg 19(2) HB(SPC) Regs
CTB Reg 9(2) CTB Regs; reg 9(2) CTB(SPC) Regs
85 Regs 1(3), definition of 'remunerative work' and 7 CB Regs

Chapter 31

National insurance contributions

This chapter covers:

Many of the benefits described in this *Handbook* are financed from the national insurance (NI) fund. Entitlement to these benefits – and sometimes the amount paid – depends upon the contribution record of the claimant or, in the case of bereavement benefits and Category B retirement pensions, of the claimant's spouse or civil partner.

Contributions are collected for the DWP by the Revenue.

Future changes[1]

- The pension age for men and women is to increase gradually to 68 over the period from 2024 to 2046.
- A single contribution condition for Category A and B retirement pension is to be introduced – contributors who reach pension age on or after 6 April 2010 will only need to have paid or been credited with sufficient contributions over 30 years to establish entitlement to a full pension.
- Home responsibilities protection is to be replaced from 6 April 2010 (see p733).

1. How decisions are made

Most decisions on national insurance (NI) contributions are made by an officer of the Revenue, and appeals against such decisions are decided by tax commissioners.[2] The appeal process is similar to appealing to the tax commissioners over a statutory payment decision (see p1153).

If you appeal against a decision on your entitlement to credited contributions or home responsibilities protection your appeal will be decided by an appeal tribunal (see Chapter 42).

See pp1094 and 1149 for details of future changes to the way appeals are to be dealt with.

2. **Contributions: liability and payment**

Classes of contribution

There are six different classes of national insurance (NI) contribution.[3] The class you pay depends on whether you are an employed or self-employed earner, or a voluntary contributor. Not all classes of contribution count for all benefits.[4] Contributions are paid for a tax year (ie, 6 April to 5 April).

Class of contribution	*Payable by*	*Giving entitlement to*
Class 1	Employed earners and their employers	All benefits with contribution conditions
Class 1A and 1B	Employers of employed earners	No benefits
Class 2	Self-employed earners	All benefits with contribution conditions except contribution-based jobseeker's allowance (see p735)
Class 3	Voluntary contributors	Widows' and bereavement benefits and retirement pensions
Class 4	Self-employed earners	No benefits

The amount of Class 1 or 4 contributions you pay depends on your earnings. You do not necessarily gain more benefit by paying higher contributions.

Employed earners and self-employed earners

An **'employed earner'** is 'a person who is gainfully employed in Great Britain (GB) either under a contract of service, or in an office (including elective office) with general earnings'.[5] This means you are an 'employed earner' if income tax is, or should be, deducted from your earnings under the Pay As You Earn scheme.

A **'self-employed earner'** is anyone 'gainfully employed in GB otherwise than in employed earner's employment'.[6] If you have two jobs it is possible to be both employed and self-employed.

Office-holders include judges, company directors and registrars of births, deaths and marriages.

It is normally clear whether you are employed or self-employed. If there is a dispute it usually concerns whether you are employed under a *contract of service* (in which case you are an employee) or a *contract for services* (in which case you are self-employed). When considering this the decision maker must take into account factors such as how closely your work is supervised, whether you can employ a substitute to do your job for you, the method of payment, whether the contract is for a fixed period, and whether you have to provide your own equipment. No one criterion is conclusive and different weight is attached to each in different cases.[7]

Certain people are deemed to be employed earners.[8] These are office cleaners, many agency workers, people employed by their spouse or civil partner for the purposes of their spouse's or civil partner's employment, lecturers, teachers and certain instructors, some entertainers and most ministers of religion. Conversely, examiners, moderators and invigilators are deemed to be self-employed.[9]

In certain circumstances you do not have to pay NI contributions – eg, if you are employed:[10]

- in your home by a close relative as long as you both live in the home and the job is not for the purposes of any trade or business carried on there. '**Close relatives**' are a parent, grandparent, step-parent, son, daughter, grandson, granddaughter, stepson, stepdaughter, brother, sister, half-brother or half-sister (step-parents and stepchildren include those relationships formed by civil partnerships);
- by your spouse or civil partner if it is not for the purposes of your spouse's or civil partner's employment;
- as a self-employed earner if you are not ordinarily self-employed.

Age limits

Contributions are intended to be paid during a normal working life. Therefore they are not payable if you are under 16[11] or over pension age (60 for women, 65 for men, but see p731 for details of credited contributions for men over 60).[12] The Revenue should send you a certificate of age exemption when you reach pension age. Ask at your local Revenue enquiry centre if it does not, or write to the National Insurance Contributions Office (see Appendix 1). Employers of employees over pension age still have to pay their contributions at the full (contracted-in) rate.

These age rules discriminate against men (and in some circumstances also against women) on the grounds of gender, but see p1167.

If you have obtained a full gender recognition certificate, the age limit for payment of your contributions will change to 60 if you have been recognised as a woman, or 65 if you have been recognised as a man.

Residence and presence in Great Britain

Class 1 contributions must usually be paid by employees who are employed in GB[13] and who are resident, present (except for temporary absence) or ordinarily resident in GB at the time.[14]

However, if you are employed by an overseas employer and are not ordinarily resident or employed in the UK, you are not liable for Class 1 contributions until you have been resident in GB for a year.[15]

If you are working abroad, you must still pay Class 1 contributions for the first year if your employer has a place of business in GB, you were resident in GB before your employment started and you are still ordinarily resident in GB.[16] After that year you are entitled, but not obliged, to pay Class 3 contributions.[17]

Class 2 contributions must be paid if you are self-employed in GB and are either ordinarily resident in GB, or have been resident here for at least 26 weeks during the last year.[18] If you are present in GB, they may be paid voluntarily if you are not required to pay them.[19] If you are self-employed outside GB, you may pay Class 2 contributions if you wish, provided you were employed or self-employed immediately before you left GB and, *either*:

- you have been resident in GB for a continuous period of at least three years at some time in the past; *or*
- you have paid contributions producing an earnings factor of at least 52 times the lower earnings limit in each of three years in the past (see pp735 and 722 for the meaning of these terms). Each set of 52 flat-rate contributions paid before April 1975 counts as satisfying that condition in respect of one year.[20]

Certain volunteer development workers who are employed abroad may be allowed to pay Class 2 contributions. These are paid at a special rate and give entitlement to contribution-based jobseeker's allowance (JSA).[21]

Class 3 contributions are always voluntary. They may be paid if you are resident in GB throughout the course of the year in respect of which you wish to pay the contributions or if:

- you arrived in GB in the year for which you want to pay contributions and either you were liable to pay Class 1 or 2 contributions earlier that year or you have been ordinarily resident for at least part of the year; *or*
- you arrived in GB in the year for which you want to pay contributions, or in the previous year, and you have been in GB for a continuous period of 26 weeks.

They may normally be paid while you are abroad if you satisfy either of the conditions which would allow you to pay Class 2 contributions, but you do not need to have been employed or self-employed before you left GB. You may also pay them if you have been paying Class 1 contributions while abroad.[22]

Class 4 contributions are payable only if you are resident in the UK for income tax purposes.[23]

If you wish to pay Class 2 or 3 contributions while abroad, leaflet NI38 contains an application form.

The meaning of the terms **'resident'** and **'present'** are explained on p1357. Members of the armed forces are deemed always to be present in GB and there are special rules for aircrew, mariners, share fishermen and offshore workers on the continental shelf.

For the factors which are taken into account in deciding where you are **'ordinarily resident'** see p1357.

Northern Ireland and Isle of Man contributions count towards British benefits, as do contributions paid in other countries in some circumstances. In particular, this may apply if you have paid contributions in the European Economic Area (including in A8 or A2 states) – see p1383. You may also be entitled to benefits from other countries while you are in this country (see Chapter 58).

Reduced liability for married women and widows

Women who were married or widowed on 6 April 1977 could choose to pay a reduced Class 1, or no Class 2, contribution, but they had to apply to do so before 12 May 1977.[24]

If you 'elected' to pay at this reduced rate you can continue to do so until you either apply to pay the full rate again (called 'revoking an election') or until the right to pay reduced contributions is automatically lost. For example, the right to pay reduced contributions is automatically lost:[25]

- at the end of the tax year in which your husband dies, or at the end of the next tax year if he dies after 30 September, if you have reduced liability when your husband dies (unless, in some circumstances, you are entitled to a widows' or a bereavement benefit);
- at the end of the tax year in which you stop receiving a widows' or bereavement benefit, unless you remarry before the end of that tax year;
- on divorce or annulment of marriage;
- after two consecutive tax years with no earnings from self-employment or on which you have had to pay Class 1 contributions.

These are examples and there are other situations when reduced liability is automatically lost.

There are disadvantages to reduced liability but it is worth thinking carefully about your position if you are considering giving it up. Once lost, the right cannot be reclaimed. The following considerations are relevant.

- Reduced contributions do not entitle you to contributory benefits and in some circumstances revoking your election may mean that you can build up your pension entitlement (see p738, but note the future changes to pensions mentioned on p717). However, even with reduced liability you may still qualify for bereavement benefits and Category B retirement pension based on your husband's record, non-contributory benefits and means-tested benefits.

- Although you could gain an additional pension under the additional state pension scheme if you started to pay full Class 1 contributions, it might be better to continue to pay reduced contributions and put the money into a private scheme instead. This is a point on which you will probably need advice from an independent financial adviser.
- A year in which you have reduced liability for contributions cannot normally be a year of home responsibilities protection (see p733).
- If your earnings are below the primary threshold but above the lower earnings limit (see below) you will normally be treated as having paid Class 1 contributions on those earnings for the purpose of entitlement to contributory benefits. However, if you have elected to pay reduced contributions you will only be treated as having paid a reduced rate of contribution on those earnings and so will not build up entitlement to contributory benefits.[26]
- You may be entitled to credited contributions if you revoke the election. If you do not, you cannot qualify for any NI credits other than credits following bereavement and starting credits (see p727).[27]

Note: if you reach pension age on or after 6 April 2010, when considering whether to revoke an election, you should also take into account forthcoming changes to pensions and home responsibilities protection (see p717).

If you are thinking of giving up your reduced liability seek independent advice (see Appendix 2).

To revoke your election, complete the form in Revenue leaflet CF9 for married women or CF9A for widows.

Class 1 contributions

Class 1 contributions are paid both by employed earners (see p718 – known as primary contributors) and their employers (secondary contributors).[28]

If you are an employed earner the amount of the Class 1 contributions you pay depends on the amount you earn in relation to the upper and lower earnings limit set for the tax year, and to the amount of that year's 'primary threshold' for payment of contributions. If your earnings are below the primary threshold you do not have to pay NI contributions on them (but if they are between the lower earnings limit and the primary threshold, you will be treated as if you had paid Class 1 NI contributions on those earnings).

If you earn more than the primary threshold you are liable to pay Class 1 contributions of 11 per cent of your earnings between the primary threshold and upper earnings limits (or 9.4 per cent if you are contracted out of the additional state pension scheme – see p476), plus 1 per cent of the earnings you have above the upper earnings limit.[29]

Year	*Lower earnings limit*	*Primary threshold*	*Upper earnings limit*
2007/08	£87	£100	£670
2008/09	£90	£105	£770

See Appendix 9 for the earnings limits and primary threshold for earlier years.

If your earnings are monthly, the earnings limits are multiplied by four-and-one-third to give monthly equivalents, and the monthly equivalent of the primary threshold for 2008/09 is £453.[30]

Example

If your weekly earnings in the tax year 2008/09 are £178, your Class 1 contribution is:

£178 – £105 = £73

11% x £73 = £8.03

If you are a member of an appropriate personal pension or stakeholder pension scheme (see p477), you pay Class 1 contributions at the contracted-in rate, but the Revenue will then pay a rebate of contributions, together with tax relief on your share of the rebate, directly into your pension scheme.[31]

If you are a married woman or widow with reduced liability for contributions (see p721), you pay 4.85 per cent of your earnings between the primary threshold and the upper earnings limit plus 1 per cent of your earnings above the upper earnings limit.[32]

Your employer should deduct your Class 1 contributions from your earnings (including from payments the Revenue has retrospectively treated as earnings under backdated tax legislation) and pay them with her/his own contributions to the Revenue.[33] See p726 for what happens if your employer does not do this.

More than one job

If you have more than one job, the basic rule is that your liability to pay Class 1 contributions is calculated for each job as if the other(s) did not exist.[34]

Example

Mary earns £60 a week working part time serving dinners at a school and £70 a week working behind the bar of a pub in the evenings. Although her total earnings are £130 a week neither she nor her employers pay any Class 1 contributions because her earnings in each job are below the lower earnings limit. As a result, Mary is not earning any entitlement to contribution-based JSA, incapacity benefit (IB) or a Category A retirement pension.

There are some exceptions to this rule – eg, if you have:[35]

- more than one job, you can claim a refund if, during a tax year, you pay more than the annual maximum;
- two different jobs for the same employer or employers who carry on business in association with each other, earnings from these jobs are normally added together and your NI contributions are based on your total earnings. This is to stop employers avoiding the liability to pay contributions.

Class 2 contributions

You must pay Class 2 contributions if you are a self-employed earner (see p718) unless you are exempt from liability. The main ground for being exempt is that you have obtained a certificate of exception because your earnings are below a certain level (£4,825 a year in 2008/09) – this is also known as a **'small earnings exception'** (see below).[36] Certain expenses are deducted when calculating your earnings.[37]

Even if you have a small earnings exception you may still choose to pay Class 2 contributions to protect your NI contribution record for IB, retirement pension and bereavement benefit.[38]

Class 2 contributions are payable at a flat rate.[39] The current and recent rates are:

2005/06 and 2006/07	£2.10 a week
2007/08	£2.20 a week
2008/09	£2.30 a week

Married women and widows with reduced liability for contributions (see p721) are not liable for Class 2 contributions.[40] Volunteer development workers employed abroad (see p720) and share fishermen pay Class 2 contributions at special rates which count towards contribution-based JSA, unlike other Class 2 contributions.[41]

If you are self-employed and also have a job as an employed earner you pay both Class 1 and Class 2 contributions, subject to a maximum.[42]

Applying for a small earnings exception

To apply for a certificate of exception you should complete Form CF10, available from local offices of the Revenue and on the Revenue's website (www.hmrc.gov.uk). You must apply promptly because a certificate can only be backdated for up to 13 weeks before the date of application, at the Revenue's discretion.[43] Usually your earnings are estimated; they will be estimated as below the minimum level if they were below that level in the previous year and there has been 'no material change of circumstances'.

You can apply for a refund of any Class 2 contributions you have paid if your earnings in that year were, in fact, sufficiently low to entitle you to an exemption from liability. The application must be made in writing after the end of the relevant tax year (ie, on or after 6 April) and must be made no later than the 31 January following the end of the relevant tax year.[44]

Class 3 contributions

Payments of Class 3 contributions are purely voluntary.[45] The introduction of home responsibilities protection (see p733) has lessened the need to pay them. They give entitlement only to bereavement benefits and retirement pension and are not payable if your earnings factor is otherwise sufficient in that tax year to meet the second contribution condition for those benefits (see pp735and 738).[46] If it is not (eg, because you have been abroad or in prison), you may wish to consider paying Class 3 contributions. Any accidental overpayment of contributions should be refunded if you make a written application.[47]

Class 3 contributions are paid at a flat rate. The current and recent rates are:[48]

2005/06	£7.35 a week
2006/07	£7.55 a week
2007/08	£7.80 a week
2008/09	£8.10 a week

If you reach pension age before 6 April 2010 you can request a state pension forecast to help you decide whether to pay Class 3 contributions, by telephoning the Pension Service (tel: 0845 300 0168 or textphone: 0845 300 0169), by completing Form BR19, available from your local Jobcentre Plus or DWP office, or by completing and submitting an application online at www.thepensionservice.gov.uk. If you reach pension age on or after 6 April 2010 changes to the contribution conditions for retirement pension will affect you (see p717), and you may not be able to obtain a pension forecast until at least autumn 2008. In this situation, seek advice before paying Class 3 contributions. If you will reach pension age on or after 6 April 2010 and you were not aware of the changes and you paid Class 3 (or voluntary Class 2) contributions between 25 May 2006 (when the Government announced these plans) and 26 July 2007 you may be able to request a refund.

Class 4 contributions

Class 4 contributions are paid by self-employed earners (see p718) when their profits in a tax year are above a certain level. They are paid in addition to Class 2 contributions, but give no extra entitlement to benefit.[49] For the tax year 2008/09, Class 4 contributions are paid on profits above £5,435. The amount paid is 8 per cent of profits between £5,435 and £40,040, plus 1 per cent of profits above £40,040. The current and recent rates are:

Year	*8% on profits between*	*1% on profits above*
2005/06	£4,895 and £32,760	£32,760
2006/07	£5,035 and £33,540	£33,540
2007/08	£5,225 and £34,840	£34,840
2008/09	£5,435 and £40,040	£40,040

The profits are those on which income tax under Schedule D is payable, and Class 4 contributions are usually collected with your income tax by the Revenue. You may apply for permission to defer payment for a specified period if the amount to be paid has not yet been established.[50]

If you are liable to pay Class 1, and/or Class 2 and Class 4 contributions, the total payable is subject to a maximum.[51]

Pre-1975 contributions

The present contribution system was introduced on 6 April 1975. Between 5 July 1948 and 5 April 1975 there were no Class 4 contributions, and Class 1 contributions were paid by a 'flat-rate stamp' in the same way as Class 2 and Class 3 contributions. Graduated contributions giving entitlement to graduated retirement benefit (see p467) were introduced in 1961, but were collected separately.

Before 6 April 1975, contribution years were not the same as tax years, as they are now. Instead, the month in which they began depended on the last letter of the contributor's NI number. There were complicated transitional arrangements in both 1948 and 1975 so that you may well have had a contribution year which was not 12 months long. That may explain what would otherwise be anomalies in your contribution record.

Non-payment or late payment of contributions

It is an offence deliberately not to pay contributions for which you are liable (unless they are voluntary).[52] It is your employer's responsibility to deduct Class 1 contributions from your earnings and pay them to the Revenue. But if you connive with your employers in order to avoid paying contributions, you too could be prosecuted.

If your employer has deducted Class 1 contributions from your earnings, but has failed to pay them to the Revenue, you are treated as though they had been paid unless you have been negligent, or consented to or connived in that arrangement.[53]

Class 2 contributions are usually paid by quarterly bill or direct debit.[54] At the end of the tax year you will know whether or not it is necessary to pay Class 3 contributions to fill any gap in your record (but see p717).

Contributions can still count for benefit purposes if paid late, provided they are paid within two years (Class 1) or six years (Class 2 or Class 3) after the end of the tax year in which they were due (but see below).[55] Students, apprentices, trainees and prisoners may pay Class 3 contributions to cover their period of education, apprenticeship or imprisonment at any time before the end of the sixth complete tax year after that period finished.[56] However, contributions paid late cannot count for benefit entitlement for a period before the date on which they were actually paid (and, in the case of contribution-based JSA or IB, contributions paid late cannot count for benefit entitlement unless they were either paid before the start of the relevant benefit year – see p736 – or, if they were paid after the start of the relevant benefit year, until six weeks after they have been paid).[57] In very limited circumstances, such as when there have been certain kinds of official error by the DWP or the Revenue, contributions paid after the above time limits may count for benefit purposes.[58] There are special rules on the treatment of Class 1 contributions paid under a tax and NI contribution anti-avoidance scheme or arrangement.[59]

Note: the Revenue has extended the deadline for payment of:

- Class 3 contributions for the tax years from 1996/97 to 2001/02 if you did not receive notice before 1 November 2003 that you were entitled to pay these. If you reach pension age:
  - before 24 October 2004 you have until 5 April 2010 to pay;
  - on or after 24 October 2004 you have until 5 April 2009 to pay;[60]
- voluntary Class 2 and Class 3 contributions for the tax years 1993/4 to 2007/8, if credits which were awarded to you as a result of an official error (as defined on p732) were removed from your contribution record on or after 1 July 2007. The time limit for payment of the missing contributions is extended to 5 April 2014. (Class 2 contributions are voluntary if you are entitled, but not liable to pay them.)[61]

See p725 for advice on whether you should pay Class 3 contributions if you will reach pension age on or after 6 April 2010.

Voluntary contributions may be paid on behalf of a contributor after her/his death provided they are paid no later than s/he would have been allowed to pay them.[62] This may be useful to gain entitlement to, or increase the rate of, widowed parent's allowance or bereavement allowance (see pp21 and 24).

3. Credits and home responsibilities protection

In some circumstances you can be 'credited' with earnings or with Class 3 contributions. Such 'credits' can help you satisfy the second contribution condition for benefits with two contribution conditions – ie, Category A and B retirement pensions, widowed parent's allowance, bereavement allowance, widowed mother's allowance, widow's pension, contribution-based jobseeker's allowance (JSA) and incapacity benefit (IB). Most kinds of credits count for all these benefits; only starting credits (see p729), credits for bereavement (see p731), credits for some tax credits (see p732), and some education and training credits (see p730) do not. You can only receive sufficient credits in any tax year to meet the minimum contribution condition for that year.[63]

Credits cannot help you to satisfy the first contribution condition for these benefits or to qualify for a bereavement payment, which has a single contribution condition.

Married women currently opting for reduced liability for contributions (see p721) normally cannot qualify for home responsibilities protection and can only qualify for starting credits (see p729) and credits following bereavement (see p731) and are not entitled to other types of credits.[64]

Home responsibilities protection (see p733) helps you satisfy the second contribution condition for retirement pension, bereavement benefits and widow's benefits by reducing the number of years for which you would otherwise have to satisfy the contribution condition.

Credits for unemployment or incapacity for work

You can be credited with earnings equal to the lower earnngs limit for *either:*[65]

- each complete week (ie, the seven days from Sunday to Saturday) for which you receive JSA (or where you would receive it but you are sanctioned because of a benefit offence – see p1047); *or*
- each complete week for which you have (either from the first day for which you are claiming credits or within a reasonable period of time) made a written claim for credits and provided the DWP with evidence that you satisfy (or satisfied), or were treated as having satisfied, the following qualifying conditions for JSA (see Chapter 15) – ie, that you are:
  - available for work; *and*
  - actively seeking work; *and*
  - not engaged in remunerative work; *and*
  - not in relevant education; *and*
  - capable of work; *and*
  - under pension age;

  or you would have been but for being incapable of work (see Chapter 28); *or*
- each complete week in which you would have satisfied the above conditions for JSA except that you are being treated as in remunerative work because you received a compensation payment – eg, pay in lieu of notice (see p653); *or*
- each complete week during which you were either:

- incapable of work or could be treated as incapable of work for IB purposes (see p263), or you would have been had you made a claim for IB or maternity allowance; *or*
- during which you were entitled to statutory sick pay.

However, you cannot qualify for credits for days on which you were treated as not incapable of work for IB purposes (or on which you would have been, had you otherwise been entitled to IB) – see p263.

(**Note**: this rule is likely to change with the introduction of employment and support allowance (ESA), planned for October 2008. See www.cpag.org.uk/esa or CPAG's *Welfare Rights Bulletin* for updates.)

Credits for incapacity for work must be claimed before the end of the benefit year (see p736) following the tax year in which you are entitled to the credit. So, for example, if you are incapable of work at any time between 6 April 2008 and 5 April 2009 the deadline for claiming credits is Saturday 1 January 2011. This time limit can be extended if it is considered reasonable to do so, given your circumstances.[66]

Entitlement to credits for unemployment is one reason why you might continue to sign on at the Jobcentre Plus office, even if you do not qualify for JSA, as this will protect your right to contributory benefits.

However, you will not get credits for unemployment for weeks in which:[67]

- you would not have been entitled to JSA (whether or not you actually claimed it) because you are involved in a trade dispute; *or*
- you are not getting JSA because you have been 'sanctioned' see p401), or you are receiving hardship payments (see p422); *or*
- if you are a member of a joint-claim couple, you are not getting JSA or your JSA is reduced because of a sanction, or you are receiving hardship payments; *or*
- you are a 16/17-year-old and are receiving JSA severe hardship payments (see p373).

Credits for caring for a disabled person

You can be credited with earnings equal to the lower earnings limit for each week in which you receive carer's allowance (CA – see Chapter 3) or would receive it, but for the loss of benefit for benefit offences rules (see p1047).[68] You also receive credits if the only reason that you do not receive CA is because you are receiving a bereavement benefit instead.

If you are looking after a disabled person but are not entitled to credits under these provisions, you may receive home responsibilities protection instead (see p733).

Starting credits

You receive Class 3 credits for the tax year in which you were 16 and for the next two years if you would otherwise have an insufficient contribution record for those years to count towards the second contribution condition for retirement pension, bereavement benefits and widows' benefits.[69]

No credits are made under this provision for years before 6 April 1975.

Education and training credits

You can be credited with earnings equal to the lower earnings limit, for contribution-based JSA and IB purposes only, for either one of the two complete tax years which fall before the relevant benefit year (see pp736 and 737) if, for any part of those tax years, you were on:

- a course of full-time training, including training to acquire occupational or vocational skills (or, if you are disabled, part-time – which is at least 15 hours a week); *or*
- a course of full-time education; *or*
- an apprenticeship.

You are only entitled to these credits if:

- in the other tax year in which you must satisfy the second contribution condition for the benefit (see p737), you have an earnings factor of 50 times the lower earnings limit without recourse to this provision; *and*
- you are at least 18, or will become 18 during the tax year in question; *and*
- you were under 21 when the course or apprenticeship started; *and*
- your course of education, training or apprenticeship has finished.[70]

You also receive such credits for all benefits for each week in which you are undertaking an approved training course provided that:[71]

- the training is full time, unless either you are disabled, when it must be for at least 15 hours a week, or it is an introductory course; *and*
- the training is not part of your job; *and*
- the training is intended to last for one year or less (except in certain circumstances if it is a course for disabled people); *and*
- you were 18 or over at the beginning of the tax year in which the week falls.

All courses run by the DWP count. Other courses are considered on their merits.

Credits for the maternity pay and adoption pay period

You can be credited with earnings equal to the lower earnings limit for each week for which you receive either statutory maternity pay (SMP) or statutory adoption pay (SAP).[72] This will be important only if you are receiving SMP or SAP at a rate below the lower earnings limit (currently £90 a week). You must claim these credits in writing before the end of the 'benefit year' (see p736) following the tax year in which the week falls, but this time limit may be extended if it is reasonable to do so.

Credits for jury service

You are entitled to be credited with earnings equal to the lower earnings limit for each week after 6 April 1988 during which you spend at least part of the week on jury service, unless you are self-employed.[73] You must claim these credits in writing before the end of the 'benefit year' (see p736) following the tax year in which the week falls (or such further period as is reasonable).

Credits following bereavement

If your entitlement to a bereavement benefit has ended, you can be credited with earnings for each year up to and including the one in which your bereavement benefit stopped, sufficient to enable you to satisfy the second contribution condition for contribution-based JSA or IB.[74] However, this rule does not apply if the reason your bereavement benefit stopped was because you married, entered into a civil partnership or started cohabiting with someone of the opposite sex. It is likely that, from the date it is introduced, this rule will also allow you to satisfy the second contribution condition for contributory employment and support allowance (see Chapter 7).

For the purpose of satisfying the second contribution condition for IB, you are also entitled to credits for each year up to and including the one in which your entitlement to widow's allowance (abolished in April 1988) or widowed mother's allowance ceased, unless those benefits stopped because you married, formed a civil partnership or started cohabiting with someone of the opposite sex.[75]

The law does not say that you are precluded from entitlement to these credits if your widows' or bereavement benefits have stopped because you have started cohabiting with someone of the same sex as if you were civil partners, although people of the opposite sex who are cohabiting are specifically precluded. The Revenue states that this is because entitlement to widows' and bereavement benefits does not end when you are cohabiting (whether with someone of the same or opposite sex), it is just that benefit is not payable to you. As your entitlement does not end, the Revenue considers that you will not qualify for credits for bereavement while cohabiting anyway.

Credits for people aged 60 or over

Women are not entitled or required to pay contributions once they are 60 or over. A man aged over 60 must continue to pay contributions if he is liable even if his contribution record is already sufficient to qualify for a full Category A retirement pension (see p719).

You can be credited with earnings (known as 'autocredits') for the tax year in which you turn 60 and for the next four years.[76] So if you are a man and you take early retirement at 60, the last five years of your 'working life' can count towards satisfying the second contribution condition for your retirement pension when you reach 65. You cannot qualify for these credits for any year in which you were abroad for more than 182 days. Also, if you are self-employed you must *either*:

- be liable for at least one Class 2 contribution in any of the above tax years; *or*
- have a small earnings exception (see p724) for at least one week in any of the above tax years,

to qualify for credits for the other weeks in those years.

Credits for tax credits

You are entitled to be credited with earnings equal to the lower earnings limit for the purpose of satisfying the second contribution condition for any benefit for each week for any part of which you receive the disability element or severe disability element of working tax credit (WTC).

Alternatively, for Category A or B retirement pension, widowed parent's allowance, bereavement allowance, widowed mother's allowance or widow's pension purposes, a credit is given for each week for which WTC is paid to you. In this case, if WTC was paid to you as a member of a couple but only one of you has earnings, the credits will be awarded to that person, otherwise they are awarded to the person to whom WTC is paid.

In both cases you will only qualify for these credits during any week in which you were *either*:[77]

- employed and earning less than the lower earnings limit for that year; *or*
- self-employed but had been granted an exemption from paying Class 2 contributions because your earnings were below the small earnings limit (see p724).

This provision also existed for working families' tax credit and disabled person's tax credit, which were abolished in April 2003 (see CPAG's *Welfare Benefits Handbook* 2002/03) and for family credit and disability working allowance (see CPAG's *Welfare Benefits Handbook* 1999/00).

Credits for a quashed conviction

If you were imprisoned or detained in legal custody after being convicted of an offence, and that conviction has subsequently been quashed by the courts, you can be credited with earnings for each week during at least part of which you were imprisoned or detained.[78] You must apply in writing to be awarded the credits.

Credits for official error

If you (or in some cases your spouse or civil partner) were wrongly awarded credits for incapacity for work or approved training in the tax years from 1993/94 to 2007/08 as a result of an official error arising from discrepancies between the DWP and Revenue's computer systems ('credits caused by official error'), then, in the following situations, you (or your spouse or civil partner) can be credited with earnings to satisfy the second contribution condition for IB, Category A or B retirement pensions and JSA.[79]

Effectively, this means that the official mistake will be rectified by ensuring you are awarded the credits which were previously given erroneously.

- You will be credited with earnings to allow you to meet the second contribution condition for IB if you have claimed IB and your current period of incapacity for work is linked to a past one (see p264) in which you were entitled to IB at least in part on the basis of credits caused by official error.
- If you claim JSA or, if you reach pension age on or before 31 May 2008, retirement pension, and you satisfy the second contribution condition for either of those benefits at least in part on the basis of credits caused by official error you will be credited with those earnings.
- If you reach pension age after 31 May 2008 and claim retirement pension on the basis of someone else's contributions (eg, your spouse's or civil partner's) and the second contribution condition would be satisfied at least in part on the basis of credits s/he was paid which were caused by official error s/he will be credited with those earnings for the purpose of your claim if either:
  - s/he reaches (or would have reached) pension age on or before 31 May 2008; *or*
  - you received bereavement allowance, widowed mother's allowance, widowed parent's allowance or widow's pension on the basis of her/his contributions.

Home responsibilities protection

From 6 April 2010 home responsibilities protection will be replaced. For each week after that date in which you have certain caring responsibilities, you will be credited with Class 3 contributions for the purpose of qualifying for Category A and B retirement pensions, widowed parent's allowance and bereavement allowance. Unless you reach pension age before 6 April 2010, each year of home responsibilities protection that you received prior to this change will be converted into credited contributions for that year (up to a maximum of 22 years, for retirement pension purposes, or half the requisite number of years for widowed parent's allowance or bereavement allowance purposes – see p738).[80]

Home responsibilities protection can help towards satisfying the second contribution condition for retirement pension, widows' benefits and bereavement benefits (see p738), by reducing the number of years over which you need to meet the condition. Years of home responsibilities protection in which you do not satisfy the contribution conditions are deducted from the requisite number of years for which you would otherwise have had to satisfy them.[81] However, home responsibilities protection can only reduce the requisite number of years to 20, or half what it would otherwise be, whichever is lower.

A year of home responsibilities protection is a tax year throughout which:[82]

- you receive child benefit for a child aged under 16; *or*

- your partner received child benefit for a child under 16 (in this situation someone counts as your partner if, throughout the year, you resided with her/him and you both shared responsibility for the child). This only applies if you reach pension age after 5 April 2008 (or for bereavement benefits, if the contributor died after that date), and if your partner's earnings for that year were sufficient to meet the second contribution condition for retirement pension, bereavement benefits and widow's benefits (and so s/he does not need to rely on home responsibilities protection her/himself for that year); *or*
- you get income support (IS) either on the basis that you are are a carer or that it is no more than eight weeks since you stopped being a carer (see p295); *or*
- you spend at least 35 hours a week looking after someone who, for at least 48 weeks in that tax year, is receiving a 'qualifying benefit' (see below); *or*
- you are an approved foster parent or foster carer (this only applies for the tax years 2003/04 onwards); *or*
- for part of the tax year you spend at least 35 hours a week caring for someone who gets a 'qualifying benefit' and for the rest you qualify on any other of the above grounds.

A **'qualifying benefit'** is the highest or middle rates of disability living allowance care component, attendance allowance or constant attendance allowance (under the industrial injuries scheme or war pensions scheme).

A year should automatically be recorded as a year of home responsibilities protection if you qualify because you receive child benefit or you receive IS while caring for a disabled person. If you qualify on any other of the above grounds, you must apply to the Revenue, using Form CF411. From April 2002 onwards, if you apply because you spend at least 35 hours a week caring for someone, you must make your application within three years of the end of the tax year in which you were looking after the disabled person if you want to get home responsibilites protection for that year.[83]

Even if your child benefit claim is not made at the start of a tax year, as long as it is backdated to the beginning of the tax year you can qualify for home responsibilities protection for that year. For tax years from 2004/05, if your child benefit cannot be backdated to the start of the tax year because someone else was receiving it for the same child, you may still qualify for home responsibilities protection if:

- that person's child benefit claim had priority over yours (see p65); *and*
- s/he notified the child benefit office that s/he wanted to give up her/his claim so that you could qualify for it; *and*
- this notification took effect at some time within the first three months of a tax year.

In this circumstance, you will normally be treated as if you were entitled to child benefit for each of the weeks in the tax year prior to the notification if child benefit would have otherwise been payable to you for those weeks.[84]

A year in which a woman has elected to have reduced liability for contributions cannot normally be a year of home responsibilities protection.[85] It may, therefore, be worth considering whether to revoke such an election (see p721).

No year before 6 April 1978 can be a year of home responsibilities protection.

4. Contribution conditions for benefits

Contributory benefits, except a bereavement payment, have two contribution conditions. To help satisfy the second condition, you may be credited with earnings or contributions to fill gaps in your contribution record (see p727). However, the first contribution condition must always be satisfied by contributions which have actually been paid.

If you are covered by European Community Regulation 1408/71 it may be possible for you to rely on the contributions you have paid in other European Economic Area states to qualify for contributory benefits (see p1339).

Earnings factors

Payment of Class 1, 2 and 3 contributions gives rise to an 'earnings factor' which is used to calculate your entitlement to contributory benefits (including the additional pension payable under the additional state pension scheme – see p476).

For Class 1 contributions, the earnings factor is the amount of earnings, excluding those earnings above the upper earnings limit, upon which those contributions have been paid. Each Class 2 and Class 3 contribution gives rise to an earnings factor equal to that year's lower earnings limit.[86]

From 6 April 2002, certain people may be deemed to have an earnings factor equal to the low earnings threshold to build up their entitlement to additional state pension (see p476).

Contribution-based jobseeker's allowance, incapacity benefit and contributory employment and support allowance

The first condition

To qualify for contribution-based jobseeker's allowance (JSA) and incapacity benefit (IB), or from the date it is introduced, contributory employment and support allowance (ESA), (apart from IB and ESA for people incapable of work in youth, which have no contribution conditions – see p266) you must have actually paid, in one tax year, the appropriate class of contributions producing an earnings factor (see above) of at least 25 times that year's lower earnings limit (eg, £2,250 in 2008/09 – 25 times £90),[87] or 25 flat-rate contributions paid before 6 April

1975.[88] The contributions must be paid before a claim for contribution-based JSA, IB or ESA is made.

Incapacity benefit and employment and support allowance

For IB, or from the date it is introduced, contributory ESA, the contributions may be either Class 1 or 2.[89] They must have been paid in one of the last three complete tax years before the relevant 'benefit year'. For IB this rule is relaxed, so that sufficient contributions paid in any one year will be enough, if you were:[90]

- entitled to carer's allowance (CA) (even if it was not paid because of the overlapping benefit rules – see p981) in the last complete tax year before the benefit year (see below) in which you became incapable of work (CA used to be called invalid care allowance);
- working and entitled to disability working allowance or disabled person's tax credit (DPTC) for more than two years immediately before becoming incapable of work (disability working allowance and DPTC have now been abolished);
- working for more than two years and entitled to the disability element or the severe disability element of working tax credit immediately before becoming incapable of work;
- receiving IB at some time in the last complete tax year before the benefit year of the new claim;
- entitled to credited contributions because you had been in prison or a detention centre and your conviction was subsequently quashed by the courts.

At the time of writing, it was not known whether this would also apply to contributory ESA.

Benefit years are almost the same as calendar years and run from the first Sunday in January.[91] The **'relevant benefit year'** for IB is the benefit year in which the period of incapacity for work (see p264) begins, unless you have been discharged from the armed forces in particular circumstances.[92] For contributory ESA, it is the benefit year in which the period of limited capability for work begins.

For IB, a widow who loses her entitlement to widowed mother's allowance for a reason other than marriage, entering into a civil partnership or cohabitation with someone of the opposite sex (ie, because her children grow up) will be deemed to have satisfied this contribution condition (and will be credited with contributions to satisfy the second condition – see p731).[93] But this help with the first contribution condition does not extend to widows, widowers or surviving civil partners who lose entitlement to bereavement benefits.

If your widowed mother's allowance stops because you have started cohabiting with someone of the same sex as if you are civil partners, the Revenue considers that you cannot be deemed to have satisfied this contribution condition. The Revenue states that this is is because your entitlement to benefit does not end when you start cohabiting (whether with someone of the same sex or the opposite sex), it is just not payable.

Contribution-based jobseeker's allowance

The contributions must be Class 1 contributions for contribution-based JSA (unless you are a share fisherman or volunteer development worker when special Class 2 contributions can count).[94] The contributions must have been paid in one of the last two complete tax years before the 'relevant benefit year'.[95] The **'relevant benefit year'** for contribution-based JSA is:[96]

- the benefit year in which the jobseeking period begins (see p339); *or, if earlier*
- the benefit year in which a period which is linked to the jobseeking period begins (see p340).

Benefit years run from the first Sunday in January.

The second condition

To qualify for contribution-based JSA and IB or, from the date it is introduced, contributory ESA you must have also either paid or been credited with contributions producing an earnings factor (see p735) equal to 50 times the lower earnings limit in each of the last two complete tax years ending before the relevant benefit year.[97] However, not all types of credited contributions count for IB and JSA or will count for ESA (see pp727 – 732 for details).

In rare cases, it may be beneficial for you to delay a claim for contribution-based JSA so that you can draw on a different year's contribution record. This is because the years in which you must meet the second contribution condition for contribution-based JSA depend on the benefit year in which your jobseeking period starts (unless your jobseeking period is linked to an earlier period – see p339). Thus, if your claim is not linked to an earlier period, and you claim before 6 January 2008 you must meet the contribution conditions in the tax years 2004/05 and 2005/06, whereas if you claim on 6 January 2008 you must meet them in 2005/06 and 2006/07.

Any day for which you do not claim does not count as part of your jobseeking period (see p339),[98] so it is easy to postpone when that period begins. However, if you claim and are refused benefit because the contribution conditions are not satisfied, your jobseeking period will have started. You would then normally have to wait for more than 12 weeks to make a fresh claim. The 12-week gap would break the jobseeking period.

Bereavement payment

The only contribution condition for a bereavement payment is that your spouse or civil partner must actually have paid in any one tax year before s/he reached pension age (or before her/his death, if s/he died before reaching pension age) contributions of Classes 1, 2 or 3, producing an earnings factor (see p735) of at least 25 times the lower earnings limit (eg, £2,250 in 2008/09 – 25 x £90).[99]

The sum of any contributions paid in any year may be counted if s/he only became liable to pay contributions in either the last complete tax year before the benefit year in which s/he reached pension age or in which s/he died (if s/he died before reaching pension age), or in the tax year before that.

The contribution condition for bereavement payment is treated as satisfied if your late spouse or civil partner had ever successfully claimed and met the first contribution condition for maternity allowance (MA) or IB.

Note: MA no longer has contribution conditions, although it did for women whose expected week of childbirth fell before 20 August 2000.[100]

The payment of 25 flat-rate contributions in a contribution year prior to 6 April 1975 also satisfies this condition.[101]

Widowed parent's allowance, bereavement allowance, widowed mother's allowance, widow's pension and Category A and B retirement pensions

Note: the contribution conditions for Category A and B retirement pensions described below only apply if the contributor reaches pension age before 6 April 2010, or, for Category B pension, if s/he dies before that date. See p717 for further details.

The first condition

The contributor must actually have paid, in any one tax year before s/he died or reached pension age, Class 1, 2 or 3 contributions with an earnings factor of 52 times that year's lower earnings limit (eg, £4,680 in 2008/09 – 52 x £90).[102] The contributor is:

- for Category A retirement pension – you, or your late spouse or late civil partner, or your former spouse or former civil partner if you are divorced or your civil partnership has been dissolved;
- for Category B retirement pension – your spouse, civil partner or your late spouse or late civil partner;
- for widowed parent's allowance or bereavement allowance – your late spouse or late civil partner;
- for widowed mother's allowance or widow's pension – your late husband.

The first condition is deemed to be satisfied if the contributor was receiving long-term IB, or from the date ESA is introduced, the support or work-related activity component of ESA (see p145) either in the year in which s/he died (if s/he died before reaching pension age) or in which s/he reached pension age, or in the preceding year.[103] Fifty flat-rate payments at any time before 6 April 1975 also satisfy this condition.[104]

The second condition

The contributor must have paid or been credited with contributions with an earnings factor of at least 52 times that year's lower earnings limit for each of the requisite number of years.[105]

The requisite number of years you need to satisfy this condition depends on the length of your 'working life'. This is the period inclusive of the tax year in which you reach the age of 16 up to but exclusive of the year in which you reach pension age or in which you die (if earlier).[106] If you have obtained a full gender recognition certificate, as your pension age will change (see p33), the length of your working life is likely to change.[107]

If you were over 16 on 5 July 1948, your working life is taken as having started either on 6 April 1948 or on 6 April of the year between 1936 and 1948 that you first started paying contributions, if you paid contributions before 5 July 1948.[108]

A year of home responsibilities protection looking after a child or a disabled person does not count as a year of your working life unless your earnings factor in that year was at least 52 times the lower earnings limit (see p723).

The requisite number of years is then calculated as follows:[109]

Length of 'working life'	*Requisite number of years*
1–10 years	Length of working life minus 1
11–20 years	Length of working life minus 2
21–30 years	Length of working life minus 3
31–40 years	Length of working life minus 4
41–50 years	Length of working life minus 5

Since contributions paid before 6 April 1975 do not produce an earnings factor (see p735), the number of years before that date in which the contribution condition is satisfied is calculated by adding together all the contributions paid or credited before 6 April 1975, and dividing the answer by 50. If that does not produce a whole number the result is rounded up, as long as that would not produce a number greater than the number of years of the working life before 6 April 1975.

If you are a widow, widower or surviving civil partner, you may be able to combine your own contribution record with that of your late spouse or civil partner, in order to claim a Category A retirement pension (see p465). You may also be able to combine your own contribution record with that of your former spouse or civil partner to qualify for a Category A retirement pension if you have been divorced or your civil partnership has been dissolved.

Insufficient contributions

Benefits are paid at a reduced rate if the second contribution condition is not satisfied for the requisite number of years, provided it is satisfied in at least 25 per cent of the requisite number. The benefit is paid at a percentage of the amount which would otherwise be paid. The percentage is calculated by expressing the number of years in which the condition is satisfied as a percentage of the requisite number of years and rounding it up to the nearest whole number.[110] Thus, if you are a widow and your husband's working life was 12 years, so that the requisite number of years is 10, and if he only satisfied the condition in eight years, you receive 80 per cent of the standard rate of widowed parent's allowance or bereavement allowance.

Increases for adult dependants are reduced in the same proportion, but increases for children, if you still qualify for these (see p691), are always paid in full.[111]

It may be possible for you to pay Class 3 contributions (see p725) to bring the number of years in which the second contribution condition is satisfied up to the 25 per cent figure needed for a minimum pension or to enhance the rate at which the pension will be paid. This can be very worthwhile. For example, if you are only one year short of the minimum number of years, payment of £421.20 (52 Class 3 contributions at £8.10 each) may secure you a pension of £22.67 a week (£90.70 x 25 per cent) uprated annually for the rest of your life. You will get your money back in a little over 18 weeks (unless you also receive mean-tested benefits).

Notes

1 PA 2007

1. How decisions are made

2 s11 SSC(TF)A 1999; Part III SSC(DA) Regs

2. Contributions: liability and payment

3 s1(2) SSCBA 1992
4 s21(1) and (2) SSCBA 1992
5 s2(1)(a) SSCBA 1992
6 s2(1)(b) SSCBA 1992
7 *Ready Mixed Concrete South East Ltd v Ministry of Pensions and National Insurance* [1968] 2 QB 497 (QBD); *Global Plant v Secretary of State for Health and Social Security* [1971] 3 All ER 385 (QBD)
8 Sch 1 paras 1-5 SS(CatE) Regs
9 Sch 1 para 6 SS(CatE) Regs
10 Sch 1 paras 7-12 SS(CatE) Regs
11 ss6(1)(a), 11(1) and 13(1) SSCBA 1992; reg 93 SS(Con) Regs
12 ss6(3) and 11(2) SSCBA 1992; regs 49(e) and 91 SS(Con) Regs
13 ss2(1)(a) and 6 SSCBA 1992
14 Reg 145(1)(a) SS(Con) Regs
15 Reg 145(2) SS(Con) Regs
16 Reg 146 SS(Con) Regs
17 Reg 146(2)(b) SS(Con) Regs
18 ss2(1)(b)and 11 SSCBA 1992; reg 145(1)(d) SS(Con) Regs
19 Reg 145(1)(c) SS(Con) Regs
20 Regs 147 and 148 SS(Con) Regs
21 Regs 149 and 151 SS(Con) Regs
22 Regs 49A, 145(1)(e), 146(2)(b), 147, 148 and 148A SS(Con) Regs
23 Reg 91(b) SS(Con) Regs
24 Reg 127 SS(Con) Regs
25 Regs 128(1) and 130 SS(Con) Regs
26 Reg 6 SSC(NPPC1C) Regs
27 s22(4) SSCBA 1992; reg 7(3), 7(A)2, 7B(3), 7C(4), 8(2), 8A(5), 8B(3), 9B(3), 9C(4) and 9D(4) and (5) SS(Cr) Regs
28 ss6 and 7 SSCBA 1992
29 ss6, 6A and 8 SSCBA 1992; ss8 and 41 PSA 1993
30 Reg 11(2)(b) and (3)(a) SS(Con) Regs
31 ss43(1) and 45(1) PSA 1993
32 s19(4) SSCBA 1992; reg 131 SS(Con) Regs

33 Sch 1 para 3 SSCBA 1992; reg 2(1) Social Security Contributions (Consequential Provisions) Regulations 2007
34 Regs 13, 14, 15 and 21 SS(Con) Regs
35 Sch 1 para 1 SSCBA 1992; regs 13, 14, 15 and 21 SS(Con) Regs
36 s11 SSCBA 1992; regs 43 and 46 SS(Con) Regs
37 Reg 45 SS(Con) Regs
38 Reg 46 SS(Con) Regs
39 s11(1) SSCBA 1992
40 Reg 127(1) SS(Con) Regs
41 Regs 125, 149, 151 and 152 SS(Con) Regs
42 Reg 21 SS(Con) Regs
43 s11(5) SSCBA 1992; reg 44 SS(Con) Regs
44 Reg 47 SS(Con) Regs
45 s13 SSCBA 1992
46 s14 SSCBA 1992
47 Reg 56 SS(Con) Regs
48 s13(1) SSCBA 1992
49 s15(1) and (3) SSCBA 1992
50 Regs 95-99 SS(Con) Regs
51 Reg 100 SS(Con) Regs
52 s114 SSAA 1992
53 Reg 60 SS(Con) Regs
54 Regs 89 and 90 SS(Con) Regs
55 Reg 4 SS(CTCNIN) Regs
56 Reg 48(3)(b) SS(Con) Regs
57 Reg 4(7) and (8) SS(CTCNIN) Regs
58 Regs 50 and 61 SS(Con) Regs; reg 6, 6A and 6B SS(CTCNIN) Regs
59 Regs 4(11) and 5A SS(CTCNIN) Regs
60 Reg 50A SS(Con) Regs; reg 6A SS(CTCNIN) Regs
61 Regs 50(B) and 61A SS(Con) Regs, but see also regs 4(1A) and 6B SS(CTCNIN) Regs
62 Reg 62 SS(Con) Regs

3. **Credits and home responsibilities protection**
63 Reg 3 SS(CR) Regs
64 Regs 7(3), 7A(2)(b), 7B(3), 7C(4), 8(2)(b), 8A(5)(e), 8B(3), 9B(3), 9C(4) and 9D(4) SS(CR) Regs
65 Regs 8A and 8B SS(Cr) Regs
66 Reg 8B(4) SS(Cr) Regs
67 Reg 8A(5) SS(Cr) Regs
68 Reg 7A SS(Cr) Regs
69 Reg 4 SS(Cr) Regs
70 Reg 8 SS(Cr) Regs
71 Reg 7 SS(Cr) Regs
72 Reg 9C SS(Cr) Regs
73 Reg 9B SS(Cr) Regs
74 Reg 8C SS(Cr) Regs
75 Reg 3(1)(b) SSB(MW&WSP) Regs
76 Reg 9A SS(Cr) Regs
77 Regs 7B and 7C SS(Cr) Regs
78 Reg 9D SS(Cr) Regs
79 Regs 8D, 8E and 8F SS(Cr) Regs
80 s23A SSCBA 1992
81 Sch 3 para 5(7) SSCBA 1992
82 Reg 2(2) and (3) SSP(HR) Regs
83 Reg 2(5)(b) and (c) SSP(HR) Regs
84 Reg 2(4B) SSP(HR) Regs
85 Reg 2(5)(a) and (6) SSP(HR) Regs

4. **Contribution conditions for benefits**
86 Sch 1 SS(EF) Regs
87 s21 and Sch 3 para 2 SSCBA 1992; ss1(2)(d) and 2 JSA 1995; Sch 1 para 1 WRA 2007
88 Reg 15 SS(STB)(T) Regs
89 s21(1) and (2) SSCBA 1992; Sch 1 para 1 WRA 2007
90 Reg 2B SS(IB) Regs
91 s21(6) SSCBA 1992
92 Sch 3 para 2(6) SSCBA 1992; reg 4 Social Security Contributions and Benefits Act 1992 (Modifications for Her Majesty's Forces and Incapacity Benefit) Regulations 2003 No.737
93 Reg 3(1) SSB(MW&WSP) Regs
94 s2 JSA 1995; regs 158 and 167 JSA Regs
95 s2(1) JSA 1995
96 s2(4) JSA 1995
97 s21 and Sch 3 para 2 SSCBA 1992; s2 JSA 1995; Sch 1 para 2 WRA 2007
98 Reg 47(3)(a) JSA Regs
99 s21and Sch 3 para 4 SSCBA 1992
100 Sch 3 paras 7 and 9 SSCBA 1992
101 Reg 13(1) SS(STB)(T) Regs
102 Sch 3 para 5 SSCBA 1992
103 Sch 3 para 5(6) SSCBA 1992; Sch 3 para 5(6A) SSCBA as inserted by Sch 3 para 9(13) WRA 2007
104 Reg 6 SS(WBRP&OB)(T) Regs
105 Sch 3 para 5(3) SSCBA 1992
106 Sch 3 para 5(8) SSCBA 1992
107 But see also *Richards v Secretary of State for Work and Pensions* C-423/04, unreported, 27 April 2006 (ECJ); R(P)1/07; *Grant v United Kingdom,* No.32570/03, unreported, 23 May 2006 (ECtHR); CP/3485/2003
108 Reg 7(7) SS(WBRP&OB)(T) Regs; s20 and Sch 3 para 5(5) SSCBA 1992
109 Sch 3 para 5(5) SSCBA 1992
110 Reg 6 SS(WB&RP) Regs
111 s60(4)-(6) SSCBA 1992; reg 6(3) SS(WB&RP) Regs

Chapter 32

Maintenance

This chapter is about maintenance and how it affects your entitlement to benefit. It covers:

How to claim maintenance for yourself or your children, and how maintenance is calculated and enforced, is beyond the scope of this *Handbook*. You may be able to claim maintenance through the courts, or, if it is for children, via the Child Support Agency (CSA). However, it is advisable to consult a solicitor if you need to claim maintenance or if maintenance is being sought from you. If you are on a low income, you may qualify for help with the costs of legal advice.

The CSA currently operates two child support schemes, in which child support is calculated in different ways and some other rules also apply differently. Some parents are covered by the new scheme (the 'new rules') and others continue to be dealt with under the old scheme (the 'old rules') (see p747).

If you need more information about child support and about dealing with the CSA , see CPAG's *Child Support Handbook*.

Changes to child support

The Government is introducing extensive reforms to child support. It intends to replace the CSA with a new body, the Child Maintenance and Enforcement Commission (C-MEC) during 2008. Other planned changes include the following.[1]

By the end of 2008

- The requirement to co-operate (which treats parents with care on income suport (IS) and income-based jobseeker's allowance (JSA) as applying for child support) will end. All reduced benefit decisions will cease and the full rate of benefit will be reinstated from the date of change.

- Parents with care on IS or income-based JSA who have maintenance calculations will be contacted by C-MEC and given the option to end these and make their own arrangements if they wish to do so.
- The child maintenance premium (effectively a £10 a week disregard of maintenance) will be extended to all parents with care on IS or income-based JSA, and the amount will be increased.

Further changes

- Parents will be encouraged to make their own arrangements.
- There will be a new simplified child support calculation based on details of gross income direct from the Revenue, using the latest tax year unless income differs by at least 25 per cent.
- The flat rate of child support paid by most non-resident parents on benefit will be increased to £7 once the simplified scheme starts.
- There will be tougher and quicker enforcement action.

New applications to the simplified assessment scheme (for people without exisiting child support cases) are not expected to be possible until 2010/11. New applications made prior to that date will be dealt with under the existing 'new rules' calculation.

1. What is maintenance

Maintenance is financial support paid for another person. In some cases, there is a legal liability to maintain (or to pay towards the maintenance of) another person. If you are, or have been, married or in a civil partnership, you may be able to get maintenance for yourself ('spousal maintenance') on a voluntary basis or under a court order. You should seek legal advice about this. You may also be able to get child maintenance for your children if you are not living with their other parent. Child maintenance may be paid voluntarily, or following a court order, or following an application to the Child Support Agency (CSA) ('child support maintenance'). For information on the rules about how child support maintenance affects your right to benefit, see p746. For further information about the child support scheme, see CPAG's *Child Support Handbook*.

Maintenance could technically be enforced while you are on income support (IS) or income-based jobseeker's allowance (JSA) because certain people are 'liable to maintain' you or your children (see p744). The DWP could take action to obtain maintenance from the liable person on your behalf if s/he does not support you or your children financially, though this is rare (see p745). If the liable person does make payments, these are called 'liable relative payments'. In practice, however, the CSA enforces most maintenance for children while you are on IS or JSA and payments are dealt with as child maintenance payments. The liable relative provision for children is expected to be removed under the changes to child maintenance.

If you have come to the UK following a formal sponsorship undertaking, your sponsor is liable to maintain you if you are not able to support yourself.

Who is liable to maintain you while you are on income support or income-based jobseeker's allowance

If someone is 'liable to maintain' you or your child(ren), s/he must pay maintenance. The Secretary of State for Work and Pensions can take proceedings against anyone who has a liability to maintain you while you are on IS or income-based JSA, although this is rare. If that person fails to maintain you, s/he can be prosecuted (see below). These rules are not used to seek maintenance for your children while you are on IS or JSA if they are qualifying children for child support. Instead, your benefit claim is currently treated as an application for child support (see p747).

While you are on IS or income-based JSA:[2]

- you must be maintained by your spouse or civil partner, if you are married, in a civil partnership or separated. Liability ceases (for social security purposes) on divorce or dissolution of a civil partnership. If you have to live apart from your spouse or civil partner because you need care or treatment (eg, in hospital or in a care home) you may be assessed and paid as separate individuals for benefit purposes (see p707). However, your spouse or civil partner is still liable to maintain you and may be asked to make a financial contribution towards your care.

While you are on IS:[3]

- your child(ren) must be maintained by both their parents. A parent is not liable to maintain children who are 20 or over, or 16 or over if they are no longer dependent for benefit purposes (**Note:** this rule is expected to be abolished during 2008, so all liability for children is covered by child maintenance law[4]);
- if you are the subject of a formal sponsorship/undertaking you must be maintained by a sponsor who has given an undertaking to support you (see p1341). This includes your ex-spouse or ex-civil partner after you are divorced or your civil partnership is dissolved.

Unless you are the subject of a formal sponsorship/undertaking (see above) your right to claim benefit is not affected by the fact that the DWP can get money back from someone who is liable to maintain you. You should not, therefore, be refused IS or income-based JSA while maintenance is being pursued. However, maintenance that is recovered might affect your benefit (see p751).

Proceedings against liable relatives

If the DWP takes proceedings to pursue a liable relative for maintenance, the magistrates' court can make an order telling the person who is liable what s/he has to pay.[5] The fact that you agreed not to ask for maintenance is not a bar to an order being made,[6] although all the circumstances must be taken into account.[7] For example, if there was a clean break settlement, the DWP will still pursue the liable relative, but may later decide it is not cost effective and cease action.[8] If you have been cruel, deserted your spouse or civil partner, or committed adultery, the DWP is unlikely to take proceedings, but if it does, the court may decide that the liable person should not have to maintain you.[9]

For how payments from a liable relative affect your benefit, see p753.

Prosecution

A person who is liable to maintain you or your child(ren) (see p744) can be prosecuted if IS or income-based JSA is paid as a result of her/his persistently refusing or neglecting to maintain you. You can even be prosecuted for failing to maintain yourself (this rarely, if ever, happens). Although the power remains in respect of children, it is very unlikely to be used given that you would usually apply for child support through the CSA if you are on these benefits (see p750) and that, during 2008, the power to prosecute parents in this situation will be removed. However, it could be used in respect of a young person for whom child support cannot currently be claimed, but whom a liable relative still legally has to maintain. In either case, the maximum penalty is three months' imprisonment or a fine of £2,500, or both.[10] If you are charged with such an offence, see a solicitor.

Amount of maintenance

CPAG's *Child Support Handbook* gives details of both the 'old' and 'new' schemes, which allow the CSA to work out how much maintenance a liable person is required to pay for children covered by the child support scheme.

There is more flexibility about how much maintenance your spouse or civil partner is required to pay for you (or for young people who are not covered by the child support scheme but who are required to be maintained) if you are on IS or income-based JSA. The 'liable relative' can negotiate with the DWP to pay an amount s/he can afford, given her/his income and outgoings.

If the DWP believes your spouse or civil partner is not paying sufficient maintenance it can take her/him to court (see p744). For how liable relative payments affect your benefit, see p753.

Collection of maintenance by the DWP

If the DWP obtains an order for maintenance for your support from a magistrates' court (including via orders made in the county court or High Court but registered in the magistrates' court), it will normally expect the liable relative to make the payments direct to you or via some other arrangement to you (eg, through a solicitor). However, payment can be paid to the DWP where there is a reason for it to collect it – eg, where maintenance is already in arrears or where you request this arrangement because you do not want any contact with the liable relative.[11]

2. **Child support maintenance**

This section applies if you do not live with your child(ren)'s other parent and are claiming (or thinking about claiming):

- income support (IS); *or*
- income-based jobseeker's allowance (JSA).

Future changes

These rules are expected to change by the end of 2008. Parents on IS or income-based JSA will no longer be required to apply to the Child Support Agency (CSA) and will not have any reduction in benefit if they decide not to do so. In addition, during 2008 the CSA will be replaced by the Child Maintenance and Enforcement Commission (C-MEC), which will start to take over the CSA's functions. The Child Maintenance and Other Payments Bill provides for other changes to the child maintenance system. See CPAG's *Welfare Rights Bulletin* for updates.

Maintenance assessed by the CSA is called 'child support maintenance'. If your child(ren) live with you but their other parent lives elsewhere and you claim or are paid IS or income-based JSA, the CSA will treat you as having made an application for child support unless you 'opt out'. The CSA calculation requires the other parent (the 'non-resident parent') to pay child support. If you are not on these benefits and you have separated from your child's other parent, you may be able to get child maintenance either voluntarily under a court order or by applying to the CSA. CPAG's *Child Support Handbook* has more information about how and when you can apply to the CSA. Child support maintenance can be paid via the CSA or directly to you, but if you are on IS or income-based JSA, payment will usually be made via the CSA.

The CSA uses the term 'non-resident parent' to mean the parent who it has decided does not provide the main day-to-day care of the child. The parent who has the main day-to-day care of the child is the 'parent with care'. Sometimes the person who has principal care of the child will not be the child's parent and is called the 'person with care'. A 'qualifying child' is a child for whom child support can be paid. This includes under-16-year-olds, 16–18-year-olds in full-time non-advanced education (see p61), and, for a short time after leaving education, young people aged 16 or 17 who are registered for work and training. The definition of 'qualifying child' is currently *not* the same as the definition of children and young people for whom child benefit can be paid. More information about who is a 'qualifying child' is in CPAG's *Child Support Handbook*. If you want to claim maintenance for a young person who is not a qualifying child, you cannot do this via the CSA. You should seek advice from a solicitor.

If you are on IS or income-based JSA and you come off these benefits – eg, because you start work, increase your hours of work or move onto pension credit (PC), you will no longer be treated as applying for child support maintenance and will have a choice about whether or not you want to pursue the other parent for maintenance and, if so, how.

When the 'old rules' apply and when the 'new rules' apply

The child support scheme that applies to you depends, in most cases, on when your child support maintenance calculation ('new rules') or assessment ('old rules') was due to take effect (this date is called the 'effective date'), as follows.[12]

- Effective date before 3 March 2003: old rules apply.
- Effective date on or after 3 March 2003: new rules apply.

The effective date is usually the date on which the non-resident parent is contacted by the CSA to notify her/him of the child support application and gather information, but it can be earlier or later.

There are some exceptions to the main rule. Some new applications will be treated under the old rules – eg, if there is a short gap between the end of an old rules case and a new application. Some old applications will be treated under the new rules if there is a connection to a new rules case.

See CPAG's *Child Support Handbook* for full details.

Applications

Under the new rules, you are taken to have applied for a maintenance calculation when you apply for benefit, unless you opt out. If you opt out, unless you can show good cause for doing this, your benefit may be reduced (see below). **'Good cause'** means that there is a 'risk of harm or undue distress' to you or a child living with you (see p748).

Even if a maintenance calculation is currently in force you may opt out – ie, ask for this to cease (see below). However, if you do this without good cause your benefit may be reduced (see p748).

Your benefit claim should not be held up by the CSA, but opting out without good cause could affect the amount of benefit you receive (see p748).

When you are on IS or income-based JSA, regardless of whether the new or old rules apply, the CSA maintenance overrides any previous maintenance agreement you have for your child(ren), including a court order.

Opting out

When you claim benefit, or at any time during your claim, you can ask the CSA not to act, regardless of whether you are covered by the new or the old rules.[13] This is known as 'opting out'.

If you request the CSA not to act, it cannot proceed with the child support case.[14] However, unless the DWP accepts that you and/or your child(ren) would be at risk of 'harm or undue distress' if you did not opt out (known as having 'good cause'), your IS or income-based JSA may be paid at a reduced rate. These benefits may also be reduced if you fail to co-operate in other ways without good cause – eg, by failing to provide information, including information to help identify and trace the non-resident parent.[15] If you come under the new rules, co-operating can include allowing yourself and/or your child to take a DNA test to establish parentage.[16] See CPAG's *Child Support Handbook* for more details of the information you can be required to provide.

The DWP (Jobcentre Plus office) will normally interview you to gather information. If good cause is not initially accepted, or you fail to contact it or to attend the interview, it will write to you explaining that your benefit could be paid at a reduced rate. You will be given at least two weeks to respond, either giving your reasons, supplying additional information or stating that you will co-operate.[17]

There is no legal definition of harm or undue distress.[18] It certainly covers situations where there is a possibility of violence or where there has been rape, sexual abuse, threats or other harassment. There does not need to have been a history of actual violence – fear of violence is enough. There are also many other situations which could potentially be accepted as good cause – eg, if the non-resident parent might stop contact with children. If you think you have a good reason for not applying to the CSA, see CPAG's *Child Support Handbook* for more information, and/or seek advice.

Each case is decided on its merits. You should give as much information as you can, but your word should be accepted without any supporting evidence unless you contradict yourself or what you say is improbable.[19]

If the DWP agrees that you or your child(ren) would be at risk of harm or undue distress, you should be notified in writing, and your benefit should not be paid at a reduced rate.

Reduced benefit decisions

If the DWP decides that you do not have good cause, it considers whether to make a '**reduced benefit decision**'.[20] Under the old rules this was known as a 'reduced benefit *direction*'. Any reduced benefit *direction* in force on 3 March 2003 is treated as if it were a reduced benefit decision made under the new rules.[21] In deciding whether to make a reduced benefit decision, the DWP must consider the welfare of any children affected.[22] If their welfare would be adversely affected in any way, it may decide not to impose a reduced benefit decision. See CPAG's *Child Support Handbook* for more information about how the welfare of children should be taken into account.

A reduced benefit decision cannot be issued if IS or income-based JSA paid to you or your partner includes a disabled child premium, a disability premium or a higher pensioner premium, or if a child tax credit (CTC) award for you or your partner includes the element for a child/young person with a disability (see pp778 and 783).[23] (This applies even if it is your partner who has the disability.) However, if you or your partner are awarded a relevant premium or element of CTC after the reduced benefit decision is imposed, the reduction still applies. If a reduced benefit decision is made, you have the right to appeal against it (see p1093).[24]

All reduced benefit decisions will stop and benefit will be reinstated when the requirement to co-operate is abolished by the end of 2008 (see p742).

The reduced rate of benefit

Once a reduced benefit decision is made, your benefit is reduced by £24.20 a week. If the reduction would take your IS or income-based JSA below 10p a week, it is adjusted to ensure you are left with this minimum amount.[25]

The reduction lasts for three years from the second benefit week after the reduced benefit decision is made.[26] At the end of the three-year period, if you still do not want to claim child support, or refuse to co-operate, another reduced benefit decision can be issued.

Only one reduced benefit decision can be in operation at any one time.[27] If you refuse to co-operate in respect of another child (whether this is a child of the same non-resident parent or not), a second reduced benefit decision can be made which replaces the original one, and lasts for a fresh three years immediately after the original decision lapses.[28]

A reduced benefit decision is **suspended** if:

- you stop getting IS or income-based JSA.[29] However, if you claim one of these benefits again within 52 weeks and you continue to opt out, the reduced benefit decision is reinstated for the remainder of the three-year period. If you make a new claim after 52 weeks, the decision is no longer valid, but if you decide to opt out again a new reduced benefit decision could be made;
- your children stop being qualifying children for child support (see p746), or you stop being the person with care. If within 52 weeks, they start to become qualifying children again (eg, they go back to school and are under 19), or you become their person with care again, the decision is reinstated for the balance of the three years;[30]
- you are paid IS or income-based JSA while in hospital or in a care home (see Chapter 26). Once the reduced benefit decision has been suspended for this reason for 52 weeks it ceases completely.[31]

When a reduced benefit decision ends early

The reduced benefit decision **terminates** early if:[32]

- you withdraw the request for the CSA not to act, or you provide information or submit to a DNA test; *or*

- the DWP decides you do not have to co-operate (eg, it accepts that you have good cause or that the welfare of children would be adversely affected); *or*
- you stop getting IS or income-based JSA permanently (eg, because you move onto PC). If the change is only temporary, the reduced benefit decision will be suspended and then reinstated, or a new one could be made when you go back onto these benefits (see above); *or*
- in Scotland only, your child(ren) successfully apply to the CSA for a maintenance calculation.

You should be notified if a reduced benefit decision ceases.[33]

Challenging a reduced benefit decision

If you disagree with a reduced benefit decision, you can:

- seek a revision or a supersession(see pp1065 and 1074);
- appeal to an appeal tribunal (see Chapter 42). Your appeal must be made against the reduced benefit decision, not against the reduced rate of your benefit.[34]

The reduction in your benefit continues whilst your challenge is being considered.

Collection of child support by the Child Support Agency

Child support maintenance can be paid via the CSA or direct from your child(ren)'s other parent to you as the person looking after the child(ren). If you claim IS or income-based JSA you will not be given the option of having payments made direct to you by the other parent, but you can request payments to be made this way, and your request should be taken into account when deciding how you are paid.[35] Payment via the CSA is useful where maintenance payments are likely to be irregular or unreliable, and/or where you do not want to be located by the other parent. If the CSA is collecting the payments for you, it should take action automatically when a payment is missed. Where payments are being made directly to you by the other parent, it is up to you to contact the CSA and the DWP when a maintenance payment does not arrive.

If you are on IS or income-based JSA and your child(ren)'s other parent is making payments to the CSA, the CSA retains the payments made and only passes onto you the amount of maintenance which you are able to receive on top of your benefit (currently up to £10 a week under the new rules only – see p862). If the CSA does not receive your child support maintenance payment, you are still entitled to the full amount of IS or income-based JSA.

3. How maintenance affects income support, income-based jobseeker's allowance, pension credit and tax credits

The following are taken into account in working out the amount of income support (IS) or income-based jobseeker's allowance (JSA) to which you are entitled:

- child maintenance (see below);
- other maintenance payments made by 'liable relatives' (see p753).

Different rules apply if you are claiming housing benefit or council tax benefit (see p763).

Note: child maintenance is ignored for **pension credit** (PC). Spousal maintenance, including maintenance from a civil partner, is taken into account as income,[36] but it does not count as qualifying income for the savings credit of PC (see p447).

Maintenance of any kind is not taken into account for tax credits (see p1268).

Child maintenance

If you receive a payment from someone who is liable to maintain a child or young person (see p746), this is dealt with in a particular way, whether or not the payments are made as a result of a Child Support Agency (CSA) application. Child maintenance includes all payments for children and young people for whom child benefit can be claimed (see p57). You may receive maintenance payments for a young person for whom child support would currently not be payable – eg, because s/he is 19.[37] If the payment is from someone who is not legally liable to maintain the child or young person, it may still be a liable relative payment (see p753); otherwise, it will be treated under the normal income rules – eg, as a voluntary payment (see Chapter 36).

If you come under the old rules, all payments of child maintenance are treated as income and are taken into account in full on a weekly basis.[38] However, you may qualify for a child maintenance bonus (see p757). If you come under the new rules, up to £10 a week of child maintenance for a qualifying child, including child support, is ignored as income.[39] This is known as the 'child maintenance premium' (see p862). This is expected to be extended to all parents, and increased, by the end of 2008.

Where payments are made monthly, multiply by 12 and divide by 52 to obtain a weekly amount. Where regular payments are made at intervals other than each week or month, the payments are spread over the period, including any part-week. Lump-sum payments of child maintenance are treated as income (rather than capital), although you may be able to argue about the period which they cover.[40]

The DWP should not calculate IS or income-based JSA on the assumption that child support maintenance payments are being made where this has not been happening.

Only actual payments made, and not the amount due under a CSA calculation, are taken into account for benefit purposes.[41] So a parent who would lose entitlement to IS or income-based JSA if payments were made can continue to receive it if the child support maintenance is not received. If you have problems getting the DWP to assess your benefit correctly, you should seek advice.

Amounts for children in income support or jobseeker's allowance

If you are not on IS or income-based JSA, any child maintenance you receive is ignored as income for the purposes of working tax credit (WTC) and child tax credit (CTC). Some parents who get child support maintenance and who still receive amounts for their children in their IS or JSA may, therefore, be better off claiming CTC. If you are considering this, you should always have a better-off calculation carried out before making this decision. You will not be able to cancel the CTC claim and go back to receiving amounts for your children in IS/JSA.

If IS/JSA stops, a parent with care no longer has to apply to the CSA and has a choice about how, or if, s/he wants to claim child maintenance. If a reduced benefit decision is in force (see p748), this will also affect any assessment of whether s/he would be better off on CTC. **Note:** the requirement for parents with care on benefits to apply to the CSA is expected to be abolished by the end of 2008, when all reduced benefit decisions will also cease.

Arrears

Arrears of child support maintenance have usually accrued by the time a child support calculation is made. Usually, these initial arrears are paid to, and retained by, the CSA if you are on IS or income-based JSA. However, if the maintenance payment is made directly to you as the person with care, any IS or income-based JSA that has been overpaid to you can be recovered by the DWP.[42] Only child support maintenance both due for and received in the weeks of your IS/income-based JSA claim can be taken into account by the DWP. A payment of child support maintenance due before, but paid after, you claim IS or income-based JSA is treated as paid in the week in which it was due.[43]

The CSA is also responsible for collecting arrears of child support maintenance which should have been paid during your claim if you are on IS or income-based JSA. The CSA retains an amount equal to the difference between the IS or income-based JSA you were actually paid, and the amount you would have been paid if maintenance had been received on time.[44] Any additional amount should be passed to you.

Other maintenance payments made by liable relatives

If a liable relative (see below) makes maintenance payments to you for your support, these are dealt with in a special way.[45]

How such a payment affects your benefit depends on whether it counts as a liable relative payment or not (see below), and if it is a liable relative payment, whether it is:

- a regular payment, known as a 'periodical payment' (see below); *or*
- a lump sum (in one go or by instalments) treated as income or capital (see p755).

You and your solicitor should look at these rules carefully *before* negotiating payments from your former partner.

Liable relative payments

Most payments from the following people (known as '**liable relatives**') count as liable relative payments:[46]

- a husband, wife or civil partner. This includes one from whom you are separated or divorced, or where your civil partnership has been dissolved;
- a parent of a child or young person under 20 for whom you claim IS/JSA or CTC (but not where they are legally liable to maintain the child or young person, when the payment counts as child maintenance, see p751);
- a parent of a young person under 20 who is claiming IS or JSA in her/his own right;
- a person who has been living with and maintaining a child or young person under 20, or maintaining a young person under 20 who is claiming IS or JSA in her/his own right and can, therefore, reasonably be treated as her/his parent;
- if you are the subject of a formal sponsorship/undertaking, a sponsor who has given an undertaking to support you financially (see p1341).

The definition of parent in the context of the liable relative rules covers any situation where the child or young person was treated as their child, or as a member of their family, and so includes step-parents.

Note: despite the term 'liable relative', not all of these people are legally liable to maintain you (see p744). The DWP can only pursue those who are liable to maintain you or your children (see p744). In addition, some payments you recieve from a liable relative may, nevertheless, not count as liable relative payments (see p756).

Periodical payments

'**Periodical payments**' are any of the following payments made by liable relatives (see above), unless they do not count as liable relative payments (see p756):[47]

- any payment made, or due to be made, regularly, whether under a court order or other formal agreement, or voluntarily where there is a pattern of making regular payments;
- any other small payment no higher than your weekly IS or income-based JSA;
- any payment made instead of one or more regular payments, either in advance or arrears. This does not include any arrears due before the beginning of your entitlement to IS or income-based JSA (see p755).

Periodical payments which are received on time are spread over a period equal to the interval between them – eg, monthly payments are spread over a month. Payments are converted to a weekly amount – eg, monthly payments are multiplied by 12 and divided by 52 to produce a weekly income figure.[48]

Arrears of periodical payments due during your claim

When a payment arrives during a claim which includes a lump sum for arrears (or advance payments) due during your claim, and nothing is specified about which period it covers, the payment is spread over a period calculated by dividing it by the weekly amount of maintenance you should have (or would have) received.[49]

Example

Tia should receive maintenance of £80 a month. It is not paid for three months and she then receives £200.

£80 a month is treated as producing a weekly income of:

$$\frac{£80 \times 12}{52} = £18.46$$

The £200 is taken into account for:

$$\frac{£200}{£18.46} = 10.83 \text{ weeks}$$

Tia is assumed to have an income of £18.46 for the next 10 weeks and six days. The maintenance payments due are still two weeks and one day in arrears (3 x £80 is £240, so she is still owed £40).

If a payment is specifically identified as being arrears of maintenance for a particular period, the DWP can:

- take it into account for a forward period from the week you report you have received it; *or*
- attribute it to the past period which it was intended to cover, unless it is 'more practicable' to choose a later week.[50] In this case the DWP can recover the full amount of extra benefit paid to you while maintenance was not being received.[51] This can still be done if you receive a payment after your claim ends

which is for arrears of maintenance that should have been paid while you were claiming.

It is important to work out how you would be financially better off. You should then argue for the payment to be spread over whichever period is more advantageous to you. This depends on the amount of IS or income-based JSA you would otherwise receive, the amount of the payment and whether any other periodical payments (see p753) are being made. You should seek advice about appealing if your argument is not accepted.

Arrears of periodical payments due before your claim

If arrears of maintenance are paid for a period before the date of your claim they do not count as periodical payments (see p753).[52] The DWP treats such payments as lump sums treated as income (see below). This means that they are spread over a future period.

Lump-sum payments

For IS and income-based JSA, in general, the rules ensure that you usually do not benefit financially from receiving lump-sum payments of maintenance. Unless they do not count as 'liable relative payments' (see p756) or can be treated as capital (see p756), lump sums are treated as income.[53] They are spread over a period so as to disqualify you from IS or income-based JSA for as long as possible.

It is only to your advantage to get a lump-sum payment if it can be treated as capital. Lump-sum payments that count as capital do not affect your IS or income-based JSA unless they take your capital over £6,000 (£10,000 if you live in a care home). See Chapter 37 for more information about the capital rules.

A lump sum is treated as capital if you are already getting 'periodical payments' (see p753) equal to or higher than the IS or income-based JSA you would otherwise receive.[54] If you stop getting periodical payments (see p753) or these decrease, any of the lump sum you still have is taken into account as income.[55]

Unless it can be treated as capital, a lump sum is treated as income and divided by the weekly IS or income-based JSA you would otherwise receive, plus £2.[56] However, if you receive periodical payments at the same time as the lump sum, and the periodical payments are less than the total of weekly IS/JSA plus £2, the lump sum is divided by the difference between that amount and the amount of the periodical payment. If you have not yet been awarded CTC for your children, the IS or income-based JSA amounts used will include amounts for your children.

See Chapter 33 for further information about how your IS or income-based JSA is calculated.

If you receive a lump sum that is treated as income, and are disqualified from receiving IS or income-based JSA under the rules described above, you should ask the DWP to recalculate the period of your disqualification whenever:

- your circumstances change so that your entitlement to IS or income-based JSA would be higher; *or*
- benefit rates increase (in April of every year).

Payments that do not count as liable relative payments

Certain types of payment from 'liable relatives' (see p753) do not count as liable relative payments.[57] They are, therefore, dealt with under the normal income and capital rules (see Chapters 36 and 37) and you are usually better off. You should ensure that your solicitor takes account of this when negotiating payments with your former partner. For example:

- some payments can be disregarded as income or capital (see pp843 and 916);
- some payments made to someone else for the benefit of you or a member of your family (or paid to you or a member of the family to pay to someone else – see p756) do not count as your income or capital (see pp844 and 916 for more information about 'notional income' and 'notional capital' that do not affect your IS or income-based JSA).

If you receive a payment which does not count as a liable relative payment, it is usually better if it can be treated as capital. If it is treated as capital it does not affect your benefit unless it takes your capital over £6,000 (£10,000 if you live in a care home). If the payment is more than the upper capital limit (see p910), whether it is capital or a lump sum treated as income (see p924), you will not receive any means-tested benefit but you might be able to reclaim sooner if the payment is capital.

The following types of payment from liable relatives (see p753) do not count as liable relative payments:[58]

- any payment arising from a 'disposition of property' (see p757) in consequence of your separation, divorce or the nullity of your marriage;
- any gifts not exceeding £250 in any period of 52 weeks (and which are not so regular as to amount to periodical payments – see p753);
- payments made after the liable relative has died;
- any payment in kind;
- any payment made to someone else for the benefit of you or a member of your family (such as mortgage capital payments), or paid to you or a member of your family to pay to someone else, which it is unreasonable to take into account – you can appeal to a tribunal which may take a different view from the DWP about what is reasonable;
- any payment to, or for, a child or young person who does not count as a member of your household for benefit purposes;

- money from a liable relative which has already been taken into account under a previous claim, or which has already been recovered out of overpaid IS or income-based JSA;
- any payment which you have used before the DWP makes its decision, provided that you did not use it for the purpose of gaining entitlement to IS or income-based JSA. It should not be taken into account if you have used it to clear debts, such as your solicitor's bill.

Disposition of property

Any payment arising from a 'disposition of property' does not count as a liable relative payment (see p756). It is, therefore, vital to distinguish between payments that arise from a disposition of property and those that do not. **'Property'** is not confined to houses and land, but includes any asset such as the contents of your former home or a building society account. There is a **'disposition'** when those contents are divided up or your former partner buys out your interest.[59] Therefore, any lump sum which is paid in settlement of a claim to a share in any property does not count as a liable relative payment. Only lump sums which are paid instead of income should be treated as income.[60] It is important to take this into account in any negotiations with your former partner. You should make sure your solicitor knows about this rule.

It is best that court orders are drawn up to make it clear that any lump sum is in settlement of a claim to an interest in property. However, this is not essential and the DWP should accept a letter from your solicitor explaining why a lump sum was asked for and agreed.

Note: the proceeds of the sale of your former home may be disregarded altogether for a period of time (see p916). Other capital, such as the home itself and its contents, may also be disregarded. There is, therefore, an advantage, while you are on benefit, to ask for a greater share of the home and accept less in the way of income or capital which would be taken into account to reduce your benefit.

4. Child maintenance bonus

A child maintenance bonus is a lump-sum payment of up to £1,000 that you may be able to get if you have been on income support (IS) or income-based jobseeker's allowance (JSA) and receiving child maintenance. You cannot accrue a child maintenance bonus if you qualify for a child maintenance premium instead (see p862). If you are getting child maintenance and later qualify for a child maintenance premium, you can claim any bonus you have already accrued, but there is a very strict time limit for doing so (see p760). The child maintenance bonus scheme will be withdrawn at the same time as the child maintenance premium is extended to all child support cases (by the end of 2008).

Child maintenance for the purposes of the child maintenance bonus is:[61]

- child support maintenance (see p746);
- maintenance paid to you for your child(ren) by agreement or under a court order;
- maintenance being deducted from the benefit of a non-resident parent (see p765) who is liable to maintain your child(ren).

Who can claim a child maintenance bonus

You qualify for a child maintenance bonus if you do not qualify for a child maintenance premium and:[62]

- you were paid (or were meant to be paid) child maintenance (see above) during a period when you or your partner were on IS or income-based JSA (what is known as your 'bonus period' – see p759); *and*
- your or your partner's entitlement to IS or income-based JSA ceases because you satisfy the 'work condition' within the time limit (see p760). Special rules apply once you qualify for a child maintenance premium (see below).

  At the time the work condition is satisfied, you must not (but see p763) be within a day of:
  - your 60th birthday if you are coming off IS; *or*
  - the day you reach pension age (60 for women and 65 for men) if you are coming off income-based JSA.

If you qualified for a child maintenance premium

If you had accrued a child maintenance bonus when you qualified for a child maintenance premium, you can still claim if:

- you qualified for a bonus before the date you qualified for a child maintenance premium (see below); *or*
- you had not yet satisified the 'work condition' when you qualified for the premium (see p760). In this case, there is a strict time limit for satisfying the work condition by a later date.

You qualify for a child maintenance premium when you:[63]

- come under the child support scheme 'new rules' (see p747); *or*
- are first paid child maintenance by agreement or under a court order, if this is on or after 3 March 2003; *or*
- are first paid voluntary maintenance (that is not paid by agreement or under a court order) on or after 16 February 2004. This type of maintenance, however, cannot help you accrue a child maintenance bonus.

If you qualified for a bonus before you qualified for the child maintenance premium

Your bonus period ends on the date you qualify for a child maintenance premium if it has not ended already (see p759). You can be paid a bonus you have already accrued if:

- a decision to pay you a bonus has not yet been made and prior to the date you qualified for the premium:
  - you satisified the 'work condition' and claimed the bonus (this includes where a late claim is accepted); *or*
  - you were someone to whom the special rules for those who reach age 60 or pension age applied (see p763). If you are someone who has to make a claim, you must have done so before that date (this includes where a late claim is accepted); *or*
- you qualified for a bonus prior to the date you qualified for the premium, but did not claim it until on or after that date. You must claim within the time limit. You can make a late claim in some circumstances (see p763).

If you do not yet satisfy the 'work condition' when you qualify for a child maintenance premium, see p760.

The bonus period

You accumulate a child maintenance bonus during a bonus period – ie, days when:[64]

- you or your partner were entitled, or treated as entitled, to IS or income-based JSA whether or not it was paid. Days when you are getting an urgent cases payment of IS or income-based JSA do not count unless you get the payment because you are a 'person subject to immigration control' (see p1344); *and*
- you are getting, or are meant to be paid, child maintenance (see p758) for a child who lives with you but whose other parent does not. Your child still counts as living with you if s/he is away temporarily, but not for more than 12 weeks. You count as getting child maintenance if:[65]
  - it is being collected by the Child Support Agency on your behalf (see p750), even if the payments are retained; *or*
  - it is being taken into account as income when working out how much IS or income-based JSA you can get (see p751).

The earliest your bonus period could start was 7 April 1997.

When a bonus period ends

When your bonus period ends, in order to qualify for a child maintenance bonus you must satisfy the 'work condition' within a strict time limit (see p760). A bonus period ends:[66]

- when the rules above no longer apply (eg, your IS or income-based JSA ceases or your child's other parent no longer has to pay maintenance to you[67]); *or*
- when the person with the care of the child dies; *or*
- if your bonus period has not already ended for one of the above reasons, once you qualify for a child maintenance premium (see p758).[68]

If your bonus period ends but you cannot claim a child maintenance bonus (eg, because you do not satisfy the work condition – see below) you do not necessarily lose out. Two bonus periods can be linked to count as one if they are separated by:[69]

- not more than 12 weeks; *or*
- a period during which you are getting maternity allowance; *or*
- not more than two years throughout which you were getting incapacity benefit, carer's allowance or severe disablement allowance.

Example

Beth stopped getting IS when her ex-partner began to pay her additional maintenance but she could not claim a child maintenance bonus as she was not working. Eight weeks later she started getting IS again. When Beth takes up full-time work the DWP should look at the child maintenance she was paid during both bonus periods when it calculates her child maintenance bonus.

Although bonus periods can link, it is best to claim your child maintenance bonus as soon as your bonus period ends and you satisfy the work condition (see below) – eg, if you are uncertain how long a temporary job will last. Remember, you must satisfy the work condition within a strict time limit after your bonus period ends. See p762 for information about how and when you must claim.

The work condition

You satisfy the work condition if you or your partner:[70]

- take up a new job or the waged option of the New Deal or return to work (but not if you return to work for the same employer at the same place of work following a trade dispute[71]); *or*
- increase your weekly hours of work and so count as in full-time paid work (see p648); *or*
- have an increase in earnings. This includes where the combined earnings of you and your partner have increased to a level at which you are no longer entitled to IS or income-based JSA.

The time limit

Unless you qualify for a child maintenance premium (see p761), you must satisfy the work condition:[72]

- within the 14 days after your bonus period ends (see p759); *or*
- within 12 weeks of whichever of the following events occurs first: a non-resident parent dies, stops being habitually resident in the UK, or is found not to be your child(ren)'s parent; *or*
- if you get maintenance for one child and s/he dies, within 12 months of her/his date of death.

The time limits within which you must satisfy the work condition are different if, before the date you qualified for a child maintenance premium, you:[73]

- claimed a bonus, but did not satisfy the work condition; *or*
- did not claim a bonus, did not satisfy the work condition and on the day before that date:
  - you or your partner were entitled to (or treated as entitled to) IS or income-based JSA; *and*
  - you were getting child maintenance or were meant to be paid child maintenance.

In either of these cases, you must satisfy the work condition:[74]

- within one month after your bonus period ends (see p759); *or*
- within 12 weeks of whichever of the following events occurs first: a non-resident parent dies, stops being habitually resident in the UK, or is found not to be your child(ren)'s parent, if the event happened before you qualified for a child maintenance premium; *or*
- if you get maintenance for one child and s/he dies before the date you qualify for a child maintenance premium, within 12 months of her/his death.

The amount of child maintenance bonus

To calculate your child maintenance bonus, the DWP looks at how much child maintenance (see p757) you were paid, or were meant to be paid, during your bonus period (see p759). Your child maintenance bonus is the lower of the following amounts:[75]

- £5 for every week when you were meant to be paid at least £5 child maintenance *plus* for each week you were meant to be paid less than £5, the amount due; *or*
- the actual amount of child maintenance you were paid. If it is not clear how much maintenance is being paid for your child(ren) because you are also getting it for yourself, £5 is taken into account as child maintenance (or all of what you are paid if this is less than £5).[76] Any child maintenance you get above what has been taken into account as income in working out your IS or income-based JSA (see p751), or what has been collected on your behalf (see p745) is not included; *or*
- £1,000.

Example

Sarah's ex-husband, Phil, was meant to pay £20 a week child maintenance during her bonus period of 100 weeks. During that time Phil actually paid her £4 a week.

£5 x 100 weeks = £500 *or*

£4 x 100 weeks = £400

Sarah gets a child maintenance bonus of £400.

If your child maintenance bonus would be less than £5, you are not paid at all.[77]

While you are on IS or income-based JSA, you are sent regular estimates of how much child maintenance bonus you might be paid were you to take up work.[78] However, you can ask for a statement at any time.

Claims

A claim for child maintenance bonus must be in writing and on the appropriate form.[79] You can get the form from the office that deals with your IS or JSA or from the DWP website (see Appendix 1). Return it to the office that deals with your IS or JSA.

You can be asked to provide information or evidence to support your claim.[80] You are given one month to do so (longer if the decision maker thinks this is reasonable). If you fail to provide the information or evidence required, your claim is decided without it.[81]

You can ask for your claim to be amended or withdrawn.[82] You must do this in writing before a decision is made about your claim.

Who should claim

If you are one of a couple, you should claim the child maintenance bonus if you are the one caring for a child for whom child maintenance is paid.[83] If both you and your partner care for different children for whom child maintenance is paid, you can both qualify for a child maintenance bonus. In this case, each of you must claim. If you separate, you count as entitled to IS or income-based JSA on days when your former partner was claiming for you.[84] If you are not one of a couple, you claim the child maintenance bonus if you are the person who accrued it.

When to claim

You can claim in the week before the week in which your or your partner's entitlement to IS or income-based JSA ceases. This is useful, for example, where you know you or your partner are returning to work. Otherwise, you must claim within the time limits as follows:[85]

- no later than 28 days after you or your partner stop getting IS or income-based JSA; *or*
- where you are claiming because you stopped getting IS/income-based JSA in the 12 weeks before you reached age 60/pension age (see p763), no later than 28 days after you reach that age.

Different rules apply if you are an appointee claiming the child maintenance bonus of someone who has died.[86]

The date of your claim

Your claim is usually treated as made on the date it is received by the benefit office.[87] Your claim can be backdated for up to six months, if you can show that you had 'good cause' for failing to claim.[88] See p207 for what counts as 'good cause' for a late claim.

Special rules if you reach age 60 or pension age, or if person with care of the child dies

You may be able to get a child maintenance bonus when you turn 60 or reach pension age, even if you do not satisfy the work condition. If someone dies, it is possible for the bonus s/he has accumulated to be paid to an appointee, or possibly help a close relative who takes over the care of the children to get a higher bonus. You should ask the benefit office about claiming a bonus in these circumstances. Further details are also in previous years' *Handbooks*.

Challenging a child maintenance bonus decision

You can apply for a revision or supersession of a child maintenance bonus decision or appeal against it (see Chapters 41 and 42).

Tax, tax credits and other benefits

The bonus is not taxable.

A child maintenance bonus is treated as capital for IS, JSA, housing benefit (HB) and council tax benefit (CTB) purposes.[89] If you are under 60 or you or your partner are on IS or income-based JSA, it is disregarded for 52 weeks for HB and CTB purposes.[90] It is disregarded as income for the purposes of working tax credit and child tax credit.[91] It does not count as income or capital for the purposes of PC, or for HB or CTB if you are 60 or over and neither you nor your partner are on IS or income-based JSA.

5. How maintenance affects housing benefit and council tax benefit

If you and your partner are under 60, the following are taken into account when working out the amount of housing benefit (HB) or council tax benefit (CTB) to which you are entitled:

- child maintenance, including child support;
- other maintenance paid for you or a member of your family (see p700 for who counts as your 'family').

If you or your partner are aged 60 or over, how maintenance is taken into account depends on whether you are claiming pension credit (PC) and, if so, whether you get any guarantee credit (see p881). If you do not get PC, income support (IS) or income-based jobseeker's allowance (JSA), child maintenance is completely disregarded. In addition, if you have a family premium included in your HB/CTB, £15 of any spousal or civil partner maintenance is disregarded (see p890).

How maintenance payments are taken into account depends on whether they are treated as income or capital (see below). It is important to remember that some payments made to someone else for the benefit of you or a member of your family (or paid to you or a member of the family to pay to someone else) do not always count as your income or your capital (see pp873 and 924 for more information about notional income and capital that does not affect your HB or CTB).

The rules on who is 'liable to maintain' you or your child(ren) (see p744) and on 'liable relatives' payments'(see p753) if you are claiming IS or income-based JSA do not apply to HB and CTB, but if you are claiming IS or income-based JSA as well as HB and CTB, you may be affected.

Disregarded maintenance

If you and your partner are under 60 and you are a lone parent, or a couple with a child, £15 of any maintenance payment (whether for you, your partner or for a child) made by your former partner, or your partner's former partner, or the parent of any child in your family is disregarded when working out the amount of your HB and CTB. If you receive maintenance from more than one person, only £15 of the total is disregarded.[92] See Chapter 36 for further information about the income rules.

How maintenance is taken into account

If you are claiming HB or CTB, and you are receiving payments of maintenance regularly, they are taken into account as income. If you are paid irregularly or in lump sums, they are taken into account as capital. See Chapters 36 and 37 for information about the income and capital rules. See pp873 and 924 for information about notional income and capital that does not affect your HB or CTB.

You are usually better off if maintenance can be treated as capital. If it is treated as capital, it does not affect your benefit unless it takes your capital over £6,000 (£10,000 if you live in a care home).

Child maintenance paid to or for your dependent child counts as your income.[93]

6. Benefits if you are contributing to someone's maintenance

If you contribute to the maintenance of an adult or child, this may have an effect on your own benefit entitlement. You may be entitled to an increase in certain benefits. If you are liable to pay child support maintenance, deductions can be made from certain benefits paid to you. If you are liable to maintain someone who is claiming income support (IS) or income-based jobseeker's allowance (JSA) and you fail to do so, the DWP may decide to pursue you for maintenance (see p744).

Non-means tested benefits if you pay maintenance

If you are 'contributing to the maintenance' of your spouse, civil partner or an adult who cares for a child, and you receive incapacity benefit (IB), severe disablement allowance (SDA), carer's allowance (CA), a Category A or C retirement pension or maternity allowance (MA), you might qualify for an increase in respect of her/him even if you do not live together. See Chapter 29 for details of the rules.

It is no longer possible to qualify for an increase in a non-means-tested benefit for a child you maintain, but if you were receiving one on 5 April 2003 you may continue to get it (see p691). These increases have been replaced by child tax credit.

If you contribute to the maintenance of a child, including paying child support, you may qualify for child benefit (see p64) and/or guardian's allowance (see p153). However, if you are not the person with whom the child lives, another claimant of child benefit may have priority over you (see p65).

If you recieve a non-means-tested benefit on the basis that you are 'contributing to the maintenance' of a dependant and fail to do so, and that person is claiming IS or income-based JSA, part of your non-means-tested benefit may be recovered. This applies if, as a result of your failure to pay, the dependant's IS or income-based JSA is increased. The extra IS or income-based JSA which would not have been paid if you had paid the maintenance can be recovered from your child benefit or guardian's allowance, or from the dependant's increase in IB, SDA, CA, Category A or C retirement pension or MA.[94]

Non-resident parents on benefit

If you are a child's non-resident parent in the child support system (see p746), a deduction for child support can be made from certain benefits. The deductions are different depending on whether you are covered by the old or new rules (see p747). If you are in arrears with child support payments, deductions can also be made from certain benefits towards the arrears in certain circumstances (see p994).

Old rules

If you are a non-resident parent on IS, income-based JSA or pension credit (PC), a deduction of £6.10 a week can be made from your benefit as a contribution towards child support maintenance for your child(ren) (see p987 for how this fits in with other deductions that can be made from your benefit).[95] If you have children from two or more different relationships, only one deduction can be made and the £6.10 is apportioned between the people who care for the children.[96]

The deduction does not apply if you:[97]

- are aged under 18;
- would qualify for a family premium (see p777) or have 'day-to-day care' of any child (see CPAG's *Child Support Handbook* for details of 'day-to-day care');
- receive:
  - IB or SDA;
  - MA;
  - statutory sick pay or statutory maternity pay;
  - attendance allowance or disability living allowance;
  - CA;
  - industrial injuries disablement benefit or a war disablement pension;
  - an Armed Forces Compensation Scheme payment or a payment from either of the Independent Living Funds.

If one of the above benefits is not paid solely because of overlapping benefit rules or an inadequate contribution record, you are still exempt from deductions.

New rules

If you are a non-resident parent and you are liable to pay the flat rate of maintenance (currently £5), a deduction of £5 can be made from certain benefits (see p993 for how this fits in with other deductions). If your current partner is also a non-resident parent with a child support maintenance application in force, and either you or your partner get IS or income-based JSA, you pay half the flat rate.[98] If you are a non-resident parent, you or your partner are on one of the benefits prescribed for the flat rate and you are regarded as having 'shared care' of your child(ren), then a nil rate calculation will apply and your benefit will not be reduced.[99] For what counts as 'shared care', and more details about who is liable to pay the flat rate, see CPAG's *Child Support Handbook*.

No deduction will be made, as you will be liable to pay the nil rate, if you:[100]

- are a student, child or prisoner;
- are a 16/17-year-old and receive (or your partner receives) IS or income-based JSA;
- receive an allowance for work-based training for young people (Skillseekers in Scotland);
- are in a care home and receive one of the prescribed benefits for the flat rate of child support or have the whole or part of the cost of your accommodation met by the local authority;
- are a patient in hospital on IS and have been a patient for more than six weeks;
- are a patient in hospital on PC and have been a patient for at least 13, but no more than 52, weeks;

- are a patient in hospital in receipt of one of the prescribed benefits for the flat rate of child support and have been in hospital for 52 weeks or more; *or*
- have a net income of less than £5 a week.

Transitional amount

You may have deductions made at a lower rate than described above for a transitional period if your old maintenance assessment converts to a new maintenance calculation. This applies if you had nothing to pay under the old rules, but under the new rules you are liable to pay the flat rate. For more information on conversion and transitional amounts, see CPAG's *Child Support Handbook*.

Challenging a decision to make deductions

If you think that a decision to make deductions for child support from your IS or income-based JSA is wrong, you can apply in writing to the DWP for a revision or a supersession (see p1056), or you can appeal (see p1093). See p987 for more information about the rules on deductions. However, you cannot do this if you disagree with a decision on your child support liability, as this is a CSA decision and you will need to challenge the CSA. If you disagree with the rate of child support applied to you, see CPAG's *Child Support Handbook*.

Notes

1 *A New System of Child Maintenance*, White Paper, December 2006

1. **What is maintenance**

2 ss78(6)-(9) and 105(3) and (4) SSAA 1992
3 ss78(6)-(9) and 105 SSAA 1992
4 s40 Child Maintenance and Other Payments Bill
5 **IS** s106 SSAA 1992
JSA s23 JSA 1995
6 *National Assistance Board v Parkes* [1955] 2 QBD 506 (QBD)
7 **IS** s106(2) SSAA 1992
JSA s23 JSA 1995; reg 169 JSA Regs
8 GAP, Liable Relatives Procedures, para 2011
9 *National Assistance Board v Wilkinson* [1952] 1 All ELR 255
10 s105(1) SSAA 1992
11 **IS** s106(4)(a) SSAA 1992
JSA s23 JSA 1995; reg 169 JSA Regs
Both GAP, Liable Relatives – Payments, para 3051

2. **Child support maintenance**

12 CSPSSA 2000
13 s6(5)CSA 1991('old rules'), as substituted by s3 CSPSSA 2000 ('new rules'); reg 31(4) CS(MCP) Regs
14 s6(5) CSA 1991 ('old rules'), as substituted by s3 CSPSSA 2000 ('new rules')
15 s46 CSA 1991 ('old rules'), as substituted by s19 CSPSSA 2000 ('new rules')
16 s46(1)(a) CSA 1991
17 GAP, CSA – good cause decision making
18 s6(2) CSA 1991

19 R(SB) 33/85. Although this case concerned social security benefits, the principle that corroboration of evidence is not a necessary requirement also applies to child support.
20 s46(5) CSA 1991 ('old rules'), as substituted by s19 CSPSSA 2000 ('new rules')
21 Reg 31(6) CS(MCP) Regs
22 s2 CSA 1991; GAP, CSA – good cause decision making, para 34893
23 Reg 35A CS(MAP) Regs ('old rules'); reg 10 CS(MCP) Regs ('new rules')
24 s20 CSA 1991 ('old rules'), as substituted by s10 CSPSSA 2000 ('new rules')
25 Reg 37 CS(MAP) Regs ('old rules'); reg 12 CS(MCP) Regs ('new rules')
26 Reg 36(2) and (4) CS(MAP) Regs ('old rules'); reg 11(2) and (3) CS(MCP) Regs ('new rules')
27 Reg 36(8) CS(MAP) Regs ('old rules'); reg 11(8) CS(MCP) Regs ('new rules')
28 Regs 36(4A) and 47 CS(MAP) Regs ('old rules'); regs 11(4) and 17 CS(MCP) Regs ('new rules')
29 Reg 38 CS(MAP) Regs ('old rules'); reg 13 CS(MCP) Regs ('new rules')
30 Reg 48 CS(MAP) Regs ('old rules'); reg 18 CS(MCP) Regs ('new rules')
31 Regs 40 and 40ZA CS(MAP) Regs ('old rules'); regs 14 and 15 CS(MCP) Regs ('new rules')
32 Reg 41 CS(MAP) Regs ('old rules'); reg 16 CS(MCP) Regs ('new rules')
33 Reg 49 CS(MAP) Regs ('old rules'); reg 19 CS(MCP) Regs ('new rules')
34 s46(7) CSA 1991 ('old rules'); s20(1)(c) CSA 1991, as amended by CSPSSA 2000 ('new rules')
35 s29(3) CSA 1991; regs 2 and 6 CS(C&E) Regs

3. **How maintenance affects income support, income-based jobseeker's allowance, pension credit and tax credits**

36 Reg 15(5)(d) SPC Regs
37 **IS** Reg 14 IS Regs
JSA Reg 76 JSA Regs
38 **IS** Reg 60B IS Regs
JSA Reg 126 JSA Regs
39 **IS** Sch 9 para 73 IS Regs
JSA Sch 7 para 70 JSA Regs
40 *Secretary of State for Work and Pensions v Menary-Smith* [2006] EWCA Civ 1689
41 **IS** Reg 60C IS Regs
JSA Reg 128 JSA Regs
42 s74(1) SSAA 1992; reg 7 SS(PAOR) Regs
43 **IS** Reg 60D(1)(aa) IS Regs
JSA Reg 129(1)(aa) JSA Regs
44 s41(2) CSA 1991; reg 8 CS(AIAMA) Regs
45 **IS** Regs 54-60 IS Regs
JSA Regs 117-124 JSA Regs
46 **IS** Reg 54 IS Regs
JSA Reg 117 JSA Regs
47 **IS** Reg 54 IS Regs, definition of 'periodical payment'
JSA Reg 117 JSA Regs, definition of 'periodical payment'
Both *Bolstridge v CAO*
48 **IS** Reg 58 IS Regs
JSA Reg 122 JSA Regs
49 **IS** Reg 58(4) IS Regs
JSA Reg 122(4) JSA Regs
50 **IS** Reg 59(1) IS Regs
JSA Reg 123(1) JSA Regs
51 s74(1) SSAA 1992; reg 7(1) SS(PAOR) Regs
52 **IS** Reg 54 IS Regs, definition of 'periodical payment'
JSA Reg 117 JSA Regs, definition of 'periodical payment'
53 **IS** Regs 54, definition of 'payment', and 55 IS Regs
JSA Regs 117, definition of 'payment', and 118 JSA Regs
54 **IS** Reg 60 IS Regs
JSA Reg 124 JSA Regs
55 **IS** Reg 60(2) IS Regs
JSA Reg 124(2) JSA Regs
56 **IS** Reg 57(1) and (2) IS Regs
JSA Reg 121(1) and (2) JSA Regs
57 **IS** Reg 54 IS Regs, definition of 'payment'
JSA Reg 117 JSA Regs, definition of 'payment'
58 **IS** Regs 54, definition of 'payment', 55 and 60(1) IS Regs
JSA Regs 117, definition of 'payment', 118 and 124(1) JSA Regs
59 CSB/1160/1986; R(SB) 1/89
60 R(SB) 1/89

4. **Child maintenance bonus**

61 Reg 1(2) SS(CMB) Regs
62 s10 CSA 1995; reg 3 SS(CMB) Regs
63 Regs 1 and 4 SS(CMPMA) Regs
64 Reg 4 SS(CMB) Regs
65 Reg 2(1) SS(CMB) Regs
66 Reg 4(7) SS(CMB) Regs
67 CIS/3544/2002
68 Reg 4(7) SS(CMB) Regs, as modified by reg 4(6) SS(CMPMA) Regs
69 Reg 4(2)-(5) SS(CMB) Regs
70 Reg 3(1) SS(CMB) Regs

71 Reg 3(2) and (3) SS(CMB) Regs
72 Reg 3(1)(f) SS(CMB) Regs
73 Reg 4(3) and (4) SS(CMPMA) Regs
74 Reg 3(3)(1)(f) SS(CMB) Regs, as modified by reg 4(5) SS(CMPMA) Regs
75 Reg 5 SS(CMB) Regs
76 Reg 1(5) SS(CMB) Regs
77 Reg 5(5) SS(CMB) Regs
78 Regs 2(2)and 6 SS(CMB) Regs
79 Reg 10(1) SS(CMB) Regs
80 Reg 10(5) SS(CMB) Regs
81 CJSA/2838/2001
82 Reg 11(1) and (2) SS(CMB) Regs
83 Reg 9 SS(CMB) Regs
84 Reg 9(4) and (5) SS(CMB) Regs
85 Reg 10 SS(CMB) Regs
86 Reg 13 SS(CMB) Regs
87 Reg 11(3) SS(CMB) Regs
88 Reg 11(4) SS(CMB) Regs
89 s10(3) CSA 1995; reg 14 SS(CMB) Regs
90 **HB** Sch 6 para 48 HB Regs
CTB Sch 5 para 50 CTB Regs
91 Reg 7 Table 3 paras 13, 16 and 17 TC(DCI) Regs

5. How maintenance affects housing benefit and council tax benefit

92 **HB** Sch 5 para 47(2) HB Regs; Sch 5 para 20(2) HB(SPC) Regs
CTB Sch 4 para 48(2) CTB Regs; Sch 3 para 20(2) CTB(SPC) Regs
93 s136(1) SSCBA 1992

6. Benefits if you are contributing to someone's maintenance

94 s74(3) SSAA1992; reg 9 SS(PAOR) Regs
95 s43 CSA 1991; regs 13 and 28 CS(MASC) Regs; Sch 9 para 7A SS(C&P) Regs
96 Reg 28(3) CS(MASC) Regs
97 Reg 28(1) and Sch 4 CS(MASC) Regs
98 Reg 4(3) CS(MCSC) Regs
99 Sch 1 CSA 1991 ('old rules'), as substituted by Sch 1 para 8 CSPSSA 2000 ('new rules')
100 Sch 1 para 5 CSA 1991; reg 5 CS(MCSC) Regs

Chapter 33

Applicable amounts

This chapter explains the amounts allowed for meeting your needs when calculating your entitlement to income support (IS), income-based jobseeker's allowance (JSA), housing benefit (HB) and council tax benefit (CTB). It covers:

The rules for assessing entitlement to **pension credit (PC)** are, for the most part, completely different, and are dealt with in Chapter 18. However, the additional amounts in the guarantee credit of PC for claimants who are **severely disabled** or **carers** have rules which are similar to those for the severe disability premium and carer's premium, and are dealt with in this chapter – see pp784 and 789.

Note: in this chapter, unless otherwise stated, references to income-based JSA are intended also to refer to joint-claim JSA.

Employment and support allowance

At the time this *Handbook* was written, a new benefit, employment and support allowance (ESA), was expected to be introduced for new claimants from October 2008. One type of ESA, income-related ESA, will use an applicable amount to calculate entitlement. The applicable amount for income-related ESA is expected to be broadly similar, though not exactly the same (in particular it will not include a disability premium), as that for IS. The applicable amounts in the HB and CTB of people on ESA will be different. See the sections on personal allowances and premiums below for more details, and see www.cpag.org.uk/esa and CPAG's *Welfare Rights Bulletin* for updates.

1. What is the applicable amount

For **income support** (IS) and **income-based jobseeker's allowance** (JSA), your applicable amount is the amount you are expected to live on each week. For **housing benefit** (HB) and **council tax benefit** (CTB), it is the amount used to see how much help you need with your rent or council tax. This chapter explains how you work out your applicable amount for these benefits. For the way benefit payable is calculated, see p299 for IS, p366 for income-based JSA, p189 for HB and p84 for CTB.

What is included in your applicable amount

For IS, income-based JSA, HB and CTB, your applicable amount is made up of:

- **personal allowances:** the amount the law says you need for living expenses (see below);
- **premiums:** the amount given for certain extra needs you or your family may have (see p775);
- for IS and income-based JSA only, **housing costs** (see Chapter 34).

When your applicable amount is reduced

Your applicable amount is reduced if, for IS/income-based JSA/HB/CTB, you are:

- receiving an urgent cases payment (see p1344);
- involved in a trade dispute (see p633);
- a couple and one of you is a 'person subject to immigration control' (see p1343);
- without accommodation (see p632);
- a prisoner (see p624);
- for IS and income-based JSA only, a patient in hospital for 52 weeks or more (see p611);
- for IS only, appealing against a decision that you are not incapable of work under the personal capability assessment[1] (see p294 for entitlement to IS in this situation and p668 for more information on the personal capability assessment);
- for income-based JSA only, getting JSA on hardship grounds (see p422);
- for income-based JSA only, if you are required to be a 'joint-claim couple', you or your partner are subject to a sanction (see Chapter 16).

2. Personal allowances

The amount of your personal allowance for income support (IS), income-based jobseeker's allowance (JSA), housing benefit (HB) and council tax benefit (CTB) depends on your age and whether you are claiming as a single person or a couple. For HB and CTB, and in some circumstances for IS and income-based JSA, you also get an allowance for each dependent child (but see below if your child has capital).

If you are polygamously married (see p702) you receive an extra amount for each additional partner in your household. However, for IS and income-based JSA, if any additional partner is under the age of 18, you only receive an extra amount if s/he is responsible for a child (see p710) or would otherwise meet the special conditions for qualifying for JSA as a 16/17-year-old (see p371).[2]

Employment and support allowance

Employment and support allowance (ESA) is expected to be introduced for new claimants from October 2008. One type of ESA, income-related ESA, will include an applicable amount to calculate entitlement. Personal allowances for income-related ESA are expected to be broadly similar to IS.[3] It is also expected that the personal allowances in the HB and CTB of ESA claimants will include an extra amount, equivalent to the value of the ESA support component or work-related activity component (whichever has been awarded).[4] See www.cpag.org.uk/esa and CPAG's *Welfare Rights Bulletin* for updates.

Personal allowances for children

For when children can be included in your claim, see p709. HB and CTB include personal allowances and premiums for dependent children. From 6 April 2004, new claims for IS and income-based JSA do not include such allowances or premiums. (But see CPAG's *Welfare Rights Bulletin* 186, p12 for doubts about this. The DWP attempted to clarify the rules from 8 September 2005.[5])

If you already get IS or income-based JSA and have a child tax credit (CTC) award, from 6 April 2004 your benefit is adjusted to remove allowances and premiums for children. However, you may be entitled to continue having them included in your claim for IS or income-based JSA for a time, in certain circumstances. This will apply if:

- you have a claim which began before 6 April 2004; *and*
- you had a dependent child(ren) included in the claim before 6 April 2004; *and*
- you have not yet been awarded CTC.

In these circumstances, if you are entitled to them, the personal allowance and premiums continue to be included in your claim until such point as you are awarded CTC.

If your child has capital

Even if you are still entitled to amounts for children in your IS/income-based JSA, if a child has over £3,000 capital you do not get any allowance or premium for that child, except for a family premium. See p844 for how a child's income affects benefit. For HB and CTB, your child's income and capital do not affect your benefit.

Rates of personal allowances (aged 18 and over)[6]

Note: some 16/17-year-olds may also be entitled to these rates (see below).

	IS/JSA/HB/CTB	*HB/CTB only – claimant or partner aged 60 or over and not claiming IS or income-based JSA*
Single claimant:		
Aged 18–24	£47.95	
Aged 25 or over	£60.50	
Aged 60–64		£124.05
Aged 65 or over		£143.80
Lone parent:		
Aged 18 or over	£60.50	
Couple:		
Both aged 18 or over	£94.95	
One or both aged 60–64		£189.35
One or both aged 65 or over		£215.50
One aged under 18 (some IS/JSA cases only – see p774 – and all HB/CTB cases)	£94.95	
One aged under 18 (other IS/JSA cases – see p774):		
either	£60.50	
or	£47.95	
Polygamous marriages, each additional qualifying partner living in the same household:[7]		
Any age	£34.45	
Claimant and all partners aged under 65		£65.30
One or more aged 65 or over		£71.70

Rates of personal allowances (16/17-year-olds)

For **IS** and **income-based JSA**, if you are single and aged 16 or 17 (including if you are a lone parent) you get the same rate as 18–24-year-olds – ie, £47.95. If you are in a couple (unless one of the special circumstances on p774 applies) and your partner is also aged under 18, or is aged 18–24, you get £47.95. If your partner is aged 25 or over, you get £60.50.

For **HB**, if you are single you get the same rate as 18–24-year-olds – ie, £47.95. If you are in a couple and your partner is also aged under 18, you get £72.35. If your partner is aged 18 or over, you get £94.95.

CTB is not payable to single people under 18, or to couples if both of you are under 18 because you cannot be liable to pay council tax at that age (see p84). If one of you is 18 or over you will get the same personal allowance as couples aged 18 to 24 (see p773).

Note: most 16/17-year-olds who have left local authority care cannot claim IS/JSA or HB (see p610).

Couples in special circumstances[8]

Note: these rules apply to IS and income-based JSA only

The amount paid to couples depends on your ages and whether one or both of you are, or would be, eligible for IS or income-based JSA (including JSA discretionary severe hardship payments – see p373) if you were a single person. For some couples the amount may be no more than that for a single person.

One partner aged 18 or over and the other under 18 *and* (for IS) entitled to IS (or would be if not a member of a couple) *or* income-based/discretionary JSA; for JSA claims, the partner under 18 must *either* be able to qualify both for income-based/discretionary JSA *and* for IS (were they to claim it) *or* be treated as responsible for a child[9]	£94.95
Both under 18 *and both* entitled to IS or income-based/discretionary JSA (or would be if not a member of a couple)	£72.35
Both under 18 and one is responsible for a child	£72.35
For IS, the claimant, or for JSA, either partner, is aged 25 or over and the other under 18 *and* not entitled to IS or income-based/discretionary JSA (even if, for IS, s/he were not a member of a couple)	£60.50
For IS, the claimant, or for JSA either partner, is aged 18–24 and the other under 18 *and* not entitled to IS or income-based/discretionary JSA (even if, for IS, s/he were not a member of a couple)	£47.95
Both under 18 in any other circumstance	£47.95

Children

Note: for IS and income-based JSA, you are only entitled to personal allowances for children in limited circumstances (see p771).

The rate for your dependent children is the same for IS, income-based JSA, HB and CTB, and is not affected by your (or your partner's) age.

Note, however, that this rate does not apply to joint-claim JSA, as you cannot claim this type of JSA if you have children.

Under 20	£52.59

3. **Premiums**

Premiums are added to your basic personal allowances and are intended to help with extra expenses caused by age, disability or, in some circumstances, children.

- **Family premium:** for housing benefit (HB) and council tax benefit (CTB), but only for income support (IS) and income-based jobseeker's allowance (JSA) in some claims (see p777).
- **Disabled child premium:** for HB and CTB, but only for IS and income-based JSA in some claims (see p778).
- **Disability premium:** for IS, income-based JSA, HB and CTB (see p779).
- **Enhanced disability premium:** for IS, income-based JSA, HB and CTB (see p781).
- **Pensioner premium:** for IS and income-based JSA, but only relevant for HB and CTB in some circumstances (see p782).
- **Higher pensioner premium:** for IS and income-based JSA, but only relevant for HB and CTB in some circumstances (see p783).
- **Severe disability premium:** for IS, income-based JSA, HB and CTB (a similar allowance applies to the guarantee credit of pension credit (PC)) – see p784.
- **Carer's premium:** for IS, income-based JSA, HB and CTB (a similar allowance applies to the guarantee credit of PC) – see p789.

See p790 for information about backdating of premiums. See the table on p776 for the premium rates.

Employment and support allowance

Employment and support allowance (ESA) is expected to be introduced for new claimants from October 2008. One type of ESA, income-related ESA, will use an applicable amount to calculate entitlement. Premiums for income-related ESA are expected to include the enhanced disability, severe disability, carer's and pensioner premiums (but not the disability premium or premiums for children), with similar rules to those described below for IS.[10] See p779 for more regarding the disability premium, and www.cpag.org.uk/esa or CPAG's *Welfare Rights Bulletin* for updates.

Premiums for families with children

For when children can be included in your claim (for any means-tested benefit), see p709. **HB** and **CTB** include premiums for families with dependent children. These are the family premium, disabled child premium and the child rate of the enhanced disability premium. From 6 April 2004, new claims for **IS** and **income-based JSA** do not include these premiums. (But see CPAG's *Welfare Rights Bulletin* 186, p12 for doubts about this. The DWP attempted to clarify the rules from 8 September 2005.)[11]

If you already get IS or income-based JSA and have a child tax credit (CTC) award, from 6 April 2004 your IS or income-based JSA no longer includes those premiums. However, you may be entitled to continue having them included in your claim for IS or income-based JSA for a time, in certain circumstances. This will apply if:

- you have a claim which began before 6 April 2004; *and*
- you had a dependent child(ren) included in the claim before 6 April 2004; *and*
- you have not yet been awarded CTC.

In these circumstances, if you are entitled to them, the premiums will continue to be included in your claim until you are awarded CTC.

If your child has capital

Even if you are still entitled to amounts for children in your IS/income-based JSA, if a child has over £3,000 capital you do not get any allowance or premium for that child, except for a family premium. See p844 for how a child's income affects benefit. For HB and CTB, your child's income and capital do not affect your benefit.

Premium rates

The rates of premiums are the same for all claimants, except for the family premium with HB/CTB if you have a child aged under one.

If you are aged 60 or over

If you are aged 60 or over and not claiming IS or income-based JSA, no lone parent increase is payable in your HB or CTB.

If you or your partner (if any) are aged 60 or over and not claiming IS or income-based JSA, your HB or CTB can only include the family, disabled child, enhanced disability for a child, severe disability and carer's premiums.[12] This is because you can get a higher personal allowance instead of a pensioner premium.

Premium rates

Where payable, the following premiums can be paid on top of any other premiums, except that the enhanced disability premium cannot be paid on top of the pensioner premium or higher pensioner premium[13] (but see p781).

Family premium	
Ordinary rate	£16.75
Higher rate if one child under one year old (for HB and CTB only)	£27.25
Disabled child premium (for each qualifying child)	£48.72
Severe disability premium	
Single (or one partner qualifies)	£50.35
Couple (both partners qualify)	£100.70

Carer's premium	
Single (or one partner qualifies)	£27.75
Couple (both partners qualify)	£55.50
Enhanced disability premium	
Child rate (for each qualifying child)	£19.60
Single	£12.60
Couple (one or both partner(s) qualify)	£18.15

We understand that, where appropriate, the DWP will pay the enhanced disability premium for a child on top of any of the pensioner premiums.

Only one of the following premiums can be paid. If you qualify for more than one you get whichever is the highest:[14]

Family premium for HB/CTB (lone parent increase)	
HB/CTB	£5.45
Disability premium	
Single	£25.85
Couple	£36.85
Pensioner, enhanced pensioner and higher pensioner premium (see p782)	
Single (not payable in IS)	£63.55
Couple	£94.40

Entitlement to some premiums depends on receipt of other benefits. Once you have qualified for a premium, if you or your partner cease to receive a qualifying benefit because of the overlapping benefit rules (ie, because you are receiving another benefit at the same or a higher rate – see p981), or because you or your partner are on an employment training course or getting a training allowance, you continue to receive the relevant premium.[15] In addition, you or your partner must be getting the benefit for yourself (or for your partner), and not on behalf of someone else – eg, as an appointee (see p955).[16]

Sometimes, you may be able to get payment of a premium backdated (see p790).

Family premium[17]

Note: for **IS** and **income-based JSA** you will only be entitled to a family premium for a time and in certain circumstances (see p775).

You are entitled to a family premium if your family includes a child (see p709). It is paid even if you are not the parent of the child and even if you do not receive a personal allowance in your IS/income-based JSA for any child because s/he has capital over £3,000.

Only one family premium is payable regardless of the number of children you have. A **higher amount is paid in HB and CTB** if at least one child in your family is under one year old.[18] This higher amount is payable to both couples and lone parents, and the additional amount for a lone parent (see below) is paid on top of the higher amount.

If a child who is being looked after by a local authority or who is in custody comes home for part of a week, your IS or income-based JSA includes a proportion of the premium, according to the number of days the child is with you.[19] For HB and CTB, you may be paid the full premium if your child who is being looked after by a local authority is part of the household for any part of the week, provided the local authority thinks it is reasonable given how often and for how long the child is at home with you.[20]

Lone parents[21]

The lone parent rate of the family premium is only payable in **HB and CTB**, and is only payable if:

- you were entitled or treated as entitled to HB/CTB and the lone parent increase on 5 April 1998; *and*
- you do not cease to be a lone parent; *and*
- you do not cease to be entitled or treated as entitled to HB/CTB; *and*
- you do not become or cease to be entitled to IS or income-based JSA; *and*
- the disability premium (see p779) or one of the pensioner premiums (see p782) does not become payable instead.

You are treated as entitled to HB and CTB on 5 April 1998 if you were entitled to the other benefit (ie, CTB or HB) as a lone parent from 5 April 1998 to the day before you eventually claim it. You are also treated as entitled to HB during any rent-free weeks.

There are no linking periods for HB and CTB, so if you lose the increase, even for a short period, you will not be able to claim it back (although a change of address does not break your entitlement).[22]

If you lose your entitlement to the lone parent increase, you may still be entitled to the ordinary rate of the family premium instead.

Disabled child premium[23]

Note: for **IS** and **income-based JSA** you will only be entitled to a disabled child premium in certain circumstances (see p775).

You are entitled to a disabled child premium for each child in your family who gets disability living allowance (DLA) (or extra-statutory payments to compensate for non-payment of DLA) or who is blind.

A child is treated as blind if s/he is registered as blind and for the first 28 weeks after s/he has been taken off the register on regaining her/his sight.[24] If DLA stops because the child has gone into hospital, see p615.

If your child is looked after by the local authority or in custody for part of the week, this premium is affected in the same way as the family premium.

For how to qualify for DLA, see Chapter 6.

For IS and income-based JSA, if your child has over £3,000 capital or has been in hospital for more than 52 weeks, you do not get this premium.[25] Your child's capital does not affect your HB or CTB.[26]

If your child dies

If your child dies, for HB and CTB only, you may be able to continue receiving the disabled child premium for eight weeks.[27] This will apply if:

- you get child benefit for the child following her/his death (see p75); *and*
- you were getting the disabled child premium included in your applicable amount for that child immediately before her/his death.

Disability premium[28]

The way in which you can get a disability premium differs depending on whether you have a partner or not (see p702). In either case, the person who satisfies the qualifying conditions set out on p780 has to be aged under 60. If you or your partner are aged 60 or over you may instead get the higher pensioner premium.

Future changes

From October 2008, alongside the introduction of ESA, the Government plans to change the rules on the disability premium. ESA itself will not include a disability premium at all. If you are already getting the premium included in your claim for IS, income-based JSA, HB or CTB at the point that ESA is introduced, it is expected to continue as long as you still satisfy the usual rules for the benefit and the premium (eg, you remain entitled to IS and you are incapable for work or are entitled to a qualifying benefit such as DLA).

If you make a new claim for any of these benefits on or after the date ESA is introduced, it is expected that you will not be able to get the disability premium on the ground of *incapacity for work*. But it is expected that you will still be able to get the disability premium in IS, income-based JSA and (if you are not on ESA) HB and CTB on grounds *other* than incapacity for work. If you are on ESA, it is expected that your HB and CTB will not include a disability premium on *any* ground, but will instead include a higher personal allowance.[29] See www.cpag.org.uk/esa or CPAG's *Welfare Rights Bulletin* for updates.

Note:

- You only qualify for the higher pensioner premium for **IS** if your partner is aged 60 or over.[30]
- For **IS and income-based JSA**, you may not be entitled to the disability premium once you or your partner have been receiving free treatment as a hospital inpatient for more than 52 weeks (see p616).
- The disability premium cannot be included in your **HB or CTB** if you or your partner are aged 60 or over and not claiming IS or income-based JSA.

You qualify for a disability premium if:

- you, or your partner (if any), are getting a qualifying benefit. These are:
  - DLA (see Chapter 6) or an equivalent benefit paid to meet attendance needs because of an injury at work (see Chapter 14) or a war injury;[31]
  - war pensioner's mobility supplement;
  - the disability element or severe disability element of working tax credit (WTC);
  - severe disablement allowance (SDA – see Chapter 20);
  - incapacity benefit (IB) paid at the long-term rate (see Chapter 12);
  - special short-term rate of IB because you are terminally ill (see p273).[32]

  Extra-statutory payments to compensate you or your partner for not getting these benefits also count.[33]

  You must be getting the qualifying benefit for yourself, not on behalf of someone else – eg, as an appointee (see p955). The same applies if it is your partner who gets the benefit.[34]

  Once you qualify for the premium, you or your partner are treated as still getting a qualifying benefit you no longer receive because of the overlapping benefit rules (see p981);[35]
- you, or your partner, are registered as blind with a local authority. If you, or your partner, regain your sight you still qualify for 28 weeks after being taken off the register;[36]
- you, or your partner, have an NHS invalid trike or private car allowance because of disability;[37]
- you, or your partner, were getting IB paid at the long-term rate (or at the short-term rate because of terminal illness) which stopped at pension age[38] or when retirement pension became payable, since when you have been continuously entitled to IS/income-based JSA/HB/CTB.[39] If it is your partner who began receiving a retirement pension, s/he must still be alive (IS/income-based JSA),[40] or still be a member of your family (HB/CTB).[41] In the case of IS or income-based JSA only, you or your partner must have previously qualified for a disability premium;[42]
- you, or your partner, were getting attendance allowance (AA) or DLA but payment of that benefit was suspended when one of you became a hospital inpatient.[43] In the case of IS and income-based JSA only, you or your partner must have previously qualified for a disability premium;
- for IS/HB/CTB, but not for income-based JSA, the DWP has decided that you are 'incapable of work' or you are treated as incapable or (for IS only) you are entitled to statutory sick pay (SSP) and you have been entitled, incapable of work or treated as incapable of work for a continuous qualifying period of:[44]
  - 196 days if you have been certified as 'terminally ill' – ie, it can reasonably be expected that you will die within six months as a consequence of a progressive disease;[45]
  - 364 days in all other cases.

Incapacity for work

To establish your incapacity for work (unless you get SSP), you should claim IB, whether you are entitled to it or not. (But see p779 if you have to claim ESA instead of IB.)

Breaks in entitlement/incapacity of up to 56 days (or 104 weeks if you are a 'welfare to work' beneficiary[46]) are ignored for the qualifying period above. See p555 for more details about SSP and 'incapacity for work'.

If you consider you have been incapable of work for 364/196 days or more, but you have not previously been certified or assessed as incapable of work, you should claim IB (see Chapter 12). You do not have to be awarded IB; you only have to show that you have been incapable of work. You should supply a medical certificate covering the whole period. This and other evidence of your incapacity can be accepted even though it relates to a past period.[47] Even if you have not yet been incapable of work for 364/196 days, it is advisable to claim IB as soon as possible so that the disability premium can be awarded to you as soon as you reach the end of the qualifying period.

Couples

If you are a couple, you get the disability premium at the couple rate provided one of you meets one of the qualifying conditions on p780, except in the case of the condition concerning SSP and incapacity for work. In that case, you do not get the premium at all unless the person who qualifies is also the claimant of the IS/HB/CTB paid to you as a couple.[48] You may, therefore, need to swap who is the claimant of your IS/HB/CTB (see pp702 and 954). This does not apply to income-based JSA because you cannot claim JSA while you are incapable of work. If your partner is incapable of work s/he should probably claim IS instead of you claiming JSA so that you may benefit from the disability premium. In this case, however, you should still consider signing on in order to get national insurance credits (see p727). **Note:** if your partner is in receipt of long-term IB the disability premium can be included in your claim for JSA.[49]

Training

If you go on a government training course or for any period you receive a training allowance, you keep the disability premium even though you may cease to receive one of the qualifying benefits, or cease to be entitled to SSP or be incapable of work during the course, as long as you continue to be entitled to IS, income-based JSA, HB or CTB. After the course, the premium continues (except for income-based JSA) if you remain entitled to SSP (for IS only), are still incapable of work, or are getting a qualifying benefit.[50]

Enhanced disability premium[51]

Note: for **IS** and **income-based JSA** you are only entitled to the child rate of this premium in certain circumstances (see p775).

This premium can be paid in addition to either or both the disability and severe disability premiums (see p776). For more details of which premiums the enhanced disability premium can be paid in addition to, see p776.

You qualify for one enhanced disability premium for each child who receives DLA highest rate care component (or extra-statutory payments to compensate for non-payment of this) and who is a member of your family (see Chapter 30 for the meaning of 'family').

You are also entitled to an enhanced disability premium for an adult (at the single or couple rate) if you or your partner receive DLA highest rate care component and are aged under 60.

Once you or your partner reach the age of 60 you will be paid the pensioner premium instead, or, for HB/CTB, the higher personal allowance.

In most cases, you (or the family member) will be treated as receiving the highest rate of DLA care component during any period when DLA is suspended while you are in hospital. The exception is if you are in one of the groups of people listed below who cannot qualify for the premium.

The following people cannot qualify:

- for **IS and income-based JSA only**, children who have been in hospital for more than 52 weeks, or with more than £3,000 in capital;[52]
- some people who have been in hospital for 52 weeks or more or, in some cases, if their partner has (see p616).

Pensioner premiums[53]

Note: for **IS** you only qualify for any of the pensioner premiums if your partner satisfies the age requirements.[54] For **HB** and **CTB** only, if you or your partner are aged 60 or over and not claiming IS or income-based JSA, no pensioner premiums are included in your HB or CTB. If you *are* on IS or income-based JSA, you get maximum HB/CTB anyway without having to calculate an applicable amount (see p190). However, HB and CTB are still included here as you may need to refer to the rules for another purpose.

There are three pensioner premiums, but they are all paid at the same rate – either a single person's rate or a couple rate. The premiums are:

- **pensioner premium** if you or your partner are aged 60–74;
- **pensioner premium** (sometimes referred to as **enhanced pensioner premium**) if you or your partner are aged 75–79;
- **higher pensioner premium** if you or your partner are aged 80 or over, or if certain other conditions are satisfied (see below).

Qualifying for the higher pensioner premium may be important, for example, because it qualifies you for a £20 earnings disregard (see p854) or because it meets one of the qualifying conditions for the disability element of WTC (see p1237).

The couple rate is paid even if only one partner fulfils the condition. You are paid the highest rate that applies to you (or your partner). If you or your partner are sick or disabled, check if you could get the higher pensioner premium instead (see below).

Higher pensioner premium

You qualify for the higher pensioner premium if:[55]

- for income-based JSA, HB and CTB, either you or your partner are aged 80 or over or, for IS, your partner is aged 80 or over;
- for IS, your partner is aged 60–79, for income-based JSA, HB and CTB, you or your partner are aged 60–79 and either of you receives a qualifying benefit (as for the disability premium – see p780 – but including AA) or are registered blind, or have an NHS trike or a private car allowance.
  If your AA or DLA stops because you go into hospital, see p613. If you stop getting IB, or if you are getting SDA, see below;
- you were getting a disability premium as part of your income-based JSA, HB or CTB before you were 60 and you have continued to claim that benefit since reaching 60. You must have been getting a disability premium at some time during the eight weeks (or 104 weeks if you are a 'welfare to work' beneficiary[56]) before you were 60 and have received that benefit continuously since you reached 60.[57] But you can have a period off that benefit of up to eight (or 104) weeks and still qualify;
- for IS, you were getting a disability premium before your partner was 60 and continue to get IS since s/he reached 60.

Note: for **IS and income-based JSA**, you may not be entitled to the higher pensioner premium once you or (for IS and joint-claim JSA) your partner has been receiving free treatment as a hospital inpatient for more than 52 weeks (see p616).

For HB and CTB, if you were entitled to a higher pensioner premium for one benefit in the previous eight (or 104) weeks you will get a higher pensioner premium with the other if you then qualify or requalify for that benefit.[58] Previous entitlement to a premium while on HB or CTB does not help you qualify for the higher pensioner premium when you claim IS or income-based JSA and vice versa. Previous entitlement while on IS helps you qualify when you claim income-based JSA,[59] but the reverse does not apply.

In the case of couples, the person who was the benefit claimant before s/he was 60 must continue to claim after that, but it is not necessary for the claimant to have been the person who qualified for the disability premium.

If you stop getting incapacity benefit

If you or your partner stop getting IB because you reach pension age[60] or get retirement pension instead, you still get a higher pensioner premium if you remain continuously entitled to the same means-tested benefit. Breaks of eight weeks (104 weeks if you are a 'welfare to work' beneficiary) or less in your entitlement are ignored.[61] In the case of HB and CTB, if you were entitled to a higher pensioner premium for one of these benefits in the previous eight or 104 weeks, you get a higher pensioner premium with the other if you then qualify or requalify for that benefit.[62] Previous entitlement within this period to the higher pensioner premium with IS will also count if you claim income-based JSA, but the reverse will not apply.[63] If your partner has changed to a retirement pension, s/he must still be alive (in the case of IS/income-based JSA), or still be a member of your family (HB and CTB).[64] In the case of IS and income-based JSA, the higher pensioner premium or a disability premium must also have been applicable to you or your partner.[65]

If you are getting severe disablement allowance

If you are getting SDA by the time you reach 65, you will be awarded it for life even if you no longer satisfy the incapacity or disability conditions. You will, therefore, continue to qualify for the higher pensioner premium.[66] This also applies even if it ceases to be paid because you get retirement pension at a higher rate.[67]

Severe disability premium and pension credit additional amount[68]

You qualify for a severe disability premium, or for the additional amount for severe disability in the guarantee credit of PC, if all of the following apply to you.

- You receive a **qualifying benefit**. This is either AA, the middle or highest rate care component of DLA, constant attendance allowance, exceptionally severe disablement allowance (or the equivalent war pension),[69] or extra-statutory payments to compensate you for not receiving any of these benefits.[70]
- For **couples**, both partners must be getting a qualifying benefit, or else one must be getting a qualifying benefit while the other is registered blind or treated as blind because s/he came off the register in the last 28 weeks. If one partner is blind, the other partner who gets the qualifying benefit must be the claimant to get the premium in IS, income-based JSA, HB or CTB. For PC, either partner can be the claimant.[71] You and your partner are treated as getting the qualifying benefit while either or both of you are still in hospital, but this is only if you are claiming the amount for severe disability on the basis that both you and your partner are receiving a qualifying benefit.[72] For IS, income-based JSA, HB and CTB, the qualifying benefit must be paid in respect of yourself/selves, receipt of benefit for someone else (eg, a child) does not count.[73] It is probably intended that the same rule should apply to PC.
- **No non-dependant aged 18 or over is 'normally residing with you'** (see p786) – eg, a grown-up son or daughter or your parents. It does not matter whose house it is, yours or the non-dependant's.[74] For IS, income-based JSA, PC and HB, someone is only counted as living with you if you share accommodation apart from a bathroom, lavatory or a communal area such as a hall, passageway or a room in common use in sheltered accommodation. If

s/he is separately liable to make payments for the accommodation to the landlord, s/he does not count as living with you.[75] This is not explicitly stated in the rules for CTB, although the same test may in practice be applied.

- **No one gets carer's allowance (CA) for looking after you**, or if you are a couple, no one gets CA for both of you (but see below for an exception when you and/or your partner go into hospital). For couples, if a person is getting CA for one (but not both) of you then you can get the amount for severe disability, but only at the single person's rate. Only actual receipt of CA counts[76] (except when it is not paid because of the loss of benefit rules – see p1047), so no account is taken of any underlying entitlement to CA if it is awarded but not paid because of the overlapping benefit rules, or of any extra-statutory payments to compensate for it not being paid. Similarly, no account is taken of any backdated payments or arrears of CA.[77] You should also argue that no account should be taken of any CA which has been overpaid and that, if you have been denied the premium because of a CA overpayment, it should be repaid to you (see p789).

Couples

Couples get the couple rate only if both of you are getting a qualifying benefit and no one gets CA for either of you. However, if your partner does not get a qualifying benefit but is registered blind (or treated as blind), or if CA is paid for one of you, you still get the single rate. (In polygamous marriages the single rate is awarded in respect of each eligible partner who gets a qualifying benefit while CA is not paid.)

Note: for couples only, you and/or your partner are treated as getting AA (or the highest or middle rate care component of DLA), even though it has stopped because you/your partner have been in hospital for more than four weeks, but the severe disability premium is paid at the single rate only. Similarly, for couples only, for IS, income-based JSA, HB or CTB, a person is treated as receiving CA even if the qualifying benefit of the person for whom s/he is caring has stopped because that person has been in hospital for more than four weeks.[78]

Note also: for **IS and JSA couples** only, if you (or your partner) temporarily move into an independent care home (see p617), although you remain members of the same household,[79] your applicable amount is the greater of:

- the normal amount for you as a couple; *or*
- the total of the applicable amounts for each of you as if you and your partner were each a single claimant (or lone parent) living in your present accommodation.[80] This means that if the person who stays at home gets a qualifying benefit, then totalling the applicable amounts separately will enable a severe disability premium to be included for her/him, even though the person in the care home cannot get the premium once her/his AA or DLA care component stops.

For PC, if you (or your partner) temporarily move into a care home, you still count as a couple if you have not been apart for substantially more than 52 weeks (see p621). So for PC, once the person in the care home loses her/his AA or DLA care component, no severe disability premium can be paid for either member of the couple even if the person at home gets a qualifying benefit.

Non-dependants[81]

The following people who live with you do *not* count as non-dependants.

For IS, income-based JSA, PC, HB and CTB:

- anyone aged under 18;
- anyone else who receives a qualifying benefit;[82]
- anyone who is registered blind (or treated as blind);[83]
- anyone staying in your home who normally lives elsewhere. In deciding whether someone normally lives with you or elsewhere it may be relevant to consider: why the residence started; the relationship and its history, if any, between those concerned; the motivations involved; the purpose for which residence has been taken up; its duration; and whether there is any other home in which residence is or could be taken up;[84]
- any person (and, for IS, income-based JSA and PC only, her/his partner) employed by a charitable or voluntary body as a resident carer for you or your partner if you pay a charge for that service (even if the charge is only nominal).[85] **Note:** these rules do not apply to a live-in carer employed directly by you (even if, for example, you are paying her/him from payments made to you by social services for that purpose under the Community Care (Direct Payments) Act 1996). For such a person to be disregarded as a non-dependant you would either have to pay a charitable or voluntary body to employ her/him for you, or prove that s/he normally lives elsewhere.

For IS, income-based JSA, HB and CTB:

- any member of your family (see p700 for who counts as part of your family). This may include any child under the age of 20 (see p709) as well as your partner, although your partner must be getting a qualifying benefit (or would be if s/he were not in hospital), or be registered or treated as blind (see p293) if you are to be paid the severe disability premium (see p784).

For IS, income-based JSA and PC:

- any person (or her/his partner) who jointly occupies (see p788) your home and is either the co-owner with you or your partner, or jointly liable with you or your partner to make payments to a landlord for occupying it. If this person is a close relative (see p788), however, s/he *will* count as a non-dependant *unless* the co-ownership or joint liability to make payments to a landlord existed either before 11 April 1988 or by the time you or your partner first moved in (but, for IS only, see transitional provisions below);

- any person (or any member of her/his household) who is liable to pay you or your partner on a commercial basis (see p788) for occupying the dwelling (eg, tenants or licensees), unless s/he is a close relative of you or your partner (but, for IS only, see transitional provisions below);
- any person (or any member of her/his household) to whom you or your partner are liable to make such payments on a commercial basis, unless s/he is a close relative of you or your partner (for IS only, see below).

In any of these situations, **for IS only** the presence of close relatives (see p788) does *not* prevent you from continuing to get the severe disability premium if you fall within the scope of the transitional provisions that applied to IS claimants entitled to this premium before 21 October 1991. These were set out in CPAG's *National Welfare Benefits Handbook* 1992/93.

Note also that, for IS, income-based JSA and PC, if someone comes to live with you in order to look after you (or your partner), and has not lived with you before, your severe disability premium or amount for severe disability remains in payment for the first 12 weeks after the carer moves in, even if s/he would otherwise count as a non-dependant.[86] After that, you lose the premium or the amount for severe disability. The carer should then consider claiming CA (see Chapter 3).

For HB only:[87]

- any person who jointly occupies your home and is either the co-owner with you or your partner, or liable with you or your partner to make payments in respect of occupying it. A joint occupier who was a non-dependant at any time within the previous eight weeks counts as a non-dependant if the local authority thinks that the change of arrangements was created to take advantage of the HB scheme;
- any person who is liable to pay you or your partner on a commercial basis for occupying the dwelling unless s/he is a close relative of you or your partner, or if the local authority thinks that the rent or other agreement has been created to take advantage of the HB scheme (but this cannot apply if the person was otherwise liable to pay rent for the accommodation at any time during the eight weeks before the agreement was made);
- any person, or any member of her/his household, to whom you or your partner are liable to make payments for your accommodation on a commercial basis unless s/he is a close relative of you or your partner.

For CTB only:[88]

- any person who is jointly and severally liable (see p788) with you to pay council tax. If s/he was a non-dependant at any time within the eight weeks before s/he became liable for council tax, s/he counts as a non-dependant if the local authority thinks that the change of arrangements was created to take advantage of the CTB scheme;

- any person who is liable to pay you or your partner on a commercial basis for occupying the dwelling unless s/he is a close relative (see below) of you or your partner, or if the local authority thinks that the liability to make payments has been created to take advantage of the CTB scheme (but this cannot apply if the person was otherwise liable to pay rent for the accommodation at any time during the eight weeks before that liability arose).

Definitions

'Close relative' is a parent, parent-in-law (including a civil partner's parent), son, son-in-law (including a son's civil partner), daughter, daughter-in-law (including a daughter's civil partner), brother, sister, step-parent (including a parent's civil partner), stepson (including a civil partner's son), stepdaughter (including a civil partner's daughter), or the partners of any of these.[89]

'Jointly occupies' has a technical meaning. It is a legal relationship involving occupation by two or more persons (whether as owner-occupiers or as tenants or licensees), with one and the same legal right.[90] It does not exist if people merely have equal access to different parts of the premises (as had previously been decided by a commissioner[91]).

'Commercial basis' has no technical meaning, and there is no requirement that there need be any intention to make a profit.[92] It may be sufficient if a 'reasonable' charge is made, even if this does not fully cover the cost of the accommodation and meals being provided.[93] The reasonableness of the charge made should be judged solely against the cost of occupying the dwelling, disregarding the additional costs of providing food, clothing and care for the claimant.[94] A useful, but not conclusive, test to apply is to consider whether the same arrangement *might* have been entered into with a lodger rather than with the claimant.[95] It is not relevant to the question of whether the arrangement is on a commercial basis to consider either whether the non-dependant depends financially on the charge being paid or if s/he would take action against the claimant if s/he did not pay.[96] These last two matters are relevant to whether there is a *liability* (see below).

'Liability' means a legal or contractual liability (as distinct from a moral or ethical obligation), although this can always be inferred from the circumstances, there being no requirement that any arrangements need be in writing.[97] It has been held, however, that even though a landlord may have expected relatives of a liable person to share her/his home in order to provide care, it cannot be inferred that they are also liable. Nor can it be assumed that someone is owed a liability in recompense merely for allowing another person to occupy her/his home, particularly if the gains (eg, when someone depends on another person for her/his care) exceed any possible loss.[98] Any liability must arise from the costs of occupying the home. People with no contractual capacity (eg, people with very severe learning disabilities) cannot establish liability under English law. A commissioner has urged a consistency of approach for England and Scotland, where the law is different in that a liability can exist even where there is no contractual capacity.[99]

Carer's premium and pension credit additional amount[100]

You qualify for this if you or your partner are entitled to CA (see Chapter 3).

You are entitled to CA even if you do not receive it because of the overlapping benefit rules (see p981) (eg, you get long-term IB or retirement pension instead).

If you stop being entitled to CA, or the person you are getting the CA for dies, your entitlement to a carer's premium will continue for a further eight weeks. This applies even if you first claim IS, income-based JSA, or (if you or your partner are aged under 60) HB or CTB in this time.[101]

A double premium is awarded if both you and your partner satisfy the conditions for it.

Carers and severe disability

Before claiming CA, you should consider how your claim may affect the entitlement to the severe disability premium, or the amount for severe disability in the guarantee credit of PC (see p784), of the disabled person you are caring for – particularly where the only financial advantage to you as the carer is the amount of the carer's premium, which may be worth considerably less than the severe disability premium (but see p784 for the rules on notional income).

Any backdated award of CA does not affect a disabled person's entitlement to the severe disability premium or the amount for severe disability in the guarantee credit of PC.[102] There may, therefore, be scope for careful planning to take advantage of this rule so that carers can be paid CA or the carer's premium for the same period that the disabled person has already received the severe disability premium or the amount for severe disability in PC.

Although the severe disability premium or amount for severe disability is not payable throughout any period during which a carer is entitled to, and receiving, CA, if it is later decided that CA has been overpaid (ie, that the carer was not in fact entitled to receive CA) you should ask for any decision denying you entitlement to the severe disability premium or the amount for severe disability to be revised. The carer must be both entitled to *and* in receipt of CA for the severe disability premium not to be payable.[103]

Other than for HB/CTB, if payment of CA stops, the severe disability premium can be backdated to the date the CA stopped.[104]

4. Backdating of premiums

To qualify for the disability premium, enhanced disability premium, higher pensioner premium, severe disability premium, disabled child premium or carer's premium, you and/or a member of your family usually have to have been awarded the qualifying benefit that applies to each premium. The date you may begin to get your premium may therefore depend on the date from which your qualifying benefit is awarded. However, because of the time it may take to deal with your claim for the qualifying benefit, or if your claim is backdated (see p964) or initially refused but awarded some time later after a revision (see p1065), supersession (see p1074) or appeal (see p1093), you may not get your premium straight away and you may have to apply for it to be backdated.

If you are already getting benefit

If you are already getting income support (IS), income-based jobseeker's allowance (JSA), housing benefit (HB) or council tax benefit (CTB), you should ask for your award of this benefit either to be revised or superseded and for your premium to be backdated either to the same date from which your qualifying benefit is awarded, or to when you first got (or claimed) IS, income-based JSA, HB or CTB if that is later. In such circumstances, there is no limit to the period for which arrears can be paid to you.[105]

If you were refused benefit

If you have previously claimed **IS** or **income-based JSA** but your claim was refused because you or a member of your family did not at that time get the qualifying benefit for the premium, you should make another IS or income-based JSA claim once the qualifying benefit is awarded. To get full backdating you should have claimed the qualifying benefit before, or no later than 10 days after, the first IS or income-based JSA claim. You must then make your second claim for IS or income-based JSA within three months of the decision awarding the qualifying benefit. The second claim is backdated, including the premium, to the date of the first IS or income-based JSA claim or to the date from which the qualifying benefit was awarded, if that is later.[106] If the qualifying benefit is initially refused, or awarded at a lower rate than you need for the premium, but is later decided in your favour, to get full backdating you must make your second IS or income-based JSA claim within three months of the date the qualifying benefit is decided in your favour on revision, supersession or appeal.[107]

For **HB** and **CTB**, the rules are different and you may be limited to a maximum of, currently, 12 months' backdating although these limits may change during 2008 (see p205).

If you lose entitlement to benefit

If you lose your existing **IS** or **income-based JSA** as a result of having your (or a member of your family's) qualifying benefit stopped or reduced, or whilst you are waiting for a claim for a qualifying benefit to be decided, and that qualifying benefit is then awarded, or reinstated on a revision, supersession or appeal (or you make a later claim for the qualifying benefit), you should make a new claim for IS or income-based JSA. Provided you claim within three months of the favourable decision on the qualifying benefit, your IS or income-based JSA is fully backdated to the date entitlement had previously ended, or to the date from which the qualifying benefit is payable if that is later.[108]

If you lose your **HB** or **CTB** because you lose entitlement to a qualifying benefit, the decision ending your HB/CTB can be revised if the qualifying benefit is reinstated. Your HB/CTB can be fully backdated in this situation. You need to tell the local authority that you have had your qualifying benefit reinstated, but you do not need to make a fresh claim for HB/CTB.[109]

Additional points to note

- Although a later award of carer's allowance may entitle you to have your carer's premium backdated, this will not affect the severe disability premium of the person you are looking after (see p784).
- For HB and CTB, if you are one of a couple and the person who is incapable of work is not the claimant, you can swap the claimant role and s/he can apply to backdate a new claim if s/he has 'good cause' (see pp207 and 92). In this way, you can get the disability premium backdated for up to 12 months (although this may be reduced to three months during 2008).[110] For IS/income-based JSA, it will not be possible to backdate your claim unless one of the specified reasons for making a late claim applies (see p967).

Backdating of pension credit

For backdating of pension credit, see p456.

Notes

1. **What is the applicable amount**
   1 Reg 22A IS Regs

2. **Personal allowances**
   2 **IS** Reg 18(2) IS Regs
   JSA Reg 84(2) JSA Regs
   3 s4 WRA 2007; Explanatory Notes to WRA 2007, para 55
   4 HB/CTB G3/2008
   5 SS(TC)A Regs
   6 **IS** Sch 2 Part I IS Regs
   JSA Sch 1 Part 1 JSA Regs
   HB Sch 3 Part I HB Regs; Sch 3 Part I HB(SPC) Regs
   CTB Sch 1 Part I CTB Regs; Sch 1 Part I CTB(SPC) Regs
   7 **IS** Reg 18(1)(b) IS Regs
   JSA Reg 84(1)(b) JSA Regs
   HB Reg 23(b) HB Regs; Sch 3 para 1 HB(SPC) Regs
   CTB Reg 13(b) CTB Regs; Sch 1 para 1 CTB(SPC) Regs
   8 **IS** Sch 2 para 1(3) IS Regs
   JSA Sch 1 para 1(3) JSA Regs
   9 CJSA/3009/2006

3. **Premiums**
   10 s4 WRA 2007; Explanatory Notes to WRA 2007, para 58; Welfare Reform Bill Draft Regulations and supporting material, available at www.dwp.gov.uk/welfarereform
   11 SS(TC)A Regs
   12 **HB** Sch 3 paras 3 and 6-9 HB(SPC) Regs
   CTB Sch 1 paras 3 and 6-9 CTB(SPC) Regs
   13 **IS** Sch 2 para 6(2) IS Regs
   JSA Sch 1 paras 7(2) and 20C(2) JSA Regs
   HB Sch 3 para 6 HB Regs
   CTB Sch 1 para 6 CTB Regs
   14 **IS** Sch 2 para 5 IS Regs
   JSA Sch 1 para 6 JSA Regs
   HB Sch 3 para 5 HB Regs
   CTB Sch 1 para 5 CTB Regs
   15 **IS** Sch 2 para 7 IS Regs
   JSA Sch 1 para 8 JSA Regs
   HB Sch 3 para 7 HB Regs; Sch 3 para 5 HB(SPC) Regs
   CTB Sch 1 para 7 CTB Regs; Sch 3 para 5 CTB(SPC) Regs
   16 **IS** Sch 2 para 14B IS Regs
   JSA Sch 1 para 19 JSA Regs
   HB Sch 3 para 19 HB Regs; Sch 3 para 11 HB(SPC) Regs
   CTB Sch 1 para 19 CTB Regs; Sch 1 para 3 CTB(SPC) Regs
   See also R(IS) 10/94
   17 **IS** Sch 2 para 3 IS Regs
   JSA Sch 1 para 4 JSA Regs
   HB Sch 3 para 3 HB Regs; Sch 3 para 3 HB(SPC) Regs
   CTB Sch 1 para 3 CTB Regs; Sch 1 para 3 CTB(SPC) Regs
   18 **HB** Sch 3 para 3(2) HB Regs; Sch 3 para 3(2) HB(SPC) Regs
   CTB Sch 1 para 3(2) CTB Regs; Sch 1 para 3(2) CTB(SPC) Regs
   19 **IS** Regs 15(3) and 16(6) IS Regs
   JSA Regs 74(4) and 78(7) JSA Regs
   20 **HB** Reg 21(4)-(5) HB Regs; reg 21(4)-(5) HB(SPC) Regs
   CTB Reg 11(3)-(4) CTB Regs; reg 11(3)-(4) CTB(SPC) Regs
   21 **HB** Sch 3 para 3 HB Regs
   CTB Sch 1 para 3 CTB Regs
   22 para BW 3.76 GM
   23 **IS** Sch 2 paras 14 and 15(6) IS Regs
   JSA Sch 1 para 16 JSA Regs
   HB Sch 3 paras 16 and 20(7) HB Regs; Sch 3 paras 8 and 12(3) HB(SPC) Regs
   CTB Sch 1 paras 16 and 20(7) CTB Regs; Sch 1 paras 8 and 12(3) CTB(SPC) Regs
   24 **IS** Sch 2 paras 12(1)(a)(iii) and (2) and 14(c) IS Regs
   JSA Sch 1 para 14(1)(h) and (2) JSA Regs
   HB Sch 3 paras 13(1)(a)(v) and (2) and 16(c) HB Regs; Sch 3 para 8(b) HB(SPC) Regs
   CTB Sch 1 paras 13(1)(a)(v) and (2) and 16(c) CTB Regs; Sch 1 para 8(b) CTB(SPC) Regs
   25 **IS** Sch 2 para 14(2)(a) IS Regs
   JSA Sch 1 para 16(2)(a) JSA Regs
   26 **HB** Reg 25(3) HB Regs; reg 23(3) HB(SPC) Regs
   CTB Reg 15(3) CTB Regs; reg 13(3) CTB(SPC) Regs

27 **HB** Sch 3 para 16 HB Regs; Sch 3 para 8 HB(SPC) Regs
CTB Sch 1 para 16 CTB Regs; Sch 1 para 8 CTB(SPC) Regs
28 **IS** Sch 2 para 11 IS Regs
JSA Sch 1 paras 13 and 14 JSA Regs
HB Sch 3 para 12 HB Regs
CTB Sch 1 para 12 CTB Regs
29 HB/CTB G3/2008
30 Reg 29(5) SPC(CTMP) Regs
31 **IS** Reg 2(1) IS Regs
JSA Reg 1(3) JSA Regs
HB Reg 2(1) HB Regs
CTB Reg 2(1) CTB Regs
All Definition of 'attendance allowance'
32 **IS** Sch 2 para 12(6) IS Regs
JSA Sch 1 para 14(1)(d) JSA Regs
HB Sch 3 para 12(7) HB Regs
CTB Sch 1 para 13(7) CTB Regs
33 **IS** Sch 2 para 14A IS Regs
JSA Sch 1 para 18 JSA Regs
HB Sch 3 para 18 HB Regs
CTB Sch 1 para 18 CTB Regs
34 **IS** Sch 2 para 14B IS Regs
JSA Sch 1 para 19 JSA Regs
HB Sch 3 para 19 HB Regs
CTB Sch 1 para 19 CTB Regs
See also R(IS) 10/94
35 **IS** Sch 2 para 7(1)(a) IS Regs
JSA Sch 1 para 8(1)(a) JSA Regs
HB Sch 3 para 7(1)(a) HB Regs
CTB Sch 1 para 7(1)(a) CTB Regs
36 **IS** Sch 2 para 12(1)(a)(iii) and (2) IS Regs
JSA Sch 1 para 14(1)(h) and (2) JSA Regs
HB Sch 3 para 13(1)(a)(v) and (2) HB Regs
CTB Sch 1 para 13(1)(a)(v) and (2) CTB Regs
37 **IS** Sch 2 para 12(1)(a)(ii) IS Regs
JSA Sch 1 para 14(1)(e) and (f) JSA Regs
HB Sch 3 para 13(1)(a)(iv) HB Regs
CTB Sch 1 para 13(1)(a)(iv) CTB Regs
38 R(IS) 7/02
39 **IS** Sch 2 para 12(1)(c)(i) IS Regs
JSA Sch 1 para 14(1)(g)(i) JSA Regs
HB Sch 3 para 13(1)(a)(ii) HB Regs
CTB Sch 1 para 13(1)(a)(ii) CTB Regs
40 **IS** Sch 2 para 12(1)(c)(i) IS Regs
JSA Sch 1 para 14(1)(g)(i) JSA Regs
41 **HB** Sch 3 para 13(1)(a)(ii) HB Regs
CTB Sch 1 para 13(1)(a)(ii) CTB Regs
42 **IS** Sch 2 para 12(1)(c) IS Regs
JSA Sch 1 para 14(1)(g) JSA Regs
43 **IS** Sch 2 para 12(1)(d) IS Regs
JSA Sch 1 para 14(1)(g)(ii) JSA Regs
HB Sch 3 para 13(1)(a)(iii) HB Regs
CTB Sch 1 para 13(1)(a)(iii) CTB Regs
44 **IS** Sch 2 para 12(1)(b) IS Regs
HB Sch 3 para 13(1)(b) HB Regs
CTB Sch 1 para 13(1)(b) CTB Regs
45 s30B(4) SSCBA 1992
46 **IS** Sch 2 para 12(1A) IS Regs
JSA Sch 1 para 12(3) JSA Regs
HB Sch 3 para 13(8) HB Regs
CTB Sch 1 para 13(8) CTB Regs
47 R(IS) 4/04
48 **IS** Sch 2 paras 11(b) and 12 IS Regs
HB Sch 3 paras 12(b) and 13 HB Regs
CTB Sch 1 paras 12(b) and 13 CTB Regs
49 Sch 1 para 14(d) JSA Regs
50 **IS** Sch 2 paras 7(1)(b) and 12(5) IS Regs
JSA Sch 1 para 8(1)(b) JSA Regs
HB Sch 3 paras 7(1)(b) and 13(5) HB Regs
CTB Sch 1 paras 7(1)(b) and 13(5) CTB Regs
51 **IS** Sch 2 para 13A IS Regs
JSA Sch 1 paras 15A and 20IA JSA Regs
HB Sch 3 para 15 HB Regs; Sch 3 para 7 HB(SPC) Regs
CTB Sch 1 para 15 CTB Regs; Sch 1 para 7 CTB(SPC) Regs
52 **IS** Sch 2 para 13A IS Regs
JSA Sch 1 para 15A JSA Regs
53 **IS** Sch 2 paras 9 and 9A IS Regs
JSA Sch 1 paras 10 and 11 JSA Regs
HB Sch 3 paras 9 and 10 HB Regs
CTB Sch 1 paras 9 and 10 CTB Regs
54 Sch 2 para 10 IS Regs
55 **IS** Sch 2 para 10 IS Regs
JSA Sch 1 para 12 JSA Regs
HB Sch 3 para 11 HB Regs
CTB Sch 1 para 11 CTB Regs
56 **IS** Sch 2 para 10(4) IS Regs
JSA Sch 1 para 12(3) JSA Regs
HB Sch 3 para 11(4) HB Regs
CTB Sch 1 para 11(4) CTB Regs
57 **IS** Sch 2 para 10(1)(b)(ii) and (3) IS Regs
JSA Sch 1 para 12(2) JSA Regs
HB Sch 3 para 11(1)(b)(ii) and (3) HB Regs
CTB Sch 1 para 11(1)(b)(ii) and (3) CTB Regs
58 **HB** Sch 3 para 11(3)(c) HB Regs
CTB Sch 1 para 11(3)(c) CTB Regs
59 Sch 1 para 12(1)(a)(ii) JSA Regs
60 R(IS) 7/02

61 **IS** Sch 2 para 12(1)(c)(i) and (1A) IS Regs
JSA Sch 1 paras 14(1)(g)(i) and 12(3) JSA Regs
HB Sch 3 para 13(1)(a)(ii) and (8) HB Regs
CTB Sch 1 para 13(1)(a)(ii) and (9) CTB Regs
62 **HB** Sch 3 para 11(3)(c) HB Regs
CTB Sch 1 para 11(3)(c) CTB Regs
63 Sch 1 para 12(2) JSA Regs
64 **IS** Sch 2 para 12(1)(c)(i) IS Regs
JSA Sch 1 para 14(1)(g)(i) JSA Regs
HB Sch 3 para 13(1)(a)(ii) HB Regs
CTB Sch 1 para 13(1)(a)(ii) CTB Regs
65 **IS** Sch 2 para 12(1)(c) IS Regs
JSA Sch 1 para 14(1)(g) JSA Regs
66 CIS/458/1992
67 **IS** Sch 2 para 7(1)(a) IS Regs
JSA Sch 1 para 8(1)(a) JSA Regs
HB Sch 3 para 7(1)(a) HB Regs
CTB Sch 1 para 7(1)(a) CTB Regs
68 **IS** Sch 2 para 13 IS Regs
JSA Sch 1 para 15 JSA Regs
PC Reg 6(4) and Sch 1 paras 1-2 SPC Regs
HB Sch 3 para 14 HB Regs; Sch 3 para 6 HB(SPC) Regs
CTB Sch 1 para 14 CTB Regs; Sch 1 para 6 CTB(SPC) Regs
69 **IS** Reg 2(1) IS Regs
JSA Reg 1(3) JSA Regs
PC Reg 1(2) SPC Regs
HB Reg 2(1) HB Regs; reg 2(1) HB(SPC) Regs
CTB Reg 2(1) CTB Regs; reg 2(1) CTB(SPC) Regs
All Definition of 'attendance allowance'
70 **IS** Sch 2 para 14A IS Regs
JSA Sch 1 para 18 JSA Regs
PC Sch 1 para 1(2)(a)(ii) SPC Regs
HB Sch 3 para 18 HB Regs; Sch 3 para 10 HB(SPC) Regs
CTB Sch 1 para 18 CTB Regs; Sch1 para 10 CTB(SPC) Regs
71 **IS** Sch 2 para 13(2A) IS Regs
JSA Sch 1 para 15(3) JSA Regs
PC Sch 1 para 1(1)(b) and (c) SPC Regs
HB Sch 3 para 13(3) HB Regs; Sch 3 para 6(3) HB(SPC) Regs
CTB Sch 1 para 14(3) CTB Regs; Sch 1 para 6(3) CTB(SPC) Regs
72 **IS** Sch 2 para 13(3A)(a) IS Regs
JSA Sch 1 paras 15(5)(a) and 20I(4)(a) JSA Regs
PC Sch 1 para 2(b) SPC Regs
HB Sch 3 para 14(5) HB Regs; Sch 3 para 6(7) HB(SPC) Regs
CTB Sch 1 para 14(5) CTB Regs; Sch 1 para 6(7) CTB(SPC) Regs
73 **IS** Sch 2 para 14B IS Regs
JSA Sch 1 para 19 JSA Regs
HB Sch 3 para 19 HB Regs; Sch 3 para 11 HB(SPC) Regs
CTB Sch 1 para 19 CTB Regs; Sch 1 para 11 CTB(SPC) Regs
See also R(IS) 10/94, upheld in *Rider v CAO, The Times*, 30 January 1996 (CA)
74 *Bate v CAO* [1996] 2 All ER 790 (HL), reported as R(IS) 12/96
75 **IS** Reg 3(4) and (5) IS Regs
JSA Reg 2(6) and (7) JSA Regs
HB Reg 3(4) HB Regs; Sch 3 para 6(7) HB(SPC) Regs
CTB Sch 1 para 14(2)(b) CTB Regs; Sch 1 para 6(7) CTB(SPC) Regs
76 **IS** Sch 2 para 13(2)(a)(iii) and (b) IS Regs
JSA Sch 1 para 15(1)(c) and (2)(d) JSA Regs
HB Sch 3 para 14(2)(a)(iii) and (b) HB Regs; Sch 3 para 6(2)(a)(iii) and (b) HB(SPC) Regs
CTB Sch 1 para 14(2)(a)(iii) and (b) CTB Regs; Sch 1 para 6(2)(a)(iii) and (b) CTB(SPC) Regs
PC Sch 1 para 1(1)(a)(iii) SPC Regs
77 **IS** Sch 2 para 13(3ZA) IS Regs
JSA Sch 1 para 15(7) JSA Regs
PC Sch 1 para 2(c) SPC Regs
HB Sch 3 para 13(6) HB Regs; Sch 3 para 6(8) HB(SPC) Regs
CTB Sch 1 para 14(6) CTB Regs; Sch 1 para 6(8) CTB(SPC) Regs
78 **IS** Sch 2 para 13(3A) IS Regs
JSA Sch 1 para 15(5) JSA Regs
PC Reg 6(5) and Sch 1 para 1(2)(b) SPC Regs
HB Sch 3 para 14(5) HB Regs; Sch 3 para 6(7) HB(SPC) Regs
CTB Sch 1 para 14(5) CTB Regs; Sch 1 para 6(7) CTB(SPC) Regs
79 **IS** Reg 16(1) IS Regs
JSA Reg 78(1) JSA Regs
80 **IS** Sch 7 para 9 IS Regs
JSA Sch 5 para 5 JSA Regs
Both R(IS) 9/02

81 **IS** Reg 3 and Sch 2 para 13 IS Regs
JSA Reg 2 and Sch 1 para 15 JSA Regs
PC Sch 1 para 2 SPC Regs
HB Reg 3 HB Regs; reg 3 HB(SPC) Regs
CTB Reg 3 CTB Regs; reg 3 CTB(SPC) Regs
82 **IS** Sch 2 para 13(3)(a) IS Regs
JSA Sch 1 para 15(4)(a) JSA Regs
PC Sch 1 para 2(2)(a) SPC Regs
HB Sch 3 para 13(4) HB Regs; Sch 3 para 6(6) HB(SPC) Regs
CTB Sch 1 para 14(4) CTB Regs; Sch 1 para 6(6) CTB(SPC) Regs
83 **IS** Sch 2 para 13(3)(d) IS Regs
JSA Sch 1 para 14(1)(h) and (2) JSA Regs
PC Sch 1 para 2(2)(b) and (c) SPC Regs
HB Sch 3 para 14(4)(b) HB Regs; Sch 3 para 6(6)(b) HB(SPC) Regs
CTB Sch 1 para 14(4)(b) CTB Regs; Sch 1 para 6(6)(b) CTB(SPC) Regs
84 CIS/14850/1996 para 10
85 **IS** Reg 3(2)(c) and (d) IS Regs
JSA Reg 2(2)(c) and (d) JSA Regs
PC Sch 1 para 2(d) and (e) SPC Regs
HB Reg 3(2)(f) HB Regs; reg 3(2)(f) HB(SPC) Regs
CTB Reg 3(2)(f) CTB Regs; reg 3(2)(f) CTB(SPC) Regs
86 **IS** Sch 2 para 13(3)(c) and (4) IS Regs
JSA Sch 1 para 15(4)(b) and (5) JSA Regs
PC Sch 1 para 2(3)-(4) SPC Regs
87 Regs 3 and 9(1) HB Regs; regs 3 and 9(1) HB(SPC) Regs
88 Reg 3 CTB Regs; reg 3 CTB(SPC) Regs
89 **IS** Reg 2(1) IS Regs
JSA Reg 1(3) JSA Regs
HB Reg 2(1) HB Regs; reg 2(1) HB(SPC) Regs
CTB Reg 2(1) CTB Regs; reg 2(1) CTB(SPC) Regs
All Definition of 'close relative'
90 *Bate v CAO* [1996] 2 All ER 790 (HL)
91 CIS/180/1989
92 R(IS) 11/98 tribunal of commissioners
93 CSIS/43/1989
94 CIS/754/1991 and R(IS) 11/98 para 12
95 R(IS) 11/98 para 8
96 R(IS) 11/98 paras 10 and 11
97 CIS/754/1991
98 CSIS/641/1995
99 CIS/754/1991, referring to CSIS/28/1992 and CSIS/40/1992
100 **IS** Sch 2 para 14ZA IS Regs
JSA Sch 1 para 17 JSA Regs
PC Reg 6(6)(a) and Sch 1 para 4 SPC Regs
HB Sch 3 para 17 HB Regs; Sch 3 para 9 HB(SPC) Regs
CTB Sch 1 para 17 CTB Regs; Sch 1 para 9 CTB(SPC) Regs
101 **IS** Sch 2 paras 7 and 14ZA(3) and (4) IS Regs
JSA Sch 1 paras 8, 17(3) (4) and 20J(3) JSA Regs
HB Sch 3 paras 7 and 17(3) and (4) HB Regs; Sch 3 paras 5 and 9(3) HB(SPC) Regs
CTB Sch 1 paras 7 and 17(3) and (4) CTB Regs; Sch 1 paras 5 and 9(3) CTB(SPC) Regs
PC Sch 1 para 4(2) and (3) SPC Regs
102 **IS** Sch 2 para 13(3ZA) IS Regs
JSA Sch 1 para 15(7) JSA Regs
PC Sch 1 para 1(2)(c) SPC Regs
HB Sch 3 para 14(6) HB Regs; Sch 3 para 6(8) HB(SPC) Regs
CTB Sch 1 para 14(6) CTB Regs; Sch 1 para 6(8) CTB(SPC) Regs
103 Sch 1B para 4(b) IS Regs
104 Reg 7(2)(bc) SS&CS(D&A) Regs

4. **Backdating of premiums**

105 **IS/JSA** Regs 3(7) and 6(2)(e) SS&CS(DA) Regs
HB/CTB Regs 4(7B) and 7(2)(i) HB&CTB(DA) Regs
106 Reg 6(16)-(18) SS(C&P) Regs
107 Reg 6(26) SS(C&P) Regs
108 Reg 6(19), (20) and (30) SS(C&P) Regs
109 Reg 4(7C) HB&CTB(DA) Regs
110 CSIS/66/1992; CIS/706/1992

Chapter 34

Housing costs

This chapter covers the rules for getting income support, income-based jobseeker's allowance and pension credit to cover your housing costs. It contains:

If you own or are buying your home, income support (IS), *income-based* jobseeker's allowance (JSA) or pension credit (PC) can include a variety of payments for your housing costs. Housing costs are not included as part of *contribution-based* JSA, but if you qualify for *income-based* JSA you can claim this to top up your contribution-based JSA.

The amount you are paid for loans is calculated in a special way (see p809) and is usually paid directly to the lender.

If you are a tenant you can get IS, income-based JSA or PC for some types of housing costs, but not for your rent.[1] This is covered by housing benefit (HB). If you live permanently in a care home, an independent hospital or for IS and JSA only, an Abbeyfield Home, you cannot get help with housing costs for your former home.[2] If you are only staying in the accommodation temporarily, you might get help with the housing costs on your normal home (see p799).

If your entitlement to IS or income-based JSA ends because you start work, or increase your hours or pay, you may be entitled to mortgage interest run-on (see p823).

In this chapter, unless otherwise stated, references to income-based JSA also refer to joint-claim JSA.

1. When you can get help with housing costs

You can get help with your housing costs if:[3]

- you or someone in your family (for income support (IS) and income-based jobseeker's allowance (JSA)), or you or your partner (for pension credit (PC)) are liable to pay the housing costs (see below). See p798 for who counts as your 'family';
- the housing costs are for the home in which you normally live (see p798);
- the type of housing costs can be met (see p802).

Liable to pay housing costs

You count as liable to pay housing costs if:[4]

- you, or your partner, are **liable** to pay them. You do not have to be legally liable.[5] However, you do not count as liable to pay housing costs if you pay these to someone who is a member of your household (see p703 for the meaning of 'household'). If you or your partner share liability with someone, you might only get help with your share of the housing costs (see p809);
- you are **treated as liable** to pay them. You are treated as liable if:
  - you share the costs with other members of your household (see p703 for the meaning of 'household'); *and*
  - at least one of those with whom you share is liable.

  In this case, you can be paid for your share,[6] as long as the people with whom you share are not 'close relatives' (see below) of you or your partner and it is reasonable to treat you as sharing;
- **someone else is liable to pay them but is not paying** so you have to meet the cost yourself in order to continue to live in your home. You must show that it is reasonable for you to pay instead of her/him – eg, if you have given up your home to live with and care for someone and s/he has now gone into a care home, or if you have separated from your partner (even if you have not lived in the home continuously since your partner left[7]).

If you are not required to pay any housing costs currently (eg, if under the terms of your mortgage you do not have to pay interest) you cannot receive IS, income-based JSA or PC for housing costs. This applies to special mortgage schemes for pensioners where the mortgage is repaid from your estate when you die rather than by you making regular monthly payments.[8]

For IS and income-based JSA only, if you are on strike, a member of your family (see p798) who is not affected by the strike is treated as liable for your housing costs.[9]

Close relative

'Close relative' means a parent, parent-in-law (including a civil partner's parent), son, son-in-law (including a son's civil partner), daughter, daughter-in-law (including a daughter's civil partner), brother, sister, step-parent (including a parent's civil partner), step-son (including a civil partner's son), step-daughter (including a civil partner's daughter), or the partners of any of these. 'Sister' or 'brother' includes a half-sister or half-brother. An adopted child ceases to be related to her/his birth family on adoption and becomes the relative of her/his adoptive family.[10]

Member of the family

For IS and income-based JSA purposes, member of the family means your partner (see p702) and any child (this includes some qualifying young people) who lives in your household and for whom you count as 'responsible' (see pp298 and 366).[11]

Costs for the home in which you normally live

Housing costs are paid for the home in which:[12]

- for IS and income-based JSA, you and your 'family' (see above) normally live;
- for PC, you and your partner normally live.

You cannot usually be paid for any other home. If you are liable to pay the mortgage on a property but have no immediate intention of living there you cannot get help with the cost.[13]

Your **'home'** is defined as the building, or part of the building, in which you live. This includes any garage, garden, outbuildings and other premises and land which it is not reasonable or practicable to sell separately.[14] You can argue that a home can consist of more than one building if you occupy more than one dwelling – eg, because your family is too large for one.[15]

There are special rules if:

- you have just moved into your home (see below);
- you are temporarily away from home (see p799);
- you are liable to pay housing costs on more than one home (see p801).

Moving home

If you have just moved into your home but were liable to pay housing costs before moving in, your IS, income-based JSA or PC can include these costs for a period of up to four weeks before your move if your delay in moving was reasonable, you claimed IS, JSA or PC before moving in, *and*:[16]

- you were waiting for adaptations to be finished to meet the disability needs of:
  - for IS and income-based JSA, you or a member of your family (see above for who counts as your family); *or*
  - for PC, you, your partner, or someone under 20 for whom you or your partner are responsible ('responsible' is not defined in the rules).

The adaptions must involve a change to the fabric or structure of the dwelling, not just decorating or furnishing (eg, carpeting) it.[17]

- you became responsible for the housing costs while you were in hospital or a care home or an independent hospital (or for IS and JSA only, an Abbeyfield Home); *or*
- you were wating for a social fund payment to help you set up home – eg, for help with removal costs or furniture and bedding (see Chapter 21). For IS and JSA only, you must have a child aged five or under, or qualify for a disability, severe disability or disabled child premium, or one of the pensioner premiums (see p775), or be getting child tax credit for a member of your family which includes a disability or severe disability element.

The amount for housing costs is not actually paid until you move in. If the earlier IS, JSA or PC claim you made before you moved was turned down you must claim again within four weeks of moving in to qualify.

Temporary absence from home

If you are temporarily away from home but are still entitled to IS, income-based JSA or PC, have not rented out your home and intend to return, your housing costs continue to be paid for a period. You can argue that you count as temporarily absent from home even if you have not yet stayed there – eg, you move your furniture and belongings in but cannot move in yourself because you have to go into hospital.[18]

You can get housing costs for up to **13 weeks** while you are away, whatever the reason. You must be unlikely to be away for longer than this.[19]

You can get housing costs for up to **52 weeks** if you are unlikely to be away for longer than this (or in exceptional circumstances, unlikely to be away for substantially longer than this) and you are:[20]

- in hospital. If you are claiming JSA, you must be treated as capable of work during a two-week period of sickness (see p345). If you are sick for longer than this you should claim IS or PC (you may have to claim the new employment and support allowance when it is introduced – see Chapter 7);
- as long as it is not in a care home or an independent hospital (or for IS and JSA only, an Abbeyfield Home):
  - receiving care (approved by a doctor) in the UK or abroad;
  - receiving medical treatment or convalescing in the UK or abroad (approved by a doctor) or your partner or a dependent child (or for PC only, a dependant under 20) is;
- attending a 'training course' away from home in the UK or abroad. Your training course counts if it is provided or approved by, or on behalf of or by arrangement with a government department, the Secretary of State, Scottish Enterprise or Highlands and Islands Enterprise;
- required to live in an approved hostel or an address away from your normal home as a condition of bail;

- for IS and PC only, in prison on remand pending trial or sentence. If you were claiming JSA before going into prison you must claim IS or PC instead to cover your housing costs. Once you are sentenced, you are no longer entitled to IS or PC;
- in a care home or an independent hospital (or for IS and JSA only, an Abbeyfield Home) for short-term or respite care. However, if you are in the accommodation for a trial period to see if you wish to move there permanently, you can only get your housing costs met for 13 weeks.[21] On the date you enter the accommodation, you must intend to return home if it is not suitable.[22] If the accommodation does not suit your needs you can have further trial periods in other homes, so long as you are not away from home for more than 52 weeks in total;
- providing care for someone living in the UK or abroad (approved by a doctor);
- caring for a child (or for PC only, someone under 20) whose parent or guardian is receiving medical treatment or care (approved by a doctor) away from home;
- away from home because of a fear of violence (see p801 if you need to claim for two homes and for what counts as violence);
- a full-time student (see p579); *and*
  - living apart from your partner but cannot get housing costs for two homes (see p801); *or*
  - a single claimant or a lone parent who is liable to pay housing costs on both a term-time and a home address.

Unless you are in a care home, independant hospital (or for IS and JSA, an Abbeyfield Home) for a trial period, your intention to return and whether or not you are unlikely to be away for longer than 13/52 weeks should be considered initially based on the circumstances on the date you leave your home.[23] If at any time after that date you no longer intend to return or it becomes likely that you will be away from home for more than the 13/52 weeks, your entitlement can be reconsidered.[24]

There is no linking rule with these provisions, which means that a new period can start if you return home even for a short stay – eg, a day or a weekend.[25]

If you have to live in temporary accommodation while essential repairs are done to your normal home and you only have to pay for housing costs for one of the homes, your IS, income-based JSA or PC covers these costs.[26] This is not subject to the normal limits on temporary absence from home.[27] If you have to pay housing costs for both homes, you may be able to claim IS, income-based JSA or PC for both for up to four weeks (see p801). After that you are only paid for one home. This could be your normal home if you are unlikely to be away for more than 13/52 weeks or your temporary home if you will be away for longer.

Housing costs for more than one home

In most cases you can only be paid housing costs for one home (see p798 for what counts as your 'home'). However, if you have to pay housing costs for two homes you can get IS, income-based JSA or PC for both:[28]

- for up to **four weeks** if you have moved into a new home and cannot avoid having to pay for the other one as well;[29]
- **indefinitely** if you left your home because of a fear of violence. Provided you left home because of this and are still away from home because of this, it does not matter if you were away from home for some other reason during this period – eg, because you were in prison.[30] You have to show that it is reasonable for you to get payment for two homes. Thus, if you do not intend to return home or someone else is paying the mortgage, you might not get IS, income-based JSA or PC for both homes.

  'Violence' means violence against you and not caused by you.[31] For the purpose of these rules, it must be fear of violence:[32]
  - in your old home. Fear of a racial attack should be covered provided the attack would take place in your home (see p798). Remember that your garden and garage, for example, count; *or*
  - for IS and income-based JSA, from a former member of your family (see p798); *or*
  - for PC, from a close relative (see p797) or former partner;
- **indefinitely** if you are one of a couple and you or your partner are a full-time student or on a training course and living away from your home (see below).

If you have to live in temporary accommodation while essential repairs are done to your normal home, see p800.

If you have to live away from your normal home because you are a **full-time student** (see p579) or on a training course (see p799):

- if you are one of a couple and have to live apart, you can get IS, income-based JSA or PC for both of your homes if it is reasonable for you to get help with both;[33]
- if you are a single person or lone parent and are having to pay housing costs for *either* your normal home *or* your term-time accommodation but not both, you can get IS, income-based JSA or PC, for the home for which you pay.[34]

If neither of the above applies you may only get help with your usual home for up to 52 weeks during a temporary absence (see p799).[35]

If you are getting IS, income-based JSA or PC for your term-time accommodation and you stop living there during a vacation, you cannot get housing costs unless you are away because you are in hospital.[36]

2. Types of housing costs that can be met

Your income support (IS), income-based jobseeker's allowance (JSA) and pension credit (PC) can include help with:

- mortgages and other loans for house purchase (see below);
- loans used to pay for certain repairs and improvements or to meet a service charge for these (see p806);
- 'other housing costs' – eg, ground rent, payments under co-ownership schemes and service charges (see p807).

Mortgages and loans

An amount for qualifying home loan payments can be included in your IS or income-based JSA applicable amount (see p299 and p368). An additional amount for home loan payments can be included in your PC appropriate minimum guarantee (see p448). However, restrictions might be made if you took out or increased the loan while entitled to IS, JSA or PC (see p803).

You must have a home loan.[37] The term **'home loan'** refers to, for example, a mortgage, a hire purchase agreement or some other loan to help you buy your home.

Loans that qualify

Your loan qualifies if it was:[38]

- **taken out to buy the home in which you live**. Loans taken out to buy an existing property as well as those to pay for materials and labour to build your own home are covered. If all or part of your loan was not taken out with the immediate intention of paying for your home (eg, it was to buy a car or set up a business), or is for deferred interest, you cannot get help with the cost even if the loan is secured on your home (but see p808);[39]
- **taken out to buy an additional interest in the home in which you live**, for example:[40]
  - by buying out your ex-partner's share in your home after you separate. However, if your ex-partner has registered a right to occupy your home (a 'Class F land charge') you cannot get help with a loan to pay her/him to remove it;[41]
  - by purchasing the freehold on a leasehold property;[42]
  - by buying your partner's share from a trustee if s/he is bankrupt;[43]
  - by buying out sitting tenants;[44]
- **taken out to repay a loan which itself would have qualified.** However, if the second loan is also for things that do not qualify for help (eg, to pay debts or for a holiday) you only get help with the amount of the original loan.

Example

Mr Clay took out a new mortgage of £60,000. £45,000 was to pay off a mortgage to buy his home and £15,000 was to pay off business debts. He gets help with the loan of £45,000.

Note: loans for costs necessary to help you buy the home or the additional interest (eg, search or valuation fees, legal fees and stamp duty) are covered.[45] If your home is used for both business and domestic purposes and neither part can be sold off separately, you can only get help with the loan for the part where you live.[46]

The rules for help with mortgages and loans changed on 2 October 1995. If you took out your loan before that date, you might still be able to get help under the old, more favourable rules (see p808).

Taking out or increasing loans while entitled to benefit

Even if your loan qualifies (see p802) you cannot usually get IS, income-based JSA or PC to help you pay the cost if you became liable for it or increased it during a 'relevant period' (see below):[47]

- for IS and PC:
  - after 1 October 1995; *or*
  - after 2 May 1994, unless you qualified for IS for it in the 26 weeks before 2 October 1995; *or*
  - in the 26 weeks before 2 October 1995, unless at the time you became liable you were not entitled to IS and neither you nor your partner became entitled to IS or income-based JSA after 1 October 1995 and within 26 weeks of your IS ceasing; *or*
- for JSA:
  - after 7 October 1996; *or*
  - after 2 May 1994, unless you qualified for IS for it in the 26 weeks before 7 October 1996; *or*
  - in the 26 weeks before 7 October 1996, unless at the time you became liable you were not entitled to IS and neither you nor your partner became entitled to IS or JSA after 6 October 1996 and within 26 weeks of your IS ceasing.

The DWP is likely to say that this also applies if you are awarded backdated IS, income-based JSA or PC for the day on which you became liable for or increased your loan.[48]

Relevant periods

A **'relevant period'** is a period:

- for IS and JSA:[49]

  - when you were entitled to IS or income-based JSA (for IS) or IS or JSA (for JSA); *or*
  - when you were living as a member of the family (see p798) of someone who was entitled to IS or income-based JSA (for IS) or IS or JSA (for JSA); *or*
  - of up to 26 weeks between two of either of the types of period above.

  Note: official guidance suggests that for JSA, the DWP might only apply this rule if you (or the family member with whom you were living) were entitled to IS or *income-based* JSA;[50]
- for PC:[51]
  - when you were entitled to IS, income-based JSA or PC; *or*
  - when your partner was entitled to IS, income-based JSA or PC; *or*
  - of up to 26 weeks between two of either of the types of period listed above.

For these purposes you and your partner are:
- treated as entitled to IS, income-based JSA or PC when you are on one of the New Deal programmes or schemes listed on p821, even if as a result you count as in full-time paid work (see p648) or have too much income to qualify for IS, JSA or PC;[52]
- *not* treated as entitled to IS or JSA under the rules described on pp820–822.[53]

Note: if you become liable for the loan during a period of 26 weeks or more between two relevant periods, you *can* get help with the cost.

Getting help with a new or increased loan

You can get IS, income-based JSA or PC for housing costs even if you became liable for your loan during a 'relevant period' (see p803) if:
- you have taken out or increased your loan to buy a home which is better suited than your former home to **the needs of a 'disabled person'** (see below).[54]
  There is no rule that says that you must buy the home or take out the loan within a certain time before or after the disabled person moves in.[55] However, the person has to qualify as disabled at the time the loan is taken out.[56] S/he does not have to be a member of your family nor to have previously lived with you;
- for IS or JSA, you have a **boy and a girl aged 10 or over**, or for PC, you are looking after a boy and a girl who live with you and are aged 10 or over but under 20, and you increased your loan and moved to a new home because you needed to provide them with separate bedrooms.[57]
  You can argue that this should apply if one of the children is aged 10 or over and the other will be 10 in the reasonably near future.[58]

'Disabled person'

For these purposes, a disabled person is:[59]

- for **IS and income-based JSA**, anyone for whom you or someone living with you is getting a disabled child, disability, enhanced pensioner or higher pensioner premium

(see p775) as well as other people living in your home who would get one of these premiums if they were on IS or JSA, or a child or young person who counts as disabled or severely disabled for the purpose of the child tax credit disability or severe disability element;
- for **PC**, anyone under 20 for whom you or your partner are responsible ('responsible' is not defined in the rules) who gets disability living allowance or who is registered blind (in Scotland, certified blind), or anyone living in your home who is aged at least 75, or who would qualify for a disability or higher pensioner premium if s/he were on IS.

For all the benefits, a person continues to count as a disabled person even if, under the incapacity rules, s/he is either disqualified from receiving benefit or is treated as capable of work (see p271).

You can get IS, income-based JSA or PC for your housing costs even if you became liable for your loan during a 'relevant period' (see p803), but the amount you get might be restricted to your former housing costs if:

- you:[60]
  - **re-mortgaged your home** to pay off your original house purchase loan; *or*
  - **sold your previous home**, paid off an original loan which you took out to buy a home or pay for repairs or improvements, and have now taken out a new loan for a new property, even if this is some time later.

  The original loan must have qualified (see pp802 and 806) and be one for which you can get IS, income-based JSA or PC even when taken out during a 'relevant period' (see p803). Unless the loan was to buy a home for a disabled person or to provide separate bedrooms for a boy and girl aged 10 or over (see p804), you cannot get help with any increase in your housing costs. Thus, if your original mortgage was £30,000 and you took out a new loan for £35,000, you can only get housing costs on £30,000 of the second loan.

  If, following divorce or separation, you buy out your former partner's share of your home, you cannot get help with the mortgage in relation to that share. Similarly, if you take out a loan or increase an existing loan to buy a home after separation, the restriction will, in principle, apply. However, you can argue that each of you should be entitled to housing costs up to the amount of the loan you were liable to pay when you were together – eg, if you were liable to pay £50,000 when you were together, you should each be entitled to housing costs on a mortgage of up to £50,000 when you separate;[61]
- you buy a home and the week before:
  - you **were in rented accommodation and getting housing benefit** (HB). To begin with you only get the amount of HB you were entitled to plus any 'other housing costs' (see p807) you were already getting;[62]
  - you **were only getting 'other housing costs'** (see p807) paid with your IS, income-based JSA or PC (eg, as ground rent).[63] To begin with you only get the amount you had been getting for those other costs.

In both cases, you get any subsequent increases in the standard rate of interest (see p810) or the 'other housing costs' and do not lose these if the interest rate or costs go down again.[64]

Loans for repairs and improvements

IS, income-based JSA and PC do not meet the cost of repairs and improvements to your home or the cost of service charges for these (although service charges for minor repairs and maintenance *can* be covered as 'other housing costs' – see p807). However, if you take out a loan to pay for the repairs and improvements or the service charge (or to pay off an earlier loan taken out for this purpose) you might get help with this.[65] See below for which repairs or improvements qualify.

You must use the loan for the repairs and improvements or service charge within six months (longer if this is reasonable). A bank overdraft that is taken to pay for the repairs or improvements counts as a loan.[66]

Repairs and improvements that qualify

You can only get help with loans for repairs or improvements to maintain your current home,[67] or any part of the building in which it is contained, in a habitable condition. See p798 for what counts as your 'home'. This includes loans towards the cost of necessary survey work.[68] You can get help with a loan for:[69]

- providing a bath, shower, toilet, wash basin and the necessary plumbing and hot water;
- repairs to your heating system;
- damp-proof measures (you can argue this includes repairs to a roof[70]);
- providing ventilation and natural lighting;
- providing drainage facilities;
- facilities for preparing and cooking food (but not for storing it[71]);
- home insulation;
- providing electric lighting and sockets;
- storage facilities for fuel or refuse;
- repairing unsafe structural defects;
- adaptations for a disabled person (see p804 for who counts);
- providing separate bedrooms for children of different sexes:
  - for IS and income-based JSA, aged 10 or over who are part of your family (see p798 for who counts as your family); *or*
  - for PC, aged 10 or over but under 20 for whom you or your partner are responsible and who live with you. 'Responsible' is not defined in the rules.

  You can argue that this should apply if one of the children is aged 10 or over and the other will be 10 in the reasonably near future.[72]

If your loan is also for other repairs and improvements, you are only paid housing costs for the proportion which relates to any of the items listed above.

Note: the rules for help with loans for repairs and improvements changed on 2 October 1995. If you took out your loan before that date, you might still be able to get help under the old, more favourable, rules (see p808).

Help with 'other housing costs'

You are paid the normal weekly charge for all 'other housing costs' covered by IS, JSA and PC.[73] These are:

- service charges (see below). Note that some service charges are excluded;
- rent or ground rent if you have a lease of more than 21 years. If your lease is of 21 years or less, the rent or ground rent might be met by HB instead (see p179);[74]
- rentcharge payments;
- payments under a co-ownership scheme;
- rent if you are a Crown tenant (minus any water charges[75]);
- payments for a tent and its pitch if that is your home.

If you pay your other housing costs annually or irregularly, the weekly amount is worked out by dividing what is payable for the year by 52.[76]

If your other housing costs have been waived because you or your partner (or for IS and income-based JSA only, a member of your family – see p798) have paid for repairs or redecoration that are not your responsibility, you can still get IS, income-based JSA or PC for them for up to eight weeks.[77]

Charges that cannot be met

The following charges cannot be met:[78]

- fuel, where this is included in your 'other housing costs'. If there is no specific charge for fuel, set deductions are made;

Heating	£15.45	Lighting	£1.25
Hot water	£1.80	Cooking	£1.80

- amounts for repairs and improvements listed on p806. You are expected to take out a loan to pay for these and can claim help with this;[79]
- ineligible services listed on p195. These are the same as for HB.[80]

Service charges

A **'service'** is something that is agreed and arranged on your behalf and for which you are required to pay. So, for example, if you own a flat and the freeholder arranges for the exterior of the building to be painted, for which you have to pay a share of the cost, your IS, income-based JSA or PC includes this as a service charge. Some service charges are specifically excluded (see p195). Some service charges only count if they relate to the provision of 'adequate accommodation'.[81]

You should bear the following in mind.

- Service charges to cover minor repairs and maintenance are eligible. However, those to cover repairs and improvements listed on p806 are not.[82]
- Payments for support services are not eligible service charges. Instead, you can get help with these via your local authority's 'Supporting People team'. See p196 for further information.
- House insurance paid under the terms of your lease can be a service charge, but insurance required by a bank as a condition of your mortgage is not.[83]
- Services provided by an authority that you arrange yourself are not covered. Thus, charges for water and sewerage paid to a water company are not met.[84]

Housing costs that are no longer paid

You can continue to get help with certain types of housing costs that could be paid with IS before 2 October 1995, but which can no longer be paid by IS or income-based JSA. These are:[85]

- accumulated arrears of interest;
- interest on a secured loan that was not for house purchase, taken out when you were one of a couple, where your partner had left and could not (or would not) pay the cost, or had died;
- interest on a loan for repairs and improvements under the pre-2 October 1995 rules.

You can continue to get help with these if they were included in your housing costs before 2 October 1995, you fulfil the qualifying conditions *and* you remain in receipt of (or are treated as in receipt of) IS or income-based JSA. You are treated as receiving IS or income-based JSA during the periods described on pp820–822. See CPAG's *National Welfare Benefits Handbook*, 1995/96 edition, pp30–32 for more details on how these costs were assessed.

Note: if you are claiming PC, you should not be worse off than you were on IS or income-based JSA. See p448 to see if you qualify for a transitional amount as part of your appropriate minimum guarantee.

3. The amount of housing costs you get

Once you have worked out which housing costs can be met by income support (IS), income-based jobseeker's allowance (JSA), or pension credit (PC) you must:

- calculate the weekly amount of:
  - housing costs for home loans. **Note:** these might be restricted if you took out or increased your loan while entitled to IS, JSA or PC (see p803);
  - housing costs for loans for repairs and improvements;
  - 'other housing costs' (see p807);

- add these amounts together;
- deduct any restrictions being made because your housing costs are too high (see p811);
- deduct any amounts for other people living in your home (known as non-dependants – see p815).

For IS and income-based JSA only, a reduced amount might also be paid during a 'waiting period' in the early weeks of your claim (see p817).

If you or your partner were getting (or treated as getting) IS, income-based JSA or PC which included help with housing costs in the 12 weeks or less before becoming entitled to another of those benefits, the same amount of housing costs are met as were when you were getting the other benefit.[86] However, if there has been a change of circumstances affecting the calculation of the housing costs, other than a reduction in the amount of your outstanding loan, they are recalculated. For IS and income-based JSA, the 12 weeks is extended to 26 weeks if you or your partner:

- were getting full housing costs but stopped getting IS or income-based JSA because you received child support maintenance, and this has now reduced as a result of child support rule changes in April 1995 or because an interim maintenance calculation has been replaced or terminated; *or*
- reclaimed IS or income-based JSA within 26 weeks of a previous claim during which you were getting housing costs and you have been receiving payments under an employment insurance policy which has since run out.

You might only get your **share of the housing costs** if you or your partner:[87]

- share liability to pay the housing costs with someone. However, if the other person is not paying her/his share you can argue that you should get help with the amount;[88] *or*
- are treated as liable for housing costs because you share the costs with someone (see p797).

How your housing costs for loans are calculated

Your IS, income-based JSA or PC housing costs for loans for house purchase and repairs and improvements are calculated using a standard rate of interest (see p810). They do not usually cover the whole of your loan payments. You cannot get help with associated insurance premiums. Thus, if you have an endowment mortgage you do not get the insurance element paid.

There can be a limit on the amount of housing costs that can be paid. If the total of your loans is more than £100,000 your housing costs might only be calculated on this figure (see p811). If your loans are lower than this but your housing costs are still thought to be excessive, your housing costs might be restricted (see p812).

There is often a shortfall between the IS, income-based JSA or PC you get for your housing costs and what you have to pay your lender. See p811 for ideas about what to do to meet the shortfall.

The formula

The weekly housing costs that you get are worked out using a special formula.[89] A standard rate of interest is used, not what you actually have to pay. The standard rate of interest is set by the DWP on the basis of the Bank of England base rate, plus 1.58 per cent.[90] At the time of writing the **standard rate of interest** was 6.83 per cent. If your repayments are higher because your lender charges a higher rate of interest, you have to meet the shortfall yourself.

The amount of your loan that qualifies (see pp802 and 806) less any restrictions that have been made (see pp805 and 811) is multiplied by the standard rate of interest. This figure is divided by 52 to reach a weekly amount.

Example

Mr and Mrs Khan have a repayment mortgage and a loan for repairs and improvements. The outstanding loans of £30,000 and £5,000 qualify. They also have a loan for a conservatory. This does not qualify. They pay interest at the rate of 7.6%.

£30,000 x 6.83% (standard interest rate) = £2,049. £5,000 x 6.83% = £341.56.

Their weekly IS housing costs are (£2,049 ÷ 52) + (£341.50 ÷ 52) = £45.97

Transitional rules

The rules for calculating housing costs changed on 2 October 1995. If you were on IS both on and after 1 October 1995 and the amount of IS or income-based JSA housing costs to which you are now entitled is less because of the rules since 2 October 1995, you can get an extra payment to make up the loss.[91] This payment is called an 'add-back' and is equal to the difference between your IS housing costs in the week including 1 October 1995 and your entitlement in the next week. If you have more than one loan, the add-back for each is calculated separately.

You continue to be paid the add-back so long as you remain entitled to IS or income-based JSA. However, you lose the add-back if you stop being entitled to (or being treated as entitled to – see p820) IS or income-based JSA for more than 12 weeks (104 weeks if you or your partner are a 'welfare to work' beneficiary – see p666) or if you cease to qualify for housing costs. If you lose the add-back but your partner makes a claim for you within 12 weeks (104 weeks if s/he is a 'welfare to work' beneficiary – see p666), s/he can continue to get the add-back to which you were entitled.

The add-back reduces if your entitlement to housing costs increases.[92] However, it does not increase if your entitlement to housing costs goes down. You lose the add-back when your entitlement equals what you used to get under the old rules.

Note: if you are claiming PC, you should not be worse off than you were on IS or income-based JSA. See p448 to see if you qualify for a transitional amount as part of your appropriate minimum guarantee.

When housing costs are recalculated

Your IS, income-based JSA or PC housing costs are usually recalculated annually, on the anniversary of the date these housing costs were first met by your benefit, even if there is a reduction in the amount of your outstanding loan.[93] If there are other changes, your housing costs are recalculated on the date of the change. However, if you are getting PC and you or your partner are at least 65, and a non-dependant has come to live with you or your non-dependant's circumstances have changed and this means the amount of housing costs to which you are entitled reduces, your housing costs are recalculated 26 weeks after the date of the change (or if there is more than one change in respect of the same non-dependant, the first of these changes).[94]

If your housing costs are not met in full

If you do not have enough money to pay your housing costs you may be in danger of losing your home, particularly if you are on IS, JSA or PC for a long time. You should inform your lender and discuss how to resolve the situation. Your lender may be prepared to accept interest-only payments for a while. It is important to discuss this in order to avoid falling into arrears and risk losing your home. You should also seek independent debt advice.

If you have to make payments towards the shortfall:

- you may be able to increase your income by taking in lodgers. See pp865 and 890 for how this affects your IS, income-based JSA or PC;
- some payments made direct to the lender by relatives, friends or a charity towards housing costs not being met (eg, capital repayments) can be ignored in calculating your entitlement to IS or income-based JSA;[95]
- if you get charitable or voluntary payments, these are ignored as income. See pp864 and 895 for further information;
- you could try finding a part-time job and benefit from an earnings disregard (see pp854 and 885), but see Chapter 27 for information about how work affects IS and JSA.

Ultimately, you may have to sell your home and buy somewhere cheaper. If you move out and put your house up for sale the capital value of your house can be disregarded for a period while you take reasonable steps to sell it (see pp916 and 937).[96] If you rent it while trying to sell, see pp866 and 891 for how the income is treated.

Restrictions if your housing costs are too high

Your housing costs can be restricted if:

- your loans exceed an upper limit (see below); *or*
- your total housing costs are considered excessive (see below).

Your housing costs can also be restricted if you take out or increase a loan while entitled to IS, JSA or PC or in a period between claims (see p803).

The upper limit

If your loans amount to more than £100,000 in total, your housing costs might not be met in full.[97] This includes all mortgages taken out to buy your home and also any loans for repairs and improvements. The restriction is applied proportionately to each loan. If a loan was taken out to adapt your home for a disabled person (see p804 for who counts), it is ignored when working out if your loans exceed the upper limit. If you are getting housing costs on more than one home (see p801) you can be paid up to the limit for each.[98]

Upper limits for loans have only existed since 2 August 1993 and have changed twice since that date. The limit has been £100,000 since 10 April 1995. There is no limit if you have been entitled to IS or income-based JSA from before 2 August 1993, unless you take out or increase a loan after that date. If you took out your loan or increased it:[99]

- after 2 August 1993 but before 12 April 1994 and have been entitled to IS or income-based JSA since 2 August 1993, your limit is £150,000;
- after 11 April 1994 but before 10 April 1995 and have been entitled to IS or income-based JSA since 11 April 1994, your limit is £125,000.

If you are getting IS or income-based JSA without an upper limit or with one greater than £100,000, but you then claim PC you should not lose out. Check to see if you qualify for a transitional amount as part of your appropriate minimum guarantee (see p448).

If you or your partner are a 'welfare to work' beneficiary (see p666) you can be treated as entitled to IS or income-based JSA for up to 104 weeks. Your old upper limit applies if you have to claim IS or income-based JSA again within that period.[100]

Excessive housing costs

Whether or not an upper limit applies to you (see above), your housing costs can be restricted if:[101]

- your home (excluding any part which you let) is too big for:
  - for IS and income-based JSA, you and your family (see p798) and any of your non-dependants (see p815) or foster children;
  - for PC, you and your partner, anyone under 20 living with you and any other non-dependants (see p815).

  When deciding if your home is too big, a comparison is made with other accommodation that would be suitable given the size of your household.

Everyone's needs must be considered – eg if a member of your family needs extra space because of a disability or you have a child or relative in a care home who regularly comes to stay with you, your need for a large home may be justified;
- the area in which you live is more expensive than other areas where there is suitable accommodation. The area should not be chosen on too wide a basis. 'Area' means something more confined, restricted and compact than a locality or district. It might be a neighbourhood or even a large block of flats;[102]
- the outgoings on your home which are met by IS, income-based JSA or PC housing costs are higher than those in other suitable accommodation in the area.

The capital value of your home cannot be taken into account.[103]

When no restriction should be made

No restriction should be made, even if suitable accommodation is available, if it is not reasonable for you and your family (for IS and income-based JSA) or you and your partner (for PC) to look for cheaper accommodation. Account should be taken of:[104]
- the general level of housing costs in the area and whether suitable accommodation is available. This means that property must be generally available, not necessarily available to you personally;[105]
- your family circumstances (for IS and income-based JSA) or your circumstances and those of the people who live with you (for PC) – eg, your employment prospects, the age and health of your family members and whether the move would have a detrimental effect on a child's or young person's education if s/he were to change schools.

These are not the only situations which count.[106] A move may not be reasonable if:
- the size of your family would make it difficult to find accommodation;
- you need to be near relatives or friends to provide (or receive) care or support;
- you have moved a number of times recently;
- it would be difficult to sell your property,[107] you have negative equity, or selling would cause you financial hardship;[108]
- you have lived in your home for many years and it is now too large because you are separated or divorced, your children have left home, or your partner has died;
- prior to your claim you were advised by the DWP that your housing costs would not be restricted;[109]
- you could not get another mortgage on a property.[110]

Even if it is reasonable for you to move, your housing costs should not be restricted in certain circumstances (see p814). If it *is* appropriate to restrict your housing costs, these are limited to help with the amount of loan you would need in order to get suitable alternative accommodation.[111] This must be assessed in practical and realistic terms. Any loans that are repayable on the sale of your home which would leave you with less money to purchase another home should be taken into account.[112] However, if the equity in your property was sufficient to buy a new home outright, without a loan, your housing costs could be nil.[113]

Delaying a restriction

Your housing costs cannot be restricted for 26 weeks if you or a member of your family (for IS and JSA – see p798), or you and your partner (for PC), were able to meet these costs when they were first taken on, and for a further 26 weeks if you are trying to find cheaper accommodation.[114] If full payment is made but later your housing costs are restricted:

- for IS and JSA, following a supersession, the 26-week periods begin from the date you are informed of the intention to restrict your costs under these provisions;[115]
- for PC, following a 'review', the 26-week periods begin from the date of the review.[116]

Periods of 12 weeks or less when you stop getting IS, income-based JSA or PC are included when calculating these periods.[117] In addition, other periods count towards the 26-week periods. These are periods when:

- for IS and JSA, your partner was in receipt of IS or income-based JSA. This only applies if:[118]
  - you have only recently become one of a couple or separated from your partner and you make a new claim within 12 weeks;
  - your partner was getting or treated as getting IS or income-based JSA for you both and you have taken over the claiming role;
  - you or your partner were on one of the New Deal programmes or schemes listed on p821, your partner was claiming IS or income-based JSA (but not joint-claim JSA) for you immediately before this and you claim IS or income-based JSA (but not joint-claim JSA) immediately after;
- for IS and JSA, someone who was not your partner was claiming IS or income-based JSA while you and a child or young person counted as a member of her/his family (see p798). This only applies if you claim IS or income-based JSA yourself, that child or young person becomes a member of your family and you claim within 12 weeks of this (104 weeks if you are a 'welfare to work' beneficiary (see p666) or 52 weeks if you qualify for a longer linking period – see p822);
- for PC, you were getting IS or income-based JSA if this was immediately before 6 October 2003 or before you or your partner turned 60.[119]

Deductions for non-dependants

If other people ('non-dependants') normally live with you in your home who are not part of your family for benefit purposes (see p700), a set deduction is usually made from your housing costs.[120] This is because it is assumed the non-dependant makes a contribution towards your outgoings, whether or not s/he does so. Examples of non-dependants are adult sons or daughters, or elderly relatives who share your home.

A person can only be treated as living with you if s/he shares rooms with you. This includes the kitchen (unless it is only used by someone else to prepare food for her/him[121]), but not a bathroom, toilet or common access areas.[122] A person who is separately liable to pay rent to a landlord is not counted as living with you.

A person does not normally live with you if s/he has not been there long enough to regard your home as her/his normal home.[123] If you think the DWP has wrongly assumed that a person is normally living with you, ask for a revision or appeal (see Chapters 41 and 42).

People who are not non-dependants

No deduction is made from your housing costs if the person living with you is not treated as a non-dependant (though any rent or lodging charges s/he pays to you affect the amount of your IS, income-based JSA or PC – see pp865 and 890). The following people do not count as non-dependants even if they normally live with you:[124]

- for IS and income-based JSA only, a member of your family for benefit purposes (see p798) as well as any child (this includes qualifying young people) living with you who is not a member of your household (see p712);
- for PC only, your partner and anyone under 20 for whom you or your partner are responsible ('responsible' is not defined in the rules);
- someone who is liable to pay you, or your partner, in order to live in your home – eg, a sub-tenant, licensee or boarder along with other members of her/his household. This does not apply if the person is a close relative of yours or your partner (see p797).
  The payment must be on a commercial basis. A low charge does not necessarily mean that the arrangement is not commercial. Nor do you have to make a profit. An arrangement between friends can be commercial;[125]
- for IS and income-based JSA only, someone other than a close relative (see p797) to whom you, or your partner, are liable to make payments on a commercial basis (ie, as a sub-tenant, licensee or boarder) in order to live in her/his property. Other members of her/his household also do not count as non-dependants;
- someone who jointly occupies your home and is a co-owner or joint tenant with you or your partner. Your joint occupier's partner is also not a non-dependant. For IS and income-based JSA only, close relatives (see p797) who

jointly occupy your home *are* treated as non-dependants unless they had joint liability prior to 11 April 1988 or joint liability existed on or before the date you first lived in the property (or your partner did if s/he is the joint owner/ tenant). However, no non-dependant deduction is made for them even though they are non-dependants (see below);

- someone who is employed by a charitable or voluntary organisation as a resident carer for you, or your partner, and who you pay for that service (even if the charge is nominal). If the carer's partner lives in your home s/he also does not count as a non-dependant.

When no deduction is made

Even if you do have a non-dependant in your home no deduction is made for her/ him if you (or your partner):[126]

- are blind or treated as blind;
- get attendance allowance (AA) (or equivalent benefits paid because of injury at work or a war injury) or the care component of disability living allowance (DLA).

In addition, no deduction is made for a non-dependant:[127]

- who is staying with you but whose normal home is elsewhere;
- who is 16 or 17 years old;
- for whom a deduction is already being made from your housing benefit (HB – see p196);
- who is under 25 years old and getting IS or income-based JSA;
- who is getting PC;
- who gets a training allowance in connection with youth training under specific provisions;[128]
- who is a full-time student during her/his period of study (see p579). Unless you are getting PC and you or your partner are 65 or over, this only applies during the summer vacation if the student is not in full-time paid work (see p648);
- who is not living with you at present because s/he:
  - has been in hospital for more than 52 weeks. Separate stays in hospital which are not more than 28 days apart are added together when calculating the 52 weeks;
  - is in prison;
- for IS and income-based JSA only, who is a close relative (see p797) and a co-owner or joint tenant with you, or your partner. For PC, no deduction is made because co-owners and joint tenants do not count as non-dependants, even if they are close relatives.

The amount of the deduction

If you have a non-dependant living with you who is 18 or over and for whom a deduction must be made, a fixed amount is deducted from your housing costs, whatever s/he pays you. Unless your non-dependant is in full-time paid work, a £7.40 deduction is made each week. If your non-dependant is in full-time paid work, the amount of the deduction depends on her/his weekly gross income.[129]

Gross weekly income	*Weekly non-dependant deduction*
£369 or more	£47.75
£296–£368.99	£43.50
£223–£295.99	£38.20
£172–£222.99	£23.35
£116–£171.99	£17.00
Less than £116	£7.40

The rules on full-time paid work are covered in Chapter 27. **Note:**

- A non-dependant who is not in (or is treated as not in) full-time paid work does not attract the higher levels of deduction even if her/his weekly gross income is £116 or more.
- For PC, if someone is getting IS or income-based JSA for more than three days in a benefit week, s/he does not count as in full-time paid work in that week.[130] This means the lower deduction (£7.40) is made (or no deduction is made, if the non-dependant is under 25).

Gross income includes wages before tax and national insurance are deducted plus any other income the non-dependant has (but not AA, DLA or certain payments from the Macfarlane Trusts, the Eileen Trust, the Fund or the Independent Living Funds, or for IS and JSA only, the Skipton Fund and the London Bombings Relief Charitable Fund – see p864 – or for PC only, payments in kind).[131]

You should try to provide information to show which deduction applies. If you cannot, ask the DWP to consider the circumstances – eg, if your non-dependant is doing a job which is normally very low paid. The DWP should not assume the worst. It should assess the likely level of your non-dependant's earnings on the evidence available.[132]

A deduction is made for each non-dependant in your home. However, if you have a non-dependant couple and a non-dependant deduction applies to both members, only one deduction is made – the highest applicable. The couple's joint income counts.

If you are a joint owner with someone other than your partner, any deductions are shared proportionally between you and the other owner(s).

4. Waiting periods

Even if your housing costs qualify, these are not usually met until you have been entitled to (or treated as entitled to) income support (IS) or jobseeker's allowance

(JSA) for a number of weeks – known as a 'waiting period'.[133] For information about when you can be treated as entitled to IS or JSA (see p820).

You can be paid straight away if:[134]

- you have already been entitled to IS or JSA for the relevant number of weeks in your waiting period when you agree to pay your loan or other housing costs (but see p803 for the rules restricting housing costs if you take out or increase a loan while entitled to IS or JSA);
- you were getting help with your housing costs when your IS or JSA ceased because:
  - you became a 'welfare to work' beneficiary (see p666); *or*
  - you started full-time paid work or training for work, or increased your hours or your pay (so long as you qualify for a longer linking period – see p822).

  This only applies if you claim IS or income-based JSA again within 104 weeks (if you are a 'welfare to work' beneficiary) or 52 weeks (if you qualify for a longer linking period);
- you or your partner are 60 or over. If you are 60 or over, you cannot claim IS, but can claim PC;
- you are claiming for payments as a Crown tenant, under a co-ownership scheme or for a tent.

In addition, if you reclaim IS or income-based JSA within 26 weeks of a previous claim during which you were getting housing costs and you have been receiving payments under an employment insurance policy which has since run out, periods when you were getting those payments are ignored in calculating the waiting periods.[135] This means that you can requalify for housing costs sooner.

All other claimants get a reduced amount of help initially. The length of your waiting period depends on when you agreed to pay your mortgage or loan or other housing costs and how long you have been entitled to (or treated as entitled to) IS or JSA (see p820). You are expected to use mortgage payment protection policy payments, savings or income to meet any shortfall. If you do not have enough to pay the shortfall you should approach your lender to discuss how you can protect your home.

Note: if you claim PC, there is no waiting period. You can get help with your housing costs straight away.

The 26-week waiting period

If you agreed to pay your loan or other housing costs before 2 October 1995 (the DWP calls these 'existing housing costs') you get:[136]

- nothing for the first eight weeks;
- 50 per cent of your housing costs for the next 18 weeks;
- full housing costs after you have been entitled (or treated as entitled) to IS or JSA for 26 weeks.

This 26-week waiting period can also apply if you agreed to pay a loan after 2 October 1995, provided it replaces a loan you agreed to pay before that date. You must have been liable for the housing costs under both the old and the new agreements and the new loan must be for the same (or lower) amount as the earlier loan.

The 39-week waiting period

If you agreed to pay your loan or other housing costs after 1 October 1995 (the DWP calls these 'new housing costs') you get:[137]

- nothing for the first 39 weeks;
- full housing costs after you have been entitled to IS or JSA for 39 weeks.

However, if the loan replaces another loan you agreed to pay before 2 October 1995, see p818.

Certain claimants are exempt from this 39-week waiting period. Instead, the 26-week waiting period applies. This is the case if you:[138]

- are a lone parent and have claimed IS or JSA because your partner has abandoned you[139] or died, unless you become one of a couple again. This includes where you have been 'constructively abandoned' – eg, your partner's behaviour was such as to give you little reasonable option but to leave her/him or require her/him to leave you;[140]
- are claiming IS or JSA; *and*
  - you are a carer getting carer's allowance; *or*
  - you are caring for someone:
    - getting AA or DLA highest or middle rate care component, or who has been awarded one of these on an advance claim but it has not yet been paid; *or*
    - who has claimed AA or DLA. This applies for 26 weeks from the date of that claim, or until it is decided if this is sooner; *or*
  - for IS only, it is not more than eight weeks since you have ceased to meet those conditions or have stopped being a carer;
- are claiming IS and are in prison awaiting trial or sentence;
- have been refused payments under a mortgage payment protection policy due to a pre-existing medical condition delete or because you are HIV positive.[141]

If you have two loans or agreements to pay other housing costs and one was agreed before and one after 1 October 1995, the relevant waiting periods apply to each.[142]

5. Treated as entitled to income support or jobseeker's allowance

You are treated as entitled to and receiving income support (IS) or jobseeker's allowance (JSA) for certain periods, even though you were not actually entitled to or receiving it. These are known as 'linking rules'. They can:

- help you get full housing costs earlier. Periods when you are treated as entitled to IS or JSA can count towards your waiting period (see p817);
- allow you to continue to receive help with certain types of housing costs that are no longer met (see p808) if there is a break in your claim.

General rules

You are treated as entitled to and getting IS for any period when you were entitled to or getting JSA.[143] You are treated as entitled to income-based JSA for any period when you were entitled to or getting IS.[144] In addition, you are treated as entitled to and getting IS or JSA:[145]

- for any period where you were getting JSA as a 'joint-claim couple' (see p381);
- during a period of 12 weeks (104 weeks if you or your partner are a 'welfare to work' beneficiary – see p666 – or 52 weeks if you qualify for a longer linking period – see p822) or less between two periods when:
  - you were entitled to, getting, or treated as getting IS or JSA; *or*
  - you were treated as entitled to IS or JSA while your income or capital were too high in the circumstances described on p821.

  The period of 12 weeks is extended to 26 weeks if you were getting full housing costs but stopped getting IS or income-based JSA because you received child support maintenance, and this has now reduced as a result of child support rule changes in April 1995 or because an interim maintenance assessment has been replaced or terminated (see CPAG's *Child Support Handbook*, 2003/04 edition for details);[146]
- during any period for which you are awarded IS or JSA after a revision, supersession or an appeal.

Couples and former couples

You are treated as entitled to and getting IS or income-based JSA:[147]

- during the time when your ex-partner was getting, or treated as getting, IS, income-based JSA (but not joint-claim JSA) or PC for you both, provided you claim IS or income-based JSA within 12 weeks of separating (104 weeks if you are a 'welfare to work' beneficiary – see p666 – or 52 weeks if you qualify for a longer linking period – see p822);
- during the time when your partner was getting or treated as getting IS or income-based JSA on her/his own, provided you make a claim for IS or income-

based JSA within 12 weeks of becoming a couple (or a 'joint-claim couple' – see p381). Unless you are a joint-claim couple, the time limit is 104 weeks if you or your partner are a 'welfare to work' beneficiary (see p666) – or 52 weeks if you qualify for a longer linking period (see p822);

- during the time when your partner was getting or treated as getting IS or income-based JSA (but not joint-claim JSA) for you both, if you take over the claiming role.

Employment and training schemes

You are treated as entitled to and getting IS or income-based JSA:[148]

- during the time when you or your partner were on one of the New Deal programmes or schemes listed below, provided your partner was claiming IS or income-based JSA (but not joint-claim JSA) for you immediately before this and you claim IS or income-based JSA (but not joint-claim JSA) immediately after;
- during periods when you stop getting IS or income-based JSA because you or your partner are:
  - on an employment training rehabilitation course;
  - on one of the New Deal programmes or schemes listed below, or an employment zone programme and as a result count as in full-time paid work (see p648), or have too much income (see Chapter 36);
- during any period when you were getting contribution-based JSA immediately before starting on one of the New Deal programmes or schemes listed below.

New Deal programmes and schemes

The self-employed employment option of the New Deal for young people
The voluntary sector option of the New Deal for young people
The environment task force option of the New Deal for young people
The 'intensive activity period' for people aged 25 or over but under 60

Other

You are treated as entitled to and getting IS or income-based JSA during the time when someone who was not your partner was entitled to IS or income-based JSA and you and a child or young person counted as a member of her/his family.[149] You must claim within 12 weeks of that child or young person becoming a member of *your* family (104 weeks if you are a 'welfare to work' beneficiary – see p666 – or 52 weeks if you qualify for a longer linking period – see p822). See p798 for who counts as a member of your family.

You are treated as entitled to IS or income-based JSA for up to 39 weeks if you were not entitled to IS or income-based JSA only because your income was too high or your capital was over £16,000 (including if your contribution-based JSA was the same as or higher than your income-based JSA applicable amount);[150] *and*

- you have been entitled to contribution-based JSA, statutory sick pay or incapacity benefit (or credits for unemployment or incapacity). A claim for IS or *income-based* JSA is not required;[151] *or*
- for IS only, you are treated as getting IS or income-based JSA; *or*
- you are a lone parent or for IS, a carer (see p294) or for JSA, a carer who is allowed to restrict the hours you are available for work (see p355) and you, or someone claiming on your behalf, has previously claimed and been refused IS or JSA. This does not apply if you or your partner count as in full-time paid work (see p649), or you are a full-time student who cannot claim IS or JSA (see p579), or are temporarily absent from Great Britain and not entitled to IS or JSA (see pp1350 and 1352).

If the above applies and you were not entitled to IS or income-based JSA only because your *income* was too high and you were getting payments under a mortgage payment protection policy, you are treated as entitled to IS or income-based JSA for *any* period for which the payments were made.[152] This could be longer than 39 weeks.

Longer linking periods

Some of the 12-week periods and time limits above are extended to 52 weeks – referred to in this *Handbook* as 'longer linking periods'. You qualify for a longer linking period if you stop getting IS or JSA because:[153]

- you or your partner:
  - start work or increase your hours; *or*
  - are taking steps to get work under certain training schemes; *or*
  - are on one of the New Deal programmes or schemes listed on p821, the full-time education and training option of the New Deal for people aged 18 or over but under 26, or an employment zone programme; *or*
  - are getting assistance in pursuing self-employment while on a training course funded under specific provisions;[154] *and*
- as a result, you or your partner count as in full-time paid work (see p648) or your earnings or your income are too high.

You only qualify for a longer linking period if, immediately before the day your entitlement to IS or income-based JSA ceased, you had served enough of your waiting period (see p817) that housing costs:[155]

- were included in your IS or income-based JSA (in full or in part); *or*
- would have been included but for a non-dependant deduction (see p815).

6. Mortgage interest run-on

When you return to work or increase your hours and so count as in full-time paid work, you no longer qualify for income support (IS) or income-based jobseeker's allowance (JSA). However, you might qualify for mortgage interest run-on. If you do, you are paid IS for your housing costs for the first four weeks after you go into full-time paid work, even if the benefit you were claiming was income-based JSA.

Who can claim mortgage interest run-on

You qualify for mortgage interest run-on if:[156]

- you or your partner take up a new job or increase your weekly hours of work and so count as in full-time paid work (see p648). You must expect the work to last for at least five weeks; *and*
- throughout the 26 weeks before the day you count as in full-time paid work, you or your partner were getting IS or income-based JSA. Periods when you were getting mortgage interest run-on do not count towards the 26 weeks;[157] *and*
- on the day before you or your partner commenced the work, your IS or income-based JSA applicable amount included any of the following housing costs:
  - mortgages and other home purchase loans (see p802); *or*
  - loans for repairs and improvements (see p806); *or*
  - 'other housing costs' (see p807); *and*
- you or your partner are still liable to pay the housing costs.

If you qualify, you are paid IS for the housing costs for the first four weeks of full-time paid work.[158] Mortgage interest run-on is paid to you, *not* direct to your lender.[159]

The amount of mortgage interest run-on

You are paid the lowest of:[160]

- the weekly amount of IS or income-based JSA housing costs that you were getting immediately before you or your partner took up full-time paid work. See p808 for information about how these costs are calculated; *or*
- your or your partner's IS or income-based JSA entitlement in the week before you took up full-time paid work (or the amount to which you would have been entitled had you not been getting a training allowance). See pp299 and 368 for information about how your IS or income-based JSA is calculated.

Your mortgage interest run-on can be adjusted if there are changes in:[161]

- the IS applicable amount (see p299);
- the amount of housing costs you can get because:

- the standard rate of interest used to calculate housing costs (see p810) or your non-dependant deductions (see p815) have changed; *or*
- you have been entitled to IS for 26 weeks.

Your earnings from the full-time paid work and any other income you get are disregarded.[162] All of your capital is also disregarded.[163]

Claims

Although you do not have to make a claim to qualify for mortgage interest run-on,[164] you must let your local DWP (or Jobcentre Plus) office know you are starting full-time paid work. Mortgage interest run-on should then be paid automatically.

Tax, tax credits and other benefits

Mortgage interest run-on is not taxable.

Mortgage interest run-on is a payment of IS. You might, therefore, get health benefits and education benefits (see p15). You might also qualify for social fund payments.

Notes

1 **IS** Sch 3 para 4(1)(a) IS Regs
JSA Sch 2 para 4(1)(a) JSA Regs
PC Sch 2 para 5(1)(a) SPC Regs
2 **IS** Sch 3 para 4(1)(b) IS Regs
JSA Sch 2 para 4(1)(b) JSA Regs
PC Sch 2 para 5(1)(b) SPC Regs

1. When you can get help with housing costs

3 **IS** Sch 3 para 1 IS Regs
JSA Sch 2 para 1 JSA Regs
PC Sch 2 para 1 SPC Regs
4 **IS** Sch 3 para 2 IS Regs
JSA Sch 2 para 2 JSA Regs
PC Sch 2 para 3 SPC Regs
5 CSB/213/1987
6 **IS** Sch 3 para 5(5) IS Regs
JSA Sch 2 para 5(5) JSA Regs
PC Sch 2 para 6(5) SPC Regs
All R(IS) 4/95
7 *Ewens v Secretary of State for Social Security*, reported as R(IS) 8/01
8 CIS/636/1992, confirmed by the Court of Appeal in *Brain v CAO*, 2 December 1993
9 **IS** Sch 3 para 2(2) IS Regs
JSA Sch 2 para 2(2) JSA Regs
10 **IS** Reg 2(1) IS Regs
JSA Reg 1(3) JSA Regs
PC Reg 1(2) SPC Regs
All R(SB) 22/87
11 **IS** s137(1) SSCBA 1992
JSA s35(1) JSA 1995
12 **IS** Sch 3 para 3(1) IS Regs
JSA Sch 2 para 3(1) JSA Regs
PC Sch 2 para 4(1) SPC Regs
13 CIS/297/1994
14 **IS** Reg 2(1) IS Regs
JSA Reg 1(3) JSA Regs
PC Reg 1(2) SPC Regs
All Definition of 'dwelling occupied as the home'; s137(1) SSCBA 1992, definition of 'dwelling'

15 *Secretary of State for Work and Pensions v Mohamed Miah*, reported as R(JSA) 9/03
16 **IS** Sch 3 para 3(7) IS Regs
JSA Sch 2 para 3(7) JSA Regs
PC Sch 2 para 4(7) SPC Regs
17 CH/1363/2006; R(H) 4/07
18 R(H) 9/05
19 **IS** Sch 3 para 3(10) IS Regs
JSA Sch 2 para 3(10) JSA Regs
PC Sch 2 para 4(10) SPC Regs
20 **IS** Sch 3 para 3(11) and (12) IS Regs
JSA Sch 2 para 3(11) and (12) JSA Regs
PC Sch 2 para 4(11) and (12) SPC Regs
21 **IS** Sch 3 para 3(8) and (9) IS Regs
JSA Sch 2 para 3(8) and (9) JSA Regs
PC Sch 2 para 4(8) and (9) SPC Regs
22 *Secretary of State for Work and Pensions v Selby District Council and Bowman* [2006] EWCA Civ 271, 13 February 2006, reported as R(H) 4/06
23 CH/1237/2004
24 CH/3893/2004
25 *R v Penwith District Council ex parte Burt* [1990] 22HLR 292, QBD
26 **IS** Sch 3 para 3(5) IS Regs
JSA Sch 2 para 3(5) JSA Regs
PC Sch 2 para 4(5) SPC Regs
27 CIS/719/1994
28 **IS** Sch 3 para 3(6) IS Regs
JSA Sch 2 para 3(6) JSA Regs
PC Sch 2 para 4(6) SPC Regs
29 CH/1911/2006
30 CIS/543/1993
31 CIS/339/1993
32 **IS** Sch 3 para 3(6)(a) IS Regs
JSA Sch 2 para 3(6)(a) JSA Regs
PC Sch 2 para 4(6)(a) SPC Regs
33 **IS** Sch 3 para 3(6)(b) IS Regs
JSA Sch 2 para 3(6)(b) JSA Regs
PC Sch 2 para 4(6)(b) SPC Regs
34 **IS** Sch 3 para 3(3) IS Regs
JSA Sch 2 para 3(3) JSA Regs
PC Sch 2 para 4(3) SPC Regs
35 **IS** Sch 3 para 3(11)(c)(viii) IS Regs
JSA Sch 2 para 3(11)(c)(viii) JSA Regs
PC Sch 2 para 4(11)(c)(viii) SPC Regs
36 **IS** Sch 3 para 3(4) IS Regs
JSA Sch 2 para 3(4) JSA Regs
PC Sch 2 para 4(4) SPC Regs

2. Types of housing costs that can be met

37 CIS/14483/1996
38 **IS** Sch 3 para 15 IS Regs
JSA Sch 2 para 14 JSA Regs
PC Sch 2 para 11 SPC Regs
39 R(IS) 14/01; CPC/3322/2007
40 R(IS) 11/94
41 R(IS) 4/95
42 R(IS) 7/93
43 R(IS) 6/94
44 R(IS) 24/95
45 R(IS) 11/94
46 **IS** Sch 3 para 5 IS Regs
JSA Sch 2 para 5 JSA Regs
PC Sch 2 para 6 SPC Regs
47 **IS** Sch 3 para 4(2) and (4) IS Regs
JSA Sch 2 para 4(2) and (4) JSA Regs
PC Sch 2 para 5(2) and (4) SPC Regs
All *Saleem v Secretary of State for Social Security*, reported as R(IS) 5/01
48 CPC/3226/2005
49 **IS** Sch 3 para 4 (4) IS Regs; reg 32 IS(JSACA) Regs
JSA Sch 2 paras 4(4) and 18(1)(c) JSA Regs
50 para 23466 DMG
51 Sch 2 para 5(2) and (4) SPC Regs
52 **IS** Sch 3 para 4(4A) IS Regs
JSA Sch 2 para 4(4A) JSA Regs
PC Sch 2 para 5(5) SPC Regs
53 **IS** Sch 3 para 4(4B) IS Regs
JSA Sch 2 para 4(4B) JSA Regs
54 **IS** Sch 3 paras 1(3) and (4) and 4(9) IS Regs
JSA Sch 2 paras 1(3) and (4) and 4(9) JSA Regs
PC Sch 2 paras 1(2)(a) and (3) and 5(10) SPC Regs
55 CIS/3295/2003
56 R(IS) 20/98
57 **IS** Sch 3 para 4(10) IS Regs
JSA Sch 2 para 4(10) JSA Regs
PC Sch 2 para 5(11) SPC Regs
All *Saleem v Secretary of State for Social Security* reported as R(IS) 5/01; CIS/1068/2003
58 CIS/14657/1996
59 **IS** Sch 3 para 1(3) and (4) IS Regs
JSA Sch 2 para 1(3) and (4) JSA Regs
PC Sch 2 para 1(2)(a) and (3) SPC Regs
60 **IS** Sch 3 para 4(6) IS Regs
JSA Sch 2 para 4(6) JSA Regs
PC Sch 2 para 5(7) SPC Regs
61 CIS/11293/1995
62 **IS** Sch 3 para 4(8) IS Regs
JSA Sch 2 para 4(8) JSA Regs
PC Sch 2 para 5(9) SPC Regs
All CIS/4712/2002
63 **IS** Sch 3 para 4(11) IS Regs
JSA Sch 2 para 4(11) JSA Regs
PC Sch 2 para 5(12) SPC Regs
64 R(IS) 8/94
65 **IS** Sch 3 para 16 IS Regs
JSA Sch 2 para 15 JSA Regs
PC Sch 2 para 12 SPC Regs
All CIS/1480/2005

66 R(IS) 22/98
67 R(IS) 5/96
68 CIS/14657/1996
69 **IS** Sch 3 para 16(2) IS Regs
JSA Sch 2 para 15(2) JSA Regs
PC Sch 2 para 12(2) SPC Regs
70 CIS/2132/1998
71 R(IS) 16/98
72 CIS/14657/1996
73 **IS** Sch 3 para 17(1) IS Regs
JSA Sch 2 para 16(1) JSA Regs
PC Sch 2 para 13(1) SPC Regs
74 CH/3110/2003; R(H) 3/07
75 **IS** Sch 3 para 17(5) IS Regs
JSA Sch 2 para 16(5) JSA Regs
PC Sch 2 para 13(5) SPC Regs
76 **IS** Sch 3 para 17(3) IS Regs
JSA Sch 2 para 16(3) JSA Regs
PC Sch 2 para 13(3) SPC Regs
77 **IS** Sch 3 para 17(4) IS Regs
JSA Sch 2 para 16(4) JSA Regs
PC Sch 2 para 13(4) SPC Regs
78 **IS** Sch 3 para 17(2) IS Regs
JSA Sch 2 para 16(2) JSA Regs
PC Sch 2 para 13(2) SPC Regs
79 CIS/15036/1996
80 **IS** Sch 3 para 17(2)(b) IS Regs
JSA Sch 2 para 16(2)(b) JSA Regs
PC Sch 2 para 13(2)(b) SPC Regs
81 R(IS) 4/91; CIS/1460/1995; CIS/15036/1996
82 **IS** Sch 3 para 17(2)(c) IS Regs
JSA Sch 2 para 16(2)(c) JSA Regs
PC Sch 2 para 13(2)(c) SPC Regs
83 R(IS) 4/92; R(IS) 19/93
84 CIS/4/1988
85 Reg 3 IS(AT) Regs

3. **The amount of housing costs you get**

86 **IS** Sch 3 para 1A IS Regs
JSA Sch 2 para 1A JSA Regs
PC Sch 2 para 7(4A)-(5) SPC Regs
87 **IS** Sch 3 para 5(5) IS Regs
JSA Sch 2 para 5(5) JSA Regs
PC Sch 2 para 6(5) SPC Regs
88 R(IS) 4/00
89 **IS** Sch 3 para 10 IS Regs
JSA Sch 2 para 9 JSA Regs
PC Sch 2 para 7(1) SPC Regs
90 **IS** Sch 3 para 12 IS Regs
JSA Sch 2 para 11 JSA Regs
PC Sch 2 para 9 SPC Regs
91 **IS** Sch 3 para 7 IS Regs
JSA Sch 2 para 18 JSA Regs
92 Sch 3 para 7(4A) IS Regs
93 **IS** Sch 3 paras 6(1A) and (1B) and 8(1A) and (1B) IS Regs; reg 7(14) and (23) and Sch 3A paras 12 and 13 SS&CS(DA) Regs
JSA Sch 2 paras 6(2) and 7(2)-(2B) JSA Regs; reg 7(18) and (23) and Sch 3A paras 12 and 13 SS&CS(DA) Regs
PC Sch 2 para 7(2) and (4C) SPC Regs; reg 7(17A) SS&CS(DA) Regs
94 Reg 7(17B) and (17C) SS&CS(DA) Regs
95 **IS** Reg 42(4)(a)(ii) IS Regs
JSA Reg 105(10)(a)(ii) JSA Regs
96 **IS** Sch 10 para 26 IS Regs
JSA Sch 8 para 6 JSA Regs
PC Sch 5 para 7 SPC Regs
97 **IS** Sch 3 para 11(4) and (5) IS Regs
JSA Sch 2 para 10(3) and (4) JSA Regs
PC Sch 2 para 8(1) and (2) SPC Regs
98 **IS** Sch 3 para 11(6) IS Regs
JSA Sch 2 para 10(5) JSA Regs
PC Sch 2 para 8(3) SPC Regs
99 Reg 4 IS(G)A No.3 Regs; reg 28 IBS(MA) Regs
100 **IS** Sch 3 para 14(3AA) IS Regs
JSA Sch 2 para 13(4A) JSA Regs
101 **IS** Sch 3 para 13 IS Regs
JSA Sch 2 para 12 JSA Regs
PC Sch 2 para 10 SPC Regs
102 R(IS) 12/91
103 **IS** Sch 3 para 13(2) IS Regs
JSA Sch 2 para 12(2) JSA Regs
PC Sch 2 para 10(2) SPC Regs
104 **IS** Sch 3 para 13(4) and (5) IS Regs
JSA Sch 2 para 12(4) and (5) JSA Regs
PC Sch 2 para 10(4) and (5) SPC Regs
105 R(SB) 7/89
106 R(SB) 6/89; R(SB) 7/89
107 R(IS) 10/93
108 CIS/347/1992
109 CSB/617/1988. This case has been reported as R(SB) 4/89, but the reported version omits the relevant paragraphs.
110 R(SB) 7/89
111 **IS** Sch 3 para 13(3) IS Regs
JSA Sch 2 para 12(3) JSA Regs
PC Sch 2 para 10(3) SPC Regs
112 CJSA/2683/2002
113 R(IS) 9/91; CJSA/2536/2000
114 **IS** Sch 3 para 13(6) IS Regs
JSA Sch 2 para 12(6) JSA Regs
PC Sch 2 para 10(6) SPC Regs
All *Secretary of State for Social Security v Julien*, reported as R(IS) 13/92; R(SB) 7/89; CIS/104/1991
115 CJSA/2536/2000
116 The term 'review' is used in Sch 2 para 10(6) SPC Regs, not the term 'revision' or 'supersession'.

117 **IS** Sch 3 para 13(7) IS Regs
JSA Sch 2 para 12(7) JSA Regs
PC Sch 2 para 10(7) and (10) SPC Regs
118 **IS** Sch 3 para 13(9) IS Regs
JSA Sch 2 para 12(9) JSA Regs
119 Sch 2 para 10(7), (9) and (10) SPC Regs
120 **IS** Reg 3 and Sch 3 para 18 IS Regs
JSA Reg 2 and Sch 2 para 17 JSA Regs
PC Sch 2 paras 1(4)-(9) and 14 SPC Regs
121 CSIS/185/1995
122 **IS** Reg 3(4) and (5) IS Regs
JSA Reg 2(6) and (7) JSA Regs
PC Sch 2 para 1(8) and (9) SPC Regs
123 CIS/14850/1996
124 **IS** Reg 3 IS Regs
JSA Reg 2 JSA Regs
PC Sch 2 para 1(4)-(7) SPC Regs
125 CSB/1163/1988
126 **IS** Sch 3 para 18(6) IS Regs
JSA Sch 2 para 17(6) JSA Regs
PC Sch 2 para 14(6) SPC Regs
127 **IS** Sch 3 para 18(7) IS Regs
JSA Sch 2 para 17(7) JSA Regs
PC Sch 2 para 14(7) SPC Regs
128 s2 ETA 1973 and s2 Enterprise and New Towns (Scotland) Act 1990
129 **IS** Sch 3 para 18(1) and (2) IS Regs
JSA Sch 2 para 17(1) and (2) JSA Regs
PC Sch 2 para 14(1) and (2) SPC Regs
130 Sch 2 para 2(6) SPC Regs
131 **IS** Sch 3 para 18(8) IS Regs
JSA Sch 2 para 17(8) JSA Regs
PC Sch 2 para 14(8) SPC Regs
132 CH/48/2006

4. **Waiting periods**
133 **IS** Sch 3 paras 6 and 8 IS Regs
JSA Sch 2 paras 6 and 7 JSA Regs
134 **IS** Sch 3 para 9 IS Regs
JSA Sch 2 para 8 JSA Regs
135 **IS** Sch 3 para 14(8) and (9) IS Regs
JSA Sch 2 para 13(10) and (11) JSA Regs
136 **IS** Sch 3 paras 1(2) and 6 IS Regs
JSA Sch 2 paras 1(2) and 6 JSA Regs
Both CJSA/2028/2000
137 **IS** Sch 3 paras 1(2) and 8 IS Regs
JSA Sch 2 paras 1(2) and 7 JSA Regs
Both CJSA/2028/2000
138 **IS** Sch 3 para 8(2) and (3) IS Regs
JSA Sch 2 para 7(3)-(6) JSA Regs
139 CIS/5177/1997; R(IS) 12/99; CIS/2790/1998; CIS/3303/1998; CIS/326/2006
140 *Secretary of State for Work and Pensions v W* [2005] EWCA Civ 570, 18 May 2005, reported as R(IS) 9/05; R(IS) 2/01
141 CJSA/679/2004
142 **IS** Sch 3 para 11(2) IS Regs
JSA Sch 2 para 10(1) JSA Regs

5. **Treated as entitled to income support or jobseeker's allowance**
143 Sch 2 para 18(1)(c) JSA Regs
144 Reg 32 IS(JSACA) Regs
145 **IS** Sch 3 para 14(1)(a) and (3A) IS Regs
JSA Sch 2 para 13(1)(a), (2A) and (4) JSA Regs
146 **IS** Sch 3 para 14(2) IS Regs
JSA Sch 2 para 13(2) JSA Regs
147 **IS** Sch 3 para 14(1)(c), (d) and (e), (3A) and (14) IS Regs
JSA Sch 2 para 13(1)(c), (d), (dd) and (e), (4) and (16) JSA Regs
148 **IS** Sch 3 para 14(1)(ee), (3), (3ZA), (3A) and (3B) IS Regs
JSA Sch 2 para 13(1)(ee), (3), (3A) and (4) JSA Regs
149 **IS** Sch 3 para 14(1)(f) and (3A) IS Regs
JSA Sch 2 para 13 (1)(f) and (4) JSA Regs
150 **IS** Sch 3 para 14(4), (5), (5A) and (5B) IS Regs
JSA Sch 2 para 13(5), (6), (7) and (8) JSA Regs
Both Reg 32 IS(JSACA) Regs; CIS/621/2004
151 CJSA/4613/2001
152 **IS** Sch 3 para 14(6) IS Regs
JSA Sch 2 para 13(9) JSA Regs
153 **IS** Sch 3 para 14(11) and (12) IS Regs
JSA Sch 2 para 13(13) and (14) JSA Regs
154 Schemes mentioned in reg 19(1)(r)(i)-(iii) JSA Regs
155 **IS** Sch 3 para 14(13) IS Regs
JSA Sch 2 para 13(15) JSA Regs

6. **Mortgage interest run-on**
156 Reg 6(5) and (8) IS Regs
157 Reg 6(7) IS Regs
158 Reg 6(6) IS Regs
159 Sch 9A para 3(9) SS(C&P) Regs
160 Sch 7 para 19A(1) IS Regs
161 Sch 7 para 19A(2) and (3) IS Regs
162 Schs 8 para 15C and 9 para 74 IS Regs
163 Sch 10 para 62 IS Regs
164 Reg 3(h) SS(C&P) Regs

35

Chapter 35

Income: non-means-tested benefits

This chapter explains the income rules for non-means-tested benefits. It covers:

1. Earnings-related income for non-means-tested benefits (except contribution-based jobseeker's allowance) (below)
2. Earnings-related income for contribution-based jobseeker's allowance (p838)

The term **'earnings-related income'** is used in this chapter to cover both earnings from employment and self-employment (see pp830 and 834) as well as payments from occupational and personal pension schemes (see p838).

This chapter explains which benefits are affected, what counts as earnings and pension payments, how they are calculated, and how they affect your entitlement. However, the rules on how your pension payments affect your entitlement to incapacity benefit are dealt with in Chapter 12.

No other form of income you, any member of your family, or anyone else receives affects your entitlement to any non-means-tested benefit you may be able to claim for yourself or anyone else.

1. Earnings-related income for non-means-tested benefits

The rules in this section apply to all non-means-tested benefits except contribution-based jobseeker's allowance (JSA). For the rules on contribution-based JSA, see p838.

Most non-means-tested benefits are not affected by income. However, some non-means-tested benefits are intended as earnings-replacement benefits and they may be affected by earnings-related income.

Benefits affected by earnings-related income

You are not entitled to any of the following benefits if you earn more than a certain amount:

- carer's allowance (CA);
- incapacity benefit (IB);
- severe disablement allowance (SDA).

Payment of an increase for an adult dependant may be affected by the earnings of your dependant, and payment for a child dependant may be affected by the earnings of your partner.

Carer's allowance

You are not entitled to CA if your earnings are above £95 a week.[1] Earnings of £95 a week or less do not affect the amount to which you are entitled. Only your own earnings count, not those of a partner. Any pension payments you get do not affect your benefit. See p832 for how earnings are worked out. For more about the earnings limit, and when all your earnings can be ignored, see p45. If you stop work and then claim CA, final earnings generally do not affect your entitlement (see p831).

Incapacity benefit and severe disablement allowance

Your IB or SDA can be affected by the following income.

- **Earnings from permitted work.** If you are entitled to IB or SDA while doing 'permitted work' (see p663) the amount you get is not reduced by your earnings but you can only be allowed permitted work if your earnings do not go above certain limits. The permitted work lower limit is £20 a week. The permitted work higher limit is £88.50 a week (this usually goes up in October). Only your own earnings count towards these limits. Pension payments do not count.
- **Councillors' allowances.** IB or SDA is paid at a reduced rate if you are a local councillor and your net allowances are more than £88.50 in a week (the limit usually goes up in October). A basic allowance and special responsibilities allowance is converted into a weekly amount in a set way (eg, if paid monthly, multiply by 12 and divide by 52).[2] Ignore any payments for expenses and, from the allowances, deduct any other expenses incurred in the relevant week in connection with your council duties,[3] but do not deduct any tax or national insurance.[4] Your IB or SDA in that week is reduced by the amount by which the net allowances exceed £88.50.[5]
- **Pensions.** If you get certain kinds of pension payments, these can affect the amount of IB to which you are entitled. See p276 for which pensions count and how they reduce your IB. Any pension payments you get do not affect the amount of SDA to which you are entitled.

It is expected that these rules will apply to contributory employment and support allowance (ESA), due to be introduced in October 2008, in the same way as they do for IB. The limits on earnings from permitted work are also expected to apply to income-related ESA.

Increases for dependants

You may not be entitled to an increase in CA, IB, maternity allowance (MA), retirement pension or SDA for an **adult dependant** if her/his earnings-related income is over the relevant earnings limit. Your adult dependant's earnings (see below) and any pension payments s/he gets (see p838) count towards the limit. For the amount of the earnings limits and more details of how entitlement is affected, see p690.

Increases for **child dependants** in non-means-tested benefits were abolished from 6 April 2003. Those already entitled can continue to get the increase for as long as they remain entitled. Payment of the increase stops if your partner's earnings-related income is over the earnings limit. Your partner's earnings (see below) and any pension payments s/he gets (see p838) count towards the limit. If payments stop for more than eight weeks then entitlement is lost altogether. See p691 for more details.

Earnings

It is important to distinguish between 'earnings' and other types of income because, apart from the rules for contribution-based JSA (see p839) and the rules on how pension payments you receive can affect your IB (see p288), only your earnings and the earnings and pension payments of adult dependants (see p838) can affect your entitlement to non-means-tested benefits.

Earnings are what you get in return for working as opposed to, for example, interest on your savings or social security benefits. What counts as earnings depends on whether you are an employee or self-employed.

Employees

If you are employed by someone else (including employment by a limited company in which you have shares) **'earnings'** means 'any remuneration or profit derived from ... employment'. The main type of income which counts as earnings is, therefore, your wages. The following are also included:[6]

- any bonus or commission (including tips);
- holiday pay (but not if it is payable more than four weeks after your job ends or is interrupted);
- compensation for unfair dismissal and certain other types of compensation under the Employment Rights Act 1996 or under trade union legislation;[7]
- any payments made by your employer for expenses not 'wholly, exclusively and necessarily' incurred in carrying out your job, including any travel

expenses to and from work, and any payments made to you for the cost of arranging care for members of your family;
- a retainer (eg, you may be paid during the school holidays if you work for the school meals service) or a guarantee payment (ie, payment for a workless period under the Employment Rights Act 1996);[8]
- maternity pay, paternity pay, adoption pay and sick pay;[9]
- certain payments at the end of a job (see below).

Note: it is the pay you actually receive which should be taken into account rather than what you may be legally entitled to,[10] so if you receive less than the national minimum wage then it is that lesser amount that counts as your 'earnings'.

The following do not count as earnings:
- periodic payments made as part of a redundancy scheme;[11]
- payments towards expenses that are 'wholly, exclusively and necessarily' incurred in the performance of your employment, such as travelling expenses during the course of your work.[12] In appropriate circumstances these could, for example, include:
  - tools or work equipment;
  - special clothing or uniform;[13]
  - telephone costs (including rental);[14]
  - postage;
  - fuel costs (including standing charges);
  - secretarial expenses;[15] *and*
  - the costs of running a car (including petrol, tax, insurance, repairs and maintenance and rental on a leased car).[16]

Where any expenditure serves a dual purpose for both business and private use it should be apportioned as appropriate to the circumstances (and any determination by the Revenue should normally be followed).[17]

Payments at the end of a job

If you stop work and claim CA, final earnings generally do not affect your benefit. The same applies if your partner stops work and you claim an increase to a non-means-tested benefit for her/him. As long as your entitlement begins after the employment ends, earnings disregarded are:[18]
- final wages, paid or due, including bonus, commission, tips and expenses that count as earnings;
- holiday pay;
- pay in lieu of notice;
- pay in lieu of remuneration (eg, loss of earnings payment to a councillor);
- statutory or contractual redundancy pay and other compensation payments (other than from an employment tribunal complaint).

Certain final payments are taken into account (unless you are retiring over pension age):

- maternity pay, paternity pay, adoption pay and sick pay;
- employment tribunal award or settlement of a complaint to a tribunal or court (ie, compensation for unfair dismissal and certain other types of compensation under the Employment Rights Act 1996 or under trade union legislation);[19]
- a retainer.

Your partner's occupational or personal pension counts if you are claiming an increase for her/him (see p838).

If you are already entitled to CA or a dependency increase while working, final earnings when you stop work are not disregarded.

For **IB** and **SDA**, if you stop doing permitted work, final earnings do count towards the earnings limit but not after your final working week (see p662).

Calculating net earnings from employment

For the earnings rules for the non-means-tested benefits in this *Handbook* (other than contribution-based JSA – see p838), your 'earnings' are your net earnings. **'Net' earnings** are your 'gross' earnings less any deductions made for income tax, Class 1 national insurance (NI) contributions (but not Class 3 voluntary contributions[20]) and half of any contribution you make towards a personal or occupational pension scheme.[21] It is the amount of your earnings calculated on a weekly basis which is important.[22] So, for example, if you are paid monthly, this figure will be multiplied by 12 and divided by 52 to arrive at a weekly figure.[23] If you are paid for a period of less than a week, this payment will be treated as a payment for a week.[24]

If your earnings fluctuate and have changed more than once, or your employment is such that you do not work every week, your weekly earnings may be averaged as follows:[25]

- if you have a regular pattern of work, over one complete 'cycle' of work. This includes periods where you do no work if this forms part of your regular pattern of work (eg, if you regularly work three weeks on and one week off, your earnings will be averaged over four weeks); *or*
- in any other case, over five weeks, or whatever other period will enable your weekly earnings to be assessed more accurately.[26]

The date from when earnings from employment are counted

You are usually treated as having received earnings on the first day of the benefit week in which they are due to be paid.[27] The **'benefit week'** is the seven days corresponding to the week for which the particular benefit you are claiming is paid (see the relevant chapter for the benefit you are claiming).[28]

The exception to this is if you are claiming:

- an increase in MA or CA for an adult dependant (see p686); *or*
- an increase in your Category A retirement pension for an adult dependant who does not live with you (see p686),

in which case earnings are treated as having been paid on the first day of the benefit week after the week in which they are due to be paid.[29]

The date that a payment is due may well be different from the date of actual payment. Earnings are due on the employee's normal payday. If your contract of employment does not reveal the date when the payment is due and there is no evidence to suggest differently, the date the payment was received should be taken as the date it was due.[30]

If your contract of employment is terminated without proper notice, outstanding wages, wages in hand, holiday pay and any pay in lieu of notice are due on the last day of employment and are treated as paid on that day, even if this does not happen.[31] (See p831 for when these final payments are disregarded.) If an employment tribunal awards you compensation for loss of earnings (eg, for being dismissed in circumstances constituting sex discrimination), the relevant date is the date when the earnings in question were due to be paid, not when the compensation was awarded.[32]

The period covered by earnings from employment

Your earnings count for a future period starting from the date worked out above. The length of that period is worked out as follows.

- Where a payment of income is made in respect of an identifiable period, it is taken into account for the number of benefit weeks corresponding to that period.[33] For example, a week's part-time earnings are taken into account for a week.
- If the payment does not relate to a particular period, the amount of the payment is divided by the amount of the weekly earnings limit (see pp690 and 829) plus one penny and then rounded down to the nearest whole number. If part of the payment should be disregarded (see p834), the weekly earnings limit is increased (for the purpose of this calculation only) by the amount of the appropriate disregard (see p834). The result of this calculation is the number of full weeks for which you will not get benefit.[34]

Example

Bob receives a Category A retirement pension with an increase for his wife, who lives with him. She receives £700 net earnings for work which cannot be attributed to any specific period of time. The £700 figure includes a tax refund of £150 paid through the PAYE system.

The earnings limit for the dependant's increase is £60.50.

The £150 tax refund is disregarded.

The period over which the income is taken into account is

£700 ÷ (£60.50 + £0.01 + £150) =
£700 ÷ 210.51 = 3.33 weeks
This means that Bob is not entitled to the dependant's increase for three weeks.

Self-employed people

If you are self-employed, your weekly earnings (including any allowance from a DWP scheme to assist you with your business[35]) are averaged over a period of a year unless:

- you have recently become self-employed; *or*
- there has been a change which is likely to affect the normal pattern of your business,

in which case, your earnings are averaged over whatever other period the decision maker considers will give the most accurate figure.[36] This means that when you first claim, the decision maker will need you to provide an up-to-date set of accounts. If you receive royalties or payments from copyrights, the period for which these payments will count is calculated in a similar way to payments made for unspecified periods to employees.[37]

The figure used for your earnings is your 'net profit' from self-employment or, if you are a member of a partnership or a share fisherman, your share of the net profit. Unless you are a childminder (in which case, see below) your 'net profit' is calculated taking your earnings over the period and deducting:[38]

- expenses incurred during the period wholly and exclusively for the purposes of the business. Where a car or telephone, for example, is used partly for business and partly for private purposes, the costs of it can be apportioned and the amount attributable to business use can be deducted.[39] Certain expenses cannot be deducted, including business entertainment, repayment of capital on a business loan, capital expenditure and depreciation, or for providing board and lodging or renting a room in your home;
- income tax and NI contributions;[40] *and*
- half of any contributions you have made during the period towards a personal pension scheme or retirement annuity contract.

Childminders are always treated as self-employed. If you are a childminder, your net profit is deemed to be one-third of your earnings less income tax, your NI contributions and half of certain pension contributions (see p832).[41] The rest of your earnings are completely ignored.

Disregarded earnings

Some of your income which might otherwise be classed as earnings is specifically disregarded and does not affect your benefit. Some care and childcare costs can also be disregarded. The same earnings disregards apply whether you are an employee or self-employed (and, if you are a childminder, they apply in addition to the other disregards explained on p834).

Earnings which can be disregarded are:[42]

- any payment made to you by someone who normally lives with you on an informal or non-contractual basis as part of her/his contribution towards shared living expenses;
- the first £20 a week of any income for renting out room(s) in your home;
- the first £20 of any income you receive each week for providing board and lodging in your home. If you get more than £20 a week, then 50 per cent of the excess is also disregarded. This disregard applies to each person who lodges with you – eg, if you are providing bed and breakfast accommodation and in one week five different people each stay for one night and pay £20 each, then the full £100 is disregarded;
- payments from a local authority or voluntary organisation for fostering or accommodating a child under formal arrangements;
- payments from a health authority, local authority or voluntary organisation for providing temporary care. There is no set time after which care is no longer temporary. In one case, a carer could not have payments disregarded for a placement that had lasted five years;[43]
- refunds of Schedule D income tax or what was formerly Schedule E income tax and now comes under IT(EP)A 2003;
- if you are an employee, any loan or advance of earnings from your employer;
- certain bounty payments made to part-time firefighters, auxiliary coastguards, members of the territorial or reserve armed forces and part-time lifeboat crews;
- unless you are abroad yourself, earnings payable abroad which cannot be brought into Great Britain (eg, because of exchange control regulations);
- unless you are abroad yourself, if your earnings are paid in another currency, any bank charges for converting them into sterling.

Childcare costs[44]

In addition to the earnings disregards, certain childcare costs may also be deducted from earnings. The following rules apply to claims for those benefits and dependency increases listed on p828 except that different rules (see p837) apply to the treatment of childcare costs if you are claiming CA (although the following rules do apply to CA dependency increases).

An allowance of up to a maximum of £60 a week may be deducted from your earnings if:

- you are a lone parent; *or*
- you are a member of a couple and both you and your partner are working (full or part time); *or*
- you are a member of a couple and your partner is incapacitated (see p836).

This will only apply if you have any child(ren) in your family under the age of 11 for whom you are paying charges for childcare (not counting charges paid by you to your partner or by your partner to you, or charges in respect of compulsory education) which is provided:

- by a registered childminder or other registered childcare provider (such as a nursery or after-school club for the under-eights); *or*
- for children aged eight or over but under 11, by a school on school premises or by a local authority (eg, an out-of-hours or holiday play scheme); *or*
- by a childcare scheme operating on Crown property; *or*
- in schools or establishments exempt from registration.[45]

Your partner counts as '**incapacitated**' if:[46]

- s/he is getting long-term IB, SDA, attendance allowance, disability living allowance (or an equivalent award under the war pensions or industrial injuries schemes), or would have been if s/he were not a hospital inpatient; *or*
- s/he is provided with an invalid carriage or other vehicle by the NHS; *or*
- you or your partner are getting housing benefit or council tax benefit and either childcare costs have been allowed for under the rules applying to claims for those benefits (see p856) or else a disability premium or higher pensioner premium for your partner has been awarded.

As childcare costs are likely to vary considerably between term time and holiday periods, a formula is used to assess the costs that will be taken into account.

Where charges are paid monthly, the amount is:

- if the charge is for a fixed amount, that amount multiplied by 12 and divided by 52; *or*
- if the charge is variable, 1/52 of the total charges over the previous 12 months.

Where charges are paid other than monthly, the amount is either:

- 1/52 of the total of:
  - the average weekly charge in the four most recent complete weeks falling in term time, multiplied by 39; *and*
  - the average weekly charge in the two most recent complete weeks falling out of term time, multiplied by 13; *or*
- if your child does not yet attend school, the average weekly charge in the four most recent complete weeks.

However, if there is no, or insufficient, information available to calculate your childcare costs in these ways (eg, you have just started to use a childminder), an estimate will be made based on the information provided by the childcare provider or, if that is not available, by the claimant.[47]

Notes on childcare costs

- Childcare allowances apply separately to each individual in respect of whom benefit is claimed. For example, the childcare costs you and your partner pay may be deducted from your earnings on your own IB, as well as on your award of an adult dependency increase of IB in respect of your partner's earnings.
- Similarly, the same childcare costs may apply to a claim for CA for yourself, as well as on a claim for a CA dependency increase. Because different rules apply, however, the same childcare costs may be allowed on one claim but not on the other (eg, if your child is over 11, your costs may be deducted from your earnings on a claim for yourself, but will not be deducted from your partner's earnings on a claim for a dependency increase).
- Whether or not childcare costs are taken into account on a claim for a non-means-tested benefit, different rules apply for claims for any means-tested benefit (see p856).

Care costs and carer's allowance[48]

If you are getting CA and because of your work you have to pay for someone (other than a 'close relative') to look after the severely disabled person you care for or to look after a child(ren) under 16 for whom you or your partner are getting child benefit, then (in addition to any disregarded earnings), those care costs can be deducted when your earnings are calculated. The maximum deduction is 50 per cent of the figure which would otherwise be your net earnings. Any disregarded income is deducted from your net earnings before calculating the 50 per cent figure. **'Close relative'** means a parent, son, daughter, brother, sister or partner (see p702) of you or the severely disabled person for whom you care. There is, therefore, no restriction on charges paid to someone who is only a close relative of the child being looked after (eg, the parent of the child if you are not married and s/he is not also your partner).

Notional earnings

You will be deemed to have notional earnings only if it is not possible to work out your earnings when your claim is decided.[49] This may apply if, for example, you have just started employment and your pay depends on your performance, or you have just started a business and there is no way of calculating what profits you will make. If so, you will be treated as earning such amount as is considered reasonable taking into account the number of hours you work and the earnings paid for comparable work in the area.

Estimates of the appropriate deductions for income tax and NI contributions, and half of any occupational or personal pension contributions, are deducted from your notional earnings, as are any earnings disregards or allowances for childcare or care costs.

Pension payments

For all claims for dependency increases, certain pension payments, including periodic payments from the Pension Protection Fund, count as earnings.[50]

All the following periodical payments of an occupational or personal pension made in connection with the ending of a person's employment count as earnings if they are paid:

- out of money provided wholly or partly by or under arrangements made by an employer; *or*
- under an approved personal pension, contract or trust scheme; *or*
- under a statutory scheme.[51]

This covers most pension payments, including early retirement schemes for those who retire early on health grounds or for other reasons,[52] or, in some cases, those who volunteer for redundancy.[53]

However, it does not include lump-sum or redundancy payments which are not related to a specific period, even if you have chosen to receive a lump sum instead of a periodical payment (although if you choose to receive payments in instalments, even if you do not have to, they will count).[54]

Only pension payments made in respect of the person for whom benefit is being claimed count. Payments made because of the ending of someone else's employment (eg, the pension received by a widow or widower on account of her/his late spouse's employment) do not count.[55]

Calculation of weekly pension payments

The amount of the pension to be taken into account is the gross amount paid less any deductions for income tax, less any compulsory reductions made by the pension scheme if the rules of the scheme require this for the purpose of acquiring additional pension rights.[56]

All pension payments are converted into equivalent weekly amounts[57] and any pension payment is counted from the first day of the benefit week in which it is actually made.

2. Earnings-related income for contribution-based jobseeker's allowance

Any earnings and pension payments you receive can affect your entitlement to contribution-based jobseeker's allowance (JSA). Any other income you receive does not affect your contribution-based JSA. Similarly, any savings you have and any income (including earnings and pension payments) or savings of any member of your family do not affect your entitlement to contribution-based JSA. For the rules on the treatment of any income or savings of yours, or any member of your family, on a claim for income-based JSA, see Chapters 36 and 37.

Earnings

The rules on the treatment of earnings for contribution-based JSA are different from the rules which apply to other non-means-tested benefits explained on p830. Although all other rules on the treatment of income are different, most of the earnings rules for income-based JSA apply in the same way to contribution-based JSA.[58] For an explanation of how each of the following applies to contribution-based JSA, you should, therefore, read the relevant section of Chapter 36 as it applies to income-based JSA:

- what counts as earnings (p848);
- how earnings are assessed (p876);
- calculating net earnings from employment (p847);
- calculating net earnings from self-employment (p852);
- working out average earnings from self-employment (p853);
- childminders (p854);
- payments at the end of a job (p849);
- converting income into a weekly amount (p877);
- the period covered by income (p878); *and*
- the date from which a payment is counted (p879).

Although these rules are the same, different rules apply to disregarded earnings and how earnings affect your contribution-based JSA. These are explained below.

Disregarded earnings

For contribution-based JSA, £5 a week of your earnings is disregarded. If you are an auxiliary coastguard, a part-time firefighter, a part-time lifeboat crewmember or a member of the territorial or reserve forces, £20 a week is disregarded.[59]

How earnings affect your benefit

Your benefit is reduced by the full amount of any earnings you receive over the amount of disregarded earnings.[60] You are not entitled to contribution-based JSA for any week in which your earnings exceed a prescribed amount (see below).[61] The days in any week when your earnings exceed the prescribed amount do not count towards your maximum 182 days of contribution-based JSA (see p367).

Calculating the 'prescribed amount'

The 'prescribed amount' is not the same for everyone. It is calculated by adding the amount of the relevant earnings disregard to the rate of contribution-based JSA paid to someone your age (see p367), and then deducting one penny.

Example

Maggie, aged 35, is entitled to contribution-based JSA of £60.50 a week. She works part time. Her earnings disregard is £5 a week. Applying the formula: (£60.50 + £5) – £0.01 = £65.49. If Maggie earns more than £65.49 a week she is not entitled to contribution-based JSA.

Pension payments

Certain pension payments you receive may also affect your contribution-based JSA.[62] Your contribution-based JSA is reduced by the amount of weekly pension *above* £50 a week, regardless of your age. A pension of £50 or less a week is ignored for contribution-based JSA.[63] In this context, **'pension payments'** means periodical payments made under:[64]

- a personal pension scheme; *or*
- a pension connected with the ending of your employment as an earner under an occupational pension scheme or a public service pension scheme; *or*
- Pension Protection Fund and Financial Assistance Scheme payments (paid when occupational schemes close because of employer insolvency).

Although the meaning of pension payments is slightly different than that applying to other non-means-tested benefits, it should still cover most periodical pension payments (including contractual redundancy/early retirement payments[65]) as explained on p838, and identical rules apply to the calculation of weekly pension payments.[66] **Note:** lump-sum payments may still count as pension payments for the purposes of JSA if they are calculated on the basis of a weekly or monthly entitlement.[67]

The amount of your pension payments may mean that you are not paid any JSA. However, unless your earnings also exceed the prescribed amount (see p839) you remain *entitled* to contribution-based JSA even though it is not paid because your pension payments are too high (so long as you also satisfy the other conditions for getting JSA – see p339). Any day on which you are entitled to JSA even if it is not paid counts towards your 182 days' entitlement to contribution-based JSA (see p367). A combination of earnings and pension payments may also mean that you are not paid any JSA, even though you may remain entitled to it.

Any pension payments you receive because of the death of the person who was a member of the pension scheme are ignored when calculating your contribution-based JSA.[68] For example, if your late partner was a member of a scheme, any payment made to you following her/his death does not affect your contribution-based JSA.

Any pension payment you receive is counted from the first day of the benefit week in which the payment is actually made to you.[69]

Example

Brian claims JSA and is entitled to contribution-based JSA from Wednesday 7 May 2008. His benefit week begins on a Friday (his signing-on day is Thursday). He starts receiving a personal pension of £68 a week from Monday 12 May 2008. £18 a week is deducted from his contribution-based JSA (£68 – £50) from the benefit week starting Friday 9 May 2007.

If your pension is increased when you are on contribution-based JSA, the change should be taken into account from the first day of the benefit week in which the increase is paid.[70]

Notes

1. **Earnings-related income for non-means-tested benefits**
   1 Reg 8 SS(ICA) Regs
   2 Reg 9 SS(IB) Regs
   3 s30E(3) SSCBA 1992
   4 R(IB) 3/01
   5 s30E(1) SSCBA 1992; reg 8 SS(IB) Regs
   6 Reg 9 SSB(CE) Regs
   7 Reg 9(1)(g) and (h) SSB(CE) Regs
   8 CIS/743/1992
   9 Reg 9(1)(j) SSB(CE) Regs
   10 R(IB) 7/03
   11 Reg 9(1)(b) SSB(CE) Regs
   12 Reg 9(3) SSB(CE) Regs; *Parsons v Hogg* [1985] 2 All ER 897 (CA), appendix to R(FIS) 4/85
   13 R(FC) 1/90
   14 CFC/26/1989
   15 R(FIS) 4/85
   16 R(IS) 13/91; R(IS) 16/93; CFC/26/1989
   17 R(U) 2/72; R(FIS) 4/85; R(FC) 1/91; R(IS) 13/91
   18 Sch 1 para 12 SSB(CE) Regs
   19 Reg 9(1)(g) and (h) SSB(CE) Regs
   20 CIS/521/1990
   21 Reg 10(4) SSB(CE) Regs
   22 Reg 6(1) SSB(CE) Regs
   23 Reg 8(1)(b)(i) SSB(CE) Regs
   24 Reg 8(1)(a) SSB(CE) Regs
   25 Reg 8(3) SSB(CE) Regs
   26 CG/4941/2003
   27 Reg 7(b) SSB(CE) Regs
   28 Reg 2(1) SSB(CE) Regs
   29 Reg 7(a) SSB(CE) Regs
   30 R(SB) 33/83
   31 R(SB) 22/84; R(SB) 11/85
   32 CIS/590/1993
   33 Reg 6(2)(a) SSB(CE) Regs
   34 Reg 6(2)(b) SSB(CE) Regs
   35 Reg 12(1) SSB(CE) Regs
   36 Reg 11(1) SSB(CE) Regs
   37 Reg 11(2) SSB(CE) Regs
   38 Reg 13(1)(a) and (b), (4) and (5) SSB(CE) Regs
   39 R(IS) 13/91; R(FC) 1/91; CFC/26/1989
   40 See also reg 14 SSB(CE) Regs
   41 Reg 13(10) SSB(CE) Regs
   42 Sch 1 SSB(CE) Regs
   43 CG/1752/2006
   44 Regs 10(2) and 13(2) and Sch 2 SSB(CE) Regs
   45 Sch 2 para 2 SSB(CE) Regs
   46 Sch 2 para 8 SSB(CE) Regs
   47 Sch 2 paras 4-7 SSB(CE) Regs
   48 Regs 10(3) and 13(3) and Sch 3 SSB(CE) Regs
   49 Reg 4(1) and (3) SSB(CE) Regs and CIB/1650/2002, disapplying reg 4(2) of these Regs
   50 s89 SSCBA 1992; Sch 2 para 9 SSB(Dep) Regs
   51 s122(1) SSCBA 1992
   52 CP/7/1987
   53 CU/66/1993
   54 R(U) 5/85
   55 para 15283 DMG

56 R(U) 4/83; para 15286 DMG
57 Reg 9A SSB(Dep) Regs; para 15290 DMG

2. **Earnings-related income for contribution-based jobseeker's allowance**

58 Reg 80 JSA Regs
59 Regs 99(3) and 101(3) and Sch 6 JSA Regs
60 Reg 80 JSA Regs
61 s2(1)(c) JSA 1995; reg 56(1) and (2) JSA Regs
62 s4(1) JSA 1995
63 Reg 81(1) JSA Regs
64 s35(1) JSA 1995
65 R(JSA) 1/01
66 Reg 81 JSA Regs; para 23931 DMG
67 R(JSA) 6/02
68 Reg 81(2)(c) JSA Regs
69 Reg 81(1A) JSA Regs
70 Reg 81(1B) JSA Regs

Chapter 36

Income: means-tested benefits

This chapter explains the rules for working out your weekly income for means-tested benefits. It covers:

1. People aged under 60 (p844)
2. People aged 60 or over (p880)

Your entitlement to income support (IS), income-based jobseeker's allowance (JSA), pension credit (PC), housing benefit (HB) and council tax benefit (CTB) and the amount you receive depends on how much income you have.

Note: if you get IS, income-based JSA or the guarantee credit of PC you do not need to work out your income again for HB or CTB purposes (see pp84 and 190).[1]

In each case some of your income may be completely ignored, *or* partially ignored, *or* counted in full. Some income may be treated as capital (see p915) and some capital may be treated as income (see p867). There are some important differences in the rules on income for urgent cases payments under the IS and income-based JSA schemes. These are set out on p1344.

The rules described in this chapter about *earnings* (as opposed to other forms of income) for income-based JSA are also relevant when applying the earnings rules for contribution-based JSA. However, for contribution-based JSA, only the claimant's earnings are relevant, and never the earnings of other members of her/his family.[2] For further information about the earnings rules for contribution-based JSA, see p838.

For information about the earnings rules for certain other non-means-tested benefits, see Chapter 35.

For the treatment of earnings and other income on claims for certain health benefits, see p172.

For the rules on income for tax credits, see Chapter 52.

Note: unless otherwise stated, references to income-based JSA are intended also to refer to joint-claim JSA.

1. People aged under 60

This part applies to:

- income support (IS) – including those over 60 with a partner under 60 claiming IS;
- income-based jobseeker's allowance (JSA) – including men aged 60 to 64;
- housing benefit (HB) and council tax benefit (CTB) if you and your partner (if you have one) are aged under 60.

The rules for IS, JSA, HB and CTB are very similar. Where there are differences these are indicated.

Note: in this part, whenever HB or CTB is referred to, this only applies to the rules for people aged under 60.

When the new **employment and support allowance** (ESA) is introduced, due in October 2008, it is expected that the rules for working out how much income you have for income-related ESA will be very similar to those for IS. For more information, see www.cpag.org.uk/esa or CPAG's *Welfare Rights Bulletin*.

Whose income counts

Income of a partner

If you are a member of a couple (see p702), your partner's income is added to yours.[3]

Note: for HB and CTB, if you or your partner (if you have one) are getting IS or income-based JSA all of your (and your partner's) income is ignored.[4]

If, for IS/income-based JSA, you receive the reduced rate of the normal personal allowance for a couple because your partner is under 18 and not eligible for IS or income-based JSA (see p773), an amount of her/his income equivalent to the reduction is ignored.[5]

Example

Kalid is 19. His partner, Kate, is 17 and is not able to claim IS or income-based JSA. Kalid's personal allowance is £47.95 (the rate for a single person aged 18–24). If Kate was eligible for IS or income-based JSA, their personal allowance would be £94.95. Up to £47 (£94.95 – £47.95) of any income that Kate has is ignored.

Income of a dependent child

The income of a dependent child does *not* affect the following benefits:

- IS or income-based JSA[6] – unless you have been getting benefit since before 6 April 2004 with a child included in your claim and you do not yet have a child tax credit (CTC) award (see p845);
- HB and CTB;[7]

- any benefit – for income of certain 16/17-year-olds who leave local authority care. They do not count as members of your family so their income is not counted in with yours.[8]

Although in the above cases a dependent child's income does not affect your benefit, if the child has left school/college and is working 24 hours a week or more, you can usually no longer get benefit for her/him (see p68).

Maintenance paid to or for a child counts as your income (see 751), but some may be disregarded (see p862).

The income of a dependent child may affect **IS and income-based JSA**, but only if you have been getting benefit since before 6 April 2004 with a child included in your claim and you do not yet have an award of CTC. Once CTC is awarded, amounts for children are no longer included in your IS or income-based JSA and any income of a dependent child is ignored.

Even when you still have a child included in your IS or JSA claim, if your child has capital of over £3,000, you do not get benefit for her/him[9] (although you can still get a family premium) and her/his income is not counted as yours.[10] If your child has capital of £3,000 or less, any income is treated as yours but may be disregarded as follows.[11]

- Earnings of a dependent child at school/college are ignored.
- Earnings from part-time work (less than 16 hours a week) of a dependent child are ignored even if s/he has left school.
- If a child has left school/college and is working 24 hours or more a week, you usually do not get benefit for her/him and her/his earnings do not count with yours. If s/he is working 16 hours or more but less than 24 hours a week, earnings are treated as your income while you are still entitled to claim for that child (eg, during the summer holidays). Ignore £5 a week and any earnings above the child's personal allowance.
- If you get a disabled child premium for your child, earnings are still treated as your income as described above, but you ignore £20 a week and any earnings above the the child's personal allowance, disabled child premium and any enhanced disability premium. All your disabled child's earnings are ignored if her/his earnings capacity is less than 75 per cent of what it would be if s/he was not disabled.[12]
- Income other than earnings and maintenance is taken into account up to the level of the child's personal allowance, and any disabled child premium and enhanced disability premium. Income above that level is ignored.[13]

What counts as income

All income is taken into account for IS and income-based JSA except for income that is specifically disregarded.

If you get IS or income-based JSA, all your income is ignored for HB and CTB. If you do not get IS or income-based JSA, all income is taken into account for HB and CTB other than income that is specifically disregarded.

The way income from employment and self-employment is treated is explained below and on p852. Some of your earnings are disregarded (see p854). Most other types of income are taken into account, less any tax due on them.[14] For HB and CTB, changes in tax and national insurance (NI) rates and in the maximum rate of CTC or working tax credit (WTC) may be ignored for up to 30 weeks,[15] as for earnings (see p847).

Income will only count if it is paid to you for your own use, and will not count if you cannot prevent it being paid to a third party – eg, under an attachment of earnings order, although other payments for you made to a third party might count (see p874).[16]

Income is converted into a weekly amount (see p877).

Income or capital?

The difference between income and capital is not defined. Payments of income are normally made in respect of a specified period or periods and form, or are intended to form, part of a regular series of payments.[17] In this way, payments of income can usually be distinguished from payments of capital. However, some income is treated as capital (see p915) and some capital is treated as income (see p867).

Earnings of employed earners

This section explains how any earnings received by you or your partner and, in some cases, a dependent child (see p844) are treated for any claim for IS, income-based JSA and, if you and your partner are aged under 60, for HB and CTB. The same rules apply to your (but not your partner's or child's) earnings if you are claiming contribution-based JSA (for further information, see p838). For the rules on earnings for non-means-tested benefits, see Chapter 35.

To work out how earnings are taken into account:

- check whether payments count as earnings (see p848). In some cases payments are treated as capital, or as income other than earnings, or ignored altogether;
- calculate net earnings (see p847);
- work out weekly earnings (see p876);
- deduct the appropriate weekly earnings disregard of £5, £10, £20 or £25 (see p854) and, for HB and CTB, if you qualify, the additional earnings disregard (see p855) and disregard for childcare costs (see p856);
- for HB and CTB, the amount worked out as above is your weekly income from earnings in the benefit assessment. For IS and income-based JSA, work out the period covered by payments of earnings (see p878). Normally a payment counts from the date it is due to be paid, for the length of time it has been paid

for – eg, a month's wages count for a month, starting from the day they are due, at the weekly rate as calculated (see p876).

There are special rules for how payments affect benefit when you leave a job (see p849).

Calculating net earnings from employment

Both your 'gross' earnings and 'net' earnings need to be calculated so that a proper assessment can be made of your income from employment.

'Gross' earnings means the amount of earnings received from your employer less deductions for any expenses wholly, necessarily and exclusively incurred by you in order to carry out the duties of your employment.[18] For example, deductions could be made for:

- tools or work equipment;
- special clothing or uniform;[19]
- telephone costs (including rental);[20]
- postage;
- fuel costs (including standing charges);
- secretarial expenses;[21]
- running a car (including petrol, tax, insurance, repairs and maintenance and rental on a leased car);[22]
- armed forces local overseas allowance (for extra overseas living expenses),[23] but not lodgings allowances if you are stationed in the UK,[24] and probably not rent allowances for police officers;[25]
- professional expenses for membership fees to an approved body if also deducted for income tax.[26]

Where any expenditure serves a dual purpose for both business and private use, it should be apportioned as appropriate to the circumstances (and any Revenue determination normally followed).[27]

'Net' earnings means your gross earnings less any deductions made for:

- income tax;
- Class 1 NI contributions (but not Class 3 voluntary contributions[28]);
- half of any contribution you make towards a personal or occupational pension scheme.[29]

For HB and CTB, if your earnings are estimated the authorities estimate the amount of tax and NI you would expect to pay on those earnings, and deduct this plus half of any pension contribution you are paying.[30]

For HB and CTB, the local authority has the discretion to ignore changes in tax or NI contributions and the maximum rate of WTC or CTC for up to 30 benefit weeks. This can be used, for example, where Budget changes are not reflected in your actual income until several months later. When the changes are eventually taken into account and your benefit entitlement is either increased or reduced accordingly, you are not treated as having been underpaid or overpaid benefit during the period of the delay.[31]

What counts as earnings

'**Earnings**' means 'any remuneration or profit derived from ... employment'.

As well as your wages, this includes:[32]

- any bonus or commission (including tips);
- holiday pay (but see p849 if your job ends or you are off work);
- for HB and CTB, any statutory sick pay (SSP) or contractual sick pay.[33] For IS and income-based JSA all sick pay is treated as income other than earnings and, therefore, does not attract an earnings disregard and is counted in full less any tax, Class 1 NI contributions and half of any pension contributions;[34]
- for HB and CTB, any statutory maternity pay (SMP), statutory paternity pay (SPP) or statutory adoption pay (SAP), or any other pay made to you by your employer while you are on maternity, paternity or adoption leave.[35] For IS and income-based JSA all maternity, paternity or adoption pay is treated as income other than earnings and therefore does not attract an earnings disregard and is counted in full less any tax that is payable, Class 1 NI contributions and half of any pension contributions;[36]
- any payments made by your employer for expenses not 'wholly, exclusively and necessarily' incurred in carrying out your job, including any travel expenses to and from work, and any payments made to you for looking after members of your family;
- a retainer (eg, you may be paid during the school holidays if you work for the school meals service[37]) or a guarantee payment (eg, if you are working short time or laid off);[38]
- certain compensation payments in respect of the termination of your employment, including employment tribunal awards and pay in lieu of notice (see p849 for the way these are treated when you stop work). For IS/JSA, compensatory refunds of contributions to an occupational scheme[39] are not treated as earnings;
- any payment of a non-cash voucher which is liable for Class 1 NI contributions.[40] Non-cash vouchers that are *not* liable for contributions are classed as payments in kind (see below).[41]

Examples of payments not counted as earnings:

- Payments in kind (eg, petrol) are ignored[42] unless you are on IS or income-based JSA and involved in a trade dispute (see p633), although the notional income rules may be applied instead (see p873).[43] Although non-cash vouchers which are liable for Class 1 NI contributions are not treated as payments in kind, vouchers which are not liable for contributions (eg, certain childcare and charitable vouchers) are treated as payments in kind and these are disregarded.[44]

- The value of any accommodation provided as part of your job is ignored for IS and income-based JSA.[45] For CTB, and for HB where job-related accommodation is in addition to the normal home, you should argue that this is payment in kind[46] and should be disregarded.
- An advance of earnings or a loan from your employer. This is treated as capital[47] (although it is still treated as earnings for IS or income-based JSA if you or your partner are involved in a trade dispute, or have been back at work after a dispute for no longer than 15 days).[48]
- Payments towards expenses that are 'wholly, exclusively and necessarily' incurred, such as travelling expenses during the course of your work.[49]
- If you are a local councillor, travelling expenses and subsistence payments are (and basic allowances may be[50]) ignored as expenses 'wholly, exclusively and necessarily' incurred in your work.
- Earnings payable abroad which cannot be brought into Britain – eg, because of exchange control regulations.[51] If your earnings are paid in another currency, any bank charges for converting them into sterling are deducted before taking them into account.[52]
- Any occupational pension.[53] This counts as income other than earnings and the net amount is taken into account in full.[54] See p839 for the occupational pension rules for contribution-based JSA.

Payments when you stop work

When you stop work and claim benefit, your final earnings are usually ignored with some exceptions. But if you were claiming benefit while working, final earnings are generally taken into account, as explained below.

Your job ends before benefit starts

If your employment ends before your entitlement to benefit begins, any payments that count as earnings (see p848) are ignored for that benefit including wages, holiday pay (but see p850) and pay in lieu of notice, except for the following payments, which are taken into account:[55]

- a retainer counts as earnings;
- if you were in full-time work, certain employment tribunal awards (and 'out of court' settlements) count as earnings, including:
  - compensation because of unfair dismissal;[56]
  - a 'protective' award when an employer fails to comply with redundancy procedures and, for JSA, a compensatory award in respect of trade union activity;[57]
  - for IS, HB and CTB, pay under a continuation of contract award or for arrears of pay in respect of a reinstatement order;[58]
  - guarantee payments while suspended from work on medical or maternity grounds;[59]

an award is usually taken into account for IS or JSA from when it is due to be paid, even if not actually paid then, for the period for which the award is made.[60] If you were in part-time work, these are all ignored for IS, HB and CTB but count for JSA;
- arrears of sick pay, maternity, paternity and adoption pay (statutory or contractual) are taken into account for IS and JSA, as income, without any earnings disregard, from when they are paid for the same length of time covered by the arrears. For HB and CTB, they are ignored;[61]
- statutory redundancy pay counts as capital;[62]
- contractual redundancy pay (deducting an amount for statutory entitlement) is ignored completely for JSA. For IS, HB and CTB, it counts as capital. unless for IS, you are part-time and have not been paid all pay in lieu of notice due, in which case it is ignored;[63]
- some redundancy schemes make periodic payments after leaving work; these are treated as income other than earnings;[64]
- *ex gratia* payments and other kinds of compensation (other than employment tribunal awards) are treated in the same way as contractual redundancy pay;
- holiday pay is usually ignored. However, if your job ends, it counts as capital if your contract provides for it to be payable more than four weeks after termination of employment (eg, in some cases if you leave without giving notice).[65]

Note: these rules only apply to benefits you claim after employment ends. So, for example, if you are already getting HB/CTB when you leave your job, but not IS or JSA, your final earnings are disregarded for IS/JSA in this way, but not for HB/CTB. See p851 for how final payments are treated when you are already getting benefit.

Example

Gina is made redundant from a full-time job on 31 May and leaves with one month's wages, her full four weeks' pay in lieu of notice, contractual redundancy pay of £5,000 and three days holiday pay. All are due to be paid on 31 May. She claims IS, HB and CTB after her job ends. Final wages, pay in lieu of notice and holiday pay are ignored. Redundancy pay is treated as capital. Her capital is below the limit, and she is entitled to benefit from 1 June.

You stop work but your job has not ended

If you stop work before your benefit begins but your employment has not ended (eg, you go on sick leave or maternity leave), statutory and contractual sick pay, maternity, paternity and adoption pay are taken into account as income without any earnings disregard for IS and JSA.[66] For HB and CTB, they count as earnings with the usual disregard.[67] If holiday pay is due to be paid more than four weeks after you stopped work, it is treated as capital (unless, for IS/JSA you are involved in a trade dispute). If it is paid earlier than this, it is ignored.[68] All other earnings are ignored, except for a retainer.[69]

Note: these rules only apply to benefits you claim after you stop work. If, for example, you are already getting HB/CTB when you stop work, but not IS/JSA, your final earnings are ignored in this way for IS/JSA but not for HB/CTB.

If you are suspended from work, any earnings are taken into account as normal.

You were working while claiming benefit

If your job ends or you stop work before your entitlement to benefit begins, any payments that count as earnings are ignored with some exceptions, as described above (see p849). If, however, you were claiming benefit while you were in work, any payments made to you when that job ends are taken into account as earnings for that benefit as follows[70] (for IS and JSA, some different kinds of payments count consecutively in the order below,[71] but for HB and CTB final earnings are averaged as normal):

- final earnings are taken into account as normal (including wages, bonuses, expenses that count as earnings);
- for IS, HB and CTB, pay in lieu of notice is taken into account; for IS starting from the day after earnings stop counting;
- contractual redundancy pay, *ex gratia* payments and other types of compensation (other than employment tribunal awards) above the level of entitlement to statutory redundancy pay:
  - for IS, are treated as capital if you work out your notice or get full pay in lieu of notice. Otherwise they are taken into account as earnings for one week only;
  - for JSA, are treated as earnings, together with pay in lieu of notice, up until the end of the fixed term contract, if you had one, or until the end of the notice period (sometimes longer if the employer says it covers a longer period). For JSA, if none of the payment covers pay in lieu of notice or early termination of a fixed-term contract, the total of these payments covers a standard number of weeks arrived at by dividing the payment by the weekly maximum statutory redundancy (£330 from February 2008) if this is shorter than the notice period;
  - for HB and CTB, are treated as capital except for any amount representing loss of income which is taken into account as earnings;
- holiday pay normally counts as earnings. However, it counts as capital if it is payable more than four weeks after employment ends or is interrupted – eg, if you are off sick before your employment ends. For IS and JSA, it counts for the number of weeks covered by the holiday pay (not the number of working weeks) starting after the period covered by other payments listed above;

- an employment tribunal award – eg, for unfair dismissal, is taken into account as earnings, usually, for IS and JSA, from when it is due to be paid, even if it is not actually paid then;
- arrears of sick pay, maternity, paternity and adoption pay count as earnings for HB and CTB, and as income other than earnings for IS and JSA;[72]
- statutory redundancy payments are treated as capital.

Example

Neelam has been getting HB and CTB while working part time. She earned £50 a week. She finishes work on 16 July and on that day is given £60 made up of £30 final wages and £30 holiday pay. For HB/CTB, the £60 wages and holiday pay are taken into account as normal, deducting the earnings disregard. She claims JSA on 17 July. For JSA, her final wages and holiday pay are ignored so none of the £60 is taken into account. Her JSA starts on 20 July after the three waiting days.

Earnings from self-employment

Even if you are an employee, any other earnings from work you do as a self-employed person are assessed under the following rules.

Calculating net earnings

Your **'net profit'** over the period before your claim must be worked out. This consists of your self-employed earnings, including any allowance from a DWP scheme to assist you with your business (unless, for IS and JSA, paid during a period of test trading to those undertaking the self-employment option of the New Deal, including the New Deal for Lone Parents),[73] *minus*:[74]

- reasonable expenses (see below); *and*
- income tax and NI contributions; *and*
- half of any premium paid in respect of a personal pension scheme contract which is eligible for tax relief.[75] For IS and income-based JSA, if you or your partner (if you have one) are aged 60 or over, you must supply certain information about the scheme if requested.[76]

If you receive payments for board and lodging charges these do not count as earnings[77] but as other income (less any disregards, see p865).

Reasonable expenses

Expenses must be reasonable and 'wholly and exclusively' incurred for the purposes of your business.[78] This involves similar considerations to those that apply in the allowances permitted in the assessment of 'gross' earnings of employed earners. Where a car or telephone, for example, is used partly for business and partly for private purposes, the costs of it can be apportioned and the amount attributable to business use can be deducted.[79]

Reasonable expenses include:[80]

- repayments of capital on loans for replacing equipment and machinery;
- repayment of capital on loans for, and income spent on, the repair of a business asset except where this is covered by insurance;
- interest on a loan taken out for the purposes of the business;
- excess of VAT paid over VAT received.

Reasonable expenses do not include:[81]

- any capital expenditure;
- depreciation, although the normal accountancy practice in valuing stock should be applied so that the 'cost of sales' (the cost of any opening stock plus purchases less any closing stock) should be set against actual sales;[82]
- money for setting up or expanding the business – eg, the cost of adapting the business premises;
- any loss incurred before the beginning of the current assessment period. If the business makes a loss, the net profit is nil. The losses of one business cannot be offset against the profit of any other business in which you are engaged, or against your earnings as an employee[83](although where two businesses or employments share expenses these may be apportioned and offset);[84]
- capital repayments on loans taken out for business purposes;
- business entertainment expenses;
- for HB and CTB, debts (other than proven bad debts) – but the expenses of recovering a debt can be deducted.

Working out average earnings from self-employment

For **IS and income-based JSA**, the weekly amount is the average of earnings:[85]

- over a period of any one year (normally the last year for which accounts are available);
- over a more appropriate period where you have recently taken up self-employment or there has been a change which will affect your business or for any other reason if a different period may enable any part or all of your income and expenditure to be calculated more accurately.[86]

If your earnings are royalties or copyright payments, the amount of earnings is divided by the weekly amount of IS or income-based JSA which would be payable if you had not received this income plus the amount that would be disregarded from those earnings.[87] You are not entitled to IS/income-based JSA for the resulting number of weeks.

For **HB/CTB** the amount of your weekly earnings is averaged out over an 'appropriate' period (usually based on your last year's trading accounts), which must not be longer than a year.[88]

For IS and JSA, if you stop doing self-employed work, any earnings from that work are disregarded except for royalties and copyright payments.[89]

Childminders

Childminders, in practice, are always treated as self-employed. Your net profit is deemed to be one-third of your earnings less income tax, your NI contributions and half of personal pension scheme contributions (see p852).[90] The rest of your earnings are completely ignored.

Disregarded earnings

Some of your earnings from employment or self-employment are disregarded and do not affect your benefit. The amount of the 'disregard' depends on your circumstances. The three main levels of disregard are £25 or £20 or £5/£10. For HB and CTB there is an additional disregard depending on the hours you work and a childcare costs disregard (see p855). These disregards are explained below.

For the amount of disregarded earnings for contribution-based JSA, see p838.

It is expected that earnings of people claiming income-related employment and support allowance (due to be introduced in October 2008) who are undertaking permitted work (see p663) will be disregarded up to the higher limit (see www.cpag.org.uk/esa or CPAG's *Welfare Rights Bulletin* for updates).

£25 disregard

Lone parents on HB or CTB have £25 of their earnings ignored.[91] This does not apply to anyone claiming IS or income-based JSA.

£20 disregard

Twenty pounds of your earnings (including those of your partner, if you have one) is disregarded if:

- for IS or income-based JSA, you are a lone parent;[92]
- you or your partner qualify for a disability premium (see p779).[93] For IS and income-based JSA, you are treated as qualifying for the premium if you would do so but for being in hospital;
- you or your partner qualify for a carer's premium (see p789). The disregard applies to the carer's earnings. For a couple, if both partners get the carer's premium, £20 is disregarded from their combined earnings. If you are the carer and you are the claimant and your earnings are less than £20, the remainder of the disregard can be used up on your partner's earnings as an auxiliary coastguard, etc (see below), or up to £5 (for HB and CTB up to £10) of it can be used up on your partner's earnings from another job – but the total disregard cannot be more than £20;[94]
- you or your partner are an auxiliary coastguard, part-time firefighter, part-time member of a lifeboat crew or member of the Territorial Army.[95] If you earn less than £20 for doing any of these services you can use up to £5 (for HB and CTB up to £10 if you have a partner) of the disregard on another job[96] or on a partner's earnings from another job;[97]

- you are a member of a couple, your benefit would include a disability premium but for the fact that one of you qualifies for the higher pensioner premium (see p783), and one of you is under 60 and either of you are in employment. For IS and income-based JSA, you are treated as qualifying for the higher pensioner premium if you would do so but for being in hospital;[98]
- you or your partner qualify for the higher pensioner premium (see p783) and, immediately before reaching age 60, you or your partner were in employment (part time for IS and income-based JSA) and you were entitled to a £20 disregard because of qualifying for a disability premium. Since reaching 60, you or your partner must have continued in employment (part time for IS and income-based JSA), although breaks of up to eight weeks when you were not getting IS or income-based JSA (or HB/CTB where you claim either of these benefits) are ignored. For IS and income-based JSA you are treated as qualifying for the higher pensioner premium even if you are in hospital.[99]

If you qualify under more than one category you still have a maximum of only £20 of your earnings disregarded.

Basic £5 or £10 disregard

If you do not qualify for a £25 or £20 disregard, £5 of your earnings is disregarded if you are single. If you claim as a member of a couple, £10 of your total earnings is disregarded – whether or not you are both working.[100]

Additional disregard for housing benefit and council tax benefit[101]

For **HB/CTB only**, whichever earnings disregard applies is increased by £16.05 if:

- you or your partner receive the 30-hour element as part of your (or your partner's) WTC (see p1237); *or*
- you or your partner are aged 25 or over and work 30 hours a week or more on average; *or*
- you or your partner work 16 hours or more a week on average and your HB/CTB includes the family premium (see p777); *or*
- you are a lone parent and work 16 hours or more a week on average; *or*
- you or your partner work 16 hours or more a week on average and your HB/CTB includes the disability or higher pensioner premium (see p779). For couples, the partner for whom the premium is awarded must be working 16 hours a week or more on average; *or*
- you or your partner get a 50-plus element in WTC, or would qualify for one if you applied for WTC (see p1239).

The additional earnings disregard does not apply where your total earnings are less than the total of £16.05 plus any earnings disregard (see p854) and childcare costs disregard (see p856). In that case, £16.05 is disregarded from any WTC which is awarded to you or your partner, but the earnings disregard is not increased.

Note: as with the ordinary earnings disregards, only one additional disregard can be allowed from your (or your partner's) earnings.

Childcare costs for housing benefit and council tax benefit

Note: for **IS and income-based JSA**, no allowance is made for any childcare charges you may have to pay.

For **HB/CTB**,[102] an allowance of up to £175 a week for one child, or up to £300 a week for two or more children, can be deducted from your (or your partner's) earnings (from employment or self-employment) in respect of childcare costs if you are:

- a lone parent working 16 hours a week or more; *or*
- a couple and both of you work 16 hours a week or more, or else one of you works 16 hours a week or more and the other is 'incapacitated' (see p857) or in hospital or prison.

Lone parents and couples can still make this deduction for childcare costs if they are off work sick, although for lone parents it stops after 28 weeks (see p857 for details).

If you or your partner (if you have one) also get WTC or CTC, in some circumstances your earnings (and, if applicable, those of your partner) and the WTC/CTC are added together before the deduction for childcare costs is made. This applies if your earnings, once other HB/CTB deductions have been taken off, are less than the deduction for childcare costs.[103]

The childcare allowance only applies to charges you pay for certain types of childcare provided for any child(ren) in your family under the age of 15 (or 16 if s/he is disabled). A child is not treated as having reached the age of 15/16 until the day before the first Monday in September *following* her/his 15th/16th birthday.[104] A child is defined as disabled if s/he is:[105]

- in receipt of disability living allowance (DLA), or payment has been suspended because s/he is a hospital inpatient; *or*
- registered as blind, or was taken off the register before the first Monday in September following her/his 16th birthday, but no more than one year and 28 weeks before then.

The childcare must be provided:[106]

- by a registered childminder or other registered childcare provider (such as a nursery or local authority daycare service); *or*
- out of school hours for children between the ages of eight and 15/16, by a school on school premises or a local authority – eg, an out-of-hours or holiday play scheme; *or*
- by another relevant childcare provider (see p1241, these are the same as for WTC).

You cannot include charges for care provided by a relative of the child in the child's own home even if s/he is a registered childminder, nor charges paid by you to your partner or by your partner to you for a child in your family. Charges for compulsory education do not count.

If you or your partner are on maternity, paternity or adoption leave you will be treated as *working*, and so be able to deduct childcare charges if you (or your partner):[107]

- were working and paying childcare charges that qualify (see p856) in the week immediately before the maternity, paternity or adoption leave began; *and*
- are entitled to SMP, SPP, SAP or maternity allowance (MA) (see Chapters 23 and 17), or are getting IS because you are on paternity leave.

You are no longer treated as working and thus cannot get childcare charges deducted any longer when:

- the maternity, paternity or adoption leave comes to an end; *or*
- if you are not receiving the childcare element of WTC, you or your partner stop getting SMP, SPP, SAP or MA, or IS because you are on paternity leave; *or*
- if you are receiving the childcare element of WTC when you stop getting SMP, SPP, SAP or MA or IS because you are on paternity leave, you stop getting the childcare element of WTC.

You can deduct charges for childcare for the new child in your family while you are still on maternity, paternity or adoption leave.

Childcare costs and ill health or disability

As long as you were working at least 16 hours a week immediately before you started getting one of the following benefits, you can still deduct charges for childcare while off work sick for the first 28 weeks while you are getting:[108]

- SSP;
- short-term lower rate incapacity benefit (IB);
- IS on incapacity grounds;
- NI credits for incapacity.

After 28 weeks, lone parents who are off work sick can no longer deduct childcare charges but couples can do so (before or after 28 weeks) if one of them works 16 hours or more a week and the other is treated as 'incapacitated'.

You (or your partner) are treated as **'incapacitated'** if:[109]

- you get short-term higher rate or long-term IB (see Chapter 12); *or*
- you get severe disablement allowance (SDA) (see Chapter 20); *or*
- you get attendance allowance (AA), DLA or constant attendance allowance (or an equivalent award under the war pensions or industrial injuries schemes) or you would receive one of these benefits but for the fact that you (or your partner) are in hospital; *or*

- you have an invalid carriage or similar vehicle; *or*
- your HB and CTB includes a disability or higher pensioner premium (see Chapter 33) for the incapacity; *or*
- you (but not your partner) have been treated as incapable of work for a continuous period of 196 days or more (disregarding any break of up to 56 days).

Calculating childcare costs[110]

The costs to be taken into account are estimated over whatever period, not exceeding a year, that will give the best estimate of the average weekly charge based on information to be provided by the childminder or care provider.

Points to note

- These rules do *not* apply to IS or JSA and *only* apply to HB and CTB. There are also separate childcare costs rules for non-means-tested benefits (see p835).
- The maximum amount that can be deducted for one child is £175, even if the actual cost of your childcare is more. Even if you have to pay for childcare for more than two children or the actual cost is more, £300 is the maximum.
- The costs of any childcare outside the child's home provided by a relative (other than your partner – but a former partner, who may even be the child's parent, is not excluded) may be allowed so long as s/he is a registered childminder.
- It is not necessary for the childcare to be provided only while you are at work, nor for it to be in any way work related, and there is no requirement for the charges to be reasonable (so the £175/£300 charge could be incurred for only one hour of childcare).

Income other than earnings

As well as income from earnings, most other forms of income are taken into account in full less any tax due. To work out the weekly income to take into account, check whether the payment can be disregarded in part or in full (see below), deduct any tax due and work out the weekly amount (see p876). Where a taxable benefit or other unearned income is not taxed at source and you have not yet had a tax assessment, ask the Revenue for a forecast of tax due on that income, otherwise the DWP itself needs to calculate how much tax to deduct.[111]

Benefits and tax credits

Benefits and tax credits that count in full:

- carer's allowance (CA);
- child benefit is taken into account:
  - in full for HB/CTB;
  - for IS and income-based JSA, but only if you have been getting IS or income-based JSA since before 6 April 2004 with a child already included in your

claim (ie, you still have amounts for children in your IS/income-based JSA) and you do not yet have an award of CTC. In this case, child benefit continues to be taken into account in IS/income-based JSA until your CTC award begins.[112] If you are getting child benefit for a child under one year old, £10.50 a week is ignored;[113]

- CTC counts in full for HB and CTB but is disregarded for IS and income-based JSA. See p861 if your CTC is reduced to recover a tax credit overpayment;
- child's payment under the Armed Forces and Reserved Forces Compensation Scheme (but if it is paid for a dependent child it is usually ignored – see p844);
- child's special allowance and war orphan's pension;
- contribution-based JSA;
- contributory employment and support allowance is expected to count;
- IB and SDA;
- industrial injuries benefits, except constant attendance allowance and exceptionally severe disablement allowance which are disregarded;
- MA;
- retirement pensions;
- SSP, SMP, SPP and SAP count for IS and income-based JSA only, less any Class 1 NI contributions and half of any pension contributions and any tax.[114] These are treated as earnings for HB and CTB and, therefore, may benefit from an earnings disregard (see p854);[115]
- widow's pension, bereavement allowance and industrial death benefit;
- WTC for IS and income-based JSA. For HB and CTB, WTC is taken into account in full (but see p861 if a tax credit overpayment is being deducted) except for those whose earnings are too low to use the whole £16.05 additional full-time earnings disregard (see p855). In this case, £16.05 is disregarded from your WTC instead of your earnings. You must satisfy the conditions for the additional earnings disregard and have earnings of less than £16.05 plus whichever other earnings disregard applies plus any childcare costs disregard.[116]

Benefits that are ignored completely:[117]

- AA;[118]
- child benefit is ignored for IS and income-based JSA[119] unless you have a child included in a pre-6 April 2004 claim and do not have a CTC award (see p858). It counts in full for HB and CTB;
- CTC is ignored completely for IS and income-based JSA.[120] CTC is taken into account in full for HB and CTB;
- constant attendance allowance, exceptionally severe disablement allowance or severe disablement occupational allowance paid because of an injury at work or a war injury;[121]
- DLA care component and mobility component;[122]
- guardian's allowance;[123]
- mobility supplement under the War Pensions Scheme;[124]

- Christmas bonus (see p9);[125]
- any extra-statutory payment made to you to compensate for non-payment of IS, income-based JSA, mobility allowance, mobility supplement, AA or DLA;[126]
- social fund payments.[127] They are also disregarded as capital indefinitely;[128]
- HB, CTB or, formerly, community charge benefit;[129]
- certain special war widows' payments[130] and any special or supplementary payments to pre-1973 war widows or widowers;[131]
- any increase for adult or child dependants who are not members of your family (see p700), where you are getting IB, MA, SDA, widowed mother's allowance, widowed parent's allowance, retirement pension, industrial injuries benefits (including unemployability supplement), CA or a service pension;[132]
- IS and income-based JSA are ignored for HB and CTB.[133] There are special HB and CTB rules for IS and income-based JSA claimants (see pp84 and 190);
- any transitional payment made to compensate you for loss of benefit due to the changes in benefit rules in April 1988, except for income-based JSA;[134]
- any payment made to the Secretary of State to compensate for the loss of HB (whether due to the 1988 changes in benefit rules or not);[135]
- any payment in consequence of a reduction in liability for council tax (or, formerly, community charge).[136]

Benefits that have £15 ignored:
- for HB/CTB only, widowed mother's allowance and widowed parent's allowance.[137]

Benefits that have £10 ignored:
- for IS and income-based JSA only, widowed mother's allowance and widowed parent's allowance;[138]
- war disablement pension;[139]
- guaranteed income payment and survivor's guaranteed income payment under the Armed Forces and Reserve Forces Compensation Scheme;[140]
- war widow's, widower's or surviving civil partner's pension;[141]
- widow's, widower's or surviving civil partner's pension payable to a spouse or civil partner of a member of the Royal Navy, Army or Royal Air Force who was disabled or died as a result of service in the armed forces;[142]
- an extra-statutory payment made instead of the above pensions;[143]
- similar payments made by another country;[144]
- a pension from Germany or Austria paid to the victims of Nazi persecution.[145]

Even if you have more than two payments which attract a £10 disregard, only £20 in all can be ignored.[146] However, the £10 disregard allowed on these war pensions is additional to the total disregard of any mobility supplement or AA (ie, constant attendance allowance, exceptionally severe disablement allowance and severe disablement occupational allowance) paid as part of a war disablement pension.

The £10 disregard may overlap with other disregards on student loans and access funds (see pp598 and 600) when a combined maximum of £20 is allowed.

Local authorities are given a limited discretion to increase the £10 disregard on war disablement, war widows' or widowers' pensions and the pension payable to widows or widowers of members of the Royal Navy, Army or Royal Air Force and the guaranteed income payment and survivor's guaranteed income payment, when assessing income for HB and CTB.[147] Some local authorities disregard the full amount of these pensions, and some do not increase the disregard at all, so you should check your own local authority's policy. It has been held that a local authority must at least consider the nature and purpose of such pensions when deciding whether or not to disregard them, and the courts have indicated that it may be appropriate to apply a disregard to retrospective awards.[148]

Benefit delays

Problems can arise where a decision maker tries to take into account a benefit you are not receiving (such as child benefit), that has been delayed. In such a case, the benefit should not be treated as income possessed by you. For IS and income-based JSA, you should get your full benefit and leave the DWP to deduct the difference from arrears of the delayed benefit when it is eventually awarded.[149]

For the treatment of payments of arrears of certain benefits and CTC and WTC, see p921.

Tax credit payments and overpayments

For **HB and CTB**, if a tax credit overpayment from a previous year is being recovered from the current year's tax credit award, it is the amount of your tax credit award less any reduction to recover the overpayment that is taken into account.[150] Because HB/CTB entitlement is based on the amount of tax credits you are actually paid at the time, local authorities do not treat you as having been underpaid HB or CTB for the earlier period when tax credits were being overpaid, so your HB/CTB award is not revised for that period.[151]

The situation where you have been overpaid in the same year as your tax credit award and your tax credits are reduced accordingly is similar – ie, it is the reduced amount that is taken into account. This is because it is the actual amount of the tax credit award still due to be paid to you that is taken into account, instalment by instalment. For example, if paid weekly or four-weekly, each tax credit instalment is taken into account for the seven or 28 days ending on the day on which the instalment is due to be paid.[152] If the Revenue gives you an additional payment (eg, because your reduced tax credit award leaves you in hardship), local authorities count this as income for HB and CTB.[153]

For **IS and income-based JSA**, the rules are less clear, but the intention seems to be to take into account the actual award paid – eg, after any overpayment has been deducted or additional payment added.[154] Take into account the total amount of WTC to be paid in the complete benefit weeks from the start of the amended tax credit award (if your IS or income-based JSA award has already started), or the complete benefit weeks starting after the beginning of the IS or income-based JSA award, to the end of the amended tax credit award. This amount is averaged over the period for which it is paid to get a weekly amount.[155]

If you stop work, WTC entitlement continues for four weeks and is treated as income if you claim IS or JSA (or HB/CTB). It sometimes happens that WTC payments wrongly continue beyond this even when you have told the Revenue that you have stopped work, and the Revenue treats this as an overpayment. If you are prevented from getting full IS or JSA because this WTC is taken into account as income after the date you informed the Revenue of your change of circumstances, you should consider appealing. Arguably, WTC should be ignored in these circumstances.[156]

Maintenance payments

There are special rules about the treatment of any payments of maintenance or child support maintenance which you or your partner receive for yourself/selves or any child(ren) in your family. These are explained in Chapter 32.

Most maintenance counts in full while you are claiming **IS or income-based JSA** (but see p757 for the rules on entitlement to a child maintenance bonus) but there is a £10 a week disregard, called a child maintenance premium (expected to increase to £20 by the end of 2008) if:[157]

- you get child maintenance under the 'new rules' child support scheme in respect of a child or young person who is a member of your family;
- you get child maintenance under an agreement or court order first paid on or after 3 March 2003;
- you get voluntary child maintenance payments (eg, pending an assessment) and you claimed IS or income-based JSA on or after 16 February 2004;
- you are already on IS or income-based JSA on 16 February 2004 and on or after that date you begin to receive voluntary child maintenance payments. You will not get the £10 disregard if you were previously getting voluntary maintenance while on IS or income-based JSA.[158]

For **HB and CTB**, at present, £15 of any maintenance payments made by your or your partner's former partner or the parent of any child in your family is disregarded, but only if you are a lone parent or a couple with a child.[159] By the end of 2008, the full amount of these maintenance payments is expected to be disregarded.

If you pay maintenance

If you *pay* maintenance to a former partner or a child not living with you, your payments are not disregarded for the purpose of calculating your income for any benefits.[160] Even if you are on IS or income-based JSA you may still have to pay child support maintenance (see p765).

Student loans and grants

For the special rules on the treatment of student grants and loans, career development loans and access fund payments paid to students, see Chapter 25.

Adoption, fostering, guardianship and residence order payments

Adoption allowance

An adoption allowance is disregarded in full for IS and income-based JSA unless your benefit still includes amounts for children as described below.[161]

An adoption allowance is taken into account for:

- IS and income-based JSA if you have been getting benefit since before 6 April 2004 with a child included in your claim and do not yet have an award of CTC;[162]
- HB and CTB.

In the two cases above, the adoption allowance is taken into account in full up to the level of the adopted child's personal allowance and any disabled child premium.[163] Above that level it is ignored. For IS and income-based JSA, if the child has capital over £3,000, you get no benefit for that child and all the adoption allowance is disregarded.[164] However, if the adoption allowance is paid for a child or young person who is not a member of your family (eg, because s/he is in custody), it is fully disregarded in England[165] but, in Scotland and Wales, only the amount you spend on the child is disregarded, while any you keep or use for yourself is taken into account.[166]

Fostering allowance

The way a fostering allowance is treated depends on whether the arrangement is official or private. If a child is placed or boarded out with you by the local authority or a voluntary organisation under specific legal provisions,[167] the child is not counted as a member of your family (see p712), so you are not entitled to any benefit for her/him; any fostering allowances you receive while the child is placed with you should be ignored altogether.[168] If the fostering arrangement is a private one, any money you receive from the child's parent(s) is counted as maintenance (see p744). If the money you receive is not from the child's parent(s), you should probably be treated as a childminder (see p854).

Residence order

If you are paid a residence order allowance by the local authority, this is treated in the same way as an adoption allowance (see above).[169] If not disregarded altogether under the rules above, arrears of residence order allowances are treated as capital for IS and income-based JSA.[170] Any payments made by the biological parents count as maintenance (see p744).

Special guardianship allowance

A special guardianship allowance (payable in England and Wales) is treated in the same way as an adoption allowance.[171]

Charitable, voluntary and personal injury payments

Payments from the Macfarlane and similar trusts

Any payments from the following trusts, including payments in kind, are disregarded in full:[172]

- the Macfarlane Trust, the Macfarlane (Special Payments) Trust, the Macfarlane (Special Payments) (No.2) Trust (for people with haemophilia infected with HIV through blood products);
- the Fund or the Eileen Trust (for others who contracted HIV through NHS products);
- either of the Independent Living Funds.

Also disregarded are payments from the Skipton Fund (for people infected with hepatitis C through blood products) and the London Bombings Relief Fund, though these are made as lump-sum capital payments.

Payments can still be disregarded if you give them to certain relatives or they inherit them from you after your death.

Any income or capital that derives from any such payment is also disregarded.

Other payments

Most other charitable or voluntary payments that are made irregularly and are intended to be made irregularly are treated as capital and are unlikely to affect your claim unless they take your capital above the limit.[173] However, if you are on IS or income-based JSA they count as income if you are involved in a trade dispute and, for IS only, for the first 15 days following your return to work after a dispute (see p633).[174]

Payments made on a regular basis

Charitable and voluntary payments and certain personal injury payments (see below) are ignored if made, or due to be made, regularly.[175]

A **'voluntary payment'** is one given without getting anything back in return.[176]

For IS and income-based JSA, these payments are not disregarded where you are involved in a trade dispute and, for IS only, for the first 15 days following your return to work after a trade dispute.

Payments from a former partner, or the parent of your child, are dealt with as maintenance (see p753).

The **personal injury payments** that qualify under the above rules are:[177]

- payments from a trust fund set up out of money paid because of any personal injury to you; *or*

- payments under an annuity purchased either under an agreement or court order set up because of any personal injury to you, or from money paid because of any personal injury to you; *or*
- payments you get under an agreement or court order because of any personal injury to you.

For the treatment of sports awards made by the Sports Council out of National Lottery funds, see p871.

See also: payments made to someone else on your behalf (p874) and payments disregarded under miscellaneous income (p871).

Concessionary coal to former British Coal workers and their surviving partners is ignored (except to strikers). Cash in lieu of coal counts in full.[178]

Income from tenants and lodgers

Lettings without board

If you let out room(s) in your home to tenants, sub-tenants or licensees under a formal contractual arrangement, £20 of your weekly charge for each tenant, sub-tenant or licensee (and her/his family) is ignored.[179] The balance counts as income.

If someone shares your home under an informal arrangement, any payment made by her/him to you for her/his living and accommodation costs is ignored,[180] but a non-dependant deduction may be made from any HB/CTB or housing costs paid with IS/income-based JSA (see pp197, 86 and 815).

Boarders

If you have a boarder(s) on a commercial basis in your own home, and the boarder or any member of her/his family is not a close relative of yours, the first £20 of the weekly charge is ignored and half of any balance remaining is then taken into account as your income.[181] For HB and CTB, this applies even if the boarder is a close relative and it is not a commercial arrangement. However, there might still be a non-dependant deduction for them (see p196). This applies for each boarder you have. The charge must normally include at least some meals.[182] If you have a business partner, even though your gross income includes just your share of the weekly charge to boarders, you still get the full disregard of £20 plus half the excess for each boarder.[183]

Note: whether you let part of your home to a tenant, sub-tenant, licensee or to a boarder, any income left after applying the above disregards may be considered to be intended to be used to meet any housing costs of your own which are not met by IS, income-based JSA or HB, and may, therefore, be offset accordingly (see p870).[184]

Tenants in other properties

If you have a freehold interest in a property other than your home and you let it out, the rent is normally treated as capital.[185] This rule also applies if you have a leasehold interest in another property which you are sub-letting. There is disagreement between commissioners as to whether it is the gross rent which should be taken into account, or only the sum left after deducting expenses.[186] The rent is treated as income if the property you let is in one of the categories where the capital value is disregarded (see p916) and, in this case, the expenses listed on p866 are deducted from the income.

Income from capital

In general, actual income generated from capital (eg, interest on savings) is ignored as income[187] but counts as *capital*[188] from the date you are due to receive it. However, income derived from the following categories of disregarded capital (see p916) is treated as income:[189]

- your home;
- your former home, if you are estranged, divorced or out of a civil partnership;
- property which you have acquired for occupation as your home but into which you have not yet been able to move;
- property which you intend to occupy as your home but which needs essential repairs or alterations;
- property occupied wholly or partly by a partner or relative of any member of your family who is 60 or over or incapacitated;
- property occupied by your former partner, but not if you are estranged, divorced or out of a civil partnership;
- property for sale;
- property which you are taking legal steps to obtain to occupy as your home;
- your business assets;
- a trust of personal injury compensation.

Some expenses are deducted from this income. Income from any of the above categories (other than your current home, business assets or a personal injuries trust) is ignored up to the amount of the total mortgage repayments (ie, capital and interest, and any payments that are a condition of the mortgage such as insurance or an endowment policy),[190] council tax and water charges paid in respect of the property for the same period over which the income is received.[191]

Tariff income from capital

If your capital is over a certain level, you are treated as having an assumed income from it, called your '**tariff income**'. You are assumed to have an income of £1 for every £250, or part of £250, by which your capital exceeds £6,000 but does not exceed £16,000.[192]

For IS, income-based JSA and HB, if you are in a care home or similar accommodation (see p910), tariff income applies between £10,000 and £16,000.

If you are underpaid because of a reduction in your capital affecting your tariff income, you should ask for a revision or supersession (see pp1065 and 1074). You should report any increase in your capital to the DWP for IS and income-based JSA,[193] and to the local authority for HB/CTB, except where the increase does not stop you getting some IS/income-based JSA.[194] If there is a change in your capital which increases the amount of your tariff income and as a result of which you are overpaid, see p1019 for IS and income-based JSA and pp1021 and 1033 for HB and CTB on recovery of overpayments.

Capital that counts as income

Sometimes the rules treat capital as though it is income.

The following count as income:

- instalments of capital outstanding when you claim benefit, if they would bring you over the capital limit. For IS and income-based JSA, the instalments to be counted are any outstanding either when your benefit claim is decided, or when you are first due to be paid benefit, whichever is earlier, or at the date of any subsequent supersession.[195] For HB and CTB it is any instalments outstanding when your claim is made or treated as made, or when your benefit is revised or superseded.[196] The outstanding instalments count as income, by spreading them over the number of weeks between each instalment.[197]
  If instalments are outstanding in this way on your child's capital, a similar rule applies for IS or income-based JSA, but only if you have been getting benefit since before 6 April 2004 with a child included in your claim and do not yet have an award of CTC. If the total of these instalments and your child's existing savings come to more than £3,000, the outstanding instalments should count as your child's income,[198] and be spread over the period between each instalment;[199]
- any payment from an annuity[200] (see p920 for when this is disregarded);
- any career development loan paid under s2 Employment and Training Act 1973[201] (see p599 for how such loans are treated);
- for IS only, a tax refund if you or your partner have returned to work after a trade dispute (see p633);[202]
- for IS and income-based JSA if you have been getting benefit since before 6 April 2004 with a child included in your claim and do not yet have an award of CTC, certain social services payments for strikers if you or your partner are involved in – or, for IS only, have returned to work after – a trade dispute. These are payments from social services to assist children in need or young people who have previously been in care or been looked after by them;[203]
- periodic payments made under an agreement or court order for any personal injury to you (see p864 for when these are disregarded);[204]
- some lump sums from liable relatives (see p753).

Capital which is counted as income cannot also be treated as producing a tariff income (see p866).[205]

For HB and CTB, a local authority sometimes treats withdrawals from a capital sum as income.[206] This is most likely where a sum was intended to help cover living expenses over a particular period – eg, a bank loan taken out by a mature student. If this is not the intended use of any capital sum, you should dispute the decision. Even where the sum is intended for living expenses, you should argue that unless it is actually paid in instalments it should be treated as capital.

Any payments of capital, or any irregular withdrawals from a capital sum, which are clearly for one-off items of expenditure and not regular living expenses, should be treated as capital. Further, whatever the intention behind the sum, if no withdrawals are in fact made, it should be treated as capital.[207]

Income tax refunds

Pay As You Earn (PAYE) income tax refunds are not payable to people receiving income-based JSA or taxable IB until the end of the tax year, or until they obtain a job, whichever comes first.

PAYE refunds (employed earners) and tax refunds under Schedule D (self-employed) are treated as capital.[208]

For IS and JSA, tax refunds paid during a trade dispute are treated as income and taken into account.[209] For IS only, if you or your partner have returned to work after a trade dispute (see p633), tax refunds are treated as income and are taken into account in full.[210]

Income from employment and training programmes

Payments from the New Deal, 'welfare to work', employment rehabilitation and other employment or training programmes under s2 Employment and Training Act 1973 or s2 Enterprise and New Towns (Scotland) Act 1990 are treated as follows.[211]

Payments taken into account:

- payments made as a substitute for IS, JSA, IB or SDA (eg, a New Deal allowance or training allowance);
- payments intended for certain living costs while you are participating in a scheme to enhance your employment prospects. Payments for food, ordinary clothing or footwear, fuel, rent met by HB, housing costs met by IS or JSA, council tax or water charges are all taken into account;
- bridging allowances paid to under-18-year-olds.

All other payments are disregarded, for example:

- travel expenses;
- training premium;
- childcare expenses;

- special needs payments;
- New Deal mandatory top-up payments;
- New Deal living away from home allowance (if rent is not met by HB);
- return-to-work credit and work search premium (paid to sick or disabled people returning to work);
- in-work credit and work search premium (paid to lone parents looking for work or starting work).

For those taking part under the 'self-employment route' of the New Deal, any payments to meet expenses 'wholly and necessarily' incurred while trading, and any payments used for the repayments of a loan necessary for the business, are also disregarded[212] (provided these payments are from a special account set up for the purposes of this programme). Once you have completed your (up to) 26-week period of 'test trading', any income you have received from trading and which has accrued in your special account is released to you. For HB/CTB, this is treated as capital.[213] For IS/income-based JSA, this is treated as income and spread over the same number of weeks in the future for which you have been receiving assistance, less any income tax due on the profits and an earnings disregard appropriate to your circumstances (see p854).[214]

Occupational pensions and annuities

The following income is **taken into account in full:**

- an occupational pension (except for any discretionary payment from a hardship fund) or income from a personal pension;[215]
- payments from an annuity, except payments under an annuity purchased either under an agreement or court order set up because of any personal injury to you, or from money paid because of any personal injury to you (see p864). However, in the case of 'home income plans', income from the annuity equal to the interest payable on the loan with which the annuity was bought is ignored if:
  - you used at least 90 per cent of the loan made to you to buy the annuity; *and*
  - the annuity will end when you and your partner die; *and*
  - you or your partner are responsible for paying the interest on the loan; *and*
  - you, or both your partner and yourself, were at least 65 at the time the loan was made; *and*
  - the loan is secured on a property which you or your partner own or have an interest in, and the property on which the loan is secured is your home, or that of your partner.

  If the interest on the loan is payable after income tax has been deducted, it is an amount equal to the net interest payment that is disregarded, otherwise it is the gross amount of the interest payment.[216]

Mortgage and insurance payments

The following income is ignored:

- for IS and income-based JSA only, payments you receive under a mortgage protection policy which you took out, and which you use, to pay the housing costs which are not being met by the DWP in your IS or income-based JSA[217] (for restrictions on housing costs see p811). However, if the amount you receive exceeds the total of:
  - the interest you pay on a qualifying loan which is not met by the DWP;
  - capital repayments on a qualifying loan; *and*
  - any premiums you pay on the policy in question and any building insurance policy,

  then the excess is counted as your income;
- for IS and income-based JSA only, and as long as you have not already used insurance payments for the same purpose, *any* money *you* receive which is given, and which *you* use to make:[218]
  - payments under a secured loan which do not qualify under the housing costs rules (see Chapter 34);
  - interest payments which are not met under the housing costs rules, even though some interest payments under the loan in question are met;
  - capital repayments on a qualifying loan;
  - payments of premiums on an insurance policy which you took out to insure against the risk of not being able to make the payments in the above three categories, and premiums on a building insurance policy;
  - payment of any rent that is not covered by HB (see Chapter 10);
  - payment of the part of your accommodation charge in a care home that exceeds that payable by a local authority;
- for HB and CTB (see above for IS/income-based JSA), payments you receive under an insurance policy you took out to insure against the risk of being unable to maintain payments on a loan secured on your home. However, anything you get above the total of the following counts as your income:
  - the amount you use to maintain your payments; *and*
  - any premium you pay for the policy; *and*
  - any premium for an insurance policy which you had to take out to insure against loss or damage to your home;[219]
- for IS, income-based JSA, HB and CTB, payments you receive under an insurance policy you took out to insure against the risk of being unable to maintain hire purchase or similar payments or other loan payments – eg, credit card debts. However, anything you get above the amount you use to make your payments and the premium for the policy counts as your income.[220]

Social services, community care and other payments

The following payments are ignored:

- a payment from a social services department under ss17, 23B, 23C or 24A Children Act 1989, or, in Scotland, a payment from a social work department under s12 Social Work (Scotland) Act 1968 or under ss29 or 30 Children (Scotland) Act 1995 – ie, payments from social services to assist children in need or young people who have been in care or been looked after by them.[221] For IS and income-based JSA, if you have been getting benefit since before 6 April 2004 with a child included in your claim and do not yet have a CTC award, such payments are not ignored if you or your partner are involved in or, for IS only, have returned to work after a trade dispute (see p633);
- any community care direct payments. Local authorities pay these to disabled people or carers to buy their own services instead of providing services directly. A direct payment is not ignored as income of the person you pay for services even if this is your partner;[222]
- any payment you receive for looking after a person temporarily in your care if it is paid under community care arrangements by a health authority, primary care trust, local authority, voluntary organisation or by the person being looked after;[223] but any HB paid to you by a local authority for that person is not ignored, although see p865 for other possible disregards;
- a lump-sum payment from the local authority to enable you to make adaptations to your home for a disabled child; this is treated as capital and ignored;[224]
- payments by a local authority for support services to help you live independently (ie, under the Supporting People programme) are ignored indefinitely.[225] Landlords receiving such payments for providing the services do not benefit from this disregard, although other disregards may apply (see p865);
- if you live in a care home and the local authority arranged your place, local authority payments towards your fees are ignored for IS and JSA. If the local authority did not arrange your place, any payment intended and used for your maintenance is fully disregarded if it is a voluntary or charitable payment, and partly disregarded if not – up to the difference between the care home fees and your applicable amount.[226]

Miscellaneous income

The following income is ignored:

- education maintenance allowances (or corresponding payments).[227] These are paid to young people staying on at school or other non-advanced education beyond school-leaving age;
- any payment to cover your expenses if you are working as an unpaid volunteer, or working unpaid for a charity or voluntary organisation;[228]

- payments in kind (unless, for IS or income-based JSA, you or your partner are involved in a trade dispute, see p633).[229] These may include food, fuel, cigarettes,[230] clothing, holidays, gifts, accommodation, transport, or nursery education vouchers (but see p873 for the rules on notional income and p848 for the rules on non-cash vouchers paid as earnings). Items for essential living needs provided from the Border and Immigration Agency to an asylum-seeking partner are ignored;
- a payment (other than a training allowance) to a disabled person under the Disabled Persons (Employment) Act 1944 to assist her/him to obtain or retain employment;[231]
- any discretionary payment made to you by an employment zone contractor while you are taking part in an employment zone scheme;[232]
- any payments, other than for loss of earnings or a benefit, made to jurors or witnesses for attending at court;[233]
- Victoria Cross or George Cross payments or similar awards;[234]
- income paid outside the UK which cannot be transferred here;[235]
- if income is paid in another currency, any bank charges for converting the payment into sterling;[236]
- fares to hospital;[237]
- payments instead of milk tokens and vitamins;[238]
- payments to assist prison visits;[239]
- for HB and CTB, if you make a parental contribution to a student's grant or loan, an equal amount of any 'unearned' income you have for the period the grant or loan is paid is ignored.[240] If your 'unearned' income does not cover the contribution, the balance can be disregarded from your earnings.[241] If you are a parent of a student under 25 in advanced education who does not get a grant or loan (or who only gets a smaller discretionary award) and you contribute to her/his living expenses, the amount of your 'unearned' income that is ignored is the amount equal to your contribution up to a maximum of £47.95 (less the weekly amount of any discretionary award the student has).[242] This is only ignored during the student's term. Again, any balance can be disregarded from your earnings;[243]
- any payment of a sports award made by the Sports Council out of National Lottery funds *except* for any part of any award which is made for 'ordinary living expenses' – ie, food, ordinary clothing or footwear, household fuel, council tax, water charges and rent (less any non-dependant deductions) for which HB could be payable or housing costs that could be met by IS or income-based JSA. Payments for clothes and shoes used just for sport, and payments for vitamins, minerals or other special dietary supplements intended to enhance performance are ignored;[244]
- any discretionary housing payments paid by a local authority.[245]

Notional income

You may, in certain circumstances, be treated as having income even if you do not possess it, or have used it up.

Deprivation of income to claim or increase benefit

If you deliberately get rid of income in order to claim or increase your benefit, you are treated as though you are still in receipt of the income.[246] The basic issues involved are the same as those for the deprivation of capital (see p924). **Note:** the rule can only apply if the purpose of the deprivation is to gain benefit for *yourself* (or your family). It should not apply if, for example, you stop claiming CA solely so that another person (who is not a member of your family) can become entitled to the severe disability premium (see p784).[247] However, if you do not claim a benefit which would clearly be paid if you did, it may be argued that you have failed to apply for income (see below).

Failing to apply for income

If you fail to apply for income to which you are entitled without having to fulfil further conditions, you are deemed to have received it from the date you could have obtained it.[248]

This does not include income from:

- a discretionary trust; *or*
- a trust set up from money paid as a result of a personal injury; *or*
- funds administered by a court as a result of a personal injury; *or*
- a rehabilitation allowance made under the Employment and Training Act 1973; *or*
- if you are under 60, a personal or occupational pension scheme or payments from the Pension Protection Fund. However, if you are 60 or over, you are treated as receiving income in certain circumstances if you defer or fail to claim your pension or purchase an annuity;[249] *or*
- WTC and CTC;[250] *or*
- the lone parent element of child benefit – but only for IS and income-based JSA if you have been on benefit since before 6 April 2004 and have amounts for a child included and you do not yet have a CTC award.

For other income or benefits it must still be certain that it would be paid upon application (and the rule ceases to apply as soon as a claim is made[251]). It may, therefore, be difficult to establish that there is 'no doubt' that CA, for example, would be paid to a carer who does not wish to claim it because of the effect on another person's severe disability premium (see p784).[252]

Any such income must also be available to *you* (or your family) *for your own benefit*. For example, in one case, income could not be attributed to the leaseholder of a shop who was forced to sublet to tenants in order to meet his liabilities to the landlord. Although the rent was technically available to the leaseholder, it was immediately passed on to the landlord so no profit was ever available.[253]

Income due to you that has not been paid

This applies to IS and income-based JSA only.[254] You are treated as possessing any income owing to you. Examples of when this rule *may* apply could include:

- when wages are legally due to you but are not paid; *or*
- an occupational pension payment that is due but has not been received. However, this does not apply where an occupational pension has not been paid, or fully paid, because the pension scheme has insufficient funds.[255]

This rule should *not* apply if:

- any social security benefit has been delayed; *or*
- you are waiting for a late payment of a pension under the Job Release Scheme, a government training allowance or a benefit from a European Economic Area country; *or*
- money is due to you from a discretionary trust, or a trust set up from money paid as a result of a personal injury; *or*
- you are owed earnings when your job has ended because of redundancy but these have not been paid to you.[256]

As above, the income must be due to *you* (or your family) and *for your own benefit*.[257]

If this rule is applied, an urgent cases payment should be considered (see p297).[258]

Unpaid wages

This applies to IS and income-based JSA only. If you have wages due to you, but you do not yet know the exact amount or you have no proof of what they will be, you are treated as having a wage similar to that normally paid for that type of work in that area.[259] If your wages cannot be estimated you might qualify for an interim payment (see p986).[260]

Income paid to someone else on your behalf

If money is paid to someone on your behalf (eg, the landlord for your rent) this can count as notional income. Even if it does count as notional income, it is still subject to the usual disregards that would apply if it were actual income – eg, a voluntary or charitable payment of income is ignored whether it is paid directly to you or to someone else on your behalf. See p929 for a description of these 'third party' rules – the notional income rules are the same as those for notional capital.

Income in kind given to a third party for you is ignored, whatever it is (eg, a food parcel used to prepare meals for you), unless you or your partner are involved in a trade dispute. However, money given to someone who uses it to buy you goods or services would count as notional income under the usual rules.

Income paid to you for someone else[261]

If you or your partner get a payment for somebody not in the 'family' (see p700 – eg, a relative living with you) it counts as your income if you keep any of it yourself or spend it on yourself or your partner.

If you have been on IS or income-based JSA since before 6 April 2004 with a dependent child included in your claim and you do not yet have a CTC award, income paid to your dependent child for someone not in the family also counts as yours in the same way as it would if it were paid to you or your partner.

The payment does not count as yours in this way if it is from the Macfarlane Trusts, the Fund, the Eileen Trust or either of the Independent Living Funds or is in the form of concessionary coal under the Coal Industry Act 1994, or if it is a grant for participating in an approved employment-related course of education, or in a New Deal programme.[262]

Note: the same exception for payments in kind applies for IS and income-based JSA as for income payments made to someone else on your behalf.

Cheap or unpaid labour

If you are helping another person or an organisation by doing work of a kind which would normally command a wage, or a higher wage, you are deemed to receive a wage similar to that normally paid for that kind of job in that area.[263]

The burden of proving that the kind of work you do is something for which an employer would pay, and what the comparable wages are, lies with the decision maker.[264]

The rule does not apply if:[265]

- you are on unpaid approved work experience, or, for IS only, you are a lone parent taking part in work experience under the New Deal for lone parents; *or*
- you are on a government employment or training programme (other than in the New Deal intensive activity period) with no training allowance or only travel or meals expenses; *or*
- you can show that the person ('person' includes a limited company[266]) cannot, in fact, afford to pay, or pay more; *or*
- you work for a charitable or voluntary organisation or as a volunteer, and it is accepted that it is reasonable for you to give your services free of charge.[267] A **'volunteer'** is someone who, without any legal obligation, performs a service for another person without expecting payment.

Sometimes it may also be reasonable to do a job for free out of a sense of community duty, particularly if the job would otherwise remain undone, and there would be no financial profit to an employer.[268] Even if you are caring for a sick or disabled relative or another person, it may be considered reasonable for her/him to pay you from her/his benefits, unless you can bring yourself within these exceptions.[269] There are, however, many arguments which carers can rely on to show that it would not be reasonable for them to be expected to be paid. It has been held, for example, that it may be more reasonable for a close relative to provide services free of charge out of a sense of family duty,[270] particularly if a charge would otherwise break up a relationship.[271] Whether it is reasonable to provide care free of charge depends on the basis on which the arrangement is made, the expectations of the family members concerned, the housing arrangements and the reasons (if appropriate) why a carer gave up any paid work. The risk of a carer losing entitlement to CA if a charge were made should also be considered,[272] as should the likelihood that a relative being looked after would no longer be able to contribute to the household expenses.[273] If there is no realistic alternative to the carer providing services free to a relative who simply will not pay, this may also make it reasonable not to charge.[274] It may also be worth arguing that carers should not charge because they will otherwise lose their statutory right to an assessment of their needs by social services.[275]

Working out weekly income

For HB and CTB, to assess your current normal weekly income:

- average your earnings over a past period (see below for earnings from employment and p853 for self-employed earnings);
- estimate income other than earnings (see p858 for what income counts) by looking at an appropriate period of up to 52 weeks. The period chosen must give an accurate assessment of your income.[276] CTC and WTC are taken into account instalment by instalment – eg, if paid weekly or four-weekly, each instalment counts for the seven or 28 days ending on the day it is due to be paid;
- for earnings from employment and income other than earnings, convert income into a weekly amount if necessary (see p877);
- deduct appropriate earnings disregard/s (see p854).

For IS and income-based JSA, as well as working out weekly income, you also need to know the period that payments cover. These rules apply to earnings from employment and income other than earnings (see p853 for how self-employed earnings are assessed):

- work out the period covered by income (see p878);
- work out the date from which to start taking the income into account (see p879);
- convert income into a weekly amount if necessary (see p877). There are special rules covering variable income, payments for less than a week and overlapping payments (see p877).

Averaging earnings for housing benefit and council tax benefit

For HB and CTB, earnings as an employee are usually averaged out over:

- the previous five weeks if you are paid weekly; *or*
- two months if you are paid monthly.[277]

If your earnings vary, or if there is likely to be, or has recently been, a change (eg, you usually do overtime but have not done so recently, or you are about to get a pay rise), the local authority may average them over a different period where this is likely to give a more accurate picture of what you are going to earn.[278]

If you are on strike, the local authority should not take into account your pre-strike earnings and average them out over the strike period.[279]

If you have only just started work and your earnings cannot be averaged over the normal period (ie, five weeks or two months) an estimate is made, based on any earnings you have been paid so far if these are likely to reflect your future average wage. If you have not yet been paid or your initial earnings do not represent what you will normally earn, your employer must provide an estimate of your average weekly earnings.[280] If your earnings change during your award, your new weekly average figure is estimated on the basis of what you are likely to earn over whatever period (up to 52 weeks) best allows an accurate estimate.[281] If averaging does not result in a weekly figure, the amount is converted (see below).

Converting income into a weekly amount

IS, income-based JSA, HB and CTB are all calculated on a weekly basis, so your earnings and other income have to be converted into a weekly amount if necessary.

The following rules apply to income from employment and income other than earnings.[282] For income from self-employment, see p852.

To convert income to a weekly amount:

- if the payment is for less than a week, it is treated as the weekly amount;
- if the payment is for a month, multiply by 12 and divide by 52;
- for IS and income-based JSA, multiply a payment for three months by four and divide by 52;
- for IS and income-based JSA, divide a payment for a year by 52;
- for all four benefits, for any other period, divide the payment by the number of days in the period then multiply by seven.

If you work on certain days but are paid monthly, it is necessary to decide whether the payment is for the days worked or for the whole month. This generally depends on the terms of your contract of employment,[283] but may depend on how your employer has arranged to make payments to you.[284]

Variable income

For IS and income-based JSA, if your income fluctuates or your earnings vary because you do not work every week, your weekly income may be averaged over the cycle, if there is an identifiable one, or, if there is not, over five weeks, or over another period if this would be more accurate.[285] If the cycle involves periods when you do no work, those periods are included in the cycle, but not other absences – eg, holidays, sickness.

Example

Ahmed works a cycle of two weeks on and one week off. He works 20 hours a week in the weeks he works, for which he is paid £120. In the third week he is paid a retainer of £30. He claims income-based JSA in the third week. His average weekly earnings are £90 a week (£120 + £120 + £30 = £270 ÷ 3 = £90) which will be taken into account in calculating his income-based JSA entitlement.

Part-weeks

For IS and income-based JSA, there are rules about the calculation of income for part-weeks.

- If income covering a period up to a week is paid before your first benefit week (normally the seven days ending with your payday for IS, or your signing-on day for JSA) and part of it is counted for that week; *or* if, in any case, you are paid for a period of a week or more, and only part of it is counted in a particular benefit week – multiply the whole payment by the number of days it covers in the benefit week, then divide the result by the total number of days covered by the payment.[286]
- If any payment of MA, IB or SDA falls partly into the benefit week, only the amount paid for those days is taken into account. For any payment of IS or JSA, that amount is the weekly amount multiplied by the number of days in the part-week and divided by seven.[287]

Overlapping payments

For IS or income-based JSA, where you have regularly received a certain kind of payment of income from one source, and in a particular benefit week you receive that payment and another of the same kind from the same source (eg, where your employer first pays you sick pay in arrears and this then overlaps with a payment in advance), the maximum amount to be taken into account is the one paid first.[288]

This does not apply if the second payment was due to be taken into account in another week, but the overlapping week is the first in which it could practically be counted (see p879).

The period covered for income support and jobseeker's allowance

For IS or income-based JSA, there are special rules for deciding the length of the period for which and the date from which payments of earnings and other income count. These rules are designed to give a clearer indication of how you are expected to make use of any earnings or other income you receive for each week of your claim for IS/income-based JSA. These rules do not, however, apply to self-employed earnings (see p852).

- If a payment of income is made in respect of an identifiable period, it is taken into account for a period of equal length.[289] For example, a week's part-time earnings are taken into account for a week.
- If the payment does not relate to a particular period, the amount of the payment is divided by the amount of the weekly IS or income-based JSA to which you would otherwise be entitled. If part of the payment should be disregarded, the amount of IS or income-based JSA is increased by the appropriate disregard. The result of this calculation is the number of weeks that you are not entitled to IS or income-based JSA.[290]

Example

Conor receives £750 net earnings for work which cannot be attributed to any specific period of time. He and his partner are both aged 28. Their rent and council tax are met by HB and CTB. Conor's income-based JSA is £94.95. As a couple they are entitled to a £10 earnings disregard.

Divide £750 by the weekly JSA (£94.95) plus the disregard (£10)

750 ÷ 104.95 = 7.1463

This is seven weeks, with 0.1463 x £104.95 left over = £15.35

This means that Conor is not entitled to income-based JSA for seven weeks and the remaining £15.35 (less a £10 earnings disregard, leaving £5.35) is taken into account in calculating his benefit for the following week.

Payments made on leaving a job are taken into account for a forward period (see p849).

There is a separate rule for **WTC**. The period over which it is taken into account depends on whether you already have an award of IS or income-based JSA when the WTC award begins or when it is amended. If you do, WTC is taken into account from the first day of the IS or income-based JSA benefit week (see below) on or after the start of the tax credits award (or amended award). If your IS or income-based JSA award begins later, WTC is taken into account from the first day of the benefit week after the date the IS or income-based JSA award begins. In either case, it counts until the last day of the benefit week on or after the end of the tax credits award.[291]

The date from when a payment is counted

For IS and income-based JSA, the date from when a payment of earnings and/or other income counts depends on when it was due to be paid. If it was due to be paid before you claimed IS or income-based JSA, it counts from the date on which it was due to be paid.[292] Otherwise it is treated as paid on the first day of the benefit week in which it is due, or on the first day of the first benefit week after that in which it is practicable to take it into account.[293]

Payments of IS, JSA, MA, IB or SDA are treated as paid on the day they are officially due.[294]

The '**benefit week**' is normally the seven days ending with the signing-on day for JSA or the payday for IS. It often overlaps two calendar weeks.[295]

The date that a payment is due may well be different from the date of actual payment. Earnings are due on the employee's normal payday. If the contract of employment does not reveal the date of due payment, and there is no evidence pointing in another direction, the date the payment was received should be taken as the date it was due.[296] If your contract of employment is terminated without proper notice, outstanding wages, wages in hand, holiday pay and any pay in lieu of notice are due on the last day of employment and are treated as paid on that day, even if this does not happen (although these are usually disregarded).[297]

If you receive compensation for, say, being dismissed in circumstances constituting sex discrimination, the relevant date is the date when the earnings in question were due to be paid, not when the compensation was awarded.[298]

If income due to you has not been paid, you may be entitled to an urgent cases payment (see p1344) or a crisis loan from the social fund (see p503).

For the treatment of payments at the end of a job, see p849.

2. People aged 60 or over

This part applies to:

- pension credit (PC);
- housing benefit (HB) and council tax benefit (CTB) if you or your partner are aged 60 or over and not getting income support (IS) or income-based jobseeker's allowance (JSA). If you do get IS or income-based JSA, all your income is ignored for HB and CTB.

If you are under 60, or you have a partner and both of you are under 60, this part does not apply – see section 1 on p844 instead. If you or your partner get IS or income-based JSA, section 1 explains how your income is treated.

The rules for PC and, if you or your partner (if you have one) are aged 60 or over, for HB and CTB, are very similar. Where there are differences, they are indicated.

Note: in this part, whenever HB or CTB are referred to, this only applies to the rules for people aged 60 or over.

Whose income counts

If you are a member of a couple (see p702), your partner's income is added to yours.[299]

The income of a dependent child does *not* affect:

- PC;
- HB or CTB.[300]

What counts as income

Pension credit

For PC, '**income**' means:

- earnings (see pp882 and 885);
- certain benefits and tax credits, including state retirement pensions and war pensions (see p888);
- maintenance (see p890);
- income from tenants and lodgers (see p890);
- income from capital (see p891);
- other specified miscellaneous income, including occupational and personal pensions (see p892);
- notional income (see p894);
- any income paid in lieu of the above.

For each type of income, some income is taken into account and some is ignored in the assessment of PC. The details are explained in this chapter. If the rules do not specify a type of income as being included in the assessment, then it is ignored and does not affect your benefit.

For the rules on 'qualifying income' for the savings credit and the 'assessed income period', both of which only apply to PC, see Chapter 18.

Housing benefit and council tax benefit

How your income affects your entitlement to HB and CTB depends on whether you are getting PC and, if you are, which type of PC.

If you get pension credit guarantee credit

If you (or your partner) are getting the guarantee credit of PC, all of your (and your partner's) income is ignored.[301] This is because entitlement to PC guarantee credit acts as a passport to maximum HB and CTB.

If you get pension credit savings credits

If you (or your partner) are only getting the savings credit of PC, your income for HB and CTB purposes is the income (and capital) figure used by the DWP to work out your PC, *plus*:[302]

- the amount of savings credit of PC;
- any income (and capital) of your partner which was not taken into account in the PC calculation (eg, where a partner abroad is no longer included for PC but is for HB/CTB); *and*

- any income of a non-dependant, but only in the very limited circumstances where her/his income can be treated as yours under the HB rules (see p200);[303]

minus[304]

- any childcare charges earnings disregard;
- the higher amount disregarded, where applicable, for:
  - lone parent earnings;
  - payments of maintenance made by your former partner (or your partner's former partner), or payments of maintenance made by the parent of a child or young person who is a member of your family, as long as that parent is neither yourself nor your partner;
- any additional full-time earnings disregard (see p887);
- any discretionary increase to the £10 disregard for war pensions, and war widows' and widowers' pensions.

If you do not get pension credit

If you or your partner are aged 60 or over and are not getting the guarantee or savings credit of PC, or IS or income-based JSA, income is defined in the same way as for PC (see p881).[305] As for PC, some income is taken into account and some disregarded but the rules on how this happens are not always the same as for PC. Any differences are explained in each relevant section.

Net weekly income

The income that is taken into account is the amount after deducting any tax or national insurance (NI) contributions.[306]

For HB and CTB, the local authority may ignore changes (eg, Budget changes) in tax or NI contributions and the maximum rate of tax credits for up to 30 benefit weeks. When the changes are eventually taken into account, you are not treated as having been underpaid or overpaid benefit during the period of the delay.[307]

Once you have worked out what income should be taken into account, this is converted into a weekly amount (see p895) and the total taken into account in the benefit assessment (see p896 for the date from when a payment is counted). Chapters 5, 10 and 18 explain how income affects the amount of CTB, HB or PC you get.

Earnings of employed earners

This section explains how any earnings received by you or your partner (see p700) are treated for PC and for HB and CTB.

Calculating net earnings from employment

It is your net earnings that are taken into account in the assessment. See p895 for how earnings are converted into a weekly amount. **'Net earnings'** means your 'gross earnings' (see p883) *minus*:

- any deductions made for income tax; *and*

- Class 1 NI contributions; *and*
- half of any contribution you make towards a personal or occupational pension scheme.[308]

If your earnings are estimated for HB or CTB, the authorities estimate the amount of tax and NI you would expect to pay on those earnings, and deduct this plus half of any pension contribution you are paying.[309]

For HB and CTB, the local authority has the discretion to ignore changes in tax or NI contributions for up to 30 benefit weeks. When the changes are eventually taken into account, you are not treated as having been underpaid or overpaid benefit during the period of the delay.[310]

'Gross earnings' means the amount of earnings received from your employer less deductions for any expenses 'wholly, necessarily and exclusively incurred' by you in order to carry out the duties of your employment.[311] A range of deductions may be made (see p847 – the provisions are the same as those for people aged under 60).

What counts as earnings

'Earnings' means 'any remuneration or profit derived from ... employment'.

As well as your wages, this includes:[312]

- any bonus or commission (including tips);
- holiday pay – but this is ignored if your employment ends before your PC entitlement starts;
- statutory sick pay (SSP) and contractual sick pay,[313] statutory maternity pay (SMP), statutory paternity pay (SPP) or statutory adoption pay (SAP) or any other pay made to you by your employer while you are on maternity leave;[314]
- any payments made by your employer for expenses not 'wholly, exclusively and necessarily' incurred in carrying out your job, including any travel expenses to and from work, and any payments made to you for looking after members of your family;
- pay in lieu of notice, or pay in lieu of remuneration except for periodic payments following redundancy. However, all earnings – including pay in lieu – are ignored if your employment ends before your PC entitlement starts;
- a retainer fee (eg, you may be paid during the school holidays if you work for the school meals service[315]) or a guarantee payment;[316]
- any payment of a non-cash voucher which is liable for Class 1 NI contributions.[317] Non-cash vouchers that are *not* liable for contributions (eg, certain childcare and charitable vouchers) are classed as payments in kind and ignored.[318]

Examples of payments not counted as earnings:

- If you become entitled to HB, CTB or PC after your employment ends, all earnings are disregarded (see p886) except certain royalties.[319]
- Payments in kind (eg, petrol) are ignored.[320]

- An advance of earnings or a loan from your employer – this is treated as capital, according to PC guidance.[321]
- The value of free accommodation provided as part of your job is ignored, according to PC guidance.[322]
- Payments towards expenses that are 'wholly, exclusively and necessarily' incurred, such as travelling expenses during the course of your work, are ignored.[323]
- If you are a local councillor, travelling expenses and subsistence payments are (and basic allowances may be[324]) ignored as expenses 'wholly, exclusively and necessarily' incurred in your work.
- If your earnings are paid in another currency, any bank charges for converting them into sterling are deducted before taking them into account.[325]
- The net amount of any occupational pension,[326] although not counted as earnings (and therefore having no earnings disregard), is still taken into account in full.[327]
- Any compensation payments made by an employment tribunal for unfair dismissal or unlawful discrimination do not count as earnings.[328]
- Any lump-sum payments made under the Iron and Steel Re-adaptation Benefits Scheme are not treated as earnings.[329]

Payments at the end of a job

Redundancy payments are treated as capital.[330]

If you leave a job, any earnings should be disregarded except[331] certain copyright royalties, payments for patents, trademarks or under the Public Lending Right Scheme.

However, these rules only apply if you leave your job before you claim benefit. If you are already getting HB/CTB or PC when you leave your job, your earnings are not disregarded for that benefit. If you are already getting HB/CTB but not PC, your earnings are disregarded for PC.

For PC, any final payment is treated as paid on the date your next regular payment of earnings would have been paid and taken into account for the same period unless the final payment is higher than the normal amount. If it is higher, the final payment is taken into account over the corresponding multiple of the regular payment period with any remainder counting for a further payment period.[332]

Example

Sandra has been getting PC and working part time. She earns £25 a week, paid on a Friday. She finishes work on Wednesday 4 August and on that day is given £35 made up of £15 final wages and £20 holiday pay. This £35 is treated as paid on Friday 6 August and taken into account for two benefit weeks – £25 in the first week and the remaining £10 in the second week.

Earnings from self-employment

Even if you are an employee, any other earnings from work you do as a self-employed person are assessed under the following rules for PC and, if you or your partner are aged 60 or over, for HB and CTB.

Calculating net earnings

Your '**net profit**' over the period before your claim must be worked out. This consists of your self-employed earnings, including any allowance from a DWP scheme to assist you with your business *minus*:[333]

- reasonable expenses (see p852 – the rules are the same as those for people under age 60 except that expenses relating to debts are not excluded); *and*
- income tax and NI contributions; *and*
- half of any premium paid in respect of a personal pension scheme which is eligible for tax relief.[334] For PC, you must supply certain information about the scheme or annuity contract to the relevant authority if requested.[335]

If you receive payments for board and lodging charges, these do not count as earnings[336] but as other income (less any disregards – see p890).

Working out average earnings from self-employment

The weekly amount is the average of earnings:[337]

- over a period of one year (normally the last year for which accounts are available);
- over a more appropriate period where you have recently taken up self-employment or there has been a change which will affect your business.

Childminders

Childminders, in practice, are always treated as self-employed. Your net profit is deemed to be one-third of your earnings less income tax, your NI contributions and half of certain pension contributions (see above).[338] The rest of your earnings are completely ignored.

Disregarded earnings

Some of your earnings from employment or self-employment are disregarded and do not affect your PC, HB or CTB. The amount of the 'disregard' depends on your circumstances. The three main levels of disregard are £25 or £20 or £5/£10, but additional disregards may apply in special circumstances. These are explained on p886.

For the treatment of childcare costs for claims for HB/CTB, see p888.

Full disregard

For HB and CTB only, the amount (or the balance of the amount) of the student parental contribution which is not disregarded under other income (see p895) is ignored.[339]

For PC, HB and CTB:

- all earnings (except royalties or other payments of earnings made for the use of, or the right to use, any copyright, patent, trademark or book registered under the Public Lending Right Scheme if you or your partner are the first owner of the copyright, patent or trademark or are the author of the book) derived from employment which ended before you claimed PC, HB or CTB are ignored;[340]
- any banking charges or commission payable for converting your earnings into sterling if you are paid in a currency other than sterling are deducted.[341]

£25 disregard

Lone parents on HB or CTB have £25 of their earnings ignored.[342] This does not apply to PC.

£20 disregard

Twenty pounds of your earnings (including those of your partner, if any) is disregarded if:

- for PC, you are a lone parent;[343]
- you or your partner are in receipt of long-term incapacity benefit (IB), severe disablement allowance (SDA), attendance allowance (AA), disability living allowance (DLA), any mobility supplement or the disability or severe disability element of working tax credit (WTC);[344]
- you or your partner are registered or certified as blind;[345]
- for HB and CTB only, you or your partner are, or are treated as, incapable of work and have been, or have been treated as, incapable of work for a continuous period of 196 days in the case of a person who is terminally ill, or 364 days in any other case;[346]
- you or your partner qualify for a carer's premium (see p789). For a couple, if both partners get the carer's premium, £20 is disregarded from their combined earnings;[347]
- you or your partner previously had an earnings disregard of £20 in (for PC) your IS or income-based JSA or in (for HB/CTB) your HB or CTB, *and* that previous award of IS, income-based JSA, HB or CTB was not more than eight weeks before (for PC) the date you or your partner first became entitled to PC or (for HB/CTB) you or your partner reached the age of 60, *and* the employment which the earnings disregard applied to continues after the end of the previous award of IS, income-based JSA or HB/CTB.[348] This £20 disregard will continue so long as there is no break of more than eight weeks in either your claim for

PC or HB/CTB or in employment. Only one £20 disregard can apply, even if both you and your partner could qualify for a £20 disregard under this rule;

- for PC only, you or your partner, immediately before reaching pensionable age, had a £20 disregard under an award of PC because you or your partner were in receipt of long-term IB or SDA.[349] This £20 disregard will continue so long as there is no break of more than eight weeks in your claim for PC. Only one £20 disregard can apply, even if both you and your partner could qualify for a £20 disregard under this rule;
- you or your partner are an auxiliary coastguard, part-time firefighter, part-time member of a lifeboat crew or member of the Territorial Army.[350] If your, or your partner's, earnings from any of these jobs come to less than £20 a week, what is left over of the £20 disregard can be used against your, or your partner's, earnings from any other employment.

If you qualify under more than one category you still have a maximum of only £20 of your earnings disregarded.

Basic £5 or £10 disregard

If you do not qualify for a £25 or £20 disregard, £5 of your earnings is disregarded if you are single. If you claim as a member of a couple, £10 of your total income is disregarded, whether or not you are both working.[351]

Additional disregard for housing benefit and council tax benefit[352]

For **HB/CTB only**, whichever earnings disregard applies is increased by £16.05 if:

- you or your partner receive the 30-hour element as part of your (or your partner's) WTC (see p1237); *or*
- you or your partner work 30 hours a week or more on average; *or*
- you or your partner work 16 hours or more a week on average and your HB/CTB includes the family premium (see p777); *or*
- you are a lone parent and work 16 hours or more a week on average; *or*
- you or your partner work 16 hours or more a week on average and one or both of you get long-term IB, SDA, AA, DLA, mobility supplement, WTC disability or severe disability element, are registered blind or have been incapable of work for 364 days (196 days if terminally ill). For couples, the partner who is disabled is the one who must be working 16 hours a week or more on average; *or*
- you or your partner get a 50-plus element in WTC, or would qualify for one if you claimed WTC (see p1239).

The only exception is where your total earnings are less than the total of £16.05 plus any earnings disregard (see p888) and childcare costs disregard (see p888). In that case, £16.05 is disregarded from any WTC that is awarded to you or your partner, but the earnings disregard is not increased.

Note: as with the ordinary earnings disregards, only one additional disregard can be allowed from your (or your partner's) earnings.

Childcare costs for housing benefit and council tax benefit

For **HB/CTB**,[353] an allowance of up to £175 a week for one child, or up to £300 a week for two or more children, can be deducted from your (or your partner's) earnings (from employment or self-employment) in respect of childcare costs in certain circumstances. The rules are the same as those for people aged under 60 (see p856), except there is one extra way you can have an allowance deducted if you are a couple: if one of you works 16 hours or more a week and the other is aged 80 or over. There is no allowance for childcare costs for PC.

Benefits and tax credits

Some benefits and tax credits are taken into account as income and others are disregarded wholly or partly.

Benefits and tax credits that count in full:

- carer's allowance (CA);
- a payment under the Armed Forces and Reserve Forces Compensation Scheme for someone aged 18 or over whose parent died and who is disabled;[354]
- child's special allowance (it counts for HB/CTB but is ignored for PC[355]) and war orphan's pension;
- contribution-based JSA;
- IB and SDA;
- industrial injuries benefits, except constant attendance allowance and exceptionally severe disablement allowance which are disregarded;
- maternity allowance (MA);
- retirement pensions;
- SSP, SMP, SPP and SAP are treated as earnings and therefore may benefit from an earnings disregard (see p854);[356]
- widow's pension, bereavement allowance and industrial death benefit;
- WTC counts for PC, and for HB and CTB. For HB and CTB if your earnings are too low to use the whole £16.05 additional full-time earnings disregard (see p887), £16.05 is disregarded from your WTC instead of your earnings.[357] If a tax credit overpayment is being recovered from your WTC award, it is the amount of the WTC award less the overpayment that is taken into account for PC, HB and CTB;
- foreign social security benefits which are similar to the benefits listed above.[358]

Benefits and tax credits that are ignored completely:[359]

- AA;[360]
- bereavement payments are ignored as income,[361] although they would be taken into account as capital;

- child benefit;[362]
- child tax credit (CTC);[363]
- constant attendance allowance, exceptionally severe disablement allowance or severe disablement occupational allowance paid because of an injury at work or a war injury;[364]
- DLA care component and mobility component;[365]
- guardian's allowance;[366]
- mobility supplement under the War Pensions Scheme;[367]
- Christmas bonus (see p9);[368]
- social fund payments;[369]
- HB or CTB;[370]
- certain special war widows' payments[371] and any special or supplementary payments to pre-1973 war widows or widowers;[372]
- increases for child dependants are ignored. Increases for adult dependants are only ignored if the dependant is not your partner.[373]

Benefits that have £15 ignored:

- for HB/CTB only, widowed mother's allowance and widowed parent's allowance.[374]

Benefits that have £10 ignored:

- for PC only, widowed mother's allowance and widowed parent's allowance;[375]
- war disablement pension;[376]
- guaranteed income payment and survivor's guaranteed income payment under the Armed Forces and Reserve Forces Compensation Scheme;[377]
- war widow's, widower's or surviving civil partner's pension;[378]
- widow's, widower's or surviving civil partner's pension payable to a spouse or civil partner of a member of the Royal Navy, Army or Royal Air Force who was disabled or died as a result of service in the armed forces;[379]
- an extra-statutory payment made instead of the above pensions;[380]
- similar payments made by another country;[381]
- a pension from Germany or Austria paid to the victims of Nazi persecution.[382]

The £10 disregard allowed on these war pensions is additional to the total disregard of any mobility supplement or AA (ie, constant attendance allowance, exceptionally severe disablement allowance and severe disablement occupational allowance) paid as part of a war disablement pension.

Local authorities have discretion to increase the £10 disregard on war disablement, war widows' or widowers' pensions and the pension payable to widows or widowers of members of the Royal Navy, Army or Royal Air Force, and on the guaranteed income payment and survivor's guaranteed income payment, when assessing income for HB and CTB.[383] Some local authorities disregard the full amount of these pensions, and some do not increase the disregard at all, so you should check your own local authority's policy. It has been held that a local authority must at least consider the nature and purpose of such pensions when deciding whether or not to disregard them, and the courts have indicated that it may be appropriate to apply a disregard to retrospective awards.[384]

Benefit delays

If you have made a claim for benefit but have not yet been paid, the benefit should not be treated as income possessed by you. For PC, you should get your full benefit and leave the DWP to deduct the difference from arrears of the delayed benefit when it is eventually awarded.[385]

For the treatment of payments of arrears of certain benefits and CTC and WTC, see p940.

Maintenance payments

For **HB and CTB**, if you have a family premium included in your HB/CTB, at present £15 of any maintenance payments for you or your partner made by your (or your partner's) spouse/civil partner or former spouse/civil partner is disregarded.[386] If you receive maintenance from more than one person, only £15 of the total is disregarded. By the end of 2008, it is expected that the full amount of this kind of maintenance will be disregarded. Other kinds of maintenance (eg, for a child) do not count as income and are ignored completely.[387]

For **PC**, any maintenance payments for you or your partner made by your (or your partner's) spouse/civil partner or former spouse/civil partner count in full as income. Maintenance for a child is ignored completely.[388]

If you *pay* maintenance to a former partner or a child not living with you, your payments are not disregarded for the purpose of calculating your income for PC, HB or CTB.[389] Even if you are on PC you may still have to pay child support maintenance (see p765).

Income from tenants and lodgers

How income from tenants is treated depends on whether or not you live in the same property.

Lettings without board

If you are the owner of a property (or the tenant of it), you live in part of the property and you have an agreement with another person allowing her/him to occupy another part of the property for which s/he pays you rent, then all the rent paid to you is ignored if the rent is less than £20 a week. If the rent is £20 a week or more, £20 of the rent is ignored.[390]

Boarders

If you have a boarder(s) in your own home, the first £20 of the weekly charge is ignored and half of any balance remaining is then taken into account as your income.[391] For PC, if the boarder is a 'close relative' (see p797) or not staying on a commercial basis, this disregard does not apply. This applies for each boarder you have. The charge must normally include at least some meals.[392] If you have a business partner, even though your gross income includes just your share of the weekly charge to boarders, you still get the full disregard of £20 plus half the excess for each boarder.[393]

Tenants in other properties

Rent from a property other than your home is not taken into account as income.[394] Instead, the value of the property (if it cannot be disregarded) is treated as producing a 'deemed income' (see p892).

Income from capital

The general rule is that capital (unless disregarded) is assumed to provide a set rate of income called 'deemed income' (see p892). Actual income generated from capital is ignored as income[395] with the exception of the following types of capital. In these cases any actual income (but no deemed income) is taken into account.[396] **Note:** for HB and CTB it is only taken into account in these cases if the total capital listed below is worth more than £6,000 or, if you live in a care home, £10,000.[397]

Actual income from the following capital is taken into account:

- the value of the right to receive a payment in the future of:
  - income under a life interest or life rent;
  - rent, unless you only have a reversionary (ie, future) interest in the property (for the way actual rent is treated, see p890);
  - the surrender value or income under an annuity;
- property held in a trust, including a discretionary trust, but not charitable trusts or, for PC, trusts set up out of payments from personal injury to you or your partner or, for HB/CTB, from the Independent Living Funds, Macfarlane Trusts, the Fund, the Eileen Trust, the Skipton Fund or the London Bombings Relief Charitable Fund.

If deemed income is taken into account, actual income from the same capital is ignored.

Example

Frank, aged 72, has savings in the bank of £12,000. Deemed income is taken into account for PC, HB and CTB of £12 a week for each benefit. Any interest from the savings is ignored as income.

There are no rules that treat capital of any kind as though it were income.

Deemed income

There is no upper capital limit for PC. If you have capital above £6,000 (or £10,000 if you live in a care home), you will be treated as having an assumed income of £1 for every £500, or part of £500, by which your capital exceeds £6,000 (or £10,000).[398]

For HB and CTB the following apply.

- If you or your partner are getting the guarantee credit of PC then all of your (and your partner's) capital is ignored.[399]
- In any other case, there is a capital limit of £16,000.[400] If you have capital above £6,000 (or £10,000 if you live in a care home), you will be treated as having an assumed income of £1 for every £500, or part of £500, by which your capital exceeds £6,000 (£10,000) but does not exceed £16,000.[401]

For PC, HB and CTB, you are not treated as having deemed income on capital that is disregarded (see p937).

Occupational and personal pensions

The following income is taken into account:[402]

- an occupational pension;
- income from a personal pension;
- income from a retirement annuity contract (including an annuity purchased for you or transferred to you on divorce;
- payments from a former employer for early retirement on the grounds of ill health or disability, unless this was under a court order or settlement of a claim;[403]
- overseas pension;
- Civil List Act pension;[404]
- payment under an equity release scheme.[405] This provides regular payments from a loan secured on your home. For some home income plans, interest on the loan can be disregarded (see p870);
- payments from the Financial Assistance Scheme and periodic payments from the Pension Protection Fund (these help some people with underfunded occupational schemes whose employer has gone out of business).

Some charitable trusts provide discretionary income to people retired from specific occupations. This is ignored for PC, HB and CTB.[406]

Specified miscellaneous income

The following rules apply.

Income counted in full:

- copyright royalties, payments for patents, trademarks or under the Public Lending Right Scheme – add these payments to your earnings (if any) if you are the first owner of the copyright or patent or author of the book and deduct the appropriate earnings disregards on p885.[407]

Income that is ignored:

- income paid outside the UK which cannot be transferred here;[408]
- if income is paid in another currency, any bank charges for converting the payment into Sterling;[409]
- income from an annuity is normally taken into account. However, an amount equal to the interest payable on the loan with which the annuity was bought is ignored if the following conditions are met:[410]
  - you used at least 90 per cent of the loan made to you to buy the annuity; *and*
  - the annuity will end when you and your partner die; *and*
  - you or your partner are responsible for paying the interest on the loan; *and*
  - you, or both your partner and yourself, were at least 65 at the time the loan was made; *and*
  - the loan is secured on a property which you or your partner own or have an interest in, and the property on which the loan is secured is your home or that of your partner.

  If the interest on the loan is payable after income tax has been deducted, it is an amount equal to the net interest payment that is disregarded, otherwise it is the gross amount of the interest payment;
- any discretionary payment made to you by trustees is ignored altogether, *except* where the payment is for the purpose of:
  - obtaining food, ordinary clothing or footwear or household fuel; *or*
  - paying rent, council tax or water charges for which you or your partner (if any) are liable. **'Rent'** means eligible rent under the HB rules, less any non-dependant deductions; *or*
  - meeting housing costs which could be met by the PC rules,

  in which case £20 of the payment is disregarded, or if the payment is less than £20 the whole of the payment is disregarded.[411] If this disregard overlaps with certain other disregards (eg, certain war pensions) then a combined maximum of £20 is allowed.[412] **Note:** this is a weekly disregard so payments spread over different or successive benefit weeks attract a £20 disregard for each.

  School uniform and sportswear are examples of clothing and footwear that are not ordinary;
- periodic payments made to you or your partner under an agreement entered into in settlement of a claim for any injury to you or your partner;[413] any payment ordered by a court to be made to you or your partner because of an accident, injury or disease suffered by you or your partner (or, for HB and CTB only, your child).[414]

Notional income

You may, in certain circumstances, be treated as having income although you do not possess it or have used it up in the PC assessment and in HB and CTB.

If you are working, but earning less than the going rate, there are no rules to treat you as though your wages were higher than those you actually get, as there are for IS.

Deprivation of income to claim or increase benefit

If you deliberately get rid of income in order to claim or increase your benefit, you are treated as though you are still in receipt of the income.[415] The basic issues involved are the same as those for the deprivation of capital (see p942). If you deferred your retirement pension to get extra increments, then take a lump sum instead, you are not treated as still having the increments (see below for what happens if you fail to apply for, or defer, your pension). **Note:** the rule can only apply if the purpose of the deprivation is to gain benefit for *yourself* (or your partner). It should not apply if, for example, you stop claiming CA solely so that another person (who is not your partner) can become entitled to the severe disability premium (see p784).[416] However, if you do not claim a benefit which would clearly be paid if you did, it may be argued that you have failed to apply for income (see below).

Failing to apply for income

Sometimes you can be treated as having pension income even though you have not applied for it.[417]

If you defer your Category A or B pension, graduated retirement benefit or any shared additional pension paid on divorce, you are *not* treated as having that income for HB and CTB before you actually claim it. However, for PC, you *are* treated as having that income. The amount that counts for PC is the pension you would expect to be entitled to if you claimed, less any overlapping benefit you get (eg, SDA or CA). If you have deferred claiming your pension for at least 12 months, the amount is based on you taking the lump sum option (there is a choice when claiming a deferred pension to take a lump sum or to take extra pension income). To take account of the time it can take to process claims, you are only treated as having this income from the date you could expect to get it if you made a claim.

For PC, HB and CTB, you are treated as having any amount of Category C or D pension and age addition that you might expect to be entitled to if you claimed (for PC, deducting any overlapping benefit you get).

You are treated as having any income from an occupational pension that you have elected to defer, as though you had claimed it (for PC, taking account of the time it might take to process and deducting any overlapping benefit). If you are aged 60 or over and entitled to money purchase benefits under an occupational or personal pension scheme and you fail to purchase an annuity (because you defer or do not apply), you are treated as having the amount of income you have foregone. If your scheme does not allow income withdrawal, you are treated as having income you could have received if you had chosen a different kind of scheme. However, if you give up a small occupational or personal pension in favour of a 'trivial commutation' lump sum (there is a limit set in law), you are not treated as having that income.[418]

Income paid to someone else on your behalf

Any money that counts as income (see p881) and is paid to someone on your behalf is normally treated as being yours and then either taken into account or ignored as income under the rules described in this chapter. The exception is for payments of income made under an occupational or personal pension scheme (or, for HB and CTB only, from the Pension Protection Fund) if you or your partner (if any) are bankrupt (or the subject of a sequestration order). In this case, if the payment is made to the trustee or other person acting on your creditors' behalf and you (and your partner) have no income other than the payment made, it is not treated as being yours.[419]

Other income

Only income that is specified in the rules can affect your benefit. That income is listed on p881 and described above. Any other kind of income is ignored. Below are some examples of income that is ignored and does not affect your benefit.

- **Student loans and grants** are disregarded.[420]
- For HB and CTB only, there is a specific disregard if you make a **parental contribution** to a student's grant or loan. An equal amount of income you have for the period the grant or loan is paid is ignored.[421] If you are a parent of a student under 25 in advanced education who does not get a grant or loan (or who only gets a smaller discretionary award) and you contribute to her/his living expenses, your contribution up to a maximum of £47.95 (less the weekly amount of any discretionary award the student has) is ignored from your income during term time.[422]
- **Adoption allowances, fostering allowances and residence order payments** are disregarded in full.[423]
- **Charitable and voluntary payments** are not taken into account as income, so if a charity or a person gives you voluntary payments, that does not reduce your benefit. Note that maintenance payments can affect your benefit (see p890).

Working out weekly income

To assess your weekly income:

- work out whether income is taken into account or fully or partly disregarded (see p880);
- if income varies, work out average income (see p896);

- convert into a weekly amount if necessary (see below);
- add any deemed weekly income from capital (see p892);
- for HB and CTB if you are working and eligible for a childcare cost disregard, deduct the eligible childcare charges (see p888).

Variable income

Where your earnings vary because you do not work the same hours every week, your weekly income may be averaged over the cycle, if there is an identifiable one.[424] Where you do not work a recognisable cycle or your income fluctuates, your income is worked out on the basis of:

- the last two payments before your claim was made or treated as made (or, where applicable, before your claim was superseded), if those payments are at least one month apart; *or*
- the last four payments before your claim was made or treated as made (or, where applicable, before your claim was superseded), if the last two payments are less than a month apart; *or*
- calculating (or estimating for HB or CTB) any other payments that would give a more accurate figure for your average weekly income.[425]

In all cases, if the cycle involves periods when you do no work, those periods are included in the cycle, but not other absences – eg, holidays, sickness.

If you are entitled to receive:

- royalties or other sums in respect of the use of any copyright, patent or trademark; *or*
- payments in respect of any book registered under the Public Lending Right Scheme 1982; *or*
- payments made on an occasional basis,

the payment is treated as if made for a period of a year.[426]

Converting income into a weekly amount

PC, HB and CTB are calculated on a weekly basis so your earnings and other income have to be converted into a weekly amount if necessary.

The following rules apply to income from employment and other income.[427] For income from self-employment, see p885.

- If the payment is for less than a week, it is treated as the weekly amount.
- If the payment is for a month, multiply by 12 and divide by 52.
- Multiply a payment for three months by four and divide by 52.
- Divide a payment for a year by 52.
- Multiply payments for any other periods by seven and divide by the number of days in the period.

The date from when a payment is counted

For PC, at the start of a claim or a new 'assessed income period' (see p458), the total weekly income is taken into account from the first day of the first 'benefit week' or new assessed income period.[428] A **'benefit week'** is the seven days starting on the day PC is payable.[429]

The general rule is that social security benefits are treated as paid on the first day of the PC benefit week in which the benefit is payable.[430] Some benefits are treated slightly differently. Contribution-based JSA, IB, SDA and MA are treated as paid on the day that benefit is payable.

For other types of income, the general rule is that changes to income take effect from the first day of the benefit week in which the change takes place.[431] If that is not practicable, the change is put into effect from the start of the next benefit week. However, where there is a change to the amount of deemed income from capital or an increase in WTC, the change is put into effect from the benefit week that starts on or after the change takes place.[432]

Notes

1 **HB** Schs 4 para 12 and 5 para 4 HB Regs; reg 26 HB(SPC) Regs
CTB Schs 3 para 12 and 4 para 4 CTB Regs; reg 16 CTB(SPC) Regs

2 Reg 80(2) JSA Regs

1. People aged under 60

3 **IS/HB/CTB** s136(1) SSCBA 1992
JSA s13(2) JSA 1995

4 **HB** Schs 4 para 12 and 5 para 4 HB Regs
CTB Schs 3 para 12 and 4 para 4 CTB Regs

5 **IS** Reg 23(4) IS Regs
JSA Reg 88(3) JSA Regs

6 **IS** Reg 23(2) IS Regs
JSA Reg 88(2) JSA Regs

7 **HB** Reg 25(3) HB Regs
CTB Reg 15(3) CTB Regs

8 **IS** Reg 14(2)(c) IS Regs
JSA Reg 76(2)(d) JSA Regs
HB Reg 19(2)(c) HB Regs
CTB Reg 9(2)(c) CTB Regs

9 **IS** Reg 17(b) IS Regs
JSA Reg 83(b) JSA Regs

10 **IS** Reg 44(5) IS Regs
JSA Reg 106(5) JSA Regs

11 **IS** Reg 44(4) and Sch 8 para 15 IS Regs
JSA Reg 106(4) and Sch 6 para 18 JSA Regs
Both Reg 1 SS(WTCCTC)(CA) Regs

12 **IS** Sch 8 paras 14 and 15 IS Regs
JSA Sch 6 paras 17 and 18 JSA Regs

13 **IS** Reg 44(4) IS Regs
JSA Reg 106(4) JSA Regs

14 **IS** Reg 40 and Sch 9 para 1 IS Regs
JSA Reg 103(1) and (2) and Sch 7 para 1 JSA Regs
HB Reg 40 and Sch 5 para 1 HB Regs
CTB Reg 30 and Sch 4 para 1 CTB Regs

15 **HB** Reg 34 HB Regs
CTB Reg 24 CTB Regs

16 R(IS) 4/01

17 *R v SBC ex parte Singer* [1973] 1 WLR 713

18 *Parsons v Hogg* [1985] 2 All ER 897 (CA), appendix to R(FIS) 4/85

19 R(FC) 1/90

20 CFC/26/1989

21 R(FIS) 4/85

22 R(IS) 13/91; R(IS) 16/93; CFC/26/1989

23 CCS/318/1995 (applying the identical provisions in child support law)

24 CCS/5352/1995

25 R(CS) 2/99, following CCS/10/1994 and R(CS) 10/98, and CCS/2561/1998, but see CCS/12769/1996 for a contrary view

26 CCS/3882/1997

27 R(FIS) 4/85; R(FC) 1/91; R(IS) 13/91

28 CIS/521/1990

29 **IS** Reg 36(3) IS Regs
JSA Reg 99(1) and (4) JSA Regs
HB Reg 36(3) HB Regs
CTB Reg 26(3) CTB Regs
30 **HB** Regs 29(2) and 36(6) HB Regs
CTB Regs 19(2) and 26(6) CTB Regs
31 **HB** Reg 34 HB Regs
CTB Reg 24 CTB Regs
Both para BW2.34
32 R(SB) 21/86
IS Reg 35(1) IS Regs
JSA Reg 98(1) JSA Regs
HB Reg 35(1) HB Regs
CTB Reg 25(1) CTB Regs
33 **HB** Reg 35(1)(i)-(j) HB Regs
CTB Reg 25(1)(i)-(j) CTB Regs
34 **IS** Regs 35(2)(b) and 40(4) and Sch 9 paras 1, 4 and 4A IS Regs
JSA Regs 98(2)(c) and 103(6) and Sch 7 paras 1, 4 and 5 JSA Regs
35 **HB** Reg 35(1)(i)-(j) HB Regs
CTB Reg 25(1)(i)-(j) CTB Regs
36 **IS** Regs 35(2)(b) and 40(4) and Sch 9 paras 1, 4 and 4A IS Regs
JSA Regs 98(2)(c) and 103(6) and Sch 7 paras 1, 4 and 5 JSA Regs
37 **IS** Reg 35(1)(e) IS Regs
JSA Reg 98(1)(d) JSA Regs
HB Reg 35(1)(e) HB Regs
CTB Reg 25(1)(e) CTB Regs
38 R(IS) 9/95
39 **IS** Reg 35(3)(a)(iv) IS Regs
JSA Reg 98(3)(d) JSA Regs
40 **IS** Reg 35(1)(j) IS Regs
JSA Reg 98(1)(h) JSA Regs
HB Reg 35(1)(k) HB Regs
CTB Reg 25(1)(k) CTB Regs
41 **IS** Reg 35(2A) IS Regs
JSA Reg 98(2A) JSA Regs
HB Reg 35(3) HB Regs
CTB Reg 25(3) CTB Regs
42 **IS** Reg 35(2)(a) and Sch 9 para 21 IS Regs
JSA Reg 98(2)(a) and Sch 7 para 22 JSA Regs
HB Reg 35(2)(a) and Sch 5 para 23 HB Regs
CTB Reg 25(2)(a) and Sch 4 para 24 CTB Regs
43 CIS/11482/1995
44 para 26095 DMG
45 **IS** Reg 35(2)(a) IS Regs
JSA Reg 98(2)(a) JSA Regs
Both para 26040 DMG
46 **HB** Reg 35(2)(a) HB Regs
CTB Reg 25(2)(a) CTB Regs
47 **IS** Reg 48(5) IS Regs
JSA Reg 110(5) JSA Regs
HB Reg 46(5) HB Regs
CTB Reg 36(5) CTB Regs
48 **IS** Reg 48(6) IS Regs
JSA Reg 110(6) JSA Regs
49 **IS** Reg 35(2)(c) IS Regs
JSA Reg 98(2)(d) JSA Regs
HB Reg 35(2)(b) HB Regs
CTB Reg 25(2)(b) CTB Regs
50 CIS/77/1993; CIS/89/1989
51 **IS** Sch 8 para 11 IS Regs
JSA Sch 6 para 14 JSA Regs
HB Sch 4 para 13 HB Regs
CTB Sch 3 para 13 CTB Regs
52 **IS** Sch 8 para 12 IS Regs
JSA Sch 6 para 15 JSA Regs
HB Sch 4 para 14 HB Regs
CTB Sch 3 para 14 CTB Regs
53 **IS** Reg 35(2)(d) IS Regs
JSA Reg 98(2)(e) JSA Regs
HB Reg 35(2)(c) HB Regs
CTB Reg 25(2)(c) CTB Regs
54 **IS** Reg 40(4) and Sch 9 para 1 IS Regs
JSA Reg 103(6) and Sch 7 para 1 JSA Regs
HB Reg 40(10) and Sch 5 para 1 HB Regs
CTB Reg 30(11) and Sch 4 para 1 CTB Regs
55 **IS** Sch 8 paras 1(1)(a), (2) and 2 IS Regs
JSA Sch 6 paras 1(1)(a), (2) and 2 JSA Regs
HB Sch 4 paras 1(b) and 2(b)(i) HB Regs
CTB Sch 3 paras 1(b) and 2(b)(i) CTB Regs
56 **IS** Reg 35(1)(g) IS Regs
JSA Reg 98(1)(f) JSA Regs
HB Reg 35(1)(g) HB Regs
CTB Reg 25(1)(g) CTB Regs
57 **IS** Reg 35(1)(h) IS Regs
JSA Reg 98(1)(g) JSA Regs
HB Reg 35(1)(h) HB Regs
CTB Reg 25(1)(h) CTB Regs
58 **IS** Reg 35(1)(h) IS Regs
HB Reg 35(1)(h) HB Regs
CTB Reg 25(1)(h) CTB Regs
59 **IS** Sch 8 para 1(2)(b)(ii) IS Regs
JSA Sch 6 para 1(2)(b)(ii) JSA Regs
HB Sch 4 para 1(b)(ii)(bb) HB Regs
CTB Sch 3 para 1(b)(ii)(bb) CTB Regs
60 **IS** Reg 31 IS Regs
JSA Reg 96 JSA Regs

61 **IS** Regs 35(2)(b) and 40(4) and Sch 9 paras 4 and 4A IS Regs; R(IS) 8/99
JSA Regs 98(2)(c) and 103(6) and Sch 7 paras 4 and 5 JSA Regs
HB Reg 35(1)(i) to (j) and Sch 4 paras 1(b) and 2(b)(i) HB Regs
CTB Reg 25(1)(i) to (j) and Sch 3 paras 1(b) and 2(b)(i) CTB Regs
62 **IS** Reg 35(3)(a)(iii) IS Regs
JSA Reg 98(2)(f) JSA Regs
HB because not listed as earnings in reg 35 HB Regs
CTB Reg 25 CTB Regs
63 **IS** Reg 35(1)(i) and (3) and Sch 8 paras 1(1)(a) and 2 IS Regs
JSA Reg 98(1)(b) and Sch 6 paras 1(1)(a) and 2 JSA Regs
HB Reg 35 HB Regs
CTB Reg 25 CTB Regs
64 **IS** Reg 35(1)(b) IS Regs
JSA Regs 98(2)(b) and 103(6)(a) JSA Regs
HB Reg 35(1)(b) HB Regs
CTB Reg 25(1)(b) CTB Regs
65 **IS** Regs 35(1)(d) and 48(3) IS Regs
JSA Regs 98(1)(c) and 110(3) JSA Regs
HB Regs 35(1)(d) and 46(3) HB Regs
CTB Regs 25(1)(d) and 36(3) CTB Regs
66 **IS** Regs 35(2)(b) and 40(4) IS Regs
JSA Regs 98(2)(c) and 103(6) JSA Regs
67 **HB** Reg 35(1)(i) to (j) and Sch 4 paras 1(c) and 2(b)(ii) HB Regs
CTB Reg 25(1)(i) to (j) and Sch 3 paras 1(c) and 2(b)(ii) CTB Regs
68 **IS** Regs 35(1)(d) and 48(3) and Sch 8 paras 1(1)(b) and 2 IS Regs
JSA Regs 98(1)(c) and 110(3) and Sch 6 paras 1(1)(b) and 2 JSA Regs
HB Regs 35(1)(d) and 46(3) and Sch 4 paras 1(c) and 2(b)(ii) HB Regs
CTB Regs 25(1)(d) and 36(3) and Sch 3 paras 1(c) and 2(b)(ii) CTB Regs
69 **IS** Sch 8 paras 1(1)(b) and 2 IS Regs
JSA Sch 6 paras 1(1)(b) and 2 JSA Regs
HB Sch 4 paras 1(c) and 2(b)(ii) HB Regs
CTB Sch 3 paras 1(c) and 2(b)(ii) CTB Regs
70 **IS** Reg 35 IS Regs
JSA Reg 98 JSA Regs
HB Reg 35 HB Regs
CTB Reg 25 CTB Regs
71 **IS** Reg 29(4) and (4C) IS Regs
JSA Reg 94(4) JSA Regs
72 **IS** Regs 35(2)(b) and 40(4) IS Regs
JSA Regs 98(2)(c) and 103(6) JSA Regs
73 **IS** Reg 37(1) IS Regs
JSA Reg 100(1) JSA Regs
HB Reg 37 HB Regs
CTB Reg 27 CTB Regs
74 **IS** Reg 38(3) IS Regs
JSA Reg 101(4) JSA Regs
HB Reg 38(3) HB Regs
CTB Reg 28(3) CTB Regs
75 **IS** Reg 2(1) IS Regs
JSA s35(1) JSA 1995
HB Regs 2(1) and 38(11) and (12) HB Regs
CTB Regs 2(1) and 28(11) and (12) CTB Regs
76 Reg 32(3) SS(C&P) Regs
77 **IS** Reg 37(2)(a) IS Regs
JSA Reg 100(2)(a) JSA Regs
HB Sch 5 para 42 HB Regs
CTB Sch 4 para 23 CTB Regs
78 **IS** Reg 38(3)(a), (4), (7) and (8)(a) IS Regs
JSA Reg 101(4) and (8) JSA Regs
HB Reg 38(3)(a), (4), (7) and (8)(a) HB Regs
CTB Reg 28(3)(a), (4), (7) and (8)(a) CTB Regs
79 R(IS) 13/91; R(FC) 1/91; CFC/26/1989
80 **IS** Reg 38(6) and (8)(b) IS Regs
JSA Reg 101(7) and (9) JSA Regs
HB Reg 38(6) and (8)(b) HB Regs
CTB Reg 28(6) and (8)(b) CTB Regs
81 **IS** Reg 38(5) IS Regs
JSA Reg 101(6) and (8) JSA Regs
HB Reg 38(5) HB Regs
CTB Reg 28(5) CTB Regs
82 R(FC) 1/96
83 **IS** Reg 38(11) IS Regs
JSA Reg 101(12) JSA Regs
HB Reg 38(10) HB Regs
CTB Reg 28(10) CTB Regs
See also R(FC) 1/93
84 CFC/836/1995
85 **IS** Reg 30 IS Regs
JSA Reg 95 JSA Regs
86 **IS** CIS/166/1994; CIS/14409/1996
JSA Regs 95(1)(b) and 101(11) JSA Regs
87 **IS** Reg 30(2) IS Regs
JSA Reg 95(2) JSA Regs
88 **HB** Regs 30(1) and 33(2) HB Regs
CTB Regs 20(1) and 23(2) CTB Regs
89 **IS** Sch 8 para 3 IS Regs
JSA Sch 6 para 4 JSA Regs
90 **IS** Reg 38(9) IS Regs
JSA Reg 101(10) JSA Regs
HB Reg 38(9) HB Regs
CTB Reg 28(9) CTB Regs

91 **HB** Sch 4 para 4 HB Regs
CTB Sch 3 para 4 CTB Regs
92 **IS** Sch 8 para 5 IS Regs
JSA Sch 6 para 6 JSA Regs
93 **IS** Sch 8 para 4(2) IS Regs
JSA Sch 6 para 5(1) and (2) JSA Regs
HB Sch 4 para 3(2) HB Regs
CTB Sch 3 para 3(2) CTB Regs
94 **IS** Sch 8 paras 6A and 6B IS Regs
JSA Sch 6 paras 7 and 8 JSA Regs
HB Sch 4 paras 5 and 6 HB Regs
CTB Sch 3 paras 5 and 6 CTB Regs
95 **IS** Sch 8 para 7(1) IS Regs
JSA Sch 6 para 9(1) JSA Regs
HB Sch 4 para 8(1) HB Regs
CTB Sch 3 para 8(1) CTB Regs
96 **IS** Sch 8 para 8 IS Regs
JSA Sch 6 para 10 JSA Regs
HB Sch 4 para 9 HB Regs
CTB Sch 3 para 9 CTB Regs
97 **IS** Sch 8 para 7(2) IS Regs
JSA Sch 6 paras 9-10 JSA Regs
HB Sch 4 para 8(2)(b) HB Regs
CTB Sch 3 para 8(2)(b) CTB Regs
98 **IS** Sch 8 para 4(3) IS Regs
JSA Sch 6 para 5(3) JSA Regs
HB Sch 4 para 3(3) HB Regs
CTB Sch 3 para 3(3) CTB Regs
99 **IS** Sch 8 para 4(4) IS Regs
JSA Sch 6 para 5(4) JSA Regs
HB Sch 4 para 3(4) HB Regs
CTB Sch 3 para 3(4) CTB Regs
100 **IS** Sch 8 paras 6 and 9 IS Regs
JSA Sch 6 paras 11-12 JSA Regs
HB Sch 4 paras 7 and 10 HB Regs
CTB Sch 3 paras 7 and 10 CTB Regs
101 **HB** Sch 4 para 17 HB Regs
CTB Sch 3 para 16 CTB Regs
102 **HB** Regs 27(1)(c) and 28 HB Regs; reg 30(1)(c) HB(SPC) Regs
CTB Regs 17(1)(c) and 18 CTB Regs; reg 20(1)(c) CTB(SPC) Regs
103 **HB** Reg 27(2) HB Regs; reg 30(2) HB(SPC) Regs
CTB 17(2) CTB Regs; reg 20(2) CTB(SPC) Regs
104 **HB** Reg 28(6) HB Regs; reg 31(6) HB(SPC) Regs
CTB Reg 18(6) CTB Regs; reg 21(6) CTB(SPC) Regs
105 **HB** Reg 28(13) HB Regs; reg 31(13) HB(SPC) Regs
CTB Reg 18(13) CTB Regs; reg 21(13) CTB(SPC) Regs
106 **HB** Reg 28(6)-(8) HB Regs; reg 31(6)-(8) HB(SPC) Regs
CTB Reg 18(6)-(8) CTB Regs; reg 21(6)-(8) CTB(SPC) Regs
107 **HB** Reg 28(14) HB Regs; reg 31(14) HB(SPC) Regs
CTB Reg 18(14) CTB Regs; reg 21(14) CTB(SPC) Regs
108 **HB** Reg 28(2)-(4) HB Regs; reg 31(2)-(4) HB(SPC) Regs
CTB Reg 18(2)-(4) CTB Regs; reg 21(2)-(4) CTB(SPC) Regs
109 **HB** Reg 28(11) HB Regs; reg 31(11) HB(SPC) Regs
CTB Reg 18(11) CTB Regs; reg 21(11) CTB(SPC) Regs
110 **HB** Reg 28(10) HB Regs; reg 31(10) HB(SPC) Regs
CTB Reg 18(10) CTB Regs; reg 21(10) CTB(SPC) Regs
111 R(IS) 4/05
112 **IS** Reg 7(4) and (5) SS(WTCCTC)(CA) Regs
JSA Reg 8(3) and (4) SS(WTCCTC)(CA) Regs
113 **IS** Reg 7(6) SS(WTCCTC)(CA) Regs
JSA Reg 8(5) SS(WTCCTC)(CA) Regs
114 **IS** Reg 35(2) and Sch 9 para 4 IS Regs
JSA Sch 7 para 5 JSA Regs
115 **HB** Reg 35(1)(i) HB Regs
CTB Reg 25(1)(i) CTB Regs
116 **HB** Sch 5 para 56 HB Regs
CTB Sch 4 para 56 CTB Regs
117 **IS** Sch 9 IS Regs
JSA Sch 7 JSA Regs
HB Sch 5 HB Regs
CTB Sch 4 CTB Regs
118 **IS** Sch 9 para 9 IS Regs
JSA Sch 7 para 10 JSA Regs
HB Sch 5 para 9 HB Regs
CTB Sch 4 para 10 CTB Regs
119 **IS** Sch 9 para 5B(2) IS Regs
JSA Sch 7 para 6B(2) JSA Regs
120 **IS** Sch 9 para 5B(1) IS Regs
JSA Sch 7 para 6B(1) JSA Regs
121 **IS** Sch 9 para 9 IS Regs
JSA Sch 7 para 10 JSA Regs
HB Sch 5 paras 6 and 9 HB Regs
CTB Sch 4 paras 7 and 10 CTB Regs
122 **IS** Sch 9 paras 6 and 9 IS Regs
JSA Sch 7 paras 7 and 10 JSA Regs
HB Sch 5 para 6 HB Regs
CTB Sch 4 para 7 CTB Regs
123 **IS** Sch 9 para 5A(1) IS Regs
JSA Sch 7 para 6A(1) JSA Regs
HB Sch 5 para 50 HB Regs
CTB Sch 4 para 51 CTB Regs
124 **IS** Sch 9 para 8 IS Regs
JSA Sch 7 para 9 JSA Regs
HB Sch 5 para 8 HB Regs
CTB Sch 4 para 9 CTB Regs

125 **IS** Sch 9 para 33 IS Regs
JSA Sch 7 para 35 JSA Regs
HB Sch 5 para 32 HB Regs
CTB Sch 4 para 33 CTB Regs
126 **IS** Sch 9 paras 7 and 8 IS Regs
JSA Sch 7 paras 8 and 9 JSA Regs
HB Sch 5 paras 7 and 8 HB Regs
CTB Sch 4 paras 8 and 9 CTB Regs
127 **IS** Sch 9 para 31 IS Regs
JSA Schs 7 para 33 and 8 para 23 JSA Regs
HB Sch 5 para 31 HB Regs
CTB Sch 4 para 32 CTB Regs
128 **IS** Sch 10 para 18 IS Regs
JSA Sch 8 para 23 JSA Regs
HB Sch 6 para 20 HB Regs
CTB Sch 5 para 20 CTB Regs
129 **IS** Sch 9 paras 5, 45 and 52 IS Regs
JSA Sch 7 paras 6, 44 and 51 JSA Regs
HB Sch 5 paras 40 and 51 HB Regs
CTB Sch 4 paras 37 and 42 CTB Regs
130 **IS** Sch 9 para 47 IS Regs
JSA Sch 7 para 46 JSA Regs
HB Sch 5 para 43 HB Regs
CTB Sch 4 para 44 CTB Regs
131 **IS** Sch 9 paras 54-56 IS Regs
JSA Sch 7 paras 53-55 JSA Regs
HB Sch 5 paras 53-55 HB Regs
CTB Sch 4 paras 53-55 CTB Regs
132 **IS** Sch 9 para 53 IS Regs
JSA Sch 7 para 52 JSA Regs
HB Sch 5 para 52 HB Regs
CTB Sch 4 para 52 CTB Regs
133 **HB** Sch 5 para 4 HB Regs
CTB Sch 4 para 4 CTB Regs
134 **IS** Sch 9 paras 40-42 IS Regs
HB Sch 5 paras 36, 37 and 48 HB Regs
CTB Sch 4 paras 38, 39 and 49 CTB Regs
135 **IS** Sch 9 para 40 IS Regs
JSA Sch 7 para 42 JSA Regs
HB Sch 5 para 36 HB Regs
CTB Sch 4 para 38 CTB Regs
136 **IS** Sch 9 para 46 IS Regs
JSA Sch 7 para 45 JSA Regs
HB Sch 5 para 41 HB Regs
CTB Sch 4 para 43 CTB Regs
137 **HB** Sch 5 para 16 HB Regs
CTB Sch 4 para 17 CTB Regs
138 **IS** Sch 9 para 16 IS Regs
JSA Sch 7 para 17 JSA Regs
139 **IS** Sch 9 para 16 IS Regs
JSA Sch 7 para 17 JSA Regs
HB Sch 5 para 15 HB Regs; Sch Part I HB&CTB(WPD) Regs
CTB Sch 4 para 16 CTB Regs; Sch Part I HB&CTB(WPD) Regs
140 **IS** Sch 9 para 16(cc) IS Regs
JSA Sch 7 para 17(aa) JSA Regs
HB Sch 5 para 15(d) HB Regs
CTB Sch 4 para 16(d) CTB Regs
141 **IS** Sch 9 para 16 IS Regs
JSA Sch 7 para 17 JSA Regs
HB Sch 5 para 15 HB Regs; Sch Part 2 HB&CTB(WPD) Regs
CTB Sch 4 para 16 CTB Regs; Sch Part 2 HB&CTB(WPD) Regs
142 **IS** Sch 9 para 16 IS Regs
JSA Sch 7 para 17 JSA Regs
HB Sch 5 para 15 HB Regs
CTB Sch 4 para 16 CTB Regs
143 **IS** Sch 9 para 16 IS Regs
JSA Sch 7 para 17 JSA Regs
HB Sch 5 para 15 HB Regs
CTB Sch 4 para 16 CTB Regs
144 **IS** Sch 9 para 16 IS Regs
JSA Sch 7 para 17 JSA Regs
HB Sch 5 para 15 HB Regs
CTB Sch 4 para 16 CTB Regs
145 **IS** Sch 9 para 16 IS Regs
JSA Sch 7 para 17 JSA Regs
HB Sch 5 para 15 HB Regs
CTB Sch 4 para 16 CTB Regs
146 **IS** Sch 9 para 36 IS Regs
JSA Sch 7 para 38 JSA Regs
HB Sch 5 para 34 HB Regs
CTB Sch 4 para 35 CTB Regs
147 ss134(8) and 139(6) SSAA 1992
HB Reg 40(3)-(4A) HB Regs
CTB Reg 30(3)-(4A) CTB Regs
148 *R v South Hams District Council, ex parte Ash, The Times*, 27 May 1999
149 s74(2) SSAA 1992
150 **HB** Reg 40(6) HB Regs
CTB Reg 30(6) CTB Regs
151 CH/1450/2005
152 **HB** Reg 32 Regs; reg 32 HB(SPC) Regs
CTB Reg 22 CTB Regs; reg 22 CTB(SPC) Regs
153 BW2.642 GM; in CIS/1064/2004, para 48, the Revenue said additional payments counted as tax credits and not extra-statutory payments.
154 CIS/1064/2004 seems to lend weight to this approach.
155 **IS** Regs 28, 31(3), 32 and 40 IS Regs
JSA Regs 93, 96(3), 97 and 103 JSA Regs
156 CIS/1813/2007, but note CIS/647/2007 and CH/1450/2005, which found the opposite for HB.
157 **IS** Sch 9 para 73 IS Regs
JSA Sch 7 para 70 JSA Regs

158 Reg 1(3) Social Security (Child Maintenance Premium) Amendment Regulations 2004 No.98
159 **HB** Sch 5 paras 14(2) and 47 HB Regs
CTB Sch 4 paras 15(2) and 48 CTB Regs
160 CIS/683/1993
161 **IS** Sch 9 para 25(1)(a) and (1A) IS Regs
JSA Sch 7 para 26(1)(a) and (1A) JSA Regs
162 Reg 1 and Schs 1 para 23(c) and 2 para 23(c) SS(WTCCTC)(CA) Regs
163 **IS** Sch 9 para 25(1)(a) and (2)(b) IS Regs
JSA Sch 7 para 26(1)(a) and (2)(b) JSA Regs
HB Sch 5 para 25(1)(a) and (3) HB Regs
CTB Sch 4 para 26(1)(a) and (3) CTB Regs
164 **IS** Sch 9 para 25(2)(a) IS Regs
JSA Sch 7 para 26(2)(a) JSA Regs
165 **IS** Sch 9 para 25(1A) IS Regs
JSA Sch 7 para 26(1A) JSA Regs
HB Sch 5 para 25(2) HB Regs
CTB Sch 4 para 26(2) CTB Regs
166 **IS** Reg 42(4)(b) IS Regs
JSA Reg 105(10)(b) JSA Regs
HB Reg 35(3)(b) HB Regs
CTB Reg 26(3)(b) CTB Regs
All para 28174 DMG
167 That is, under ss23(2)(a) or 59(1)(a) CA 1989 or (in Scotland) s26 C(S)A 1995 or reg 9 Fostering of Children (Scotland) Regulations 1996.
168 **IS** Sch 9 para 26 IS Regs
JSA Sch 7 para 27 JSA Regs
HB Sch 5 para 26 HB Regs
CTB Sch 4 para 27 CTB Regs
169 **IS** Sch 9 para 25(1)(c) and (2) IS Regs
JSA Sch 7 para 26(1) JSA Regs
HB Sch 5 para 25(1)(b) and (3) HB Regs
CTB Sch 4 para 26(1)(b) and (3) CTB Regs
170 **IS** Reg 48(8) IS Regs
JSA Reg 110(8) JSA Regs
171 **IS** Sch 9 para 25(1)(e) IS Regs
JSA Sch 7 para 26(1) JSA Regs
HB Sch 5 para 25(1)(d) HB Regs
CTB Sch 4 para 26(1)(d) CTB Regs
172 **IS** Sch 9 para 39 IS Regs
JSA Sch 7 para 41(1) JSA Regs
HB Sch 5 para 35 HB Regs
CTB Sch 4 para 36 CTB Regs
173 **IS** Reg 48(9) IS Regs
JSA Reg 110(9) JSA Regs
HB Reg 46(6) HB Regs
CTB Reg 36(6) CTB Regs
174 **IS** Reg 48(10)(a) IS Regs
JSA Reg 110(10) JSA Regs
175 **IS** Sch 9 para 15 IS Regs
JSA Sch 7 para 15 JSA Regs
HB Sch 5 para 14 HB Regs
CTB Sch 4 para 15 CTB Regs
All See *Secretary of State for Work and Pensions v Perkins and Ryedale District Council* [2004] EWCA Civ 1671 if it is not clear for what the payments are intended or used.
176 R(H) 5/05 explains the difference between a loan and a voluntary payment.
177 **IS** Sch 9 para 15(5A) IS Regs
JSA Sch 7 para 15(5A) JSA Regs
HB Sch 5 para 14 HB Regs
CTB Sch 4 para 15 CTB Regs
178 para 28102 DMG
179 **IS** Sch 9 para 19 IS Regs
JSA Sch 7 para 20 JSA Regs
HB Sch 5 para 22 HB Regs
CTB Sch 4 para 22 CTB Regs
180 **IS** Sch 9 para 18 IS Regs
JSA Sch 7 para 19 JSA Regs
HB Sch 5 para 21 HB Regs
CTB Sch 4 para 21 CTB Regs
181 **IS** Sch 9 para 20 IS Regs
JSA Sch 7 para 21 JSA Regs
HB Sch 5 para 42 HB Regs
CTB Sch 4 para 23 CTB Regs
182 **IS** Reg 2(1) IS Regs
JSA Reg 1(3) JSA Regs
HB Sch 5 para 42(2) HB Regs
CTB Sch 4 para 23(2) CTB Regs
All Definition of 'board and lodging accommodation'
183 CIS/521/2002
184 CIS/13059/1996
185 **IS** Reg 48(4) IS Regs
JSA Reg 110(4) JSA Regs
HB Reg 46(4) HB Regs
CTB Reg 36(4) CTB Regs
All *CAO v Palfrey and Others, The Times*, 17 February 1995; R(IS) 26/95
186 R(IS) 26/95
187 **IS** Sch 9 para 22(1) IS Regs
JSA Sch 7 para 23 JSA Regs
HB Sch 5 para 17(1) HB Regs
CTB Sch 4 para 18(1) CTB Regs
188 **IS** Reg 48(4) IS Regs
JSA Reg 110(4) JSA Regs
HB Reg 46(4) HB Regs
CTB Reg 36(4) CTB Regs
189 **IS** Sch 9 para 22(1) IS Regs
JSA Sch 7 para 23(2) JSA Regs
HB Sch 5 para 17(1) HB Regs
CTB Sch 4 para 18(1) CTB Regs
190 CFC/13/1993

191 **IS** Sch 9 para 22(2) IS Regs
JSA Sch 7 para 23(2) and (3) JSA Regs
HB Sch 5 para 17(2) HB Regs
CTB Sch 4 para 18(2) CTB Regs
192 **IS** Reg 53 IS Regs
JSA Reg 116 JSA Regs
HB Reg 52 HB Regs
CTB Reg 42 CTB Regs
193 **IS** Reg 32(1B) SS(C&P) Regs
JSA Reg 24(7) JSA Regs
194 **HB** Reg 88 HB Regs
CTB Reg 74 CTB Regs
195 **IS** Reg 41(1) IS Regs
JSA Reg 104(1) JSA Regs
196 **HB** Reg 41(1) HB Regs
CTB Reg 31(1) CTB Regs
197 **IS** Reg 29(2)(a) IS Regs
JSA Reg 94(2)(a) JSA Regs
HB Reg 33 HB Regs
CTB Reg 23 CTB Regs
198 **IS** Reg 44(1) and (5) IS Regs
JSA Reg 106(1) and (5) JSA Regs
199 **IS** Reg 32(1) IS Regs
JSA Reg 97(1) JSA Regs
200 **IS** Reg 41(2) IS Regs
JSA Reg 104(2) JSA Regs
HB Reg 41(2) HB Regs
CTB Reg 31(2) CTB Regs
201 **IS** Reg 41(6) IS Regs
JSA Reg 104(5) JSA Regs
HB Reg 41(4) HB Regs
CTB Reg 31(4) CTB Regs
202 Regs 41(4) and 48(2) IS Regs
203 **IS** Reg 41(3) IS Regs
JSA Reg 104(3) JSA Regs
204 **IS** Reg 41(7) IS Regs
JSA Reg 104(6) JSA Regs
HB Reg 41(5) HB Regs
CTB Reg 31(5) CTB Regs
205 **IS** Sch 10 para 20 IS Regs
JSA Sch 8 para 25 JSA Regs
HB Sch 6 para 22 HB Regs
CTB Sch 5 para 22 CTB Regs
206 *R v SBC ex parte Singer* [1973] 1 All ER 931; *R v Oxford County Council ex parte Jack* [1984] 17 HLR 419; *R v West Dorset DC ex parte Poupard* [1988] 20 HLR 295
207 *R v West Dorset DC ex parte Poupard* [1988] 20 HLR 295
208 **IS** Reg 48(2) IS Regs
JSA Reg 110(2) JSA Regs
HB Reg 40(2) HB Regs
CTB Reg 31(2) CTB Regs
209 **IS** s126(5) SSCBA 1992
JSA s5(2)(c) JSA 1995
210 Regs 41(4) and 48(2) IS Regs
211 **IS** Sch 9 para 13 IS Regs
JSA Sch 7 para 14 JSA Regs
HB Sch 5 para 13 HB Regs
CTB Sch 4 para 14 CTB Regs
212 **IS** Sch 9 para 64 IS Regs
JSA Sch 7 para 62 JSA Regs
HB Sch 5 para 58 HB Regs
CTB Sch 4 para 58 CTB Regs
All Reg 18 SS(NDP) Regs
213 **HB** Reg 46(7) HB Regs
CTB Reg 36(7) CTB Regs
214 **IS** Regs 39C and 39D IS Regs
JSA Regs 102C and 102D JSA Regs
215 **IS** Reg 40(4) IS Regs
JSA Regs 98(2)(e) and 103(6) JSA Regs
HB Reg 40(10) HB Regs
CTB Reg 30(11) CTB Regs
All Definition of 'occupational pension' in reg 2(1) of each of those Regs or reg 1 for JSA
216 **IS** Reg 41(2) and Sch 9 para 17 IS Regs
JSA Reg 104(2) and Sch 7 para 18 JSA Regs
HB Reg 41(2) and Sch 5 para 18 HB Regs
CTB Reg 31(2) and Sch 4 para 64 CTB Regs
217 **IS** Sch 9 para 29 IS Regs; para 28240 DMG
JSA Sch 7 para 30 JSA Regs
218 **IS** Sch 9 para 30 IS Regs
JSA Sch 7 para 31 JSA Regs
Both R(IS) 13/01
219 **HB** Sch 5 para 29 HB Regs
CTB Sch 4 para 30 CTB Regs
220 **IS** Sch 9 para 30ZA IS Regs
JSA Sch 7 para 31A JSA Regs
HB Sch 5 para 29 HB Regs
CTB Sch 4 para 30 CTB Regs
221 **IS** Sch 9 para 28 IS Regs
JSA Sch 7 para 29 JSA Regs
HB Sch 5 para 28 HB Regs
CTB Sch 4 para 29 CTB Regs
222 **IS** Sch 9 para 58 IS Regs
JSA Sch 7 para 56 JSA Regs
HB Sch 5 para 57 HB Regs
CTB Sch 4 para 57 CTB Regs
All *Casewell v Secretary of State for Work and Pensions*, an appeal from CIS/1068/2006, due to be heard on 10/11 March 2008
223 **IS** Sch 9 para 27 IS Regs
JSA Sch 7 para 28 JSA Regs
HB Sch 5 para 27 HB Regs
CTB Sch 4 para 28 CTB Regs

224 **IS** Sch 10 para 8(b) IS Regs
JSA Sch 8 para 13(b) JSA Regs
HB Sch 6 para 10(b) HB Regs
CTB Sch 5 para 10(b) CTB Regs
225 **IS** Sch 9 para 76 IS Regs
JSA Sch 7 para 72 JSA Regs
HB Sch 5 para 63 HB Regs
CTB Sch 4 para 63 CTB Regs
226 **IS** Sch 9 paras 15, 30A and 66 IS Regs
JSA Sch 7 paras 15, 32 and 64 JSA Regs
227 **IS** Sch 9 para 11 IS Regs
JSA Sch 7 para 12 JSA Regs
HB Sch 5 para 11 HB Regs
CTB Sch 4 para 12 CTB Regs
228 **IS** Sch 9 para 2 IS Regs
JSA Sch 7 para 2 JSA Regs
HB Sch 5 para 2 HB Regs
CTB Sch 4 para 2 CTB Regs
229 **IS** Sch 9 para 21 IS Regs
JSA Sch 7 para 22 JSA Regs
HB Sch 5 para 23 HB Regs
CTB Sch 4 para 24 CTB Regs
230 para BW2 Annex B para 13 GM
231 **IS** Sch 9 para 51 IS Regs
JSA Sch 7 para 50 JSA Regs
HB Sch 5 para 49 HB Regs
CTB Sch 4 para 51 CTB Regs
232 **IS** Sch 9 para 72 IS Regs
JSA Sch 7 para 69 JSA Regs
HB Sch 5 para 61 HB Regs
CTB Sch 4 para 61 CTB Regs
233 **IS** Sch 9 para 43 IS Regs
JSA Sch 7 para 43 JSA Regs
HB Sch 5 para 39 HB Regs
CTB Sch 4 para 41 CTB Regs
234 **IS** Sch 9 para 10 IS Regs
JSA Sch 7 para 11 JSA Regs
HB Sch 5 para 10 HB Regs
CTB Sch 4 para 11 CTB Regs
235 **IS** Sch 9 para 23 IS Regs
JSA Sch 7 para 24 JSA Regs
HB Sch 5 para 24 HB Regs
CTB Sch 4 para 25 CTB Regs
236 **IS** Sch 9 para 24 IS Regs
JSA Sch 7 para 25 JSA Regs
HB Sch 5 para 33 HB Regs
CTB Sch 4 para 34 CTB Regs
237 **IS** Sch 9 para 48 IS Regs
JSA Sch 7 para 47 JSA Regs
HB Sch 5 para 44 HB Regs
CTB Sch 4 para 45 CTB Regs
238 **IS** Sch 9 para 49 IS Regs
JSA Sch 7 para 48 JSA Regs
HB Sch 5 para 45 HB Regs
CTB Sch 4 para 46 CTB Regs
239 **IS** Sch 9 para 50 IS Regs
JSA Sch 7 para 49 JSA Regs
HB Sch 5 para 46 HB Regs
CTB Sch 4 para 47 CTB Regs
240 **HB** Sch 5 para 19 HB Regs
CTB Sch 4 para 19 CTB Regs
241 **HB** Sch 4 para 11 HB Regs
CTB Sch 3 para 11 CTB Regs
242 **HB** Sch 5 para 20 HB Regs
CTB Sch 4 para 20 CTB Regs
243 **HB** Sch 4 para 11 HB Regs
CTB Sch 3 para 11 CTB Regs
244 **IS** Sch 9 para 69 IS Regs
JSA Sch 7 para 67 JSA Regs
HB Sch 5 para 59 HB Regs
CTB Sch 4 para 59 CTB Regs
245 **IS** Sch 9 para 75 IS Regs
JSA Sch 7 para 71 JSA Regs
HB Sch 5 para 62 HB Regs
CTB Sch 4 para 62 CTB Regs
246 **IS** Reg 42(1) IS Regs
JSA Reg 105(1) JSA Regs
HB Reg 42(1) HB Regs
CTB Reg 32(1) CTB Regs
247 paras 28608-16 DMG; see also CIS/15052/1996
248 **IS** Reg 42(2) IS Regs
JSA Reg 105(2) JSA Regs
HB Reg 42(2) HB Regs
CTB Reg 32(2) CTB Regs
249 **IS** Reg 42(2ZA) and (2A) IS Regs
JSA Reg 105((2B) and (3) JSA Regs
HB Reg 42(3) HB Regs
CTB Reg 32(3) CTB Regs
250 **IS** Reg 42(2)(e)-(f) IS Regs
JSA Reg 105(2)(d) JSA Regs
HB Reg 42(2)(f)-(g) HB Regs
CTB Reg 32(2)(f)-(g) CTB Regs
251 CIS/16271/1996
252 paras 28608-16 DMG
253 CIS/15052/1996, para 11
254 **IS** Reg 42(3) IS Regs
JSA Reg 105(6) JSA Regs
255 **IS** Reg 42(3A) and (3B) IS Regs
JSA Reg 105(7)(a), (8) and (9) JSA Regs
256 **IS** Reg 42(3C) IS Regs
JSA Reg 105(7)(d) JSA Regs
257 CIS/15052/1996, para 10
258 **IS** Reg 70(2)(b) IS Regs
JSA Regs 147-149 JSA Regs
259 **IS** Reg 42(5) IS Regs
JSA Reg 105(12) JSA Regs
260 Reg 2 SS(PAOR) Regs
261 **IS** Reg 42(4ZA) IS Regs
JSA Reg 105(10A) JSA Regs
HB Reg 42(7) HB Regs
CTB Reg 32(7) CTB Regs

262 **IS** Reg 42(4)(b) IS Regs
JSA Reg 105(10)(b) JSA Regs
HB Reg 42(6)(c) HB Regs
CTB Reg 32(6)(c) CTB Regs
263 **IS** Reg 42(6) IS Regs; CIS/191/1991
JSA Reg 105(13) JSA Regs
HB Reg 42(9) HB Regs
CTB Reg 32(9) CTB Regs
264 R(SB) 13/86
265 **IS** Reg 42(6A) IS Regs
JSA Reg 105(13A) JSA Regs
HB Reg 42(10) HB Regs
CTB Reg 32(10) CTB Regs
266 R(SB) 13/86
267 **IS** Reg 42(6A)(a) IS Regs
JSA Reg 105(13A)(a) JSA Regs
HB Reg 42(10)(a) HB Regs
CTB Reg 32(10)(a) CTB Regs
268 CIS/147/1993
269 *Sharrock v CAO*, 26 March 1991 (CA); CIS/93/1991
270 CIS/93/1991
271 CIS/422/1992
272 CIS/701/1994
273 CIS/422/1992
274 CIS/701/1994
275 s1(3)(a) Carers (Recognition and Services) Act 1995 excludes those who care 'by virtue of a contract of employment or other contract' which, according to policy guidance issued by the Department of Health, means 'anyone who is providing personal assistance for payment either in cash or in kind'.
276 **HB** Reg 31 HB Regs
CTB Reg 21 CTB Regs
277 **HB** Reg 29(1)(a) HB Regs
CTB Reg 19(1)(a) CTB Regs
278 **HB** Reg 29(1)(b) HB Regs
CTB Reg 19(1)(b) CTB Regs
Both para BW2.53 GM
279 *R v HBRB of the London Borough of Ealing ex parte Saville* [1986] 18 HLR 349
280 **HB** Reg 29(2) HB Regs
CTB Reg 19(2) CTB Regs
281 **HB** Reg 29(3) HB Regs
CTB Reg 19(3) CTB Regs
282 **IS** Reg 32(1) IS Regs
JSA Reg 97 JSA Regs
HB Reg 33 HB Regs
CTB Reg 23 CTB Regs
283 R(IS) 3/93
284 R(IS) 10/95
285 **IS** Reg 32(6) IS Regs
JSA Reg 97(6) JSA Regs
286 **IS** Reg 32(2) and (3) IS Regs
JSA Reg 97(2) and (3) JSA Regs
287 **IS** Reg 32(4) IS Regs
JSA Reg 97(4) JSA Regs
288 **IS** Reg 32(5) and Sch 8 para 10 IS Regs
JSA Reg 97(5) and Sch 6 para 13 JSA Regs
289 **IS** Reg 29(2)(a) IS Regs
JSA Reg 94(2)(a) JSA Regs
290 **IS** Reg 29(2)(b) IS Regs
JSA Reg 94(2)(b) JSA Regs
291 **IS** Reg 31(3) IS Regs
JSA Reg 96(3) JSA Regs
see also CIS/1064/2004
292 **IS** Reg 31(1)(a) IS Regs
JSA Reg 96(1)(a) JSA Regs
293 **IS** Reg 31(1)(b) IS Regs
JSA Reg 96(1)(b) JSA Regs
294 **IS** Reg 31(2) IS Regs
JSA Reg 96(2) JSA Regs
295 **IS** Reg 2(1) IS Regs
JSA Reg 1(3) JSA Regs
296 R(SB) 33/83
297 R(SB) 22/84; R(SB) 11/85
298 CIS/590/1993

2. **People aged 60 or over**

299 **HB/CTB** s136(1) SSCBA 1992
PC s5 SPCA 2002
300 **HB** Reg 23(3) HB(SPC) Regs
CTB Reg 13(3) CTB(SPC) Regs
301 **HB** Regs 25 and 26 HB(SPC) Regs
CTB Regs 15 and 16 CTB(SPC) Regs
302 **HB** Reg 27(4) HB(SPC) Regs
CTB Reg 17(4) CTB(SPC) Regs
303 **HB** Reg 24 HB(SPC) Regs
304 **HB** Reg 27(4)(b) and (c) HB(SPC) Regs
CTB Reg 17(4)(b) and (c) CTB(SPC) Regs
305 **HB** Reg 29 HB(SPC) Regs
CTB Reg 19 CTB(SPC) Regs
306 **PC** Reg 17(10) SPC Regs
HB Reg 33(12) HB(SPC) Regs
CTB Reg 23(12) CTB(SPC) Regs
307 **HB** Reg 34 HB(SPC) Regs
CTB Reg 24 CTB(SPC) Regs
308 **PC** Regs 17(10) and 17A(4A) SPC Regs
HB Reg 36(2) and (4) HB(SPC) Regs
CTB Reg 26(2) and (4) CTB(SPC) Regs
309 **HB** Reg 36(5) HB(SPC) Regs
CTB Reg 26(5) CTB(SPC) Regs
310 **HB** Reg 34 HB(SPC) Regs
CTB Reg 24 CTB(SPC) Regs
311 *Parsons v Hogg* [1985] 2 All ER 897 (CA), appendix to R(FIS) 4/85
312 **PC** Reg 17A(2) SPC Regs
HB Reg 35(1) HB(SPC) Regs
CTB Reg 25(1) CTB(SPC) Regs

313 **PC** Reg 17A(h) and (k) SPC Regs
HB Reg 35(1)(h) and (k) HB(SPC) Regs
CTB Reg 25(1)(h) and (k) CTB(SPC) Regs
314 **PC** Reg 17A(h)-(k) SPC Regs
HB Reg 35(1)(h)-(k) HB(SPC) Regs
CTB Reg 25(1)(h)-(k) CTB(SPC) Regs
315 **PC** Reg 17A(2)(e) SPC Regs
HB Reg 35(1)(e) HB(SPC) Regs
CTB Reg 25(1)(e) CTB(SPC) Regs
316 R(IS) 9/95
317 **PC** Reg 17A(2)(g) SPC Regs
HB Reg 35(1)(g) HB(SPC) Regs
CTB Reg 25(1)(g) CTB(SPC) Regs
318 **PC** Reg 17A(4) SPC Regs
HB Reg 35(3) HB(SPC) Regs
CTB Reg 25(3) CTB(SPC) Regs
319 **PC** Sch 6 para 6 SPC Regs
HB Sch 4 para 8 HB(SPC) Regs
CTB Sch 2 para 8 CTB(SPC) Regs
320 **PC** Reg 17A(3)(a) SPC Regs
HB Reg 35(2)(a) HB(SPC) Regs
CTB Reg 25(2)(a) CTB(SPC) Regs
321 para 86058 DMG
322 para 86054 DMG
323 **PC** Reg 17A(3)(b) SPC Regs
HB Reg 35(2)(b) HB(SPC) Regs
CTB Reg 25(2)(b) CTB(SPC) Regs
324 CIS/77/1993; CIS/89/1989
325 **PC** Sch 6 para 7 SPC Regs
HB Sch 4 para 10 HB(SPC) Regs
CTB Sch 2 para 10 CTB(SPC) Regs
326 **PC** Reg 17A(3)(c) SPC Regs
HB Reg 35(2)(c) HB(SPC) Regs
CTB Reg 25(2)(c) CTB(SPC) Regs
327 **PC** s15(1)(c) SPCA 2002
HB Reg 29(1)(c) HB(SPC) Regs
CTB Reg 19(1)(c) CTB(SPC) Regs
328 **PC** Reg 17A(3)(e) SPC Regs
HB Reg 35(2)(e) HB(SPC) Regs
CTB Reg 25(2)(e) CTB(SPC) Regs
329 **PC** Reg 17A(3)(d) SPC Regs
HB Reg 35(2)(d) HB(SPC) Regs
CTB Reg 25(2)(d) CTB(SPC) Regs
330 para 86162 DMG
331 **PC** Sch 6 para 6 SPC Regs
HB Sch 4 para 8 HB(SPC) Regs
CTB Sch 2 para 8 CTB(SPC) Regs
332 Reg 17ZA SPC Regs
333 **PC** Reg 17B(5) SPC Regs; reg 13(1) and (4) SSB(CE) Regs
HB Reg 39(1)-(3) HB(SPC) Regs
CTB Reg 29(1)-(3) CTB(SPC) Regs
334 **PC** Reg 17B(1) SPC Regs; regs 2 and 13(4) SSB(CE) Regs
HB Regs 2(1) and 39(2) and (11) HB(SPC) Regs
CTB Regs 2(1) and 29(2) and (11) CTB(SPC) Regs
335 Reg 32(3) SS(C&P) Regs
336 **PC** Reg 17B(4)(b) SPC Regs; reg 12(2) SSB(CE) Regs
HB Reg 38(2)(a) HB(SPC) Regs
CTB Reg 28(2)(a) CTB(SPC) Regs
337 **PC** Reg 17B SPC Regs; reg 11(1) SSB(CE) Regs
HB Reg 37(1) HB(SPC) Regs
CTB Reg 27(1) CTB(SPC) Regs
338 **PC** Reg 17B(5)(b) SPC Regs; reg 13(10) SSB(CE) Regs
HB Reg 39(8) HB(SPC) Regs
CTB Reg 29(8) CTB(SPC) Regs
339 **HB** Sch 4 para 6 HB(SPC) Regs
CTB Sch 2 para 6 CTB(SPC) Regs
340 **PC** Sch 6 para 6 SPC Regs
HB Sch 4 para 8 HB(SPC) Regs
CTB Sch 2 para 8 CTB(SPC) Regs
341 **PC** Sch 6 para 7 SPC Regs
HB Sch 4 para 10 HB(SPC) Regs
CTB Sch 2 para 10 CTB(SPC) Regs
342 **HB** Sch 4 para 2 HB(SPC) Regs
CTB Sch 2 para 2 CTB(SPC) Regs
343 Sch 6 para 1 SPC Regs
344 **PC** Sch 6 para 4(1)(a) SPC Regs
HB Sch 4 para 5(1)(a) HB(SPC) Regs
CTB Sch 2 para 5(1)(a) CTB(SPC) Regs
345 **PC** Sch 6 para 4(1)(b) SPC Regs
HB Sch 4 para 5(1)(b) HB(SPC) Regs
CTB Sch 2 para 5(1)(b) CTB(SPC) Regs
346 **HB** Sch 4 para 5(1)(c) HB(SPC) Regs
CTB Sch 2 para 5(1)(c) CTB(SPC) Regs
347 **PC** Sch 6 paras 3 and 4A SPC Regs
HB Sch 4 para 4 HB(SPC) Regs
CTB Sch 2 para 4 CTB(SPC) Regs
348 **PC** Sch 6 para 4(2) SPC Regs
HB Sch 4 para 5(2) HB(SPC) Regs
CTB Sch 2 para 5(2) CTB(SPC) Regs
349 Sch 6 para 4(3) SPC Regs
350 **PC** Sch 6 para 2 SPC Regs
HB Sch 4 para 3 HB(SPC) Regs
CTB Sch 2 para 3 CTB(SPC) Regs
351 **PC** Sch 6 para 5 SPC Regs
HB Sch 4 para 7 HB(SPC) Regs
CTB Sch 2 para 7 CTB(SPC) Regs
352 **HB** Sch 4 para 9 HB(SPC) Regs
CTB Sch 2 para 9 CTB(SPC) Regs
353 **HB** Reg 30(1)(c) HB(SPC) Regs
CTB Reg 20(1)(c) CTB(SPC) Regs
354 **PC** Reg 15(5)(ab) SPC Regs
HB Reg 29(1)(h) HB(SPC) Regs
CTB Reg 19(1)(h) CTB(SPC) Regs

355 Reg 15(1)(f) SPC Regs
356 **PC** Reg 17A(2)(h)-(j) SPC Regs
HB Reg 35(1)(h)-(j) HB(SPC) Regs
CTB Reg 25(1)(h)-(j) CTB(SPC) Regs
357 **PC** s15(1)(b) SPCA 2002
HB Sch 5 para 21 HB(SPC) Regs
CTB Sch 3 para 21 CTB(SPC) Regs
358 **PC** Reg 15(2) SPC Regs
HB Reg 29(1)(k) HB(SPC) Regs
CTB Reg 19(1)(k) CTB(SPC) Regs
359 **PC** Reg 15(1) SPC Regs
HB Reg 29(1)(j) HB(SPC) Regs
CTB Reg 19(1)(j) CTB(SPC) Regs
360 **PC** Reg 15(1)(b) SPC Regs
HB Reg 29(1)(j)(ii) HB(SPC) Regs
CTB Reg 19(1)(j)(ii) CTB(SPC) Regs
361 **PC** Reg 15(1)(n) SPC Regs
HB Reg 29(1)(j)(xiii) HB(SPC) Regs
CTB Reg 19(1)(j)(xiii) CTB(SPC) Regs
362 Reg 15(1)(j) SPC Regs
363 s15 SPCA 2002
364 **PC** Reg 15(1)(c) and (e) and Sch 4 para 2 SPC Regs
HB Reg 29(1)(j)(iii) and (v) and Sch 5 para 2 HB(SPC) Regs
CTB Reg 19(1)(j)(iii) and (v) and Sch 3 para 2 CTB(SPC) Regs
365 **PC** Reg 15(1)(a) SPC Regs
HB Reg 29(1)(j)(i) HB(SPC) Regs
CTB Reg 19(1)(j)(i) CTB(SPC) Regs
366 **PC** Reg 15(1)(g) SPC Regs
HB Reg 29(1)(j)(vii) HB(SPC) Regs
CTB Reg 19(1)(j)(vii) CTB(SPC) Regs
367 **PC** Sch 4 para 3 SPC Regs
HB Sch 5 para 3 HB(SPC) Regs
CTB Sch 3 para 3 CTB(SPC) Regs
368 **PC** Reg 15(1)(k) SPC Regs
HB Reg 29(1)(j)(x) HB(SPC) Regs
CTB Reg 19(1)(j)(x) CTB(SPC) Regs
369 **PC** Reg 15(1)(i) SPC Regs
HB Reg 29(1)(j)(ix) HB(SPC) Regs
CTB Reg 19(1)(j)(ix) CTB(SPC) Regs
370 **PC** Reg 15(1)(l) and (m) SPC Regs
HB Reg 29(1)(j)(xi) and (xii) HB(SPC) Regs
CTB Reg 19(1)(j)(xi) and (xii) CTB(SPC) Regs
371 **PC** Sch 4 para 17 SPC Regs
HB Sch 5 para 23 HB(SPC) Regs
CTB Sch 3 para 22 CTB(SPC) Regs
372 **PC** Sch 4 paras 4-6 SPC Regs
HB Sch 5 paras 4-6 HB(SPC) Regs
CTB Sch 3 paras 4-6 CTB(SPC) Regs
373 **PC** Reg 15(1)(h) SPC Regs
HB Reg 29(1)(j)(viii) HB(SPC) Regs
CTB Reg 19(1)(j)(viii) CTB(SPC) Regs
374 **HB** Sch 5 paras 7 and 8 HB(SPC) Regs
CTB Sch 3 paras 7 and 8 CTB(SPC) Regs
375 Sch 4 paras 7 and 7A SPC Regs
376 **PC** Sch 4 para 1(a) SPC Regs
HB Sch 5 para 1(a) HB(SPC) Regs; Sch Part 1 HB&CTB(WPD) Regs
CTB Sch 3 para 1(a) CTB(SPC) Regs; Sch Part 1 HB&CTB(WPD) Regs
377 **PC** Sch 4 para 1(cc) SPC Regs
HB Sch 5 para 1(d) HB(SPC) Regs
CTB Sch 3 para 1(d) CTB(SPC) Regs
378 **PC** Sch 4 para 1(b) SPC Regs
HB Sch 5 para 1(b) HB(SPC) Regs; Sch Part 1 HB&CTB(WPD) Regs
CTB Sch 3 para 1(b) CTB(SPC) Regs; Sch Part 1 HB&CTB(WPD) Regs
379 **PC** Sch 4 para 1(c) SPC Regs
HB Sch 5 para 1(c) HB(SPC) Regs
CTB Sch 3 para 1(c) CTB(SPC) Regs
380 **PC** Sch 4 para 1(d) SPC Regs
HB Sch 5 para 1(e) HB(SPC) Regs
CTB Sch 3 para 1(e) CTB(SPC) Regs
381 **PC** Sch 4 para 1(e) SPC Regs
HB Sch 5 para 1(f) HB(SPC) Regs
CTB Sch 3 para 1(f) CTB(SPC) Regs
382 **PC** Sch 4 para 1(f) SPC Regs
HB Sch 5 para 1(g) HB(SPC) Regs
CTB Sch 3 para 1(g) CTB(SPC) Regs
383 ss134(8) and 139(6) SSAA 1992
384 *R v South Hams District Council, ex parte Ash*, *The Times*, 27 May 1999
385 s74(2) SSAA 1992
386 **HB** Sch 5 para 20 HB(SPC) Regs
CTB Sch 3 para 20 CTB(SPC) Regs
387 **HB** Reg 29(1)(o) HB(SPC) Regs
CTB Reg 19(1)(o) CTB(SPC) Regs
388 Reg 15(5)(d) SPC Regs
389 CIS/683/1993
390 **PC** Sch 4 para 9 SPC Regs
HB Sch 5 para 10 HB(SPC) Regs
CTB Sch 3 para 10 CTB(SPC) Regs
391 **PC** Sch 4 para 8 SPC Regs
HB Sch 5 para 9 HB(SPC) Regs
CTB Sch 3 para 9 CTB(SPC) Regs
392 **PC** Reg 1(2) SPC Regs
HB Reg 2(1) HB(SPC) Regs
CTB Reg 2(1) CTB(SPC) Regs
All Definition of 'board and lodging accommodation'
393 CIS/521/2002
394 **PC** s15(1)(i) SPCA 2002
HB Reg 29(1)(i) HB(SPC) Regs
CTB Reg 19(1)(i) CTB(SPC) Regs
395 **PC** Sch 4 para 18 SPC Regs
HB Sch 5 para 22 HB(SPC) Regs
CTB Sch 3 para 24 CTB(SPC) Regs
396 **PC** s15(1)(i) SPCA 2002; reg 15(6) and Sch 4 para 18 SPC Regs
HB Reg 29(1)(i) HB(SPC) Regs
CTB Reg 19(1)(i) CTB(SPC) Regs

397 **HB** Sch 5 para 24 HB(SPC) Regs
CTB Sch 3 para 23 CTB(SPC) Regs
398 s15(2) SPCA 2002; reg 15(6) SPC Regs
399 **HB** Regs 25 and 26 HB(SPC) Regs
CTB Regs 15 and 16 CTB(SPC) Regs
400 **HB** Reg 43 HB(SPC) Regs
CTB Reg 33 CTB(SPC) Regs
401 **HB** Reg 29(2) HB(SPC) Regs
CTB Reg 19(2) CTB(SPC) Regs
402 **PC** ss15(1)(c) and 16(1)SPCA 2002; reg 16 SPC Regs
HB Reg 29(1)(c) HB(SPC) Regs
CTB Reg 19(1)(c) CTB(SPC) Regs
403 **PC** Reg 16 SPC Regs
HB Reg 29(1)(s) HB(SPC) Regs
CTB Reg 19(1)(s) CTB(SPC) Regs
404 **PC** Reg 16 SPC Regs
HB Reg 29(1)(t) HB(SPC) Regs
CTB Reg 19(1)(t) CTB(SPC) Regs
405 **PC** Reg 16 SPC Regs
HB Reg 29(1)(w) HB(SPC) Regs
CTB Reg 19(1)(w) CTB(SPC) Regs
406 para 85136 DMG
407 **PC** Reg 17(9) SPC Regs
HB Reg 33(8) HB(SPC) Regs
CTB Reg 23(8) CTB(SPC) Regs
408 **PC** Sch 4 para 15 SPC Regs
HB Sch 5 para 16 HB(SPC) Regs
CTB Sch 3 para 16 CTB(SPC) Regs
409 **PC** Sch 4 para 16 SPC Regs
HB Sch 5 para 17 HB(SPC) Regs
CTB Sch 3 para 17 CTB(SPC) Regs
410 **PC** Sch 4 para 10 SPC Regs
HB Sch 5 para 11 HB(SPC) Regs
CTB Sch 3 para 11 CTB(SPC) Regs
411 **PC** Sch 4 para 11 SPC Regs
HB Sch 5 para 12 HB(SPC) Regs
CTB Sch 3 para 12 CTB(SPC) Regs
412 **PC** Sch 4 para 11(3)(b) SPC Regs
HB Sch 5 paras 12(3) HB(SPC) Regs
CTB Sch 3 paras 12(3) CTB(SPC) Regs
413 **PC** Sch 4 para 14 SPC Regs
HB Sch 5 para 15 HB(SPC) Regs
CTB Sch 3 para 15 CTB(SPC) Regs
414 **PC** Sch 4 para 13 SPC Regs
HB Sch 5 para 14 HB(SPC) Regs
CTB Sch 3 para 14 CTB(SPC) Regs
415 **PC** Reg 18(6) SPC Regs
HB Reg 41(8) HB(SPC) Regs
CTB Reg 31(8) CTB(SPC) Regs
416 paras 28608-16 DMG; see also CIS/15052/1996
417 **PC** Reg 18(1)-(5) SPC Regs
HB Reg 41(1)-(7) HB(SPC) Regs
CTB Reg 31(1)-(7) CTB(SPC) Regs
418 **PC** Reg 18(9) SPC Regs
HB Reg 41(11) HB(SPC) Regs
CTB Reg 31(11) CTB(SPC) Regs
419 **PC** Reg 24 SPC Regs
HB Reg 42 HB(SPC) Regs
CTB Reg 32 CTB(SPC) Regs
420 The rules do not include grants and loans in the definition of 'income'.
421 **HB** Schs 4 para 6 and 5 para 18 HB(SPC) Regs
CTB Schs 2 para 6 and 3 para 18 CTB(SPC) Regs
422 **HB** Sch 5 para 19 HB(SPC) Regs
CTB Sch 3 para 19 CTB(SPC) Regs
423 **PC** s15 SPCA 2002; regs 15 and 17B(2) SPC Regs
HB Regs 29 and 38(2) HB(SPC) Regs
CTB Regs 19 and 28(2) CTB(SPC) Regs
424 **PC** Reg 17(2)(b)(i) SPC Regs
HB Reg 33(2)(b)(i) HB(SPC) Regs
CTB Reg 23(2)(b)(i) CTB(SPC) Regs
425 **PC** Reg 17(2)(b)(ii) SPC Regs
HB Reg 33(2)(b)(ii) HB(SPC) Regs
CTB Reg 23(2)(b)(ii) CTB(SPC) Regs
426 **PC** Reg 17(4) SPC Regs
HB Reg 33(4) HB(SPC) Regs
CTB Reg 23(4) CTB(SPC) Regs
427 **PC** Reg 17(1) SPC Regs
HB Reg 33(1) HB(SPC) Regs
CTB Reg 23(1) CTB(SPC) Regs
428 para 85030 DMG
429 Reg 1(2) SPC Regs
430 Reg 13B SPC Regs
431 Sch 3B para 2 SS&CS(DA) Regs
432 Sch 3B paras 1(b) and 3 SS&CS(DA) Regs

Chapter 37

Capital

This chapter explains how capital affects your entitlement to any means-tested benefit. It covers:

How much capital you have may affect your entitlement to any of the means-tested benefits. The phrase 'means-tested benefits' is used to refer to income support (IS), income-based jobseeker's allowance (JSA), pension credit (PC), housing benefit (HB) and council tax benefit (CTB).

Similar rules on the treatment of capital, and different capital limits, apply to social fund payments (Chapter 22), grants and loans (Chapter 21), and certain health benefits (Chapter 9). The different rules are explained in those chapters.

There are no capital rules for non-means-tested benefits. Your entitlement to any non-means-tested benefit is not affected by any capital you may have.

The first part of this chapter applies to IS, income-based JSA and if you and your partner (if you have one) are aged under 60, to HB and CTB.

The second part applies to PC and, if you or your partner (if you have one) are aged 60 or over, to HB and CTB.

Note: unless otherwise stated, references to income-based JSA are intended also to refer to joint-claim JSA.

1. People aged under 60

This part applies to:

- income support (IS) – including if you are over 60 and your partner is claiming IS for you;
- income-based jobseeker's allowance (JSA) – including men aged 60 to 64;
- housing benefit (HB) and council tax benefit (CTB) if you and your partner (if you have one) are aged under 60.

If you get **IS or income-based JSA**, you do not need to work out your capital again for HB and CTB purposes because you receive your maximum HB or CTB,[1] less any deductions for non-dependants (see pp86 and 196).

Note: in this part, whenever HB or CTB are referred to, this only applies to the rules for people aged under 60.

When the new **employment and support allowance** (ESA) is introduced, due in October 2008, it is expected that the rules for working out how much capital you have for income-related ESA will be very similar to those for IS. For more information, see www.cpag.org.uk/esa or CPAG's *Welfare Rights Bulletin*.

The capital limits

There is a lower and upper limit:[2]

- the lower limit is £6,000;
- the upper limit is £16,000.

If you have over £16,000 you are not entitled to benefit (but for CTB, see p89 for second adult rebate). The first £6,000 is ignored and does not affect your weekly benefit at all. If you have between £6,000.01 and £16,000 you may be entitled to benefit but some income from your capital is assumed. This is 'tariff income' (see p866) which is assumed to be £1 for every £250, or part of £250, of your capital within those limits. The lower limit is £10,000 if you live in a care home (see below).

There are some important differences in the rules on capital for urgent cases payments under the IS and income-based JSA schemes (see p1345).

Whichever capital limit applies, some capital is disregarded (see p916), but you may also be treated as having some capital which you do not actually possess (see p924).

Care homes

If you live permanently in a care home or similar accommodation:

- the lower limit goes up to £10,000;
- the upper limit stays at £16,000.

Tariff income starts above £10,000.

You cannot claim **CTB** if you are permanently in a care home because you are not liable for council tax so these limits do not apply to CTB.

For **HB**,[3] the £10,000 lower limit applies if you live permanently in one of the limited categories of care home for which HB is payable, referred to on p624. Some temporary absences (see p185) are ignored.

For **IS and income-based JSA**[4] the £10,000 lower limit applies if you live permanently in:

- a care home or independent hospital (as defined in ss2 and 3 Care Standards Act 2000 and including, in Scotland, a care home service, independent hospital or private psychiatric hospital under s2(3), (5)(a) and (b) Regulation of Care (Scotland) Act 2001); *or*
- an Abbeyfield Home; *or*

- a home provided under the Polish Resettlement Act in which you are receiving personal care.

Note: you are treated as living permanently in one of these homes during periods of absence of up to 13 weeks.

Whose capital counts

Your partner's capital

Your partner's capital is added to yours – ie, it counts as yours.[5]

Your child's capital

Your child's capital is not added to yours and does not affect your benefit, with one exception that applies only to some people who have been getting IS or income-based JSA since before 6 April 2004.[6]

For **IS and income-based JSA**, if you are entitled to have children included in your claim (ie, you have an award that includes a child that began before 6 April 2004 and you have not yet been awarded child tax credit (CTC)), your child's capital is not added to yours, but if your child's capital is over £3,000 you will not get benefit included for that child[7] (although the family premium is still payable – see p777). If that applies, any income of the child will not be counted as yours either.[8]

What counts as capital

The term 'capital' is not defined. In general, it means lump-sum or one-off payments rather than a series of payments[9] – eg, it includes savings, property and statutory redundancy payments.

Capital payments can normally be distinguished from income because they are not payable in respect of any specified period or periods, and they do not form, nor are intended to form, part of a regular series of payments[10] (although capital can be paid by instalments).

However, some capital is treated as income (see p867), and some income is treated as capital (see p915).

Savings

Your savings generally count as capital – eg, cash you have at home, premium bonds, stocks and shares, unit trusts and money in a bank account or building society.

Your savings from past earnings can only be treated as capital when all relevant debts, including tax liabilities, have been deducted.[11] Savings from other past income (including social security benefits – see p921) are treated as capital after the period for which the income was paid has lapsed (so that, for example, a weekly payment of child benefit will become capital a week after it is paid and a monthly occupational pension will become capital after a month).[12] There is no provision for disregarding money put aside to pay bills.[13] If you have savings just below the capital limit, it may be best to pay bills (eg, for fuel or telephone) by monthly standing order, or using a budget account, to prevent your capital going above the limit.

Fixed-term investments

Capital held in fixed-term investments counts. However, if in reality it is presently unobtainable, it may have little or no value. If you can convert the investment into a realisable form, sell your interest, or raise a loan through a reputable bank using the asset as security, its value counts. If it takes time to produce evidence about the nature and value of the investment, you may be able to get an interim payment of IS, JSA or HB[14] (see p217) or a crisis loan from the social fund (see p503).

Property and land

Any property or land that you own counts as capital. Many types of property are disregarded (see p916). See also 'proprietary estoppel' on p913.

Loans

A loan usually counts as money you possess. However, a loan granted on condition that you only use the interest but do not touch the capital should not be counted as part of your capital because the capital element has never been at your disposal.[15] Where you have been paid money to be used for a particular purpose on condition that the money must be returned if not used in that way, it should not be treated as part of your capital.[16] If you have bought a property on behalf of someone else who is paying the mortgage,[17] or if you are holding money in your bank account on behalf of another person which is to be returned to them at a future date,[18] the capital should not count as yours.

For HB and CTB, some loans might be treated as income even if they were paid as a lump sum (see p867).

Trusts

A trust is a way of owning an asset. In theory, the asset is split into two notional parts: the legal title owned by the trustee, and the beneficial interest owned by the beneficiary. A trustee can never have use of the asset, only the responsibility of looking after it. An adult beneficiary, on the other hand, can ask for the asset at any time. Anything can be held on trust – eg, money, houses, shares, etc.

If you are the adult beneficiary of:

- a non-discretionary trust, you can obtain the asset from the trustee at any time. You effectively own the asset, and so its market value counts as your capital;
- a discretionary trust, you cannot insist on receiving payments from the trust. Payments are at the discretion of the trustee within the terms of the trust. Any payments made are treated in full as income or capital depending on the

nature of the payment. The trust asset itself would not normally count as your capital because you cannot demand payment (of either income or capital);
- a trust which gives you the right to receive payments in the future – eg, on reaching 25. This is a right that has a present capital value, unless disregarded (see p920).

If you only have a life interest (or, in Scotland, a life rent) in an asset (ie, if you have the right to enjoy an asset in your lifetime, but the asset will pass on to someone else when you die), the value of your right to receive income is disregarded[19] (see p920), but not the income itself if you get any.

If the beneficiary is under 18, even with a non-discretionary trust, s/he has no right to payment until s/he is 18 (or later if that is what the trust stipulates). Her/his interest may nevertheless have a present value.[20]

If you hold an asset as a trustee, it is not part of your capital. You are only a trustee either if someone gives you an asset on the express condition that you hold it for someone else (or use it for their benefit), or if you have expressed the clearest intention that your own asset is for someone else's benefit, and renounced its use for yourself.[21] Assets other than money may need to be transferred in a particular way to the trust.

It is not enough only to intend to give someone an asset. However, in the case of property and land, **'proprietary estoppel'** may apply. It could arise where you lead someone to believe that you are transferring your interest in some property to her/him, but fail to do so (eg, it is never properly conveyed). If that person acts on the belief that s/he has ownership (eg, s/he improves or repairs it, or takes on a mortgage), it would then be unfair on her/him were s/he to lose out if you insisted that you were still the owner.[22] In this case, you can argue the capital asset has been transferred to her/him, and you are like a trustee. Thus, you can insist that it is not your capital asset, but the other person's, when claiming benefit.

If money (or another asset) is given to you to be used for a special purpose, it may be possible to argue that it should not count as your capital. This is called a **'purpose trust'**.[23]

Payments of personal injury compensation

A payment that does not come from a trust and is made because of personal injury to you or your partner is disregarded for 52 weeks.[24] This gives you time to spend some or all of the payment, or put it into a trust, before your benefit is affected. The 52 weeks starts from when you receive the payment. As you spend it, the disregard goes down to the level of the payment you have left. A subsequent payment for the same injury is not disregarded unless it is put into a trust.

Where a trust fund has been set up out of money paid because of a personal injury to yourself or your partner, the value of the trust fund is ignored without time limit.[25] The 52-week disregard does not apply to lump-sum payments you then get from the trust (see p914 for how payments from trust funds are treated).

If the personal injury was to your partner and s/he has since died, you cannot carry over the remainder of the 52-week disregard, or if the payment is in a trust fund, it is no longer ignored.[26] If the personal injury was to a child, income or capital belonging to the child does not count as yours, with one exception, so compensation paid for the child should not affect your benefit. The exception is for IS and JSA if your claim began before 6 April 2004 and you still get amounts for a child included (ie, you have not yet transferred to CTC). In this case, the value of a personal injury trust for a child is not ignored and you should seek advice about whether it is in your interests to transfer to CTC.

For the payment to be disregarded, it is not necessary for the trust to be set up by a formal deed. The important point is that the person who is awarded the compensation should not be able to have any direct access to it.

In this context, **'personal injury'** includes not only accidental and criminal injuries, but also any disease and injury as a result of a disease. Therefore, a trust fund for someone who has had both legs amputated following meningitis and septicaemia could be disregarded.[27]

Trust funds administered by a court[28]

The value of a trust fund is also ignored where damages are awarded in respect of personal injury (or, for minors under the age of 18, as compensation for the death of one or both parents), and the money paid into a special fund to be administered by, or under the control of, a court (eg, the Court of Protection). As well as ignoring the capital value, income from these funds is also ignored.[29]

Note: the notional income and capital rules (see pp873 and 924) cannot apply to trusts or funds administered by a court which, in either case, have been set up as a result of a personal injury.

Payments from trust funds

Payments made from a trust fund *not* set up from money for a personal injury to you or your partner:

- from a discretionary trust count as income or capital depending on the nature of the payment.[30] Capital payments are taken into account in full but income from the trust would generally be treated as a voluntary payment and ignored;[31]
- from a non-discretionary trust count in full as capital whatever the nature of the payment.[32]

Payments made to you from a discretionary or non-discretionary trust set up from money for a personal injury to you or your partner are treated either as income or capital depending on the nature of the payment. Income is disregarded but capital payments count in full.[33]

Trustees may have a discretion to use such funds to purchase items that would normally be disregarded as capital, such as personal possessions (see p919) – eg, a wheelchair, car, new furniture – or to arrange payments that would normally be disregarded as income – eg, ineligible housing costs. Similarly, they may have discretion to clear debts or pay for a holiday, leisure items or educational or medical needs. See p864 for the treatment of voluntary payments and pp864 and 874 for the treatment of payments made to third parties.

Money held by your solicitor

Money held by your solicitor will normally count as your capital. This includes compensation payments, other than for personal injury, before a trust fund has been set up.[34] A payment for personal injury to you or your partner is ignored for 52 weeks from when you receive it (see p913). If it is sent to your solicitor first, it is likely the 52 weeks will start from when the solicitor receives it. Where money is held by your solicitor pending quantification of any statutory charge due to the Legal Services Commission it does not count as your capital, as it is not possible to identify the capital which belongs to you until any statutory charge has been quantified and deducted.[35]

Income treated as capital

Certain payments which appear to be income are nevertheless treated as capital. These are:[36]

- income from capital (eg, interest on a building society account) and income from rent on property let to tenants (see p865). However, income from the first five disregarded property bullet points listed on p916, trust funds administered by a court (see p914), income from the home of a partner, former partner or relative in the circumstances described on p918, income from the home you normally live in and income from business assets or personal injury trusts counts as income not capital;
- a lump sum or 'bounty' paid to you not more than once a year as a part-time firefighter or part-time member of a lifeboat crew, or as an auxiliary coastguard or member of the Territorial Army;
- unless involved in a trade dispute (for IS or income-based JSA) or returning to work after a dispute (for IS) (see p633);
  - an advance of earnings or loan from your employer;
  - holiday pay which is not payable until more than four weeks after your employment ends or is interrupted;
  - income tax refunds;
  - irregular (one-off) charitable or voluntary payments;
- for IS only, the part, or the whole, of a compensation payment for loss of employment that is treated as capital under the IS rules;[37]
- for IS and income-based JSA only, a discharge grant paid on release from prison;
- for IS and income-based JSA only (where these are still taken into account, see p863), arrears of residence order payments from a local authority;

- for HB and CTB only, any arrears of CTC or working tax credit (WTC);[38]
- arrears of subsistence allowance paid as a lump sum. The arrears are ignored (as capital) for 52 weeks.[39] A 'subsistence allowance' is an allowance paid by an employment zone contractor to a person participating in the employment zone programme, and is equivalent to the weekly amount of income-based JSA which would be payable to that person less 50p;[40]
- for HB and CTB, the gross receipts from work carried out under the self-employment route of the New Deal.

Disregarded capital

Your home

If you own the home you normally live in, its value is ignored.[41]

The value of your home

Your '**home**' includes any garage, garden, outbuildings and land, together with any premises that you do not occupy as your home but which it is impractical or unreasonable to sell separately – eg, croft land.[42] This disregard applies to any home you are treated as normally living in (eg, because you are only temporarily living away from it – see p799), although if you own more than one property, only the value of the one normally occupied is disregarded under this rule.[43] Although the home may consist of more than one unit of accommodation,[44] both units will only count as the home if you (as opposed to a member of your family) normally have to occupy both units (ie, where one unit is treated as an extension or annexe of the other).[45]

Disregards

The value of the property can be disregarded even if you do not normally live in it in the following circumstances.

- **If you have left your former home following a marriage or relationship breakdown**, the value of the property is ignored for six months from the date you left. It may also be disregarded for longer if any of the steps below are taken. If it is occupied by your former partner who is a lone parent its value is ignored as long as s/he lives there.[46]
- **If you have sought legal advice or have started legal proceedings in order to occupy property** as your home, its value is ignored for six months from the date you first took either of these steps.[47] The six months can be extended, if it is reasonable to do so, where you need longer to move into the property.
- **If you are taking reasonable steps to dispose of any property**, its value is ignored for six months from the date you *first* took such steps.[48] This may include a period before you claimed benefit.[49] The definition of '**property**' here includes land on its own, even if there are no buildings on it.[50] Putting the property in the hands of an estate agent or getting in touch with a prospective purchaser should constitute 'reasonable steps',[51] as might taking ancillary

relief proceedings to resolve financial issues in a divorce before putting a property up for sale.[52] The test for what constitutes 'reasonable steps' is an objective one. Any period when the house is advertised at an unrealistic sale price would not count.[53] But if you need longer to dispose of the property, the disregard can continue for years if it is reasonable – eg, where a husband or wife attempts to realise her/his share in a former matrimonial home but the court orders that it should not be sold until the youngest child reaches a certain age.

- **If you are carrying out essential repairs or alterations** which are needed so that you can occupy a property as your home, the value of the property is ignored for six months from the date you first began to take steps to carry them out.[54] 'Steps' may include applying for planning permission, or a grant or loan to make the property habitable, employing an architect or finding someone to do the work.[55] If you cannot move into the property within that period because the work is not finished, its value can be disregarded for as long as is necessary to allow the work to be carried out.
- **If you have acquired a house or flat for occupation** as your home but have not yet moved in, its value is ignored if you intend to live there within six months of acquisition.[56] If you cannot move in by then, the value of the property can be ignored for as long as seems reasonable.
- **If you sell your home** and intend to use the money from the sale to buy another home, the capital is ignored for six months from the date of the sale.[57] This also applies even if you do not actually own the home but, for a price, you surrender your tenancy rights to a landlord.[58] If you need longer to complete a purchase, the authorities can continue to ignore the capital if it is reasonable to do so. You do not have to have decided within the six months to buy a *particular* property. It is sufficient if you intend to use the proceeds to buy *some* other home within the six-month (or extended) period,[59] although your 'intention' must involve more than a mere 'hope' or 'aspiration'.[60] There must be an element of 'certainty' which may be shown by evidence of a practical commitment to another purchase, although this need not involve any binding obligation.[61] If you intend to use only part of the proceeds of sale to buy another home, only that part is disregarded even if, for example, you have put the rest of the money aside to renovate your new home.[62]
- **If your home is damaged or you lose it altogether**, any payment in consequence of that, including compensation, which you intend to use for its repair, or for acquiring another home, is ignored for a period of six months, or longer if it is reasonable to do so.[63]
- If you have taken out a **loan or been given money for the express purpose of essential repairs and improvements** to your home, it is ignored for six months, or longer if it is reasonable to do so.[64] If it is a condition of the loan that the loan must be returned if the improvements are not carried out, you should argue that it should be ignored altogether.[65]

- If you have **deposited money with a housing association as a condition of occupying your home**, this is ignored indefinitely.[66] If money which was deposited for this purpose is now to be used to buy another home, this is ignored for six months, or longer if reasonable, in order to allow you to complete the purchase.[67]
- **Grants made to local authority tenants to buy a home or do repairs/ alterations** to it can be ignored for up to 26 weeks, or longer if reasonable, to allow completion of the purchase or the repairs/alterations.[68]

When considering whether it is reasonable to extend the period of any disregard, as provided for under some of the rules above, all the circumstances should be considered – particularly your and your family's personal circumstances, any efforts made by you to use or dispose of the home[69] (if relevant) and the general state of the market (if relevant). In practice, periods of around 18 months are not considered unusual.

It is possible for property to be ignored under more than one of the above paragraphs in succession.[70]

Some income generated from property which is disregarded is ignored (see p866).

The home of a partner, former partner or relative

The value of a home (see p916) is also ignored if it is occupied wholly or partly as her/his home by:[71]

- *either*
  - your partner[72] – ie, your husband/wife/civil partner, provided you are both still treated as living in the same household (see p702) or your cohabitee, provided you are still treated as living together as husband and wife or civil partners (see p704); *or*
  - a relative of yours, or any member of your family,

  who in either case, is aged 60 or over or is incapacitated (see p919);
- your former partner from whom you are not estranged, divorced or out of a civil partnership. This means your husband/wife/civil partner where you are not still treated as living in the same household or your former cohabitee where you are not still treated as living together as husband and wife or civil partners;
- your former partner from whom you are estranged, divorced or out of a civil partnership if s/he is a lone parent. If your former partner is not a lone parent, the value of the home is ignored for 26 weeks from the date you ceased to live in the home.[73]

It has been held that this disregard only applies to a property which you previously occupied yourself.[74]

'Incapacitated' is not defined, but guidance suggests it refers to someone who is getting an incapacity or disability benefit, or who is sufficiently incapacitated to qualify for one of those benefits.[75] However, you should argue for a broader interpretation, if necessary.

'Relative' includes: a parent, son, daughter, step-parent/son/daughter (including the civil partner of a parent and the son or daughter of a civil partner), or parent/son/daughter-in-law (including the parent of a civil partner and the civil partner of a son or daughter); brother or sister; or a partner of any of these people; or a grandparent or grandchild, uncle, aunt, nephew or niece.[76] It also includes half-brothers and sisters and adopted children.[77]

Personal possessions

All personal possessions, including items such as jewellery, furniture or a car, are ignored.[78] A personal possession has been defined as any physical asset not used for business purposes, other than land.[79] For example, in one case, a static caravan on a non-residential site was treated as a personal possession. (However, a home that you own but do not live in would not normally be a personal possession but would count as capital – see p916.) Personal possessions are not ignored if you have bought them in order to be able to claim or get more benefit (in which case the sale value, rather than the purchase price, is counted as actual capital, and the difference is treated as notional capital[80] – see p924).

Compensation for damage to, or the loss of, any personal possessions, which is to be used for their repair or replacement, is ignored for six months, or longer if reasonable.[81]

Business assets

If you are self-employed, your business assets are ignored for as long as you continue to work in that business.[82] If you cannot work because of physical or mental illness, but intend to work in the business when you are able, the disregard operates for 26 weeks from the date of claim, or for longer if reasonable in the circumstances.[83] If you stop working in the business, you are allowed a reasonable time to sell these assets without their value affecting your benefit. It is sometimes difficult to distinguish between personal and business assets. The test is whether the assets are 'part of the fund employed and risked in the business'.[84] Where the assets of a business partnership (eg, plant and machinery) have been sold but the partnership has not yet been dissolved, the proceeds of sale can still count as business assets.[85] **Note:** letting out a single house does not constitute a business.[86] For the treatment of business assets if you are taking part in the self-employment route of the New Deal, see p923.

Tax rebates

Tax rebates for the tax relief on interest on a mortgage or loan obtained for buying your home or carrying out repairs or improvements are ignored.[87]

Personal pension schemes

The value of a fund held under a personal pension scheme is ignored.[88]

Insurance policy and annuity surrender values

The surrender value of any life assurance or endowment policy is ignored.[89] **Note:** the life assurance aspect need not be the sole or even the main aspect of the policy (although the other features of any policy may still be considered under the actual or notional income and capital rules – see pp924 and 926). The surrender value of any annuity is also ignored (see pp866 and 910). Any actual income the surrender value generates for you, and which is not disregarded as income, can be taken into account as income.[90] Any payment under the annuity counts as income[91] (but see p871 for when this is ignored).

Future interests in property

A future interest in most kinds of property is ignored.[92] A **'future interest'** is one which will only revert to you, or become yours for the first time, when some future event occurs.

However, this does not include a freehold or leasehold interest in property which has been let *by you* to tenants. If you did not let the property to the tenant (eg, because the tenancy was entered into before you bought the property), then your interest in the property should be ignored as a future interest in the normal way. In addition, in one case it was suggested that if you grant someone an '*irrevocable* licence' to occupy property, your interest in that property is a future one and should be ignored.[93]

An example of a future interest is where someone else has a life interest in a fund and you are only entitled after that person has died.

The right to receive a payment in the future

If you know you will receive a payment in the future, you could sell your right to that payment at any time so it has a market value and therefore constitutes an actual capital resource. The value of this is ignored if it is a right to receive:

- income under a life interest or, in Scotland, a life rent;[94]
- an occupational or personal pension;[95]
- any rent if you are not the freeholder or leaseholder.[96] Any actual income which the right to receive such rent in the future generates for you, and which is not disregarded as income, can be taken into account as income;
- any payment under an annuity (see p871).[97] Any actual income generated by the right to receive income from an annuity in the future, and which is not disregarded as income, can be taken into account as income;
- any earnings or income that is ignored because it is frozen abroad;[98]
- any outstanding instalments where capital is being paid by instalments;[99]
- any payment under a trust fund that is disregarded.[100]

Benefits and other payments

Arrears of benefits and tax credits

The general rule is that arrears of specified benefits and other payments (see below) are ignored for:[101]

- 52 weeks after they are received by you; *or*
- longer in some cases of official error. If arrears are £5,000 or over and are paid to make good or compensate for an official error (see p1069), they are ignored until the end of your (or your partner's) award. If you or your partner go on to claim the same benefit again (ie, IS, income-based JSA, HB or CTB), or go from IS to income-based JSA or the other way around, they continue to be ignored for the whole of this next and any subsequent awards if there is no gap between awards.[102]

The benefit arrears that are ignored under the general rule described above are:

- attendance allowance (AA), mobility supplement, disability living allowance (DLA), income-based JSA, IS, HB, CTB, CTC, WTC and discretionary housing payments (as well as the former supplementary benefit, family income supplement, family credit, working families' tax credit, disabled person's tax credit and mobility allowance) or concessionary payments instead of any of these.

Also ignored for 52 weeks from the date you receive the payment are:

- arrears of certain war widows' and war widowers' payments;[103]
- for HB and CTB only, any child maintenance bonus (see p757);[104]
- fares to hospital;[105]
- payments in place of milk tokens or vitamins;[106]
- payments to assist prison visits.[107]

Other payments

The following payments are ignored:

- social fund payments are ignored indefinitely;[108]
- refunds on council tax (or, formerly, community charge) liability are ignored for 52 weeks from the date you receive the arrears;[109]
- a payment to a disabled person under the Disabled Persons (Employment) Act 1944 (other than a training allowance or training bonus) to assist with employment, or a local authority payment to assist blind homeworkers;[110]
- any payments made to holders of the Victoria or George Cross;[111]
- certain compensatory payments made because of the 1988 changes to the means-tested benefits scheme, are ignored indefinitely;[112]
- payments by a local authority or the National Assembly for Wales for support services to help you live independently from the Supporting People team are ignored indefinitely.[113]

For the treatment of payments for taking part in the New Deal programme, see p923.

Personal injury payments

A personal injury payment can be disregarded for a grace period of 52 weeks after you first receive it and when it is held in a trust (see p913).

World War Two compensation payments

The way these compensation payments are treated is described on p941. The rules are the same as for people aged 60 or over.

Creutzfeldt-Jakob disease payments

Payments made to you or your partner out of government trust funds for people with variant Creutzfeldt-Jakob disease (CJD) are ignored for varying periods if you or your partner have CJD (it is ignored for life), or were the partner of someone with CJD when s/he died (it is ignored for life), or are the parent (it is ignored for two years) or dependent child of someone with CJD (it is ignored until s/he leaves full-time education or reaches 20 or for two years from the date of payment, whichever is the latest).[114] You can also give money from your payment to a partner, parent or dependent child or leave them money from the payment after you die, and it will be disregarded for their benefit claim for the same varying periods.

Charitable payments

Any payment in kind by a charity is ignored.[115]

All payments from the Macfarlane Trusts, the Fund, the Skipton Fund, the Eileen Trust and the London Bombings Relief Charitable Fund (see p864) are ignored.[116] Payments from these trusts and funds do not have to be declared for HB and CTB at all, or for all other benefits, if they are kept separately from the claimant's other capital and income.[117] Certain payments from money that originally came from them are also ignored. All payments from either of the Independent Living Funds are ignored.

Any sports award made by the Sports Council out of National Lottery funds, *except for* any part of the award which is made in respect of ordinary living expenses (for definition see p872), is disregarded for 26 weeks.[118]

Payments in other currencies

Any payment in a currency other than sterling is taken into account after disregarding banking charges or commission payable on conversion to sterling.[119]

Payments by social services[120]

A payment under s17 Children Act 1989 from a social services department or, in Scotland, a payment from a social work department under s12 Social Work

(Scotland) Act 1968 is ignored. Payments made by local authorities to young people who have previously been in care or been looked after by social services (in England and Wales under ss23C, 24, 24A or 24B Children Act 1989, in Scotland under ss29 or 30 Children (Scotland) Act 1995) are also ignored. But if you or your partner are involved in a trade dispute or, for IS, it is paid during the first 15 days following your return to work after the dispute, it counts as income for IS and income-based JSA.

Also ignored indefinitely are:

- community care direct payments;[121]
- special guardianship allowances (payable in England and Wales);[122]
- payments under ss2, 3 or 4 Adoption and Children Act 2002.[123]

Payments to jurors and witnesses

For IS and income-based JSA, any payments made to jurors or witnesses for attending at court are ignored, except for payments for loss of earnings or of benefit.[124]

Employment and training programme payments

A payment under s2 Employment and Training Act 1973 or s2 Enterprise and New Towns (Scotland) Act 1990 is ignored,[125] but only for a year from the date it is received.

Employment zone payments

A payment made by an employment zone contractor to a person taking part in an employment zone scheme[126] is ignored for 52 weeks. Payments to help you in self-employment are treated in the same way as described below for the New Deal.

Education maintenance allowances

An education maintenance allowance is ignored indefinitely.[127]

New Deal payments

Any sum of capital acquired for the purpose of participating under the 'self-employment route' of the New Deal is ignored for 52 weeks,[128] and any capital assets acquired for such purposes are ignored for as long as you are receiving assistance for taking part in the programme[129] and, after you have ceased trading, for as long as is reasonable in order to dispose of the assets.[130]

For the treatment of payments under the New Deal as income, notional income and notional capital, see pp868, 873 and 924.

Capital treated as income

Some payments which appear to be capital are treated as income. See p867 for the detailed rules.

Any capital treated as income is ignored as capital.[131]

Notional capital

In certain circumstances, you are treated as having capital which you do not in fact possess. This is called '**notional capital**'.[132] There is a similar rule for notional income (see p873). Notional capital counts in the same way as capital you actually do possess except that a 'diminishing notional capital rule' (see p926) may be applied so that the value of the notional capital you are treated as having will be considered to reduce over time.

You may be treated as having notional capital if:

- you deliberately deprive yourself of capital in order to claim or increase benefit (see below);
- you fail to apply for capital which is available to you (see p928);
- someone makes a payment of capital to a third party on your behalf or on behalf of a member of your family (see p929);
- you (or a member of your family) receive a payment of capital on behalf of a third party and, instead of handing it on, you (or the member of your family) use or keep the capital (see p930);
- you are a sole trader or a partner in a business which is a limited company (see p930).

Note: the 'diminishing notional capital rule' (see p926) can only apply if you are treated as having notional capital under the first circumstance.

Deprivation of capital in order to claim or increase benefit

If you deliberately get rid of capital in order to claim or increase your benefit, you are treated as still possessing it.[133] The same applies if your partner got rid of capital even if s/he did it before you became a couple.[134] You are likely to be affected by this rule if, at the time of using up your money, you know that you may qualify for benefit (or more benefit) as a result, or qualify more quickly. It should not be used if you know nothing about the effect of using up your capital (eg, you do not know about the capital limit for claiming benefit),[135] or if you have been using up your capital at a rate which is reasonable in the circumstances. Knowledge of capital limits can be inferred from a reasonable familiarity with the benefit system as a claimant,[136] but if you fail to make enquiries about the capital limit, this does not constitute an intention to secure benefit. This is because you cannot form the required intention if you do not know about the capital rules.[137]

Why was the capital got rid of?

Even if you do know about the capital limits, it still has to be shown that you intended to obtain, retain or increase your benefit.[138] For example, where a claimant, facing repossession of his home, transferred ownership to his daughter (who, he feared, would otherwise be made homeless), in spite of having been warned by DWP staff that he would be disqualified from benefit if he did so, it was held that, under the circumstances, he could not be said to have disposed of the property with the intention of gaining benefit.[139] The longer the period that has elapsed since the disposal of the capital, the less likely that it was for the purpose of obtaining benefit.[140] However, no matter how long it has been since you may have disposed of an asset, there is no set 'safe' period after which it may be said that benefit can be claimed without the need for further enquiry.[141]

A person who uses up her/his resources may have more than one motive for doing so. Even where qualifying for benefit is only a subsidiary motive for your actions, and the predominant motive is something quite different (eg, ensuring your home is in good condition by spending capital to do necessary repairs and improvements) you may still be counted as having deprived yourself of a resource in order to gain benefit.[142]

Examples of the kinds of expenditure that could be caught by the rule are an expensive holiday and putting money in trust.[143] (For IS and income-based JSA, putting money in trust for yourself does not constitute deprivation if the capital being put in trust came from compensation paid for any personal injury.[144]) But the essential test is not the kind of item that the money has been spent on but the *intention* behind the expenditure.

Gifts and paying off debts

If you pay off a debt which you are required by law to repay immediately, you may not be counted as having deprived yourself of money in order to gain benefit.[145] But it is the facts of your case which are most important: if you paid off an immediately repayable debt when you thought it would not actually be called in for some time, it may be that you will be held to have deprived yourself of money in order to get benefit. However, even if you pay off a debt which you are not required by law to repay immediately, it is still for the decision maker to prove that you did so in order to get benefit – again, it is the facts of your case which are important.[146]

Intention to get benefit

In practice, arguing successfully that you have not deprived yourself of capital to get or increase benefit may boil down to whether you can show that you would have spent the money in the way you did (eg, to pay off debts or reduce your mortgage), regardless of the effect on your benefit entitlement. Where this is unclear, the burden of proving that you did it in order to get benefit lies with the decision maker.

In one case, a man lost over £60,000 speculating on the stock market. Because of his wife's serious illness, which affected his own health and judgement, he did not act to avoid losses when the stock market crashed. It was held that the decision maker had not proved that this had been done to obtain IS.[147] In another case, a council house was bought at a discount using a loan from a relative secured by a trust deed over the property. In effect, the relative was being given the value of the discount. When the owner fell ill he had to be re-housed so that the relative acquired the property. A claim for HB was initially refused on the grounds that the claimant had deprived himself of the value of the property he had bought. A court later rejected this decision on the grounds that there was no evidence of intention, as it was clear that the sole purpose of the arrangement was so that the relative would be gifted the discount value.[148]

Calculation of notional capital

If you are treated as possessing notional capital, it is calculated in the same way as if it were actual capital[149] and the same disregards usually apply. The only possible exception is that you may not be able to rely on the disregard for the 26 weeks (or longer) you would otherwise be allowed to take steps to dispose of a property, even if the new owner is trying to sell it. However, there is conflicting caselaw on this.[150]

Note: where a disposal of capital is not effective (eg, where there is a disposal between the serving of a bankruptcy notice and the appointment of a trustee in bankruptcy) the notional capital rules do not apply (but the actual capital rules will apply if you still own the asset in question).[151] If, on the other hand, a person acting on your behalf as your attorney has misspent your money for her/his own benefit, the amount spent cannot be notional capital (because the disposal was unlawful) or actual capital (because you no longer have it), but your right to recover the money may still have an actual capital value.[152]

Other points on deprivation of capital

Where an intentional deprivation has been found for the purposes of obtaining IS, it does not necessarily follow that there has also been any intention to gain HB and CTB. Nor can a deprivation for the purposes of gaining income-based JSA be treated as a deprivation for IS (although a deprivation for IS can be treated as one for income-based JSA). Each decision maker must reach her/his own decision on each benefit. Even decisions on deprivation for HB must be made independently of decisions for CTB.[153] This may result in different conclusions being drawn on any disposal for each benefit. And even where intent is found in two different benefits, there may be different views about the amount of capital that has been intentionally disposed of.

However, if you are held to have deprived yourself of capital for the purposes of claiming HB and CTB, and you then submit a successful claim for IS, the notional capital rules for HB and CTB should be put in abeyance for as long as IS remains in payment.[154]

The diminishing notional capital rule

This rule provides a calculation for working out how your notional capital may be treated as *spent*.[155] It only applies if you have deliberately deprived yourself of capital.[156] The rule starts to operate from the first week or part-week after the week in which it is first decided that the notional capital is to be taken into account.

- **If your benefit has been refused altogether** because of your notional capital, the amount of your notional capital is reduced by the weekly total of any of the following benefits (or the additional amounts of the benefits, unless it is IS or income-based JSA) that you would have been entitled to but for the notional capital rule for:

IS	IS, HB and CTB
Income-based JSA	Income-based JSA, HB and CTB
HB	IS, income-based JSA, HB and CTB
CTB	IS, income-based JSA, HB and CTB
Pension credit (PC)	PC, HB and CTB

  In order to ensure that account is taken of as many other benefits as possible, it is important (where you are not already doing so) to make a claim for any of the other benefits (where appropriate) as soon as the notional capital rule has been applied. Any notice you are then given of any amounts of benefits you have 'lost' can then be supplied as evidence of the total weekly aggregate that should be taken into account.
- **Where your means-tested benefit is reduced because of tariff income from your notional capital**, that capital is diminished by the amount of that reduction each week (or part-week). For example, if your notional capital is £6,750, giving a tariff income of £3 a week, the reduction is £3 a week until it reaches £6,500, when it will be £2 and so on.

  For HB and CTB, the amount of your notional capital is also reduced by the weekly aggregate of the following benefits (or any additional amounts of these benefits, unless it is IS or income-based JSA) which you would have been entitled to but for the notional capital rule for:

HB	IS, income-based JSA and CTB
CTB	IS, income-based JSA and HB

- **The reduction in your notional capital is calculated on a weekly basis.** However, where your benefit has been stopped altogether because of the notional capital rule, the amount is fixed for a period of at least 26 weeks. Even if the amount you would have been entitled to increases during this period, there will be no change in the amount by which the capital is reduced (except for HB and CTB where guidance[157] states that in circumstances not related to capital – eg, you have married or a baby has been born – a new assessment can be made). The aggregate of your benefit entitlement can, however, be recalculated from the end of this 26-week period when you reclaim benefit, and is increased if it is more than it was before, but it stays the same as in the earlier assessment if it is unchanged or less. You do not have to reclaim at the end of every 26-week period but there can be no recalculation unless and until you do. However, you cannot renew a claim until at least 26 weeks (IS, income-based JSA, HB and CTB) have passed since the last assessment. Once the amount of reduction has been recalculated in this way, it is again fixed for the same period.

For IS, PC or income-based JSA, you should ask the DWP for a forecast of when your notional capital will reduce to a point where a further claim might succeed, but the onus will be on you to re-claim when it is to your advantage to do so[158] – ie, when you may qualify for an increased assessment, or because you have requalified for benefit. Timing is important. If you delay you may lose out as new assessments cannot take effect before you reclaim. However, if you reclaim too soon you have to wait until the fixed periods have lapsed before you can apply for a fresh determination.

- **Where you have both actual and notional capital**, you may have to draw on your actual capital to meet your living expenses, which may include (and will probably exceed) amounts equivalent to benefits you have 'lost'. There is no reason why this should affect the amount by which your notional capital is diminished, even if this effectively results in double-counting. Any reduction in your actual capital should be taken into account in calculating any tariff income arising from your combined actual and notional capital, unless you have spent it at such a rate and in such a way that it raises questions of intent, when you may find that the notional capital rules are applied all over again.

Failing to apply for capital[159]

The benefit rules treat you as having capital you could get if you applied for it. Examples of failure to apply could be where money is held in court which would be released on application, or even an unclaimed premium bond win. However, this does not include money held by your solicitor pending quantification of any statutory charge due to the Legal Services Commission, as until any statutory charge due has been quantified it is impossible to identify what part of the capital will remain yours.[160] You are only treated as having such capital from the date you could obtain it.

This rule does not apply if you fail to apply for:

- capital from a discretionary trust; *or*
- capital from a trust (or fund administered by the court) set up from money paid as a result of a personal injury; *or*
- capital from a personal pension scheme or, if you are aged under 60, from an occupational pension scheme or payment from the Pension Protection Fund; *or*
- a loan which you could only get if you gave your home or other disregarded capital (see p916) as security; *or*
- for HB and CTB only, CTC or WTC.[161]

Capital payments made to a 'third party' on your behalf

If someone else pays an amount to a 'third party' (eg, an electricity company or a building society) for you or a member of your family (if any), this may count as your capital.[162] It counts if the payment is to cover certain of your or your family's normal living expenses – ie, food, household fuel, council tax or ordinary clothing or footwear. (School uniforms and sportswear are not ordinary clothing;[163] nor are, for example, special shoes needed because of a disability.[164])

It also counts if it is to cover:

- rent for which HB could be payable (less any non-dependant deductions) or water charges;
- for IS and income-based JSA only, housing costs which could be met by IS or income-based JSA.

If the payment is for other kinds of expenses (eg, a TV licence, accommodation charges above the IS/income-based JSA limit, or mortgage capital repayments) it does not count. Payments from the Macfarlane Trusts, the Fund, the Skipton Fund, the Eileen Trust, the London Bombings Relief Charitable Fund or either of the Independent Living Funds do not count, whatever their purpose.

Payments for participating in any of the employment, education or training options of the New Deal also do not count, whatever they are for.[165]

Payments made, for instance, for food or clothes for any member of the family count as the capital of the member of the family in respect of whom they are paid. Since a child's capital is not counted as belonging to the claimant, a payment to, for example, a clothes shop for your child, should count as the child's notional capital and not yours.

Payments from an occupational or personal pension scheme or from the Pension Protection Fund to a third party count as yours regardless of whether or not the payments are used, or intended to be used, for ordinary living expenses.[166] They are disregarded, however, if:

- you (or the member of your family on whose behalf the payments are made) are bankrupt (or the subject of a sequestration order), the payment is made to the trustee or other person acting on your creditors' behalf and you (and your family) have no other income other than the payment made;[167] *or*
- the payments do nothing to support you financially (and therefore do not reduce or remove your need to be supported by IS, income-based JSA, HB or CTB) – eg, deductions from an occupational pension made under an attachment of earnings order.[168]

For IS and income-based JSA only, payments *derived* from certain social security benefits (including war disablement pensions, war widows' pensions and Armed Forces Compensation Scheme payments) and paid to a third party count:

- as yours, if you are entitled to the benefit; *and*

- as a member of your family's, if it is the family member who is entitled to the benefit.[169]

For IS and income-based JSA, there are different rules if you could be liable to pay maintenance as a liable relative (see p744).

Capital payments paid to you for a 'third party'[170]

If you or a member of your family get a payment for someone not in your family (eg, a relative who does not have a bank account) it only counts as yours if it is kept or used by you. Payments from the Macfarlane Trusts, the Fund, the Skipton Fund, the Eileen Trust, the London Bombings Relief Charitable Fund, either of the Independent Living Funds or any of the New Deal payments referred to on p929 do not count at all.

Companies run by sole traders or a few partners

You will also be treated as possessing notional capital if, as a sole trader or a small partnership, you have registered your business as a limited company. For IS and income-based JSA, the value of your shareholding is ignored but you are treated as possessing a proportionate share of the capital of the company.[171] This does not apply while you are doing any work on the company's business.[172] Even if you only do a little work for the company – eg, taking messages, this will suffice.[173] It has, however, been held that a 'sleeping partner' in a business managed and worked exclusively by others may not benefit from this disregard. As well as having a financial commitment to the business, you must also be involved or engaged in it in some practical sense as an earner.[174]

For HB and CTB, the local authority has a discretion whether to apply the same rules as for IS and income-based JSA, but if it decides to, it must apply them all.[175]

How capital is valued

Market value

Your capital is valued at its current market or surrender value.[176] This means the amount of money you could raise by selling it or raising a loan against it. The test is the price that would be paid by a willing buyer to a willing seller on a particular date.[177] So if an asset is difficult or impossible to realise, its market value should be very heavily discounted or even nil.[178]

In the case of a house, an estate agent's figure for a quick sale is a more appropriate valuation than the District Valuer's figure for a sale within three months.[179]

It is not uncommon for an unrealistic assessment to be made of the value of your capital. You should consider challenging any decision you disagree with (see Chapters 41 and 42).

Expenses of sale

If there would be expenses involved in selling your capital, 10 per cent is deducted from its value for the cost of sale.[180]

Debts

Deductions are made from the 'gross' value of your capital for any debt or mortgage secured on it.[181] If a creditor (eg, a bank) holds the land certificate to your property as security for a loan and has registered notice of deposit of the land certificate at the Land Registry, this counts as a debt secured on your property.[182] Where a single mortgage is secured on a house and land, and the value of the house is disregarded for benefit purposes, the whole of the mortgage can be deducted when calculating the value of the land.[183]

If you have debts which are not secured against your capital (eg, tax liabilities), these cannot be offset against the value of your capital.[184] However, once you have paid off your debts your capital may well be reduced. You can be penalised if you deliberately get rid of capital in order to get benefit (see p924).

Capital that is jointly owned under a joint tenancy

If you jointly own any capital asset (except as a partner in a company when the rules explained on p930 will apply instead) under a joint tenancy you are treated as owning an equal share of the asset with all other owners.[185] For example, if two of you own the asset, you will each be treated as having a 50 per cent share of it. This rule does not apply, however, if you jointly own the capital asset as tenants in common.[186]

The key differences between a joint tenancy and a tenancy in common are that with a joint tenancy each co-owner owns the whole of the capital asset jointly and severally and if one of the joint tenants were to die her/his interest in the asset would pass automatically to the other joint tenant(s), whereas with a tenancy in common each co-owner owns a discrete share in the asset and this share can be passed on by the deceased on her/his death to whoever s/he wishes.

If the rule does apply, the value of your deemed share should be calculated in the same way as your actual capital. However, it is only the value of your deemed share looked at in isolation which counts, and this will usually be worth rather less than the same proportion of the value of the whole asset. If the asset is a house, for example, the value of any deemed share may be very small or even worthless, particularly if the house is occupied and there is a possibility that the sale of the property cannot be forced. This is because even a willing buyer could not be expected to pay much for an asset s/he would have difficulty making use of or selling on to someone else.[187] Whether a sale can be forced will depend on individual circumstances, and valuations should take into account legal costs and the length of time it could take to gain possession of the property.[188] A valuation should set out details of the valuer's expertise (where relevant), describe the property in sufficient detail to show that all factors relevant to its value have been taken into account, and should state any assumptions on which it is based.[189] You may need to challenge any decision (see Chapters 41 and 42) based on an inadequate valuation.

The rule applies regardless of whether the capital asset in question is in the UK or abroad[190] (see p933 for the particular valuation rules which also apply to assets abroad).

If the rule does not apply to you because you jointly own the capital asset under a tenancy in common, it is your actual share in the asset which has to be valued.

Treatment of assets after a relationship breakdown

When partners separate, assets such as their former home or a building society account may be in joint or sole names. For example, if a building society account is in joint names, under the rule about jointly-owned capital, you and your former partner are treated as having a 50 per cent share each (see p931). On the other hand, a former partner may have a right to some, or all, of an asset that is in your sole name – eg, s/he may have deposited most of the money in a building society account in your name. If this is established, then you may well, depending on the circumstances, be treated as not entitled to the whole of the account but as holding part of it as trustee for your former partner.[191] You cannot be treated as having any interest in a capital asset (eg, the former matrimonial home) under the Matrimonial Causes Act 1973 unless and until an Order (eg, a decree of divorce) has actually been made under that Act.[192]

Shares

Shares are valued at their current market value less 10 per cent for the cost of sale[193] and after deducting any 'lien' held by brokers for sums owed for the cost of acquisition and commission. Market value should be calculated in accordance with guidance from the Revenue, which is based on the bid price plus a quarter of the difference between this and the offer price (rather than *Financial Times* figures, which rely on the mean between the bid and offer prices).[194] Fluctuations in price between routine reviews of your case are normally ignored. If you have a minority holding of shares in a company, the value of the shares should be based on what you could realise on them, and not by valuing the entire share capital of the company and attributing to you an amount calculated according to the proportion of shares held.[195]

Unit trusts

These are valued on the basis of the 'bid' price quoted in newspapers. No deduction is allowed for the cost of sale because this is already included in the 'bid' price.[196]

The right to receive a payment in the future

The value of any such right that is not ignored (see p920) is its market value – what a willing buyer will pay to a willing seller.[197] For something which is not yet realisable this may be very small.

Overseas assets

If you have assets abroad, and there are no exchange controls or other prohibitions that would prevent you transferring your capital to this country, your assets are valued at their current market or surrender value in that country.[198] If there are problems getting benefit because it is difficult to get the assets valued, you may be able to get an interim payment of IS or income-based JSA (see p986), or a 'payment on account' of HB (see p217).

If you are not allowed to transfer the full value of your capital to this country, you are treated as having capital equal to the amount that a willing buyer in this country would give for those assets.[199] It seems likely that the price such a person (if there is one) would be willing to pay may bear little relation to the actual value of the assets.

The same deductions of 10 per cent if there are expenses of sale, and for any debts or mortgage secured on the assets abroad, are made. If the capital is realised in a currency other than sterling, charges payable for converting the payment into sterling are also deducted.[200]

2. People aged 60 or over

This part applies to:

- pension credit (PC);
- housing benefit (HB) and council tax benefit (CTB) if you or your partner (if you have one) are aged 60 or over and not getting income support (IS) or income-based jobseeker's allowance (JSA).

If you get IS or income-based JSA, you do not need to work out your capital again for HB and CTB purposes because you receive your maximum HB or CTB,[201] less any deductions for non-dependants (see pp196 and 86).

This part does not apply to IS or income-based JSA even if you or your partner are over 60. If you get IS or income-based JSA, see p909 for the rules on how your capital is treated.

Note: in this part, whenever HB or CTB are referred to, this only applies to the rules for people aged 60 or over.

How capital is taken into account

Unlike other benefits, for **PC** there is no upper limit on your capital beyond which you are excluded from benefit. Instead, your capital above the lower limit (see p934) is taken into account in the assessment as follows.

- Actual income from capital (eg, interest or regular payments) is only taken into account for some specific kinds of capital.[202] This includes the value of the right to receive certain kinds of payment in the future, and capital in a trust unless the trust is set up out of personal injury payments to you or your partner or is a charitable trust (see p891).
- Any other capital, unless it is specifically disregarded, is assumed to provide you with a set rate of income called 'deemed income' (see p892). Some capital can be ignored for a time or ignored permanently. This part explains which payments can be disregarded. If deemed income is taken into account, then any actual income, such as interest, is ignored.[203]

If any actual income is taken into account – eg, payments from a trust, the capital is ignored when working out how much deemed income to include.

For **HB and CTB** there is an upper capital limit. If your capital is over £16,000 you are not eligible for HB or CTB unless you get PC guarantee credit. Capital between the lower limit (see below) and the upper limit is taken into account in the assessment in the same way as described above for PC.

The capital limits

Different capital limits apply depending on which benefit you claim and on whether you are living in a care home.

Pension credit

For PC:

- there is no upper capital limit;
- the lower limit is £6,000 (£10,000 if you live in a care home – see p935).

Capital of £6,000 or less is ignored altogether. If you have capital above £6,000 (or £10,000 if you are in a care home), you will be treated as having a deemed income of £1 for every £500, or part of £500, by which your capital exceeds £6,000 (£10,000 if you are in a care home).[204]

Housing benefit and council tax benefit

- If you or your partner are getting the guarantee credit of PC, all of your (and your partner's) capital is ignored.[205] This means that you can get HB or CTB even if your capital is above £16,000.
- If you or your partner get IS or income-based JSA, you do not need to work out your capital again for HB or CTB because you get maximum HB or CTB.

- In any other case, there is a capital limit of £16,000,[206] but capital of £6,000 or less (£10,000 if you live in any of the care homes listed below) is ignored altogether. If you have capital above £6,000 (or £10,000 if you are in a care home), you will be treated as having a deemed income of £1 for every £500, or part of £500, by which your capital exceeds that amount. (If you get the savings credit, but not the guarantee credit, of PC see p178.)[207]

Care homes

There are higher capital limits if you live permanently in a care home or similar accommodation.

For **PC**, as usual there is no upper limit. However, deemed income starts at above £10,000 instead of £6,000[208] if you live permanently in:

- a care home or independent hospital (as defined in the Care Standards Act 2000 including, in Scotland, a care home service, independent hospital or private psychiatric hospital under s2(3), (5)(a) and (b) Regulation of Care (Scotland) Act 2001); *or*
- an Abbeyfield Home; *or*
- a home provided under the Polish Resettlement Act in which you receive personal care.

For **HB** the upper limit remains at £16,000. Also, deemed income starts at above £10,000 (instead of £6,000). You cannot claim CTB if you are permanently in a care home because you will not be liable for council tax. For HB,[209] the higher limits apply if you live permanently in one of the limited categories of care home for which HB is payable, referred to on p624. Some temporary absences (see p185) are ignored.

Whose capital counts

Your partner's capital is added to yours – ie, it counts as yours.[210]

The capital of any dependent child will not affect your PC as you cannot claim for any children in your PC (see p447).

For HB and CTB, your child's capital is not added to yours[211] and does not affect your claim. You can get benefit included for your child, including premiums, even though her/his capital is over £3,000.

What counts as capital

The term 'capital' is not defined. In general, it means lump-sum or one-off payments rather than a series of payments[212] – eg, it includes savings, investments and property. The rules below apply to PC and, if you or your partner are aged 60 or over, to HB and CTB.

Savings

Your savings generally count as capital – eg, cash you have at home, premium bonds, stocks and shares, unit trusts, and money in a bank account or building society.

Savings from past income (including social security benefits – see p940) are treated as capital after the period for which the income was paid has lapsed. There is no provision for disregarding money put aside to pay bills.[213] If you have savings just below the capital limit, it may be best to pay bills (eg, for gas, electricity and telephone, by monthly standing order or using a budget account) to prevent your capital going above the limit.

Fixed-term investments

Capital held in fixed-term investments counts. However, if in reality it is presently unobtainable, it may have little or no value. If you can convert the investment into a realisable form, sell your interest, or raise a loan through a reputable bank using the asset as security, its value counts. If it takes time to produce evidence about the nature and value of the investment, you may be able to get an interim payment of PC (see p986) or HB[214] (see p217) or a crisis loan from the social fund (see p503).

Property and land

Any property or land that you own counts as capital. Many types of property are disregarded (see p937). See also 'proprietary estoppel' on p913.

Loans

A loan usually counts as money you possess. However, in some limited cases you can argue that a loan should be disregarded (see p912).

Trusts

Money or property held in a trust for the benefit of you or your partner is ignored when working out deemed income (see p934). You are not assumed to have a fixed income from the trust.[215] This applies to both discretionary and non-discretionary trusts. However, payments actually made from the trust can be taken into account. If made regularly, payments are treated as income. For discretionary trusts, regular payments are either disregarded in full or in part (see p892). If payments are not made regularly they would be taken into account as capital.

The rules are different if the trust is set up out of personal injury payments (see below). Payments made from certain charitable trusts are specifically ignored (see p941).

Payments of personal injury compensation

Any money paid because of a personal injury to you or your partner is ignored whether or not it has been placed into a trust.[216] Neither deemed income (see p934) nor actual income from the fund is taken into account. The capital value will not be ignored if it was paid in respect of someone who is no longer a member of your family (eg, because s/he has died).[217]

Trust funds administered by a court[218]

The value of a trust fund is also ignored where damages are awarded in respect of personal injury and the money paid into a special fund to be administered by, or under the control of, a court (eg, the Court of Protection). Payments out of these funds are ignored completely both as capital and income.[219]

Disregarded capital

Some kinds of capital are ignored in the assessment of PC, HB and CTB.

Your home

If you own the home you normally live in, its value is ignored.[220] The value of your home is disregarded for the purposes of the deemed income rule (see p934).[221]

The value of your home

Your '**home**' includes any garage, garden, outbuildings and land, together with any premises that you do not occupy as your home but which it is impractical or unreasonable to sell separately – eg, croft land.[222] This disregard applies to any home you are treated as normally living in (eg, because you are only temporarily living away from it – see p799), although if you own more than one property, only the value of the one normally occupied is disregarded under this rule.[223] Although the home may consist of more than one unit of accommodation,[224] both units will only count as your home if you (as opposed to any member of your family) normally have to occupy both units (ie, where one unit is treated as an extension or annexe of the other).[225]

Disregarding property

The value of the property can be disregarded, even if you do not normally live in it, in the following circumstances.

- **If you have left your former home following a marriage or relationship breakdown**, the value of the property is ignored for six months from the date you left. It may also be disregarded for longer if any of the steps below are taken. If it is occupied by your former partner who is a lone parent its value is ignored as long as s/he lives there.[226]
- **If you have sought legal advice or have started legal proceedings in order to occupy property** as your home, its value is ignored for six months from the date you first took either of these steps.[227] The six months can be extended, if it is reasonable to do so, where you need longer to move into the property.

- **If you are taking reasonable steps to dispose of any property**, its value is ignored for six months (which may start before you claimed benefit) from the date you *first* took such steps.[228] The steps you take must be objectively 'reasonable' so, for example, advertising at an unrealistic sale price would not count. Placing the property with an estate agent or contacting a possible buyer should count,[229] as might taking ancillary proceedings to resolve financial issues in a divorce.[230] The disregard can continue beyond six months, even for years if it is reasonable – eg, if a husband or wife cannot sell because a court orders that the former matrimonial home should not be sold until the children grow up.
- **If you are carrying out essential repairs or alterations** which are needed so that you can occupy a property as your home, the value of the property is ignored for six months from the date you first began to take steps to carry them out.[231] 'Steps' may include applying for planning permission or a grant or a loan to make the property habitable, employing an architect or finding someone to do the work.[232] If you cannot move into the property within that period because the work is not finished, its value can be disregarded for as long as is necessary to allow the work to be carried out.
- **If you have acquired a house or flat for occupation** as your home but have not yet moved in, its value is ignored if you intend to live there within six months of acquisition.[233] If you cannot move in by then, the value of the property can be ignored for as long as seems reasonable.
- **Any amounts paid to you or deposited in your name for the sole purpose of buying a home for you to live in or carrying out essential repairs or alterations to your home or the home you intend to occupy** are ignored for a year from the date you were paid them, or for PC only, until the end of the assessed income period (p458), if there is one, if this is longer.[234]
- **Any compensation paid under an insurance policy because of loss or damage to your home** is ignored for a year from the date it is paid to you, or for PC only, until the end of the assessed income period, if there is one, if this is longer.[235]

When considering whether to increase the period of any disregard, all the circumstances should be considered – particularly your and your family's personal circumstances, any efforts made by you to use or dispose of the home[236] (if relevant) and the general state of the market (if relevant). In practice, periods of around 18 months are not considered unusual.

It is possible for property to be ignored under more than one of the above paragraphs in succession.[237]

The home of a former partner or relative

The value of a home (see p937) is also ignored if it is occupied wholly or partly as her/his home by:[238]

- a relative of yours or your partner (see p919 for who this includes)[239] who is aged 60 or over or is incapacitated (see below);
- your former partner from whom you are not estranged, divorced or out of a civil partnership. This means your husband/wife/civil partner where you are not still treated as living in the same household or your former cohabitee where you are not still treated as living together as husband and wife or civil partners;
- your former partner from whom you are estranged, divorced or out of a civil partnership if s/he is a lone parent. If your former partner is not a lone parent, the value of the home is ignored for 26 weeks from the date you ceased to live in the home.[240]

It has been held that this disregard only applies to a property which you previously occupied yourself.[241]

'Incapacitated' is not defined, but guidance suggests it refers to someone who is getting an incapacity or disability benefit, or who is sufficiently incapacitated to qualify for one of those benefits.[242] However, you should argue for a broader interpretation, if necessary.

Personal possessions

All personal possessions, including items such as jewellery, furniture or a car, are ignored.[243]

Compensation paid under an insurance policy for damage to or loss of your personal possessions is ignored for a year from the date you were paid the compensation or, for PC only, until the end of the assessed income period (if there is one) if that is longer.[244]

Business assets

If you are self-employed, your business assets are ignored for as long as you continue to work in that business.[245] If you cannot work because of physical or mental illness, but intend to work in the business when you are able, the disregard operates for 26 weeks from the date of claim, or for longer if reasonable in the circumstances.[246]

Insurance policy and annuity surrender values

The surrender value of any life assurance or endowment policy is ignored.[247] **Note:** the life assurance aspect need not be the sole or even the main aspect of the policy (although the other features of any policy may still be considered under the actual or notional income and capital rules – see p894).

The surrender value of any annuity is also ignored for the purposes of the deemed income rule (see p892). Any actual income the surrender value generates for you, and which is not disregarded as income, can be taken into account as income.[248] Any payment under the annuity counts as income[249] (but see p892 for when this is ignored).

Future interests in property

A future interest in most kinds of property is ignored.[250] A **'future interest'** is one which will only revert to you, or become yours for the first time, when some future event occurs. For more about this, see below.

The right to receive a payment in the future

If you know you will receive a payment in the future, you could sell your right to that payment at any time so it has a market value and therefore constitutes an actual capital resource. The value of this is ignored where it is a right to receive:

- income under a life interest or, in Scotland, a life rent.[251] However, it is only ignored for the purposes of the deemed income rule (see pp892 and 934);
- an occupational or personal pension;[252]
- any rent if you are not the freeholder or leaseholder.[253] However, it is only ignored for the purposes of the deemed income rule (see pp892 and 934). Any actual income which the right to receive such rent in the future generates for you, and which is not disregarded as income, can be taken into account as income;
- any payment under an annuity (see p892).[254] However, that is only ignored for the purposes of the deemed income rule (see pp892 and 943). Any actual income generated by the right to receive income from an annuity in the future, and which is not disregarded as income, can be taken into account as income.

Benefits and other payments

Arrears of specified benefits (see below) are ignored for:[255]

- one year after they are received by you or, for PC only, until the end of the assessed income period (if there is one) if that is longer; *or*
- for the remainder of the award if the payment is £5,000 or more for arrears or late payment of a specified benefit (see below), which was made to rectify or compensate for an official error, and which you received in full since becoming entitled to PC, HB or CTB. If you got the compensation before then, it is still disregarded if your current award follows on immediately from a previous award of IS, income-based JSA, HB or CTB (or PC for current awards of HB and CTB) in which the compensation was disregarded, or it is still being disregarded in an award of one of those benefits.

The **specified benefits** are:

- attendance allowance, disability living allowance, income-based JSA, IS, PC, HB, CTB, child tax credit, constant attendance allowance and exceptionally severe disablement; *and*
- for PC only, child benefit and social fund payments; *and*

- for HB and CTB only, working tax credit and discretionary housing payments; *or*
- concessionary payments (ie, compensation) made instead of any of the above benefits or payments made in lieu of any of these benefits.

Also ignored for one year from when you get the payments are:
- payments made by a local authority under s91 Local Government Act 2003 (the 'Supporting People' scheme) or under s91 Housing (Scotland) Act 2001.

Ignore indefinitely the amount of a lump-sum state retirement pension if you deferred your pension and chose a lump sum rather than increased income.[256]

World War Two compensation payments

There are two ways in which such compensation payments may be disregarded.
- **Former Japanese prisoners of war:** £10,000 is ignored indefinitely if you received an *ex gratia* payment from the Secretary of State because during World War Two the Japanese imprisoned or interned you, your partner, your deceased spouse/civil partner or your partner's deceased spouse/civil partner.[257] Arguably the £10,000 disregard can be set against other capital if the payment itself has been spent.
- **Victims of World War Two:** any payment (except for a war pension) made to compensate for the fact that, during World War Two, you, your partner, your deceased spouse/civil partner or your partner's deceased spouse/civil partner was a slave or forced labourer, lost property or suffered a personal injury, or was the parent of a child who died, is ignored for an indefinite period.[258]

Creutzfeldt-Jakob disease payments

Payments made out of trust funds established from funds provided by the Secretary of State for people with variant Creutzfeldt-Jakob disease (CJD) are ignored as capital for varying periods.[259] See p922 for details.

Funeral plan payments[260]

The value of any funeral plan contract is ignored indefinitely.

A funeral plan contract is a contract under which:
- you make at least one payment to another person;
- that person undertakes to provide, or ensure you are provided with, a funeral in the UK on your death; *and*
- the sole purpose of the plan is to provide, or ensure that you are provided with, a funeral on your death.

Charitable payments

All payments from the Macfarlane Trusts, the Skipton Fund, the Fund, the Eileen Trust, the London Bombings Relief Charitable Fund and either of the Independent

Living Funds are ignored.[261] Certain payments from money that originally came from any of these trusts and funds, other than the Independent Living Funds, are also ignored.

Payments in other currencies

Any payment in a currency other than sterling is taken into account after disregarding banking charges or commission payable on conversion to sterling.[262]

Notional capital

In certain circumstances, you are treated as having capital which you do not, in fact, possess. This is called **'notional capital'**.[263] There is a similar rule for notional income (see p894). Notional capital counts in the same way as capital you actually do possess except that a 'diminishing notional capital rule' (see p926) may be applied so that the value of the notional capital you are treated as having will be considered to reduce over time.

For PC and, if you or your partner are aged 60 or over, for HB and CTB, you are treated as having notional capital if you:

- deliberately deprive yourself of capital in order to claim or increase benefit (see below);
- are a sole trader or a partner in a business which is a limited company (see below).

Note: the 'diminishing notional capital rule' (see p926) can only apply where you are treated as having notional capital under the first circumstance.

Deprivation of capital in order to claim or increase benefit

If you deliberately get rid of capital in order to claim or increase your benefit, you are treated as still possessing it.[264] See p924 for when you are likely to be affected by this rule. It applies in the same way as for people aged under 60 except that you will not be treated as having deprived yourself of capital if:

- you pay off or reduce a debt which you owe; *or*
- you pay for goods or services if the purchase of those goods or services was reasonable in the circumstances of your case.[265]

Companies run by sole traders or a few partners

You are also treated as possessing notional capital if, as a sole trader or a small partnership, you have registered your business as a limited company. The value of your shareholding is ignored, but you are treated as possessing a proportionate share of the capital of the company.[266] This does not apply while you are doing any work on the company's business.[267] Even if you do very little work for the company – eg, taking messages, this will suffice.[268] It has, however, been held that a 'sleeping partner' in a business managed and worked exclusively by others may not benefit from this disregard. As well as having a financial commitment to the business, you must also be involved or engaged in it in some practical sense as an earner.[269]

How capital is valued

There are a number of issues to consider when valuing capital.

- **Market value.** Capital is valued at its current market or surrender value,[270] which could be very low if it is difficult to sell. See p930 for more information (the rules are the same as those for people under age 60).
- **Expenses of sale.** If there would be expenses involved in selling your capital, 10 per cent is deducted from its value for the cost of sale.[271]
- **Debts.** Deductions are made from the 'gross' value of your capital for any debt or mortgage secured on it.[272] For more information, see p931 (the rules are the same as those for people aged under 60).
- **Capital that is jointly owned under a joint tenancy.** If you jointly own any capital asset (except as a partner in a company, when the rules explained on p942 will apply instead) under a joint tenancy you are treated as owning an equal share of the asset with all other owners.[273] For example, if two of you own the asset, then you will each be treated as having a 50 per cent share of it. This rule does not apply, however, if you jointly own the capital asset as tenants in common.[274] For more information, see p931.
- **Treatment of assets after a relationship breakdown.** There are no specific rules about this, but there is some guidance and caselaw. For information, see p932 (the information there applies equally to people aged 60 or over).
- **Shares** are valued at their current market value less 10 per cent for the cost of sale[275] and after deducting any 'lien' held by brokers for sums owed for the cost of acquisition and commission. See p932 for more details (the rules are the same as those for people aged under 60).
- **Unit trusts** are valued on the basis of the 'bid' price quoted in newspapers. No deduction is allowed for the cost of sale because this is already included in the 'bid' price.[276]
- **The right to receive a payment in the future.** The value of any such right that is not ignored (see p940) is its market value – what a willing buyer would pay to a willing seller.[277] For something which is not yet realisable, this may be very small.
- **Overseas assets.** If you have assets abroad, and there are no exchange controls or other prohibitions that would prevent you transferring your capital to this country, your assets are valued at their current market or surrender value in that country.[278] If you are not allowed to transfer your capital, you are treated as having capital equal to the amount that a willing buyer in this country would give (which might not be very much).[279] Deduct any debts or mortgage secured on the assets, 10 per cent for any expenses of sale and any charges for converting the payment into sterling.[280]

Notes

1. **People aged under 60**

1 **HB** Sch 6 para 5 HB Regs
CTB Sch 5 para 5 CTB Regs
2 **IS** Regs 45 and 53 IS Regs
JSA Regs 107 and 116 JSA Regs
HB Regs 43 and 52 HB Regs
CTB Regs 33 and 42 CTB Regs
3 Reg 52(3), (4), (5), (8) and (9) HB Regs
4 **IS** Reg 53(1A), (IB) and (1C) IS Regs
JSA Reg 116(1A), (1B) and (1C) JSA Regs
5 **IS/HB/CTB** s136(1) SSCBA 1992
JSA s13(2) JSA 1995
6 **IS** Reg 23(2) IS Regs
JSA Reg 88(2) JSA Regs
HB Reg 25(3) HB Regs
CTB Reg 15(3) CTB Regs
7 **IS** Reg 17(1)(b) IS Regs
JSA Reg 83(b) JSA Regs
8 **IS** Reg 44(5) IS Regs
JSA Reg 106(5) JSA Regs
9 para BW1.72 GM; para 29020 DMG
10 *R v SBC ex parte Singer* [1973] 1 WLR 713
11 R(SB) 2/83; R(SB) 35/83; R(IS) 3/93
12 R(IS) 3/93 para 22
13 R(IS) 3/93
14 **IS/JSA** Reg 2 SS(PAOR) Regs
HB Reg 93(1) HB Regs
15 R(SB) 12/86
16 R(SB) 53/83; R(SB) 1/85
17 R(SB) 49/83
18 R(SB) 12/86
19 **IS** Sch 10 para 13 IS Regs
JSA Sch 8 para 18 JSA Regs
HB Sch 6 para 15 HB Regs
CTB Sch 5 para 15 CTB Regs
20 *Peters v CAO,* reported as appendix to R(SB) 3/89
21 R(IS) 1/90; CSIS/639/2006
22 R(SB) 23/85; CSIS/639/2006
23 *Barclays Bank v Quistclose Investments Ltd* [1970] AC 567; R(SB) 49/83; CFC/21/1989
24 **IS** Sch 10 para 12A IS Regs
JSA Sch 8 para 17A JSA Regs
HB Sch 6 para 14A HB Regs
CTB Sch 5 para 14A CTB Regs
25 **IS** Sch 10 para 12 IS Regs
JSA Sch 8 para 18 JSA Regs
HB Sch 6 para 14 HB Regs
CTB Sch 5 para 14 CTB Regs
26 R(IS) 3/03
27 R(SB) 2/89
28 **IS** Sch 10 paras 44 and 45 IS Regs
JSA Sch 8 paras 42 and 43 JSA Regs
HB Sch 6 paras 45 and 46 HB Regs
CTB Sch 5 paras 47 and 48 CTB Regs
29 **IS** Sch 9 paras 15 and 22 IS Regs
JSA Sch 7 paras 15 and 23 JSA Regs
HB Sch 5 paras 14 and 17 HB Regs
CTB Sch 4 paras 15 and 18 CTB Regs
30 **IS** Reg 48(4) IS Regs
JSA Reg 110(4) JSA Regs
HB Reg 46(4) HB Regs
CTB Reg 36(4) CTB Regs
31 **IS** Sch 9 para 15 IS Regs
JSA Sch 7 para 15 JSA Regs
HB Sch 5 para 14 HB Regs
CTB Sch 4 para 15 CTB Regs
32 **IS** Sch 9 para 15 IS Regs
JSA Sch 7 para 15 JSA Regs
HB Sch 5 para 14 HB Regs
CTB Sch 4 para 15 CTB Regs
All para 29239 DMG
33 CIS/25/1989
34 *Thomas v CAO,* appendix to R(SB) 17/87
35 CIS/984/2002
36 **IS** Reg 48 IS Regs
JSA Reg 110 JSA Regs
HB Reg 46 HB Regs
CTB Reg 36 CTB Regs
37 Reg 48(11) IS Regs
38 **HB** Reg 46(9) HB Regs
CTB Reg 36(9) CTB Regs
39 **IS** Sch 10 para 59 IS Regs
JSA Sch 8 para 54 JSA Regs
HB Sch 6 para 53 HB Regs
CTB Sch 5 para 55 CTB Regs
40 **All** Reg 2(1) IS/JSA/HB/CTB Regs
41 **IS** Sch 10 para 1 IS Regs
JSA Sch 8 para 1 JSA Regs
HB Sch 6 para 1 HB Regs
CTB Sch 5 para 1 CTB Regs
42 **IS** Reg 2(1) IS Regs, meaning of 'dwelling occupied as the home'; R(SB) 3/84; CIS/427/1991 and R(IS) 3/96
JSA Reg 1(3) JSA Regs, meaning of 'dwelling occupied as the home'
HB Sch 6 para 1 HB Regs
CTB Sch 5 para 1 CTB Regs
43 **IS** Sch 10 para 1 IS Regs
JSA Sch 8 para 1 JSA Regs
HB Sch 6 para 1 HB Regs
CTB Sch 5 para 1 CTB Regs

44 R(JSA) 9/03
45 R(SB) 10/89
46 **IS** Sch 10 para 25 IS Regs
JSA Sch 8 para 5 JSA Regs
HB Sch 6 para 25 HB Regs
CTB Sch 5 para 25 CTB Regs
47 **IS** Sch 10 para 27 IS Regs
JSA Sch 8 para 7 JSA Regs
HB Sch 6 para 27 HB Regs
CTB Sch 5 para 27 CTB Regs
48 **IS** Sch 10 para 26 IS Regs
JSA Sch 8 para 6 JSA Regs
HB Sch 6 para 26 HB Regs
CTB Sch 5 para 26 CTB Regs
All CIS/6908/1995; R(IS) 4/97
49 CIS/562/1992
50 R(IS) 4/97
51 R(SB) 32/83
52 R(IS) 5/05
53 R(IS) 4/97, para 22
54 **IS** Sch 10 para 28 IS Regs
JSA Sch 8 para 8 JSA Regs
HB Sch 6 para 28 HB Regs
CTB Sch 5 para 28 CTB Regs
55 *R v London Borough of Tower Hamlets Review Board ex parte Kapur*, 12 June 2000, unreported
56 **IS** Sch 10 para 2 IS Regs
JSA Sch 8 para 2 JSA Regs
HB Sch 6 para 2 HB Regs
CTB Sch 5 para 2 CTB Regs
57 **IS** Sch 10 para 3 IS Regs
JSA Sch 8 para 3 JSA Regs
HB Sch 6 para 3 HB Regs
CTB Sch 5 para 3 CTB Regs
58 R(IS) 6/95
59 R(IS) 7/01
60 CIS/685/1992
61 CIS/8475/1995; CIS/15984/1996
62 R(SB) 14/85
63 **IS** Sch 10 para 8(a) IS Regs
JSA Sch 8 para 13(a) JSA Regs
HB Sch 6 para 10(a) HB Regs
CTB Sch 5 para 10(a) CTB Regs
64 **IS** Sch 10 para 8(b) IS Regs
JSA Sch 8 para 13(b) JSA Regs
HB Sch 6 para 10(b) HB Regs
CTB Sch 5 para 10(b) CTB Regs
65 *Barclays Bank v Quistclose Investments Ltd* [1970] AC 567; CSB/975/1985
66 **IS** Sch 10 para 9(a) IS Regs
JSA Sch 8 para 14(a) JSA Regs
HB Sch 6 para 11(a) HB Regs
CTB Sch 5 para 11(a) CTB Regs
67 **IS** Sch 10 para 9(b) IS Regs
JSA Sch 8 para 14(b) JSA Regs
HB Sch 6 para 11(b) HB Regs
CTB Sch 5 para 11(b) CTB Regs
68 **IS** Sch 10 para 37 IS Regs
JSA Sch 8 para 9 JSA Regs
HB Sch 6 para 38 HB Regs
CTB Sch 5 para 38 CTB Regs
69 CIS/4757/2003
70 CIS/6908/1995
71 **IS** Sch 10 para 4 IS Regs
JSA Sch 8 para 4 JSA Regs
HB Sch 6 para 4 HB Regs
CTB Sch 5 para 4 CTB Regs
72 **IS** Reg 2(1) IS Regs
JSA Reg 1(3) JSA Regs
HB Reg 2(1) HB Regs
CTB Reg 2(1) CTB Regs
All definition of 'partner'
IS/HB/CTB s137(1) SSCBA 1992
JSA s35 JSA 1995, definition of 'couple'
73 **IS** Sch 10 para 25 IS Regs
JSA Sch 8 para 5 JSA Regs
HB Sch 6 para 25 HB Regs
CTB Sch 5 para 25 CTB Regs
74 R(IS) 3/96
75 para 29437 DMG
HB/CTB para BW1.Annex A, A1.01 GM
76 **IS** Reg 2(1) IS Regs
JSA Reg 1(3) JSA Regs
HB Reg 2(1) HB Regs
CTB Reg 2(1) CTB Regs
77 CSB/209/1986; CSB/1149/1986; R(SB) 22/87
78 **IS** Sch 10 para 10 IS Regs
JSA Sch 8 para 15 JSA Regs
HB Sch 6 para 12 HB Regs
CTB Sch 5 para 12 CTB Regs
79 CH/3700/2006
80 CIS/494/1990 and CIS/2208/2003
81 **IS** Sch 10 para 8(a) IS Regs
JSA Sch 8 para 13(a) JSA Regs
HB Sch 5 para 10(a) HB Regs
CTB Sch 5 para 10(a) CTB Regs
82 **IS** Sch 10 para 6(1) IS Regs
JSA Sch 8 para 11(1) JSA Regs
HB Sch 6 para 8(1) HB Regs
CTB Sch 5 para 8(1) CTB Regs
83 **IS** Sch 10 para 6(2) IS Regs
JSA Sch 8 para 11(2) JSA Regs
HB Sch 6 para 8(2) HB Regs
CTB Sch 5 para 8(2) CTB Regs
84 R(SB) 4/85
85 CIS/5481/1997
86 CFC/15/1990
87 **IS** Sch 10 para 19 IS Regs
JSA Sch 8 para 23 JSA Regs
HB Sch 6 para 21 HB Regs
CTB Sch 5 para 21 CTB Regs

88 **IS** Sch 10 para 23A IS Regs
JSA Sch 8 paras 28 and 29 JSA Regs
HB Sch 6 para 32 HB Regs
CTB Sch 5 para 32 CTB Regs
89 **IS** Sch 10 para 15 IS Regs
JSA Sch 8 para 20 JSA Regs
HB Sch 6 para 17 HB Regs
CTB Sch 5 para 12 CTB Regs
All R(IS) 7/98
90 **IS** Sch 10 para 11 IS Regs
JSA Sch 8 para 16 JSA Regs
HB Sch 5 para 13 HB Regs
CTB Sch 5 para 13 CTB Regs
91 **IS** Reg 41(2) IS Regs
JSA Reg 104(2) JSA Regs
HB Reg 41(2) HB Regs
CTB Reg 31(2) CTB Regs
All *Beattie v Secretary of State for Social Security* [2001] EWCA Civ 498, *The Times*, 3 May 2001, upholding CIS/114/1999, reported as R(IS) 10/01
92 **IS** Sch 10 para 5 IS Regs
JSA Sch 8 para 10 JSA Regs
HB Sch 6 para 7 HB Regs
CTB Sch 5 para 7 CTB Regs
93 CIS/635/1994
94 **IS** Sch 10 para 13 IS Regs
JSA Sch 8 para 18 JSA Regs
HB Sch 6 para 15 HB Regs
CTB Sch 5 para 15 CTB Regs
95 **IS** Sch 10 para 23 IS Regs
JSA Sch 8 para 28 JSA Regs
HB Sch 6 para 31 HB Regs
CTB Sch 5 para 31 CTB Regs
96 **IS** Sch 10 para 24 IS Regs
JSA Sch 8 para 30 JSA Regs
HB Sch 6 para 33 HB Regs
CTB Sch 5 para 33 CTB Regs
97 **IS** Sch 10 para 11 IS Regs
JSA Sch 8 para 16 JSA Regs
HB Sch 6 para 13 HB Regs
CTB Sch 5 para 13 CTB Regs
98 **IS** Sch 10 para 14 IS Regs
JSA Sch 8 para 19 JSA Regs
HB Sch 6 para 16 HB Regs
CTB Sch 5 para 16 CTB Regs
99 **IS** Sch 10 para 16 IS Regs
JSA Sch 8 para 21 JSA Regs
HB Sch 6 para 18 HB Regs
CTB Sch 5 para 18 CTB Regs
100 **IS** Sch 10 para 12 IS Regs
JSA Sch 8 para 17 JSA Regs
HB Sch 6 para 14 HB Regs
CTB Sch 5 para 13 CTB Regs
101 **IS** Sch 10 para 7 IS Regs
JSA Sch 8 para 12 JSA Regs
HB Sch 6 para 9 HB Regs
CTB Sch 5 para 9 CTB Regs
102 **IS** Sch 10 para 7(2) IS Regs
JSA Sch 8 para 12(2) JSA Regs
HB Sch 6 para 9(2) HB Regs
CTB Sch 5 para 9(2) CTB Regs
103 **IS** Sch 10 para 41 IS Regs
JSA Sch 8 para 39 JSA Regs
HB Sch 6 para 9 HB Regs
CTB Sch 5 para 39 CTB Regs
104 **HB** Sch 6 para 48 HB Regs
CTB Sch 5 para 50 CTB Regs
105 **IS** Sch 10 para 38 IS Regs
JSA Sch 8 para 36 JSA Regs
HB Sch 6 para 40 HB Regs
CTB Sch 5 para 40 CTB Regs
106 **IS** Sch 10 para 39 IS Regs
JSA Sch 8 para 37 JSA Regs
HB Sch 6 para 41 HB Regs
CTB Sch 5 para 41 CTB Regs
107 **IS** Sch 10 para 40 IS Regs
JSA Sch 8 para 38 JSA Regs
HB Sch 6 para 42 HB Regs
CTB Sch 5 para 42 CTB Regs
108 **IS** Sch 10 para 18 IS Regs
JSA Sch 8 para 23 JSA Regs
HB Sch 6 para 20 HB Regs
CTB Sch 5 para 20 CTB Regs
109 **IS** Sch 10 para 36 IS Regs
JSA Sch 8 para 35 JSA Regs
HB Sch 6 para 37 HB Regs
CTB Sch 5 para 37 CTB Regs
110 **IS** Sch 10 paras 42 and 43 IS Regs
JSA Sch 8 paras 40 and 41 JSA Regs
HB Sch 6 paras 43 and 44 HB Regs
CTB Sch 5 paras 43 and 44 CTB Regs
111 **IS** Sch 10 para 46 IS Regs
JSA Sch 8 para 44 JSA Regs
HB Sch 6 para 47 HB Regs
CTB Sch 5 para 49 CTB Regs
112 **IS** Sch 10 paras 31-33 IS Regs
JSA Sch 8 para 33 JSA Regs
HB Sch 6 paras 29, 30 and 42 HB Regs
CTB Sch 5 paras 29, 30 and 44 CTB Regs
113 **IS** Sch 10 para 66 IS Regs
JSA Sch 8 para 59 JSA Regs
HB Sch 6 para 57 HB Regs
CTB Sch 5 para 59 CTB Regs
114 **IS** Sch 10 para 64 IS Regs
JSA Sch 8 para 57 JSA Regs
PC Sch 5 para 13 SPC Regs
HB Sch 6 para 55 HB Regs; Sch 6 para 14 HB(SPC) Regs
CTB Sch 5 para 57 CTB Regs; Sch 4 para 14 CTB(SPC) Regs
115 **IS** Sch 10 para 29 IS Regs
JSA Sch 8 para 31 JSA Regs
HB Sch 6 para 34 HB Regs
CTB Sch 5 para 34 CTB Regs

116 **IS** Sch 10 para 22 IS Regs
JSA Sch 8 para 27 JSA Regs
HB Sch 6 para 24 HB Regs
CTB Sch 5 para 24 CTB Regs
117 **IS** para 29462 DMG
HB Reg 86(1) and (3) HB Regs
CTB Reg 72(1) and (3) CTB Regs
118 **IS** Sch 10 para 56 IS Regs
JSA Sch 8 para 51 JSA Regs
HB Sch 6 para 50 HB Regs
CTB Sch 5 para 52 CTB Regs
119 **IS** Sch 10 para 21 IS Regs
JSA Sch 8 para 26 JSA Regs
HB Sch 6 para 23 HB Regs
CTB Sch 5 para 23 CTB Regs
120 **IS** Sch 10 para 17 IS Regs
JSA Sch 8 para 22 JSA Regs
HB Sch 6 para 19 HB Regs
CTB Sch 5 para 19 CTB Regs
121 **IS** Sch 10 para 67 IS Regs
JSA Sch 8 para 60 JSA Regs
HB Sch 6 para 58 HB Regs
CTB Sch 5 para 60 CTB Regs
122 **IS** Sch 10 para 68A IS Regs
JSA Sch 8 para 61A JSA Regs
HB Sch 6 para 60 HB Regs
CTB Sch 5 para 62 CTB Regs
123 **IS** Sch 10 para 68 IS Regs
JSA Sch 8 para 61 JSA Regs
HB Sch 6 para 59 HB Regs
CTB Sch 5 para 61 CTB Regs
124 **IS** Sch 10 para 34 IS Regs
JSA Sch 8 para 34 JSA Regs
125 **IS** Sch 10 para 30 IS Regs
JSA Sch 8 para 32 JSA Regs
HB Sch 6 para 35 HB Regs
CTB Sch 5 para 35 CTB Regs
126 **IS** Sch 10 para 58 IS Regs
JSA Sch 8 para 53 JSA Regs
HB Sch 6 para 52 HB Regs
CTB Sch 5 para 64 CTB Regs
127 **IS** Sch 10 para 63 IS Regs
JSA Sch 8 para 52 JSA Regs
HB Sch 6 para 51 HB Regs
CTB Sch 5 para 53 CTB Regs
128 **IS** Sch 10 para 52 IS Regs
JSA Sch 8 para 47 JSA Regs
HB Sch 6 para 49 HB Regs
CTB Sch 5 para 51 CTB Regs
129 **IS** Sch 10 para 6(3) IS Regs
JSA Sch 8 para 11(3) JSA Regs
HB Sch 5 para 8(3) HB Regs
CTB Sch 5 para 7(3) CTB Regs
130 **IS** Sch 10 para 6(4) IS Regs
JSA Sch 8 para 11(4) JSA Regs
HB Sch 6 para 8(4) HB Regs
CTB Sch 5 para 8(4) CTB Regs
131 **IS** Sch 10 para 20 IS Regs
JSA Sch 8 para 25 JSA Regs
HB Sch 6 para 22 HB Regs
CTB Sch 5 para 22 CTB Regs
132 **IS** Reg 51(6) IS Regs
JSA Reg 113(6) JSA Regs
HB Reg 49(6) HB Regs
CTB Reg 39(6) CTB Regs
133 **IS** Reg 51(1) IS Regs
JSA Reg 113(1) JSA Regs
HB Reg 49(1) HB Regs
CTB Reg 39(1) CTB Regs
134 R(IS) 7/07
135 CIS/124/1990; CSB/1198/1989
136 R(SB) 9/91
137 CIS/124/1990
138 CIS/40/1989
139 CIS/621/1991. See also CJSA/3937/2002
140 CIS/264/1989
141 R(IS) 7/98, para 12(3)
142 R(SB) 38/85; R(IS) 1/91; R(H) 1/06
143 para BW1.714 GM
144 **IS** Reg 51(1) IS Regs
JSA Reg 113(1) JSA Regs
145 R(SB) 12/91; *Verna Jones v Secretary of State for Work and Pensions* [2003] EWCA Civ 964, 10 July 2003, unreported (CA)
146 CIS/2627/1995; *Verna Jones v Secretary of State for Work and Pensions* [2003] EWCA Civ 964, 10 July 2003, unreported (CA)
147 CIS/236/1991
148 *R v Caerphilly CBC HBRB ex parte Jones*, 1 February 1999, unreported
149 CIS/634/1992
150 CIS/12403/1996
151 **IS** Reg 51(6) IS Regs
JSA Reg 113(6) JSA Regs
HB Reg 49(4) HB Regs
CTB Reg 39(4) CTB Regs
152 CIS/30/1993, but other commissioners have taken a different view (see for example, CIS/25/1990 and CIS/81/1991)
153 para BW1.870 GM
154 para BW1.831 GM
155 **IS** Reg 51A IS Regs
JSA Reg 114 JSA Regs
PC Reg 22 SPC Regs
HB Reg 50 HB Regs and reg 50 HB Regs as amended by reg 11 HB(LHA&IS)A Regs; reg 48 HB(SPC) Regs and reg 48 HB(SPC) Regs as amended by reg 11 HB(SPC)(LHA&IS)A Regs
CTB Reg 40 CTB Regs; reg 38(SPC) Regs

156 **IS** Reg 51A(1) IS Regs
JSA Reg 114(1) JSA Regs
PC Reg 22(1) SPC Regs
HB Reg 49(1) HB Regs; reg 48(1) HB(SPC) Regs
CTB Reg 40(1) CTB Regs; reg 38(1) CTB(SPC) Regs
157 para BW1.795 GM
158 R(IS) 9/92
159 **IS** Reg 51(2) IS Regs
JSA Reg 113(2) JSA Regs
HB Reg 49(2) HB Regs
CTB Reg 39(2) CTB Regs
160 CIS/984/2002
161 **HB** Reg 49(2) HB Regs
CTB Reg 39(2) CTB Regs
162 **IS** Reg 51(3)(a)(ii) and (8) IS Regs
JSA Reg 113(3)(a)(ii) JSA Regs
HB Reg 49(3)(a) and (7) HB Regs
CTB Reg 39(3)(a) and (7) CTB Regs
163 **IS** Reg 51(8) IS Regs
JSA Reg 113(8) JSA Regs
HB Reg 49(7)(b) HB Regs
CTB Reg 39(7) CTB Regs
164 **IS/JSA** para 29866 DMG
165 **IS** Reg 51(3A) IS Regs
JSA Reg 113(3A) JSA Regs
HB Reg 49(4)(b) HB Regs
CTB Reg 39(4)(c) CTB Regs
166 **IS** Reg 51(3)(a)(ia) IS Regs
JSA Reg 113(3)(a)(ia) JSA Regs
HB Reg 49(3)(a) HB Regs
CTB Reg 39(3)(a) CTB Regs
167 **IS** Reg 51(3A)(c) IS Regs
JSA Reg 113(3A)(c) JSA Regs
HB Reg 49(4)(c) HB Regs
CTB Reg 39(4)(c) CTB Regs
168 R(IS) 4/01
169 **IS** Reg 51(3)(a)(i) IS Regs
JSA Reg 113(3)(a)(i) JSA Regs
170 **IS** Reg 51(3)(b) IS Regs
JSA Reg 113(3)(b) JSA Regs
HB Reg 49(3)(c) HB Regs
CTB Reg 39(3)(c) CTB Regs
171 **IS** Reg 51(4) IS Regs
JSA Reg 113(4) JSA Regs
HB Reg 49(5) HB Regs
CTB Reg 39(5) CTB Regs
172 **IS** Reg 51(5) IS Regs
JSA Reg 113(5) JSA Regs
HB Reg 49(6) HB Regs
CTB Reg 39(6) CTB Regs
173 **IS/JSA** para 29879 DMG; see also R(IS) 13/93
174 R(IS) 14/98
175 **HB** Reg 49(5) HB Regs
CTB Reg 39(5) CTB Regs
176 **IS** Reg 49(a) IS Regs
JSA Reg 111(a) JSA Regs
HB Reg 47(a) HB Regs
CTB Reg 37(a) CTB Regs
177 R(SB) 57/83; R(SB) 6/84
178 R(SB) 18/83
179 R(SB) 6/84
180 **IS** Reg 49(a)(i) IS Regs
JSA Reg 111(a)(i) JSA Regs
HB Reg 47(a)(i) HB Regs
CTB Reg 37(a)(i) CTB Regs
181 **IS** Reg 49(a)(ii) IS Regs
JSA Reg 111(a)(ii) JSA Regs
HB Reg 47(a)(ii) HB Regs
CTB Reg 37(a)(ii) CTB Regs
182 CIS/255/1989
183 R(SB) 27/84
184 R(SB) 2/83; R(SB) 31/83
185 **IS** Reg 52 IS Regs
JSA Reg 115 JSA Regs
HB Reg 51 HB Regs
CTB Reg 41 CTB Regs
186 *Hourigan v Secretary of State for Work and Pensions* [2002] EWCA Civ 1890 reported as R(IS) 4/03
187 CIS/15936/1996; CIS/263/1997; CIS/3283/1997 (joint decision); R(IS) 26/95
188 R(IS) 3/96
189 R(JSA) 1/02
190 CIS/2575/1997
191 R(IS) 2/93
192 R(IS) 1/03
193 **IS** Reg 49(a) IS Regs
JSA Reg 111(a) JSA Regs
HB Reg 47(a) HB Regs
CTB Reg 37(a) CTB Regs
194 R(IS) 18/95
195 R(SB) 18/83; R(IS) 2/90
196 **IS/JSA** para 29681 DMG
HB/CTB para C2.184 GM
197 *Peters v CAO* (appendix to R(SB) 3/89)
198 **IS** Reg 50(a) IS Regs
JSA Reg 112(a) JSA Regs
HB Reg 48(a) HB Regs
CTB Reg 38(a) CTB Regs
199 **IS** Reg 50(b) IS Regs
JSA Reg 112(b) JSA Regs
HB Reg 48(b) HB Regs
CTB Reg 38(b) CTB Regs
200 **IS** Sch 10 para 21 IS Regs
JSA Sch 8 para 26 JSA Regs
HB Sch 6 para 23 HB Regs
CTB Sch 5 para 23 CTB Regs

2. **People aged 60 or over**

201 **HB** Sch 6 para 5 HB Regs
CTB Sch 5 para 5 CTB Regs

202 **PC** s15 SPCA 2002; Sch 5 paras 24-28 SPC Regs
HB Reg 29(1)(i) and Sch 6 paras 27-30 HB(SPC) Regs
CTB Reg 19(1)(1) and Sch 4 paras 27-30 CTB(SPC) Regs
203 **PC** Sch 4 para 18 SPC Regs
HB Reg 29(2) HB(SPC) Regs
CTB Reg 19(2) CTB(SPC) Regs
204 s15(2) SPCA 2002; reg 15(6) SPC Regs
205 **HB** Regs 25 and 26 HB(SPC) Regs
CTB Regs 15 and 16 CTB(SPC) Regs
206 **HB** Reg 43 HB(SPC) Regs
CTB Reg 33 CTB(SPC) Regs
207 **HB** Reg 29(2) HB(SPC) Regs
CTB Reg 19(2) CTB(SPC) Regs
208 Reg 15(6) SPC Regs
209 Reg 29(2) and (6) HB(SPC) Regs
210 **PC** s5 SPCA 2002
HB/CTB s136(1) SSCBA 1992
211 **HB** Reg 23(3) HB(SPC) Regs
CTB Reg 13(3) CTB(SPC) Regs
212 para C2.21 GM
213 R(IS) 3/93
214 **PC** Reg 2 SS(PAOR) Regs
HB Reg 74(1) HB(SPC) Regs
215 **PC** Sch 5 para 28 SPC Regs
HB Sch 6 para 30 HB(SPC) Regs
CTB Sch 4 para 30 CTB(SPC) Regs
216 **PC** Sch 5 para 16(1) SPC Regs
HB Sch 6 para 17(1) HB(SPC) Regs
CTB Sch 4 para 17(1) CTB(SPC) Regs
217 R(IS) 3/03
218 **PC** Sch 5 para 16(2)(a) and (b) SPC Regs
HB Sch 6 para 17(2)(a) and (b) HB(SPC) Regs
CTB Sch 4 para 17(2)(a) and (b) CTB(SPC) Regs
219 **PC** Schs 4 paras 13 and 14 and 5 para 16(2) SPC Regs
HB Schs 5 paras 14 and 15 and 6 para 17(2) HB(SPC) Regs
CTB Schs 3 paras 14 and 15 and 4 para 17(2) CTB(SPC) Regs
220 **PC** Sch 5 para 1A SPC Regs
HB Sch 6 para 26 HB(SPC) Regs
CTB Sch 4 para 26 CTB(SPC) Regs
221 **PC** Reg 17(8) SPC Regs
HB Reg 33(11) HB(SPC) Regs
CTB Reg 23(11) CTB(SPC) Regs
222 **PC** Reg 1(2) SPC Regs
HB Reg 2(1) HB(SPC) Regs
CTB Reg 2(1) CTB(SPC) Regs under the definition of 'dwelling occupied as the home'
223 **PC** Sch 5 para 1A SPC Regs
HB Sch 6 para 26 HB(SPC) Regs
CTB Sch 4 para 26 CTB(SPC) Regs
224 R(JSA) 9/03
225 R(SB) 10/89
226 **PC** Sch 5 para 6(1) SPC Regs
HB Sch 6 para 6(1) HB(SPC) Regs
CTB Sch 4 para 6(1) CTB(SPC) Regs
227 **PC** Sch 5 para 2 SPC Regs
HB Sch 6 para 2 HB(SPC) Regs
CTB Sch 4 para 2 CTB(SPC) Regs
228 **PC** Sch 5 para 7 SPC Regs
HB Sch 6 para 7 HB(SPC) Regs
CTB Sch 4 para 7 CTB(SPC) Regs
All CIS/6908/1995; R(IS) 4/97
229 R(SB) 32/83
230 R(IS) 5/05
231 **PC** Sch 5 para 3 SPC Regs
HB Sch 6 para 3 HB(SPC) Regs
CTB Sch 4 para 3 CTB(SPC) Regs
232 *R v London Borough of Tower Hamlets Review Board ex parte Kapur*, 12 June 2000, unreported
233 **PC** Sch 5 para 1 SPC Regs
HB Sch 6 para 1 HB(SPC) Regs
CTB Sch 4 para 1 CTB(SPC) Regs
234 **PC** Sch 5 paras 17 and 19 SPC Regs
HB Sch 6 paras 18 and 20 HB(SPC) Regs
CTB Sch 4 paras 18 and 20 CTB(SPC) Regs
235 **PC** Sch 5 paras 17 and 18 SPC Regs
HB Sch 6 paras 18 and 19 HB(SPC) Regs
CTB Sch 4 paras 18 and 19 CTB(SPC) Regs
236 CIS/4757/2003
237 CIS/6908/1995
238 **PC** Sch 5 para 4 SPC Regs
HB Sch 6 para 4 HB(SPC) Regs
CTB Sch 4 para 4 CTB(SPC) Regs
239 **PC** Reg 1(2) SPC Regs
HB Reg 2(1) HB(SPC) Regs
CTB Reg 2(1) CTB(SPC) Regs
All Definition of 'close relative'
240 **PC** Sch 5 para 6 SPC Regs
HB Sch 6 para 6 HB(SPC) Regs
CTB Sch 4 para 6 CTB(SPC) Regs
241 R(IS) 3/96
242 para 84444 DMG
HB/CTB para BP1.Annex A, A1.01 GM
243 **PC** Sch 5 para 8 SPC Regs
HB Sch 6 para 8 HB(SPC) Regs
CTB Sch 4 para 8 CTB(SPC) Regs

244 **PC** Sch 5 paras 17 and 18 SPC Regs
HB Sch 6 paras 18 and 19 HB(SPC) Regs
CTB Sch 4 paras 18 and 19 CTB(SPC) Regs
245 **PC** Sch 5 para 9 SPC Regs
HB Sch 6 para 9 HB(SPC) Regs
CTB Sch 4 para 9 CTB(SPC) Regs
246 **PC** Sch 5 para 9A SPC Regs
HB Sch 6 para 10 HB(SPC) Regs
CTB Sch 4 para 10 CTB(SPC) Regs
247 **PC** Sch 5 para 10 SPC Regs
HB Sch 6 para 11 HB(SPC) Regs
CTB Sch 4 para 11 CTB(SPC) Regs
All R(IS) 7/98
248 **PC** Sch 5 para 26 SPC Regs
HB Sch 6 para 29 HB Regs
CTB Sch 4 para 29 CTB Regs
249 **PC** s15(1)(d) SPCA 2002
HB Reg 29(1)(d) HB(SPC) Regs
CTB Reg 19(1)(d) CTB(SPC) Regs
All R(IS) 10/01
250 **PC** Sch 5 para 5 SPC Regs
HB Sch 6 para 5 HB(SPC) Regs
CTB Sch 4 para 5 CTB(SPC) Regs
251 **PC** Sch 5 para 24 SPC Regs
HB Sch 6 para 27 HB(SPC) Regs
CTB Sch 4 para 27 CTB(SPC) Regs
252 **PC** Sch 5 para 22 SPC Regs
HB Sch 6 para 24 HB(SPC) Regs
CTB Sch 4 para 24 CTB(SPC) Regs
253 **PC** Sch 5 para 25 SPC Regs
HB Sch 6 para 28 HB(SPC) Regs
CTB Sch 4 para 28 CTB(SPC) Regs
254 **PC** Sch 5 para 26 SPC Regs
HB Sch 6 para 29 HB(SPC) Regs
CTB Sch 4 para 29 CTB(SPC) Regs
255 **PC** Sch 5 paras 17, 20 and 20A SPC Regs
HB Sch 6 paras 18, 21 and 22 HB(SPC) Regs
CTB Sch 4 paras 18, 21 and 22 CTB(SPC) Regs
256 **PC** Sch 5 para 23A SPC Regs
HB/CTB amendments made by regs 11(4) and 12(4) SS (DRPSAPGRB)(MP) Regs were omitted in error from HB(SPC) Regs and CTB(SPC) Regs, but have effect by virtue of reg 2 HB&CTB(CP) Regs
257 **PC** Sch 5 para 12 SPC Regs
HB Sch 6 para 13 HB(SPC) Regs
CTB Sch 4 para 13 CTB(SPC) Regs
258 **PC** Sch 5 para 14 SPC Regs
HB Sch 6 para 15 HB(SPC) Regs
CTB Sch 4 para 15 CTB(SPC) Regs
259 **PC** Sch 5 para 13 SPC Regs
HB Sch 6 para 14 HB(SPC) Regs
CTB Sch 4 para 14 CTB(SPC) Regs
260 **PC** Sch 5 para 11 SPC Regs
HB Sch 6 para 12 HB(SPC) Regs
CTB Sch 4 para 12 CTB(SPC) Regs
261 **PC** Sch 5 para 15 SPC Regs
HB Sch 6 para 16 HB(SPC) Regs
CTB Sch 4 para 16 CTB(SPC) Regs
262 **PC** Sch 5 para 21 SPC Regs
HB Sch 6 para 23 HB (SPC) Regs
CTB Sch 4 para 23 CTB (SPC) Regs
263 **PC** Reg 21 SPC Regs
HB Reg 47 HB(SPC) Regs
CTB Reg 37 CTB(SPC) Regs
264 **PC** Reg 21(1) SPC Regs
HB Reg 47(1) HB(SPC) Regs
CTB Reg 37(1) CTB(SPC) Regs
265 **PC** Reg 21 SPC Regs
HB Reg 47(2) HB(SPC) Regs
CTB Reg 37(2) CTB(SPC) Regs
266 **PC** Reg 21(3) SPC Regs
HB Reg 47(3) HB(SPC) Regs
CTB Reg 37(3) CTB(SPC) Regs
267 **PC** Reg 21(4) SPC Regs
HB Reg 42(4) HB(SPC) Regs
CTB Reg 37(4) CTB(SPC) Regs
268 R(IS) 13/93
269 R(IS) 14/98
270 **PC** Reg 19(a) SPC Regs
HB Reg 45(a) HB(SPC) Regs
CTB Reg 35(a) CTB(SPC) Regs
271 **PC** Reg 19(a)(i) SPC Regs
HB Reg 45(a)(i) HB(SPC) Regs
CTB Reg 35(a)(i) CTB(SPC) Regs
272 **PC** Reg 19(a)(ii) SPC Regs
HB Reg 45(a)(ii) HB(SPC) Regs
CTB Reg 35(a)(ii) CTB(SPC) Regs
273 **PC** Reg 23 SPC Regs
HB Reg 49 HB(SPC) Regs
CTB Reg 39 CTB(SPC) Regs
274 R(IS) 4/03
275 **PC** Reg 19(a) SPC Regs
HB Reg 45(a) HB(SPC) Regs
CTB Reg 35(a) CTB(SPC) Regs
276 **PC** para 84772 DMG
HB/CTB para BP1.530 GM
277 *Peters v CAO* (appendix to R(SB) 3/89)
278 **PC** Reg 20(a) SPC Regs
HB Reg 46(a) HB(SPC) Regs
CTB Reg 38(a) CTB(SPC) Regs
279 **PC** Reg 20 SPC Regs
HB Reg 46(b) HB(SPC) Regs
CTB Reg 36(b) CTB(SPC) Regs
280 **PC** Sch 5 para 21 SPC Regs
HB Sch 6 para 23 HB(SPC) Regs
CTB Sch 4 para 23 CTB (SPC) Regs

Part 5

Benefit claims, decisions and challenges

Chapter 38

Claims, backdating and getting paid

This chapter covers:

This chapter deals with benefits administered by the DWP, and with child benefit and guardian's allowance which are administered by the Revenue. (For tax credits see Chapter 52.) This chapter does not cover statutory sick pay (see Chapter 24), statutory adoption pay, statutory maternity pay or statutory paternity pay (see Chapter 17), bonuses, the health benefits discussed in Chapter 9 or payments from the social fund (see Chapters 21 and 22).

This chapter does not cover the main rules for housing benefit (HB) or council tax benefit (CTB). For those rules, see Chapters 10 and 5. However, the rules on the national insurance (NI) number requirement and suspensions are the same for HB and CTB as for other benefits. Therefore, the description of those rules here also applies to HB and CTB.

You should look at this chapter if you are claiming:

- attendance allowance (AA);
- child benefit;
- CTB – but only regarding the NI number requirement and suspensions (otherwise, see Chapter 5);
- disability living allowance (DLA);
- guardian's allowance;
- HB – but only regarding the NI number requirement and suspensions (otherwise, see Chapter 10);
- incapacity benefit;

- income support;
- industrial injuries benefits;
- carer's allowance (CA);
- jobseeker's allowance;
- maternity allowance;
- pension credit (PC);
- retirement pension;
- widows' benefits or bereavement benefits.

Many of the benefits listed above are dealt with at a telephone contact centre when you first make your claim and thereafter at a regional benefit delivery centre. However, there are exceptions:

- HB and CTB are administered by your local authority at their own local offices;
- PC and retirement pension are administered by the Pension Service in regional pension centres;
- claims are administered in units for:
  - child benefit and guardian's allowance by the Revenue (see Appendix 1);
  - AA and DLA by regional disability centres and/or (depending on where you live) by the Disability Contact and Processing Units in Blackpool;
  - CA by a central unit in Preston.

You can find your appropriate local Jobcentre Plus office by looking in the telephone directory for business and service numbers, or the Jobcentre Plus website at www.jobcentreplus.gov.uk, which may also contain details of contact centres and benefit delivery centres. Details of the regional pension centres are on the Pension Service website at www.thepensionservice.gov.uk, or in the telephone directory. See Appendix 1 for the addresses of the central units.

1. Who should claim

You should claim benefit for yourself and any adult or child dependants. If you cannot do so, another person can claim on your behalf – eg, an appointee (see p955) or your parent if you are a child claiming disability living allowance.

Couples and children

If you are part of a **couple**, for some non-means-tested benefits you may be the claimant and claim for an adult dependant (see Chapter 29), and for most means-tested benefits you may be assessed as a couple, but still only one of you actually makes the claim (see Chapter 30). You can sometimes choose which one of you claims income support for both of you.[1] Couples can also choose which person claims pension credit.[2] For housing benefit (HB) and council tax benefit (CTB), see p204. Check to see how the decision on which one of you claims makes you better or worse off. In the case of jobseeker's allowance (JSA), there are special provisions for joint claims by couples (see below).

If you have **children**, except for HB and CTB, they are not included in a new claim for benefit, although in some circumstances they continue to be included in a pre-existing claim (see Chapters 29 and 30). Also, you can claim child benefit, but other people might also be entitled (see p64).

Appointees

Someone else (eg, a friend or relative), called an 'appointee', can be authorised to act on your behalf if you cannot claim for yourself – eg, you are mentally ill.[3] This is not necessary if a court has already appointed someone to look after your affairs. The appointee takes on all your rights and responsibilities as a claimant. For example, s/he must notify changes in your circumstances. Normally, this only applies from the date the appointment is agreed, but if someone acts on your behalf before becoming your official appointee her/his actions can be validated in retrospect by her/his appointment.[4] To become an appointee, a person must normally apply in writing. However, if s/he has already been made an appointee by the local authority for HB or CTB purposes, the DWP can, by agreement, make her/him an appointee without a written application, and vice versa.[5] S/he must be over 18.

If you are an appointee for a claimant who dies, you must re-apply for appointee status in order to settle any outstanding benefit matters.[6] An executor under a will can also pursue an outstanding claim or appeal on behalf of a deceased claimant even if the decision was made before the formal grant of probate.[7]

Joint claims for jobseeker's allowance

In some cases, both members of a couple are subject to the labour market conditions for entitlement to income-based JSA (see Chapter 1) and must make a joint claim (see p381).

2. How to make a claim

To qualify for a benefit you must usually make a claim.[8] There are exceptions to this rule. Where there is a delay in making a claim, you may be able to get an **interim payment** of benefit (see p986). You do not have to make a claim for retirement allowance (see p330) and certain retirement pensions if you are already receiving certain other retirement pensions or widows' benefits (see p474), or for bereavement payment if you are over pension age (see p33).[9]

Starting your claim

You usually need to make your claim in writing. Income support (IS) and jobseeker's allowance (JSA) *must* eventually be claimed on an official claim form.[10] However, in many cases, in particular if you are aged under 60, your claim is actually started by telephone (see below).

For details on how to start a claim for any of the following benefits, which are claimed from central or regional units, see the relevant chapter on the benefit concerned:

- attendance allowance (AA);
- child benefit;
- disability living allowance (DLA);
- housing benefit (HB) and council tax benefit (CTB);
- guardian's allowance;
- pension credit (PC).
- retirement pension.

For many other benefits, administered by the DWP through Jobcentre Plus, you are encouraged to start your claim by telephoning a contact centre before being sent either written details to confirm or a claim form to fill in. This applies in particular if you are aged under 60.

There is no rule that you *must* start your claim by telephone – eg, Jobcentre Plus offices can still accept your claim if it is made direct on a claim form and posted. Claim forms should still be available and some can be downloaded from the DWP website. However, in practice it is best to make your claim in the way the DWP prefers if you can.

If starting your claim by telephone is either impractical or impossible for you, tell the Jobcentre Plus and ask to claim in an alternative way. For example:

- if speaking in English is difficult, an interpreter can be arranged;
- another person may be able to make the call on your behalf, especially if you are there to help;
- a 'face-to-face' interview could take place at the Jobcentre Plus office;
- a home visit could be arranged;
- if none of the above is suitable, a claim form could be completed and sent in.

Claiming via a telephone contact centre

The DWP prefers you to start your claim for certain benefits administered by Jobcentre Plus by making a telephone call to a contact centre. In particular, it encourages you to do this if you are aged under 60 and claiming **IS, JSA** or **incapacity benefit (IB)**. For these benefits, you can also start your claim online at www.dwp.gov.uk/eservice. However, remember that this is not the same as actually making a claim. If you do not receive a quick reply, seek advice. It is also expected that Jobcentre Plus will prefer claims for the new **employment and**

support allowance (expected to be introduced in October 2008) to be started by telephone.

Claims for some other benefits can also be started by telephone, although in practice you are sent a claim form for these benefits even if you do start your claim via the contact centre. These benefits are: **bereavement benefits, carer's allowance (CA), industrial injuries benefits** and **maternity allowance**.

There is a national 0800 number for making your claim, which routes your call to the relevant contact centre. The number is telephone 0800 0 55 66 88, textphone 0800 0 23 48 88, Welsh language 0800 0 12 18 88. These numbers are free if you are using a landline, but not if you are using a mobile telephone. Your local Jobcentre Plus office should have a 'warm phone' that you can use free of charge, although you might need to queue. When you make your call, the contact centre will take the details for your claim (it may need to call you back) and will then either:

- send you a 'written statement' for you to confirm the details (IS, JSA and IB claims only); *or*
- send you a claim form (claims for other benefits).

The contact centre will also arrange your first jobseeker's interview if you are claiming JSA (see p380) or your initial work-focused interview, if applicable (see p971). If you are sent a written statement, you are asked to bring that along to the work-focused interview where it will be finalised and signed, and so become your written claim. (If no work-focused interview is considered appropriate, you are asked to confirm the statement and return it by post.) If you are sent a claim form, you are asked to complete it and return it to the address given with the form.

Claim forms, the internet and other ways of claiming

It is still possible to start claims by filling in and returning a claim form (but see above for when Jobcentre Plus may encourage you to telephone a contact centre, even if you do send in a claim form). You may be able to get claim forms from your local DWP office or (for child benefit and guardian's allowance) the Revenue. You may also be able to download forms from www.dwp.gov.uk or www.hmrc.gov.uk.

Some benefits can be claimed using the internet and a few (mainly if you are aged 60 or over) may be claimed by telephone or in person at a DWP, local authority or 'alternative' office (see p958).

See the relevant chapter of this *Handbook* for more details on the benefit you are claiming.

Where to claim

If you are aged under 60 you are normally expected to start your claim for most benefits, except those listed below, by telephoning a contact centre (see p956).

If are aged 60 or over or are claiming:

- AA;
- DLA;
- child benefit;
- guardian's allowance;
- CA;
- bereavement benefits;
- PC; *or*
- retirement pension,

you should usually send a claim form to the relevant office, even if you do start off by telephoning a contact centre. If you are aged 60 or over, you may be able to claim a few benefits by telephone or in person at a DWP or local authority office, or at an alternative office (see below). For information about where you should get and return your claim form, see the relevant chapter in this *Handbook*.

Claiming at alternative offices

If you are aged 60 or over, you can claim certain benefits not only from the relevant DWP office, but also at designated local authority HB/CTB offices, at other 'alternative offices' and, in England only, from designated county councils.[11] You can also claim at such offices if you are aged under 60 and are claiming DLA, CA, IB or IS. You do not have to use the local authority or alternative office, but you can claim there in writing or in person. A claim for PC, however, must be in writing. Even if you do not make your claim at the local authority office, you can give information and evidence relating to the claim, and get advice about it there (but you cannot do this at alternative offices).

The alternative offices include some local advice centres and local authority HB offices identified by the DWP.

The offices can deal with claims for AA, bereavement benefits, CA, DLA, IB, IS, PC, retirement pension and winter fuel payments.

When to claim

You should claim as soon as you think you might be entitled to benefit, even if it might take you time to collect all the information required on the form. See p963 for further information about your date of claim.

Very occasionally, it may be in your interests to wait for the next 'benefit year' to claim **IB** or **JSA** on the basis of a better record of national insurance (NI) contributions (see p735). In some limited circumstances your claim can be backdated (see p964).

Amending or withdrawing your claim

You can **amend** your claim by writing to the office handling your claim.[12] If your letter is received before a decision is made, the decision maker can treat your claim as being amended from the date it was initially made.

You can **withdraw** your claim at any time before a decision is made.[13] Once a decision is made, the claim may not be withdrawn in respect of a period before the date of the decision, but it may be possible to withdraw it in respect of a future period even if you have ongoing entitlement.[14]

Making sure your claim is valid

Your claim for benefit must be valid. Usually, this means that your claim must be in writing, even if you start the claim by telephoning a contact centre, and be made on the appropriate form (this can be a written statement sent after the telephone call). There are exceptions:

- PC does not have to be claimed in writing unless you are specifically required to do so (although you are eventually sent something to sign). If you claim by telephone, you must supply any information requested within one month, or longer if that is considered reasonable;
- for IS and JSA, there is an additional 'evidence requirement' (see p960).

For claims other than for IS and JSA, the decision maker may decide to treat any letter or other written communication as being a valid claim.[15] Also, if you just write a letter or send the wrong form, you can be sent the appropriate form to fill in. If you do not fill in the form properly, it can be returned to you. If you subsequently return it correctly filled in within a month, you count as having made a valid claim on the date of your first letter or form.[16] The decision maker can extend this one-month period if s/he thinks this is reasonable – eg, because you were ill. See p964 for other situations when your claim can be backdated.

Claims for IS and JSA must *always* be made on the appropriate form – this can be the 'written statement' that is sent to you if you start your claim by telephone at a contact centre.

If your claim is valid, it is referred to a decision maker to decide if you are entitled to benefit. The decision maker can ask you to provide further information to support your claim (see p961) or even ask you to attend a medical examination before s/he makes a decision (see pp668 and 676). This should not prevent a decision being made on your claim (but see below). If you are asked to provide information after a decision has been made on your claim, see p985.

If your claim is not accepted as valid

If your claim is not accepted as valid, the decision maker will not make a decision on your entitlement to benefit. The DWP or the Revenue may tell you that the claim is not valid, and give you some time to return a properly completed claim form. Except for IS, PC not claimed in advance and JSA, however, it does not have to do this.[17] The time allowed for this is one month but, except for written claims for PC,it can be extended.

In any case, if the DWP or the Revenue does not accept that your claim is valid, you should still be given a decision saying so. You have the right of appeal against such decisions.[18] If your claim *is* accepted as valid, the decision maker must make a decision on your entitlement to benefit.[19]

Work-focused interviews

The Government is introducing schemes that make entitlement to certain benefits dependent on attending interviews about work. In these schemes, the general rule is that you must, as part of your claim, attend a 'work-focused interview' with an adviser. If you are part of a couple, in some cases your partner may have to attend a work-focused interview as well. See p971 for further information about the schemes.

Evidence required for income support and jobseeker's allowance

It is your responsibility to:[20]

- complete your claim form fully and correctly; *and*
- produce information and evidence to verify your claim.

This is also known as the 'onus of proof' rule. See p380 (for JSA) and p303 (for IS) for the information you can be asked to provide.

If you do not fill in the form properly or provide all the information and evidence required, the DWP must notify you that your claim is defective and contact you to put things right.[21] It might telephone or write to you or, in the case of IS, visit you to get the information or evidence. But it might simply return your claim form. You should provide the information or evidence or complete the form and return it to your local office within one month of your initial contact (or that of someone contacting the DWP on your behalf). If you do not, you might lose benefit (see p964 for when your claim can be backdated). In any case, if the DWP does not accept your claim is valid, you should be given a decision saying so, and you have the right of appeal against that decision.[22]

Exemptions from the evidence requirement

You are exempt from the evidence requirement if:[23]

- you could not complete the form or get the information or evidence required because of a physical, mental, learning or communication difficulty. You must also show that it is not reasonably practicable for you to find someone to help you complete the form or get the proof on your behalf. However, you can argue that someone else is not expected to take the initiative in offering you assistance;[24] *or*
- the information or evidence required does not exist; *or*

- you could not get the information or evidence required without serious risk of physical or mental harm. You must also show that it is not reasonably practicable to get it in another way; *or*
- you could only get the information or evidence required from a third party and it is not reasonably practicable to get it from her/him; *or*
- the decision maker thinks sufficient proof has been provided to show that you are not entitled to IS or JSA (eg, because your capital or income is too high) so it would be inappropriate to require further information or evidence.

If you are unable to complete your claim form or provide the required information or evidence for one of the reasons listed above, you should give your local office notice of this as soon as possible, ideally by explaining this on the claim form or by ringing or visiting the benefit or Jobcentre Plus office. The DWP says that such notice must be given within one month of the date when you first contacted it. Explain your circumstances fully. You can provide supporting letters – eg, from a social worker or a solicitor. If the DWP accepts you are exempt from the evidence requirement, it might:

- help you to fill in the form; *or*
- give you longer to complete it; *or*
- collect evidence or information on your behalf; *or*
- tell you that you do not have to provide the information after all.

If you are claiming JSA, you are normally required to attend an interview at which a properly completed claim form is signed. Your claim is then treated as being made on the date you first notified your intention to claim (usually when you picked up the form and made the appointment for the interview), or the first date in respect of which your claim is made if this is later.[25] If you fail to attend the interview or hand in a properly completed form you might lose benefit.

Remember that the decision maker can ask you for further information or evidence even after s/he has accepted your claim as valid. However, this should not change the date from which you can be paid. If s/he eventually decides you are entitled to benefit you should still be paid from your date of claim. See pp963 and 964 for more information about your date of claim.

Further information to support your claim

Once your claim has been accepted as valid, you may be required to provide additional documentation and evidence relevant to your claim and you can be asked for an interview to discuss your circumstances if this is reasonable.[26] You may be able to claim travelling expenses for this.[27] Where a local authority has used information on your claim for HB or CTB and has passed that to the DWP because it is relevant to your claim for another benefit, in most cases the DWP must use that information without checking it further.[28]

The national insurance number requirement

When you claim benefit (including HB and CTB) you must usually satisfy the NI number requirement:[29]

- by providing an NI number and information or evidence to show that it is yours; *or*
- by providing evidence or information to enable the DWP (or the Revenue) to trace your NI number, if you do not know it; *or*
- by applying for an NI number if you do not have one and providing enough information and evidence to allow one to be allocated to you.

For a few benefits, you do not need to make a claim (see p955), in which case the NI number requirement should not apply. If you cannot satisfy the NI number requirement straight away, you may be able to claim an interim payment of benefit (see p986). If you are refused an NI number, you have the right of appeal against that decision, including where you are refused benefit as a result.[30]

Exemptions

You are exempt from the NI number requirement if:

- you are under 16 and the benefit is DLA;[31]
- the benefit is statutory adoption pay, statutory maternity pay, statutory paternity pay, statutory sick pay or social fund payments;
- you made your claim before the test was introduced for the particular benefit in question. See p1059 of CPAG's *Welfare Benefits Handbook* 2000/01 for a list of dates;
- the benefit is HB and you live in a hostel.[32]

Members of your family

If you are claiming a means-tested benefit as a couple (see p702), your partner must also satisfy the NI number requirement.[33] That is the case even where s/he is a 'person subject to immigration control' and no extra benefit would be paid for her/him.[34]

The same applies if you are claiming extra benefit for an adult dependant with your non-means-tested benefit (see p686) in relation to that dependant.[35]

A child under the age of 16 does not need to satisfy the NI number requirement.[36]

Proof of identity

In addition to requiring you to satisfy the NI number requirement, you may be asked to produce further documents or evidence that prove your identity. If you are claiming for your partner or an adult dependant (see p686) you must also prove her/his identity.

You can prove your identity with a passport, a national identity card issued by a European Economic Area member state, or a letter issued by the Home Office acknowledging your application for asylum. You could also produce your birth certificate, full driving licence, a travel pass with a photograph, a local council rent card or tenancy agreement or even paid fuel or telephone bills.

Note:

- It is important to provide details of any other people who can confirm what you have stated – eg, your solicitor or other representative, a support group or official organisation.
- You should not be refused benefit simply because you do not have any documents, especially where it is unreasonable for you to have or obtain them. Ask the decision maker to make a decision on your claim and you can then appeal.

In some cases, the decision maker may refuse to accept evidence that you are who you say you are. Some claimants may have particular difficulty supplying evidence, or believe they are being discriminated against. Press the decision maker to be clear about what is required and why, and complain if you consider any requests for information are unreasonable (see p1180). You may also wish to approach your local race equality council if you feel you have experienced race discrimination.

3. The date of your claim

You are not usually entitled to benefit for any day before your date of claim. See the chapter in this *Handbook* about the benefit you are claiming for information about this. In addition, remember:

- you might be able to claim in advance if you know you are not entitled now but will be later – eg, you are coming out of hospital;
- your claim might be backdated in certain circumstances (see p964);
- if you claim the wrong benefit, your claim can be treated as one for the right benefit (see below).

If you claim the wrong benefit

If you have claimed the wrong benefit but are in fact entitled to another benefit, your original claim can sometimes be treated as a claim for the right benefit.[37] This might be a way around the strict backdating rules (see p964). To find out which claims can interchange, see below. See also information in the chapter about the benefit you should have claimed.

Interchange of claims[38]

Benefit claimed	*May be treated as a claim for*
Incapacity benefit	Severe disablement allowance; maternity allowance
Severe disablement allowance	Incapacity benefit; maternity allowance
Maternity allowance	Incapacity benefit; severe disablement allowance
Widows' benefits; bereavement benefits	Retirement pension
Retirement pension	Widows' benefits; bereavement benefits
Income support	Carer's allowance
Attendance allowance	Disability living allowance
Disability living allowance	Attendance allowance

In addition, a claim for:

- child benefit can be treated as a claim for guardian's allowance and vice versa;[39]
- attendance allowance (AA) or disability living allowance (DLA) can be treated as a claim for an increase in disablement pension where constant attendance is needed (see p326) and vice versa.

If you claim a non-means-tested benefit (other than child benefit) but are not entitled to it, your claim may be treated as a claim by someone else for an increase in her/his benefit for you (see p696).

If you claim an increase of a non-means-tested benefit for an adult dependant but are not entitled to it, the claim may be treated as a claim by someone else who is entitled.[40] An increase of incapacity benefit (IB) can be treated as an increase of severe disablement allowance (SDA) and vice versa.

The decision maker does not have to accept your claim for one benefit as a claim for another. You cannot appeal if this is refused. Your only remedy is to seek a judicial review (see p1129).

In addition, for all benefits except income support (IS) and income-based jobseeker's allowance (JSA) there is a general power to treat any written document as a claim for benefit.[41] You may be able to argue that the claim form for the wrong benefit should be treated in that way. Again, if the relevant office refuses to do so, you cannot appeal and your only remedy is to seek a judicial review (see p1129).

Backdating your claim

There are strict time limits for claiming benefits.[42] However, if you miss the time limit for claiming, your claim can sometimes be backdated for up to three months (12 months for pension credit (PC) and retirement pension, although for PC this may be reduced to three months during 2008 – see CPAG's *Welfare Rights Bulletin* for updates). The backdating period is longer for most benefits if you are reclaiming following the award of a 'qualifying benefit' (see p968).

In general:

- if you want your claim to be backdated you must ask for this to happen, otherwise it will not be considered;[43]
- some benefits can be backdated without special reasons (see below);
- claims for IS and JSA can only be backdated in limited circumstances (see p966);
- special rules apply if you are claiming backdated JSA because your entitlement ceased when you failed to attend an interview or sign on (see p391);
- extra backdating of most benefits is allowed after awards of qualifying benefits (see p968);
- claims for AA and DLA can never be backdated;[44]
- different rules apply to housing benefit (HB) and council tax benefit (CTB) (see p206);
- if you claim the wrong benefit, your claim can sometimes be treated as a claim for the benefit you should have claimed (see p963).

For the main exceptions to the rules, see the chapter in this *Handbook* about the benefit you are claiming.

If you are prevented from receiving backdated benefit because of an error on the part of the DWP (or, in child benefit and guardian's allowance cases, the Revenue) you should write and request an *ex gratia* payment or extra-statutory payment as compensation (see p1186). The intervention of an MP or the Ombudsman (see p1183) may help in these circumstances.

If you satisfy the conditions for getting benefit it should be paid from your date of claim. If backdating is refused you have a right to appeal (see Chapter 42). Payment should not be held up because you are challenging the decision on backdating.

Benefits that can be backdated without special reasons

Claims for the following benefits can be backdated without the need for special reasons for up to three months or, where stated, for up to 12 months:[45]

- IB (Chapter 12);
- industrial injuries benefits (Chapter 14);
- child benefit (Chapter 4);
- guardian's allowance (Chapter 8);
- increase of non-means-tested benefit for an adult (Chapter 29);
- retirement pension (12 months) (Chapter 19);
- PC (12 months, although this may be reduced to three months during 2008 – see CPAG's *Welfare Rights Bulletin* for updates) (Chapter 18);
- bereavement benefits (except for bereavement payment which can be backdated for 12 months) (Chapter 2). The time limit can be extended in some cases – eg, when you did not know your partner had died (see p37);
- maternity allowance (p435); *and*
- carer's allowance (CA – Chapter 3).

If you want backdated benefit for a period before your actual date of claim (see p963) you must show that you would have qualified for the benefit had you claimed at the time. For example, if you want to claim three months' backdated IB, you must show that you have been incapable of work (see p661) for the past three months.

You can only ask for benefit to be backdated for up to three months (12 months for PC, retirement pension and bereavement payment). If you ask for backdating for a longer period, the decision maker must treat the request as if it were for the maximum possible.[46]

There are exceptions to the rules. If you are claiming backdated **child benefit** after being awarded refugee status, see p1347. If you miss the time limit for claiming **disablement benefit** for occupational deafness or occupational asthma (see p318) or bereavement payment (see p20), you may lose your right to benefit altogether.

Backdating income support and jobseeker's allowance

For IS or JSA, your claim can be backdated for up to one or three months in particular circumstances, or longer periods after the award of a qualifying benefit.

If you are claiming benefit late, it is important to explain why. If you can, provide evidence or information that backs this up – eg, a copy of the letter from your adviser or information from your employer which misled you (see p967). If you have been misled, misinformed or given insufficient advice by an officer of the DWP, explain how and when this happened and where possible, give the name and a description of the officer concerned. Where relevant, you should explain why there is no one else who could help you make your claim.

One month's backdating of income support or jobseeker's allowance

The decision maker is required to backdate your claim for up to one month, if one or more of the following applies (or has applied) and because of which you could not reasonably have been expected to make your claim any earlier:[47]

- your claim is late because the office where you are supposed to claim was closed (eg, because of a strike) and there were no other arrangements for claims to be made;
- you could not get to the DWP office because there were difficulties with the type of transport you normally use and there was no reasonable alternative;
- there were adverse postal conditions – eg, bad weather, a postal strike, or the post office failed to act under its agreement to deliver under-stamped mail to the DWP;[48]
- you (or your partner) stopped getting another benefit but you (or your partner) were not informed before your entitlement ceased so you could not claim IS or JSA in time;
- you claimed IS or JSA in your own right within one month of separating from your partner;

- a close relative of yours died in the month before your claim. **'Close relative'** in these circumstances means your partner, parent, son, daughter, brother or sister;
- you were unable to notify the DWP of your intention to make a claim because the telephone lines to the office were busy or not working.

Three months' backdating of income support or jobseeker's allowance

Your claim can be backdated for up to three months if you can show it was not reasonable to expect you to claim earlier than you did for one of the following reasons.[49] (If more than one reason applies to you, the combined effect of all of them must be considered in deciding whether it was reasonable to expect you to claim earlier.[50])

- You were given information by an officer of the DWP and as a result thought your claim would not succeed. This includes situations where:
  - you were given incorrect information or the wrong claim form and this led you to claim the wrong benefit – eg, you were advised to claim IB although you did not qualify and you should have claimed IS instead;[51] *or*
  - someone with authority to act on your behalf was given incorrect information;[52] *or*
  - you were told your claim would not be accepted;[53] *or*
  - you were told you did not have to fill in a claim form;[54] *or*
  - the refusal of, or failure to respond to,[55] an earlier claim for the same[56] or a different[57] benefit led you to believe that you were not entitled; *or*
  - the information was incomplete in that it failed to include advice to claim when it should have done.[58]

  'Officer' includes anyone carrying out public functions at the benefit office (eg, a security guard).[59] It does not matter if the information you received was correct or reasonable on the basis of any information that you gave to the officer about your circumstances, as long as the officer's advice caused you to think that a claim would fail.[60]
- You were given advice in writing by a Citizens Advice Bureau or other advice worker, a solicitor or other professional adviser (eg, an accountant), a doctor or a local authority and as a result thought your claim would not succeed. 'Advice in writing' includes leaflets, emails[61] or information on a website, provided it is directed at claimants in your position. Your claim should be backdated if you are given written confirmation of advice that was originally given to you orally,[62] provided that this is done before the decision maker decides whether you are entitled to backdating.[63] The written advice must also be given to you and so it will not be enough if your adviser records a note of oral advice unless you are provided with a copy.[64]
- You or your partner were given written information about your income or capital by your employer or former employer, or a bank or building society, and as a result you thought your claim would not succeed.

- You could not get to the DWP office because of bad weather.

In addition, you can have your claim backdated if you comply with any of the following conditions *and* it was not 'reasonably practicable' for you to seek help to make your claim from anyone else.[65] If you are mentally ill, this will not necessarily mean you cannot be expected to seek assistance.[66] However, another person is not expected to take the initiative in offering assistance.[67] The conditions are:

- you have learning, language or literacy difficulties; *or*
- you are deaf or blind *or* were sick or disabled (but not if you are claiming JSA); *or*
- you were caring for someone who is sick or disabled; *or*
- you were dealing with a domestic emergency which affected you.

Even if one of these applies, you might be paid less than three months' arrears if you claim because of a new interpretation of the law (see p1087).

If a person has been formally appointed by a court or the DWP to act on your behalf, it is your appointee (see p955), not you, who must show that it was not reasonable to expect her/him to claim sooner than s/he did for one of the reasons listed above.[68] If someone is informally acting on your behalf, you must show this. You must also show that it was reasonable for you to delegate responsibility for your claim and that you took care to ensure the person helping you did it properly.[69]

Extra backdating after awards of qualifying benefits

Most benefits, if refused on an original claim, can be backdated if they are then reclaimed after the award of a 'qualifying benefit'. A **'qualifying benefit'** is, in general, any benefit which gives you entitlement to another benefit, or makes another benefit payable at a higher rate.[70] For example, depending on the facts in your case, you may not be entitled to IS until you also become entitled to DLA.

For **CA**, there is a special rule that means that if you claim it within three months of the disabled person being awarded a qualifying benefit (eg, AA) on a new claim, the date of your claim is the first day for which the qualifying benefit is payable. (For this rule, the qualifying benefit is any of those in the third bullet point on p43.) The **general** rule is that you can get backdating if:

- your original claim (eg, for IS or JSA) is refused while you (or your dependent child or your partner) are waiting to hear about a qualifying benefit (eg, DLA); *and*
- you claimed that qualifying benefit no later than 10 days after your original claim; *and*
- the qualifying benefit is then awarded; *and*

You should notify changes promptly to the office handling your claim. That office might be at a benefit delivery centre or other benefit processing unit (eg, for income support), a central or regional unit (eg, for disability living allowance), or a local Jobcentre Plus office. Check the information sent to you about your benefit award, but seek advice if you are in doubt. For child benefit and guardian's allowance, the rules say that the office handling your claim includes the Revenue child benefit office (see Appendix 1), any Revenue enquiry centre and any Jobcentre Plus office. It is always best to check that the child benefit office has been notified.

Notification can be in writing or by telephone. It is always best to notify changes in writing so that you have a record of what you have reported. If you do report a change by telephone, note the time and date of your call and confirm what was said in writing. Keep a copy of any letters you send reporting changes. If you give the original to an officer, ask her/him to stamp your copy to confirm s/he has received the original.

If you do not promptly report any change which it is your duty to notify, any resulting overpayment may be recoverable from you (see Chapter 39). If you are considered deliberately to have acted falsely or dishonestly, you may also be guilty of an offence (see Chapter 40).

5. Work-focused interviews and benefit

There are schemes, mostly for people making new claims for benefit, that make entitlement to certain benefits conditional on attending 'work-focused interviews'. The interviews are supposed to help and encourage you to keep in contact with the employment market and eventually to begin full-time work. Claimants who are not required to attend the interivew can still take part in the schemes on a voluntary basis. At the interview, job opportunities, training and rehabilitation are discussed. There are three main schemes.

- The **Jobcentre Plus** scheme. For new claimants of certain benefits of working age and in some cases their partners.
- The **Pathways to Work** scheme. For people claiming benefits for incapacity for work (mostly new claimants only) and for claimants of the new employment and support allowance when it is introduced (expected to be in October 2008).
- The **lone parent** scheme, a nationwide scheme for lone parents claiming income support (IS).

Jobcentre Plus

The scheme is run from Jobcentre Plus offices. If you are a member of a couple, similar but not identical rules may apply to your partner (see p972). In the

Jobcentre Plus scheme, people of working age who make a new claim for benefit are required to attend work-focused interviews as a condition of claiming and continuing to receive:[83]

- IS;
- incapacity benefit (IB).

You do not have to attend an interview if you are:

- in remunerative work (ie, at least 16 hours a week); *or*
- claiming jobseeker's allowance (JSA); *or*
- aged 60 or over.[84]

At the interview, you first see a benefits specialist (called a 'financial assessor'), who deals with your benefit claim and queries, before the actual work-focused interview, which is conducted by the personal adviser.

You can be required to take part in an interview as part of your ongoing entitlement to benefit if you have already had a work-focused interview, are an existing claimant of IS, IB or severe disability allowance (SDA) and certain conditions (called 'trigger points') apply.[85] These are:

- if you are a lone parent aged at least 18 and are not on IB or SDA, and your youngest child is aged over five, six months have passed since your last interview or you were last due to have one; *or*
- if you are a lone parent aged at least 18 and are not on IB or SDA and your youngest child is aged under five, a year has passed – but only until 28 April 2008 and in any case the first repeat interview is after six months have passed; *or*
- in any other case, if:
  - you have been found incapable of work following assessment under the personal capability assessment;
  - you are no longer entitled to carer's allowance (CA), but are still entitled to IS, IB or SDA;
  - you have stopped or started part-time work (ie, any work which does not count as full-time work);
  - you have stopped education or training that was arranged by your personal adviser;
  - you have reached the age of 18 and have had a work-focused interview before;
  - you have not been required to take part in an interview for three years.

Work-focused interviews for partners

If you are a member of a couple and are entitled to benefit in a Jobcentre Plus area, your partner may be required to take part in a work-focused interview (as well as you, where you are required to do so). This will apply if:[86]

- you and your partner are both aged 18 or over but under 60; *and*

- you are getting one of the benefits listed below from a Jobcentre Plus office; *and*
- you have been continuously entitled to the benefit for 26 weeks or more; *and*
- the benefit is paid to you at a higher rate because of your partner (this includes where you get an increase for an adult dependant).

However, your partner does not have to take part in an interview under these rules if s/he is entitled to one of the benefits listed below as a claimant in her/his own right.[87]

The benefits (claimed by you) that the work-focused interviews for partners rules apply to are:

- IS;
- income-based JSA (but not joint-claim JSA);
- IB;
- SDA;
- CA.

If these rules apply, your partner has to take part in work-focused interviews as a condition of you receiving the full amount of the benefit. There is no specified time or 'trigger points' at which further such interviews must take place.[88]

The interviews themselves and the consequences of failing to take part are much the same as for the work-focused interviews that apply to you as a claimant (see p975). The main differences are:[89]

- the only consequence for your partner failing to take part in an interview is a reduction in your benefit (of £12.10 a week);
- your partner is not required to draw up an 'action plan';
- if your benefit is reduced because you partner fails to take part in an interview, income-based JSA is the first benefit in the list to be reduced, and SDA is reduced before CA; *and*
- both you and your partner are notified of and have the right to appeal against the decision on failure to take part and on 'good cause' for not taking part.

Pathways to Work

You will come under the work-focused interview part of this scheme compulsorily if:[90]

- you live in a Pathways to Work area (the scheme is expected to have national coverage by April 2008); *and*
- you are aged 18 or over but under 60; *and*
- you make a new claim for IB or IS on the basis of incapacity for work (**Note:** the Government intends that all *existing* claimants of IB aged under 25 will come under the scheme at some point.[91] See CPAG's *Welfare Rights Bulletin* for updates); *or*

- you claim employment and support allowance (ESA) when it is introduced (expected to be in October 2008) and you are not in the 'support group' of claimants with a severe condition or disability.[92] **Note:** at the time this *Handbook* was written, the rules had not been finalised. See www.cpag.org.uk/esa or CPAG's *Welfare Rights Bulletin* for updates.

In addition, you may be affected by Pathways to Work even if you are not making a new claim for benefit. We call this the **'Pathways to Work extension scheme'**. You will come under this scheme if:[93]

- you live in a Pathways to Work extension scheme area; *and*
- you were aged 18 or over but under 60 on 7 February 2005; *and*
- you are not exempt from the personal capability assessment on the basis of a severe condition (see p669); *and*
- you made a successful claim for IB, SDA or IS on the basis of incapacity for work at some point in the six years before or, in certain areas, at any time before the Pathways to Work pilot scheme was introduced in your area, and are still on the benefit. More areas may be introduced in the future.

The work-focused interviews in the Pathways to Work scheme are much the same as in the main Jobcentre Plus work-focused interviews, as described on p975. The most important differences are:

- after your initial work-focused interview, unless you are exempt from the personal capability assessment on the basis of a severe condition (see p669) you must attend an additional five interviews at monthly intervals (or two additional interviews if you come under the Pathways to Work extension scheme);
- after that, you must attend further interviews whenever you are again assessed as being incapable of work, if you stop being entitled to CA, if you start or stop part-time work, or if you have been on DWP-arranged education, training or rehabilitation and that comes to an end;
- the only sanction for failing to take part in an interview (that includes not drawing up an action plan) is a reduction in your benefit of £12.10 a week.

The Pathways to Work pilots also include a 'return-to-work credit' of £40 a week, payable for 52 weeks for certain people returning to work and earning less than £15,000 a year, and grants to help with work expenses.[94] If you are in the Pathways to Work extension scheme (see p974), you can also be offered a 'job preparation premium' of £20 a week if you actually carry out some of the steps set out in your action plan. See CPAG's *Welfare Rights Bulletins* 175 and 182 for full details.

There are likely to be a few differences in the Pathways to Work scheme for ESA claimants who are required to take part, in particular with regard to work-focused interviews (see p975).

Work-focused interviews for lone parents

Some lone parents have to attend work-focused interviews under the Jobcentre Plus scheme (see p971). However, a similar scheme exclusively aimed at lone parents claiming IS operates on a national basis. In the scheme, entitlement to IS is dependent on attending work-focused interviews.

The requirement to attend interviews under the lone parent scheme applies to you if you are a lone parent and are responsbile for and living in the same household as a child. It applies both if you make a new claim for IS or if you are already on it.[95]

In most cases, if you come under this scheme you are required to attend a **repeat work-focused interview** every six months. (Where your last interview was due between 28 April 2007 and 30 October 2007, the *first* of these repeated interviews is one year after that.[96]) However, in certain cases you may be required to attend every 13 weeks. This applies if:[97]

- your youngest child is aged either 11, 12 or 13; *and*
- you have been continuously entitled to IS for at least 12 months; *and*
- you live in an area specified in the lone parents rules.

In any case, however, you are not required to attend a work-focused interview under this scheme if you are a lone parent and:[98]

- are aged under 18; *or*
- are aged 60 or over; *or*
- are subject to the Jobcentre Plus or Pathways to Work scheme.

Work-focused interviews – general rules

You will be informed when your interview is to take place. In the Jobcentre Plus and Pathways to Work schemes, if you claim IB, or IS on the basis of incapacity for work (or get IS because you are appealing a decision on your capacity for work) your initial interview takes place eight weeks after your claim. Otherwise, the initial interview takes place 'as soon as reasonably practicable'.[99]

Note: if you are claiming the new ESA (expected to be introduced in October 2008), the Pathways to Work interviews are expected to work in much the same way as they do for benefits for incapacity for work, although there wlll be a few differences concerning taking part in an interview and in benefit penalties for failing to take part (see p977). See www.cpag.org.uk/esa or CPAG's *Welfare Rights Bulletin* for updates.

The interview normally takes place at the local DWP office, but you can ask your personal adviser to interview you at home if going to the office would cause undue inconvenience or endanger your health (but there is no right of appeal).[100]

Interviews are compulsory and, in general, you are not exempt from them even if you are, for example, exempt from the personal capability assessment. You may have the requirement to attend an interview 'waived' (ie, cancelled) or 'deferred' (ie, put off to another date) if it is considered that an interview would not be of assistance or appropriate. There are no definitions of when these might apply, but possible situations are likely to include where you are too ill, or if there has been a domestic emergency or adverse weather conditions. There is no right of appeal.[101]

The basic process is similar in all the work-focused interview schemes. There are three basic stages.

- Initial contact, where you indicate that you want to claim benefit, forms are issued and basic information is taken.
- Initial work-focused interview – this is a part of the benefit claim.
- Repeat work-focused interviews at various times (called 'trigger points') during your claim.

Usually, at the interview you are first seen by a 'financial assessor' to deal with your benefit claim and other potential benefit entitlement before the work-focused interview itself, which is carried out by a personal adviser.

Taking part in an interview

You must 'take part' in the work-focused interview. If you do not, unless you can show 'good cause', a benefit penalty may be imposed on you.[102]

'Taking part' means that you must:[103]

- turn up at the place and time notified;
- 'participate in discussions' with the personal adviser about your employability;
- answer questions, where asked, about your educational qualifications, employment history, any current work and your future hopes for working, vocational training, employment skills and abilities, medical conditions which affect your chances of getting a job, and caring or childcare responsibilities;
- discuss and assist in completing an 'action plan' which includes any action you and the personal adviser agree is reasonable and you are willing to take. (If there is nothing you reasonably can do, you will not have failed to take part. There is nothing which says you actually have to take the steps in the action plan);
- in further interviews, discuss your progress, any action you 'might have taken' under the action plan, how the action plan might be amended and any further support that might be available to you;
- in further interviews, answer questions, where asked, about reports (usually called 'capability reports') on medical aspects of your employability drawn up following the personal capability assessment being applied to you, and your opinion about the effect of your medical condition on your ability to find work.

In the Jobcentre Plus scheme, if you are under 18, 'taking part' also requires you to attend an interview with the Careers Service or Connexions.[104] If you are claiming the new ESA, you must also take part in a 'work-focused health-related assessment', which is expected to be similar to the capability report mentioned in the last bullet on p976.[105]

Benefit penalties for failing to take part

Usually, when you make a new claim for benefit you are required to attend an initial work-focused interview. If the decision maker decides that you did not take part, unless you have 'good cause' for not doing so (see p978), in the **Jobcentre Plus** and **lone parent** schemes you will be treated as not having made a claim and hence will not be entitled to benefit.[106] You will have to make a new claim before you can become entitled to benefit.[107] In the **Pathways to Work** scheme (including for ESA claimants from October 2008) you are not required to take part in an interview unless you are entitled to benefit, and so the benefit penalty is always a reduction in your benefit – the rules are the same as those described below.[108]

Following an initial interview, you may then be required to attend further work-focused interviews. If you fail to take part without 'good cause' (see p978), a benefit reduction of £12.10 will be applied to one of your benefits (IS in the **lone parent** scheme; IS, IB and SDA in the **Pathways to Work** scheme).[109] If you are a claimant of the new ESA from October 2008, the benefit reduction is expected to be 50 per cent of the work-related activity component for the first four weeks of the reduction, then 100 per cent of the component for each following week.[110] In all the schemes, the deduction continues to apply until you take part in an interview.[111] In the **Jobcentre Plus** scheme, if you are entitled to more than one of the following benefits, the deduction is normally made in the following order of priority, but you must be left with at least 10p per week of the reduced benefit:[112]

- IS;
- IB;
- any bereavement benefit;
- CA;
- SDA.

The reduction should stop from the point that you do take part in the interview. The consequences also cease to apply if you are no longer required to take part in work-focused interviews of the scheme you are in (eg, in the lone parent scheme, you cease to be a lone parent), or if you reach the age of 60. The consequences *also* cease to apply if, within a month of the date of the decision that you failed to take part in the interview or that you did not have 'good cause' (see p978) for not taking part, you:

- notify new facts which show you had good cause; *and*
- you could not reasonably have notified those facts within five working days of the date of the interview.[113]

You have a right of appeal against a decision that you did not take part in an interview and that you did not have 'good cause' (see p978). However, the rules have the effect that you will need to have tried to show good cause within five working days of the date on which the interview was to take place. The decision may also be revised or superseded on normal grounds (see Chapters 41 and 42).[114] Rules on appeals and good cause in ESA decisions had not been finalised at the time this *Handbook* was written, although it is understood they will not require you to have attempted to show good cause within five working days.

Good cause for failing to take part

To avoid a penalty, you must show good cause within five working days following the date on which the interview was to take place.[115] However, you may still be able to demonstrate good cause up to a month after the decision that you did not take part was notified to you, if the facts you rely on could not have been brought to the personal adviser's attention within five days.[116]

In deciding whether you have good cause, the decision maker will consider all the circumstances but must take the following into account:[117]

- any misunderstanding on your part because of learning, literacy or linguistic difficulties, or misleading information given by the benefit authority;
- attending a doctor or dentist appointment or accompanying a person for whom you are caring, where the appointment could not reasonably have been rearranged;
- difficulties with transport where no reasonable alternative was available;
- the practice of your religion that prevented you attending at the fixed time;
- attending a job interview;
- the need to work in your business if you are trying to become self-employed;
- if you or a person for whom you are caring had an accident, illness or relapse;
- attending a funeral of a close friend or relative;
- a disability that makes attendance impracticable.

6. Getting paid

The DWP (or the Revenue) decides how benefit is paid to you.[118] In practice, this normally means that you are paid by direct credit transfer ('direct payment') into a bank, building society or similar account. There is no right of appeal about the way in which you are paid.

Direct payments

Payment by direct credit transfer into a bank account, building society account or similar account is the normal method of payment on new claims for benefit. The Government calls this **'direct payment'**. If that is not suitable for you, you may be able to get your benefit paid by cheque (see p979).

The Government has said that all benefit recipients will, at the appropriate time, be given information setting out the various account options.[119] If you experience difficulty getting your money as a result of these new arrangements, complain to the DWP or the Revenue. You could also contact your MP.

Payment by cheque

If you cannot open or manage an account, then it should be possible for you to be paid by a cheque which can be cashed at a post office. However, there are no rules that say that you must be paid in this way. If you cannot open or manage an account, make sure the DWP or the Revenue know this, and ask to be paid by cheque.

Account options

When you are paid by direct payment, there are five main options you have regarding the accounts that your benefit is paid into:

- an existing bank or building society current or savings account;
- a new current account at a bank or building society;
- a new 'basic bank account' at a bank or building society (sometimes this is called an 'introductory' or 'starter' account);
- a Post Office card account; *and*
- in some cases, a credit union account.

All of these accounts (excepting some credit unions) are suitable for direct payment, and you can withdraw cash without charge. But they are not all the same. For example, you cannot access all current accounts at post offices, basic bank accounts and Post Office card accounts do not offer cheque books or overdrafts, and you cannot pay bills by direct debit with a Post Office card account. The Government contract for providing Post Office card accounts is due to expire in 2010 and at the moment the future of the accounts after that date is unknown.[120] The DWP or the Revenue should write to you with details of your options, including how to open an account.

Direct payment means that you can get your benefit in the way you get other money in your account – eg, by cheque or via a cash machine at bank branches and at supermarket checkouts with a 'cashback' facility. If you do want to get your money at a post office, the following will apply to direct payments.

- You may be able to access your bank or building society current account at a post office. However, not all bank and building societies have this facility – check with your bank, building society or the DWP/Revenue.
- You can use a PIN number at a post office if you have a basic bank account. Not all banks and building societies offer these accounts – check with your bank, building society or the DWP/Revenue.

- You can use a PIN number at a post office if you have a Post Office card account. If you have a card account, you can nominate someone else to collect your benefit for you, in which case that person will be issued with a card her/himself.

If someone collects your benefit for you

It should be possible, if necessary, to arrange for someone you trust to be able to access your account in order to so. If you already have a bank or building society account, ask the bank or building society about this. If you use a Post Office card account, a second card can be issued to the person who collects your benefit.

If you lose or forget your PIN

If you lose or forget your PIN, you need to contact the bank to change the PIN and issue you with a new one as soon as possible. If you cannot access your benefit, contact the benefit office for advice about what to do.

If you use a Post Office card account and you lose or forget your PIN, call the customer service helpline number on 08457 22 33 44 (or textphone 08457 22 33 55). You will get a replacement PIN within four working days. Again, if you cannot access your benefit in the meantime, contact the benefit office for advice.

If all else fails, you may be invited to claim a crisis loan (see p503) while the problem is sorted out. If you cannot get access to your benefit, and the DWP/the Revenue refuses to remedy the situation, seek advice (see Appendix 2).

When you are paid

How, when and how often your benefit is paid depends on the benefit you have claimed.[121] You are sometimes paid in advance and sometimes in arrears. For further information, see the chapter in this *Handbook* about the benefit you are claiming.

Who is paid

Payment is usually made directly to you, but there are some circumstances in which payments can be made to other people or organisations on your behalf.

- If you are unable to manage your own money or if you die, your benefit is paid to a person appointed to act on your behalf (see p955).[122]
- If it is in the interests of you, your partner or your children, the decision maker can pay your benefit to another person.[123] For example, if your partner is refusing to support you, all or part of her/his benefit can be paid to you. If you are neglecting your children even though benefit is being paid for them, it might be paid to another person to help look after them.
- If you are claiming income support (IS), pension credit (PC) or income-based jobseeker's allowance (JSA) and are getting help with your housing costs (see Chapter 34), these are usually paid directly to your lender on your behalf (see p989).

- If you are claiming IS, PC or JSA, and are in certain types of debt, payments can be made to your creditors on your behalf (see p988).[124]

Overlapping benefits

Special rules mean that sometimes you cannot be paid more than one non-means-tested benefit at the same time (see below). These are the **'overlapping benefit' rules**. These rules also apply where more than one person is claiming for the same child or adult dependant (see p983), where you are getting child benefit, guardian's allowance or an increase in your non-means-tested benefit for your child (see p983), and where you are entitled to an increase in your non-means-tested benefit for an adult dependant who is getting one or more certain benefits her/himself (see p983).

Disability living allowance (DLA) care component and attendance allowance (AA) overlap with constant attendance allowance.[125] Otherwise AA, DLA, disablement benefit (see p324), reduced earnings allowance (see p326) and retirement allowance (see p330) can be received in addition to any of the other benefits described in this *Handbook* – eg, you may receive incapacity benefit (IB), both components of DLA and disablement benefit all at once.

You might qualify for IS, PC, income-based JSA, housing benefit (HB) or council tax benefit (CTB) in addition to your non-means-tested benefit, although the non-means-tested benefit is usually taken into account as income (see p858).

Earnings replacement benefits

Some benefits are available to compensate you for your inability to work through unemployment, sickness, pregnancy or old age. These are 'earnings replacement' benefits. You cannot usually receive more than one of the following 'earnings replacement' benefits at a time.

- Contributory benefits:
  - contribution-based JSA;
  - IB;
  - maternity allowance (MA, which counts as contributory for the purposes of this rule);
  - retirement pension;
  - widow's or bereavement pension;
  - widowed mother's or widowed parent's allowance.
- Non-contributory benefits:
  - severe disablement allowance (SDA);
  - carer's allowance(CA).

Where there is an entitlement to more than one of the benefits above the following rules apply.[126]

- A contributory benefit is paid in preference to a non-contributory benefit. However, this is topped up by any balance of a non-contributory benefit due.

- Weekly benefits are paid and topped up by any balance of daily benefit (unless the claimant makes an application to receive the daily benefit in full) – see the chapter in this *Handbook* about the benefit you are claiming to see if it is a daily or a weekly benefit.
- The highest rate benefit is paid, or if the rates are the same, one benefit is paid.

Special rules apply if you are entitled to widows' benefits or bereavement benefits and to IB at the same time. See p277 for further information.

Other adjustments

If you are getting a training allowance paid by a government department or training agency, your earnings replacement benefit is reduced by the amount of the training allowance.[127]

If you are getting unemployability supplement under the industrial injuries scheme or war pensions scheme, your earnings replacement benefit – other than MA – is reduced by the amount of the unemployability supplement.

You cannot usually get more than one retirement pension at a time. However, there are special rules if you are a widow or widower entitled to both a Category A (see p465) and a Category B retirement pension (see p465) and your Category A pension would be paid at a reduced rate because you have not paid enough contributions (see p738). In this situation your basic Category A pension is increased by either:

- the amount of the shortfall between your Category A pension and the full Category A amount of £90.70; *or*
- the amount of your Category B pension,

whichever amount is less.[128]

You are also entitled to an additional pension on your own contribution record and one on your spouse or civil partner's record up to the maximum additional pension a person could theoretically receive on one contribution record.[129]

Earnings-related additions to non-means-tested benefits

Additional pensions under the additional state pension scheme (see p100) and graduated retirement benefit (see p467) do not overlap with non-means-tested benefits. However, if two or more benefits would otherwise be payable with an additional pension and graduated retirement benefit, only the higher or highest total of additional pension and graduated retirement benefit payable in addition to one of those benefits is due.[130]

There are exceptions to this rule if you are a Category B retirement pensioner whose own contribution records would entitle you to a Category A retirement pension or if you are a widow who receives transitional long-term IB (see p278).

An age addition paid with IB, SDA or retirement pension overlaps with another age addition.[131]

Increases to non-means-tested benefits for adult dependants

Only one person may receive an increase of benefit in respect of the same dependant, except when one of you receives an increase because the dependant is someone employed by you to look after your child(ren) and the dependant does not live with you (in this case, both of you can claim). Equally, you may only receive one increase in respect of an adult dependant. If, apart from those rules, more than one increase would be payable, only the higher or highest total is paid.[132] See p686 for who can claim increases for dependants.

An increase for an adult dependant also overlaps with certain earnings replacement benefits (see p981) or training allowances which are payable to that dependant – eg, you are claiming an increase of retirement pension for your partner, but s/he is claiming IB in her/his own right.[133] If the increase is less than or equal to the benefit payable to your dependant, the increase is not paid. If the increase is greater than the basic benefit, you get the difference. This does not apply if the adult is not residing with you and is employed by you to care for a child.

Increases to non-means-tested benefits for child dependants

Since 6 April 2003, no increases to non-means-tested benefits for child dependants are payable, although some people already entitled to them on 5 April 2003 will still be paid them (see p691).

Only one person may receive child benefit or an increase to a non-means-tested benefit for a child dependant for the same child (see pp56 and 691).

The standard rate of child benefit (see p68) does not overlap with any other benefit. However, if you receive the higher amount payable for your eldest child (see p68), any other benefit (except guardian's allowance) or increase paid for the same child is reduced by £2.10.[134]

All increases for children and child's special allowance overlap with guardian's allowance and industrial death benefit for children and are reduced by the level of guardian's allowance you get for the child.[135]

Missing payments

If you are entitled to benefit you must be paid it.[136] If your benefit is not paid into your account or you are not issued with a cheque, the DWP or the Revenue must rectify that.

If you have lost or forgotten your PIN number, see p980. If there is a long delay, the DWP/Revenue may refer to a rule (applying to benefits paid by the DWP) that says your entitlement to payment is lost 12 months after the date it was due to be paid into your account. However, the rule should only apply where you have actually been allocated benefit, not where you have not been paid it.[137] If necessary, seek advice (see Appendix 2).

Suspension of payments of benefit

A decision maker can suspend payment of part or all of your benefit in certain circumstances (see below). In some of these circumstances, s/he can ask you to provide further information or evidence or submit to a medical examination to help her/him decide if you are still entitled to benefit (or are getting it at the correct rate). It is very important that you provide the information that is required or submit to the medical examination. Your entitlement to benefit could be terminated if you fail to do so (see p986).

Local authorities are able to suspend HB in similar circumstances.[138]

Suspension while an appeal is pending

Your benefit can be suspended if the DWP (or, in child benefit and guardian's allowance cases, the Revenue) or local authority is appealing (or considering an appeal) against:[139]

- a decision of a tribunal, commissioner or court to award *you* benefit; *or*
- a decision of a commissioner or court about *someone else's case*, but only if the issue in the appeal could affect your claim (and for HB, only where the other case is about an HB issue).

But, except for HB, the DWP/Revenue must give you written notice of the intention either to request the statement of reasons for the tribunal's decision, to apply for leave to appeal or to appeal, whichever is the first of those that is yet to be done. It must do that as soon as is 'reasonably practicable'.[140]

The decision maker must then actually go on to do one of those things within the usual time limits for doing so (see Chapter 42 for the details of time limits). If s/he does not, the suspended benefit must be paid to you. The suspended benefit must also be paid to you if the decision maker withdraws an application for leave to appeal, withdraws the appeal or is refused leave to appeal and it is not possible for her/him to renew the application for leave to appeal.[141]

Suspension in other circumstances

Your benefit can also be suspended if:[142]

- a question has arisen about your entitlement.[143] In this case, all or part of the benefit due to you can be suspended pending a revision, supersession or appeal of the decision about your entitlement;
- you have been getting JSA and a question has arisen about whether you are available for or actively seeking work. Your JSA must be suspended until this matter is resolved;[144]
- it looks as though your award of benefit should be superseded or revised;[145]
- the DWP (or, in child benefit and guardian's allowance cases, the Revenue) thinks you are being (or may have been) overpaid.[146] All or part of your benefit may be withheld while the possible overpayment is investigated;
- you are not living at the last address you notified;[147]

- for child benefit and guardian's allowance, the bank account or other account details which you have given to the Revenue are incorrect;[148]
- for HB, a recoverable overpayment may have occurred.[149]

In some cases, your benefit can also be suspended if you fail to provide information or submit to a medical examination (see below).

Providing information and evidence

You can be required to supply information or evidence (including evidence of your incapacity for work[150]) if the decision maker needs this to determine whether your award of benefit should be revised or superseded (see pp1065 and 1074).

You can be required to provide information and evidence if:[151]

- your benefit has been suspended in the circumstances described above; *or*
- you apply for a revision or supersession (see pp1065 and 1074); *or*
- you fail to provide certificates, documents, evidence and other information about the facts of your case as required;[152] *or*
- your entitlement to benefit is conditional on you being incapable of work.

You must be notified in writing if the decision maker wants you to provide information or evidence. Within one month of being sent the request, you must:

- supply the information or evidence.[153] You can be given more time than this if you satisfy the decision maker that this is necessary; *or*
- satisfy the decision maker that the information does not exist or you cannot obtain it.[154]

If the decision maker has not already done so, your benefit can be suspended if you do not provide the information or evidence within one month of the request.[155] To find out if your entitlement to benefit can be terminated, see p986.

Medical examinations

Most benefits can be suspended if you fail to submit to a medical examination on two consecutive occasions without 'good cause' (there is no specific rule for child benefit, guardian's allowance, HB or CTB).[156] This applies where:

- the decision maker is looking at whether you should still be getting a benefit (or whether you are getting it at the correct rate); *or*
- you apply for a revision or a supersession (see pp1065 and 1074) and the decision maker thinks a medical examination is necessary in order to make a decision.

This rule does not apply where the issue is whether you are incapable of work. For information about the rules on medical examinations when your incapacity for work is being assessed, see p676.

To find out if your entitlement to benefit can be terminated, see p986.

Challenging decisions to suspend benefit

The decision maker may be willing to continue to pay your benefit, or at least some of it, if you can show that you will experience hardship otherwise. If you receive a letter telling you that your benefit has been suspended, you can write back explaining how the suspension will affect you and asking the DWP, the Revenue or local authority to reconsider. It may be wise to get advice (see Appendix 2) before writing.

You cannot appeal to a tribunal against the decision to suspend your benefit. The only ways to change the decision are to negotiate to get your benefit reinstated or to challenge the decision in the courts by judicial review (see p1129). Aside from getting the decision changed, you could also ask for an interim payment (see below). Seek advice (see Appendix 2).

Termination of entitlement to benefit

Your entitlement to benefit can be terminated if:

- your benefit was suspended *in full* in the circumstances described on p984 and you are required to provide information or evidence and fail to do so within one month of the request;[157]
- your benefit was suspended *in full* because you failed to provide information in the circumstances described on p985, but only if it is more than one month since your benefit was suspended.[158]

The termination of entitlement to benefit takes effect from the date payment was suspended (or an earlier date if you ceased to be entitled for another reason).[159]

Your entitlement to most benefits (although there is no specific rule for child benefit, guardian's allowance, HB or CTB) can also be terminated if you fail to submit to a medical examination, but only if it is more than one month since your benefit was suspended on this ground.[160] This is discretionary.

If you disagree with a decision to terminate your benefit you can seek a revision (see p1065) or appeal (see Chapter 42).[161]

Interim payments

If your claim or payment of your benefit is delayed, you can ask for an interim payment. However, it may be that you cannot get an interim payment pending an appeal unless the DWP considers that there is entitlement to benefit.[162]

An interim payment can be made where it seems that you are or may be entitled to benefit and where:[163]

- there is a delay in your making a claim, including being able to satisfy straight away the national insurance number requirement; *or*
- you have claimed it but not in the correct way (eg, you have filled in the wrong form, or filled in the right form incorrectly or incompletely – see p960) and

you cannot put in a correct claim immediately (eg, because the DWP office is closed); *or*

- you have claimed it correctly, but it is not possible for the claim, or for a revision or supersession which relates to it, to be dealt with immediately; *or*
- you have been awarded benefit, but it is not possible to pay you immediately other than by means of an interim payment.

You cannot appeal to a tribunal if you are refused an interim payment. It may be possible to apply for judicial review (see p1129). If you are refused an interim payment, see Chapter 21 to find out if you can get a crisis loan. You could contact your MP to see if s/he can help to get the decision to refuse you an interim payment reconsidered. You could also try using the emergency service (see below).

An interim payment can be deducted from any later payment of benefit and if it is more than your actual entitlement, the overpayment can be recovered.[164] You should be notified of this in advance, unless it is an interim payment of:

- IS made because you have not received child support maintenance (see p746). In this case, any overpayment is recovered from the arrears of maintenance rather than your benefit; *or*
- DLA and you are terminally ill or have an invalid vehicle.

Emergencies

If you have lost all your money or there has been a similar crisis, it is possible to get help at any time. Any local police station should have a contact number for DWP staff on call outside normal office hours.

If you are unable to contact the DWP, your local social services office may be able to help. The police station should have a contact number.

If you need money urgently, it is important that you provide as much information as you can to support your claim. It may help if you can get an advice agency or third party (such as a health visitor or social worker, doctor or MP) to support you.

7. Deductions and payments to third parties

Your benefits are usually paid directly to you but there are some circumstances when money can be deducted and paid to a third party on your behalf. The majority of these deductions can usually only be made from income support (IS), pension credit (PC) and income-based jobseeker's allowance (JSA). They can also be made from contribution-based JSA or from other benefits, but only in limited circumstances.

What deductions can be made

Amounts can be deducted from your IS, PC or *income-based* JSA to pay for:[165]

- housing costs paid to your lender under the mortgage payment scheme (p989);
- other housing costs (p990);
- rent arrears (p991);
- residential accommodation charges (p991);
- hostel payments (p991);
- fuel (p991);
- water charges (p992);
- council tax arrears (p992);
- community charge arrears (p992);
- fines (p992);
- repayment of eligible loans (see p992);
- child support maintenance (p993); *and*
- integration loans paid to refugees and others (p993).

Except for council tax and community charge arrears and fines, if you are on IS or PC and the amount of benefit is not enough to cover the deduction, deductions can also be made from your incapacity benefit (IB), severe disablement allowance (SDA) or retirement pension, if they are paid in combination with your IS or PC.

You may also have deductions made for the recovery of **social fund loans** (p502) and **overpayments** (p1019).

Deductions from contribution-based jobseeker's allowance

Deductions can be made from your *contribution-based* JSA for the payments listed above if you have an 'underlying entitlement' to income-based JSA. This means that if you were not entitled to contribution-based JSA, you would be entitled to income-based JSA of at least the same rate (see example below).[166]

Deductions can also be made from contribution-based JSA if you have no underlying entitlement to income-based JSA, but only for community charge arrears, council tax arrears, fines and child support maintenance arrears.

Example

Tina is 27 and receives contribution-based JSA of £60.50 a week. She has no other income and no savings. The amount of the income-based JSA she would receive if she was not getting contribution-based JSA would also be £60.50 a week.

Deductions can be made from Tina's contribution-based JSA as if she were receiving income-based JSA.

Deductions from other benefits

Deductions can only be made from other benefits to repay certain loans (see p992) and child support maintenance that you owe (see p993).

When deductions can be made

Deductions and direct payments to third parties can only be made if you or your partner are liable to make the payments.[167] If there is a doubt about whether you or your partner are liable, deductions should only be made if there is evidence that you are liable – eg, the bill is in your name or your partner's name.

Do you have to agree to deductions?

If you do not get child tax credit (CTC), your consent is required before direct payments are made for housing costs arrears, rent arrears, service charges for fuel and water, fuel costs (including arrears), water charges (including arrears), repayment of integration and other loans, *and* the *total* to be deducted for these payments exceeds 25 per cent of your family's applicable amount (see Chapter 33) or, in the case of PC, 25 per cent of your minimum guarantee (see p448), before housing costs.

If you (or your partner) do get CTC, your consent is required if the above deductions amount to more than 25 per cent of the total of your applicable amount/PC minimum guarantee before housing costs, plus your CTC and child benefit.[168] Any housing costs included in your applicable amount (see Chapter 34) should not be taken into account when calculating the 25 per cent.

The DWP can make deductions without your agreement if they are made for:

- community charge or council tax arrears;
- fines;
- child support maintenance;
- current housing costs;
- current mortgage interest;
- nursing home charges or hostel charges not included in your housing benefit (HB).

Consent is not needed for these deductions even if the total amount deducted exceeds the 25 per cent referred to above.[169]

The deductions

Deductions are made at the DWP office before you receive your regular benefit payment. If you want to have deductions made to help you clear any arrears or debts, ask at the DWP office dealing with your claim. If you disagree with a decision about deductions, you can appeal (see Chapter 42).

The mortgage payment scheme

When you claim IS, PC or income-based JSA, you may get help with your housing costs (see Chapter 34). The general rules for payment of housing costs are as follows.

- Once you qualify for help with housing costs, the amount for mortgage interest or interest on loans for repairs and improvements is usually paid directly to your lender for each complete week that you are on benefit.[170]
- The main exceptions to this are where your lender is not covered by, or has opted out of, the mortgage payments scheme.[171] The DWP should tell you if this is the case and you must pay your own mortgage.
- Also, if you receive PC, if you are entitled only to the savings credit and not to the guarantee credit, then direct payments will only be made where a written request has been made and the DWP agrees that it is in the best interests of you or your family.[172]

Your housing costs are deducted from your total IS, PC or income-based JSA entitlement and you get the balance.[173] If you are on IS or PC and the amount of benefit is not enough to cover the deduction, then deductions can also be made from your IB, SDA or retirement pension, if they are paid in combination with your IS or PC. You have to make up any difference between what the DWP pays to your lender and the amount you owe it. This could include such things as mortgage capital, non-dependant deductions or a restriction due to excessive housing costs. If you do not have enough benefit to meet the full cost, all but 10p of your benefit is paid over and you must pay the rest yourself.[174]

Payments are made four-weekly in arrears[175] even if your payments are due on a calendar month basis.

If you are in mortgage arrears, no amount towards the arrears can be deducted from your benefit if your lender is covered by the mortgage payments scheme.

Except in the case of PC, if you have a mortgage protection policy the amount of mortgage interest paid directly is reduced. The reduction is the amount of income from the insurance policy which is taken into account.[176]

If an overpayment of mortgage interest is paid to your lender, see p1018.

Other housing costs[177]

The IS, PC or income-based JSA for your mortgage interest is usually paid directly to your lender under the mortgage payments scheme (see p989). If this applies to you (or would if your lender had not opted out of the scheme) the deductions under this provision only cover payments for other types of housing costs (see p807).[178]

If your current IS, PC or income-based JSA includes money for such housing costs and you are in debt for these costs (excluding payments for ground rent or feu duty unless paid with your service charges or for a tent[179]), deductions can be made from your benefit both to clear the debt and to meet current payments. Deductions are made if it would be 'in the interests' of you or your family to do so.

You only qualify for direct deductions if you owe more than half of the annual total of the relevant housing cost. This condition can be waived if it is in the 'overriding interests' of you or your family that deductions start as soon as possible – eg, repossession of your home is imminent.[180]

In the case of mortgage payments, the decision maker must be satisfied there are arrears.[181] You must have paid less than eight weeks' full payments in the last 12 weeks.[182] The amount of mortgage interest taken into account is the amount after deductions for non-dependants (see p815).

Rent arrears and arrears of hostel payments[183]

If you are in arrears with your rent (including any inclusive water, fuel and service charges) while on benefit, or are £100 or more in arrears of hostel payments (see below) an amount can be deducted from your IS, PC or JSA and paid directly to your landlord.

Rent arrears do not include the amount of any non-dependant deductions (see above), but can cover any water charges or service charges payable with your rent and not met by HB. Fuel charges included in your rent cannot be covered by direct deductions if they change more than twice a year.

To qualify for direct deductions, your rent arrears must amount to at least four times your full weekly rent. If you have not paid your full rent for more than eight weeks, direct deductions can be made automatically if your landlord asks the DWP to make them.[184] If your arrears relate to a shorter period, deductions can only be made if it is in the overriding interests of your family to do so.[185] In either case, the decision maker must be satisfied that you are in rent arrears. Even if you are, you can ask her/him not to make direct deductions – eg, where you are claiming compensation from your landlord because of the state of repair of your home.[186] Once your arrears are paid off, direct payments can continue for any fuel and water charges inclusive in your rent.[187]

Residential accommodation charges[188]

Deductions can be made from your IS, PC or income-based JSA to meet your accommodation charges if you have failed to budget for the charges and it is considered to be in your interest for deductions to be made.

Hostel payments[189]

If you (or your partner) live in a hostel *and* you have claimed HB to meet your accommodation costs *and* your payments to the hostel cover fuel, meals, water charges, laundry and/or cleaning of your room, part of your IS, PC or JSA can be paid directly to the hostel for these items. You do not have to be in arrears for this to apply (see above for arrears). These costs are all items which cannot be covered by HB (see p193) and which you must meet from your IS, PC or JSA. Fuel costs are not paid directly if the charge varies according to actual consumption, unless the charge is altered less than three times a year.

Fuel debts[190]

If you are in debt, an amount can be deducted from your benefit each week and paid over to the fuel company (mains gas or mains electricity) in instalments –

usually once a quarter. This is **'fuel direct'**. In return, the fuel company agrees not to disconnect you. Deductions can be made where:[191]

- the amount you owe is £60.50 or more (including reconnection or disconnection charges if you have been disconnected); *and*
- you continue to need the fuel supply; *and*
- it is in your interest to have deductions made.

An amount is deducted for the fuel you use each week (your current consumption) as well as for the arrears you owe. The amount deducted for current consumption is whatever is necessary to meet your current weekly fuel costs. This is adjusted if the cost increases or decreases. Deductions for current consumption can be continued after the debt has been cleared.[192]

Water charges[193]

If you get into debt with charges for water and sewerage, direct deductions might be made. Debt includes any disconnection, reconnection and legal charges. If you pay your landlord for water with your rent, deductions are made under the arrangements for rent arrears (see p991).[194]

Deductions can be made if you failed to budget and it is in the interests of your family to make deductions.[195] If you are in debt to two water companies you can only have a deduction for arrears made to one of them at a time. Your debts for water charges should be cleared before your debts for sewerage costs, but the amount paid for current consumption can include both water and sewerage charges.[196]

Council tax and community charge arrears[197]

Deductions for council tax or community charge arrears can be made from IS, PC or JSA if the local authority gets a liability order from a magistrates' court (in Scotland, a summary warrant or decree from a sheriff's court) and applies to the DWP for recovery to be made in this way. Deductions can be made for arrears and any unpaid costs or penalties imposed.

Fines, costs and compensation orders[198]

Magistrates' courts (any court in Scotland) can apply to the DWP for a fine, costs or compensation order to be deducted from your IS, PC or JSA. Only one court application can be dealt with at a time – if a second application is made it is not dealt with until the first debt is paid.

Deductions can only be made if you are 18 or over, on IS, PC or JSA, and you have defaulted on payments. Payments continue until the debt is paid off, or your IS, PC or JSA ceases or is too low to cover the repayments.

Repayment of eligible loans[199]

Deductions can be made from your IS, JSA, PC and (if necessary) your IB, retirement pension or carer's allowance (CA) towards repaying certain 'eligible' loans if you have not kept up with the repayments. This applies only to loans made by certain 'not-for-profit' lenders, such as community development financial institutions, credit unions and charities. When taking out the loan, you must have given your agreeement that, were your repayments to fall behind, your lender could send your details to the DWP so that deductions could be made from your benefit. The loan must be unsecured, not made for business purposes and not made by means of a credit card.

Deductions can be made if you have failed to make payments for at least 13 weeks and have not started making them again. They can only be made where your lender has agreed that no interest or other charges will be added from the point the deductions start, and where you do not have deductions for repayment of a benefit overpayment or social fund loan. Only one deduction for repayment of certain loans can be made.

Repayment of integration loans[200]

Deductions can be made from your benefit to repay an integration loan – ie, those paid to refugees, people granted humanitarian protection under the immigration rules and dependants of such people. You must have been told when repayment will start and that it will be by deduction from your benefit.

Child support maintenance

The rules that apply depend on whether the child support maintenance is payable under the old rules that applied up to 3 March 2003, or the new rules that apply from that date (see Chapter 32 and CPAG's *Child Support Handbook* for more details).

At the time this *Handbook* was written the Child Support Agency (CSA), the Government agency that makes child support maintenance assessments under the old or new rules, was expected to be replaced by a new agency, the Child Maintenance and Enforcement Commission (C-MEC) in 2008. C-MEC will not insist that parents with care on benefit apply to or otherwise continue to use it.

But *where the child support assessment made by the CSA remains in force*, it is expected that deductions will continue to be made from the non-resident parent's benefit as described below.

This may change again when C-MEC begins to offer calculations under more new assessment rules, but this is not expected to be until 2010/11. See CPAG's *Welfare Rights Bulletin* for updates.

Under the **old rules**, deductions can be made from a non-resident parent's IS, PC or income-based JSA as a contribution towards the maintenance of her/his child(ren). Currently, the maximum deduction is £6.10 a week. Deductions cannot be made in certain circumstances (see p752) and may be reduced where deductions are also being made for debts of other payments (see p996).[201]

Under the **new rules**, if you are a non-resident parent on benefit and liable to pay child support maintenance at the flat-rate (see p765) deduction of £5 a week (this is expected to increase to £7 a week, but it is not clear if this will be in 2008/09 – see CPAG's *Welfare Rights Bulletin* for updates), this can be made from the following benefits paid to you:[202]

- bereavement allowance;
- retirement pension;
- IB;
- CA;
- SDA;
- industrial injuries benefit;
- widowed mother's allowance/widowed parent's allowance;
- widow's pension;
- a training allowance (other than Work-Based Learning for Young People or Skillseekers);
- contribution-based JSA;
- war widow's or war disablement pension;

or any of the following benefits paid either to you or your partner:

- IS, income-based JSA or PC.

The whole of the maintenance may be deducted from one of the benefits listed above.[203] If more than one partner in a couple or polygamous marriage is liable to pay maintenance at the flat rate, £5 is deducted from any IS or income-based JSA s/he is receiving.[204]

Deductions may be also made from some benefits for **arrears** for child support maintenance.[205] In old rules cases, deductions may be made only from your contribution-based JSA. In new rules cases (including where the case is converted from the old rules), deductions may be made from any of the benefits above paid to you *except* IS, income-based JSA or PC.

How much can be deducted

Deductions are made to pay off the debt or current weekly costs, or both.[206] Deductions are made from your IS, PC and any IB, retirement pension or SDA paid with it. They are also made from your JSA. For repayment of eligible loans, deductions can be made from your IS, JSA, PC, IB, retirement pension or CA. You must be left with at least 10p.[207] Council tax and community charge arrears can be deducted from IS, PC and JSA only.[208]

For **arrears of child support maintenance**, in old rules cases deductions can be made from your *contribution-based* JSA if no deductions are being made for community charge arrears, council tax arrears or fines.[209] The maximum deduction is one-third of the weekly amount of JSA for a person of your age. In new rules cases, the deduction is £1 per week from any of the benefits paid to you in the bullet points listed above, *except* IS, income-based JSA or PC.[210]

If deductions are being made from your **IS, PC or income-based JSA** (or contribution-based JSA where you have an underlying entitlement to income-based JSA – see p988), maximum deductions are shown below.

Type of arrears	*Deduction for arrears*	*Deduction for ongoing cost*
Mortgage direct payments*	Nil	Current weekly cost
Housing costs*	£3.05 each housing debt (maximum of £9.15 payable)	Current weekly cost
Rent/hostel payment arrears	£3.05	Nil (met by HB)
Fuel	£3.05 each fuel debt (maximum of £6.10 payable)	Estimated amount of current consumption
Water charges	£3.05 (adjusted every 26 weeks)	Estimated costs
Council tax	£3.05	Nil (met by council tax benefit)
Community charge	£3 (single person) £4.75 (couple)	Not applicable
Fines	Nil	£3.05
Repayment of eligible loans	Nil	£3.05
Repayment of integration loans	Nil	£3.05
Child support maintenance	Nil	£5 (new rules – may increase to £7) £6.10 (old rules)
Residential accommodation charges	Nil	The accommodation allowance (for those in local authority homes); all but £20.45 of your IS, PC or JSA (for those in private or voluntary homes)
Hostel charges	Nil	Weekly amount assessed by local authority

*If you have more than one type of housing cost and these are not met in full because of a restriction on the amount that can be covered (see p811) or a non-dependant deduction (see p815), the direct payment to meet current weekly costs is reduced as follows:[211]
Multiply the amount of the restriction and/or deduction by the amount of the item of housing costs to be paid directly and then divide by the amount of total housing costs. This ensures that such reductions are shared proportionately between different items of housing costs.

More than one debt

For **IS, PC** and **income-based JSA** deductions for arrears can be made for more than one debt. However:

- the maximum amount that can be deducted from your benefit for arrears (excluding community charge arrears) and for current child support maintenance under the old rules is £9.15 a week.[212] The *total* amount deducted from benefit may be more than that if you are having deductions made for current costs as well as for arrears. If the total amount of deductions for arrears would exceed £9.15 a week, the deductions are made in a set order of priority (see below);
- if deductions of £6 would be due for arrears and for current child support maintenance under the old rules, only half of the child support maintenance deduction is made – ie, £3;
- in the case of fuel, rent, water charges, housing costs arrears and repayment of certain loans, if the combined cost of deductions for arrears and current consumption is more than 25 per cent of your total applicable amount (see p771) or, in the case of PC, more than 25 per cent of your minimum guarantee (see p448) before housing costs, the deductions cannot be made without your consent.[213]

Where there is no underlying entitlement to income-based JSA, the maximum amount that can be deducted in total (for debts) from **contribution-based JSA** for community charge or council tax, fines and child support maintenance arrears is one-third of the age-related amount of contribution-based JSA payable to you.

Priority between deductions

If you have more debts or current charges than can be met within the limits for direct payments (see p994), they are paid in the following order of priority:[214]

- 1st: housing costs not covered by the mortgage payment scheme;
- 2nd: rent arrears (and related charges);
- 3rd: fuel charges;
- 4th: water charges;
- 5th: council tax and community charge arrears;
- 6th: unpaid fines, costs and compensation orders;
- 7th: payments for child support maintenance under the old rules. **Note:** payments due under the new rules are always payable whatever other deductions are being made;
- 8th: repayment of integration loans;
- 9th: repayment of eligible loans.

If you owe both gas and electricity arrears, the DWP chooses which one to pay first, depending on your circumstances. If you have arrears for both council tax and community charge, only one application can be dealt with at a time and the earliest debt should be dealt with first.[215]

If you have been overpaid benefit or given a social fund loan, you may have to repay these too by having deductions from your benefit.[216] You should argue that these deductions should take a lower priority.

8. Sanctions for breach of community orders and for benefit offences

Breach of community orders

Under a pilot scheme in Derbyshire, Hertfordshire, Teeside and West Midlands there are sanctions on claimants who fail to comply with community orders.[217] What follows is a summary of the main rules. Seek further advice (see Appendix 2) if you are affected.

The sanctions will be applied if:[218]

- a court has decided that you have failed to comply with the requirements of the order without reasonable excuse; *and*
- the Secretary of State is notified of the determination; *and*
- you otherwise satisfy the conditions of entitlement to benefit.

The sanction is that specified benefits (income support, jobseeker's allowance (JSA) and certain training allowances paid with Work-Based Learning for Adults and the New Deal) will not be payable in full or in some cases at all for a period of four weeks.[219] Even if you are sanctioned, you are treated as if you are still in receipt of income-based or joint-claim JSA for housing benefit or council tax benefit.[220]

Benefit offences

If you are convicted of one or more benefit 'offences' (ie, in connection with fraud) in two separate proceedings within a three-year period, sanctions may be imposed on certain of your benefits, with the result that they may be paid at a reduced rate or not at all (see Chapter 40).

9. Recovery of benefits from compensation payments

If you are seeking compensation from someone (a defendant) through the courts (eg, because you have been unfairly dismissed or because you have had a personal injury) you might be awarded damages to compensate you for your loss. However, if, as the result of a defendant's action, you have had to claim benefit, the amount of damages to be awarded is reduced by the amount of benefit you received.

Employment cases

In a wrongful or unfair dismissal case, your claim for loss of earnings is reduced by the amount of jobseeker's allowance (JSA) you received.[221] The DWP is able to recover an equivalent sum from your employer if it is an unfair dismissal case dealt with in an industrial tribunal,[222] but not if there is a settlement or it is a wrongful dismissal case dealt with by a court.

Personal injury cases

If you are paid compensation in respect of an accident, injury or disease after 6 October 1997, those compensating you can reduce compensation paid to you when you have received benefit in respect of a particular loss for which the compensation is paid. They must then pay money back to the Compensation Recovery Unit (CRU), which is part of the DWP. It does not matter whether the payment is voluntary, with or without legal proceedings, or by order of a court. A reduction is not made if the compensation is paid for pain and suffering, because benefits are not paid for this. You are, therefore, able to keep all compensation paid for that reason. However, because the right to reduce your compensation can reduce it quite considerably, it is important to be aware of the law governing the CRU's rights of recovery.

The CRU is not entitled to recover all the benefits you have received. It may only recover those listed in the right-hand column of the table on p1000, and only then if you were paid the benefit as a consequence of the accident (see p999).

Note: the rules described here apply to payments made from 6 October 1997 onwards. The rules that applied under the old scheme are described in CPAG's *Rights Guide to Non-Means-Tested Benefits*, 20th edition, 1997/98, pp230–32.

Which benefits can be recovered

The recoverable benefit consists of all benefits paid to you 'in consequence' of the injury or disease from which you have suffered during the 'relevant period' (see p999).

Before you are paid compensation, those compensating you must apply to the DWP for a 'certificate of recoverable benefits'.[223] The certificate tells them which benefits are recoverable.

Those compensating you become liable to pay the DWP for the total amount of recoverable benefit 14 days after the certificate is issued.[224] It is the compensator's obligation, not yours, and so if the compensator fails to pay, the CRU cannot pursue you for the money. The compensator remains liable even if it fails to apply for a certificate.[225]

When benefit is paid 'in consequence'

The following rules apply.

- If both the relevant event (cause A) and some unrelated problem (cause B) led you to be entitled to benefit, then provided that cause A is at least partially to blame for your illness or disability, the benefit is recoverable.[226]
- However, if cause A would not have led you to be entitled to benefit by itself, but cause B did do so, then the benefit is not recoverable.[227]
- It is common, particularly in back injury cases, for doctors to say that you have 'aggravated' or 'exacerbated' pre-existing damage to your body which you may not have been aware of prior to the accident. They often say that after a certain period of time, say two years, you would have been experiencing the same level of pain even had the accident not happened. In such a case, after that period of time the benefit is not being paid in consequence of the accident but as a result of your underlying problem.[228]

The CRU must look at the reality of your state of health when deciding whether benefit was paid 'in consequence' of your accident or illness and may not simply look at the opinions given by DWP doctors at the time of awarding you benefit.[229] It can help if you think about the effects of the CRU scheme on your compensation while the case is still proceeding and get your solicitor to ask appropriate questions of the medical experts in your case. You can then use the evidence of the medical expert if you want to challenge the CRU certificate.

Compensators can argue that you were wrongly paid benefit, and that where this is accepted, the benefit was not 'paid in respect of' an injury, accident or disease. Where that is the case, the money will not be recoverable from the compensator. Also, where the compensator has shown that you were not entitled to benefit, the DWP can consider whether your benefit award should be revised or superseded, and if any overpayment is recoverable from you (see Chapter 39 for overpayments and when they can be recovered).[230] If you are asked to repay an overpayment in this situation, seek advice (see Appendix 2). Although you can argue that money already recovered from the compensator is not also recoverable from you,[231] this may not help you if the compensator has been refunded.

The relevant period

The **'relevant period'** is usually the period of five years from the date:[232]

- of your accident or injury if you are claiming compensation for an accident or injury; *or*
- you first claimed a recoverable benefit because of the disease (see above) if you are claiming compensation in respect of a disease.

The relevant period ends if those compensating you make a final payment of compensation or an agreement is made under which compensation already paid is accepted as being in final payment.[233]

Offsetting against your compensation

Before the compensator pays your compensation, it is allowed to deduct the recoverable benefits paid during the relevant period (see p999) from certain types of compensation.[234] The type of compensation is shown in the left-hand column and the relevant benefits in the right-hand column of the table below.

Compensation	*Recoverable benefits*
Loss of earnings	Disability working allowance, disablement benefit, incapacity benefit, income support, invalidity pension, jobseeker's allowance, reduced earnings allowance, severe disablement allowance, sickness benefit, statutory sick pay (paid before 6 April 1994), unemployment benefit, unemployability supplement, invalidity allowance
Cost of care	Attendance allowance, disability living allowance care component, disablement benefit paid for constant attendance (see p326) or exceptionally severe disablement (see p326)
Loss of mobility	Mobility allowance, disability living allowance mobility component

Example

Gary receives a £30,000 compensation payment consisting of £15,000 for loss of earnings, £5,000 for pain and suffering, and £10,000 for the cost of care. By the time the award is made he has received £20,000 of incapacity benefit and £5,000 disability living allowance care component. The award for loss of earnings is reduced to nil. Gary will receive the full award for pain and suffering, but his award for the cost of care is reduced by £5,000. The compensator is liable to pay the DWP recoverable benefits of £25,000, and pays Gary a net award of £10,000 (£5,000 pain and suffering + £5,000 care).

Any compensation reduced by this method is treated as being paid to you. Those compensating you must give you a statement showing how the payment has been calculated, even if the recovery of benefits reduces a particular type of compensation to nil. If the recoverable benefit (see above) exceeds the compensation paid to you for a particular loss, those compensating you still have to pay the balance to the DWP.

Exempt payments

The recovery rules apply to all claims, no matter how small. However, certain compensation payments are exempt.[235] These include:

- payments under the Fatal Accident Act 1996, the Vaccine Damage Act 1979 and the NHS industrial injury scheme;
- payments under the Pneumoconiosis Compensation Scheme and certain payments for loss of hearing;
- criminal injuries compensation;

- contractual sick pay and redundancy payments;
- payments from insurance companies from policies agreed before the accident; *and*
- payments from certain trusts – eg, the Macfarlane Trust, Eileen Trust, UK Asbestos Trust and the EL Scheme Trust.

Challenging a recovery decision

A decision maker may look at a certificate of recoverable benefit (see p998) again if s/he is satisfied that it was issued in ignorance of or was based on a mistake about a material fact, or if there was an error in its preparation – eg, a miscalculation.[236] You and those compensating you can both appeal against the certificate but not until the compensation payment has been made and the benefit paid back to the DWP. There are only two possible grounds for appeal:[237]

- that the amount, rate, or period of benefit specified on the certificate is wrong; *or*
- that the benefits specified were not paid because of an accident, injury or disease.

Appeals are heard by an appeal tribunal[238] (see p1093). Further appeals can be made to a commissioner in the usual way (see p1120).[239]

Other sources of information

Details of the procedures to be followed and other advice can be obtained from the CRU (see Appendix 1). A guide to the procedures, *Social Security Recovery of Benefits: procedures for liaison with Compensation Recovery Unit – a guide for companies and solicitors*, is available free from the DWP.

Notes

1. **Who should claim**
   1 Reg 4(4) SS(C&P) Regs
   2 Reg 4D(7) and (8) SS(C&P) Regs
   3 **CB/GA**Reg 28 CB&GA(Admin) Regs
   Other benefits Reg 33 SS(C&P) Regs
   4 R(SB) 5/90
   5 Reg 33(1A) SS(C&P) Regs
   HB Reg 82(5) HB Regs; reg 63(5) HB(SPC) Regs
   CTB Reg 68(5) CTB Regs; reg 52(5) CTB(SPC) Regs
   6 CIS/642/1994
   7 CIS/379/1992

2. **How to make a claim**
   8 s1 SSAA 1992
   9 Reg 3 SS(C&P) Regs
   10 **CB/GA**Reg 5 CB&GA(Admin) Regs
   Other benefits Reg 4 SS(C&P) Regs
   11 Regs 4(6A)-(6CC) and 4D SS(C&P) Regs; Memo Vol 1 06/03 DMG
   12 **CB/GA**Reg 8 CB&GA(Admin) Regs
   Other benefits Reg 5(1) SS(C&P) Regs
   13 **CB/GA**Reg 8 CB&GA(Admin) Regs
   Other benefits Reg 5(2) SS(C&P) Regs

14 CJSA/3979/1999
15 Reg 4 SS(C&P) Regs
16 Reg 4 SS(C&P) Regs
17 Regs 4(7) and 4D(10)-(12) SS(C&P) Regs
18 Sch 2 SS&CS(DA) Regs and Sch 2 CB&GA(DA) Regs do not include such decisions in the list of decisions against which no appeal lies.
19 s8 SSA 1998
20 Reg 4(1A) SS(C&P) Regs
21 Reg 4(7A) SS(C&P) Regs
22 Sch 2 SS&CS(DA) Regs and Sch 2 CB&GA(DA) Regs do not include such decisions in the list of decisions against which no appeal lies.
23 Reg 4(1B) SS(C&P) Regs
24 CIS/2057/1998
25 Reg 6(4A) SS(C&P) Regs
26 **CB/GA** Reg 7 CB&GA(Admin) Regs
Other benefits Regs 7 and 8(2) SS(C&P) Regs; reg 23 JSA Regs
27 s180 SSAA 1992
28 The Social Security (Claims and Information) Regulations 2007 No.2911
29 s1(1A) and (1B) SSAA 1992; reg 2A IS Regs
30 CIS/345/2003
31 Reg 1A SS(DLA) Regs
32 Reg 4(a) HB Regs; reg 4(a) HB(SPC) Regs
33 Reg 2A IS Regs; reg 2A JSA Regs
34 *Secretary of State for Work and Pensions v Wilson* [2006] EWCA Civ 882, reported as R(H) 7/06
35 Reg 2A SS(IB) Regs; reg 2A SS(ICA) Regs; reg 1A SS(MA) Regs; reg 1A SS(WB&RP) Regs; reg 2A SS(SDA) Regs
36 Reg 2A IS Regs; reg 2A JSA Regs; reg 2A SS(IB) Regs; reg 2A SS(ICA) Regs; reg 1A SS(MA) Regs; reg 1A SS(WB&RP) Regs; reg 2A SS(SDA) Regs

3. **The date of your claim**

37 **CB/GA** Reg 11 CB&GA(Admin) Regs
Other benefits Reg 9(1) and Sch 1 SS(C&P) Regs
38 Sch 1 SS(C&P) Regs
39 Reg 11 CB&GA(Admin) Regs
40 Reg 9(4) and (5) SS(C&P) Regs
41 **CB/GA** Reg 5(1)(b) CB&GA(Admin) Regs
Other benefits Reg 4(1) SS(C&P) Regs
42 Reg 19 and Sch 4 SS(C&P) Regs
43 R(SB) 9/84
44 ss65(4) and (6) and 76 SSCBA 1992
45 **CB/GA** Reg 6 CB&GA(Admin) Regs
Other benefits Reg 19(2) and (3) and Sch 4 SS(C&P) Regs
46 CJSA/3994/1998
47 Reg 19(6) and (7) SS(C&P) Regs
48 CIS/4901/2002
49 Reg 19(4) and (5) SS(C&P) Regs
50 CIS/2484/1999
51 CIS/1721/1998; CIS/3749/1998; CSIS/256/1999
52 CJSA/4573/1999
53 CJSA/4066/1998
54 CIS/610/1998
55 CJSA/3084/2004
56 CIS/4354/1999
57 CIS/4490/1999
58 CJSA/0580/2003
59 CIS/610/1998
60 CIS/3994/1998
61 CIS/5430/1999
62 CJSA/1136/1998
63 CIS/5430/1999
64 CIS/5430/1999
65 Reg 19(5) SS(C&P) Regs; C12/98 (IS)
66 C12/98 (IS)
67 CIS/2057/1998
68 R(SB) 17/83; R(IS) 5/91; CIS/812/1992
69 R(P) 2/85
70 Reg 6(22) SS(C&P) Regs
71 Reg 6(16)-(26) SS(C&P) Regs
72 Reg 6(22)-(25) SS(C&P) Regs
73 Reg 6(19) SS(C&P) Regs
74 Reg 6(19)-(21A) SS(C&P) Regs
75 Reg 6(30) SS(C&P) Regs
76 CG/1479/1999
77 Reg 1(3) SS&CS(DA) Regs

4. **How your claim is dealt with**

78 s8 SSA 1998
79 R(SB) 29/83
80 **CB/GA** Reg 15 CB&GA(Admin) Regs
Other benefits Reg 17 SS(C&P) Regs
81 Decisions on invalid claims are not excluded from appeal rights: Sch 2 para 5 SS&CS(DA) Regs; Sch 2 para 6 CB&GA(DA) Regs
82 Reg 32(1A) and (1B) SS(C&P) Regs; reg 24 JSA Regs

5. **Work-focused interviews and benefit**

83 Reg 2(1) SS(JPI) Regs
84 Reg 8 SS(JPI) Regs
85 Reg 4 SS(JPI) Regs
86 s2AA SSAA 1992
87 Reg 7 SS(JPIP) Regs
88 s2AA SSAA 1992; regs 3 and 4 SS(JPIP) Regs
89 Regs 10, 11 and 14 SS(JPIP) Regs

90 Reg 3 SS(IBWFI) Regs 2003
91 *Opportunity, Employment and Progression: making skills work*, Cm 7288, November 2007
92 ESA(WFI) Regs (draft)
93 Reg 2(a)(ii)and Sch Parts 1, 2 and 6 SS(IBWFI) Regs
94 HB/CTB A1/2008
95 Reg 1(3) SS(WFILP) Regs
96 Reg 2(6)(a) and (b) SS(WFILP) Regs; memo DMG 04/08
97 Reg 2B SS(WFILP) Regs
98 Reg 4 SS(WFILP) Regs
99 Reg 5(a) SS(JPI) Regs; reg 3(3) SS(IBWFI)Regs; reg 2(2) SS(WFILP) Regs
100 Reg 10(2) SS(JPI) Regs; reg 2(3) SS(WFILP) Regs; reg 5(3) SS(IBWFI) Regs
101 Regs 6 and 7 SS(JPI) Regs; regs 5 and 6 SS(WFILP) Regs; regs 6 and 7 SS(IBWFI) Regs
102 Regs 12 and 14 SS(JPI) Regs; regs 3 and 7 SS(WFILP) Regs; regs 10 and 11 SS(IBWFI) Regs
103 Reg 11(2)-(2B) SS(JPI) Regs; reg 3(2)-(2B) SS(WFILP) Regs; reg 9(2)-(3) SS(IBWFI) Regs
104 Reg 3(3) SS(JPI) Regs
105 ESA(WFHRA) Regs (draft)
106 Reg 12(2)(a) SS(JPI) Regs; reg 7(3)(a) SS(WFILP) Regs
107 Reg 12(10) SS(JPI) Regs; reg 7(6) SS(WFILP) Regs
108 Reg 10 SS(IBWFI) Regs; reg 4 ESA(WFI) Regs (draft); reg 2 ESA(WFHRA) Regs (draft)
109 Reg 12(2)(c) to (8) SS(JPI) Regs; reg 8 SS(WFILP) Regs; reg 10 SS(IBWFI) Regs
110 Reg 12 ESA(WFI) Regs (draft); reg 8 ESA(WFHRA) Regs (draft)
111 Reg 12(9) SS(JPI) Regs; reg 8(3)(c) SS(WFILP) Regs; reg 10(10) SS(IBWFI) Regs; reg 14 ESA(WFI) Regs (draft); reg 10 ESA(WFHRA) Regs (draft)
112 Reg 12(3)-(5) SS(JPI) Regs
113 Regs 12(12) and 13 SS(JPI) Regs; reg 10(12) SS(IBWFI) Regs; reg 8(3)(a) and (b) SS(WFILP) Regs
114 Reg 15 SS(JPI) Regs; reg 9 SS(WFILP) Regs; reg 12 SS(IBWFI) Regs
115 Reg 11(4) SS(JPI) Regs; reg 7(1)(b) SS(WFILP) Regs; reg 9(4) SS(IBWFI) Regs
116 Regs 12(12) and 15(1) SS(JPI) Regs; reg 7(2) SS(WFILP) Regs; reg 10(12) SS(IBWFI) Regs
117 Reg 14 SS(JPI) Regs; reg 7(5) SS(WFILP) Regs; reg 11 SS(IBWFI) Regs

6. **Getting paid**

118 **CB/GA** Reg 16 CB&GA(Admin) Regs
Other benefits Reg 20 SS(C&P) Regs
119 House of Commons *Hansard*, 6 November 2002, col 288W
120 House of Commons *Hansard*, 19 January 2006, col 937
121 **CB/GA** Regs 16-20 CB&GA(Admin) Regs
Other benefits Regs 22-26A SS(C&P) Regs
122 **CB/GA** Regs 27 and 28 CB&GA(Admin) Regs
Other benefits Regs 30 and 33 SS(C&P) Regs
123 **CB/GA** Reg 33 CB&GA(Admin) Regs
Other benefits Reg 34 SS(C&P) Regs
124 Reg 35 SS(C&P) Regs
125 Reg 6 SS(OB) Regs
126 Reg 4(5) SS(OB) Regs
127 Reg 6 SS(OB) Regs
128 s52(2) SSCBA 1992
129 s16(1), (2) and (6) SSCBA 1992; reg 2 SS(MAP) Regs
130 Reg 4(4) SS(OB) Regs
131 Reg 4(3) SS(OB) Regs
132 Reg 9 SS(OB) Regs
133 Reg 10 SS(OB) Regs
134 Reg 8 SS(OB) Regs
135 Reg 7 SS(OB) Regs
136 **CB/GA** Reg 18 CB&GA(Admin) Regs
Other benefits Reg 20 SS(C&P) Regs
137 Reg 38(1)(bb) SS(C&P) Regs; CDLA/2609/2002 commented on the way a similar rule applied to payment by giro/order book
138 Reg 11 HB&CTB(DA) Regs
139 **HB/CTB** Sch 7 para 13(2) CSPSSA 2000; reg 11(2)(b) HB&CTB(DA) Regs
CB/GA Reg 18(3) CB&GA(DA) Regs
Other benefits ss21(2)(c) and (d) SSA 1998; reg 16(3)(b) SS&CS(DA) Regs
140 **CB/GA** Reg 18(4) and (5) CB&GA(DA) Regs
Other benefits Reg 16(4) SS&CS(DA) Regs
141 **CB/GA** Reg 21 CB&GA(DA) Regs
Other benefits Reg 20(2) and (3) SS&CS(DA) Regs
142 **CB/GA** Reg 18(2) CB&GA(DA) Regs
HB/CTB Sch 7 para 13(2)(a) CSPSSA 2000
Other benefits ss21(2)(a) and (b), 22 and 24 SSA 1998

143 **CB/GA** Reg 18(2)(a) CB&GA(DA) Regs
HB/CTB Reg 11(2)(a)(i) HB&CTB(DA) Regs
Other benefits Reg 16(3)(a)(i) SS&CS(DA) Regs
144 Reg 16(2) SS&CS(DA) Regs
145 **CB/GA** Reg 18(2)(b) CB&GA(DA) Regs
HB/CTB Reg 11(2)(a)(ii) HB&CTB(DA) Regs
Other benefits Reg 16(3)(a)(ii) SS&CS(DA) Regs
146 **CB/GA** Reg 18(2)(c) CB&GA(DA) Regs
HB/CTB Reg 11(2)(c)(i) and (ii) HB&CTB(DA) Regs
Other benefits Reg 16(3)(a)(iii) SS&CS(DA) Regs
147 Reg 16(3)(a)(iv) SS&CS(DA) Regs
148 Reg 18(e) CB&GA(DA)Regs
149 Reg 11(2)(c) HB&CTB(DA) Regs
150 Reg 17(6) SS&CS(DA) Regs
151 **CB/GA** Reg 19 CB&GA(DA) Regs
Other benefits Reg 17(2) SS&CS(DA) Regs
152 As required under reg 32(1) SS(C&P) Regs or for CB/GA reg 23 CB&GA(Admin) Regs
153 **CB/GA** Reg 19(2) CB&GA(DA) Regs
HB/CTB Reg 13(4)(a) HB&CTB(DA) Regs
Other benefits Reg 17(4)(a) SS&CS(DA) Regs
154 **CB/GA** Reg 19(2)(b) CB&GA(DA) Regs
HB/CTB Reg 13(4)(b) HB&CTB(DA) Regs
Other benefits Reg 17(4)(b) SS&CS(DA) Regs
155 **CB/GA** Reg 19(5) CB&GA(DA) Regs
HB/CTB Reg 13(4) HB&CTB(DA) Regs
Other benefits Reg 17(5) SS&CS(DA) Regs
156 s24 SSA 1998; reg 19(2) SS&CS(DA) Regs
157 **CB/GA** Reg 20(1)(a) CB&GA(DA) Regs
HB/CTB Reg 14(1)(a) HB&CTB(DA) Regs
Other benefits Reg 18(1)(a), (2) and (4) SS&CS(DA) Regs
158 **CB/GA** Reg 20(1)(b) CB&GA(DA) Regs
HB/CTB Reg 14(1)(b) HB&CTB(DA) Regs
Other benefits Reg 18(1)(b), (3) and (4) SS&CS(DA) Regs
159 **CB/GA** Reg 20(2) CB&GA(DA) Regs
HB/CTB Reg 14(1) HB&CTB(DA) Regs
Other benefits Reg 18(1) SS&CS(DA) Regs
160 Reg 19(3) and (4) SS&CS(DA) Regs
161 para 04130 DMG; CH/402/2007 (regarding HB and CTB)
162 Reg 2(1A) SS(PAOR) Regs. It is unclear whether in cases involving EC law there would be a breach in not making an interim payment pending an appeal.
163 Reg 2 SS(PAOR) Regs
164 Regs 3 and 4 SS(PAOR) Regs

7. **Deductions and payments to third parties**

165 Regs 34A and 35 and Sch 9 SS(C&P) Regs; CC(DIS) Regs; CT(DIS) Regs; F(DIS) Regs
166 Sch 9 para 1 SS(C&P) Regs
167 Sch 9 para 2(1) SS(C&P) Regs
168 Sch 9 para 8(2) and (4) SS(C&P) Regs
169 Sch 9 para 8 SS(C&P) Regs
170 Reg 34A and Sch 9A para 2 SS(C&P) Regs
171 Sch 9A paras 8 and 9 SS(C&P) Regs
172 Regs 34A(1A) and 34B and Sch 9A para 2A SS(C&P) Regs
173 Sch 9A para 3 SS(C&P) Regs
174 Sch 9A paras 1 and 3 SS(C&P) Regs
175 Sch 9A para 6 SS(C&P) Regs
176 Sch 9A para 3(4) SS(C&P) Regs
177 Sch 9 para 3 SS(C&P) Regs
178 Sch 9 para 3(5) SS(C&P) Regs
179 Sch 9 para 1 SS(C&P) Regs
180 Sch 9 para 3(4) SS(C&P) Regs
181 CIS/15146/1996
182 Sch 9 para 3(4) SS(C&P) Regs
183 Sch 9 para 5 SS(C&P) Regs
184 Sch 9 para 5(1)(c)(i) SS(C&P) Regs
185 Sch 9 para 5(1)(c)(ii) SS(C&P) Regs
186 Sch 9 para 5(6) SS(C&P) Regs; R(IS) 14/95
187 Sch 9 para 5(7) SS(C&P) Regs
188 Sch 9 para 4 SS(C&P) Regs
189 Sch 9 para 4A SS(C&P) Regs
190 Sch 9 para 6 SS(C&P) Regs
191 Sch 9 para 6(1) SS(C&P) Regs
192 Sch 9 para 6(4)(b) SS(C&P) Regs
193 Sch 9 paras 1 and 7 SS(C&P) Regs
194 Sch 9 para 7(1) SS(C&P) Regs
195 Sch 9 para 7(2) SS(C&P) Regs
196 Sch 9 para 7(7) SS(C&P) Regs
197 CC(DIS) Regs; CT(DIS) Regs; CIS/11861/1996
198 F(DIS) Regs
199 Sch 9 para 7C SS(C&P) Regs
200 Sch 9 para 7D SS(C&P) Regs; reg 9 The Integration Loans for Refugees and Others Regulations 2007 No.1598
201 s43 CSA 1991; Sch 9 paras 7A and 7B SS(C&P) Regs

202 Sch 1 para 4(I)(b) CSA 1991; Sch 9B para 2 SS(C&P) Regs
203 Sch 9B para 2 SS(C&P) Regs
204 Sch 9B paras 4-6 SS(C&P) Regs
205 Schs 9 para 7B and 9B para 3(1) SS(C&P) Regs
206 Sch 9 SS(C&P) Regs
207 Sch 9 paras 1 and 2(2) SS(C&P) Regs
208 Reg 2 CC(DIS) Regs; regs 2 and 3 CT(DIS) Regs
209 Sch 9 para 7B SS(C&P) Regs
210 Sch 9B para 3 SS(C&P) Regs
211 Sch 9 para 3(2A) SS(C&P) Regs
212 Sch 9 para 8(1) SS(C&P) Regs
213 Sch 9 paras 5(5) and (5A), 6(6) and (6A), 7(8) and (9), and 8(2) and (2A) SS(C&P) Regs
214 Sch 9 para 9 SS(C&P) Regs
215 Reg 4 CC(DIS) Regs; reg 8 CT(DIS) Regs
216 Regs 15 and 16 SS(PAOR) Regs; reg 3 SF(RDB) Regs

8. **Sanctions for breach of community orders and for benefit offences**

217 Child Support, Pensions and Social Security Act 2000 (Commencement No.10) Order 2001 No.2619(C.86); SS(BCO) Regs
218 s62(1) CSPSSA 2000
219 s62(2) CSPSSA 2000; reg 2 SS(BCO) Regs
220 **HB** Reg 2(3)(d) HB Regs; reg 2(3)(d) HB(SPC) Regs
CTB Reg 2(4)(d) CTB Regs; reg 2(4)(d) CTB(SPC) Regs

9. **Recovery of benefits from compensation payments**

221 *Nabi v British Leyland (UK) Ltd* [1980] 1 WLR 529 (CA)
222 EP(RUB&SB) Regs
223 s4 SS(RB)A 1997
224 s6(4) SS(RB)A 1997
225 s7 SS(RB)A 1997
226 CCR/5336/1995
227 CCR/5336/1995
228 CCR/4/1993; CCR/2129/1999
229 CCR/12532/1996
230 R(CR) 1/02
231 CSIS/37/1994
232 s3 SS(RB)A 1997
233 s3(4) SS(RB)A 1997
234 s8 and Sch 2 SS(RB)A 1997
235 s1 and Sch 1 SS(RB)A 1997; reg 2 SS(RB) Regs
236 s10 SS(RB)A 1997
237 s11 SS(RB)A 1997
238 s12 SS(RB)A 1997
239 s13 SS(RB)A 1997; reg 13 SS(RB)App Regs

Chapter 39

Overpayments

This chapter covers all the rules about overpayments of benefit. It contains:

If you are paid more benefit than you are entitled to, then an **overpayment** occurs. You may have to repay the overpayment – including, in some cases, where there was no fault on your part. If you have been overpaid a social fund payment (see Chapters 21 and 22) you may have to repay that too.

If it is considered that an overpayment was made because of **fraud**, as well as the overpayment being recovered you may be prosecuted, or you may be offered the option of paying a penalty as an alternative to going to court. You should seek advice before agreeing to pay. See Chapter 40 for further information.

If you were paid too much income support, pension credit or jobseeker's allowance, this could mean that you were also paid too much housing benefit and council tax benefit. If you are in this situation, see p1021.

Note: for overpayments of **tax credits**, see Chapter 55.

1. Ordinary overpayments of benefits

Most overpayments are recoverable only in certain circumstances. These are referred to in this *Handbook* as ordinary overpayments'. Different rules apply if:

- you have been paid too much income support (IS), income-based jobseeker's allowance (JSA) or pension credit (PC) because other income was paid late (see p1017);
- too much mortgage interest has been paid direct to your lender (see p1018);
- too much benefit has been paid into your bank account by mistake (see p1017);
- you have been paid too much housing benefit (HB) or council tax benefit (CTB) (see pp1021 and 1033).

Benefits covered by these rules

This section covers the rules that allow recovery of overpayments of:

- all the benefits (not tax credits) covered in this *Handbook*, other than HB and CTB. HB and CTB are paid by local authorities and special rules apply (see pp1021 and 1033);
- Sure Start maternity grants, funeral expenses, cold weather and winter fuel payments (see pp513, 515, 521 and 523 for the rules of entitlement to these payments);
- payments from the discretionary social fund (see Chapter 21) paid after 5 October 1998. The DWP has said that it only intends to exercise these powers if you were overpaid because you fraudulently claimed another benefit. It should not use these rules to recover a payment if:[1]
  - you are given a loan or grant for an item but use the money to buy something else instead; *or*
  - one social fund officer (SFO) decides to give you a loan or grant but, for example following a request for a review, another SFO interprets the guidance (see p486) differently.

Overpayments made before 6 April 1987

The old law still applies if the overpayment which the DWP (or, for child benefit or guardian's allowance, the Revenue) is seeking to recover from you was made before 6 April 1987.[2] See CPAG's *Rights Guide to Non-Means-Tested Benefits*, 9th edition, 1986/87, p8 or, regarding overpaid supplementary benefit from this period, CPAG's *National Welfare Benefits Handbook*, 1986/87.

From whom an overpayment can be recovered

An overpayment can be recovered from you if it was caused by you *failing to disclose* or *misrepresenting* a material fact.[3] The DWP/Revenue may try to argue that it can recover the overpayment from you even if you are *not* the claimant or were not otherwise paid the benefit. However, it is arguable that, at least, overpayments caused by failure to disclose are only recoverable from you if you are the claimant.[4]

If you are an appointee (see p955), in general the overpayment can be recovered either from you or the claimant, or both of you. Exactly who the overpayment is recoverable from will depend on the individual facts of the case – ie, who misrepresented or failed to disclose a material fact. The DWP or the Revenue should issue a decision that deals with the liability of both the appointee and the claimant.[5] There are two exceptions to this rule.

- If the overpaid benefit has not been given to the claimant, the overpayment cannot be recovered from the claimant, unless s/he contributed to the misrepresentation of or failure to disclose a material fact.

- If the overpayment was caused by misrepresentation of a material fact by an appointee, the overpayment cannot be recovered from the appointee if s/he used 'due care and diligence' in making the representation.

Having power of attorney is not the same as being an appointee. Unless you are an appointee, a benefit overpayment caused by your actions cannot be recovered from the claimant. Depending on the facts, however, such an overpayment may be recoverable from you.[6] You should seek advice if you are in this situation.

An overpayment can be recovered from a claimant's estate if s/he dies.[7] However, no recovery may be made until a grant either of probate (where the claimant has a will) or of letters of administration (where the claimant has no will) has been made.[8]

When an overpayment can be recovered

Before an overpayment can be recovered, a number of conditions must usually be fulfilled.[9] Unless it can be shown that all of them are present in your case, the benefit cannot be recovered from you.[10] The conditions are that:

- the decisions awarding you benefit have been changed (see below); *and*
- you *failed to disclose* or *misrepresented* a material fact (see p1009); *and*
- as a result of your failure to disclose or misrepresentation, the overpayment was made (see p1014); *and*
- the whole amount is in fact recoverable (see p1014).

The DWP sometimes claims it can recover overpayments outside these rules under common law, although this may not be correct (see p1020).

The decisions awarding you benefit have been changed

In order for you to be paid benefit, a decision maker will have made a decision to award you that benefit. If it later turns out that you have been overpaid benefit, the decision must be changed before the benefit is recoverable. Any overpayment from a period for which your benefit award has not been changed is not be recoverable.[11] There are, therefore, two decisions. First, there is a decision which alters previous decisions awarding you benefit. Second, there is a decision that the overpayment is recoverable.

If both decisions are not made, it is not possible to recover the overpayment from you.[12] Moreover, during the period for which you were overpaid, there may have been more than one decision awarding you benefit, and unless they are *all* changed, the overpayment cannot be recovered.[13]

If this rule is not complied with, you should appeal to a tribunal (see p1093) against the decision that the overpayment is recoverable. The tribunal should decide that the decision is of no effect. In this case, the DWP (or, in child benefit or guardian's allowance cases, the Revenue) can usually try again to recover the overpayment by complying with this formality.[14] However, sometimes a tribunal will go further and say that an overpayment is not recoverable, in which case the tribunal's decision will be final (unless the DWP or the Revenue appeals or the decision can be altered in some other way – see pp1118, 1120 and 1066).

How a decision is changed

A decision to alter your benefit award should have been made by an officer called a 'decision maker'. A decision maker can change a decision by carrying out a revision or a supersession of the decisions to award you benefit (see pp1065 and 1074 for more details).

Special cases

The way in which the decision to award benefit is changed differs in some cases.

- If you are 16 or 17 and have been overpaid discretionary JSA to avoid severe hardship (see p373), the Secretary of State must 'revoke' your award of JSA before you can be asked to repay the overpayment.[15] You cannot appeal against the revocation, which can only be challenged by a judicial review.[16] If you are in this situation, seek advice.
- Decisions to make awards from the discretionary social fund are made by 'appropriate officers' (see p485). Such officers will make the initial decision to revise the award.[17]

Did you fail to disclose or misrepresent a material fact?

You have a duty to report your circumstances correctly when you first claim, and to notify the DWP (or, in the case of child benefit or guardian's allowance, the Revenue) when they have changed[18] (see p1076 and the section 'Change of circumstances' in the relevant benefit chapter of this *Handbook*).

Even if you innocently misrepresented your situation or you failed to tell the relevant office certain facts because you did not understand how the benefit scheme works, you can still be required to repay the benefit provided you failed to disclose or misrepresented a material fact.[19]

A material fact

Overpayments can only usually be recovered if you failed to disclose (see p1010) or misrepresented (see p1012) a 'material fact'. A **'material fact'** is one which is relevant to how much benefit you should be paid.[20] Sometimes there can be a difference between a statement of your honest opinion and a statement of a material fact.[21] For example, it may well be that your statement about the distance you can walk should be taken merely as your honest opinion of your ability, rather than as a statement of fact.[22] If the decision maker has simply come to a different *conclusion* about the facts than you, you can argue that an overpayment should not be recovered.[23]

Facts	*Conclusions about the facts*
You have arthritis	You are incapable of work
A friend of the opposite sex is sharing your flat	You are living together as husband and wife
You have a bad back	Your mobility is severely restricted most of the time

Failure to disclose

Failure to disclose occurs where you do not give the relevant office material facts – eg, you forget to tell it that you or your partner's working hours or pay have increased. It must be shown that you:

- knew of the material fact (see p1011); *and*
- did not inform the relevant office about the material fact by making a 'valid disclosure' (see below); *and*
- should have reported the material fact (see p1011).

Have you made a valid disclosure?

Generally, to make a valid disclosure you have to disclose to the 'relevant office' the material fact in sufficiently clear terms so that how it affects your claim can be examined. Note the following.

- Where you have been told that you need to report a certain fact, the 'relevant office' is the one that handles the benefit that you are claiming.[24] This may be a local office or a benefit delivery centre (eg, for IS), or a central office (eg, for disability living allowance). Much will depend on what you have been told officially about who is dealing with your claim.[25]
- Where you have not been told to report a certain fact, but could reasonably have been expected to know that your benefit might be affected, the law says that the relevant office is any DWP office or, in JSA cases, a specified DWP office. But it is always best to tell the office handling your claim if you can. For child benefit and guardian's allowance you can disclose such changes in your circumstances to the Revenue Child Benefit Office, DWP Jobcentre Plus office or any Revenue enquiry centre.[26] Again, it is best to ensure that you tell the Revenue, as it (and not the DWP or local authority) administers your claim.
- If the office already *actually* knew about the fact, you cannot have 'failed to disclose' the fact to it.[27]
- You can usually notify changes in writing or by telephone – but it is best to do so in writing.[28]
- If you filled in a form while giving information, a tribunal should not just look at what you said on the form, but also consider whether you gave the necessary information in another way.[29] If you fail to fill in a form correctly, but give the relevant information in the wrong place, you have disclosed the facts.[30]

- If you have made a statement in person or over the telephone but the decision maker says there is no record of this, you only have a case to answer once the decision maker has shown, 'on the balance of probabilities', that there would be a record of the conversation at the local office if it had taken place. In order to do this, the decision maker must give a tribunal information on:[31]
  - the instructions which should have applied for recording and attaching information to a claimant's file;
  - whether the appropriate administrative arrangements were in place to enable these instructions to be carried out;
  - to what extent *in practice* these instructions are, or are not, carried out.
- You should usually make the disclosure yourself,[32] unless you have an appointee acting for you (see p955). To be effective, disclosure by someone else on your behalf must be made to the right office with your knowledge and you must think that there is no need to repeat the disclosure yourself. However, if someone else makes the disclosure to an office not handling your claim, but s/he reasonably believes that the information will be passed on to the correct office, that may count as disclosure.[33]
- Once you have made a disclosure, you are not normally expected to repeat it.[34] However, if you give the information to the wrong person and subsequently become aware that it has not been acted upon, you are obliged to take further steps to make a proper disclosure.[35] A short time may elapse before you can reasonably be expected to realise that the original information has not been acted on.[36]

When you must report a fact

You will have failed to disclose a fact if you did not report it and:[37]

- you were clearly told by the DWP or the Revenue, for example, in your benefit award letter, that you needed to disclose the fact. The instruction must be absolutely clear and leave no room for doubt;[38] *and*
- you knew about the material fact; *or*
- you were *not* clearly told of the need to disclose the fact, but:
  - you knew about the fact; *and*
  - the fact was a change in your circumstances; *and*
  - it was reasonable to expect you to know that your benefit might be affected.

You should, therefore, report anything you have been told you need to report *and* any changes that might affect your benefit. If you are alleged to have failed to disclose, note the following.

- You may be able to argue that the test of whether you were clearly informed of your need to report a certain fact depends on whether it was reasonable for you to understand the instructions from the DWP or the Revenue, including if you were mentally unwell.[39]

- In general, you cannot rely on one DWP/Revenue office telling another about the fact. But if the office handling your claim already *actually* knew about the fact, you can argue that you did not fail to disclose it. If the office *should* have known about the fact because of an automatic computer interface between it and another DWP office (but not for any other reason), you may be able to argue that any failure in your part did not cause the overpayment, although that is not yet clear.[40]
- In any case, remember there is still discretion on whether or not the overpayment should actually be recovered from you (see p1021).

If you did not know about the fact, whether or not it was a change in your circumstances, you have not 'failed' to disclose it.[41] You cannot have failed to disclose something you did not know about unless:

- there is some reason why you should have been aware of it;[42] *or*
- it was reasonable for you to make enquiries which would have revealed the information to you;[43] *or*
- you had been aware of it, but simply forgot.[44]

If you were not told what to report

If you were not clearly told that you needed to report a certain fact, the overpayment is not recoverable *unless* the fact was a change in your circumstances *and* you could reasonably have been expected to know that your benefit might be affected.[45] What was reasonable will depend on the details of your case. For example, if you were told by the DWP or a lawyer that your benefit would not be affected, or if you were too ill to have realised that it might be, arguably you could not reasonably have been expected to have known that your benefit might be affected.[46] If there is no obvious connection between the fact and the allegedly overpaid benefit, you could argue that it was not reasonable to expect you to know your benefit might be affected.

Misrepresentation

Misrepresentation occurs if you have provided information that is inaccurate – eg, you gave an incorrect answer to a specific question on the claim form. It will not apply to a failure to give information, unless you do so deliberately and with an intention to mislead.[47] The following principles apply.

- It does not matter whether a reasonable person would have also given the information inaccurately. No 'failure' on your part needs to be shown.[48]
- It does not matter if you honestly believed the information you gave to be correct – once it is shown to be incorrect, you have misreprented it. But you would not be guilty of misrepresentation if you add the phrase 'not to my knowledge' to your statement.[49]
- A written misrepresentation may be qualified by an oral one so that, if you fill in a form incorrectly but explain the situation to an officer when handing in

the form, the explanation has to be taken into account when deciding whether what is stated on the form amounts to a misrepresentation.[50] Similarly, if you give incorrect information in one document but correct information in another, there may not be a relevant misrepresentation.[51] However, if you have declared a fact on a previous claim but inadvertently give incorrect information on a later claim, you have misrepresented. The decision maker is not required to check back for you.[52]

- If you are incapable of managing your affairs but nevertheless sign a claim form which is incorrectly completed, you cannot argue later, to avoid recovery, that you were not capable of making a true representation of your circumstances.[53] However, arguably there cannot be recovery from you on the basis of the misrepresentation if:[54]
  - you had a disability or an incapacity – this may include non-medical things such as illiteracy or poor understanding of English; *and*
  - you thought that you were signing something different from what you were signing, or you did not understand the effect of your signature; *and*
  - you took precautions to understand what you were signing – eg, you should ensure a form is checked for accuracy before you sign it.[55]

Decision makers often rely on general statements you have signed to argue that a failure to disclose facts can later become a misrepresentation. This can occur:[56]

- when you sign the claim form. Some claim forms end with a statement: 'I declare that the information I have given is correct and complete'. If you gave correct answers but left out relevant information because you were unaware of it, the information is incomplete and you have failed to disclose. You can argue that signing the declaration does not convert this into a misrepresentation as the declaration means 'complete insofar as I have knowledge of the material facts';[57]
- when you cashed a giro or an order book. Each time you did this you signed a declaration that you reported any facts which could affect the amount of your benefit. This is different from a 'failure to disclose'. If you knew a fact but failed to declare it (eg, if you were claiming IS, then start getting incapacity benefit (IB) so became entitled to less IS but did not tell the IS section about your IB award) you misrepresented each time you signed the declaration because you incorrectly declared that you had reported relevant facts. Arguably, the overpayment is recoverable because of the misrepresentation. However, a court case has cast doubt on whether such misrepresentations actually cause the overpayment.[58] This might mean that the overpayment is not recoverable.

However:

- if you did not declare a fact because you were unaware of it, signing the declaration does not amount to a misrepresentation because all you are declaring is that you have correctly disclosed those facts *which were known to you*;[59]

- if you were told by the DWP (or, in the case of child benefit and guardian's allowance, the Revenue) that certain facts are irrelevant to your claim, signing the declaration cannot be a misrepresentation if you fail to disclose those facts;[60]
- if someone else disclosed a fact to an office not handling your claim but s/he reasonably believed it would be passed on to the correct office, it may be that disclosure has been made, and therefore you signing the declaration does not amount to a misrepresentation.[61]

Did an overpayment result?

Even if there is information that you failed to disclose or misrepresented your circumstances, you might still be able to argue that this was not the cause of the overpayment. If something else caused the overpayment, it should not be recovered. The following applies.

- If the relevant office has been given the correct information to decide your claim by someone else, but fails to act on it, you could argue that any overpayment did not arise because of your failure.[62] If one office of the DWP fails to inform another about *other* changes in your circumstances (eg, an increase in your earnings), that does not prevent the overpayment resulting from your failure to disclose that to the second office yourself.[63]
- In any case, if you have not actually disclosed a relevant fact to the relevant office and you then sign a declaration on a giro or order book that you have reported the relevant facts, this will be a misrepresentation. If you are overpaid, the DWP (or in child benefit and guardian's allowance cases, the Revenue) may argue that the misrepresentation caused the overpayment. However, a court case has cast doubt on whether such declarations actually cause the overpayment.[64]
- If what you say on your claim form is obviously incorrect and the decision maker does not check this, the overpayment is due to official error, not your misrepresentation, and you do not have to pay it back. For example, if you say you pay ground rent and are a freeholder, the decision maker should recognise that this must be incorrect and check before paying you benefit.[65]

How much is repayable

DWP policy is not to recover overpayments of £65 or less (although the law sets no limit).[66] It is always worth checking how the overpayment has been calculated, as you may be asked to repay too much by mistake. Ask for more information if you need it. To calculate the amount of the overpayment, you should:

- determine the dates between which the overpayment is recoverable;
- work out the total amount of benefit you were paid over the period;

- work out the correct amount of benefit you should have received during the period;
- deduct this from the total amount of benefit you were paid.

No interest charges may be added to the amount of the overpayment.

The amount of the overpayment is the difference between what you were paid and what you should have been paid.[67] The decision maker works out what you should have been paid using the information you originally gave her/him, plus any facts you misrepresented or did not disclose.

Except for child benefit and guardian's allowance,[68] the decison maker should deduct (offset) from the overpayment any underpaid IS, PC or income-based JSA you should have been paid – but not underpayments of any other benefit.[69]

If your benefit claim contained sufficient information to alert the decision maker to your potential need, but s/he did not investigate this fully, you can argue that the underpayment should be offset against the overpayment. It does not matter if the overpayment was for a different period, so long as there was sufficient information to alert the decision maker to your need for extra benefit.[70]

If additional facts are needed to prove you were underpaid IS or income-based JSA, you cannot offset the underpayment of those benefits against the overpayment.[71] However, if you have been getting IS or income-based JSA, you can ask the DWP to revise or supersede your award (see pp1065 and 1074). It could then withhold any arrears owed to you to reduce the overpayment.

If you were overpaid IS or income-based JSA because you had too much capital (see p910), the overpayment is calculated taking account of the fact that, had you received no benefit, you would have had to use your capital to meet everyday expenses. For each 13-week period, the DWP assumes your capital is reduced by the amount of overpaid benefit.[72] This is known as the 'diminishing capital' rule, and if your capital goes below the capital limit any subsequent overpayment will not be recoverable. However, if there are any increases or decreases in your actual capital during the overpayment period these are also taken into account.[73]

Example

Nina received IS of £100 a week for a period of 30 weeks. She has capital of £20,000. After 13 weeks, the rule means that she is treated as having spent 13 x 100 = £1,300 and her capital is deemed to be £18,700. After a further 13 weeks, her capital is deemed to be £17,400.

After 26 weeks of the period, Nina paid £5,000 towards credit card arrears after the credit card company threatened her with court proceedings. Provided that obtaining benefit was not a significant purpose for her making that payment (see p924), her capital is then deemed to be £12,400.

Although your capital is treated as reducing for these purposes, if you re-claim benefit your full capital counts (see p926).

Apart from checking that the overpayment has been calculated correctly, you should claim any other benefits or tax credits to which you may be entitled and ask for these to be backdated (see p964 for benefits and p1281 for tax credits) so you can repay the overpayment. You should not delay in making the claims or you could lose out.

If you were overpaid a benefit which overlaps with another benefit you claimed but were not being paid (see p981 for the overlapping benefit rules), you should seek a revision or supersession of that benefit and ask for it to be paid instead (see p1065).

If you were overpaid a benefit, but in fact were entitled to another benefit, check whether the claim for the benefit you were overpaid can be treated as a claim for the other (see p963).

Example

Maxine should not have been receiving IS because her partner is in full-time paid work (see p648). However, she is caring for her aunt who is disabled and receiving attendance allowance. Maxine should ask the DWP to treat her claim for IS as a claim for carer's allowance (CA) and offset arrears of CA against the IS she has been overpaid.

Challenging an overpayment decision

Whether or not you are the claimant, you can appeal if you:[74]

- disagree that an overpayment has occurred; *or*
- disagree that an overpayment can be recovered; *or*
- disagree with the amount to be recovered.

You can also appeal if the decision concerns a payment from the *regulated* social fund (see Chapter 22). If you have been overpaid a payment from the *discretionary* social fund (see Chapter 21), you can instead seek a review by a social fund officer and then a further review by a social fund inspector (see pp1156 and 1160).

Do not pay back any of the money until your appeal has been decided. If you do so, and then successfully appeal the decision that the overpayment is recoverable from you, then arguably the DWP should reimburse you. If it does not do so, you may be entitled to recover the money in court proceedings because you repaid the money on the basis of a mistake. You should write to the DWP (or, in child benefit or guardian's allowance cases, the Revenue) and explain that you do not intend to repay any of the money until your appeal has been decided. If the DWP is already making deductions from your benefit (see p502) you should ask it to stop doing this straight away.

The decision actually to recover an overpayment is discretionary, so you can ask that it is not recovered (see p1021).

2. Late receipt of other income

This section only applies to payments of **income support (IS)**, **income-based jobseeker's allowance (JSA)** and **pension credit (PC)**.

Sometimes you receive too much IS, income-based JSA or PC because money owing to you does not arrive on time. When you get your arrears, you must repay the IS, income-based JSA or PC that you would not have received if the other income had been paid on time.[75] This is to prevent a duplication of payment.

The rule applies to any income that affects the amount of your IS, income-based JSA or PC. This includes:

- other social security benefits (remember though, that arrears of some benefits are treated as capital and ignored for 52 weeks – see Chapter 37);
- arrears of child support maintenance paid to you for the period from your application to the date it is assessed by the Child Support Agency (or its intended replacement, the Child Maintenance and Enforcement Commission);
- benefits paid by other European Economic Area member states.[76]

The decision to make you pay back the money is a discretionary decision, and does not carry the right of appeal. You can still ask the DWP not to recover the overpayment, even though it can. See p1021 for further information about how to do this. See p1019 for how the overpayment can be recovered.

However, you are entitled to appeal about whether an overpayment has occurred, and how it has been calculated.[77]

3. Excess benefit credited to your account

Your benefit may be paid by direct credit transfer into a bank or other account – eg, a building society. If you are credited with too much benefit because of the direct credit transfer system itself, the excess benefit can be recovered in certain circumstances (see below).[78] This is the case even if the rules for recovery of ordinary overpayments do not apply.

Recovery under this rule can only happen if the overpayment was caused by the direct credit transfer system itself. Even though you may be paid by direct credit transfer, that does not automatically mean that the overpayment was caused by the system itself.

Excess benefit credited to your bank or other account can only be recovered if:[79]

- you were notified in writing before you agreed to your benefit being paid into a bank or other account that excess benefit could be recovered; *and*
- it has been certified that you were paid excess benefit because of the direct credit transfer system itself.

If excess benefit cannot be recovered under the rules described above, it could still be recoverable under the 'ordinary' overpayment rules (see p1006) or those for recovery following late payment of income (see p1017).

Challenging decisions

You can appeal to a tribunal against a decision to recover excess benefit credited to your bank or other account.[80]

4. Mortgage interest paid to a lender

This section only applies to payments of **income support** (IS), **income-based jobseeker's allowance** (JSA) and **pension credit** (PC).

If you are getting help with your housing costs in your IS, income-based JSA or PC (see Chapter 34) your mortgage interest is usually paid directly to your lender. Any overpayment of mortgage interest paid directly to your lender must be sent back to the DWP by that lender if it arose because:[81]

- you ceased to be entitled to IS, income-based JSA or PC, but only if the DWP asks for repayment within four weeks of your entitlement ceasing; *or*
- the DWP failed to reduce your mortgage direct payments, even though you were entitled to less IS, income-based JSA or PC because there was a reduction in:
  - the amount of your outstanding loan; *or*
  - the standard interest rate (see p810); *or*
  - your actual mortgage interest rate. If you have a deferred interest mortgage, the relevant interest rate is the one that you are liable to pay, not the one being charged by your lender (which under the terms of such a mortgage you have to repay later on). If the Secretary of State pays the latter rate by mistake, there is no power to recover.[82]

In this case, your mortgage account should simply be corrected, but where you come off IS, income-based JSA or PC and interest is recovered, you will be in arrears unless you have started to make payments yourself.

In practice, the DWP often stops sending your lender your ongoing housing costs until it has recovered the overpayment, rather than asking a lender to return what was overpaid. However, the DWP should not do this if you are put into arrears as a result.[83] If you go arrears, you should seek advice immediately to avoid losing your home.

You can appeal to a tribunal (see p1094) if, for example, you think the rules do not apply to you, if the DWP has not revised or superseded your IS, income-based JSA or PC properly (see p1093), or if you dispute the amount being recovered.[84] If you are not to blame for the overpayment, or would experience hardship, you can also ask the Secretary of State to use her/his discretion not to ask your lender to repay the overpayment.

The DWP can also recover overpaid mortgage interest under the rules for 'ordinary' overpayments[85] described on p1006 – eg, if it fails to ask your lender to repay within four weeks of you coming off IS, income-based JSA or PC. If it tries to do this, you should make sure that those rules actually apply.

5. Recovery of overpaid benefit

This section does not apply to recovery of overpayments of housing benefit (HB) or council tax benefit (CTB). See pp1021 and 1033.

Methods of recovery

There are a number of different ways in which overpayments can be recovered.

Deductions from benefit

Which deductions are allowed

If an overpayment of benefit must be repaid, it can be done through deductions from most of the benefits in this *Handbook*. However, no deduction can be made from guardian's allowance (except for recovery of overpaid guardian's allowance), child benefit (except for recovery of overpaid child benefit), HB or CTB.[86] Remember that recovery is discretionary (see p1021). Except in the case of income support (IS), income-based jobseeker's allowance (JSA) or pension credit (PC), deductions can only be made from the benefit of the person who has to repay the overpayment (see p1006).

For IS, income-based JSA and PC overpayments, as long as a couple are married or living together as husband and wife, or are civil partners or living together as if they were civil partners, the amount overpaid can be recovered from either partner's IS, income-based JSA or PC.[87]

If an overpayment of IS, income-based JSA or PC occurred because of a duplication of payment, the DWP normally deducts any overpaid IS, income-based JSA or PC from the arrears owing to you.[88] However, if it omits to do so you can still be asked to repay even if you have spent the money.

Maximum deductions from benefit

The following are the maximum weekly amounts that can be deducted from IS, income-based JSA,contribution-based JSA (but only if you would be entitled to income-based JSA at the same rate) and PC:[89]

- £12 if you have agreed to pay a penalty (see p1050), admitted fraud or been found guilty of fraud; *or*
- £9.15 in any other case.

The deduction can be increased by half of any:[90]

- earnings subject to the £5, £10 or £15 disregard (see p854); *or*
- charitable income subject to a disregard (see p864); *or*
- benefit subject to a disregard (see p858).

If you have been overpaid *contribution-based* JSA but are not entitled to *income-based* JSA, the maximum deduction is one-third of the personal allowance for someone of your age (see p773).[91] However, this depends on whether any other deductions are being made from your JSA.

Remember, the above amounts are maximum amounts. The DWP might be persuaded to deduct less, especially if you have other direct deductions made from your benefit.

If you have been overpaid a benefit other than IS, income-based JSA or PC, the rules limiting the maximum payment that can be deducted do not apply. The DWP usually wants to deduct one-third of your weekly benefit. However, you can argue that your rate of repayment should be less than this.

Overpaid benefit cannot be recovered by withholding tax credits.[92]

Other methods of recovery

Benefit may also be recovered by enforcement proceedings in the county court in England or Wales or the sheriff's court in Scotland.[93] The DWP (or, in child benefit or guardian's allowance cases, the Revenue) might use these proceedings – eg, if you have gone back to work and are no longer claiming benefit.

Once a decision of a decision maker, tribunal or commissioner is produced, the court has to enforce it unless you persuade the court to delay enforcement (what is known as a 'stay of execution') while you appeal against the relevant decision. If you are in this situation you should seek advice.

Overpayments can also be recovered from arrears of benefit you are owed, except arrears where the benefit has previously been suspended (see p984).[94]

Recovery under common law

Sometimes the DWP claims to be entitled to recover overpayments of benefit not under the rules described in this chapter, but by relying instead on what it claims are its rights under 'common law'.

Under 'common law' it is possible for someone to reclaim money through the courts from someone to whom it has been paid as a result of a mistake. If the DWP does retain its common-law rights then it would be entitled to use this procedure to recover overpayments, even where there has been no misrepresentation (see p1012) or failure to disclose (see p1010) and, indeed, even if the overpayment was entirely caused by its own mistake rather than yours.

If you are in this situation, you should seek urgent advice and ask your adviser to contact CPAG, as the DWP's approach is being challenged by CPAG in the courts. We understand that pending the outcome of this challenge, the DWP will cease sending letters seeking to recover using the common law.[95] You can argue that:

- the rules about overpayments are in the Social Security Acts. These rules replace the 'common law' as far as overpayments of benefit are concerned;
- the Social Security Acts say it is a decision maker (see p1057) who must decide whether there has been an overpayment and that you have a right to appeal to a tribunal against the decision – on this basis, a court would have no jurisdiction to decide the point.

If the DWP or the Revenue takes you to court under the 'common law', you should get advice from a solicitor immediately. Tactically the best course may be to apply for judicial review of the decision to proceed in this way (see p1129). Alternatively, you may simply wish to defend the action in the county court.

The discretion to recover

The DWP (or, in child benefit and guardian's allowance cases, the Revenue) does not have to recover an overpayment even where it is recoverable. It has the discretion not to recover all or part of the overpayment. Proper exercise of this discretion is important in avoiding harshness.[96]

DWP guidance states that in practice it will be rare for recovery not to be made,[97] but that the DWP can apply discretion, particularly if a claimant acted in good faith, and recovery would cause hardship or be detrimental to the health of the claimant or her/his family. If you agree to repay the overpayment or do not ask for recovery not to be made, in almost all cases the DWP will recover the overpayment from you.

You cannot appeal against a refusal to exercise discretion in your favour. Your only possible legal recourse is judicial review (see p1129), but it may also help to involve your MP. A tribunal cannot 'write off' part of the overpayment even if there are mitigating circumstances. It can only decide if it is recoverable and, if so, how much is repayable.

If you have been underpaid in the past but cannot now get arrears – eg, because of the rules on backdating (see p964) – ask the DWP/Revenue to reduce the amount to be recovered by this sum if it will not write it off altogether.

6. Overpayments of housing benefit and council tax benefit

Although this section refers mainly to housing benefit (HB), the rules about recovery of overpayments of council tax benefit (CTB) are generally the same. The references given cover both HB and CTB. See p1033 for the exceptions to the rules for CTB.

If you have been overpaid income support (IS) or income-based jobseeker's allowance (JSA) you may also have been overpaid HB. This is because your automatic passport to maximum HB ceases when you are no longer entitled to IS or income-based JSA. If you are in this situation, you should inform the local authority dealing with your HB claim.

To see from whom an overpayment can be recovered, see p1025.

What is an overpayment

An **'overpayment'** is an amount of HB which has been paid, and to which the local authority later decides you were not entitled under the HB rules.[98] Being **'paid'** includes payment to you, your landlord or somebody else, and also includes HB credited to your local authority rent account (see p214).[99]

Arrears of benefits and tax credits

In general, if you are paid arrears of income, including **benefit** income, this is treated as if the income was paid at the time when it was due, and this may lead to a decision that you have been overpaid HB.[100] However, remember that arrears of some benefits are treated as capital and ignored for 52 weeks (see p858).

Arrears of **tax credits** are treated as capital.[101] They are ignored as capital for 52 weeks (see pp921 and 940).

If your arrears are treated as capital, unless the arrears mean your capital is increased above a relevant capital limit (see p910), you will not have been overpaid HB.

When an overpayment can be recovered

An overpayment can only be recovered if the local authority has taken the following five steps. It must:

- decide whether the overpayment is legally recoverable (see below);
- decide from whom recovery of the overpayment can be made, and whether recovery should actually be made (see p1025);
- work out how much of the overpayment is repayable and for what period (see p1027);
- decide how the overpayment should be recovered and at what rate (see p1028);
- notify you of all the above decisions regarding the overpayment (see p1031) and give you an opportunity to request further information or a review (see p208).

Step one: is the overpayment recoverable?

The general rule is that all overpayments of HB are recoverable except, in certain circumstances, those caused by 'official error' (see p1023). However, some overpayments are always recoverable (see p1023). An overpayment may be recoverable even if it was caused by an innocent mistake on your part or was somebody else's fault. Remember that in most cases, the local authority has the discretion to decide whether or not to recover an overpayment (see p1028).

For the differences for overpayments of CTB, see p1033.

Overpayments that are always recoverable

There are two types of overpayments that are always recoverable:

- an overpayment that is the result of the local authority overestimating your HB when making an interim payment (see p217). When the local authority decides how much HB you should actually get, it is obliged to recover any excess you were paid from future HB payments.[102] However, if you stop getting HB before the local authority decides, this rule does not apply. In this case, the overpayment can only be recovered under the other rules described in this section;
- an overpayment of HB relating to a future payment is credited to your rent account. In this case, the overpayment can be recovered even if it was made as a result of an 'official error' (see below).[103] If an overpayment of HB caused by an official error has been credited to your account for a *past* period, see below to find out if it is recoverable.

Overpayments caused by official error

Overpayments that do not fall into the above category are not recoverable if you can show that:[104]

- the overpayment was caused by an official error (see below); *and*
- no 'relevant person' caused the official error to be made (see p1024); *and*
- no relevant person could reasonably be expected to have realised that an overpayment was being made (see p1025).

An **'official error'** is defined as a mistake, whether in the form of an act or omission, by:

- the appropriate authority; *or*
- an officer of the authority; *or*
- a person acting for that authority. This would include a person employed by a private organisation providing services to the local authority or to a ONE office (although those offices ceased to exist from April 2007); *or*
- an officer of the DWP or the Revenue acting as such.[105]

It therefore includes:

- a mistake made by the local authority in calculating your entitlement;
- a failure by the local authority to reduce your HB when you inform it of a change of circumstances. It is always best to notify changes in writing and keep a copy. If you notify the local authority by telephone there may be a dispute about whether you actually called or what you said. In such disputes, what you

say should not be rejected solely on the evidence of local authority recording procedures, unless it is accepted that those procedures are infallible;[106]
- a failure by an officer of another department of the local authority, such as a social worker, to pass on details of a change of circumstances, where s/he has promised to do so. This is an official error because the definition does not require the mistake to be made by an officer in the department handling HB. A mistake by any local authority officer will be an official error if it results in an overpayment;
- similar mistakes by somebody carrying out functions relating to HB on behalf of the local authority – eg, a private agency to whom work has been contracted;
- a mistake made by the DWP in calculating your entitlement to IS or income-based JSA which results in an incorrect calculation of your entitlement to HB. However, it is not an official error for the local authority to fail to check with the DWP about the correctness of your IS or income-based JSA entitlement, unless it has information that shows the award is wrong or fraudulent;[107]
- a failure by the DWP to pass on information to the local authority;[108]
- incorrect advice given to you by an officer of the local authority, the DWP or the Revenue, provided that s/he is acting as an officer at the time (rather than, say, as a friend giving you informal advice).

The list above is not exhaustive. The official error does not have to be the sole cause of the overpayment. However, even if an official error has occurred, if the primary cause of the overpayment was something that you did or failed to do, the overpayment is likely to be recoverable.[109]

No relevant person caused the official error

An official error does not prevent the overpayment being recoverable if the error was partially or wholly caused by a 'relevant person'. You are a relevant person if you are:
- the HB claimant; *or*
- a person acting on the HB claimant's behalf, whether because s/he is unable to deal with her/his affairs or because s/he has asked the authority in writing to deal with you on her/his behalf; *or*
- a person to whom the payment was made, including a different person acting on the HB claimant's behalf or a landlord.

The relevant person must have caused the *error*, not the overpayment.[110]

The local authority might say it only needs to show that *any* relevant person caused the official error but it does not have to pursue that person for the overpayment.[111] If the local authority tries to recover an overpayment from you but it was another person who caused the official error, you should argue that recovery must be sought from the person causing the official error. You could also argue that the authority should exercise its discretion to recover from that person instead. See below for information about who overpayments can be recovered from.

No one realised an overpayment was being made

Even if the official error was not caused by a relevant person, an overpayment is still recoverable if any relevant person (see p1024) knew, or ought reasonably to have known, that an overpayment had been made. The test is whether or not you could reasonably have been be expected to *know* (not merely suspect) that an overpayment had occured. Much depends on what could reasonably have been expected of you given the information available to you, in particular the extent to which the local authority has advised you about the scheme or your duties and obligations, particularly about your duty to notify changes of circumstances.[112] You should always argue that, as a claimant, you cannot be expected to know the intricacies of the HB rules and that, unless it was glaringly obvious a change of circumstances would reduce your HB, you should be given the benefit of the doubt.

If you or some other 'relevant person' could only have realised that there was an overpayment at some point during the period of the overpayment, the overpayment is only recoverable from that date.

Step two: from whom can the overpayment be recovered?

General rules

The general rule is that a recoverable overpayment (not all overpayments are recoverable – see p1023) can be recovered from the person to whom it was paid – eg, you, the claimant.[113]

An overpayment can also be recovered from someone other than the person to whom it was paid, including you as the claimant. This applies if:[114]

- the overpayment was caused by misrepresentation or failure to disclose a material fact (these are not specifically defined for HB/CTB, but are likely to be the same as for ordinary overpayments – see p1006). In this case it must be recovered from the person who misrepresented or failed to disclose the fact *instead of* the person to whom it was paid; *or*
- the overpayment was caused by an official error (see p1023) and you as the claimant (or someone acting your behalf) or any other person to whom the HB was paid could reasonably have been expected to have realised that there was an overpayment at the time. In this case it must be recovered from whoever should have so realised *instead of* the person to whom it was paid; *or*
- neither of the above two bullet points apply, in which case the overpayment is also recoverable from the claimant. In such a case, the overpayment *may* be recovered from you as the claimant *as well as* the person to whom it was paid. (In such cases, it can also be recovered from your partner, although in practice it would be recovered from you before your partner.)

If you think you have been wrongly chosen under these rules (eg, because you did not fail to disclose a material fact) you can appeal to an appeal tribunal. But if the overpayment *can* be recovered from you under these rules, you cannot appeal simply because you think the local authority should recover from another liable person instead.[115]

In the event of the death of the person from whom recovery is being sought, local authorities may consider recovering any outstanding overpayment from that person's estate.[116]

For the differences for overpayments of CTB, see p1033.

Recovery from your landlord

If a recoverable overpayment has been paid to your landlord, in general s/he can be required to pay it back, as s/he is the person to whom the overpayment was made. Where your benefit has been calculated using the local housing allowance, your landlord cannot be required to pay back more than s/he actually received – so any amount above that may be recoverable from you.[117]

However, it can be recovered from another person, including you as the claimant, in certain circumstances (see p1025). In any case, the overpayment *cannot* be recovered from your landlord if:[118]

- s/he was receiving the payment; *and*
- s/he wrote to the local authority notifying it of the possible overpayment; *and*
- it appears to the local authority that the overpayment was not caused by you ceasing to live in the property as your home; *and*
- it appears to the local authority that either there are grounds for action to be taken for fraud (see p1044) or that the overpayment was caused by a deliberate failure to report a relevant change of circumstances; *and*
- s/he has not colluded with you (ie, the claimant) or otherwise contributed to the overpayment.

The local authority's discretion to recover

Apart from certain interim payments of HB on account (see p217), the local authority has a discretion whether to recover an overpayment, even where the law says it can do so.[119] However, the decision to recover an overpayment does not carry the right of appeal. A policy of always recovering all recoverable overpayments could be challenged by judicial review (see p1129). If you have been overpaid and you think the overpayment might not be recoverable from you, you should consider challenging the decision either by asking for a revision (see Chapter 41) or making an appeal (see Chapter 42). Remember that even if the decision does prove to be recoverable from you, you can still ask the local authority not to recover the overpayment, especially if recovery would cause you hardship.

If the overpayment was caused by someone else, you could suggest that recovery is made from her/him (but where this is your landlord, see p1032).

You may be asked to repay a non-recoverable overpayment on a voluntary basis. You are under no legal obligation to do so.

Step three: how much is repayable and for what period?

Check the amount of an overpayment to ensure the local authority has calculated it correctly. The local authority should distinguish between parts of an overpayment that are recoverable and those that are not. To calculate the amount of the overpayment, it should:

- determine the dates between which you have been paid too much benefit;
- identify the period or periods over which the local authority is entitled to recover;
- work out the total amount of HB you were paid over the period(s) during which the local authority can recover;
- work out the correct amount of HB you should have received during the period(s) of the overpayment. The local authority must award you whatever amount of HB you would have received if it had been aware of your true circumstances (this applies even if the overpayment occured before the rules were changed in October 2000). If necessary, it should ask you for any necessary information or evidence to do this. However, the local authority does not include a change of your address when doing this;[120]
- deduct the HB you should have been paid from what you were paid.[121]

The authority is not allowed to add any interest charges to the amount of the overpayment.[122]

For the differences for overpayments of CTB, see p1033.

Deductions from the overpayment

Besides any amount of HB which you should have been paid (see above), the local authority must deduct other amounts from the overpayment (this is known as 'offsetting'). These are:

- extra rent paid into your rent account. If you have been getting HB during the overpayment period and, for some reason, have paid more into your rent account than you should have paid according to your original (incorrect) benefit assessment, the extra rent you paid can be deducted from any overpayment made during that period. The local authority might not apply this rule where you paid extra rent to repay rent arrears;[123]
- reductions under the 'diminishing capital rule' (see below).

You are not entitled to have other amounts deducted.

If you were overpaid HB because you had too much capital, the overpayment is calculated taking into account the fact that had you received no HB, you would have used your capital. This is known as the '**diminishing capital rule**'. This only applies if:[124]

- you were overpaid for more than 13 weeks; *and either*
- the overpayment was caused by a misrepresentation of or a failure to disclose the amount of your capital (see p1009 for the meaning of 'misrepresentation' and 'failure to disclose'); *or*
- the overpayment was caused by an error (other than an 'official error' – see p1023) about your capital (or that of a member of your family – see p700).

For each 13-week period, the local authority assumes that your capital is reduced by the amount of overpaid HB.[125] However, although your capital is treated as reducing for these purposes, if you reclaim benefit your full capital counts (see p911).

Step four: how is the overpayment recovered?

A local authority can decide how much of a recoverable overpayment it will actually recover. It can ask for the whole amount at once or recover it by instalments. When an overpayment is recovered from your landlord, you should take careful note of how that affects your liability to pay rent (see p1032). Overpayments of HB can be recovered:

- from payments of HB (see below);
- from other benefits (see p1029);
- for local authority tenants only, by adjusting your rent account (see p1030);
- through the courts (see p1030).

The methods used by the authority and the rates of recovery should be consistent between groups of claimants. For example, council tenants should not be required to repay overpayments in a lump sum (ie, the whole overpayment is debited to their account), where private tenants can repay by instalment (eg, by weekly deductions made to their HB).

For the differences for overpayments of CTB, see p1033.

Recovery from payments of housing benefit

A local authority is entitled to recover an overpayment by deducting sums from HB payable to any person from whom an overpayment can be recovered (see p1025).[126] As well as yourself, this could be your partner (see p1029) or your landlord (see p1029). Deductions can be made from both future payments of HB and any arrears of HB that are owing.

Also, if you have moved home, your local authority may be able to recover an overpayment of HB from your previous home by altering the HB paid at your new home.

It can decide to do this if:[127]

- the overpayment occured after you moved; *and*
- the same local authority that paid you the overpayment is paying your HB at your new home.

In these circumstances, the local authority can deduct all the weekly HB for your new home to recover the overpayment, for however many weeks it was that you were overpaid at your previous home.

Recovery from your partner

If you were overpaid HB while you were a claimant, the local authority may recover an overpayment from payments of HB made to your partner but only if:[128]

- the overpayment was made to you, rather than to your landlord or someone acting on your behalf; *and*
- you and your partner were living in the same household (see p703) at the time of the overpayment *and* when the deduction is made. You must have been living together for the whole period of the overpayment, not just for part of it.

Recovery from a landlord

If you have been overpaid HB, the local authority may recover the overpayment from:

- HB paid to your landlord personally, as a claimant;[129]
- HB paid directly to your landlord on your behalf.[130] The notification of the overpayment (see p1031) should make it clear from whom the authority is recovering;
- HB paid directly to your landlord on behalf of other claimants.[131]

When HB is recovered from a landlord in this way, there are special rules on how this affects your liability to pay rent (see p1032).

The rate of recovery

The same weekly rates apply as those for IS and income-based JSA (see p1019).[132] They apply to future entitlement (but not to arrears owed to you). However, you may argue that the rate will cause you hardship and in your particular circumstances a lesser amount should be recovered. You should also ask the local authority to take into account any other debts, financial commitments or health problems you may have.[133] Complain if the rate of recovery is causing you hardship and suggest an amount you think you can afford.

Recovery from other benefits

The local authority can ask the DWP to recover an overpayment by making deductions from most of the benefits in this *Handbook (except* guardian's allowance).[134] Overpayments of HB cannot be recovered by deductions from CTB (and vice versa).[135]

An overpayment can also be recovered from benefits paid to your landlord personally.[136]

Deductions can only be made if:[137]

- a recoverable overpayment has been made as a result of a misrepresentation or failure to disclose (see p1009) a material fact by you, on your behalf or by or on behalf of some other person to whom HB has been paid; *and*
- the local authority is unable to recover that overpayment from any HB entitlement; *and*
- the person who misrepresented or failed to disclose is receiving enough of at least one of the relevant benefits to allow deductions to be made.

There are no rules limiting the maximum amount that can be deducted. However, you can argue that your rate of repayment should be reasonable. If you are on IS or income-based JSA, you should argue that the weekly maximums for those benefits should apply (see p1019). You should make representations to the DWP if deductions cause hardship.

If deductions stop because you are no longer entitled to a particular benefit, or the amount to which you are entitled is insufficient for deductions to be made, the DWP notifies the local authority which, once again, becomes responsible for any further recovery action.

Adjustment of a rent account

If you are a local authority tenant, the local authority can recover an overpayment by adding it as a debt to your rent account. If a local authority recovers overpaid HB by adjusting your rent account, the overpayment should be separately identified and you should be informed that the amount being recovered does not represent rent arrears.[138]

If the local authority is seeking possession of your home on the grounds of rent arrears, you should obtain advice. It cannot argue you owe it rent arrears if you have only been overpaid HB. Local authorities are reminded in DWP guidance that overpayments of HB in respect of their own tenants are not rent arrears and should not be treated as such.[139]

An overpayment cannot be recovered in this way if you have a private or housing association landlord. However, an overpayment can be recovered from your landlord (see p1029). If the local authority recovers from your landlord, you might count as being in rent arrears (see p1012).

Court action

If a local authority cannot use any of the above methods of recovery and you cannot agree on repayments, it can try to recover the money you owe through the county court (sheriff's court in Scotland) if it thinks you could afford to make repayments. You have one month to ask for a revision or appeal against a decision that an overpayment is recoverable. This should be borne in mind when local authorities are deciding when to start proceedings.

A local authority should not use court proceedings to recover an overpayment if it has not followed the correct procedure (see p1022). The correct procedure has not been followed if, for example, the local authority has not issued the correct notification (see below).[140]

An authority may use one of two means of recovering through the courts. It can:

- sue you for the debt created by the overpayment.[141] If the correct procedure (see p1022) has not been followed, you can use this as a defence to the authority's claim.[142] You may also be able to claim compensation in certain circumstances (see p1022). However, you are not allowed to say that you should have received more HB – you must seek a review instead;[143]
- use the special rules to register the overpayment as a debt which can then be recovered using a court procedure.[144] Seek advice if you think the local authority is not entitled to do this.

If the local authority is successful in using court proceedings against you, you may have to pay legal costs and interest as well as the overpayment. Remember that court procedures often require you to take action within a very short period of time. If the local authority is threatening to use court proceedings, seek urgent advice.

Step five: notification of overpayments

If the local authority decides that a recoverable overpayment has occurred, it must write to the person from whom recovery is being sought (see p1025) within 14 days if possible, notifying her/him accordingly.[145] This notification must state:[146]

- the fact there is an overpayment that is legally recoverable;
- the reason why there is a recoverable overpayment;
- the amount of the recoverable overpayment;
- how the amount of the overpayment was calculated;
- the benefit weeks to which the overpayment relates;
- if recovery is to be made from future benefit, how much the deduction will be;
- if recovery is to be made from your landlord by deduction from direct payments of HB of a claimant other than you (if you were overpaid – see p1029), your identity and the claimant whose HB will be deducted;[147]
- that you have a right to ask for a further written explanation of any of the decisions the local authority has made regarding the overpayment, how you can do this and the time limit for doing so;
- that you have a right to ask the local authority to reconsider any of the decisions it has made regarding the overpayment, how you can do this and the time limit for doing so.

It may also include any other relevant matters. Local authorities have guidance that states they should issue a single notification to all relevant parties (eg, landlord and tenant) saying who the overpayment is recoverable from and who it is not.[148]

If you write and ask the local authority for a more detailed written explanation of any of the decisions it has made regarding an overpayment, it must send you this within 14 days or, if this is not reasonably practicable, as soon as possible after that.[149]

If a notification sent to you is a clear decision that there is an overpayment which is recoverable from you, but does not contain all of the matters set out in the bullets above, it will only be valid if the omissions do not put you at a disadvantage.[150] If, for example, it does not set out your rights to seek a revision so that you do not do so until it is too late, you will have been put at a disadvantage and so can argue that the overpayment is not recoverable. But if the decision is not about recoverability at all, and is only about the fact that you have been overpaid, then you can argue that there is no decision saying that you must repay the overpayment.[151]

If your local authority does not give proper notification, you should write and point out the decision to recover the overpayment is not valid until you are given proper notification. No recovery should be sought until after you have been notified and the one month time period for asking for a revision or appealing has passed.[152]

The effect of recovery from your landlord

If you are a private or housing association tenant, an overpayment of HB recovered from your landlord (see p1029) could leave your landlord claiming money from you. This could put you in difficulty, particularly if the landlord claims that you are in arrears of rent as a result and seeks possession of your home.

Whether HB was paid directly to your landlord or not, s/he may still try to claim that even if you owe no rent, you nevertheless owe a debt under common law, which is probably not correct. If s/he threatens to sue you, seek advice straight away.

If you are a local authority tenant, these rules do not apply. However, the local authority can recover an overpayment of HB by making deductions from your rent account. To see how these rules might affect you, see p1029.

If you were overpaid HB after 4 November 1997 and HB was paid directly to your landlord, the following rules apply.

- If you are overpaid, and the local authority recovers the overpayment from your landlord by making deductions from direct payments of **other tenants' HB** (see p1028), the other tenants are treated as having paid the amount of the deduction towards their rent.[153]
- If you are overpaid, and the local authority recovers the overpayment from your landlord by making deductions from direct payments of **your HB**, you are treated as having paid the amount of the deduction towards your rent if your landlord is convicted of an offence or agrees to pay a penalty (see p1050) in relation to that overpayment.[154]

If the local authority decides to recover under this rule, it must notify both your landlord and you that you are to be treated as having paid your rent.[155]

In these situations, it is clear that your landlord cannot claim that you are in arrears of rent. It is also much easier to argue that your landlord cannot sue you under common law for a debt (see p1031).

The law does not make clear what happens in other cases where deductions are made from your HB. If you are in this position you could try to argue that the rules do not say what happens in your case and so the same rules apply as before the law was introduced. If this is right, you should be treated as having paid your rent. However, because there is a risk of you losing your home if your landlord were to seek possession, you should seek advice *immediately*.

If you were overpaid HB before 4 November 1997, see the different rules on pp1119–20 of the *Welfare Benefits Handbook* 2000/01 and seek advice.

Challenging an overpayment decision

You can seek a revision or appeal (see Chapters 41 and 42) if you want to dispute:

- the decision that you have been overpaid;
- the amount of the overpayment;
- the decision that it is a recoverable overpayment;
- that the overpayment is to be recovered from you under the rules set out on p1025 – ie, on the grounds that those rules do not allow recovery from you.

Do not pay back any of the money until your challenge has been dealt with. Local authority guidances states that overpayments should not be recovered while under appeal.[156] If the local authority is already making deductions from your HB (see p1027) or deductions are being made from your other benefits (see p1029) you should ask it to stop this straight away.

If the local authority thinks an overpayment was made because of fraud, as well as recovering the overpayment it can prosecute you or offer you the option of paying a penalty as an alternative to going to court. You should seek advice before agreeing to pay. See Chapter 40 for further information.

Overpayments of council tax benefit

An overpayment of council tax benefit (CTB) is called **'excess benefit'**.[157] The rules about recovery are the same as for housing benefit (HB) (see p1021), with the following exceptions.

Is the overpayment recoverable?

The criteria for when an overpayment is recoverable are the same as for HB (see p1021), except that the following are always recoverable:

- an overpayment of CTB credited to your council tax account that relates to a future period, even if it was made as a result of an 'official error' (see p1023);[158]

- an overpayment that has arisen because you were paid CTB, but then your council tax liability was reduced because of a disability reduction, discount, transitional relief or charge-capping;[159]
- an overpayment that results from the local authority changing the levels of council tax for the financial year.[160]

The amount of the overpayment

The amount overpaid is the difference between what you were actually paid and what you should have received. However, there are two possible variations of what should have been paid – either a reduced amount of main CTB (see p81), or a second adult rebate (see p81) if you are eligible for this and it would have been higher than the revised amount of main CTB.

When assessing the amount overpaid, the local authority should do both calculations (see pp84 and 89) and can only recover the balance between the higher of the two figures and the amount which you in fact received. It is always worth checking that the second adult rebate calculation has been done and that the correct amount is being recovered.

From whom benefit can be recovered?

Recovery of a CTB overpayment is always from the CTB claimant or the person to whom benefit was paid – eg, your partner or an appointee. There can be no recovery from any other person, even if s/he caused the overpayment.[161]

CTB is recoverable by the same methods as HB (see p1027), except that:

- the overpayment can be recovered by increasing your outstanding council tax liability;[162]
- there are no limits for the maximum amount of CTB that can be recovered in each week;[163]
- the local authority cannot use the special court procedures for recovering the overpayment (see p1030). If it wishes to recover through the courts, it must sue you instead. It may not start proceedings for 21 days after it notifies you of the amount due.[164]

Notes

1. **Ordinary overpayments of benefits**

1 paras 8 and 9 *Social Fund Bulletin* 17/98, 9 September 1998
2 *Plewa v CAO* [1995] 1 AC 248 (HL)
3 s71(3) SSAA 1992
4 *B v Secretary of State for Work and Pensions* [2005], EWCA Civ 929, reported as R(IS) 9/06, which says that overpayments for failure to disclose are actually recoverable because of a breach of duty by a claimant of reg 32 SS(C&P) Regs; CIS/1996/2006; CIS/2125/2006
5 CIS/2178/2001. This tribunal of commissioners' decision was intended to resolve the conflict between the earlier CIS/332/1993 and R(IS) 5/2000, and preferred the latter.
6 CA/1014/1999; CSDLA/1282/2001
7 *Secretary of State for Social Services v Solly* [1974] 3 All ER 922; R(SB) 21/82
8 CIS/1423/1997
9 s71 SSAA 1992
10 R(SB) 34/83
11 s71(5A) SSAA 1992; CIS/3228/2003; R(IS) 13/05. See CPC/3743/2006 for where not all the overpayment period has been covered by the change of the award.
12 R(SB) 7/91
13 CSIS/45/1990
14 R(SB) 7/91; R(IS) 13/05. But see CIS/3228/2003 in cases where a decision changing the award is defective but has been certified.
15 s71A SSAA 1992
16 Sch 2 para 1 SSA 1998
17 s38(1)(b) SSA 1998
18 Reg 32 SS(C&P) Regs; reg 24 JSA Regs
19 *Page and Davis v CAO, The Times*, 4 July 1991 (CA)
20 CSB/1006/1985
21 CDLA/5803/1999
22 CDLA/1823/2004
23 R(S) 4/86; R(I) 3/75
24 R(SB) 15/87; *Hinchy v Secretary of State for Work and Pensions*, 3 March 2005 (HL), reported as R(IS) 7/05
25 CIS/1887/2002
26 Reg 23(5) CB&GA(Admin) Regs
27 CIS/1887/2002
28 Reg 32(1B) SS(C&P) Regs requires notification in writing or by telephone, unless the DWP specifically requires otherwise.
29 R(SB) 18/85
30 CWSB/2/1985
31 CSB/347/1983; R(SB) 10/85
32 R(SB) 15/87
33 CDLA/6336/1999
34 R(SB) 15/87
35 R(SB) 54/83
36 CSB/393/1985
37 *B v Secretary of State for Work and Pensions* [2005] EWCA Civ 929, reported as R(IS) 9/06. The effect of the decison is that recovery is under reg 32 SS(C&P) Regs and, presumably, under the equivalent rules in reg 24 JSA Regs and reg 23 CB&GA(Admin) Regs
38 *Hooper v Secretary of State for Work and Pensions* [2007] EWCA Civ 495, reported as R(IB) 4/07. See also official guidance in Memo DMG 26/07.
39 CDLA/1823/2004; CDLA/2328/2006 suggests that a claimant's 'mental state' may be relevant.
40 R(IS) 13/05; CG/5631/1999; CG/2888/2000; CIS/1887/2002
41 R(SB) 21/82
42 R(SB) 54/83; CSB/296/1985
43 CG/190/1999
44 R(SB) 21/82
45 Reg 32(1B) SS(C&P) Regs; reg 24(7) JSA Regs; reg 23(4) CB&GA(Admin) Regs
46 CSB/510/1987; CIS/545/1992; CIS/1769/1999. However, these decisions arose from the old test of failure to disclose and it is not clear that they apply now.
47 CIS/5117/1998
48 R(SB) 9/85
49 *Jones and Sharples v CAO* [1994] 1 All ER 225 (CA); R(SB) 9/85
50 R(SB) 18/85
51 R(SB) 2/91
52 R(SB) 3/90
53 *Sheriff v CAO, The Times*, 10 May 1995 (CA), reported as R(IS) 14/96

54 CG/4494/1999 suggests the principle may apply in social security; R(IS) 4/06 is more doubtful but does not rule it out.
55 CIS/3846/2001
56 *Jones and Sharples v CAO* [1994] 1 All ER 225 (CA); *Franklin v CAO, The Times*, 29 December 1995 (CA); CIS/674/1994; CIS/583/1994
57 CIS/674/1994
58 This was an obiter (not binding) comment by the Court of Appeal in *Hinchy v Secretary of State for Work and Pensions* [2003] EWCA Civ 138 (CA). The point was not approved or disapproved by the further decision in *Hinchy v Secretary of State for Work and Pensions*, 3 March 2005 (HL), now reported as R(IS) 7/05
59 *Franklin v CAO, The Times*, 29 December 1995 (CA)
60 CIS/583/1994
61 CDLA/6336/1999
62 CIS/159/1990; CS/11700/1996; CSIS/7/1994; CG/5631/1999
63 *Duggan v CAO, The Times*, 18 December 1989 (CA); CG/662/1998; CG/4494/1999; *Hinchy v Secretary of State for Work and Pensions* [2003] EWCA Civ 138 (CA)
64 This was an obiter (not binding) comment by the Court of Appeal in *Hinchy v Secretary of State for Work and Pensions* [2003] EWCA Civ 138 (CA). It was not approved or disapproved by the House of Lords in *Hinchy v Secretary of State for Work and Pensions*, 3 March 2005 (HL), now reported as R(IS) 7/05
65 CIS/222/1991
66 Letter from DWP Corporate Customer Affairs to welfare rights organisations, 20 December 2007
67 R(SB) 20/84; R(SB) 24/87
68 Reg 43 CB&GA(Admin) Regs
69 Reg 13 SS(PAOR) Regs
70 R(IS) 5/92
71 *Commock v CAO*, reported as an appendix to R(SB) 6/90; CSIS/8/1995
72 Reg 14 SS(PAOR) Regs
73 CIS/5825/1999
74 s12 SSA 1998

2. **Late receipt of other income**
75 s74 SSAA 1992
76 R(SB) 3/91
77 See for example, the appeals in R(SB) 28/85 and R(IS) 6/02

3. **Excess benefit credited to your account**
78 s71(4) SSAA 1992; reg 11 SS(PAOR) Regs; reg 35 CB&GA(Admin) Regs
79 Reg 11 SS(PAOR) Regs; reg 35 CB&GA(Admin) Regs
80 Sch 2 para 20(d) SS&CS(DA) Regs

4. **Mortgage interest paid to a lender**
81 Sch 9A para 11 SS(C&P) Regs
82 *R v Secretary of State for Social Security ex parte Craigie* [2000] EWCA Civ 329, 15 December (CA)
83 *R v Secretary of State for Social Security ex parte Golding* [1996] 1 July, unreported (CA)
84 CIS/5206/1995
85 CIS/5206/1995

5. **Recovery of overpaid benefit**
86 Regs 15 and 16 SS(PAOR) Regs
87 Reg 17 SS(PAOR) Regs
88 s74(2)(b) SSAA 1992
89 Reg 16(4), (4A), (5) and (6) SS(PAOR) Regs
90 Reg 16(6) SS(PAOR) Regs
91 Reg 16(5A) SS(PAOR) Regs
92 There is no provision allowing this.
93 s71(10) SSAA 1992
94 Reg 16(3) SS(PAOR) Regs
95 See CPAG's *Welfare Rights Bulletin* 196, p6. At time of writing, CPAG was proceeding with court action against the DWP's approach.
96 *B v Secretary of State for Work and Pensions* [2005] EWCA Civ 929 reported as R(IS) 9/06
97 *Guide to Waiver* (DWP internal document). See the article in CPAG's *Welfare Rights Bulletin* 190 for details.

6. **Overpayments of housing benefit and council tax benefit**
98 **HB** Reg 99 HB Regs; reg 80 HB(SPC) Regs
CTB Reg 82 CTB Regs; reg 67 CTB(SPC) Regs
99 **HB** Reg 99 HB Regs; reg 80 HB(SPC) Regs
CTB Reg 82 CTB Regs; reg 67 CTB(SPC) Regs
100 **HB** Reg 79(7) HB Regs; reg 59(7) HB(SPC) Regs
CTB Reg 67(9) CTB Regs; reg 50(9) CTB(SPC) Regs
101 **HB** Reg 46(9) HB Regs; reg 44(3) HB(SPC) Regs
CTB Reg 36(9) CTB Regs; reg 34(3) CTB(SPC) Regs

102 Reg 93(3) HB Regs; reg 74(3) HB(SPC) Regs
103 Reg 100(4) HB Regs; reg 81(4) HB(SPC) Regs
104 **HB** Reg 100(2) HB Regs; reg 81(2) HB(SPC) Regs
CTB Reg 83(2) CTB Regs; reg 68(2) CTB(SPC) Regs
105 **HB** Reg 100(3) HB Regs; reg 81(3) HB(SPC) Regs
CTB Reg 83(3) CTB Regs; reg 68(3) CTB(SPC) Regs
106 CH/4065/2001
107 CH/571/2003. See also CH/5485/2002, which makes a similar finding.
108 CH/939/2004; see also *R on the application of Sier v Cambridge CC* [2001], unreported (QBD), as upheld by the Court of Appeal [2001] EWCA 1523, 8 October 2001; CH/3761/2005
109 *Duggan v CAO, The Times*, 18 December 1989 (CA); *R on the application of Sier v Cambridge CC* [2001], unreported (QBD), as upheld by the Court of Appeal [2001] EWCA 1523, 8 October 2001; CH/571/2003; CH/3761/2005
110 *R on the application of Sier v Cambridge CC* [2001] (QBD), as upheld by the Court of Appeal, [2001] EWCA 1523, 8 October 2001
111 *Warwick DC v Freeman* [1994] 27 HLR 616 (CA)
112 *R v Liverpool City Council ex parte Griffiths* [1990] 22 HLR 312; CH/2554/2002
113 s75(3)(a) SSAA 1992
114 Reg 101(2) HB Regs; reg 82(2) HB(SPC) Regs. See also the article in CPAG's *Welfare Rights Bulletin* 193, p4
115 RH 6/06
116 HB/CTB Overpayments Guide, para 4.115
117 Reg 101(2A) HB Regs; reg 82(2A) HB (SPC) Regs
118 Reg 101(1) HB Regs; reg 82(1) HB(SPC) Regs
119 **HB** s75(1) SSAA 1992
CTB Reg 84 CTB Regs; reg 69 CTB(SPC) Regs
120 **HB** Reg 104 HB Regs; reg 85 HB(SPC) Regs
CTB Reg 89 CTB Regs; reg 74 CTB(SPC) Regs
Both *Adan v London Borough of Hounslow and Secretary of State for Work and Pensions* [2004] EWCA Civ 101, 19 February 2004, reported as R(H) 5/04 (CA); CH/4943/2001; HB/CTB Circular A13/2006
121 **HB** Reg 104(1) HB Regs; reg 85 HB(SPC) Regs
CTB Reg 89(1) CTB Regs; reg 74 CTB(SPC) Regs
122 *R v Kensington and Chelsea RBC ex parte Brandt* [1995] 28 HLR 528 at 537 (QBD)
123 **HB** Reg 104(3) HB Regs; reg 85(3) HB(SPC) Regs
CTB Reg 89(3) CTB Regs; reg 74(3) CTB(SPC) Regs
124 **HB** Reg 103 HB Regs; reg 84 HB(SPC) Regs
CTB Reg 88(1) CTB Regs; reg 73 CTB(SPC) Regs
125 **HB** Reg 103(1)(a) and (b) HB Regs; reg 84(1)(a) and (b) HB(SPC) Regs
CTB Reg 88(1)(a) and (b) CTB Regs; reg 73 CTB(SPC) Regs
126 **HB** Reg 102 HB Regs; reg 83 HB(SPC) Regs
CTB Reg 86 CTB Regs; reg 71 CTB(SPC) Regs
Both s75 SSAA 1992
127 Reg 102(1A) HB Regs; reg 83(1A) HB(SPC) Regs
128 **HB** Reg 101(2) HB Regs; reg 82(2) HB(SPC) Regs
CTB Reg 85(2) CTB Regs; reg 70(2) CTB(SPC) Regs
129 s75(5)(a) SSAA 1992; reg 106 HB Regs; reg 87 HB(SPC) Regs
130 s75(5)(b) SSAA 1992; reg 106 HB Regs; reg 87 HB(SPC) Regs
131 s75(5)(c) SSAA 1992; reg 106 HB Regs; reg 87 HB(SPC) Regs
132 Reg 102 HB Regs; reg 83 HB(SPC) Regs; HB/CTB Circular A42/00
133 HB/CTB Overpayments Guide, para 4.281
134 Reg 105(1)(a) HB Regs
135 **HB** Reg 105 HB Regs; reg 86 HB(SPC) Regs
CTB Reg 90 CTB Regs; reg 75 CTB(SPC) Regs
136 s75(5)(a) SSAA 1992; reg 106 HB Regs; reg 87 HB(SPC) Regs
137 **HB** Regs 102 and 105 HB Regs; regs 83 and 86 HB(SPC) Regs
CTB Regs 86(3) and 90 CTB Regs; regs 71 and 75 CTB(SPC) Regs
138 *R v Haringey LBC ex parte Azad Ayub* [1992] 25 HLR 566 (QBD)
139 paras A7.360 GM
140 *Warwick DC v Freeman* [1994] 27 HLR 616 (CA)
141 Reg 87 CTB Regs; reg 72 CTB(SPC) Regs; para A7.361 GM

142 *Warwick DC v Freeman* [1994] 27 HLR 616 (CA)
143 *Plymouth CC v Gigg* [1997] 30 HLR 284 (CA)
144 s75(7) SSAA 1992
145 **HB** Reg 90(1)(b) HB Regs; reg 71(1)(b) HB(SPC) Regs
CTB Reg 76(1)(b) CTB Regs; reg 61 CTB(SPC) Regs
146 **HB** Sch 9 paras 2, 3, 6 and 15 HB Regs; Sch 8 paras 2, 3, 6 and 15 HB(SPC) Regs; para A7.222 GM
CTB Sch 8 paras 2, 3, 6 and 16 CTB Regs; Sch 7 paras 2, 3, 6 and 16 CTB (SPC) Regs
147 **HB** Sch 9 para 15 HB Regs; Sch 8 para 15 HB(SPC) Regs
CTB Sch 8 para 16 CTB Regs; Sch 7 para 16 CTB(SPC) Regs
148 HB/CTB Circular A13/2006
149 **HB** Reg 90(4) HB Regs; reg 71(4) HB(SPC) Regs
CTB Reg 76(2) and (3) CTB Regs; reg 61 CTB(SPC) Regs
150 *Haringey LBC v Awaritefe* [1999] 32 HLR 517 (CA)
151 CH/1395/2006
152 para A7.230-233 GM; HB/CTB Circular A13/2006
153 s75(6) SSAA 1992
154 s75(6) SSAA 1992; reg 107 HB Regs; reg 88 HB(SPC) Regs
155 Reg 107(3) HB Regs; reg 88(3) HB(SPC) Regs
156 HB/CTB Overpayments Guide, paras 4.07 and 6.25; HB/CTB Circular A13/2006
157 Reg 82 CTB Regs; reg 67 CTB(SPC) Regs
158 Reg 83(5) CTB Regs; reg 68 CTB(SPC) Regs
159 Regs 82(a) and 83(4) CTB Regs; regs 67(a) and 68(4) CTB(SPC) Regs
160 Regs 82(b) and 83(4) CTB Regs; regs 68(4) and 76(b) CTB(SPC) Regs
161 Reg 85(1) CTB Regs; reg 70(1) CTB(SPC) Regs
162 Reg 86(2)(b) CTB Regs; reg 71(2)(b) CTB(SPC) Regs
163 HB/CTB Circular A42/00
164 Reg 87 CTB Regs; reg 72 CTB(SPC) Regs

Chapter 40

Fraud

This chapter covers the rules about fraud. It contains:

Child benefit and guardian's allowance

The Revenue makes decisions about child benefit and guardian's allowance as well as tax credits. However, references to the Revenue in this chapter only apply to decisions about child benefit and guardian's allowance. For information about tax credit and fraud, see Chapter 56.

When you claim benefit you must give correct and complete information to the DWP, the Revenue or local authority. You might commit an offence if you deliberately mislead them. You are also required to report changes in your circumstances that could affect your entitlement to benefit. You might commit an offence if you fail to notify the relevant office of such changes promptly, or cause or allow another person to fail to do so. These offences are referred to as 'fraud' in this chapter.

If the DWP, the Revenue or the local authority believe you have committed fraud:

- you may be at risk of being prosecuted (see p1044);
- your benefit could be reduced or removed if you are prosecuted for committing an offence twice within a three-year period (see p1047);
- you might be given the option of paying a penalty instead of being taken to court (see p1050);
- for benefits dealt with by the DWP you may be given the option of accepting a formal caution (see p1052).

If you are accused of fraud you should seek urgent advice before taking any action or making any statements.

This chapter does *not* cover:
- child tax credit or working tax credit (for these, see Chapter 56); *or*
- statutory sick pay, statutory maternity pay, statutory paternity pay or statutory adoption pay; *or*
- the benefits in Chapter 9 .

1. Investigating claims

The DWP, the Revenue or local authority may start an investigation into your benefit claim for a variety of reasons. It does not have to tell you straight away about the enquiries it is making. It normally waits until it has gathered more information and then asks you to attend an interview to explain matters.

Powers to seek information

The DWP and the Revenue can seek information from:
- tax authorities;[1]
- government departments (this provision relates in particular to issues about passports, immigration, emigration, nationality and prisoners);[2]
- the Registration Service, which is under an additional duty to report particulars of deaths to the Secretary of State for social security purposes;[3]
- local authorities.[4]

Local authorities have no specific powers to seek information from the above bodies themselves but may be supplied with any information held by the DWP or the Revenue.[5]

Local authorities, the Revenue and the DWP can require information about redirected post and have undelivered social security post returned to them.[6]

All information gathered is confidential to the bodies concerned with administration of benefit, including private companies contracted to carry out such functions. Unauthorised disclosure of such information is a criminal offence.[7]

The **Data Protection Act 1998** restricts the use of accessible personal data held on computer or in a relevant filing system in written form. The DWP has a code of practice for data matching which applies to all information held or sought by it.[8] If local authorities, the Revenue or the DWP make a request for information based on either the information-seeking provisions above, or the investigative powers on p1041, which is inappropriate or unreasonable, the matter can be referred to the Information Commissioner. The Data Protection Act covers written records but most manual data which was held in a relevant filing system before 24 October 1998 was exempted from full compliance until 2007.

Powers of investigation

The Secretary of State can appoint 'authorised officers' to investigate possible benefit fraud.[9] Authorised officers have certain special powers to obtain information.[10] Where an investigation into housing benefit (HB) or council tax benefit (CTB) fraud by an authorised officer has begun, local authorities also have the power to investigate fraudulent claims for income support, jobseeker's allowance, incapacity benefit, pension credit and (when it is introduced) employment and support allowance. Local authorities in England and Wales also have the discretion to prosecute offences concerning these benefits (as well as HB and CTB).[11]

'Authorised officers' can be:

- officials of any government department (not just the DWP or the Revenue);
- employees of local authorities carrying out HB or CTB functions; *or*
- employees of organisations that perform contracted-out HB and CTB functions.

Authorised officers can carry out investigations, enter premises and require information and documents for the 'authorised purpose'[12] of:

- establishing whether benefit is or was payable in a particular case;
- investigating the circumstances of an accident, injury or disease which may give rise to a claim for industrial injury or other benefit in a particular case;
- ascertaining whether social security provisions are or were being contravened;
- preventing, detecting or gathering evidence about social security offences.

The first two purposes above relate to individual claimants and claims, but the second two apply to cases 'whether by particular persons or more generally'. Therefore, investigators can require employers to produce classes of information, such as lists of employees and wages. However, information sought in connection with fraud investigation must be 'reasonably required'.

Authorised officers can write to the following (including by email) to obtain any information or documents they reasonably suspect them to hold and which the officer 'reasonably requires' for an 'authorised purpose':[13]

- employers and employees;
- self-employed earners;
- people running agencies offering goods or services through people other than their own employees;
- local authorities acting as grantors of any licence;
- trustees or managers of pension schemes;
- people liable to make compensation payments.

Under these provisions, authorised officers can require people to make copies of documents or extracts of such, or to create documents, such as lists of casual staff, where no such documents currently exist.

For the purpose of obtaining information about specified individuals, authorised officers can also require information from:[14]

- banks and the Director of National Savings;
- credit providers;
- insurance companies;
- credit reference agencies;
- fraud agencies;
- money transfer businesses;
- water or sewerage authorities;
- gas and electricity suppliers and distributors;
- telecommunication services;
- educational establishments and bodies that deal with admissions to such establishments;
- student loans companies; *or*
- any servant or agent of any of the above.

Authorised officers should have regard to a Code of Practice when obtaining information from any of the above.[15] No information can be requested that is the subject of 'legal privilege' – ie, confidential communications between a legal adviser and her/his client for the purpose of giving or receiving legal advice.[16]

The information must be required because it is suspected that a person has committed, is committing or is going to commit a benefit offence, or is the family member of such a person (see p700 for who counts as your family).[17] If any of the bodies listed above keep electronic records, they can be required to allow an authorised officer access to them.[18]

Although, in general, information must relate to specific people identified by name or description, authorised officers can:

- require the water, electricity and gas suppliers and distributors to provide information about whether, and in what quantities, these services are being or have been supplied to specified residential premises;[19]
- require information from telecommunications companies about the subscriber's use of that service, as well as any other information held about her/him. The actual contents of any communications are excluded from investigation (eg, phone tapping is not permitted), as is identifying the person, apparatus and location to or from which a communication is sent.[20] However, information can be required from a telecommunication service about the identity and postal address of a person identified solely by reference to a phone number or electronic address.[21]

Authorised officers have powers to enter, at a reasonable time, places which they have reasonable grounds for suspecting are premises:[22]

- which are a person's place of employment;
- where a trade or business is carried out;

- where documents relating to a business are kept;
- where someone operating a compensatory scheme may be found;
- where a person on whose behalf a compensatory payment may be made can be found.

This may include someone's home. The authorised officer must show a certificate of appointment if asked for it and enter only at a 'reasonable time'. S/he can interview anyone on the premises, and require, if reasonable, any documents or copies of documents.

Authorised officers can use ongoing surveillance to investigate social security fraud (eg, observing people entering or leaving premises). Any surveillance must be authorised by an officer of the appropriate level. Authorisation is only given where surveillance is necessary for the purposes of preventing or detecting crime and where the authorised surveillance activity is proportionate to the outcome the investigator is seeking to achieve.[23]

Authorised officers cannot come into your home without your permission (except if your home is also where you run a business – see above) and they cannot detain you. They cannot make you give information or answer questions in such a way as to confess that you, or your spouse/civil partner, are guilty of an offence.[24]

Fraud investigators are 'persons charged with the duty of investigating offences or charging offenders' and are, therefore, bound by codes of practice under the Police and Criminal Evidence Act 1984.[25] If the codes are breached, this may restrict the use of evidence they have obtained.[26] If you think the officers have acted unfairly, you should seek advice.

Interviews

During investigations, fraud investigators may carry out fact-finding interviews to gather information. If you are suspected of fraud, officers should carry out a formal interview, known as an 'interview under caution'. You should always be cautioned before the interview if there are grounds to suspect that you have committed an offence. If the authorised officer fails to do so, the interview may not be admissible in court. If you do not understand the caution, its meaning should be explained to you.

You do not have to answer any questions put to you, but if you fail to answer questions after you have been cautioned this might be taken as a sign of guilt. If you are interviewed under caution, you may make a written statement if you wish to explain matters further.

You might not be told why the interview is happening. Failure to inform claimants of the purpose of a fraud interview has occasionally been successfully challenged in the courts as an attempt to mislead suspects into admitting an offence before realising the possibility of prosecution. Although not a breach of the codes of practice, it may result in an unfairness and a court may rule that the interview is inadmissible as evidence. The DWP issued guidance to local authority fraud officers suggesting that all letters inviting claimants to interviews under caution should broadly state why an interview is being held and the possibility of criminal prosecution.[27]

If you think fraud officers may interview you, you should seek advice before you attend the interview. Free legal advice may be available from a solicitor. Try to take someone (eg, a solicitor, adviser or friend) to the interview with you. Although they cannot speak for you, they can support you and take notes. Although it can be very distressing to be accused of committing an offence, remain calm and listen carefully to the questions you are asked. If you do not understand anything, ask for clarification. You must answer the questions yourself. Think carefully about the implications of the answers you give.

If you think you can explain why the situation has arisen, you should probably do so, since if you do not mention it at the interview your explanation is less likely to be believed if you are prosecuted.[28] In addition, if you are able to explain matters, your benefit is less likely to be taken away (see p1053). However, do not confess to something that you did not do just to finish the interview or to try to prevent your benefit being stopped.

A formal interview is either taped or someone writes down what you say. You should be asked to read through the notes of the interview afterwards and sign that they are accurate. It is important to check them carefully and challenge anything you think is wrong, since it may be difficult to do so later. If you do not have anyone with you at the interview, try to write down shortly afterwards as much as you can remember about what was said because it may be difficult to remember later.

2. **Prosecution of offences**

Benefit offences can broadly be divided into two categories, based on the severity of the penalty that you can potentially be given. For information about:

- false representations for claiming benefit, see below; *and*
- dishonest representations for claiming benefit, see p1046.

In addition, you can also be charged with offences under the Theft Act 1968.[29]

If you are found guilty of the offence of false representations or dishonest representations, you can be fined or imprisoned, or both. The maximum fine is £5,000, but can be smaller. Any fine that you have to pay is in addition to any overpayment that is found to be recoverable from you (see Chapter 39).

False representations for claiming benefit

False representations for claiming benefit are considered to be the less serious of the benefit offences. You commit these offences if you:

- for the purpose of claiming a benefit or payment for yourself or someone else or for any other purpose relating to the benefit rules:[30]
  - make a statement which you know to be false; *or*
  - give information or produce documents that you know to be false (or knowingly cause or allow someone else to do so).

  It does not have to be shown that you intended to obtain benefit to which you were not entitled;[31]
- fail to notify the DWP, the Revenue or local authority promptly of a change of circumstances which you are required to notify and which you know affects your entitlement to benefit or other payment.[32] This also applies to appointees and other third parties receiving benefit on your behalf. You count as notifying a change promptly if you do so as soon as reasonably practicable after the change occurs;[33]
- cause or allow another person to fail to notify a change of circumstances to the DWP, the Revenue or local authority promptly which is required to be notified and which you know affects her/his entitlement to benefit or other payment.[34]

You do not 'know' something if you are merely careless about whether or not something is true, or if you fail to find out.[35] You will not have committed an offence if you fail to notify a change of circumstance that did not affect your entitlement to benefit.[36] The maximum penalty for these offences is a £5,000 fine or three months in prison, or both.[37]

Duty to report a change in circumstances

The DWP/Revenue should inform you of the main kinds of changes in your circumstances that you need to report but might not actually list them all. In any case, it is your duty to report *any* change in your circumstances which you might reasonably be expected to know might affect your right to, the amount of, or the payment of your benefit.[38] You will only be liable of committing an offence if you fail to report a change which you know affects benefit, but, in order to avoid potential allegations of fraud or prosecution, you should report all changes promptly and in writing or by telephone (for housing benefit and council tax benefit, you must report changes in writing[39]).

In individual cases, notification in a form other than in writing or by telephone may be accepted. However, it will usually be best to notify changes in writing and to keep a copy of your letter.

Advisers and other third parties

The offences of allowing or causing a claimant to fail to notify a change of circumstances or knowingly allowing or causing someone to give false information do not place any additional duty on advisers to notify the DWP, the Revenue or local authority of a claimant's change of circumstances. In order for an offence to be committed there must be some sort of implied permission given to the person, under a duty to notify or to give information, not to do so.[40] You do not 'allow' somebody to do something unless you are able to stop them doing it. If you are an adviser you should not be liable if you have advised your client fully of the law and the requirement to notify a change of circumstances and provide truthful information. You should do nothing to help facilitate a misrepresentation or failure to notify a change of circumstances (eg, help complete a claim or review form which you know is inaccurate).

Dishonest representations for claiming benefit

Dishonest representations for claiming benefit are considered to be the more serious of the benefit offences. You commit these offences if you commit any of the acts subject to the offence of false representations for claiming benefit (see p1044) and you act dishonestly ('knowingly' in Scotland) in doing so.[41] This means that in committing the offence you do something that most people would consider dishonest and that you must have known this was dishonest.[42]

The maximum penalty for these offences if you are convicted in a magistrates' court is a £5,000 fine or six months in prison, or both. If you are convicted in the Crown Court, you can receive an unlimited fine, or seven years in prison, or both.[43]

Will you be prosecuted?

Not all cases where there is evidence to justify a prosecution are taken to court. In some cases you may be given the chance to pay a penalty (see p1050) or accept a formal caution instead (see p1052). In some cases no fraud action is taken at all. The factors taken into account include the strength of the evidence, the amount of benefit involved, whether an offence was planned and your personal circumstances.

There are time limits for prosecutions of the offences of false representations for claiming benefit (see p1044). A prosecution must be started either within three months of the date the DWP, the Revenue or local authority (or in Scotland the Procuator Fiscal) thinks it has enough evidence to prosecute you, or within 12 months of the date you committed the offence, whichever is later.[44]

Prosecutions of the offences of dishonest representations for claiming benefit (see above) may be started at any time.

What to do if you are prosecuted

The most important thing to do if you are prosecuted is to get advice. You may be entitled to free legal help from a solicitor and representation in court. You should check carefully that the DWP, the Revenue or local authority is able to prove all the parts of the offence with which you are charged. Do not plead guilty until you have obtained advice.

3. Loss of benefit for benefit offences

You can have sanctions imposed on certain benefits known as 'sanctionable' benefits (see below) if:[45]

- you are convicted of one or more benefit offences (see p1044) in two separate sets of proceedings; *and*
- the later offence occurs within three years of the date on which you were first convicted of an offence (this period is expected to increase from three to five years.[46] See CPAG's *Welfare Rights Bulletin* for updates); *and*
- those offences have not previously been taken into account.

The DWP sometimes refers to this as the 'two strikes' rule.

The benefit offence must have been committed after 1 April 2002:[47]

- in connection with a claim for a 'disqualifying' benefit (see below); *or*
- in connection with the receipt or payment of an amount of a 'disqualifying' benefit; *or*
- for the purpose of facilitating the commission (whether or not by the same person) of a benefit offence; *or*
- having consisted of an attempt or conspiracy to commit a benefit offence.

Disqualifying benefits

All social security benefits (including pension credit – PC) as well as war pensions are 'disqualifying' benefits for the purposes listed above, except statutory sick pay, statutory maternity pay and maternity allowance.[48]

Sanctionable benefits

Sanctions can be imposed on sanctionable benefits. These are all the disqualifying benefits except retirement pension, graduated retirement benefit, disability living allowance, attendance allowance, child benefit, guardian's allowance, constant attendance allowance, exceptionally severe disablement allowance, mobility supplement, social fund payments, Christmas bonus and bereavement payments.[49] Joint-claim jobseeker's allowance (JSA) is also not a sanctionable benefit. However, it can still be removed or reduced (see below).[50]

The sanctions

If the 'loss of benefit for benefit offences' rules apply, sanctionable benefits are not paid during the sanction period unless the benefit is income support (IS), income-based JSA, joint-claim JSA, PC, housing benefit (HB) or council tax benefit (CTB).[51] These benefits are instead paid at a reduced rate during the sanction period in some circumstances (see below).

The **sanction period** is 13 weeks and can be applied to any benefit claim for a sanctionable benefit within a three-year period following the later conviction.[52]

While benefits are sanctioned, an underlying entitlement remains in place to ensure the link between benefits and other entitlements (eg, free school meals and free prescriptions) remains.

Income support

IS is paid at a reduced rate during the sanction period if you or a member of your family (see p700) are the benefit offender.[53] The reduction is 20 per cent of the appropriate IS personal allowance for a single person of the offender's age (see p773) if you or a member of your family are pregnant or seriously ill, or the offender's IS has already been reduced while s/he is appealing against a decision that s/he is capable of work under the personal capability assessment (see p293). In all other cases, the reduction is 40 per cent of the appropriate IS personal allowance for a single person of the offender's age (see p773).[54]

Payment cannot be reduced to below 10p a week. No reduction is made if IS is already being restricted because you breached a community order (see p997). If the rate of IS to which you are entitled changes, the reduction is recalculated and takes effect from the first day of the first benefit week following the change.

Income-based jobseeker's allowance

Income-based JSA is paid at a reduced rate during the sanction period if you or a member of your family (see p700) are the benefit offender, and you are a 'person in hardship'. This means that you are in a 'vulnerable group' or a decision maker is satisfied that you or your partner would face hardship if a payment were not made.[55] The rules for who counts as in a 'vulnerable group' and on deciding hardship are the same as for JSA sanctions (see p426).[56]

If you do not fall into a vulnerable group, you are not paid reduced rate JSA until the 15th day of the sanction period.[57]

You do *not* count as a 'person in hardship':[58]

- if you or your partner are entitled to IS or fit into one of the groups of people who can claim IS (see p292). In this case, you or your partner can claim IS instead of JSA; *or*
- during any period when JSA is not payable to you because you have been given an employment-related or a New Deal, training or employment programme-related sanction (see Chapter 16); *or*
- during any week in the sanction period when your benefit has been restricted because you breached a community order (see p997).

The reduction is 20 per cent of the appropriate JSA personal allowance for a single person of your age (see p773) if you or a member of your family are pregnant or seriously ill.[59] If you are a member of a couple, one of you is 18 or over and the other is not entitled to income-based JSA as an under-18-year-old or to severe hardship payments, the reduction is 40 per cent of the appropriate JSA personal allowance for a single person aged 25 or over. In all other cases, the reduction is 40 per cent of the appropriate JSA personal allowance for a single person of your age (see p773).

Joint-claim jobseeker's allowance

If you are a member of a joint-claim couple, joint-claim JSA is not paid at all if the 'loss of benefit for benefit offences' rules apply to:

- both you and your partner;[60] *or*
- one of you, while:
  - the other has been given an employment-related or a New Deal, training or employment programme-related sanction (see Chapter 16);[61] *or*
  - the other's benefit has been restricted because s/he breached a community order (see p997).[62]

In other cases, if one of you is sanctioned, the other person is paid at the rate of:[63]

- contribution-based JSA, if s/he satisfies the rules for claiming it (see p341); *or*
- hardship payments, if you and your partner qualify (see p422); *or*
- income-based JSA calculated as if s/he is a single person (see p368), although any income or capital either of you have is taken into account in the calculation (see Chapters 35 and 36).

Housing benefit and council tax benefit

If you or a member of your family (see p700) are entitled to IS or income-based JSA during a sanction period, your HB and CTB (or that of your family member if s/he is the IS or income-based JSA claimant) is unaffected by any sanction.[64] Otherwise, any HB/CTB payable to you is reduced rather than removed during the sanction period if you or a member of your family are the benefit offender.

The reduction is 20 per cent of the appropriate personal allowance for a single person of the offender's age (see p773) if you or a member of your family are pregnant or seriously ill. In all other cases, the reduction is 40 per cent of the appropriate personal allowance for a single person of the offender's age (see p773).[65] If the rate of HB/CTB to which you are entitled changes, the reduction is recalculated and takes effect from the first day of the first benefit week following the change.

Pension credit

PC is paid at a reduced rate during the sanction period if you or a member of your family (see p700) are the benefit offender. The reduction is 20 per cent of the 'relevant amount' if you or a member of your family are pregnant or seriously ill. In all other cases it is 40 per cent of the 'relevant amount'.[66]

The 'relevant amount' where a member of your family is the offender and s/he is under 25, is the appropriate IS personal allowance for a single person of her/his age (see p771). In all other cases, the reduction is the IS personal allowance for a single person aged 25 (see p771).

Payment cannot be reduced to below 10p a week. If the rate of PC to which you are entitled changes, the reduction is recalculated and takes effect from the first day of the first benefit week following the change.

4. Penalties

The DWP, the Revenue or local authority may offer you the option of agreeing to pay a financial penalty, instead of being prosecuted.

The penalty is 30 per cent of the amount of the overpayment that is recoverable from you.[67] The overpayment must have been caused by an offence you committed after 18 December 1997.[68]

The penalty is added to the overpayment of benefit and is recoverable in the same way as the overpayment[69] (see pp1019 and 1028). Guidance from the DWP to local authorities suggests that where an overpayment is being recovered from weekly benefits, deductions to recover the penalty should be instituted after the overpayment is fully recovered.[70]

The option of paying a penalty

You can *only* be offered the option of paying a penalty if:[71]

- an overpayment has been found to be recoverable from you. The DWP, the Revenue or local authority must have gone through the process of revising or superseding your award of benefit and issuing a decision that the overpayment is recoverable; *and*
- the overpayment was due to an act or omission on your part. This act or omission must have occurred after 18 December 1997;[72] *and*
- there are grounds for prosecuting you for an offence relating to the overpayment.

The DWP, the Revenue or local authority issues you with a notice which must set out how the scheme works and give you information about how you agree to pay a penalty or notify your withdrawal of your agreement.[73] If you are not issued with a proper notice, it may not be possible for the DWP, the Revenue or local authority to enforce the penalty.

The notice is sent with an invitation to an interview to discuss accepting the penalty. The interview should not be carried out by the same officer who gave the interview under caution.[74] The interview relates only to the offering of a penalty. You are not able to use it to add to or alter any statement that you made about the alleged offence in an interview under caution. If you are unable to decide whether or not to accept the caution at the interview, you should be allowed five days to make up your mind.[75]

Remember the following.

- If you agree to pay a penalty you are immune from prosecution for any offence relating to the overpayment.[76] However, this does not stop you being prosecuted in the future if you commit another offence, or one relating to a different overpayment.
- If it is found on revision or appeal that the overpayment is not due or not recoverable, any penalty you have paid must be repaid to you.[77] This does not affect the existence of the agreement, so you are still immune from prosecution.
- If the amount of the overpayment is changed on review or appeal, the agreement is cancelled, so you lose your immunity from prosecution and any penalty you have paid must be repaid to you. However, if you enter into a fresh agreement:
  - you are again immune from prosecution; *and*
  - the amount of penalty you have already paid can be offset against the new penalty rather than being repaid to you.[78]
- If you decline to accept the penalty, the DWP, the Revenue or local authority considers whether to prosecute you.

Changing your mind

If you enter into an agreement to pay a penalty, you are entitled to change your mind so long as you notify the DWP, the Revenue or local authority within 28 days, on a form provided for the purpose as specified on the penalty notice.[79] You lose your immunity, but you do not have to pay the penalty and if you have paid any part of it, it must be refunded to you.

Whether to accept the penalty

It can be difficult deciding whether to accept a penalty or to risk facing prosecution. You should seek advice and consider your options carefully. In considering what to do, bear the following in mind.

- You might be invited to pay a penalty when there is insufficient evidence to prosecute you. If you are offered a penalty, make sure that you are told what evidence the DWP, the Revenue or local authority has against you.
- The fraud officer can only recommend that your case be considered for prosecution. The DWP, the Revenue or local authority legal department decides whether to prosecute (see p1044). You are not automatically prosecuted if you refuse to accept a penalty.
- If you are prosecuted and found guilty, you might be offered community service rather than a fine. On the other hand, you could get a large fine or even a prison sentence.
- A penalty of 30 per cent of the overpayment may be a substantial amount of money. For minor offences, a fine imposed on you could be less than the penalty.

5. Formal cautions

The DWP operates a system of 'cautioning' for social security offences. This system only applies within the DWP, although some local authorities have similar systems of their own. Scottish local authorities use 'administrative cautions', similar in the way they operate to the cautioning system in England and Wales. However, since Scottish law does not recognise cautions as anything other than an administrative measure, these administrative cautions cannot be cited in the Scottish courts. Instead, the administrative caution may be referred to in the report submitted to the procurator fiscal, who considers it when looking at whether to prosecute for any later offence. The cautioning system is not laid down in regulations but is based on guidance modelled on the established guidelines for the police practice of cautioning.[80]

A formal caution can only be offered when you have been interviewed under caution (see p1043), an overpayment has been calculated and the fraud officer believes there is sufficient evidence to prosecute you for an offence. Cautions are generally only offered in less serious fraud where the value of an overpayment is low.

The procedure is as follows.

- You attend a formal caution interview, where you are asked to sign a record admitting the offence and accepting the caution. If you accept a caution you are immune from prosecution for the offence that you have admitted. This may encompass overpayments of more than one benefit.
- A caution certificate is sent to the DWP and the caution is recorded on a central database. The record is kept initially for five years. It is subject to data protection rules. Information about the caution can be disclosed to other bodies in some circumstances – eg, to local authorities for use in housing benefit (HB) and council tax benefit matters or to the police for use in criminal investigations.
- In England and Wales, a properly recorded formal caution may be cited in court if you are successfully prosecuted for a subsequent offence. It may then become part of a criminal record.
- If you refuse to admit the offence and accept a formal caution, your case is considered for prosecution.

Whether to accept a caution

In can be difficult deciding whether to accept a caution or to risk facing prosecution. You should seek advice and consider your options carefully. In considering what to do, bear the following in mind.

- A formal caution may be offered in circumstances where there is insufficient evidence to prosecute you for an offence. You are not necessarily prosecuted

just because you refuse to accept a caution. You should not admit to something that you did not do just to avoid the threat of prosecution.
- Accepting a formal caution is an admission of guilt. Once you have accepted a caution you cannot change your mind.
- Although accepting the formal caution means that you are immune from prosecution for offences specified on the caution certificate, you may be prosecuted for related offences not specified, such as an HB overpayment.
- If you are subsequently found guilty of another benefit offence in court, your formal caution could be cited and may mean that you get a stiffer sentence.

6. The effect of fraud investigation on benefit

Your benefit cannot be stopped just because of fraud. However, the DWP, the Revenue or local authority is entitled to suspend or withhold your benefit in some circumstances (eg, if it has a doubt about whether you are entitled or there is a possibility that you are being overpaid). See p984 for further information about when payments of benefit can be suspended.

The DWP, the Revenue or local authority can ask you to provide information and evidence about your claim. If you do not do so within a specified time limit, your claim can be terminated (see p985).[81] If you still believe that you are entitled to benefit, make a new claim.

You may have difficulties in getting your benefit reinstated during a fraud investigation or after you have been prosecuted. However, the DWP, the Revenue or local authority should not withhold your benefit indefinitely without making a decision on whether or not you are, in fact, entitled. If you think an investigation is taking too long, you should complain (see p1181). If that brings no results, seek legal advice about forcing the DWP, the Revenue or local authority to make a decision.

Being under investigation for fraud can be very distressing. Fraud officers can take your papers away from the DWP, the Revenue or local authority section that normally deals with your claim and it can sometimes be difficult to find out what is happening. You might be put under pressure by the fraud officer to withdraw your benefit claim. You should not do so unless you know that you are not entitled to benefit. Fraud officers cannot make decisions on your entitlement to benefit. They merely pass on evidence to decision makers (some local authority fraud officers may also be decision makers). Always insist on a proper decision from a DWP, Revenue or local authority decision maker.

The decision on whether you should be prosecuted is separate from a decision to recover an overpayment of benefit (see Chapter 39). Whether you are entitled to benefit, and the amount and recoverability of any overpayment, is decided by the DWP, the Revenue or local authority decision maker without regard to your honesty of intention. These decisions can be appealed, revised or superseded in the usual way (see Chapters 41 and 42). The fraud investigation department decides whether your actions were fraudulent and recommends whether action should be taken to prosecute, award penalties or caution you. The two processes are independent and have different tests. Therefore:

- a decision or appeal relating to your claim does not have to be delayed while waiting for the outcome of a criminal prosecution, and is only likely to be delayed if the particular circumstances of your case show that it should be;[82] *and*
- a court-awarded fine does not prevent separate action for overpayment recovery. However, successful prosecution of a fraudulent offence alters the burden of proof in an overpayment appeal and if you have made payments under a compensation order to the DWP, the Revenue or local authority, it cannot also recover that amount as an overpayment.[83]

Whatever the result of an investigation or prosecution, the DWP, the Revenue or local authority may take more time assessing your future claims because they may check out your circumstances thoroughly. If they take too long to make a decision, you should complain (see p1181). You should not be prevented from making a fresh claim during a fraud investigation if your circumstances have changed. You could also apply for interim payments (see p986) or help from the social fund (see Chapter 21).

Notes

1. **Investigating claims**

1 ss122 and 122ZA SSAA 1992
2 s122B SSAA 1992
3 ss124 and 125 SSAA 1992
4 ss122D and 122E SSAA 1992
5 s122C SSAA 1992
6 ss182A and 182B SSAA 1992; HB Fraud Circular HB/CTB F5/98
7 s123 and Sch 4 SSAA 1992
8 DWP *Code of Practice for Data Matching*, August 2000, available free of charge from the DWP website
9 s109A SSAA 1992
10 s110A SSAA 1992
11 ss116 and 116A SSAA 1999; regs 2 and 3 SS(LAIP) Regs. In Scotland, the Procurator Fiscal is responsible for all prosecutions.
12 ss109A(2) and 110A(2) SSAA 1992
13 s109B(2) SSAA 1992
14 s109B(2A) SSAA 1992
15 s3(6) SSFA 2001
16 s109B(5)(b) SSAA 1992; DWP *Code of Practice on Obtaining Information*, s2.11
17 s109B(2C) SSAA 1992
18 ss109BA and 110AA SSAA 1992
19 s109B(2D) SSAA 1992
20 s109B(2E) SSAA 1992
21 s109B(2F) SSAA 1992
22 s109C SSAA 1992
23 s28(2) Regulation of Investigatory Powers Act 2000
24 ss109B(5) and 109C(6) SSAA 1992
25 s67(9) PACEA 1984

26 s78(1) PACEA 1984; *DHSS v McKee* [1995] 6 *Bulletin of NI Law* 17 (NI Crown Court)
27 HB Fraud Circular HB/CTB F5/97
28 s34 CJPOA 1994

2. **Prosecution of offences**
29 *Osinunga v DPP, The Times*, 26 November 1997 (DC)
30 s112(1) SSAA 1992
31 *Clear v Smith* [1981] 1 WLR 399 (DC)
32 s112(1A) SSAA 1992
33 s112(1C)-(1F) SSAA 1992
34 s112(1B) SSAA 1992
35 *Taylor's Central Garages v Roper* [1951] 115 JPR 445
36 *R v Passmore* [2007] EWCA Crim 2053
37 s112(2) SSAA 1992
38 Reg 32(1A) and (1B) SS(C&P) Regs
39 Reg 4 SS(NCC) Regs
40 *R v Chainey* [1914] 1 KB 137 at 142 (DC)
41 s111A SSAA 1992
42 *R v Ghosh* [1982] QB 1053 at 1064D-G (CA)
43 s111A(3) SSAA 1992
44 s116(2), (2A) and (7) SSAA 1992

3. **Loss of benefit for benefit offences**
45 s7(1) SSFA 2001
46 s49 WRA 2007
47 s7(8) SSFA 2001, definition of 'benefit offence'
48 s7(8) SSFA 2001, definition of 'disqualifying benefit'
49 s7(8) SSFA 2001, definition of 'sanctionable benefit'; reg 19 SS(LB) Regs
50 s8 SSFA 2001
51 s7(2)-(5) SSFA 2001
52 s7(6) SSFA 2001; reg 2 SS(LB) Regs
53 ss7(3)and 9(3) SSFA 2001
54 Reg 3 SS(LB) Regs
55 ss7(4)and 9(4) SSFA 2001; regs 6-9 SS(LB) Regs
56 Reg 5(1)-(2) SS(LB) Regs
57 Reg 7 SS(LB) Regs
58 Reg 5(3) SS(LB) Regs
59 Reg 10 SS(LB) Regs
60 s8(2)(a) SSFA 2001
61 s8(2)(b)(i) SSFA 2001; s20A JSA 1995
62 s8(2)(b)(ii) SSFA 2001; s62(2) CSPSSA 2000
63 s8(3) SSFA 2001
64 s7(5) SSFA 2001; reg 18 SS(LB) Regs
65 s7(5) SSFA 2001; reg 17 SS(LB) Regs
66 Reg 3A SS(LB) Regs

4. **Penalties**
67 s115A(3) SSAA 1992
68 s25(7) SSA(F)A 1997
69 s115A(4)(a) SSAA 1992
70 HB Fraud Circular F4/98, para 44(e) and (f)
71 s115A(1) SSAA 1992
72 s25(7) SSA(F)A 1997; Art 2(1)(b) SSA(F)AO No.5
73 s115A(2) SSAA 1992; reg 2(1) and (2) SS(PN) Regs
74 HB Fraud Circular F4/98, para 24
75 HB Fraud Circular F4/98, para 48
76 s115A(4)(b) SSAA 1992
77 s115A(6) SSAA 1992
78 s115A(7) SSAA 1992
79 s115A(5) SSAA 1992

5. **Formal cautions**
80 Cautions guidance issued by DWP to local authorities (not currently available in published form).

6. **The effect of fraud investigation on benefit**
81 Regs 17 and 18 SS&CS(DA) Regs
82 *Mote v Secretary of State for Work and Pensions and Chichester District Council* [2007] EWCA Civ 1324, 14 December 2007, unreported
83 CIS/683/1994

Chapter 41

Decisions, revisions and supersessions

This chapter covers:

Once you have made a valid claim for benefit, a decision must be made by a decision maker.[1] The DWP calls this an 'outcome decision'. See pp959 and 202 for what counts as a valid claim and p959 if your claim is not accepted as valid.

If you want more information about a decision, you can ask for an explanation (see p1060). In many cases, you can also ask for written reasons for a decision (see p1061). If you disagree with the decision, you can ask the decision maker to change it by seeking a revision or a supersession. In many cases, you can also challenge a decision by appealing to a tribunal (see Chapter 42). You may also be able to seek a supersession if your circumstances change after a decision is made.

Child benefit and guardian's allowance

The Revenue makes decisions about child benefit and guardian's allowance as well as tax credits. However, references to the Revenue in this chapter only apply to decisions about child benefit and guardian's allowance.

This chapter does *not* cover:

- child tax credit or working tax credit. For these, see Chapters 54 and 57; *or*
- statutory sick pay and statutory maternity, adoption and paternity pay. For these, see Chapter 43; *or*
- payments from the *discretionary* social fund. For these, see Chapter 44; *or*
- the health benefits in Chapter 9 or the other types of financial help on pp14-16; *or*

- discretionary housing payments of housing benefit and council tax benefit. For these see p224.

This chapter covers the other benefits in this *Handbook*, including payments from the *regulated* social fund.

1. Decisions

In this *Handbook* those who make decisions about benefits and the social fund are referred to as **'decision makers'**. Decisions about:

- benefits and the social fund (other than child benefit, guardian's allowance, housing benefit (HB) and council tax benefit (CTB)) are made by the Secretary of State for Work and Pensions. In practice, such decisions are made by the Secretary of State's representatives who are civil servants in the DWP;
- child benefit and guardian's allowance are made by officers of the Revenue;
- HB and CTB are made by officers of the local authority.

Some issues – eg, whether you are or can be treated as incapable of work or are terminally ill for benefit purposes, are decided by the Secretary of State for Work and Pensions, even if the main benefit decision is made by another authority (eg, the local authority).[2]

Employment officers (EOs) work in Jobcentre Plus offices. They are sometimes called personal advisers. If you are claiming jobseeker's allowance (JSA), their job is to agree with you the steps you are willing to take to get back to work, keep a check on those steps and to offer practical help and advice.They are involved in work-focused interviews which you (and your partner) may have to attend. See p971 for further information.

Making a decision

The decision maker may need further information before making a decision. You can be asked to provide this (see pp203 and 961). In some cases, if you fail to do so, payment of your benefit could be suspended or your award terminated (see p985), or the decision maker might draw adverse conclusions and make a decision based on these. In addition, if your claim:

- involves medical issues, the decision maker can refer you to a 'healthcare professional' (see p1058) for a medical examination and a report.[3] The health care professional can ask you to submit to a medical examination. If you fail to do so without 'good cause' the decision maker must decide against you. Remember that different rules apply if you fail to attend a medical examination about your incapacity for work (see p678) or if a decision maker requires you to attend for a medical examination to see if a decision to award you benefit

should be revised or superseded (see p985) or if a chair of a tribunal refers you to a 'healthcare professional' for a medical examination (see p1112);
- involves issues about your national insurance contributions, the decision maker can refer these to the Revenue. See below for further information about the special procedure;
- for disablement benefit, involves whether you may have a prescribed disease or have a disablement (and if so the extent of it), the decision maker can refer the issue to a health care professional for a report;[4]
- involves a question about the facts where special expertise is needed, the decision maker can get assistance from experts.[5]

Healthcare professionals

A 'healthcare professional'[6] is a registered medical practitioner (eg, a doctor), registered nurse or registered occupational therapist or phsyiotherapist, or a member of a profession regulated by a body mentioned in s25(3) of the National Health Service Reform and Health Care Professions Act 2002 (eg, an optician, osteopath or chiropracter).

If the decision maker needs more evidence or information to make a decision, s/he can make a decision in the meantime in certain circumstances. A decision is made on the basis that the evidence or information needed is adverse to you, if:[7]
- for income support (IS), JSA and social fund payments only, it is needed to decide:
  - whether you should be paid less benefit because you (or a member of your family) are involved in a trade dispute (see p633); *or*
  - whether you are in relevant education (see p576);
- for IS, social fund payments and pension credit (PC) only, it is needed to decide whether you are entitled to a severe disability premium (additional amount for PC) (see p784);
- for retirement pension only, you deferred claiming your pension, but when you did claim you had not yet elected whether to take a lump sum or an increased pension. When you make the election, the decision maker must revise the decision (see p1072).

For IS, PC and social fund payments only, if further evidence or information is needed to decide what housing costs you can be paid (see Chapter 34), a decision is made on the basis of the evidence or information the decision maker already has.[8]

If you do not fill in your claim form properly, you are given time to do so (see pp203 and 202). If your claim is for IS or JSA, your claim is treated as defective if all the required information is not provided (see p960).

A decision maker may withhold making a decision if there is a test case pending. See p1088 for further information.

If you think a decision is wrong, you can seek a revision or supersession or appeal against it. The position is different if you are given wrong advice by an employee of the DWP, local authority or Revenue. See p1186 for information about seeking compensation.

Special procedure

Certain questions are dealt with by a special procedure. These are to do with contributions and a person's employment – eg, whether you:[9]

- are an 'employed earner' for the purposes of paying contributions or entitlement to industrial injuries disablement benefit; *or*
- are liable to pay a particular class of contributions or have paid contributions for a particular period.

The decision maker refers matters that are the Revenue's responsibility to the Revenue for a decision, which is then binding on the decision maker.[10] The decision maker can continue to deal with other issues relating to your claim, but can defer making a decision on it. Note that the decision maker should also refer matters to the Revenue if s/he decides your claim on the basis of facts which do not appear to be under dispute – eg, it appears you do not satisfy the contribution conditions for the benefit, but you apply for a revision or supersession of the decision, or appeal against it (eg, because you think your contribution record is wrong).

You can appeal against the decision. Appeals on most Revenue issues are dealt with by tax appeal commissioners.[11] You must appeal in writing within 30 days after the date on which a decision notice is issued.[12] The time limit can be extended if you have a reasonable excuse for not making your appeal within it and your appeal was made without unreasonable delay.[13]

Appeal tribunals can also require the DWP to refer matters that are the Revenue's responsibility, that are relevant to a benefit appeal, to the Revenue for a decision.[14] The Secretary of State may revise the decision on your claim as a result; if not, the matter goes back to the tribunal.

Note: the decision maker can also refer to the Revenue some issues to do with whether you satisfy the conditions for receipt of home responsibilities protection and whether you can be credited with earnings or contributions.[15] You can appeal to a tribunal about these.

Delays

The DWP and the Revenue have target times for dealing with claims. These are available at your benefit or Jobcentre Plus office. Local authorities must make a decision on your claim for HB or CTB within 14 days or, if that is not reasonably practicable, as soon as possible after that (see p216).

If you have been waiting more than the relevant time for a decision, contact the DWP, local authority or Revenue. First check that your claim has been received. If it has not, let the office have a copy of your claim or fill out a new form and refer to the claim form you sent earlier. If the DWP, local authority or Revenue does not accept that you made the claim, you may have to claim again and ask for it to be backdated if possible (see pp964 and 206).

If your claim has been received but not dealt with, ask why. If you are not satisfied with the explanation for the delay, make a complaint (see Chapter 46). In extreme cases, it might be possible to make an application for judicial review (see p1129).

If a decision cannot be made on your claim straight away:

- you should ask the office to make interim payments (see p986). If the benefit is HB and you are a private or housing association tenant, in most cases you *must* be given an interim payment (see p217);
- if your claim is for a non-means-tested benefit, you may be able to claim IS, income-based JSA or PC in the meantime. The amount of any of these paid to you may be deducted from arrears of social security benefits which you subsequently receive;[16]
- you may be able to claim a crisis loan from the social fund if you have inadequate resources.

Correcting a decision

Unless the benefit is child benefit or guardian's allowance, if the decision maker makes an accidental error in her/his decision, this can be corrected.[17] You must be sent written notice of the correction as soon as it is practicable. To see how the time limit for seeking an 'any grounds' revision or appealing against the decision can be extended when a decision has been corrected, see pp1067 and 1099.

Information about decisions

You must be given a written notice of a decision against which you have a right of appeal (see p1095). These are sometimes called 'decision notices'. You must be informed of:[18]

- your right to appeal against the decision; *and*
- your right to a written statement of reasons for the decision (if this is not already included) – see p1061.

You may want to know more about a decision or want a breakdown of how your benefit has been calculated. To find out more about a decision, you can also ask for an explanation. **Note:** you do *not* have to ask for an explanation or a written statement of reasons in order to seek a revision or a supersession, or to appeal.

Explanations

You can ask for an explanation of any decision maker's decision, in writing, in person or over the telephone. Contact the office that made the decision. Ask about anything that is unclear to you and point out any errors you think the decision maker made.

At the end of the explanation, you should be asked whether you are happy with the decision and whether or not you want it to be looked at again. If you are not happy with a decision, say so. The decision maker should then advise you about your right to seek a revision (see p1065) or to appeal (see Chapter 42). S/he may refer to this as a dispute or a request for a reconsideration but you should use the term 'revision'.

Explanations are usually given orally and it can sometimes be difficult to take in or remember what has been said. However, you have a right to a written statement of reasons for a decision if it is one against which you can appeal (see below).

The time limit for seeking an 'any grounds' revision or appealing is very strict. It runs from the date you are sent the decision with which you disagree, *not* the date of the explanation (see pp1067 and 1099). You should, therefore, ensure you seek a revision or appeal within the time limit even if an explanation for the decision has not yet been given to you.

Written reasons for a decision

Whether or not you asked for an explanation, you may want to see the reasons for a decision in writing. You have a right to a written statement of reasons for a decision against which you have a right of appeal if these have not already been provided with the decision. This is especially useful if you are considering seeking a revision or supersession, or appealing to a tribunal.

If the decision is about **HB or CTB**, there is no time limit for asking for a written statement of reasons. However, as the time limit for seeking a revision or appealing is very strict, you should seek one within the time limit even if you decide to ask for a written statement of reasons later. If you ask for a written statement of reasons (where this has not already been provided), the local authority must provide one within 14 days if this is practicable.[19] Days between the date the local authority receives your request for the statement and the date on which it is provided to you are ignored when calculating the one-month time limit for seeking an 'any grounds' revision and appealing (see pp1067 and 1099).

If the decision is about **other benefits**, you must ask for a written statement of reasons within one month of being sent the decision.[20] The decision maker must then provide one within 14 days or as soon as practicable afterwards. Your time limit for seeking a revision or appealing is automatically extended if you ask for a written statement of reasons, but only where these have not already been provided. See pp1067 and 1099 for further information.

'Month' means a complete calendar month running from the day after the day you have been sent or given a decision.[21] For example, a decision sent on 24 July has a time limit that expires at the end of 24 August.

The DWP says a written statement of reasons for a decision is provided automatically with a decision about some benefits (see below). Although you may believe a written statement of reasons has not been included with your decision or that what has been provided is inadequate, the DWP, local authority or Revenue could disagree. In these cases, the DWP is likely to argue that your time limit for seeking an 'any grounds' revision or appealing cannot be extended.

If you are in any doubt about the situation, you should presume your time limit for seeking an 'any grounds' revision or appealing has *not* been extended. If you miss the time limit in this situation, you should argue that the rules that allow a late application for a revision or a late appeal apply (see pp1067 and 1129). Remember that the time limit for seeking a revision or appealing is strict.

Automatic statements of reasons

The DWP says that written statements of reasons are automatically provided with decisions about: bereavement benefits, incapacity benefit, maternity allowance, retirement pension, severe disablement allowance, and social fund funeral payments, cold weather payments and Sure Start maternity grants.

Remember: read and consider the reasons carefully to ensure you understand why the decision maker made her/his decision. You are then better prepared to argue why the decision should be changed if you seek a revision or appeal.

If you disagree with a decision maker's decision

If you think a decision maker's decision is wrong (eg, because the decision maker got the facts or law wrong, or your circumstances have changed) you can:

- seek a revision of the decision (see p1065); *or*
- seek a supersession of the decision (see p1074).

In many cases, you also have a right to appeal to a tribunal (see Chapter 42).

The time limits for seeking what is known as an 'any grounds' revision or appealing are strict – normally only one month (see pp1067 and 1099). For information about how an application for a revision could affect your appeal rights and the time limit for appealing, see p1103.

You can seek a revision or a supersession of a decision that you cannot appeal to a tribunal (see p1097). If you are still dissatisfied you should seek advice about whether you can apply for judicial review (see p1129).

Checklist for challenging a decision

1. To get more information about a decision, ask for an explanation or a written statement of reasons (if this has not already been provided – see p1061).
2. Decide whether to seek a revision (see p1065) or appeal (see Chapter 42). Get advice as soon as possible if you need this (see Appendix 2).
3. Ensure you keep within the time limit (see p1067 for revisions and p1099 for appeals).

If you disagree with an employment officer's decision

You cannot appeal against an EO's decision to issue a jobseeker's direction (see p406), but if you are sanctioned by a decision maker for failing to comply with it you can appeal against the sanction.

If you cannot reach an agreement with your EO about the terms of your jobseeker's agreement or whether your jobseeker's agreement should be changed you can ask for it to be referred to a decision maker for a decision. See p362 for details of the procedure. If you disagree with the decision maker's decision, you can seek a revision (see p1065) or appeal (see Chapter 42).

Note: if you want to challenge decisions about work-focused interviews, see p976.

Contacting benefit offices

Writing to the DWP, local authority or the Revenue is nearly always the best way to have your case dealt with. It ensures there is a record of what you said and enables you to cover all the points you want to make. Always keep a copy of the letters, forms and other documents you send as well as copies of those sent to you. Such a record may help you or your adviser to challenge decisions.

It may be necessary to telephone the DWP, local authority or Revenue. If you do this, make a note of the date and what is said. If the information is important, follow up the telephone call with a letter confirming what was said.

Visiting the DWP or local authority office enables you to have a detailed conversation with an officer. You can ask for a private interview. Follow up any important meeting with a letter confirming the points you or the officer have made or ask the officer to confirm in writing any advice to you.

If you cannot get to an office (eg, because of your age, health or a disability) an officer may be able to make a home visit if your case cannot be dealt with by telephone. If you are refused a visit and are not satisfied with the reason you are given, ask to speak to a supervisor or the customer services manager.

2. General information

If you are getting benefit but you cease to satisfy the conditions of entitlement, or the amount of benefit to which you are entitled should be reduced or increased, the decision awarding you benefit can be changed either by a revision or a supersession. In some cases, this can only be done if one of the grounds for revision or supersession applies (see pp1068 and 1075).

Whoever wants a revision or supersession has to show that there are grounds.[22] It is best to ask for a revision or supersession in writing, giving the reasons why you think one should take place. For housing benefit (HB) and council tax benefit (CTB), you *must* ask for a revision or supersession in writing.[23] Claims for benefit or questions about your entitlement can be treated as requests for a revision or a supersession.[24]

If you are trying to get arrears going back several years, it can be difficult to identify the grounds for a revision or supersession, particularly if the DWP, local authority or the Revenue has destroyed old papers relating to your claim. If you are the one who wants the revision or supersession, the onus is on you to show that there are grounds. You might not be able to rely on the DWP's, local authority's or Revenue's lack of evidence where they failed to retain it.[25] However, check to see if your papers have simply been stored (archived), rather than actually destroyed.

After you seek a revision or supersession

When considering whether to carry out a revision or a supersession, the decision maker decides what further evidence is needed in order to come to a decision, and how to collect this. You can be asked to have a medical examination (see p985). Note that for HB and CTB, the local authority *cannot* ask you to have a medical examination.

The decision maker can ask you for more evidence or information if s/he thinks this is needed to consider all the issues raised by your application for a revision or supersession.[26] You must provide this information within one month of the request. The decision maker can allow longer than this. If you do not provide the information, your application is decided on the basis of the information and evidence the decision maker already has.

Remember, in some cases if you fail to provide information or have a medical examination, payment of your benefit could be suspended and your entitlement terminated (see p986).

If a decision is changed

If a decision is changed in your favour, you can receive arrears of benefit. You usually get more arrears with a revision than a supersession. For this reason it is best to apply for a revision if you can. If you are in any doubt about how you would be better off, seek advice. See pp1074 and 1079 for when a revision or supersession takes effect.

If you were underpaid benefit because of a clear error by the DWP, local authority or Revenue you could apply for compensation as well as getting arrears (see p1186).

If a decision is *not* in your favour, you may have been overpaid. The decision maker decides whether or not to recover the overpayment (see Chapter 39). There is no limit on how far back an overpayment can be recovered.

The risks of revision and supersession

Following a revision or a supersession, the original decision may:

- remain the same; *or*
- be changed either to increase or decrease the amount of your benefit or take away your entitlement altogether.

Thus, your benefit can go down as well as up. If the revision or supersession reduces the amount of benefit to which you are entitled, it may mean that you have been overpaid. See Chapter 39 for information about overpayments and when they can be recovered.

You should seek advice before you seek a revision or supersession if you are concerned about what could happen in your case. However, you must notify changes in your circumstances that could affect your benefit.

Disability living allowance

As well as the risks described above, you should seek advice if you want to seek a revision or supersession because:

- you have not been awarded one component of DLA when you are already in receipt of the other; *or*
- of the rate you have been awarded of one component of DLA when you are quite satisfied with the rate you have been awarded of the other.

In these circumstances the decision maker may consider the component which is not the subject of the revision or supersession, although s/he does not have to do so.

If you have been awarded one component of DLA for an indefinite period (see p130), the decision maker can reconsider the rate of that component, or the length of time for which it has been awarded, although s/he does not have to do so. However, suggest that s/he should not do so unless you ask for a revision or supersession on that basis.[27]

3. Revisions

If you disagree with a decision maker's decision (including a decision superseding an earlier decision), you can seek a revision.[28] If you seek a revision, the decision maker must look at the decision again to see if it can be changed. The DWP, local authority and Revenue often refer to your request as a dispute or a request for a reconsideration. However, you should use the term 'revision'. Seeking a revision is only one of the ways of getting a decision changed. See p1098 for help in deciding whether to seek a revision or supersession, or to appeal.

In some cases, if you can show grounds, you can seek a revision even if the decision was made a long time ago (see p1068). Revisions can, therefore, be a way around the strict time limit for appealing to a tribunal (see p1099).

Following a revision, your benefit could be increased, but it could also be decreased or stopped altogether. See p1065 for what you should consider before seeking a revision.

For information on how to seek a revision, see p1073. To find out when a revision takes effect, see p1074.

When a decision can be revised

You can ask for a decision to be revised or the decision maker can decide to do this.[29] There are two types of revision:

- 'any grounds' revisions where all you have to do is say you disagree with the decision (see below); *and*
- 'any time' revisions where you must show that certain grounds apply (see p1068).

A decision maker can only revise a decision on the basis of your circumstances at the time the decision:[30]

- took effect; *or*
- in the case of advance awards for benefits other than housing benefit (HB) and council tax benefit (CTB), was made.

If your circumstances have since changed, you should instead make a fresh claim or ask for the decision to be superseded (see p1074).

If you want to seek a revision of a decision about attendance allowance (AA) or disability living allowance (DLA) because you (or the person on whose behalf you are claiming) are terminally ill (see p121), you must specify this.[31] If you do not do so, the decision maker cannot revise the decision on this ground.

'Any grounds' revisions

You can ask for a revision on any grounds if you do so within a strict time limit, normally one month.[32] The decision maker may refer to this as the dispute period. You do not have to show specific grounds for a revision, so it is enough if you simply think a decision is wrong. However, you should still explain why you disagree with the decision and provide information and evidence which supports this.

You do not have to seek a revision and can appeal to a tribunal instead. However, if you seek a revision rather than appealing you get two bites at the cherry because if your application for a revision is turned down, there are special rules about time limits that allow you to appeal to a tribunal against the original decision (but see p1074).

If you are uncertain whether your request for a revision of a decision is being acted on, you should appeal against the decision within the time limit (see p1099). However, your appeal could lapse if the decision maker revises the decision, even if you do not get everything you want (see p1103).

In addition, for benefits other than HB and CTB, a decision maker can decide to revise a decision her/himself, on any ground, within one month of the date you are sent the decision.[33] For HB and CTB, a decision maker can also decide to revise a decision within one month of the date you are sent or given it, but only if s/he has information which shows that there was a mistake about the facts of your case or the decision was made in ignorance of relevant facts.[34]

Time limit for seeking an 'any grounds' revision

If you want an 'any grounds' revision you must ask for one:

- in the case of a **Sure Start maternity grant or a social fund funeral expenses payment**, within one month of the date you were sent the decision or within the time limit for claiming the payment (see pp513 and 515) if this is later;[35]
- in the case of **HB and CTB**, within one month of the date you were sent the decision.[36] If a written statement of reasons has not already been included with the decision, days between the date you request the statement and the date on which it is provided to you are ignored when calculating the one month;[37]
- in all **other cases**:[38]
  - within one month of the date you were sent the decision; *or*
  - within one month and 14 days of the date you were sent the decision, if you requested a written statement of reasons (see p1061) and it is provided within the month; *or*
  - within 14 days of a written statement of reasons being provided, if you requested one within one month of the date you were sent the decision, but it is not provided within that one-month period.

For benefits (other than a Sure Start maternity grant or a social fund funeral expenses payment, child benefit or guardian's allowance), if an accidental error in a decision has been corrected (see p1060), any day falling before the day on which the correction is notified to you is ignored in calculating the one-month period.[39]

Late requests for an 'any grounds' revision

You can ask for an 'any grounds' revision outside the time limit in limited circumstances. You must do so within an absolute time limit of 13 months from the date you were sent the decision.[40] However, if you requested a written statement of reasons within one month of the date you were sent the decision:

- for HB and CTB, days between the date you requested the statement and the date on which it was provided are ignored; *or*
- for other benefits, if the statement of reasons is provided:
  - within one month of the date you were sent the decision, the 13 months are extended by 14 days; *or*
  - during a period later than one month after the date you were sent the decision, the 13 months are extended by 14 days, plus the number of days in that period.

Your application outside the time limit must contain:[41]

- enough details about the decision with which you disagree for it to be identified. You should say which benefit you are disagreeing about and the date the DWP, local authority or Revenue sent you the decision; *and*
- a summary of your reasons for applying for a revision late. You must show that:[42]
  - it is reasonable to grant your request; *and*
  - your application for a revision has merit; *and*
  - there are special circumstances which mean that it was not practicable for you to request a revision within the time limit.

The longer you have delayed seeking a revision, the more compelling the special circumstances have to be.[43]

When deciding whether it is reasonable to grant your application, the decision maker cannot take account of the fact that:[44]

- a court or commissioner has interpreted the law in a different way than previously understood and applied;
- you (or anyone acting for you) misunderstood or were unaware of the relevant law, including the time limits for seeking a revision.

You cannot appeal against the decision maker's refusal or failure to let you seek a revision outside the time limit.[45] The only remedy is judicial review. However, you might be able to make a late appeal against the original decision (see Chapter 42).

'Any time' revisions

If you can show there are specific grounds (see p1069) you can ask for a revision at any time (an 'any time' revision in this *Handbook*). There is no time limit for seeking an 'any time' revision. In practice, if you ask for a revision and it is within one month of you being sent the decision, the DWP, local authority or Revenue treats your application as one for an 'any grounds' revision (see p1066).

If a decision maker refuses to do an 'any time' revision, see p1074.

The main grounds for revision

There are a number of grounds for an 'any time' revision. The main ones are where there has been:

- an official error (see below);
- a mistake about or ignorance of facts (see p1070);
- an award of a 'qualifying benefit' (see p1070);
- an appeal against a decision (see p1071).

Other grounds for revision are on p1072.

Official error

You can ask for an 'any time' revision if there was an official error.[46] For **benefits, other than child benefit and guardian's allowance**, this means an error made by an officer of the DWP or the Revenue or a local authority or someone acting on behalf of, or providing services to, a local authority.[47] Other than for HB and CTB, it also includes errors made by someone providing services to the DWP. For **child benefit and guardian's allowance**, it means an error made by an officer of the Revenue or a person providing services to the Revenue.[48]

If the official error was made before the Social Security Act 1998 took effect (see CPAG's *Welfare Benefits Handbook* 1999/00, p2:649) by an adjudication officer, you can argue that the decision can be revised.[49]

Note: a decision to award you bereavement allowance, contribution-based jobseeker's allowance (JSA), incapacity benefit, retirement pension, widowed mother's allowance, widowed parent's allowance or widow's pension cannot be revised on this ground if the official error arose from discrepancies between the DWP and Revenue's computer systems and you were previously wrongly credited with earnings for incapacity for work or approved training in the tax years from 1993/94 to 2007/08 (see p732). This only applies if this has resulted in a more advantageous award than if the error had not been made.

You should argue that the following count as official errors.

- The decision maker made an error of law (see p1121).[50] However, this does not apply if the decision maker was only shown to have made an error of law after a later decision of a commissioner or a court. In this case, you could make a fresh claim or ask for a supersession, but the 'anti-test case rule' could apply (see p1087).
- There is specific evidence which the decision maker had, but which s/he failed to take into account even though it was relevant. You should argue this applies even if the evidence does not conclusively prove your entitlement, so long as it raised a strong possibility that you were entitled.
- There is documentary or other written evidence of your entitlement which the DWP, local authority or Revenue had, but failed to give to the decision maker dealing with your claim when the earlier decision was made.

In all cases, if someone else (eg, you, your partner or your representative) caused or materially contributed to the error, it does not count as an official error. This includes where the way your claim pack was completed contributed to the error.[51]

Mistake about or ignorance of facts

An 'any time' revision can be done if there was a mistake about the facts of your case or the decision was made in ignorance of relevant facts. However, this is only the case if, as a result of the mistake or ignorance about the facts, the decision was more favourable to you than it would have been – eg, you were awarded too much benefit.[52]

The rules are different if there was a mistake about, or ignorance of, facts related to your disability or incapacity, and the decision is:[53]

- a disability decision about AA, DLA, severe disablement allowance, industrial injuries disablement benefit; *or*
- an incapacity decision about your incapacity for work under the personal capability assessment (see p668) or whether you can be treated as incapable of work or there are exceptional circumstances (see p673).

In this case, in addition it must be shown that, at the time of the decision, you (or the person being paid the benefit) knew, or could reasonably have been expected to know, about the fact and that it was relevant to your benefit. If the disability benefit is a qualifying benefit for another benefit (see below) and revision of the disability or incapacity decision means your entitlement to the other benefit is affected, the decision about the other benefit takes effect on the same date.[54]

If this ground for revision applies, you will have been overpaid benefit and the decision maker may seek to recover the overpayment (see Chapter 39).

If the mistake about or ignorance of facts means you should be entitled to more benefit:

- a decision can be superseded on this ground (see p1076);
- a decision can be revised on 'any ground' if you apply in time (see p1066);
- a decision maker can decide to revise a decision her/himself within one month of the date you are sent the decision. For HB and CTB, this only applies if s/he has information that shows that there was a mistake about the facts of your case or the decision was made in ignorance of relevant facts.[55]

Awards of a 'qualifying benefit'

If you are awarded a benefit (eg, income support (IS) or HB) and for a period which includes the date that award took effect, **you or a member of your family are awarded a 'qualifying benefit'** (eg, DLA or carer's allowance) or the qualifying benefit is increased, the decision awarding you benefit can be revised.[56] See p700 for who counts as your family.

A decision to end your entitlement to HB or CTB because your (or a member of your family's) qualifying benefit ceases can also be revised at any time. This only applies if the qualifying benefit is later reinstated following a revision, supersession or appeal.[57] For other benefits, see p968 to see how a new claim can be backdated.

For IS or pension credit (PC) only, if you have a non-dependant living with you (see p786) and since you were awarded IS or PC, **your non-dependant has been awarded a 'qualifying benefit'** for a period which includes the date the award took effect, and this means that you are now entitled to a severe disability premium (for IS) or a severe disability additional amount (for PC), the decision awarding benefit can be revised.[58]

See p1085 for further information. If you are only entitled to a benefit once a qualifying benefit is awarded, see pp968 and 205.

A decision that has been appealed

If you appealed against a decision, and you:

- appealed within the time limit or were allowed a late appeal (see pp1099 and 1130) and the appeal has not yet been determined, a decision maker can look at the decision again and carry out a revision.[59] This includes where a tribunal has adjourned the hearing or where a commissioner has sent a case back to a tribunal to make a new decision; *or*
- make a fresh claim or seek a supersession when your circumstances change (eg, because a tribunal cannot, in general, take changes into account – see p1114), a decision maker can revise the new decision once the appeal against the first decision has been determined. This only applies if:
  - for **benefits other than HB and CTB**, you appealed against a decision to a tribunal;[60] *and*
    - a fresh claim is decided or the decision is superseded before your appeal is determined; *and*
    - the tribunal then makes its decision; *and*
    - the decision maker would have made her/his decision differently if s/he had been aware of the appeal decision at the time her/his decision was made; *or*
  - for **HB and CTB** only, you appealed against a decision to a tribunal, a commissioner or court;[61] *and*
    - a fresh claim is decided or the decision is changed (eg, by a supersession – see p1074); *and*
    - the decision maker would have made her/his decision differently if s/he had been aware of the appeal decision at the time her/his decision was made.

Note: if you have appealed a decision, your appeal could lapse if a decision maker revises the decision, even if you do not get everything you want (see p1103).

Other grounds for revision

There are a number of other situations when a decision maker can do an 'any time' revision. This includes where the decision is one against which you have no right of appeal (see p1097).[62]

Incapacity for work

If you have been **found capable of work under the personal capability assessment** and a decision to terminate your IS is made, it can be revised if the decision about your capacity for work is revised, or if you appeal and are therefore entitled to IS at a reduced rate.[63] If you win your appeal (or your appeal lapses – see p1103), the decision to pay you IS at a reduced rate can then itself be revised.[64] A decision that you are not entitled to a disability premium with your IS because you are not incapable of work can also be revised if the decision about your capacity for work is revised or you win your appeal.[65]

A decision to award you IB can be revised if:[66]

- when you first claimed, you were **not treated as incapable of work while waiting for a personal capability assessment** because you had been found capable of work in the last six months (see p669);
- you were awarded IB when six months had passed; *and*
- you have since been found incapable of work under the personal capability assessment.

This means that you can be paid arrears for the period between when you claimed and when you were awarded IB.

Other

Other decisions that can be revised at 'any time' are certain decisions:

- that JSA is not payable because asanction applies (see Chapter 16);[67]
- refusing reduced earnings allowance (see p326) because of a decision about your entitlement to industrial injuries disablement benefit;[68]
- about you (or your partner) failing to take part in a work-focused interview (see p971) or show good cause for this;[69]
- sanctioning you because you failed to comply with a community order (see p997) or stopping or restricting your benefit under the loss of benefit for benefit offences rules (see p1047);[70]
- about HB, where your maximum rent (see p247) increases because of a rent officer re-determination (see p243) or because a local housing allowance (see p236) or a broad rental market area has been amended because of a rent officer's error, or where, (in Scotland) a no rent payable order or notice is revoked following an appeal;[71]
- about retirement pension, PC, HB and CTB, where you or your partner deferred claiming a pension, then change your option from a higher pension to a lump sum (or, for retirement pension only, vice versa).[72]

How to seek a revision

Apply for a revision to the office that sent you the decision with which you disagree.[73] For benefits (other than child benefit, guardian's allowance, HB and CTB) if you are a person who is required to attend a work-focused interview as a condition of getting benefit, you can also apply to the Jobcentre Plus office. The DWP, local authority or Revenue can treat a request for a supersession (see p1074) as a request for a revision.[74]

For **benefits other than HB and CTB**, you do not have to ask for a revision in writing, although it is always best to do so. This ensures that the decision maker understands that you are asking for a revision, not just seeking an explanation or complaining about the rules.

Example

Stan is awarded IS, but the DWP says he is not entitled to help with his housing costs. He telephones the benefit office and complains that he has not got enough money to live on. The benefit office takes no action because it thinks Stan is simply letting off steam, not seeking a revision. Stan should have made it clear he wanted a revision. He can still ask for one (or appeal) but only if he is within the time limit (see pp1067 and 1099).

For **HB** and **CTB**, you *must* apply for a revision in writing.[75] A late application for a revision must also be in writing.[76]

A decision maker does not have to consider any issue not raised by your application for a revision or which caused her/him to act on her/his own initiative.[77] You should, therefore, ensure you:

- tell the decision maker all the points about the decision with which you disagree;
- provide any information or evidence that supports your case. This includes, for example, medical evidence from a GP, consultant or other health worker if this is relevant. If you are claiming AA or DLA, evidence or information from your carer or a diary of your walking, supervision or care needs over a period may be equally useful.

It is worth following up your request for a revision with the DWP, local authority or Revenue to check that your application has been received. This is to ensure that you do not miss the time limit for seeking an 'any grounds' revision or for appealing.

The revised decision

After a decision maker considers a revision, s/he can decide there are:

- grounds for revision and that the original decision was correct or should be changed; *or*

- no grounds for revision and refuse to change the original decision.

For information about challenging the decision, see below.

When a revision takes effect

The date a revision takes effect is important. This is the date from which you are paid arrears if you are entitled to more benefit, or have been overpaid if you are entitled to less benefit. A revision takes effect from:

- the date the decision with which you disagree took (or would have taken) effect[78] – eg, your date of claim or the date a supersession took effect; *or*
- the correct date, if the date on which the original decision took effect was found to be wrong.[79]

It is important to make it clear that you want payment for the past period. You might get less backdating if the 'anti-test case rule' applies (see p1087).

Note: in the case of retirement pension only, a revision takes effect on the later of 1 October 1998, or the date on which you reached pension age (if you claimed a Category A retirement pension) or your spouse or civil partner reached pension age (if you claimed a Category B retirement pension). This only applies if you made a late claim and this was refused because you or your spouse/civil partner had not paid enough national insurance contributions in the tax years 1996/97 to 2001/02 and you (s/he) were invited by the DWP to make these up by paying voluntary contributions and have since done so.[80]

Challenging a revision

If a decision is revised or the decision maker refuses to revise a decision, you are notified of this in writing. If the original decision is one against which you have a right of appeal (see p1095), you can appeal to a tribunal against the revised decision (or in the case of a refusal to do an 'any grounds' revision, against the original decision). Your time limit for appealing (see p1099) runs from the date you are sent or given the notification.[81]

If a decision maker refuses to do an 'any time' revision (see p1068) – eg, because s/he does not accept that an official error was made, you cannot appeal against the refusal.[82] However, you could make a late request for an 'any grounds' revision or try to make a late appeal against the original decision, if you are still within the absolute time limit for these.

4. Supersessions

If your circumstances have changed since a decision was made, you can seek a supersession.[83] You can also seek a supersession if you think a decision is wrong, but you must show there are grounds (see below). You can seek a supersession of an original decision or one superseding an earlier decision.

You can seek a supersession even if the decision was made a long time ago. However, the arrears of benefit you are paid can be limited (see p1079). It is usually better to try for a revision or appeal if you can (see p1065 and Chapter 42).

Following a supersession, your benefit could be increased, but it could also be decreased or stopped altogether. See p1063 to see what you should consider before seeking a supersession.

For information on how to seek a supersession, see p1079. To find out when a supersession takes effect, see p1079.

When a decision can be superseded

You can ask for a decision to be superseded or the decision maker can decide to do this.[84] However, there must be grounds for a supersession. See below for the main grounds and for other grounds see p1077.

Note: if a decision could be revised (see p1065) it cannot be superseded unless there are grounds for supersession that are not covered by the revision rules.[85]

The main grounds for supersession

There are a number of grounds for supersession. The main grounds are:

- changes of circumstance (see below);
- mistakes about or ignorance of facts (see p1076);
- where a decision is legally wrong (see p1077);
- where a qualifying benefit has been awarded (see p1077).

For other grounds for supersession, see p1077.

Change of circumstances

A decision can be superseded if, since it had effect (or in the case of advance awards for benefits other than housing benefit (HB) and council tax benefit (CTB), since it was made), your circumstances have changed or it is anticipated that they will do so and this means the decision might no longer be correct.[86] This is what is known as a relevant change of circumstances. If the change means that you could be entitled to more benefit, there is a strict time limit for reporting the change in order to get all the arrears of benefit to which you are entitled (see p1080).

You should bear the following in mind.

- An amendment to the law counts as a change of circumstances, but a decision of a court or commissioner that the law has been wrongly interpreted does not.[87]
- A new medical opinion is not a change of circumstances, but a new medical report following an examination might give evidence of such a change.[88]
- For income support (IS) and jobseeker's allowance (JSA), the repayment of a student loan does not count as a relevant change of circumstance.[89]

- For attendance allowance (AA) and disability living allowance (DLA), you or the person claiming on your behalf must specify that you are terminally ill in the application for a supersession for this to count as a relevant change of circumstances.[90]
- In respect of your assessed income period for pension credit (PC), the only change of circumstance that is relevant for these purposes is that the period has ended for one of the reasons listed on p460.[91]
- In deciding whether there has been a change of circumstances, it is necessary to compare the circumstances as they were at the time of the decision and as they are at the time of the supersession. So, in considering a supersession of a tribunal's decision to award a benefit, a decision maker may have difficulty showing that there has been a change of circumstances if there is no statement of reasons for the tribunal's decision.[92]

The decision maker might say that a change of circumstances you have reported is not a relevant one and refuse to consider a supersession. If this happens, see p1085.

Note: it is your duty to report any change in your circumstances which may affect your right to, the amount of, or payment of, your benefit.

Change of circumstances after benefit is refused

If you were correctly refused benefit but your circumstances are now different, you *cannot* seek a supersession on the grounds of a change of circumstances. You must instead make a fresh claim (unless you are seeking a supersession because there has been a 'recrudescence' of a prescribed disease – see p320).[93]

Even if you are appealing against the decision refusing or stopping your benefit, you should make a fresh claim when your circumstances change and appeal if you are still refused. If you do not, you could lose out. This is because if you appeal to a tribunal against a decision refusing benefit or terminating your award, the tribunal cannot take a change of circumstances into account if it happens after the decision with which you disagree (but see p1114).

Mistake about or ignorance of facts

A decision can be superseded if there was a mistake about the facts of your case or if it was made in ignorance of relevant facts.[94] However, if, as a result of this, a decision is more favourable to you than it would have been (ie, you were being overpaid), a decision maker can, instead, do an 'any time' revision (see p1070).

For HB and CTB, if the decision can be revised on this ground, a local authority must do a revision, rather than a supersession.[95] For other benefits, a decision maker cannot do a supersession on this ground unless the time limit for seeking an 'any grounds' revision (or any longer period allowed) has passed (see p1067).[96]

Note:

- There must have been a mistake about the facts or the decision maker must not have had all the facts, but it does not matter how the mistake came about or whether you could have produced evidence sooner than you did.
- The mistake or ignorance must be in respect of facts, not conclusions or opinions about the facts. See p1010 for some examples.

Decisions that are legally wrong

A decision can be superseded if it was made by a decision maker (not a tribunal or commissioner) and was legally wrong.[97] This is what is known as an error of law (see p1121). If you think a tribunal or commissioner's decision is legally wrong, you need to appeal against it.

For HB and CTB, if the decision can be revised on this ground, a local authority must do a revision, rather than a supersession.[98] For other benefits, a decision maker cannot do a supersession on this ground unless the time limit for seeking an 'any grounds' revision (or any longer period allowed) has passed (see p1067).[99]

Awards of qualifying benefits

If you are awarded a benefit (eg, IS or HB) but, from a later date than the entitlement began, **you or a member of your family become entitled to a 'qualifying benefit'** (eg, DLA or carer's allowance (CA)) or the qualifying benefit is increased, the decision awarding you benefit can be superseded.[100] See p700 for who counts as your family.

For IS or PC only, if you have a non-dependant living with you (see p786) and since you were awarded IS or PC, **your non-dependant has been awarded a 'qualifying benefit'** for a period after the date the award took effect, and this means that you are now entitled to a severe disability premium (for IS) or a severe disability additional amount (for PC), the decision awarding you benefit can be superseded.[101]

See p1085 for further information. If you are only entitled to a benefit once a qualifying benefit is awarded, see pp968 and 205.

Other grounds for supersession

There are a number of other situations when a decision maker can do a supersession. This includes where the decision is one against which you have no right of appeal (see p1097).[102]

Incapacity for work

A decision to award you benefit or national insurance (NI) credits on the basis that you are incapable of work can be superseded if it has been determined that you satisfy the personal capability assessment (see p668), you can be treated as incapable of work, or there are exceptional circumstances (see p673) and since the decision:[103]

- you have been examined by a doctor approved by the Secretary of State; *and*
- the doctor has provided medical evidence on your capacity for work.

However, your benefit (or NI credits) cannot be stopped unless the decision maker considers whether, and shows that, you are no longer incapable of work.[104] If you have told the decision maker that your condition has not improved since your last personal capability assessment or you have a variable condition, you can argue that reference should be made to earlier assessments and decisions on your claim.[105]

Note:

- If this ground for supersession is not satisfied, a decision to award you benefit might still be superseded on the grounds of a change of circumstances.
- This ground for supersession is not available for HB and CTB.

Other

Other decisions that can be superseded are certain decisions:

- about payment of JSA where a sanction applies;[106]
- about benefits other than HB and CTB, child benefit and guardian's allowance, where you (or your partner) failed to take part in a work-focused interview or where you (or s/he) no longer have to take part;[107]
- of a tribunal to terminate your IS because you were not incapable of work, but another tribunal subsequently decides that you are;[108]
- about HB, where the 'local housing allowance' rules apply and the local authority must redetermine your maximum rent (see p238) because a year has passed since it last did so, or where the 'local reference rent' rules apply and the local authority has referred your tenancy to a rent officer to make determinations because a previous reference was made more than 52 weeks ago. See Chapter 11 for information about these rules;[109]
- about HB, where your maximum rent (see p238) decreases because of a rent officer re-determination (see p243). Note that a decrease in your maximum rent because a local housing allowance (see p236) or a broad rental market area has been amended because of a rent officer's error is dealt with as a change of circumstance;[110]
- awarding you IS or JSA, where you have since failed to comply with a community order (see p997) or where the loss of benefit for benefit offences rules apply (see p1047).[111] An HB or CTB decision which is affected by such a decision can also be superseded;[112]
- about PC, HB and CTB, where you or your partner deferred claiming a pension and you are paid a lump sum or change your option to a pension increase;[113]
- about PC, where your assessed income period has ended or is about to end (see p458);[114]
- of a tribunal or a commissioner while a test case was pending where the test case eventually goes in your favour (see p1108).[115]

How to seek a supersession

Apply for a supersession to the office that made the decision with which you disagree. The DWP, local authority or Revenue can treat a request for a revision as a request for a supersession.[116] The DWP and local authority can also treat a notification of a change in circumstances as a request for a supersession. Claims for benefit or questions about your entitlement can be treated as requests for a supersession.[117]

For benefits other than HB and CTB, you do not have to ask for a supersession in writing although it is always best to do so. For HB and CTB, you *must* ask the local authority for a supersession in writing.[118]

The decision maker does not have to consider any issue not raised by your application for a supersession or which caused her/him to act on her/his own initiative.[119] You should, therefore, ensure you:

- tell the decision maker all the points about the decision with which you disagree;
- provide any information or evidence that supports your case. This includes medical evidence from a GP or consultant if this is relevant. If you are claiming AA or DLA, evidence or information from your carer or a diary of your walking, supervision or care needs over a period may be equally useful.

The new decision

After a decision maker carries out a supersession s/he makes a new decision. S/he can decide that:

- the original decision should continue; *or*
- the original decision should be replaced.

For information about challenging a decision, see p1084. If the decision maker refuses to consider a supersession, see p1085.

When a supersession takes effect

The date a supersession takes effect is important. This is the date from which you are paid arrears if you are entitled to more benefit, or you have been overpaid if you are entitled to less benefit. The date a supersession takes effect, in some cases, depends on the grounds for the supersession. It is important to make it clear that you want payment for the past period. You might get less backdating if the 'anti-test case rule' applies (see p1087).

The general rule

The general rule is that, if a decision is superseded, the new decision takes effect from the date you applied for the supersession or, if the decision maker decides to do one on her/his own, the date the decision is made.[120]

There are a number of situations when the general rule does not apply. These depend on the grounds for supersession. For exceptions to the rules, see below and the chapter in this *Handbook* about the benefit you are claiming.

Changes in your circumstances

For benefits other than child benefit and guardian's allowance, if the change of circumstances is that there has been a change in the legislation that affects your benefit, the decision takes effect from the date the legislation took effect.[121] Otherwise, the supersession takes effect as set out below.

It is important to remember that if you fail to notify a change of circumstances in time, and the change means you are entitled to less benefit, you will have been overpaid. The DWP, local authority or Revenue might seek to recover the overpayment (see Chapter 39).

Housing benefit and council tax benefit

For HB or CTB, in most cases the new decision takes effect from the Monday after the week in which the change occurs.[122] This applies whether or not a decision is advantageous to you. For further information about the general rule on when changes in circumstances take effect and exceptions to this rule, see p219.

However, if the change is one you are required to notify to the local authority (other than, if you get PC, one of the exceptions to the rules described on p220) and it is advantageous to you, the change must be notified within one month of it taking place.[123] The one-month period can be extended in certain circumstances (see p1082). If you notify the change outside the one-month period (or any longer period allowed by the local authority) the date you notify the change is treated as if that is the date the change occurred.

Other benefits

If you are claiming a benefit on the basis that you are incapable of work and you are covered by the own occupation test (see p667), the decision maker can anticipate a change in your circumstances as a result of information gathered for a personal capability assessment and do a supersession. The new decision takes effect the day after the day on which the own occupation test ceases to apply to you.[124] Otherwise, when the change takes effect depends on whether or not the new decision is advantageous to you.

If the new decision is **advantageous** to you, the supersession takes effect as follows.

- If you apply for the supersession and the decision is about AA or DLA[125] *and*:
  - the change means you are now entitled to a particular rate of benefit, the supersession takes effect from the first benefit payday after you satisfy the conditions of entitlement to that rate. You must notify the DWP of the change within one month of doing so;

  - the change makes a difference to whether benefit is payable to you (eg, you go into, or leave, hospital or a care home), the supersession takes effect from the first benefit payday after the change. You must notify the DWP of the change within one month of it taking place.

  In both cases, the one-month period can be extended in certain circumstances (see p1082).
- If you apply for the supersession and the decision is *not* about AA or DLA, the supersession takes effect from the date of the change so long as the DWP or the Revenue is notified of the change within one month of it taking place.[126] To see if the one-month period can be extended, and when a supersession takes effect if it is not, see p1082.
- For benefits other than HB or CTB, if the change of circumstances is that your carer has stopped being paid CA, the supersession takes effect the day after the last day for which CA was paid. This means that if you are now entitled to the severe disability premium with your IS or income-based JSA (or the severe disability additional amount with PC), this can be backdated to when your carer stopped getting CA for looking after you.[127]
- If the decision maker decides to do a supersession her/himself, it takes effect from the date s/he first took action with a view to doing a supersession.[128]

If a decision is **not advantageous** to you, the supersession usually takes effect from the date of the change of circumstances.[129] This does not apply to certain disability and incapacity decisions.

If a decision is a disability decision about AA, DLA, severe disablement allowance (SDA), industrial injuries disablement benefit or a decision about your incapacity for work under the personal capability assessment (see p668) or whether you can be treated as incapable of work or there are exceptional circumstances (see p673), and the change related to your disability or incapacity, the supersession takes effect from the date you (or the person being paid the benefit) ought to have notified the change if:[130]

- the change was one you were required to notify; *and*
- you (or the person being paid the benefit) failed to notify the change when you knew that you should have, or could reasonably be expected to have known that you should have, done so.

However, if this does not apply and the decision is a disability decision, the general rule applies (see p1079) – ie the supersession takes effect from the date you applied for it, or the date the decision was made.[131] So if your condition is found to have improved in the past, you will not have been overpaid benefit.

Note: if the benefit is a qualifying benefit (see p1077) and the supersession means your entitlement to another benefit is affected, the decision about the other benefit takes effect on the same date.[132]

Late notification of a change of circumstances

If you fail to notify a change within the one-month periods above, you can apply for an extension of time in limited circumstances.[133] You must do so within an absolute time limit of 13 months from the date the change occurs. Your application must contain:[134]

- details of the relevant change of circumstances; *and*
- the reasons why you failed to notify the change in time. You must show that:[135]
  - it is reasonable to grant your request; *and*
  - the change of circumstances is relevant to the decision you want changed; *and*
  - there are special circumstances which mean that it was not practicable for you to notify the change within the time limit.

The longer you have delayed notifying a change, the more compelling the special circumstances have to be. When deciding whether it is reasonable to grant your application, the decision maker cannot take account of the fact that:[136]

- a court or commissioner has interpreted the law in a different way than previously understood and applied;
- you (or anyone acting for you) misunderstood or were unaware of the relevant law, including the time limits for seeking a supersession.

If your application for an extension of time is refused, the supersession takes effect:

- for benefits (other than AA, DLA, HB and CTB), from when you notified the change;[137] *or*
- for AA or DLA, from the date you applied for the supersession;[138] *or*
- for HB and CTB, usually from Monday after the date when you notified the change (see p219).[139]

Mistake about or ignorance of facts

Where there has been a mistake about or ignorance of facts, the general rule usually applies (see p1079). However, there are exceptions to this rule.

If a tribunal or commissioner made a decision in ignorance of relevant facts or made a mistake about the facts and, as a result, the decision was more advantageous to you than it would otherwise have been, the supersession takes effect from the date the tribunal's or commissioner's decision took effect.[140] However, if it is a disability decision about AA, DLA, SDA, industrial injuries disablement benefit or a decision about your incapacity for work under the personal capability assessment (see p668) or whether you can be treated as incapable of work or there are exceptional circumstances (see p673), this only happens if you (or the person being paid the benefit) knew, or could reasonably have been expected to know, the fact in question and that it was relevant to the decision.

For HB and CTB, if a decision was made in ignorance of facts or there was a mistake about the facts and the new decision is advantageous to you, the supersession takes effect from the start of the benefit week in which:[141]

- you applied for the supersession; *or*
- if you did not apply for a supersession, the local authority had sufficient information to show that the original decision was wrong.

Other grounds for supersession

There are a large number of other exceptions to the general rule. The main ones are as follows.

- If you are entitled to a benefit at a higher rate because you, a member of your family or a non-dependant were awarded a **qualifying benefit**, the supersession takes effect on the date of entitlement to the qualifying benefit or to an increase in its rate, or if you are now entitled to a severe disability premium with IS (additional amount with PC), the date a non-dependant ceases to live with you. See p1085 for further information.[142]
- If the decision is that you are entitled to be paid **IB at the long-term rate** because you have become entitled to the highest rate of the care component of DLA (see p273), even though you have been incapable of work for less than a year, the supersession takes effect from the date you became entitled to the highest rate of the care component.[143]
- If your award of IS, PC or JSA is being superseded to include help with **mortgage interest** (see p802) or **interest on a loan for repairs and improvements** (see p806), the supersession can be backdated for up to eight weeks. This can only be done if the supersession could not take place sooner because your lender did not supply the DWP with your mortgage details.[144]
- If a decision about your benefit is being superseded because of a decision by a commissioner or court in another case – a **test case** – the supersession is effective from the date of the commissioner's or court's decision, even if you did not realise it was relevant to your case until some time later.[145] This could help you get considerable arrears of benefit. See p1087 for further information about the 'anti-test case rule'.
- For benefits other than HB and CTB, if a decision was made on your claim for benefit or to make a revision or a supersession, but your benefit was suspended while a **test case was pending** (see p984) and the test case is eventually decided against you (in whole or in part), the supersession takes effect from the date the earlier decision took effect.[146]
- If you appealed to a tribunal while a **test case was pending**, a tribunal or commissioner determines your appeal as if the test case had been decided in the way most unfavourable to you and the test case eventually goes in your favour (see p1108), the supersession takes effect from the date it would have taken effect had the decision maker made it in accordance with the decision in the test case.[147]

- For HB only:
  - if the local authority has determined your maximum rent (see p238) under the **local housing allowance rules** because a year has passed since it last did so, the new decision usually takes effect from the first day of the benefit week following the one in which the determination was made. However, if the determination was made on the first day of a benefit week, the new decision takes effect on the day it was made;[148]
  - if the local authority has referred your tenancy to the **rent officer** to make **determinations** (see p243) because more than 52 weeks has passed since it last made a reference, unless your entitlement to HB ceases, the new decision takes effect:[149]
    - if the determination is the same or has increased, from the end of the period covered by the previous determinations; *or*
    - if the determination has decreased, from the first day of the benefit week after the local authority receives it;
  - if your **maximum rent** (see p238) has **decreased** because of a rent officer redetermination (see p242), the new decision usually takes effect from the start of the benefit week after the date of the determination.[150]

There are other exceptions, where a decision is superseded:
- to apply a sanction to your JSA;[151]
- if you are 16 or 17, to disapply a sanction to your JSA severe hardship payments because you have been given a 'certificate of good cause';[152]
- where you (or your partner) failed to take part in a work-focused interview without good cause (see p971);[153]
- because you are awarded IB or SDA on the grounds that you are exempt from the personal capability assessment (see p668);[154]
- for IS and JSA, to sanction you because you failed to comply with a community order (see p997);[155]
- to stop or restrict benefit under the loss of benefit for benefit offences rules (see p1047);[156]
- for PC, when your assessed income period has ended or is about to end;[157]
- where a tribunal terminated your IS because you were not incapable of work but another tribunal subsequently decides that you are;[158]
- for PC, HB and CTB, where you or your partner deferred claiming a pension and you are paid a lump sum or change your option to a pension increase.[159]

Challenging a supersession

Following your application for a supersession, or a decision maker deciding to do a supersession on her/his own, a new decision is issued in writing. If you do not get all that you wanted from the supersession, you can seek a revision of the superseded decision (see p1065). If the decision is one against which you have a right of appeal (see p1095) you can appeal to a tribunal. If you have a right of appeal against the decision, you must be told about this.

If the decision maker has said there are no grounds for a supersession, you must show why there are, as well as saying what you think the new decision should be. If the decision maker has done a supersession, but you do not agree that s/he had grounds for this, you should explain why.

If a decision maker refuses to consider a supersession

When you apply for a supersession, a decision maker must, in almost all cases, make a decision. There are two possibilities. Your application for a supersession contains a ground for supersession that is potentially relevant to the amount of benefit you can be paid or the length of time you can be paid it, and:

- the decision maker agrees that there is a reason to change your award – eg, you are claiming HB and notify the decision maker that your non-dependant has moved out and so are entitled to more benefit. In this situation, the decision maker does a supersession; *or*
- the decision maker does not think there is a reason to change your award – eg, you are getting DLA care component at the lowest rate, feel your condition has deteriorated and want to claim middle rate instead. However, the decision maker thinks you do not qualify for the middle rate. In this situation, the decision maker issues a decision refusing to do a supersession.

In either situation, you can seek a revision of the decision maker's decision or appeal against it.[160] The only situations where a decision maker does not have to make a decision is where an application has not been made properly and, therefore, cannot possibly lead to a supersession or where an application is transparently not on a potentially relevant ground for supersession or is otherwise misconceived. In these cases, there is no decision against which you can seek a revision or appeal.

5. Revisions and supersessions after a 'qualifying benefit' award

There are special revision and supersession rules, known as 'qualifying benefit' rules. They help where, because of delays in assessing entitlement to a qualifying benefit (eg, attendance allowance (AA), disability living allowance (DLA), carer's allowance (CA) or child benefit):

- you did not get certain premiums paid with your income support (IS), jobseeker's allowance (JSA), housing benefit (HB) or council tax benefit (CTB) (eg, disability, disabled child or carer's premium), or additional amounts paid with your pension credit (PC) or allowances for your children. For IS and

PC, this includes where there are delays in assessing your non-dependant's entitlement to a qualifying benefit (see below); *or*

- a non-dependant deduction was made from your IS, JSA or PC housing costs, or from your HB or CTB.

Note: you can only ask for a revision or supersession on this ground if you are already entitled to IS, JSA, PC, HB or CTB.[161] It is, therefore, *essential* to make a claim for these at the same time as the claim for a qualifying benefit. If you only qualify for one of these when the qualifying benefit is awarded, see p1087.

You or a member of your family

If you, or a member of your family (see p700), are awarded a qualifying benefit or an increase in its rate, and arrears of the qualifying benefit are payable, your award of IS, JSA, PC, HB or CTB can be increased on revision or supersession and arrears paid for the same length of time.[162] This applies where you are now entitled to premiums (or if the qualifying benefit is child benefit, allowances for your children paid with your benefit). It also applies where no non-dependant deduction should now be made from your IS, JSA or PC housing costs (or from your HB or CTB) because you are now entitled to AA or the care component of DLA (see pp816 and 198).

Note that for IS or PC only, if you had a non-dependant living with you while you were waiting for a decision on your claim for a qualifying benefit, your IS or PC award can be superseded to include the severe disability premium (additional amount), from the date s/he ceased to reside with you, if this was after the date from which the qualifying benefit is payable.[163]

Example

Gus has been getting IS, HB and CTB for two months. His IS does not include any premiums and because his uncle lives with him and his partner, Tanya, a non-dependant deduction is being made from his HB and CTB. He claims DLA, and his partner claims CA on 15 July. Six months later, Gus is awarded DLA highest rate care component and Tanya is awarded CA, both payable from 15 July. Gus is now entitled to the disability, enhanced disability and carer's premiums with his IS and a non-dependant deduction should not be made from his HB and CTB. His IS, HB and CTB awards are superseded and and he is paid six months arrears, backdated to 15 July.

Your non-dependant

For IS or PC only, if you have a non-dependant living with you (see p786) and, but for this, a severe disability premium (additional amount for PC) would be paid, your award of IS or PC can be increased on revision or supersession to include this premium (additional amount) from the date the non-dependant is awarded a qualifying benefit (eg, AA or middle or highest rate DLA care component).[164]

If you only qualify when the qualifying benefit is awarded

If you only qualify for IS, JSA or PC when the qualifying benefit is awarded, you should make a second claim as soon as you hear about the qualifying benefit. See p968 for further information.

If you only qualify for HB or CTB when the qualifying benefit is awarded, see p205. If you lose benefit because of the way the rules operate, ask the local authority for compensation.

Remember, if you only claim for the first time after you hear about the qualifying benefit:

- for IS or JSA, you can only get arrears if you satisfy the backdating rules on p966;
- for PC, your claim can only be backdated for up to 12 months (see p456);
- for HB or CTB, your claim can be backdated for up to 12 months, but if you are under 60 or either you or your partner are getting IS or income-based JSA, only if you can show 'good cause' for your late claim (see p206).

Note: the Government intends to reduce the time for which PC, HB and CTB can be backdated to three months. See CPAG's *Welfare Rights Bulletin* for updates.

There are similar rules that help you get extra backdating if your entitlement to IB, SDA or CA depends on whether you (or in the case of CA, the person for whom you care) are entitled to a qualifying benefit. See p968 for information.

6. The 'anti-test case rule'

There is a rule – known as the 'anti-test case rule' – which says that some court and commissioners' decisions should be ignored when decision makers are considering your entitlement to benefit for periods before the court or commissioners' decisions were given. This is intended to prevent you from taking advantage of a test case. If the anti-test case rule applies, you get arrears of benefit, but only going back to the date of the decision in the test case.

How the anti-test case rule operates

If a commissioner or court decides that a decision maker in a totally different case (the test case) has made an error of law (see p1121), and you make a claim, or seek a revision or a supersession (whether before or after the test case decision), your decision maker must decide any part of *your* claim (or revision or supersession) which relates to the period *before* the test case decision as if that decision had been found by the commissioner or court in question not to have been wrong.[165] The anti-test case rule only applies if the test case is the first authoritative decision on the issue, and not merely a later decision which confirms an earlier decision.[166]

The test case decision only has to be disregarded for the period before it was made if it found the decision maker to have been wrong, not if it found her/him to be right.

You can avoid the anti-test case rule by appealing rather than seeking a revision or supersession. This means that in cases where the anti-test case rule might apply, and you are still within the absolute time limit for appealing, it may be better to appeal first (applying for permission out of time if necessary – see p1129) and only ask for a revision or supersession if you cannot appeal.

What happens while a test case is pending

If a test case is pending, the decision maker can postpone making a decision on your claim or request for a supersession or revision.[167] This prevents you appealing until a decision is made in the test case. If you already have a decision in your favour, the decision maker can suspend payment of your benefit (see p984).

If you would be entitled to benefit even if the test case were decided against you, the decision maker can make a decision.[168] This is done on the assumption that the test case has been decided in the way that is most unfavourable to you. However, this does mean that you are at least paid something while you wait for the result of the test case.

If the decision on your claim or request for a revision or supersession is postponed, once a decision has been made in the test case, the decision maker then makes the decision in your case. If the test case goes in your favour, you are paid the extra benefit you are owed.[169]

If you have already appealed to a tribunal, see p1108. If payment of your benefit was suspended pending the test case, see p984.

Notes

1 R(SB) 29/83; R(SB) 12/89; CIS/807/1992; R(H) 3/05

1. **Decisions**

2 Reg 11 SS&CS(DA) Regs
3 s19 SSA 1998
4 Reg 12 SS&CS(DA) Regs
5 **HB/CTB** Sch 7 para 5 CSPSSA 2000
Other benefits s11(2) SSA 1998
6 s39(1) SSA 1998
7 Regs 13(2) and (3), 13A and 15 SS&CS(DA) Regs
8 Reg 13(1) SS&CS(DA) Regs
9 s8 SSC(TF)A 1999
10 s10A SSA 1998; reg 11A SS&CS(DA) Regs
11 s11 SSC(TF)A 1999
12 s12(1) SSC(TF)A 1999
13 Reg 9 SSC(DA) Regs; s49 TMA 1970
14 s24A SSA 1998; reg 38A SS&CS(DA) Regs
15 s17 SSC(TF)A 1999; Sch 3 paras 16 and 17 SSA 1998
16 s74 SSAA 1992; regs 7-10 SS(PAOR) Regs
17 **HB/CTB** Reg 10A HB&CTB(DA) Regs
Other benefits Reg 9A SS&CS(DA) Regs
18 **CB/GA** Reg 26(1) CB&GA(DA) Regs
HB/CTB Reg 10(1) HB&CTB(DA) Regs
Other benefits Reg 28(1) SS&CS(DA) Regs
19 Reg 10(2) HB&CTB(DA) Regs
20 **CB/GA** Regs 3 and 26(1)(b) and (2) CB&GA(DA) Regs
Other benefits Regs 2 and 28(1)(b) and (2) SS&CS(DA) Regs
21 R(IB) 4/02

2. **General information**

22 CSB/376/1983; R(I) 1/71; CI/11/1977
23 Regs 4(8) and 7(7) HB&CTB(DA) Regs
24 R(I) 50/56
25 R(IS) 11/92
26 **CB/GA** Regs 7(2) and (3) and 14(3) CB&GA(DA) Regs
HB/CTB Regs 4(5) and 7(5) HB&CTB(DA) Regs
Other benefits Regs 3(2) and 6(4) SS&CS(DA) Regs
27 ss9(2) and 10(2) SSA 1998

3. **Revisions**

28 **HB/CTB** Sch 7 para 3 CSPSSA 2000
Other benefits s9 SSA 1998
29 **CB/GA** s9(1) SSA 1998; regs 5, 8, 10 and 11 CB&GA(DA) Regs
HB/CTB Sch 7 para 3(1) CSPSSA 2000; reg 4 HB&CTB(DA) Regs
Other benefits s9(1) SSA 1998; reg 3 SS&CS(DA) Regs
30 **CB/GA** Reg 5(3) CB&GA(DA) Regs
HB/CTB Reg 4(10) HB&CTB(DA) Regs
Other benefits Reg 3(9)(a) SS&CS(DA) Regs
31 Reg 3(9)(b) SS&CS(DA) Regs
32 **CB/GA** Reg 5(2)(b) CB&GA(DA) Regs
HB/CTB Reg 4(1)(a) HB&CTB(DA) Regs
Other benefits Reg 3(1)(b) SS&CS(DA) Regs
33 **CB/GA** Reg 5(2)(a) CB&GA(DA) Regs
Other benefits Reg 3(1)(a) SS&CS(DA) Regs
34 Reg 4(1)(b) HB&CTB(DA) Regs
35 Reg 3(3) SS&CS(DA) Regs
36 Regs 2 and 4(1)(a) HB&CTB(DA) Regs
37 Reg 4(4) HB&CTB(DA) Regs
38 **CB/GA** Regs 3 and 5(2)(b) CB&GA(DA) Regs
Other benefits Regs 2 and 3(1)(b) SS&CS(DA) Regs
39 **HB/CTB** Reg 10A(3) HB&CTB(DA) Regs
Other benefits Reg 9A(3) SS&CS(DA) Regs
40 **CB/GA** Reg 6(3)(c) CB&GA(DA) Regs
HB/CTB Reg 5(3)(b) HB&CTB(DA) Regs
Other benefits Reg 4(3)(b) SS&CS(DA) Regs
41 **CB/GA** Regs 5(2)(b) and 6(3)(a) and (b) CB&GA(DA) Regs
HB/CTB Reg 5(3)(a) HB&CTB(DA) Regs
Other benefits Regs 3(1)(b)(iv) and 4(3)(a) SS&CS(DA) Regs
42 **CB/GA** Reg 6(4) CB&GA(DA) Regs
HB/CTB Reg 5(4) HB&CTB(DA) Regs
Other benefits Reg 4(4) SS&CS(DA) Regs

43 **CB/GA** Reg 6(5) CB&GA(DA) Regs
HB/CTB Reg 5(6) HB&CTB(DA) Regs
Other benefits Reg 4(5) SS&CS(DA) Regs
44 **CB/GA** Reg 6(6) CB&GA(DA) Regs
HB/CTB Reg 5(5) HB&CTB(DA) Regs
Other benefits Reg 4(6) SS&CS(DA) Regs
45 R(TC) 1/05
46 **CB/GA** Reg 10(2)(a) CB&GA(DA) Regs
HB/CTB Reg 4(2)(a) HB&CTB(DA) Regs
Other benefits Reg 3(5)(a) SS&CS(DA) Regs
47 **HB/CTB** Reg 1(2) HB&CTB(DA) Regs
Other benefits Reg 1(3) SS&CS(DA) Regs
48 Reg 10(3) CB&GA(DA) Regs
49 R(CS) 3/04; CG/2122/2001
50 para 03257 DMG
51 CDLA/393/2006
52 **CB/GA** Reg 10(2)(b) CB&GA(DA) Regs
HB/CTB Reg 4(2)(b) HB&CTB(DA) Regs
Other benefits Reg 3(5)(b) and (d) SS&CS(DA) Regs
53 Regs 3(5)(c) and 7A(1) SS&CS(DA) Regs
54 Reg 7A(2) SS&CS(DA) Regs
55 Reg 4(1)(b) HB&CTB(DA) Regs
56 **CB/GA** Reg 11 CB&GA(DA) Regs
HB/CTB Reg 4(7B) HB&CTB(DA) Regs
Other benefits Reg 3(7) SS&CS(DA) Regs
57 Reg 4(7C) HB&CTB(DA) Regs
58 Reg 3(7ZA) SS&CS(DA) Regs
59 **CB/GA** Reg 8(2) CB&GA(DA) Regs
HB/CTB Reg 4(1)(c) HB&CTB(DA) Regs
Other benefits Reg 3(4A) SS&CS(DA) Regs
60 **CB/GA** Reg 8(3) CB&GA(DA) Regs
Other benefits Reg 3(5A) SS&CS(DA) Regs
61 Reg 4(7) HB&CTB(DA) Regs
62 **CB/GA** Reg 9 CB&GA(DA) Regs
HB/CTB Reg 4(6) HB&CTB(DA) Regs
Other benefits Reg 3(8) SS&CS(DA) Regs
63 Reg 3(7C) SS&CS(DA) Regs
64 Reg 3(7B) SS&CS(DA) Regs
65 Reg 3(7F) SS&CS(DA) Regs
66 Reg 3(5B) SS&CS(DA) Regs
67 Reg 3(6) SS&CS(DA) Regs
68 Reg 3(7A) SS&CS(DA) Regs
69 Reg 3(6A) SS&CS(DA) Regs
70 **HB/CTB** Reg 4(7A) HB&CTB(DA) Regs
Other benefits Reg 3(8A) and (8B) SS&CS(DA) Regs
71 Reg 4(3), (7E) and (7F) HB&CTB(DA) Regs; reg 18A(1) and (3) HB Regs; reg 18A(1) and (3) HB(SPC) Regs
72 **RP** Reg 3(7E) SS&CS(DA) Regs
PC Reg 3(7D) SS&CS(DA) Regs
HB/CTB Reg 4(7D) HB&CTB(DA) Regs
73 **CB/GA** Reg 2(1) CB&GA(DA) Regs, definition of 'appropriate office'
HB/CTB Reg 4(8) HB&CTB(DA) Regs
Other benefits Reg 3(11) SS&CS(DA) Regs
74 **CB/GA** Reg 7(1) CB&GA(DA) Regs
HB/CTB Reg 4(9) HB&CTB(DA) Regs
Other benefits Reg 3(10) SS&CS(DA) Regs
75 Reg 4(8) HB&CTB(DA) Regs
76 Reg 5(2) HB&CTB(DA) Regs
77 **HB/CTB** Sch 7 para 3(2) CSPSSA 2000
Other benefits s9(2) SSA 1998
78 **HB/CTB** Sch 7 para 3(3) CSPSSA 2000
Other benefits s9(3) SSA 1998
79 **CB/GA** Reg 12 CB&GA(DA) Regs
HB/CTB Reg 6 HB&CTB(DA) Regs
Other benefits Reg 5(1) SS&CS(DA) Regs
80 Reg 5(2) SS&CS(DA) Regs
81 **CB/GA** Reg 28(2) CB&GA(DA) Regs
HB/CTB Sch 7 para 3(5) CSPSSA 2000; reg 18(3) HB&CTB(DA) Regs
Other benefits s9(5) SSA 1998; reg 31(2) SS&CS(DA) Regs
82 R(IS) 15/04; *Beltekian v Westminster City Council and Another* [2004] EWCA Civ 1784, 8 December 2004, reported as R(H) 8/05

4. **Supersessions**
83 **HB/CTB** Sch 7 para 4 CSPSSA 2000
Other benefits s10 SSA 1998
84 **CB/GA** Reg 13(1) CB&GA(DA) Regs
HB/CTB Reg 7(2) HB&CTB(DA) Regs
Other benefits Reg 6(2) SS&CS(DA) Regs
85 **CB/GA** Reg 15 CB&GA(DA) Regs
HB/CTB Reg 7(4) HB&CTB(DA) Regs
Other benefits Reg 6(3) SS&CS(DA) Regs
86 **CB/GA** Reg 13(2)(a) CB&GA(DA) Regs
HB/CTB Regs 7(2)(a) and (3) and 7A(4) HB&CTB(DA) Regs
Other benefits Reg 6(2)(a) SS&CS(DA) Regs
All *Wood v Secretary of State for Work and Pensions* [2003] EWCA Civ 53 reported as R(DLA) 1/03; *Saker v Secretary of State for Social Services*, reported as R(I) 2/88; CIB/2338/2000
87 *CAO v McKiernon*, 8 July 1993 (CA)

88 *Cooke v The Secretary of State for Social Security* [2001], reported as R(DLA) 6/01; R(S) 4/86; R(IS) 2/98; CIB/7899/1996; CIS/856/1994
89 Reg 6(6)(a) SS&CS(DA) Regs
90 Reg 6(6)(c) SS&CS(DA) Regs
91 Reg 6(8) SS&CS(DA) Regs
92 CSDLA/637/2006; CSDLA/822/2006
93 **HB/CTB** Sch 7 para 2 CSPSSA 2000
Other benefits s8(2) SSA 1998; reg 12A SS&CS(DA) Regs
94 **CB/GA** Reg 13(2)(b)(i) and (c)(i) CB&GA(DA) Regs
HB/CTB Reg 7(2)(b) and (d) HB&CTB(DA) Regs
Other benefits Reg 6(2)(b)(i) and (c) SS&CS(DA) Regs
95 Reg 7(2)(b)(i) HB&CTB(DA) Regs
96 **CB/GA** Reg 13(2)(b)(ii) CB&GA(DA) Regs
Other benefits Reg 6(2)(b)(ii) SS&CS(DA) Regs
97 **CB/GA** Reg 13(2)(b)(i) CB&GA(DA) Regs
HB/CTB Reg 7(2)(b) HB&CTB(DA) Regs
Other benefits Reg 6(2)(b)(i) SS&CS(DA) Regs
98 Reg 7(2)(b)(i) HB&CTB(DA) Regs
99 **CB/GA** Reg 13(2)(b)(ii) CB&GA(DA) Regs
Other benefits Reg 6(2)(b)(ii) SS&CS(DA) Regs
100 **CB/GA** Reg 13(2)(e) CB&GA(DA) Regs
HB/CTB Reg 7(2)(i) HB&CTB(DA) Regs
Other benefits Reg 6(2)(e) SS&CS(DA) Regs
101 Reg 6(2)(ee) SS&CS(DA) Regs
102 **CB/GA** Reg 13(2)(d) CB&GA(DA) Regs
HB/CTB Reg 7(2)(e) HB&CTB(DA) Regs
Other benefits Reg 6(2)(d) SS&CS(DA) Regs
103 Regs 6(2)(g) and 7A(1) SS&CS(DA) Regs. Note that the reference to a 'doctor' in reg 6(2)(g) SS&CS(DA) Regs has not been amended; CIB/4033/2003; R(IB) 2/05
104 CSIB/377/2003; CIB/1509/2004 ; R(IB) 5/05
105 CIB/1972/2000; CIB/3179/2000; CIB/3985/2001
106 Reg 6(2)(f) SS&CS(DA) Regs
107 Reg 6(2)(h) SS&CS(DA) Regs
108 Reg 6(2)(n) SS&CS(DA) Regs
109 Reg 7A(2) and (3) HB&CTB(DA) Regs
110 Reg 7(2)(c) HB&CTB(DA) Regs; reg 18A(2) HB Regs; reg 18A(2) HB(SPC) Regs
111 Reg 6(2)(i)-(k) SS&CS(DA) Regs
112 Reg 7(2)(g) and (h) HB&CTB(DA) Regs
113 **PC** Reg 6(2)(o) SS&CS(DA) Regs
HB/CTB Reg 7(2)(j) HB&CTB(DA) Regs
114 Reg 6(2)(l) and (m) SS&CS(DA) Regs
115 **CB/GA** Reg 13(2)(c)(ii) CB&GA(DA) Regs
HB/CTB Reg 7(2)(d)(ii) HB&CTB(DA) Regs
Other benefits Reg 6(2)(c)(ii) SS&CS(DA) Regs
116 **CB/GA** Reg 14(1) CB&GA(DA) Regs
HB/CTB Reg 7(6) HB&CTB(DA) Regs
Other benefits Reg 6(5) SS&CS(DA) Regs
117 R(I) 50/56
118 Reg 7(7) HB&CTB(DA) Regs
119 **HB/CTB** Sch 7 para 4(3) CSPSSA 2000
Other benefits s10(2) SSA 1998
120 **HB/CTB** Sch 7 para 4(5) CSPSSA 2000
Other benefits s10(5) SSA 1998
121 **HB/CTB** Reg 8(10) HB&CTB(DA) Regs
Other benefits Reg 7(9)(a)(ii) and (30) SS&CS(DA) Regs
122 Reg 8(2) HB&CTB(DA) Regs
123 Reg 8(3) HB&CTB(DA) Regs
124 Reg 7(31) and (32) SS&CS(DA) Regs
125 Reg 7(9) SS&CS(DA) Regs
126 **CB/GA** Reg 16(3)(a) CB&GA(DA) Regs
Other benefits Reg 7(2)(a) SS&CS(DA) Regs
127 Reg 7(2)(bc) and (bd) SS&CS(DA) Regs
128 **CB/GA** Reg 16(4) CB&GA(DA) Regs
Other benefits Reg 7(2)(bb) and (9)(a) SS&CS(DA) Regs
129 **CB/GA** Reg 16(5) CB&GA(DA) Regs
Other benefits Reg 7(2)(c)(iv) and (v) SS&CS(DA) Regs
130 Regs 7(2)(c)(ii)and 7A(1) SS&CS(DA) Regs
131 Reg 7(2)(c)(v) SS&CS(DA) Regs
132 Reg 7A(2) SS&CS(DA) Regs
133 **CB/GA** Reg 17 CB&GA(DA) Regs
HB/CTB Reg 9 HB&CTB(DA) Regs
Other benefits Reg 8 SS&CS(DA) Regs
134 **CB/GA** Reg 17(3) CB&GA(DA) Regs
HB/CTB Reg 9(2) HB&CTB(DA) Regs
Other benefits Reg 8(3) SS&CS(DA) Regs

135 **CB/GA** Reg 17(4) and (5) CB&GA(DA) Regs
HB/CTB Reg 9(3) and (4) HB&CTB(DA) Regs
Other benefits Reg 8(4) and (5) SS&CS(DA) Regs
136 **CB/GA** Reg 17(6) CB&GA(DA) Regs
HB/CTB Reg 9(5) HB&CTB(DA) Regs
Other benefits Reg 8(6) SS&CS(DA) Regs
137 **CB/GA** Reg 16(3)(b) CB&GA(DA) Regs
Other benefits Reg 7(2)(b) SS&CS(DA) Regs
138 Reg 7(9)(d) SS&CS(DA) Regs
139 Reg 8(3) HB&CTB(DA) Regs
140 **CB/GA** Reg 16(7) CB&GA(DA) Regs
HB/CTB Reg 8(7) HB&CTB(DA) Regs
Other benefits Reg 7(5) SS&CS(DA) Regs
141 Reg 8(4) HB&CTB(DA) Regs
142 **CB/GA** Reg 16(10) CB&GA(DA) Regs
HB/CTB Reg 8(14) HB&CTB(DA) Regs
Other benefits Reg 7(7) SS&CS(DA) Regs
143 Reg 7(10) SS&CS(DA) Regs
144 Reg 7(12) and (13) SS&CS(DA) Regs
145 **CB/GA** Reg 16(9) CB&GA(DA) Regs
HB/CTB Reg 8(8) HB&CTB(DA) Regs
Other benefits Reg 7(6) SS&CS(DA) Regs
146 **CB/GA** Reg 16(9A) CB&GA(DA) Regs
Other benefits Reg 7(6A) SS&CS(DA) Regs
147 **CB/GA** Reg 16(8) CB&GA(DA) Reg
HB/CTB Reg 8(11) HB&CTB(DA) Regs
Other benefits Reg 7(33) SS&CS(DA) Regs
148 Reg 8(15) HB&CTB(DA) Regs
149 Reg 8(6A) HB&CTB(DA) Regs
150 Reg 8(2) and (6) HB&CTB(DA) Regs
151 Reg 7(8) SS&CS(DA) Regs
152 Reg 7(24) SS&CS(DA) Regs
153 Reg 7(25) SS&CS(DA) Regs
154 Reg 7(11) SS&CS(DA) Regs
155 Reg 7(27) SS&CS(DA) Regs
156 **HB/CTB** Reg 8(9) HB&CTB(DA) Regs
Other benefits Reg 7(28) SS&CS(DA) Regs
157 Reg 7(29) and (29A)-(29C) SS&CS(DA) Regs
158 **CB/GA** Reg 16(9A) CB&GA(DA) Regs
Other benefits Reg 7(34) SS&CS(DA) Regs
159 **PC** Reg 7(7A) SS&CS(DA) Regs
HB/CTB Reg 8(14A) HB&CTB(DA) Regs
160 *Wood v Secretary of State for Work and Pensions* [2003] EWCA Civ 53, reported as R(DLA) 1/03

5. **Revisions and supersessions after a 'qualifying benefit' award**
161 **IS/JSA/PC** s8(2) SSA 1998
HB/CTB Sch 7 para 2 CSPSSA 2000
162 **IS/JSA/PC** Regs 3(7), 6(2)(e) and 7(7) SS&CS(DA) Regs
HB/CTB Regs 4(7B) and (7C), 7(2)(i) and 8(14) HB&CTB(DA) Regs; CIS/1178/2001
163 Reg 7(7)(b) SS&CS(DA) Regs
164 Regs 3(7ZA)and 6(2)(ee) and 7(7) SS&CS(DA) Regs

6. **The 'anti-test case rule'**
165 **HB/CTB** Sch 7 para 18 CSPSSA 2000
Other benefits s27 SSA 1998
All *CAO and Another v Bate* [1996] 2 All ER 790 (HL)
166 R(FC) 3/98; R(I) 1/03
167 **HB/CTB** Sch 7 para 16 CSPSSA 2000
Other benefits s25 SSA 1998
168 **CB/GA** s25(3) SSA 1998; reg 22 CB&GA(DA) Regs
HB/CTB Sch 7 para 16(3) CSPSSA 2000; reg 15 HB&CTB(DA) Regs
Other benefits s25(3) SSA 1998; reg 21 SS&CS(DA) Regs
169 **HB/CTB** Sch 7 para 18(2) CSPSSA 2000
Other benefits s27(2) SSA 1998

Chapter 42

Appeals

This chapter covers:

You can appeal to an appeal tribunal if you disagree with certain decisions made by the DWP, local authority and the Revenue about the benefits in this *Handbook* or payments from the regulated social fund (see Chapter 22). See p1095 for information about the decisions you can appeal. In addition, you can appeal against some decisions about your national insurance contributions (see p1059).

The Revenue

The Revenue makes decisions about child benefit and guardian's allowance as well as tax credits. The references to the Revenue in this chapter apply to decisions about child benefit and guardian's allowance but *not* to child tax credit (CTC) and working tax credit (WTC). The rules for appeals about CTC and WTC are covered in Chapter 57. However, many of the rules for appeals about CTC and WTC are the same as those described in this chapter. Chapter 57 refers you to this chapter where relevant. The footnotes in this chapter contain references to the CTC and WTC legislation where applicable.

This chapter does *not* cover:

- statutory sick pay, statutory maternity pay, statutory adoption pay or statutory paternity pay. For these, you can appeal to the tax appeal commissioners (see Chapter 43); *or*
- payments from the *discretionary* social fund. You *cannot* appeal to an appeal tribunal. Instead you can seek a review (see Chapter 44); *or*
- the benefits in Chapter 9 or on p14; *or*
- discretionary housing payments of housing benefit or council tax benefit (see p224).

You can seek a revision (see p1065) prior to appealing against a decision. If you want to seek a revision or appeal you should not delay. The time limit for doing this is very strict (see pp1099 and 1067). For information about the advantages and disadvantages of revisions or appeals, see p1098. Appeals can take time. If your circumstances change while you are waiting for your appeal to be heard, you may need to make a fresh claim for benefit or seek a supersession (see p1114).

Future changes

From October 2008, the way tribunals and the commissioners are organised, and the procedural rules for appeals, will change. Although the new rules were not available when this *Handbook* was written, it is understood that the following are likely to be key features of the new scheme.

- 'Judges' (currently called 'legally qualified tribunal members') and 'members' drawn from the social entitlement chamber of a new 'first-tier tribunal' will hear benefit (and tax credit) appeals. The make-up of tribunals hearing individual appeals may change. Medical members of tribunals will include doctors as well as other qualified health professionals, such as nurses and psychologists.
- Commissioners will be members of a new 'upper tribunal' and will also be renamed 'judges'. As well as dealing with appeals from the 'first-tier tribunal', they will have powers to deal with delegated judicial review work.
- The 'first-tier tribunal' and the 'upper tribunal' will have new powers to review their own decisions.
- Common procedural rules – eg, on time limits for appealing, permission to appeal and striking out appeals will be introduced for both the new tribunals.

See CPAG's *Welfare Rights Bulletin* for updates.

1. Appeal rights

You can appeal to an appeal tribunal against some decisions of the DWP, local authority or the Revenue.

- There is a **strict time limit** for appealing – normally one month (see p1099).
- You must appeal **in writing** and normally on the appropriate form (see p1100).
- Your **appeal must be valid** and contain all the information required. If it is not valid, it might not go ahead (see p1100).

Send or deliver your completed appeal form to the office that made the decision with which you disagree. That office passes your appeal to the Tribunals Service (TS – see p1109) along with its submission on your appeal. A decision maker can ask you to provide further information about your appeal, but it is a legally qualified tribunal member who decides if your appeal is valid, not the DWP, local authority or the Revenue (see p1101).

Who can appeal

You can appeal to an appeal tribunal if you are the claimant. However, certain other people can also appeal.

- If you are appealing about a **benefit other than housing benefit (HB) or council tax benefit (CTB)**, you also have a right to appeal if you are:[1]
  - an appointee claiming on someone's behalf (see p955);
  - claiming attendance allowance (AA) or disability living allowance (DLA) on behalf of someone who is terminally ill (see p121), even if this is without her/his knowledge;
  - a person from whom an ordinary overpayment of a benefit or social fund payment or a duplication of payment of income support (IS), pension credit (PC) or income-based jobseeker's allowance (JSA) (see p1017) can be recovered. This is the case even if you were not the person who claimed the benefit that was overpaid;[2]
  - the partner of a claimant, if the decision concerns whether *you* failed to take part in a work-focused interview without good cause (see p972);[3]
  - a person appointed by the DWP or the Revenue to proceed with a claim for benefit made by someone who has since died or to make a claim for (and who has now claimed) benefit for someone who has died.[4]
- If you are appealing about **HB or CTB**, you have a right to appeal if you are a person affected by that decision – ie, your rights, duties or obligations are affected by the decision, and you are:[5]
  - a claimant;
  - someone acting for a claimant who is unable to act for her/himself – eg, an appointee (see p955);
  - someone from whom the local authority decides to recover an overpayment (including a landlord);[6] *or*
  - a landlord or agent, where the decision concerns whether or not to make a direct payment of HB to you.

In all cases, if the person who appealed dies, the DWP, local authority or the Revenue can appoint some other person to proceed with the appeal.[7]

Decisions you can appeal

You can appeal to an appeal tribunal against *most* decisions taken by the Secretary of State, a local authority officer or an officer of the Revenue (known as decision makers – see p1057).[8] You can appeal against an original decision (even if you have first sought a revision) or a decision made after an application for a supersession (see pp1074 and 1084).

You must be given a written notice of any decision against which you can appeal.[9] The notice must give you information about your right to appeal against the decision and your right to request a written statement of reasons for it if this has not been included (see below).

Sometimes, a decision maker refuses to make a decision on your claim. If this happens, it effectively prevents you having the right to appeal. However, a decision maker must make a decision on every valid claim.[10] See pp959 and 202 for what counts as a valid claim. You can then appeal and it is up to the tribunal to decide whether the decision is correct. **Note:** if the decision maker does not accept that your claim is valid, you should be given a decision saying so. You can appeal to a tribunal and ask it to decide if your claim is valid.

A decision maker can sometimes postpone making a decision if there is a test case pending (see p1088).

Examples of decisions against which you can appeal

All benefits

Whether you are entitled to a benefit.

Whether you have been overpaid benefit and if it is recoverable.

Whether your claim has been validly made or can be backdated.

Whether benefit is payable under the overlapping benefit rules.[11]

A refusal to allocate you a national insurance number.[12]

Whether you are incapable of work.

Whether you satisfy the habitual residence test.

Whether you satisfy the disability conditions for benefit.

Jobseeker's allowance only

Whether you are available for or actively seeking work.

Whether you have left a job voluntarily or have lost it through misconduct.

Whether you have given up or lost your place on a training scheme.

Whether you should be sanctioned and how long a sanction should last.

Whether you can be paid hardship payments.

Whether a jobseeker's agreement is reasonable or your refusal or failure to carry out a jobseeker's direction was reasonable.

If you are uncertain whether you can appeal against a decision, you should seek advice immediately. There is a strict time limit for appealing (see p1099).

You can seek a revision (see p1065) before you appeal, but you do not have to do so. See p1098 before deciding what to do.

Reasons for the decision maker's decision

You can ask why a decision was made, but remember that there is a one-month time limit for making an appeal (see p1097). For information about explanations, see p1060, and for written statements of reasons for a decision, see p1061. These could help you decide if it is worth challenging the decision.

Sometimes it might not be clear whether you have been given a written statement of reasons with your decision, or you might not receive it before your time limit for appealing expires. In both of these situations, you should appeal within the one-month time limit to protect your position.

If the decision is about:

- **HB or CTB**, there is no time limit for asking for a written statement of reasons.[13] However, the time limit for appealing is very strict. If you want to appeal you should remember to do so within the time limit, even if you decide to ask for a written statement of reasons later. If you ask for a written statement of reasons, these must be provided by the local authority within 14 days if this is practicable;
- **benefits other than HB or CTB**, you must ask for a written statement of reasons within one month of being sent a decision. The DWP or the Revenue must then provide the written statement of reasons within 14 days, or as soon as it is practicable.[14]

See p1100 for information about how your time limit is extended if you ask for a written statement of reasons.

On receiving the written statement of reasons, if there are grounds for a revision or supersession (see pp1065 and 1075), you may decide it is worth asking for one of these rather than appealing immediately (but see p1098). In any case, if you appeal, a decision maker should look at the decision again and could decide to revise it (see p1102).

Decisions you cannot appeal

You cannot appeal to a tribunal against some decisions made by decision makers.[15] You *can* ask for a revision or a supersession of these (see pp1065 and 1075). You do not have to have specific grounds for the revision or supersession. However, if the decision maker refuses to revise or supersede the decision, your only legal remedy is to apply for judicial review (see p1129).

Examples of decisions against which you cannot appeal

Who should be the claimant when a couple is unable to decide.

Whether a claim for one benefit can be treated as (or in addition to) a claim for another benefit.

Whether to demand recovery of an overpayment, and the amount of weekly deductions.

Whether to suspend payment of benefit.

Whether to take action against people who are liable to maintain claimants (see p744).

Whether to appoint a person as an appointee (see p955).

Whether to issue or replace cheques.

Whether to make an interim payment.

If you are uncertain whether you can appeal against a decision, you should seek advice straight away. If a decision maker says you cannot appeal against a refusal to do an 'any time' revision, or to consider a supersession, see pp1074 and 1085.

Revision, supersession or appeal?

Revisions, supersessions and appeals are all ways of getting decisions changed. If you can seek a revision or supersession as well as appealing you need to be careful which one you choose. For more information about revisions and supersessions, see Chapter 41.

Advantages

The advantages of applying for an **'any grounds' revision** include that you:

- could receive a decision more quickly if you seek a revision;
- get two bites at the cherry because if your application for a revision is turned down you can still appeal against the original decision.

You do not have to seek a revision and can appeal straightaway. However, if the decision maker agrees that a decision is wrong, s/he might revise it anyway and your appeal could lapse (see p1103).

Example

Lindsey fails to satisfy the 'personal capability assessment' and her incapacity benefit ceases. She asks the DWP to revise the decision because she has a new medical report that shows she cannot walk far without severe discomfort. The DWP considers the new medical evidence but refuses to revise its decision. Lindsey can still appeal to an appeal tribunal.

An advantage of seeking an **'any time' revision** is that there is no time limit for doing so (see p1068). You can ask for an 'any time' revision even if the time limit for appealing has expired. However, you cannot appeal against a refusal to do an 'any time' revision (see p1074).

An advantage of seeking a **supersession** is that, in most cases, there is no time limit for doing so – eg, where there has been a mistake about the facts or where a test case is decided in your favour.

Disadvantages

The disadvantages of applying for a **revision** include:

- the time limit for appealing continues to run while the decision maker considers your application for a revision. If you are unsure if the DWP, local authority or the Revenue has received your request, appeal within the time limit to protect your position;
- the arrears of benefit you get could be limited if the 'anti-test case' rule applies (see p1087).

There is a major disadvantage to applying for a **supersession**. You generally get less arrears of benefit if you seek a supersession rather than a revision or an appeal, even if you are successful. See p1079 for information about when a supersession takes effect.

When deciding whether to ask for a supersession or to appeal, you should consider all the factors that might lead to arrears of benefit being limited, including:

- the length of time since the original decision; *and*
- whether the 'anti-test case' rule (see p1087) applies to you.

If you think there is a risk that you will not obtain all the arrears you are due you should seek a revision (see p1065) or appeal instead of applying for a supersession if you can.

There is not usually any risk attached to making an **appeal**. However, in some cases, you should seek advice before you appeal. Because the tribunal looks at your case afresh, there is a risk you could lose benefit. For example, if your appeal is about a benefit that can be paid at different rates (eg, AA, DLA or industrial injuries disablement benefit), the rate could go down. If you are appealing about an overpayment, the amount could increase.

The time limit for appealing

Your appeal, including all the information described on p1101, must arrive at the relevant office within one month of the date the written decision was sent to you.[16] It is important that you provide all the information required within the time limit. Your appeal is not valid until you do. The time limit can be extended and you can appeal outside the one-month time limit in limited circumstances (see p1100) .

'Month' means a complete calendar month running from the day after the day you have been sent or given a decision.[17] For example, a decision sent on 24 July has an appeal time limit that expires at the end of 24 August.

Remember:

- unless it is a decision about child benefit or guardian's allowance, if an accidental error in a decision has been corrected (see p1060), any day falling before the day on which the correction is notified to you is ignored in calculating the one-month period;[18]
- it is a legally qualified tribunal member, *not* the DWP, local authority or Revenue who decides whether your appeal has been made within the time limit.[19] If you think your appeal has been made within the time limit, you should explain why when you appeal.

If the decision maker revises or supersedes a decision (and in some cases if s/he refuses to do so), the one-month time limit runs from the date you are sent the new decision.[20] However, if the decision maker refuses to do an 'any time' revision or to consider a supersession and says you cannot appeal, you should appeal against the original decision within the time limit (if this has not already passed) and seek advice.

Extending the time limit

If you ask for a written statement of reasons for a decision where one has not already been given to you (see p1061), your time limit is automatically extended. If the decision is about:

- **HB or CTB**, the days between the date you request the statement and the date on which it is given to you are ignored when calculating the one-month time limit;[21]
- **other benefits**, you must appeal within:[22]
  - one month and 14 days of the date you were sent the decision, if you requested a written statement of reasons and it is provided within the month; *or*
  - 14 days of a written statement of reasons being provided, if you requested one within one month of the date you were sent the decision, but it is not provided within that one-month period.

If you miss the one-month time limit

You can appeal outside the one-month time limit in limited circumstances. However, you must appeal within an absolute time limit. This is one year from the date the one-month time limit for appealing expired. See p1129 for further information about late appeals.

You could also make a late application for an 'any grounds' revision in limited circumstances (see p1067). If you can show grounds you can ask for an 'any time' revision or a supersession (see pp1068 and 1075).

How to appeal

You must appeal in writing, preferably using the appropriate appeal form.[23] For **HB and CTB**, you should use the form approved by your local authority.[24] For **other benefits**, the appeal form is in leaflet GL24 (CH24A for child benefit or guardian's allowance), *If You Think Our Decision is Wrong*. The leaflets are available at DWP offices, the Revenue, some Citizens Advice Bureaux and advice centres. In addition, the form for child benefit and guardian's allowance is on the Revenue website and the form for other benefits is on the DWP website (see Appendix 1 for the addresses). If you do not use the appropriate form, your appeal can be accepted provided it is in writing and includes all the information required (see p1101). There is no guarantee of this, so use the form wherever possible.

You must sign the appeal form. For benefits other than HB and CTB, if you have provided written authority, your representative can sign it on your behalf.[25] You should send or deliver your appeal to the office of the DWP, local authority or Revenue that sent you the decision.[26]

If you want the tribunal to deal with your appeal quickly, make this clear on your appeal form, explaining why. You could also telephone the DWP, local authority or Revenue or write to the TS, asking it to intervene.

Making sure your appeal is valid

For your appeal to be valid, it must contain all the information required. If you do not use the correct appeal form, your appeal can still be valid, so long as you provide the information.[27] It is a legally qualified tribunal member who decides if your appeal is valid, not the DWP, local authority or the Revenue (see p1102).

When you appeal you must provide:[28]

- sufficient details about the decision with which you disagree for it to be identified. For example, the DWP appeal form asks you for:
  - the name of the benefit you are appealing about – eg, IS or carer's allowance; *and*
  - the date you were sent the decision with which you disagree; this is on the letter notifying you of the decision;
- a summary of your reasons for believing the decision was wrong. You should not simply say you think the decision was wrong, but explain why.

Examples

'The decision says I have been overpaid income-based jobseeker's allowance because I failed to disclose that my wife had started working part time, but I wrote to you as soon as she started work and told you what her take-home pay would be.'

'The Revenue says I should not get child benefit for my son because he left school in June. This decision is wrong because my son decided to stay on at school and do his A levels.'

'You say I cannot get DLA care component. This decision is wrong because you have not taken into account the amount of help I need due to incontinence problems.'

It is also helpful to include information and evidence that supports your appeal because a decision maker looks at the decision again before the appeal hearing and might revise it (see p1103).

What happens if you do not provide sufficient information

If you do not include sufficient information on your appeal form or letter, a decision maker can return it, asking you to provide the information you left out.[29] You must be given at least 14 days to return this. Be sure to complete the form properly and return it or provide the information required within the time allowed. Otherwise you might not count as having made your appeal within the time limit.

Your one-month time limit for appealing (see p1099) is extended if you are asked to complete your appeal form or provide information. The one-month time limit is extended by:[30]

- 14 days from the date your appeal form is returned to you for completion, if the completed form is received back within 14 days;
- 14 days from the date you are asked for further information, if you provide this within 14 days of the request;
- the length of time you are given to complete a form or provide information, if this is longer than 14 days.

If you fail to complete the form properly or provide the information required in time, your appeal, along with any relevant documents and evidence, is forwarded to the TS. A legally qualified tribunal member then considers whether your appeal is valid and can go ahead.[31] If you complete and return the form or provide the information before s/he makes a decision, any further details you provide must be taken into account.[32]

If your appeal is not accepted as valid, you can try to make a late appeal (see p1129).

What happens after you appeal

After you appeal, the DWP, local authority or the Revenue:

- prepares the appeal papers – known as the decision maker's submission (see p1104) – and sends a copy to you (and your representative if you have one); *and*
- sends you a questionnaire (called an enquiry form) asking you whether you want an oral hearing and, if so, when you and your representative (if you have one) are available to attend; *and*
- forwards your appeal to the TS office, along with a copy of the decision maker's decision and submission.

You should be sent a postage-paid envelope in which to return the enquiry form to the TS. You must return it within 14 days.[33] Your appeal could be struck out if you do not return the enquiry form in time (see p1105).

You might find that your appeal is not dealt with if there is a test case pending that deals with the same issues (see p1108).

If the decision maker does not forward your appeal

Your appeal should not be held up unduly while the decision maker considers whether s/he should carry out a revision (see p1103). You are entitled to have your appeal heard within a reasonable period of time, so your appeal should be processed promptly and passed to the TS without delay.[34] Following a complaint, an Ombudsman said the local authority should forward an appeal to the TS within 28 days.[35] The decision maker can still consider revising the decision pending the appeal being heard.

You cannot usually bypass the normal procedures. However, if the decision maker does not forward your appeal within a reasonable period, forward a copy of it to the TS yourself. Although you cannot usually expect the tribunal to deal with your appeal before the decision maker has had a chance to prepare her/his submission and assemble the appeal papers, the tribunal is free to allow matters to be handled differently if circumstances require it.[36]

When your appeal can lapse

After you appeal, a decision maker looks at the decision you are appealing about again and might revise it – eg, on the basis of any facts, information or evidence you provided with your appeal form. If this happens, your appeal could lapse, even if you do not get everything you want, and you have to appeal again.[37]

Your appeal lapses where the revised decision is more advantageous to you than the original decision – eg, the decision:[38]

- awards you benefit at a higher rate or for a longer period;
- lifts a refusal or disqualification of benefit or a JSA sanction (in whole or in part);
- reverses a decision to pay benefit to a third party (see p987);
- means you gain financially from the revised decision;
- says an overpayment of benefit is not recoverable or that less should be recovered; *or*
- reverses a decision that an accident was not an industrial accident.

If the revised decision is *not* more advantageous to you, your appeal must go ahead, but against the revised decision.[39] You have one month from the date the decision is sent to you to make further representations.[40] At the end of that period (or earlier if you agree in writing), your appeal proceeds unless the decision is revised again and is now more advantageous to you.[41]

If your appeal lapses, you must make a fresh appeal. Your time limit for appealing (see p1099) runs from the date the revised decision is sent to you.[42]

Oral or paper hearings

If you want an **oral hearing**, you must state this on the enquiry form (see p1102).[43] You are more likely to win your appeal if you attend an oral hearing, particularly where your appeal concerns a medical issue or your disability, or where there is an argument about the facts of your case. The DWP, local authority or the Revenue can also ask for an oral hearing. If you (or the DWP, local authority or Revenue) do so, you must be given one, unless your appeal has been struck out (see p1105).[44] Even if no one wants an oral hearing, the chair of the tribunal may decide one should take place.[45] If this happens, you should be given an opportunity to attend.

If there is not an oral hearing, the tribunal makes its decision by looking at what you said on your appeal form, any evidence or other information you provided to support your appeal, and the decision maker's submission (see p1104). This is known as a **paper hearing**.

If you opt for a paper hearing, but decide you want an oral hearing after all, you may be able to change your mind. You must tell the clerk to the tribunal before the tribunal makes its decision.

You may not want to attend an oral hearing – eg, because you are worried about speaking for yourself or would have difficulty getting there. You can seek advice before you decide what to do, but remember:

- if you attend an oral hearing, you can explain your side of the story to the tribunal and you are more likely to win;
- you can ask someone to represent you at the hearing;[46] your chances of winning are much higher if you do. You can also take a friend, relative or adviser with you for support. You can have more than one person if the chair of the tribunal agrees;[47]
- the TS aims to provide a qualified interpreter if you need one. If you do, tell the clerk to the tribunal in advance of the hearing;
- if you or your representative cannot be physically present at an oral hearing (eg, because of a disability), one might be arranged at a venue you can get to (see p1112), or you might be able to be present via a video link if the chair of the tribunal agrees.[48] Contact your TS office to see if this can be arranged;
- you, an interpreter (if needed) and any witnesses may be able to get expenses paid – eg, you can claim for travel (including the extra costs involved for disabled people), meals, loss of earnings and childcare costs.[49]

If you opt for a paper hearing, you should think about what other information and evidence you can get to support your appeal, and send it to the tribunal. Make sure that everything you want to say in support of your appeal has been put in writing and that there are no other documents which you would like the tribunal to see. You must send this to the clerk to the tribunal as soon as possible as paper hearings often take place soon after you return your enquiry form. You are not given notice of the date. See p1133 for information about sorting out the facts and checking the law that applies in your case.

The decision maker's submission

The DWP, local authority or Revenue prepares a detailed explanation of the reasons for its decision – known as the decision maker's submission – and this is sent to you along with a bundle of papers relevant to your appeal. If your appeal involves a medical issue or one about your disability, a record of medical examinations you have had in connection with your claim is usually included.

You should read through the whole submission carefully to find out the case being made against you. Be sure to take the submission with you to the hearing.

Providing other information

You may want to provide additional information to support your appeal. For example, you may want to get independent medical evidence or provide supporting statements from witnesses. Otherwise, the decision maker's submission and the bundle of papers s/he prepares are the only written information the tribunal has to consider in reaching its decision.

If your appeal is to be dealt with at a paper hearing, you should provide this information as soon as possible after being sent the decision maker's submission. Even if you are going to have an oral hearing, it is important to provide information in advance. See p1133 for information about how to prepare an appeal.

Information you must provide

A legally qualified tribunal member (see p1109) or clerk to the tribunal might issue directions requiring you or the DWP (or local authority or the Revenue) to provide further information or documents.[50] You or the decision maker can also apply to the clerk to ask a legally qualified tribunal member to issue directions.[51] This can be useful, for example, if you are having trouble getting documents or information from the decision maker.

If you are given a direction to provide information or evidence within a specific period, it is important that you comply with it. If you do not, your appeal can be struck out (see below), or the tribunal might conclude that the information or evidence was adverse to you. If you miss the deadline in the directions, try to provide what has been requested as soon as possible. The tribunal should still consider the information or evidence – eg, if you provide it at the hearing.[52]

When your appeal can be struck out

Your appeal can be struck out, but only in certain circumstances. This cancels your appeal and it does not go ahead. Your appeal can only be struck out if:[53]

- the **tribunal does not have 'jurisdiction'** to deal with it (ie, you do not have a right to appeal against the decision – see p1097).[54] You must have been notified that it may be struck out; *or*
- there is **want of prosecution** (ie, you do not appear to be pursuing it) including where you have not appealed within the absolute time limit (see p1129); *or*
- you **fail to comply with a direction** given to you by a legally qualified tribunal member or clerk to the tribunal – eg, you fail to provide information or documents as required. You must be notified that a failure to do so could lead to your appeal being struck out; *or*
- you **fail to notify the clerk to the tribunal whether or not you want an oral hearing** within the 14-day time limit (see p1102) – ie, you fail to return the tribunal enquiry form. The form must inform you that a failure to do so could lead to your appeal being struck out.[55]

The procedure for striking out an appeal

Your appeal can be struck out by the clerk to the tribunal or by a legally qualified tribunal member. In practice, the clerk to the tribunal only strikes out appeals where you fail to notify her/him whether or not you want an oral hearing. In all other cases, it is a legally qualified tribunal member.[56] If the clerk to the tribunal strikes out your appeal, you must be notified and told how you can apply for your appeal to be reinstated (see below).[57]

Getting your appeal reinstated

If your appeal is struck out, you may be able to get it reinstated. A clerk to the tribunal can reinstate the appeal if:[58]

- it has been struck out because you failed to notify the clerk to the tribunal whether or not you wanted an oral hearing within the 14-day time limit; *and*
- the clerk is satisfied that there are reasonable grounds for it to be reinstated.

You must apply in writing to the clerk to the tribunal, within one month of the order to strike out your appeal being issued. You must say why you think your appeal should not have been struck out. If the clerk is not satisfied that there are reasonable grounds for your appeal to be reinstated, your application must be passed to a legally qualified tribunal member to make a decision.

A legally qualified tribunal member can reinstate your appeal if s/he is satisfied that:[59]

- there are reasonable grounds for it to be reinstated. You must apply in writing to the clerk to the tribunal within one month of the order to strike out your appeal being issued, saying why your appeal should not be struck out; *or*
- it is not an appeal which can be struck out (see p1105); *or*
- it is not in the interests of justice for your appeal to be struck out.

If the tribunal member refuses to reinstate your appeal, you may be able to make a fresh appeal.[60] See p1099 for the time limit for appealing and p1129 for late appeals. You cannot appeal to a commissioner against the decision to strike out your appeal or to refuse to reinstate it; your only remedy is judicial review (see p1129).[61]

Withdrawing an appeal

If you change your mind about appealing, you can withdraw your appeal.[62] If your appeal has not yet been passed to the TS, you should write to the DWP, local authority or Revenue, saying that you do not wish your appeal to go ahead. Your authorised representative can write on your behalf.

If your appeal has been passed to the TS, you must apply in writing to the clerk to the tribunal. S/he must allow you to withdraw your appeal. You can also withdraw your appeal at an oral hearing.

Once an appeal has been withdrawn it cannot be reinstated.[63] So if you decide that you want to go ahead after all, you could try to make a late appeal (but see p1129).[64]

The oral hearing

You must be sent notice of the oral hearing at least 14 days before it is to take place unless you agree to less notice than this.[65] However, the TS aims to give you longer notice than 14 days.

If you have not been given the correct notice (you can argue this includes the decision maker's submission and evidence as well as the time and date of the hearing) the tribunal can only go ahead if you agree.[66] If you give up your right to notice – eg, because you want your appeal to be dealt with quickly and are happy for it to be listed at short notice, the tribunal can go ahead with the hearing even if you are not there.[67]

An appeal is heard in public unless the chair thinks it should be in private for certain specified reasons.[68]

If you want your hearing to be in private, ask the chair of the tribunal to consider this. In practice, it is extremely rare for members of the public to attend.

Postponements and adjournments

If the hearing date is inconvenient or you want more time to prepare your case, you can ask for it to be **postponed**. You must apply in writing to the clerk to the tribunal, before the hearing date, saying why you want your appeal to be postponed.[69] Make it clear that you do not want the hearing to go ahead in your absence. You should apply as soon as you decide that you want a postponement. Clerks and tribunal members can postpone your oral hearing even if this is not requested.[70]

If you are refused a postponement, you should be given written notice and your request and the refusal is put to the tribunal.[71] You should *not* presume that a postponement will be granted. You should telephone before the hearing is due to take place to check if it has been agreed. Be ready to attend the hearing if it goes ahead. If you have a representative, s/he should warn you that your application might not be successful.[72]

If you do not attend and have not asked for a postponement, the tribunal can hear the appeal without you,[73] and you are less likely to succeed. If you do not attend the hearing, the tribunal should consider whether to adjourn the hearing, even if you have been refused a postponement.[74] A hearing should be **adjourned** if:

- there is doubt about whether you received notice of the oral hearing;[75] *or*
- you have advised the tribunal that you cannot attend, have a good reason for not attending and have asked for another hearing date;[76] *or*

- you are unable to attend the hearing (eg, you are in prison) but your evidence could be expected to play an important part in the tribunal reaching its decision;[77] *or*
- you want to be represented at the oral hearing, but your representative is not available on the date it has been listed and has made a reasonable request for a postponement. Your representative should explain why s/he cannot attend and why no one else can represent you in her/his place;[78] *or*
- you need to get a representative – eg, because it is difficult for you to represent yourself, or the decision with which you disagree concerns a large overpayment.[79]

If the tribunal makes a decision in your absence with which you disagree, you can try to appeal to a social security commissioner (see p1120) or you can ask for the decision to be set aside (but see p1118).

Even if an oral hearing is underway, it can be adjourned – eg, if you or the DWP, local authority or the Revenue asks for an adjournment, or if the tribunal itself thinks this is the best course – eg, if more evidence is required.[80] You should consider asking for an adjournment if the tribunal says it is going to consider whether you should get a lower rate of benefit than you are getting currently, to allow you to prepare your case and make representations. A tribunal might postpone or adjourn your case if there is a test case pending which deals with the same issues as your appeal (see p1108).

You can only appeal against a tribunal's decision to adjourn if it is a 'final decision' – eg, there are no major issues to resolve or it is inevitable what the tribunal will eventually decide.[81]

What happens if a test case decision is pending

If a test case is pending that deals with issues raised in your case (your appeal is then known as a 'look-alike' case), the DWP, local authority or Revenue can suspend payment of your benefit or even postpone making a decision about your claim (see p1088). This means you will not be able to appeal until a decision is made about the test case.

For benefits other than HB and CTB, if a decision is pending in a test case against a commissioner's or court's decision and you have already appealed to a tribunal or commissioner in a 'look-alike' case, the decision maker can serve notice requiring the tribunal or commissioner in *your* appeal:[82]

- not to make a decision and to refer your case back to her/him;
- to postpone making a decision until the test case is decided; *or*
- to decide your appeal as if the test case had been decided in the way most unfavourable to you, but only if this is in your interests. If this happens, and the test case eventually goes in your favour, the decision maker has to make a new decision superseding the decision of the tribunal or commissioner in the light of the decision in the test case.[83]

If the decision on your appeal has been postponed, once a decision has been made in the test case, the decision is made on your appeal.

The paper hearing

You are not sent notice of a paper hearing. The tribunal makes its decision in your absence and you are then notified of its decision (see p1115).

2. Tribunal procedures

The appeals described in this chapter are dealt with by tribunals drawn from an independent panel of tribunal members (led by the President), appointed by the Lord Chancellor. Social security tribunals are organised by region, with a chair for each region who is responsible for the recruitment and training of tribunal members.

The administration of the work of tribunals is the responsibility of the Tribunals Service (TS), an executive agency of the Ministry of Justice. The TS officials who deal with the day-to-day work of social security tribunals are known as tribunal clerks.

People present at hearings

The tribunal consists of a **chair** and up to two other **members**. The chair makes a note of what is said by you, your representative, the DWP (or local authority or the Revenue) and any witnesses. The chair records the tribunal's decision and the reasons for its decision – known as a 'statement of reasons'. Where a tribunal has more than one member, the chair has the casting vote.[84] See p1115 for information about decisions. To see which members make up a tribunal, see below.

If the tribunal thinks your appeal involves particularly difficult issues, it can ask another member of the panel of tribunal members – known as an **expert** – to assist.[85] The expert can be asked either to attend the hearing and give evidence or provide a written report. Any written report should be sent to every party to the proceedings. The expert cannot take part in making the decision.

The **clerk to the tribunal** is there in an administrative capacity – eg, to pay expenses. The clerk takes no part in making the decision on your appeal and should not express any views on the case.

A **presenting officer** sometimes attends – eg, when an appeal is considered complicated. S/he represents the decision maker. S/he is not necessarily the person who made the decision you are appealing about. S/he explains the reasons for the decision, but is not there to defend it at all costs. S/he may provide information which helps your case.[86] If there is no presenting officer, the tribunal can consider and decide your appeal, although it might adjourn and request a presenting officer to attend a new hearing. The DWP has agreed to send a presenting officer to a hearing where directed to do so by the tribunal.[87]

You can have a **representative** with you at the hearing.[88] S/he can help you understand the procedures, present your case to the tribunal and ensure the tribunal is aware of all the relevant issues and the law.

The tribunal members

Tribunals are made up of one, two or three members.[89] The people who hear your appeal are drawn from a panel of doctors, lawyers, people with experience of disability and people with financial expertise – eg, accountants. One of the tribunal members must be legally qualified. S/he acts as the chair of the tribunal.

The types of tribunal appropriate to hear a particular kind of appeal are set out in the rules as follows.[90]

- A three-member tribunal hears disability living allowance (DLA) and attendance allowance (AA) appeals – a lawyer, a doctor and a person with experience of disability.[91]
- A two-member tribunal (a lawyer and a doctor) hears appeals about whether you are incapable of work under the 'personal capability assessment' (see p668).[92]
- A two-member tribunal (a lawyer and a financial expert) hears appeals involving difficult financial issues which involve consideration of, for example, profit and loss accounts, balance sheets and the accounts of trust funds. Only complex cases are dealt with in this way.[93]
- A two- or three-member tribunal (a lawyer and one or two doctors) hears appeals about industrial injuries benefits (see Chapter 14) or severe disablement allowance (SDA), unless the only issue is whether there should be a declaration of an industrial accident (see p314).[94] If your appeal also involves difficult financial issues, your appeal is heard by a three-member tribunal – a financial expert is substituted for one of the two doctors.
- A one-member tribunal (a lawyer) hears all other appeals.[95]

A doctor *cannot* be a member of your tribunal if s/he has ever attended, advised or prepared a report about you or any other person whose medical condition is relevant to your appeal.[96] You cannot argue that a doctor should not be a member of a tribunal even if s/he regularly provides medical reports about benefit claimants to the DWP.[97] You *can* argue that a tribunal should not rely on evidence from a DWP doctor who sits on tribunals at other times; this depends on how often and how recently this has happened.[98]

Procedure at an oral hearing

When the tribunal is ready to hear your case, you (and your representative if you have one) are taken in with the presenting officer (see p1109). There are no strict rules of procedure. The chair decides how the hearing is conducted.[99]

The chair should introduce the members of the tribunal and everyone else present. The presenting officer, if at the hearing, may be asked to summarise the decision maker's submission (see p1104). You may be asked to explain your position.

The tribunal members ask you (and the presenting officer) questions. The chair may allow you and the presenting officer to question each other.

If you think there are mistakes in the tribunal papers, point them out. You can call any witnesses and can ask questions of the presenting officer's witnesses.[100] See p1133 for information about preparing for your appeal and presenting your case.

The tribunal considers all the facts, evidence (see p1133) and law (see p1135) before it makes a decision. It should not bargain with you by 'offering' to allow part of your appeal if you agree to drop other parts – eg, by offering you one component of DLA if you agree not to argue for the other.[101]

Medical examination at the oral hearing

Tribunals cannot carry out physical examinations unless your appeal is related to the assessment of your disablement for SDA or industrial injuries disablement benefit, or whether you have a prescribed disease or injury.[102] Studying X-ray evidence does not count as a physical examination so you can ask the tribunal to consider this.[103] Although there is no 'walking test' for the DLA mobility component, the tribunal may take its observation of you into account. It should not, however, attach undue weight to its observations[104] and you should be given the opportunity to comment on them. The tribual should remember that what it sees may only be relevant to your condition on that day and not in general.[105] It should check, for example, whether you have just taken medication or have been resting for some time in the waiting area.

The tribunal decides whether to carry out a physical examination. It should let you know at the hearing if it thinks one is not nececssary so you can make representations.[106] The examination usually takes place after the main hearing in a separate room in the absence of everyone else. You can have someone with you as a chaperone or if, for example, you need help undressing. Make sure you tell the member(s) of the tribunal examining you if you are in pain or discomfort. It is also a good idea to provide a full list of any medicines you are taking. After the examination, you should be invited to make further representations to the tribunal if you wish.

Appeals about disability or incapacity for work

You should tell the tribunal how your disability or incapacity affects you at work or in your daily life at home. You should be completely straightforward with the tribunal, neither underplaying nor overplaying your symptoms. If you feel better on some days than others, explain how and how often they occur, and tell the tribunal whether they are seeing you on a good day or a bad day.

The tribunal listens and asks you questions. It considers all of the medical and other evidence relevant to your case, and tries to draw out the evidence about your disabilities, perhaps with the help of questioning from the doctor or consultant members. This may confirm the opinions expressed in medical reports with which you disagree, or it may support your view. See p1135 for further information about medical evidence.

The tribunal should not restrict itself to accepting the medical evidence about you given in written reports.[107] If there is conflict between what is said in a report and what you have said about your disability or incapacity in writing – eg, on your claim form, the tribunal should not accept the evidence in the report without first listening to what you have to say about how your condition affects you.[108] You should ensure that you explain any inconsistences. The tribunal should be particularly careful not to accept automatically the findings in electronically produced medical reports.[109]

A chair can adjourn the hearing and refer you to a healthcare professional (eg, a doctor or a nurse) for a medical examination and report if your appeal concerns:[110]

- whether you are entitled to AA or DLA, the appropriate rate of benefit or the period for which you are entitled;
- whether you are entitled to SDA;
- whether you are incapable of work;
- the extent of your disablement for SDA or industrial injuries disablement benefit purposes; *or*
- whether you have a prescribed disease or injury (see p318) or a loss of faculty as a result of an industrial accident (see p320).

A medical examination may take place in your home or at a DWP medical examination centre. Alternatively, a report may be requested from your GP or other medical adviser. The written decision to adjourn for a report should make clear why the tribunal adjourned and what sort of medical evidence is being sought.[111]

Remember that although you cannot be compelled to undergo a medical examination by the chair, the tribunal might draw negative conclusions if you refuse.

Domiciliary hearings

Most appeal venues have access for disabled people and the TS may meet the cost of special transport to get there, or arrange the hearing at another venue. However, if you are unable to attend a tribunal hearing at the venue, it is possible to hold the hearing in your home. This is known as a 'domiciliary hearing'. You should include a letter from your doctor with your request, confirming that you are unable to travel at all (eg, even by taxi). You cannot appeal against a decision to refuse you a domiciliary hearing, but if the refusal meant that your appeal was unfair, you may be able to appeal against the tribunal's decision on your appeal.[112]

Note: you may be able to be present via a video link if the chair of the tribunal agrees.[113] Contact your TS office to see if this can be arranged.

What the tribunal considers

The tribunal should consider an issue if it is in the appeal papers or in any representations you make, or if the evidence before the tribunal should lead it to believe it is relevant to your appeal.[114] You (or the DWP, local authority or Revenue) can even raise an issue at the hearing.[115] However, the tribunal might then adjourn to give the other side a chance to meet the point. You do not necessarily have to raise an issue with the tribunal for it to be something it should consider, even if you have a representative. However, the issue must be one which in some way obviously demands attention.[116] If you have a representative, the tribunal may decide not to investigate matters that s/he does not raise on your behalf.[117]

A tribunal does not have to consider issues that are 'not raised by' your appeal.[118] However, it can consider issues even if neither you nor the DWP, local authority or Revenue raises them.[119] The tribunal should exercise its discretion fairly.

Difficulties may arise – eg, where you are appealing about not being awarded one component of DLA when you are already in receipt of the other, or against the rate of one component of DLA when you are satisfied with the rate you receive of the other, or where you ask for a higher rate of DLA or AA than you are already getting. In these circumstances the tribunal *does not have to* consider issues which are not the subject of your appeal. If it *does* decide to consider both components of DLA, or if it decides to consider whether you should get a lower rate of DLA or AA than you are already getting, the tribunal:

- should give you notice of this and a chance to prepare your case and make representations or to consider withdrawing your appeal.[120] Ask for the hearing to be adjourned if you need time to do this or want someone to represent you;
- if your appeal is being dealt with at a paper hearing, give proper notice that this is being considered and offer you a chance to attend an oral hearing or to withdraw your appeal;[121]
- should explain why it decided to use its discretion in this way in the statement of reasons for its decision.[122]

Note: if you are concerned about what might happen in your appeal, you can withdraw it at any time before the tribunal makes its decision (see p1106).

Faulty revisions and supersessions

If your appeal involves a revision or a supersession decision which is faulty, the tribunal can remedy any defect and make any decision that the decision maker could have taken.[123] This includes where the decision maker:

- carried out a supersession but failed to state the ground or to identify the correct ground for doing so; *or*
- carried out a supersession when s/he should have conducted a revision (and *vice versa*).

In addition, the tribunal can carry out an 'any time' revision where no decision has been made on the matter by a decision maker (either to revise the decision or refuse to do so) – ie, if you are appealing because the decision maker refused to carry out a supersession.[124]

If errors in the decision making are extensive, you can try to argue that the tribunal should adjourn the hearing, point out the errors to the decision maker and invite her/him to reconsider, rather than making any corrections itself.[125]

Changes of circumstances after you appeal

When a tribunal hears your appeal, it considers whether the decision with which you disagree was correct when it was made. If your circumstances change after the decision, the tribunal cannot take this into account.[126] This includes where a change occurs between the date a decision is made on a renewal claim for DLA and the date that decision takes effect, unless you are appealing about a revision or supersession of that decision.[127]

Any evidence you get after the decision with which you disagree could still be relevant to your appeal.[128] If the evidence relates to the period before the decision you are disputing was made, or to a past event that was relevant to the decision, it must be taken into account.[129]

Repeat claims

It is important as a *general* rule for you to consider making a fresh claim (or seeking a supersession) every time your circumstances change, and appeal if you are unhappy with the subsequent decision. This is particularly so where your appeal is about:

- whether you are incapable of work, or qualify for AA or DLA and your condition has worsened;
- whether you satisfy the 'habitual residence' test (see Chapter 59); *or*
- how much income or capital you have, and this changes.

If you wait until the tribunal makes its decision and this goes against you, you could lose out. You could only get arrears from the date your circumstances changed if you make a fresh claim (or seek a supersession) and ask for benefit to be backdated. See pp964 and 1079 for how far your benefit can be backdated.

Example

Ravi has been getting incapacity benefit (IB) for some time. A decision maker decides he is fit for work and stops his IB. He appeals. While awaiting his appeal hearing, his health deteriorates, he makes a fresh claim and is awarded IB. When the tribunal hears his appeal against the original decision it upholds the decision maker's decision. However, because Ravi made a fresh claim when his circumstances changed, he has not lost out.

If you make a fresh claim (or seek a supersession), you can ask the decision maker to wait until your appeal has been determined before making a decision. However, if the decision maker decides the fresh claim (or supersession) and you disagree with the decision:

- you can appeal against the new decision. Consider whether it is in your interests to ask for all of the appeals to be heard together by the same tribunal;[130] *or*
- whether or not you appeal against the new decision, you can ask the decision maker to revise it once your first appeal is determined (see p1071).

Example

Ali claims income support (IS) but the decision maker says he does not satisfy the 'habitual residence test' and refuses his claim. He appeals against the decision and makes a fresh claim for IS on 8 July 2007. The fresh claim is refused. Ali wins his appeal. Because he did not appeal the new decision, the tribunal can only award IS up to 8 July 2007. However, the decision maker does an 'any time' revision and awards IS from that date.

The decision

Usually you are told the tribunal's decision at the hearing and you are given a decision notice confirming it.[131] If the tribunal is unable to come to a unanimous decision, it makes a majority decision.

The decision notice may include a summary of the tribunal's reasons for its decision. If it is not given at the hearing or you opted for a paper hearing, the decision notice is sent to you later by the clerk. You must be informed of:[132]

- your right to request a statement of reasons for the tribunal's decision (see p1116); *and*
- the conditions for appealing to a commissioner (see p1120).

A decision can be corrected or set aside (see p1118).

Record of proceedings

A record of the tribunal proceedings is made by the chair of the tribunal. It must be sufficient to indicate the evidence taken by the appeal tribunal. The record is kept by the tribunal clerk for six months from the date of the tribunal's decision or for six months from various other specific dates.[133] You must apply in writing for a copy within the six-month period. You can apply for a typed copy if the original is difficult to read. If you are considering an appeal to a commissioner it is a good idea to ask for a copy. If you foresee disputes about what happened at the hearing, you should also make and keep your own notes.

The statement of reasons

You have a right to apply for a statement of reasons for the tribunal's decision.[134] If you lose your appeal and want to appeal to a commissioner (see p1120) you must generally have one (but see p1122). It may otherwise be difficult to show that the tribunal made an error of law (see p1121).

A chair may give you a statement of reasons at the hearing or tell you s/he will send one to you later. If not, and you request one, this must then be given to you as soon as it is 'practicable'.

Your request for a statement of reasons must be:[135]

- in writing; *and*
- received by the clerk to the tribunal within one month (see p1099) of you being sent or given the tribunal's decision notice. Late applications can be allowed in limited circumstances (see below).

If an accidental error in the tribunal's decision is corrected or you applied for the tribunal's decision to be set aside and this has been refused, the one-month period runs from the date you are sent notice of this.[136] However, this does not apply where the decision was not set aside because of a refusal to extend the time limit for applying for one.

Note:

- If the decision is not unanimous, the statement of reasons must give the reasons why a tribunal member disagreed.[137]
- If you mistakenly ask the chair of the tribunal for permission to appeal to a commissioner (see p1122) instead of asking for a statement of reasons, s/he should treat this as a request for a statement of reasons.[138]
- If you apply for the tribunal's decision to be set aside and this is refused, the legally qualified tribunal member can treat your application as a request for a statement of reasons.[139]
- If the chair fails wrongly to provide a statement of reasons, you may have grounds for appeal to a commissioner.

The DWP (or local authority or Revenue) can also ask for a statement of reasons. If this happens, it means it is considering appealing to a commissioner.

Late applications for a statement of reasons

You can make a late application for a statement of reasons in limited circumstances, but must do so within an absolute time limit of three months.[140]

If an accidental error in the tribunal's decision has been corrected or you applied for the tribunal's decision to be set aside (see p1118) and this has been refused, the three-month period runs from the date you are sent notice of this. However, this does not apply where a decision was not set aside because of a refusal to extend the time limit for applying for one.

The chair does not have to give you a statement of reasons if you apply outside the time limit.[141] However, s/he might consider giving one on a discretionary basis.

A late application for a statement of reasons can only be allowed if it is 'in the interests of justice' for it to be allowed late.[142] It can only be in the interests of justice if it was not practicable for you to apply in time because:[143]

- you, your partner or a dependant has died or had a serious illness;
- you are not resident in the UK;
- normal postal services were disrupted; *or*
- there are other special circumstances (see p1131)

The longer you have delayed in applying, the more compelling the special circumstances need to be.[144] When deciding if it is in the interests of justice to allow your application, the tribunal member cannot take into account the fact that:[145]

- a court or commissioner has interpreted the law in a different way than previously understood and applied;
- you (or anyone acting for you) misunderstood or were unaware of the relevant law, including the time limits for applying.

After the hearing

If you have won your appeal, the DWP (or local authority or Revenue) ought to carry out the tribunal's decision straight away. It can do this on the basis of the decision notice (see p1115). However, if the DWP (or local authority or Revenue) disagrees with the decision it might consider seeking permission to appeal against it to a social security commissioner (see p1120). In this case, you are not normally paid while it decides what to do. See p984 for details of what the DWP (or local authority or the Revenue) must do before it can suspend your benefit. If the DWP (or local authority or Revenue) decides to appeal, you are not normally paid until the commissioner decides the case.[146] However, you can ask the DWP, local authority or Revenue to pay you if you are left in financial hardship. If you are left without any money, you might be able to get a crisis loan.

If you disagree with the tribunal's decision

A tribunal's decision is final. However:

- if the decision notice contains an **accidental error** this **can be corrected** by the clerk to the tribunal or a legally qualified tribunal member. This only applies if it is a genuine error such as a typing or spelling mistake, not an error of law on an important issue in your appeal – eg, a change of the date of onset of an industrial disease;[147]

- it **can be superseded**, if there are grounds (see p1074). However, if the tribunal made a mistake about the law you must appeal to a social security commissioner;
- you or the DWP (or local authority or Revenue) can **appeal to a social security commissioner** (see p1120);
- a decision **can be set aside**, which means the decision is cancelled and your appeal is heard again (see below).

If you are considering an appeal to a social security commissioner remember to ask for the tribunal's statement of reasons within the one-month time limit (see p1116). You should do so even if you are first going to apply for the tribunal's decision to be set aside.

When a decision can be set aside

A tribunal decision can only be set aside in limited circumstances. You must apply, in writing, to the clerk to the tribunal within one month of being sent or given:[148]

- the decision notice (see p1115); *or*
- the tribunal's statement of reasons (see p1116), if this is later.

The application should be signed by you. If you have provided written authority, your representative can sign it on your behalf. You must include your reasons for applying for the decision to be set aside. You can make a late application in limited circumstances (see p1119).

A copy of the application for a decision to be set aside is sent to all the parties involved in the appeal.[149] The other parties are given the chance to make representations.

A legally qualified tribunal member can set aside a decision if s/he thinks it is 'just' and:[150]

- you, your representative or the DWP (or local authority or Revenue) were not sent or did not receive appeal papers or other relevant documents, or the tribunal that made the decision did not receive them in sufficient time before the hearing; *or*
- you, your representative or the DWP, local authority or the Revenue were not present at the hearing. However, if you or the presenting officer chose not to attend it may not be 'just' to set the decision aside. If you did not ask for an oral hearing, the decision cannot be set aside for this reason unless it would undoubtedly be in the 'interests of justice'.

In some circumstances, a tribunal decision can also be set aside when you (or the DWP, local authority or Revenue) seek the permission of the tribunal chair to appeal to a commissioner (see p1120).

Sometimes there are 'procedural irregularities' which lead to an obvious unfairness. If, as a result, it would be in the 'interests of justice' for a tribunal decision to be set aside, you can try to argue that there is also a power to do this.[151] If the tribunal refuses to do so, you could try to appeal to a commissioner against the tribunal's original decision on the grounds that there was a breach of the rules of natural justice (see p1121).

Applications for a decision to be set aside are normally decided without a hearing, so make sure you give a full explanation of your reasons when you apply.[152] If the tribunal's decision is set aside, your appeal is then referred back to be heard by another tribunal.

You must be sent a written notice of the decision on your application as soon as it is practicable.[153] The notice must include a statement of the reasons for the decision. If the legally qualified tribunal member refuses to set aside the decision, s/he can treat your application to set aside as an application for a statement of reasons for the tribunal's decision, subject to the usual time limits.[154]

If a decision is wrongly set aside, any subsequent re-hearing by a tribunal is invalid. The second tribunal could thus refuse to re-hear the case if there was no power to set aside the previous decision.[155]

Late applications for a decision to be set aside

The time limit for applying for a decision to be set aside can be extended by up to one year.[156] You must apply in writing. In addition to the reasons for your application, you must explain your reasons for lateness, including details of any special circumstances.[157]

A late application can only be accepted if there is a reasonable chance that the tribunal's decision will be set aside and it is 'in the interests of justice' for the time limit for applying to be extended.[158] It can only be in the interests of justice if it was not practicable for you to apply in time because:[159]

- you, your partner or a dependant has died or had a serious illness;
- you are not resident in the UK;
- normal postal services were disrupted; *or*
- there are other special circumstances that are 'wholly exceptional' (see p1131).

The longer you have delayed in applying for a decision to be set aside, the more compelling the special circumstances need to be.[160]

You cannot appeal against the refusal to allow your late application[161] but you may be able to apply to the High Court for judicial review if the decision is clearly unreasonable.

If the decision is not set aside

You cannot appeal against a refusal to set aside, but you may be able to apply for judicial review (see p1129).[162] You could also try to appeal to a commissioner (see below) against the tribunal's original decision. If, after you are sent the tribunal's statement of reasons, your application for the tribunal's decision to be set aside is refused, the one-month time limit for appealing to a commissioner runs from the date you are sent notice of this.[163] However, this does not apply where a decision was not set aside because of a refusal to extend the time limit for applying for one.

If you seek permission to appeal to a commissioner

A tribunal decision can also be set aside if:[164]

- you (or the DWP, local authority or Revenue) seek the permission of the tribunal chair to appeal to a commissioner (see p1122); *and*
- the person considering your application also thinks the tribunal made an 'error of law' (see p1121).

The tribunal decision *must* be set aside if you and the DWP (or local authority or Revenue) agree that the tribunal made an 'error of law' (see p1121).[165]

If the DWP (or local authority or Revenue) seeks permission to appeal to the commissioner, the TS must send you a copy of the application.[166] This gives you the chance to let the tribunal chair know if you agree the tribunal made an 'error of law'. However, there is no such requirement if *you* seek permission. In this case, if you think that the DWP (or local authority or Revenue) might agree the tribunal made an 'error of law', you should send a copy of your application to them. However, there is no guarantee that they will take any action on this.

If the tribunal decision is set aside, you should be given the opportunity to ask for an oral hearing, even if your appeal was originally decided at a paper hearing.[167]

Commissioners have the discretion to set aside decisions in similar circumstances when applications for permission to appeal are made directly to them (see p1125).

3. Appealing to a commissioner

Both you and the DWP (or local authority or Revenue) have a right of appeal to a social security commissioner against a decision of an appeal tribunal. There is only one possible ground for appeal: that the tribunal has made an 'error of law' (see p1121).[168] You must first apply for, and obtain, permission to appeal and there is a strict time limit for applying (see p1122).

If you have evidence, it might enable you to apply for a supersession of the tribunal's decision (see p1074) and you can do so while your appeal is pending.

Bear in mind that the amount of arrears you can get with a supersession are limited, so you need to continue with your appeal at the same time.

Error of law

The tribunal made an error of law if:[169]

- it got the **law wrong** or misinterpreted it – eg, it misunderstood the particular benefit rule concerned. **Note:** if the tribunal sets out the reasons for its decision in the decision notice (see p1115) and these indicate that the tribunal did not apply the law correctly, the decision notice is likely to be a more reliable statement of the tribunal's reasons than a later conflicting explanation in a statement of reasons (see p1116);[170]
- there is **no evidence** to support its decision. In addition, if a tribunal gave you a physical examination when it was not permitted to do so (see p1111), it made an error of law if its decision is based on evidence obtained from that examination.[171] However, a tribunal has not necessarily made an error of law if it fails to take account of evidence that was not before it at the hearing – ie, where you (or the DWP, local authority or Revenue) only produce evidence when your appeal is before a commissioner,[172] or if it accepts evidence that was not challenged at the hearing (eg, where the DWP, local authority or the Revenue choose not to attend);[173]
- the **facts it found** are such that, had it acted reasonably and interpreted the law correctly, it could not have made the decision it did. This argument can be used where the facts are inconsistent with the decision – eg, a tribunal finds that a man and a woman live in separate households, but decides they are living together as husband and wife. The tribunal also made an error of law if it took things into account which it should not have taken into account, or refused or failed to take into account things which it should have taken into account;
- there is a **breach of the rules of natural justice**. This includes where:
  - the procedure followed by the tribunal leads to unfairness. Whether or not this is so depends on the facts of the case, but examples include if:
    - you are not allowed to call witnesses to support you; *or*
    - the tribunal refuses to postpone or adjourn a hearing (see p1107) even though you cannot attend for a good reason and have told it so; *or*
    - the standard of interpretation is not adequate and the tribunal does not take appropriate action;[174] *or*
    - the tribunal pressurises you into giving up your right to a fair hearing – eg, it bargains with you by 'offering' you one component of disability living allowance (DLA) if you agree not to argue for the other;[175] *or*

- you did not get notice of the hearing and the result is that you lost without having a chance to put your case properly, even if you could have applied for the tribunal's decision to be set aside instead;[176]
- you (or the DWP, local authority or Revenue) asked for an oral hearing but one did not take place;[177]
- you did not receive the decision maker's submission or receive it in sufficient time before the hearing and were not given an opportunity to read it properly;[178]
- the tribunal removed your entitlement to benefit at a paper hearing without warning you or giving you the chance to make representations;[179]

- it does not give **proper findings of fact**. The tribunal can rely on the summary of the facts given in the decision maker's submission (see p1104), but only if these are not in dispute and s/he has covered all relevant issues.[180] If you and the DWP (or local authority or Revenue) disagree about the facts the tribunal must explain which version it prefers and why;
- it does not provide **adequate reasons** for its decision (see p1116). If a delay in writing the reasons indicates that they are unreliable as an accurate statement of the tribunal's reasoning, you can argue the reasons are inadequate.[181] The tribunal must not simply say what its decision was. It must give sufficient reasons so that you can see why, on the evidence, it reached the conclusion it did. **Note:** a tribunal does not have to give its reasons for refusing to adjourn an appeal hearing.[182]

Note: a tribunal will *not* have erred in law simply because a different tribunal or a commissioner might have come to a different conclusion.[183]

How to appeal to a commissioner

You must first obtain permission ('leave') to appeal to a commissioner.[184] This means you have to show there has possibly been an error of law (see p1121) and you have the beginnings of a case. There is a strict time limit for applying for permission to appeal. If you wish to appeal:

- you must usually have the tribunal's statement of reasons (see p1116). You may find it difficult to show that the tribunal made an error of law without one;
- you first have to apply for permission to appeal to the chair of the tribunal. If the chair refuses (or rejects) your application, you can apply for permission direct to a commissioner.

Applying to the chair of the tribunal

You apply for permission to appeal, in the first instance, to the chair of the tribunal.[185] You should first apply for a statement of reasons for the tribunal's decision (see p1116).

Your application for permission to appeal must:[186]

- be in writing. You must sign the application yourself. However, if you have given written authority to your representative, s/he can sign it on your behalf; *and*
- contain details of your grounds for appeal and sufficient information about the tribunal's decision for it to be identified. If you are making a late application you must also give your grounds for this.

Bear in mind that the person considering your application might not be the chair of your tribunal.[187]

You do not have to attach a copy of the statement of reasons to your application because the chair of the tribunal already has one. However, if there is no statement of reasons for the tribunal's decision – eg, because you did not apply for one in time or one has not been provided, your application for permission to appeal must be rejected.[188] However, you may make a fresh application to the commissioner (see below).

If the DWP (or local authority or Revenue) applies for permission to appeal you are sent a copy of the application. You can make comments on the application if you want to – eg, why you think it does not have grounds for appeal, but these do not have to be taken into account.[189] If you and the DWP (or local authority or Revenue) agree that the tribunal made an 'error of law', the chair of the tribunal must set the decision aside (see p1120).

The time limit for applying

Your application for permission to appeal must be received by the clerk to the tribunal at the Tribunals Service (TS) office within one month (see p1099) of you being sent the tribunal's statement of reasons.[190] If, after you are sent the statement of reasons, an accidental error in the decision notice is corrected or your application for the tribunal's decision to be set aside is refused, the one-month period runs from the date you are sent notice of this.[191] However, this does not apply where a decision was not set aside because of a refusal to extend the time limit for applying for one. If you do not have a statement of reasons, see below.

Outside the one-month time limit, an application for permission to appeal can only be considered if a legally qualified tribunal member thinks there are special reasons for doing so.[192] However, you must apply within an absolute time limit. This is one year from the date the one-month limit expired. See p1129 for further information about late appeals.

Note: if you have not been sent a statement of reasons, the time limit for applying for permission to appeal effectively does not start to run and the chair of the tribunal must reject your application.[193] However, you must make an application to her/him before you can make a fresh application to a commissioner and must do so within 13 months of the date of the tribunal's decision (see p1124). Otherwise the commissioner cannot consider your application.

If the chair refuses or rejects your application

If the chair refuses you permission to appeal or rejects your application (eg, because your application was late or you did not apply for a statement of reasons) you may make a fresh application to a commissioner. You must apply in writing. You should use Form OSSC1, available from your TS office, the Commissioners' Office (see Appendix 1) or at www.osscsc.gov.uk. Your application must include:[194]

- your name and address;
- the reasons for your appeal – ie, the error of law you think the tribunal made. If your application is late, you must also give your reasons for this;
- copies of the tribunal's decision, its statement of reasons (if you have one – see below) and the notice of the chair's refusal, or rejection of, your application for permission.

The commissioner can waive any irregularities in your application for permission to appeal.[195] Therefore, if you do not have a statement of reasons, your application can still be considered. However, you must still show that the tribunal made an error of law (see p1121) without it – ie, if what is said in the decision notice is sufficient to do so.[196] The failure of the chair of the tribunal to provide a statement of reasons where s/he has a duty to do so is in itself an error of law.[197]

You can send your application by post, fax or email, or deliver it in person. However, you can only send it by email if you have been given written permission in advance.[198]

The Commissioners' Office obtains the file of your appeal papers from the TS regional office. The commissioner considers these as well as what you say in your application before reaching a decision. The DWP (or local authority or Revenue) plays no part in the procedure at this stage.

You are sent a written notice of the commissioner's decision on your application for permission to appeal, including the reasons for the decision. You cannot appeal against a commissioner's refusal to grant you permission to appeal, but you might be able to apply for the decision to be set aside[199] (see p1126) or for judicial review (see p1129).

The time limit for applying

Your application for permission to appeal must be sent to the Commissioners' Office within one month (see p1099) of the date the chair of the tribunal's refusal (or rejection) was sent to you.[200]

A late application may be accepted if there are special reasons. This is the case even if you made a late application to the chair (or one is rejected) so long as you applied within 13 months of the tribunal's decision (or of being sent the tribunal's statement of reasons if this is later).[201] There is no absolute time limit for applying to a commissioner.

See p1129 for further information about late appeals.

What happens when you get permission to appeal

If you have been granted leave to appeal by the chair, you must send a 'notice of appeal' within one month of being sent notice of this.[202] You are sent a form on which to do this. The time may be extended for special reasons (see p1131).[203] As well as the notice of appeal, you must send a copy of the notice telling you that your application for permission to appeal has been granted, the tribunal's decision and its statement of reasons (if you have one), along with your details and your reasons for appealing against the decision. Where you have applied for permission to appeal direct to a commissioner on Form OSSC1 (see p1124), you are usually told your notice of application has been treated as a notice of appeal. In this case, you do not have to send in another.[204]

The DWP (or local authority or Revenue) might agree with you that the tribunal made an error of law (see p1121). If this happens a commissioner can:[205]

- set aside the tribunal's decision;
- refer your appeal back to be heard by another tribunal; *and*
- issue a direction to the tribunal, which will hear your appeal again. You or the DWP (or local authority or Revenue) can ask a commissioner to do this and suggest what the direction should say.

If a test case is pending

If a test case is pending that deals with issues raised in your appeal, you may find that your appeal is delayed. See p1108 for further information.

The written procedure

The Commissioners' Office sends you a copy of the appeal file, asks for submissions and sets a timetable for providing them. The decision maker is asked to provide a submission first, then you are given the chance to reply to this. You may find the decision maker supports your appeal and asks the commissioner to consider referring it back to be heard by a different tribunal.

You are given one month in which to reply to the decision maker's submission, although the commissioner may extend the time limit.[206] If you have nothing to add and do not want to reply at any stage, tell the Commissioners' Office. A commissioner has the power to strike out an appeal that appears to have been abandoned, although you can apply for it to be reinstated.[207]

When the commissioner has all the written submissions, if your appeal is not dealt with by agreement without a detailed decision, s/he decides whether or not there should be an oral hearing of the appeal. If you ask for an oral hearing, the commissioner holds one unless s/he considers the case can be dealt with properly without one.[208] Occasionally, a commissioner decides to hold an oral hearing even if you have not asked for one. If there is no oral hearing, the commissioner reaches a decision on the basis of written submissions and other documents.

Note: because of the length of time you usually have to wait before your case is dealt with, you should make a fresh claim for benefit (or seek a supersession) if, for example, your circumstances change (but see p1114).

Oral hearings

Oral hearings are usually held at the Commissioners' Office in London or Edinburgh, or at the law courts in Bury, Cardiff or Doncaster. Oral hearings can also be held at other court centres – eg, if it is difficult for you to travel to the usual venues. You are told the date in good time and your fares are paid in advance.

Unless there are more than two parties involved in the appeal, you and your representative may be able to participate in the oral hearing via a video conferencing link – eg, if your disability makes it difficult for you to travel, or to avoid travel costs and time.[209] These are available in a number of areas.

Usually, one commissioner hears your case. However, if there is a 'question of law of special difficulty', the hearing may be before a tribunal of three commissioners,[210] but the procedure is the same.

The commissioner might ask you to provide a summary of the arguments you are going to make (a 'skeleton argument') in advance of the hearing. If s/he does so, you must provide one.[211] See p1133 for information about how to prepare an appeal.

The hearing is more formal than that before a tribunal, but the commissioner lets you say everything you want to. Commissioners usually intervene a lot and ask questions so you need to be prepared to argue your case without your script. A full set of commissioners' decisions (see p1137) and the statute law (see p1136) are available for your use. The DWP (or local authority or Revenue) is usually represented by a lawyer, so you should also consider obtaining representation.

The decision

The decision is always given in writing.[212] It may be a number of weeks before it is sent to you.

If the commissioner agrees an appeal tribunal's decision was wrong, the case is often sent back to another tribunal with directions on how to reconsider the issues.[213] However, if the commissioner thinks the tribunal's statement of reasons for its decision contains all the material facts, or s/he considers it expedient to make any extra findings of fact, the commissioner makes the final decision.[214] It is unusual for a commissioner not to send a case back to a tribunal if there is a dispute about facts that were not determined by the original tribunal, unless all the evidence points in one direction.[215]

If you disagree with a commissioner's decision

A commissioner's decision is final. However:

- a commissioner may **correct or set aside** her/his decision.[216] A decision can be set aside if s/he thinks it is just and:

  - you, your representative or the DWP (or local authority or Revenue) were not sent papers or other relevant documents, or did not receive them in sufficient time, or the commissioner who made the decision did not receive them in sufficient time; *or*
  - you, your representative or the DWP (or local authority or Revenue) were not present at the hearing.

  Sometimes there are 'procedural irregularities' which lead to an obvious unfairness and as a result, it would be in the 'interests of justice' for a decision to be set aside. You can try to argue that there is also a power to do this.[217]

  You must apply for a decision to be set aside within one month of being given the decision. A commissioner can extend this time limit.[218] All the parties involved in the appeal are sent a copy of the application and are given a change to make representations;
- it can be **superseded** in the normal way – eg, where new facts have come to light since the decision was made or there was a mistake about the facts (see p1074). However, if the commissioner made a mistake about the law you must appeal to a court (see below);
- you or the DWP (or local authority or Revenue) can **appeal** to the Court of Appeal (in Scotland, the Court of Session) – see below.

4. Appealing to the courts

You might consider appealing to a court if you want to:
- appeal against a commissioner's decision (see below); *or*
- seek a judicial review (see p1129).

Appeals from social security commissioners

You may appeal against a commissioner's decision to the Court of Appeal (in Scotland, the Court of Session). You can only do this if the commissioner made an error of law (see p1121) and you must first obtain permission to appeal.[219] The DWP (or local authority or Revenue) has the same rights of appeal as you.

The procedure in the Court is strict, formal and far less flexible than the procedure before a tribunal or a commissioner. For an outline of the procedure, see p1128.

The DWP (or local authority or Revenue) will be represented by a barrister at the hearing. You should consider obtaining legal advice from a solicitor before appealing. See p1129 for information about meeting the cost of going to court.

Note: before making *any* application you should seek advice about whether you could be liable for your opponent's costs if you were to lose your case.

England and Wales

In England and Wales, an application for permission to appeal to the Court of Appeal must first be made to a commissioner in writing within three months of the date when you were sent the commissioner's decision.[220] You must clearly identify the commissioner's error of law in your application.[221]

If an accidental error in the commissioner's decision has been corrected or you applied for the decision to be set aside (see p1126) and this has been refused, the time limit runs from the date you are sent notice of this.[222] This does not apply where your application for a set aside was refused because it was made outside the time limit for this.

The commissioner may extend the time limit.[223] If the commissioner refuses to extend it, the Court of Appeal cannot hear your appeal and you can only proceed by applying to the High Court for judicial review of the refusal to grant a late appeal (see p1129).[224]

If the commissioner refuses to give you permission to appeal (for reasons other than being outside the time limit), you can apply direct to the Court of Appeal.[225] Your notice of application should be lodged with the Civil Appeals Office within six weeks of being sent notification of the commissioner's refusal.[226] The court may extend the time limit.[227]

Generally, the Court of Appeal first considers your application for permission to appeal without an oral hearing. If permission is refused, you may renew your application in open court by writing to the court office but must do this within seven days.[228]

If permission to appeal is granted by a commissioner or the Court of Appeal, you must serve a notice of appeal on the relevant parties. There are strict time limits for doing this.[229] Seek advice immediately if you are in this position. The DWP solicitor will accept service on behalf of the DWP. The solicitor to the Revenue will accept service on behalf of the Revenue (see Appendix 1 for the addresses). Ask your local authority who will accept service on its behalf.

If the Court of Appeal refuses you permission to appeal after an oral hearing, you cannot appeal further, nor apply for a judicial review.

You cannot appeal to the Court of Appeal against a commissioner's refusal to grant you permission to appeal against a tribunal's decision, but you can apply to the High Court for judicial review of such a decision.[230]

Scotland

In Scotland the procedures for appealing to the Court of Session are similar to those for England and Wales but there are a number of crucial differences.

If the commissioner refuses you permission to appeal to the Court of Session you have six weeks from the date of notification to lodge a further application for permission to appeal with the Court of Session.

The Court of Session hears applications for permission to appeal in open court rather than making the decision simply by reading the papers as in England and

Wales. The DWP (or local authority or the Revenue) may agree that the application for permission and the appeal itself are heard at the same time.

Applying for judicial review

Occasionally it is possible to challenge decisions with which you disagree by going to court for a judicial review. Judicial review is a means of challenging the decisions of any form of tribunal, government department or local authority.

For example, you can apply for a judicial review of a decision:

- made by a decision maker, if it is a decision against which you do not have a right of appeal (see p1097); *or*
- made by a legally qualified tribunal member to strike out your appeal or refusing to grant you a late appeal to a tribunal; *or*
- made by a social security commissioner refusing to grant you permission to appeal late; *or*
- refusing you a payment from the discretionary social fund (see Chapter 21); *or*
- made by a local authority about discretionary housing payments of housing benefit and council tax benefit (see p222).

You cannot usually go to court for a judicial review if you have another independent means of appeal, such as to a tribunal.

You need the services of a solicitor, law centre or legal advice centre to apply for a judicial review. You must apply to the High Court promptly and within three months of the decision you want to challenge. In Scotland, you apply to the Court of Session. There is no time limit but you should make your application as soon as possible.[231]

Meeting the cost of going to court

Free legal help from a solicitor is available for cases in the Court of Appeal, the High Court and the Court of Session and you should consider obtaining legal advice and representation for these. If you are not eligible for free legal help you are likely to have to pay court fees and if you want to be represented by a lawyer, her/his fees. It may be a worthwhile investment if your claim is worth hundreds of pounds.

Note: before making *any* application to a court you should seek advice about whether you could be liable for your opponent's legal costs if you were to lose your case.

5. **Late appeals**

If you miss the time limit for lodging an appeal, a late appeal can be accepted in certain circumstances by:

- a legally qualified tribunal member or a decision maker, if you are appealing to a tribunal (see below);
- a legally qualified tribunal member or a commissioner, if you are seeking permission to appeal to the commissioner against a tribunal's decision (see p1131);
- a commissioner or the Court of Appeal (in Scotland, the Court of Session), if you are seeking permission to appeal to the Court against a commissioner's decision (see p1127).

The rules for making a late appeal to a tribunal are much more strict.

Late appeals to tribunals

You need permission ('leave') to appeal if you miss the time limit (see p1099) and this can be difficult to get. It might be simpler to ask for a revision or supersession of the decision maker's decision instead of making a late appeal, so long as there are grounds for doing this and this would give you everything to which you are entitled (see pp1065 and 1074). However, you often get less arrears of benefit if you seek a supersession (see p1079).

No appeal can be allowed outside an absolute time limit. This is one year from the date your time limit for appealing expired.[232] You must apply in writing. In addition to the information you must provide on your appeal form (see p1100), you must explain your reasons for lateness, including details of any special circumstances (see p1131).[233]

A late appeal can only be allowed if:[234]

- a decision maker is satisfied that it is in the 'interests of justice'. The decision maker's submission tells you if the decision maker has given you permission to appeal.[235] If the decision maker does not give you permission to appeal, s/he *must* pass your application to the Tribunals Service for a legally qualified tribunal member to decide; *or*
- a legally qualified tribunal member:
  - is satisfied that it is in the 'interests of justice'; *or*
  - the appeal has reasonable prospects of success.

It can only be in the interests of justice to allow a late appeal if it was not practicable for you to appeal in time because:[236]

- you, your partner or a dependant has died or had a serious illness;
- you are not resident in the UK;
- normal postal services were disrupted; *or*
- there are other special circumstances that are 'wholly exceptional' (see p1131)

The longer you have delayed appealing, the more compelling the special circumstances need to be.[237] When deciding if it is in the interests of justice to allow your application, account cannot be taken of the fact that:[238]

- a court or commissioner has interpreted the law in a different way than previously understood and applied;
- you (or anyone acting for you) misunderstood or were unaware of the relevant law, including the time limits for appealing.

You must be sent a written summary of the tribunal member's decision as soon as it is practicable.[239]

If you are refused a late appeal because you are outside the absolute time limit for appealing, you cannot appeal to a commissioner against the refusal.[240] However, if you were within the absolute time limit, you can try to argue that you *can* appeal to a commissioner.

Late appeals to commissioners

An application to a **tribunal chair** for permission to appeal to the commissioner can only be considered outside the one-month time limit (see p1122) if a legally qualified tribunal member thinks there are 'special reasons' for doing so.[241] No application can be allowed outside an absolute time limit. This is one year from the date the one-month limit expired.

If your application is refused or rejected, you can apply direct to a **commissioner** for permission to appeal. If you apply outside the one-month limit (see p1124), your application can be accepted if there are special reasons.[242] This is also the case where you have already made an unsuccessful late application to the tribunal chair, so long as you applied to her/him within 13 months of being given the tribunal's decision (or statement of reasons if this is later).

In this context – and in contrast to late appeals to tribunals – potentially anything can count as a special reason as long as it is special enough.[243] In particular, special reasons do not have to relate to why the appeal was late[244] (although they may do so). See below for information about what might count as a special reason.

The decision whether or not to allow a late appeal must be made bearing in mind the merits of the appeal and the consequences for the claimant (and the DWP, local authority or the Revenue). If you are refused permission for a late appeal to a commissioner, you do not have a right of appeal against the decision. The only other possible remedy is judicial review (see p1129).

Special reasons and circumstances

What may or may not be a special reason or circumstance cannot be defined in advance. It depends on the circumstances of each case and the commissioner or tribunal chair (or decision maker) has to make her/his decision on an individual, case-by-case basis.

You should stress reasons or circumstances that are personal to you. Permission to appeal is sometimes refused because the reasons given are general ones – ie, ones that apply in a large number of cases rather than special ones that apply specifically to you.

There are no hard and fast rules about what should be taken into account but the following are all relevant.

- Explaining the **reasons for the delay** is important in any application for a late appeal. Make sure you explain these as clearly and as fully as possible. Do not worry if some or all of the delay is your fault. Almost any explanation is better than none at all. The worst situation is where you knew the time limit, but simply ignored it, but even then it may be possible to say something favourable. Say if things have been difficult at home or you were confused by the rules or just assumed that the DWP (or local authority or Revenue) were the experts and had got it right until, for example, you were advised otherwise or read an article in a newspaper. Reasons for the delay could include the fact that:
  - you did not receive the decision;
  - you made a reasonable mistake in calculating the time limit;
  - you posted your appeal in time but it went astray in the post;
  - you were ill;
  - a mistake was made by your advisers. It should not make any difference that you might be able to sue your advisers for negligence. Professional advisers are not normally negligent and if yours does make an error then that is special to your case;
  - you were given wrong advice or otherwise misled by the DWP (or local authority or Revenue) – eg, you were discouraged from appealing by a decision maker who advised you incorrectly that an appeal would be doomed to fail.

  If you have been badly advised by the DWP (or local authority or Revenue) and lose money because you are refused a late appeal you should consider claiming compensation (see Chapter 46).
- The **length of the delay**. Short delays are likely to be easier to justify than long delays. However, the usual approach is that time limits have to be kept to, and there has to be good reason for not doing so. So even a short delay may be difficult to justify without good reason.
- The **merits of your appeal**. The more likely your appeal is to succeed, the greater the injustice in refusing to allow an extension of time. A strong case is particularly useful if there has been a very long delay and permission is usually granted where there has been a 'clear error', which would have long-term continuing effects unless corrected.[245]
- The **amount of money at stake**. Even if there has been no clear error, permission to appeal may be granted if there is a lot of money at stake.[246]
- A **decision in a test case**. The fact that there has been a decision in a test case, establishing that an earlier decision was incorrect can amount to a special reason, at least in some circumstances (but see p1130).[247] In any case, if there

are other reasons why a late appeal should be granted these should be emphasised, as well as the decision in the test case. Such appeals often involve large sums of money and (given the test case) a clear error in the decision which is being appealed against. Both of these have been accepted as special reasons in other contexts – usually when it is the DWP (or local authority or Revenue) that wishes to appeal late rather than you.

6. How to prepare an appeal

Appeals are taken on all sorts of issues – disputes about facts or the law or both – so the advice given here can only be general. You usually need to think about both the facts and the law because they are connected. The law tells you which facts are relevant and the facts tell you which parts of the law you need to consider. Always try, if possible, to link the facts of your case and your arguments to the rules laid down in the Acts and regulations (see p1136).

Sorting out the facts

You are likely to know more than anyone else about the facts of your case. Your key task is to pass your knowledge on to the tribunal. A tribunal is a complete re-hearing of your case, so fresh facts and arguments can be put by either side.

Remember to:

- check through the appeal papers carefully to work out what evidence the DWP (or local authority or Revenue) used in support of the decision. This helps you decide what evidence you need to win your case;
- study the DWP's (or local authority's or Revenue's) evidence and think about your arguments – eg, to show how it may have got the wrong impression;
- gather evidence to back up what you are saying. If you want to give any evidence or information to the tribunal, send it to the clerk as soon as possible before your oral hearing. Otherwise the tribunal might decide to adjourn your appeal (see p1107). The clerk sends a further copy to the DWP (or local authority or Revenue), who might then decide to support your appeal;
- ask any witnesses who support your case to attend the hearing. Both you and the DWP (or local authority or Revenue) can ask witnesses to give information. Chairs have the power to refuse to hear witnesses who are not relevant, but they should always be fair to you and generally allow witnesses to speak, even if it looks like they may have nothing useful to say.[248]

Evidence

Evidence includes:

- oral evidence – what you (and any witnesses or others) actually say at the hearing; *and*

- written evidence – any documents you (or the DWP, local authority or Revenue) produce, including medical evidence.

The tribunal considers all the evidence and decides what weight it should be given.[249]

The DWP (or local authority or Revenue) might use video evidence – eg, if you are appealing about entitlement to incapacity benefit or disability living allowance. You cannot prevent the DWP (or local authority or Revenue) doing so.[250] However, you should insist you are given time to view and consider the evidence in advance of the tribunal hearing and, if relevant, that the person who made the video is called as a witness.

Oral evidence

You are usually expected to give your own oral evidence at the hearing, if you can. Your representative is generally not allowed to give it for you. However, s/he can assist the tribunal in gathering evidence from you,[251] and can give her/his *own* evidence based on her/his observations.[252] A tribunal cannot dismiss oral evidence without a proper explanation of why it has done so.[253]

Witnesses can also give oral evidence at the hearing. You or the DWP (or local authority or Revenue) can call witnesses.[254]

If s/he is at the hearing, the presenting officer (see p1109) puts the DWP's (or local authority's or Revenue's) case but is not necessarily the person who actually made the decision on your claim. Unless giving her/his own evidence (eg, because s/he was directly involved in the decision on your claim), her/his submissions are not evidence.[255]

You, your representative and the presenting officer can report what other people have said. This is called **hearsay evidence**. Tribunals can accept hearsay evidence, but they must carefully weigh up its value, given that the person who originally made the statement is not present at the hearing.[256]

Written evidence

Written evidence includes letters, medical and other reports, wage slips, bank statements, birth certificates and anything else that helps prove the facts. If, for example, the DWP (or local authority or Revenue) says you failed to disclose an increase in your earnings and you have been overpaid, you could explain to the tribunal how and when you told it. It is even better to produce a copy of the letter you sent informing it of the change. It is not unknown for the DWP (or local authority or the Revenue) to fail to include copies of relevant letters from you or other parties in the decision maker's submission. You should check the submission carefully and submit copies you have of any missing documents to the tribunal as soon as you can. If you do not have copies, insist that the decision maker provides these.

Most evidence relied on by the DWP (or local authority or Revenue) is written and you can point out that you have not had the opportunity of questioning the witnesses. You are not entitled to insist on the presence of any particular witness,[257] but you should argue that the tribunal should not place any weight on the written evidence of, say, an interviewing officer if you are disputing the interview, or an investigating officer if you are disputing what s/he heard or saw.

Medical evidence

Your medical evidence should deal with the points in dispute if that is possible and also with the dates relevant to the decision with which you disagree. If your doctor does not know about the effect of your disability on your everyday life, tell her/him about it and ask her/him to confirm that this is consistent with the degree of your disability. Your evidence or that of a friend or relative may also be of use.

Where medical evidence might be useful, you can ask your doctor to provide it, or ask an advice agency to write to your doctor. Your doctor may charge for such evidence, but an advice agency or solicitor might be able to get a report free. If possible, the report should be sent to the tribunal in advance of the hearing. Send a copy of the letter to your doctor with the report as this will help to show that s/he is expressing her/his own opinion about your case. You could also ask your doctor to supply a copy of her/his notes about you over the last few years.

The tribunal can refer you for an examination and obtain a report if it thinks this is necessary (see p1111). If the lack of a report is causing you difficulties at a tribunal hearing, you could remind the tribunal of this power to obtain one itself.

You may have problems at the hearing if your opinion about the effect of your ill-health or disabilities is contradicted by evidence from a doctor, or where there is evidence from more than one doctor and the doctors disagree. The tribunal should weigh all the evidence on its own merits. It should not automatically assume one piece of evidence is the best. If a doctor does not know you or how you are affected by your condition (for instance, if s/he only gave you a very short examination), this should be taken into account.[258] Point out how long the doctor has known you and what s/he knows about your day-to-day living activities or walking abilities. You should seek further medical evidence to support your view in advance of the hearing if you foresee any such conflict of evidence.

Note: a tribunal should not rely on evidence from a DWP doctor with whom it sits on tribunals at other times. This depends on how often and on how recently this has happened.[259]

Checking the law

If you know what the law says, you know what facts you have to prove. The primary sources of social security law are statute law and caselaw decided by commissioners and courts. It is easy to find both once you know what you are looking for. The footnotes in this *Handbook* point you in the right direction. There are also a number of books that explain the law and refer you to relevant legislation and cases (see Appendix 3).

You should also look carefully at the decision maker's submission (see p1104), as this refers to the statute law and caselaw which s/he thinks is relevant. The DWP (or local authority or Revenue) does not always get the law right and you should emphasise a point that it has overlooked or got wrong.

Statute law

The law consists of Acts of Parliament and regulations. The Acts set out the main framework and empower the Secretary of State to make regulations covering the details. These regulations are known as statutory instruments.

The best way to look up the relevant statute law is to read one of the annotated volumes of legislation, listed in Appendix 3. Remember that in rare cases, the books do not contain all the regulations that are relevant. You can purchase regulations individually from The Stationery Office. Many Acts and regulations are also available at www.opsi.gov.uk/legislation/index.htm. The Acts and regulations are sometimes amended, so you must confirm that the rules in the books or obtained individually are up to date.

If you are trying to discover the current law or chase up a reference, unless your appeal is an old one and the law has changed since the relevant time, you can refer to *The Law Relating to Social Security* – known as the 'Blue Volumes'. These are available at www.dwp.gov.uk/advisers/docs/lawvols/bluevol/index.asp. Your local DWP office should also have a copy. Make sure it is up to date. CPAG's *Welfare Benefits and Tax Credits Law Online* includes up-to-date social security legislation, caselaw and commissioners' decisions, plus the text of this *Handbook*, with links to the relevant law. For information, see Appendix 3.

Benefit law is complicated and the staff who administer benefits are issued with guidance manuals and circulars. The DWP (or local authority or Revenue) and tribunals are only bound by what the law says, not by the guidance. Nevertheless, it is sometimes useful to check the guidance. See Appendix 3 for a list of what is available.

If the statute law is ambiguous

If the statute law (see above) is ambiguous, the courts, including tribunals and commissioners, can look at statements made to Parliament by ministers when the law was first made.[260] It may, therefore, be worth checking the House of Commons' and House of Lords' official reports (known as *Hansard*) to see what was said in Parliament when the rules were first introduced. You can find *Hansard* at www.publications.parliament.uk/pa/pahansard.htm. You can also check the transcripts of debates in the Standing Committee on Delegated Legislation at www.publications.parliament.uk/pa/cm/othstn.htm. Other important sources of information are the Social Security Advisory Committee (www.ssac.org.uk) and the Industrial Injuries Advisory Council (www.iiac.org.uk).

Caselaw

When a commissioner or a court decides an appeal, the decision sets a precedent, which a decision maker or appeal tribunal deciding a similar case must follow.[261] Unreported decisions must be followed in the same way as reported ones.[262]

The decision maker's submission often refers to caselaw. You should also use caselaw to support your appeal if possible. To help you decide which cases to use, see p1138.

Identifying commissioners' decisions

All commissioners' decisions have file numbers – eg, CU/255/1984. The last numbers indicate the year in which the appeal was lodged. The second letter indicates the type of benefit involved in the decision. See below for the full list. An extra 'S' after a 'C' denotes a Scottish case, as in CSIB/721/2004. Significant decisions are highlighted on the social security commissioners' website (see p1139).

The most important cases are reported by the Chief Commissioner. These 'reported decisions' are given a new number – eg, CU/255/1984 became R(U) 3/86. All reported cases since 1951 begin with an 'R'. Again, the second letter denotes the type of benefit. The last numbers indicate the year in which the case was published.

Commissioners' decision references

A	Attendance allowance
AF	War pensions
CR	Compensation recovery
CS	Child support
CTF	Child trust funds
DLA	Disability living allowance
DWA	Disability working allowance
F	Child benefit and family allowance
FC	Family credit
FG	Forfeiture – widows' benefits and bereavement benefits
FIS	Family income supplement
FP	Forfeiture – retirement pension
G	General (all benefits not covered in other categories)
H	Housing benefit and council tax benefit
HR	Home responsibilities
I	Industrial injuries benefits
IB	Incapacity benefit
IS	Income support
JSA	Jobseeker's allowance
M	Mobility allowance
P	Retirement pensions

PC	Pension credit
S	Severe disablement allowance, sickness benefit and invalidity benefit
SB	Supplementary benefit
SMP	Statutory maternity pay
SSP	Statutory sick pay
TC	Working tax credit, child tax credit, working families' tax credit and disabled person's tax credit
U	Unemployment benefit

Identifying court decisions

Court decisions are identified by the names of the parties involved in the appeal. The first name is usually the party who has appealed and the second name is the other party. In judicial review cases, the case citation begins with 'R'.

Examples of court decisions

Mallinson v Secretary of State for Social Security, 21 April 1994 (HL) is a House of Lords decision.

Hockenjos v Secretary of State for Social Security [2004] EWCA Civ 1749, 21 December 2004 is a Court of Appeal decision.

R v South Tyneside MBC ex parte Tooley [1997] QBD and *R (Reynolds) v Secretary of State for Work and Pensions* [2002] EWHC Admin 426 are decisions following applications for judicial review.

Which cases to use

Caselaw can seem less precise than statute law and frequently cases seem to contradict each other. Very often there are small differences in the facts of the cases, which justify the different results. Find cases where the facts are similar to yours. If cases appear to be against you, look at the facts of those cases and see whether any differences justify a different decision in your case (known as 'distinguishing' cases). One distinction may simply be that what seemed reasonable in the 1950s does not seem fair in the 2000s.[263] Remember that most appeals before April 1987 were decided when there was a right of appeal to commissioners on questions of fact as well as law so tribunals may not necessarily be erring in law if they take a different view from a commissioner in an older decision.

If there have been amendments to the statute law since a case was decided, it might only apply to the previous version of the law. You need to ensure that the caselaw is still relevant to the decision you are appealing.

Where there is an irreconcilable conflict between two or more decisions, a tribunal has to choose which decision to follow. It normally follows a reported commissioner's decision in preference to an unreported one, and must follow a decision of a tribunal of commissioners in preference to a decision of a single commissioner.[264] Decisions of the House of Lords, the Court of Appeal or the High Court on an application for judicial review, or in Scotland the Court of Session, take precedence over all commissioners' decisions.[265]

Commissioners have more freedom than a tribunal. A commissioner:

- does not have to follow the decision of another single commissioner if satisfied that the earlier decision was wrong;[266]
- must follow a decision of a tribunal of commissioners although, if s/he thinks it may be wrong, s/he can ask the Chief Commissioner to appoint another tribunal to reconsider the point;
- where two earlier decisions conflict, should follow the latest decision if it fully considers the earlier one, unless satisfied it was wrong.[267]

A tribunal of commissioners does not have to follow the decision of another tribunal, but usually does so.[268]

Note: it is worth checking the decisions referred to in the decision maker's submission (see p1104). Sometimes they rely on only part of a decision and fail to mention another part which is more favourable to you. To find other cases relevant to your own, you can use the footnotes in this *Handbook* or any of the books listed in Appendix 3.

Obtaining commissioners' and court decisions

Since September 2000, reported **commissioners' decisions** have been published in a loose-leaf format, available on subscription. All reported decisions from 1991 onwards are also available on the DWP website (see Appendix 1). Reported decisions are published from time to time in bound volumes which are sometimes available in law libraries.

Summaries of reported commissioners' decisions, most highlighted decisions and important court decisions are published in CPAG's *Welfare Rights Bulletin*. These, together with the full decisions are also available on CPAG's *Welfare Benefits and Tax Credits Law Online*. It is important to use the full decision, not just the summary, at the appeal hearing. Many decisions are available at www.osscsc.gov.uk and on the Rightsnet website at www.rightsnet.org.uk. Reported and unreported commissioners' decisions may be purchased from the Commissioners' Office (see Appendix 1).

If an unreported decision is to be used at a tribunal hearing by the DWP (or local authority or Revenue), a copy should be supplied to you. Similarly, if you wish to use one, you should supply copies to everyone, preferably by sending one to the tribunal clerk in advance of the hearing.

Many **court decisions** are now available on the internet. A useful link to these is at www.bailii.org/databases.html. In addition, where there has been an appeal against a commissioner's decision, it is usually reported (see p1137) with the court decision attached.

Presenting your case to the tribunal

Each case is different and hearings are informal, so there is no set pattern for presenting cases. If you want to make a presentation on your appeal, make this clear to the tribunal as soon as possible – eg, tell the clerk to the tribunal before the hearing starts and ask her/him to let the chair of the tribunal know.

It is a good idea to send any detailed submissions and medical reports before the hearing. Some claimants like to use a written submission at the hearing and to read directly from it. However, tribunals usually ask questions so it is necessary to be able to talk about your case without the script.

It is helpful to make it clear at the beginning which parts of the decision maker's submission are in dispute. It is, then, usually best to tell the tribunal about the facts and to call any witnesses before turning to legal arguments.

It is the tribunal's job to help you to say everything you want by putting you at your ease and asking the right questions. However, you must also be prepared for some searching questions. If you forget to say something when it is your turn to speak, do not hesitate to add it at the end of the hearing.

Advice and representation

There are a number of agencies which can advise you and help you prepare your case for the hearing (see Appendix 2). Some can also represent you at hearings if you feel that someone else would put your case better than you. Remember that many non-lawyer advisers know more about social security law than lawyers and their advice and representation are usually free.

Meeting the costs of going to a tribunal or commissioner

You cannot normally get free legal help from a solicitor to cover representation before tribunals (but see above for help from non-lawyers). However, if you are on income support, income-based jobseeker's allowance, the guarantee credit of pension credit or have a very low income, you might be able to get free legal advice and assistance to cover not only advice but also preparatory work for a hearing, such as obtaining medical reports and writing submissions. If you have a solicitor acting for you in an industrial injury or personal injury claim, s/he may have medical and other reports and evidence which you can use for your benefit claim. If you are not eligible for free advice and assistance, or you want to be represented by a lawyer at an oral hearing, you are likely to have to pay. It may be a worthwhile investment if your claim is worth hundreds of pounds.

If you are resident in Scotland, free legal help is available for appeals to commissioners. This includes help preparing for paper as well as oral hearings. If you are resident in England or Wales, free legal help for appeals to commissioners is available in exceptional cases, if authorised by the Lord Chancellor. If you are granted funding, you must send a copy of the funding notice (in Scotland, the legal aid certificate) to the Commissioners' Office.[269] You must also let the other parties involved in your appeal know that you have been granted funding. The Commissioners' Office says it sends a copy to them and that this counts as adequate notification.[270]

Notes

1. **Appeal rights**
   1 **CB/GA** Reg 24 CB&GA(DA) Regs
   Other benefits s12 SSA 1998; reg 25 SS&CS(DA) Regs
   2 s12(4) SSA 1998
   3 Reg 14 SS(JPIP) Regs
   4 Reg 30(5) and (6)-(6B) SS(C&P) Regs
   5 Sch 7 para 6(3) and (6) CSPSSA 2000; reg 3 HB&CTB(DA) Regs
   6 R(H) 3/04
   7 **CB/GA** Reg 33 CB&GA(DA) Regs
   HB/CTB Reg 21 HB&CTB(DA) Regs
   Other benefits Reg 34 SS&CS(DA) Regs
   8 **CB/GA** s12 and Schs 2 and 3 SSA 1998; reg 25(2) CB&GA(DA) Regs
   HB/CTB Sch 7 para 6 CSPSSA 2000
   Other benefits s12 and Schs 2 and 3 SSA 1998; reg 26 SS&CS(DA) Regs
   9 **CB/GA** Reg 26 CB&GA(DA) Regs
   HB/CTB Reg 10 HB&CTB(DA) Regs
   Other benefits Reg 28 SS&CS(DA) Regs
   10 R(SB) 29/83; R(SB) 12/89; CIS/807/1992; R(H) 3/05
   11 *Secretary of State for Work and Pensions v Adams* [2003] EWCA Civ 796, 18 June 2003 (EWCA), reported as R(G) 1/03
   12 CIS/0345/2003
   13 Reg 10(1)(b) and (2) HB&CTB(DA) Regs
   14 **CB/GA** Reg 26(1)(b) and (2) CB&GA(DA) Regs
   Other benefits Reg 28(1)(b) and (2) SS&CS(DA) Regs
   15 **CB/GA** Sch 2 SSA 1998; reg 25 and Sch 2 CB&GA(DA) Regs
   HB/CTB Sch 7 para 6(2) CSPSSA 2000; reg 16 and Sch to HB&CTB(DA) Regs
   Other benefits Sch 2 SSA 1998; reg 27 and Sch 2 SS&CS(DA) Regs
   16 **CB/GA** Reg 28(1)(a) and (2) CB&GA(DA) Regs
   HB/CTB Reg 18(1)-(3) HB&CTB(DA) Regs
   Other benefits Reg 31(1)(a) and (2) SS&CS(DA) Regs
   17 R(IB) 4/02
   18 **HB/CTB** Reg 10A(3) HB&CTB(DA) Regs
   Other benefits Reg 9A(3) SS&CS(DA) Regs
   19 **CB/GA** Reg 28(3) CB&GA(DA) Regs
   HB/CTB Reg 18(4) HB&CTB(DA) Regs
   Other benefits Reg 31(4) SS&CS(DA) Regs
   20 **CB/GA** Reg 28(2) CB&GA(DA) Regs
   HB/CTB Reg 18(3) HB&CTB(DA) Regs
   Other benefits Reg 31(2) SS&CS(DA) Regs
   21 Reg 18(2) HB&CTB(DA) Regs
   22 **CB/GA** Reg 28(1)(b) and (c) CB&GA(DA) Regs
   Other benefits Reg 31(1)(b)-(c) SS&CS(DA) Regs
   23 **CB/GA** Reg 31(1) CB&GA(DA) Regs
   HB/CTB Reg 20(1)(a) HB&CTB (DA) Regs
   Other benefits Reg 33(1) SS&CS(DA) Regs
   24 Reg 20(1)(a) HB&CTB(DA) Regs
   25 **CB/GA** Reg 31(1)(b) CB&GA(DA) Regs
   HB/CTB Reg 20(1)(b) HB&CTB(DA) Regs
   Other benefits Reg 33(1)(a) SS&CS(DA) Regs
   26 **CB/GA** Regs 2(1), definition of 'appropriate office' and 31(1)(c) CB&GA(DA) Regs
   HB/CTB Reg 20(1)(c) HB&CTB(DA) Regs
   Other benefits Reg 33(1) and (2) SS&CS(DA) Regs

27 **CB/GA** Reg 31(1)(a) CB&GA(DA) Regs
HB/CTB Reg 20(1)(a) HB&CTB(DA) Regs
Other benefits Reg 33(1) SS&CS(DA) Regs

28 **CB/GA** Reg 31(1)(d) and (e) CB&GA(DA) Regs
HB/CTB Reg 20(1)(d) and (e) HB&CTB(DA) Regs
Other benefits Reg 33(1)(c) and (d) SS&CS(DA) Regs

29 **CB/GA** Reg 31(2)-(6) CB&GA(DA) Regs
HB/CTB Reg 20(2)-(6) HB&CTB(DA) Regs
Other benefits Reg 33(3)-(7) SS&CS(DA) Regs

30 **CB/GA** Reg 31(6) CB&GA(DA) Regs
HB/CTB Reg 20(6) HB&CTB(DA) Regs
Other benefits Reg 33(7) SS&CS(DA) Regs

31 **CB/GA** Reg 31(7) CB&GA(DA) Regs
HB/CTB Reg 20(7) HB&CTB(DA) Regs; para C7/7.133 GM
Other benefits Reg 33(8) SS&CS(DA) Regs; para 06114 DMG

32 **CB/GA** Reg 31(8) CB&GA(DA) Regs
HB/CTB Reg 20(8) HB&CTB(DA) Regs
Other benefits Reg 33(9) SS&CS(DA) Regs

33 **HB/CTB** Reg 23 HB&CTB(DA) Regs
Other benefits Reg 39(1) and (3) SS&CS(DA) Regs
TC Reg 12(1) and (3) TC(A)(No.2) Regs

34 Art 6 European Convention on Human Rights; s6 HRA 1998; CH/3497/2005

35 Complaint 01/C/13400 against Scarborough BC

36 R(H) 1/07

37 **HB/CTB** Sch 7 para 3(6) CSPSSA 2000
Other benefits s9(6) SSA 1998

38 **CB/GA** Reg 27(1) and (5) CB&GA(DA) Regs
HB/CTB Reg 17(1) and (2) HB&CTB(DA) Regs
Other benefits Reg 30(1) and (2) SS&CS(DA) Regs

39 **CB/GA** Reg 27(2) CB&GA(DA) Regs
HB/CTB Reg 17(3) HB&CTB(DA) Regs
Other benefits Reg 30(3) SS&CS(DA) Regs

40 **CB/GA** Reg 27(3) CB&GA(DA) Regs
HB/CTB Reg 17(4) HB&CTB(DA) Regs
Other benefits Reg 30(4) SS&CS(DA) Regs

41 **CB/GA** Reg 27(4) CB&GA(DA) Regs
HB/CTB Reg 17(5) HB&CTB(DA) Regs
Other benefits Reg 30(5) SS&CS(DA) Regs

42 **CB/GA** Reg 28(2) CB&GA(DA) Regs
HB/CTB Reg 18(3) HB&CTB(DA) Regs
Other benefits Reg 31(2) SS&CS(DA) Regs

43 **HB/CTB** Reg 23 HB&CTB(DA) Regs
Other benefits Reg 39 SS&CS(DA) Regs
TC Reg 12 TC(A)(No.2) Regs

44 **HB/CTB** Reg 23 HB&CTB(DA) Regs
Other benefits Reg 39(4) SS&CS(DA) Regs
TC Reg 12(4) TC(A)(No.2) Regs

45 **HB/CTB** Reg 23 HB&CTB(DA) Regs
Other benefits Reg 39(5) SS&CS(DA) Regs
TC Reg 12(5) TC(A)(No.2) Regs

46 **HB/CTB** Reg 23 HB&CTB(DA) Regs
Other benefits Reg 49(8) SS&CS(DA) Regs
TC Reg 18(9) TC(A)(No.2) Regs

47 **HB/CTB** Reg 23 HB&CTB(DA) Regs
Other benefits Reg 49(9)(d) SS&CS(DA) Regs
TC Reg 18(10)(d) TC(A)(No.2) Regs

48 **HB/CTB** Reg 23 HB&CTB(DA) Regs
Other benefits Reg 49(7)(b) SS&CS(DA) Regs
TC Reg 18(8)(b) TC(A)(No.2) Regs

49 Sch 1 para 4 SSA 1998

50 **HB/CTB** Reg 23 HB&CTB(DA) Regs
Other benefits Reg 38 SS&CS(DA) Regs
TC Reg 11TC(A)(No.2) Regs

51 **HB/CTB** Reg 23 HB&CTB(DA) Regs
Other benefits Reg 38(2) SS&CS(DA) Regs
TC Regs 7 and 11(2) TC(A)(No.2) Regs

52 CIB/4253/2004

53 **HB/CTB** Reg 23 HB&CTB(DA) Regs
Other benefits Reg 46 SS&CS(DA) Regs

54 **CB/GA** Reg 1(3) SS&CS(DA) Regs, definition of 'out of jurisdiction appeal', as modified by reg 36 CB&GA(DA) Regs; reg 25 CB&GA(DA) Regs
Other benefits Reg 1(3) SS&CS(DA) Regs, definition of 'out of jurisdiction appeal'
All Reg 46(1)(a) SS&CS(DA) Regs

55 **HB/CTB** Reg 23 HB&CTB(DA) Regs
Other benefits Reg 39(2) SS&CS(DA) Regs

56 **HB/CTB** Reg 23 HB&CTB(DA) Regs
Other benefits Reg 46(3) SS&CS(DA) Regs
TC Reg 16(3) TC(A)(No.2) Regs
All House of Commons, *Hansard*, 8 December 2004, col 15

57 **HB/CTB** Reg 23 HB&CTB(DA) Regs
Other benefits Reg 46(2) SS&CS(DA) Regs
TC Reg 16(2) TC(A)(No.2) Regs
58 **HB/CTB** Reg 23 HB&CTB(DA) Regs
Other benefits Reg 47(1) SS&CS(DA) Regs
TC Reg 17(1) TC(A)(No.2) Regs
59 **HB/CTB** Reg 23 HB&CTB(DA) Regs
Other benefits Reg 47(2) SS&CS(DA) Regs
TC Reg 17(2) TC(A)(No.2) Regs
60 R(IS) 5/94
61 *Secretary of State for Work and Pensions v Morina and Anr* [2007] EWCA Civ 749 (23 July 2007) (CA), reported as R(IS) 6/07
62 **CB/GA** Reg 32 CB&GA(DA) Regs
HB/CTB Regs 20(9) and 23 HB&CTB(DA) Regs
Other benefits Regs 33(10) and 40 SS&CS(DA) Regs
63 *Rydqvist v Secretary of State for Work and Pensions* [2002] EWCA Civ 947, 24 June 2002, *The Times* 8 July (CA)
64 R(IS) 5/94
65 **HB/CTB** Reg 23 HB&CTB(DA) Regs
Other benefits Reg 49(2) SS&CS(DA) Regs
TC Reg 18(2) TC(A)(No.2) Regs
66 **HB/CTB** Reg 23 HB&CTB(DA) Regs
Other benefits Reg 49(2) SS&CS(DA) Regs
TC Reg 18(3) TC(A)(No.2) Regs
All CH/3594/2002
67 **HB/CTB** Reg 23 HB&CTB(DA) Regs
Other benefits Reg 49(3)-(5) SS&CS(DA) Regs
TC Reg 18(4)-(6) TC(A)(No.2) Regs
68 **HB/CTB** Reg 23 HB&CTB(DA) Regs
Other benefits Reg 49(6) SS&CS(DA) Regs
TC Reg 18(7) TC(A)(No.2) Regs
69 **HB/CTB** Reg 23 HB&CTB(DA) Regs
Other benefits Reg 51(1) SS&CS(DA) Regs
TC Reg 20(1) TC(A)(No.2) Regs
70 **HB/CTB** Reg 23 HB&CTB(DA) Regs
Other benefits Reg 51(3) SS&CS(DA) Regs
TC Reg 20(3) TC(A)(No.2) Regs
71 **HB/CTB** Reg 23 HB&CTB(DA) Regs
Other benefits Reg 51(2) SS&CS(DA) Regs
TC Reg 20(2) TC(A)(No.2) Regs
72 CDLA/1290/2004
73 **HB/CTB** Reg 23 HB&CTB(DA) Regs
Other benefits Reg 49(4) SS&CS(DA) Regs
TC Reg 18(5) TC(A)(No.2) Regs
74 CDLA/3680/1997
75 CDLA/5413/1999
76 CIS/566/1991; CS/99/1993
77 CIS/2292/2000
78 CIS/6002/1997; *R v Social Security Commissioner ex parte Angora Bibi* [2000] 23 May 2000, unreported (HC); CIB/1009/2004; CIB/2058/2004
79 CIS/3338/2001
80 **HB/CTB** Reg 23 HB&CTB(DA) Regs
Other benefits Reg 51(4) SS&CS(DA) Regs
TC Reg 20(4) TC(A)(No.2) Regs
81 CDLA/557/2001
82 s26 SSA 1998
83 s26(5) SSA 1998

2. **Tribunal procedures**

84 s7(3) SSA 1998
85 **HB/CTB** Reg 23 HB&CTB(DA) Regs
Other benefits Reg 50 SS&CS(DA) Regs; s7(4) and (5) SSA 1998
TC Reg 19 TC(A)(No.2) Regs
86 para 06429 DMG; para C7/7.380 GM
87 R(IS) 17/04
88 **HB/CTB** Reg 23 HB&CTB(DA) Regs
Other benefits Reg 49(8) SS&CS(DA) Regs
TC Reg 18(9) TC(A)(No.2) Regs
All CIB/1009/2004; CIB/2058/2004
89 s7(1) and (2) SSA 1998
90 s7(6) SSA 1998
91 Reg 36(6) SS&CS(DA) Regs
92 Reg 36(2)(a) SS&CS(DA) Regs
93 **HB/CTB** Reg 22(1)(a) HB&CTB(DA) Regs
Other benefits Reg 36(3) SS&CS(DA) Regs
94 Reg 36(2)(b) SS&CS(DA) Regs
95 **HB/CTB** Reg 22(1)(b) HB&CTB(DA) Regs
Other benefits Reg 36(1) SS&CS(DA) Regs
96 Reg 36(8) SS&CS(DA) Regs
97 *Gillies v Secretary of State for Work and Pensions* [2006] UKHL 2, 26 January 2006, reported as R(DLA) 5/06
98 *Secretary of State for Work and Pensions v Cunningham* [2004] 211, 6 August 2004 (ScotCS), reported as R(DLA) 7/04; R(DLA) 3/07

99 **HB/CTB** Reg 23 HB&CTB(DA) Regs
Other benefits Reg 49(1) SS&CS(DA) Regs
TC Reg 18(1) TC(A)(No.2) Regs
100 **HB/CTB** Reg 23 HB&CTB(DA) Regs
Other benefits Reg 49(11) SS&CS(DA) Regs
TC Reg 18(12) TC(A)(No.2) Regs
All CDLA/2014/2004
101 CSDLA/606/2003
102 s20(3) SSA 1998; reg 52 SS&CS(DA) Regs; R(DLA) 5/03
103 R(IB) 2/06
104 R(DLA) 1/95, qualified by CM/2/1994
105 R(DLA) 8/06
106 CI/3384/2006
107 CM/527/1992; CIB/3074/2003
108 CIB/5586/1999
109 CIB/476/2005; CIB/511/2005. For further information about electronic incapacity reports, see CPAG's *Welfare Rights Bulletin* 189, pp4-5
110 s20(2) SSA 1998; reg 41 SS&CS(DA) Regs
111 ITS President's Circular No.1 para 9, June 1997
112 CIB/2751/2002; CDLA/1350/2004
113 **HB/CTB** Reg 23 HB&CTB(DA) Regs
Other benefits Reg 49(7)(b) SS&CS(DA) Regs
114 *Mongan v Department for Social Development* [2005] NICA 16, 13 April 2005, reported as R3/05 (DLA)
115 CH/1229/2002
116 *Mooney v Secretary of State for Work and Pensions* [2004] SLT 1141, 23 April 2004, reported as R(DLA) 5/04; *Mongan v Department for Social Development* [2005] NICA 16, 13 April 2005, reported as R3/05 (DLA); *Secretary of State for Work and Pensions v Hooper* [2007] EWCA Civ 495, reported as R(IB) 4/07
117 CSDLA/336/2000; CSIB/160/2000; R(H) 1/02
118 **HB/CTB** Sch 7 para 6(9)(a) CSPSSA 2000
Other benefits s12(8)(a) SSA 1998
119 CH/1229/2002; R(IB) 2/04
120 CI/531/2000; CDLA/1000/2001; CH/1229/2002; R(IB) 2/04
121 CDLA/4184/2004
122 R(IB) 2/04
123 R(IB) 2/04; CH/3009/2002
124 CDLA/1707/2005
125 R(IB) 2/04; R(IB) 7/04; CIS/1675/2004
126 **HB/CTB** Sch 7 para 6(9)(b) CSPSSA 2000
Other benefits s12(8)(b) SSA 1998
TC s12(8)(b) SSA 1998; reg 4(6) TC(A) Regs
127 R(DLA) 4/05
128 ITS President's Circular No.15, July 1998
129 R(DLA) 2/01; R(DLA) 3/01; CJSA/2375/2000
130 R(SB) 4/85
131 **HB/CTB** Reg 23 HB&CTB(DA) Regs
Other benefits Reg 53(1) SS&CS(DA) Regs
TC Reg 21(1) TC(A)(No.2) Regs
132 **HB/CTB** Reg 23 HB&CTB(DA) Regs
Other benefits Reg 53(3) SS&CS(DA) Regs
TC Reg 21(3) TC(A)(No.2) Regs
133 **HB/CTB** Reg 23 HB&CTB(DA) Regs
Other benefits Reg 55 SS&CS(DA) Regs
TC Reg 23 TC(A)(No.2) Regs
134 **HB/CTB** Reg 23 HB&CTB(DA) Regs
Other benefits Reg 53(4) SS&CS(DA) Regs
TC Reg 22(5) TC(A)(No.2) Regs
All CCS/1664/2001
135 **CB/GA** Reg 3(1)(a) CB&GA(DA) Regs; reg 53(4) SS&CS(DA) Regs
HB/CTB Regs 2(a) and 23 HB&CTB(DA) Regs
Other benefits Regs 2(a) and 53(4) SS&CS(DA) Regs
TC Regs 2(a) and 21(4) TC(A)(No.2) Regs
All CIB/3937/2000
136 **HB/CTB** Reg 23 HB&CTB(DA) Regs
Other benefits Reg 53(4A) SS&CS(DA) Regs
TC Reg 21(4A) TC(A)(No.2) Regs
137 **HB/CTB** Reg 23 HB&CTB(DA) Regs
Other benefits Reg 53(5) SS&CS(DA) Regs
TC Reg 21(6) TC(A)(No.2) Regs
All CDLA/572/2001
138 R(IS) 11/99; CDLA/5793/1997
139 **HB/CTB** Reg 23 HB&CTB(DA) Regs
Other benefits Reg 57(4A) SS&CS(DA) Regs
TC Reg 25(4A) TC(A)(No.2) Regs
140 **HB/CTB** Reg 23 HB&CTB(DA) Regs
Other benefits Reg 54(1) SS&CS(DA) Regs
TC Reg 22(1) TC(A)(No.2) Regs
141 CH/2553/2005

142 **HB/CTB** Reg 23 HB&CTB(DA) Regs
Other benefits Reg 54(4) SS&CS(DA) Regs
TC Reg 22(4) TC(A)(No.2) Regs
143 **HB/CTB** Reg 23 HB&CTB(DA) Regs
Other benefits Reg 54(5) and (6) SS&CS(DA) Regs
TC Reg 22(5) and (6) TC(A)(No.2) Regs
144 **HB/CTB** Reg 23 HB&CTB(DA) Regs
Other benefits Reg 54(7) SS&CS(DA) Regs
TC Reg 22(7) TC(A)(No.2) Regs
145 **HB/CTB** Reg 23 HB&CTB(DA) Regs
Other benefits Reg 54(8) SS&CS(DA) Regs
TC Reg 22(8) TC(A)(No.2) Regs
146 **HB/CTB** Sch 7 para 13 CSPSSA 2000; reg 11 HB&CTB(DA) Regs
Other benefits s21 SSA 1998; reg 16 SS&CS(DA) Regs
147 **HB/CTB** Reg 23 HB&CTB(DA) Regs
Other benefits Reg 56 SS&CS(DA) Regs
TC Reg 24 TC(A)(No.2) Regs
All CI/3887/1999
148 **HB/CTB** Reg 23 HB&CTB(DA) Regs
Other benefits Reg 57(3) SS&CS(DA) Regs
TC Reg 25(3) TC(A)(No.2) Regs
149 **HB/CTB** Reg 23 HB&CTB(DA) Regs
Other benefits Reg 57(4) SS&CS(DA) Regs
TC Reg 25(4) TC(A)(No.2) Regs
150 **HB/CTB** Reg 23 HB&CTB(DA) Regs
Other benefits Reg 57 SS&CS(DA) Regs
TC Reg 25 TC(A)(No.2) Regs
151 **HB/CTB** Sch 7 para 19(2) CSPSSA 2000
Other benefits s28(2) SSA 1998
TC s28(2) SSA 1998; reg 11(1) TC(A) Regs
All *Lloyd v McMahon* [1987] AC 625, 702-703
152 CSB/172/1990
153 **HB/CTB** Reg 23 HB&CTB(DA) Regs
Other benefits Reg 57(5) SS&CS(DA) Regs
TC Reg 25(5) TC(A)(No.2) Regs
154 **HB/CTB** Reg 23 HB&CTB(DA) Regs
Other benefits Reg 57(4A) SS&CS(DA) Regs
TC Reg 25(4A) TC(A)(No.2) Regs
155 CI/79/1990; CIS/373/1994
156 **HB/CTB** Reg 23 HB&CTB(DA) Regs
Other benefits Reg 57(6) SS&CS(DA) Regs
TC Reg 25(6) TC(A)(No.2) Regs
157 **HB/CTB** Reg 23 HB&CTB(DA) Regs
Other benefits Reg 57(7) SS&CS(DA) Regs
TC Reg 25(7) TC(A)(No.2) Regs
158 **HB/CTB** Reg 23 HB&CTB(DA) Regs
Other benefits Reg 57(8) SS&CS(DA) Regs
TC Reg 25(8) TC(A)(No.2) Regs
159 **HB/CTB** Reg 23 HB&CTB(DA) Regs
Other benefits Reg 57(9) and (10) SS&CS(DA) Regs
TC Reg 25(9) and (10) TC(A)(No.2) Regs
160 **HB/CTB** Reg 23 HB&CTB(DA) Regs
Other benefits Reg 57(11) SS&CS(DA) Regs
TC Reg 25(11) TC(A)(No.2) Regs
161 **HB/CTB** Reg 23 HB&CTB(DA) Regs
Other benefits Regs 57(12) and 57A(2) SS&CS(DA) Regs
TC Reg 25(12) TC(A)(No.2) Regs
162 **HB/CTB** Reg 23 HB&CTB(DA) Regs
Other benefits Reg 57A(2) SS&CS(DA) Regs
TC Reg 26(2) TC(A)(No.2) Regs
163 **HB/CTB** Reg 23 HB&CTB(DA) Regs
Other benefits Reg 58(1A) SS&CS(DA) Regs
TC Reg 27(1A) TC(A)(No.2) Regs
164 **HB/CTB** Sch 7 para 7(2) CSPSSA 2000
Other benefits s13(2) SSA 1998
TCs13(2) SSA 1998; reg 5(1) TC(A) Regs
All CIS/4533/2003
165 **HB/CTB** Sch 7 para 7(3) CSPSSA 2000
Other benefits s13(3) SSA 1998
166 **HB/CTB** Reg 23 HB&CTB(DA) Regs
Other benefits Reg 58(2) SS&CS(DA) Regs
TC Reg 27(2) TC(A)(No.2) Regs
167 CIB/4193/2003

3. **Appealing to a commissioner**

168 **HB/CTB** Sch 7 para 8(1) CSPSSA 2000
Other benefits s14(1) SSA 1998
TC s14(1) SSA 1998; reg 6(1) and (2) TC(A) Regs
169 R(A) 1/72; R(SB) 11/83; R(IS) 11/99; R(I) 2/06
170 CIS/2345/2001; CH/4065/2001
171 CDLA/433/1999
172 CDLA/ 7980/1995; CH/5221/ 2001; CH/396/2002
173 CIB/2977/2002
174 CDLA/2748/2002
175 CSDLA/606/2003
176 CS/1939/1995; CDLA/5413/1999; CIB/ 303/1999

177 CDLA/3224/2001
178 CH/3594/2002
179 CDLA/1480/2006
180 R(IS) 4/93
181 CJSA/322/2001; R(IS) 5/04
182 *Carpenter v Secretary of State for Work and Pensions* [2003] EWCA Civ 33, reported as R(IB) 6/03
183 CDLA/1456/2002; R(H) 1/03
184 **HB/CTB** Sch 7 para 8(1) CSPSSA 2000
Other benefits s14(10) SSA 1998
TC s14(10) SSA 1998; reg 6(1) TC(A) Regs
185 **HB/CTB** Sch 7 para 8(7) CSPSSA 2000
Other benefits s14(10) SSA 1998
All benefits Reg 9(1) SSCP Regs
TC s14(10) SSA 1998; reg 6(1) TC(A) Regs; reg 7(1) SSCP(TCA) Regs
186 **HB/CTB** Reg 23 HB&CTB(DA) Regs
Other benefits Reg 58(1)(b)-(e) SS&CS(DA) Regs
TC Reg 27(1)(b)-(e) TC(A)(No.2) Regs
187 **HB/CTB** Reg 23 HB&CTB(DA) Regs
Other benefits Reg 58(6) SS&CS(DA) Regs
TC Reg 27(5) TC(A)(No.2) Regs
188 R(IS) 11/99
189 **HB/CTB** Reg 23 HB&CTB(DA) Regs
Other benefits Reg 58(2) SS&CS(DA) Regs
TC Reg 27(2) TC(A)(No.2) Regs
190 **HB/CTB** Reg 23 HB&CTB(DA) Regs
Other benefits Regs 2(a) and 58(1)(a) SS&CS(DA) Regs
TC Regs 2(1) and 27(1A) TC(A)(No.2) Regs
191 **HB/CTB** Reg 23 HB&CTB(DA) Regs
Other benefits Reg 58(1A) SS&CS(DA) Regs
TC Reg 27(1A) TC(A)(No.2) Regs
192 **HB/CTB**Reg 23 HB&CTB(DA) Regs
Other benefits Reg 58(5) SS&CS(DA) Regs
TC Reg 27(4) TC(A)(No.2) Regs
193 R(IS) 11/99
194 **Benefits** Reg 10 SSCP Regs
TC Reg 8 SSCP(TCA) Regs
All CSDLA/1207/2000
195 **Benefits** Reg 27 SSCP Regs
TC Reg 22 SSCP(TCA) Regs
196 R(IS) 11/99; CDLA/5793/1997
197 CCS/1664/2001
198 **Benefits** Reg 8(2) SSCP Regs
TC Reg 6(2) SSCP(TCA) Regs
199 Regs 31 and 32 SSCP Regs; CDLA/3432/2001
200 **Benefits** Regs 8 and 9(2) SSCP Regs
TC Regs 6 and 7 SSCP(TCA) Regs
201 **Benefits** Reg 9(3) and (4) SSCP Regs
TC Reg 7(3) and (4) SSCP(TCA) Regs
202 **Benefits** Regs 12 and 13(1) SSCP Regs
TC Regs 10 and 11(2) SSCP(TCA) Regs
203 **Benefits** Reg 13(2) SSCP Regs
TC Reg 11(3) SSCP(TCA) Regs
204 **Benefits** Reg 11(2) SSCP Regs
TC Reg 9(2) SSCP(TCA) Regs
205 **HB/CTB** Sch 7 para 8(3) CSPSSA 2000
Other benefits s14(7) SSA 1998
TC s14(7) SSA 1998; reg 6(1) TC(A) Regs
206 **Benefits** Regs 5(2)(a), 18, 19 and 20 SSCP Regs
TC Regs 3(2)(a), 14, 15 and 16 SSCP(TCA) Regs
207 **Benefits** Reg 5(3)-(5) SSCP Regs
TC Reg 3(3)-(5) SSCP(TCA) Regs
208 **Benefits** Reg 23 SSCP Regs
TC Reg 18 SSCP(TCA) Regs
209 **Benefits** Regs 4(1), definition of 'live television link' and 24(6A) and (6B) SSCP Regs
TC Regs 2(1), definition of 'live television link' and 19(6A) and (6B) SSCP(TCA) Regs
210 **HB/CTB** Sch 7 para 10(5) CSPSSA 2000
Other benefits s16(7) SSA 1998
TC s16(7) SSA 1998; reg 9(1) TC(A) Regs
211 R(I) 1/03
212 **Benefits** Reg 28 SSCP Regs
TC Reg 23 SSCP(TCA) Regs
213 **HB/CTB** Sch 7 para 8(5)(c) CSPSSA 2000
Other benefits s14(8)(b) SSA 1998
TC s14(8)(b) SSA 1998; reg 6(1) TC(A) Regs
214 **HB/CTB** Sch 7 para 8(5)(a) CSPSSA 2000
Other benefits s14(8)(a) SSA 1998
TC s14(8)(a) SSA 1998; reg 6(1) TC(A) Regs
215 *Innes v CAO* 19 November 1986, unreported (CA)
216 **Benefits** Regs 30 and 31 SSCP Regs
TC Regs 24 and 25 SSCP(TCA) Regs
217 **HB/CTB** Sch 7 para 19(2) CSPSSA 2000
Other benefits s28(2) SSA 1998
TC s28(2) SSA 1998; reg 11(1) TC(A) Regs
All *Lloyd v McMahon* [1987] AC 625, 702-703
218 **Benefits** Reg 5(2)(a) SSCP Regs
TC Reg 3(2)(a) SSCP(TCA) Regs

4. **Appealing to the courts**

219 **HB/CTB** Sch 7 para 9 CSPSSA 2000
Other benefits s15 SSA 1998
All benefits Reg 33 SSCP Regs
TC s15 SSA 1998; reg 8 TC(A) Regs; reg 27 SSCP(TCA) Regs

220 **Benefits** Reg 33(1) SSCP Regs
TC Reg 27(1) SSCP(TC) Regs

221 *Fryer-Kelsey v The Secretary of State for Work and Pensions* [2005] EWCA Civ 511, 21 April 2005, reported as R(IB) 6/05

222 **Benefits** Reg 33(2) SSCP Regs
TC Reg 27(2) SSCP(TCA) Regs

223 **Benefits** Regs 5(2) and 33(1) SSCP Regs
TC Regs 3(2) and 27(1) SSCP(TCA) Regs

224 *White v CAO* [1986] 2 All ER 905 (CA), also reported as R(S) 8/85

225 **HB/CTB** Sch 7 para 9(2)(b) CSPSSA 2000
Other benefits s15(2)(b) SSA 1998
TC s15(2)(b) SSA 1998; reg 8 TC(A) Regs

226 Practice Direction 52 para 21.5

227 r3.1(2)(a) and r52.6 Civil Procedure Rules

228 Practice Direction 52 paras 4.11 and 4.14

229 r52.4 Civil Procedure Rules; Practice Direction 52 paras 5.1 and 21.5

230 *Bland v CSBO* [1983] 1 WLR 262 (CA), reported as R(SB) 12/83

231 See *Hanlon v Traffic Commission* [1988] SLT 802 and *Perfect Swivel v Dundee District Licensing Board* (No.2) [1993] SLT 112

5. **Late appeals**

232 **CB/GA** Reg 29(1) CB&GA(DA) Regs
HB/CTB Reg 19(1) and (2) HB&CTB(DA) Regs
Other benefits Reg 32(1) SS&CS(DA) Regs
TC Reg 5(1) TC(A)(No.2) Regs

233 **CB/GA** Reg 29(4) CB&GA(DA) Regs
HB/CTB Reg 19(4) HB&CTB(DA) Regs
Other benefits Reg 32(3) SS&CS(DA) Regs
TC Regs 5(3) and 6 TC(A)(No.2) Regs

234 **CB/GA** Reg 29(5) CB&GA(DA) Regs
HB/CTB Reg 19(5) HB&CTB(DA) Regs
Other benefits Reg 32(4) SS&CS(DA) Regs
TC Reg 5(4) TC(A)(No 2) Regs

235 HB/CTB Circular A28/02, as amended by HB/CTB Circular A31/02 paras 40-43. It is understood that DWP decision makers have been given similar internal guidance.

236 **CB/GA** Reg 30(1) and (2) CB&GA(DA) Regs
HB/CTB Reg 19(6) and (7) HB&CTB(DA) Regs
Other benefits Reg 32(5) and (6) SS&CS(DA) Regs
TC Reg 5(5) and (6) TC(A)(No.2) Regs

237 **CB/GA** Reg 30(4) CB&GA(DA) Regs
HB/CTB Reg 19(8) HB&CTB(DA) Regs
Other benefits Reg 32(7) SS&CS(DA) Regs
TC Reg 5(7) TC(A)(No.2) Regs

238 **CB/GA** Reg 30(5) CB&GA(DA) Regs
HB/CTB Reg 19(9) HB&CTB(DA) Regs
Other benefits Reg 32(8) SS&CS(DA) Regs
TC Reg 5(8) TC(A)(No.2) Regs

239 **CB/GA** Reg 29(7) and (8) CB&GA(DA) Regs
HB/CTB Reg 19(11) and (12) HB&CTB(DA) Regs
Other benefits Reg 32(10) and (11) SS&CS(DA) Regs
TC Reg 5(10) and (11) TC(A)(No.2) Regs

240 *Secretary of State for Work and Pensions v Morina and Anr* [2007] EWCA Civ 749 (23 July 2007) (CA), reported as R(IS) 6/07

241 **HB/CTB** Reg 23 HB&CTB(DA) Regs
Other benefits Reg 58(5) SS&CS(DA) Regs
TC Reg 27(4) TC(A)(No.2) Regs

242 **Benefits** Reg 9(3) and (4) SSCP Regs
TC Reg 7(3) and (4) SSCP(TCA) Regs

243 *R(Howes) v Social Security Commissioner* [2007] EWHC 559 (Admin)

244 R(M) 1/87

245 R(M) 1/87; R(I) 5/91

246 R(M) 1/87

247 CIS/147/1995

6. **How to prepare an appeal**

248 R(SB) 6/82

249 CDLA/2014/2004

250 R(DLA) 4/02

251 CIB/2058/2004

252 **HB/CTB** Reg 23 HB&CTB(DA) Regs
Other benefits Reg 49(8) and (11) SS&CS(DA) Regs
All CDLA/1138/2003; CDLA/2462/2003

253 R(SB) 33/85; R(SB) 12/89

254 **HB/CTB** Reg 23 HB&CTB(DA) Regs
Other benefits Reg 49(1) SS&CS(DA) Regs
TC Reg 18(1) TC(A)(No.2) Regs
All CDLA/2014/2004
255 R(SB) 10/86; R(IS) 6/91
256 CIS/4901/2002
257 R(SB) 1/81
258 See CPAG's *Welfare Rights Bulletin* 183, pp4-5 for a discussion on tribunals and medical evidence.
259 *Secretary of State for Work and Pensions v Cunningham* [2004] 6 August, ScotCS 211, reported as R(DLA) 7/04; R(DLA) 3/07
260 *Pepper v Hart* [1992] 3 WLR 1032, *The Times*, 30 November 1992
261 R(I) 12/75
262 R(SB) 22/86
263 *Nancollas v Insurance Officer* [1985] 1 All ER 833 (CA), also reported as R(I) 7/85
264 R(I) 12/75
265 *CSBO v Leary*, reported as R(SB) 6/85; see generally CS/140/1991
266 R(G) 3/62; R(U) 4/88
267 R(IS) 13/01
268 R(U) 4/88
269 **Benefits** Reg 8A SSCP Regs
TC Reg 6A SSCP(TCA) Regs
270 SSCSC Practice Memorandum No. 5, 1 March 2005

Chapter 43

Challenging decisions on statutory payments

This chapter covers:

This chapter explains the rules for challenging decisions on entitlement to statutory sick pay (SSP), statutory maternity pay (SMP), statutory paternity pay (SPP) and statutory adoption pay (SAP). The conditions of entitlement to these benefits are detailed in Chapters 23 and 24. The rules explained in this chapter do not apply to challenging decisions on other benefits.

SSP, SMP, SPP and SAP is normally paid by your employer and your employer should make the initial decision on your entitlement. If you disagree with your employer's decision on your entitlement, or if your employer has failed to make a decision, you can request that the Revenue decides whether you are entitled to SSP, SMP, SPP or SAP.

In certain circumstances, the Revenue can vary or supersede its own decision. You or your employer also have the right to appeal to the tax commissioners against the Revenue's decision on your entitlement.

If you are considering challenging your employer's decision on your entitlement to SSP, SMP, SPP or SAP it is advisable to consider how this might affect your employment. Before making a decision to proceed, you may wish to consult an employment adviser to discuss your employment rights.

Future changes: the Tribunals, Courts and Enforcement Act 2007

The Tribunals, Courts and Enforcement Act 2007 will introduce changes to the way appeals against decisions on SSP, SMP, SPP and SAP are dealt with. These changes are unlikely to come into force before April 2009. See CPAG's *Welfare Rights Bulletin* for updates.

1. Information from your employer

If your employer decides it is not liable to pay you statutory sick pay (SSP), statutory maternity pay (SMP), statutory paternity pay (SPP) or statutory adoption pay (SAP), it should provide you with details of its decision and the reasons for it within certain time limits. (This also applies to a former employer for SMP, SPP and SAP.)[1] This should happen if you have either:

- for SSP notified your employer of your incapacity for work; *or*
- given your employer (or ex-employer):
  - the necessary notice of when you expect your entitlement to SMP to begin (see p542); *or*
  - the information necessary to establish your entitlement to SPP or SAP (see pp544 and 545).

For SSP, your employer should give you the information about its decision on Form SSP1 or on its own computerised form if it contains the same information as Form SSP1. (Your employer should also provide you with one of these forms if it has been paying you SSP but your period of entitlement has come to an end or is due to come to an end.) For SMP, SPP and SAP, the employer normally gives the information on Form SMP1, Form SPP1 or Form SAP1 respectively. The employer should also return certain evidence to you, such as your MATB1 form or evidence you have provided to establish your SPP or SAP entitlement.

In connection with your entitlement to SSP or SMP you can also request a written statement from your employer, detailing in respect of the period before your request:[2]

- the days (or for SMP, weeks) for which your employer considers you are entitled to SSP or SMP;
- the daily rate of SSP, or the weekly rate of SMP, to which your employer thinks you are entitled;
- the reason why SSP is not payable for other days, or SMP is not payable for other weeks.

For SMP you also have the right to request this information from a former employer. If your request is reasonable your employer (or former employer) should provide this information within a reasonable time.

If you disagree with your employer's decision on your entitlement to SSP, SMP, SPP or SAP, or if your employer has failed to make a decision, you can ask the Revenue to make a formal decision on your entitlement.

2. Involving the Revenue

If you are dissatisfied with your employer's decision, or your employer has failed to make a decision, you can request that the Revenue makes a decision on your entitlement to statutory sick pay (SSP), statutory maternity pay (SMP), statutory paternity pay (SPP) or statutory adoption pay (SAP).[3]

It can take some time to get a final decision on your entitlement to SSP, SMP, SPP or SAP so it is worth considering whether there are other benefits you can claim in the interim (see pp549 and 568). As well as considering your entitlement to means-tested benefits or tax credits, you should claim incapacity benefit (IB – see Chapter 12), or (from when it is introduced) employment and support allowance (ESA – see Chapter 7) while you are waiting for a decision on your entitlement to SSP, or maternity allowance (MA – see Chapter 17) while you are waiting for a decision on your SMP. Although the DWP will not normally make a decision on your entitlement to IB or MA until the Revenue has decided on your entitlement to SSP or SMP (because you will not qualify for IB if you are entitled to SSP, nor for MA if you are entitled to SMP) it is important not to delay your claim for IB or MA as you may lose benefit if you do.

Applying for a decision

Your application to the Revenue for a decision on your entitlement should normally be made on an SSP14 form (for SSP), SMP14 (for SMP), SPP14 (for SPP) or SAP14 (for SAP) and should be sent to the Statutory Payments Disputes Team (see Appendix 1) or to your local Revenue enquiry centre (the address should be in the telephone directory or can be obtained from www.hmrc.gov.uk). You can obtain these forms from the Statutory Payments Disputes Team.

Your application must be made within six months of the earliest date for which your entitlement to SSP, SMP, SPP or SAP is in dispute. If it is approaching the six-month deadline and you are unable to obtain and return the form before the deadline, you should apply for a decision by letter. Your letter *must* contain details of the period in respect of which your entitlement to SSP, SMP, SPP or SAP is at issue and the grounds (if any) on which your employer is refusing payment.[4]

If possible, you should send with your application a copy of the SSP1, SMP1, SPP1 or SAP1 form that your employer has given you and evidence of your entitlement (eg, a medical certificate if you have been sick for more than seven days for SSP, a MATB1 form for SMP or SPP(birth), or the 'matching certificate' from the adoption agency for SAP or SPP(adoption)). However, do not delay your application if you do not have this information.

If the Revenue requests information from you

If the Revenue is making a decision on your entitlement to SSP or SMP, it may request information from you. You must provide such information within 10 days of receiving the Revenue's request. For SPP or SAP, the Revenue may request information from you, or from your spouse or partner and such information must be provided within 30 days of receiving the Revenue's request.[5]

Although the Revenue has the power to impose a financial penalty on you if you do not provide the information or documents which it reasonably needs to decide on your entitlement to SSP, SMP, SPP or SAP, it is only likely to do so if you fraudulently or negligently make incorrect statements.[6]

Note: at the time of writing, the Government was considering changing the SSP and SMP rules to give you 30 days to provide requested information. See CPAG's *Welfare Rights Bulletin* for updates.

For SPP and SAP, notification sent to the Revenue in a properly addressed and pre-paid letter is treated as having been given on the day it is put in the post.[7]

The Revenue's decision

On receiving your application, the Revenue may contact you for further information and is likely to send a form to your employer to complete.

The Revenue may then try to negotiate between you and your employer to settle the dispute. In order to do this, before it issues a formal decision on your application, it may send both you and your employer a written opinion on your entitlement to SSP, SMP, SPP or SAP. As this is an opinion on your entitlement rather than a decision, the Revenue states that you have no right of appeal at this stage. Instead, if you disagree with the Revenue's opinion, you should write to the Revenue, giving your reasons. The Revenue may give you a deadline to object to its written opinion, before it issues a formal decision. The Revenue will consider any new information you or your employer have provided and should then issue a formal decision on your entitlement.

The Revenue states that, in some cases, it might not issue a formal decision, but that this should only occur if it has issued a written opinion in your favour, and does not receive an objection from your employer, and your employer has paid the amount owed. If you disagree with this, it is important that you write to the Revenue informing them of this, asking for a formal decision. It is arguable that, unless you have withdrawn your application, a formal decision should always be issued.

In some cases, the Revenue sends the formal decision without first issuing a written opinion. The Revenue's formal decision is legally binding on the employer (see p1155 for the time limits for complying with a decision). However, both you and your employer have a right to appeal against the Revenue's formal decision (see p1153).

3. Varying or superseding a decision

The Revenue can change one of its own decisions by varying or superseding the decision.[8] It can **vary** its decision if it believes that the decision was wrong at the time it was made. The new decision may take effect from the date that the original decision would have had effect if the reason for the variation had been known. If you or your employer have appealed against a decision, the Revenue may vary that decision at any time before the appeal is determined. If the Revenue varies its decision it must notify you and your employer of the new decision in writing.

The Revenue can **supersede** an earlier decision if the decision has become incorrect for any reason – eg, if your circumstances have changed. The new decision will take effect from the date of your change in circumstances.

If the Revenue varies or supersedes an earlier decision either you or your employer can appeal against the new decision (see below).

4. Appealing against a Revenue decision

Both you and your employer have the right to appeal to the tax commissioners if you do not agree with the Revenue's decision.[9] Your appeal should be made in writing and should include your reasons for appealing.[10] An appeal form (Form DAA3) is included with the Revenue's formal decision letter and you may wish to use this to make your appeal. Your appeal should reach the Revenue within 30 days of the date the Revenue's decision was issued.[11] This time limit can be extended if there is a reasonable excuse for you not having made your appeal within the time limit and your appeal was made without unreasonable delay.[12] If the Revenue does not accept that a reasonable excuse exists, it must refer the application to the tax commissioners. If the tax commissioners refuse the application, that decision can only be challenged by judicial review (see p1129).

The Revenue can try to settle the appeal through the consent of all the parties at any time before the determination of the tax commissioners. If, before the appeal is decided, an agreement is reached between the Revenue and you (if you have appealed), or your employer (if your employer has appealed), the appeal will lapse.[13]

You can withdraw your appeal at any time before it is decided by notifying the Revenue and your employer that you wish to do so. Your employer and the Revenue have 30 days to object to your request and if no objection is made your appeal will lapse.[14]

Your appeal will normally be decided by general commissioners (see p1154). You can ask for the appeal to be heard by special commissioners instead – eg, if you think there are complex legal issues involved (see p1154). The appeal can be transferred to (or from) the special commissioners if both you and your employer agree, or if the commissioners themselves decide that is appropriate.[15]

Appeals to the general commissioners

If your appeal is dealt with by general commissioners it will be decided by a minimum of two, but normally three, lay people assisted by a clerk, who is usually a solicitor. They hear appeals arising within a geographical tax division. Your appeal can be dealt with in the tax division in which you work or live – you should state which you would prefer when you make your appeal.[16]

Appeals to the special commissioners

The special commissioners are full-time, legally qualified adjudicators who hear cases in London or Manchester (for England and Wales), Edinburgh (for Scotland) and Belfast (for Northern Ireland). However, you can apply to the clerk for the case to be heard locally – eg, on the grounds of a disability or sickness.

Appealing further

You, your employer and the Revenue have the right to appeal against the decision of the tax commissioners to the High Court (or the Court of Session in Scotland) on a point of law (ie, on the grounds that the commissioners have interpreted the law incorrectly).[17]

The time limits for making such applications differ depending on whether you are appealing against a decision of the general commissioners or a decision of the special commissioners. You should appeal:

- within 30 days of the date on the notification of a decision of the general commissioners. If you were told the decision at the hearing of your appeal, the 30-day period runs from the date you were told rather than the date of the notice;
- within 56 days of the date on the notification of a decision of the special commissioners (42 days in Scotland) or, if you were told the decision at the hearing, within 56 days of the date of the hearing (42 days in Scotland).

There is a fee for lodging an appeal against the decision of the general or special commissioners. You can get further information on the appeals procedure in the leaflet *Tax Appeals: a guide to appealing against decisions of Her Majesty's Revenue and Customs on income tax and other direct tax matters*. You can obtain a copy of this leaflet from a Revenue enquiry centre, or from the guidance section of the general commissioners' website (www.generalcommissioners.gov.uk).

Seek advice from a solicitor, law centre or legal advice centre if you are considering appealing against the decision of a tax commissioner.

If you win your appeal

If it is decided that your employer should pay you a statutory payment, your employer should pay you within the time limits detailed below, unless it has appealed against the decision. Your employer does not have to pay you until a final decision is given on appeal.

Time limits for payment

When it is decided by the Revenue or the tax commissioners that you are entitled to a statutory payment and no appeal against this decision has been made (or the matter has been finally determined), your employer should pay you on or before the first payday after either:[18]

- the day on which the employer is notified that the appeal has been disposed of; *or*
- the day the employer receives notification that leave to appeal has been refused, and there is no further opportunity to apply for leave; *or*
- in any other case, the day the time limit for appeal expires.

If, because of your employer's payroll methods, it is not practical for you to be paid at this time your employer should pay you on or before your next payday after this date.

If your employer does not pay

If your employer does not pay you within the above time limits, the Revenue should pay you (although the Revenue states it would contact your employer first to try to get it to pay).[19] You should write to the Revenue's Statutory Payments Disputes Team (see Appendix 1) asking for payment. The Revenue should also pay you if your employer was liable to pay, but is insolvent.[20]

Notes

1. **Information from your employer**
 1 ss130 and 132 SSAA 1992; reg 15 SSP Regs; reg 25A SMP Regs; reg 11 SPPSAP(A) Regs
 2 ss14(3) and 15(2) SSAA 1992

2. **Involving the Revenue**
 3 s8 SSC(TF)A 1999
 4 Reg 3 SSP&SMP(D) Regs; reg 13 SPPSAP(A) Regs
 5 Reg 14 SSP Regs; reg 25 SMP Regs; reg 14 SPPSAP(A) Regs
 6 s11(1) and (2) Employment Act 2002; s113A SSAA 1992
 7 Reg 47 SPPSAP(G) Regs

3. **Varying or superseding a decision**
 8 s10 SSC(TF)A 1999; regs 5 and 6 SSC(DA) Regs

4. **Appealing against a Revenue decision**
 9 s11(2)(a) SSC(TF)A 1999
 10 s12(3) SSC(TF)A 1999
 11 s12(1) SSC(TF)A 1999
 12 s49 TMA 1970; reg 9 SSC(DA) Regs
 13 Reg 11 SSC(DA) Regs
 14 Reg 11(5) SSC(DA) Regs
 15 s44(3) TMA 1970
 16 Reg 7 SSC(DA) Regs
 17 Reg 12 SSC(DA) Regs
 18 Reg 9 SSP Regs; reg 29 SMP Regs; reg 42 SPPSAP(G) Regs
 19 ss151(6), 164(9)(b), 171ZD(3) and 171ZM(3) SSCBA 1992; reg 9A SSP Regs; reg 7 SMP Regs; reg 43 SPPSAP(G) Regs
 20 Reg 9B SSP Regs; reg 7(3) and (4) SMP Regs; reg 43(2) and (3) SPPSAP(G) Regs

Chapter 44

Social fund reviews

This chapter covers:

1. Internal reviews (below)
2. Social fund inspector reviews (p1160)

The social fund (SF) review system only covers decisions on the discretionary SF (see Chapter 21) – ie, community care grants (CCGs), budgeting loans (BLs) and crisis loans (CLs). Decisions on the regulated SF (see Chapter 22) – ie, funeral, maternity, cold weather and winter fuel payments – can be challenged by revision, supersession or appeal, in the same way as for most other benefits (see p1094).

There is no right of appeal against CCG, BL and CL decisions. There is, instead, a review system, which is divided into two distinct stages.

- First, an internal review is carried out by a reviewing officer at the DWP office which made the decision.
- Second, an applicant has a right to request a further review by a social fund inspector (SFI). SFIs are part of the Independent Review Service (see Appendix 1), which conducts second-tier reviews independently of the DWP.

1. **Internal reviews**

Powers of review

The law on internal reviews is set out in legislation and legally binding social fund (SF) directions.[1] All decisions on community care grants (CCGs), budgeting loans (BLs) and crisis loans (CLs) made by decision makers are subject to review,[2] including:

- the refusal of a CCG or loan;
- the amount awarded;
- payment to a third party or in instalments;
- refusal to determine a repeat application (see p486);
- refusal to treat an application for a CL as an application for a CCG;
- overpayment decisions (see p1159).

Decisions about the repayment of loans are not subject to review, but can still be challenged (see p502).

A reviewing officer ***must*** review a decision if:

- you apply for a review within the time limit (see below);[3] *or*
- a decision was based on a mistake about the law, the directions or a material fact, or was given in ignorance of a material fact. This can be conducted at any time.[4]

A reviewing officer *may* review a decision:

- if you misrepresented or failed to disclose a material fact, in which case any overpayment is recoverable;[5] *or*
- in such other circumstances as s/he thinks fit.[6]

In both of the above cases, the reviewing officer can conduct a review at any time. The second case offers wide (but discretionary) scope for reviews on any grounds, and at any time (eg, if you have missed the time limit for a mandatory review) with or without an application.

Procedure

Applying for a review

You must apply for a review of a decision by writing to the office where the decision was made within 28 days of the date the decision was issued to you.[7] Your application must include your grounds for requesting a review.[8] If somebody is making an application on your behalf, it must be accompanied by your written authority (unless the person is your appointee – see p955).[9]

Late applications can be accepted for 'special reasons'.[10] 'Special reasons' are not defined. They could include reasons why the application is late (eg, ill health, domestic crisis, wrong advice) or any other reasons (eg, you will experience hardship without a review). If the DWP does not accept there are special reasons, get advice. You may have to threaten judicial review if its refusal is unreasonable (see p1129).

If your application is out of time, you can also ask a reviewing officer to conduct a discretionary review (see above).

The DWP can ask you to submit further information in connection with your application if reasonably required.[11]

You can withdraw your application in writing at any time.[12]

See p1159 for reviews relating to overpayment decisions.

Review interviews

If a decision is not wholly revised in your favour, you will be offered a phone interview but if this is difficult for you, you can ask for an interview in person instead.[13] Whichever it is, you can have someone with you to help explain your situation.

During the interview you must be given an explanation of the reasons for the review decision and an opportunity to make representations and submit any additional evidence.[14] The reviewing officer must make an accurate written record of the interview, including your representations, which must be agreed with you.[15]

Due to a backlog of SF reviews, temporary measures are being introduced where only one attempt will be made to contact you to offer you an interview. If you do not respond, the review will be carried out without you. At the time of writing it was envisaged that these measures will be in place until the end of May 2008.

Decisions

You are entitled to a written decision on your application for review (whether or not you have had an interview), which must include notification of your right to request a further review by a social fund inspector (SFI).[16] There are no legal time limits for carrying out reviews and notifying decisions. The SF Independent Review Service has stated that all reviews should be carried out within 10 working days, and a review of a crisis loan decision relating to urgent living expenses should be completed on the day the request is received.[17] If there are unreasonable delays, you should complain to the SF manager and, if necessary, ask your MP or an advice agency to assist.

How review decisions are made

Community care grants and crisis loans

When carrying out a review about a CCG or CL, a reviewing officer must take into account all the circumstances of each case, and in particular:[18]

- the nature, extent and urgency of the need;
- the existence of resources which could meet the need;
- whether any other person or body could, wholly or partly, meet the need;
- the district budget (see p485);
- the SF directions (see p485);
- national and local guidance (see p486); *and*
- in the case of CLs, the likelihood of repayment and the time it would take.

The High Court has ruled that need and the priority of an application should be assessed before budgeting considerations are taken into account.[19]

The reviewing officer must also:[20]

- check whether the decision was correctly arrived at (eg, sustainable on the evidence, based on all relevant considerations and a correct interpretation of the law);
- check that the decision maker acted fairly and reasonably and exercised discretion properly;
- check that you were given the opportunity to put your case and that there was no bias;

- take into account all the circumstances which existed at the time of the original decision and any new evidence and relevant changes in circumstances since the decision was made.

The reviewing officer does not have to take into account any issue not raised by the application for review.[21]

Budgeting loans

When carrying out a review about a BL decision, a reviewing officer must have regard to the same factors as decision makers (see p500).[22] This means that s/he is bound by the factual criteria set out in the directions (see p485).

The reviewing officer must also take into account:[23]

- whether the decision was correctly arrived at and whether you had sufficient opportunity to put your case;
- your personal circumstances – ie, whether you are single or have a partner and whether you have children;
- any new loan debt you have;
- the district budget and the maximum amounts payable, from the time of the original decision up to the date of the review decision.

The reviewing officer does not have to take into account any issue not raised by the application for review.[24]

The above legal duties and restrictions mean that the scope for revision of a decision is very limited. In practical terms, unless your circumstances have changed, or there has been an increase in the district budget and maximum awards, the decision will merely be confirmed by the reviewing officer.

Overpayments

A decision to award you a CCG or a loan can be reviewed at any time if you misrepresented or failed to disclose a material fact (see p1009). Any resulting overpayment is recoverable. An overpayment decision is most likely to be triggered by a decision that you were not entitled to a qualifying benefit when you applied for a CCG or BL. You are entitled to a written decision of any overpayment and can ask for a further review by a reviewing officer.[25]

The reviewing officer must:[26]

- check whether the decision was correctly arrived at and based on the evidence and law; *and*
- take into account all the circumstances of the misrepresentation or non-disclosure and any new evidence which has been produced.

You will then receive a new decision. If you are still dissatisfied, you can request a further review by an SFI (see p1160).[27]

Tactics

- You should always consider requesting a review if you are dissatisfied with a decision. Although you could end up with a less favourable decision, any CCG you have received is only recoverable if you misrepresented or failed to disclose a material fact (see p1009), while a review decision to award you a lower loan, or no loan, has no practical effect if you have already been paid.
- You should also bear in mind the limited scope for a successful review of a BL decision (see p499) so, as an alternative, consider re-applying for a BL.
- Your application for review must be in writing and you should retain a copy. If your application is late, you should give your special reasons why it should be considered out of time (see p1157) or ask the reviewing officer to conduct a discretionary review (see p1157).
- You should explain, as fully as possible, why you disagree with a decision. Make it clear that your application *is* for one of the allowable purposes (see p489) and why it should be given high priority. If you are unhappy about the amount awarded, you should explain and justify the reasonableness of the amount you asked for.
- Most review interviews are carried out on the phone but you can insist on an interview in person if this is easier for you. You can also have someone speak on the phone for you, though you will need to be present as well. Always insist on an interpreter if you need one.
- You should be prepared to receive a negative review decision and to pursue your case by requesting a further review by an SFI (see below).

2. Social fund inspector reviews

Powers of review

The law relating to reviews by social fund inspectors (SFIs) is set out in legislation and legally binding SFI directions.[28]

All decisions which have been reviewed by a reviewing officer are subject to further review by an SFI (see p1161).[29]

The SFIs conduct their reviews independently of the DWP. They are part of the Independent Review Service for the social fund (SF) (see Appendix 1).

SFIs can:[30]

- confirm the decision of the reviewing officer; *or*
- substitute their own decision; *or*
- refer the case back to a reviewing officer at the DWP for re-determination (in practice, this happens in very few cases).

Procedure

Applying for a further review

You must apply for a further review in writing within 28 days of the date the review decision was issued to you.[31] You can apply on Form IRS1, *How to ask for an Independent Review,* available from your local Jobcentre Plus office, or in a letter. Your application must include your grounds for requesting a further review (see p1162).[32] If somebody is applying on your behalf, you must send your written authority (unless the person is your appointee).[33] You should specifically authorise the person to make an application for further review by an SFI on your behalf. You need to do this even if you supplied written authority when you first applied for an internal review. Late applications can be accepted for 'special reasons' (see p1157).[34] If your case is urgent, state this and explain why.

You must send your application directly to the SFI office in Birmingham.[35]

Process

Reviews are almost always conducted on the basis of written information (papers received from the local DWP and any new evidence submitted). You have no right to an oral hearing, although an SFI can interview you, if necessary, at a mutually convenient location.[36]

Within a few days of receiving an application, the SFI dealing with your case should write to you setting out the main issues and facts of the case and any additional information s/he needs. You should also be sent copies of your application form, the decisions made by the SF decision maker and reviewing officer, and the local guidance on priorities. You will normally be given eight days to make any further comments or supply further information or evidence to the SFI (either by telephone or on the reply form provided). It is important to look through the papers carefully and add anything relevant. You can request more time if you need it. The SFI will then decide the case.[37]

Decisions

You should receive a detailed written decision from the SFI. The Independent Review Service says it aims to clear all cases within 12 working days (23 days if further investigation is necessary). Crisis loan reviews should be dealt with more quickly (those relating to urgent living expenses should be dealt with within 24 hours).[38] If you are unhappy about an SFI decision, get advice. There is no right of appeal, but you can ask an SFI to reconsider her/his decision – eg, because it is unreasonable or wrong in law.[39] You can also apply for a judicial review of the decision in the High Court (see p1129).

If a case is referred back to the DWP for another internal review, the SFI should identify the factors which need further consideration. A decision maker must re-determine the case and send you a new decision, with a full explanation of how this was reached, taking into account the SFI's comments.[40] If you are dissatisfied with the new decision, you have the right to request a further review by an SFI.

How social fund inspectors' decisions are made

When carrying out a further review, SFIs must take into account the same factors as reviewing officers must when conducting internal reviews (see p1156).[41] This means they must exercise individual discretion in community care grant and crisis loan reviews, but they are bound by the weighting rules in budgeting loan reviews. See p1159 for reviews of overpayment decisions.

The High Court has ruled that it must be clear from an SFI's decision that s/he has taken the Secretary of State's guidance into account.[42] In another case, the Court ruled that the SFI must apply the law at the time of the SFI decision, not the law at the time of the original SF officer's decision.[43]

SFI decision making tends to be of a much higher standard. SFIs are more independent and thorough and tend to be less bound by local budgets and guidance. You should note, however, that the SFI is primarily concerned with ensuring that the DWP decision was 'reasonable' rather than 'right' – ie, that discretion was exercised reasonably and in accordance with the law.[44]

Notes

1. **Internal reviews**
1 s38 SSA 1998; SF Dirs 31-39
2 s66 SSAA 1992; s38 SSA 1998
3 s38(1)(a) SSA 1998
4 SF Dir 31
5 s38(1)(b) SSA 1998; s71ZA SSAA 1992; SF Dir 43
6 s38(1)(c) SSA 1998
7 Reg 2(1)(a) and (2)(a) SF(AR) Regs
8 Reg 2(4) SF(AR) Regs
9 Reg 2(6) SF(AR) Regs
10 Reg 2(3) SF(AR) Regs
11 Reg 2(5) SF(AR) Regs
12 SF Dir 37
13 SF Dir 33
14 SF Dir 34
15 SF Dir 35
16 SF Dir 36
17 IRS *Journal*, Issue 28, Summer 2004
18 s38 SSA 1998
19 *R v SFI ex parte Taylor* [1998] COD 152 (HC)
20 SF Dirs 32 and 39
21 s38 SSA 1998
22 s66(6)(b) SSAA 1992; s38(7) SSA 1998
23 SF Dirs 32 and 39
24 s66(5A) SSAA 1992; s38(6) SSA 1998
25 SF Dir 44
26 SF Dirs 45 and 46
27 SF Dir 47

2. **Social fund inspector reviews**
28 s38 SSA 1998; SFI Dirs
29 s38(3) SSA 1998
30 s38(4) SSA 1998
31 Reg 2(1)(b) and (2)(b) SF(AR) Regs
32 Reg 2(4) SF(AR) Regs
33 Reg 2(6) SF(AR) Regs
34 Reg 2(3) SF(AR) Regs
35 Reg 2(1)(b)(ii)(bb) SF(AR) Regs
36 part 7 para 14 SFG
37 IRS *Journal*, Spring 2002 and Summer 2004
38 IRS *Journal*, Summer 2004
39 s38(5) SSA 1998
40 SF Dir 38
41 s38 SSA 1998; SFI Dirs 1-5
42 *R v IRS ex parte Connell* 3 November 1994, unreported (HC)
43 *R v SFI ex parte Ledicott* [1995] CO/2492/94 (HC)
44 SF Commissioner's Advice on SFI Dirs 1 and 2, 2 January 2002

Chapter 45

Discrimination and human rights

This chapter looks at European rules which prohibit discrimination between men and women in matters of social security and considers the Human Rights Act and its possible application to social security law. It covers:

1. European law and discrimination between men and women

Social security benefits are not governed by British law alone. There are also Regulations and Directives made by the European Community (EC) which apply directly in the UK and throughout the European Economic Area (EEA) (see Chapter 61).

In particular, there are a number of Directives which are designed to ensure that (subject to limited exceptions) social security benefits, occupational pensions, pay and other benefits from employment are received on an equal basis by both men and women.

British courts (including decision makers, tribunals and social security commissioners) are obliged to apply EC law as well as domestic British law and although British law has been amended to take these Directives into account, the EC rules override the British rules where the two still conflict.[1] Cases which involve new points of EC law may be referred to the European Court of Justice (ECJ) in Luxembourg for a ruling. The ECJ is not the same as the European Court of Human Rights (ECtHR), which is an institution of the Council of Europe and operates from Strasbourg.

There has been a vast amount of caselaw in the ECJ and national courts on these anti-discrimination provisions and this *Handbook* cannot begin to cover the subject comprehensively.[2] What follows is an outline of the general principles and a discussion of what they mean in practical terms for people claiming benefits. If you think there is a chance that you may benefit from the principle of equal treatment, you should get advice (see Appendix 2).

2. The principle of equal treatment

The 'principle of equal treatment' established by Council Directive 79/7 is that:

> There shall be no discrimination whatsoever on ground of sex either directly, or indirectly by reference in particular to marital or family status.[3]

'Discrimination' simply means treating one person less favourably than another. Indirect discrimination occurs when a rule appears to be neutral but in practice can be complied with by fewer members of one sex than the other and that rule cannot be justified for reasons other than discrimination based on sex.

For example, a rule which said that applicants for a job have to be at least 6'3" tall would be indirectly discriminatory even though it applied equally to women and men. This is because, in practice, fewer women than men would qualify. Such a rule would be unlawful unless the employer could show a good, non-discriminatory, reason for employing only tall people.

It is often necessary to rely on statistical evidence to prove indirect discrimination. Governments may not rely upon purely financial reasons to justify a discriminatory practice.[4]

The principle of equal treatment only prohibits discrimination 'on ground of sex'. It does not prevent a government from discriminating on the ground of marital or family status unless that amounts to a form of indirect discrimination on the ground of sex. So a rule is not necessarily contrary to the Directive just because it differentiates between married (or cohabiting) people and single people.[5] On the other hand, a rule which differentiates between married men and married women or single men and single women is directly discriminatory on grounds of sex.

If the principle of equal treatment applies to you, your claim for benefit should be decided using the rules which would have applied had you been a member of the opposite sex where those rules would be more favourable.[6]

However, this broad general principle is subject to a number of limitations and exceptions (known as 'derogations'). In practice, this means that you have to ask three questions before you can know whether the principle of equal treatment applies in your case.

- Is the benefit you are claiming (or your liability to pay contributions) covered by the Directive? Only schemes for benefits which cover certain risks are subject to the principle of equal treatment. This is sometimes referred to as the 'material scope' of the Directive.
- Does the Directive apply to you? You are only entitled to benefit from the principle of equal treatment if you are a member of the working population (see p1166). This is sometimes referred to as the 'personal scope' of the Directive.
- Does the Directive include a derogation which applies in your case? If so, the Government is allowed to discriminate against you even if you are within both the personal and material scope of the Directive.

3. **Which benefits are covered**

Directive 79/7 applies to schemes for state benefits which are designed to protect against:[7]

- sickness;
- invalidity;
- old age;
- accidents at work and occupational diseases;
- unemployment.

Most contributory benefits are covered by the Directive. However, whether or not a benefit is contributory is not the crucial factor in deciding whether it falls within the scope of the Directive. Certain non-contributory benefits, such as carer's allowance (previously invalid care allowance), severe disablement allowance and industrial injury benefit are within the scope of the Directive.[8]

The Directive can also apply to means-tested benefits (sometimes referred to as 'social assistance') to the extent that they are intended to supplement or replace the schemes referred to above.[9] For example, a commissioner decided that income-based jobseeker's allowance is covered as it is a benefit that protects against the risk of unemployment.[10] A similar approach has been taken by the Court of Appeal.[11] A commissioner has also held that pension credit falls within the scope of the Directive as an old-age benefit.[12]

Income support, housing benefit and council tax benefit are not within the scope of the Directive.

Certain risks are specifically excluded from the Directive – in particular, positive discrimination for maternity allowances and the different pension ages for men and women. Widows' and widowers' benefits are also not covered. Family benefits, such as child benefit and child tax credit, are also excluded from the scope of the Directive.

The fact that the Directive applies only to state schemes means that other schemes (such as occupational pension schemes) are beyond its scope. These are, however, covered by a later Directive.[13]

4. Who is covered

Directive 79/7 applies to you if you are a member of the working population. There is no requirement to have moved from one member state to another in order to fall within the scope of the Regulation. If you are not a member of the working population then you cannot use the Directive to stop the Government discriminating against you, even if the benefit which you are claiming is covered by the Directive.

The **'working population'** is defined as being:[14]

- workers (ie, people in employment);
- the self-employed;
- people seeking employment;
- workers and self-employed people whose jobs have been interrupted by illness, accident or involuntary unemployment;
- workers and self-employed people who have retired or become unable to work because of invalidity.

This means that to be covered by the Directive you must have been either working or actively looking for work when you became affected by one of the risks set out on p1165.[15] So, for example, the Directive does not apply to you if:

- you have been so ill or disabled since before you reached the age of 16 that you have never been able to contemplate working or looking for work; *or*
- you stopped working for a reason which is not included in the list of risks on p1165 (eg, because you were pregnant) and before you began to look for work again you became too ill to work.

It is not, however, necessary for the risks to be experienced by you personally. In one case, a woman who gave up work to look after her severely disabled mother was held to be a member of the working population because her work had been interrupted by invalidity, even though it was the invalidity of her mother and not her own.[16]

5. Exceptions to the principle of equal treatment

The Directive permits member states to adopt or continue discriminatory rules on certain aspects of entitlement to benefits even if they are within its scope.

The types of discriminatory rule which may be lawful are those which:[17]

- set a different age for men and women to become entitled to retirement pensions. This also covers rules which deal with the possible consequences for other benefits of having different pensionable ages;
- allow people who have looked after children to claim retirement pensions and other benefits on advantageous terms;
- allow special treatment for people who, before 22 December 1984, opted 'not to acquire rights or incur obligations under a statutory scheme'. This is intended to cover the rules on the married woman's reduced national insurance contribution (see p721).

European Economic Area states are supposed to keep these discriminatory rules under review to ensure that they are still justified in the light of social developments,[18] and to notify the European Commission of the measures that they have taken to do so.[19]

Perhaps more importantly, the European Court of Justice has repeatedly held that the elimination of discrimination based on sex is a fundamental right which it has a duty to protect. In the past it, therefore, scrutinised very carefully the validity of rules which rely on the derogations to ensure that the principle of proportionality was observed.[20]

This meant that it did not follow that a discriminatory rule was lawful just because it had one of the effects allowed by the derogations. In each case, it was for the government of the member state which made the rule to establish that the discriminatory means adopted were an appropriate way of achieving the ends permitted by the derogation.

6. Equal treatment and social security benefits

In British social security law, one of the most important issues has been the scope of the derogation allowing for 'the possible consequences' of different retirement ages for other benefits.[21] What this means is whether it is lawful to withdraw or reduce earnings replacement benefits (eg, contribution-based jobseeker's allowance (JSA), incapacity benefit, severe disablement allowance (SDA), carer's allowance (CA) and reduced earning allowance (REA)) when a claimant reaches pensionable age – with the effect, in most cases, that women are denied benefits which would be paid to a man of the same age.

It is clear that not just any connection between a benefit and pensionable age is sufficient for the derogation to apply. The question is on how close the link must be before it is covered.

This question has been the subject of a number of European Court of Justice (ECJ) decisions. In the *Thomas*[22] case the Court ruled that different pensionable ages for men and women in non-contributory benefits such as CA and SDA were contrary to EC Directive 79/7 and, therefore, unlawful. As a result, British law was amended to bring the rules on non-contributory benefits into line with the law as declared by the ECJ.

In the *Equal Opportunities Commission (EOC)*[23] case, the Court held that inequality in the amount of contributions required to be paid in order to be entitled to a full retirement pension was justified. Men could be required to pay contributions for 44 years but women only for 39 years for the same amount of benefit.

The decision in the *Graham*[24] case was that the DWP could lawfully:

- reduce invalidity benefit (now abolished) to pension rate at 60 for women and 65 for men;
- take invalidity benefit away altogether from women at 60 and men at 65; *and*
- pay extra benefit to men who became incapable of work between the ages of 55 and 60 and not to women in the same position.

A commissioner has considered whether the same discriminatory age rules contravene the Directive.[25] The commissioner held that there was a possible contravention of the Directive in spite of the ECJ judgment in *Graham*. It was significant in the case before the commissioner that incapacity had arisen after pension age. This was important because it may not be lawful to limit the contributions that a claimant has paid to those paid before pension age where that age is different for women than for men. However, to enforce that right the claimant would be required to pay outstanding contributions after age 60.

By contrast, in the *Richardson*[26] case it was held that the discriminatory treatment of men in respect of free prescriptions for those over retirement age unlawfully discriminated against men, since there was no necessary or objective link to pensionable ages. The Court followed a similar line in the *Taylor*[27] case where it was held that the refusal of winter fuel payments to men aged between 60 and 64 was in breach of Directive 79/7, as men were unlawfully discriminated against.

The combined effect of these cases is that, in order to be covered by the derogation for 'the possible consequences for other benefits' of setting different pensionable ages for men and women, the discriminatory rule must be necessary *either*:

- to avoid disturbing the financial equilibrium of the social security system; *or*
- to ensure coherence between the retirement pension scheme and other benefit schemes.

Applying these tests, the Court has held (in general terms) that for contributory benefits (*Graham*) or the liability to pay national insurance contributions (*EOC*), a discriminatory link to pensionable age is lawful, but for non-contributory benefits (*Thomas*) such discrimination is unlawful.

The ECJ has considered the discriminatory rules in respect of REA. REA is not contributory, although the requirement that the claimant must have been an 'employed earner' at the time of the industrial accident or the onset of the prescribed disease means that, in practice, many REA claimants would actually have been paying, or liable to pay, Class 1 contributions.[28] Although the Advocate-General gave an opinion that was favourable, the ECJ held that the discrimination within the REA regulations is objectively justified and, therefore, exempted from the prohibition on discrimination under Directive 79/7.[29]

Income-based jobseeker's allowance

More recent cases have focused on discrimination in the income-based JSA rules. For example, in one case before the social security commissioners[30] a woman successfully argued that a student who was pregnant and temporarily gave up her course could claim income-based JSA. The UK regulations which excluded her from benefit were discriminatory as they would have far greater impact on women. However, the decision has subsequently been overturned by the Court of Appeal.[31] The Court decided that the JSA regulations were not directly discriminatory against pregnant women or against women generally and were not, for that reason, in breach of the Directive. The regulations made no express distinction between men and women, nor did they seek to deal with whether a woman was pregnant or not. What they did was to define student status in such a way that any full-time student who interrupted her/his course was deemed to remain a student, and so was ineligible for JSA until the last day of the course or such earlier date as s/he abandoned it or was dismissed from it. The claimant's ineligibility for JSA derived from the fact that she was a student, not from the fact that she was pregnant.

In another case, a commissioner considered whether the requirement to be available for work for 40 hours a week in order to qualify for JSA was indirectly discriminatory. The commissioner found that the rule could not be discriminatory because the JSA regulations allowed certain people to be exempt from this condition. In particular, those with caring responsibilities can be exempt from the 40 hours a week requirement provided the restrictions are reasonable.[32]

A more successful outcome was found in a number of joined cases which looked at the discriminatory effect of the JSA rules on part-time staff employed in schools and colleges. The rules meant that these people were treated as working during periods when they received no pay. Consequently, they were unable to claim income-based JSA. The commissioners found this rule to be incompatible with Article 4 of Directive 79/7 and decided that it should be struck down.[33] The same discriminatory rules operate within the income support (IS) regulations, but as IS is not within the scope of the Directive it is not possible to challenge them in the same way.

Shared care

In the case of *Hockenjos* before the Court of Appeal[34] it was argued that the income-based JSA rules discriminated against a man who had shared care of his two children with his separated partner. Although the children spent equal periods of time with each parent, only the mother received an additional amount of income-based JSA for the children because she was the parent who received child benefit for them. For couples, the child benefit regulations give priority to women claimants. Where a couple subsequently separate, it was argued that the rules favour the person already in receipt of child benefit and, therefore, discriminate against men and are contrary to the Directive. The Court of Appeal referred the case back to the commissioners to decide on the discrimination point. The commissioner subsequently held that where a person is able to rely on Directive 79/7, receipt of child benefit should not be the determining factor in deciding who has responsibility for a child.[35] The case was further appealed to the Court of Appeal. The Court has now held that in genuine shared care cases, linking increases in JSA to child benefit for dependent children for whom there is shared responsibility is discriminatory and, therefore, contrary to Directive 79/7. Consequently, in such cases both parents are entitled to the child addition of income-based JSA for their children. The Court further held that a person would be considered to be sharing the care of her/his child if s/he is caring for her/him 104 nights or more a year.

The Secretary of State applied for leave to appeal to the House of Lords but it was refused.

In theory, anyone in a similar position to Mr Hockenjos is now entitled to an additional amount of income-based JSA. However, the judgment is unlikely to affect other claimants apart from those with outstanding appeals.

A fresh claim for the addition is not likely to succeed because the child additions for income-based JSA have been abolished for claims made after April 2004. Instead, claimants are expected to claim child tax credit (CTC). In theory, it would be possible to make a similar argument in respect of CTC, but CTC does not fall under this area of EC law and, therefore, the discrimination argument would have to be made by relying on human rights law. This is more difficult and the Courts have been largely unsympathetic to human rights challenges in social security.

Claimants who are already in receipt of income-based JSA are also unlikely to succeed in a claim. In order to claim the child addition the claimant would need to seek a revision of the original decision. However, in such cases the 'anti-test case' rules mean that where an established interpretation of the law is overturned by a decision of a court or commissioner, the effect of that decision is retrospective only so far as the individual litigant is concerned. Other claimants can only gain the benefit of such a ruling on a revision or fresh claim with effect from the date of the new decision. As there are no longer any child additions, claimants seeking a revision will not benefit from the judgment.

It might be argued that the anti-test case rules cannot operate to deny rights in EC law and they too should be disapplied. Such an approach has been applied by the ECJ. In the case of *Emmott*[36] the ECJ disapplied a national rule on the limitation period for instituting judicial review proceedings. However, the ECJ has also considered the UK anti-test case provisions in *Johnson*. The case concerned a woman who successfuly argued that the rules which restricted her entitlement to SDA were contrary to Directive 79/7. She sought to challenge the anti-test case rules which restricted the amount of backdated benefit that she could receive. The ECJ considered that the anti-test case provisions were not in breach of EC law.[37] A tribunal of commissioners has recently considered the application of UK time limits for claims and the anti-test case rule. At the time of writing, the decision had not been given.[38]

The implications of the *Hockenjos* judgment in respect of other benefits such as CTC, housing benefit/council tax benefit and IS are also limited. These benefits are not covered by the Directive so any challenges would have to be made by relying on human rights legislation.

7. The Human Rights Act

Key aspects of the Act

The Human Rights Act 1998 (HRA) came into effect on 2 October 2000. It only applies to decisions made on or after 2 October 2000.[39] It incorporates into UK law most of the Articles of the European Convention on Human Rights.[40] For social security purposes, all of the relevant provisions of the Convention now form part of our domestic law.

An appeal tribunal, social security commissioner or court must take account of any relevant caselaw of the European Court of Human Rights (ECtHR) when deciding an appeal in which a human rights issue arises.[41] However, where there is a conflict between a UK court and the ECtHR, the decision of the UK court should generally be followed.[42]

In addition, all legislation must be read and given effect, *so far as it is possible to do so*, in a way which is compatible with the Convention.[43] This duty applies to all social security decision makers (eg, Secretary of State decision makers, appeal tribunals and the commissioners),[44] and applies regardless of whether the legislation in question was made before October 2000 or after. This interpretative obligation is a strong one. It may require words to be 'read into' the statutory provision concerned in order to remove a breach of the Convention (as long as this stops short of creating a new and different legal rule) and decision makers should strive to find a Convention-compatible reading of the statute or regulations in issue.[45]

Relevant Articles of the Convention

The Articles of the Convention which are most likely to be relevant in social security are:

- Article 6(1): right to a fair trial;
- Article 8: right to respect for private and family life, home and correspondence;
- Article 1 of the First Protocol: protection of property;
- Article 14: prohibition of discrimination (though not a free-standing right).

In addition, Article 2 of Protocol 1 (right to education) could be relevant.

Note: Article 14 will often be needed in social security cases to supplement the other Articles because of the difficulty of bringing social security within those Articles.

Key aspects of relevant Articles

Article 6(1) provides:

In the determination of his civil rights and obligations or any criminal charge against him, everyone is entitled to a fair and public hearing within a reasonable time by an independent and impartial tribunal established by law.

- This article should cover any social security benefit where there is no element of discretion. Whether the benefit is contributory or non-contributory, or means-tested or non-means-tested, should not matter.[46] Child tax credit and working tax credit fall within Article 6.[47]
- The discretionary social fund may be excluded, but this is not certain because the discretion which appropriate officers have is very constrained (especially for budgeting loans). However, *ex gratia* payments made by the Secretary of State and discretionary housing payments are almost certainly excluded.
- The term 'fair ... hearing' has been widely interpreted, and means that a claimant must:
  - have real and effective access to a court. Although access to a court or tribunal may be restricted in a particular case or class of cases,[48] any restriction must not impair the very essence of the right and must both be proportionate and pursue a legitimate aim;[49]
  - have a real opportunity of presenting her/his case;
  - be given a reasoned decision; *and*
  - have 'equality of arms' with her/his opponent.[50] This includes the right to have a representative. In an appropriate case, there may be a right to *paid* representation.[51] However, the test here is a broad one. 'Equality of arms' only requires that a claimant is not placed under a *substantial* disadvantage compared to her/his opponent (eg, the Secretary of State or the Revenue).[52] This rule has been held to have been breached when the DWP failed to ensure the attendance of one of its staff as a witness at an appeal hearing[53] and when it failed to provide an appeal tribunal with previous personal capability assessments in respect of the appellant.[54]

- 'Public hearing' includes the concept of a right to an oral hearing, but this will usually be confined to a hearing by a fact-finding body.[55]
- 'Within a reasonable time' has not been interpreted very beneficially as far as social security cases are concerned, with the ECtHR only finding breaches of this criterion with delays of four years and above[56] and the social security commissioners finding delays of seven months[57] and one year[58] for hearing of appeals not unreasonable. However, much will depend on the circumstances and, in particular, the benefit in question.
- 'Independent and impartial tribunal' includes the *appearance* of impartiality. The test of bias is 'real possibility of bias'.[59] This is an objective test based on the circumstances of the case and whether these would lead a fair-minded observer to conclude that there was a real possibility of bias.[60]

Note: a breach of Article 6 may be rectified by access to a review or appellate court, if that court itself complies with Article 6.[61]

Article 8 provides:
Everyone has the right to respect for his private and family life, his home and his correspondence.

There shall be no interference by a public authority with the exercise of this right except such as is in accordance with the law and is necessary in a democratic society in the interests of national security, public safety or the economic well-being of the country, for the prevention of disorder or crime, for the protection of health or morals, or for the protection of the rights and freedoms of others.

- This article may impose a positive obligation on the state to ensure effective respect for private or family life – eg, by regulating the conduct of people. This does not extend to an obligation to provide any particular social security benefit.
- Benefits that promote respect for family life or the home may be covered by Article 8.[62] However, the income support (IS) and jobseeker's allowance schemes are not, in general, covered by Article 8.[63]
- 'Family life' extends beyond formal and legitimate relationships.[64]
- 'Private life' covers the right to develop personally as well as create relationships with others,[65] and can include protection of a person's physical and psychological integrity.[66] However, it is not a breach of the right to respect for private life to film a disability living allowance claimant in public to check whether s/he is entitled to the benefit.[67]

Note: wide discretion is given to national governments in deciding how the right in question should be 'respected', and Article 8(2) provides a get-out for governments where there is a *prima facie* breach of Article 8(1).

Note also: once the decision of the ECtHR in *Stec* has been confirmed to be correct by the House of Lords (see below), Article 8 should not need to be used in most social security challenges.

Article 1 of the First Protocol provides:
Every natural or legal person is entitled to the peaceful enjoyment of his possessions. No one shall be deprived of his possessions except in the public interest and subject to the conditions provided for by law and by the general principles of international law.

The preceding provisions shall not, however, in any way impair the right of a State to enforce such laws as it deems necessary to control the use of property in accordance with the general interest or to secure the payment of taxes or other contributions or penalties.

- This Article will be breached if:
  - the state interferes with the peaceful enjoyment of the claimant's possessions; *or*
  - the claimant has been deprived of possessions by the state; *or*
  - the claimant's possessions have been subjected to control by the state.
- The critical issue in social security is whether benefits constitute 'possessions' under this Article. The answer to this question used to be dependent on whether the benefit in question was contributory or non-contributory. Contributory benefits were (and remain) possessions,[68] and it did not matter whether the contributions were paid by the claimant or her/his spouse.[69] Non-contributory benefits, however, were not possessions.[70] However, recently, in the case of *Stec* the ECtHR has ruled decisively that any social security benefits to which a person has a right should count as possessions regardless of whether the right to the benefit arises in a contributory or non-contributory scheme.[71] But until *Stec* is confirmed by the House of Lords as being correct, it seems likely that decision makers, appeal tribunals and the social security commissioners will have to follow an earlier decision of the Court of Appeal (*Reynolds*[72]) which held that non-contributory benefits are not possessions.[73]
- Even if your benefit is a 'possession', this Article provides no general right to be paid it at a particular rate unless the reduction in your benefit is of such a substantial amount that it affects 'the very substance of the right'.[74] In a case concerning the reduction of retirement pension for hospital inpatients, the following factors were listed as helping to determine whether there was deprivation:[75]
  - Did the provision in question reduce a benefit previously in payment?
  - Was the provision in force throughout the time when the claimant was paying relevant contributions?
  - How close was the link between the benefit and payment of contributions?
  - The amount of the reduction in benefit.

Note: as with Article 8, states have a wide get-out in accordance with the 'public interest' or 'general interest'.

Article 14 provides:
The enjoyment of the rights and freedoms set forth in this Convention shall be secured without discrimination on any ground such as sex, race, colour, language, religion, political or other opinion, national or social origin, association with a national minority, property, birth or other status.

- It is important to note that this Article only comes into play if one of the other Articles applies, though it is not necessary to demonstrate that the other Article has been breached. It includes a long list of different sorts of discrimination, with a catch-all 'or other status'. This covers 'age',[76] and 'residence'[77] and should also cover discrimination on the grounds of disability; but the 'status' must amount to a personal characteristic.[78]
- It covers indirect, as well as direct, discrimination. The test for indirect discrimination is whether the effect of the rule on the particular group is 'disproportionately prejudicial'.[79]
- However, only different treatment of people 'placed in an analogous situation' falls within Article 14.
- It will be breached if a measure creates differential treatment which does not pursue a legitimate aim, or if it is disproportionate to the aim pursued.[80] Administrative convenience may not amount to a legitimate aim.[81] Although very weighty reasons are needed to justify discrimination based on race or sex,[82] that has to be balanced against the fact that judgments about econcomic and social strategy are generally for governments to make and so may only be disagreed with by courts or tribunals if the judgment is 'manifestly without reasonable foundation'.[83]

Article 2 of the First Protocol provides:
No person shall be denied the right to education. In the exercise of any functions which it assumes in relation to education and to teaching, the State shall respect the right of parents to ensure such education and teaching in conformity with their own religious and philosophical convictions.

- This Article applies to both school education and further and higher education, which may provide new scope for arguments in respect of the problems created for students by the IS and housing benefit (HB) rules in particular.[84]
- The Article, however, is expressed in the negative, so it probably does not create any duty on a state to subsidise education.

Using the Human Rights Act

For most social security cases, there are no special courts or procedures which need to be used if you want to bring a challenge relying on the HRA. Therefore, HRA arguments can be used in front of appeal tribunals, social fund inspectors and the commissioners, and the ordinary time limits for bringing such challenges will continue to apply (see Chapters 41 and 42).[85] In addition, guidance has been issued concerning social security (and child support) appeals, which recommends the following.

- Any HRA challenges should be raised at as early an opportunity as possible (eg, in the grounds of appeal).
- Such grounds of appeal need to:
  - identify the rule, regulation or practice which it is alleged breaches the HRA and the Article(s) of the Convention;
  - set out the Articles of the Convention which it is claimed have been breached, and explain why they have been breached; *and*
  - set out the relevant supporting caselaw (and provide copies of the cases).
- Grounds of appeal which fail to do the above and merely state that the decision is in breach of the Convention are unlikely to succeed.
- Raising an argument relying on the Convention for the first time at the hearing, when it could have reasonably been raised in advance, will almost certainly lead to an adjournment of the appeal.[86]

The starting point for any appeal tribunal (or other relevant decision-making body) considering an HRA challenge is to decide whether the statute, regulation, rule or practice which is in issue on the appeal is compatible with the relevant Articles of the Convention, or can be read 'so far as it is possible to do so' in such a way to make it compatible with the Convention. However, if the legislation cannot be interpreted in a way which makes it compatible with the Convention,[87] then the following two considerations apply.

- If the legislation is contained in an Act of Parliament, the appeal tribunal, commissioner or social fund inspector has to apply it as it stands.[88] Even the higher courts (High Court, Court of Appeal (Court of Session in Scotland) and House of Lords) are limited to issuing what is termed a 'declaration of incompatibility' in this situation,[89] which does not change the legislation[90] and simply requires the government minister to consider amending the legislation.[91]
- If the legislation in question is contained in a regulation, then the appeal tribunal, commissioner or social fund inspector may disapply the (incompatible) regulation,[92] unless the Act under which the regulation was made is so prescriptive that it required an incompatible regulation to be made. In this latter case, the appeal tribunal, commissioner or social fund inspector cannot disapply the regulation,[93] and the remedy here is again limited to seeking a declaration of incompatibility from the higher courts.

Challenges in social security using the HRA and the Convention are difficult and may call for specialist input. In these circumstances, if you have a case in which an HRA argument arises, you should think very seriously about seeking specialist advice (see Appendix 2).

Notes

1. **European law and discrimination between men and women**
   1 s2 ECA 1972
   2 For a detailed account see McCrudden (ed), *Equal Treatment Between Women and Men in Social Security*, Butterworths, 1994

2. **The principle of equal treatment**
   3 Art 4(1) Directive 79/7/EEC
   4 *M A De Weerd (nee Roks) & Others v Bestuur van de Bedrijfsvereniging voor de Gezondheid, Geestelijke en Maatschappenlijke Belangen & Others* C-343/92 24 February 1994, unreported (ECJ)
   5 R(SB) 6/91, *Blaik v Department of Health & Social Security* 19 July 1990, unreported (CA)
   6 For example, see *Cotter and McDermott v Minister for Social Welfare and Another* C-286/85 24 March 1987, unreported (ECJ)

3. **Which benefits are covered**
   7 Art 3(1)(a) Directive 79/7/EEC
   8 *Thomas v Secretary of State for Social Security* C-328/91 30 March 1993, unreported (ECJ)
   9 Art 3(1)(b) Directive 79/7/EEC
   10 R(JSA) 3/02
   11 *Hockenjos v Secretary of State for Social Security* [2001] EWCA Civ 624 (CA)
   12 Directive 86/378/EEC (*Official Journal of the European Communities* No. L225, 12 August 1986, p40)
   13 CPC/4177/2005

4. **Who is covered**
   14 Art 2 Directive 79/7/EEC
   15 *Achterberg-te Riele & Others v Social Verzekeingsbank* C-48/88, C-106-107/88 [1989] (ECJ)
   16 *Drake v CAO* C-150/85 24 June 1986, unreported (ECJ)

5. **Exceptions to the principle of equal treatment**
   17 Art 7(1) Directive 79/7/EEC
   18 Art 7(2) Directive 79/7/EEC
   19 Art 8(2) Directive 79/7/EEC
   20 *Johnston v Chief Constable of the Royal Ulster Constabulary* [1986] ECR 723 (ECJ)

6. **Equal treatment and social security benefits**
   21 Art 7(1)(a) Directive 79/7/EEC
   22 *Thomas v Secretary of State for Social Security* C-328/91 30 March 1993, unreported (ECJ)
   23 *Graham v Secretary of State for Social Security* C-92/94 11 August 1995, unreported (ECJ)
   24 *Graham v Secretary of State for Social Security* C-92/94 11 August 1995, unreported (ECJ)
   25 R(IB) 5/04
   26 *R v Secretary of State for Health ex parte Richardson* C-137/94 19 October 1995, unreported (ECJ)
   27 *R v Secretary of State ex parte Taylor* C-382/98 16 December 1999, unreported (ECJ)
   28 It is possible to be an employed earner but not liable to pay NI contributions if you are in part-time or low-paid work and earn less than the lower earnings limit.
   29 *Hepple and Others v CAO* C-196/98, 23 May 2000, unreported (ECJ), reported as R(I) 2/00
   30 R(JSA) 3/02
   31 *Secretary of State for Social Securityv Walter* [2001] EWCA Civ 1913 [2002] ICMLR 794, reported as R(JSA) 3/02
   32 R(JSA) 4/02; regs 6 and 13(4) JSA Regs
   33 R(JSA) 4/03
   34 *Hockenjos v Secretary of State for Social Security* [2001] EWCA Civ 624 (CA)
   35 R(JSA) 1/05; R(JSA) 2/05
   36 *Emmott v Minister for Social Welfare* C-208/90 [1991] ECR 1-4569
   37 *Johnson v Chief Adjudication Officer* C-410/92 [1994] ECR I-5483
   38 CSP/503/2007;CP/1425/2007;CP/2862/2007

7. **The Human Rights Act**
   39 ss7(1)(b) and 22(4) HRA 1998
   40 s1(2) HRA 1998

Notes

41 s2(1) HRA 1998
42 *Leeds City Council v Price* [2006] UKHL 10
43 s3(1) HRA 1998
44 See definition of 'public authority' in s6(3) HRA 1998
45 *Ghaidan v Godin-Mendoza* [2004] UKHL 30, 3 All ER 411
46 *Salesi v Italy* [1998] 26 EHRR 187 (ECtHR); R(IS) 6/04
47 CTC/2162/2005
48 See for example, the categories of non-appealable decisions in Sch 2 SS&CS(DA) Regs
49 *Tolstoy Miloslavsky v United Kingdom* [1995] 20 EHRR 441 (ECtHR); R(IS) 6/04
50 *Neumeister v Austria* [1968] 1 EHRR 91 (ECtHR); CDLA/5413/1999
51 *Airey v Ireland* [1979] 2 EHRR 305 (ECtHR); see also CJSA/5101/2001 in which the commissioner confirmed that there is no general right to (paid) legal representation before an appeal tribunal.
52 *De Haes and Gijsels v Belgium* [1997] 24 EHRR 1 (ECtHR)
53 CJSA/5100/2001
54 CIB/3985/2001
55 *Schuler-Zgraggen v Switzerland* [1993] 16 EHRR 405 (ECtHR)
56 *Deumeland v Germany* [1986] 8 EHRR 448 (ECtHR) and *Schouten and Meldrum v Netherlands* [1995] 19 EHRR 432 (ECtHR)
57 R(IS) 1/04
58 R(IS) 2/04
59 *Porter and another v Magill* [2001] UKHL 67, [2002] 1 All ER 465 (HL)
60 In social security this test has been adopted in relation to EMPs sitting on and providing reports to appeal tribunals (see CSDLA/1019/1999 (*Gillies*) and CSDLA/444/2002 - though the claimant's challenge in the *Gillies* case failed on further appeals to the Court of Session and the House of Lords).
61 *Runa Begum v LB Tower Hamlets* [2003] UKHL 5, 1 All ER 731 (HL); but see also *Tsfayo v United Kingdom,* Application No.60860/00, 14 November 2006, unreported (ECtHR)
62 *R (Hooper and others) v Secretary of State for Work and Pensions* [2003] EWCA Civ 813, [2003] 3 All ER 673, para 18; *Petrovic v Austria* [2001] 33 EHRR 14 (ECtHR); CH/4574/2003 and *Esfandiari* (R(IS) 11/06). But note, in contrast, CH/663/2003 and *Langley v Secretary of State for Work and Pensions* [2004] EWCA Civ 1343, 15 October 2004).
63 *R (Reynolds) v Secretary of State for Work and Pensions* [2003] EWCA Civ 797, [2003] All ER 577, para 28
64 *Marckx v Belgium* [1979] 2 EHRR 330 (ECtHR); *X, Y and Z v UK* [1997] 24 EHRR 143 (ECtHR)
65 *Niemitz v Germany* [1992] 16 EHRR 97 (ECtHR)
66 *Botta v Italy* [1998] 26 EHRR 241 (ECtHR)
67 R(DLA) 4/02
68 *Willis v United Kingdom* Application No.36042/97, 11 June 2002, unreported (ECtHR); *R (Reynolds) v Secretary of State for Work and Pensions* [2003] EWCA Civ 797, 3 All ER 577
69 *Willis v United Kingdom* Application No.36042/97, 11 June 2002, unreported (ECtHR), effectively overruling the contrary view in *Hooper and others v Secretary of State for Work and Pensions* [2002] EWHC Admin 191
70 *R (Reynolds) v Secretary of State for Work and Pensions* [2003] EWCA Civ 797, All ER 577, para 28
71 *Stec and others v UK,* Application Nos.65731/01 and 65900/01, 5 September 2005
72 *R (Reynolds) v Secretary of State for Work and Pensions* [2003] EWCA Civ 797, 3 All ER 577
73 See *R (Couronne) v Crawley BC and Secretary of State for Work and Pensions and others* [2007] EWCA Civ 1086 and CIS/1757/2006, both of which follow the rule in *Leeds v Price* [2006] UKHL 10 and the Court of Appeal's decision in *Reynolds* in preference to the ECtHR's decision in *Stec.*
74 *Müller v Austria* (Commission) (1975) 3 D and R 25
75 CP/5084/2001
76 *R (Reynolds) v Secretary of State for Work and Pensions* [2003] EWCA Civ 797, All ER 577, para 28
77 *R (Carson) v Secretary of State for Work and Pensions* [2003] EWCA Civ 797, 3 All ER 577

78 *R (S) v Chief Constable of the South Yorkshire Police* [2004] 1 WLR 2196, and *Carson and Reynolds v Secretary of State for Work and Pensions* [2005] UKHL 37, 26 May 2005
79 *Esfandiari* (R(IS)11/06)
80 *Belgian Linguistics Case (No.2)* [1968] 1 EHRR 252 (ECtHR)
81 *Darby v Sweden* [1990] 13 EHRR 774 (ECtHR)
82 *Schmidt v Germany* [1994] 18 EHRR 513 (ECtHR)
83 *Stec and others v United Kingdom,* Application Nos.65731/01 and 65900/01, final judgment, 12 April 2006 (ECtHR)
84 See *Douglas v North Tyneside Metropolitan Borough Council* [2003] EWCA Civ 1847, [2004] 1 All ER 709 and *Sahin v Turkey*[2007] 44 EHRR 5 (ECtHR)
85 s7(5) HRA 1998
86 President's Protocol No.6, *Handling Questions Under the Human Rights Act 1998,* 14 July 2000
87 For example, the pre-April 2000 rules on widows' benefits arguably conflicted with the Convention because the benefits were only available to women who had been widowed, and not men. However, the relevant part of the legislation referred to women and wives (as being entitled), and such specific and deliberate references cannot be interpreted as applying also to men and husbands. *Hooper and others v Secretary of State for Work and Pensions* [2003] EWCA Civ 813, 3 All ER 673. This part was not contested on the further appeal to the House of Lords.
88 s3(2)(b) HRA 1998
89 s4 HRA 1998
90 s4(6) HRA 1998
91 s10(2) HRA 1998
92 On the basis that the Minister acted outside the powers given to him in the Act to made such regulations (referred to as the *ultra vires* rule), following the House of Lords' decision in *CAO v Foster* [1993] 1 All ER 705 (HL)
93 s3(2)(c) HRA 1998

Chapter 46

Complaints

This chapter covers:

The procedures for revision, supersession and appeal (see Chapters 41 and 42) allow you to challenge decisions about your entitlement to benefit (including the refusal of benefit). However, in some circumstances you may want to make a complaint simply about the way in which your benefit claim was handled.

You might want to complain about:

- a delay in dealing with your claim;
- poor administration in the benefit office – eg, it keeps losing your papers, or you can never get through on the telephone;
- poor or negligent advice from the DWP, Revenue, local authority or the Tribunals Service (TS) staff;
- the behaviour of members of staff – eg, staff rudeness, or sexist or racist remarks.

If you think you have lost out because you were badly advised by an independent adviser, such as a Citizens Advice Bureau or law centre, you should seek legal advice about taking action for negligence.

You should ask your local office for any written information on the standards and levels of service that you can expect. This may include targets for the time it should take to deal with your claim. You can also visit the DWP, Revenue and TS websites (see Appendix 1) for information about standards and complaints. All the agencies should also be able to provide you with written details about how to complain if you are not getting the service you think you should be.

Whenever you write to the DWP, Revenue, TS or local authority you should quote your national insurance number and, if you are not writing to the office that is handling your claim, the name and address of that office. You should explain exactly what you are complaining about, any costs you have incurred as a result of this problem and what you would like to see done to resolve your complaint. Always keep a copy of any letters you send or receive and take the name of anyone you speak to on the phone.

Note: for details of complaints about the Child Support Agency, see CPAG's *Child Support Handbook*.

1. Complaining to the DWP

The DWP has separate complaints policies for each of its agencies and each agency has its own complaints procedure. The individual agencies are:

- The Pension Service;
- Jobcentre Plus;
- The Child Support Agency;
- The Disability and Carers Service.

Note: the Pension Service and the Disability and Carers Service were to be merged on 1 April 2008 to create a new DWP agency, the Pension, Disability and Carers Service, but for the time being, all contact with claimants will continue to be made by the Pension Service and the Disability and Carers Service and their procedures will remain the same.

If you want to complain about how a particular agency of the DWP has dealt with your individual case, you should first contact the office that dealt with your claim. If you are still dissatisfied, you can contact the manager of the agency. S/he investigates your complaint and should respond within seven days. Further details on how to make a complaint are contained in the DWP leaflet GL22 *Tell Us How to Improve our Service.* If you not satisfied, you can complain to the Independent Case Examiner (see below). You may also have grounds to make a complaint to the Ombudsman.

2. Complaining to the Independent Case Examiner

The Independent Case Examiner's Office (ICE) was set up in 1997 to deal with complaints about the Child Support Agency, but its role was extended in April 2007 to deal with complaints about all other agencies of the DWP.

A complaint can only be made to the ICE if you have already completed the complaints procedure of the particular agency concerned. This usually means you have had a response from the Chief Executive or a senior manager. Complaints can be made in writing or by telephoning (see Appendix 1). There is a form attached to the ICE leaflet, *Our Service and Standards,* that can be used. You need to give all relevant information, including the agency you are complaining about.

The ICE will first consider whether or not it can accept the complaint. If it can, it will attempt to settle the complaint by suggesting ways in which the agency concerned and the complainant can come to an agreement. If this fails, the ICE prepares a formal report, setting out how the complaint arose and how it believes it should be settled. The ICE considers whether there has been maladminstration; it cannot deal with matters of law or cases that are subject to judicial review or under appeal.

A complaint should be made no later than six months after the final response from the agency you are complaining about. Further details of the ICE are available at www.ind-case-exam.org.uk.

3. Complaining to the Revenue

If you want to complain about how the Revenue has dealt with your tax credit claim or with your national insurance credits or contributions, it is best to raise the complaint with the officer dealing with your case, or the named contact person on any letters you have received, to ask her/him to sort the matter out. This can be done verbally or in person, but it is advisable to put the complaint in writing. If you are still not satisfied you can write to the customer services manager at the Revenue. If s/he cannot resolve the matter satisfactorily, you can write to the director of that office (see Appendix 1). The customer services manager should provide you with the director's details. S/he should reply to your letter within seven days. The Revenue's complaints procedure is set out in its factsheet, *Complaints and Putting Things Right* (C/FS), available on its website (see Appendix 1). The Revenue's target for answering correspondence is 15 days.

If you are not happy with the Revenue's reply you can ask the independent Adjudicator to look into it and recommend appropriate action (see below).

4. Complaining to the Adjudicator

The Adjudicator's Office was set up in 1993 to investigate complaints about the way in which the Revenue deals with people's tax matters. It now also covers a number of areas, including complaints about tax credits and the Public Guardianship Office (see Appendix 1). The Adjudicator is similar in nature to the

Ombudsman (see p1184). Therefore, complaints can be made about delays, inappropriate staff behaviour, misleading advice or any other form of maladministration. The Adjudicator cannot, however, investigate disputes about matters of law. The Adjudicator will only investigate a complaint if you have first exhausted the Revenue's internal complaints procedure. A complaint should be made within six months of the final correspondence with the Revenue.[1]

The Adjudicator can recommend that compensation is paid, and the Revenue has undertaken to follow her/his recommendations in all but exceptional circumstances. If you are unhappy with the Adjudicator's response to your complaint you can ask your MP to put your complaint to the Ombudsman. As well as looking at your complaint about the Revenue, the Ombudsman may also look into the way in which the Adjudicator has investigated your complaint.[2] Further information about the Adjudicator can be found at www.adjudicatorsoffice.gov.uk

5. Complaining to a local authority

Most local authorities have a complaints procedure and you should ask for details of how this works. If there is no formal procedure, you should begin by writing to the supervisor of the person dealing with your claim, making it clear why you are dissatisfied. If you do not receive a satisfactory reply, you should take the matter up with someone more senior in the department and ultimately the principal officer. Send a copy of the letter to your ward councillor and to the councillor who chairs the council committee responsible for housing benefit/council tax benefit – local authority officers are always accountable to the councillors. If this does not produce results, or if the delay is causing you severe hardship, you should consider a complaint to the local government Ombudsman (see p1185) or court action.

Government departments also monitor local authorities, so you could contact your MP or write to the relevant minister – eg, the Secretary of State for Work and Pensions. If a minister believes there is a widespread problem with maladministration in the local authority, s/he can ask the Benefit Fraud Inspectorate to report on the authority's administration.

6. Complaining to the Tribunals Service

Complaints about the administration of your appeal

The Tribunals Service (TS) provides administrative support to appeal tribunals. If you have a complaint about the administration of your appeal you should complain to the TS. Initially you should raise your complaint with the person who has been dealing with your appeal. Her/his name and telephone number should be on all correspondence that you have received. If you are not satisfied with the response you receive to your complaint, you can ask to be referred to the customer services manager. If you remain dissatisfied, you should complain in writing to the Chief Executive of the TS.

Complaints about the conduct of panel members

If you are unhappy about the way in which you were treated by a tribunal member (eg, because s/he was discourteous or racist) you should raise the matter initially by writing to the regional chair of the region in which the tribunal was heard. The chair will then investigate the complaint. You should receive an acknowledgement of your complaint within five working days of the complaint being received. The regional chair will contact all of the people involved and then write, telling you whether or not the complaint is upheld and, if so, what action is to be taken.[3]

If the complaint is about the conduct of the regional chair it should be made to the President of the TS. If your complaint is about the President it should be made to the Lord Chancellor.

6. Using your MP

If you are not satisfied with the reply from the officers to whom you have written, the next step is to take up the matter with your MP.

Most MPs have 'surgeries' in their areas where they meet constituents to discuss problems. You can get the details from your local library or Citizens Advice Bureau. You can either go to the surgery or write to your MP with details of your complaint.

Your MP will probably want to write to the benefit authorities for an explanation of what has happened. If you are not satisfied with the reply, the next stage is to complain to the Ombudsman, via your MP.

7. Complaining to the Ombudsman

The system of the Ombudsman was introduced to the UK in 1967 with the appointment of the Parliamentary Commissioner for Administration (PCA). The role of the Ombudsman is to investigate complaints from members of the public who believe they have experienced an injustice because of maladministration by a government department.[4] Maladministration means poor administration and can include avoidable delays, failure to advise about appeal rights, refusal to answer reasonable questions or respond to correspondence, discourteousness, racism or sexism.

As the name suggests, the PCA is concerned with complaints about central government. In 1974 local government also became subject to the scrutiny of the Ombudsman with the creation of the Commissioner for Local Administration.[5]

The Ombudsman will not usually investigate a complaint unless you have first exhausted the internal complaints procedure. However, if the authority is not acting upon your complaint, or there are unreasonable delays, this delay may also form part of your complaint. The time limit for lodging a complaint with the Ombudsman is 12 months from the date you were notified of the matter complained about.

The Parliamentary Commissioner for Administration

The PCA deals with complaints about all central government departments. This includes the DWP and the Revenue as well as any agencies carrying out functions on behalf of these departments. It also includes both the Tribunals Service and the Office of the Social Security and Child Support Commissioners. In order to make a complaint it is necessary to write to your MP, who will then refer the complaint to the Ombudsman. The Ombudsman can only investigate complaints of maladministration and not complaints about entitlement, which should be dealt with by an appeal tribunal. The Ombudsman has extensive powers to look at documents held by the benefit authority on your claim. You may be interviewed to check any facts. The Ombudsman can recommend financial compensation if you have been unfairly treated or experienced a loss as a result of the maladministration.

The Commissioner for Local Administration

If you have tried to sort out your complaint with the local authority but you are still not satisfied with the outcome, you can apply to the Commissioner for Local Administration (more commonly known as the local government Ombudsman). The Ombudsman can investigate any cases of maladministration by local authorities, but not matters of entitlement, which can be dealt with by an appeal tribunal.

You may apply to the Ombudsman by writing to the appropriate local office (see Appendix 1). The Ombudsman has extensive powers to look at documents held by the local authority on your claim. You may be interviewed to check any facts. Straightforward cases can be dealt with in about three months. The Ombudsman can recommend financial compensation if you have been unfairly treated or experienced a loss as a result of the maladministration. A complaint may also make the authority review its procedures, which could benefit other claimants.

8. Compensation payments

You should expect prompt, courteous and efficient service from staff dealing with your claim. If you are dissatisfied with the way your claim has been administered you can seek compensation.

The DWP, the Revenue and local authorities sometimes pay compensation if you can show that you have lost out through their error or delay and the loss cannot be made good by a revision, supersession, appeal or backdating a claim (see Chapters 41 and 42). For instance, if you failed to claim carer's allowance because you were misled by the DWP and you could not have the benefit backdated for more than three months you could claim compensation.

The DWP uses a guide, *Guide to Financial Redress for Maladministration*, to help it decide when and how much compensation (known as an 'extra statutory' or *ex gratia* payment) should be paid. The guide is available from The Stationery Office or can be obtained from the DWP website (see Appendix 1). The Revenue has a code of practice (COP1), *Complaints and Putting Things Right* (C/FS) which sets out when it will make compensatory or consolatory payments.

You should ask for a payment equal to the money you have lost, but you could also ask for additional amounts to cover interest on arrears and extra expenses you had to pay out, and to compensate you for any hardship or distress experienced because of the mistake. Payments are discretionary so, in order to ensure payment, you should stress the DWP, Revenue or local authority error and the fact that you have suffered as a consequence of official negligence. If your loss was as a clear result of incorrect advice or negligence on the part of the agency, you may be able to bring a court action for damages.[6] You will need the help of an advice agency or solicitor to do this. Tactically, it is probably better to pursue a payment under this scheme before making a complaint to the Ombudsman. This is because if the Ombudsman does not uphold your complaint, the particular benefit authority is likely to resist making a compensation payment.

9. Delays

All benefit authorities should act promptly to process a claim. A failure to do so can lead to you making a complaint and possibly obtaining compensation.

Local authorities should process housing benefit claims within 14 days as long as you have given them all the information they have asked for.[7] Most do not. Complaining may be one way to get your claim processed more quickly, although threatening legal action may be more effective. The local government Ombudsman often orders compensation to be paid where there have been long delays which are not your fault.

The Revenue has no official targets for processing tax credit claims. It also has no guidelines for when it will pay compensation. However, many claimants have experienced long delays and errors in their claims and as a consequence have experienced financial hardship. In such cases, claimants should consider making a complaint to the Adjudicator (see p1182) and/or the Ombudsman (see p1184).

DWP offices have target times for dealing with claims, but they are not always able to meet these. If there is a long delay (eg, in assessing your entitlement or paying you benefit) you may be entitled to compensation if:[8]

- a significant reason for the delay was DWP error or delay; *and*
- the amount of benefit involved was more than £100; *and*
- the delay in payment was more than a set length of time (known as a 'delay indicator' – see below); *and*
- any compensation would be £10 or more.

Delay indicator	*Benefit*
Two months	Income support, pension credit and bereavement payment
Three months	Jobseeker's allowance, community care grants and budgeting loans
Four months	Incapacity benefit, bereavement allowance and widowed parent's allowance
Five months	Maternity allowance and social fund funeral expenses payments
Seven months	Attendance allowance and disability living allowance (two months if claimed under the special rules)
Eight months	Retirement pension
Nine months	Carer's allowance and renewal claims for disability living allowance
One year	Industrial injuries disablement benefit

You are not automatically awarded compensation, although the DWP should automatically consider whether it should be paid where you are owed arrears of benefit. You should still write to your local DWP office and ask. If you do not get a sympathetic response you could ask your MP to write on your behalf or to take up your case with the social security minister.

10. **Legal action**

It is not possible to sue a benefit authority for negligence in the way it decides your claim.[9] Instead, if a decision is wrong, you can seek a revision or supersession or appeal against it. However, it is possible to seek compensation through the courts if there has been:

- misadvice – ie, if an employee of a benefit authority or the Tribunals Service gives wrong advice which leads to some financial loss for you;
- unpaid benefit – ie, if your benefit claim has been determined but you have not received payment;

- a breach of human rights.

Although it is possible to seek compensation through the courts it should never be the first course of action and should only ever be considered after seeking legal advice.

If a benefit authority refuses to process your claim you may have grounds for a judicial review. Contact CPAG for further details.

Notes

4. **Complaining to the Adjudicator**
   1 For further details, see CPAG's *Welfare Rights Bulletin* 180
   2 See also CPAG's *Welfare Rights Bulletin* 180

6. **Complaining to the Tribunals Service**
   3 President's Protocol 2

7. **Complaining to the Ombudsman**
   4 s5(1)(a) Parliamentary Commissioner Act 1967
   5 ss23 and 24 Local Government Act 1974

8. **Compensation payments**
   6 *Haringey LBC v Cotter* [1996] 29 HLR 682 (CA)

9. **Delays**
   7 Reg 89(2) HB Regs; reg 70(2) HB(SPC) Regs
   8 DWP leaflet, *Guide to Financial Redress for Maladministration*

10. **Legal action**
   9 *Jones v Department of Employment* [1989] QB 1 (CA)

Part 6

Tax credits

Chapter 47

Introduction: tax credits

This chapter covers:

1. Tax credits

You may be entitled to one or both of:

- child tax credit; *and*
- working tax credit.

These tax credits are administered by Her Majesty's Revenue and Customs (referred to in this *Handbook* as the Revenue).

The rules are mainly separate from the benefit rules that are described elsewhere in this *Handbook*, although tax credits can be paid with most benefits. This chapter outlines the basic rules for tax credits and the way they affect benefits. Detailed rules on other matters are described in the chapters that follow this one.

Child tax credit[1]

This is an income-based credit for low-income and middle-income families who are in or out of work and who have responsibility for a child(ren) under 16, or under 20 if in full-time non-advanced education or approved training (or enrolled on or accepted to undertake approved training) – see p61 for details. See Chapter 48 for more details.

Working tax credit[2]

This is an income-based credit for working adults. To be eligible to claim, you or your partner must:

- work 16 hours or more a week; *and*
  - have responsibility for a child; *or*
  - have a disability that puts you at a disadvantage in getting a job; *or*
  - qualify for a 50-plus element (see p1239); *or*

- work 30 hours or more a week; *and*
  - be 25 or over.

See Chapter 49 for more details.

2. **Impact on benefits**

Benefits – general

Tax credits can be paid with the benefits described in this *Handbook*, including child benefit, income support (IS) and income-based jobseeker's allowance (JSA). Child benefit is ignored as income when calculating entitlement to tax credits. However, see Chapter 52 for how benefits count as income when calculating your entitlement to tax credits.

Means-tested benefits

Income support and income-based jobseeker's allowance

From 6 April 2004 the amounts for children in IS and income-based JSA are not included in new claims, leaving only the amounts in respect of adults and housing costs (see p709). If you are in this situation, you will have to claim child tax credit (CTC) as well as child benefit in order to get money for them.

You may be entitled to both CTC and IS or income-based JSA if you are not working 16 hours (or 24 in the case of a partner) or more a week. If you claim both CTC and IS or income-based JSA, CTC does not count as income for these benefits from 6 April 2004.[3] Working tax credit (WTC) counts as income at all times.

You only have child amounts included in your IS or income-based JSA if your current claim included a child before 6 April 2004 and you have not yet been awarded CTC. But see the note in CPAG's *Welfare Rights Bulletin* 186 p12 for some possible doubts about this. The DWP attempted to clarify the rules from 8 September 2005.[4] People who still have child amounts included in their IS or income-based JSA will have the child part of their claim transferred to CTC at a date to be announced.[5] At the point the child part of the claim is transferred to CTC, the IS or income-based JSA will cease to include amounts for children. While an award of IS or income-based JSA includes child amounts, any child benefit you receive counts in full as income for IS and income-based JSA (with a £10.50 disregard if you are getting child benefit for a child under one).[6]

Pension credit

If you are aged 60 or over and are responsible for a child(ren) you will have to claim CTC as well as pension credit (PC). Only WTC, not CTC, counts as income when claiming PC.[7] WTC does not count as qualifying income for the purposes of calculating any savings credit to which you may be entitled (see Chapter 18).[8]

Housing benefit and council tax benefit

Housing benefit (HB) and council tax benefit (CTB) continue to include amounts for children. You can claim HB and CTB and tax credits at the same time. The local authority is not allowed to take unclaimed or unawarded tax credits into account as income.[9] CTC and WTC count as income for HB and CTB and only from the date they are awarded. However, CTC does not count as income for calculating HB and CTB for those aged 60 or over.

If your award of tax credits includes the 30-hour or 50-plus elements of WTC (or would include the 50-plus element were you to apply for it), or the disability or severe disability element of WTC, £16.05 of your earnings is disregarded when calculating your HB and CTB.[10]

Your HB and CTB are normally based on the amount of tax credits you actually receive. Also, any arrears of tax credits are treated as capital[11] – the capital is ignored for 52 weeks.[12]

If your tax credit is reduced in order to recover an overpayment of tax credits, your HB/CTB entitlement is based on that reduced amount (see p858).

Non-means-tested benefits

Child benefit can be paid in addition to CTC and WTC. It is ignored as income for the purposes of calculating CTC and WTC.[13]

Other non-means-tested benefits to which you are entitled can be paid in addition to any tax credits you are getting. Getting certain non-means-tested benefits can help you qualify for, or increase an award of, WTC or CTC. However, see Chapter 52 for how these benefits may count as income when claiming tax credits.

Example

Merlene is in receipt of disability living allowance (DLA). She starts work for more than 16 hours week. She may be entitled to WTC as a person with a disability and CTC and child benefit if she has responsibility for a child(ren). If she has a mortgage for her main home she will not qualify for any IS housing costs (as she works over 16 hours a week and so is not entitled to IS), but she might get some CTB.

If she is in rented accommodation she may qualify for HB and/or CTB. She will still get her DLA, as long as she continues to satisfy the conditions of entitlement.

For more details of which benefits and/or tax credits you should claim see p5.

Increases for child dependants

CTC replaced increases for child dependants previously available with some non-means-tested benefits from April 2003 (see p691).[14] However, you can continue to get an increase if you were entitled to an increase for a child dependant on

5 April 2003 (or have claimed an increase after 6 April 2003 and your entitlement is backdated to include 5 April).

This 'transitional protection' will be lost once your entitlement to an increase for a child dependant ceases (or your increase stops being paid for 58 days or more because your partner's earnings exceed the earnings limit). If the benefit you are paid the increase with is terminated, your increase will also stop. You keep your transitional protection, however, as long as you reclaim the benefit and the increase within three months of the date the benefit is re-awarded on revision, supersession or appeal.[15]

3. **Passported benefits**

Tax credits may provide you with an automatic entitlement – a 'passport' – to the following:

- Sure Start maternity grant (see p513);[16]
- social fund funeral expenses payment (see p515);[17]
- free school meals (see p15);[18]
- health benefits (see p163);[19]
- help under the Healthy Start scheme (see p168).

Notes

1. **Tax credits**

1 s8 TCA 2002; regs 3-5 CTC Regs
2 s10 TCA 2002; reg 4 WTC(EMR) Regs

2. **Impact on benefits**

3 Regs 1 and 7 SS(WTCCTC)(CA) Regs
4 SS(TC)A Regs
5 House of Commons *Hansard* 6 December 2006, col 15WS
6 Regs 7(6) and 8(5) SS(WTCCTC)(CA) Regs
7 s15(1) SPCA 2002
8 Reg 9 SPC Regs
9 **HB** Reg 42(2)(f) and (g) HB Regs
CTB Reg 32(2)(f) and (g) CTB Regs
10 **HB** Sch 4 para 17(3)(c) HB regs; Sch 4 para 9(3)(c) HB(SPC) Regs
CTB Sch 3 para 16(3)(c) CTB Regs; Sch 2 para 9(3)(c) CTB(SPC) Regs
11 **HB** Reg 46(9) HB Regs
CTB Reg 36(9) CTB Regs
12 **HB** Sch 6 para 9(1)(e) HB Regs; Sch 6 paras 18 and 21(2)(h) and (l) HB(SPC) Regs
CTB Sch 5 para 9(1)(e) CTB Regs; Sch 4 paras 18 and 21(2)(h) and (l) CTB(SPC) Regs
13 Reg 7(3) TC(DCI) Regs
14 s1(3)(e) TCA 2002
15 Art 3 TCA(No.3)O

3. **Passported benefits**

16 Reg 5(1) SFM&FE Regs
17 Reg 7(1)(a)(i) SFM&FE Regs
18 s512ZB(4) Education Act 1996; s53(3) Education (Scotland) Act 1980
19 NHS(TERC) Regs; NHS (TERC)(S) Regs; NHS(CDA) Regs; NHS(CDA)(S) Regs; NHS(CDA)(W) Regs; NHS(DC) Regs; NHS(DC)(S) Regs; NHS(OCP) Regs; NHS(OCP)(S) Regs; WF Regs

Chapter 48

Child tax credit

This chapter covers:

Child tax credit (CTC) is paid to families with children (this includes some qualifying young people). It is paid whether or not you are in full-time paid work. CTC does not count as income for income support, income-based jobseeker's allowance or pension credit purposes and can be paid in addition to those benefits.

CTC is administered by the Revenue.

You do not have to have paid national insurance contributions to qualify for CTC.

1. Who can claim child tax credit

You qualify for child tax credit (CTC) if:[1]

- you (or your partner) have at least one dependent child for whom you are responsible (see p1196);
- your income is sufficiently low (see Chapter 52);
- you are 'present' and 'ordinarily resident' in the UK. You can be treated as present and ordinarily resident in the UK in some circumstances – eg, if you are temporarily away. You can be treated as not being in the UK if you claim CTC for the first time on or after 1 May 2004 and do not have a 'right to reside' here. See Chapter 60 for further information;
- you are not a 'person subject to immigration control' (see Chapter 60).

2. **The rules about your age**

You (and your partner) must be aged at least 16 to make a claim for child tax credit (CTC), but there is no upper age limit.[2] If you are under 16, someone else (eg, your parent or the adult with whom you normally live) may be able to claim CTC for you *and* your child (see p1198).

3. **Who is included in your claim**

You can only claim child tax credit (CTC) if you are responsible for one or more children. Some qualifying young people continue to count as children until they are 20 – see below.

If you are a **member of a couple**, you must claim CTC jointly with your partner.[3] If you are not a member of a couple, you claim for yourself.[4] For information about who counts as a couple for tax credit purposes, see p1211. The rules are the same as for working tax credit. See Chapter 53 for further information about joint claims for CTC.

If you are a couple:

- when working out how much CTC you get, your partner's income is added to yours (see Chapter 52);
- CTC is paid to the person who is the main carer for your children (see p1280).

Children

To qualify for CTC, you must be 'responsible' for a child or qualifying young person.[5] The terms 'child' or 'children' in this chapter include these qualifying young people. You do not have to be the child's parent. You could, for example, be the grandparent, sister or brother. See p1198 for when you count as responsible for a child and p1199 for when you do not count as responsible.

Who counts as a child

Someone counts as a child until the 1st of September following her/his 16th birthday.[6] In some circumstances, a young person aged under 20 also counts as a child. The Revenue refers to her/him as a **'qualifying young person'**.

A young person counts as a child during any period from the 1st of September following her/his 16th birthday when s/he is:[7]

- under 20 and in full-time non-advanced education (see p1197) or 'approved training' (see p61) or has been enrolled or accepted to undertake approved training. This does not apply if s/he is getting the education or training because of her/his own employment. The education or training must have begun before s/he reached 19, or s/he must have been enrolled or accepted to undertake the education or training before that age;

- under 18, has ceased full-time education or 'approved training' (see p61) and it is not more than 20 weeks since s/he did so. S/he must notify the Revenue within three months of ceasing full-time education or 'approved training' that s/he has registered for work or training with the Careers or Connexions Service. This rule can apply again if s/he goes back into full-time education or 'approved training' and ceases again.

When working out whether a young person counts as in full-time education or 'approved training', the Revenue ignores:[8]

- an interruption of up to six months, whether it began before or after the young person turned 16; *and*
- an interruption of any length which is due to the young person's illness or disability 'of the mind or body'.

This only applies if the Revenue thinks it is reasonable to do so.

You should let the Revenue know if the above applies to ensure that you continue to get CTC for your child.

Full-time non-advanced education[9]

'**Education**' means education at a recognised educational establishment or elsewhere, if the education is recognised by the Secretary of State, the Revenue or the Scottish Ministers. Education counts as **full time** if it is for more than 12 hours a week, on average, in normal term time including instruction or tuition, supervised study, exams, practical work and experiments or projects provided for in the curriculum but excluding meal breaks and unsupervised study.

For examples of what counts as **non-advanced** education, see p61.

When a young person does not count as a child

A young person cannot count as a child during any period from the 1st of September following her/his 16th birthday:

- in which s/he has ceased full-time education or 'approved training' but has not registered for work or training with the Careers or Connexions Service (see above); *or*
- which includes a week in which, having ceased full-time education or 'approved training', s/he is in full-time paid work.[10] This means work of 24 hours or more per week. For information about:
  - what counts as paid work, see p1224;
  - how the hours are calculated, see p1224;
  - situations when the young person is not treated as in full-time paid work, see p1230.

  The rules for what counts as full-time paid work are the same as for working tax credit; *or*

- which includes a period in which s/he gets income support or income-based jobseeker's allowance in her/his own right.[11] **Note:** you might not count as *responsible* for a child 16 or over if s/he gets CTC or incapacity benefit in her/his own right (see p1199).

Being responsible for a child

For tax credits purposes, a child can only count as the responsibility of one claimant (or joint-claim couple).[12] You are treated as 'responsible' for a child if:[13]

- s/he normally lives with you. The Revenue calls this the 'normally living with test'; *or*
- you have the main responsibility for her/him. The Revenue calls this the 'main responsibility test'. This test only applies if you and another person (or couple) make competing claims for CTC for the same child.

If a child for whom you are treated as responsible has a child of her/his own who normally lives with her/him, you also count as responsible for that child.[14] This does not apply if your child is 16 or over and is awarded CTC in her/his own right.[15]

The 'normally living with test'

The rules do not define when a child counts as 'normally living with' you. The Revenue says it means that your child 'regularly, usually, typically' lives with you and that this allows for temporary or occasional absences.[16] So if your child counts as normally living with you, s/he should also count as doing so even if s/he is away from home – eg, because s/he is away at school or for a temporary period on holiday or in hospital. You can argue that a child is normally living with you if s/he spends more time with you than with anyone else.[17]

Your child can count as normally living with you even if s/he also lives with someone else or only lives with you for part of the week, and lives for part of the week with someone else (eg, your child's other parent). This means that more than one person could claim CTC for the child. However, CTC can only be paid to one claimant (or joint-claim couple). If more than one claims, see below.

The 'main responsibility test'

Even though you may be sharing responsibility for a child and s/he normally lives with you for part of the week, you might not qualify for CTC because the rules might not treat you as having the main responsibility. There is currently no provision for allowing CTC to be split between parents where a child divides her/his time between their homes. However, if you share actual responsibility for the child (eg, you share responsibility with your ex-partner) and are a 'substantial minority carer' (ie, you have the child with you for at least 104 nights a year), then following a court decision it may be arguable that you should be regarded as responsible for the child.[18] Seek advice and see CPAG's *Welfare Rights Bulletins* 185 pp9–10 and 194 pp5–6 for further information.

Where you (and your partner, if you have one) and at least one other person (or couple) with whom the child also normally lives claim CTC for the same child, you only qualify for CTC for the child if you can show *you* have the 'main responsibility' for her/him. The main responsibility test applies if:[19]

- your child normally lives with *both* you *and*:
  - at least one other person in another household (eg, with you and with the child's other parent from whom you have separated); *or*
  - someone who is not your partner in the same household (eg, with you and with the child's grandparent where you live together).

  It also applies if it is a combination of these situations. 'Household' is not defined. See p703 for ideas about what might count as a household; *and*
- you and at least one of the other people with whom your child normally lives claim CTC.

You and the other CTC claimant(s) can decide which of you should count as having 'main responsibility'. If you cannot agree, a decision maker decides.[20] You can challenge the decision (see p1200).

'Main responsibility' is not defined in the rules. The decision maker is likely to consider things like:[21]

- whether there are any court orders in existence that set out where your child is to live or who is to care for her/him;
- how many days of the week a child lives with you compared with the number of days s/he lives elsewhere;
- who pays for your child's food and clothes and who is responsible for giving her/him pocket money;
- where your child's clothes and toys are kept;
- who is the main contact or registered address for the school or college, nursery or child care provider;
- who does the child's laundry;
- who looks after your child when s/he is ill and who arranges appointments to see a doctor.

If you share responsibility for your child(ren) equally with the other CTC claimant(s), it may be difficult to decide who has the *main* responsibility. In this case you can argue that the decision maker should regard you as having the main responsibility if you would be entitled to more CTC than the other claimant(s).[22]

When you do not count as responsible for a child

Even if a child normally lives with you or, where the main responsibility test applies, you have the 'main responsibility' for her/him, you do *not* count as responsible for the child and cannot claim CTC for her/him during any period when s/he is:[23]

- provided with or placed in accommodation and the accommodation or the child's maintenance is funded wholly or partly by the local authority under s23 Children Act 1989, s26 Children (Scotland) Act 1995 or out of other public funds. This includes children staying with foster carers who get foster payments for them from the local authority.
  This does not apply if your child is staying in certain forms of residential accommodation and this is only necessary because your child has a disability or because her/his health would be significantly impaired or further impaired if s/he was not staying in the accommodation. You must have been treated as responsible for her/him immediately before s/he went into the accommodation;[24] *or*
- being looked after by a local authority and has been placed with you because you want to adopt her/him. This only applies if the local authority is paying for the child's accommodation or maintenance or both under s23 Children Act 1989 or s26 Children (Scotland) Act 1995; *or*
- in custody. This only applies if your child:
  – is serving a life or unlimited sentence; *or*
  – is serving a term of more than four months; *or*
  – has been detained 'during Her Majesty's pleasure'; *or*
- at least 16 and is awarded CTC in her/his own right for a child for whom s/he is responsible; *or*
- at least 16 and receives working tax credit in her/his own right (including in a joint claim); *or*
- at least 16 and entitled to and receiving incapacity benefit (IB) in her/his own right. There were transitional rules where a child was getting IB before 6 April 2004. See p1204 of CPAG's *Welfare Benefits and Tax Credits Handbook* 2007/08 for details.

Note: a young person does not count as a child if s/he gets income support or income-based jobseeker's allowance in her/his own right (see p1197).

Challenging a decision

The Revenue might say that:

- your child does not normally live with you or that you are not the person with main responsibility for your child so you are not entitled to CTC;
- someone else has claimed CTC for your child(ren) and now satisfies the 'main reponsibility test' when you have been getting CTC for the same child(ren). In this case, your entitlement to CTC ends and you may have been overpaid.

If you think a decision is wrong and it affects your tax credits, you can appeal.[25] See Chapter 57 for more information about revisions and appeals.

It is possible that the DWP, local authority and the Revenue might reach different conclusions about whether your child(ren) can be included in your claims. If so, you should appeal *all* the decisions with which you disagree.

Whether or not you appeal, you should apply immediately for any other benefits or tax credits for which you might qualify. You may be able to get a social fund crisis loan in the meantime (see p503).

Change of circumstances

There are changes of circumstances that you must report to the Revenue (see p1288). If you do not do so, you could incur a recoverable overpayment and a penalty. Those that relate to couples and children (including qualifying young people) are:[26]

- you were claiming as a single person and you become part of a couple; *or*
- you were claiming as a couple and you cease to be a member of a couple; *or*
- you or your partner lose your right to reside in the UK or no longer count as ordinarily resident here; *or*
- you or your partner are no longer treated as responsible for a child; *or*
- a child for whom you or your partner are responsible dies; *or*
- you or your partner notifed the Revenue that your child was expected to become a qualifying young person (eg, by staying on at school to do 'A' levels) but s/he does not; *or*
- a qualifying young person for whom you or your partner are responsible ceases to be one other than by turning 20.

Note: the first three of the above changes also end your entitlement to CTC and you have to make a fresh claim as a couple or single person as the case may be.

If you are entitled to CTC for a child (or would have been had you made a claim) and the child dies, you continue to be entitled to CTC for the child for eight weeks immediately following the death (or to the date your child would have turned 20 if this is earlier).[27] After that period, you may still continue to qualify for CTC – ie, if you are responsible for any other child(ren) and still satisfy the means test.

There are other changes of circumstances connected with your child(ren) you may wish to report – eg, to enable your award of CTC to be increased. These include circumstances where a child:

- starts normally living with you or becomes your 'main responsibility'; *or*
- returns to full-time non-advanced education or gets a place on an 'approved training' programme.

4. The amount of child tax credit

The amount of child tax credit (CTC) you get depends on:

- your maximum CTC. This is made up of a combination of 'elements' (see below);
- how much income you have; *and*
- the 'income threshold figure' that applies to you.

The elements and thresholds can be increased every April. If you do not qualify for CTC currently, you might qualify if the rates go up.

If you are on income support, income-based jobseeker's allowance or pension credit

Entitlement to income support, income-based jobseeker's allowance or pension credit acts as an automatic passport to maximum CTC.[28] You, therefore, do not need to work out your income or capital. In these circumstances, CTC = maximum CTC.

If you are not on income support, income-based jobseeker's allowance or pension credit

- **Step one:** work out your 'relevant period' (see pp1233 and 1245).
- **Step two:** work out your maximum entitlement for the relevant period. This involves working out your maximum CTC for your relevant period (see p1245).
- **Step three:** work out your relevant income (see p1245).
- **Step four:** compare your income with the 'income threshold figure' for the relevant period – currently £15,575.[29] If your maximum amount of tax credits includes any element of working tax credit as well as elements of CTC, an 'income threshold figure' of £6,420 is used.[30] See p1246 for further information.
- **Step five:** calculate CTC entitlement for the relevant period (see p1246). If your income is less than the 'income threshold figure', CTC = maximum CTC. If your income exceeds the 'income threshold figure', your maximum CTC is reduced by 39 per cent of the excess. **Note:** this was 37 per cent in claims before the 2008/09 tax year.

  Note: your maximum CTC is not reduced below the level of the family element (including the baby element if you are entitled to this) unless your annual income is higher than £50,000.

For full details of the calculation, see Chapter 51.

Maximum child tax credit

Your maximum CTC is calculated by adding together all of the elements that apply to you.[31] These are:[32]

- child element (£2,085 a year) – one for each child;
- disability element (£2,540 a year) – one for each child who qualifies;
- severe disability element (£1,020 a year) – one for each child who qualifies;
- family element (£1,090 including the baby element a year; £545 if not).

For details of how you qualify for the above elements, see Chapter 51.

5. Claims and backdating

This section gives an outline of the rules about claims for child tax credit (CTC). For more information about claiming and how your award can be renewed at the end of the year, see Chapter 53.

Making a claim

Your first claim for CTC must be made in writing on the approved or authorised form. You use the same form for CTC and for working tax credit (WTC). See p1274 for further information.

You should send the completed form directly to the Tax Credit Office (TCO) of the Revenue in the pre-paid envelope provided with the claim form. The claim form can also be sent, if necessary, to any Jobcentre Plus office, DWP office or Revenue enquiry centre office.[33] Keep a copy of your claim form in case queries arise. You can amend or withdraw your claim at any time before the claim has been decided.[34]

Information to support your claim

When you claim CTC, you must satisfy the national insurance (NI) number requirement. In most cases this means you must provide your NI number, as well as your partner's. You may also be asked to provide proof of your identity and information to support your claim.[35] See p1275 for further details. It is important that you provide all the information required. If you do not do so, a decision might not be made on your claim.

When you claim CTC you must provide:

- your child benefit reference number. This can be found on your child benefit order book or on any letters about child benefit that you have received;
- details of your (and your partner's) income for the previous tax year (see p1253);
- details of a bank or building society account into which CTC can be paid. If you do not have an account, you need to open one within eight weeks of making your claim. See pp1276 and 1280 for further information.

If you are also claiming WTC there is other information you must also provide (see p1215). The Revenue might need further information before it makes a decision on your claim. See p1276 for details of the time you must be given to provide the information and what happens if you fail to do so.

Who should claim

If you are a member of a couple, you must make a joint claim with your partner. If you are not a member of a couple, you claim for yourself. For information about who counts as a couple for tax credit purposes, see p1211. If, exceptionally, you are unable to claim for yourself, the decision maker may authorise someone else (eg, a friend or relative) to act on your behalf.

When to claim

The general rule is that your claim runs from the date it is received by the Revenue.[36] You cannot make a claim in advance of the tax year for which you are claiming. See p1204 for information on how and when claims can be backdated.

Awards of CTC are always based on annual income (see p1253). The Revenue bases the initial award of CTC on your (and your partner's) *previous* tax year's income. If you think your income for the current tax year is likely, eventually, to be low enough for you to qualify for CTC (for instance, you know your income is going to fall or has fallen), you may wish to consider making a claim (including a request for your claim to be backdated if relevant), even if you know you will be given what is known as a 'nil award'. This protects your position because you can then ask the Revenue to amend the award on the basis of a change in your income (seep1254). The amended award would then run from your original date of claim (or the date to which your claim was backdated). However, see pp1290–1292 before deciding what to do.

How your claim is dealt with

Once you have claimed CTC and provided all the information required, the Revenue makes a decision on your claim. You receive an award notice telling you how much CTC you are entitled to and when payment will start.

Backdating your claim

It is important to claim in time. A claim for CTC can usually only be backdated for a maximum of three months.[37] You only need to show that you qualified for CTC during that period. Unlike for most means-tested benefits, you do not have to show any reasons for your delay. See p1281 for further information.

Note: there is an exception to this rule if you were not paid CTC (ie, you were given a 'nil award') because your child did not receive disability living allowance at the time of your claim. Under this rule your CTC can be backdated more than three months.

Renewal awards

At the end of the tax year in which you claimed CTC, you (and your partner if you are a member of couple), receive a 'final notice' from the Revenue asking you to confirm that your income and/or your household circumstances are as stated for the previous tax year (see p1285). The Revenue then makes a final decision, based on your actual income during the tax year. It decides whether you were entitled to CTC and if so, the amount of your award. This is known as the 'end of year review'. The Revenue also uses the information about your income and household circumstances for the last tax year to renew your award for the next tax year.[38]

Example

Joe is a lone parent who is in full-time paid work. He claims CTC in October 2007. His initial award is based on his income during the 2006/07 tax year. In May 2008, he is sent a final notice. He sends the Revenue details of his actual income for 2007/08. The Revenue uses this information to work out whether his CTC award was correct. Joe's actual income for 2007/08 is now the previous year's income in respect of Joe's CTC claim for 2008/09. The Revenue uses this income to make an initial decision to award Joe CTC and set payments for 2008/09.

6. Getting paid

This section gives an outline of the rules about payment of child tax credit (CTC). For more information about getting paid, see p1280.

Payments of CTC are usually made directly into the bank or building society account or post office card account of whoever is deemed to be the main carer of your children (see p1280). CTC can be paid into the account every week or every four weeks, whichever is more convenient for you.[39] However, you might be paid by cheque while your account arrangements are finalised.

If your award of CTC (or the combination of CTC and working tax credit (WTC)) is £2 a week or less, it is paid in a single lump sum into your account to cover the whole year.[40] **Note:** if your entitlement to CTC (or the combination of CTC and WTC) is less than £26 for the whole of the tax year, no award is made and you are not paid at all.[41]

Length of award

Your award of CTC runs from the date your claim is received by the Revenue (or from the date to which your claim can be backdated) to the end of the tax year.[42] However, changes in your circumstances can be taken into account during the tax year. In some cases, you *must* report changes of circumstances. See p1206 and Chapter 54 for details.

Delays and complaints

If payment of your CTC is delayed, or you wish to complain about how your claim has been dealt with, see p1182. You might be able to claim compensation (see p1186). If the delay is causing hardship, ask the Revenue to make 'immediate payments'.

Change of circumstances

Your award of CTC is made on the basis of your (and your partner's) previous year's income and your personal circumstances on the date of your claim. If your current year's income or your personal circumstances change, your award of CTC can be amended. Remember the following.

- There are some changes you *must* report to the Revenue (see p1288). If you fail to do so within one month, you might be given a financial penalty. Some of these end your entitlement to CTC and you have to make a fresh claim.
- Unless it is a change that you must report, it is optional to report changes that affect your maximum entitlement to CTC – eg, when you have a baby or one of your children stops getting disability living allowance (DLA) (see p1289) – but see below. However, changes that increase your maximum entitlement to CTC can generally only be backdated three months from when you notify the Revenue. Changes that decrease your entitlement always take effect from the date of the change so an overpayment can occur if you delay.
- There is a special rule that allows an increase in your entitlement to CTC to be backdated *more* than three months if you were waiting to hear about a DLA claim for your child when you claimed CTC, this has now been awarded and the disability or severe disability elements should now be included in your CTC entitlement. You must notify the Revenue within three months of the date the DLA is awarded (see p1290).
- It is optional to report changes in your income (see p1290). These are always taken into account at the end of the tax year, but you may want to consider reporting these sooner to avoid an overpayment or underpayment of CTC.

Overpayments and fraud

If you are overpaid CTC, you may have to repay it. The rules on overpayments are covered in Chapter 55. In some cases, interest can be added to the overpayment. For information on fraud see Chapter 56. In some cases, you can be given a financial penalty.

7. Challenging a child tax credit decision

You can apply for a revision of, or appeal against, many child tax credit decisions (see Chapter 57).

8. **Tax, tax credits and benefits**

Child tax credit (CTC) is not taxable.

Tax credits

If you are in full-time paid work, you might qualify for working tax credit (WTC). CTC is not taken into account as income for WTC.

Means-tested benefits

If you (and your partner) are not in full-time paid work, you might qualify for income support (IS) or income-based jobseeker's allowance (JSA). If you are 60 or over, whether or not you (or your partner) are in full-time paid work, you might qualify for pension credit (PC). CTC is not taken into account as income for IS, income-based JSA or PC.

If you pay rent or council tax, you might qualify for housing benefit (HB) or council tax benefit (CTB). Unless you are on IS or income-based JSA or are 60 or over, the amount of CTC you are paid *is* taken into account as income for HB and CTB.

If you get arrears of CTC, these count as capital and can be disregarded in some circumstances (see pp921 and 940).

Non-means-tested benefits

CTC can be paid in addition to any non-means-tested benefits to which you (or your partner) are entitled, including child benefit. See Chapter 52 for which of these benefits may be taken into account as income for CTC. If your child qualifies for disability living allowance, you might qualify for the disability or severe disability elements of CTC.

Passports and other sources of help

If you are entitled to CTC you may also qualify for:

- health benefits such as free prescriptions (see Chapter 9). You do not have to satisfy the means test if you are getting CTC and your gross annual income is below a set amount (see p163); *and*
- education benefits such as free school meals. You do not have to satisfy the means test if you are getting CTC (but not WTC) and your gross annual income is below £15,575.

You may also qualify for a Sure Start maternity grant or a social fund funeral expenses payment (see Chapter 22).

Notes

1. **Who can claim child tax credit**
 1 ss3(3) and (7), 8 and 42 TCA 2002; regs 3-5 CTC Regs; reg 3 TC(R) Regs; reg 3 TC(Imm) Regs

2. **The rules about your age**
 2 s3(3) TCA 2002

3. **Who is included in your claim**
 3 s3(3)(a) and (5A) TCA 2002; reg 2(1) CTC Regs; CTC/3864/2004; CSTC/724/2006
 4 s3(3)(b) TCA 2002
 5 s8(1) TCA 2002
 6 s8(3) TCA 2002; regs 2(1) and 4 CTC Regs
 7 s8(4) TCA 2002; regs 2, definition of 'qualifying young person' and 5(1)-(3A) CTC Regs
 8 Reg 5(7) CTC Regs
 9 Regs 2(1), definition of 'advanced education' and 5(5) and (6) CTC Regs
 10 Regs 2, definition of 'remunerative work' and 5(4)(a) CTC Regs
 11 Reg 5(4)(c) CTC Regs
 12 Reg 3(1) rule 2.2 CTC Regs
 13 s8(2) TCA 2002; reg 3(1) rules 1 and 2 CTC Regs
 14 Reg 3(2) CTC Regs
 15 Reg 3(1) rules 4 and 4.1 Case D CTC Regs
 16 para 02201 TCTM, 'Normally lives with you'
 17 CFC/1537/1995
 18 *Hockenjos v Secretary of State for Social Security* [2004] EWCA Civ 1749, 21 December 2004 (*Times Law Report* 4 January 2005), applies only to JSA. However, it may support arguments concerning CTC and WTC based on the Human Rights Act.
 19 Reg 3(1) rules 2, 2.1 and 2.2 CTC Regs
 20 Reg 3 rules 3 and 3.1 CTC Regs
 21 para 02201 TCTM, 'Shared responsibility'
 22 CTC/4390/2004
 23 Reg 3(1) rule 4.1 CTC Regs
 24 Reg 3(1) rule 4.2 CTC Regs; reg 9 CB Regs
 25 CTC/2090/2004
 26 s3(4) and (7) TCA 2002; reg 21 TC(CN) Regs
 27 s8(5) TCA 2002; reg 6 CTC Regs

4. **The amount of child tax credit**
 28 ss7(2)and 13 TCA 2002; reg 4 TC(ITDR) Regs
 29 Reg 3(3) TC(ITDR) Regs
 30 Reg 3(2) TC(ITDR) Regs
 31 s9(2) TCA 2002
 32 Reg 7 CTC Regs

5. **Claims and backdating**
 33 Regs 2 and 5 TC(CN) Regs
 34 Reg 5(7) TC(CN) Regs; R(IS) 3/05
 35 Reg 5(3)-(6) TC(CN) Regs
 36 s5(2) TCA 2002
 37 Reg 7 TC(CN) Regs
 38 Regs 11 and 12 TC(CN) Regs

6. **Getting paid**
 39 Regs 8 and 13 TC(PC) Regs
 40 Reg 10 TC(PC) Regs
 41 Reg 9 TC(ITDR) Regs
 42 s5(2) TCA 2002

Chapter 49

Working tax credit

This chapter covers:

Working tax credit (WTC) is paid to low-paid workers. It tops up your wages if you are in 'remunerative work'. In this *Handbook* this is referred to as full-time paid work.

WTC is administered by the Revenue.

You do not have to have paid national insurance contributions to qualify for WTC.

1. Who can claim working tax credit

You qualify for working tax credit (WTC) if:[1]

- you (or your partner) are in full-time paid work (see below);
- your income is sufficiently low (see Chapter 52);
- you are 'present' and 'ordinarily resident' in the UK. You can be treated as present and ordinarily resident in the UK in some circumstances – eg, if you are temporarily away. See Chapter 60 for further information;
- you are not a 'person subject to immigration control' (see Chapter 60).

Full-time paid work

You count as in full-time paid work if:[2]

- you (or your partner) are responsible for a child and you work at least 16 hours a week (see p1196 for who counts as a child);

- you have a physical or mental disability that puts you at a disadvantage in getting a job, you qualify for a disability element (see p1237) and you work at least 16 hours a week;
- you are aged 25 years or over and you work at least 30 hours a week;
- you (or your partner) are at least 50, work at least 16 hours a week and qualify for a 50-plus element of WTC (see p1239).

In addition, you must be actually working at the date of your claim or have accepted an offer of work which is expected to start within seven days from the date of your claim, and the work must be expected to last for at least four weeks.

In some circumstances you can be treated as in full-time paid work when you are not, or treated as not being in full-time paid work even if you are. For further information about full-time paid work, see Chapter 50.

2. The rules about your age

You (and your partner) must be aged at least 16 to make a claim for working tax credit.[3] There is no upper age limit.

3. Who is included in your claim

If you are a member of a couple, you must claim working tax credit (WTC) jointly with your partner.[4] If you are not a member of a couple, you claim for yourself.[5] For information about who counts as a couple for tax credit purposes, see below. WTC includes elements for you and your partner and for the special needs of either of you (see Chapter 51). When working out how much WTC you get, your partner's income is added to yours (see Chapter 52). See Chapter 53 for further information about joint claims for WTC.

If you are responsible for one or more children:

- you (or your partner) need only do paid work of 16 hours a week to qualify for WTC (see Chapter 50);
- if you are a couple and one of you works at least 16 hours a week, your hours of work can be added to those of your partner to enable you to qualify for the 30-hour element (see p1237);
- you (and your partner) might qualify for the childcare element of WTC if you pay for childcare (see p1240).

See p1196 for who counts as a child. The rules are the same as for child tax credit (CTC).[6] Some young people can continue to count as children for a period. The Revenue calls them 'qualifying young people'. The terms 'child' or 'children' in this chapter include these qualifying young people.

To see when you count as responsible for a child see p1198. The Revenue uses the same test as for CTC.[7]

Couples

You and your partner count as a 'couple' if you are:[8]

- a man and woman and are:
  - married, unless you are separated and this is under a court order or is likely to be permanent (see below); *or*
  - not married and are 'living together as husband and wife' (see p1212); *or*
- the same sex as your partner and are:
  - registered as civil partners, unless you are separated and this is under a court order or is likely to be permanent (see below); *or*
  - not civil partners and are living together as if you are – ie, you would be regarded as 'living together as husband and wife' if you were a different sex from your partner (see p1212).[9]

Married couples and civil partners

You must claim tax credits jointly with your partner if you are married to her/him or you are registered as civil partners. You continue to count as a couple while you and your partner are **temporarily separated**. It does not matter how long the temporary separation lasts (but see p1212 if you or your partner go abroad).

If you and your partner are **permanently separated** or are separated under a court order, you can claim tax credits as a single person immediately. This is the case even if you are still living under the same roof and whether or not you are taking steps to divorce your partner or dissolve your civil partnership. The test is whether you are 'separated in circumstances in which the separation is likely to be permanent' and this depends on your (and your partner's) intentions.[10] If you and your partner are having a trial separation and there is at least a 50 per cent chance of reconciliation, the Revenue is likely to say you still count as a couple.[11]

You count as a 'polygamous unit' if you are a member of a couple married under a law which permits polygamy and either you or your partner are also married to another person (unless any of you are separated and this is under a court order or is likely to be permanent).[12]

Special rules apply if you are a member of a 'polygamous unit'.[13]

- You must make a claim jointly with *all* your partners and the income of all of these is taken into account.
- An increased maximum award of WTC is allowed to take all your partners' needs into account.
- Your entitlement to tax credits ceases if you are a married or unmarried couple and become a member of a polygamous unit or if you are claiming as a polygamous unit and there is any change in the people who are members of that unit.

Living together as husband and wife

You must claim tax credits jointly with your partner if:

- you are 'living together as husband and wife'; *or*
- you are not civil partners but are living together as if you are, in circumstances where you would be regarded as 'living together as husband and wife' if you were a different sex from your partner.

In determining whether or not you count as living together as husband and wife, the Revenue is likely to consider:[14]

- whether you live in the same household;
- if you have a sexual relationship;
- your financial arrangements;
- whether your relationship is stable;
- whether you have children;
- how you appear in public;
- if you are living apart, the length of time you have been doing so.

See p704 for more information about the situations when you might count as living together as husband and wife.

No one factor need in itself be conclusive, as it is your 'general relationship' as a whole which is of paramount importance.[15] Just as relationships between couples may often vary considerably, so each case depends on all its own particular facts and circumstances.

People with no sexual relationship who live together might sometimes still be treated as a couple. People who provide mutual support and share household expenses should not necessarily be treated as a couple – this is also the case where friends share a home.[16]

Decision makers often apply too narrow an interpretation of the test. There is no rule, for example, that if your partner stays with you for three nights or more a week you are *automatically* to be treated as a couple living together.

If you and your partner stop living together, you can claim tax credits as a single person immediately. Note that if you and your partner are only temporarily living apart (eg, one of you is in hospital or in respite care), you may still be treated as a couple.

If you or your partner go abroad

If you or your partner go abroad, either permanently or for more than a set period of time (see p1379), you cease to satisfy the residence conditions. In this case, you must terminate your joint claim. Failure to do this may result in a penalty (see p1308). The person still in the UK may be able to make a new claim as a single person.

Challenging a decision

In some cases you may have to prove that you are a couple – eg, if you want to claim WTC instead of income support (IS) and you are not in full-time paid work yourself, but your partner is. In other cases you may have to prove that you are not a couple – eg, if your former partner's income is being taken into account when working out your tax credits.

If you think a decision about whether or not you count as a couple is wrong and it affects your tax credits, consider appealing. It is possible that the DWP, local authority and the Revenue might reach different conclusions about whether you are a couple. If so, you should appeal *all* the decisions with which you disagree.

Whether or not you appeal, you should apply immediately for any other benefits or tax credits for which you might qualify. You may be able to get a social fund crisis loan in the meantime (see p503).

Change of circumstances

There are changes of circumstances that you must report to the Revenue (see p1288). If you do not do so, you could incur a recoverable overpayment and a penalty. Those that relate to couples and children (including qualifying young people) are:[17]

- you were claiming as a single person and you become part of a couple; *or*
- you were claiming as a couple and you cease to be a member of a couple; *or*
- you or your partner no longer count as ordinarily resident in the UK; *or*
- you or your partner are no longer treated as responsible for a child; *or*
- a child for whom you or your partner are responsible dies; *or*
- you or your partner notifed the Revenue that your child was expected to become a qualifying young person (eg, by staying on at school to do 'A' levels) but s/he does not; *or*
- a qualifying young person for whom you or your partner are responsible ceases to be one other than by turning 20.

Note: the first three of the above changes also end your entitlement to WTC and you have to make a fresh claim as a couple or single person, as the case may be.

If you are claiming WTC and you only qualify for the lone parent or childcare element because you (or your partner) are responsible for a child and the child dies, you are paid WTC for a further eight weeks (or to the date your child would have turned 20 if this is earlier) as if this had not happened.[18] This is only the case if you would have continued to qualify for the lone parent or childcare element but for the child's death. After that period, you may continue to qualify for WTC – eg, if you still satisfy the means test and work sufficient hours to count as in full-time paid work.

For further information about changes of circumstances and whether you should or must report them, see Chapter 54.

4. The amount of working tax credit

The amount of working tax credit (WTC) you get depends on:

- your maximum WTC. This is made up of a combination of 'elements' (see p1215);
- how much income you have; *and*
- the 'income threshold figure' that applies to you.

The elements and threshold can be increased every April. If you do not qualify for WTC currently, you might qualify if the rates increase.

If you are on income support, income-based jobseeker's allowance or pension credit

Entitlement to income support (IS), income-based jobseeker's allowance (JSA) or pension credit (PC) acts as an automatic passport to maximum WTC.[19] You, therefore, do not need to work out your income and capital. In these circumstances, WTC = maximum WTC.

Remember that, in practice, there are not many situations when you can claim IS or income-based JSA at the same time as WTC because you cannot claim IS or JSA if you or your partner are in full-time paid work for those purposes. But you might be able to claim both – eg, if you are a 'term-time only' worker or if you are off sick (see p657). WTC counts in full as income for IS, income-based JSA and PC.

If you are not on income support, income-based jobseeker's allowance or pension credit

- **Step one:** work out your 'relevant period' (see pp1233 and 1245).
- **Step two:** work out your maximum entitlement for the relevant period. This involves working out your maximum WTC for your relevant period (see p1245).
- **Step three:** work out your relevant income (see p1245).
- **Step four:** compare your income with the 'income threshold figure' for the relevant period – currently £6,420 for WTC.[20]
- **Step five:** calculate WTC entitlement for the relevant period (see p1246). If your income is less than the 'income threshold figure', WTC = maximum WTC. If your income exceeds the 'income threshold figure', your maximum WTC is reduced by 39 per cent of the excess. **Note:** this was 37 per cent in claims before the 2008/09 tax year.

For full details of the calculation, see Chapter 51.

Maximum working tax credit

Your maximum WTC is calculated by adding together all the elements that apply to you.[21] These are:[22]

- basic element (£1,800 a year);
- disability element (£2,405 a year);
- lone parent/couple element (£1,770 a year);
- 30-hour element (£735 a year);
- severe disability element (£1,020 a year);
- 50-plus element (£1,235 a year for 16–29 hours work; £1,840 a year for 30 or more hours work);
- childcare element (see Chapter 51 for how this is calculated).

If you are a member of a couple, more than one disability element, severe disability element and 50-plus element can be included – eg if both you and your partner qualify, two are included. For details of how you qualify for the above elements, see Chapter 51.

5. Claims and backdating

This section gives an outline of the rules about claims for working tax credit (WTC). For more information about claiming and how your award can be renewed at the end of the year, see Chapter 53.

Making a claim

Your first claim for WTC must be made in writing on the approved or authorised form. You use the same form for WTC and for child tax credit (CTC). See p1274 for further information.

You should send the completed form directly to the Tax Credit Office (TCO) of the Revenue in the pre-paid envelope provided with the claim form. The claim form can also be sent, if necessary, to any Jobcentre Plus office, DWP office or the Revenue enquiry centre office.[23] Keep a copy of your claim form in case queries arise. You can amend or withdraw your claim at any time before the claim has been decided.[24]

Information to support your claim

When you claim WTC, you must satisfy the national insurance number requirement. In most cases this means you must provide your national insurance number, as well as your partner's. You may also be asked to provide proof of your identity and information to support your claim.[25] See p1275 for further details. It is important that you provide all the information required. If you do not do so, a decision might not be made on your claim.

When you claim WTC you must provide:

- details of your (and your partner's) income for the previous year (see Chapter 52);
- details of the work that you do, including your usual hours;
- if you are self-employed, your tax reference number and the date you became self-employed;
- if you have childcare expenses, your childcare provider's name, address, phone number, approval or registration details and the average weekly cost;
- details of a bank or building society account into which your WTC can be paid. If you do not have an account, you need to open one within eight weeks of making your claim. See pp1276 and 1280 for further information.

If you are also claiming CTC you must provide additional information (see p1203).

The Revenue may need further information before it makes a decision on your claim. See p1276 for details of the time you must be given to provide the information and what happens if you fail to do so.

Who should claim

If you are a member of a couple, you must make a joint claim with your partner. If you are not a member of a couple, you claim for yourself. For information about who counts as a couple for tax credit purposes, see p1211. If, exceptionally, you are unable to claim for yourself, the decision maker may authorise someone else (eg, a friend or relative) to act on your behalf.

When to claim

The general rule is that your claim runs from the date it is received by the Revenue.[26] You cannot make a claim in advance of the tax year in which you are claiming. You *can* claim WTC in advance of starting work, provided that you expect to start work within seven days and will be entitled to WTC within seven days of starting work.[27] See p1217 for information on how and when claims can be backdated.

Awards of WTC are always based on annual income. The Revenue bases the initial award of WTC on your (and your partner's) *previous* tax year's income. If you think your income for the current tax year is likely, eventually, to be sufficiently low for you to qualify for WTC (for instance, you know your income is going to fall or has fallen), you may wish to consider making a claim (including a request for your claim to be backdated if relevant), even if you know you will be given what is known as a 'nil award'. This protects your position because you can then ask the Revenue to amend the award on the basis of a change in your income (see p1254). The amended award would then run from your original date of claim (or the date to which your claim was backdated). However, see pp1290–1291 before deciding what to do.

How your claim is dealt with

Once you have claimed WTC and provided all the information required, the Revenue makes a decision on your claim. You receive an award notice telling you how much WTC you are entitled to and when payment will start.

Backdating your claim

It is very important to claim in time. A claim for WTC can usually only be backdated for a maximum of three months.[28] You only need to show that you qualified for WTC during that period. Unlike for most means-tested benefits, you do not have to show any reasons for your delay. See p1281 for further information.

Note: there is a special backdating rule if you are refused WTC because you do not receive a qualifying benefit (eg, disability living allowance) and make a second claim when the qualifying benefit is awarded (see p1281). Under this rule your WTC can be backdated more than three months.

Renewal awards

At the end of the tax year in which you claimed WTC, you (and your partner if you have one), receive a 'final notice' from the Revenue asking you to confirm that your income and/or household circumstances are as stated for the previous tax year (see p1285). The Revenue then makes a final decision, based on your actual income during the tax year. It decides whether you were entitled to WTC and, if so, the amount of your award. This is known as the 'end of year review'. The Revenue also uses the information about your income and household circumstances for the last tax year to renew your award for the next tax year.[29]

Example

Louise, aged 37, works 30 hours a week. She claims WTC in June 2007. Her initial award is based on her income during the 2006/07 tax year. In May 2008, she is sent a 'final notice'. She sends the Revenue details of her actual income for 2007/08. The Revenue uses this information to work out whether her WTC award was correct. Louise's actual income for 2007/08 is now the previous year's income in respect of Louise's WTC claim for 2008/09. The Revenue uses this income to make an initial decision to award Louise WTC and set payments for 2008/09.

6. Getting paid

This section gives an outline of the rules about payment of working tax credit (WTC). For more information about getting paid, see p1280.

Payments of WTC are usually made directly into your bank or building society account, or post office card account. If you make a joint claim, any WTC to which you are entitled towards your childcare expenses is paid to whoever is decided to be the main carer of your child(ren) (see p1280 for how this is worked out). WTC can be paid into the account every week or every four weeks, whichever is more convenient for you.[30] You might be paid by cheque while your account arrangements are finalised.

If your award of WTC (or the combination of WTC and child tax credit (CTC)) is £2 a week or less, it is paid in a single lump sum into your account to cover the whole year.[31] **Note:** if your entitlement to WTC (or the combination of WTC and CTC) is less than £26 for the whole of the tax year, no award is made and you are not paid at all.[32]

Length of award

Your award of WTC runs from the date your claim is received by the Revenue (or from the date to which your claim can be backdated) to the end of the tax year.[33] However, changes in your circumstances can be taken into account during the tax year. In some cases, you *must* report changes of circumstance. See below and Chapter 54 for details.

Delays and complaints

If payment of your WTC is delayed or you wish to complain about how your claim has been dealt with, see p1182. You might be able to claim compensation (see p1186). If the delay is causing hardship, ask the Revenue to make 'immediate payments'.

Change of circumstances

Your award of WTC is made on the basis of your (and your partner's) previous year's income and your personal circumstances on the date of your claim. If your current year's income or your personal circumstances change, your award of WTC can be amended. Remember the following.

- There are some changes you *must* report to the Revenue (see p1288). If you fail to do so within one month, you may receive a financial penalty. Some of these end your entitlement to WTC and you have to make a fresh claim.
- Unless it is a change that you must report, it is optional to report changes that affect your maximum entitlement to WTC – eg, when your hours increase to 30 or more so you would qualify for a 30-hour element (see p1289) – but see below. However, changes that increase your maximum entitlement to WTC can generally only be backdated three months from when you notify the Revenue. Changes that decrease your entitlement always take effect from the date of the change so an overpayment can occur if you delay.
- There is a special rule that allows an increase in your entitlement to WTC to be backdated more than three months if you were waiting to hear about a qualifying benefit claim when you claimed WTC. Once this has been awarded

the disability or severe disability elements should be included in your WTC entitlement. You must notify the Revenue within three months of the date the qualifying benefit is awarded (see p1289).

- It is optional to report changes in your income (see p1290). These are always taken into account at the end of the tax year, but you may want to consider reporting these sooner to avoid an overpayment or underpayment of WTC.

Overpayments and fraud

If you are overpaid WTC, you may have to repay it. The rules on overpayments are covered in Chapter 55. In some cases, interest can be added to the overpayment. For information on fraud, see Chapter 56. In some cases, you can be given a financial penalty.

7. Challenging a working tax credit decision

You can apply for a revision of, or appeal against, many working tax credit decisions (see Chapter 57).

You cannot appeal decisions about which member of a couple is paid.

8. Tax, tax credits and benefits

Working tax credit (WTC) is not taxable.

Tax credits

If you have dependent children you might qualify for child tax credit (CTC). WTC is not taken into account as income for CTC.

Means-tested benefits

WTC counts as income for income support (IS), pension credit (PC), income-based jobseeker's allowance (JSA), housing benefit (HB) and council tax benefit (CTB). However, for HB and CTB, see p1220.

If you get arrears of WTC, these count as capital and can be disregarded (see pp921 and 940).

Income support or income-based jobseeker's allowance

Sometimes you may be able to claim IS/income-based JSA or WTC. For example, you may be able to claim IS if your partner works more than 16 but less than 24 hours a week. If you have to pay housing costs (see Chapter 34), in some cases you might be better off financially if you claim IS or income-based JSA. You may be able to claim both IS/income-based JSA and WTC at the same time in some circumstances. However, your earnings and WTC are taken into account as income in working out how much IS or income-based JSA you can get.

Pension credit

There is no rule that prevents you or your partner doing full-time paid work while claiming PC. This means that you can claim WTC at the same time as PC. However, your earnings and WTC are taken into account as income in working out how much PC you can get.

Housing benefit and council tax benefit

If you pay rent or council tax you might qualify for HB or CTB. The amount of WTC you are paid is taken into account as income. However, in some circumstances you get an additional earnings disregard. See pp855 and 887 for details.

Non-means-tested benefits

WTC can be paid in addition to any non-means-tested benefits to which you (or your partner) are entitled. See Chapter 52 for which of these benefits may be taken into account as income for WTC. Qualifying for certain non-means-tested benefits means you may also qualify for the disability element or severe disability element of WTC.

Passports and other sources of help

If you are entitled to WTC you may also qualify for health benefits, such as free prescriptions (see Chapter 9).You do not have to satisfy the means test if your gross annual income is below a set amount (see p163) and you are getting WTC which includes a disability element or a severe disability element, or CTC with your WTC.

You may also qualify for a Sure Start maternity grant or a social fund funeral expenses payment (see Chapter 22).

Notes

1. **Who can claim working tax credit**
   1 ss3(3) and (7), 10 and 42 TCA 2002; regs 4-8 WTC(EMR) Regs; reg 3 TC(R) Regs; reg 3 TC(I) Regs
   2 Reg 4 WTC(EMR) Regs

2. **The rules about your age**
   3 s3(3) TCA 2002

3. **Who is included in your claim**
   4 s3(3)(a) and (5A) TCA 2002; CTC/3864/2004; R(TC) 1/07
   5 s3(3)(b) TCA 2002
   6 Reg 2 WTC(EMR) Regs, definition of 'child' and 'qualifying young person'
   7 Reg 2(2) WTC(EMR) Regs
   8 s3(5A) TCA 2002; reg 2(1) WTC(EMR) Regs, definition of 'couple'
   9 s48(2) TCA 2002
   10 s3(5A)(a)(ii) and (c)(ii) TCA 2002
   11 R(TC) 2/06
   12 ss3(6A)and 43 TCA 2002; reg 2 TC(PM) Regs
   13 See the TC(PM) Regs
   14 *Crake and Butterworth v SBC* [1982] 1 All ER 498; R(SB) 17/81; CTC/3864/2004
   15 R(SB) 17/81; R(G) 3/71; CIS/87/1993
   16 CSSB/145/1983
   17 s3(4) and (7) TCA 2002; reg 21 TC(CN) Regs
   18 Reg 19 WTC(EMR) Regs; reg 6 CTC Regs

4. **The amount of working tax credit**
   19 ss7(2) and 13 TCA 2002; reg 4 TC(ITDR) Regs
   20 Reg 3(2) TC(ITDR) Regs
   21 s11 TCA 2002
   22 Regs 3 and 20 and Sch 2 WTC(EMR) Regs

5. **Claims and backdating**
   23 Regs 2 and 5 TC(CN) Regs
   24 Reg 5(7) TC(CN) Regs; R(IS) 5/05
   25 Reg 5(3)-(6) TC(CN) Regs
   26 s5(2) TCA 2002
   27 Reg 10 TC(CN) Regs
   28 Reg 7 TC(CN) Regs
   29 Regs 11 and 12 TC(CN) Regs

6. **Getting paid**
   30 Regs 8 and 13 TC(PC) Regs
   31 Reg 10 TC(PC) Regs
   32 Reg 9 TC(ITDR) Regs
   33 s5(2) TCA 2002

Chapter 50

Work and tax credits

This chapter covers:

Full-time paid work (the Revenue calls this 'remunerative work') affects working tax credit (WTC). If you or your partner are in full-time paid work you can claim WTC.[1] This chapter covers the rules about full-time paid work for this purpose. If neither you nor your partner are in full-time paid work you might be able to claim income support (IS) or jobseeker's allowance (JSA). You might be able to choose whether to claim IS/JSA or WTC. In some situations, you might be able to claim both IS/JSA and WTC (eg, if you are a 'term-time only' worker or are off sick and getting statutory sick pay). This is because different rules for what counts as full-time paid work apply for WTC and IS/JSA. See p657 for information about what you should consider.

Whether or not you are in full-time paid work, you might be able to claim child tax credit (CTC) or pension credit. However, you cannot get CTC for a qualifying young person for any period that includes a week in which s/he:[2]

- has left full-time education or 'approved training' (see pp1197 and 61); *and*
- is in full-time paid work of 24 hours or more. Even if s/he is, see p1230 to see if s/he can be treated as not being in full-time paid work. The rules are the same as for WTC claimants.

Entitlement to many benefits is also affected by issues to do with work and employment. For further information, see Chapter 27.

1. The full-time paid work rule

If you work full time and are paid for the work, you count as being in what the Revenue calls 'remunerative work'. This is called 'full-time paid work' in this *Handbook*. See p1223 for what counts as full-time work, p1224 for what counts as paid work and p1224 for how your hours are calculated. 'Work' includes self-employment and work which is done from home.

In some circumstances you may be treated as not being in full-time paid work even if you are (see p1230). In others, you may be treated as if you are in full-time paid work when you are not (see p1229). If you are unsure if you are in full-time paid work, see p1227.

Remember that your income from work affects your entitlement to working tax credit (WTC). This means that although your (or your partner's) hours of work are high enough for you to qualify, you might not satisfy the means test. Although full-time paid work does not affect entitlement to child tax credit, your income from work affects the amount you can be paid.

What counts as full-time work

You can only get WTC if you or your partner are in full-time paid work. For the purpose of WTC, you count as being in full-time work if:[3]

- you (or your partner) are responsible for a child or qualifying young person (see p1198), and you work at least 16 hours a week; *or*
- you have a physical or mental disability which puts you at a disadvantage in getting a job, you qualify for a disability element (see p1237) and you work at least 16 hours a week; *or*
- you (or your partner) are at least 50, work at least 16 hours a week and qualify for a 50-plus element (see p1239). Note that this can only apply for up to 12 months; *or*
- you are 25 or over and you work at least 30 hours a week.

If you are under 25, you can only claim WTC if you count as being in full-time work under any of the first three categories.

If your circumstances change and you are no longer responsible for a child or qualifying young person, or no longer qualify for a disability or a 50-plus element, you may now have to increase your hours to 30 or more per week to continue to qualify for WTC. See Chapter 54 for more information on changes of circumstances.

At the date of your claim, you must:[4]

- be working; *or*
- have accepted an offer of work which is expected to start within seven days. In this case, you only count as being in full-time paid work when the work begins.

The work must be expected to continue for at least four weeks after you make your claim (or if you have accepted an offer of work, after the work starts).[5]

If you normally work at least 16 (or 30) hours a week, but are off sick or on maternity, paternity or adoption leave you might be able to claim WTC (see p1229). You might also be able to claim income support (IS) or jobseeker's allowance (JSA).

Note: you can continue to count as in full-time work for four weeks after you leave work (see p1230).

What counts as paid work

'Paid work' includes work for which you are paid or expect to be paid.[6] The information on p649 about what counts as paid work for IS, JSA, pension credit (PC), housing benefit and council tax benefit also applies to WTC.

How your hours are calculated

How you calculate your hours depends on if you are employed or self-employed.

You count as **employed** if you are employed under a contract of service or apprenticeship and your earnings are taxable as employment income under certain provisions of the Income Tax (Earnings and Pensions) Act 2003.[7] You count as **self-employed** if you are carrying out a trade profession or vocation.[8]

To work out whether you are in full-time paid work:[9]

- if you are employed, include all the hours:
  - you normally work under your contract, if you are an apprentice or employee; *or*
  - you normally perform in the office in which you are employed, if you are an office holder; *or*
  - for which you are normally paid by the employment agency with whom you have a contract, if you are an agency worker; *or*
- if you are self-employed, include all the hours you normally do for payment or for which you expect to be paid.

Paid meal and refreshment breaks count towards the total hours you work.[10] Also included is any time allowed for visits to a hospital, clinic or other establishment, but only if this is for the treatment or monitoring of your disability and if you are paid, or expect to be paid, for the time.[11] Your total hours from more than one job are added together.

Periods when you are on a customary or paid holiday from work are ignored in calculating your hours.[12] Likewise, unpaid meal and refreshment breaks are ignored.

Hours you normally work

Whether you are employed or self-employed, the measure for WTC purposes is the number of hours you normally work.[13] 'Normally' is not defined in the WTC rules. The Revenue says you should calculate your hours based on what is 'usual or typical' and that the number of hours you normally work might not be the number of hours specified in your contract of employment.[14] The hours that are relevant are those you *actually* work. If you routinely do paid overtime, try to argue that these are hours you normally work and that they should be included. See p1225 if your hours fluctuate.

Example

Harriet is a cashier in a supermarket. Her partner stays at home to look after their children. She is contracted to work 14 hours a week over a two-day week but she does 3.5 hours overtime almost every week. She gets an unpaid half-hour lunch break. When Harriet and her partner claim WTC she has just returned from two weeks' paid holiday.

Harriet normally works 14 + 3.5 = 17.5 hours a week. Unpaid lunch breaks and the time she was on paid holiday are not taken into account. As Harriet and her partner are responsible for children, she need only work 16 hours or more a week. Harriet therefore counts as being in full-time paid work.

In working out your normal hours if you are self-employed, the Revenue says you can include not only the hours you spend providing orders or services but also those that are necessary to your self-employment. These include things like trips to the wholesalers, visits to potential clients, time spent on advertising or canvassing, cleaning the business or vehicles used as part of the business, book-keeping and research work.[15]

If your hours fluctuate

Working out the number of hours you normally work is straightforward if:

- you do the same number of hours each and every week; *or*
- your hours vary, but you always do at least enough hours each week to count as being in full-time paid work (16 or 30, as the case may be).

However, if your weekly hours fluctuate, it can be more complicated. Unless you are a term-time only worker (ie, you have a recognisable cycle of work that lasts for a year with periods where you are not required to work – eg, in an educational establishment – see p1226), there is no rule to tell you how to average your hours. If your hours fluctuate:

- over a regular short-term cycle (eg, you work two weeks on and two weeks off), the Revenue says you can average your hours over that cycle;[16]
- but there is no regular pattern to your hours, and in some weeks you do not do enough hours each week (16 or 30 as the case may be), working out the number of hours you 'normally' work is a question of judgement.

If you are in any doubt about what your normal hours are, contact the Revenue and seek advice. If you are unsure if you are in full-time paid work (eg, if your hours are changeable), see p1227.

Examples

Shane works in a residential project. He works three weeks on and one week off. When he is on, he works 40 hours a week. His average hours are 40 x 3 ÷ 4 = 30 hours a week. Shane can try to argue that he normally works 30 hours or more a week. As Shane is aged 45, does not have a physical or mental disability and has no children, he must work at least 30 hours a week. He therefore counts as being in full-time paid work.

Narindar is contracted to do 15 hours a week. However, she gets regular overtime of three hours every other week. Her average hours are 15 + 18 ÷ 2 = 16.5 hours. Narindar can try to argue that she normally works 16 hours or more per week. As Narindar is a lone parent, she need only work 16 hours or more a week. She therefore counts as being in full-time paid work.

You should appeal if you think your average hours have been calculated unfairly (see Chapter 57). You should work out first whether you are better off claiming IS/JSA or WTC (see p657).

'Term-time only' workers

If you have a recognisable cycle of work that lasts for a year (eg, in a school or an educational establishment where you have periods of school holidays or similar vacations where you do not work), the 'term-time only' worker rule applies.[17] The periods when you are not working are ignored in deciding whether you are in full-time paid work. Note that this rule can also apply to other seasonal workers. However, if you work casually or intermittently – eg, you are a seasonal worker who works in the summer but you are unemployed the rest of the year, the Revenue might say that your work 'cycle' is that part of the year in which you are working and that you do not count as in full-time work when you are unemployed.[18]

In practice, if the hours of work you do during term-time mean you are in full-time paid work during term-time, you also count as being in full-time paid work over the holidays. You should be able to claim WTC during this period if your normal hours of work are 16/30 hours a week during term time. If you are not paid for the holidays, you might also be able to claim JSA during these periods if you satisfy the other qualifying conditions.

Example

Dee is 35 years old and has no children. She is a cleaner at a local college and works 35 hours a week, 32 weeks of the year. She does not work (and is not paid) when the students are on study leave or on holiday. The periods when Dee does not work are ignored. She is in full-time paid work during term-time because she works 30 hours or more a week. She therefore counts as being in full-time paid work throughout the year and can claim WTC.

Sometimes it might not be clear whether you have a cycle of work that lasts a year – eg, if you have only started your job recently or have a fixed-term contract that finishes at the end of the school term, or are employed on a casual or relief basis.[19] It can take time before it can be said that you have a yearly cycle of work.[20] However, if you have an indefinite contract to work in term-time only, you can argue that you have a yearly work cycle from the start.[21]

Students

You are not excluded from claiming WTC simply because you are a student. However, you must count as in full-time paid work under the rules described in this chapter. So if, for example, you do sufficient hours of paid work (16 or 30 as the case may be) in addition to your studies or during the holidays, you can qualify for WTC. **Note:** the work must be expected to last for four weeks.

Any work you do in studying for a degree or other qualification does not count as full-time paid work – any grant or loan you receive is for your maintenance and not paid in return for work done on the course. You will not be considered to be in full-time paid work if you are a student nurse because the NHS bursary and other grants or loans you get are not payments for work done on the course and do not count as income for tax credit purposes.[22] However, if you are paid in return for the work you do – eg, you are paid by an employer during a work placement, you can argue that you are in full-time paid work. There are a number of situations when you do not count as in full-time paid work even if you are – eg, if you are on a government training scheme being paid a training allowance. See p1230.

When calculating how much WTC you can get, student loans and most other student income is disregarded. See p1262 for what income counts.

Foster carers

If you are working sufficient hours as a foster carer, you can claim WTC. The Revenue generally treats foster carers as self-employed. It says that the hours of work you declare on your claim form should be accepted.[23] If you do more than one job, the total hours are added together. So if you are doing work in addition to foster caring, the hours from the other work can be added in.

Fostering allowances which qualify for tax relief are generally ignored in calculating your WTC and child tax credit. See p1268 for further information.

Note: for IS and JSA purposes, if you are a foster carer receiving a payment for fostering a child from a local authority, voluntary organisation or a care authority (in Scotland) you are treated as not being in full-time paid work (see p655). You may wish to consider how you would be better off financially.

If you are unsure whether you are in full-time paid work

If you are unsure if the number of hours you normally work are 16/30 hours or more at the **date of your claim,** contact the Revenue and seek advice. Consider making a further claim for WTC in a week when you are certain. Bear in mind that a claim for WTC can be backdated for three months automatically (see p1281) so there is scope to postpone claiming WTC until you are certain. If time is running out and you are still uncertain, consider making a claim to protect your position.

Note that if you are refused WTC because neither you nor your partner are in full-time paid work for WTC purposes and within 14 days of that decision you claim IS or JSA, your claim for IS or JSA can be backdated to the date you claimed WTC.[24]

If your **circumstances change** while you are claiming WTC, consider the following.

- If you are now uncertain about whether you are still in full-time paid work (eg, your weekly hours change), keep a record of the hours you work each week.
  - If it appears that you no longer normally work 16/30 hours each week (or if you have a partner, neither of you normally works 16/30 hours each week), you are no longer entitled to WTC.
  - If you have a partner and are getting a childcare element because *both* of you are in full-time paid work and it appears that one of you no longer normally works 16 hours each week, you may no longer be entitled to a childcare element (see p1240).

  In both cases, you must report your change in hours to the Revenue within one month. See Chapter 54 for more information on changes of circumstances.
- If you are no longer responsible for a child or qualifying young person (note that you must report this to the Revenue within one month), or no longer qualify for a disability or a 50-plus element, you may now have to increase your hours to 30 or more hours per week to continue to qualify for WTC.
- If you no longer count as being in full-time paid work, check to see if you qualify for IS or JSA and make a claim if this is possible. Remember that claims for IS and JSA can only be backdated in limited circumstances (see p966).
- If you are 60 or over, whether or not you are in full-time paid work, check to see if you qualify for PC. There is no full-time paid work rule for PC, but earnings and WTC count as income.
- If your hours change, but you still count as being in full-time paid work, the amount of WTC to which you are entitled could be affected by:
  - a change in your earnings. If these increase, you may wish to report this to the Revenue to avoid an overpayment at the end of the year. If these decrease, you can get increased WTC if you report the change. You may wish to consider waiting until the end of the year (see p1290);
  - whether or not you are entitled to have a 30-hour element (see p1237) or the lower or higher rate of the 50-plus element (see p1239) included in calculating your WTC. If your entitlement decreases, you must report your change in hours to the Revenue within one month. Any increase in your entitlement to WTC can only be backdated three months from the date you notify the Revenue of the change (see p1289).

2. Treated as being in full-time paid work

You or your partner are treated as being in full-time paid work:

- during any period when:[25]
  - you are being paid statutory maternity pay (SMP), statutory paternity pay (SPP), statutory adoption pay (SAP) or maternity allowance (MA); *or*
  - you are absent from work during ordinary maternity leave, paternity leave or ordinary adoption leave, or during the first 13 weeks of additional maternity or adoption leave.

  If you are an employee, you are treated as in full-time paid work from the start of the period, so long as you are in full-time paid work for working tax credit (WTC) purposes (16 or 30 hours a week) immediately before the period begins. However, if this is not the case – eg, you are under 25, or are 25 or over but working less than 30 hours a week and the child you and your partner are having (or adopting) is your first child – you are treated as in full-time paid work from the date of birth (or adoption). You must have been working at least 16 hours a week immediately before the period begins.[26]

  If you are self-employed, you count as in full-time paid work during any period when the above would have applied had the work done in the week before the period began been done as an employee.

  If you do not return to work when your SMP, SPP, SAP or MA ceases or your leave ends, you are no longer treated as being in full-time paid work under this rule; *and*
- during any period when:[27]
  - you are being paid statutory sick pay (SSP) or short-term lower rate incapacity benefit (IB); *or*
  - you are being paid income support (IS) because you are incapable of work (including where this because of pregnancy) or are getting national insurance credits because you are incapable of work. This only applies for 28 weeks. **Note:** this rule may change when the employment and support allowance rules take effect (see Chapter 7).

  You must have been in full-time paid work for WTC purposes (16 or 30 hours a week) immediately before the period began.

  If you are self-employed, you count as in full-time paid work during any period when the above would have applied had the work done in the week before the period began been done as an employee.

  If you do not return to work when your SSP or short-term lower rate IB ceases (or if you are being paid IS, after 28 weeks), you no longer count as being in full-time paid work under this rule.

Even though you continue to count as in full-time paid work, you should consider letting the Revenue know if you are in any of the above situations. This is because any MA and short-term lower rate IB are ignored as income, as is the first £100 of any SMP, SPP and SAP. You are entitled to maximum WTC if you are on IS.

You or your partner are also treated as being in full-time paid work:

- for the four weeks immediately after you stop work, or your hours reduce to less than 16 a week. You must have been in full-time paid work for WTC purposes (16 or 30 hours a week) immediately before the start of the four-week period. This means you continue to qualify for WTC for the four-week period - sometimes called **'WTC run-on'**. **Note:** you must report the change in your circumstances to the Revenue within one month;[28]
- if you were **in full-time paid work within the past seven days.**[29] This means you can make a new claim or continue to qualify for WTC – eg, during a short period between jobs or when you are on jury service;
- during any period when you are **on strike** or are **suspended from work** while complaints or allegations against you are investigated, so long as you were in full-time paid work for WTC purposes (16 or 30 hours a week) immediately before the start of the period. You must not be on strike for longer than 10 consecutive days when you should have been working.[30]

3. Treated as not being in full-time paid work

You or your partner are treated as *not* being in full-time paid work during any period when you are receiving pay in lieu of notice after you stop work, unless you continue to qualify under the four-week, working tax credit (WTC) 'run-on' rule (see above).[31] In addition, you or your partner are treated as *not* being in full-time work if:[32]

- you are a volunteer, or are working for a charity or voluntary organisation and are giving your services free (except for your expenses);
- you are providing care for someone who is staying with you temporarily but who is not normally a member of your household; *and*
  - the only payment you receive is from a health authority, a local authority, a voluntary organisation, a primary care trust or from the person her/himself for caring for her/him; *and*
  - the payment is disregarded as a tax-free payment under the Revenue's 'rent-a-room' scheme (see p1266).

  Note that if you are an adult placement carer who has *not* opted for the 'rent-a-room' scheme, you *can* count as in full-time paid work.[33]
- you are on certain goverment schemes – ie:
  - you are working on a government training scheme and are being paid a training allowance (see p1231) or you are participating in the 'intensive activity period' of the New Deal (see p412), unless the training allowance, or

the money you are being paid by the DWP, is subject to income tax as a profit from work;[34]
- the only payment you receive, or expect to receive, is a sports award from a Sports Council;
- you are on an employment zone programme and are only being paid discretionary payments (eg, fees and grants) that are disregarded (see p1268), or training premiums;

Note that if you are on any other employment scheme and you are paid for your services, if you do sufficient hours (16 or 30 a week) you can count as being in full-time paid work;[35]

- you are working while a sentenced or remand prisoner. This means you cannot qualify for WTC even if the work you do is outside the prison – eg, while you are on temporary release.

Training allowance

A 'training allowance' is an allowance paid to maintain you or a member of your family:[36]
- by a government department or by or on behalf of the Secretary of State or Scottish Enterprise or Highlands and Islands Enterprise; *and*
- for the period or part of a period during which you are on a course provided or approved by or under arrangements made by any of these.

Allowances paid to or in respect of you by a government department or the Scottish Executive are not included if these are paid because you are a trainee teacher or on a full-time course of education, unless this is under arrangements made under s2 Employment and Training Act 1973.

4. Working tax credit, income support and jobseeker's allowance

Sometimes it is difficult to show that you count as being in full-time paid work and the differences between the rules for **working tax credit** (WTC) and **out-of-work benefits** (income support (IS) or jobseeker's allowance (JSA)) mean that in some situations you may have a choice about whether to claim WTC or out-of-work benefits. In some situations, you might be able to claim both IS or income-based JSA and WTC (eg, if you are a 'term-time only' worker or are off sick and getting statutory sick pay). See p657 for further information.

Notes

1 s10(1) TCA 2002
2 Regs 2, definition of 'remunerative work' and 5(4)(a) CTC Regs

1. The full-time paid work rule

3 Reg 4(1) (second condition) WTC(EMR) Regs
4 Reg 4(1) (first condition) WTC(EMR) Regs
5 Reg 4(1) (third condition) WTC(EMR) Regs
6 Reg 4(1) (fourth condition) WTC(EMR) Regs
7 Reg 2(1) WTC(EMR) Regs; s5 IT(EP)A 2003, application to offices and office-holders
8 Reg 2(1) WTC(EMR) Regs
9 Reg 4(3) WTC(EMR) Regs
10 Reg 4(4)(b) WTC(EMR) Regs
11 Reg 4(5) WTC(EMR) Regs
12 Reg 4(4)(b) WTC(EMR) Regs
13 Reg 4(3) WTC(EMR) Regs
14 para 02405 TCTM
15 para 02405 TCTM
16 para 02405 TCTM
17 Reg 7 WTC(EMR) Regs; *Stafford and Banks v CAO* [2001] UKHL 33 (HL), reported as R(IS) 15/01
18 R(JSA) 1/07
19 R(JSA) 8/03
20 CIS/914/1997; CJSA/2759/1998
21 R(JSA) 5/02
22 R(FIS) 1/83; R(FIS) 1/86; para 02403 TCTM
23 para 02404 TCTM
24 Reg 6(28) SS(C&P) Regs

2. Treated as being in full-time paid work

25 Reg 5 WTC(EMR) Regs
26 Reg 5A WTC(EMR) Regs
27 Reg 6 WTC(EMR) Regs
28 Reg 7D WTC(EMR) Regs
29 Reg 8 WTC(EMR) Regs
30 Regs 7A and 7B WTC(EMR) Regs

3.Treated as not being in full-time paid work

31 Reg 7C WTC(EMR) Regs
32 Reg 4(2) WTC(EMR) Regs
33 para 02404 TCTM
34 Reg 4(2)(c) and (d) and (2A) WTC(EMR) Regs
35 para 02404 TCTM
36 Reg 2(1) WTC(EMR) Regs

Chapter 51

The amount of tax credit

This chapter covers:

The amount of tax credit to which you are entitled depends on your family circumstances and your income. There are no limits on the amount of savings or other capital that you might have. If you are entitled to income support (IS), income-based jobseeker's allowance (JSA) or pension credit (PC – guarantee and/ or savings element), you are automatically entitled to the maximum amount of tax credit that you could receive. If you are not entitled to IS, income-based JSA or PC, you may receive less than your maximum amount of tax credit, depending on the level of your income. Your maximum amount of child tax credit depends on the size of your family, the ages of the children in your family and whether any child in your family has a disability. The amount of working tax credit you can get depends on whether you are single with no dependants, a lone parent, or a member of a couple, the hours you work, whether you (or your partner if you have one) are disabled, whether you are returning to work aged 50 or above, and whether you have eligible childcare costs.

The basic steps in calculating the amount of tax credit are as follows.

- Work out the number of days in your 'relevant period'.
- Work out your 'maximum amount'.
- Work out your 'relevant income'.
- Compare this income with the 'threshold figure'.
- Calculate entitlement.

1. The relevant period

The amount of tax credit you can receive is based on your entitlement during a 'relevant period'. Tax credit awards are calculated by reference to a maximum *annual* amount that you could receive. If you claim at the beginning of the new tax year, your award will usually be calculated on the basis that you will be entitled to tax credit for the whole of that tax year (6 April–5 April), and your relevant period will, therefore, be one year.[1] Your annual entitlement is calculated and then paid to you over the course of that year.

If you claim a tax credit after the beginning of a tax year your award is calculated for a period beginning with the date on which you make your claim and ending at the end of that tax year, unless you are able to have your claim backdated to an earlier period (see p1281). Similarly, if your circumstances change in the course of the year, and your award is amended, a new relevant period will begin. The new relevant period is calculated on the basis that it will end at the end of the tax year.[2] In both of these cases, you will be entitled to tax credit for less than a year, and so only a proportion of the annual amount can be paid.

In order to work out your maximum amount of tax credit, therefore, you need to know the length of your relevant period.

A **'relevant period'** is:

- for child tax credit (CTC), a period of an award during which your maximum amount remains the same;[3]
- for working tax credit (WTC), a period during which the elements making up your maximum amount of tax credit (apart from the childcare element) remain the same, *and:*
  - during which there is no change in the childcare you use; *and*
  - your average weekly childcare charge does not change by £10 or more, or reduce to nil.[4]

If you are entitled to both CTC and WTC, a relevant period is one during which both of the above conditions are satisfied.[5]

2. The maximum amount of child tax credit

The maximum amount of child tax credit (CTC) you can get is calculated by adding together each of the 'elements' which apply to you.[6] The amount of each element is set at a yearly rate. If you are entitled to CTC for a period of less than a year, or if your entitlement changes part of the way through the year, the amount of each of these elements is adjusted so that the correct proportion of your annual maximum amount is paid to you.[7] How entitlement is calculated when entitlement changes part of the way through a tax year is explained on p1249.

The elements are:[8]

Element	*Annual rate*
Family element (not including baby element)	£545
Family element (including baby element for child under one)	£1,090
Child element	£2,085
Disability element (for a child)	£2,540
Severe disability element (for a child)	£1,020

- One family element is payable for your family, and the amount is not affected by whether you are a single parent or one of a couple (see p1210 for who counts as your family). The basic rate is £545. If your family includes at least one child under the age of one, you receive an additional baby element, which brings your total family element to £1,090. (This higher amount is not increased if your family includes more than one child under the age of one.)
- You get a child element for each child in your family (see p1196 for when a child or young person can count as a member of your family).
- You get a disability element for any child in your family who gets disability living allowance (DLA), or is registered blind, or who has been taken off the register in the last 28 weeks. The element still applies if DLA has stopped because your child is in hospital.[9] It is paid in addition to the child element for that child.
- You get a severe disability element for each child in your family who gets the highest rate of the care component of DLA. The element still applies if DLA has stopped because your child is in hospital.[10] It is paid in addition to the child element and disability element for that child.

The Revenue uses the term 'family element' to cover both rates at which the family element is paid, and uses the term 'child element' to cover the child element *plus* any related disability and severe disability element for that child.

Example

Tracy is a single parent with two children aged five and three. The annual elements used when calculating her maximum amount are as follows:

Family element	£545
Child element for three-year-old child	£2,085
Child element for five-year-old child	£2,085

3. The maximum amount of working tax credit

The maximum amount of working tax credit (WTC) you get is calculated by adding together each of the 'elements' which apply to you.[11] The amount of each element, with the exception of the childcare element, is set at a yearly rate. The amount of the childcare element is set using your average *weekly* childcare costs.[12] See p1240 for how your childcare element is calculated.

If you are entitled to WTC for a period of less than a year, or if your entitlement changes part of the way through the year, the amount of each of these elements is adjusted so that the correct proportion of your annual maximum amount is paid to you.[13] See p1249 for an explanation of how entitlement is calculated when entitlement changes part of the way through a tax year.

There are eight elements.[14]

Element	*Annual rate*
Basic element	£1,800
Lone parent element	£1,770
Couple element	£1,770
30-hour element	£735
Disability element	£2,405
Severe disability element	£1,020
50-plus element:	
– 16–29 hours	£1,235
– 30+ hours	£1,840
Childcare element:	*Weekly rate*
– maximum eligible cost for two or more children per week	£300
– maximum eligible cost for one child per week	£175
– percentage of eligible costs covered	80%

Basic element

One basic element is paid with each award of WTC. To be entitled to this element you must be engaged in 'qualifying remunerative work'. In this *Handbook* we call this 'full-time work'.[15] For the definition of full-time work, see Chapter 50. Unless you qualify for the basic element of WTC you cannot qualify for any of the other elements.[16]

Couple element

You get the couple element if you are one of a couple making a joint claim (see p1273) unless:

- either you or your partner are aged 50 or over; *and*

- either you or your partner are entitled to the 50-plus element; *and*
- neither you nor your partner are engaged in full-time work for at least 30 hours a week.[17] However, if either you or your partner are responsible for a child or qualifying young person, or are entitled to the disability element, then you will not be prevented from receiving the couple element simply because you do not work for at least 30 hours a week.[18] This means that if you or your partner are aged 50 or above, and are entitled to the 50-plus element, and are *either*:
  - responsible for a child or qualifying young person; *or*
  - entitled to the disability element,

  you can still have the couple element included in your maximum tax credit.

You cannot get the couple element if your partner is serving a prison sentence of more than 12 months, unless either you or your partner are responsible for a child or qualifying young person.[19] You can only have one couple element included in your maximum amount.[20] For when you count as a couple, see p1211.

Lone parent element

You get the lone parent element if you are a lone parent.[21]

30-hour element

You get a 30-hour element if you are:[22]

- a single claimant who works for at least 30 hours a week; *or*
- making a joint claim and either or both of you work for at least 30 hours a week; *or*
- making a joint claim and at least one of you is responsible for a child or qualifying young person *and*:
  - you are both engaged in remunerative work; *and*
  - at least one of you works for at least 16 hours a week; *and*
  - your joint hours of work total at least 30 hours a week.

You can only have one 30-hour element included in your maximum amount.[23]

Disability element

You get a disability element if you work for at least 16 hours a week *and* have a disability which puts you at a disadvantage in getting a job.[24] This means you must pass a disability test (see Appendix 10). If you are claiming as a couple, at least one of you must satisfy all these conditions.

If you pass the disability test and meet one of the following conditions, a disability element can be included in your maximum amount in an existing award of tax credit (see p1249), or in a new award of tax credit. (It does not matter that you did not satisfy any of these conditions in any previous claim, or that you are part of the way through an award of tax credit which until now has not included a disability element.) You must:[25]

- receive (or for at least one day in the 182 days immediately preceding your claim have been in receipt of):
  - the higher rate of short-term incapacity benefit (IB); *or*
  - long-term IB; *or*
  - severe disablement allowance (SDA); *or*
  - a higher pensioner premium or disability premium paid with income support (IS), income-based jobseeker's allowance (JSA), housing benefit (HB) or council tax benefit (CTB); *or*
- receive disability living allowance (DLA), attendance allowance (AA) or a mobility supplement or constant attendance allowance payable with a war pension or industrial injuries disablement benefit. If your qualifying benefit stops, you are no longer entitled to the disability element on these grounds;[26] *or*
- have an invalid carriage or similar vehicle; *or*
- have received for at least 140 days forming a single period of incapacity for work (see Chapter 28) (the last of which must have fallen within the 56 days of the date of the claim) statutory sick pay (SSP), occupational sick pay, short-term IB at the lower rate, or IS on account of incapacity, or credits for incapacity for a period of 20 weeks; *and*
  - have a disability at the date of the claim which is likely to last for at least six months (or for the rest of your life, if your death is expected within that time); *and*
  - have gross earnings which are less than they were before the disability began by at least the greater of 20 per cent and £15 a week; *or*
  - have undertaken 'training for work' for at least one day in the 56 days immediately preceding the claim, *and* are receiving long-term IB, SDA or the higher rate of short-term IB within the 56 days before that training started. For an explanation of what 'training for work' means, see p266.

Employment and support allowance

Employment and support allowance (ESA) will replace IB and IS paid on the grounds of incapacity for work for new claimants (see Chapter 7). This is expected to be in October 2008. ESA is expected to affect the rules on qualifying for tax credits paid on the basis of incapacity for work. For ESA the 'incapacity for work' test is to be replaced with a 'limited capacity for work' test. See www.cpag.org.uk/esa or CPAG's *Welfare Rights Bulletin* for updates.

If there is a break in your claim

If you make a further claim for WTC within 56 days of the day your previous award ended, *and* in that earlier claim you qualified for the disability element *either*:

- because you received (or for at least one day in the 182 days immediately preceding that earlier claim had been in receipt of):
  - the higher rate of short-term IB;

  - long-term IB;
  - SDA;
  - a higher pensioner premium or disability premium paid with IS, income-based JSA, HB or CTB; *or*
- because you have undertaken training for work for at least one day in the previous 56 days and had received the higher rate of short-term IB, long-term IB or SDA within the 56 days preceding that training; *or*
- because you received for at least 140 days (the last of which must have fallen within the 56 days of the date of the earlier claim) SSP, occupational sick pay, short-term IB at the lower rate, IS, or credits for incapacity for a period of 20 weeks; *and*
  - you had a disability at the date of that earlier claim which was likely to last for at least six months (or for the rest of your life, if your death was expected within that time); *and*
  - you have gross earnings which are less than they were before the disability began by at least the greater of 20 per cent and £15 a week; *and*
  - you continue in full-time paid work for at least 16 hours a week,

you will be treated as though you still met those conditions, and can continue to receive the disability element in your new award.

You can still benefit from this linking rule if your income was too high for you to receive any WTC within the previous 56 days, as long as your maximum amount of WTC would have included the disability element on one of the above grounds.[27]

If both you and your partner meet the above conditions, then two disability elements can be paid.[28]

Severe disability element

You get a severe disability element if you receive the highest rate of the care component of DLA or the higher rate of AA, or if payment of either of these has been suspended because you are in hospital.[29] If you have a partner who meets these conditions, a severe disability element can also be included for them.[30]

50-plus element

You get a 50-plus element if:[31]

- you are aged 50 or over; *and*
- you are engaged in full-time paid work (see Chapter 50) of at least 16 hours a week *and either*:
  - for consecutive periods (that is, periods separated by no more than 12 weeks) which add up to six months and end immediately before you start work, you have been getting IS, JSA, IB, SDA, state retirement pension plus pension credit (PC), or a training allowance paid under the 'work-based learning for adults' or 'training for work' schemes; *or*

- for an uninterrupted period of at least six months immediately before you started work you have been getting IS, JSA, IB, SDA, state retirement pension plus PC, or a training allowance paid under the 'work-based learning for adults' or 'training for work' schemes; *or*
- for at least six months immediately before you started work someone else was getting an increase for you in their IS, JSA, IB, SDA, or state retirement pension (which must have been paid with PC); *or*
- for at least six months immediately before you started work you were entitled to be credited with national insurance (NI) contributions or earnings.

If any of the last three conditions above applies, but for a period of less than six months, you can still qualify for the 50-plus element if immediately before you started satisfying one of these three conditions, you or your partner were getting carer's allowance, bereavement allowance or widowed parent's allowance and this period, plus one of the last three periods described above, add up to at least six months.

This element is only payable for a 12-month period starting when you return to work. This can be one period of 12 months, or periods separated by 26 weeks or less that add up to 12 months. A lower rate is payable if you work for between 16 and 29 hours, and a higher rate is paid if you work for 30 hours a week or more. If you have a partner who also meets these conditions, a 50-plus element can be paid for her/him too.[32]

Childcare element

If you have 'eligible childcare costs', your maximum amount of WTC can include a childcare element.[33] This is added to the other elements you are entitled to. For the definition of eligible childcare costs, and an explanation of how these are calculated, see pp1241–1244.

4. The childcare element of working tax credit

Your maximum amount of working tax credit (WTC) can include a childcare element, to help meet the cost of 'relevant childcare' (see p1241).[34] This element is 80 per cent of actual childcare costs of up to £175 a week for one child, or £300 a week for two or more children (ie, up to £140 or £240 a week).[35]

To get the childcare element of WTC, you or your partner must be 'responsible for' at least one child.[36] You do not have to be the child's parent. **'Responsible for'** has the same meaning for WTC as it does for child tax credit (CTC) (see p1198).[37]

The childcare element is just a part of the maximum WTC calculation and cannot be claimed on its own, or as part of CTC.[38]

This element can be included to help meet the costs of childcare if you are incurring charges for relevant childcare and you are:[39]

- a lone parent engaged in full-time paid work; *or*
- a member of a married or unmarried couple, or living with your registered civil partner (or living with someone as if you were registered civil partners); *and either:*
  - you are both engaged in full-time paid work; *or*
  - one of you is engaged in full-time paid work and the other is incapacitated (see below); *or*
  - one of you is engaged in full-time paid work and the other is in hospital or in prison (serving a sentence or remanded in custody).

Incapacitated

You or your partner are treated as incapacitated if:[40]

- you get short-term higher rate or long-term incapacity benefit (IB); *or*
- you get severe disablement allowance; *or*
- you get attendance allowance, disability living allowance (DLA) (or an equivalent award paid as an increase under the war pensions or industrial injuries disablement scheme) or would be getting it but for the fact that you are in hospital; *or*
- you get industrial injuries disablement benefit with constant attendance allowance; *or*
- you have an award of housing benefit or council tax benefit which includes a disability premium or a higher pensioner premium in respect of incapacity; *or*
- you have an invalid carriage or similar vehicle.[41]

You can claim the childcare element for a new baby while you are on statutory maternity, paternity or adoption leave, as well as for any other children for whom you are responsible.

Relevant childcare charges can be for any child in your family up to the last day of the week in which 1 September falls, following the child's 15th birthday, or her/his 16th birthday if s/he is disabled.[42] **'Disabled child'** means a child who:[43]

- receives DLA, or whose DLA has been suspended because s/he is a hospital inpatient; *or*
- has been registered blind; *or*
- ceased to be registered blind in the 28 weeks immediately preceding the WTC claim.

Relevant childcare

In order to be **'relevant childcare'** the childcare must be provided by:[44]

- a registered childminder; *or*

- another registered childcare provider such as a nursery, after-school club and local authority daycare service; *or*
- a school or establishment exempt from registration; *or*
- an out-of-hours club on school premises run by the school or the local authority for children up to age 15 (or 16 if the child is disabled). The child counts as 15 (or 16) up to the last day of the week in which 1 September falls, following the child's 15th/16th birthday; *or*
- a foster parent or foster carer under specified fostering regulations – but not in respect of a child who is being fostered by that foster parent; *or*
- in England only and in your own home, a person approved to provide care for children (including someone approved under the Childcare Approval Scheme before 1 October 2007, where now properly registered - check if unsure), a domiciliary worker or nurse employed by an agency registered for that purpose, or someone registered under the Vountary Registration Scheme; *or*
- in England and Wales, for children aged 8 or over on other domestic premises, someone approved under the Childcare Approval Scheme (in England this was abolished on 1 October 2007 but you should remain covered if the childcare provider is properly registered – check if unsure). **'Domestic premises'** means any premises used wholly or mainly as a private dwelling.[45] You cannot claim help under this scheme for childcare provided in the home of a relative of your child, where the care is usually provided only for children to whom that childcare provider is a relative;[46] *or*
- in Wales only, a domiciliary care worker registered under the Domiciliary Care Agencies (Wales) Regulations 2004, or someone approved to provide care for children, including under the Welsh Childcare Approval Scheme; *or*
- in Scotland only, or arranged through a childcare agency which is required to be registered.

Your childcare provider must be properly registered or approved – check with the Revenue if unsure. A registered childminder, childcare scheme or nursery, or an approved home childcare provider means one which is registered or approved:

- (in England) by Ofsted, the National Care Standards Commission or, in the case of a childminder approved under the Childcare Approval Scheme, by Nestor Primecare Services Ltd;[47]
- (in Wales) by the National Assembly for Wales (via the Care Standards Inspectorate for Wales);
- (in Scotland) by the Scottish Commission for the Regulation of Care;
- (in Northern Ireland) by a Health and Social Services Trust.

Some schemes run on school premises may be approved by local authorities or local education authorities. You can also claim help with the costs of childcare in these schemes.

You cannot claim help with the costs of childcare provided in your own home if that care is provided by a relative of your child. '**Relative**' means parent, grandparent, aunt or uncle, brother or sister, whether related by blood, marriage or affinity. By affinity, we understand that the Revenue means people who are related through partners, rather than husbands or wives. For example, if childcare is provided in your home by your partner's mother, she is related to the child by affinity, even if your partner is not the child's parent, and so you cannot claim for the cost of paying her.

You can only claim for charges that you are actually paying. If you will not be making payments for childcare until some time after you have claimed WTC, you cannot receive a childcare element for these until you actually start making the payments. If you have made an arrangement with a childcare provider to pay childcare costs, you can claim for these costs up to a week before the childcare is provided.[48]

The amount of the childcare element

The amount of the element is calculated as follows.

Step one: work out your relevant period

Add up the number of days in your relevant period (see p1233). If you are making a claim for tax credits before the beginning of a new tax year, your award is usually based on entitlement at the same rate for a whole tax year, and your relevant period is one year. The tax year 2008/09 has 365 days.

Step two: calculate your relevant childcare charge

Your '**relevant childcare charge**' is your average weekly charge. The way in which your average weekly charge is calculated depends on whether you pay for childcare weekly, monthly, or at some other interval, and on whether the amount you pay varies over time.[49]

- If you pay for childcare on a weekly basis and the charge is a fixed weekly amount, add together the charges in the most recent four weeks before the claim and divide by four.
- If you pay for childcare on a weekly basis, have paid for childcare for at least 52 weeks and the charge varies over time, add together the charges in the 52 weeks before the claim and divide by 52.
- If you pay on a monthly basis and the charge is a fixed monthly amount, multiply that monthly amount by 12 and divide the total by 52.
- If you pay on a monthly basis and the charge varies from month to month, add together the charges for the last 12 months and divide the total by 52.
- If there is not enough information for the Revenue to establish your average weekly charge by any of the above methods, the charge will be calculated by the Revenue on the basis of information which you provide about your childcare costs, using any method which, in its opinion, is reasonable.

- If you have entered into an agreement to pay for childcare, which will be provided during the period of your award, your average weekly childcare costs will be calculated on the basis of your own written estimate of these costs. In practice, you provide this estimate on your tax credit claim form.

When you have calculated your average weekly childcare charges by one of these methods, round the figure up to the nearest whole pound.

Step three: calculate your actual childcare costs for the relevant period

The weekly amount found in step two is now converted to an amount covering your relevant period. Multiply the weekly charge by 52 to calculate the annual amount. Divide this figure by the number of days in the current tax year to find the daily rate, and then multiply this daily rate by the number of days in your relevant period. This gives your childcare costs for the relevant period.[50]

Step four: calculate your maximum eligible childcare costs for the relevant period

Divide the maximum eligible weekly childcare cost which applies to you by seven, to find the daily rate. The maximum eligible weekly cost is £175 for one child, and £300 for two or more children. Round this figure up to the nearest penny and then multiply this daily rate by the number of days in the relevant period.

Step five: calculate the childcare element for the relevant period

Take the lower of the two figures found in steps three and four, and calculate 80 per cent of that figure. Round the amount up to the nearest penny. This gives your childcare element for the relevant period.

Example

Tracy paid a fixed amount of £200 every week in eligible childcare costs for her two children during each of the four weeks before her application for tax credits was made. She makes an application for WTC in advance of the new tax year. She will continue to pay £200 a week for the same childcare. Her childcare element for the whole of a tax year is calculated as follows.

Step one

Tracy's relevant period is one year (365 days).

Step two

Her relevant childcare charge is £200. (This is her average weekly charge.)

Step three

£200 x 52 = £10,400

(£10,400 ÷ 365) x 365 = £10,400

Step four

The maximum weekly eligible childcare cost for Tracy is £300, as she has two children.

The daily rate is £300 ÷ 7 = £42.86 (rounded up to the nearest penny).

The annual rate is £42.86 x 365 = £15,643.90

Step five

The lower figure from Steps three and four is £10,400

Childcare element is 80% x £10,400 = £8,320

Tracy's childcare element for the relevant period (in this case, one whole tax year) is £8,320

5. How to calculate the amount of tax credit

If you are not receiving income support, income-based jobseeker's allowance or pension credit

The following steps describe how your entitlement is worked out if you are *not* receiving income support (IS), income-based jobseeker's allowance (JSA) or pension credit (PC).

Step one: work out your relevant period

Add up the number of days in your relevant period (see p1233). If you are making a claim for tax credit at the beginning of a new tax year, your award will be based on entitlement at the same rate for a whole tax year, and your relevant period will be one year. The tax year 2008/09 has 365 days.

Step two: find your maximum entitlement for the relevant period

First, identify the different elements of each tax credit you are eligible for. Take the daily rate of each element *apart from the childcare element of working tax credit (WTC)* – see pxvii for the daily rates.

For each element, multiply this daily rate by the number of days in the relevant period. Add the adjusted amounts of each element together. Next, calculate your childcare element for the relevant period as described on p1243.

Add the childcare element for the relevant period to the other elements for the relevant period to find your maximum entitlement for the relevant period.

Step three: find your relevant income

The income used in the tax credit calculation is your relevant income (see p1246).

The usual procedure which the Revenue uses is to base the calculation on your previous tax year's income. (In some cases, it may be to your advantage to have an estimate of your current tax year's income used in the calculation instead – see p1254.)

Divide this income by the number of days in the tax year to which your claim for tax credits relates to find the daily rate, and then multiply this daily rate by the number of days in the relevant period. Round this amount down to the nearest penny. This is your relevant income.

At the end of the tax year, when determining whether your entitlement during that year should have been based on the current year's income or the previous year's income, the Revenue will compare the two amounts, to see whether there is a difference of £25,000 or more between the two.[51]

- If your income in the current tax year exceeds your income in the previous tax year by £25,000 or less, the previous year's income will be used.
- If your income in the current tax year exceeds your income in the previous tax year by more than £25,000, your current year's income minus £25,000 will be used.
- If your income in the current tax year is less than or the same as your income in the previous tax year, your current year's income will be used.

Step four: compare your income with the threshold for the relevant period

Find the annual threshold which applies to you.

- If you are entitled to WTC only, the annual threshold is £6,420.
- If you are entitled to WTC *and* CTC, the annual threshold is £6,420.
- If you are entitled to CTC only, and not to WTC, the annual threshold is £15,575.

Divide the threshold which applies to you by the number of days in the current tax year, and then multiply this figure by the number of days in the relevant period. Round this amount up to the nearest penny. This figure is your threshold for the relevant period.

Step five: calculate tax credit entitlement for the relevant period

- If your income is less than the threshold that applies to you, you are entitled to receive the maximum amount of tax credit(s).
- If your income is greater than the threshold which applies to you, subtract the threshold figure from your relevant income to find your excess income. Calculate 39 per cent of this excess income and round this figure down to the nearest penny. Finally, reduce your maximum amount of tax credit(s) by this amount.
- The different elements of your maximum tax credit are tapered away in a set order.
  - First, the elements of WTC except for the childcare element are reduced.
  - Next, the childcare element is reduced.
  - Third, the child elements of CTC plus any disability or severe disability elements for your children are reduced.

– The family element of CTC will not be reduced unless you have income for a tax year in excess of the second income threshold of £50,000. At this point, the family element will be reduced by £1 for every £15 of income in excess of £50,000 (ie, at a rate of 6.67 per cent).

It is expected that in a small number of cases, a claimant's maximum amount of tax credit will be so high that the child element of CTC will not have been tapered away completely by the time income for the tax year has reached £50,000. In these cases, the child element will continue to be tapered away at a rate of 37 per cent until this element is exhausted, and then the family element will be tapered away at the rate of £1 for every £15 of excess income.

If you are entitled to CTC only, or WTC only, and the calculation results in entitlement of less than £26, no award of tax credit will be made. If you are entitled to both CTC and WTC, and the total entitlement from both adds up to less than £26, no award will be made.[52]

To find out how much your weekly payment will be, divide the total found in step five above by the number of days in your relevant period to find the daily rate and then multiply this daily rate by seven. If your credit is paid four-weekly, multiply the daily rate by 28, to calculate the amount of your payments.

Example

Tracy claims tax credits at the beginning of the tax year 2008/09. During the tax year 2007/08 she worked 20 hours a week and earned £8 an hour, gross. During the tax year 2008/09, she continues to work the same hours, for the same rate of pay. Tracy's entitlement to tax credits is calculated as follows:

Step one: work out the relevant period

Tracy's relevant period is 365 days.

Step two: find maximum entitlement for the relevant period

CTC	Family element	£547.50
	Child element for three-year-old child	£2,087.80
	Child element for five-year-old child	£2,087.80
WTC	Basic element	£1,803.10
	Lone parent element	£1,770.25
	Childcare element	£8,320.00
Total maximum amount of tax credit		£16,616.45

Note: although Tracy's annual period is one year, the figures for each element do not equal the annual amount of each element. For example, the annual amount of the family element is £545, but the calculation above shows Tracy's family element during her relevant period of one year as being £547.50. This is because when the annual amount has been divided by 365 the figure produced is *rounded up* to the nearest penny, before being multiplied by the number of days in the tax year. This rounding up has the effect of increasing Tracy's annual maximum amount.

Step three: find relevant income

Tracy earned £8,342.85 during the tax year 2007/08. (She is paid £8 an hour, gross, and works 20 hours a week.) This total is calculated as follows:

((£8 x 20) ÷ 7) x 365 = £8,342.85

She continues to be paid at the same rate during the tax year 2008/09. During the year in which tax credits are paid (2008/09), her income for the year 2007/08 is used.

Tracy's income for the relevant period is therefore:

(£8,342.85 ÷ 365) x 365 =£8,342.85, rounded down to the nearest penny.

Step four: compare income with the threshold for the relevant period

As Tracy will receive both WTC and CTC, her annual threshold figure is £6,420.

The threshold for the relevant period is therefore:

(£6,420 ÷ 365) x 365 = £6,420, rounded up to the nearest penny.

Step five: calculate tax credit entitlement for the relevant period

Tracy has excess income of £1,922.85 (income of £8,342.85 minus the threshold figure of £6,420).

Apply the taper of 39 per cent to this excess income:

39% x £1,922.85 = £749.91

Tracy's maximum tax credit (£16,616.45) will be reduced by this amount. Her total tax credit entitlement will be:

£16,616.45 – £749.91= £15,866.54

The reduction is first applied to the elements of her WTC apart from the childcare element (ie, the basic element of £1,803.10 plus the lone parent element of £1,770.25 = £3,573.35):

£3,573.35 – £749.91 = £2,823.44

Tracy's tax credits for the tax year 2008/09 will, therefore, be:

WTC (not including childcare element)	£2,823.44
Childcare element	£8,320.00
CTC	£4,723.10
Total tax credits	**£15,866.54**

To find the weekly rate of payment, this figure is divided by 365 (the number of days in Tracy's relevant period) and multiplied by 7.

(£15,866.54 ÷ 365) x 7 = £304.28

If you are receiving income support, income-based jobseeker's allowance or pension credit

If you are entitled to IS, income-based JSA or PC, you are automatically entitled to the maximum amount of CTC or WTC you could receive.[53] You calculate this by adding together the elements of each tax credit you qualify for, over your relevant period, as described above. Your maximum amount is not subject to any reduction during the period you are receiving IS, income-based JSA or PC.

6. Entitlement after a change of circumstances

There are three different ways in which your circumstances can change that will affect your entitlement to tax credits.

- If your circumstances change in a way that affects your maximum entitlement, a new relevant period begins. For example, if a disability benefit which gives entitlement to a disability element is awarded to you or someone included in your claim, this changes your maximum amount of tax credit and starts a new relevant period.
- Other changes, such as a change in the number of adults heading your household, will bring your award to an end, and you will have to make a fresh claim for tax credit, if you remain entitled. This will also start a new relevant period.
- Finally, some changes, which do not affect your maximum entitlement and do not bring your existing award to an end, will affect the amount of tax credit which is payable to you. For example, if your existing award has been based on your current tax year's income, and you have a significant rise in your income during that tax year, you may be overpaid tax credit unless you report the change at once, enabling your award to be recalculated.

See p1287 for a description of the changes of circumstances which bring one relevant period to an end and start another, for changes which end your current award, and for changes which will affect the amount of your award.

In any of these circumstances, your tax credit award will need to be recalculated. This is done by working through steps one to five as described on pp1245–1246, for each relevant period.

Example

Tracy claims disability living allowance (DLA) for her five-year-old child and this is awarded (middle rate of the care component) from day 201 of the tax year 2008/09. She therefore has two relevant periods during this tax year. The first is 200 days long, and the second, from the date her daughter is awarded DLA, 165 days long.

Her entitlement during the first 200 days is calculated as follows:

Step one: work out the relevant period

The first relevant period is 200 days long.

Step two: find maximum entitlement for the relevant period

Maximum entitlement to all of the elements of tax credits for the relevant period of 200 days, apart from the childcare element, is calculated.

Child tax credit (CTC)	Family element	£300
	Child element for three-year-old child	£1,144
	Child element for five-year-old child	£1,144

Working tax credit (WTC) (not including childcare element)	Basic element	£988
	Lone parent element	£970

Next, the childcare element for the relevant period is calculated, as described above.

Childcare element	£4,558.92

Tracy's total maximum amount of tax credit for this relevant period is therefore £9,104.92 (£4,546 + £4,558.92).

Step three: find relevant income

Tracy's annual income is £8,342.85. This is adjusted for the relevant period by dividing by the number of days in the tax year, and multiplying by the number of days in the relevant period.

(£8,342.85 ÷ 365) x 200 = £4,571.42

Step four: compare income with the threshold for the relevant period

As Tracy receives both WTC and CTC, her annual threshold figure is £6,420. The threshold figure is also adjusted to cover the relevant period.

(£6,420 ÷ 365) x 200 = £3,517.81

Step five: calculate tax credit entitlement for the relevant period

Tracy has excess income of £1,053.61 (relevant income of £4,571.42 minus the threshold figure of £3,517.81).

Apply the taper of 39 per cent to this excess income:

39% x £1,053.61 = £410.90

Tracy's maximum tax credit 9,104.92) will be reduced by this amount. Her total tax credit entitlement will be:

£9,104.92 – £410.90 = £8,694.02

This reduction of £410.90 is first applied to the elements of her WTC apart from the childcare element (ie, the basic element of £988 plus the lone parent element of £970 = £1,958).

£1,958 – £410.90 = £1,547.10

Tracy's tax credits for the first 200 days will be made up as follows:

WTC (not including childcare element)	£1,547.10
Childcare element	£4,558.92
CTC	£2,588.00
Total tax credits	**£8,694.02**

Tracy's total tax credit entitlement for the first 200 days is therefore £8,694.02.

To find the weekly rate of payment, this figure is divided by 200 and multiplied by 7.

(£8,694.02 ÷ 200) x 7 = £304.29

Her entitlement for the second relevant period is calculated as follows:

Step one: work out relevant period

The second relevant period is 165 days long.

Step two: find maximum entitlement for the relevant period

Maximum entitlement to all of the elements of tax credits for the relevant period of 165 days, apart from the childcare element, is calculated:

CTC	Family element	£247.50
	Child element for three-year-old child	£943.80
	Child element for five-year-old child	£943.80
	Disability element for five-year-old child	£1,148.40
WTC (not including childcare element)	Basic element	£815.10
	Lone parent element	£800.25
Total		£4,898.85

Next, the childcare element for the relevant period is calculated, as described above.

	Childcare element	£3,761.10

Tracy's total maximum amount of tax credit for this relevant period is therefore £8,659.95 (£4,898.85 + £3,761.10).

Step three: find relevant income

Tracy's annual income is £8,342.85. This is adjusted for the relevant period by dividing by the number of days in the tax year, and multiplying by the number of days in the relevant period.

(£8,342.85 ÷ 365) x 165 = £3,771.42

Step four: compare income with the threshold for the relevant period

As Tracy receives both WTC and CTC, her annual threshold figure is £6,420. The threshold figure is also adjusted to cover the relevant period.

(£6,420 ÷ 365) x 165 = £2,902.20

Step five: calculate tax credit entitlement for the relevant period

Tracy has excess income of £869.22 (relevant income of £3,771.42 minus the threshold figure of £2,902.20).

Apply the taper of 39 per cent to this excess income.

39% x £869.22 = £338.99

Tracy's maximum tax credit (£8,659.95) will be reduced by this amount. Her total tax credit entitlement will be:

£8,659.95 – £338.99 = £8,320.96

The reduction is first applied to the elements of her WTC apart from the childcare element (ie, the basic element of £815.10 plus the lone parent element of £800.25 = £1,615.35).

£1,615.35 – £338.99 = £1,276.36

Tracy's tax credits for the second 165 days will be made up as follows:

WTC (not including childcare element)	£1,276.36
Childcare element	£3,761.10
CTC	£3,283.50
Total tax credits	**£8,320.96**

Tracy's total tax credit entitlement for the second 165 days is therefore £8,320.96.

To find the weekly rate of payment, this figure is divided by 165 and multiplied by 7.

(£8,320.96 ÷ 165) x 7 = £353.01

Notes

1. **The relevant period**
   1 s5(1) TCA 2002
   2 s5(2) TCA 2002
   3 Reg 8(2) TC(ITDR) Regs
   4 Reg 7(2) TC(ITDR) Regs
   5 Reg 8(2) TC(ITDR) Regs

2. **The maximum amount of child tax credit**
   6 Reg 7 CTC Regs
   7 Regs 7 and 8 TC(ITDR) Regs
   8 Reg 7 CTC Regs
   9 Reg 8(1) and (2) CTC Regs
   10 Reg 8(1) and (3) CTC Regs

3. **The maximum amount of working tax credit**
   11 Reg 20 WTC(EMR) Regs
   12 Reg 15 WTC(EMR) Regs
   13 Regs 7 and 8 TC(ITDR) Regs
   14 Reg 20 WTC(EMR) Regs
   15 Reg 4 WTC(EMR) Regs
   16 Reg 3(2) WTC(EMR) Regs
   17 Reg 11(2) WTC(EMR) Regs
   18 Reg 11 WTC(EMR) Regs
   19 Reg 11 WTC(EMR) Regs
   20 Reg 3 WTC(EMR) Regs
   21 Reg 12 WTC(EMR) Regs
   22 Reg 10 WTC(EMR) Regs
   23 Reg 3 WTC(EMR) Regs
   24 Reg 9 WTC(EMR) Regs
   25 Reg 9 WTC(EMR) Regs
   26 CTC/643/2005
   27 Reg 9(8) WTC(EMR) Regs
   28 Reg 3(3) WTC(EMR) Regs
   29 Reg 17 WTC(EMR) Regs
   30 Reg 3(3) WTC(EMR) Regs
   31 Reg 18 WTC(EMR) Regs
   32 Reg 3(3) WTC(EMR) Regs
   33 Reg 13 WTC(EMR) Regs

4. **The childcare element of working tax credit**
   34 Regs 3 and 13 WTC(EMR) Regs
   35 Reg 20(3) WTC(EMR)Regs
   36 Reg 14(1) WTC(EMR) Regs
   37 Reg 14(1) WTC(EMR) Regs
   38 Reg 20 WTC(EMR) Regs
   39 Reg 13(1) WTC(EMR) Regs
   40 Reg 13(4) WTC(EMR) Regs
   41 Reg 13(8) WTC(EMR) Regs
   42 Reg 14(3) WTC(EMR) Regs
   43 Reg 14(4) WTC(EMR) Regs
   44 s12(5) TCA 2002; reg 14(2) WTC(EMR) Regs; TC(ACCP)S; Childcare (Voluntary Registration) Regulations 2007 No.730; Tax Credits (Approval of Childcare Providers) (Wales) Scheme 2007 No.226 (W20)
   45 Art 2 TC(ACCP)S
   46 Art 5 TC(ACCP)S
   47 Arts 2 and 3 TC(ACCP)S
   48 Revenue leaflet WTC5
   49 Reg 15 WTC(EMR) Regs
   50 Reg 7(3) TC(ITDR) Regs, steps 7-10

5. **How to calculate the amount of tax credit**
   51 s7(3) TCA 2002; reg 5 TC(ITDR) Regs
   52 Reg 9 TC(ITDR) Regs
   53 ss7(2) and 13 TCA 2002; reg 4 TC(ITDR) Regs

Chapter 52

Income: tax credits

This chapter explains how to work out your annual income for child tax credit and working tax credit. It covers:

The amount of tax credit to which you are entitled depends on how much income you have. Chapter 51 explains how income affects the amount of tax credit you get. In general, most taxable income is taken into account in the assessment, while non-taxable income is ignored, but there are exceptions. This chapter explains what income is taken into account and what income is disregarded.

For tax credits, your **savings or other capital** are not taken into account in the assessment, although interest or other income earned from savings or capital does count. There is no capital limit as there is for social security benefits. You are eligible for tax credits whatever the level of your capital.

Note: in this chapter, unless otherwise stated, references to income-based jobseeker's allowance (JSA) also refer to joint-claim JSA.

1. Annual income

The assessment is always based on income over a full tax year (6 April to 5 April) except during a time when you are getting income support (IS), income-based jobseeker's allowance (JSA) or pension credit (PC) (see p1254). If the tax credit award only runs for part of the year, the full year's income is reduced on a *pro-rata* basis as explained on p1245.

At the start of your claim, your tax credit is calculated based on income for the previous tax year.

At the end of the tax year the Revenue finalises entitlement by comparing income over the year of the award ('current year's income') with that in the previous tax year. If the current year's income is less, your final entitlement is based instead on the current year's income. If the current year's income is more than £25,000 higher than in the previous year, your final entitlement is based on the current year's income, but with £25,000 disregarded (see p1255). Thus, your final entitlement may be less or more than the award originally made.

The original award can be revised during the year, with the calculation based instead on an estimate of your current year's income if you tell the Revenue about the change in income.

Note: while you are on IS, income-based JSA or PC, you are entitled to maximum tax credits without any income test, so the level of your income in the previous or current year is not relevant. When IS, income-based JSA or PC stops, the tax credit award is again based on annual income.

When you claim

When claiming for all or part of the tax year 6 April 2008 to 5 April 2009, your award is based initially on your income for the year 6 April 2007 to 5 April 2008. This is the case even if you know at the outset that your income during the year of the award will be different. If your income in the previous year is too high to qualify for tax credits, but you satisfy the other qualifying conditions, the decision will be to award tax credits at a nil rate. If you think your income will be lower or significantly higher in the current year, you can ask for the award, including a nil-rate award, to be revised (see below).

If your income has changed since the previous year

Any decrease in income in the current year compared with the previous year, however small, affects your final tax credit entitlement. An increase in income affects final entitlement only if your income is more than £25,000 higher than in the previous year. Increases of less than this do not affect your award until the following year. (For awards up to the year 2005/06, increases of over £2,500 affected final entitlement.)

If you do not tell the Revenue about your change in income, your award continues at the same rate until the end of the tax year if other circumstances stay the same. At that point you must give full details when the Revenue sends you the annual review pack and it will recalculate your final entitlement for that year. Because this can take some months, if your income has gone up, even if the increase is not enough to affect your award this year, you should tell the Revenue by 6 April to avoid being overpaid from the start of your renewed award. If you have not given up-to-date income details by 6 April, the Revenue starts your renewed award assuming your income went up in line with average earnings.

If you tell the Revenue during the year about an increase in income of more than £25,000 compared with the previous year, your award can be revised based on an estimate of the current year's income less a disregard of £25,000. This is advisable if you want to reduce the risk of overpayments at the end of the year.

If you expect your income to be *less* in the current year than in the previous year, you should tell the Revenue so it can base your award on what you expect your earnings to be in the current year. You should take particular care to tell the Revenue quickly if you later think your estimate was too low so it can readjust your award. If you do not, you could end up with an overpayment. The £25,000 disregard only applies to an increase in income compared with the previous year, not to an increase compared with an earlier current year's estimate.

You can phone the Tax Credit Helpline or write to the Tax Credit Office with details of your current year's income (or you can pass them to a Revenue enquiry centre, Jobcentre Plus or other DWP office). There is no special form to fill in so you need to take care to give full details of *all* your (and your partner's) relevant income for the current year.

At the end of the tax year

At the end of the tax year, the Revenue finalises your entitlement. It sends you an annual review form to see whether your income in the current year is any different from that in the previous year.

The previous year means the tax year that ended immediately before the year of the award – eg, 6 April 2007 to 5 April 2008 for awards in the tax year 6 April 2008 to 5 April 2009.

Your final entitlement is based on:[1]

- the current year's income, if income in the current year is less than the previous year's income;
- the current year's income less £25,000 if income in the current year has gone up by more than £25,000;
- the previous year's income if income has stayed the same or gone up by no more than £25,000.

Examples

From 6 April 2007 to 5 April 2008 Izzy worked part time and earned a total of £5,000. Since then she has worked full time and earned £12,500 in the current year of the award from 6 April 2008 to 5 April 2009. Her tax credit award is initially based on income of £5,000. Because her income went up by just £7,500 in the current year – below the £25,000 threshold – her final entitlement is also based on income of £5,000.

From 6 April 2007 to 5 April 2008, Marsha and Bill, who are claiming as a couple, had total income of £11,000 from Bill's wages. In the current year of the award from 6 April 2008 to 5 April 2009, Marsha has gone back to work and they earned £37,000 between them. Their tax credit award is initially based on the previous year's income of £11,000. Because their income went up by £26,000 in the current year (£37,000 – £11,000), their final entitlement is based on income of £12,000 (£37,000 – £25,000). For the next year, 6 April 2009 to 5 April 2010, their award will be based on income of £37,000.

Estimating income

There are no special rules for how to estimate income. Using, for instance, payslips and benefit award letters, work out how much income you have already received in the current year and estimate how much you will receive for the remainder of the year. Tax credits are always worked out using annual income, so you must include all income received or estimated for the whole tax year, 6 April to 5 April, even if you are asking for an award to be adjusted part-way through the year.

If you are self-employed, the Revenue's Self-assessment Helpline (0845 9000 444) can advise you how to work out your business profits. You need to estimate your profits for the accounting period relevant to the current tax year. This might be different from your current earnings, particularly if your accounting year-end is early in the tax year.

2. Whose income counts

If you are a member of a couple (see p1211), your partner's income is added to yours.[2] Otherwise, only your own income counts.

If you were previously part of a couple, but now are single or a lone parent, only your income counts, not that of your former partner, even where the previous year's income is used in the assessment.

If you were single or a lone parent but are now in a couple, your joint income is assessed, whether entitlement is based on the current or previous tax year.

Children's income

Children's income is ignored. However, if you have transferred money under a trust to your child and tax rules treat that income as still belonging to you, it may also be treated as yours for tax credits.[3]

3. What income counts

In general, taxable social security benefits are taken into account, and gross earnings (before tax and national insurance (NI)) and business profits are taken into account less your pension contributions. Most other income, such as pensions and interest on savings, is added together and taken into account only to the extent that the total exceeds £300 a year. The rules specify what income must be taken into account and what is disregarded.

If you have a special exemption from income tax, your income is calculated as though you were liable for tax.[4] People such as foreign military personnel, officials of international organisations or consular staff may have an exemption.

Types of income

Income to be taken into account falls into certain categories and within each category certain amounts may be disregarded. There is also a general list of income that is disregarded (see p1267).

The income taken into account in the assessment is worked out as follows.[5]

Add together your income, or your joint income if you are a couple, from:

- social security benefits (see below);
- income from employment (see p1259);
- taxable profits from self-employment (see p1262);
- student income (see p1262);
- miscellaneous income (see p1263).

Add together your income, or your joint income if you are a couple, from:

- pension income (see p1263);
- income from investments (see p1264);
- income from property (see p1266);
- foreign income (see p1266);
- notional income (see p1269).

If the total income in the last group of five categories is less than £300 it is ignored completely, otherwise deduct £300 and add the remainder to your income under the first group of five categories. **Note:** couples share one £300 disregard.[6]

This gives you the total income that is taken into account – subject to any disregards described later in this chapter.

Example

Mr and Mrs Killean renew their claim for child tax credit (CTC) and working tax credit (WTC) from April 2008. The Revenue assesses their claim on their joint income for the year 6 April 2007 to 5 April 2008. In 2007/08 Mrs Killean earned £13,500 before tax and NI contributions. Mr Killean received taxable long-term incapacity benefit (IB) totalling £4,500 and an occupational pension of £500. Income taken into account is:

Employment income = £13,500

IB = £4,500

Occupational pension = £200 (ie, £500 less £300 disregard)

Total income = £18,200

Benefits

Generally, benefits are taken into account if they are taxable and ignored if they are not. However, increases for child dependants, although not taxable themselves, are nevertheless taken into account if paid with a taxable benefit.

Disregarded benefits

The following benefits are disregarded:[7]

- attendance allowance;
- back-to-work bonus;
- bereavement payment;
- child benefit;
- Christmas bonus;
- council tax benefit;
- disability living allowance;
- discretionary housing payment;
- an *ex gratia* supplement to IB for those over pension age;
- guardian's allowance;
- housing benefit (HB);
- income support (IS), except to strikers;
- income-based jobseeker's allowance (JSA);
- income-related employment and support allowance (ESA) (expected to be disregarded);
- industrial injuries benefit (except industrial death benefit);
- maternity allowance;
- pension credit (guarantee and savings credit);[8]
- severe disablement allowance;
- short-term lower rate IB;
- social fund payments;
- transitional long-term IB (see p278);
- any payment to compensate for the loss of IS, JSA or HB;
- any payment in lieu of milk tokens or vitamins;
- increases for a child[9] or adult dependant[10] paid with any of the above.

Tax credits themselves are disregarded. Statutory sick pay (SSP), statutory maternity pay (SMP), statutory adoption pay (SAP) and statutory paternity pay (SPP) are treated as employment income (see p1259). Retirement pensions, widowed mother's allowance, widowed parent's allowance, widow's pension, industrial death benefit and war pensions are treated as pension income (see p1263).

Benefits taken into account

Any benefits not in the list above are taken into account in full. This includes:

- bereavement allowance;
- carer's allowance (CA);
- contribution-based JSA;[11]
- long-term IB (but the non-taxable transitional long-term IB paid to those who transferred from invalidity benefit in 1995 is not taken into account);
- short-term higher rate IB;
- increases for a child or adult dependant paid with the above;

- contributory ESA (expected to be taken into account).

It is the amount of benefit payable that is taken into account. Arrears of benefit or any *ex gratia* payment in connection with a benefit are taken into account as income for the year in which the payment of arrears is made.[12]

Each year the DWP should give you a statement of the taxable benefits you received in the previous tax year. You can ask the local benefit office for a replacement if you did not get one. If you get any increase for a child dependant paid with CA or IB (or widowed mother's or widowed parent's allowance), this will not be included in the statement but it is taken into account as income so you should include it when completing your tax credit claim form.

Employment income

For tax credits, it is your **'gross'** pay that is taken into account.[13] This means your pay before any income tax or NI contributions are deducted.

Income counts whether received in the UK or elsewhere.[14]

What counts as employment income

'Employment income' means the following income received in the tax year:[15]

- 'any earnings from an office or employment, including:[16]
  - wages;
  - fees;
  - bonuses;
  - commission;
  - overtime pay;
  - tips or gratuities;
  - goods or assets that can be converted into money – eg, gifts of drink, clothes and fuel (the taxable value is shown on Form P9D or P11D, which your employer gives you at the end of the tax year);
  - payments made on your behalf – eg, rent paid by your employer direct to your landlord (amounts are shown on Form P9D or P11D);
- taxable expenses (see p1260 for expenses that do not count as earnings);[17]
- any taxable cash voucher, non-cash voucher or credit token (eg, company credit card).[18] Vouchers spent on allowable expenses are ignored.[19] Disregard 15p a day from meals vouchers. (Taxable values are shown on Form P9D or P11D);[20]
- taxable payments in connection with the termination of your employment or with a change in your duties or wages, including non-statutory and statutory redundancy payments, pay in lieu of notice and employment tribunal awards for unfair dismissal. The first £30,000 of the total of such payments is ignored;[21]
- SSP;[22]
- SMP above £100 a week. The first £100 a week is ignored;[23]
- SPP and SAP above £100 a week;[24]

- strike pay from your trade union (even though this is non-taxable);[25]
- the cash equivalent of the benefit of a company car for private use and car fuel benefits if you earn £8,500 or more or you are a company director. (These amounts are shown in Form P11D, which your employer should give you.)[26] Other expenses in connection with the car are ignored.[27] However, if you are a disabled employee with an adapted or automatic company car, the car is exempt from income tax and ignored for tax credits;[28]
- payments for agreeing to restrict your future conduct or activities;[29]
- taxable income from an employee share scheme;[30]
- payment for work done while sentenced or on remand in prison.[31]

Payments not counted as earnings

Some payments do not count as earnings and are disregarded in the tax credits assessment. In so far as they are exempt from income tax, ignore the following:[32]

- expenses incurred 'wholly, exclusively and necessarily' in the course of your employment.[33] **Note:** if you are a volunteer with a charity or voluntary organisation, all your expenses are ignored.[34] If you earn less than £8,500 a year, generally all your expenses are ignored. However, any that are taxable would be taken into account – eg, 'round sum' expense allowances payable irrespective of how you might spend it;[35]
- approved mileage allowance;[36]
- fixed-sum deductions for maintaining work tools;[37]
- homeworkers' additional household expenses;[38]
- travel expenses, but not to and from work[39] unless you are a disabled employee or need transport home because of irregular late-night working or disrupted car sharing arrangements;[40]
- the first £8,000 of relocation expenses;[41]
- car parking payments for a space near your work;[42]
- the use of, or vouchers for, sports or recreational facilities;[43]
- incidental overnight expenses up to £5 a night in the UK (£10 overseas);[44]
- travel and subsistence allowance when public transport is disrupted by industrial action;[45]
- small gifts of goods or vouchers below £250 from a donor (who cannot be your employer) a year;[46]
- childcare vouchers or credit tokens for 'relevant childcare' (see p1241) (but any childcare element in your WTC will be based on the lower subsidised childcare costs);[47]
- 15p a day of meals vouchers.[48] (The taxable value of meals vouchers that is taken into account for tax credits is shown on Form P9D or P11D from your employer.) Vouchers for staff canteens are ignored;[49]
- one tax-free mobile phone;[50]
- expenses for personal security;[51]
- an award under a staff suggestion scheme below the taxable limit;[52]

- any fees to approved professional bodies;[53]
- premium payments for professional indemnity insurance or towards liability claims made against you;[54]
- deduct from earnings or from a benefit or pension[55] any charity payments under a payroll giving scheme;[56]
- payment for work-related training or individual learning account training;[57]
- job grant, return-to-work credit, in-work credit or DWP payment under the Employment Retention and Advancement Scheme or Working Neighbourhoods Pilot;[58]
- payment of re-training course expenses for people leaving their employment;[59]
- amount of salary given up under the Home Computer Initiative;[60]
- travel, accommodation and subsistence costs for work outside the UK, including travel for a spouse and child where your absence lasts at least 60 days;[61]
- travel expenses for work inside the UK if you live outside the UK.[62]

Some groups of workers have special income tax exemptions. The following are ignored as earnings for tax credits:

- armed forces' travel facilities for going to and returning from leave;[63]
- armed forces' food, drink and mess allowances and reserve forces' training allowances;[64]
- armed forces operational allowance for service in specified areas;[65]
- armed forces council tax relief payment;[66]
- free coal to miners, or former miners, or cash in lieu;[67]
- if you are an actor or performer, the tax-free amount of agents' fees;[68]
- expenses for mainland transfers for offshore oil and gas workers;[69]
- Crown employees' foreign service allowance;[70]
- expenses of a minister of religion, including a rent deduction;[71]
- European Commission daily subsistence allowance to seconded national experts.[72]

Deduct pension contributions

Deduct any contributions you make to a personal or occupational pension that is approved by the Revenue.[73]

If you pay contributions through your employer, your P60 or P45 should show your wages after the contributions have been deducted, so there is no further deduction to make.

If you pay the pension contributions directly, deduct the gross annual contributions. Because tax relief is given on personal pension contributions, your actual contributions are less than the gross amount included in the pension plan. It is the higher gross amount that you should deduct from your employment income. Your pension provider should supply you with annual statements of contributions received.

If you have no income from employment but are still making pension contributions, deduct the contributions from any other income you may have.

Income from self-employment

Your taxable profits from any 'trade', 'profession' or 'vocation' are taken into account for the relevant year.[74] If you have a business partner, it is taxable profits from your share of the business income that count.[75] This includes trading outside the UK. It also includes profits from renting out property if this is conducted as a business. (If property income comes from a 'trade', then income counts without the £300 disregard that would otherwise apply to such income.) If renting property is not conducted as a business, see p1266.

Taxable profits are shown on your tax return for the relevant year. If you have not yet submitted a tax return, the notes that accompany the tax credit claim form (TC600) explain how to work out your profit. You should deduct allowable business expenses from annual turnover to arrive at a profit figure. The Revenue's Self-assessment Helpline (0845 9000 444) should be able to give advice. See also p1256. **Note:** the provision allowing artists, farmers and market gardeners to average out fluctuating profits across two tax years does not apply; it is the actual taxable profit in the relevant year that counts.[76]

Business losses

If your business is run on a commercial basis and has made a loss, your income is nil for that tax year unless you have other income that counts in the assessment. If you do have other income, you should deduct the amount of the loss from that income (from joint income if you are claiming as a couple).[77] If you do not have enough income to offset the full amount, any left over can be carried forward and deducted from profits of the same trade in the next and later tax years.

Deduct pension contributions

Deduct the gross amount of any contributions you make to an approved personal pension scheme or a retirement annuity (see p1261).

Student income

Take into account an adult dependants' grant and, in Scotland, a lone parents' grant.[78] In general, other student grants and loans are ignored.

Student income disregarded

Apart from the grants above, other kinds of student support are ignored – eg:

- student loan;
- any supplementary grant from the local authority or Student Awards Agency for Scotland (SAAS), except for an adult dependants' grant and lone parents' grant;

- postgraduate award from research councils, the British Academy or SAAS;
- adult learning grant;
- Care to Learn grant and childcare grant;
- career development loan, except any amount applied for or paid in respect of living expenses for the period supported by the loan;[79]
- education maintenance allowance;[80]
- English Opportunity bursary;
- hardship funds;
- NHS or Scottish Executive Health Department bursary;
- Northern Irish higher education bursary;
- parents' learning allowance;
- 'scholarship', 'exhibition, bursary or any other similar educational endowment' if you are 'receiving full-time instruction' at an educational institution;[81]
- social work bursary;
- Welsh Assembly learning grant;
- young student's bursary;
- interest paid to you for an amount of student loan recovered then repaid by the Student Loan Company.[82]

Note: unlike means-tested benefits, students are not excluded from WTC and CTC. So long as you satisfy the eligibility rules, you can qualify. Another key difference from means-tested benefits is that your student loan and most other student income is ignored in the assessment, so if you are eligible you may well qualify for a tax credit throughout the year, not just in the long vacations.

Miscellaneous income

Any income that does not fit into any of the other nine categories on p1257 is taken into account if it is taxable under Revenue 'sweep up' provisions in Part 5 Income Tax (Trading and Other Income) Act 2005.[83] This includes copyright royalties if your writing does not amount to a trade or profession.

Pension income

Pension income taken into account

Take into account the following pension income. The first £300 a year is ignored from the total of your pension and any income from savings, investments, property or foreign or notional income.

- **State retirement pensions** and **graduated retirement benefit.**[84] (**Note:** the Christmas bonus and winter fuel payment are ignored.) The Revenue says that as well as your pension, it takes into account any additional state pension, incapacity addition, adult dependant addition and child dependant addition paid with your pension.[85] Include as income any lump sum you become entitled to through deferring your state pension.

- **Personal and occupational pensions.**[86] It is the gross amount before tax is deducted that counts. Your pension provider should give you a certificate each year showing how much pension was paid and how much tax taken off. If you retired because of work-related illness or disability caused by injury on duty, only count the amount of pension that you would have been paid if you had retired on non-work-related ill-health grounds. Any extra amount paid is ignored.[87] Tax-free lump sums paid under a personal pension scheme, retirement annuity contract or tax exempt pension scheme are ignored completely.[88] If you give up a small pension in favour of a trivial commutation lump sum, or you get a winding-up lump sum when your occupational pension scheme winds up, these lump sums count.
- **Widow's pension, widowed mother's** and **widowed parent's allowance**, including any increases for a child or adult dependant.[89]
- **Industrial death benefit.**[90]
- **Survivor's guaranteed income payment** and **child's payment** under the Armed Forces Compensation Scheme.[91]

Pension income disregarded

Ignore the following **war pensions**:[92]

- war disablement pension including constant attendance allowance and mobility supplement;
- war widow's or widower's pension under the War Pensions Scheme;
- annuity or additional pension to holders of theVictoria Cross, George Cross and certain other medals;
- wounds, injury or disablement pensions to members of the armed forces – eg, guaranteed income payment;
- death in service pensions for service in the armed forces or war injuries. If the death in service pension is overlapped by another pension, ignore an equivalent amount from the other pension;
- increase for a non-family dependant paid with a pension under the Service Pensions Order.

Investment income

There is no capital limit in the tax credit assessment as there is with means-tested benefits. The value of your savings is ignored completely. However, taxable *income*from savings and investments is taken into account. For example, the amount of savings in a bank account is ignored, but the interest on those savings is taken into account.

Investment income is taken into account as described on p1265. The first £300 a year is ignored from the total of your investment income and any income from pensions or property, or foreign or notional income.

Investment income taken into account

Take into account the following amounts before tax is deducted:[93]

- interest on invested money, including outside the UK – eg, interest on savings in a bank account;[94]
- dividends from shares of a company, resident in the UK (including the tax credit payable by the company with the dividend);[95]
- income from government stocks and bonds;[96]
- taxable payments from a life assurance policy, life annuity contract or capital redemption policy;[97]
- discounts on securities (ie, the profit from trading in securities such as government stocks and bonds);[98]
- payments from a trust;[99]
- payments from the estate of a deceased person;[100]
- interest arising from a debt owed to you.[101]

Investment income disregarded

Certain investment income is disregarded:

- interest, dividend or bonus from an ISA;[102]
- any dividend on a PEP. If you have cash held in a PEP (rather than shares) you can withdraw up to £180 interest and this is disregarded. If you withdraw more than this, the whole amount of interest is taken into account;[103]
- interest under a certified SAYE (save as you earn) scheme;[104]
- income from savings certificates and tax reserve certificates;[105]
- £70 per tax year of interest on deposits with National Savings and Investments;[106]
- investment income from tax-exempt annual payments – eg, from a covenant;[107]
- winnings from betting, pools, lotteries and games with prizes;[108]
- certain compensation payments to World War II victims;[109]
- interest on damages awarded through the courts for personal injuries or periodical payments of personal injury damages;[110]
- periodical payments from the Thalidomide Trust;[111]
- annuity payments under a Criminal Injuries Compensation Scheme award;[112]
- interest on the first £30,000 of a 'home income plan' loan taken out before 9 March 1999 to buy a life annuity;[113]
- interest on compensation to a child under 18 for the loss of a parent;[114]
- payments from the variant Creutzfeldt-Jakob disease government-funded trust, the Macfarlane Trusts, Independent Living Funds and the Eileen Trust. These are disregarded for the lifetime of the recipient, or for two years if paid to the disabled person's parent (or someone acting in place of a parent). If you inherit money from the estate of a disabled person who received such a payment, that inheritance is ignored, up to a maximum of the value of the original trust payment, for your lifetime if you were her/his partner or for two years if you were her/his parent;[115]

- capital element of a purchased life annuity;[116]
- tax-free health and employment insurance or immediate needs annuity payments.

Property income

The capital value of the property is ignored but rental income from the property is taken into account unless this is exempt from tax under the 'rent-a-room' scheme.[117] This scheme allows you to rent furnished accommodation in your own home earning up to £4,250 a year tax free.[118]

If you are not within the 'rent-a-room' scheme – eg, you rent out a property that you do not live in yourself, the amount of rent taken into account is the same as that agreed for income tax purposes. You can deduct from the rent received, expenses wholly and exclusively incurred in running the property – eg, repairs, council tax (if you, rather than your tenant, are liable to pay), water charges, insurance premiums and mortgage interest (but not capital repayments of a mortgage).[119] You can offset any losses against property income in the following tax year.

The first £300 a year is ignored from the total of your property income and any pensions, investment income, foreign or notional income.

If you rent property as a business (eg, you run a hotel or guesthouse), count this as income from self-employment (see p1262).[120]

Income from property outside the UK counts as 'foreign income' (see below).

Income from outside the UK

Although earnings from abroad are taken into account in the same way as UK earnings, other 'foreign income' – eg, from pensions, property or investments (other than taxable gains from an overseas insurer, which fall within the definition of 'investment income'), is taken into account subject to the following rules.[121]

The following are disregarded:[122]

- a banking charge or commission for converting currency to pounds sterling;[123]
- social security payments from outside the UK that are equivalent to tax-free UK benefits (see p1257);
- certain pensions or compensation for victims of Nazi persecution;
- one-tenth of the amount of any overseas pension or of a pension payable in the UK by the governments of certain countries;
- tax-free lump-sum payments under an overseas pension scheme;
- personal injury damages from a court outside the UK;
- certain education allowances payable to workers in the public sector of some countries outside the UK;

- property losses in one tax year that can be offset against property income in the following year;[124]
- maintenance payments;
- income that you are prevented from transferring to the UK by law or by the government of the country where the income arises or because you cannot get foreign currency in that country; other income that remains abroad is counted.[125]

The first £300 a year is disregarded from the total of your 'foreign income' and any pensions, investment, property or notional income.

Income from outside the UK is still taken into account even if you would normally have tax relief on that income in the UK to avoid double taxation in both countries (such income is treated as though it were taxable in the UK in the normal way).[126]

Converting currency

If your income is in another currency, the Revenue converts it to pounds sterling using a 12-month average of exchange rates for the tax year in which the income is paid.[127] Where your tax credit award is based on an estimate of current year's income, the rate of conversion will be adjusted once the exchange rate average is available at the end of the tax year. These rates are published on the Revenue's website (see Appendix 1).

General income disregards

All of the following income is disregarded in the tax credit assessment.[128]

Employment and training programmes

Ignore the following income:

- New Deal 50-plus employment credit;[129]
- mandatory top-up payment on a New Deal voluntary sector option, environment task force option or under a written agreement for your participation in the intensive activity period of the New Deal 25 plus (or the pilots) or the preparation for employment programme (where these are not taxable as profits);[130]
- discretionary payment for special needs on a New Deal full-time education and training option;[131]
- childcare expenses while you are participating in training on a New Deal option, or on the intensive activity period of the New Deal pilots for 25 plus or a preparation for employment programme (where these are not taxable as profits);[132]
- travelling expenses, a living away from home allowance and a training grant if you are participating in training under s2 Employment and Training Act 1973 or, in Scotland, under s2 Enterprise and New Towns (Scotland) Act 1990 or, in

Northern Ireland, under s1 Employment and Training Act (Northern Ireland) 1950, or attending a course at an employment rehabilitation centre (where these are not taxable as profits);[133]
- if you are aged 25 or over and getting JSA while on a 'qualifying course', a discretionary payment to help meet your special needs;[134]
- a payment to a disabled person under s2 Employment and Training Act 1973 or s15 Disabled Persons (Employment) Act 1944 (or equivalent Northern Ireland Acts) to assist disabled people to get or keep employment;[135]
- education maintenance allowance;[136]
- training premium or discretionary payment paid to you by an employment zone contractor for your participation in an employment zone programme.[137]

See also p1261 for other disregarded credits and payments.

Maintenance and children

Any maintenance you receive from an ex-partner is ignored, whether it is paid under a court order or not. Any child support you receive from your child's other parent (who is not now your partner) is ignored.[138]

If you pay maintenance to your ex-husband or ex-wife and one of you was born before 6 April 1935, you may qualify for tax relief. An amount equal to these qualifying maintenance payments is disregarded from your income in the tax credit assessment.[139]

If you foster a child placed with you by a local authority, independent fostering provider or, in Northern Ireland, an HSS trust, all your income from foster care (eg, the fostering allowance) is ignored, provided the annual amount is no more than £10,000 plus £200 a week for each child under 11 and £250 a week for each child aged 11 or over. If fostering income is over this limit, only the taxable amount is taken into account – ie, the amount above this limit or the actual net profit.[140]

Note: a foster child may not count as a member of your family for tax credits, so you may not get CTC for her/him (see p1199).

An **adoption allowance**,[141] **residence order allowance**[142] or **special guardianship payment**[143] for a child who is a member of your household is ignored completely. Other payments made by a local authority under the Children Act 1989 (CA 1989) or Children (Scotland) Act 1995 (C(S)A 1995) – eg, a payment for a child or family in need under s17 CA 1989 or s22 C(S)A 1995 or to a care leaver under s24 CA 1989 or s29 C(S)A 1995, are ignored.[144]

Other income

The following is ignored from your income:
- any contribution you make to an approved personal or occupational pension scheme (see p1261);[145]
- payments for fares to hospital;[146]

- payments to assist prison visits;[147]
- community care direct payments;[148]
- payments under the Supporting People programme;[149]
- payment or voucher for a former asylum seeker or dependant;[150]
- trade union provident benefits – eg, sickness or accident benefit or funeral payment;[151]
- payment for expenses incurred if you are an unpaid volunteer with a charity or voluntary organisation;[152]
- jury or witness payments if this is not compensation for loss of earnings or loss of benefit;[153]
- a payment to you for someone you are caring for temporarily made by a health authority, local authority, voluntary organisation, primary care trust or by the person themselves under the local authority's financial assessment, or, in Northern Ireland,[154] by a training school. This disregard only applies if the payment would be tax free under the Revenue's 'rent-a-room' scheme (see p1266);[155]
- any payment under an insurance policy taken out to insure against the risk of being unable to maintain mortgage repayments or other payments on a loan secured on your home. However, any payment you get above the amount you use to maintain the repayments plus the premiums on that policy or buildings insurance premiums required as a condition of the mortgage counts as your income;[156]
- any payment under an insurance policy taken out to insure against the risk of being unable to maintain repayments under a hire purchase, regulated or conditional sale agreement. However, any payment above the amount you use to maintain the repayments and the premiums on that policy counts as your income;[157]
- the gross amount of any 'gift aid' donation to charity;[158]
- a sports award for anything other than living expenses. Living expenses count as your income. Ignore parts of the award for dietary supplements and living away from home accommodation costs.[159]

4. Notional income

Sometimes you are treated as though you have income that you do not actually have. This is called **'notional income'**.[160] There are four kinds of notional income:

- income you have deprived yourself of to get or increase tax credits;
- income that would be available to you if you applied for it;
- a reasonable rate for work you have done for less than the going rate;
- income you are treated as having through certain provisions for preventing tax avoidance or when tax law treats capital as income and charges it to income tax.

Deprivation of income

You are treated as having income you have deprived yourself of for the purpose of getting a tax credit or a higher tax credit.[161] See p924 for details of when this rule might affect you.

Failing to apply for income

You are treated as having income that would become available to you if you applied for it.[162] This does not include:

- income under a trust set up from a personal injury payment;
- income from a personal pension scheme;
- interest on damages awarded through the courts for personal injury;
- a rehabilitation allowance;
- Category A or B retirement pension;
- graduated retirement benefit;
- a deferred shared additional pension.

Cheap or unpaid labour

If you work or provide a service for less than the going rate, you are treated as getting a reasonable rate for the job if the person has the means to pay.[163]

This does not affect you if you are a volunteer and the Revenue is satisfied that it is reasonable for you to provide your services free of charge. Nor does it apply if you are on an employment or training programme under s2 Employment and Training Act 1973 where no training allowance is payable (with the exception of the intensive activity period and preparation for employment programme).

Sometimes carers looking after disabled people have been expected to charge the person they care for under a similar provision affecting means-tested benefits. If you are in this position, see p875 for more details.

Preventing tax avoidance and treatment of capital as income

If income is treated as yours under certain prevention of tax avoidance provisions or where tax law treats capital as income, it also counts as your income for tax credits.[164]

Notes

1. **Annual income**
   1 s7(3)(a) and (b) TCA 2002; reg 5 TC(ITDR) Regs

2. **Whose income counts**
   2 s7(5) TCA 2002
   3 Reg 14(2)(b)(vii) TC(DCI) Regs

3. **What income counts**
   4 Reg 3(6) TC(DCI) Regs
   5 Reg 3(1) TC(DCI) Regs
   6 Reg 3(1) Step One TC(DCI) Regs
   7 Reg 7(3) TC(DCI) Regs
   8 PC paid under SPCA 2002 is by definition not counted as social security income under reg 7(1) TC(DCI) Regs.
   9 Reg 7(4) TC(DCI) Regs
   10 Regulations make no mention of the treatment of increases for adults. However, these are non-taxable if paid with a non-taxable benefit and the intention is that tax credits follow suit. See the Revenue's *Employment Income Manual*, para 76102.
   11 s674 IT(EP)A 2003
   12 Reg 7(1)(c) and (d) TC(DCI) Regs
   13 Reg 4 TC(DCI) Regs
   14 Reg 4(1) TC(DCI) Regs
   15 Reg 4 TC(DCI) Regs
   16 Regs 2(2) and 4(1)(a) TC(DCI) Regs; *Employment Income Manual*, para 00520
   17 Reg 4(1)(b) TC(DCI) Regs
   18 Reg 4(1)(c)-(e) TC(DCI) Regs
   19 ss362 and 363 IT(EP)A 2003; reg 4(4) Table 1 para 11D and (5) TC(DCI) Regs
   20 Reg 4(4) Table 1 para 8 TC(DCI) Regs
   21 Reg 4(1)(f) TC(DCI) Regs
   22 Reg 4(1)(g) TC(DCI) Regs
   23 Reg 4(1)(h) TC(DCI) Regs
   24 Reg 4(1)(h) TC(DCI) Regs
   25 Reg 4(1)(k) TC(DCI) Regs
   26 Reg 4(1)(i) TC(DCI) Regs
   27 Reg 4(4) Table 1 paras 14B, 14C and 14D TC(DCI) Regs
   28 Reg 4(4) Table 1 para 2B TC(DCI) Regs
   29 Reg 4(1)(j) TC(DCI) Regs
   30 Reg 4(1)(l) TC(DCI) Regs
   31 Reg 4(1)(m) TC(DCI) Regs
   32 Reg 4(4) TC(DCI) Regs
   33 Reg 4(5) TC(DCI) Regs; s336 IT(EP)A 2003
   34 Reg 19 Table 7 para 1 TC(DCI) Regs
   35 Reg 4(1)(b) TC(DCI) Regs
   36 Reg 4(5) TC(DCI) Regs; s231 IT(EP)A 2003
   37 Reg 4(5) TC(DCI) Regs; s367 IT(EP)A 2003
   38 Reg 4(4) Table 1 para 17 TC(DCI) Regs
   39 Reg 4(5) TC(DCI) Regs; ss337 and 338 IT(EP)A 2003
   40 Reg 4(4) Table 1 paras 2A and 2C TC(DCI) Regs
   41 Reg 4(4) Table 1 para 1 TC(DCI) Regs
   42 Reg 4(4) Table 1 para 4 TC(DCI) Regs
   43 Reg 4(4) Table 1 para 5 TC(DCI) Regs
   44 Reg 4(4) Table 1 para 6 TC(DCI) Regs
   45 Reg 4(4) Table 1 para 13 TC(DCI) Regs
   46 Reg 4(4) Table 1 para 14 TC(DCI) Regs
   47 Reg 4(4) Table 1 para 15 TC(DCI) Regs
   48 Reg 4(4) Table 1 para 8 TC(DCI) Regs
   49 Reg 4(4) Table 1 para 11E TC(DCI) Regs
   50 Reg 4(4) Table 1 para 11F TC(DCI) Regs
   51 Reg 4(5) TC(DCI) Regs; s377 IT(EP)A 2003
   52 Reg 4(4) Table 1 para 12 TC(DCI) Regs
   53 Reg 4(5) TC(DCI) Regs; s343 IT(EP)A 2003
   54 Reg 4(5) TC(DCI) Regs; s346 IT(EP)A 2003
   55 Regs 5(3) and 7(5A) TC(DCI) Regs
   56 Reg 4(5) TC(DCI) Regs; s713 IT(EP)A 2003
   57 Reg 4(4) Table 1 para 11C TC(DCI) Regs
   58 Reg 4(4) Table 1 paras 16 and 16A TC(DCI) Regs
   59 Reg 4(4) Table 1 para 18 TC(DCI) Regs
   60 Reg 4(4) Table 1 para 19 TC(DCI) Regs
   61 Reg 4(5) TC(DCI) Regs; ss370, 371 and 376 IT(EP)A 2003
   62 Reg 4(5) TC(DCI) Regs; s373 IT(EP)A 2003
   63 Reg 4(4) Table 1 para 3 TC(DCI) Regs
   64 Reg 4(4) Table 1 para 7 TC(DCI) Regs
   65 Reg 4(4) Table 1 para 3A TC(DCI) Regs
   66 Reg 4(4) Table 1 para 3B TC(DCI) Regs
   67 Regs 4(4) Table 1 para 9 and 5(2) Table 2 para 11 TC(DCI) Regs
   68 Reg 4(5) TC(DCI) Regs; s352 IT(EP)A 2003
   69 Reg 4(4) Table 1 para 11A TC(DCI) Regs
   70 Reg 4(4) Table 1 para 11B TC(DCI) Regs

71 Reg 4(5) TC(DCI) Regs; s351 IT(EP)A 2003
72 Reg 4(4) Table 1 para 11 TC(DCI) Regs
73 Reg 3(7)(c) TC(DCI) Regs
74 Reg 6(a) TC(DCI) Regs
75 Reg 6(b) TC(DCI) Regs
76 Reg 6 TC(DCI) Regs
77 Reg 3(1) Step 4 TC(DCI) Regs
78 Reg 8 TC(DCI) Regs
79 Reg 19(c) Table 8 para 2 TC(DCI) Regs
80 Reg 19 Table 6 para 5(a) TC(DCI) Regs
81 Reg 9 TC(DCI) Regs
82 Reg 9 TC(DCI) Regs
83 Reg 18 TC(DCI) Regs
84 Reg 5(1)(a) TC(DCI) Regs
85 TC600 Notes
86 Reg 5(1)(b)-(o) TC(DCI) Regs
87 Reg 5(2) Table 2 para 9 TC(DCI) Regs
88 Reg 5(2) Table 2 para 10 TC(DCI) Regs
89 Reg 5(1)(a) TC(DCI) Regs
90 Reg 5(1)(a) TC(DCI) Regs
91 Reg 5(1)(b) TC(DCI) Regs
92 Reg 5(2) Table 2 paras 1-8 TC(DCI) Regs
93 Reg 10(1) TC(DCI) Regs
94 Reg 10(1)(a) TC(DCI) Regs
95 Reg 10(1)(d) TC(DCI) Regs
96 Reg 10(1)(c) TC(DCI) Regs
97 Reg 10(1)(e) TC(DCI) Regs
98 Reg 10(1)(b) TC(DCI) Regs
99 Reg 10(1)(a) TC(DCI) Regs
100 Reg 10(1)(a) TC(DCI) Regs
101 Reg 10(1)(a) TC(DCI) Regs
102 Reg 10(2)(a) Table 4 paras 1(b) and 2 TC(DCI) Regs
103 Reg 10(2)(a) Table 4 para 1(a) TC(DCI) Regs
104 Reg 10(2)(a) Table 4 para 3 TC(DCI) Regs
105 Reg 10(2)(c) TC(DCI) Regs
106 Reg 10(2)(d) TC(DCI) Regs
107 Reg 10(2)(e) TC(DCI) Regs
108 Reg 10(2)(a) Table 4 para 4 TC(DCI) Regs
109 Reg 10(2)(a) Table 4 paras 5 to 7 TC(DCI) Regs
110 Reg 10(2)(a) Table 4 para 8 TC(DCI) Regs
111 TCTM para 4619
112 Reg 10(2)(a) Table 4 para 9 TC(DCI) Regs
113 Reg 10(2)(a) Table 4 para 10 TC(DCI) Regs
114 Reg 10(2)(a) Table 4 para 11 TC(DCI) Regs
115 Reg 10(2)(b) Table 5 TC(DCI) Regs
116 Reg 10(2)(a) Table 4 para 12 TC(DCI) Regs
117 Reg 11 TC(DCI) Regs
118 See Revenue Help Sheet IR 223
119 para 04700 TCTM
120 para 04700 TCTM
121 Reg 12(1) TC(DCI) Regs
122 Reg 12(3) TC(DCI) Regs
123 Reg 3(7)(a) TC(DCI) Regs
124 Reg 12(4) TC(DCI) Regs
125 Reg 3(3) TC(DCI) Regs
126 Reg 3(5A) TC(DCI) Regs
127 Reg 3(6A) TC(DCI) Regs
128 Reg 19 TC(DCI) Regs
129 Reg 19 Table 6 para 1 TC(DCI) Regs
130 Reg 19 Table 6 para 3 TC(DCI) Regs
131 Reg 19 Table 6 para 4 TC(DCI) Regs
132 Reg 19 Table 7 para 2(d) TC(DCI) Regs
133 Reg 19 Table 7 para 2(a)-(c) TC(DCI) Regs
134 Reg 19 Table 8 para 1 TC(DCI) Regs
135 Reg 19 Table 6 para 2 TC(DCI) Regs
136 Reg 19 Table 6 para 5 TC(DCI) Regs
137 Reg 19 Table 6 para 6 TC(DCI) Regs
138 Reg 19 Table 6 para 10 TC(DCI) Regs
139 Reg 19 Table 6 para 8 TC(DCI) Regs
140 Reg 19 Table 6 para 9 TC(DCI) Regs
141 Reg 19 Table 6 para 11(a) TC(DCI) Regs
142 Reg 19 Table 6 para 11(b) TC(DCI) Regs
143 Reg 19 Table 6 para 11(bb) TC(DCI) Regs
144 Because they are not defined as income under reg 3 TC(DCI) Regs
145 Reg 3(7)(c) TC(DCI) Regs
146 Reg 19 Table 6 para 12 TC(DCI) Regs
147 Reg 19 Table 6 para 13 TC(DCI) Regs
148 Reg 19 Table 6 para 14 TC(DCI) Regs
149 Reg 19 Table 6 para 14A TC(DCI) Regs
150 Reg 19 Table 6 para 15 TC(DCI) Regs
151 Reg 19 Table 6 para 16 TC(DCI) Regs
152 Reg 19 Table 7 para 1 TC(DCI) Regs
153 Reg 19 Table 8 para 6 TC(DCI) Regs
154 Reg 19 Table 8 para 4(b) TC(DCI) Regs
155 Reg 19 Table 8 paras 3 and 4 TC(DCI) Regs
156 Reg 19 Table 8 para 5(a) TC(DCI) Regs
157 Reg 19 Table 8 para 5(b) TC(DCI) Regs
158 Reg 3(7)(b) TC(DCI) Regs
159 Reg 19 Table 8 para 7 TC(DCI) Regs

4. **Notional income**

160 Reg 13 TC(DCI) Regs
161 Reg 15 TC(DCI) Regs
162 Reg 16 TC(DCI) Regs
163 Reg 17 TC(DCI) Regs
164 Reg 14 TC(DCI) Regs

Chapter 53

Claims, backdating and getting paid: tax credits

This chapter covers:

This chapter deals with who can claim child tax credit and working tax credit, how and when to make a claim, how your claim is dealt with and how you are paid. Tax credits are administered by the Revenue. Claims are dealt with by the Tax Credit Office.

1. Who should claim

You must be at least 16 years old to claim a tax credit.[1]

If you are a member of a married couple or registered civil partnership, or live with someone as if you were married or civil partners, you must claim jointly with your partner. This is known as a 'joint claim'.[2] See p1211 for when you count as a member of a married or unmarried couple, as registered civil partners, or are treated as someone's civil partner. Both partners must claim the tax credits jointly but there are special rules about who receives payment of the different tax credits. Note, however, that if you or your partner go abroad, either permanently or for more than a set period of time (see p1379), you cease to be able to make a joint claim and instead must make a new claim as a single person. Failure to notify the Revenue of this may result in a penalty (see p1308).

If you are a single person, you make a 'single claim'.

If you made a joint claim and are no longer part of a couple, or if you made a single claim and are now part of a couple, your award stops. You need to make a new claim.[3] You should tell the Tax Credit Office (TCO) as soon as possible. If you do not, you could be overpaid. You could also incur a financial penalty if you fail to notify the change within one month. When you contact the TCO, you should be invited to make a fresh claim and advised to request backdating if necessary. If you do not make a new claim within three months of the change, you will lose out on tax credits.

Appointees

The following people can make a claim on your behalf if you are unable to make the claim yourself:[4]

- a receiver appointed by the Court of Protection with power to make a claim for tax credits on your behalf;
- in Scotland, a tutor, curator or other guardian acting or appointed in terms of law who is administering your estate;
- in Northern Ireland, a controller appointed by the High Court with power to make a tax credit claim on your behalf;
- a person who is your 'appointee' (see p955) for social security purposes; *or*
- if there is no one who satisfies the above, a person aged 18 or over who applies to the Revenue in writing to act on your behalf and is appointed by the Revenue in that capacity.

2. **How to make a claim**

You have no entitlement to tax credits unless you make a claim.[5] You claim both child tax credit (CTC) and working tax credit (WTC) on one claim form. If you are entitled to receive pension credit (PC), in some circumstances you can be treated as having made a claim for CTC and do not have to fill in a claim form.

You must claim the tax credits in writing on Form TC600, unless the above exception applies or you are renewing a claim (see p1276). In practice, the Revenue accepts written applications not on a claim form only in a few exceptional circumstances, although the regulations provide for discretion on this. You can get forms from Revenue enquiry centres, advice centres and directly from the Tax Credit Office (TCO – see Appendix 1), which can be contacted by telephone or in writing. The Revenue's Tax Credit Helpline can issue claim forms and answer questions about tax credits on 0845 300 3900 (textphone: 0845 300 3909).

If you are just starting work after being unemployed, you can ask a Jobcentre Plus personal adviser to give you the form. Alternatively, you can get one from your local DWP office. Staff can help you complete the claim form.

If you cannot complete all the details asked for on the claim form, you should phone the Helpline for further advice. You should send the completed claim form directly to the TCO in the pre-paid envelope provided with the claim form (or see

Appendix 1 for the address). It is always best to return your form to the TCO. However, your claim may be sent instead, if necessary, to any Jobcentre Plus, DWP office or Revenue enquiry centre office.[6] Keep a copy of your claim form in case queries arise.

If you have sent your claim form to the Revenue and you later realise that the details on it need to be amended, you should contact the TCO as soon as possible. You can amend or withdraw your claim at any time before the claim has been decided.[7] Even if your claim has been decided, there are certain circumstances when your entitlement to tax credits can be amended. Once your claim has been decided and an award made, however, you cannot withdraw it.[8] For more details of when these changes in circumstances apply, see Chapter 54.

Information to support your claim

Your claim must contain all of the information requested on the claim form, unless the Revenue decides otherwise.[9] If you do not supply all the requested information, a decision may not be made on your claim until the required information is provided. If you need advice about the information required, contact the Helpline (see p1274).

National insurance number requirement

In particular, your claim must, in respect of each person for whom a claim is made, include:[10]

- her/his national insurance (NI) number plus information or evidence establishing that it is her/his NI number; *or*
- information or evidence to enable the Revenue to find her/his NI number; *or*
- an application for an NI number, with the necessary evidence or information to allow one to be allocated.

You do not need to meet the NI number requirement if the Revenue believes you have a reasonable excuse.

Income

If you are receiving income support (IS), income-based jobseeker's allowance or PC when you claim tax credits, you only need to inform the Revenue of this, and you do not need to provide any other income details.

Otherwise, when you make a claim for tax credits, you need to provide details of your income during the previous tax year. If you are part of a couple and making a joint claim, your award is based on your joint income during the previous tax year, even in situations where you may not have been living as a couple during that tax year. For details of what counts as income, see Chapter 52.

If you think that your current tax year's income is going to be substantially different to the previous tax year's income, you should still complete the claim form with details of your previous tax year's income. When the Revenue makes a decision on your claim, you will be sent an award notice which tells you how to notify it of your estimated income for the current year. You can also request that your award be adjusted at any time during the year of the award. Where appropriate, the Revenue will then adjust your award of tax credits, using your estimated figure of your current year's income.

If you worked as an employee throughout the previous tax year, your P60 for that year will have details of your taxable income. If you received any payments in kind from your employer, you should have details of these on Form P9D or P11D, which your employer should give you. If you were self-employed throughout the previous tax year, you can use your tax return as the basis for your taxable income. If you were in receipt of taxable social security benefits, you should be able to get a statement of taxable benefit income from the DWP.

Bank account details

You are required to provide details of a bank, building society or Post Office card account into which the tax credits can be paid. This is because entitlement is dependent on having a bank or other account.[11] See p1280 if you do not have a bank or similar account.

Further information and evidence

The Revenue might need further information or evidence before making a decision (including one on a claim or revision). The information or evidence can be required from you or from your employer or childcare provider. If material is required, the Revenue gives notice to you (or another relevant person) that you are required to provide it within a specified time limit. In all cases except responses to final notices, you must be given at least 30 days. For responses to final notices there is an absolute time limit (see p1286).[12] The basic rule is that you can be required to provide any further information or evidence which the Revenue considers necessary. If you do not provide the material requested, you might be refused tax credit. If you provide incorrect information or fail to comply with requirements to provide information or evidence, you may be subject to a financial penalty or, in cases where you are considered to have acted fraudulently, a fine or imprisonment or both (see Chapter 56).

Renewing your claim

After 5 April the Revenue reviews all tax credit awards, including those where no award was put into payment because the amount awarded was too low, where there was a nil award because the claimant's income was too high or where the award ended before 5 April. This review process also invites you to renew your claim for tax credits. The Revenue will send you an annual review pack. You can give the information asked for in the pack by returning the forms in the envelope provided or by phoning the Tax Credit Helpline (see p1284).

During the annual review process, tax credits continue to be paid on a provisional basis. If the Revenue does not have up-to-date income details, these payments are based on the assumption that your income for the tax year just ended went up in line with average earnings. If your income went up by more than this, you may be overpaid until the review is complete. Therefore, it is best to provide income details as soon as possible and not wait for the forms.

Annual review

If you claimed tax credits for the tax year 2007/08, the Revenue should write to you between April and July 2008, enclosing an annual review form (TC603R). Unless you have an ongoing award of the family element only of CTC or a nil award, you should also receive an annual declaration form (TC603D – see p1278). Even if you did not actually receive any tax credits following your claim because your income was too high or the award too low, the Revenue should still write to you.

If you made more than one claim for tax credits during the previous tax year (eg, because you separated from your partner during that year and had to make a new claim for tax credits as a single person), you will receive a separate annual review form and annual declaration form, if required, for each claim. If you are sent more than one set of forms covering different claims, you should reply to each separately, even if they both ask for the same information. If an annual declaration is required, each member of a former couple is required to reply unless there are exceptional circumstances.

If you are sent an annual review form, but not an annual declaration form, you will be asked to check that all of the details on this form about your claim for the previous year are correct and to notify the Revenue of any changes of circumstances. You are also asked to confirm that your income for the tax year 2008/09 is likely to remain within the range indicated on the form. If your personal circumstances have not changed and you do not consider that your income in the coming tax year is likely to increase or drop below the amounts shown in your annual review form, you do not have to do anything further. You will then be deemed to have confirmed that all the details in the form are correct. The final decision on the award for 2007/08 and a new initial decision on an award for 2008/09 are as set out on the annual review form. However, you should always check the form and the notes accompanying it to see whether you need to return the forms.

If you do need to reply to the annual review form, you must do so by the date specified on the form – this is 31 July.

If the details set out on the forms sent to you about your claim and income are not correct and you fail to reply within the time allowed, you may not receive the correct amount of tax credit. If you are overpaid as a result, you may have to repay the overpayment. If you fail promptly to notify certain changes of circumstances, you may have to make a penalty payment(s) (see p1287).

Annual declaration

You may receive an annual declaration form (TC603D) which asks for details of your income in the previous tax year. Anyone whose 2007/08 award was more than just a family element of CTC or whose award ended before 5 April 2008 should get an annual declaration form.

If you are sent an annual declaration form you must always complete and return it by the date specified in the accompanying annual review form, usually 31 July. If you do not, your tax credit payments will stop, you may have to repay any tax credit paid since 6 April and you may have to pay a penalty payment(s). You must also tell the Revenue of any changes in personal circumstances from those set out in the annual review form.

If, before this date, you do not know what your total income is for the period in question, you should not delay returning your forms. Instead, you should provide an estimate for the Revenue and then send details of your actual income as soon as you can. You must do this before the deadline given on the form or you may lose out on backdating (see below).

If you return your annual declaration form before the 31 July deadline, your renewal claim will be backdated to 6 April 2008. If you do not return it before 31 July but, having been sent a notice that your payments of tax credits have ceased, return it within 30 days following the date on the notice, yoru renewal claim will be backdated to 6 April 2008. If neither of those apply, but you return your annual declaration form before 31 January 2009, and you have 'good cause' for returning it late, your renewal claim will be backdated to 6 April 2008.[13] Good cause is not defined but the Revenue says it includes 'very exceptional reasons' like serious illness or bereavement, and not that you were too busy or did not understand what to do.[14] If your reasons are not accepted as good cause, you can appeal.

However, this rule allowing late return of your declaration does not apply if:

- your previous claim was on the basis that you were single, and you are now a member of a couple; *or*
- your previous claim was made on the basis that you were a member of a couple, and you are now single.[15]

If you return your annual declaration form between 31 July and 31 January, but your reasons for being late are not accepted as good cause, you must make a new claim and it can only be backdated for three months. If you return your form after 31 January, you must make a new claim and it can only be backdated for three months whatever your reason for the delay.

Final award notice

The Revenue aims to process your completed forms within 30 days of receiving them. You should receive a final notice confirming whether your award for 2007/08 was correct. If you did not have an annual declaration form to complete, the final notice is as set out in your annual review form (unless, having read your annual review form, you find that you have a change of circumstance to report, in which case the Revenue will send you details of your new award after it has dealt with the reported change).

The Revenue will also send you an initial award notice (TC602) setting out your award for the tax year 2008/09.

If you are notified that you have been overpaid tax credits, see Chapter 55.

3. When to claim

You cannot make a claim for tax credits in advance of the tax year for which you are claiming.[16] The general rule is that claims for tax credits will run from the date they are received by the Revenue until the end of the tax year in which the claim is made.[17] Your claim can be backdated for a period of up to three months before the date it is received by the Revenue if you would have been entitled to tax credits throughout that period. Backdating is possible for a period of longer than three months where you become entitled to tax credit(s) following an award of disabilty living allowance or another qualifying benefit (see p1281).

Once a claim for tax credits has been made, it can automatically be renewed at the end of that tax year (see p1276).

4. How your claim is dealt with

Once you have made your claim for tax credits, the Revenue must make a decision on whether you are entitled to either of the tax credits, and if so, at what rate.[18] The Revenue may first require you, or your partner if you are making a joint claim, to provide any information or evidence that is needed to make a decision.[19]

You are notified of your award on Form TC602. You are asked to check the details on your award notice using a checklist (TC602(SN)). You should contact the Tax Credit Office if any of the details shown on the award notice are wrong or have changed. If you do not, and an overpayment results, the Revenue may expect you to pay it back (see p1298).

The first decision made after your claim is called the 'initial decision'. You can amend, verbally or in writing, the details you have provided when making your claim at any time until the Revenue makes its initial decision and your date of claim will remain the same.

The initial decision is usually made on the basis of your circumstances at the date you make your claim and on your previous tax year's income. If your income or circumstances do not change, the award will run at the amount awarded on the initial decision until the end of the tax year. If the Revenue has not been able to make a decision on a renewal claim for tax credits by 6 April, your payment will continue until a decision on the new claim is made, as described on p1276.[20] Certain changes in circumstances can mean that the initial decision will be changed. For more information on decisions and changes in circumstances, see Chapter 54.

5. Getting paid

The Revenue is responsible for making payments of tax credits.[21]

In some cases, if you are entitled only to a small amount of tax credit(s), your award will be paid as a lump sum. This will generally apply if payment to you would be less than £2 a week.[22]

Who is paid

If you make a single claim, the general rule described above applies.

If you make a joint claim, child tax credit (CTC) and the childcare element of working tax credit (WTC) is paid to whoever is the 'main carer' of the children.[23] The '**main carer**' can be either you or your partner, depending on which one of you both of you agree should be paid CTC. If you and your partner are living at the same address and either you do not identify which one of you should be paid, or you cannot agree, the Revenue will decide. Where you and your partner are not currently living at the same address, or one of you is temporarily absent from that address, the Revenue will decide which of you will be paid.[24] If the main carer changes following an award of tax credits, the Revenue, if it considers it reasonable, can make the payments to that person instead.[25]

If you claim WTC as part of a joint claim and one of you is working, the payment of WTC (apart from any childcare amount payable) is made to the person who is engaged in full-time paid work (see Chapter 50). If you are both in full-time paid work you can decide who will receive the payment between you, or if you cannot agree, the Revenue will decide. If you both agree, you can write to the Revenue requesting that payment be made to the other person.[26]

If you make a joint claim and your partner subsequently dies, you receive any outstanding amount of tax credits which would have been paid to your partner.[27]

If an appointee (see p955) has claimed tax credits on your behalf, payment is made to the appointee.

How and when payments are made

Payments of tax credits are made by direct credit transfer into a bank, building society (or similar) or Post Office card account.[28] The claim packs for tax credits should include a leaflet from the Financial Services Authority that explains the different types of account that you can open and how to do this. You can decide whether you want the payments to be made into your account every week or every four weeks, but CTC and the childcare element of WTC must be paid at the same time and at the same intervals.[29]

Where it is not considered appropriate for payments to be made into an account, the Revenue can decide on the manner and timing of payment by other means.[30] However, this will only take place in exceptional circumstances.[31] We understand that the Revenue may pay you by cheque while your account is being set up or if there are problems with your account. There is a general rule that if details of an account are not supplied, your claim will cease until you supply the relevant details.[32] If you do not provide account details, the Revenue should write to you, giving you eight weeks to supply information on the account into which you want the tax credits to be paid. If you then require an authority from the Revenue to open an account, you have three weeks from the date that the Revenue supplies you with the authority to provide details of your account. These periods can be extended if you have a 'reasonable excuse' for not being able to provide the details within the time limits.[33] 'Reasonable excuse' is not defined in the regulations but the Revenue says it can include if you were ill or abroad, or were switching bank accounts. If you have not been able to provide details of an account within the time allowed, you should explain the reason.

Postponement of payment

Payment of tax credits may be postponed if you have lodged an appeal against a decision of the Revenue, or when there is an appeal for another tax credit claim lodged which may affect your own award.[34] The award may also be postponed if the details of the account into which you want the tax credits paid or your address appear to be incorrect.[35]

6. Backdating your claim

In general, your claim for tax credits can be backdated for up to three months (but see below), provided you would have satisfied the rules of entitlement throughout the three-month period.[36] The Revenue will look at your claim form for evidence of possible backdating. However, it is best to be clear and ask for your claim to be backdated to when you think your entitlement began (subject to the three-month limit).

If you were awarded tax credits but no payment was made because you failed to provide sufficient details of an account into which tax credits could be paid and you subsequently provide the necessary details, your award can be backdated for up to three months from the date that you supply the information.[37]

Backdating of your claim for tax credit(s) for more than three months is possible following an award of a disability benefit. This rule applies where your claim for tax credit is refused because you or a child included in your claim do not receive a qualifying disability benefit, and at the time of your tax credit claim you had made a claim for a qualifying benefit which had not been decided.

The Revenue asks you to include a letter with your tax credit claim to say you are waiting for a decision on a qualifying benefit and giving the date you claimed it. If that benefit is subsequently awarded, you should make a second tax credit claim within three months of the award of the disability benefit. Your tax credit claim will then be backdated to either the date that the disability benefit was awarded from or the date of your first tax credit claim, whichever is the later.[38]

See p1378 for backdating if you are granted refugee status.

Notes

1. **Who should claim**
   1 s3(3) TCA 2002
   2 s3(3)(a) and (8) TCA 2002
   3 s3(4) TCA 2002
   4 Regs 17 and 18 TC(CN) Regs

2. **How to make a claim**
   5 S3(1) TCA 2002
   6 Reg 5(2) TC(CN) Regs
   7 Reg 5(7) TC(CN) Regs
   8 R(IS) 3/05
   9 Reg 5(3) TC(CN) Regs
   10 Reg 5(4) TC(CN) Regs
   11 Reg 14 TC(PC) Regs
   12 ss14, 15, 16, 17,18,19 and 22 TCA 2002; regs 30-33 TC(CN) Regs
   13 Reg 11 TC(CN) Regs
   14 TCTM, 'Renewal Miscellaneous'
   15 Reg 11 TC(CN) Regs

3. **When to claim**
   16 Reg 9 TC(CN) Regs
   17 s5(2) TCA 2002

4. **How your claim is dealt with**
   18 s14(1) TCA 2002
   19 s14(2) TCA 2002
   20 s24(4) TCA; reg 7 TC(PC) Regs

5. **Getting paid**
   21 s24 TCA 2002
   22 Reg 10 TC(PC) Regs
   23 Reg 3 TC(PC) Regs
   24 Reg 3(3) TC(PC) Regs
   25 Reg 3(6) TC(PC) Regs
   26 Reg 4 TC(PC) Regs
   27 Reg 5 TC(PC) Regs
   28 Reg 13(1) TC(PC) Regs
   29 Reg 8(2) and (2A) TC(PC) Regs
   30 Reg 9 TC(PC) Regs
   31 Reg 14(3) TC(PC) Regs
   32 Reg 14(1) TC(PC) Regs
   33 Reg 14(4) TC(PC) Regs
   34 Reg 11(2) TC(PC) Regs
   35 Reg 11(3) TC(PC) Regs

6. **Backdating your claim**
   36 Reg 7 TC(CN) Regs
   37 Reg 14(2) TC(PC) Regs
   38 Regs 8, 26 and 26A TC(CN) Regs

Chapter 54

Decisions and changes in circumstances: tax credits

This chapter covers:

This chapter deals with the main tax credit decisions that are made on your claim – the initial and final decisions. Your award of tax credits may be affected by changes in your circumstances. This chapter also looks at those changes and when you should report them. This chapter does not deal with revisions or appeals (see Chapter 57), with how your tax credit award is calculated (see Chapter 51) or with decisions about penalties (see Chapter 56).

1. Making a decision

Decisions about tax credits are made by the Commissioners for Her Majesty's Revenue and Customs.[1] In practice, decisions are made by civil servants in the Revenue.

An **'initial decision'** is made at the start of your claim and is based on an estimate of your tax credit entitlement in the coming tax year (which runs from 6 April to 5 April). You are then sent a tax credits award notice setting out your award. A **'final decision'** is made after the end of the tax year in which your claim is made. It is based on your actual circumstances during the year and thus is the decision that confirms what your entitlement actually was. Again, you are sent a tax credits award notice.

Unless the decision on your entitlement is changed either on revision or on appeal, the initial decision and the final decision are the only decisions on your claim that you will get. Revisions and appeals are described in Chapter 57.

Information and evidence

The Revenue can require you to provide certain information and evidence for making a decision (see p1275). If you provide incorrect information or fail to comply with requirements to provide information or evidence, you may be subject to a financial penalty or, in cases where you are considered to have acted fraudulently, a fine or imprisonment or both (see Chapter 56).

Delays, negligence and complaints

It is not possible to sue the Revenue for negligence in the way in which your claim is decided.[2] If a decision is wrong, you can seek a revision or appeal against it. If you are given wrong advice by an employee of the Revenue, you may be able to seek compensation either through the courts or through the internal complaints procedure. See p1186 for information about seeking compensation.

If your claim has been received but not dealt with, ask why. If you are not satisfied with the explanation for the delay, make a complaint to the Revenue (see Chapter 46). You can also complain if, for example, you have been treated badly or your case has been mishandled. In some cases, you can seek a judicial review (see p1129). If there are unreasonable delays in processing your claim, you may be able to make a complaint to the Ombudsman.

If you disagree with a decision or your circumstances change

Most decisions about your entitlement to tax credits can be revised or appealed. If you think a decision is wrong you can seek a revision or appeal to a tribunal (see Chapter 57).

If you want to seek a revision or appeal against a decision, you should not delay. The time limit for appeals in particular is strict – normally 30 days. Some changes in your circumstances must be notified to the Revenue within one month. If you want your tax credit entitlement increased in full because of a change in your circumstances (other than a fall in your expected income), you normally have to report the change within three months (see p1287).

2. Contacting the Revenue

Phoning the Tax Credit Helpline (0845 300 3900 (textphone: 0845 300 3909)) can be the quickest way to have your case dealt with. Be ready to give your name, address and national insurance (NI) number. Always keep a note of the date and time of your call, with a brief note of what is said and, if you can, the name and title of the person you speak to. It is best to follow up your call with a letter confirming the information you have provided and the advice given by the Helpline. Write to the Tax Credit Office at the address on the award notice, and include your name, address, NI number and the date. Always try to make a copy of your letter to keep. If you are appealing, disputing recovery of an overpayment or making a complaint, it is best to use the relevant form or put it in writing.

If you notify a change of circumstances, the Revenue should send you a new award notice (if the change affected your award) within 30 days. It is important to contact it again if you have not had a notice within this time. If you do not, the Revenue may expect you to pay back any overpayment that has built up.

3. Initial decisions

On receiving an application for tax credits, the Revenue must make an initial decision on whether an award should be made and, if so, the amount.[3] The claim form does not distinguish between child tax credit and working tax credit, so the Revenue must also decide on entitlement to both types of credit.

The main evidence on which this decision is based is that on your claim form, unless you supply further evidence before the decision is made. You can be required to provide extra information or evidence (see p1275).

The evidence used normally relates to your income in the tax year *previous* to the year in which you are claiming, but to your circumstances (eg, if you have a partner and/or children) in the *current* tax year (ie, the one in which you are claiming). See Chapter 52 for more details about income.

You must be notified of the initial decision. The notice must include the date on which it is given and your right of appeal against it.[4] If you had already claimed tax credits in the previous year, your initial decision for the coming year may be included in the final notice (see p1286).[5] The initial decision sets the amount of tax credit you are due to receive until the final decision is made, unless it is changed on revision or appeal.

4. Final decisions

After the end of the tax year in which you claimed, the Revenue must make a final decision on whether you were entitled to tax credit and, if so, the amount of your award.[6] Therefore, the final decision can establish one of three things: that the initial decision was correct, that you were underpaid tax credit or you were overpaid tax credit.

Underpayments established in a final decision are paid to you as a lump sum. **Overpayments** are usually recovered from you (see Chapter 55). **Note:** you do not have the right of appeal against a decision that an overpayment is to be recovered from you (although you can ask the Revenue not to recover it). If you do not agree that you have been paid too much tax credit, it is important that you appeal against the lower award notified to you in the final decision.

The final decision is made in two main stages.

- A final notice is issued to gather information and evidence about what your income and circumstances were in the year.
- The information from the final notice is used to make a final decision on your entitlement for the year.

Final notice

At the end of the tax year in which you claimed, a final notice is sent to you.[7] Your response to the final notice forms the basis of an automatic renewal of your claim for the following year (see p1276).

The notice either:

- requires you to confirm that the circumstances taken into account by the Revenue in your award were correct. If they were not correct, you must specify in what way they were not correct; *or*
- informs you that unless you reply within the time allowed, you will be deemed to have confirmed that the circumstances were correct.[8]

The notice also asks about your income (see below). You are required to respond by 31 July. Replying in time is important, not just to ensure your entitlement for the previous year is correct but also to renew your claim. If you reply after 31 July, but before 31 January 2009, you can still be treated as having replied in time for the purpose of renewing your claim (for more details see p1276).[9]

Current year's income

The final notice asks about your actual income for the tax year just ended. In the assessment of tax credits for that year, this was referred to as '**current year's income**'. The initial decision for that year was based on income in the previous year, or may have been revised according to an estimate of current year's income. For the final decision, the Revenue needs to compare that figure with your actual income. It is, therefore, very important that you tell the Revenue if your current year's income was different from that used to make the initial decision or any subsequent revision.

Sometimes you may only be able to provide an estimate of what your actual income was in the tax year just ended. The final notice allows for this. If you use an estimate of your current year's income, the final notice must inform you that your estimate will be treated as the actual amount of your current year's income, unless within the time allowed you state what it actually was.[10]

You may be asked to provide information about, or make a declaration about, your current year's income, or be informed that unless you respond you will be treated as having confirmed your income.[11]

Previous year's income

The final notice may ask you to confirm your actual income for the tax year before the one that has just ended. This is referred to as '**previous year's income**'. When making a decision, the Revenue may have used an estimate of previous year's income, or confirmation that it fell within a specified range. If so, you are either required to make a declaration, or are informed that the amount given in the final notice will be used unless you respond within the time allowed.[12]

Responding to the final notice

Responses to the final notice must usually be on a form provided by the Revenue. Alternatively, you can phone the Tax Credit Helpline. If you are unable to respond to the final notice (eg, because of illness) then responses can be accepted from receivers and people who are appointees for tax credit or benefit purposes.[13]

Final decision

Once a final notice has been issued, the Revenue must make a final decision, which is the decision on your actual entitlement to tax credits for the year. A final decision cannot be made before you have responded to the final notice, unless the time allowed for you to make such a response has passed. Once this decision is made, it is usually the final decision on your entitlement for the tax year concerned, unless it is changed either on revision or appeal. However, in addition to the usual revision and appeal rules, if you have responded to a final notice and a final decision has been made on or before the final date for your response, the final decision can be revised if you make a new response, as long as that new response is made on or before the final date you were given for your original response.[14]

You must be notified of a final decision.[15] However, your final notice may have said what the final decision will be and the date on which it will be made, unless you respond and say that the circumstances or income on which the decision is based are incorrect. If you did not reply to such a final notice the Revenue need not send you a separate notice of the final decision.[16] For more information about the way in which a final decision is made on your claim, see Chapter 53.

5. Change of circumstances after a claim

Changes in your family circumstances, childcare charges or income during your award may lead to changes in your entitlement. If changes do affect your entitlement, this can be changed either soon after the change has occurred, or at the end of the year when the final decision is made and the Revenue makes a final check on your details. However, certain changes must be notified to the Revenue within one month or you may incur a penalty. Some other changes which *increase* your entitlement must be notified within three months if your increased award is to be backdated in full.

Once an initial decision has been made, there are three types of change which can affect your entitlement to tax credits:

- changes which must be notified to the Revenue;
- changes which affect your maximum entitlement to tax credits;
- changes in income.

Changes that must be notified to the Revenue

Some changes must be notified to the Revenue within one month of the date of the change or the date you became aware of the change, if this was later. The requirement is that the notification is 'given' to the appropriate office (see p1292).[17] If you do not do this the Revenue may impose a financial penalty on you (see p1308). You must notify the Revenue within one month if:

- you were claiming as a single person but are now part of a couple. Your tax credit entitlement comes to an end from the time the change occurred, and you must make a new claim;
- you were claiming as a couple but are no longer part of that couple. Your entitlement comes to an end from the date the change occurred, and you must make a new claim;
- you or your partner leave the UK permanently, or go abroad for more than a set period (see p1379). Entitlement comes to an end from the date of change, and you must make a new claim. If it is your partner who is abroad, you must make a new claim as a single person (and when s/he comes back, claim again as a couple);
- for child tax credit (CTC) only, you lose your right to reside in the UK (see p1361);
- there has been a decrease of £10 a week or more over four consecutive weeks in your or your partner's childcare costs or the childcare costs have stopped;
- you or your partner stop normally working at least 16 or 30 hours a week (see p1222 for rules about work). You can still count as being in work in some situations – eg, in some cases of illness or maternity. If you stop work, you may get a four-week run-on of working tax credit (WTC) (see p1230);
- for couples with children, you and your partner stop normally working a combined total of 30 hours a week. You no longer qualify for a 30-hour element;
- you or your partner cease to be responsible for one or more of your children (see p1198 for when you count as responsible);
- a child for whom you or your partner are responsible dies (see p1198 for who counts as a child);
- a child you or your partner are responsible for stops counting as a child or qualifying young person, other than by reaching age 20 (see p1196 for who

counts as a child). In this case, you must notify the Revenue within one month of the date the change actually occurred, rather than when you became aware of the change.

New relevant period

If any of these changes occur, the way your tax credits are calculated changes. All such changes mean either that your entitlement to tax credit has ceased or that a new 'relevant period' is started from the time the change is treated as taking effect. This means that a new calculation of your entitlement for that period is made (see p1249).

Changes that affect your maximum entitlement

There are certain other changes in circumstances which affect your maximum entitlement to tax credits – ie, they affect the tax credit elements to which you are entitled (see Chapter 51).

You do not have to notify the Revenue of these changes when they occur. If you choose to, you can notify instead at the end of the year when you are issued with your final notice. Some changes can be notified up to a week in advance (see p1292). However, most changes which *increase* your entitlement are only backdated for a maximum of three months from the time that you make the notification. The only exception concerns the disability and severe disability elements (see below). Changes that *decrease* your entitlement always take effect from the date of change, no matter when you notify the Revenue of them.[18] Delaying notifying these changes can, therefore, lead to you being underpaid or overpaid. Note that overpayments will usually be recovered from you (see Chapter 55).

The sorts of changes to which these rules apply include:

- if you have a new baby, or another child joins your family;
- if you or your partner start normally working at least 16 or 30 hours a week;
- if your childcare costs increase by £10 or more a week for at least four weeks in a row. The change takes effect from the first week in which your costs increase, as long as you provide notification of the increase within three months of the first day of the first week in which the increase occurs. If you do not provide notification of the increase in your costs within that time, the change takes effect from three months before the date that you do notify the Revenue.[19] You can report an increase of £10 or more a week as soon as one occurs, as long as you expect it to last for at least four weeks. For how your childcare costs are calculated, see p1240.

Entitlement to the disability or severe disability element of working tax credit

The rules on when your increased entitlement takes effect from are different in this circumstance. This applies where since your original claim for WTC, or since you asked for a revision to have the disability or severe disability element included in your claim, you have become entitled to a qualifying benefit which means you are now entitled to one or both of those elements. See p1281 regarding claims and p1317 regarding revisions.

Entitlement to the disability or severe disability element of child tax credit

A similar rule applies to CTC entitlement. If a child for whom you are responsible is awarded disability living allowance, you may be entitled to the severe disability element and/or the disability element with your award of CTC. This could increase the amount of CTC you get or mean that you now qualify for CTC when previously you had not qualified because your income was too high. See p1281 for claims and p1317 for revisions.

New relevant period

If any of these changes occur, the way your tax credits are calculated changes.[20] This is because a new 'relevant period' is started from the time the change is treated as taking effect. This means that a new calculation of your entitlement is made. For example, an increase in your childcare costs of the sort described above results in a new relevant period, so there will be a new calculation of your entitlement for the new period in which your childcare element may be increased. See p1249 for details of the calculation.

Changes in income

The initial decision on your award of tax credit is usually based on your previous year's income. Your award can be changed to reflect:

- any expected fall in your annual income compared with that used to make the initial decision (eg, where your earnings fall during the year); *and*
- any expected rise in your income compared with that used to make the initial decision, where that rise is more than £25,000 a year.

This £25,000 disregard only applies to increases in annual income in the current year compared to the previous year. If you ask the Revenue to base your award on current year's income because of an expected decrease, then *any* subsequent increase in your estimate will affect your award. See Chapter 52 for how income affects your award.

You should consider carefully whether to notify the Revenue during the year of changes in income. Whether or not you are better off doing so depends on your circumstances, and it is worth seeking advice. Consider the general points in the following two sections. However, if you have not done so already, you should always tell the Revenue about an increase in income before the end of the tax year so that provisional payments for the new tax year starting in April will be accurate. Payment of tax credits continues during the renewal process on the assumption that your income has gone up in line with average earnings. If your income went up by more than this, you may be overpaid.

If you expect your annual income to fall

- If you notify the Revenue of this during the year, your tax credit award is increased. However, if you get housing benefit (HB) or council tax benefit (CTB), those benefits could be reduced as tax credits count as income (see Chapter 36).
- HB and CTB are based on the amount of tax credit you actually *receive*. At the end of the year it may turn out that your income did not fall as you predicted and, as a result, you have been overpaid tax credit, which you may have to repay. In these circumstances, HB and CTB are *not* increased for the period during which you were overpaid tax credit. Not only will you have been overpaid tax credit, you may have lost out on the additional HB and CTB which you would have been able to claim had you been receiving a lower award of tax credit.
- If you do *not* notify the Revenue of an expected fall in income during the year, your tax credit entitlement is not adjusted until the final decision at the end of the year. In this instance, you will have been underpaid tax credit for the year, and this will be paid to you as a lump sum. This lump sum counts as capital and is ignored for 52 weeks after you have received it. You will not, therefore, have been overpaid HB or CTB as a result of receiving these arrears.

If you expect your annual income to rise by more than £25,000

- If you notify the Revenue of this during the year, your tax credit award is decreased. This may mean that you prevent an overpayment of tax credit building up further during the year (see Chapter 55). Your HB and CTB, if you are still entitled to any, can then be increased to take account of the lower award of tax credit.
- If you do *not* notify the Revenue of such an expected rise in your income during the year, you will keep being paid the 'extra' tax credit during the year, and will incur an overpayment. The overpaid tax credit is usually recoverable from you by a reduction in the tax credit you are paid in the following year, in which case your HB and CTB in that year are likely to increase.
- There is no penalty for incurring an overpayment of tax credit on the basis of an increase in income.
- All this, however, does not mean that you are always better off building up such an overpayment. You will not know for sure exactly how much you have been overpaid and at what rate it will be recovered from you until the final decision at the end of the year. Although the reduced tax credit entitlement in the following year may increase your HB and CTB, your increased earnings will also have the effect of reducing these benefits, and any further fluctuations in your income could complicate matters further.

- Ultimately, whether you are better off not notifying the Revenue of such an expected rise during the year depends on matters such as the amount of the likely overpayment, how recovery is likely to affect your HB and CTB in the next year, whether your income is likely to rise or fall again, and how comfortable you feel with building up a recoverable overpayment.

Notifying changes in circumstance

The notification may be given either orally or in writing. The rules also state that it must be given to an 'appropriate office', which is defined as an office of the Revenue or the DWP.[21] In practice, you should ensure that the Revenue has been informed, in order to be safe. The Revenue encourages claimants to telephone the helpline with queries or to report a change (see p1284). In practice, however, it is advisable to confirm the notification in writing to the Tax Credit Office and to keep a copy. That way, you have a record of what you have said and when you said it.

Notification must be given by the person who claimed the tax credit. In joint claim cases, it can be given by either member of the couple.[22]

Some changes of circumstances can be notified up to a week in advance. These are:[23]

- if you have accepted an offer of work and expect to start work within seven days;
- if you have arranged childcare and will incur childcare costs during the current tax year;
- if there is going to be a change in your weekly childcare costs of £10 a week or more.

You can also notify in advance if you expect your child to stay on in full-time, non-advanced education or approved training from 1 September after her/his 16th birthday.

You can amend the notification at any time before the initial award is revised, in which case the amended notification is taken as being notified at the time that your original notification was sent.[24]

Notes

1. **Making a decision**
   1 s2 TCA 2002
   2 *Jones v Department of Employment* [1989] QB 1 (CA)

3. **Initial decisions**
   3 s14(1) TCA 2002
   4 s23 TCA 2002
   5 s23(3) TCA 2002

4. **Final decisions**
   6 s18 TCA 2002
   7 s17(1) TCA 2002
   8 s17(2) TCA 2002
   9 Reg 11 TC(CN) Regs
   10 s17(8) TCA 2002
   11 s17(4) TCA 2002
   12 s17(6) TCA 2002
   13 Regs 34-36 TC(CN) Regs
   14 s18 TCA 2002
   15 s23 TCA 2002
   16 s23(3) TCA 2002

5. **Change of circumstances after a claim**
   17 ss3(4), 6(3) and 32(3) TCA 2002; reg 21 TC(CN) Regs
   18 Regs 20 and 25 TC(CN) Regs
   19 Reg 16(5)(a) WTC(EMR) Regs
   20 Regs 7(2) and 8(2) TC(ITDR) Regs
   21 Regs 2 and 22 TC(CN) Regs
   22 Reg 23 TC(CN) Regs
   23 Reg 27 TC(CN) Regs
   24 Reg 24 TC(CN) Regs

Chapter 55

Overpayments of tax credits

This chapter covers the rules on overpayments of tax credits. It contains:

For the rules on overpayments of benefits, see Chapter 39.

1. What is an overpayment of tax credits

The main rules are the same for child tax credit (CTC) and working tax credit (WTC).[1] If you (and your partner, if you are making a joint claim) are paid more tax credit for a tax year than you are entitled to, the extra amount is regarded as an overpayment. The Revenue can decide to adjust your award during the year of your current tax credit award to prevent an overpayment building up (an **'in-year overpayment'**), and/or recover all or some of the overpayment from you after the end of the tax year (an **'end-of-year overpayment'**). There is no right of appeal, although you can appeal against a decision that your entitlement to tax credit has changed. This means that by challenging the new decision on your entitlement, you can, in effect, challenge the finding that there is an overpayment or challenge the amount of the overpayment.

When an overpayment occurs

The most likely causes of an overpayment are:

- your income rose by more than £25,000[2] in the current tax year, compared with the previous tax year;
- you did not tell the Revenue in time about a change of circumstances reducing your entitlement (see p1287);
- the information you gave to the Revenue was incorrect;
- none of the above applies, but an overpayment occurred anyway because the Revenue made a mistake – ie, there was an 'official error'.

In-year overpayments

These are overpayments that arise during the year of your current tax credit award. Decisions on in-year overpayments can be made during the course of the tax year concerned, in the following circumstances.[3]

- If the Revenue thinks that there is likely to be an overpayment, it can adjust the award (or an award of another tax credit) in order to reduce or wipe out the overpayment. This may mean that your award is reduced for the rest of the year.
- If an award is terminated on the grounds that you did not satisfy the basic conditions for entitlement, the Revenue may decide that the amount already paid to you, or some of it, is to be regarded as an overpayment. The basic conditions of entitlement are, for CTC, that you are responsible for a child (see p1196) and, for WTC, that you are engaged in full-time work (see p1223).

End-of-year overpayments

These are overpayments that are identified at or after the end of the tax year concerned – ie, after your award for that year has been finalised. The Revenue can decide that there has been an end-of-year overpayment when it makes:[4] a final decision (see p1285), an enquiry decision (see p1319), a decision on discovery (see p1320) or a revision for official error (see p1320).

Notification of overpayments

To decide that you have been overpaid, the Revenue must change the decision on your entitlement to tax credits. When it makes a new decision on your entitlement, it must notify you of the new decision.[5] Remember that you have the right of appeal against any decision regarding the amount of your entitlement to tax credit (see p1322). So if you think that the new decision on your entitlement is wrong and that, therefore, you have not been overpaid as much as the Revenue says, or that you have not been overpaid at all, appeal against the new decision on your entitlement. If your appeal against the new decision on your entitlement is outside the 30-day time limit because you did not realise that you needed to appeal until you received a detailed calculation, argue that that is a reasonable excuse for the appeal being late.[6]

You may only find out about an **in-year overpayment** when the Revenue writes to you to say that your entitlement has changed and your payment has been adjusted. If the Revenue is going to recover an **end-of-year overpayment** from you, it must also give you notice of that, how much it is and how it is to be recovered from you. It usually does this at the same time as it writes to you about the final decision on your entitlement for the tax year. There is no right of appeal against the decision to recover an overpayment.[7] For what you can do, see p1301.

2. Recovery of overpayments

The basic rule is that the Revenue can recover all or part of any overpayment.

The Revenue can recover the overpayment by:

- adjusting (ie, reducing) your current award, in the case of an in-year overpayment; *and*
- requiring you to repay the overpayment, in the case of an end-of-year overpayment.

However, it does not have to recover an overpayment and should exercise discretion. The official policy is that an overpayment may be written off in whole or in part where the Revenue has failed to meet its 'responsibilities' (ie, official error) or where recovery would cause hardship (see p1298). According to official guidance the Revenue will **suspend recovery** of overpayments if you dispute (see p1301) the decision to recover it from you, either on Form TC846, or in writing, or by telephoning 0845 300 3900.[8]

You must be given notice that you must repay an end-of-year overpayment. The notice must also say how much the overpayment is, and how it is to be recovered from you.[9] There is no right of appeal against the decision to recover an overpayment.[10] For what you can do, see p1301.

Also, the Revenue does not ask you if recovering an overpayment will cause you hardship, or if you think the overpayment should not be recovered from you. Instead, you have to tell it about such things. It is, therefore, important to contact the Revenue as soon as possible.

Overpayments and award notices

The tax credit award notices that the Revenue sends out can be very complicated. You should be sent a checklist with your award notice with information used in the calculation for you to check. You can request an award calculation notice (Form TC647) from the Revenue which gives more detail about how your payment has been worked out. Where it is still unclear, you can write to the Tax Credit Office (its address will be at the top of the award notice) requesting a 'tailored reply'.

If you still do not receive a satisfactory response, consider taking up the matter with your MP, or making a complaint (see Chapter 46).

From whom an overpayment can be recovered

In-year overpayments are recovered from you by reducing the ongoing tax credit award (see p1297). An end-of-year overpayment can be recovered from the person or persons to whom the tax credit award was made. This means:[11]

- if you made a claim as a single person, the overpayment can be recovered from you;

- if you made a joint claim with your partner, the overpayment can be recovered from one or both of you. If you have separated from your partner, the Revenue practice is first to ask you both to repay the overpayment equally. If you wish, you and your ex-partner may agree to each pay different amounts. If the Revenue can only contact one person it may ask her/him to repay the whole amount.[12]

How much is recoverable

In-year overpayments

The Revenue adjusts the amount you are paid during the year, so that you receive less money and so in effect repay the overpayment.[13] Usually the reduction is limited to 10 per cent of your award if you receive the maximum tax credits which you could be entitled to (ie, with no reduction for income), or 25 per cent otherwise (ie, so that you are left with either 90 per cent or 75 per cent of your payment). But if you only receive the family element of child tax credit (CTC), 100 per cent of your award may be used. We understand that these limits will normally apply even where you are having both an in-year and end-of-year overpayment recovered (ie, there are not two reductions in your payments). If you do not want the limit to apply, you should say so. Remember that you can appeal against any new decision on your entitlement (see p1322).

You can ask the Revenue to reduce your award by less than the above or not reduce it at all – eg, because you think the overpayment has been caused by **official error** or would cause you **hardship** (see p1298 for more on these), although in hardship cases the Revenue may prefer instead to pay you additional payments (see p1299). Also, according to official guidance[14] it may **offset** (ie, reduce) the amount of the overpayment by the amount of any tax credit to which you actually were entitled if the overpayment was caused by:

- you ceasing to count as a single claimant and becoming part of a couple (you will need details of your partner's income); *or*
- you ceasing to count as part of a couple and counting instead as a single claimant; *and in either case*
- you would have had some tax credit entitlement following the change in your status.

Note: the official guidance also states that such offsets will only be made where you made a 'genuine error', rather than just delayed reporting your change of circumstance. The Revenue regards 'genuine error' as meaning that you reasonably thought that you had made a correct claim, taking into account the wording on the claim form and the notes that come with it. But you should ask the Revenue to consider any factors you think are relevant.

End-of-year overpayments

The Revenue may recover all or part of an end-of-year overpayment, but does not have to.[15] Normally though, it wants to recover all of the overpayment. For how the overpayment is recovered including how your payments may be reduced, see p1300. The main exception is where **official error** (ie, Revenue failure to meet responsibilities) or **hardship** is involved (see below). However, it may also **offset** an end-of-year overpayment in the same way that it would an in-year overpayment (see p1297).

If for any reason you think you will have difficulty repaying, tell the Revenue and ask it to use its discretion not to recover all or some of the overpayment. Rather than do this, the Revenue might prefer to pay you additional payments (see p1299). It may be worth checking that the overpayment has been calculated correctly, especially if you are doubtful of the figures that have been used or do not understand how it has been worked out. Remember that you can appeal against any decision on your entitlement (see p1322). Seek advice (see Appendix 2) if you think you may need help with any of this.

Official error, responsibilities and hardship

If an overpayment has been caused by official error (the Revenue calls this failing to meet its 'responsibilities'), or where recovery would cause hardship (the Revenue calls this being unable to meet your 'essential living expenses'), the Revenue may decide not to recover all or part of an overpayment, or in hardhsip cases may make additonal payments.

These decisions are discretionary and do not carry the right of appeal. You need to explain your circumstances and ask the Revenue to exercise its discretion in your favour. If you remain unhappy with the decision, see p1301 for what you can do. In any case, remember that if you want recovery suspended while the Revenue considers the matter, it is best to dispute the decision to recover the overpayment (see p1301).

'**Official error**' and '**responsibilities**' are not used or defined in the law, but the official guidance applied to all decisions on recoverability from 31 January 2008[16] is that the Revenue will not ask you to repay an overpayment at all if it accept that:

- the overpayment was caused by the Revenue failing to meet its 'responsibilities'; *and*
- you have met all of your 'responsibilities'.

For decisions made before the 31 January 2008 version of the guidance was introduced, in official error cases the Revenue used a test of whether you 'reasonably believed' the award was corrrect (see Chapter 54 of the 2007/08 edition of this *Handbook*). However, if the Revenue thinks it has met all its responsibilities but you have not met all of yours, it will normally recover the overpayment. If it thinks that both itself and you have failed to meet responsibilities, it will look at the circumstances and may write off parts of the overpayment.

The Revenue regards its responsibilities as: giving you correct advice based on your information; accurately recording your information and paying the correct amount; putting right mistakes you tell it about and sending you a corrected award notice; accurately recording your notification of changes in your circumstances and sending you a new award notice within 30 days of having all the necessary information.

The Revenue regards your responsibilities as: providing accurate, complete and up-to-date information; reporting changes of circumstances throughout the year; using the checklist sent with your award notice to tell the Revenue if anything is wrong or incomplete; checking that your payments match the amount given on the award notice; telling the Revenue of any errors on your award notice, normally within one month (although it may think longer was reasonable depending on the facts). Although unclear, the Revenue also seems to regard it as your responsibility to tell it if you do not get a revised award notice within one month of you telling it about a change in your circumstances.

'Hardship', or not being able to meet your 'essential living expenses', is not defined either, and there is little official guidance. Old versions of the guidance used to say that the following should be considered: your income and living expenses; savings and investments; other debts that you might have (eg, rent arrears and repayment of social security overpayments); how long it would take you to repay the overpayment; other payments you are due to make to the Revenue; your previous payment history; whether repaying would mean you could not afford essentials like gas, electricity or water; whether you have children aged under five, or a chronically sick or disabled person in the family whose health could be affected; any other relevant factors.

Again, all will depend on the circumstances. It is in your interest to show how repayment would leave you unable to meet your essential living expenses.

Additional payments

If recovery of an overpayment causes you hardship, the Revenue may also pay you some extra tax credits, called additional payments, to increase your payments slightly and so recover the overpayment more slowly. However, the Revenue also has the discretion to write off some or all of the overpayment in such cases. If you think that the Revenue has not exercised its discretion properly, tell it so. If you remain unhappy, seek further advice (see Appendix 2), and consider making a complaint (see Chapter 46).

If you get additional payments

If you get additional payments, when your award for the year is finalised, the Revenue will usually treat them as an end-of-year overpayment because they limited the amount of repayments you made on an in-year overpayment. You can still ask the Revenue not to recover the end-of-year overpayment from you. You will have strong grounds for this if recovery of the overpayment would cause you hardship or if the overpayment actually resulted from an official error (see p1298), especially if the Revenue already accepted this during the year, when making the additional payments.

For the effect of additional payments on any means-tested benefit you receive, see p861. Additional payments do not affect non-means-tested benefits.

How the overpayment is recovered

The Revenue recovers **in-year overpayments** by adjusting your payments during the year, so that you receive less money. You should be notified of the new decison on your entitlement.[17] Usually, the Revenue limits the reduction in your payments (see p1297). For **end-of-year overpayments**, the Revenue must notify you (and your partner if it is also being recovered from her/him) of the amount to be repaid, and how the overpayment is to be repaid.[18]

There are two main ways in which it can require you to repay.[19]

- Deductions from ongoing payments of any tax credit (see below). This is the Revenue's preferred method of repayment, and the amount that is deducted is usually limited.
- Directly to the Revenue. If you are no longer entiteld to tax credits at all, or one tax credit award has ended and another started due to a change in your household (eg, you started or stopped being part of a couple) the Revenue requires you to repay in this way. This may be in addition to deductions to repay an in-year overpayment.[20] You may pay in 12 monthly instalments if you wish. The Revenue will consider repayment over a longer period, or delay starting recovery, if that is too difficult, but you should explain why that is.

Deductions from ongoing payments

The law only deals with end-of-year overpayments, but in practice the Revenue takes the same approach with in-year overpayments. The *maximum* amounts by which the Revenue can reduce your payments are:[21]

- 10 per cent of the award if you are receiving the maximum tax credits to which you could be entitled (ie, with no reduction for income);
- 100 per cent of the award if you receive only the family element of CTC;
- 25 per cent of the award if neither of the above apply.

Note that these are maximum amounts, although the Revenue applies them automatically. If you accept that you should repay but cannot afford to repay at these rates, contact the Revenue and ask it to accept repayment at a lower rate. In order to persuade the Revenue, you may need to show why it would cause you hardship (see p1298) to pay at the maximum rate. Even then, the Revenue is likely to pay you additional payments (see p1299) rather than use a lower rate.

We understand that overpayments of WTC will normally be recovered from payments of WTC, and overpayments of CTC will normally be recovered from payments of CTC. Different parts of the overpayment can be recovered using different methods of recovery, as described above. Revised notices of overpayments, changing the method of recovery, can be issued at any time.[22]

Disputing recovery and negotiating repayment

Disputing recovery

There is no right of appeal against a decision to recover an overpayment, although you can dispute it with the Revenue. However, you do have the right of appeal against a decision on your entitlement to tax credits, including the amount of your entitlement. Do not assume that the Revenue always gets decisions on your entitlement right. If you have been overpaid and are unclear why, check the decisions about your entitlement (see p1296 for more on this). For more on appeals, see p1322.

The Revenue is only likely not to recover an overpayment in cases involving failure to meet its responsibilities (ie, official error) or hardship – for more about those, see p1298. You can ask the Revenue to use its discretion not to recover an overpayment (the Revenue usually calls this a dispute.) Disputing recovery should ensure that recovery is suspended while the dispute is dealt with. (Some Revenue letters may say you only have three months to dispute recovery. That is wrong as there is no such rule.) To dispute recovery, complete Form TC846 (available at www.hmrc.gov.uk/taxcredits/forms-leaflets.htm), write to the Revenue, or telephone the Tax Credit Helpline on 0845 300 3900.

The only way to make a legal challenge to a decision to insist on recovering an overpayment is by judicial review in the courts. Usually, judicial review is only possible in extreme cases – eg, where the Revenue insists on making you repay an overpayment that was clearly caused by an official error, you could not reasonably have known that you were being overpaid, and there is some urgency in the need to make the Revenue change its decision. For more about judicial review, see p1129.

The only other way of making the Revenue change its mind is by making a complaint. You first need to use the Revenue's own complaints procedure. If you remain dissatisfied, you can complain to the Independent Adjudicator or to the Parliamentary Ombudsman (see Appendix 1 for the addresses and Chapter 46 for the details of making a complaint). They can recommend action and order financial compensation, but both are likely to take time to complete their investigaton. Both the Adjudicator and the Ombudsman can deal with complaints about tax credits, but it may be most appropriate to go to the Adjudicator with complaints about the Revenue's use of discretion (eg, on whether to recover an overpayment), and the Ombudsman about maladministration (eg, severe delays).

Overpayments – what to do

- Check your **award notices** to see if your entitlement is correct (see p1296).
- Consider if the overpayment was caused by **official error** (failure to meet **responsibilities**) or if recovery would cause you **hardship** (see p1298); and

consider **disputing** the decision to recover the overpayment with the Revenue (see above).

- Check if the overpayment might be **offset** (see p1297), or if you can **negotiate** repayment (see below).
- If the Revenue will not do as you ask regarding the overpayment, consider making a **complaint** and if necessary taking your case to the Adjudicator's Office (see Chapter 46).
- In extreme cases, seek advice about making a legal challenge to the decision to recover the overpayment by making an application for **judicial review** (see p1301).

Negotiating repayment

If you have difficulty repaying, the Revenue may agree to you repaying the overpayment over a longer period than normal, by making a repayment instalment plan. Contact the Tax Credit Helpline on 0845 300 3900. Usually, the Revenue would look to you paying something straight away, and the rest over a later period. It will take into account all the relevant circumstances, including your income, savings, other debts and outgoings.

Other methods of recovery

If the Revenue is not satisfied with recovery using the methods described above, including agreeing a repayment instalment plan with you, then it will consider taking legal action. Further action will follow if the Revenue considers that you are refusing to repay, or neglecting to keep to an agreement to repay. All the circumstances will be taken into account before taking such action, but the Revenue may:[23]

- seize and sell your personal possessions. However, unless you let the Revenue into your property, authorised Revenue officers cannot enter your home and seize your personal possessions unless they have a warrant from the court; *or*
- take court action against you, including bankruptcy proceedings.

---

3. Interest on overpayments

In certain circumstances, the Revenue can add interest to the overpayment, with the effect of increasing the amount you have to repay.

When interest is added

Interest may be added to an overpayment being recovered from you (and/or your partner if you have a joint claim) if the Revenue considers that the overpayment is due to 'fraud or neglect' on the part of you (and/or your partner).[24]

If interest is added, it is added from 30 days after whichever of the following dates apply:[25]

- where you (or your partner) were treated during the tax year concerned as being overpaid due to termination of your award because of not satisfying the basic conditions of entitlement (see p1295), the date of the decision terminating the award; *or*
- if that did not apply, the date in the final notice that you were given until to confirm your actual income for the tax year.

When added to the overpayment, the interest is treated as if it were part of the overpayment. This means that it is subject to the same rules as the overpayment itself.[26]

How much interest is added

The amount of interest added to the penalty is 6.5 per cent a year or, if that is different from the average lending rate of the main banks, the bank lending rate plus 2.5 per cent.[27]

Challenging an interest decision

Decisions adding interest to an overpayment carry the right of appeal. For example, you might wish to argue on appeal that you did not act fraudulently or negligently, or that the amount of the interest is wrong. You (and/or your partner if s/he is subject to the decision) must be given notice of a decision adding interest to an overpayment. The notice must be dated and include details of your right of appeal against the decision.[28] See Chapter 57 for appeals.

Notes

1. **What is an overpayment of tax credits**
   1 s28 TCA 2002
   2 Reg 5 TC(ITDR) Regs
   3 s28(5) and (6) TCA 2002
   4 s28(1) TCA 2002
   5 s23 TCA 2002
   6 The Revenue used to say as much in pre-April 2007 versions of Revenue Code of Practice COP 26, *What Happens if We Have Paid You Too Much Tax Credit?*
   7 ss29(1) and (2) and 38 TCA 2002

2. **Recovery of overpayments**
   8 Revenue Code of Practice COP 26, *What Happens if We Have Paid You Too Much Tax Credit?*
   9 ss28(1) and 29 TCA 2002
   10 s38 TCA 2002
   11 s28(3) and (4) TCA 2002
   12 Revenue Code of Practice COP 26, *What Happens if We Have Paid You Too Much Tax Credit?*
   13 Revenue Code of Practice COP 26, *What Happens if We Have Paid You Too Much Tax Credit?'*
   14 Tax Credits Claimant Compliance Manual, paras 15605, 15630 (available at www.hmrc.gov.uk/manuals/ccmmanual)
   15 s28(1) TCA 2002
   16 Revenue Code of Practice COP 26, *What Happens if We Have Paid You Too Much Tax Credit?*
   17 ss23 and 28(5) TCA 2002
   18 s29(1) and (2) TCA 2002
   19 s29(3)-(5) TCA 2002
   20 Revenue Code of Practice COP 26, *What Happens If We Have Paid You Too Much Tax Credit?*
   21 Reg 12A TC(PC) Regs; Revenue Code of Practice COP 26, *What Happens if We Have Paid You Too Much Tax Credit?*
   22 s29(2) TCA 2002
   23 s29(3) TCA 2002 (overpayment of tax credit may be treated as if it were outstanding tax)

3. **Interest on overpayments**
   24 s37(1) TCA 2002
   25 s37(2)-(3) TCA 2002
   26 s37(6) TCA 2002
   27 Reg 4 TC(IR) Regs
   28 ss37(4) and 38(1)(d) TCA 2002

Chapter 56

Investigations, penalties and fraud: tax credits

This chapter covers the rules about tax credit investigations, penalties and fraud. It contains:

The Revenue has wide powers to investigate your claim and in certain circumstances a financial penalty may be imposed on you. Also, if you are considered deliberately to have acted fraudulently, then you may be subject to a fine or imprisonment, or both.

1. Investigation of claims

The Revenue has powers to ask you to supply information and evidence and to gather evidence to help it check whether your claim is correct, and to investigate fraud. The Revenue refers to investigations into the accuracy of awards as **'examinations'** and **'enquiries'**. Examinations are carried out on some claims *during* the year in order to check that they are correct. Enquiries may be carried out *after* the year concerned to check that you were paid the correct amount. More serious investigations into **fraud** may also be carried out.

The Revenue might ask you to provide things like bank statements or your rent book, but will usually explain why it needs them and give you reasonable time to produce them. You can seek professional advice (eg, from a welfare rights adviser or a solicitor) and can be accompanied at meetings you have with the Revenue.

Not all investigations are fraud investigations. Fraud investigations tend only to happen in the more serious cases and, in such cases, the Revenue has additional powers (see p1307).

Examinations

During the course of your award, or sometimes before your claim is decided, the Revenue may telephone or write to you requiring information or evidence. It may request a meeting with you in connection with your claim. Normally, the Revenue will write to you to say that it is examining your claim. The Revenue produces a leaflet, WTC/FS2, giving a basic outline of the procedure.[1] If the examination is started before your claim is decided, normally you will not be paid before the examination is complete. If it starts while you are already receiving tax credits, normally you will continue to be paid while the examination is being carrried out.

If you prefer, the Revenue will deal with someone else on your behalf – eg, an adviser, accountant or a relative. The Revenue will need a short signed letter from you to confirm that that is what you want. However, you will still be regarded as personally responsible for the information provided.

The Revenue may request a meeting to discuss the examination with you, and ask and answer questions. A short leaflet, WTC/FS4, giving a basic description of meetings is available. You do not have to attend, but remember that the Revenue has powers to seek information or evidence (see p1307). The Revenue says that it will always arrange for an interpreter for a meeting if required.[2] At the meeting, the Revenue will take notes – it should let you have a copy later, when they have been typed up. If you do not co-operate with the examination (eg, by refusing to provide information) your claim might be refused or your award stopped, and you may be subject to a penalty (see p1308).

In some cases, the Revenue may ask you to sign the notes as an accurate record of the meeting. You do not have to sign this. Such signed notes may be used by the Revenue as evidence, so be very sure that you point out anything you disagree with in the notes before signing. If the Revenue finds your claim is incorrect or that you have not notified a change of circumstances that you must report, it might ask you to confirm the information by signing a Certificate of Full Disclosure. Be sure you are satisfied of the accuracy of information in such a certificate, as the Revenue will take a very serious view if you sign it when you know it is wrong.

You cannot stop an examination taking place, but if you are unhappy with the way you are being treated you can make a complaint (see Chapter 46).

Enquiries

After your tax credit award is finalised at the end of the tax year, the Revenue may carry out an enquiry into the award (a 'local office' enquiry). (Normally, this will not be until the following May or June, at the earliest. There is a deadline by which the Revenue must have initiated the enquiry – see p1319.) The Revenue must write to you about this. The Revenue produces a leaflet, WTC/FS1, giving a basic outline of the procedure.[3]

If you prefer, the Revenue will deal with someone else on your behalf – eg, an adviser, accountant or a relative. The Revenue will need a short signed letter from you to confirm that that is what you want. However, you will still be regarded as personally responsible for the information provided.

The Revenue may request a meeting with you. The same points apply to such meetings as they do to meetings in connection with examinations (see p1306).

You can stop the enquiry by requesting the Revenue to complete it by making a decision on your tax credit entitlement for the year in question. If the Revenue wishes to continue making the enquiry, it will pass your request to an independent appeal tribunal. You can also appeal to the tribunal if you are unhappy with the decision following the enquiry. For more on when tribunals deal with requests and decisions regarding enquiries, see p1319.

Powers to seek information

The Revenue can require you (and/or your partner if you have a joint claim) to provide information or evidence if during the course of your award it believes your award may be wrong – eg, for the purpose of an examination. It can also require information or evidence after your award has been finalised, for the purpose of an enquiry.

It can also do this if it is necessary for a decision relating to an initial claim (see Chapter 53), a revision during an award (see Chapter 57), a final notice and final decision (see Chapter 54), or (if you are an employee) regarding your employer's responsibility to pay you working tax credit.[4] You must be given at least 30 days to provide the information.[5] The Revenue does not have to suspect you of fraud in order to require information or evidence from you.

It is important that you co-operate with requests for information or evidence as far as you can. Even though you may not be the subject of a fraud investigation, the Revenue might refuse your claim or reduce your award (possibly to nil), and there are a number of circumstances in which you can be subject to a financial penalty or even a prosecution if you refuse to supply information and evidence, or supply material which you know to be incorrect (see p1308). It is important that you are as truthful as possible when responding.

The Revenue can also require your employer or childcare provider to provide information. They must be given at least 30 days to provide it. If they are subject to these requirements, they can also be subject to penalties (see p1308). They can be required to provide information and evidence relating to your claim or, for the purpose of a revision during an award or an enquiry (see pp1316 and 1322), your award.[6]

If fraud is suspected

Fraud investigations are normally carried out by the Special Compliance Office of the Revenue. **Note:** if fraud is suspected, the Revenue will usually explain to you why your claim is being investigated, and that you can seek professional advice from someone who can attend any meetings you have with the Revenue. It is advisable to seek professional advice (eg, from a solicitor) if you are investigated on suspicion of fraud. If you are being investigated you should seek advice as quickly as possible. You are likely to be interviewed under caution.

In addition to the powers described above, the Revenue has specific powers when investigating fraud.[7] Where the Revenue has 'reasonable grounds' for suspecting fraud, a court can make an order requiring that documents containing relevant evidence be delivered by you (or any other person who has them) to the Revenue within the time specified in the court order.

Where a court is satisfied that there is 'reasonable ground' for suspecting serious fraud, it can issue a warrant giving the Revenue authority to enter and search premises for evidence within 14 days. The Revenue can only apply for such a warrant where it is satisfied that asking the person in possession of the evidence to deliver it up might 'seriously prejudice' the investigation. Under the warrant, the Revenue can remove any things that there is 'reasonable cause' to believe may be required as evidence, and search any person on the premises of whom there is 'reasonable cause' to believe is in possession of such evidence.[8]

2. **Penalties**

The Revenue can impose a financial penalty on you if:[9]

- you have fraudulently or negligently made an **incorrect statement** or **declaration**, or supplied **incorrect information or evidence**; *or*
- you have **failed to comply** with requirements.

If you do not think a penalty should be imposed on you – eg, because you had a reasonable excuse for not declaring a change in circumstances, or you cannot get the information they asked for, tell the Revenue. If a penalty is imposed, then the Revenue will contact you to tell you.[10] You have the right of appeal against the imposition of a penalty (see p1328).

In making its decision, the Revenue will consider things like how much you have co-operated and the seriousness of the changes that need to be made. Here, we describe the rules on penalties and interest as they apply to you. However, in certain circumstances, these rules can also apply in the same way to your employer or your childcare provider (see p1307).

Incorrect statements and information

The Revenue can impose a financial penalty of up to £3,000 (it does not have to impose the maximum) on you if you have acted fraudulently or negligently and you have:[11]

- made an **incorrect statement or declaration** in connection with a claim, or a notification of a change of circumstances (see p1287) or in a response to a final notice (see p1286); *or*
- given **incorrect information or evidence** in connection with an initial decision (see p1285), a requirement to provide information or evidence during the course of your award, a revision during an award (see p1316), a final decision (see p1285), an enquiry (see p1319) or (if you are an employee) regarding your employer's responsibility to pay you working tax credit (WTC).

The Revenue regards 'negligence' as not taking 'reasonable care'.[12] If you think you have acted with reasonable care, tell the Revenue and ask that a penalty is not imposed.

Penalties for incorrect statements and information

The maximum penalty is £3,000 (the Revenue does not have to impose the maximum). You must be notified of the penalty, including the date on which it is given, and your right of appeal. The penalty is payable 30 days after the date you were notified of it.[13] The amount of the penalty may be increased by the addition of interest (see p1311).

If you are a member of a joint-claim couple (see p1273), the penalty may be imposed or partly imposed on your partner, unless s/he could not reasonably have been expected to have been aware that you had fraudulently or negligently made an incorrect statement or provided incorrect information or evidence. However, even if the penalty is imposed or partly imposed on your partner, the total penalty for the same incorrect statement cannot amount to more than £3,000.

If you are acting for someone else in connection with her/his claim and you fraudulently or negligently make an incorrect statement, the penalty applies to you.

Failure to comply

The Revenue can impose a financial penalty on you of up to £300 (it does not have to impose the maximum):[14]

- if you **fail to provide information or evidence** for a decision on an initial claim (see p1285), a requirement to provide information or evidence during the course of your award, a revision during an award (see p1316), a final decision (see p1285), an enquiry (see p1319) or (if you are an employee) regarding your employer's responsibility to pay you WTC; *or*
- if you **fail to comply with a requirement regarding a final notice** (see p1286); *or*
- if you **fail to notify a specified change of circumstances** within one month of the change or, except in the last case below, the date you became aware of the change if that is later.[15] These are:

- a decrease of £10 a week or more over four weeks in a row in your or your partner's childcare costs or a stop in the childcare costs; *or*
- you have stopped being counted as a single claimant; *or*
- you were claiming as a couple but are no longer part of that couple. This includes where you or your partner leave the UK permanently, or go abroad for more than a set period (see p1379); *or*
- you (or your partner) lose your right to reside in the UK or stop being regarded as being in the UK; *or*
- your or your partner's hours of work fall to less than 16 or 30 hours a week; *or*
- if you have a joint claim and get the 30-hour element of WTC because your joint hours total at least 30 hours a week, your joint total hours fall to less than 30 hours a week; *or*
- you or your partner cease to be responsible for one or more of your children (see p1198 for when you count as responsible); *or*
- a child you or your partner are responsible for dies (see p1198 for when you count as responsible for a child); *or*
- a child you or your partner are responsible for stops counting as a child (other than by reaching their 20th birthday), including where they were due to continue counting as a child by remaining in full-time education or training, but did not do so – see p1196 for who counts as a child.

The Revenue says that it will not impose a penalty if you had 'reasonable excuse' for not telling it about the change. Tell the Revenue if you think that applies. However, the Revenue will not accept as a reasonable excuse the fact that you did not know you had to inform it.[16]

Penalties for failure to comply[17]

The maximum penalty for this is £300. If the penalty is for failure to provide information or evidence there is a further daily penalty of up to £60 a day for each further day you continue to fail to comply. You must be notified of the penalty, including the date on which it is given, and your right of appeal. The penalty is payable 30 days after the date you were notified of it.[18] The amount of the penalty may be increased by the addition of interest (see p1311).

However, if the penalty is for failure to provide information or evidence, or for a failure regarding a final notice, then the Revenue cannot apply the penalty itself. Instead, it must write to the Tribunals Service, which will then summons you to an appeal tribunal where it will decide whether the penalty should be applied.[19] You can appeal against the tribunal's decision to a commissioner (see p1327).

Once you have provided the information or evidence, a penalty cannot be imposed on you. You have not failed to provide information or evidence if you did so within any time that the Revenue has allowed you to, or if you had a 'reasonable excuse' for the failure, or if having had a reasonable excuse you later actually provided the information or evidence without unreasonable delay.

If you are a member of a joint-claim couple, and a £300 penalty has been imposed for failure to comply with a requirement regarding a final notice or for failure to report the specified change of circumstances, the total of that penalty applied to either or both of you is a maximum of £300.

If your employer fails to make correct payments of tax credits to you, s/he may be subject to a financial penalty up to a maximum of £3,000.[20]

Interest added to penalties

If a penalty is imposed on you, the Revenue has the power to apply interest to the penalty. Although the Revenue does not have to apply interest, it can do so even where you are not considered to have acted fraudulently or negligently (ie, where the penalty is for failure to comply). The amount of the interest becomes part of the penalty and is recoverable in the same way as the penalty itself.[21]

The amount of interest added to the penalty is 6.5 per cent per annum or, if that is different from the average of the lending rates of the main banks, the bank lending rate plus 2.5 per cent.[22]

You can appeal against the penalty itself and the amount of the penalty. However, the way the law is written suggests that there is no right of appeal regarding the addition of interest.[23]

Separately from the above rules, if the Revenue considers that an overpayment has arisen because of 'fraud or neglect' on your part (or, if you are a member of a joint-claim couple, on the part of one or both of you), it can decide to apply interest to all or some of the overpayment (see p1302).

Recovery of penalties

The Revenue has discretion about whether to impose a penalty and – subject to the maximum amounts given above – the amount. Also, although the penalty itself can only be altered on appeal, the Revenue has discretion about whether actually to insist that you pay all or some of the penalty.[24] If you tried your best to fulfil all your obligations, or if the penalty would cause you hardship, tell the Revenue this and ask it to exercise its discretion not to recover all or some of the penalty.

If the Revenue does decide that a penalty may be imposed upon you, it will try to come to an agreement with you which involves you offering to pay the agreed amount. If you agree, it will send you a final letter setting out the agreement, which the Revenue regards as a 'legally binding contract'.[25] It may be best to try to come to an agreement because if the Revenue is not able to reach such an agreement with you, it may use its legal powers to recover the penalty. However, if you think you may want to challenge the penalty (see p1312) check to see if the contract means that the Revenue will not actually issue a decision imposing the penalty because if you do not have a decision you will not be able to challenge it on an appeal. If the Revenue uses its legal powers to recover a penalty, it can:

- seize and sell your personal possessions. However, *unless you let them into your property or they are are otherwise easily able to get in*, authorised officers cannot enter your home and seize your personal possessions unless they have a warrant from the court; *or*
- take court action against you, including bankruptcy proceedings.[26]

Challenging a penalty

You can tell the Revenue that you disagree with the penalty and/or the additon of interest to it (eg, when it contacts you to tell you that you are liable for a penalty). It can remove the penalty and/or the interest. The Revenue will decide whether to issue a formal decision, so that you can appeal if you still disagree.[27] Once a formal penalty decision has been made, it cannot be altered except on appeal. You have the right of appeal against all penalties. The appeal right includes the right of appeal against the determination that a penalty has been incurred and the amount of the penalty, although not against any addition of interest.

Note: subject to the maximum, a tribunal can increase as well as decrease the amount.

For more information on appeals, see p1322, and for more on penalty appeals, see p1328.

3. Fraud

You are regarded as having committed the offence of fraud if you deliberately take part in fraudulent activity in order to get a tax credit for you or anyone else. If you are convicted by a court, you are liable to a fine or to imprisonment, or both.[28]

Fines or imprisonment for fraud

If a court convicts you of fraud in connection with tax credits and:[29]

- you are convicted in a magistrates' court, you are liable to a maximum of six months' imprisonment or a maximum fine of £5,000, or both; *or*
- you are convicted in a Crown Court, you are liable to a maximum of seven years' imprisonment or a fine of an unlimited amount, or both.

Will you be prosecuted?

Whether or not you will be prosecuted is a discretionary decision. Not all cases of fraud end in prosecution. The Revenue may investigate your claim under civil investigation procedures – ie, without a view to prosecuting you. If you are being investigated by the Special Compliance Office *without* a view to prosecuting you, you are normally told about this. However, this does not mean that the Revenue cannot change its mind and decide that a prosecution should be made.

The factors that it may take into account are likely to include the strength of the evidence, the amount of tax credit involved, whether an offence was planned and your personal circumstances.

Official policy[30] (on all of the Revenue's work, not specifically tax credits) indicates that criminal investigations are more likely if, for example:

- there is organised or systematic fraud including conspiracy;
- false statements are made or false documents given during a civil investigation;
- deliberate concealment, deception, conspiracy or corruption is suspected;
- false or forged documents have been used;
- the person involved has committed previous offences or there is a repeated course of unlawful conduct or previous civil action;
- there is a link to suspected wider criminality.

Note: this is not a complete list (even of that in the official policy) and ultimately all depends on the circumstances of your case.

What to do if you are prosecuted

The most important thing to do is to get advice. You may be entitled to legal help and have a solicitor or barrister represent you in court. You should check carefully that the Revenue is able to prove all the parts of the offence you are charged with. Do not plead guilty until you have been able to get advice.

4. The effect of an investigation on tax credits

There is nothing to stop payment of your tax credits specifically because an investigation, whether for fraud or not, is underway. However, the Revenue can:

- revise a current award if it has 'reasonable grounds' for believing it is wrong (see p1316). Note that the Revenue might do this if you do not provide information or evidence that it has requested;
- change an award at the end of the tax year for which the award was made, when the final decision is made (see p1319);
- revise an award via an 'enquiry' or a 'decision on discovery' after the end of the tax year for which the award was made (see p1319);
- postpone payment where an appeal is pending on your claim or a similar claim, or it appears that your address or bank account details are incorrect (see p1281).

Also, the Revenue can ask you and, in certain cases, other people to provide information or evidence in connection with an award (see pp1308 and 1312), and impose a penalty (see p1308) if you do not respond within the given time.

The decision on whether you should be prosecuted is separate from a decision to recover an overpayment (see Chapter 55). Whether or not you are entitled to tax credits, the amount and recoverability of any overpayment is decided by the Revenue without regard to dishonesty of intention. Decisions on entitlement can in most cases be appealed (see p1322).

Whatever the result of an investigation or prosecution, the Revenue may take more time assessing future claims because it may check out your circumstances thoroughly. Again, if it takes too long for it to make a decision, you should complain. You could also apply for help from the social fund (see Chapter 21 or 22).

Notes

1. **Investigation of claims**

1 ss14(2),15(2) and 16(2) and (3) TCA 2002; leaftlet available at www.hmrc.gov.uk/leaflets/wtcfs.pdf
2 Information given at www.hmrc.gov.uk/taxcredits/exams-enqs.htm
3 s19 TCA 2002; leaflet available at www.hmrc.gov.uk/leaflets/wtcfs1.pdf
4 ss14(2),15(2),16(3),17, 19(2) and 22 TCA 2002
5 Reg 32 TC(CN) Regs
6 ss14(2)(b),15(2)(b),16(3)(b) and 19(2)(b) TCA 2002; regs 30 and 31 TC(CN) Regs
7 s36 TCA 2002
8 s36(2) TCA 2002

2. **Penalties**

9 ss31 and 32 TCA 2002
10 Revenue leaflet WTC7, *Tax Credits Penalties*
11 s31 TCA 2002
12 Revenue leaflet WTC7, *Tax Credits Penalties*
13 Sch 2 para 1 TCA 2002
14 s32 TCA 2002
15 ss3(4), 6(3) and 32(3) TCA 2002; reg 21(2) TC(CN) Regs
16 Revenue leaflet WTC7, *Tax Credits Penalties*
17 s32(2)(a)-(6) TCA 2002
18 Sch 2 para 1 TCA 2002
19 Sch 2 paras 1 and 3 TCA 2002
20 s33 TCA 2002
21 s37(5) and (6) TCA 2002
22 Reg 4 TC(IR) Regs
23 ss37(5)-(6) and 38 TCA 2002
24 Sch 2 paras 1 and 5 TCA 2002
25 Revenue leaflet WTC7, *Tax Credits Penalties*
26 Sch 2 para 7 TCA 2002
27 Revenue leaflet WTC7, *Tax Credits Penalties*

3. **Fraud**

28 s35(1) TCA 2002
29 s35(2) TCA 2002
30 The Revenue's criminal investigation policy, available at www.hmrc.gov.uk/prosecutions/crim-inv-policy.htm

Chapter 57

Revisions and appeals: tax credits

This chapter covers revisions and appeals for child tax credit and working tax credit. It contains:

Decisions on tax credit entitlement can be changed by revision by the Revenue or by appeal to an independent tribunal. This chapter explains how and when your award can be changed by revision or appeal.

If you are overpaid tax credits, there may be two decisions: one deciding how much you are entitled to and one deciding to recover the overpayment. A decision on entitlement can be changed by revision or appeal, but a decision to recover an overpayment cannot be changed this way. Instead, you should ask the Revenue to use its discretion not to recover all or part of the overpayment (see p1301) and use the complaints procedures if necessary (see p1182).

Rules for revising tax credit decisions are different from those for social security benefits. This chapter covers tax credit revisions in detail.

Tax credit appeals are heard by the same appeal tribunals that deal with social security benefits, and are administered by the Tribunals Service. Many of the appeal rules are the same for tax credits as they are for social security benefits. Chapter 42 covers appeals for social security benefits. This chapter refers you to Chapter 42 where tax credit rules are the same as benefit rules. The footnotes in Chapter 42 also contain references to the child tax credit and working tax credit legislation where applicable.

1. **Revisions**

If you disagree with a decision, you may be able to have it revised by the Revenue. The circumstances in which a revision can be made depend on whether the decision with which you disagree is:

- an 'initial decision' on a claim (see below);
- a 'final decision' after the tax year has ended following an annual review (see p1319); *or*
- a decision of an appeal tribunal (see p1322).

Revision or appeal?

Most decisions carry a right of appeal. An appeal must be made within 30 days after the date on which notice of the decision was given, although late appeals may be allowed in some circumstances. Unless you are simply reporting a change in circumstances, it is generally better to appeal than ask for a revision. You could be at a disadvantage if you ask for a revision before asking for an appeal because if the Revenue does not revise the award, you may have missed the deadline for appeal. On the other hand, if the Revenue does revise the award but you are still not happy with it, you have another 30 days to appeal. Asking for an appeal without first trying to have the decision revised does not mean your case will necessarily have to go to a tribunal. There is an opportunity to settle the dispute first with the Revenue (see p1324).

You do not have a choice between revision and appeal if you have missed the appeal deadline and cannot get a late appeal. In this situation, you may still be able to put your case to the Revenue and ask it to revise its decision. See below for which decisions can be revised.

Revising an initial decision during an award

When you claim a tax credit, the Revenue must decide whether to make an award and the rate at which to award it.[1] This is called an 'initial decision'. If you disagree with it, you have the right to appeal (see p1322) or you may be able to ask the Revenue to revise the decision as described below. Your award can also be revised if your circumstances change.

Your claim is refused or award stopped

If your claim has been turned down altogether or your award has been terminated, you do not have the option to ask for the decision to be revised. You must appeal within 30 days if you want the decision to be changed. If you do not appeal or your appeal is unsuccessful, you need to make a fresh claim to get any further tax credit in that tax year.[2]

No award because your income too high

If your income in the previous year is too high to qualify for a tax credit, but you satisfy the other qualifying conditions, you are awarded a tax credit at a nil rate. This nil-rate award can be revised if your income is estimated to be lower in the current year.[3]

You disagree with an award

If you have been awarded a tax credit but you disagree with the amount, the initial decision can be revised if:

- your **circumstances have changed** so that you should get an additional or higher element (see below); *or*
- the Revenue has **reasonable grounds** for believing that you are entitled to a different rate of tax credit or that you are not entitled to a tax credit at all (see p1318); *or*
- there has been an **official error** (see p1318).

Changes in circumstances that increase entitlement to a tax credit element

If your circumstances change so that you should be getting an element you were not getting before, or a higher rate of an element, your award may be revised.[4] For example, if you have a new baby your child tax credit (CTC) award can be revised to include another child element and a baby element.

If you notify the Revenue of the change within three months, the increase in the award can be fully backdated.[5] There are specific rules dealing with the date from which an award is recalculated where there is a change in childcare charges or childcare provided (see p1289).

The increase in the award cannot be backdated for more than three months before the date you provide notification of the change, except in the following cases relating to the **disability or severe disability element of CTC and working tax credit** (WTC).

- If you claim disability living allowance (DLA) for a child, tell the Revenue straight away. Do not wait till it is awarded. Tell the Revenue again within three months of the decision that DLA has been awarded so that the disability or severe disability element of CTC is fully backdated to the date from when DLA is payable or, if later, the date you told the Revenue you had claimed DLA.
- If you are already getting WTC when you claim one of the benefits that would entitle you to a WTC disability or severe disability element (eg, DLA, see p1237), do not wait until it is awarded before notifying the Revenue. If you tell the Revenue that you are waiting for a decision on the benefit claim, once it is awarded, the disability or severe disability element can be backdated to the date you first notified the Revenue that you had claimed benefit or, if later, the start of the benefit award. You must notify the Revenue within three months of the date the claim for benefit is decided.[6]

If you disagree with a revised decision, you have the right of appeal within 30 days to an appeal tribunal (see p1322) or to ask for another revision on 'reasonable grounds' (see below) or for official error (see p1320).

Reasonable grounds

The Revenue has the power to amend or terminate an award on its own initiative. It can do this if it has 'reasonable grounds for believing' that:[7]

- you are entitled to a different rate of tax credit; *or*
- you are not entitled to WTC or you are not entitled to CTC.

This could happen, for example, because you tell the Revenue about an income change or wrong information is used in deciding your claim. Or it could happen because it has decided to examine your claim and has found errors (see p1306).

If the rate of tax credit is changed, the Revenue revises your award taking into account any changes in circumstance from the date they arose unless:

- it is a change that increases entitlement to tax credit elements, which can only be backdated for up to three months (see p1317);
- childcare charges go down by £10 a week or more. In this case there is a four-week run-on at the same rate before the award is reduced (see p1288);[8]
- there is a four-week run-on because you stop work or reduce your hours below 16 a week (see p1230).

Decisions can only be revised in this way during the period of the award, not after an award has been terminated, nor after a final decision has been made.[9]

Example

Pauline provides an estimate of her income for the current year and this is less than the previous year's income on which the award was based. The initial decision can be revised and her award recalculated based on the current year's income. The estimate she provides must be sufficient to give the Revenue 'reasonable grounds for believing' that her entitlement should change.

The Revenue is not obliged to revise even when there are grounds. It could leave changes to be dealt with at the annual review – eg, if it is late in the year and the change is minor.[10]

If you disagree with the revised rate of tax credit, you can appeal within 30 days to an appeal tribunal (see p1322) or ask for another revision. However, if you disagree with a decision to end your tax credit entitlement, you have the right to appeal, but not to a further revision.

Official error

An initial award can be revised if it is incorrect because of an official error.[11] See p1320 for details.

Annual review

After 5 April, the Revenue reviews your tax credit award for the year just ended and makes a final decision on your entitlement for that year. It sends you an annual review form which details the circumstances on which the award was based and usually an annual declaration form, giving your income for the tax year just passed (see p1277).

If the Revenue sends you an annual declaration form, you must complete and return it by the deadline given on the form (31 July for most cases). The Revenue finalises your entitlement for the year just passed.

A final decision is conclusive unless it is changed on appeal or in the following circumstances.

- If you **change your statement** about your income or circumstances before the deadline (see below), the final decision can be changed.
- Once a final decision is made, there is a period during which the Revenue can enquire into your entitlement. See below for details of **revision on enquiry**.
- Outside the period of enquiry, a final decision can be revised on 'discovery' of certain information to do with your tax liability or to do with fraud or neglect. There is a deadline for such revisions. See p1320 for details of **revision on discovery**.
- A final decision can be revised because of **official error** (see p1320).

Changing your statement

If you reply to the annual review notice but then wish to change your statement, you may do so. If it is before the deadline given in the notice for replying (31 July in most cases), but the Revenue has already made a final decision, the final decision may be revised.[12]

If the Revenue only had an estimate of your income for the current year (eg, because you are self-employed and have not yet finalised your accounts), you will have a later deadline (usually 31 January) in which to give details of your actual income for that year. If you do so, the Revenue must make a new final decision.[13] It can revise the new decision if you change your statement before the later deadline.[14] If you do not give further details of actual income, the Revenue must nevertheless make a new final decision once the later deadline is passed.

Revision on enquiry

The Revenue has the power to enquire into entitlement for any reason,[15] but it must begin its enquiry by giving you notice by a certain date. That is a year after the deadline by which you were to reply to the annual review notice, or a year after the later deadline for self-employed people or others to supply actual income details where only an estimate had been provided.[16] If you are required to submit an income tax return, the enquiry must begin by the day your tax return becomes final.

When the enquiry is completed, the Revenue makes a fresh decision on whether you are entitled and how much the award should be.

Only one enquiry into entitlement can be conducted for any one tax year.[17]

For more details, see p1306.

If you disagree with an enquiry decision

If you disagree with the decision you have the right of appeal within 30 days to an appeal tribunal (see p1322). Alternatively, it may be revised if it is incorrect because of an official error (see below).[18] The Revenue may also revise an enquiry decision by a 'revision on discovery' (see below).

Revision on discovery

If it is too late to 'enquire' into your entitlement, the Revenue can still revise a final decision, but only in specific circumstances, and there are further time limits by when such a revision must take place. A final decision or an enquiry decision may be revised outside the period allowed for an enquiry where the Revenue has 'reasonable grounds for believing' that tax credit entitlement is wrong:

- because of a revision of your income tax liability. The revision of your tax credit entitlement must take place within a year of your income tax liability being revised;[19] *or*
- for reasons attributable to fraud or neglect (see below).

There is nothing to stop the Revenue going through this process more than once.[20] Where a final decision, enquiry decision or discovery decision has been revised for official error, that too can be further revised in this way.[21]

Fraud or neglect

A decision can be revised if the Revenue has reasonable grounds for believing that an incorrect decision on tax credit entitlement is attributable to fraud or neglect.[22] The fraud or neglect may be on your part, or your partner's if it is a joint claim, or on the part of anyone acting for you (see p1274 for when a person may act for you).

Your tax credit entitlement in a tax year cannot be revised on this ground after five years from the end of the tax year.[23] For example, a tax credit award for 2007/08 cannot be revised after 5 April 2013.

If you disagree with a discovery decision

You have the right of appeal within 30 days to an appeal tribunal (see p1322). Alternatively, the decision may be revised if it is incorrect because of an official error (see below).

Official error

An initial decision, final decision, enquiry decision or discovery decision can be revised in your favour if it is incorrect because of an official error.[24] The decision can be revised at any time up to five years after the end of the tax year to which the decision relates.

'Official error' means an error relating to a tax credit made by a Revenue or DWP officer or a person providing tax credit services for them. If you, or someone acting for you, materially contributed to the error, it does not count as an official error. An error of law can count as an official error. It would not count, however, if it was only shown to be an error of law because of a later decision of a commissioner or court.

How to seek a revision

If your circumstances change, there are rules (described below) on how the Revenue should be notified. In other cases, there are no set rules to follow.

You, or your partner if you have a joint claim, must make the notification.[25] In some circumstances another person can act for you. If you have an appointee, either for tax credits or benefits, or someone legally appointed to act for you (see p1274), s/he can provide notification of the change on your behalf if you are unable to do it yourself.[26]

You should notify the Tax Credit Office. Your notification can also be accepted at any Revenue or DWP office. The notification need not be in writing; you can phone or tell the office in person.[27]

The date on which you notify the Revenue may be important – eg, for changes in circumstances that you are obliged to tell the Revenue about, or where the award can only be backdated for three months from the date of notification. The **'date of notification'** is the date on which notification is given to the Revenue.[28] If you want to change any of the details, you can do so at any time before the Revenue has made a decision.[29] Your notification will still be taken as made on the original date.[30]

Keep a copy of any letter you send to the Revenue. If you call the Tax Credit Helpline it may be advisable to keep a log of your calls: the date and time you made the call, information provided and what was agreed.

Normally you must provide notification of the change in circumstance after it has happened, but there are some changes you can notify in advance (see p1292).

What happens after you seek a revision

Before making its decision, the Revenue may ask you to provide more information or evidence if it considers it needs this to help in the decision.[31] The Revenue may also contact your employer if it needs information from her/him too.[32]

It is very important that you respond to a request for information by the date given in the letter. If you do not provide the required information, you may have to pay a penalty of up to £300 and, if you still do not comply, a further daily penalty of up to £60 a day could be imposed. See p1308 for more details of how these penalties are applied.

The Revenue must give notice of the decision to you, and to your partner if it is a joint claim. This must include details of your right to appeal.[33]

2. Appealing to a tribunal

Tax credit appeals are heard by the same appeal tribunals that deal with social security benefits and are administered by the Tribunals Service (TS).[34]

Many of the tax credit appeals rules are the same as those for social security benefits (see Chapter 42). This chapter refers you to Chapter 42 where tax credit rules are the same as benefit rules.

Note: changes to the appeals structure and to the rules for appealing are due, starting from October 2008, under the Tribunals, Courts and Enforcement Act 2007.

Who can appeal

The following people have the right of appeal:[35]

- you, the tax credit claimant. For joint claimants, both or either of you can make the appeal. If only one appeals, the tribunal decision still applies to both so long as you are both given the right to a tribunal hearing;[36]
- for appeals about penalties, the person subject to the penalty;
- an appointee, if you are unable to make the appeal yourself (see p1274). If you do not have an appointee, the person (who must be 18 or over) who is to act on your behalf in the appeal should write to the Revenue asking to be appointed;
- a receiver appointed by the Court of Protection with the power to make a tax credit claim for you;
- in Scotland, a judicial factor or guardian under the Adults With Incapacity (Scotland) Act 2000 who has the power to claim tax credits for you and is administering your estate.[37]

Decisions you can appeal

You can appeal against:[38]

- an initial decision;
- a final decision;
- a revised decision (for change in circumstances, on reasonable grounds or for official error);
- an enquiry decision;
- a discovery decision;
- a Revenue decision imposing a penalty;
- a decision charging interest on an overpayment.

If the Revenue decides you have been overpaid tax credit, it can recover all or part of it at its discretion, and you cannot appeal against the decision. You can, however, appeal against the amount of the award. In some cases the Revenue may use its discretion not to recover an overpayment, or to reduce the amount – eg, where it was caused by official error or where recovery would cause hardship (see p1298). You can complain to the Revenue if you are unhappy with the way your claim has been handled, and if your complaint is not resolved to your satisfaction you can ask the Independent Adjudicator to look into it (see p1182).

Time limit for appealing

Your appeal, including the details specified below, must be given to the Revenue within 30 days after the date given on the decision letter.[39]

You may not get a separate initial or final decision notice where the annual review notice states what the decision will be and the date on which it will be made, usually 31 July. This may apply where your award is made up of just the family element of child tax credit (CTC) and your circumstances have not changed. In this case your appeal must be made within 30 days after the date the annual review notice gives as the date on which the decision is made – eg, by 30 August if the decision date is given as 31 July.

Late appeals

You can appeal outside this 30-day time limit in limited circumstances. These circumstances are the same for tax credits as they are for benefits. You must appeal within an absolute time limit. This is one year after the date the 30-day time limit expired. See p1129 for details of late appeals, but note the following differences for tax credits:

- where the benefit rules refer to a one-month limit, that should be taken to be 30 days;
- where the benefit rules refer to a 13-month limit, that should be taken to be one year plus 30 days;
- your application for an extension to the time limit must be in writing, be signed by you (or on your behalf – eg, by an appointee) and include sufficient details to identify you (eg, your name and national insurance (NI) number), identify your appeal and your grounds for asking for an extension.[40]

There is no provision to ask for written reasons for a decision or to extend the time limit if you do. Nor is the time limit extended if you try unsuccessfully to get the decision revised by the Revenue before making an appeal.

How to appeal

You can appeal on the form inside the Revenue leaflet WTC/AP, *How to Appeal Against a Tax Credits Decision or Award*. Alternatively, you can write a letter, but you must include the following details:[41]

- sufficient information to identify you (eg, your name and NI number);

- sufficient information to identify the decision being appealed – eg, the date of the decision and whether it is CTC or working tax credit (WTC);
- the grounds of your appeal – ie, you must say why the decision is wrong. If there is more than one reason why the decision is wrong, specify each one if you can. However, the tribunal may allow you to raise new grounds later if it considers that missing them out from this appeal notice was not 'wilful or unreasonable';[42]
- your signature (or someone can sign it on your behalf – eg, an appointee).

Send your appeal to the Revenue at the address given on the decision notice.

What happens after you appeal

Settling the appeal

The Revenue will usually want to settle the appeal without going to an appeal tribunal.[43] You can point out to the Revenue where you think its decision is wrong and supply information or arguments you want it to consider. The Revenue may offer you terms on which to settle the appeal. Your appeal can only be settled with your consent. If you do not agree to the settlement, the appeal must proceed to a tribunal.

If you agree to settle the appeal, the Revenue must write to you setting out the terms of the agreement – eg, giving a new amount for your award. Your appeal then lapses unless you write to the Revenue within 30 days from the date of the written notice of agreement saying you have changed your mind and wish to proceed with your appeal.

If you are asked to settle the appeal, check first whether the proposed agreement gives you everything to which you think you are entitled. Seek advice if you are not sure whether to agree. If in doubt, you should exercise your right to continue with the appeal.

Asking for a hearing

If your appeal is not settled, the Revenue prepares the appeal papers (its 'submission'). It sends a copy to you and a copy to your representative if you have one and forwards your appeal to the TS. At the same time, it sends you an enquiry form asking whether you want an oral hearing or not. You must return the form within 14 days of the date it was issued.[44] The clerk to the tribunal can extend this time limit but otherwise if you do not return the form in time, your appeal can be struck out.

For information and issues to consider when deciding whether to opt for an oral hearing, see p1103.

You are entitled to have your appeal heard within a reasonable period of time. If the Revenue does not forward your appeal to the TS, you can complain to the Revenue (see p1182) and consider taking up the issue with your MP (see p1184). Before you do, check that the decision is one that carries a right of appeal. In particular, a decision to recover an overpayment cannot be appealed to a tribunal but is challenged using a different procedure (see p1301).

Appeal not heard by the end of the year

If your appeal has not been heard by the time you get the Revenue's final decision on entitlement after the end of the year, you should put in another appeal against the final decision.[45]

When your appeal can be struck out

Your appeal may be struck out:[46]

- 'for want of prosecution' – ie, you do not pursue the appeal; *or*
- if you do not comply with a direction and were warned that it could be struck out as a result – eg, you do not provide information requested to support your appeal; *or*
- if you do not return a pre-hearing enquiry form to tell the clerk whether or not you want an oral hearing, and were warned that the appeal could be struck out.

The decision to strike out may be made by the tribunal clerk, but the clerk could refer it to a legally qualified tribunal member to decide.

Reinstatement

If your appeal was struck out because you did not reply saying whether you wanted an oral hearing, you can write to the tribunal clerk to ask for your appeal to be reinstated. You must do so within a month of the decision to strike out the appeal, saying why you think it should not have been struck out. If the clerk is not satisfied that there are reasonable grounds to reinstate the appeal, s/he must pass your application to a legally qualified tribunal member. If the appeal was struck out for any other reason, you should still write to the clerk saying why it should not have been struck out. In either case, the tribunal member can reinstate the appeal if:

- your application was made within the month and there are reasonable grounds to reinstate; *or*
- there were not proper grounds for striking out the appeal; *or*
- although there were proper grounds for striking out the appeal, it is not in the interests of justice for it to be struck out.[47]

Withdrawing an appeal

You can ask to withdraw the appeal if you decide not to go ahead with it. You can tell the Revenue in writing or phone the Helpline. However, the Revenue can refuse to let you withdraw the appeal by writing to you within 30 days. If it has not written to you within 30 days, then the appeal is withdrawn.[48]

The hearing

The appeal tribunal holds an oral hearing if you have asked for one. Otherwise there is a paper hearing in your absence. For details of these and information on requesting a postponement or adjournment of the hearing, see p1107. The tax credit rules are the same as those for benefits except that there are no special 'test case' provisions for tax credits that can block your appeal or affect its outcome (although payment can be postponed while there is an appeal pending in another case that could affect your own award).[49]

Tribunal procedures

Chapter 42 describes tribunal procedures for benefits and looks at:
- who is present at the hearing;
- what happens at an oral hearing;
- domiciliary hearings (hearings at home);
- what the tribunal can consider;
- changes in circumstances after you appeal;
- the tribunal decision;
- after the hearing;
- if you disagree with the tribunal's decision;
- when a decision can be set aside.

See pp1109–1120 for details. The tax credit rules are the same, with the following exceptions.
- **Medical examination.** The tribunal cannot refer you to a doctor for a medical examination.[50] However, if your appeal concerns a disability question it may be important to get your own medical evidence (see p1135).
- **What the tribunal can consider.** The rules on what tribunals need and need not consider are stricter for tax credits. They must consider grounds that you specified in your written application for appeal. After that, they may allow you to raise other issues if they are satisfied that it was not 'wilful or unreasonable' of you to have missed them out from the appeal notice.[51]
- **Changes in circumstance after you appeal.** These rules apply to tax credits in the same way as they do to benefits except:
  - wherever Chapter 42 refers to 'supersession' this should read 'revision' for tax credits;
  - if you re-claim or ask for a revision because of a change in circumstance after you appeal, there is no specific provision for a decision maker to revisit her/his decision on that claim/revision once the appeal has been heard on the grounds that s/he would have made a different decision had s/he known what the tribunal's decision would be.
- **After the hearing.** If the Revenue is considering an appeal to the commissioners or has decided to appeal, you are normally not paid until the commissioner

decides the case. The Revenue has the power to 'postpone' payment in these circumstances, without any extra rules about notifying you of its intention (as there are for suspending benefits).[52]

- **If you disagree with the tribunal's decision.** A tribunal decision cannot be 'superseded' (because supersessions only apply to benefits, not to tax credits) but it can be revised in any of the ways described in this chapter except for official error (see p1316).

  If a tribunal made an error of law, you can appeal to the social security commissioners as you can in benefit appeals. For tax credits, the Revenue is not prevented from revising the tribunal's decision on 'reasonable grounds' which could also include an error of law (if it is still within the tax year of the award).
- **When a decision can be set aside.** If you appeal to the commissioners, there is no provision obliging a legally qualified tribunal member to set aside the decision where both you and the Revenue agree the tribunal made an error of law.[53]

Tribunal members

The tribunal is made up of one, two or three members depending on the type of issue under appeal.

- A lawyer, a doctor and someone with experience of disability hears your appeal if it is about:
  - the disability element or severe disability element of WTC or CTC;
  - for eligibility to WTC, whether you have a disability that puts you at a disadvantage in getting a job;
  - for the childcare element, the incapacity of a partner or disability of a child.[54]
- A lawyer and someone with financial expertise hears your appeal if it involves difficult financial issues about profit and loss accounts, revenue accounts, balance sheets, and accounts of trust funds.[55]
- A lawyer alone hears your appeal in any other case.

The lawyer acts as chair. The chair has the casting vote.[56] See p1110 for restrictions on the involvement of doctors known to you or to the tribunal members.

3. Appealing to a commissioner

You can appeal to the social security commissioners against a decision of an appeal tribunal, but only if the appeal tribunal made an error of law. In some penalty appeals, you can also appeal about the amount of the penalty (see p1328).

Chapter 42 explains what an error of law is and how to go about making your appeal (see p1121). The rules for tax credits are the same as those for benefits described in Chapter 42, except that if you disagree with a commissioner's decision it cannot be 'superseded', but it can be revised in any of the ways described above, except for revision for official error (see p1316).

4. Appealing to the courts

You can appeal to the Court of Appeal (in England and Wales) or to the Court of Session (in Scotland) against a decision of a social security commissioner, but only if there is an error of law. You have three months in which to apply (see Chapter 42).

5. How to prepare an appeal

Suggestions for how to prepare your appeal and present your case are given in Chapter 42. Information in that chapter applies equally to tax credit appeals.

6. Penalty appeals

You have the right to appeal against a decision imposing a penalty. For information on penalties, see p1308.

For most types of penalty, the Revenue has the power to make its own decision on imposing one. You can appeal against this decision to an appeal tribunal in the normal way, with any further appeal going to the commissioners under the usual rules.[57] However, to impose a penalty of up to £300 for failing to provide required information or evidence, the Revenue cannot make the decision itself but must take 'proceedings' to an appeal tribunal. You have an opportunity to attend a hearing where the tribunal decides whether to apply a penalty. Your right of appeal then lies with the social security commissioners.[58]

In these penalty appeals to the commissioners (ie, where the decision was made by an appeal tribunal under penalty proceedings), you can appeal on a question of law *or* on the amount of the penalty.[59] You can appeal to the commissioners without needing leave to do so and you have a right to an oral hearing if you want one.[60] Send your notice of appeal directly to the commissioners' office. Because of a mistake in the way the law was drafted, there is no time limit for these appeals, although the usual time limits apply to other penalty appeals. However, it is advisable to appeal without delay.

Notes

1. **Revisions**
  1 s14(1) TCA 2002
  2 s3(2) TCA 2002
  3 The Revenue intends to use the power in s14(3) TCA 2002 to award at a nil rate in these circumstances.
  4 s15(1) TCA 2002
  5 Reg 25 TC(CN) Regs; reg 16(5)(a) WTC(EMR) Regs
  6 Reg 26(3) TC(CN) Regs
  7 s16(1) TCA 2002
  8 Reg 16(5)(b) WTC(EMR) Regs
  9 s16(1) TCA 2002
  10 CTC/2662/2005; CTC/3981/2005
  11 s21 TCA 2002
  12 s18(5) TCA 2002
  13 s18(6) TCA 2002
  14 s18(9) TCA 2002
  15 s19(1) TCA 2002
  16 s19(4) TCA 2002
  17 s19(11) TCA 2002
  18 s21 TCA 2002
  19 s20(1) and (3) TCA 2002
  20 s20(6)(a) TCA 2002
  21 s20(6)(b) TCA 2002
  22 s20(4) TCA 2002
  23 s20(5) TCA 2002
  24 s21 TCA 2002; reg 3 TC(OE) Regs
  25 Reg 23 TC(CN) Regs
  26 Regs 28 and 29 TC(CN) Regs
  27 Reg 22(3) TC(CN) Regs
  28 Reg 19 TC(CN) Regs
  29 Reg 22(4) TC(CN) Regs
  30 Reg 24 TC(CN) Regs
  31 ss15(2)(b),16(3)(b) and 19(2)(b) TCA 2002
  32 Reg 30 TC(CN) Regs
  33 s23 TCA 2002

2. **Appealing to a tribunal**
  34 s63(2) TCA 2002
  35 s12 SSA 1998, as amended by reg 4 TC(A) Regs
  36 CTC/2612/2005
  37 Reg 3 TC(A)(No.2) Regs
  38 s38 TCA 2002
  39 ss23(2) and 39(1) TCA 2002
  40 Reg 6 TC(A)(No.2) Regs
  41 Reg 2 TC(NA) Regs
  42 s39(2) and (5) TCA 2002
  43 Reg 3 TC(A) Regs; s54 TMA 1970
  44 Reg 12(3) TC(A)(No.2) Regs
  45 CTC/2662/2005; CTC/3981/2005
  46 Reg 16 TC(A)(No.2) Regs
  47 Reg 17 TC(A)(No.2) Regs
  48 s54 TMA 1970
  49 Reg 11 TC(PC) Regs
  50 The power to refer to a doctor in s20 SSA 1998 does not apply to tax credits.
  51 s39(5) TCA 2002
  52 Reg 11 TC(PC) Regs
  53 Reg 5(2) TC(A) Regs
  54 Reg 9(2) TC(A)(No.2) Regs
  55 Reg 9(3) TC(A)(No.2) Regs
  56 s7 SSA 1998; s63(10) TCA 2002

6. **Penalty appeals**
  57 s38 TCA 2002
  58 s63 and Sch 2 para 4(1) TCA 2002
  59 Sch 2 para 4(1) TCA 2002
  60 Reg 18 SSCP(TCA) Regs

Part 7

Immigration and residence rules for benefits and tax credits

Chapter 58

Coming from and going abroad: benefits

This chapter contains the rules on claiming benefits when you either come from or go abroad. It covers:

This chapter deals with the rules on social security benefits, with only some brief references to tax credits. For full details of the immigration rules that apply to tax credits, see Chapter 60.

1. Immigration status

It is important to know your immigration status before making a claim for benefit. This is because your immigration status determines your right to social security benefits and a claim for benefit can sometimes affect your right to remain in the UK. If you are unsure about your immigration status you should seek specialist advice.

Most people, apart from British citizens, are subject to immigration control. This means that you cannot freely enter the UK, but are subject to scrutiny by the immigration authorities. The degree of control varies according to your nationality – eg, European Community law means European Economic Area (EEA) nationals (see Chapter 61) do not need leave to enter or remain in the UK. If you are subject to immigration control you require leave, or permission, to enter or remain. Such leave can be:

- limited leave to enter or remain;

- indefinite leave to enter or remain;
- exceptional leave to enter or remain.

If you have limited leave you are only permitted to remain in the UK for a limited period of time. Certain conditions are frequently attached to limited leave. For example, a restriction may be made on you working or claiming benefits. If you breach these conditions you may put your right to remain in the UK at risk.

The interrelationship between immigration and social security law is extremely complex and your immigration status may not always be clear. There are close links between the benefit authorities and the Border and Immigration Agency. Making a claim for benefit could alert the immigration authorities to the fact that you are here unlawfully, or that you have broken your conditions of entry by claiming 'public funds'. It is vitally important, therefore, to get specialist advice before claiming if you are unsure about your position. You can get advice from your local law centre, Citizens Advice Bureau or other advice agency that deals with immigration problems.

Immigration status and benefit entitlement

Benefits affected by immigration status[1]

Attendance allowance
Carer's allowance
Child benefit
Council tax benefit
Disability living allowance
Housing benefit
Incapacity benefit for incapacity in youth[2]
Income-based jobseeker's allowance
Income support
Pension credit
Severe disablement allowance
Social fund payments

Entitlement to social security benefits is increasingly linked to your immigration status and nationality. The law defines certain people as a 'person subject to immigration control'. This phrase has a special meaning for benefit purposes. If you fall within the definition you can be excluded from entitlement to the above benefits unless you fall within certain exempt categories. For details about who is exempt, see p1340 for non-contributory benefits and p1339 for means-tested benefits.

You are defined as a '**person subject to immigration control**' if you are not an EEA national and:

- you require leave to enter or remain but do not have it;

- you have leave to enter or remain with a public funds restriction (see below);
- you have leave to enter or remain and are the subject of a formal undertaking (see p1341).

Some people who come within the general definition of a 'person subject to immigration control' may nevertheless be eligible for some benefits because regulations exempt them from the definition of a 'person subject to immigration control'. The exemptions vary according to the benefit involved. For details about who may be eligible for benefit, see p1340 for non-contributory non-means-tested benefits, p1340 for means-tested benefits and p1344 for urgent cases payments of income support (IS) and income-based jobseeker's allowance (JSA). There are also some transitional regulations that provide entitlement to some claimants. For details about tax credits see Chapter 60.

Note: even though an EEA and Swiss national and her/his family members are not defined as a 'person subject to immigration control', s/he can still be excluded from entitlement to some benefits under the habitual residence and the right to reside tests. See Chapter 59 for more details.

Public funds

Most people admitted to the UK with limited leave, such as spouses/civil partners or visitors, are given limited leave to stay on condition they do not have recourse to 'public funds'. If you have recourse to public funds in breach of your permission to stay (your 'leave conditions') you could be liable to be deported, have further leave refused and be prosecuted. You should therefore always seek advice before claiming. This is particularly important if your spouse or civil partner is applying for leave to remain, as leave could be refused.

'Public funds' is defined in the immigration rules as:[3]

- attendance allowance (AA);
- carer's allowance (previously invalid care allowance);
- child benefit;
- child tax credit (CTC);
- council tax benefit (CTB);
- disability living allowance (DLA);
- housing benefit (HB);
- IS;
- income-based JSA;
- pension credit (PC);
- social fund payments;
- working tax credit (WTC).

Only the benefits that appear on the list are public funds.

Some people coming from abroad with limited leave and subject to a public funds prohibition are nevertheless allowed to claim benefits and tax credits if they meet certain conditions. The immigration rules have been amended so that a person entitled to claim benefits or tax credits under social security or tax credit law is treated as not having recourse to public funds under the Home Office immigration rules despite her/his immigration status.[4] This applies to couples, where one person is a 'person subject to immigration control', but the other is not (see below).

Couples with different immigration statuses

If you are a British citizen or have settled status and you have a partner who is a 'person subject to immigration control', you may claim benefits for yourself but you should not claim any additional benefit for your partner. The rules for tax credits are different (see p1378).

Some benefits provide for this situation. For IS and income-based JSA if you have a partner who is a 'person subject to immigration control' you are paid benefit at the single person rate rather than the couple rate. You are, however, still treated as a couple when income or capital is assessed. Therefore, no additional benefit is paid for your partner. Other benefits, such as DLA and AA, can also be claimed because no extra benefit is paid for a partner.

The position with PC is slightly different. For PC, a partner who is a 'person subject to immigration control' does not count as a part of your household. Therefore, you get no PC for her/him and her/his income and capital do not affect your benefit.[5]

For HB and CTB, the position is more complicated. No additional benefit is payable for your partner if you receive IS, income-based JSA or the guarantee credit of PC because you are already receiving maximum HB or CTB. If you do not receive these benefits, HB/CTB includes allowances for all members of your family and, therefore, could result in an additional amount of benefit being paid for the 'person subject to immigration control'.[6]

Once your spouse or civil partner is here and has been given limited leave (for the trial two-year period), s/he should receive a letter from the Border and Immigration Agency explaining that the British, or settled, spouse/civil partner can claim any benefit to which s/he is entitled in her/his own right.

You should also always seek advice before claiming a 'public funds' benefit. This is particularly important if your spouse or civil partner is applying for leave to remain, as leave could be refused if you are unable to maintain yourselves without recourse to 'public funds'. It would be wise to avoid claiming a 'public funds' benefit at a time when seeking to extend or vary leave because receipt of benefit indicates that you are unable to maintain your partner.

Limited leave and public funds

'Limited leave' means that you only have permission to enter, or remain in, the UK for a specified period of time, but see p1342 if you have been given exceptional leave to enter or remain for a specific period.

Having recourse to 'public funds' in breach of your leave conditions could make you liable to be deported, refused further leave and prosecuted. See p1335 for further information. Claiming urgent cases payments of IS or JSA, however, is safe (see p1344).

European Economic Area nationals

Nationals of EEA states (see p1383) do not require leave to enter or remain in the UK and are not 'persons subject to immigration control'.[7] This also includes Swiss nationals and family members of EEA nationals, whatever their nationality.[8] In practice, a non-EEA family member will need to obtain an EEA family permit in order to enter the UK. Family permits are usually given for 12 months, but do not count as periods of limited leave. This is simply an administrative process. There is no limit on the period of the person's stay and no conditions can be placed on her/his entry.[9] Once the family member is in the UK, s/he can apply for a residence card.

EEA nationals and their family members are generally not subject to the public funds requirement, but certain family members of self-sufficient EEA nationals are.

However, the right of EEA nationals to claim certain benefits may be affected by the 'habitual residence' and the 'right to reside' tests (see Chapter 59). For further information on the rights of EEA nationals, see p1386.

2. National insurance numbers and contributions

In order to claim most social security benefits you must satisfy the national insurance (NI) number requirement. [10] You satisfy this requirement if you:

- provide an NI number for yourself and any person that you are claiming for (apart from a child) and evidence to show that the number is yours; *or*
- provide evidence or information to enable your NI number to be traced; *or*
- apply for an NI number and provide sufficient information or evidence for one to be allocated.

Note: you do not have to satisfy the right to reside test (see p1361) when applying for an NI number. This test only applies at the point of claiming benefit.

If you do not satisfy the NI number requirement you are not eligible for benefit. This requirement applies to both the claimant and any person for whom you are claiming benefit, except any child or young person.

An application for an NI number can be made at a local social security office on Form CA5400 and must be accompanied by sufficient documentary evidence of identity. This might include, for example, a birth or marriage certificate, a passport or an identity card. It could also include a letter from your solicitor or adviser, or a statement from someone who knows you. A person without sufficient documentation should be interviewed to establish whether an NI number should be issued. This can take several weeks.

From December 2006, some people from abroad are required to provide specific documents in order to obtain an NI number. The specified documents include passports or other Home Office/Border and Immigration Agency documents, and birth and marriage certificates.[11]

Where couples have different immigration statuses, the member of the couple who is not a 'person subject to immigration control' may be refused benefit because her/his partner does not have an NI number. This is the case even where the couple are not entitled to benefit for the person who is a 'person subject to immigration control'. However, even in this situation your partner must also satisfy the NI number requirement.[12]

Tactics for obtaining a national insurance number

- Provide the benefit authority with as much documentary evidence of your identity as you can. This could include passports, identity cards, birth or marriage certificates or Home Office documents. If you do not have any of these formal types of documents, think about what else you can provide that will help prove your identity – eg, a letter from your solicitor or a statement from a teacher, doctor or advice worker.
- If you are having difficulty obtaining your documents or confimation of your identity from the Home Office, consider making a request under the Data Protection Act. If you do this, the Home Office must comply within a fixed period of time. There is, however, a small charge.
- If the benefit authority refuses to accept the evidence you have provided, ask for written reasons for the refusal and information about what evidence would be acceptable – this may lead to a reconsideration of the decision and can be useful for later complaints or legal action.
- If you have provided sufficient evidence of your identity but the benefit authority refuses to allocate an NI number or refuses to interview you for one, you should take legal advice about the possibility of seeking a judicial review.
- Consider making a complaint (see p1180) and pursue this through to the Ombudsman if necessary. However, this can take many months, so you should not delay in taking any legal action against the authority.
- You can appeal against a refusal of an NI number including if you are refused benefit because you do not have an NI number.[13] However, you may have to wait several months for an appeal hearing. It may, therefore, be wise also to consider a judicial review of the refusal of the NI number.
- If you are a member of a couple and have been refused benefit because your partner is unable to obtain an NI number, there may be scope for arguing that

this is a breach of Article 8 of the Human Rights Act (right to respect for family life) because arguably the only way in which the person who is not a 'person subject to immigration control' can qualify for benefit is if s/he separates from her/his partner.

- It may be possible to get an interim payment of benefit (see p986).
- Consider making a complaint to the Commission for Human Rights and Equality on the basis that the current application of the NI number requirement discriminates against Black and minority ethnic claimants. If it receives sufficient complaints it may decide to investigate.
- Complain to your MP.
- In all the cases CPAG is aware of, when threatened with judicial review, the DWP has eventually allocated an NI number.

National insurance contributions

If you have recently arrived in the UK you may not have paid sufficient NI contributions to qualify for certain benefits. However, if you are a European Economic Area (EEA) national or a family member of an EEA national and have worked in another EEA state, you can rely on any contributions you have paid in those countries to qualify for UK benefits (see Chapter 61).[14] This applies to *all* EEA nationals, including A8 and A2 nationals (see p1401) even if they have been paid in a country prior to it joining the European Union. Contributions can also be taken into account if they have been paid in a country with which the UK has a reciprocal agreement.[15]

If you have returned from abroad you could ask the DWP for a copy of your contributions record. In some cases it is possible to make up a shortfall in your record by making voluntary contributions.

There are residence and presence conditions attached to NI contributions and you can remain liable for payment in some cases even if you go abroad to work (see p720).

3. Non-means-tested benefits

Contributory benefits

Your immigration status does not, by itself, prevent you from getting contributory benefits, but in practice you may have paid insufficient contributions (see p720) to be entitled. Moreover, to qualify for contributory benefits (see p722), you will normally have had to have worked in the UK. However, if you are a European Economic Area (EEA) national (including an A8 or an A2 national – see p1383) or a Swiss national, contributions paid in other member states can be used to help you qualify for contributory benefits in the UK. Contributions made in another EEA state before that state joined the European Union count towards your contribution record.

Non-contributory benefits

You should be aware of your immigration status before claiming non-contributory benefits – ie, attendance allowance (AA), child benefit, disability living allowance (DLA) and carer's allowance (CA). These are 'public funds' (see p1335) and a claim could have serious consequences for your immigration status. Incapacity benefit (IB) for incapacity in youth is not listed as a 'public funds' benefit but some people subject to immigration control are excluded from claiming it.

Certain in-work benefits are not affected by your immigration status, but may be difficult to access because you need to work in order to qualify. These are industrial injuries benefits, maternity allowance, statutory maternity pay, statutory adoption pay, statutory paternity pay and statutory sick pay.

You are *not* excluded from getting **AA, child benefit**, **DLA**, **CA** and **non-contributory IB** by your immigration status if:[16]

- you are a person with indefinite leave to remain and you are subject to a formal undertaking (see p1342);
- you are a family member of an EEA national regardless of your nationality or whether or not your partner is a 'worker' (see p1394);
- you are a family member of a Swiss national;[17]
- you or (if you are living with her/him) a member of your family are lawfully working (see p1403) in Great Britain and are a citizen of a state with which the European Community has an agreement concerning equal treatment in social security. This applies to citizens of Algeria, Morocco, San Marino, Tunisia and Turkey (see p1402) and could apply to asylum seekers from these countries;
- in the case of AA, DLA and child benefit you are covered by a reciprocal arrangement;
- you are a person who is protected by the1996 transitional rules for asylum seekers and others with limited leave.

4. Means-tested benefits

You should be aware of your immigration status before claiming means-tested benefits. Most of the benefits in this section, apart from pension credit (PC), are listed in the immigration rules as 'public funds' (see p1335). Claiming additional public funds could affect your right to stay in the UK.

You are *not* excluded from getting **income support (IS)**, **income-based jobseeker's allowance (JSA)**, **housing benefit (HB)**, **council tax benefit (CTB)**, **social fund payments** and **PC** by your immigration status if:[18]

- you are a person with indefinite leave and are the subject of a formal undertaking that was given five or more years ago and you have been in the UK for five years or more (see p1342);

- you are the subject of a formal undertaking given within the past five years but the person who gave the undertaking has died;
- you have limited leave and there is a 'public funds' restriction attached to your stay and your funds from abroad are temporarily disrupted (see p1335);
- you are an asylum seeker who has transitional protection. In some cases this can include the separated partner or grown-up children of the asylum seeker;
- for PC, you are an asylum seeker who, prior to reaching pension age, was entitled to IS. (**Note:** if you are in this position and you have dependent children, there is no provision for any additional sum for your children. Instead, PC claimants who are protected asylum seekers are entitled to child tax credit for children for whom they are responsible);
- you are a national of a country that has ratified the European Convention on Social and Medical Assistance or the Council of Europe Social Charter (1961) (Croatia, Macedonia or Turkey) and you are lawfully present in the UK (see below);
- for the social fund, you are lawfully working in Great Britain and are a national of Algeria, Morocco, Tunisia, San Marino or Turkey.

European Economic Area (EEA)/European Union (EU) and Swiss nationals are not excluded by their immigration status from claiming these benefits, but they may be excluded if:

- they do not have a right to reside (see p1361); *or*
- they have a right to reside, but do not satisfy the habitual residence test (see p1367).

If you qualify for benefit, it is usually paid at the normal rate. However, if you qualify for IS or income-based JSA on the basis that funds from abroad are disrupted, your sponsor has died or because you are an asylum seeker with transitional protection, you receive benefit at the urgent cases rate (see p1344). If you qualify for PC it will be paid at the normal rate.

Sponsorship and undertakings

Many people who enter the UK are admitted on the condition that they can maintain and accommodate themselves without recourse to public funds. A relative or friend in the UK can act as a sponsor to help satisfy this condition.

In some cases, sponsors are required to give a written undertaking under the terms of the Immigration Act 1971 (on a special form – RON 112 or SET (F)) that they will provide maintenance and accommodation. Such undertakings are only usually required for dependent elderly relatives and *not* for spouses or civil partners. They may be required for children over 16. Other sorts of voluntary or informal sponsorships that are commonly used to support applications to enter the UK are *not* undertakings (this distinction is often misunderstood by the DWP).

'**Formal undertakings**' affect entitlement to means-tested benefits. If you have been resident in the UK and were admitted subject to a mandatory sponsorship undertaking, you are not entitled to benefit for the first five years unless your sponsor dies within that period. In the case of IS or income-based JSA the amount payable is the urgent cases rate of benefit. PC is paid at the normal rate. After five years you qualify for all means-tested benefits in the ordinary way and, in the case of IS and income-based JSA, it is paid at the ordinary rate. The five-year period does not have to be one continuous period. If you go abroad for a temporary period you may be able to add together periods towards the five-year limit.[19]

A commissioner has held that a formal undertaking ceases to have effect if the sponsored immigrant becomes a British citizen.[20]

Formal undertakings do not affect non-means-tested benefits.

Different rules apply to EEA nationals. If you are a family member of an EEA national, but you are not an EEA national, and you are subject to an undertaking you can override the restriction to benefit if your partner has worker status or is covered by EC Regulation 1408/71 (see p1400). See Chapter 61 for more details.

'Leave outside the rules'

In some circumstances, you may not fit within the immigration rules, but the Home Office grants you leave to remain in the UK outside the rules. This could be by granting 'exceptional leave' to enter or remain or, for asylum seekers, humanitarian protection or discretionary leave. Leave outside the rules is granted on humanitarian grounds and could be because of poor health or needing to care for a relative. The DWP sometimes wrongly refuses benefit to people with exceptional leave because it mistakenly thinks they have limited leave (see p1333). **Exceptional leave** may initially be given for a limited period but this does not count as 'limited leave'. A person applying for an extension of her/his exceptional leave continues to be treated as a person with exceptional leave, provided her/his application was made before their original leave had expired.[21]

Some asylum seekers who are refused refugee status are nonetheless allowed to remain in the UK by the Home Office because it accepts that conditions in their country of origin and/or an individual's circumstances warrant being granted leave to remain. In the past, asylum seekers were granted exceptional leave, usually for four years, after which an application for indefinite leave could be made. However, on 1 April 2003 the Home Office introduced two new types of leave to replace exceptional leave for asylum seekers. Exceptional leave will continue for non-asylum cases.

Humanitarian protection is granted for three years or less. It is awarded to people who have been refused refugee status but who the Home Office believes cannot be returned to their country of origin as they face a serious risk to life or person because of the death penalty, unlawful killing, torture, inhumane or degrading treatment or punishment. After three years the case will be reviewed and if there is still a risk to the person s/he can be granted indefinite leave.

Discretionary leave is also awarded to people who are refused refugee status, but who do not fulfil the criteria for humanitarian protection. The Home Office intends to award it in very limited circumstances. It will be granted for three years and then reviewed. At this point a further three years may be granted and after six years of discretionary leave the person can apply for indefinite leave.

For benefit purposes a person with exceptional leave, humanitarian protection or discretionary leave is not excluded from entitlement to any benefits or tax credits.

If you are granted exceptional leave to enter or remain in the UK, humanitarian protection or discretionary leave, you are entitled to claim IS, income-based JSA or PC under the normal rules. You do not have to satisfy the 'habitual residence' (see p1367) or the 'right to reside' test (see p1361).[22] There is normally no prohibition on claiming 'public funds' (see p1335) if you are granted exceptional leave to remain.

Couples and families

The following rules apply if one or more members of your family (see Chapter 30) are 'persons subject to immigration control'.

- If you are a 'person subject to immigration control', you are not entitled to IS, JSA, HB, CTB or PC for yourself or for any members of your family, unless you qualify under one of the exemptions on p1334.[23]
- Foreign fiancé(e)s and spouses who are admitted for settlement on the condition that they can maintain and accommodate themselves, count as 'persons subject to immigration control' and are not entitled to IS/JSA and PC until they are granted indefinite leave to remain in the UK. They must apply for indefinite leave before their limited leave expires.
- If you are not a 'person subject to immigration control' but your partner is, you can claim IS/JSA under the normal rules but you do not receive any benefit for your partner.[24] You are still treated as a couple (see p702), so your joint resources are taken into account. For HB and CTB you receive benefit at the couple rate, but there may be public funds implications.
- For PC the rules are similar to IS/income-based JSA in that couples with different immigration status can receive benefit paid at the single person rate. However, there is one important difference – for PC, a 'person subject to immigration control' is not treated as being a member of the household.[25] Therefore, any income or work undertaken will not affect the benefit entitlement of the person who is not subject to immigration control.
- A claimant who is a 'person subject to immigration control' cannot claim benefit for children, even if the children are not 'subject to immigration control'.

- If one member of a couple is a 'person subject to immigration control' but the other is not, the person who is not a 'person subject to immigration control' can claim child benefit for a child.
- If a child is a 'person subject to immigration control' but her/his parent(s) are not, the parent can claim IS/income based-JSA for her/him. The child's immigration status does not affect the parent's entitlement to benefit; it is the parent's immigration status that is important.
- A person can qualify for JSA without having to satisfy the joint claims rules (see p381) if her/his partner is a 'person subject to immigration control'.

5. Urgent cases payments

Urgent cases payments are payments of income support (IS) and income-based jobseeker's allowance (JSA) at a reduced rate. There is no equivalent of urgent cases payments for pension credit (PC). A 'person subject to immigration control' who qualifies for PC receives it at the full rate.

If you are not entitled to normal rate IS or income-based JSA because you are a 'person subject to immigration control' (see p1334), you may be entitled to urgent cases payments if:

- you have limited leave to remain in the UK on the condition that you do not have recourse to 'public funds' (see p1335), but you are temporarily without money;[26] *and*
  - you have supported yourself without recourse to public funds during your limited leave; *and*
  - you are temporarily without funds because remittances from abroad have been disrupted; *and*
  - there is a reasonable expectation that your supply of funds will be resumed

  or
- you have been in the UK subject to a sponsorship undertaking for less than five years and your sponsor has died (see p1341); *or*
- you are an asylum seeker entitled to benefit under transitional protection rules

How to claim

There is no special procedure for claiming urgent cases payments. You claim IS or income-based JSA in the normal way (see p378). You do not have to make a separate claim for an urgent cases payment. In practice, you may need to request the urgent cases payment and should not rely on the DWP to decide automatically whether you are entitled.

Amount of the payment

Urgent cases payments of IS and income-based JSA are paid at a reduced rate. Your 'applicable amount' (see p770) is:

- a personal allowance for you and possibly your partner.[27] It is paid at 90 per cent of the personal allowance that would have been paid had you qualified for benefit in the normal way; *plus*
- full personal allowances for your children if your claim continues to include these (see p773); *plus*
- premiums (see p775) and housing costs (see Chapter 34) or residential allowance (see p775).

Income

All of your income counts, except for the following, which is ignored:[28]

- any tariff income from capital (see p866). However, as all capital is taken into account this concession is of very little assistance;
- any arrears of urgent cases payments of IS or income-based JSA;
- concessionary urgent cases payments of IS or income-based JSA;
- any housing benefit (HB) and/or council tax benefit;
- any payment made to compensate you for the loss of entitlement to HB;
- social fund payments;
- any payment from any of the Macfarlane Trusts, the Eileen Trust, the Fund, or the Independent Living Funds;
- payments made by people with haemophilia to their partners or children out of money originally provided by one of the Macfarlane Trusts. If the person with haemophilia has no partner or children, payments made to a parent, step-parent or guardian are also disregarded, but only for two years. These payments are also disregarded if the person with haemophilia dies and the money is paid out of the estate;
- payments arising from the Macfarlane Trusts which are paid by a person to a partner who has haemophilia, or to their child(ren).

Capital

Your capital is calculated in the usual way (see Chapter 37) but the usual disregards do not apply to urgent cases payments. Any capital taken into account affects your urgent cases payment, not just that over the capital limit (see p916). However, arrears of urgent cases payments are disregarded.

6. Asylum seekers and refugees

Asylum seekers

The system of support for asylum seekers was the subject of radical reform on 3 April 2000. Prior to this date the type of assistance available depended on where an application for asylum was made. Those claiming asylum at the port of entry or 'on arrival' continued to qualify for the main means-tested benefits, whereas those claiming asylum 'in-country' could receive assistance from the local authority under the National Assistance Act if they were destitute. Since April 2000 most asylum seekers have been excluded from entitlement to benefits and must instead claim asylum support.

Some asylum seekers, however, may still be entitled to benefits because of transitional protection (see below), or they may qualify because they fall within one of the exemptions for a particular benefit, or because they are a family member of a person who is entitled to benefit.

You are treated as an **'asylum seeker'** while you are waiting for a Home Office decision on an application for refugee status (see p1347). If you apply for asylum when you arrive in the UK, you normally are given 'temporary admission' while your case is considered (although you can be detained or removed in certain circumstances). You may also have applied for asylum while you were in the UK with limited leave or as an illegal entrant or overstayer.

If your application for asylum is refused you have the right of appeal. It can take a long time before your application is finally decided, although the Government has now introduced quicker procedures and curtailed appeal rights for many asylum seekers.

An asylum seeker will usually be issued with an application registration card (ARC). This is the current identity document confirming that the person has claimed asylum. However, many asylum seekers have a standard acknowledgement letter (SAL), the previously used identity document. Some asylum seekers who are granted temporary admission are issued with an IS96 rather than an ARC.

Claiming income support (IS), jobseeker's allowance (JSA) or other 'public funds' benefits (see p1335) will not affect your application for asylum because asylum seekers are not subject to the condition not to claim 'public funds'. However, in most cases, you are excluded from entitlement by the benefit rules. See p1347 if you have been recognised as a refugee.

Transitional protection

There are two types of transitional protection for asylum seekers and other people from abroad who were entitled to benefit:

- the first applies to those who are protected because they were entitled to benefit on 4 February 1996, or 6 October 1996 for child benefit ('the 1996 rules');
- the second applies to those who are protected because they applied for asylum on or before 2 April 2000 ('the 2000 rules').

For full details of the transitional rules, see the 2005/06 edition of this *Handbook*.

Other help available

If you are no longer entitled to benefit you may be eligible for asylum support either from the Border and Immigration Agency or your local authority. You will only qualify for support if you are destitute. If you are not eligible for asylum support or benefits you should ask your local authority for help. If you have children, support can be provided by social services departments under the Children Act 1989. If you are sick or disabled you can ask for help under the National Assistance Act 1948.

The Nationality Immigration and Asylum Act 2002 excludes from entitlement to some social services support:[29]

- European Economic Area (EEA) nationals who are not 'workers';
- people who have been granted refugee status in another EEA state, but who are not EEA nationals;
- people who have been refused asylum and who have failed to comply with removal directions or have exhausted all appeal rights.

However, the Act makes clear that a local authority is *not* prevented from supporting one of the above groups where there would otherwise be a breach of European Community (EC) law or where a refusal of support would lead to a breach of any rights under the European Convention on Human Rights. Therefore, a refusal of support, particularly where children are involved, may well be challengable. Equally, the provisions regarding EEA nationals indirectly discriminate against non-British EEA nationals and consequently may be in breach of EC law. In such circumstances you should seek legal advice.

In some circumstances a couple who are both asylum seekers will be in the situation where one of the couple is receiving urgent cases payments (see p1344) and the other is receiving asylum support. They may, however, qualify for urgent cases payments paid at the couple rate (see p1344). Asylum support is taken into account as income in respect of any housing benefit (HB) and council tax benefit (CTB), your partner receives, but it is not taken into account for IS or income-based JSA. However, any IS or income-based JSA that you receive is taken into account as income for asylum support purposes.

Refugees

The UK is a signatory to the 1951 United Nations Convention on the Status of Refugees which gives refugees certain rights in a foreign country, including the right to public relief and assistance. A refugee is defined under the Convention as someone who is unable or unwilling to return to her/his own country because of a '... well-founded fear of persecution for reasons of race, religion, nationality, membership of a particular social group or political opinion ...'

If the Home Office accepts you are a refugee, you and your family are entitled to remain in the UK and claim IS or income-based JSA and any other benefits under the normal rules and at the full rate (see Chapters 13 and 15) from the date you are recorded as a refugee by the Secretary of State.[30] You do not have to satisfy the 'habitual residence' (see p1367) or 'right to reside' tests (see p1361).

Backdating benefit

Before June 2007, people granted refugee status could make a backdated claim for IS, HB, CTB, child benefit and child tax credit (CTC) to the date of their asylum application. This has now been abolished for IS, HB and CTB[31] and replaced with a system of discretionary loans.[32] Child benefit and CTC can still be backdated. Information on these can be found at the Home Office, Border and Immigration Agency website at www.ind.homeoffice.gov.uk/lawandpolicy/refugeeintegration/integrationloan.

The new rules, however, do not apply to anyone accepted as a refugee on or before 14 June 2007.

7. Benefits when you go abroad

Many benefits have residence and presence conditions that mean that if you go abroad the particular benefit is no longer payable. Some benefits have no residence and presence conditions, and may always be payable abroad – eg, some retirement pensions. Despite being subject to residence and presence conditions, it may be possible to receive some benefits during temporary absences. Other benefits can be paid once you return from a temporary absence abroad. The rules in this section relate to UK law only. If you are a European Economic Area (EEA) national and you are travelling to another EEA state different rules apply see p1357.

Whether an absence is temporary is a question which depends on the circumstances of each individual case. An absence does not cease to be temporary because no date is fixed for your return, but the absence must be for a limited period only.[33] If you spend longer abroad than the permitted periods you may no longer satisfy the residence condition for your benefit. The residence conditions for benefits are described on pp1358–1361. For the meaning of presence, residence, and ordinarily resident, see pp1357–1358.

Payment of benefit while you are abroad

It is not usually possible to have your British benefits paid to you while you are abroad, unless you can rely on either a reciprocal agreement (see p1354) or European Community (EC) law (see p1382). However, there are some circumstances in which UK rules do allow for payment while you are abroad. This is only possible in the circumstances listed below.

If a particular benefit is payable abroad (outside the EEA), the rate is usually fixed at the level of benefit received at the time you went abroad. Benefits are usually uprated if you move to another EEA state.

Attendance allowance, disability living allowance and carer's allowance

As long as you remain 'ordinarily resident' (see p1358) in GB, a temporary absence does not affect your entitlement to disability living allowance (DLA), attendance allowance or carer's allowance and you can continue to receive benefit for up to 26 weeks. However, on your return you may experience difficulties re-qualifying for benefit if your absence has been for more than 26 weeks. This is because you must have been present in GB for 26 of the last 52 weeks in order to satisfy the residence conditions (see p1358). In some circumstances you can be treated as being present in GB even though you are abroad (see p1357).

Bereavement benefits, retirement pensions and guardian's allowance

These are payable while you are abroad, but your benefit is not normally uprated each year once you have ceased to be 'ordinarily resident' (see p1358) in GB unless you can rely on reciprocal agreements of EC law.[34] You cannot 'de-retire' (see p468) while abroad.[35]

In the case of bereavement payment (see p20) there are two further conditions:[36]

- you or your spouse or civil partner must have been in GB when your spouse or civil partner died; *or*
- the contribution conditions for widowed parent's allowance, widow's pension or bereavement allowance are satisfied (see p19).

Child benefit

If you are claiming child benefit (see Chapter 4), your benefit could be affected if you spend more than eight weeks abroad or the child spends more than 12 weeks abroad (see p1359).

Disablement benefit, reduced earnings allowance and retirement allowance

Disablement benefit (except constant attendance allowance and exceptionally severe disablement allowance) and retirement allowance are unaffected while you are abroad[37] (see also p1350 for information on severe disablement allowance (SDA) abroad).

Constant attendance allowance and exceptionally severe disablement allowance are payable during a temporary absence for up to six months, or such longer period as the Secretary of State may allow.[38]

Reduced earnings allowance (REA) is payable during a temporary absence if:[39]

- you have been away for less than three months, or a longer period if agreed by the Pension Service; *and*
- your absence is not for work purposes; *and*
- you claim before you leave; *and*

- you are entitled to the benefit before you leave.

REA has now been abolished and if you break your claim you will no longer be eligible for benefit.

Housing benefit and council tax benefit[40]

While you are temporarily out of the country you may be entitled to housing benefit to cover your rent, and council tax benefit towards your council tax (see pp185 and 83). If your income support (IS) stops, you must notify the local authority. You can be treated as temporarily absent for up to 13 (and in some cases 52) weeks. For further details of the rules on temporary absence, see p185.

If your partner goes abroad temporarily you will continue to be treated as a couple unless:

- you do not intend to resume living together; *or*
- your absence from one another is likely to exceed 52 weeks.

Incapacity benefit and severe disablement allowance

Incapacity benefit (IB – see Chapter 12) and SDA (see Chapter 20) are payable during the first 26 weeks of any temporary absence if the Secretary of State has agreed and:[41]

- your absence from GB is for the specific purpose of being treated for an illness or industrial injury (see p314) which began before you left this country; *or*
- when you left this country you had been continuously incapable of work (see p661) for six months and you have been continuously incapable since your departure.

If you are due to have a medical examination this can be arranged abroad.

Note: SDA was abolished for new claimants in April 2001. A person who is getting SDA and who goes abroad for more than 26 weeks will not re-qualify on her/his return to GB. You may qualify for IB for incapacity in youth (see p271) but you will have to re-satisfy the residence test.

Income support

Once you have established your right to IS in GB, it is possible to claim during temporary absences abroad. You can get IS **indefinitely** if:[42]

- you were entitled to IS immediately before going abroad; *and*
- your absence is temporary and for the purpose of receiving NHS treatment at a hospital or other institution outside GB.

You can get IS for up to **four weeks** if:

- you were entitled to IS immediately before going abroad;
- your absence is temporary;
- the temporary absence is unlikely to exceed 52 weeks;

- you continue to satisfy the other rules for getting IS described in Chapter 13 while you are away;

and:[43]

- you are going to Northern Ireland; *or*
- you and your partner are both abroad and your partner qualifies for a pensioner, enhanced pensioner, higher pensioner, disability or severe disability premium (see p784); *or*
- you are incapable of work (see p661); *and*
  - you have been continuously incapable for the previous 28 weeks and you are terminally ill or receiving the highest rate of disability living allowance care component; *or*
  - you have been continuously incapable for 364 days.

  Two or more periods when you are incapable of work are joined together to form a single period if they are separated by less than eight weeks; *or*
- you are incapable of work (see p661) and are going abroad specifically for treatment of the incapacity from an appropriately qualified person. Before you go you should check that the DWP accepts that this rule applies to you; *or*
- you fit into one of the groups of people who can claim IS (see p292). However, you must *not* be:
  - in 'relevant education' (see p576);
  - involved in a trade dispute, or in the first 15 days after you have returned to work following the dispute (see p633);
  - a 'person subject to immigration control' and receiving an urgent cases payment of IS (see p1344);
  - incapable of work other than situations as above or appealing a decision of the DWP not to treat you as incapable of work (see p681).

You can get IS for up to **eight weeks** if:

- you were entitled to IS immediately before going abroad;
- your absence is temporary and unlikely to exceed 52 weeks;
- you continue to satisfy the other rules for getting IS described in Chapter 13 while you are away;
- you are taking a child abroad specifically for medical, physiotherapy or similar treatment from an appropriately qualified person. The child must count as part of your family (see p709).

Your partner is abroad

If your partner is abroad temporarily you may still be treated as a couple for IS purposes (see p707).[44] This can apply even if you have not lived together in the UK because the rules concern absence from each other, not absence from home. You will not be treated as a couple if:

- you do not intend to resume living together; *or*
- your absence from one another is likely to be for 52 weeks or more.

If your partner is waiting for entry clearance to come to the UK, you can argue that because this is a lengthy process and refusal rates are high, your separation is likely to exceed 52 weeks and you should not be treated as a couple (see p707).[45] Alternatively, you can argue that you should not be treated as a couple because your intention to live together depends on entry clearance being granted.[46]

Payment of income support while abroad

If you qualify for IS under the four- or eight-week rule, your benefit is normally paid to you on your return, but if you are a member of a couple and you are the claimant, you can ask for it to be paid to your partner during your absence. If you are not entitled to IS while abroad or you have already used up your four- or eight-week entitlement, your partner has to make a claim in her/his own right (see p301).

If your partner goes abroad, your benefit is reduced after four weeks (eight weeks if your partner is taking a child abroad for medical treatment). You are then paid as if you were a single claimant or lone parent, but your partner's income and capital are still taken into account.[47]

Jobseeker's allowance[48]

You cannot normally get jobseeker's allowance (JSA) if you are not in GB. However, JSA can be paid when you are temporarily absent absent from GB:[49]

- **indefinitely** if you are entitled to JSA immediately before going abroad and your absence is for NHS treatment at a hospital or other institution outside GB;
- for up to **four weeks** if you satisfy the conditions for being treated as available for work (see p349) and your partner satisfies the conditions for one of the pensioner premiums, a disability premium or a severe disability premium (see p775) or you are in Northern Ireland;
- for up to **eight weeks** if you are taking a child or young person abroad for treatment and the child or young person is a member of your family (see p709);
- for up to **seven days** if you are attending a job interview;
- for up to **three months** if you are unemployed and looking for work in another EEA country (see p1383).

Maternity allowance

Maternity allowance (MA – see p435) can be paid to you abroad. You should tell the DWP before you leave.

The rules for remaining entitled to MA while abroad are identical to those for IB (see p1350) except that MA is currently only payable for a period of 26 weeks.

Pension credit

In order to qualify for pension credit (PC) you must be present in GB.[50] However, regulations allow for entitlement to continue during periods of temporary absence and set out situations in which a person can be treated as being present or not present in GB.[51] In addition, there are strong grounds to argue that PC is an 'old-age' benefit for EC law purposes (see p1390) and, therefore, fully exportable.

In order to be present in GB, you must be 'habitually resident' (see p1367).[52] You are exempt from this requirement, however, if you are:

- an EEA 'worker' (see p1394);
- an 'A8 national' in registered work or an 'A2 national' in authorised work (see p1401);
- a refugee;
- a person with exceptional leave to remain, humanitarian protection or discretionary leave;
- a person who has been deported or expelled from another country to the UK.

You can be treated as satisfying the presence test for PC during certain temporary absences. These are:

- for a period of **four weeks** if the absence is unlikely to exceed 52 weeks and while absent from GB you continue to satisfy the other conditions of entitlement to PC;
- for a period of **eight weeks** if the period of absence is unlikely to exceed 52 weeks and you continue to satisfy the other conditions of entitlement to PC and you are accompanying a young person solely in connection with arrangements for the treatment of her/him for a disease or bodily or mental disablement and those arrangements are for treatment:
  - outside GB;
  - during the period in which you are temporarily absent from GB;
  - by, or under supervision of, a person appropriately qualified to carry it out.

If you or your partner are receiving treatment in a hospital or other institution outside GB and the treatment is being provided under certain NHS provisions, you can be treated as being present in GB for as long as the treatment continues.[53] However, this only applies if you satisfied the conditions for entitlement to PC immediately before you or your partner left GB.

A person is treated as not being a member of the same household as you if s/he is living away from you *and*:

- s/he does not intend to resume living with you; *or*
- her/his absence is likely to exceed 52 weeks.

Statutory sick pay, statutory maternity pay, statutory paternity pay and statutory adoption pay

There is no requirement to be present or resident for statutory sick pay (see Chapter 24) or statutory maternity pay (see Chapter 23). You remain entitled if you are abroad, as long as you meet the normal entitlement rules.[54] The same applies for statutory paternity pay and statutory adoption pay.[55]

Returning to Great Britain

If you want to claim means-tested benefits on your return to GB, you will probably have to show that you have a right to reside and that you are still 'habitually resident' (see p1367).

8. Reciprocal agreements

There are several countries with which Great Britain (GB) has reciprocal agreements. These mean that you receive some British benefits while in the other country and vice versa.

Each reciprocal agreement is different from the others. For further details of a particular agreement, see CPAG's *Migration and Social Security Handbook* or contact CPAG.

Northern Ireland, the Isle of Man and the Channel Islands

Technically, the rules described in this *Handbook* apply only to GB. GB consists of England, Wales and Scotland. It does not include Northern Ireland, the Isle of Man or the Channel Islands, which have their own social security legislation.

However, because of the close links between GB, Northern Ireland and the Isle of Man, you do not lose any non-means-tested benefit by moving between them[56] and national insurance contributions (see p717) paid in one jurisdiction count as if they were paid in any other. For most practical purposes the systems in GB, Northern Ireland and the Isle of Man may be treated as identical.

The Channel Islands, Jersey and Guernsey (including Alderney, Herm and Jethou) have their own social security systems, but there is a reciprocal agreement under which you can receive some British benefits (see DWP leaflet SA4, available from the Overseas Branch).[57] You also remain entitled to benefits (other than jobseeker's allowance) under British legislation while in any part of the Channel Islands.[58]

Notes

1. Immigration status

1 s115 IAA 1999
2 Reg 16 SS(IB) Regs
3 para 6 Immigration Rules HC 395, as amended by para 1 HC 324
4 para 6B Immigration Rules HC 395
5 Regs 3 and 5(1)(h) SPC Regs
6 *Secretary of State for Work and Pensions v Wilson* [2006] EWCA Civ 882, 29 June 2006
7 s115(9) IAA 1999

8 EC Regs 1408/71 and 1612/68
9 Reg 10 Immigration (European Economic Area) Regulations 2000 No.2326

2. **National insurance numbers and contributions**
10 Email to CPAG from the Products and Services Management Division, Benefit and Integrity JCOP, 23 January 2008
11 Reg 2 Social Security (National Insurance Numbers) Amendment Regulations 2008 and Immigration (Restrictions on Employment) Order 2007
12 *Secretary of State for Work and Pensions v Wilson* [2006] EWCA Civ 882, reported as R(H) 7/06
13 CIS/345/2003
14 EC Reg 1408/71
15 s179 SSAA 1992

3. **Non-means-tested benefits**
16 s115(9) IAA 1999; regs 2 and 12 and Sch Part II SS(IA)CA Regs; reg 16(1)(b) SS(IB)(MA) Regs
17 Since June 2002 Swiss nationals have had the same rights as EEA nationals in respect of free movement and access to social security benefits.

4. **Means-tested benefits**
18 s115(9) IAA 1999; regs 2 and 12 and Sch Part I SS(IA)CA Regs
19 CIS/1077/1999; CIS/6608/1999
20 R(PC) 2/07
21 s3C IA 1971
22 s115(9) IAA 1999
23 s115(1) and (9) IAA 1999; reg 21(3) and Sch 7 para 16A IS Regs
24 Sch 7 para 16A IS Regs
25 Reg 5(1)(h) SPC Regs

5. **Urgent cases payments**
26 Reg 70 IS Regs; reg 147 JSA Regs; reg 2 SS(IA)CA Regs
27 Since April 2000 the DWP interpretation of the regulations is that you can claim for a partner who was living with you prior to April 2000, but if you are joined by a partner after that date you will not be eligible.
28 **IS** Reg 72(1) IS Regs
JSA Reg 149(1) JSA Regs

6. **Asylum seekers and refugees**
29 Sch 3 The Nationality, Immigration and Asylum Act 2002
30 Reg 21ZB IS Regs
31 The Asylum and Immigration (Treatment of Claimants, etc.) Act 2004 (Commencement No.7 and Transitional Provisions) Order 2007 No.1602
32 The Integration Loans for Refugees and Others Regulations 2007 No.1598

7. **Benefits when you go abroad**
33 *Akbar, The Times*, 6 November 1992
34 Reg 4(2A) SSB(PA) Regs
35 Reg 6 SSB(PA) Regs
36 Reg 4(2)(a) SSB(PA) Regs
37 Reg 9(3) SSB(PA) Regs
38 Reg 9(4) SSB(PA) Regs
39 Reg 9(5) SSB(PA) Regs
40 **HB** Reg 7 HB Regs; reg 7 HB(SPC) Regs
CTB Reg 8 CTB Regs; reg 8 CTB(SPC) Regs
41 Reg 2 SSB(PA) Regs
42 Reg 4(3A) IS Regs
43 Reg 4(2)(c) IS Regs
44 Reg 16 IS Regs
45 CIS/13805/1996
46 CIS/508/1992; CIS/13805/1996
47 Sch 7 paras 11 and 11A IS Regs
48 Reg 50 JSA Regs
49 Reg 50(6AA) JSA Regs
50 s1(2) SPCA 2002
51 s5(5) SPCA 2002
52 Reg 2 SPC Regs
53 This applies where treatment is provided under ss3 or 23 NHSA 1977 or Sch 2 para 13 NHSCCA 1990
54 Reg 10 SSP(MAPA) Regs; reg 2A SMP(PAM) Regs
55 SPPSAP(PAM) Regs

8. **Reciprocal agreements**
56 Reg 2 and Sch 1 SS(NIRA) Regs; Art 2 and Sch 1 SS(IoM)O
57 Sch 1 SS(J&G)O
58 Reg 12(1) SSB(PA) Regs

Chapter 59

Residence rules: benefits

This chapter covers the residence rules that apply to some benefits. It covers:

Many benefits have residence conditions. Generally, such conditions mean you have to live in the UK for a period of time before you can get that benefit, or you have to show you have a right of residence. Equally, if you go abroad, the particular benefit is usually no longer payable. The rules are complicated and vary according to the benefit involved. However, there are often exceptions to the general rules. You may also be able to rely on enhanced rights under European Community law or on reciprocal arrangements (see Chapter 61).

The type of residence condition varies according to the type of benefit claimed, but you may be required to:

- be present (see p1357);
- be resident (see p1357);
- be ordinarily resident (see p1357);
- have a right to reside (see p1361);
- be habitually resident (see p1367).

There are residence conditions for the following benefits:

- attendance allowance (see p1358);
- carer's allowance (see p1358);
- child benefit (see p1359);
- disability living allowance (see p1358);
- guardian's allowance (see p1360);
- Category D retirement pension (see p1361);
- income support, income-based jobseeker's allowance, pension credit, housing benefit and council tax benefit (see p1361);
- incapacity benefit for incapacity in youth (see p1358).

For the rules on tax credits, see Chapter 60.

1. Present, resident and ordinarily resident

Present

To be **'present'**, you must prove that you were present throughout any day in question – ie, from midnight to midnight.[1] **'Absent'** is the opposite of present. If the decision maker seeks to disqualify you because you are absent from Great Britain (GB), the burden is upon her/him to prove that you were absent throughout any day in question.[2]

For the purpose of satisfying the presence conditions for attendance allowance, disability living allowance, carer's allowance and incapacity benefit for incapacity in youth you still count as being in GB if you are:[3]

- a member of the armed forces serving abroad; *or*
- a spouse, civil partner, son, stepson, daughter, stepdaughter, parent, parent-in-law or step-parent of a member of the armed forces serving abroad and living with her/him; *or*
- a master, member of crew or other person employed on board a ship under a contract entered into in the UK; *or*
- a pilot or member of crew or other person employed on board an aircraft under a contract entered into in the UK; *or*
- a person employed on an oil or gas rig on the continental shelf.

European Community (EC) law can assist European Economic Area (EEA) nationals and their families to meet the condition of presence. If you have worked in an EEA state, the time you have spent elsewhere within the EEA can count towards presence in the UK.

The EC also has social security agreements with a limited number of countries outside the EEA (known as association agreements). Such agreements, which are similar but not identical to EC Regulation 1408/71 (see p1389) exist with Algeria, Morocco, San Marino, Tunisia and Turkey (see p1402).

EC law can also help members of your family who are not living in the UK to meet the presence test. For example, it is possible to receive child benefit and child tax credit for children who are living in another member state, including A8 and A2 states, or one of the association countries. The same principle can be applied to dependants' additions for those benefits that include a dependant's addition.[4]

EC law, therefore, effectively treats your family as if they are residing with you in the UK. See Chapter 61 for more details of EC law.

Resident and ordinarily resident

You are usually **'resident'** in the country where you have your home for the time being.[5] It is possible to be resident in more than one place at a time, but it is unusual.[6] You can remain resident in a place during a temporary absence, but this depends on the circumstances.[7] If you go abroad to work on one particular project of limited duration, intending to return on its completion, you remain resident in GB. But if you go abroad for a considerable period, you may not remain resident in GB even if you do expect to return eventually. Important factors in deciding the issue are where your family lives, the sort of accommodation you have (eg, a hotel does not suggest residence) and where your furniture and other personal effects are kept. If you move, intending to settle at your new address, you are regarded as resident there from the very first day.

You are '**ordinarily resident**' if there is a degree of continuity about your residence so that it can be described as settled.[8] If you live mostly in GB, but also live elsewhere from time to time, you remain ordinarily resident in GB throughout the shorter periods of residence elsewhere.

Residence in another EEA country (see p1383) may count as residence in GB. Some reciprocal agreements with other countries (see p1354) contain similar rules.

2. **Residence rules and benefits**

Note: you may be able to rely on enhanced rights under European Community (EC) law or on reciprocal arrangements (see Chapter 61).

Attendance allowance, disability living allowance, carer's allowance and incapacity benefit for incapacity in youth

To qualify for attendance allowance (AA), disability living allowance (DLA), carer's allowance (CA) and incapacity benefit for incapacity in youth you must:[9]

- be ordinarily resident in Great Britain (GB – see p1357); *and*
- be present in GB (see p1357); *and*
- have been present in GB for a total of 26 weeks in the last 12 months.

People claiming DLA or AA on the basis that they are terminally ill (see p121) are exempt from the rule that they have to have been present in GB for a total of 26 weeks in the last 12 months.[10] There are exemptions from the presence tests for, among others, serving members of the armed services and their families, mariners and off-shore workers.[11] If claims are made for DLA for babies who are less than six months old they only have to have been present for 13 out of 26 weeks.[12]

For DLA and AA, you are treated as being present during any temporary absence of less than 26 weeks, and during any further absence for the purpose of treatment if you obtain a certificate from the Secretary of State to say that the further absence is reasonable.[13]

For CA, you are treated as being present during any temporary absence of up to four weeks. You are also treated as present during any temporary absence for the purpose of caring for a person, provided that the person's DLA care component, AA or constant attendance allowance is still payable.[14]

If you have come from or are going to another European Economic Area member state, you may be able to rely on EC law to continue to receive benefit while abroad or to satisfy the 26-week presence test (see Chapter 61).

Child benefit

In order to claim child benefit you and the child for whom you are claiming must be present and ordinarily resident in the UK. Since 1 May 2004, your entitlement to child benefit also depends on you having a right to reside (see p1361).

EC law can allow you to receive child benefit for a child living in another member state and can also help you to meet the residence conditions (see Chapter 61).

Residence conditions for the claimant

You are treated as not present and, therefore, not eligible for child benefit if:

- you are not ordinarily resident in GB;[15]
- you do not have a right to reside (see p1361) in the UK and your claim for child benefit was made after 1 May 2004;
- you are out of the country for longer than the permitted periods.

Regulations treat you as satisfying the presence test if you are:

- a Crown servant, or a partner of a Crown servant, posted overseas;[16] *and*
  - immediately prior to your posting abroad you were ordinarily resident in the UK; *or*
  - immediately prior to your posting you were in the UK in connection with that posting; *or*
- a person who is in the UK as a result of you having been deported or legally removed from another country.[17]

If you remain ordinarily resident in the UK and your absence is unlikely, from the start of the absence, to exceed 52 weeks, child benefit continues to be paid during:[18]

- the first eight weeks of any temporary absence; *or*
- the first 12 weeks of any period when you are temporarily absent from the UK if that absence, or any extension to that period of absence, is in connection with:
  - the treatment of an illness or disability of you, your partner, a child for whom you are responsible, or another relative of either you or your partner; *or*
  - the death of your partner, a child for whom you are responsible, or another relative of you or your partner.

Residence conditions for the child

Generally, in order to claim child benefit the child for whom you are claiming must be present in the UK. However, a child will be treated as present if her/his absence abroad is temporary, during:[19]

- the first 12 weeks of any period of absence; *or*
- any period during which the child is absent for the specific purpose of being treated for an illness or physical or mental disability which commenced before her/his absence began; *or*
- any period when s/he is in GB; *or*
- any period during which the child is absent only because:
  - s/he is receiving full-time education at a school or college in another EEA member state (including the A8 and A2 states) or in Switzerland; *or*
  - s/he is engaged in an educational exchange or visit made with the written approval of the school or college which s/he normally attends.

A child will also be treated as present in the UK if s/he is living in another EEA state while you are working in the UK, provided no equivalent of child benefit is paid in that EEA state.[20] If a child is born outside the UK during a period in which the mother could be treated as present in the UK, the child will also be treated as present.

Guardian's allowance

Entitlement to guardian's allowance depends on entitlement to child benefit, so the above conditions must be satisfied.

A further condition of entitlement to guardian's allowance is that at least one of the child's parents must have been born in the UK or have, at some time after reaching the age of 16, spent a total of 52 weeks in any two-year period in the UK.[21] Time spent in other EEA states (including the A8 and A2 states) can count toward this period.

Maternity allowance

There is no residence or presence test as such because entitlement is based on past employment. Maternity allowance (MA) is not subject to a right to reside test.

Pregnant EEA nationals (including A8 and A2 nationals) can rely on employment in other EEA states in order to qualify for MA.

Bereavement benefits

Bereavement benefits are payable even if you go abroad. However, uprating of the benefit applies only to those who are ordinarily resident in GB. People living in the EEA can also qualify for full uprating under EC law.[22] You cannot qualify for a bereavement payment if your spouse or civil partner was not in GB when s/he died unless:[23]

- you were in GB on the date of your spouse/civil partner's death; *or*

- you returned to GB within four weeks of her/his death; *or*
- your spouse/civil partner's national insurance contribution record is sufficient for you to satisfy the contribution conditions for widowed parent's allowance and bereavement allowance; *or*
- your spouse/civil partner died while abroad in another EEA state (see p1383).

Category D pension

You are only entitled to Category D pension if you are over 80 and are not entitled to any other pension in excess of the present rate of this pension.[24] The residence conditions are:[25]

- you must have been resident (see p1357) in GB for at least 10 years in any continuous period of 20 years ending on or after your 80th birthday; *and*
- you were ordinarily resident (see p1357) in GB either on the day you reached the age of 80, or on the date of the claim.

Income support, income-based jobseeker's allowance, housing benefit and council tax benefit

For all of these benefits you must be present in GB, you must have a right to reside (see p1361) and you must be habitually resident in the 'common travel area' (UK, Republic of Ireland, Channel Islands and the Isle of Man). In some circumstances if you go abroad these benefits can be payable for short periods (see Chapter 58).

Pension credit

In order to qualify for pension credit (PC) you must be present in GB.[26] In order to satisfy the presence test you must be habitually resident (see p1367) and, from 1 May 2004, you must also have a right to reside (see below).[27] However, regulations allow for entitlement to continue during periods of temporary absence from GB and set out situations when you can be treated as being present or not present in GB. You can be treated as satisfying the presence test for PC during certain temporary absences (see p1352).

3. The right to reside test

Note: the right to reside test is complex and subject to constant change. What follows is only a basic outline. For more detailed information, see CPAG's online briefing at www.cpag.org.uk. See also Chapter 61 on European Community (EC) law.

The following benefits can only be paid if the person has a right to reside:

- income support(IS);
- income-based jobseeker's allowance (JSA);
- pension credit;
- housing benefit (HB);

- council tax benefit (CTB);
- child benefit;
- child tax credit (CTC). For more information on CTC, see Chapter 60.

For child benefit and CTC, the test operates as part of the existing presence test for these. For all of the other benefits, the requirement to have a right to reside forms part of the habitual residence test.

UK legislation treats the following people as having the right to reside:[28]

- European Economic Area (EEA) nationals who are employed or self-employed 'workers' for the purposes of EC Directive 2004/38 (see below for who is a 'worker');
- former 'workers' who are temporarily incapable of work or who have worked in the UK and are now signing on for JSA;
- EEA students who are able to support themselves at the start of their studies;
- EEA nationals who are self-supporting;
- workseekers who are signing on for JSA;
- family members of any of the above;
- refugees;
- claimants with exceptional leave to enter or remain;
- a person who has aquired a permanent right to reside;
- a person who has been granted humanitarian protection;
- claimants who have been deported, expelled or otherwise been legally removed from another country to the UK (but this does not apply to a 'person subject to immigration control' – see p1334);
- claimants who left Montserrat after 1 November 1995 because of the volcanic eruption.

The test has caused most problems for EEA nationals. This is because although under EC law any EEA national can lawfully come to the UK, the fact that the EEA national may be in the UK lawfully does not necessarily mean s/he has a right of residence under EC law. A person only has residence under EC law if s/he is exercising a treaty right such as if s/he is working, studying, self-employed or if s/he is a family member of such a person. You do not necessarily lose your right to reside if you stop working, but there are conditions attached to retaining your right to reside if you stop work, which vary depending on the reason you stop work.

Who has a right to reside

European Economic Area nationals

Workers

If you are from an EEA state and you are working in the UK you will usually have a right to reside. You will not lose this right purely because of a temporary interruption of work due to ill health or unemployment. However, if you are unemployed, you must sign on for JSA rather than claim IS.[29] Other former workers also retain rights to reside. For full details of who is a worker or a former worker, see p1394. Additional conditions apply to A8 and A2 nationals (see p1401). For full details of the rights of workers, see p1394.

Self-employed

Self-employed EEA nationals (including A8 and A2 nationals) have virtually the same rights as workers (see p1362). They are deemed to have a right to reside and satisfy the habitual residence.

Receiving or providing services

If you are 'providing services' you should be treated in a similar way to if you were self-employed. 'Receiving services' can include tourists or people paying for healthcare or education. Someone falling within this category is entitled not to be discriminated against. Prior to 2006 the EC residence rules were contained in the same EC Directive as for self-employed people. The UK regulations reflected this and exempted service-providers from both the habitual residence test and the right to reside test. The new residence Directive does not clearly cover service providers, other than providing an initial right of residence for the first three months after entry. See the briefing on CPAG's website at www.cpag.org.uk for further details.

Workseekers

Workseekers are people who have not worked in the UK but who are signing on for JSA and looking for work. You cannot generally be a workseeker unless you sign on for JSA. If you have previously worked in the UK, you may be a former worker and, therefore, have more rights than a workseeker.

If you are an EEA national workseeker (other than an A8 or A2 national required to register or authorise any work), you have the right to reside, but you do not automatically satisfy the habitual residence test (see below and p1365).[30]

As a workseeker your right to reside will continue as long as you continue to sign on, even if you have been signing on and looking for work for more than six months. Your search for work must be genuine and the work you are seeking 'effective'. The way in which this is judged is by you signing on. A commissioner has held that in order for work to be 'effective' the person must be seeking work that will generate an income equivalent to the amount of her/his rent and applicable amount.[31] In CPAG's view this is wrong. See p1394 for further details about 'genuine and effective' work.

The DWP sometimes tries to argue that a person seeking work only has EC rights for a period of six months. This stems from a ruling by the European Court of Justice in the case of *Antonissen*.[32] The Court held that the six-month limit contained in UK immigration rules at the time did not breach EC law. However, the Court went on to say that if a person showed s/he had a genuine chance of finding work, s/he could not be required to leave that member state.

Students

EEA students have a right to reside as long as they have sufficient resources at the start of their studies and have sickness insurance. See p1399 for further details.

European Economic Area nationals who are not economically active

If you have never worked and are not seeking work in the UK you will generally have few rights under EC law unless you are a family member of a worker or workseeker. Your rights can be significantly improved by getting work as an employee or self-employed even if this is part time.

All EEA nationals have an initial right of residence during the first three months of their arrival in the UK.[33] However, this does not give you the right of access to benefits (apart from child benefit and CTC) unless you are economically active. After the initial three-month period of residence you will no longer have a right of residence unless you have found a job or become economically active in some other way.

Family members

Family members of EEA nationals will generally have a right of residence if the EEA national has a right of residence. See p1400 for further details of the rights of family members.

A8 nationals

A8 nationals are nationals of the Czech Republic, Estonia, Hungary, Latvia, Lithuania, Poland, Slovakia and Slovenia. All eight countries are now part of the European Union (EU), but nationals from these states do not immediately have full EC rights. There are no restrictions on an A8 national entering or living in the UK. However, for benefit purposes, unless you are working and have registered that work with the Home Office, you will be treated as not having the right to reside and, therefore, will not qualify for certain benefits. If you want to work as an employee you have to comply with certain conditions under the Workers Registration Scheme.[34]

A8 nationals are required to register their first 12 months of employment under the Workers Registration Scheme. This should be done within one month of taking up employment on a Workers Registration Scheme form. There is a fee of £90. You will then be sent a registration certificate, relating to the specific employment and a registration card, relating to you. Changes in employment should be notified to the Border and Immigration Agency within a month and a new registration certificate will then be issued.

After 12 months' employment, an A8 national is entitled to the same rights as other EEA nationals.

Self-employed A8 nationals do not need to register. Non-EEA family members of A8 nationals during the first 12 months of employment must apply for a residence stamp by completing Form FMRS.

The following A8 nationals are not required to register their work:[35]

- self-employed people;
- anyone who had leave to enter or remain in the UK on 30 April 2004 that was not subject to any condition restricting employment;
- anyone who had been working legally for a continuous period of 12 months on 30 April 2004;
- anyone who has been working legally for a continuous period of 12 months, either partly or wholly after 30 April 2004;
- anyone who has been registered for 12 months or more.

A2 nationals

Bulgaria and Romania (known as the A2 states) joined the EU on 1 January 2007 and from that date nationals of both states have the right freely to enter the UK. However, in line with EC law and for a transitional period, the UK is allowed to limit access to both work and benefits.[36]

The benefit rights of A2 nationals largely mirror that of A8 nationals, but there are differences, particularly in respect of how they access work.

People from Bulgaria and Romania who want to work in the UK must, unless they are exempt, obtain a work authorisation document before they take up employment. They will then be issued with an Accession Work Card. These are purple cards that authorise employment for workers offered employment in one of 10 listed areas of employment (eg, as au pair placements or domestic workers). In addition, A2 nationals may work in the UK under the Seasonal Agricultural Workers Scheme or apply for an Accession Work Card having obtained a work permit or a letter of approval from an employer under the work permit scheme. This application is made on a BR3 form.

Purple Accession Work Cards are also issued to EEA family members of A2 nationals who have (or who are applying for) an Accession Work Card or yellow registration card. They are not limited in the type of work they can undertake, but can only work for a named employer. Non-EEA family members must apply for 'family residence stamps' on a BR6 form and there are no restrictions on employment.

You are not required to apply for an Accession Work Card and can apply for a blue registration card on a BR1 form to provide evidence of this if:[37]

- you are a highly skilled migrant who has been issued with a registration certificate that includes a statement that you have unconditional access to the UK labour market;
- you are in the UK and were entitled to work without restriction on 1 January 2007;

- you were working lawfully in the UK on 1 January 2007 after completing 12 months' continuous employment;
- you are providing services in the UK on behalf of an employer established in another EEA state;
- you are a family member of an EEA national (from other member states) or a spouse/civil partner of a British national or a person with indefinite leave to remain;
- you are a person with a permanent right of residence in the UK;
- you are a family member of an EEA national who has a right to reside in the UK;
- you are a student who intends to work less than 20 hours a week and you have a registration certificate confirming you have access to the labour market.

A2 nationals enjoy other freedom of movement rights including rights to self-employment. Self-employed or self-sufficient A2 nationals or students who wish to work do not need to register, but may apply for yellow registration certificates on the BR1 form.

Employment cannot start until the required documentation has been issued and if you wish to move jobs you will first have to obtain another Accession Work Card specific to that employment. If you take up work without obtaining an Accession Work Card you may be guilty of a criminal offence.

Only work in certain types of employment entitles you to an Accession Work Card – ie:

- work in the food processing industry;
- seasonal agricultural work.

Access to benefit for A8 and A2 nationals

A8 nationals in registered work and A2 nationals who are actually working in authorised work can claim any benefits to which they are entitled. Benefit can be paid as soon as you take up work. However, if you become unemployed before first completing 12 months of registered or authorised work, you will lose your entitlement to benefit.

If you are an A8 national who has completed 12 months of registered work or an A2 national who has completed 12 months of authorised work, you will be issued with a certificate to show that you now have unrestricted access to the UK labour market. Thereafter, you are treated in the same way as other EU nationals and will have access to any type of work and can claim benefits freely.

If you are an A2 national and exempt from the requirement to authorise your work because you are highly skilled, you must obtain a certificate confirming this from the Home Office. The certificate will state that you have unconditional access to the UK labour market. A2 nationals with this type of certificate can sign on for JSA even though they may not have worked in the UK.

Self-employed A8 and A2 nationals

A8 and A2 nationals who are self-employed are treated in exactly the same way as any other EU national. The fact that you are self-employed gives you a right of residence.

British and Irish nationals, and Commonwealth citizens with right of abode

British citizens, Irish nationals and Commonwealth citizens have rights to reside under UK immigration rules and, therefore, should not be affected by the right to reside test. However, some people may have some difficulty in proving their status.

Non-European Economic Area nationals

Non-EEA nationals living in the UK may have a right to reside under UK law – eg, if they have indefinite leave to remain. People granted temporary leave, such as a spouse or student, also have a right to reside, but in most cases these groups are excluded from access to benefits as they are defined as being subject to immigration control (see p1334).

Transitional protection

If you were entitled to one of the affected benefits (apart from child benefit and CTC) on the day the new rules came into force on 1 May 2004, you are protected against the new rules. This transitional protection is lost if there is a break in your period of claiming. However, simply retaining entitlement to any of the affected benefits, such as HB or CTB, means that you retain entitlement to any of the other benefits, apart from child benefit and CTC.

4. The habitual residence test

For some benefits you must satisfy the habitual residence test. The benefits affected are:

- income support (IS);
- income-based jobseeker's allowance (JSA);
- pension credit (PC);
- housing benefit (HB);
- council tax benefit (CTB).

You are not entitled to IS, income-based JSA, PC, HB or CTB unless you are habitually resident, or are treated as habitually resident, in the **'common travel area'** which comprises the Republic of Ireland, the Channel Islands, the Isle of Man and the UK. If you do not satisfy the habitual residence test, you are classed as a 'person from abroad' and like those 'subject to immigration control' you become ineligible for benefit (see p1334).[38]

There are two stages in the habitual residence test:

- establishing whether or not a person has a right to reside (see p1361);
- establishing whether or not a person is habitually resident.

If a decision maker decides that you do not have a right to reside, you are deemed to have failed the habitual residence test. If it is decided that you do have a right to reside, the decision maker will go on to decide if you satisfy the habitual residence test.

The habitual residence test is applied to all claimants of the above benefits including British citizens (but not partners or dependants). The following people, however, are automatically treated as habitually resident in the UK:[39]

- European Economic Area (EEA) 'workers';
- EEA 'former workers';
- EEA self-employed workers;[40]
- A8 nationals who are in registered work if they are required to be in registered work;
- A2 nationals who are in authorised work if they are required to be in authorised work;
- EEA nationals with a permanent right of residence;
- refugees or people who have been granted leave outside the immigration rules. This includes exceptional leave to enter or remain in the UK and humanitarian protection (see pp1334 and 1342);
- people in Great Britain who left Montserrat after 1 November 1995 because of the volcanic eruption;
- people who have been deported, expelled or compulsorily removed from another country to the UK. However, this exemption does not apply to 'people subject to immigration control';
- for HB and CTB purposes, people who are entitled to IS and income-based JSA.[41]

Workseekers, however, do not automatically satisfy the habitual residence test.[42]

If you are entitled to urgent cases rates of IS or income-based JSA, you are not usually subject to the habitual residence test, but you are not specifically exempt by legislation.

Habitual residence

The term **'habitually resident'** is not defined in the benefit regulations, but it has now been the subject of a substantial body of caselaw. The leading decision is that of *Nessa*[43] by the House of Lords. Also significant is the judgment by the European Court of Justice in *Swaddling*.[44] There are also numerous commissioners' decisions on the term which remain significant and DWP guidance now reflects this caselaw. What has emerged from the caselaw is that there is no absolute definition or list of factors that determines a person's habitual residence. Whether a person is habitually resident is a question of fact to be decided by looking at all the circumstances in each case. This means it is very important for claimants and advisers to put in detailed submissions to the DWP, local authority or tribunal.

To be habitually resident in a country, you must have a **'settled intention'** to reside, which means you intend to make your home here for a temporary or permanent period. Events subsequent to your arrival can help confirm that your intentions were settled from the outset. You must show some evidence of your intention to reside – eg, by bringing possessions, doing everything necessary to establish residence before coming, having a right of abode, seeking to bring family, having 'durable ties' with the country of intended residence.[45] These are only examples and other factors may be relevant to your case. Cutting your links with your previous country of residence may help – eg, travelling on a one-way ticket or selling a home abroad.

You must, unless you are able to rely on EC law, be actually resident for an 'appreciable period of time' before you become habitually resident. What counts as an appreciable period of time depends on the facts of each case. There is no minimum period, although it would appear that, in general, habitual residence cannot be immediately acquired. There is no set time limit after which you establish habitual residence; it could be as little as two or three weeks, but the longer you are here the easier it will be to show that you are habitually resident. In one case, a commissioner held that, in general, the period will lie between one and three months and that cogent reasons would need to be given by a tribunal supporting a decision in which a significantly longer period had been required.[46]

If you go abroad for a temporary period, you may retain your habitual residence in the UK, so that you will be habitually resident from the first day of your return. People who are re-establishing ties in the UK may be able to resume their habitual residence immediately. Other claimants may have enhanced rights because they are able to rely on EC law.

The way in which you might challenge a decision that you are not habitually resident very much depends on your circumstances.

It is always worth checking whether you fall into one of the categories of people who are exempt, such as EEA workers, refugees, and those with exceptional leave to enter or remain, humanitarian protection or discretionary leave (see p1333).

European Economic Area nationals

Some EEA nationals are exempt from the test (see p1367). Those not specifically exempt may be able to rely on EC Regulation 1408/71 to claim IS, income-based JSA or PC (see p1361). HB and CTB do not fall under the scope of EC Regulation

1408/71. However, UK HB rules exempt from the test a person who is entitled to IS, income-based JSA or PC.[47]

EEA nationals relying on Regulation 1408/71 must have worked in an EEA state, but not necessarily the UK. To be eligible under this category you have to show that you have strong ties with the UK and that you have a settled intention to reside here and that this country is the one in which you have your centre of interest.[48] This would almost certainly include most British citizens who have returned to the UK, but would also apply to other EEA nationals who may or may not have lived in the UK but nonetheless have ties – eg, other family or friends in the UK. The *Swaddling* judgment (see p1368) concerned a British citizen, but the principles established can also apply to other EEA nationals.

Returning residents

If you have lived in the UK in the past and you are resuming your residence you may be able to be treated as habitually resident immediately.

In a decision issued post-*Nessa* and *Swaddling* (see p1368) a commissioner held that in order to establish whether a person is resuming a previous residence it is necessary to conduct a three-stage inquiry.[49] This involves looking at:

- the circumstances in which the claimant's earlier habitual residence was lost;
- the links between the claimant and the UK while abroad;
- the circumstances of the claimant's return to the UK.

The commissioner explained that the fact that a person's absence was only temporary, albeit for a long time, may be a point in favour of the claimant resuming habitual residence immediately on return. On the other hand, if the claimant left the UK with no intention of returning, that may be a point against resuming habitual residence on return. If the person remained abroad for longer than anticipated because of circumstances outside her/his control, that also might be a feature in favour of resuming habitual residence. The ties and contacts retained or established by the claimant while abroad must also be considered. The person must also show that s/he intends resettling in the UK for the time being. Where the intention to settle is very strong, the period of actual residence becomes shorter. It is also clear that if you have previously lived in the UK and are now returning to live here for the foreseeable future, you can be treated as habitually resident immediately.

By contrast, in a later case another commissioner considered the position of returning residents and held that it is necessary for a claimant to be habitually resident for an appreciable period, even where the claimant is resuming residence.[50] The case involved a British citizen who had worked in Britain for many years and who had spent no more than 11 months in Britain in the five years before the claim for benefit. The commissioner found that although the claimant had once been habitually resident, he had ceased to be so over that five-year period. A claim for benefit had been made three days after his arrival in the UK. On that basis, the commissioner held that he had not become habitually resident by the time of the claim. The commissioner found, however, that the claimant was habitually resident five weeks after arrival.

Returning after a temporary absence

If you have been abroad for a temporary period and prior to your absence you were habitually resident, you do not lose your habitual residence.[51] The distinction between the categories of temporary absence and returning resident is not entirely clear and there is some overlap. Temporary absence is more likely to cover short periods of absence – eg, for holidays or to visit relatives or to work. As a returning resident you may have been abroad for a longer period.

People coming to the UK for the first time

People in this situation will have to satisfy the habitual residence test. This means showing you have been resident for an appreciable period of time, you have a settled intention to remain and that you have durable ties with the country of intended residence. The period, however, can be very short and in family caselaw it has been held that as little as a month may constitute an appreciable period. Even if you are found not to be habitually resident at the time of the decison, the decision maker should consider whether you are likely to become habitually resident in the near future. If so, a prospective award of benefit should be made.[52]

5. Tactics if you fail the habitual residence or right to reside tests

- If you are refused benefit because of the habitual residence or right to reside tests, you can request a revision, supersession, or appeal to a tribunal (see p1063 and p1094). You can ask for an expedited hearing of your appeal if you are experiencing hardship. Always ask for an oral hearing, so that you can explain your circumstances in person.
- Establish whether you have failed the habitual residence test because you do not have a right to reside. The arguments you make may differ under each test.
- Always check to see if you fall into one of the exempt categories (see p1369-1371).
- Check whether you can get a job. If your status is a 'worker', you have significantly more rights, even if your work is part time.
- If you are a family member of an European Economic Area (EEA) national who is economically active, you may have rights derived from the family member.
- Only the claimant is subject to the habitual residence and right to reside tests. If you cannot satisfy the tests, your partner could be the claimant if s/he would

satisfy the tests (eg, s/he has been in the UK longer than you) or would be exempt (eg, as an EEA worker – see p1394).

- Since the habitual residence and right to reside tests operate to exclude you from income support (IS), income-based jobseeker's allowance (JSA), pension credit (PC), housing benefit and council tax benefit, the onus of proof lies with the DWP or local authority to establish that you are *not* habitually resident.[53] It is vital, nevertheless, that you produce as much evidence as possible to show that you *are* habitually resident, taking into account the above points on the meaning of the term. You should prepare your case thoroughly before attending a DWP or local authority interview or a tribunal.
- A local authority should make its own decision On whether you are habitually resident. Even if you are refused a benefit by the DWP under the habitual residence test, the local authority should not simply follow that decision.
- If a claimant is in receipt of IS, income-based JSA or PC a local authority should not apply the habitual residence or right to reside test.[54]
- If you fail the test, you may be able to satisfy it at a later date, particularly if there is a change in your circumstances, or simply through the passage of time. In this situation, the decision maker should consider whether or not a future award can be made. You will need to make repeated claims, perhaps every two to four weeks. This is now essential because tribunals cannot take into account circumstances between the date of the appeal hearing and the date of the original decision (see p1114). Repeated claims for benefit can highlight your determination to remain in the UK, as well as the unfairness of the test. Some local offices are refusing to accept repeat claims if there is an appeal pending. This is wrong – the local office should accept the claim and make a decision.
- If you have no money to live on because you have failed the habitual residence test, you could:
  - if you have children, apply to your local social services department for support under the Children Act;
  - if you do not have children but are in need of 'care and attention' – eg, because of ill-health, ask your local authority for help under the National Assistance Act;
  - if you need help with rent or a deposit, ask the local authority to provide financial assistance under s2 Local Government Act 2000;
  - apply for a social fund crisis loan (see p503). Although you have to be able to repay a loan, if you are likely to be counted as habitually resident in the near future you will then qualify for benefit and will be in a position to repay the loan.

Note: the Nationality, Immigration and Asylum Act 2002 excludes the following people from some social services support:[55]

- EEA nationals who are not 'workers';

- people who have been granted refugee status in another EEA state, but who are not EEA nationals;
- a person who has been refused asylum and who has failed to comply with removal directions.

However, the Act makes clear that a local authority is *not* prevented from supporting one of the above groups where there would otherwise be a breach of EC law or where a refusal of support would lead to a breach of any rights under the European Convention on Human Rights. Therefore, a refusal of support, particularly where children are involved, may well be challengeable. Equally, the provisions regarding EEA nationals indirectly discriminate against non-British EEA nationals and consequently may be in breach of EC law. In such circumstances you should seek legal advice.

Notes

1. **Present, resident and ordinarily resident**

1 R(S) 1/66
2 R(S) 1/66
3 Reg 2(2) SS(AA) Regs; reg 2(2) SS(DLA) Regs; reg 6(2) SS(GA) Regs; reg 9(3) SS(ICA) Regs; reg 3(2) SS(SDA) Regs; reg 16 SS(IB) Regs
4 These rights stem from the co-ordination provisions of EC Regulation 1408/71 and apply to all of the association agreements apart from Turkey. The Turkish Agreement does not allow for co-ordination of social security but does prevent discriminatory treatment in respect of social security.
5 R(P) 1/78
6 R(G) 2/51
7 CG/204/1949
8 R(P) 1/78

2. **Residence rules and benefits**

9 Reg 2(1) SS(AA) Regs; reg 2(1) SS(DLA) Regs; reg 9(1) SS(ICA) Regs; reg 16 SS(IB) Regs
10 Reg 2(4) SS(DLA) Regs
11 Reg 2(2) SS(AA) Regs; reg 2(2) SS(DLA) Regs
12 Reg 2(5) SS(DLA) Regs
13 Reg 2(2)(d) and (e) SS(AA) Regs; reg 2(2)(d) and (e) SS(DLA) Regs
14 Reg 9(2) SS(ICA) Regs
15 'Ordinary residence' means the place that you have made your place of abode.
16 Regs 30 and 31 CB Regs
17 Reg 23 CB Regs
18 Reg 24 CB Regs
19 Reg 21 CB Regs
20 Art 73 EC Reg 1408/71
21 Reg 9 SS(GA) Regs
22 Art 10(1) EC Reg 1408/71
23 WRP(PABWW) Regs. These did not come into force until 20 August 2001, but anyone who was refused a payment because her/his spouse died outside GB may be able to receive an *ex gratia* payment.
24 s78(3) SSCBA 1992
25 Reg 10 SS(WB&RP) Regs
26 s1(2) SPCA 2002
27 Regs 2 and 3 SPC Regs

3. **The right to reside test**

28 **IS** Reg 21AA(3) IS Regs
JSA Reg 85A JSA Regs
PC Reg 2 SPC Regs
HB Reg 10 HB Regs
CTB Reg 7 CTB Regs
29 Art 7(3) EC Directive 2004/38
30 The right to reside is by virtue of Art 39 EC Treaty.
31 CH/3314/2005; CIS/3315/2005
32 *R v IAT ex parte Antonissen* [1991] ECR 1-745
33 Art 6 EC Directive 2004/38
34 A(IWR) Regs
35 Reg 2(5) A(IWR) Regs
36 A(IWR) Regs
37 A(IWR) Regs

4. **The habitual residence test**

38 **IS** Reg 21(3) IS Regs
JSA Reg 85 JSA Regs
HB Reg 10(2) HB Regs; reg 10(2) HB(SPC) Regs
CTB Reg 7(2) CTB Regs; reg 7(2) CTB(SPC) Regs
39 **IS** Regs 21(3) and 21AA IS Regs
JSA Regs 85(4) and 85A JSA Regs
PC Reg 2 SPC Regs
HB Reg 10(2), (3) and (3A) HB Regs; reg 10(2), (3), (4) and (4A) HB(SPC) Regs
CTB Reg 7(2), (4) and (4A) CTB Regs; reg 7(2), (4) and (4A) CTB(SPC) Regs
40 Reg 21AA(4) IS Regs
41 **HB** Reg 10(3)(a) and (b) HB Regs; reg 10(3)(a) HB(SPC) Regs
CTB Reg 7(4)(a) and (b) CTB Regs; reg 7(4)(a) CTB(SPC) Regs
42 *Collins* C-138/02
43 *Nessa v CAO* [1999] 4 All ER 677, 21 October 1999 (HL)
44 *Swaddling* C-90/97 25 February 1999, unreported (ECJ)
45 *Nessa v CAO* [1999] 4 All ER 677, 21 October 1999 (HL)
46 CIS/4474/2003
47 **HB** Reg 10(3B)(k) HB Regs; reg 10(4A)(k) HB(SPC) Regs
CTB Reg 7(4A)(k) CTB Regs; reg 7(4A)(k) CTB(SPC) Regs
48 Art 10a EC Reg 1408/71; *Di Paolo* C-76/76 17 February 1977, unreported (ECJ); *Swaddling* C-90/97 25 February 1999, All ER(EC) 217 [1999] ECRI-1075; [1999] 2 CMLR 679
49 CIS/1304/97 and CJSA/5394/98
50 CIS/376/2002
51 R(IS)6/96
52 *Secretary of State for Work and Pensions v Bhakta*, 15 February 2006 (CA)

5. **Tactics if you fail the habitual residence or right to reside tests**

53 R(IS) 6/96 para 15
54 **HB** Reg 10(3)(a) and (b) HB Regs; reg 10(3)(a) HB(SPC) Regs
CTB Reg 7(4)(a) and (b) CTB Regs; reg 7(4)(a) CTB(SPC) Regs
55 ss17, 23C, 24A and 24B CA 1989; s2 Local Government Act 2000; ss21 and 29 NAA 1948

Chapter 60

Immigration and residence rules: tax credits

This chapter contains the immigration and residence conditions for tax credits. It covers:

Many of the rules and terms used are similar to those for benefits. Therefore, for an overview of terms such as public funds and sponsorship, see Chapter 58 and for the rights of European Economic Area nationals, see Chapter 61.

1. Introduction

Before making a claim for tax credits it is important to know your immigration status. This is because your immigration status determines your right to tax credits. If you are unsure about your immigration status you should seek specialist advice.

Most people, apart from British citizens, are subject to some form of immigration control. This means you cannot freely enter the UK, but will be subject to scrutiny by the immigration authoritites. The degree of control varies according to your nationality. European Economic Area (EEA) nationals have enhanced rights from European Community law (see Chapter 61). They do not need leave to enter or remain and consequently cannot be subject to a public funds restriction. They can only be removed on very limited grounds and there are clear appeal rights against any attempts to remove them. They, therefore, have much greater security, particularly in respect of claims for benefit, than other migrants.

If you are subject to immigration control you require leave, or permission, to enter or remain. Such leave can be:

- limited leave to enter or remain;
- indefinite leave to enter or remain;

- exceptional leave to enter or remain;
- humanitarian protection or discretionary leave (see Chapter 58).

If you have limited leave you are only permitted to remain in the UK for a limited period of time. Certain conditions are frequently attached to a grant of limited leave. For example, a restriction may be made on you working or claiming certain benefits. If you breach these conditions you may put your right to remain in the UK at risk.

National insurance number

In order to claim tax credits you must satisfy the national insurance (NI) number requirement (see p1275). This rule often causes problems for people from abroad (see p1338). However, for tax credits there is an important difference from the general rule for social security benefits: the Revenue has the discretion not to apply the NI number requirement if it is satisfied that you had a reasonable excuse for making a claim which failed to comply with it.[1]

Public funds

Working tax credit (WTC) and child tax credit (CTC) are listed as public funds.[2] However, the Immigration Rules state that a person who is eligible for tax credits will be treated as not having had recourse to public funds. Therefore, if you have a partner who is not subject to immigration control, you will as a couple be able to claim without affecting your right to remain in the UK. However, if you are single and you are subject to a public funds restriction, you will be defined as a 'person subject to immigration control' and are subject to the public funds restriction.

Status of tax credits in European Community law

CTC is a family benefit for European Community (EC) Regulation 1408/71. This means that you can claim for family members who are living elsewhere in the EEA (see p1389). Both CTC and WTC are covered by EC Regulation 1612/68 and considered a 'social advantage' (see p1394).

2. The immigration status condition

You are not eligible for tax credits if you are a 'person subject to immigration control'.[3] This has the same meaning as for social security benefits (see p1334).[4] As with social security benefits, there are certain groups who are exempt from the definition.

A **'person subject to immigration control'** is defined as someone who:

- requires leave to enter or remain but does not have it; *or*
- has leave to enter or remain in the UK which is subject to a public funds restriction (see p1335); *or*
- has leave to enter or remain which has been given as a result of a maintenance undertaking (see p1341).

For both child tax credit (CTC) and working tax credit (WTC) you are exempt from the definition if:

- you are a person with indefinite leave who is subject to a maintenance undertaking but the person who sponsored you has died, or you have been resident in the UK for a period of at least five years from the date of the undertaking or the date you arrived, whichever is later; *or*
- you are a person who has limited leave with a public funds restriction and you are temporarily without funds because money from abroad has been disrupted and there is a reasonable expectation that your supply of funds will resume. The maximum period during which tax credits can be paid under this rule is 42 days in any period of leave.

There is a further exemption for CTC if:

- you are a person who is lawfully working in Great Britain and are a citizen of a state with which the European Community has an agreement concerning equal treatment in social security. (This applies to citizens of Algeria, Morocco, San Marino, Tunisia and Turkey.)

There is a further exemption for WTC if:

- you are a person who is lawfully present (see p1357) in the UK and you are either a national of a state which has ratified the European Convention on Social and Medical Assistance or a national of a state which has ratified the Council of Europe Social Charter of 1961. (This includes all European Economic Area (EEA) countries, Croatia, Macedonia and Turkey.)

In addition, the following people can never be 'persons subject to immigration control':

- EEA nationals, whether or not they are 'workers';
- refugees;
- people with leave to enter or remain outside the immigration rules (exceptional, humanitarian or discretionary leave);
- British citizens;
- family members of EEA workers, whatever their nationality.

There are also some important differences that arise for certain groups.

- Couples, where one of the couple has settled status or is a British or EEA national but the other member of the couple is a 'person subject to immigration control', are eligible to claim (see below). This will not contravene any public funds requirement. But see the rules on residence on p1379.

- Asylum seekers who are currently receiving income support (IS) because of transitional protection (see p1345) will be eligible for CTC when all IS claimants who receive a child element in their IS are migrated onto CTC at a future date to be announced.
- Asylum seekers who receive pension credit (PC) because of transitional protection to means-tested benefits are entitled to CTC.[5]

Couples and families

If you are a 'person subject to immigration control', you are not entitled to any tax credits for yourself or for any members of your family, unless you qualify under one of the exemptions above (see p1376). However, if a couple have different immigration statuses, one of which allows the person to claim, the claim is determined as though both members of the couple are *not* subject to immigration control.[6] This means that you can make a couple claim (see p1273) and you will be eligible for the second adult element of the tax credit. However, if you and your partner have different immigration statuses and your partner is exempt from the 'person subject to immigration control' definition for CTC but not WTC, you will only be able to qualify for CTC. Equally, if your partner is only exempt from the 'person subject to immigration control' definition for WTC, you will only qualify for WTC.[7]

However, if you and your partner have different immigration statuses you may not be able to use the disability route to qualify for WTC. This is because this usually depends on qualifying for incapacity or disability benefits and people who are subject to immigration control are usually excluded from entitlement to these. Therefore, the disability element will not be met if the relevant person is a 'person subject to immigration control' (see p1377) or is subject to immigration control but is in one of the exempt categories for tax credits.

The immigration status of your children does not affect your entitlement. If you are eligible you can claim for any children regardless of their immigration status.

Refugees and asylum seekers

If you are granted **refugee status**, humanitarian protection or discretionary leave you can qualify for tax credits in the same way as a UK national. If you are granted refugee status you can backdate your claim to the date you applied for asylum. You must claim within three months of being notified that you have been granted refugee status.[8]

Asylum seekers are generally excluded from entitlement to tax credits unless they fall within one of the exemptions listed above or they have a partner who has a different immigration status who is not excluded from entitlement.

However, if you were entitled to IS urgent cases payments under transitional rules (see p1346), you will be entitled to CTC instead of the child allowances in IS when IS claimants are migrated to CTC at a future date to be announced.[9] Asylum seekers not entitled to child benefit should also receive an additional payment in lieu of child benefit to top up their CTC.[10]

If you are an asylum seeker entitled to urgent cases payments of IS between 22 August 2003 and 8 September 2003 and are over 60 and now entitled to PC, you are also entitled to CTC for any children for whom you are responsible.[11]

3. Residence conditions

Tax credits, like most social security benefits, have residence and presence conditions. This means that if you have recently arrived in the UK you may not qualify for tax credits immediately and if you go abroad the particular tax credit may no longer be payable. Special rules apply to both Crown servants (see p1380) and European Economic Area (EEA) nationals; the latter may be protected by European Community (EC) law (see Chapter 61).

In order to claim tax credits you must be 'present' (see p1357) in the UK at the time of your claim and you must also be 'ordinarily resident' (see p1357) in the UK.

You must also have a right of residence in order to qualify for tax credits. The rules on residence ar similar to those for income support and other benefits. For details on who has a right of residence see Chapter 59 and for further details of the rights of EEA nationals see Chapter 61. A key difference with tax credits, however, is that you have a right to reside during the first three months after entry to the UK, whatever your purpose in the UK. You can, therefore, qualify for tax credits during this period, subject to meeting all the other conditions of entitlement.[12]

General rules on presence, residence and temporary absence

It is possible to be treated as present and ordinarily resident during some temporary absences.

If you remain ordinarily resident in the UK and your absence is unlikely to exceed 52 weeks, tax credits continue to be paid during:

- the first eight weeks of any temporary absence;
- the first 12 weeks of any period when you are temporarily absent from the UK if that absence (or any extension to that period of absence) is in connection with:
  - the treatment of an illness or disability of you, your partner, a child for whom you are responsible, or another relative of either you or your partner; *or*

- the death of your partner, a child for whom you are responsible, or another relative of you or your partner.

This means that you not only continue to satisfy the residence conditions for entitlement to tax credits during the period of an award, but you could also make a fresh or renewal claim while abroad (but see p1380 if you are a member of a couple). If you spend longer abroad than certain permitted periods[13] you may no longer satisfy the residence condition for your tax credit.

If you are not entitled to tax credits while abroad or you have exceeded the permitted period for payment while you are abroad, your partner has to make a claim in her/his own right.

Crown servants[14]

You are exempt from the presence test if you are:

- a Crown servant posted overseas; *and*
  - immediately prior to your posting abroad you were ordinarily resident in the UK; *or*
  - immediately prior to your posting you were in the UK in connection with that posting; *or*
- you are the partner of a Crown servant posted overseas and you have accompanied her/him to the country where s/he is posted or you are temporarily absent from that country for one of the reasons set out on p1379.

Couples

If your partner remains in the UK and you are no longer ordinarily resident, temporarily absent for more than the period allowed, or lose your right to reside, you or your partner must terminate the joint claims.[15] This is because to make a joint claim you must both be treated as being in the UK. The person who remains in the UK, who remains ordinarily resident or who has a right to reside can make a fresh single claim if s/he meets the conditions for getting working tax credit (WTC) and/or child tax credit. If either member of the couple fails to report that one of them has been temporarily absent for more than the allowed period and does not terminate the couple claim, the couple may be overpaid as a result and be subject to a penalty (see p1309). The single claim will be calculated on the basis of your past income, not that of your partner's. If your partner is abroad (even for a temporary absence and for no more than eight or 12 weeks) and s/he was the earning partner, you may lose entitlement to WTC if it is decided that s/he no longer satisfies the test of normally being in full-time work (see p1223). If you continue to claim as a couple after this period you may be overpaid tax credits.

Notes

1. **Introduction**
   1 Reg 5(6) TC(CN) Regs
   2 Immigration Rules para 6 HC395

2. **The immigration status condition**
   3 Reg 3(1) TC(Imm) Regs
   4 s115(9) IAA 1999
   5 Regs 2(4)(c) and 7 Immigration and Asylum (Consequential Amendment) Regulations 2000 No.636
   6 Reg 3(2) TC(Imm) Regs
   7 Reg 3(3) TC(Imm) Regs
   8 Reg 3 TC(Imm)Regs
   9 Reg 5 TC(Imm) Regs
   10 At the time of writing there were no Regulations available, but we understand this to be the position.
   11 Reg 5 TC(Imm) Regs

3. **Residence conditions**
   12 Reg 3 TC(R) Regs
   13 Reg 7(1) TC(R) Regs
   14 Reg 3 TC(R) Regs
   15 S3 TCA 2002

Chapter 61

European Community law

This chapter covers the rights to benefit in the European Economic Area. It contains:

1. Introduction

This chapter concerns the rights to which you may be entitled if you are travelling to, from or around the European Economic Area (EEA). It describes the rights you may have as a citizen of a country in the EEA, or as a dependant of a citizen.

Social security benefits are not governed by British law alone. There are also laws made by the European Community (EC) that apply directly in the UK and throughout the EEA. EC law plays an important role in the UK benefit system, particularly since the introduction of the 'right to reside' test (see Chapter 59). It is not possible in this *Handbook* to cover all aspects of EC law and what follows in this chapter is an outline. For more detailed information on EC law and the right to reside test, see CPAG's briefing at www.cpag.org.uk.

Most EEA nationals have enhanced rights under EC law, but the exact nature of those rights varies according to the activity of the EEA national.

If there is a conflict between rights given in EC law and the UK social security system, EC law takes precedence.[1]

EEA nationals are in a far better position than other non-EEA migrants. They do not require leave to enter or remain in the UK and, therefore, there is no leave to curtail. Any attempt to deport or remove an EEA national is subject to a set procedure and subject to appeal. Furthermore, any such removal would not be indefinite. Therefore, an EEA national who wants to claim benefits does not put her/his immigration position at risk.

EC law can also help to give your family members, who are not themselves EEA nationals, rights – in particular, to enter and reside in the UK and to qualify for benefits. Such rights can be retained if a couple separate[2] or, in some circumstances, if you divorce or end a civil partnership, or your spouse/civil partner dies.[3]

EC law helps to override or reduce the impact of the residence and presence tests.

It allows you to qualify for contribution-based benefits on the basis of contributions paid elsewhere in the EEA and to claim certain benefits, such as child benefit and child tax credit, for family members who live in another EEA state (including A8 and A2 states).

Note: the major issue for EEA nationals in respect of benefit claims is currently the right to reside test. The rules on this test are covered in Chapter 59 and on p1396, but it is not possible to cover the subject in detail. For more detailed information on right to reside and current caselaw, see our online publication www.cpag.org.uk/briefings.

2. Countries in the European Union and European Economic Area

Member states of the **European Union** (EU) are: Austria, Belgium, Bulgaria, Cyprus, the Czech Republic, Denmark, Estonia, Finland, France, Germany, Greece, Hungary, Ireland, Italy, Latvia, Lithuania, Luxembourg, Malta, the Netherlands, Poland, Portugal, Romania, Slovakia, Slovenia, Spain, Sweden and the UK (including Gibraltar for this purpose).

Member states of the **European Economic Area** (EEA) are: Iceland, Liechtenstein, Norway and all the EU member states.

From 1 June 2002 most European Community (EC) rights also apply to Switzerland.

Most EC rules apply to all 31 countries, but they also extend beyond the actual territory of the member states and apply to countries 'for whose external relations a member state is responsible'. Therefore, Spain includes the Balearic and Canary Islands. Portugal includes Madeira and the Azores. In the UK, Gibraltar is covered but the Isle of Man and the Channel Islands are not.

The EU expanded significantly in May 2004. Eight of the new member states are referred to as 'A8 states' and their nationals as 'A8 nationals'. The **A8 states** are the Czech Republic, Estonia, Hungary, Latvia, Lithuania, Poland, Slovakia and Slovenia.

Two more countries joined the EU in January 2007 and these are referred to as 'A2 states' and their nationals as 'A2 nationals'. The **A2 states** are Bulgaria and Romania.

Both A8 and A2 nationals have some restrictions on their EC rights, in particular during their first 12 months of employed work.

3. Using European Community law

European Community (EC) law consists of various Treaties, Regulations and Directives, as well as caselaw from the European Court of Justice (ECJ) and from UK courts and commissioners.

All EC rights stem from the **EC Treaty**, the primary legislation of the European Union (EU). These are expanded on in a variety of Regulations and Directives. An **EC Regulation** is different from a UK regulation. In UK law, regulations are secondary legislation made by a minister using powers given by statute. Courts and commissioners can consider the validity of a set of regulations and, in some circumstances, declare them unlawful and 'strike them down'. In EC law, a Regulation is not secondary legislation; it is more like UK primary legislation. It has direct effect and overrides conflicting domestic legislation. This is the case even if an EC Regulation is in conflict with a UK statute. If there is an EC Regulation, there is no need for member states to legislate in the same area. The Regulation stands as part of the legislation.

The Court of Appeal has recently held that social security benefits are not within the scope of the EC Treaty.[4] In CPAG's view this is wrong. The Treaty itself makes explicit reference to social security[5] and the ECJ has ruled on the matter in numerous cases.[6]

An **EC Directive** is also an instrument of EC law, but it is different to an EC Regulation in that it acts as an instruction to member states to change the law in a particular area. For example, the EC Residence Directive sets out the rights of residence for EU nationals.[7] Member states are usually given a period of two years in which to incorporate a Directive into domestic legislation. If the member state fails to incorporate a Directive fully into domestic legislation, you may rely on the Directive itself.

In addition to the rules laid down in the Treaties and secondary EC legislation the ECJ has developed certain general principles in the way in which it interprets Community law. One such principle is that of 'proportionality'. The principle of proportionality is that the individual should not have her/his freedom of action limited beyond the degree necessary for the public interest.[8]

In respect of the rights of free movement, the Court has held that while Article 39 of the EC Treaty provides for the free movement of workers between member states, Article 39(3) allows for exceptions that can be justified on grounds of public policy. The ECJ has held that this provision only applies in cases of a genuine and sufficiently serious threat to the requirements of public policy.[8]

One of the primary purposes of EC law is to allow free movement of people between different EU states. An EU national has a right of entry into the UK, but this right of entry does not provide a right of residence (see p1396).

Only EU nationals who are exercising (or who have exercised) 'Treaty rights' have certain rights that assist with claims for benefit. Generally, a person is exercising Treaty rights if s/he is:

- employed (see p1394);
- self-employed (see p1398);
- looking for work and signing on for jobseeker's allowance (see p1398);
- providing services (similar to self-employed)(see p1398);
- receiving services – eg, as a tourist or paying for education or healthcare (see p1398);
- a student who is self-sufficient at the start of her/his studies;
- someone who is not economically active but who is self-supporting.

Your right to claim benefit depends on what you are doing in the UK. People who are currently working or who are self-employed have the most rights, so, if possible, an EEA national should take up work. The rights of service users and providers have been less explored. In the past, the rights of service users/providers were set out in the same EC legislation as for self-employed people. This is no longer the case and UK law reflects this, giving fewer rights to service users/providers. Students and non-economically active people also have fewer rights because they are required to be self-supporting. If a person has worked, s/he may have continuing rights – eg, if s/he is temporarily sick. Even if you have not worked, if you are a family member of someone who is working or who has worked in the past, you may have some EC rights.

EC law provides protection for people who are temporarily unable to work because of unemployment, illness or injury. It also provides protection for people who have worked in a member state and who are retired or permanently sick (see p1396). It co-ordinates the various social security schemes throughout the EU/European Economic Area (EEA) so that certain benefits can be taken to other EEA states, and contributions or periods of employment spent in other EEA states can be relied on in order to qualify for certain benefits (see p1389). It also allows for certain family benefits (eg, child benefit and child tax credit) to be claimed in a member state even though the family members are living in another member state.

4. Rights under the European Community Treaty

There are a number of important principles underlying European Community (EC) law which stem from the EC Treaty. These are:

- no discrimination (Article 12) – see below;
- right of residence for all European Union (EU) citizens (Article 18) – see p1387;
- right of free movement for workers (Article 39) – see p1388;
- right of free movement for self-employed people (Article 43) – see p1389;
- right of free movement for receivers or providers of services (Article 49) – see p1389.

No discrimination

Article 12 of the EC Treaty specifies that there must be no discrimination on grounds of nationality. This is a general statement of non-discrimination which applies to any matter that falls within the scope of the Treaty, including social security benefits and tax credits. It should only be applied where there is no other relevant area of EC law that allows for non-discrimination. There is a body of caselaw from the European Court of Justice (ECJ) in which the Court has held that EU nationals who are living lawfully in a member state are entitled to be treated equally with nationals of that state in respect of access to benefits. Caselaw from the ECJ also suggests that Article 12 applies where a person has previously had a right of residence. There is a growing body of caselaw from the UK courts and commissioners on this issue, which has sought to limit the scope of Article 12 only to situations where a person has a right of residence and/or is, at the time of seeking to rely on Article12, exercising a Treaty right.[10] Where caselaw is conflicting, decisions from the ECJ take precedence, but it is difficult to persuade a tribunal to accept a decision from the ECJ in preference to one from a UK court or commissioner.

In one case,[11] the ECJ decided that a Spanish national who was living in Germany and who was economically inactive could not be denied a social security benefit paid to German nationals because to do so would be in breach of Article 12 of the EC Treaty. The Court took the view that the person may not have had a right of residence under EC law, but she was living in that member state lawfully under national law and, therefore, could rely on the anti-discrimination provision in Article 12. It was also significant that in this case the claimant was a national of a state which was a signatory to the European Convention on Social and Medical Assistance. This specifies that a person cannot have her/his right of residence withdrawn simply because s/he claims benefits.[12]

In another case,[13] the ECJ considered whether a French national who was a student in Belgium was entitled to a Belgian social security benefit. Belgian law stipulated that non-Belgian European Economic Area (EEA) nationals were only entitled to benefit if they were 'workers'. The student was not a worker, he was a student. The relevant residence Directive requires students to be self-supporting. However, despite this requirement, the Court held that the student did have rights to benefit. The Court held that a Belgian national in the same situation would be entitled to benefit and denying benefit was contrary to Article 12 of the Treaty. The Court did make the point that the requirement for a student to be self-supporting applied at the start of her/his studies rather than throughout the period of study and that this is in contrast to the position for non-economically active EEA nationals.

A similar approach was taken in a later case,[14] in which the Court found that a person who was not economically active might not have a right to reside under Article 18 of the EC Treaty but, nonetheless, was entitled to claim social security benefits under Article 12. The Court ruled that while member states may make the residence of a citizen of the EEA who is not economically active conditional on her/him having sufficient resources, that does not mean that such a person cannot, during her/his lawful residence in the host member state, benefit from the fundamental principle of equal treatment as laid down in Article 12. The Court went on to say that a person who is not economically active may rely on Article 12 if s/he has been lawfully resident in the host member state for a period of time or if s/he possesses a residence permit. However, it is also clear that a person can only rely on Article 12 if s/he is in a situation governed by EC law.[15] This means that s/he must, for example, have worked, been self-employed or economically active in some other way. A person who is not exercising, or has not exercised in the past, a Treaty right cannot rely on the non-discrimination rule of Article 12. The matter must also be covered by EC law and it is clear that this includes social security.

In the UK, a tribunal of commissioners found that although the right to reside test was indirectly discriminatory, the discrimination was justified and, therefore, allowed.[16] On appeal, the Court of Appeal decided that as there was no right to reside, Article 12 could not be relied on. The Court also held that social security is not within the scope of Article 12. However, the Treaty makes express reference to social security and the ECJ has ruled on numerous occasions on this.[17]

The right to move and reside

Article 18 of the EC Treaty gives every citizen of the EEA the right to move and reside freely within the territory of the member states. The rights that stem from Article 18 are also referred to in the EC Residence Directive.[18] However, the right of residence under Article 18 is subject to the person satisfying certain conditions.

If you are not economically active, you must:

- have sickness insurance;[19] *and*

- have sufficient resources to avoid becoming an unreasonable burden on the social assistance system of the member state in which you are residing during your period of residence.

The conditions are similar for students, who are also required to show that they have sufficient resources at the start of their studies. This is done by students making a declaration on their ability to support themselves at the start of their studies.

What are sufficient resources?

The issue of what consititutes 'sufficient resources' is far from clear. A commissioner has held that sufficient resources means the equivalent to your applicable amount for income support (IS) plus your rent liability.[20] This decision is, however, at odds with EC law, which specifies that, although members states are required to take account of a person's situation, they cannot set a fixed amount which they regard as sufficient resources.[21] Furthermore, the amount must not be higher than the threshold below which nationals of the host state become eligible for social assistance. This would seem to imply that the most 'sufficient resources' could amount to is the UK applicable amount for IS.

The ECJ has held that any limits and conditions must comply with EC law and, in particular, must be a proportionate measure. This means that any national laws must be necessary and appropriate to attain the objective pursued. UK commissioners have decided that the test is a proportionate response but their decision should be confined to cases with similar facts.[22] In other cases involving similar benefits the ECJ has held that it was a disproportionate measure to deny benefit to a person simply because he was not self-supporting.[23]

In another case, the ECJ decided that a French national who was not economically active but living in the UK did have a right to a student loan. The loan had been refused on the basis that the young person did not have a right of residence. The ECJ, however, found that the young person had residence under Article 18 of the Treaty and, as such, had a right to a student loan under Article 12 of the Treaty.[24] Although this case involved a student loan, the same principle could be applied in respect of benefits.

The UK courts and commissioners have largely taken the approach that a claim for benefit means that a person cannot claim to have residence under Article 18. However, a commissioner recently held that a French national who had been working, but who had given up her job to care for her seriously ill husband, retained a right of residence under Article 18.[25]

The right of free movement for workers

Article 39 of the EC Treaty gives EU nationals the right to enter another member state and to reside in that state while working or looking for work. The detailed rules on this are in Regulations and Directives.

The right of residence under Article 39 does not apply to accession state nationals during any period in which they are required to register or authorise their work (see p1401).[26]

The rights of free movement for people who are self-employed, or receiving or providing a service[27]

Article 43 in the EC Treaty allows for people who are self-employed to enter and reside freely in any member state. A self-employed EU/EEA national is entitled to be treated equally in respect of benefits and has a right of residence. That right of residence is not lost if there is a temporary illness. There are no restrictions on accession state nationals becoming self-employed (see p1400). **Article 49** of the EC Treaty gives similar rights to a person who is providing or receiving a service. A person providing services is similar to someone who is self-employed. A person receiving services includes a tourist and someone paying for education or medical treatment.[28] Until recently, the rules for service users/providers were in the same EC legislation as those for the self-employed. The new residence Directive does not explicitly refer to services and UK legislation now reflects this, giving service users/providers fewer rights than the self-employed.[29]

5. The co-ordination of social security systems

European Community (EC) law co-ordinates all the social security systems within the European Economic Area (EEA).[30] The main source of these rules is EC **Regulation 1408/71**. The co-ordination rules:

- allow you to rely on periods of employment, residence and contributions paid in one EEA state towards entitlement to benefit in others. For example, contributions paid in another EEA state could be used to allow an EEA national who has worked only briefly in the UK to claim contribution-based jobseeker's allowance (JSA) or incapacity benefit (IB), or periods of employment could be used to claim a benefit such as maternity allowance (MA) and periods of residence used to overcome residence tests such as those for disability living allowance (DLA);
- prohibit discrimination on nationality grounds, in terms of access to or the rate of payment of benefits covered;
- allow you to take certain benefits abroad with you to another EEA state;
- allow you to claim family benefits, such as child benefit and child tax credit (CTC), for family members living elsewhere in the EEA.

Who is covered

In order to rely on Regulation 1408/71 you must be an EEA national, a refugee or a stateless person. European Union (EU) accession state nationals (see p1401) are fully covered by this Regulation. You must also be an employed or self-employed person or a student. This is not the same as the term 'worker' for other areas of EC law. You will be treated as an employed or self-employed person if you are insured under a national social security scheme. In the UK this means that you pay, have previously paid, or ought to pay national insurance contributions. If you are covered by the Regulation, members of your family are also covered, whatever their nationality. Refugees and stateless people are only covered if they have moved within the EEA.

Which benefits are covered

Regulation 1408/71 applies to state benefits which are designed to protect against certain risks. Each member state must declare which benefits fall within these risks. In the UK the relevant benefits are:

Risk	*UK benefit*
Sickness and maternity	DLA care component, attendance allowance (AA), carer's allowance (CA), IB, MA, statutory sick pay (SSP), statutory maternity pay (SMP), statutory adoption pay, statutory paternity pay
Invalidity	IB, severe disablement allowance
Old age	Retirement pension, graduated retirement pension, Christmas bonus
Survivors' benefits and death grants	Bereavement benefits
Accidents at work and occupational diseases	Industrial disablement benefit, reduced earnings allowance
Family benefits	Child benefit, guardian's allowance, child dependency increases, CTC
Unemployment	JSA

Special non-contributory benefits

Regulation 1408/71 also applies to what are known as 'special non-contributory benefits'.

The UK Government states that the following are special non-contributory benefits:

- DLA mobility component;
- income support (IS);
- income-based JSA;
- pension credit (PC).

Special non-contributory benefits cannot be exported (see p1391) but they do attract all the other rights contained in the Regulation, such as non-discrimination. You receive these benefits from the state in which you are resident rather than where you last worked. Under EC law 'resident' means the place where you are 'habitually resident'. The term 'habitual residence' has a slightly different meaning to that of the UK definition. When deciding whether you are habitually resident, the ECJ held that account has to be taken of factors such as:

- the nature of your occupation;
- the reasons for moving to another state;
- the length of your residence before you moved.

The Court has also held that stable employment could outweigh other factors in determining habitual residence.[31] In a later case, it adopted a similar approach, with the exception that there was much less emphasis on stable employment.[32]

Exporting benefits

Under EC law, certain benefits can be 'exported'. This means that you can continue to receive the benefit at the full rate while living in another member state, for as long as you continue to satisfy the conditions for that benefit. However, only certain benefits can be fully exported to another member state. These are for 'invalidity, old age or survivors, pensions for accidents at work or occupational diseases and death benefits'. For other benefits, such as for unemployment and sickness, there are only limited rights to export. Also, the DWP sometimes disputes that certain benefits fall within an exportable category.

Benefits that are fully exportable:

- long-term IB;
- retirement pension;
- graduated retirement pension;
- Christmas bonus;
- cold weather payments;
- bereavement benefits;
- industrial injuries benefits.

Benefits with limited exportability:

- AA;
- CA;
- child benefit;
- CTC;
- DLA care component;
- guardian's allowance;
- JSA;
- SSP;
- short-term IB;
- SMP;
- MA.

Benefits about which there is a dispute on the degree of exportability:
- income-based JSA;
- AA;
- CA;
- DLA;
- PC.

Unemployment benefits can be exported but only for a maximum period of three months. You must register as unemployed for at least four weeks before you leave the state in which you are living and must register in the second EEA state within seven days. At present, the UK Government considers that only contribution-based JSA can be exported. However, a commissioner and the Court of Appeal have held that income-based JSA is an 'unemployment benefit' for the purposes of EC law.[33] These cases relate to a different area of EC law,[34] but they do give grounds for challenging a refusal by the DWP to allow you to export income-based JSA.

Maternity and sickness benefits. EC law allows these benefits to be exported if you move to live in another member state. They are also payable during a temporary absence provided that your condition requires immediate medical attention or you have authorisation to go abroad for treatment. If you fall sick while claiming exportable unemployment benefits, you can be paid sickness benefits for the balance of the three months. It is, however, often possible to get these benefits without recourse to EC law – eg, you can get UK IB for temporary absences provided the Secretary of State agrees it is consistent with the proper administration of the benefit system and you satisfy certain other conditions.

Family benefits cannot be exported, but they can be paid for family members living in another member state. For example, you may be able to get child benefit for a child who is not living with you but is residing elsewhere in the EEA. You may also be able to get dependants' additions of benefits even though your partner is living elsewhere in the EEA.

AA, DLA and CA. The ECJ recently ruled on exporting these benefits. Unfortunately, the decision raises more questions than it provides answers. The background to the case is that prior to 1 June 1992, AA, DLA and CA were fully exportable, but after that date the Government listed these benefits as special non-contributory benefits, with the effect that they were not exportable. There is some transitional protection and if you were receiving AA, DLA or CA prior to 1 June 1992 and you are an insured person by virtue of having worked in the UK, you retain the right to take your AA/DLA/CA to another EEA state indefinitely. DWP guidance on this point has been wrong in the past and some people may have been misadvised about their right to export benefit. The removal of the right to export these benefits has been the subject of a legal challenge and failed.[35] Two subsequent judgments by the ECJ[36] called into question the legality of the change in status of these benefits and this led to the European Commission taking action to remedy this. The ECJ held[37] that AA, CA and DLA care component are all sickness benefits under the Regulation. This means that in some circumstances it is possible to export them, but the rules are complex. Ring CPAG's advice line if you are in this situation.

Overcoming residence tests

One of the practical effects of Regulation 1408/71 is that if you, or a family member, are covered by the Regulation, it can override certain residence tests. The way in which this is achieved varies according to the benefit involved. Generally, if you have last worked in the UK you should be entitled to be paid any of the benefits covered immediately without having to satisfy any residence tests. However, commissioners have held that a person cannot rely on EC Regulation 1408/71 to overcome the right to reside test if s/he does not have a right of residence.[38]

If you have worked elsewhere in the EEA, but have not worked in the UK, you can become eligible for UK benefits and override residence conditions, but again the rules vary according to the benefit involved. For any of the special non-contributory benefits, you are entitled if you are 'resident' in the UK. This is an EC concept which has been defined by the ECJ in *Di Paolo*.[39] The Court held that account had to be taken of factors such as the nature of a person's occupation, the reasons for moving to another state to work, and the length of residence before the person moved. The Court also held that stable employment could outweigh other factors in determining habitual residence.[40] In *Swaddling* the ECJ adopted a similar approach, with the exception that there was much less emphasis on stable employment.[41]

Aggregating national insurance contributions and periods of employment or residence

Regulation 1409/71 allows you, where necessary, to rely on contributions paid and periods of employment or residence elsewhere in the EEA in order to qualify for benefit in the state in which you are now residing. This applies even if the period in question was prior to the state joining the EU.[42] Therefore, a person who has worked briefly in the UK may be able to qualify for contribution-based or employment-related benefits, such as IB or maternity benefits. This can be particularly important for accession state nationals.

6. **Rights of workers and former workers**

Workers

Regulation 1612/68 expands upon the right to free movement of workers. It applies to people who are currently employed or who have been employed in the past. European Economic Area (EEA) nationals who are covered by this Regulation:

- are exempt from the habitual residence test (see p1367);[43]
- are exempt from the right to reside test (see p1361);
- have a right to claim all benefits with no discrimination.[44]

If you are a UK national, you will not have workers' rights in the UK unless:[45]

- you have travelled to another EEA state; *and*
- you went to that member state to use an Economic Community (EC) right there; *and*
- you later returned to the UK.

In addition, a child of a 'worker' has a right to education and the right to reside while in education. A former worker can also retain a right to reside if s/he is no longer working but her/his child is in education.[46]

If you are a 'worker' you are entitled to the same tax, housing and social advantages as nationals of the member state. The courts have ruled that this term applies to social security benefits, including means-tested benefits such as income support. Therefore, if you are a worker you cannot be denied a benefit such as income-based jobseeker's allowance on the basis of your nationality, and your worker status allows you to override any residence tests (see Chapter 59).

Who is a worker

The term **'worker'** is not defined in EC legislation and there is no precise length of time that you must work before being considered to be a worker. It is clear, however, that many people who are not actually working or who are working part time are still classed as workers. An EEA national who has not worked in the UK cannot be a worker. If an EEA national is signing on and looking for work, however, s/he does have a right of residence under Article 39 of the EC Treaty (see p1361).[47] You should be treated as a worker for the purposes of Regulation 1612/68 if you are an EEA national (other than a UK national) and:

- you are working in the UK, whether full or part time. Any 'genuine' and 'effective work' should count, so long as it is not so irregular and limited that it is a purely marginal and ancillary activity.[48] A commissioner has held that the need to look at whether work is, or would be, effective should be limited to cases where the person is not actually in work and has placed restrictions on her/his availability;[49] *or*

- you have worked in the UK (at any time and even for a short period) but have become involuntarily unemployed and you are signing on for work;[50] *or*
- you are temporarily incapable of work;[51] *or*
- you have taken up vocational training. If you are voluntarily unemployed, the vocational training must be linked to your previous job;[52] *or*
- you have been temporarily laid off work and are seeking to return to work with the same employer in the UK.[53]

If you are a UK national, you only have rights as a 'worker' if you have been involved in some economic activity in another EEA state apart from the UK.

You should not lose your worker status if you have stopped work for a temporary period because of pregnancy or because you have recently given birth.[54] However, pregnant women and women who have recently given birth often have problems showing that they have retained worker status. Workers who are temporarily incapable of work retain worker status, but pregnancy in itself is not an incapacity. If you are on maternity leave and still under your employment contract it should be clear that you remain a worker. The situation is more difficult for women who have been working in casual work and are no longer under a contract. If the intention is to return to work, it should be argued that you retain your worker status and a right to reside during the period when you are temporarily caring for your child. There is little caselaw on this issue but the Residence Directive does state that continuity of residence is not affected by absences because of pregnancy or childbirth. The absence appears to apply to absences abroad, but it would be illogical for an absence from work because of pregnancy not to apply to a person who remains in the UK rather than travels to another state.

EC Directive 92/85 on the protection of pregnant workers appears to assist the argument that women should continue to be treated as workers during a maternity period even if no longer employed. This may help with the right to reside test. The Directive states that member states (including A8 and A2 states) must ensure that pregnant workers are entitled to a period of maternity leave of at least 14 weeks and that entitlement to adequate allowances must be ensured.[55] This gives grounds to say that a pregnant woman who has acquired worker status, whether or not an A8 or A2 national, who is dismissed or whose employment ends should continue to be treated as a worker with a consequent right to reside.

UK regulations deem a woman to be incapable for work for any period in which there would be a serious risk to her or the baby's health and, in all cases, for a period of six weeks prior to the expected week of childbirth and two weeks after the actual birth. In such cases, a woman can argue that she is temporarily incapable of work and thus retains worker status.

Former workers

Certain former workers who are incapacitated or retired have the right to remain in the state where they have worked.

You are covered if:

- you have given up work in the UK because of permanent incapacity *and either*:
  - you had resided continuously in the UK for at least two years when you gave up work; *or*
  - your incapacity resulted from an industrial injury or disease (see p314) which entitles you to a disability benefit or IB (see Chapters 7 and 12); *or*
- you retired on or after pension age *and either*:
  - you had resided continuously in the UK for at least three years and were employed in the UK for at least 12 months immediately before retiring; *or*
  - your partner is (or was before marrying you) British.[56]

As a former worker you are entitled to equal treatment in respect of all social security benefits and tax credits. The rights given to the former worker also apply to family members, irrespective of whether or not they are themselves EEA nationals.

Note:[57]

- Absences from the UK of up to three months a year (or longer for military service) are ignored when calculating your period of residence.
- Periods of unemployment recorded by Jobcentre Plus and absences from work because of illness or accident are ignored when calculating your period of employment.
- Your continuity of residence should not be affected by periods of absence from work because of pregnancy or childbirth.[58]
- Periods of employment as a 'frontier worker' in another EEA state can count if you returned to your home in the UK at least once a week.

7. Rights of residence

European Community (EC) Directive 2004/38 came into force on 30 April 2006 and replaced all other EC residence Directives. The content of the Directive is very similar but not identical to the various former residence Directives. A significant change is that it does not appear to apply to service users/providers, other than to provide an initial right of residence. The new Directive applies to all European Union (EU) citizens.

The Directive gives all EU nationals a right of residence during the first three months of arrival in a member state. However, UK rules treat you as not having a right of residence for income support, income-based jobseeker's allowance (JSA), housing benefit, council tax benefit and pension credit (unless you are economically active) during the first three months of residence. The rules are different for child benefit and child tax credit and it is possible to claim these in the first three months of residence. This restriction on benefit in the first three months does not conflict with EC law because a person in the initial three-month period of residence who is not working or economically active in some other way is not entitled to equal treatment in respect of benefits and tax credits.

A person has a continued right of residence after the three-month period under the Directive if s/he:

- is a worker or self-employed; *or*
- s/he has sufficient resources for her/himself and her/his family members not to become a burden on the social security system of the host member state during the period of residence, and s/he has comprehensive sickness insurance cover in the host state; *or*
- is a student and has comprehensive sickness insurance cover in the host member state and can show at the start of her/his studies that s/he has sufficient resources for her/himself and her/his family not to become a burden on the social system of the host state.

The Directive recognises the right of residence of family members of a European Economic Area (EEA) worker. **'Family member'** includes:

- a spouse or civil partner;
- an unmarried partner where there is evidence of a durable relationship;
- children up to the age of 21 or older if still dependent. It also includes children of a spouse, civil partner or unmarried partner;
- dependent parents or grandparents of the EEA national or her/his spouse, civil partner or unmarried partner;
- other dependent relatives.

Your right to reside in the UK can be confirmed by a residence card, but the lack of such a document does not negate that right.[59] You do not lose your right of residence if:

- you have worked in the UK (at any time and even for a short period) but have become involuntarily unemployed and you are signing on for work;[60]
- you are temporarily incapable of work;[61]
- you have taken up vocational training. If you are voluntarily unemployed, the vocational training must be linked to your previous job;[62]
- you have been temporarily laid off and are seeking to return to work with the same employer in the UK.[63] You should also retain a right to reside if you have given up work, but you have children in education (you retain the right to reside by virtue of your children).[64]

However, the UK commissioners have taken the approach that this right has been limited since the introduction of the new residence Directive. See CPAG's online briefing on the right to reside at www.cpag.org.uk for more details.

Workers

Workers have a right of residence under Article 39 of the Treaty and under the residence Directive. That right of residence is not lost if you become unemployed, but you must sign on for jobseeker's allowance to retain a right of residence. See p1394 for further details of the rights of workers.

Pregnancy and childbirth

If you are pregnant and on maternity leave and you are still under your employment contract and intend to return to work, you should retain your right of residence. The residence Directive specifies that you do not lose your continuity of residence for periods when you are absent because of pregnancy or childbirth. This is intented to cover someone who leaves a member state during such time, but arguably, it should be applied to an absence from the labour market because of pregnancy and childbirth.

EC Directive 92/85 on the protection of pregnant workers appears to assist the argument that women should continue to be treated as workers during a maternity period even if no longer employed. This may help with the right to reside test. The Directive states that member states must ensure that pregnant workers are entitled to a period of maternity leave of at least 14 weeks and that entitlement to adequate allowances must be ensured.[65] There is no derogation from this Directive for A8 or A2 nationals. This may provide grounds for a pregnant woman who has acquired worker status, whether or not an A8 or A2 national, and who is dismissed or whose employment ends to continue to have worker status for at least 14 weeks.

Self-employed people

European Union (EU) nationals, including A8 and A2 nationals (see p1383), who are self-employed in the UK have the same rights as those with worker status. To become self-employed, you simply need to notify the Revenue and submit your tax returns. You can fall within this category while searching for self-employed work and are still covered if the work is part time.

Workseekers

Workseekers are EEA nationals who are seeking employment. A person seeking work has a right of residence under Article 39 of the EC Treaty, apart from A2 nationals who require worker authorisation and A8 nationals who are required to register their work. Workseekers are not currently able to override the habitual residence test, but they do have a right of residence. However, a commissioner has held that a person who was a workseeker who then became ill and claimed IS does not have a right to reside.[66]

Receiving or providing services

A person who is providing or 'receiving services' has a right of residence.[67] This is perhaps the least explored area of EC law. However, the European Court of Justice

(ECJ) has held that a person who is a tourist, as well as a person receiving medical treatment, education or business, is receiving a service.[68] Prior to the latest residence Directive that came into force in May 2006, the EC rules on service providers and receivers were within the same residence Directive as for self-employed people. The new residence Directive does not appear to cover services and this may cause problems for people in this area. A commissioner has held that in order to rely on the services provision you must have arranged the service before coming to the UK.[69] The new residence Directive does not make any express reference to service providers/users. In the past, rights of residence were governed by the same Directive that applied to self-employed people. Consequently, UK law treated the two categories in the same way. For example, both self-employed people and service providers/users were exempt from the habitual residence test. Since the new residence Directive, this is no longer the case. However, a person may be in the UK in some other capacity – eg, as a worker or student, but then may change to be a service-provider or receiver and should have an equivalent right to reside. 'Services' is, however, intended to be a temporary category so if someone is established s/he should fall under another category within the Treaty.

Students

If you are an EEA student you have a right of residence if you:

- are enrolled as a student in a college accredited by the host member state;
- have comprehensive sickness insurance;
- provide an assurance at the start of your studies that you have sufficient resources for yourself and your family members not to become a burden on the social assistance system of the member state during the period of residence.

Under the Directive, you must possess sufficient resources to avoid becoming a burden on the public finances of the host member state and must be adequately insured against sickness costs. However, these limitations and conditions must be applied in compliance with the general principles of EC law, in particular the principle of proportionality.[70] One crucial difference between the rights of residence of students and those of self-supporting EU nationals is that students are only required to provide an assurance that they are self-supporting at the start of their studies.

In one case, the ECJ held that a student was entitled to a minimum subsistence benefit that was only payable to non-Belgian EU nationals who were workers under EC Regulation 1612/68.[71] The case involved a student who initially had been self-supporting but later tried to claim a social security benefit. The claim was refused on the basis that he was not an EC worker in accordance with Regulation 1612/68. The Court found that even though an EU student is required by the relevant Directive to be self-supporting, s/he cannot be refused benefit if a national of that state would have qualified for benefit because to do so would be in breach of Article 12 of the EC Treaty.

Permanent residence

The following groups have a permanent right of residence and are exempt from the habitual residence test and the right to reside test:

- EEA nationals who have lived in the UK for a continuous period of five years;
- family members who have lived in the UK for five years with a right of residence during the five-year period. This only appears to apply, however, to non-EEA family members;
- family members of a worker who has died;
- a worker or self-employed person who is permanently incapable of work, but who has resided in the UK for two years or more.

Residence in the UK prior to April 2006 can count towards the period of continuous residence.[72]

Accession state nationals

Nationals of accession states have some limits on their right of residence for a limited period. For full details of the rights of accession state nationals, see p1401.

8. Rights of family members of European Economic Area nationals

European Community (EC) law may assist you even if you are not a European Economic Area (EEA) national – eg, if you are a family member of an EEA national. Family members of EEA nationals generally do not require leave to remain in the UK and are, therefore, admitted without a public funds restriction. This is the case whatever the nationality of the family member. Therefore, they do not fall into the definition of a 'person subject to immigration control' and consequently are not excluded from claiming any benefits. Family members include a spouse, civil partner, unmarried partner where there is evidence of a durable relationship, children under 21, dependent older children, dependent grandchildren, dependent parents, grandparents and great-grandparents of the EEA national or her/his partner. Other relatives are also included if they are dependent on the EEA national. The Court of Appeal has held that 'dependent relatives' means dependent in the country from which they have come.[73]

In some circumstances a family member may have limited leave and/or a public funds restriction attached to her/his stay. This could be, for example, because s/he was in the UK with another status – eg, as an asylum seeker or visitor and s/he has recently married the EEA national. In such circumstances, it can be argued that her/his right to reside stems from her/his status as an EEA dependant and that this overrides any UK restrictions. Furthermore, EC Regulation 1408/71 gives entitlement to benefits to an EEA national and her/his family members, whatever the nationality of the family member(s).

Retaining the right to reside

Family members of EEA nationals who are themselves EEA nationals do not lose their right of residence simply because of the departure or death of the other person. If the person who has left or who died had already acquired a right of residence, a family member continues to enjoy a right of residence in her/his own right. Family members can also aquire permanent residence after they have completed five years' continuous residence (see p1400).

A non-EEA family member of an EEA national will not lose her/his rights to rely on EC law if the EEA national dies, provided the non-EEA national had been living with the person in the host state for at least one year prior to her/his death. It is also possible to retain rights under EC law if a couple separate.[74] If a couple divorce or dissolve a civil partnership EC rights can continue if the non-EEA spouse/civil partner is the primary carer of the couple's children who are under the age of 19 (and in some circumstances under 22) and who are attending an educational course in the UK. This will also apply if the EEA national has left the UK and the non-EEA national is left behind to care for the children.[75] However, a commissioner has held that the fact that EC Directive 2004/38 has chosen not to provide a right of residence to someone who has a child in education means that the Directive has qualified the caselaw from the ECJ on the point.[76]

9. Rights of accession state nationals

Accession state nationals (A8 and A2 nationals – see p1383) are excluded from access to some European Community (EC) provisions. These restrictions (or derogations) are limited to certain areas of EC law and are specific. The intention of the derogations is to limit access to the labour market. Consequently, A8 and A2 nationals do not have complete freedom to take up employment and, instead, certain procedures have to be complied with.

Unlike other European Union (EU) nationals, an A8 or A2 national who is a workseeker (see p1363) does not automatically have the right to work in the UK.

An A8 national who becomes employed must apply to the Home Office within one month of taking up employment to have that work registered.[77] Once employed and registered, A8 nationals, in effect, gain worker status and have the same rights as nationals from other EU states. The work rules for A2 nationals are more restrictive. An A2 national must apply to the Home Office to authorise her/his work, but s/he is only able to work in very limited types of employment. If the work is authorised s/he will be issued with an authorised work card, giving her/him access to all benefits. Certain highly skilled A2 nationals are able to take up work in any field and they are issued with a document stating that they have unlimited access to the labour market. A2 nationals with unlimited access to the labour market can sign on for jobseeker's allowance.

UK rules specify that if an A8 or A2 national becomes unemployed before s/he has worked continuously for 12 months, s/he loses the right of residence in the UK and the right to worker status. This approach may well contravene EC law because the UK regulations go further than the derogations allowed by EC law. EC law allows a derogation only from Articles 1–6 of EC Regulation 1612/68. It is Article 7 of Regulation 1612/68 which gives the right to the same 'tax and social advantage' as nationals. A person who has worked in the UK should be treated as a worker and, therefore, should not be denied access to benefit. The Northern Ireland Court of Appeal held that this restriction is allowed for in EC law. The case is being appealed to the House of Lords.[78]

It is also important to remember that the restrictions that apply to A8 and A2 nationals are limited only to certain areas of EC rights. There may be other areas of EC law that can assist an A8 national. An A8 or A2 national who is self-employed is covered by EC Directive 2004/38. This gives her/him the right to reside under EC law and entitlement to all social security benefits. It also provides these rights to the family members of a self-employed person.

A8 and A2 nationals can also rely on EC Regulation 1408/71 (see p1389) in order to access benefits. In particular, if they become sick or unemployed, national insurance contributions paid in another member state, including A8 and A2 states prior to their joining the EU, can be taken into account to get a contributory benefit.

10. **Association and co-operation agreements**

The European Community (EC) has made agreements with a number of countries outside the European Economic Area, which specify that there should be equal treatment in social security. The agreements are very similar to EC Regulation 1408/71 and are often referred to as 'association' or 'co-operation agreements'. Such agreements exist with Algeria, Morocco, San Marino, Slovenia, Tunisia and Turkey.

In order to be covered by these agreements you must be 'lawfully working' in a member state. In one decision, a commissioner held that a Turkish asylum seeker who had worked in the UK was covered by the Turkish association agreement.[79] In this case the claimant had been denied benefit under UK rules on the basis that, as an asylum seeker, he was not eligible. However, the commissioner held that the benefit in question – family credit – was a family benefit for the purposes of the agreement and as a person within the scope of the agreement he could not be denied the benefit. In another case a commissioner found that a Moroccan man was able to claim a dependant's addition to his invalidity benefit for his wife who had remained living in Morocco.[80]

The benefits covered by the agreements are the same as those under EC Regulation 1408/71 (see p1389). There is, however, some debate as to whether the 'special non-contributory benefits' which include income support (IS) and possibly income-based jobseeker's allowance (JSA) are covered by the agreements. There is some positive caselaw which suggests that benefits such as IS are covered.[81] However, in another decision, a commissioner chose to distinguish the Turkish agreement and held that IS was not within its scope.[82] The position of income-based JSA is much stronger because there is a growing body of caselaw which holds that income-based JSA is an unemployment benefit for EC purposes. However, these mainly relate to EC Directive 79/7 (see p1165).[83] The Directive differs from EC Regulation 1408/71 because there is no concept of special non-contributory benefits.

From 1 October 2007, there is also a Convention on social security between the UK and Ireland.[84] It applies to people moving between Ireland and the UK to whom EC Regulation 1408/71 does not apply. It relates to sickness benefit, maternity allowance, invalidity benefits, survivors' benefits and benefits for industrial accidents and diseases.

Lawfully working

The DWP considers that a person is lawfully working in Great Britain (GB) if s/he is:

- working in GB; *and*
- has been given permission to enter GB; *and*
- does not have restrictions on taking employment in GB.

Furthermore, the DWP guidance also states that a person will continue to be treated as covered by the association agreements if s/he:

- has retired from work in GB on or after pension age; *or*
- has given up work in GB because of sickness or invalidity; *or*
- has given up work in GB because of pregnancy; *or*
- has given up work in GB because of bereavement; *or*
- has given up work in GB because of an accident at work or an industrial disease; *or*
- has become unemployed after working in the UK; *or*
- has given up work in the UK to look after children.

Notes

1. **Introduction**
1 s2 ECA 1972
2 *Diatta* C-267/83 ECR 567; Art 13 EC Directive 2004/38
3 Arts 13 and 14 EC Directive 2004/38

3. **Using European Community law**
4 *Abdirahman v Secretary of State for Work and Pensions* [2007] EWCA Civ 657, 5 July 2007 (CA), reported in R(IS) 8/07
5 Art 42 EC Treaty
6 See for example, *Collins v Secretary of State for Work and Pensions* C-138/02 (ECJ); *Martinez Sala* C-85/96 [1988] ECR 1-2691 (ECJ); *Trojani v Centre Public d'aide Sociale de Bruxelles* C-456/07 (ECJ); *Snares v Adjudication Officer* C-20/96 [1997] All ER (EC) 886 (ECJ), [1997] ECR 1-6057, [1998] CMLR 897 (ECJ)
7 EC Directive 2004/38
8 *Internationale Handelsgesellschaft v EV St* [1970] ECR 1125, [1972] CMLR 255 (ECJ)
9 *Rutili v French Minister of the Interior* C-36/75 [1975] ECR 1219 (ECJ) and *R v Bouchereau* C-30/77 [1977] ECR 1999, [1977] 2 CMLR 800 (ECJ)

4. **Rights under the European Community Treaty**
10 *Abdirahman v Secretary of State for Work and Pensions* [2007] EWCA Civ 657, 5 July 2007 (CA), reported in R(IS) 8/07
11 *Martinez Sala* C-85/96 [1988] ECR I-2691; *Trojani v Centre Public d'aide Sociale de Bruxelles* C-456/02 7 September 2004, unreported (ECJ); *Baumbast and another v Secretary of State for the Home Department* C-413/99 [2002] (ECJ)
12 Signatories to ECSMA are Belgium, Denmark, Estonia, France, Germany, Greece, Iceland, Ireland, Italy, Luxembourg, Malta, Netherlands, Norway, Portugal, Spain, Sweden, Turkey and United Kingdom.
13 *Grzelczyk v Centre Public d'aide Sociale d'Ottignies-Louvain-la-Neuve* C-184/99 [2001] (ECJ)
14 *Trojani v Centre Public d'aide Sociale de Bruxelles* C-456/02 7 September 2004, unreported (ECJ)
15 *Cowan* C-186/87 (ECJ)
16 CIS/3573/2005
17 Art 42 EC Treaty and cases such as *Grzelczyk* C-184/99 (ECJ)
18 EC Directive 2004/38
19 There is little information regarding the issue of sickness insurance but some experts have said that it should be taken to mean a person entitled to a European Health Insurance Card (EHIC). The EHIC replaced the E111 and most EU nationals are entitled to this.
20 CH/3314/2005 and CIS/3315/2005
21 EC Directive 2004/38
22 para 16 to the preamble of EC Directive 2004/38
23 *Grzelczyk v Centre Public d'aide Sociale d'Ottignies-Louvain-la-Neuve* C-184/99 [2001] (ECJ)
24 *Bidar* C-209/03 (ECJ)
25 CIS/408/2006
26 The Accession Treaty
27 Art 49 EC Treaty
28 *Cowan* C-186/87 (ECJ)
29 For example, from May 2006, a self-employed EEA national is exempt from the habitual residence rule under UK law, but a service provider/user is not. Before May 2006 both were exempt.

5. **The co-ordination of social security systems**
30 EC Reg 1408/71 and Art 42 EC Treaty
31 *Di Paulo v Office National de l'Emploi* C-76/76 [1977] ECR 315, but see also R(U) 8/88 which provides a useful analysis
32 *Swaddling v Adjudication Officer* C-90/97 [1999] (ECJ)
33 R(JSA) 3/02; *Hockenjos v Secretary of State for Social Security* [2001] EWCA Civ 624, 2 May 2001 (CA)
34 The cases deal with the question of whether income-based JSA is an 'unemployment benefit'. There are some difficulties in reading this argument across but there is still the basis of an argument.

35 *Snares* C-20/96 (ECJ) and *Partridge* C-297/96 (ECJ)
36 In the cases of *Jauch* C-215/99 and *Leclere* C43/99 the ECJ casts doubt on the validity of its judgments in *Snares* and *Partridge*.
37 *Commission v European Parliament and Council of the EU* C-299/05, unreported
38 CIS 3182/05
39 *Di Paolo v Office National de l'Emploi* C-76/76 [1977] ECR 315, but see also R(U) 8/88 which provides a useful analysis.
40 *Di Paolo v Office National de l'Emploi* C-76/76 [1977] ECR 315, but see also R(U) 8/88 which provides a useful analysis.
41 *Swaddling v Adjudication Officer* C-90/97 [1999] (ECJ)
42 Art 94(2) EC Reg 1408/71

6. **Rights of workers and former workers**

43 **IS** Reg 21(3) IS Regs
JSA Reg 85(4) JSA Regs
PC Reg 2 SPC Regs
HB Reg 10(2) HB Regs; reg 10(2) HB(SPC) Regs
CTB Reg 7(2) CTB Regs; reg 7(2) CTB(SPC) Regs
44 Art 7(2) EC Reg 1612/68
45 *Singh* C-370/90 [1992] ECRI 4265 (ECJ)
46 Art 12 EC Reg 1612/68
47 Art 39 EC Treaty
48 *Levin* C-53/81 [1982] ECR 1035; *Kempf* C-139/85 [1986] ECR 1741; *Raulin* C-357/89 [1992] ECR 1027
49 CJSA/1475/2006
50 Art 7(3)(b) and (c) EC Directive 2004/38
51 Art 7(3)(a) EC Directive 2004/38
52 Art 7(3)(d) EC Directive 2004/38; *Raulin* C-357/89 [1992] ECR 1027
53 *Lair* C-39/86 [1988] ECR 3161; Art 7(1) EC Reg 1612/68
54 Art 16(3) EC Directive 2004/38. (This part of the Directive deals with continuity of residence in respect of the right to permanent residence and, therefore, is not strictly about the retention of worker status.)
55 Art 11(2)(b) EC Directive 92/85
56 Art 7 EC Directive 2004/38
57 Arts 2(c) and 4 EC Reg 1251/70
58 Art 16(3) EC Directive 2004/38

7. **Rights of residence**

59 *Roye* [1976] ECR 497; *Echternach and Moritz v Minister van Onderwijs* C-389 and C-390/87 [1989] ECR 723; *Raulin* C-357/89 [1992] ECR 1027
60 Art 7(3)(b) and (c) EC Directive 2004/38
61 Art 7(3)(a) EC Directive 2004/38
62 Art 7(3)(d) EC Directive 2004/38; *Raulin* C-357/89 [1992] ECR 1027
63 *Lair* C-39/86 [1988] ECR 3161; Art 7(1) EC Reg 1612/68
64 Art 12 EC Reg 1612/68
65 Art 11(2)(b) EC Directive 92/85
66 CIS/2036/2006
67 Art 49 EC Treaty
68 *Cowan* C-186/87 [1989] ECR 195 (ECJ)
69 CIS/3877/2000 and CH/1400/2000
70 Opinion of the Advocate General in *Bidar* C-209/03 (ECJ), para 32
71 *Grzelczyk* C-184/99 (ECJ)
72 Sch 4 para 6 EEA Regs 2006

8. **Rights of family members of European Economic Area nationals**

73 *KG and AK v Secretary of State for the Home Department*, 25 January 2008, unreported
74 *Diatta* C-267/83; CIS/2431/2006
75 *Baumbast* C-413/99; Art 13 EC Directive 2004/38
76 CIS/3444/2006; CIS/623/2007; CIS/1121/2007

9. **Rights of accession state nationals**

77 A(IWR) Regs
78 *Zalewska v Department of Social Development*, 9 May 2007 (NICA)

10. **Association and co-operation agreements**

79 R(FC) 1/01
80 R(S) 1/00
81 See in particular, *Babahenini* C-113/97 [1998] EC 1998, I-183; R(JSA) 7/02
82 CIS/5707/1999
83 The position of Directive 79/7 is different because there is no concept of special non-contributory benefits. The UK Government has declared income-based JSA to be a special non-contributory benefit and the ECJ held that where such declarations exist benefits will be special non-contributory benefits because the declaration forms part of the Regulation itself.
84 The Social Security (Ireland) Order 2007 No.2122

Appendices

Appendix 1

Useful addresses

The President and Appeals Service Centres of the Tribunals Service

The President
5th Floor
Fox Court
14 Grays Inn Road
London WC1X 8HN
Tel: 0203 206 0619
www.tribunals.gov.uk

Chief Executive designate
Peter Handcock CBE
4 Abbey Orchard Street
London SW1 P 2HT
Tel: 020 7210 0044

The President (Northern Ireland)
Mr C G MacLynn
Cleaver House
3 Donegal Square North
Belfast BT1 5GA
Tel: 028 9051 8518

Appeals Service Centres

Birmingham
Auchinleck House
Broad Street
Birmingham B15 1DL
Tel: 0121 634 7200
Textphone: 0121 634 7218

Cardiff
Eastgate House
Newport Road
Cardiff CF24 0YP
Tel: 02920 662 180
Textphone: 02920 440 596

Glasgow
Wellington House
134–136 Wellington Street
Glasgow G2 2XL
Tel: 0141 354 8400
Textphone: 0141 354 8413

Leeds
York House
York Place
Leeds LS1 2ED
Tel: 0113 251 9500
Textphone: 0113 251 9570

Liverpool
36 Dale Street
Liverpool L2 5UZ
Tel: 0151 243 1400
Textphone: 0151 243 1450

Newcastle
Manorview House
Kings Manor
Newcastle upon Tyne NE1 6PA
Tel: 0191 201 2300
Textphone: 0191 201 2350

Nottingham
The Pearson Building
57 Upper Parliament Street
Nottingham NG1 6AZ
Tel: 0115 909 3600
Textphone: 0115 909 3692

Sutton
Copthall House
9 The Pavement
Grove Road
Sutton SM1 1DA
Tel: 020 8710 2900
Textphone: 020 8710 2966

The Commissioners Office

England and Wales
Procession House
55 Ludgate Hill
London EC4M 7JW
Tel: 020 7029 9850
Minicom: 020 7029 9820
www.osscsc.gov.uk

Scotland
George House
126 George Street
Edinburgh EH2 4HH
Tel: 0131 271 4310
www.ossc-scotland.org.uk

Northern Ireland
Office of the Social Security Commissioner and Child Support Commissioners
Headline Building
10–14 Victoria Street
Belfast BT1 3GG
Tel: 028 9033 2344
www.courtsni.gov.uk/en-GB/Services/Tribunals

HM Revenue and Customs (tax credits)

England, Scotland and Wales
HM Revenue and Customs
Tax Credit Office
Preston PR1 0SB
www.hmrc.gov.uk/taxcredits

Northern Ireland
HM Revenue and Customs
Tax Credit Office
Dorchester House
52-58 Great Victoria Street
Belfast BT2 7WF

Tax Credit Helpline
Tel: 0845 300 3900
Textphone: 0845 300 3909

HM Revenue and Customs (child benefit and guardian's allowance)

England, Scotland and Wales
Child Benefit Office
PO Box 1
Newcastle upon Tyne NE88 1AA
Tel: 0845 302 1444
Textphone: 0845 302 1474
www.hmrc.gov.uk/childbenefit

Northern Ireland
Child Benefit Office
Windsor House
9–15 Bedford Street
Belfast BT2 7UW
Tel: 0845 603 2000
Textphone: 0845 607 6078

HM Revenue and Customs (Solicitor's Office)

Somerset House
Strand
London WC2R 1LB
Tel: 020 7438 7417/7590

HM Revenue and Customs (National Insurance Contributions Office)

Benton Park View
Newcastle upon Tyne NE98 1ZZ
Tel: 0845 302 1479
Textphone: 0845 915 3296
www.hmrc.gov.uk/nic

HM Revenue and Customs (Statutory Payments Disputes Team)

Benton Park View
Newcastle upon Tyne NE98 1ZZ
Tel: 0191 225 5221

Department for Work and Pensions (benefits)

Quarry House
Quarry Hill
Leeds LS2 7UA
Tel: 0113 232 4000
www.dwp.gov.uk

Department for Work and Pensions (policy)

The Adelphi
1–11 John Adam Street
London WC2N 6HT
Tel: 020 7962 8000

Department for Work and Pensions (Office of the Solicitor)

New Court
48 Carey Street
London WC2A 2LS
Tel: 020 7962 8000

Department for Work and Pensions (Decision Making and Appeals Unit)

Quarry House
Quarry Hill
Leeds LS2 7UB
Tel: 0113 232 4855

Disability and Carers Service

5th Floor
Whitehall 2
Whitehall Quay
Leeds LS1 4HR
www.direct.gov.uk/en/disabledpeople/financial support

Note: the Pension Service and the Disability and Carers Service were due to be merged on 1 April 2008 to create a new DWP agency, the Pension, Disability and Carers Service. It is expected that, for the time being, all contact with claimants will continue to be made by the Pension Service and the Disability and Carers Service and their contact details will remain the same.

Benefit Enquiry Line

Tel: 0800 88 22 00
Textphone: 0800 24 33 55

Disability Contact and Processing Unit

Attendance Allowance Unit and Disability Living Allowance Unit
Warbreck House
Warbreck Hill
Blackpool FY2 0YE
Tel: 08457 12 34 56
Textphone: 08457 22 44 33

Carer's Allowance Unit

Palatine House
Lancaster Road
Preston PR1 1HB
Tel: 01253 85 61 23
Textphone: 01772 89 94 89

Child Support Agency

Benton Park View
Benton Park Road
Newcastle upon Tyne NE98 1YX
Tel: 08457 133 133
Textphone: 084 7 138 924

Jobcentre Plus

Caxton House
Tothill Street
London SW1H 9NA
Tel: 020 723 6006/6102
www.jobcentreplus.gov.uk

The Pension Service

PO Box 50101
London SW1P 2WU
Tel: 0845 60 60 265
Textphone: 0845 60 60 285
www.thepensionservice.gov.uk

Note: the Pension Service and the Disability and Carers Service were due to be merged on 1 April 2008 to create a new DWP agency, the Pension, Disability and Carers Service. It is expected that, for the time being, all contact with claimants will continue to be made by the Pension Service and the Disability and Carers Service and their contact details will remain the same.

NHS Business Services Authority

Sandyford House
Archbold Terrace
Newcastle upon Tyne NE2 1DB
Tel: 0845 850 1166
www.ppa.nhs.uk

Department for Education and Skills

Sanctuary Buildings
Great Smith Street
London SW1P 3BT
Tel: 0870 000 2288
Textphone: 01928 794 274
www.dfes.gov.uk

Under-Eighteens Support Team (UEST)

Level 4
Steel City House
West Street
Sheffield S1 2GQ
Tel: 01253 848 000

Compensation Recovery Unit

England, Scotland and Wales

Durham House
Washington
Tyne and Wear NE38 7SF
Tel: 0191 213 5000
Textphone: 0191 225 2003
www.dwp.gov.uk/cru

Northern Ireland
Magnet House
81-93 York Street
Belfast BT15 1SS
Tel: 028 90545 833/855

Independent Review Service for the Social Fund

4th Floor
Centre City Podium
5 Hill Street
Birmingham B5 4UB
Freephone: 0800 096 1926
Textphone: 0800 096 1929
www.irs-review.org.uk

Local Government Ombudsman

England
Tony Redmond
10th Floor
Millbank Tower
Millbank
London SW1P 4QP
Tel: 020 7217 4620
www.lgo.org.uk
London boroughs north of the Thames (including Richmond, but excluding Harrow), Essex, Kent, Surrey, Suffolk, East and West Sussex, Berkshire, Buckinghamshire, Hertfordshire and Coventry

Anne Seex
Beverley House
17 Shipton Road
York YO30 5FZ
Tel: 01904 380200
Birmingham, Solihull, Cheshire, Debyshire, Nottinghamshire, Lincolnshire, Warwickshire and North of England (except Lancaster, Manchester and York)

Jerry White
The Oaks
Westwood Way
Westwood Business Park
Coventry CV4 8JB
Tel: 024 7682 0000
London boroughs south of the Thames (except Richmond), London Borough of Harrow, Trafford, Lancaster, Manchester, York and rest of England not covered by above offices

Scotland
4 Melville Street
Edinburgh EH3 7NS
Tel: 0800 377 7334
www.spso.org.uk

Wales
1 Ffordd yr Hen Gae
Pencoed CF35 5LJ
Tel: 01656 641 150
www.ombudsman-wales.org.uk

The Parliamentary and Health Service Ombudsman

Millbank Tower
Millbank
London SW1P 4QP
Tel: 0845 0154 033
www.ombudsman.org.uk

The Independent Adjudicator

Dame Barbara Mills
Adjudicator's Office
Euston Tower
286 Euston Road
London NW1 3US
Tel: 0300 057 1111
www.adjudicatorsoffice.gov.uk

Appendix 2

Information and advice

Independent advice and representation

If you want advice or information on a benefit or tax credit issue, the following may be able to assist.

- Citizens Advice Bureaux (CAB). You can find out where your local CAB is from the Citizens Advice website at www.citizensadvice.org.uk (England and Wales) or www.cas.org.uk (Scotland).
- Law centres. You can find your nearest law centre at www.lawcentres.org.uk.
- Other independent advice centres.
- Local authority welfare rights services.
- Local organisations for particular groups of claimants may offer help. For instance, there are unemployed centres, pensioners groups and centres for people with disabilities.
- Solicitors can give free legal advice to people on low incomes under the 'Legal help' scheme. This does not cover the cost of representation at an appeal hearing but can cover the cost of preparing written submissions and obtaining evidence such as medical reports.

You can find details of advice centres and lawyers in the phone book either under 'advice' or in the 'community' section at the front of the book. Your library or community centre may have details of where to get advice in your area. Community Legal Advice has a list of many organisations who provide advice in different areas of law including welfare benefits. You can phone them on 0845 345 4345 or visit www.clsdirect.org.uk and search the 'directory' for advisers and lawyers within.

Advice from CPAG

Unfortunately, CPAG is unable to deal with enquiries directly from members of the public, but if you are an adviser you can phone the advice line from 2pm to 4pm, Monday to Friday on 020 7833 4627.

Organisations based in Scotland can contact CPAG in Scotland at Unit 9, Ladywell, 94 Duke Street, Glasgow G4 0UW or email advice@cpagscotland.org.uk. A phone line is open for Scottish advisers Monday to Thursday from 10am to 12 noon on 0141 552 0552.

Advice from the DWP

The phone book should list contact details for your local DWP office. See also Appendix 1 of this *Handbook* for contact details for the DWP and the Revenue. If you are disabled, you can obtain free telephone advice on benefits on 0800 882 200; minicom: 0800 243 355 (in Northern Ireland 0800 220 674; minicom: 0800 243 787). This is for general advice and not specific queries on individual claims.

Finding help on the internet

CPAG's online subscription services (aimed at advisers) contain comprehensive in-depth information on welfare benefits, tax credits and child support. The text of the *Welfare Benefits and Tax Credits Handbook* is updated on a rolling basis throughout the year and is available with direct links to all of the relevant updated legislation and commissioners' decisions. Information on this and other online information packages is at http://onlineservices.cpag.org.uk

Some information about benefits and tax credits, including a selection of leaflets and forms is available on the DWP website at www.dwp.gov.uk and the Revenue website at www.hmrc.gov.uk. The DWP website also has links to the executive agencies of the DWP (see p). You may also find some useful information at www.direct.gov.uk.

CPAG's website (www.cpag.org.uk) has some articles and briefings, and information about its publications, training and campaigning activities.

The RightsNet website (aimed at advisers) at www.rightsnet.org.uk has details of new legislation, some caselaw and guidance. It also has links to other useful sites.

Most Acts and Regulations can be found on the government information website at www.opsi.gov.uk.

You can find decisions of the Social Security Commissioners at www.osscsc.gov.uk.

Appendix 3

Useful publications

Many of the books listed here will be in your local public library. Stationery Office books are available from Stationery Office bookshops or ordered by post, telephone, fax or email from The Stationery Office, Post Cash Department, PO Box 29, Norwich NR3 1GN (tel: 0870 600 5522; fax: 0870 600 5533; email: customer.services@tso.co.uk; web: www.tso.co.uk). Many publications listed are available from CPAG; see below for order details, or order from www.cpag.org.uk/publications. Details of CPAG's new online subscription services are given below.

1. Caselaw and legislation

Social Security Case Law – Digest of Commissioners' Decisions
D Neligan (Stationery Office, looseleaf in two vols).

CPAG's Welfare Benefits and Tax Credits Law Online
Includes all social security and tax credits legislation updated and consolidated throughout the year; over 3,000 commissioners' decisions, some with commentary; the *Welfare Benefits and Tax Credits Handbook* updated throughout the year with links to the relevant legislation, decisions and caselaw. Annual subscription £48 + VAT per concurrent user (bulk discounts available). More information and free seven-day trial from http://onlineservices.cpag.org.uk

CPAG's Child Support Law Online
Includes all child support legislation updated and consolidated throughout the year; the *Child Support Handbook* updated once a year in line with the print edition, with links to the relevant legislation, commissioners' decisions and caselaw. Annual subscription £29 + VAT per concurrent user (bulk discounts available). More information at http://onlineservices.cpag.org.uk

CPAG's Housing Benefit and Council Tax Benefit Law Online
Includes complete housing benefit and council tax benefit legislation, updated and consolidated throughout the year; commentary from *CPAG's Housing Benefit & Council Tax Benefit Legislation* (Findlay), updated twice a year in line with the print edition, with links to commissioners' decisions, court

cases and other relevant material. Annual subscription £100 + VAT per concurrent user (bulk discounts available). More information at http://onlineservices.cpag.org.uk

The Law Relating to Social Security
(Stationery Office, looseleaf, 12 vols) All the legislation but without any comment. Known as the 'Blue Book'. Also available at www.dwp.gov.uk/advisers.

Social Security Legislation, Volume I: Non-Means-Tested Benefits
D Bonner, I Hooker and R White (Sweet & Maxwell) Legislation with commentary. 2008/09 edition (October 2008): £86 for the main volume, reduced to £77.50 if you are a CPAG member and order from CPAG before 30 June 2008, or at full price from July.

Social Security Legislation, Volume II: Income Support, Jobseeker's Allowance, State Pension Credit and the Social Fund
J Mesher, P Wood, R Poynter, N Wikeley and D Bonner (Sweet & Maxwell) Legislation with commentary. 2008/09 edition (October 2008): £86 for the main volume, reduced to £77.50 if you are a CPAG member and order from CPAG before 30 June 2008, or at full price from July.

Social Security Legislation, Volume III: Administration, Adjudication and the European Dimension
M Rowland and R White (Sweet & Maxwell) Legislation with commentary. 2008/09 edition (October 2008): £86 for the main volume, reduced to £77.50 if you are a CPAG member and order from CPAG before 30 June 2008, or at full price from July.

Social Security Legislation, Volume IV: Tax Credits, Child Trust Funds and Employer-Paid Social Security Benefits
N Wikeley and D Williams (Sweet & Maxwell) Legislation with commentary. 2008/09 edition (October 2008): £86 for the main volume, reduced to £77.50 if you are a CPAG member and order from CPAG before 30 June 2008, or at full price from July.

Social Security Legislation – updating supplement to Volumes I, II, III & IV
(Sweet & Maxwell) The spring 2009 update to the 2008/09 main volumes: £58, reduced to £54 if you are a CPAG member and order from CPAG before 30 June 2008, or at full price from July.

CPAG's Housing Benefit and Council Tax Benefit Legislation
L Findlay, R Poynter, S Wright and C George (CPAG) Legislation with detailed commentary. 2008/09 (21st) edition (December 2008): £97 including Supplement. Reduced to £90 per set if ordered before 30 June 2008. The 20th edition (2007/08) is still available, £95 per set. Available as part of *CPAG's Housing Benefit and Council Tax Law Online* (see p1416).

Child Support: The Legislation
E Jacobs and G Douglas (Sweet & Maxwell) 8th edition main volume (August 2007): £85.

2. Official guidance

Decision Makers Guide(14 volumes, memos and letters) Available at www.dwp.gov.uk/advisers

Handbook for Delegated Medical Practitioners
(Stationery Office, 1988)

Housing Benefit and Council Tax Benefit Guidance Manual
(Stationery Office, looseleaf) Available at www.dwp.gov.uk/ advisers

Industrial Injuries Handbook for Adjudicating Medical Authorities
(Stationery Office, looseleaf)

Income Support Guide
(Stationery Office, looseleaf, 8 vols) Procedural guide issued to DWP staff.

Notes on the Diagnosis of Prescribed Diseases (except pneumoconiosis and related occupational diseases and occupational deafness)
(Stationery Office, 1991)

Tax Credit Technical Manual
Available at www.hmrc.gov.uk/ manuals/

The Social Fund Guide
(Stationery Office, looseleaf 2 vols) Available at www.dwp.gov.uk/ advisers/#guides

3. Leaflets

The DWP publishes many leaflets available free from your local DWP or Jobcentre Plus office. To order large numbers of leaflets, or receive information about new leaflets, contact Publicity Register, Freepost, NWW 1853, Manchester M2 9LU, tel: 0845 602 44 44, fax: 0870 241 2634, email: publicity-Register@dwp.gsi.gov.uk. Leaflets on HB/CTB are available from your local council.

4. Periodicals

Welfare Rights Bulletin
(CPAG, bi-monthly) Covers developments in social security law, including commissioners' decisions, and updates this *Handbook* between editions. The annual subscription is £30 but it is sent automatically to CPAG Rights/Rights Online and Comprehensive/Comprehensive Online members (contact CPAG for details).

Articles on social security can also be found in *Legal Action* (Legal Action Group), *The Adviser* (Citizens Advice) and the *Journal of Social Security Law* (Sweet & Maxwell).

5. Other publications – general

Child Support Handbook
£25 (16th edition, summer 2008) (£6.50 for claimants). Also available as part of *CPAG's Child Support Law Online.*

Personal Finance Handbook
£15 (2nd edition, October 2007)

Paying for Care Handbook
£19.50 (6th edition, late 2008)

Student Support and Benefits Handbook: England, Wales and Northern Ireland
£12.50 (6th edition, October 2008)

Benefits for Students in Scotland Handbook
£12.50 (6th edition, October 2008)
Available free online at: www.scottishhandbooks.cpag.org.uk, funded by the Scottish Government.

Council Tax Handbook
£16 (7th edition, November 2007)

Debt Advice Handbook
£20 (8th edition, autumn 2008)

Fuel Rights Handbook
£17 (14th edition, March 2008)

Migration and Social Security Handbook
£17 (14th edition, March 2008)

Children's Handbook Scotland: benefits for children living away from their parents
£12 (1st edition, summer 2008)

Guide to Housing Benefit and Council Tax Benefit
£24 (summer 2008)

Disability Rights Handbook
£21 (May 2008)

The Young Persons Handbook
£15.95 (3rd edition, September 2007)

Welfare to Work Handbook
£20.95 (4th edition, late 2008)

For CPAG publications and most of those in Sections 1 and 5 contact:
CPAG, 94 White Lion Street, London N1 9PF, tel: 020 7837 7979, fax: 020 7837 6414. Enquiries: email bookorders@cpag.org.uk. Order forms are available at www.cpag.org.uk/publications. Postage and packing: free for online subscriptions and orders up to £10 in value; for order value £10.01–£100 add a flat rate charge of £3.99; for order value £100.01–£400 add £5.99; for order value £400+ add £9.99.

Appendix 4

Disabilities that may make a person incapable of work

Schedule to the Social Security (Incapacity for Work) (General) Regulations 1995

(1) *Activity*	*(2)* *Descriptor*		*(3)* *Points*
Part 1. Physical disabilities			
1. Walking on level ground with a walking stick or other aid if such aid is normally used.	*1(a)*	Cannot walk at all.	15
	(b)	Cannot walk more than a few steps without stopping or severe discomfort.	15
	(c)	Cannot walk more than 50 metres without stopping or severe discomfort.	15
	(d)	Cannot walk more than 200 metres without stopping or severe discomfort.	7
	(e)	Cannot walk more than 400 metres without stopping or severe discomfort.	3
	(f)	Cannot walk more than 800 metres without stopping or severe discomfort.	0
	(g)	No walking problem.	0
2. Walking up and down stairs.	2(a)	Cannot walk up and down one stair.	15
	(b)	Cannot walk up and down a flight of 12 stairs.	15
	(c)	Cannot walk up and down a flight of 12 stairs without holding on and taking a rest.	7
	(d)	Cannot walk up and down a flight of 12 stairs without holding on.	3
	(e)	Can only walk up and down a flight of 12 stairs if he goes sideways or one step at a time.	3
	(f)	No problem in walking up and down stairs.	0
3. Sitting in an upright chair with a back, but no arms.	3(a)	Cannot sit comfortably.	15
	(b)	Cannot sit comfortably for more than 10 minutes without having to move from the chair [*because the degree of discomfort makes it impossible to continue sitting].	15

(1) Activity	*(2) Descriptor*		*(3) Points*
	(c)	Cannot sit comfortably for more than 30 minutes without having to move from the chair [*because the degree of discomfort makes it impossible to continue sitting].	7
	(d)	Cannot sit comfortably for more than 1 hour without having to move from the chair [*because the degree of discomfort makes it impossible to continue sitting].	3
	(e)	Cannot sit comfortably for more than 2 hours without having to move from the chair [*because the degree of discomfort makes it impossible to continue sitting].	0
	(f)	No problem with sitting.	0
4. Standing without the support of another person or the use of an aid except a walking stick.	4(a)	Cannot stand unassisted.	15
	(b)	Cannot stand for more than a minute before needing to sit down.	15
	(c)	Cannot stand for more than 10 minutes before needing to sit down.	15
	(d)	Cannot stand for more than 30 minutes before needing to sit down.	7
	(e)	Cannot stand for more than 10 minutes before needing to move around.	7
	(f)	Cannot stand for more than 30 minutes before needing to move around.	3
	(g)	No problem standing.	0
5. Rising from sitting in an upright chair with a back but no arms without the help of another person.	5(a)	Cannot rise from sitting to standing.	15
	(b)	Cannot rise from sitting to standing without holding on to something.	7
	(c)	Sometimes cannot rise from sitting to standing without holding on to something.	3
	(d)	No problem with rising from sitting to standing.	0
6. Bending and kneeling.	6(a)	Cannot bend to touch his knees and straighten up again.	15
	(b)	Cannot either bend or kneel, or bend and kneel as if to pick up a piece of paper from the floor and straighten up again.	15
	(c)	Sometimes cannot either bend or kneel, or bend and kneel as if to pick up a piece of paper from the floor and straighten up again.	3
	(d)	No problem with bending or kneeling.	0

(1) *Activity*	*(2)* *Descriptor*		*(3)* *Points*
7. Manual dexterity.	7(a)	Cannot turn the pages of a book with either hand.	15
	(b)	Cannot turn a sink tap or the control knobs on a cooker with either hand.	15
	(c)	Cannot pick up a coin which is 2.5cm or less in diameter with either hand.	15
	(d)	Cannot use a pen or pencil.	15
	(e)	Cannot tie a bow in laces or string.	10
	(f)	Cannot turn a sink tap or the control knobs on a cooker with one hand but can with the other.	6
	(g)	Cannot pick up a coin which is 2.5cm or less in diameter with one hand but can with the other.	6
	(h)	No problem with manual dexterity.	0
8. Lifting and carrying by the use of the upper body and arms (excluding all other activities specified in Part I of this Schedule).	8(a)	Cannot pick up a paperback book with either hand.	15
	(b)	Cannot pick up and carry a 0.5 litre carton of milk with either hand.	15
	(c)	Cannot pick up and pour from a full saucepan or kettle of 1.7 litre capacity with either hand.	15
	(d)	Cannot pick up and carry a 2.5 kilogramme bag of potatoes with either hand.	8
	(e)	Cannot pick up and carry a 0.5 litre carton of milk with one hand, but can with the other.	6
	(f)	Cannot pick up and carry a 2.5 kilogramme bag of potatoes with one hand, but can with the other.	0
	(g)	No problem with lifting and carrying.	0
9. Reaching.	9(a)	Cannot raise either arm as if to put something in the top pocket of a coat or jacket.	15
	(b)	Cannot raise either arm to his head as if to put on a hat.	15
	(c)	Cannot put either arm behind back as if to put on a coat or jacket.	15
	(d)	Cannot raise either arm above his head as if to reach for something.	15
	(e)	Cannot raise one arm to his head as if to put on a hat, but can with the other.	6
	(f)	Cannot raise one arm above his head as if to reach for something, but can with the other.	0
	(g)	No problem with reaching.	0

(1) *Activity*	*(2)* *Descriptor*		*(3)* *Points*
10. Speech.	10(a)	Cannot speak.	15
	(b)	Speech cannot be understood by family or friends.	15
	(c)	Speech cannot be understood by strangers.	15
	(d)	Strangers have great difficulty understanding speech.	10
	(e)	Strangers have some difficulty understanding speech.	8
	(f)	No problems with speech.	0
11. Hearing with a hearing aid or other aid if normally worn.	11(a)	Cannot hear sounds at all.	15
	(b)	Cannot hear well enough to follow a television programme with the volume turned up.	15
	(c)	Cannot hear well enough to understand someone talking in a loud voice in a quiet room.	15
	(d)	Cannot hear well enough to understand someone talking in a normal voice in a quiet room.	10
	(e)	Cannot hear well enough to understand someone talking in a normal voice on a busy street.	8
	(f)	No problem with hearing.	0
12. Vision in normal daylight or bright electric light with glasses or other aid to vision if such aid is normally worn.	12(a)	Cannot tell light from dark.	15
	(b)	Cannot see the shape of furniture in the room.	15
	(c)	Cannot see well enough to read 16 point print at a distance greater than 20 centimetres.	15
	(d)	Cannot see well enough to recognise a friend across the room at a distance of at least 5 metres.	12
	(e)	Cannot see well enough to recognise a friend across the road at a distance of at least 15 metres.	8
	(f)	No problems with vision.	0
13. Continence (other than enuresis (bed wetting)).	13(a)	No voluntary control over bowels.	15
	(b)	No voluntary control over bladder.	15
	(c)	Loses control of bowels at least once a week.	15
	(d)	Loses control of bowels at least once a month.	15
	(e)	Loses control of bowels occasionally.	9
	(f)	Loses control of bladder at least once a month.	3
	(g)	Loses control of bladder occasionally.	0
	(h)	No problem with continence.	0

(1) *Activity*	*(2)* *Descriptor*		*(3)* *Points*
14. Remaining conscious without having epileptic or similar seizures during waking moments.	14(a)	Has an involuntary episode of lost or altered consciousness at least once a day.	15
	(b)	Has an involuntary episode of lost or altered consciousness at least once a week.	15
	(c)	Has an involuntary episode of lost or altered consciousness at least once a month.	15
	(d)	Has had an involuntary episode of lost or altered consciousness at least twice in the 6 months before the day in respect to which it falls to be determined whether he is incapable of work for the purposes of entitlement to any benefit, allowance or advantage.	12
	(e)	Has an involuntary episode of lost or altered consciousness once in the 6 months before the day in respect to which it falls to be determined whether he is incapable of work for the purposes of entitlement to any benefit allowance or advantage.	8
	(f)	Has had an involuntary episode of lost or altered consciousness once in the 3 years before the day in respect to which it falls to be determined whether he is incapable of work for the purposes of entitlement to any benefit, allowance or advantage.	0
	(g)	Has no problems with consciousness.	0
Part 2. Mental disabilities			
15. Completion of tasks.	15(a)	Cannot answer the telephone and reliably take a message.	2
	(b)	Often sits for hours doing nothing.	2
	(c)	Cannot concentrate to read a magazine article or follow a radio or television programme.**	1
	(d)	Cannot use a telephone book or other directory to find a number.	1
	(e)	Mental condition prevents him from undertaking leisure activities previously enjoyed.	1
	(f)	Overlooks or forgets the risk posed by domestic appliances or other common hazards due to poor concentration.	1

(1) Activity	*(2) Descriptor*		*(3) Points*
	(g)	Agitation, confusion or forgetfulness has resulted in potentially dangerous accidents in the 3 months before the day in respect to which it falls to be determined whether he is incapable of work for the purposes of entitlement to any benefit, allowance or advantage.	1
	(h)	Concentration can only be sustained by prompting.	1
16. Daily living.	16(a)	Needs encouragement to get up and dress.	2
	(b)	Needs alcohol before midday.	2
	(c)	Is frequently distressed at some time of the day due to fluctuation of mood.	1
	(d)	Does not care about his appearance and living conditions.	1
	(e)	Sleep problems interfere with his daytime activities.	1
17. Coping with pressure.	17(a)	Mental stress was a factor in making him stop work.	2
	(b)	Frequently feels scared or panicky for no obvious reason.	2
	(c)	Avoids carrying out routine activities because he is convinced they will prove too tiring or stressful.	1
	(d)	Is unable to cope with changes in daily routine.	1
	(e)	Frequently finds there are so many things to do that he gives up because of fatigue, apathy or disinterest.	1
	(f)	Is scared or anxious that work would bring back or worsen his illness.	1
18. Interaction with other people.	18(a)	Cannot look after himself without help from others.	2
	(b)	Gets upset by ordinary events and it results in disruptive behavioural problems.	2
	(c)	Mental problems impair ability to communicate with other people.	2
	(d)	Gets irritated by things that would not have bothered him before he became ill.	1
	(e)	Prefers to be left alone for 6 hours or more each day.	1
	(f)	Is too frightened to go out alone.	1

* On whether the wording 'because the degree of discomfort makes it impossible to continue sitting' in 3(b)–(e) should apply see CIB/1239/2004; CIB/3397/2004; CSIB/148/05; CSIB/169/2005; and CIB/1205/2005. However these decisions must be applied in the light of the approach taken in R(IB)2/07.
** On whether the wording 'or television' should apply see both CIB/2821/2004 and CSIB/279/2005. However these decisions must be applied in the light of the approach taken in R(IB)2/07.

Appendix 5

Statutory maternity pay, statutory paternity pay (birth) and maternity allowance

If your baby is expected during the week which begins on Sunday	*the 15th week before the EWC begins on Sunday+*	*and the earliest week for which you can get SMP or MA begins on Sunday++*	*Your 66-week test period for MA begins on Sunday*
30.3.08	16.12.07	13.1.08	24.12.06
6.4.08	23.12.07	20.1.08	31.12.06
13.4.08	30.12.07	27.1.08	7.1.07
20.4.08	6.1.08	3.2.08	14.1.07
27.4.08	13.1.08	10.2.08	21.1.07
4.5.08	20.1.08	17.2.08	28.1.07
11.5.08	27.1.08	24.2.08	4.2.07
18.5.08	3.2.08	2.3.08	11.2.07
25.5.08	10.2.08	9.3.08	18.2.07
1.6.08	17.2.08	16.3.08	25.2.07
8.6.08	24.2.08	23.3.08	4.3.07
15.6.08	2.3.08	30.3.08	11.3.07
22.6.08	9.3.08	6.4.08	18.3.07
29.6.08	16.3.08	13.4.08	25.3.07
6.7.08	23.3.08	20.4.08	1.4.07
13.7.08	30.3.08	27.4.08	8.4.07
20.7.08	6.4.08	4.5.08	15.4.07
27.7.08	13.4.08	11.5.08	22.4.07
3.8.08	20.4.08	18.5.08	29.4.07
10.8.08	27.4.08	25.5.08	6.5.07
17.8.08	4.5.08	1.6.08	13.5.07
24.8.08	11.5.08	8.6.08	20.5.07
31.8.08	18.5.08	15.6.08	27.5.07
7.9.08	25.5.08	22.6.08	3.6.07
14.9.08	1.6.08	29.6.08	10.6.07

If your baby is expected during the week which begins on Sunday	*the 15th week before the EWC begins on Sunday+*	*and the earliest week for which you can get SMP or MA begins on Sunday++*	*Your 66-week test period for MA begins on Sunday*
21.9.08	8.6.08	6.7.08	17.6.07
28.9.08	15.6.08	13.7.08	24.6.07
5.10.08	22.6.08	20.7.08	1.7.07
12.10.08	29.6.08	27.7.08	8.7.07
19.10.08	6.7.08	3.8.08	15.7.07
26.10.08	13.7.08	10.8.08	22.7.07
2.11.08	20.7.08	17.8.08	29.7.07
9.11.08	27.7.08	24.8.08	5.8.07
16.11.08	3.8.08	31.8.08	12..8.07
23.11.08	10.8.08	7.9.08	19.8.07
30.11.08	17.8.08	14.9.08	26.8.07
7.12.08	24.8.08	21.9.08	2.9.07
14.12.08	31.8.08	28.9.08	9.9.07
21.12.08	7.9.08	5.10.08	16.9.07
28.12.08	14.9.08	12.10.08	23.9.07
4.1.09	21.9.08	19.10.08	30.9.07
11.1.09	28.9.08	26.10.08	7.10.07
18.1.09	5.10.08	2.11.08	14.10.07
25.1.09	12.10.08	9.11.08	21.10.07
1.2.09	19.10.08	16.11.08	28.10.07
8.2.09	26.10.08	23.11.08	4.11.07
15.2.09	2.11.08	30.11.08	11.11.07
22.2.09	9.11.08	7.12.08	18.11.07
1.3.09	16.11.08	14.12.08	25.11.07
8.3.09	23.11.08	21.12.08	2.12.07
15.3.09	30.11.08	28.12.08	9.12.07
22.3.09	7.12.08	4.1.09	16.12.07
29.3.09	14.12.08	11.1.09	23.12.07
5.4.09	21.12.08	18.1.09	30.12.07
12.4.09	28.12.08	25.1.09	6.1.08
19.4.09	4.1.09	1.2.09	13.1.08
26.4.09	11.1.09	8.2.09	20.1.08
3.5.09	18.1.09	15.2.09	27.1.08
10.5.09	25.1.09	22.2.09	3.2.08
17.5.09	1.2.09	1.3.09	10.2.08
24.5.09	8.2.09	8.3.09	17.2.08
31.5.09	15.2.09	15.3.09	24.2.08
7.6.09	22.2.09	22.3.09	2.3.08
14.6.09	1.3.09	29.3.09	9.3.08

If your baby is expected during the week which begins on Sunday	*the 15th week before the EWC begins on Sunday+*	*and the earliest week for which you can get SMP or MA begins on Sunday++*	*Your 66-week test period for MA begins on Sunday*
21.6.09	8.3.09	5.4.09	16.3.08
28.6.09	15.3.09	12.4.09	23.3.08
5.7.09	22.3.09	19.4.09	30.3.08
12.7.09	29.3.09	26.4.09	6.4.08
19.7.09	5.4.09	3.5.09	13.4.08
26.7.09	12.4.09	10.5.09	20.4.08
2.8.09	19.4.09	17.5.09	27.4.08
9.8.09	26.4.09	24.5.09	4.5.08
16.8.09	3.5.09	31.5.09	11.5.08
23.8.09	10.5.09	7.6.09	18.5.08
30.8.09	17.5.09	14.6.09	25.5.08
6.9.09	24.5.09	21.6.09	1.6.08
13.9.09	31.5.09	28.6.09	8.6.08
20.9.09	7.6.09	5.7.09	15.6.08
27.9.09	14.6.09	12.7.09	22.6.08
4.10.09	21.6.09	19.7.09	29.6.08
11.10.09	28.6.09	26.7.09	6.7.08
18.10.09	5.7.09	2.8.09	13.7.08
25.10.09	12.7.09	9.8.09	20.7.08
1.11.09	19.7.09	16.8.09	27.7.08
8.11.09	26.7.09	23.8.09	3.8.08
15.11.09	2.8.09	30.8.09	10.8.08
22.11.09	9.8.09	6.9.09	17.8.08
29.11.09	16.8.09	13.9.09	24.8.08
6.12.09	23.8.09	20.9.09	31.8.08
13.12.09	30.8.09	27.9.09	7.9.08
20.12.09	6.9.09	4.10.09	14.9.08
27.12.09	13.9.09	11.10.09	21.9.08
3.1.10	20.9.09	18.10.09	28.9.08

\+ EWC is the expected week of childbirth. The 15th week before the EWC is relevant to the continuous employment rule and the earnings condition for statutory maternity pay and statutory paternity pay (birth). See Chapter 23 for more information.

++ This is the 11th week before the baby is due (unless your baby is born earlier. See Chapters 17 and 23 for possible exceptions).

Appendix 6

Pensionable age for women aged between 40 and 45 on 6 April 1995

Date of birth	*Pensionable age (in years/months)*	*Date pensionable age reached*
06.04.50 – 05.05.50	60.1 – 60.0	06.05.2010
06.05.50 – 05.06.50	60.2 – 60.1	06.07.2010
06.06.50 – 05.07.50	60.3 – 60.2	06.09.2010
06.07.50 – 05.08.50	60.4 – 60.3	06.11.2010
06.08.50 – 05.09.50	60.5 – 60.4	06.01.2011
06.09.50 – 05.10.50	60.6 – 60.5	06.03.2011
06.10.50 – 05.11.50	60.7 – 60.6	06.05.2011
06.11.50 – 05.12.50	60.8 – 60.7	06.07.2011
06.12.50 – 05.01.51	60.9 – 60.8	06.09.2011
06.01.51 – 05.02.51	60.10 – 60.9	06.11.2011
06.02.51 – 05.03.51	60.11 – 60.10	06.01.2012
06.03.51 – 05.04.51	61.0 – 60.11	06.03.2012
06.04.51 – 05.05.51	61.1 – 61.0	06.05.2012
06.05.51 – 05.06.51	61.2 – 61.1	06.07.2012
06.06.51 – 05.07.51	61.3 – 61.2	06.09.2012
06.07.51 – 05.08.51	61.4 – 61.3	06.11.2012
06.08.51 – 05.09.51	61.5 – 61.4	06.01.2013
06.09.51 – 05.10.51	61.6 – 61.5	06.03.2013
06.10.51 – 05.11.51	61.7 – 61.6	06.05.2013
06.11.51 – 05.12.51	61.8 – 61.7	06.07.2013
06.12.51 – 05.01.52	61.9 – 61.8	06.09.2013
06.01.52 – 05.02.52	61.10 – 61.9	06.11.2013
06.02.52 – 05.03.52	61.11 – 61.10	06.01.2014
06.03.52 – 05.04.52	62.0 – 61.11	06.03.2014
06.04.52 – 05.05.52	62.1 – 62.0	06.05.2014
06.05.52 – 05.06.52	62.2 – 62.1	06.07.2014

Appendix 6: Pensionable age for women aged between 40 and 45 on 6 April 1995

Date of birth	*Pensionable age (in years/months)*	*Date pensionable age reached*
06.06.52 – 05.07.52	62.3 – 62.2	06.09.2014
06.07.52 – 05.08.52	62.4 – 62.3	06.11.2014
06.08.52 – 05.09.52	62.5 – 62.4	06.01.2015
06.09.52 – 05.10.52	62.6 – 62.5	06.03.2015
06.10.52 – 05.11.52	62.7 – 62.6	06.05.2015
06.11.52 – 05.12.52	62.8 – 62.7	06.07.2015
06.12.52 – 05.01.53	62.9 – 62.8	06.09.2015
06.01.53 – 05.02.53	62.10 – 62.9	06.11.2015
06.02.53 – 05.03.53	62.11 – 62.10	06.01.2016
06.03.53 – 05.04.53	63.0 – 62.11	06.03.2016
06.04.53 – 05.05.53	63.1 – 63.0	06.05.2016
06.05.53 – 05.06.53	63.2 – 63.1	06.07.2016
06.06.53 – 05.07.53	63.3 – 63.2	06.09.2016
06.07.53 – 05.08.53	63.4 – 63.3	06.11.2016
06.08.53 – 05.09.53	63.5 – 63.4	06.01.2017
06.09.53 – 05.10.53	63.6 – 63.5	06.03.2017
06.10.53 – 05.11.53	63.7 – 63.6	06.05.2017
06.11.53 – 05.12.53	63.8 – 63.7	06.07.2017
06.12.53 – 05.01.54	63.9 – 63.8	06.09.2017
06.01.54 – 05.02.54	63.10 – 63.9	06.11.2017
06.02.54 – 05.03.54	63.11 – 63.10	06.01.2018
06.03.54 – 05.04.54	64.0 – 63.11	06.03.2018
06.04.54 – 05.05.54	64.1 – 64.0	06.05.2018
06.05.54 – 05.06.54	64.2 – 64.1	06.07.2018
06.06.54 – 05.07.54	64.3 – 64.2	06.09.2018
06.07.54 – 05.08.54	64.4 – 64.3	06.11.2018
06.08.54 – 05.09.54	64.5 – 64.4	06.01.2019
06.09.54 – 05.10.54	64.6 – 64.5	06.03.2019
06.10.54 – 05.11.54	64.7 – 64.6	06.05.2019
06.11.54 – 05.12.54	64.8 – 64.7	06.07.2019
06.12.54 – 05.01.55	64.9 – 64.8	06.09.2019
06.01.55 – 05.02.55	64.10 – 64.9	06.11.2019
06.02.55 – 05.03.55	64.11 – 64.10	06.01.2020
06.03.55 – 05.04.55	65.0 – 64.11	06.03.2020
06.04.55	65.0	06.04.2020

Appendix 7

Prescribed degrees of disablement

Schedule 2 to the Social Security (General Benefit) Regulations 1982 SI No.1408

	Description of injury	*Degree of disablement %*
1	Loss of both hands or amputation at higher sites	100
2	Loss of a hand and a foot	100
3	Double amputation through leg or thigh, or amputation through leg or thigh on one side and loss of other foot	100
4	Loss of sight to such an extent as to render the claimant unable to perform any work for which eyesight is essential	100
5	Very severe facial disfiguration	100
6	Absolute deafness	100
7	Forequarter or hindquarter amputation	100
Amputation cases – upper limbs (either arm)		
8	Amputation through shoulder joint	90
9	Amputation below shoulder with stump less than 20.5 cms from tip of acromion	80
10	Amputation from 20.5 cms from tip of acromion to less than 11.5 cms below tip of olecranon	70
11	Loss of a hand or of the thumb and 4 fingers of 1 hand or amputation from 11.5 cms below tip of olecranon	60
12	Loss of thumb	30
13	Loss of thumb and its metacarpal bone	40
14	Loss of 4 fingers of 1 hand	50
15	Loss of 3 fingers of 1 hand	30
16	Loss of 2 fingers of 1 hand	20
17	Loss of terminal phalanx of thumb	20
Amputation cases – lower limbs		
18	Amputation of both feet resulting in end-bearing stumps	90
19	Amputation through both feet proximal to the metatarso-phalangeal joint	80
20	Loss of all toes to both feet through the metatarso-phalangeal joint	40
21	Loss of all toes of both feet proximal to the proximal inter-phalangeal joint	30
22	Loss of all toes of both feet distal to the proximal inter-phalangeal joint	20
23	Amputation at hip	90
24	Amputation below hip with stump not exceeding 13 cms in length measured from tip of great trochanter	80

	Description of injury	Degree of disablement %
25	Amputation below hip and above knee with stump exceeding 13 cms in length measured from tip of great trochanter, or at knee not resulting in end-bearing stump	70
26	Amputation at knee resulting in end-bearing stump or below knee with stump not exceeding 9 cms	60
27	Amputation below knee with stump exceeding 9 cms but not exceeding 13 cms	50
28	Amputation below knee with stump exceeding 13 cms	40
29	Amputation of 1 foot resulting in end-bearing stump	30
30	Amputation through 1 foot proximal to the metatarso-phalangeal joint	30
31	Loss of all toes of 1 foot through the metatarso- phalangeal joint	20
Other injuries		
32	Loss of 1 eye, without complications, the other being normal	40
33	Loss of vision of 1 eye, without complications or disfigurement of the eyeball, the other being normal	30
Loss of fingers of right or left hand		
Index finger:		
34	Whole	14
35	2 phalanges	11
36	1 phalanx	9
37	Guillotine amputation of tip without loss of bone	5
Middle finger:		
38	Whole	12
39	2 phalanges	9
40	1 phalanx	7
41	Guillotine amputation of tip without loss of bone	4
Ring or little finger:		
42	Whole	7
43	2 phalanges	6
44	1 phalanx	5
45	Guillotine amputation of tip without loss of bone	2
Loss of toes of right or left foot		
Great toe:		
46	Through metatarso-phalangeal joint	14
47	Part, with some loss of bone	3
Any other toe:		
48	Through metatarso-phalangeal joint	3
49	Part, with some loss of bone	1
2 toes of 1 foot, excluding great toe:		
50	Through metatarso-phalangeal joint	5
51	Part, with some loss of bone	2
3 toes of 1 foot, excluding great toe:		
52	Through metatarso-phalangeal joint	6
53	Part, with some loss of bone	3
4 toes of 1 foot, excluding great toe:		
54	Through metatarso-phalangeal joint	9
55	Part, with some loss of bone	3

The degree of disablement due to occupational deafness is assessed using tables and a formula to be found in reg 34 and Sch 3 Social Security (Industrial Injuries) (Prescribed Diseases) Regulations 1985, as amended.

Appendix 8

Prescribed industrial diseases

Part I of Schedule 1 to the Social Security (Industrial Injuries) (Prescribed Diseases) Regulations 1985 as amended

Prescribed disease or injury	*Occupation*
A – Conditions due to physical agents	**Any occupation involving:**
A1 Leukaemia (other than chronic lymphatic leukaemia) or cancer of the bone, female breast, testis or thyroid.	Exposure to electro-magnetic radiations (other than radiant heat), or to ionising particles, where the dose is sufficient to double the condition.
A2 Cataract.	Frequent or prolonged exposure to radiation from red-hot or white-hot material.
A3 Dysbarism, including decompression sickness, barotrauma and osteonecrosis.	Subjection to compressed or rarified air or from molten or red-hot material.
A4 Task-specific focal dystonia.	Prolonged periods of handwriting, typing or other repetitive movements of the fingers, hand or arm.
A5 Subcutaneous cellulitis of the hand.	Manual labour causing severe or prolonged friction or pressure on the hand.
A6 Bursitis or subcutaneous cellulites arising at or about the knee due to severe or prolonged external friction or pressure at or about the knee.	Manual labour causing severe or prolonged external friction or pressure at or about the knee.
A7 Bursitis or subcutaneous cellulites arising at or about the elbow due to severe or prolonged external friction or pressure at or about the elbow.	Manual labour causing severe or prolonged external friction or pressure at or about the elbow.
A8 Traumatic inflammation of the tendons of the hand or forearm, or of the associated tendon sheaths.	Manual labour, or frequent or repeated movements of the hand or wrist.
Deleted text	

Prescribed disease or injury	*Occupation*
A10 Sensorineural hearing loss amounting to at least 50dB in each ear, being the average of hearing losses at 1, 2 and 3 kHz frequencies, and being due in the case of at least one ear to occupational noise (occupational deafness).	Any occupation involving the use of, or work wholly or mainly in the immediate vicinity of the use of, a: *(a)* band saw, circular saw or cutting disc to cut metal in the metal founding or forging industries, circular saw to cut products in the manufacture of steel, powered (other than hand powered) grinding tool on metal (other than sheet metal or plate metal, pneumatic percussive tool on metal, pressurised air arc tool to gouge metal, burner or torch to cut or dress steel based products, skid transfer bank, knock out and shake out grid in a foundry, machine (other than a power press machine) to forge metal including a machine used to drop stamp metal by means of closed or open dies or drop hammers, machine to cut or shape or clean metal nails, or plasma spray gun to spray molten metal; *(b)* pneumatic percussive tool to drill rock in a quarry, on stone in a quarry works, used underground, for mining coal, for sinking a shaft, or for tunnelling in civil engineering works; *(c)* vibrating metal moulding box in the concrete products industry, or circular saw to cut concrete masonry blocks; *(d)* machine in the manufacture of textiles for weaving man-made or natural fibres (including mineral fibres), high speed false twisting of fibres, or the mechanical cleaning of bobbins; *(e)* multi-cutter moulding machine on wood, planing machine on wood, automatic or semi-automatic lathe on wood, multiple cross-cut machine on wood, automatic shaping machine on wood, double-end tenoning machine on wood, vertical spindle moulding machine (including a high speed routing machine) on wood, edge banding machine on wood, bandsawing machine (with a blade width of not less than 75 millimetres) on wood including one operated by moving the blade towards the material being cut, or chain saw on wood; *(f)* jet of water (or a mixture of water and abrasive material) at a pressure above 680 bar, or jet channelling process to burn stone in a quarry;

Prescribed disease or injury	*Occupation*
	(g) machine in a ship's engine room, or gas turbine for performance testing on a test bed, installation testing of a replacement engine in an aircraft, or acceptance testing of an Armed Service fixed wing combat aircraft; *(h)* machine in the manufacture of glass containers or hollow ware for automatic moulding, automatic blow moulding, or automatic glass pressing and forming; *(i)* spinning machine using compressed air to produce glass wool or mineral wool; *(j)* continuous glass toughening furnace; *(k)* firearm by a police firearms training officer; *(l)* shot-blaster to carry abrasives in air for cleaning.
A11 *(a)* Intense blanching of the skin, with a sharp demarcation line between affected and non-affected skin, where the blanching is cold-induced, episodic, occurs throughout the year and affects the skin of the distal with the middle and proximal phalanges, or distal with the middle phalanx (or in the case of a thumb the distal with the proximal phalanx), of: (i) in the case of a person with 5 fingers (including thumb) on one hand, any 3 of those fingers; *or* (ii) in the case of a person with only 4 such fingers, any 2 of those fingers; *or* (iii) in the case of a person with less than 4 such fingers, any one of them or, as the case may be, the one remaining finger, where none of the person's fingers was subject to any degree of cold-induced, episodic blanching of the skin prior to the person's employment in an occupation described in the second coumn in relation to this paragraph; *or* *(b)* significant, demonstrable reduction in both sensory perception and manipulative dexterity with continuous	*(a)* The use of hand-held chain saws on wood; *or* *(b)* the use of hand-held rotary tools in grinding or in the sanding or polishing of metal, or the holding of material being ground, or metal being sanded or polished by rotary tools; *or* *(c)* the use of hand-held percussive metal-working tools, or the holding of metal being worked upon by percussive tools, in riveting, caulking, chipping, hammering, fettling or swaging; *or* *(d)* the use of hand-held powered percussive drills or hand-held powered percussive hammers in mining, quarrying, demolition, or on roads or footpaths, including road construction; *or* *(e)* the holding of material being worked upon by pounding machines in shoe manufacture.

Prescribed disease or injury	*Occupation*
numbness or continuous tingling all present at the same time in the distal phalanx of any finger (including thumb) where none of the person's fingers was subject to any degree of reduction in sensory perception, manipulative dexterity, numbness or tingling prior to the person's employment in a occupation described in the second column in relation to this paragraph, where the symptoms in paragraph (a) or paragraph (b) were caused by vibration.	
A12 Carpal tunnel syndrome.	*(a)* the use, at the time the symptoms first develop, of hand-held powered tools whose internal parts vibrate so as to transmit that vibration to the hand; *or* *(b)* repeated palmar flexion and dorsiflexion of the wrist for at least 20 hours per week for a period or periods amounting in aggregate to at least 20 hours per week for a period or periods amounting in aggregate to at least 12 months in the 24 months prior to the onset of symptoms, where 'repeated' means once or more often in every 30 seconds.
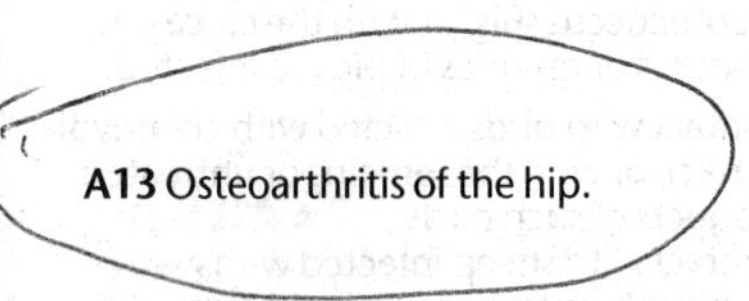**A13** Osteoarthritis of the hip.	Work in agriculture as a farmer or farm worker for a period of, or periods which amount in aggregate to, 10 years or more.
B – Conditions due to biological agents	
B1 Anthrax.	Any occupation involving: *(a)* Contact with anthrax spores, including contact with animals infected by anthrax; *or* *(b)* handling, loading, unloading or transport of animals of a type susceptible to infection with anthrax or of the products or residues of such animals.
B2 Glanders.	Contact with equine animals or their carcasses.
B3 Infection by leptospira.	*(a)* Work in places which are, or are liable to be, infested by rats, field mice or voles, or other small mammals; *or* *(b)* work at dog kennels or the care or handling of dogs; *or* *(c)* contact with bovine animals or pigs or their meat products.
B4 Ankylostomiasis.	Contact with a source of ankylostomiasis.
B5 Tuberculosis.	Contact with a source of tuberculous infection.

Prescribed disease or injury	*Occupation*
B6 Extrinsic allergic alveolitis (including farmer's lung).	Exposure to moulds or fungal spores or heterologous proteins by reason of employment in: (*a*) agriculture, horticulture, forestry, cultivation of edible fungi or malt-working; *or* (*b*) loading or unloading or handling in storage mouldy vegetable matter or edible fungi; *or* (*c*) caring for or handling birds; *or* (*d*) handling bagasse.
B7 Infection by organisms of the genus brucella.	Contact with: (*a*) animals infected by brucella, or their carcasses or parts thereof, or their untreated products; *or* (*b*) laboratory specimens or vaccines of, or containing, brucella.
B8(*a*) Infection by hepatitis A virus.	Contact with raw sewage.
(*b*) Infection by hepatitis B or C virus.	Contact with: (*a*) human blood or human blood products; *or* (*b*) any other source of hepatitis B or C virus.
B9 Infection by streptococcus suis.	Contact with pigs infected by streptococcus suis, or with the carcasses, products or residues of pigs so infected.
B10(*a*) Avian chlamydiosis.	Contact with birds infected with chlamydia psittaci, or with the remains or untreated products of such birds.
(*b*) Ovine chlamydiosis.	Contact with sheep infected with chlamydia psittaci, or with the remains or untreated products of such sheep.
B11 Q fever.	Contact with animals, their remains or their untreated products.
B12 Orf.	Contact with sheep, goats or with the carcasses of sheep or goats.
B13 Hydatidosis.	Contact with dogs.
B14 Lyme disease.	Exposure to deer or other mammals of a type liable to harbour ticks harbouring Borrelia bacteria.
B15 Anaphylaxis.	Employment as a healthcare worker having contact with products made with natural rubber latex.
C – Conditions due to chemical agents	**Any occupation involving:**
C1(*a*) Anaemia with a haemoglobin concentration of 9g/dl or less, and a blood film showing punctate basophilia. (*b*) Peripheral neuropathy. (*c*) Central nervous system toxicity.	The use or handling of, or exposure to the fumes, dust or vapour of, lead or a compound of lead, or a substance containing lead.

Prescribed disease or injury	*Occupation*
C2 Central nervous system toxicity characterised by parkinsonism.	The use or handling of, or exposure to the fumes, dust or vapour of, manganese or a compound of manganese, or a substance containing manganese.
C3 Poisoning by phosphorus or an inorganic compound of phosphorus or pseudo anti-cholinesterase action of organic phosphorus compounds.	The use or handling of, or exposure to the fumes, dust or vapour of, phosphorus or a poisoning due to the anti-cholinesterase or containing phosphorus.
C4 Primary carcinoma of the bronchus or lung.	Exposure to the fumes, dust or vapour of arsenic, a compound of arsenic or a substance containing arsenic.
C5*(a)* Central nervous system toxicity characterised by tremor and neuropsychiatric disease.	Exposure to mercury or inorganic compounds of mercury for a period of, or periods which amount in aggregate to, 10 years or more.
(b) Central nervous system toxicity characterised by combined cerebellar and cortical degeneration.	Exposure to methylmercury.
C6 Peripheral neuropathy.	The use or handling of, or exposure to carbon disulphide (also called carbon disulfide).
C7 Acute non-lymphatic leukaemia.	Exposure to benzene.
C12*(a)* Peripheral neuropathy. *(b)* Central nervous system toxicity.	Exposure to methyl bromide (also called bromomethane).
C13 Cirrhosis of the liver.	Exposure to chlorinated naphthalene.
C16*(a)* Neurotoxicity. *(b)* Cardiotoxicity.	Exposure to the dust of gonioma kamassi.
C17 Chronic beryllium disease.	Inhalation of beryllium or a compound of beryllium.
C18 Emphysema.	Inhalation of cadmium fumes for a period of, or periods which amount in aggregate to, 20 years or more.
C19*(a)* Peripheral neuropath. *(b)* Central nervous system toxicity.	Exposure to acrylamide.
C20 Dystrophy of the cornea (including ulceration of the corneal surface) of the eye.	Exposure to quinone or hydroquinone.
C21 Primary carcinoma of the skin.	Exposure to arsenic or arsenic compounds, tar, pitch, bitumen, mineral oil (including paraffin) or soot.
C22*(a)* Primary carcinoma of the mucous membrane of the nose or paranasal sinuses. *(b)* Primary carcinoma of a bronchus or lung.	Work before 1950 in the refining of nickel involving exposure to oxides, sulphides or water-soluble compounds of nickel.
C23 Primary neoplasm of the epithelial lining of the urinary tract (renal pelvis, ureter, bladder and urethra), including papilloma carcinoma-in-situ and invasive carcinoma.	*(a)* The manufacture of 1-naphtylamine, 2-naphthylamine, benzidine, auramine, magenta or 4 aminobiphenyl (also called biphenyl-4-ylamine);

Prescribed disease or injury	*Occupation*
	(b) work in the process of manufacturing methylenebis-orthochloroanile (also called MbOCA) for a period of, or periods which amount in aggregate to, 12 months or more; *(c)* exposure to 2-naphtylamine, benzidine, 4-aminobiphenyl (also called MbOCA) for a period of, or periods which amount in aggregate to, 12 months or more; *(d)* exposure to orthotoluidine, 4-chloro-2-methylaniline or salts of those compounds; *or* *(e)* exposure for a period of, or periods which amount in aggregate to, 5 years or more, to coal tar pitch volatiles produced in aluminium smelting involving the Sodeberg process (that is to say, the method of producing aluminium by electrolysis in which the anode consists of a paste of petroleum coke and mineral oil which is baked in situ).
C24*(a)* Angiosarcoma of the liver. *(b)* Osteolysis of the terminal phalanges of the fingers. *(c)* Sclerodermatous thickening of the skin of the hand. *(d)* Liver fibrosis, due to exposure to vinyl chloride monomer.	Exposure to vinyl chloride monomer in the manufacture of polyvinyl chloride.
C24A Raynaud's phenomenon due to exposure to vinyl chloride monomer.	Exposure to vinyl chloride monomer in the manufacture of polyvinyl chloride before 1st January 1984.
C25 Vitiligo.	The use or handling of, or exposure to, para-tertiary-butylphenol (also called 4-tert-butylphenol), para-tertiary-butylcatechol (also called 4-tert-butylcatechol), para-amyl-phenol (also called p-pentyl phenol isomers), hydroquinone monobenzyl ether of hydroquinone (also called 4-benzyloxyphenol), mono-benzyl ether of hydroquinone (also called 4-benzyloxyphenol) or mono-butyl ether of hydroquinone (also called 4-butoxyphenol).
C26*(a)* Liver toxicity. *(b)* Kidney toxicity.	The use of or handling of, or exposure to, carbon tetrachloride (also called tetrachloromethane).
C27 Liver toxicity.	The use of or handling of, or exposure to the fumes of, or vapour containing, trichloromethane (also called chloroform).

Deleted text

Prescribed disease or injury	*Occupation*
C29 Peripheral neuropathy.	The use of or handling of, or exposure to, n-hexane or n-butyl methyl ketone.
C30(*a*) Dermatitis. (*b*) Ulceration of the mucous membrane or the epidermis.	The use or handling of, or exposure to, chromic acid, chromates or dichromates.
D – Miscellaneous conditions **D1** Pneumoconiosis.	Any occupation involving: [Occupations specified in reg 2(b) of, and Part II of Schedule 1 to, the Social Security (Industrial Injuries) (Prescribed Diseases) Regulations 1985 which are too numerous to set out here. They are all occupations involving exposure to dust, such as mining, quarrying, sand blasting, grinding, making china or earthenware, boiler-sealing and other work involving the use of stone, asbestos, etc.]
D2 Byssinosis.	Work in any room where any process up to and including the weaving process is performed in a factory in which the spinning or manipulation of raw or waste cotton or of flax, or the weaving of cotton or flax, is carried on.
D3 Diffuse mesothelioma (primary neoplasm of the mesothelium of the pleura or of the pericardium or of the peritoneum).	Exposure to asbestos, asbestos dust or any admixture of asbestos at a level above that commonly found in the environment at large.
D4 Allergic rhinitis which is due to exposure to any of the following agents: (*a*) isocyanates; (*b*) platinum salts; (*c*) fumes or dusts arising from the manufacture, transport or use of hardening agents (including epoxy resin curing agents) based on phthalic anhydride, tetrachlorophthalic anhydride, trimellitic anhydride or triethylenetetramine; (*d*) fumes arising from the use of rosin as a soldering flux; (*e*) proteolytic enzymes; (*f*) animals including insects and other anthropods used for the purposes of research or education or in laboratories; (*g*) dusts arising from the sowing, cultivation, harvesting, drying, handling, milling, transport or storage of barley, oats, rye, wheat or maize, or the handling, milling, transport or storage of meal or flour made therefrom; (*h*) antibiotics; (*i*) cimetidine; (*j*) wood dust; (*k*) ispaghula; (*l*) castor bean dust;	Exposure to any of the agents set out in column 1 of this paragraph.

Prescribed disease or injury	*Occupation*
(m) ipecacuanha; *(n)* azodice-bonamide; *(o)* animals including insects and other arthropods or their larval forms, used for the purposes of pest control or fruit cultivation, or the larval forms of animals used for the purposes of research, education or in laboratories; *(p)* glutaraldehyde; *(q)* persulphate salts or henna; *(r)* crustaceans or fish or products arising from these in the food processing industry; *(s)* reactive dyes; *(t)* soya bean; *(u)* tea dust; *(v)* green coffee bean dust; *(w)* fumes from stainless steel welding; *(x)* products made with natural rubber latex.	
D5 Non-infective dermatitis of external origin (excluding dermatitis due to ionising particles or electro-magnetic radiant heat).	Exposure to dust, liquid or vapour or any other external agent except chromic acid, chromates or bi-chromates capable of irritating the skin (including friction or heat but excluding ionising particles or electromagnetic radiations other than radiant heat).
D6 Carcinoma of the nasal cavity or associated air sinuses (nasal carcinoma).	*(a)* Attendance for work in or about a building where wooden goods are; *or* *(b)* attendance for work in a building used for the manufacture of footwear or components of footwear made wholly or partly of leather or fibre board; *or* *(c)* attendance for work at a place used wholly or mainly for the repair of footwear made wholly or partly of leather or fibre board.
D7 Asthma which is due to exposure to any of the following agents: *(a)* isocyanates; *(b)* platinum salts; *(c)* fumes or dusts arising from the manufacture, transport or use of hardening agents (including epoxy resin curing agents) based on phthalic anhydride, tetrachlorophthalic anhydride, trimellitic anhydride or triethylenetetramine; *(d)* fumes arising from the use of rosin as a soldering flux; *(e)* proteolytic enzymes; *(f)* animals including insects and other anthropods used for the purposes of research or education or in laboratories;	Exposure to any of the agents set out in column 1 of this paragraph.

Prescribed disease or injury	*Occupation*
(g) dusts arising from the sowing, cultivation, harvesting, drying, handling, milling, transport or storage of barley, oats, rye, wheat or maize, or the handling, milling, transport or storage of meal or flour made therefrom; *(h)* antibiotics; *(i)* cimetidine; *(j)* wood dust; *(k)* ispaghula; *(l)* castor bean dust; *(m)* ipecacuanha; *(n)* azodicarbonamide; *(o)* animals including insects and other arthropods or their larval forms, used for the purposes of pest control or fruit cultivation, or the larval forms of animals used for the purposes of research, education or in laboratories; *(p)* glutaraldehyde; *(q)* persulphate salts or henna; *(r)* crustaceans or fish or products arising from these in the food processing industry; *(s)* reactive dyes; *(t)* soya bean; *(u)* tea dust; *(v)* green coffee bean dust; *(w)* fumes from stainless steel welding; *(wa)* products made with natural rubber latex; *(x)* any other sensitising agent (occupational asthma).	
D8 Primary carcinoma of the lung where there is accompanying evidence of asbestosis.	*(a)* The working or handling of asbestos or any admixture of asbestos; *or* *(b)* the manufacture or repair of asbestos textiles or other articles containing or composed of asbestos; *or* *(c)* the cleaning of any machinery or plant used in any of the foregoing operations and of any chambers, fixtures and appliances for the collection of asbestos dust; *or* *(d)* substantial exposure to the dust arising from any of the foregoing operations.

Prescribed disease or injury	*Occupation*
D8A Primary carcinoma of the lung.	Exposure to asbestos in the course of– *(a)* the manufacture of asbestos textiles; *or* *(b)* spraying asbestos; *or* *(c)* asbestos insulation work; *or* *(d)* applying or removing materials containing asbestos in the course of shipbuilding, where all or any of the exposure occurs before 1st January 1975, for a period of, or periods which amount in aggregate to, five years or more, or otherwise, for a period of, or periods which amount in aggregate to, ten years or more.
D9 Unilateral or bilateral diffuse pleural thickening with obliteration of the costophrenic angle.	*(a)* The working or handling of asbestos; or any admixture of asbestos; *or* *(b)* the manufacture or repair of asbestos textiles or other articles containing or composed of asbestos; *or* *(c)* the cleaning of any machinery or plant used in any of the foregoing operations and appliances for the collection of asbestos dust; *or* *(d)* substantial exposure to the dust arising from any of the foregoing operations.
D10 Primary carcinoma of the lung.	*(a)* Work underground in a tin mine; *or* *(b)* exposure to bis(chloromethyl) ether produced during the manufacture of chloromethyl methyl ether; *or* *(c)* exposure to zinc chromate, calcium chromate or strontium chromate in their pure forms.
D11 Primary carcinoma of the lung where there is accompanying evidence of silicosis.	Exposure to silica dust in the course of: *(a)* the manufacture of glass or pottery; *(b)* tunnelling in or quarrying sandstone or granite; *(c)* mining metal ores; *(d)* slate quarrying or the manufacture of artefacts from slate; *(e)* mining clay; *(f)* using silicous materials as abrasives; *(g)* cutting stone; *(h)* stone masonry; *or* *(i)* work in a foundry.

Prescribed disease or injury	*Occupation*
D12 Except in the circumstances specified in regulation 2(d): *(a)* chronic bronchitis; *or* *(b)* emphysema; *or* *(c)* both, where there is accompanying evidence of a forced expiratory volume in one second (measured from the position of maximum inspiration with the claimant making maximum effort) of: i) at least one litre below the mean value predicted, obtained from the following prediction formulae which give the mean values predicted in litres: For a man, where the measurement is made without back-extrapolation, (3.62 x Height in metres) – (0.031 x Age in years) – 1.41; or, where the measurement is made with back-extrapolation, (3.71 x Height in metres) – (0.032 x Age in years) – 1.44. For a woman, where the measurement is made without back-extrapolation, (3.29 x Height in metres) – (0.029 x Age in years) – 1.42; or where the measurement is made with back-extrapolation, (3.37 x Height in metres) – (0.030 x Age in years) – 1.46; or ii) less than one litre.	Exposure to coal dust by reason of working underground in a coal mine for a period of, or periods amounting in the aggregate to, at least 20 years (whether before or after 5 July 1948) and any such period or periods of incapacity while engaged in such an occupation.
D13 Primary carcinoma of the nasopharynx	Exposure to wood dust in the course of the processing of wood or the manufacture or repair of wood products, for a period or periods which amount in aggregate to at least 10 years.

Appendix 9

Upper and lower earnings limits

Year	*Lower earnings limit (£)*	*Primary threshold (£)*	*Upper earnings limit (£)*
1975/76	11.00		69.00
1976/77	13.00		95.00
1977/78	15.00		105.00
1978/79	17.50		120.00
1979/80	19.50		135.00
1980/81	23.00		165.00
1981/82	27.00		200.00
1982/83	29.50		220.00
1983/84	32.50		235.00
1984/85	34.00		250.00
1985/86	35.50		265.00
1986/87	38.00		285.00
1987/88	39.00		295.00
1988/89	41.00		305.00
1989/90	43.00		325.00
1990/91	46.00		350.00
1991/92	52.00		390.00
1992/93	54.00		405.00
1993/94	56.00		420.00
1994/95	57.00		430.00
1995/96	58.00		440.00
1996/97	61.00		455.00
1997/98	62.00		465.00
1998/99	64.00		485.00
1999/00	66.00		500.00
2000/01	67.00	76.00	535.00
2001/02	72.00	87.00	575.00
2002/03	75.00	89.00	585.00
2003/04	77.00	89.00	595.00
2004/05	79.00	91.00	610.00
2005/06	82.00	94.00	630.00
2006/07	84.00	97.00	645.00
2007/08	87.00	100.00	670.00
2008/09	90.00	105.00	770.00

Appendix 10

Disability which puts a person at a disadvantage in getting a job

Schedule 1 Regulation 9(1) to the Working Tax Credit (Entitlement and Maximum Rate) Regulations 2002

PART 1

1. When standing he cannot keep his balance unless he continually holds onto something.

2. Using any crutches, walking frame, walking stick, prosthesis or similar walking aid which he habitually uses, he cannot walk a continuous distance of 100 metres along level ground without stopping or without suffering severe pain.

3. He can use neither of his hands behind his back as in the process of putting on a jacket or of tucking a shirt into trousers.

4. He can extend neither of his arms in front of him so as to shake hands with another person without difficulty.

5. He can put neither of his hands up to his head without difficulty so as to put on a hat.

6. Due to lack of manual dexterity he cannot, with one hand, pick up a coin which is not more than $2\frac{1}{2}$ centimetres in diameter.

7. He is not able to use his hands or arms to pick up a full jug of 1 litre capacity and pour from it into a cup, without difficulty.

8. He can turn neither of his hands sideways through 180 degrees.

9. He-

(a) is registered as blind or registered as partially sighted in a register compiled by a local authority under section 24(9)(g) of the National Assistance Act 1948;

(b) has been certified as blind or as partially sighted and, in consequence, registered as blind or partially sighted in a register maintained by or on behalf of a council constituted under the Local Government (Scotland) Act 1994; or

(c) has been certified as blind and in consequence is registered as blind in a register maintained by or on behalf of a Health and Social Services Board in Northern Ireland.

10. He cannot see to read 16 point print at a distance greater than 20 centimetres, if appropriate, wearing the glasses he normally uses.

11. He cannot hear a telephone ring when he is in the same room as the telephone, if appropriate, using a hearing aid he normally uses.

12. In a quiet room he has difficulty in hearing what someone talking in a loud voice at a distance of 2 metres says, if appropriate, using a hearing aid he normally uses.

13. People who know him well have difficulty in understanding what he says.

14. When a person he knows well speaks to him, he has difficulty in understanding what that person says.

15. At least once a year during waking hours he is in a coma or has a fit in which he loses consciousness.

16. He has a mental illness for which he receives regular treatment under the supervision of a medically qualified person.

17. Due to mental disability he is often confused or forgetful.

18. He cannot do the simplest addition and subtraction.

19. Due to mental disability he strikes people or damages property or is unable to form normal social relationships.

20. He cannot normally sustain an 8 hour working day or a five day working week due to a medical condition or intermittent or continuous severe pain.

PART 2

21. As a result of an illness or accident he is undergoing a period of habilitation or rehabilitation.

Appendix 11

Abbreviations used in the notes

AC	Appeal Cases
All ER	All England Reports
Art(s)	Article(s)
CA	Court of Appeal
CCLR	Community Care Law Reports
CS	Court of Session
DC	Divisional Court
EC Reg	European Community Regulation
ECJ	European Court of Justice
ECR	European Court Reports
ECtHR	European Court of Human Rights
EHRR	European Human Rights Reports
ELR	Education Law Reports
EWCA	England and Wales Court of Appeal
EWHC	England and Wales High Court
FLR	Family Law Reports
HC	High Court
HL	House of Lords
HLR	Housing Law Reports
ICR	Industrial Cases Reports
IRS	Independent Review Service for the Social Fund
JPR	Justice of the Peace Reports
para(s)	paragraph(s)
QB	Queen's Bench Reports
QBD	Queen's Bench Division
r	rule
reg(s)	regulation(s)
s(s)	section(s)
Sch(s)	Schedule(s)
SLT	Scots Law Times
UKHL	United Kingdom House of Lords
WLR	Weekly Law Reports

Acts of Parliament

CA 1989	Children Act 1989
C(LC)A 2000	Children (Leaving Care) Act 2000
C(S)A 1995	Children (Scotland) Act 1995
CJPOA 1994	Criminal Justice and Public Order Act 1994
CPA 2004	Civil Partnership Act 2004
CSA 1991	Child Support Act 1991
CSA 1995	Child Support Act 1995
CSPSSA 2000	Child Support, Pensions and Social Security Act 2000
ECA 1972	European Communities Act 1972
ETA 1973	Employment and Training Act 1973
GRA 2004	Gender Recognition Act 2004
HRA 1998	Human Rights Act 1998
IA 1971	Immigration Act 1971

IA 1978	Interpretation Act 1978
IAA 1999	Immigration and Asylum Act 1999
ICTA 1988	Income and Corporation Taxes Act 1988
IT(EP)A 2003	Income Tax (Earnings and Pensions) Act 2003
JSA 1995	Jobseekers Act 1995
LGFA 1992	Local Government Finance Act 1992
MCA 1973	Matrimonial Causes Act 1973
NAA 1948	National Assistance Act 1948
NHSA 1977	National Health Service Act 1977
NHS(S)A 1978	National Health Service (Scotland) Act 1978
NHSCCA 1990	National Health Service and Community Care Act 1990
NIA 1965	National Insurance Act 1965
PA 1995	Pensions Act 1995
PA 2007	Pensions Act 2007
PACEA 1984	Police and Criminal Evidence Act 1984
PSA 1993	Pension Schemes Act 1993
SPCA 2002	State Pension Credit Act 2002
SS(RB)A 1997	Social Security (Recovery of Benefits) Act 1997
SSA 1998	Social Security Act 1998
SSA(F)A 1997	Social Security Administration (Fraud) Act 1997
SSAA 1992	Social Security Administration Act 1992
SSC(TF)A 1999	Social Security Contributions (Transfer of Functions, etc) Act 1999
SSCBA 1992	Social Security Contributions and Benefits Act 1992
SSFA 2001	Social Security Fraud Act 2001
SW(S)A 1968	Social Work (Scotland) Act 1968
TCA 1999	Tax Credits Act 1999
TCA 2002	Tax Credits Act 2002
TMA 1970	Taxes Management Act 1970
WRA 2007	Welfare Reform Act 2007
WRPA 1999	Welfare Reform and Pensions Act 1999

Regulations and other statutory instruments

Each set of regulations has a statutory instrument (SI) number and a date. You ask for them by giving their date and number.

A(IWR) Regs	The Accession (Immigration and Worker Registration) Regulations 2004 No.1219
C(LC)(E) Regs	The Children (Leaving Care) (England) Regulations 2001 No.2874
C(LC)(W) Regs	The Children (Leaving Care) (Wales) Regulations 2001 No.2189 (W151)
C(LC)SSB Regs	The Children (Leaving Care) Social Security Benefits Regulations 2001 No.3074
C(LC)SSB(S) Regs	The Children (Leaving Care) Social Security Benefits (Scotland) Regulations 2004 No.747
CB Regs	The Child Benefit (General) Regulations 2006 No.223
CB(R) Regs	The Child Benefit (Rates) Regulations 2006 No.965

CB&GA(AA) Regs	The Child Benefit and Guardian's Allowance (Administrative Arrangements) Regulations 2003 No.494
CB&GA(Admin) Regs	The Child Benefit and Guardian's Allowance (Administration) Regulations 2003 No.492
CB&GA(DA) Regs	The Child Benefit and Guardian's Allowance (Decisions and Appeals) Regulations 2003 No.916
CC(DIS) Regs	The Community Charge (Deductions from Income Support) Regulations 1990 No.107
CS(AIAMA) Regs	The Child Support (Arrears, Interest and Adjustment of Maintenance Assessments) Regulations 1992 No.1816
CS(C&E) Regs	The Child Support (Collection and Enforcement) Regulations 1992 No.1989
CS(MAP) Regs	The Child Support (Maintenance Assessment Procedure) Regulations 1992 No.1813
CS(MASC) Regs	The Child Support (Maintenance Assessments and Special Cases) Regulations 1992 No.1815
CS(MCP) Regs	The Child Support (Maintenance Calculation Procedure) Regulations 2000 No.2001/157
CS(MCSC) Regs	The Child Support (Maintenance Calculations and Special Cases) Regulations 2000 No.2001/155
CT(DD)O	The Council Tax (Discount Disregards) Order 1992 No.548
CT(DIS) Regs	The Council Tax (Deductions from Income Support) Regulations 1993 No.494
CTB Regs	The Council Tax Benefit Regulations 2006 No.215
CTB(SPC) Regs	The Council Tax Benefit (Persons who have Attained the Qualifying Age for State Pension Credit) Regulations 2006 No.216
CTC Regs	The Child Tax Credit Regulations 2002 No.2007
DFA Regs	The Discretionary Financial Assistance Regulations 2001 No.1167
EE(A) Regs	The Employment Equality (Age) Regulations 2006 No.1031
EP(RUB&SB) Regs	The Employment Protection (Recoupment of Unemployment Benefit and Supplementary Benefit) Regulations 1977 No.674
ESA(LCWRA) Regs	The Employment and Support Allowance (Limited Capability for Work-related Activity) Regulations 2007 Draft
ESA(WFHRA) Regs	The Employment and Support Allowance (Work-focused Health-related Assessment) Regulations 2007 Draft
ESA(WFI) Regs	The Employment and Support Allowance (Work-focused Interviews) Regulations Draft
F(DIS) Regs	The Fines (Deductions from Income Support) Regulations 1992 No.2182
GA(Gen) Regs	The Guardian's Allowance (General) Regulations 2003 No.495

HB Regs	The Housing Benefit Regulations 2006 No.213
HB(LHA&IS)A Regs	The Housing Benefit (Local Housing Allowance and Information Sharing) Amendment Regulations 2007 No.2868
HB(LHA,M&C)A Regs	The Housing Benefit (Local Housing Allowance, Miscellaneous and Consequential) Amendment Regulations 2007 No.2870
HB(SPC) Regs	The Housing Benefit (Persons who have Attained the Qualifying Age for State Pension Credit) Regulations 2006 No.214
HB(SPC)(LHA&IS)A Regs	The Housing Benefit (State Pension Credit)(Local Housing Allowance and Information Sharing) Amendment Regulations 2007 No.2869
HB&CTB(CP) Regs	The Housing Benefit and Council Tax Benefit (Consquential Provisions) Regulations 2006 No.217
HB&CTB(DA) Regs	The Housing Benefit and Council Tax Benefit (Decisions and Appeals) Regulations 2001 No.1002
HB&CTB(WPD) Regs	The Housing Benefit and Council Tax Benefit (War Pension Disregards) Regulations 2007 No.1619
HSS&WF(A) Regs	The Healthy Start Scheme and Welfare Food (Amendment) Regulations 2005 No.3262
HSS(DHSF)(W)	The Healthy Start Scheme (Description of Healthy Start Food)(Wales) Regulations 2006 No.3108
IBS(MA) Regs	The Income-related Benefits Schemes (Miscellaneous Amendments) Regulations 1995 No.516
IS Regs	The Income Support (General) Regulations 1987 No.1967
IS(AT) Regs	The Income Support (General) Amendment and Transitional Regulations 1995 No. 516
IS(G)A Regs	The Income Support (General) Amendment No.3 Regulations 1993 No.1679
IS(JSACA) Regs	The Income Support (General)(Jobseeker's Allowance Consequential Amendments) Regulations 1996 No.206
JSA Regs	The Jobseeker's Allowance Regulations 1996 No.207
NHS(CDA) Regs	The National Health Service (Charges for Drugs and Appliances) Regulations 2000 No.620
NHS(CDA)(S) Regs	The National Health Service (Charges for Drugs and Appliances) (Scotland) Regulations 2008 No.27
NHS(FP&CDA)(W)Regs	The National Health Service (Free Prescriptions and Charges for Drugs and Appliances) (Wales) Regulations 2007 No.121
NHS(DC) Regs	The National Health Service (Dental Charges) Regulations 1989 No.394
NHS(DC)(S) Regs	The National Health Service (Dental Charges) (Scotland) Regulations 1989 No.363
NHS(DC)(W) Regs	The National Health Service (Dental Charges) (Wales) Regulations 2007 No.121
NHS(GOS) Regs	The National Health Service (General Ophthalmic Services) Regulations 1986 No.975

NHS(OCP) Regs	The National Health Service (Optical Charges and Payments) Regulations 1997 No.818
NHS(OCP)(S) Regs	The National Health Service (Optical Charges and Payments) (Scotland) Regulations 1998 No.642
NHS(TERC) Regs	The National Health Service (Travelling Expenses and Remission of Charges) Regulations 2003 No.2382
NHS(TERC)(S) Regs	The National Health Service (Travelling Expenses and Remission of Charges) (Scotland) (No.2) Regulations 2003 No.460
NHS(TERC)(W) Regs	The National Health Service (Travelling Expenses and Remission of Charges Regulations)(Wales) 2007 No.1104
PAL Regs	The Paternity and Adoption Leave Regulations 2002 No.2788
RO(HBF)AO	The Rent Officers (Housing Benefit Functions) Amendment Order 2007 No.2871
RO(HBF)O	The Rent Officers (Housing Benefit Functions) Order 1997 No.1984
RO(HBF)(S)O	The Rent Officers (Housing Benefit Functions) (Scotland) Order 1997 No.144
RR(CA)O	The Regulatory Reform (Carer's Allowance) Order 2002 No.1457
SF(App) Regs	The Social Fund (Applications) Regulations 1988 No.524
SF(AR) Regs	The Social Fund (Application for Review) Regulations 1988 No.34
SF(Misc) Regs	The Social Fund (Miscellaneous Provisions) Regulations 1990 No.1788
SF(RDB) Regs	The Social Fund (Recovery by Deductions from Benefits) Regulations 1988 No.35
SFCWP Regs	The Social Fund Cold Weather Payments (General) Regulations 1988 No.1724
SFM&FE Regs	The Social Fund Maternity and Funeral Expenses (General) Regulations 2005 No.3061
SFWFP Regs	The Social Fund Winter Fuel Payment Regulations 2000 No.729
SMP Regs	The Statutory Maternity Pay(General) Regulations 1986 No.1960
SMP(ME) Regs	The Statutory Maternity Pay (Medical Evidence) Regulations 1987 No.235
SMP(PAM) Regs	The Statutory Maternity Pay (Persons Abroad and Mariners) Regulations 1987 No.418
SMPSS(MA) Regs	The Statutory Maternity Pay, Social Security (Maternity Allowance) and Social Security (Overlapping Benefits) (Amendment) Regulations 2006 No.2379
SPC Regs	The State Pension Credit Regulations 2002 No.1792
SPC(CTMP) Regs	The State Pension Credit (Consequential, Transitional and Miscellaneous Provisions) Regulations 2002 No.3019

SPP(A)&SAP(AO)(No.2) Regs	The Statutory Paternity Pay (Adoption) and Statutory Adoption Pay (Adoptions from Overseas) (No.2) Regulations 2003 No.1194
SPP(A)&SAP(AO)(PAM) Regs	The Statutory Paternity Pay (Adoption) and Statutory Adoption Pay (Adoptions from Overseas) (Persons Abroad and Mariners) Regulations 2003 No.1193
SPPSAP(A) Regs	The Statutory Paternity Pay and Statutory Adoption Pay (Administration) Regulations 2002 No.2820
SPPSAP(G) Regs	The Statutory Paternity and Statutory Adoption Pay (General) Regulations 2002 No.2822
SPPSAP(G)(A) Regs	The Statutory Paternity Pay and Statutory Adoption Pay (General) and the Statutory Paternity Pay and Statutory Adoption Pay (Weekly Rates) (Amendment) Regulations 2006 No.2236
SPPSAP(PAM) Regs	The Statutory Paternity Pay and Statutory Adoption Pay (Persons Abroad and Mariners) Regulations 2002 No.2821
SPPSAP(WR) Regs	The Statutory Paternity Pay and Statutory Adoption Pay (Weekly Rates) Regulations 2002 No.2818
SS(AA) Regs	The Social Security (Attendance Allowance) Regulations 1991 No.2740
SS(BCO) Regs	The Social Security (Breach of Community Order) Regulations 2001 No.1395
SS(CatE) Regs	The Social Security (Categorisation of Earners) Regulations 1978 No.1689
SSCBA(MHMFIB) Regs	The Social Security Contributions and Benefits Act 1992 (Modifications for Her Majesty's Forces and Incapacity Benefit) Regulations 2003 No.737
SS(CMB) Regs	The Social Security (Child Maintenance Bonus) Regulations 1996 No.3195
SS(CMPMA) Regs	The Social Security (Child Maintenance Premium and Miscellaneous Amendments) Regulations 2000 No.3176
SS(Con) Regs	The Social Security (Contributions) Regulations 2001 No.1004
SS(C&P) Regs	The Social Security (Claims and Payments) Regulations 1987 No.1968
SS(Cr) Regs	The Social Security (Credits) Regulations 1975 No.556
SS(CTCNIN)Regs	The Social Security (Crediting and Treatment of Contributions, and National Insurance Numbers) Regulations 2001 No.769
SS(DLA) Regs	The Social Security (Disability Living Allowance) Regulations 1991 No.2890
SS(DRPSAPGRB)(MP) Regs	The Social Security (Deferral of Retirement Pension, Shared Additional Pension and Graduated Retirement Benefit)(Miscellaneous Provisions) Regulations 2005 No.2677
SS(EEEIIP) Regs	The Social Security (Employed Earners' Employment for Industrial Injuries Purposes) Regulations 1975 No.467

SS(EF) Regs	The Social Security (Earnings Factor) Regulations 1979 No.676
SS(EoFCoEF) Regs	The Social Security (Effect of Family Credit on Earnings Factors) Regulations 1995 No.2559
SS(GA) Regs	The Social Security (Guardian's Allowance) Regulations 1975 No.515
SS(GB) Regs	The Social Security (General Benefits) Regulations 1982 No.1408
SS(GRB) No.2 Regs	The Social Security (Graduated Retirement Benefit) (No.2) Regulations 1978 No.393
SS(HIP) Regs	The Social Security (Hospital In-Patients) Regulations 2005 No.3360
SS(IA)CA Regs	The Social Security (Immigration and Asylum) Consequential Amendments Regulations 2000 No.636
SS(IB) Regs	The Social Security (Incapacity Benefit) Regulations 1994 No.2946
SS(IB)MA Regs	The Social Security (Incapacity Benefit) Miscellaneous Amendments Regulations 2000 No.3120
SS(IB)(T) Regs	The Social Security (Incapacity Benefit) (Transitional) Regulations 1995 No.310
SS(IB-ID) Regs	The Social Security (Incapacity Benefit – Increases for Dependants) Regulations 1994 No.2945
SS(IBWFI) Regs	The Social Security (Incapacity Benefit Work-focused Interviews) Regulations 2003 No.2439
SS(ICA) Regs	The Social Security (Invalid Care Allowance) Regulations 1976 No.409
SS(IFW) Regs	The Social Security (Incapacity for Work) (General) Regulations 1995 No.311
SS(II&D)MP Regs	The Social Security (Industrial Injuries and Diseases) Miscellaneous Provisions Regulations 1986 No.1561
SS(IIPD) Regs	The Social Security (Industrial Injuries) (Prescribed Diseases) Regulations 1985 No.967
SS(IIRE) Regs	The Social Security (Industrial Injuries) (Regular Employment) Regulations 1990 No.256
SS(IoM)O	The Social Security (Isle of Man) Order 1977 No.2150
SS(J&G)O	The Social Security (Jersey and Guernsey) Order 1992 No.1735
SS(JPI) Regs	The Social Security (Jobcentre Plus Interviews) Regulations 2002 No.1703
SS(JPIP) Regs	Social Security (Jobcentre Plus Interviews for Partners) Regulations 2003 No.1886
SS(LAIP) Regs	Social Security (Local Authority Investigation and Prosectutions) Regulations 2008 No.463
SS(LB) Regs	The Social Security (Loss of Benefit) Regulations 2001 No.4022
SS(MAP) Regs	The Social Security (Maximum Additional Pension) Regulations 1978 No.949
SS(MatA) Regs	The Social Security (Maternity Allowance) Regulations 1987 No.416

SS(MatA)(E) Regs	The Social Security (Maternity Allowance) (Earnings) Regulations 2000 No.688
SS(MatA)(WA) Regs	The Social Security (Maternity Allowance) (Work Abroad) Regulations 1987 No.417
SS(ME) Regs	The Social Security (Medical Evidence) Regulations 1976 No.615
SS(NCC) Regs	The Social Security (Notification of Change of Circumstances) Regulations 2001 No.3252
SS(NDP) Regs	The Social Security (New Deal Pilot) Regulations 2000 No.3134
SS(NIRA) Regs	The Social Security (Northern Ireland Reciprocal Arrangements) Regulations 1976 No.1003
SS(OB) Regs	The Social Security (Overlapping Benefits) Regulations 1979 No.597
SS(PAOR) Regs	The Social Security (Payments on Account, Overpayments and Recovery) Regulations 1988 No.664
SS(PN) Regs	The Social Security (Penalty Notices) Regulations 1997 No.2813
SS(RB) Regs	The Social Security (Recovery of Benefits) Regulations 1997 No.2205
SS(RB)App Regs	The Social Security (Recovery of Benefits) (Appeals) Regulations 1997 No.2237
SS(STB)(T) Regs	The Social Security (Short-term Benefits) (Transitional) Regulations 1974 No.2192
SS(TC)A Regs	The Social Security (Tax Credits) Amendment Regulations 2005 No.2294
SS(WB&RP) Regs	The Social Security (Widow's Benefit and Retirement Pensions) Regulations 1979 No.642
SS(WBRP&OB)(T) Regs	The Social Security (Widow's Benefit, Retirement Pensions and Other Benefits) (Transitional) Regulations 1979 No.643
SS(WFILP) Regs	The Social Security (Work-focused Interviews for Lone Parents) and Miscellaneous Amendments Regulations 2000 No.1926
SS(WTCCTC)(CA) Regs	The Social Security (Working Tax Credit and Child Tax Credit)(Consequential Amendments) Regulations 2003 No.455
SSA(F)AO No.5	The Social Security Administration (Fraud) Act 1997 (Commencement No.5) Order 1997 No.2766
SSB(CE) Regs	The Social Security Benefit (Computation of Earnings) Regulations 1996 No.2745
SSB(Dep) Regs	The Social Security Benefit (Dependency) Regulations 1977 No.343
SSB(MW&WSP) Regs	The Social Security (Benefit) (Married Women and Widows' Special Provisions) Regulations 1974 No.2010
SSB(PA) Regs	The Social Security Benefit (Persons Abroad) Regulations 1975 No.563
SSB(PRT) Regs	The Social Security Benefit (Persons Residing Together) Regulations 1977 No.956

SSBU(No.2)O	The Social Security Benefits Up-rating Order 1991 No.2910
SSC(DA) Regs	The Social Security Contributions (Decisions and Appeals) Regulations 1999 No.1027
SSC(NPPC1C)	The Social Security Contributions (Notional Payment of Primary Class 1 Contributions) Regulations 2000 No.747
SSCBA(AAO) Regs	The Social Security Contributions and benefits Act 1992 (Application of Parts 12ZA and 12ZB to Adoptions from Overseas) Regulations 2003 No.499
SSCP Regs	The Social Security Commissioners (Procedure) Regulations 1999 No.1495
SSCP(TCA) Regs	The Social Security Commissioners Procedure (Tax Credit Appeals) Regulations No 2002 No.3237
SS&CS(DA) Regs	The Social Security and Child Support (Decisions and Appeals) Regulations 1999 No.991
SSFA(PM) Regs	The Social Security and Family Allowances (Polygamous Marriages) Regulations 1975 No.561
SSP Regs	The Statutory Sick Pay (General) Regulations 1982 No.894
SSP(HR) Regs	The Social Security Pensions (Home Responsibilities) Regulations 1994 No.704
SSP(MAPA) Regs	The Statutory Sick Pay (Mariners, Airmen and Persons Abroad) Regulations 1982 No.1349
SSP&SMP(D) Regs	The Statutory Sick Pay and Statutory Maternity Pay (Decisions) Regulations 1999 No.776
TC(A) Regs	The Tax Credits (Appeals) Regulations 2002 No.2926
TC(A)(No.2) Regs	The Tax Credits (Appeals) (No.2) Regulations 2002 No.3196
TC(ACCP)S	The Tax Credits (Approval of Child Care Providers) Scheme 2005 No.93
TC(CN) Regs	The Tax Credits (Claims and Notifications) Regulations 2002 No.2014
TC(DCI) Regs	The Tax Credits (Definition and Calculation of Income) Regulations 2002 No.2006
TC(Imm) Regs	The Tax Credits (Immigration) Regulations 2003 No.653
TC(IR) Regs	The Tax Credits (Interest Rate) Regulations 2003 No.123
TC(ITDR) Regs	The Tax Credits (Income Thresholds and Determination of Rates) Regulations 2002 No.2008
TC(NA)Regs	The Tax Credits (Notice of Appeal) Regulations 2002 No.3119
TC(OE) Regs	The Tax Credits (Official Error) Regulations 2003 No.692
TC(PC) Regs	The Tax Credits (Payment by the Commissioners) Regulations 2002 No.2173
TC(PM) Regs	The Tax Credits (Polygamous Marriages) Regulations 2003 No.742
TC(R) Regs	The Tax Credits (Residence) Regulations 2003 No.654

TCA(No.3)O	The Tax Credits Act 2002 (Commencement No.3 and Transitional Provisions and Savings) Order 2003 No.938
WF Regs	The Welfare Foods Regulations 1996 No.1434
WRP(PABWW) Regs	The Welfare Reform and Pensions (Persons Abroad: Benefits for Widows and Widowers) (Consequential Amendments) Regulations 2001 No.2618
WRPA(No.9)O	The Welfare Reform and Pensions Act 1999 (Commencement No.9, Transitional Provisions and Savings) Order 2000 No.2958
WTC(EMR) Regs	The Working Tax Credit (Entitlement and Maximum Rate) Regulations 2002 No.2005

Other information

DMG	*Decision Makers Guide*, vols 1-14
GM	*The Housing Benefit and Council Tax Benefit Guidance Manual*
GAP	Guidance and Procedures Volume
SF Dir/SFI Dir	Direction(s) on the discretionary social fund. They are available in the *Social Fund Guide*, Sweet and Maxwell's *Social Security Legislation* and on the DWP website.
SFG	*The Social Fund Guide*
TCTM	*Tax Credits Technical Manual*

References like CIS/142/1990 and R(IS) 1/07 are references to commissioners' decisions.

Index

How to use this Index

Because the Handbook is divided into separate sections covering the different benefits, many entries in the index have several references, each to a different section. Where this occurs, we use the following abbreviations to show which benefit each reference relates to:

AA	Attendance allowance	I-JESA	Income-related employment and support allowance
CA	Carer's allowance	I-JSA	Income-based jobseeker's allowance
C-ESA	Contributory employment and support allowance	JSA	Jobseeker's allowance
C-JSA	Contribution-based jobseeker'sallowance	MA	Maternity allowance
CTB	Council tax benefit	NI	National insurance
CTC	Child tax credit	PC	Pension credit
DLA	Disability living allowance	SAP	Statutory adoption pay
ESA	Employment and support allowance	SDA	Severe disablement allowance
HB	Housing benefit	SF	Social fund
IB	Incapacity benefit	SMP	Statutory maternity pay
IIDB	Industrial injuries disablement benefit	SPP	Statutory paternity pay
		SSP	Statutory sick pay
IS	Income support	WTC	Working tax credit

Entries against the bold headings direct you to the general information on the subject, or where the subject is covered most fully. Sub-entries are listed alphabetically and direct you to specific aspects of the subject.

U

EVALUATION FORM

Please give us your views about this *Handbook* and help us to plan the next edition.
Please tick the relevant boxes – more than one if appropriate.

Who are you?

- ☐ claimant
- ☐ local authority adviser
- ☐ CAB worker
- ☐ other advice centre worker
- ☐ probation worker
- ☐ trade union official
- ☐ social worker
- ☐ health visitor
- ☐ lawyer
- ☐ tribunal member
- ☐ other, please specify: ______________________________

Are you or your organisation:

- ☐ a CPAG member?
- ☐ a non-member?

How did you obtain this Handbook?

- ☐ in a CPAG membership mailing
- ☐ from a bookshop
- ☐ purchased by mail order
- ☐ provided by employer

How easy do you find this Handbook to use?

- ☐ very easy
- ☐ OK
- ☐ difficult

Did you find the contents met your needs?

- ☐ sufficiently
- ☐ insufficiently

What information could have been added?

What information (or section) was not useful to you?

Which section(s) was most useful, and why?

Any further suggestions for improvements?

Please tick boxes for information about:

☐ CPAG publications and online services

☐ CPAG membership schemes

Name:
Organisation:
Address:

Postcode:
Tel:
Email:

Please send the completed form to:
Peter Ridpath, CPAG, 94 White Lion Street, London N1 9PF. Fax: 020 7837 6414.

ank you for your help. For information about our full range of books, training s and other CPAG activities, please see our website: **www.cpag.org.uk**

ORDER FORM

for more copies of this or other CPAG Handbooks

WELFARE BENEFITS AND TAX CREDITS HANDBOOK, 2008/09 edition

The definitive comprehensive guide to all benefits and tax credits. See overleaf for details of how to access this Handbook online.

April 2008 978 1 906076 12 2 £36.00

(£8.50 post free for individual benefit claimants – direct from CPAG)

CHILD SUPPORT HANDBOOK, 2008/09 edition

Fully updated to cover the latest information on the child support scheme.

Summer 2008 978 1 906076 14 6 £25.00

(£6.50 post free for individual claimants – direct from CPAG)

DEBT ADVICE HANDBOOK, 8th edition

The only comprehensive one-volume practitioner's guide to the processes and practice of money advice in England and Wales. This is the first revised and updated edition since 2006.

Autumn 2008 978 1 906076 21 4 £20.00

PAYING FOR CARE HANDBOOK, 6th edition

The standard guide to services, charges and welfare benefits for adults in need of care in the community or in care homes. This is the first revised and updated edition since 2005.

Late 2008 978 1 906076 20 7 £19.50

FUEL RIGHTS HANDBOOK, 14th edition

This standard practical guide to coping with fuel bills, debt and related problems with fuel supply. Fully updated with all major changes since the previous (2005) edition.

March 2008 978 1 906076 05 4 £17.00

COUNCIL TAX HANDBOOK, 7th edition

This authoritative guide to all aspects of the tax is fully updated with all changes since the previous (2005) edition.

November 2007 978 1 906076 06 1 £16.00

Payment with order

_______ Welfare Benefits and Tax Credits Handbook @ £36.00 each £_______
_______ Child Support Handbook @ £25.00 each £_______
_______ Debt Advice Handbook @ £20.00 each £_______
_______ Paying for Care Handbook @ £19.50 each £_______
_______ Fuel Rights Handbook @ £17.00 each £_______
_______ Council Tax Handbook @ £16.00 each £_______

Postage & packing: For orders up to £100 in value, add £3.99 flat fee;
£100.01–£400, add £5.99;
over £400, add £9.99. P&P: £_______
Total: £_______

I enclose a cheque/PO for £_______ payable to Child Poverty Action Group

Title _______ First Name _______ Last Name _______

Organisation _______ Dept _______

Address _______

_______ Postcode _______

Return form with payment to: **CPAG, Dept HBK, 94 White Lion Street, London N1 9PF**

For details of ordering by credit/debit card or for other information see CPAG's website: www.cpag.org.uk

CPAG Online Information Services

CPAG's online services contain the web's most comprehensive in-depth information on welfare benefits, tax credits and child support. Accessed with a simple username and password, they make it easy for subscribers to find the information they need. Annual subscriptions can include any or all of the four packages:

- ***CPAG's Welfare Benefits and Tax Credits Online*** (basic version)
  The main *Handbook* text, updated throughout the year. For users who want an updated, searchable online *Handbook* but don't need access to legislation/caselaw. Price per concurrent user for annual subscription: £36 + VAT (£42.30 inc)
- ***CPAG's Welfare Benefits and Tax Credits Law Online***
  Includes the *Handbook* text updated throughout the year, with consolidated social security and tax credit legislation plus commissioners' decisions and caselaw. Footnotes in the *Handbook* link directly to the relevant law. Price per concurrent user for annual subscription: £48 + VAT (£56.40 inc)
- ***CPAG's Child Support Law Online***
  Consists of the *Child Support Handbook* text linked to legislation and caselaw. The *Handbook* text is updated once a year in line with the print edition, but the legislation and caselaw are updated throughout the year. Price per concurrent user for annual subscription: £29 + VAT (£34.08 inc)
- ***CPAG's Housing Benefit and Council Tax Benefit Law Online***
  This has the commentary from *CPAG's Housing Benefit and Council Tax Benefit Legislation* (Findlay), updated twice a year in line with the print edition, linked to legislation, commissioners' decisions and caselaw updated throughout the year. Price per concurrent user for annual subscription: £100 + VAT (£117.50 inc)

Visit the online services homepage (http://onlineservices.cpag.org.uk) to get more information on the packages, see the latest updates and sign up for a free 7-day trial.

Bulk discounts: 10% off for 10 or more users and 20% off for 25 or more users. Please contact Ldawson@cpag.org.uk if you have 50 or more users.

Payment with order

No. users

_____ *CPAG's Welfare Benefits and TC Online* (basic) @ £36.00 + VAT (£42.30 inc) each £_________

_____ *CPAG's Welfare Benefits and TC Law Online* @ £48.00 + VAT (£56.40 inc) each £_________

_____ *CPAG's Child Support Law Online* @ £29.00 + VAT (£34.08 inc) each £_________

_____ *CPAG's Housing Benefit and Council Tax Benefit Law Online* @ £100.00 + VAT (£117.50 inc) each £_________

Total: £_________

I enclose a cheque/PO for £_________ payable to Child Poverty Action Group

Title _________ First Name _________________ Last Name _________________

Organisation _________________ Dept _________________

Address ____

____Postcode _________

' (to receive your online password): _________________________

'ʻ *form to:* **CPAG, Dept HBK, 94 White Lion Street, London N1 9PF**

CPAG COURSES

CPAG courses provide comprehensive rights training for advisers and detailed coverage of up-to-the-minute legislative changes. Our tutors are experts in their areas of work and draw on the extensive training experience of CPAG's Citizens Rights Office.

CPAG courses range from introductory, to technical and legal courses for advisers with more knowledge and experience. We also run courses with a skills base, or where the emphasis is on campaigning or challenging decisions.

We have yet again added to our extensive training programme. New titles for this year include: The Revised PCA Test for ESA and Local Housing Allowances and Housing Costs Explained.

Our courses can also be tailored to meet the needs of specific groups, including those not normally concerned with welfare rights. We are happy to discuss your requirements for 'in-house' training to meet the internal needs of your organisation. For further information, contact Sarah Kerridge or Betty Kelly at the numbers given below.

CPAG's London-based courses are Law Society and Bar Council accredited and carry continuing education points. They are also approved by the Institute of Legal Executives and the UK College of Family Mediators. Courses in Scotland have Law Society Scotland accreditation.

For a full programme please contact:

London: Judy Allen, Training Co-ordinator,
Tel: 020 7812 5228
email: training@cpag.org.uk

Scotland: Betty Kelly, Administrator, Tel: 0141 552 3303
email: bkelly@cpagscotland.org.uk

Training information is also available on the CPAG website: **www.cpag.org.uk**; an online booking service is available.

Welfare Rights Bulletin

The ***Bulletin*** is essential reading for welfare rights advisers. One of its unique roles is to provide a cross-referenced bi-monthly update to the *Welfare Benefits and Tax Credits Handbook.*

Contents in 2008/09 will include the fullest coverage of: the new employment and support allowance and the work capability assessment; the new local housing allowance for housing benefit; developments regarding overpayments of benefits and tax credits; right to reside issues; social security commissioners' decisions; court decisions, including the latest test cases.

The ***Welfare Rights Bulletin*** is the best value in the field – and compulsory reading for any adviser needing the very latest benefits and tax credits information.

£30.00 for a full year's subscription (6 issues)
ISSN 0263 2098
Sent to CPAG Rights and Comprehensive members as well as Bulletin subscribers.

For quick and easy access to the Handbook – become a CPAG 'Rights' or 'Rights Online' member

As a 'Rights' member (£57 per year) you receive automatically:

- The *Welfare Benefits and Tax Credits Handbook,* mailed to you as soon as it's published.
- Six issues of the *Welfare Rights Bulletin* – keeping you up-to-date with benefit and tax credit developments and caselaw throughout the year.

You will save £9 on the retail price of these publications, and postage is free. Your membership entitles you to further benefits:

- Regular mailings, including CPAG's *Poverty* journal and newsletter, training brochure and other useful information.
- Special offers on social security, tax credits and child support legislation – potential saving nearly £50 this year.

'The easiest way to obtain (the Handbook) annually is to become a member of CPAG and receive the equally valuable bi-monthly Welfare Rights Bulletin.' – **FAMILY LAW**

Or become a 'Rights Online' member (£72 per year inc £7 VAT), with all the benefits shown above except that instead of a printed *Handbook* you get a single-user subscription to *Welfare Benefits and Tax Credits Law Online* (see previous page for details).

Send cheques/POs payable to Child Poverty Action Group to:
CPAG, Dept HBK, 94 White Lion Street, London N1 9PF

(This is for new members only – if you are already a Rights member, please wait for your renewal form from CPAG)

Help CPAG to make a difference: make a donation

Child Poverty Action Group is an independent registered charity providing advice and support to ensure families have access to their full benefit entitlement. We campaign to bring about positive change for families with children in poverty, in the UK. Please add a donation to your order: your support (as an individual or an organisation) allows us to continue to speak up for vulnerable families and fight the injustice of poverty. Thank you.